COBOL

Jon Wessler, et al

SAMS

Unleashed

COBOL Unleashed

International Standard Book Number: 0-672-31254-9

Library of Congress Catalog Card Number: 98-84091

Printed in the United States of America

First Printing: September 1998

00 99 98   4 3 2 1

Trademarks

Warning and Disclaimer

Executive Editor
Tracy Dunkelberger

Acquisitions Editors
Tracy Dunkelberger
David Mayhew
Steve Straiger

Development Editor
Anthony Amico

Managing Editor
Jodi Jensen

Senior Editor
Susan Ross Moore

Copy Editor
Fran Blauw

Indexer
Greg Pearson

Technical Editor
Jim Eber

Software Development Specialist
John Warriner

Team Coordinator
Michelle Newcomb

Interior Designer
Gary Adair

Cover Designer
Aren Howell

Production
Michael Henry
Linda Knose
Tim Osborn
Staci Somers
Mark Walchle

Contents at a Glance

Contents

About the Authors

Lead Author

Jon Wessler graduated from Valparaiso University in 1967 with a bachelor of science degree in mathematics. He earned a masters degree in computer science from Purdue University in 1970. He has developed, implemented, and maintained financial applications in COBOL on mainframes, mid-range platforms, and PCs. He has developed, installed, and supported systems software and even dabbled in project management, supervision, and middle management.

Jon has taught Advanced COBOL at the University of Indianapolis and served on the Technical Committee X3J4 on COBOL for the American National Standards Institute. He is currently a programming consultant in the Indianapolis area.

Jon enjoys spending time with his wife Barb, three children, and four grandchildren. His hobbies are bowling, reading, and fishing and he can be reached through the publisher or at wessler@in.net.

Contributing Authors

Simon Cordingley is Development Manager at Casegen Systems, where he has been responsible for managing a small team building sophisticated COBOL tools since 1991. Prior to this, he taught programming in COBOL, CICS, DB2, and Telon and provided technical support as a software consultant. His early career in the industry included almost ten years with IBM, which involved a variety of jobs from hardware engineering to CICS, DB2, and COBOL support. His career has included several overseas assignments in Europe, India, and North America.

Simon lives in a small village in the English countryside with his wife, Marianne, where they enjoy walking, travelling, and visiting friends and family. On rare occasions when he can be persuaded to leave the Casegen office, he is often to be found sailing on the English coast or in the Greek or Turkish waters of the Mediterranean. Simon wrote Chapter 24, "Client/Server Transaction Interface."

Howard Hinman became one of the first computer scientists to work on porting mainframe COBOL programs to desktop microcomputers when he joined SoloSystems Inc. in 1982 after working as an IBM mainframe systems programmer and database administrator. When SoloSystems disbanded in 1985, Micro Focus quickly acquired Howard as a key person in its new VS COBOL Workbench product to work directly with early adopting customers who sought to offload mainframe development to PC workstations.

Howard spent 12 years at Micro Focus before becoming a private consultant in 1996. During this time, Howard became the Senior Product Manager and Corporate Evangelist for the COBOL/2 Workbench product line, including the IMS and CICS mainframe compatibility add-ons. Howard later rose to become the Senior Technical Advisor to Micro Focus' President and Chairman, working on researching new technologies and how to best incorporate them into the COBOL realm, and as a one-person SWAT team to work directly with customers to resolve complex problems. Howard additionally assisted in dealing with other software vendors involved in strategic relationships. Howard is well versed in a number of new technologies, including the Web, but his first love remains as the ongoing evolution and modernization of the COBOL development platform. During Howard's tenure at Micro Focus, the COBOL/2 Workbench Product line became the highest revenue grossing development platform available on the PC, at nearly $100 million, surpassing the revenues of Borland's entire languages division and even Microsoft's C/C++ development platform revenues at the time.

In 1994, Howard, then a single parent, decided to leave the hectic Silicon Valley area and relocate back to his original home area in southern Indiana with his five children. Howard married Kate in late 1997 after spending eight years as a single parent. Howard, Kate, and children enjoy a true family lifestyle while Howard continues to impact the COBOL world as a consultant to Fujitsu, among other customers. You can drop Howard a line at hhinman@smithville.net. He wrote Chapter 26, "Messages, Events, and GUI."

Thane Hubbell has been programming in COBOL for 15 years. He got his start in computer operations and rapidly moved into programming. He has worked on a variety of platforms, from the PC up to large MVS mainframe systems. Along the way he has had the opportunity to develop new systems ranging in size from small isolated programs to large interactive, enterprise-driving systems.

He has designed and written applications ranging from a full CICS security and menuing system in COBOL to a VSAM dataset inquiry and reporting tool. Thane is a pilot and one of his more interesting projects was a system to translate FAA formatted aviation weather reports into English.

Thane makes his home in Texas and is married to a wonderful woman, Darlene, who kindly tolerates the spare time he spends programming on his computer after work. Occasionally he will even take on a custom programming project for her.

Thane can be reached via e-mail at redsky@ibm.net, and frequents the comp.lang.cobol Internet news group. He wrote Chapter 7, "Advanced Techniques Using Indexed Files."

Carl E. Krause is the owner and president of Computers & Common Sense, a training company for information technology professionals. Carl has been teaching programming classes and programming in COBOL, CICS, DB2, IMS, and Visual Basic during his thirty years in the information technology field. Carl formed Computers & Common Sense in 1990 in order to combine the power of the mainframe and the ease of use of the personal computer. The Internet was not in mind in 1990 but is now and will evolve to become the user interface of choice for the COBOL, CICS, and DB2 systems that our corporations and country depend upon. The result of this combination of power and ease of use can be found at `http://www.ccsense.com`.

Carl enjoys spending time with his wife and three children, and is looking forward to his first grandchild in late 1998. Carl lives in St. Louis, Missouri and follows the Blues, Cardinals, and Rams. Carl can be reached at `carl@ccsense.com`. He wrote Chapter 23, "CICS Transaction Interface (IBM)."

Ralf Lammel is a research assistant in the Department of Computer Science at Rostock University in Germany, and is currently completing his Ph.D. in reusability of (declarative) programs based on meta-programming. His programming interests include compiler construction, formal specification, and software engineering. Since 1990 he has worked as a developer and consultant for SLG (Systemberatung Linkenbach GmbH), a software development company located in Hamburg (Germany) with huge business programming projects (mainly import/export). Ralf has given courses on COBOL at Rostock University and in the context of professional training, and has written a number of research papers on compiler correctness, program composition, and formal language definition and has been a guest researcher over the years in groups in Amsterdam, Linkoeping (Sweden), Riga (Latvia), and Paris. Ralf wrote Chapters 27, "Object-Oriented COBOL—Concepts," and 28, "Object-Oriented COBOL—Implementation."

Judson McClendon is a computer consultant with thirty years' programming experience. In 1968, while studying to be a physicist, he discovered computer programming and was immediately hooked. He has written several million lines of code in over forty computer languages, but mostly in COBOL. He has designed or programmed some sixty computer systems as diverse as accounting, election tallying, high-precision calculator programs, and even written a compiler in COBOL. He has also spent substantial time writing and teaching programming standards.

Jud enjoys spending time with his wife, five children, three grandchildren, and an increasing number of children-in-law. He lives in Alabama, and his favorite hobbies are reading, Bible study, helping people in programming newsgroups, and doing computer support for his church. Jud wrote Chapters 6, "Data Structures and Sequential I/O," 8, "Special-Purpose Files—Relative and Extended Structures," and 25, "Character- and Screen-Based Interfaces."

William Pierce is a system programmer with eighteen years of experience. He has been involved in the design, development, programming, and implementation of numerous systems and applications. His programming experiences have involved numerous languages with MASM, assembly language of Unisys mainframes, being his favorite. He enjoys System Administration work on Hewlett-Packard and Sun UNIX computers.

Bill enjoys spending time with his wife Jody and son Jonathan. He lives in Indiana, and enjoys reading, movies, computer programming, and his wife has made yard work one of the enjoyable tasks in his life. Bill contributed to Chapter 17, "UNIX-Based Platforms."

John Piggott is a computer consultant with thirty years' experience. He studied mathematics and languages at Cambridge before computer programming discovered him by accident and made him its willing slave. He has been writing code ever since in several computer languages, but mainly in COBOL.

John lives in London with his wife and two children. His particular interests are modern classical music, theatre, contemporary arts, reading, trying to speak foreign languages, and walking in the English countryside or elsewhere in Europe. John wrote Chapter 9, "The Report Writer Module."

Leif Svalgaard has been a participant in the COBOL community for a number of years. He has been director of development for T.O.S.C. International, Inc. in Houston, TX and was responsible for development and maintenance of the ETK (Easy ToolKit) Product. ETK is a large (1,000,000 lines) application written in COBOL that generates COBOL code that will run on any platform that has a COBOL compiler. He wrote more than half of ETK itself. Because ETK's primary goal is to generate business applications he is very familiar with business applications, having served several times as a consultant for clients producing such large-scale applications. He's also very familiar with generating and using screens in interactive applications, including generating HTML-based Web pages directly in your COBOL programs.

Meghraj Thakkar works as a Senior Technical Analyst at Oracle Corporation. He has a masters degree in computer science and a bachelors degree in electronics engineering. He has several industry vendor certifications including Microsoft Certified Systems Engineer (MCSE), Novell Certified ECNE, and Lotus Certified Notes Consultant. He has taught several courses at the University of California, Irvine. He has presented two papers at the ECO'98 held in New York City, NY in March 1998.

Meghraj has co-authored several books: *Special Edition: Using Oracle8*, *Oracle8 Server Unleashed*, and *Oracle8 for DBAs* from Macmillan Computer Publishing. He has developed, and presented several times, a two-day course "Supporting Oracle on Windows NT" to internal Oracle employees. He has been working with various Oracle products for the past six years. Meghraj would like to give a special thanks to his parents for their love and caring. He wrote Chapter 21, "Using COBOL with Oracle."

Judy Tobias is a technical writer at IBM Corporation, where she has been working for sixteen years. She has spent the past 10 years doing software development, testing, and documentation for the DB2 relational database products.

Judy and her husband live in San Jose, California. Judy wrote Chapter 20, "Writing DB2 Applications in COBOL."

Karl Wagner, P.Eng (kwagner@netron.com, http://www.netron.com) is Customer Support Manager for Netron Inc., a leading provider of application frameworks and software development solutions. He specializes in software reuse, business systems architectures, and application development on a wide variety computing platforms. Karl wrote Chapter 29, "COBOL and the Web."

Neal Walters has been an IDMS programmer and database administrator since 1982, having worked in Fortune 100 companies, government agencies, IDMS software utilities development, and as a consultant. Specific experience includes supporting and enhancing Allen Systems Group's DBOL and TRACER products.

He is currently developing an animated IDMS CD-ROM tutorial for IDMS and also developed and markets a Hebrew language tutorial program. For more information on these products and Web-hosting services, his Web site is http://www.amerisoftinc.com. Neal wrote Chapter 22, "IDMS."

Kim Watson has been working with computers for 13 years, and 10 of those have been as a Technical Writer (most recently as a Senior Associate Technical Writer with the IBM Toronto Lab). After arriving home from working as an au pair (nanny) in France, Kim pursued an interest in computers that had been sparked years earlier by an aptitude test that had been sent in the mail. After obtaining her Computer Programming/Analysis diploma, she started her first job as a Computer Operator/Programmer, where she wrote several COBOL applications for the computer operations department. Shortly after that she moved into technical writing where she has documented such products as application development tools, networking tools, database products, and most recently, COBOL.

In her spare time, Kim enjoys sewing, sailing, and looking after her dog Pepper. She also volunteers her time as Treasurer of the East York chapter of the Schizophrenia Society of Ontario. Kim wrote Chapters 30, "The Technical Problem and Dealing With It," 31, Managing a Year 2000 Project for Success," and 32, "What Will Really Happen."

Michael Wessler is an undergraduate at Purdue University, West Lafayette, Indiana, majoring in Computer Technology (CPT). He looks forward to working with database and telecommunications technologies after his graduation in December 1998. He can be reached at `wessler@in.net`. Mike would like to thank C.J. Kloote and the Purdue University CPT department for their support. Michael contributed to Chapter 17, "UNIX-Based Platforms."

Daniel Wilson is a Principal Consultant with Oracle Corporation with the Indianapolis practice. His background includes UNIX Systems Administration and Oracle Database Administration in both SMP and clustered environments. He has programmed in C, C++, COBOL, and SQL. He graduated from Ball State University, Muncie, Indiana in 1984. He currently lives outside of Indianapolis, Indiana with his wife Angela, and their two children, Tim and Emily.

Dan has participated as an author in the following books: *UNIX Unleashed Systems Administrators Edition*, *Oracle Unleashed 2nd Edition*, *Using UNIX*, and *COBOL Unleashed*. He contributed to Chapter 17, "UNIX-Based Platforms."

Dedication

I would like to dedicate this book to my wife Barbara. Her loving patience and understanding have been a real blessing during the past six months while I've been juggling work and the book. It seems like we've hardly seen each other during this time but she's always been there to support me and has selflessly taken on the many little household chores which I've put off or ignored while working on the book. Believe it or not, I have noticed and greatly appreciate it.

Acknowledgments

I would like to extend a special thank you to my son Dan Wilson and my good friend Tony Amico for getting me involved in this project. This is not a project I would have actively pursued on my own, but when Tony, who is our Development Editor and whom I've known for more than 30 years, and Dan presented the ideas for this book, the opportunity was just too good to pass up. Their continued support and encouragement has kept me going through a long and difficult process of getting ideas together, organizing them, and setting them down in a form which can hopefully be useful to others.

The folks at Macmillan Computer Publishing have been a great help. It's amazing how many different things must all be handled properly in order to publish a book and MCP knows its business. In addition to Tony who was our Development Editor, I'd like to thank our Acquisition Editors Tracy Dunkelberger, Steve Straiger, and David Mayhew, Executive Editor Tracy Dunkelberger, Project Editor Susan Moore, and our Technical Editor Jim Eder. Thanks also to the people behind the scenes who take our rough sketches and poor grammar and turn them into the finished product.

Thanks to Micro Focus for the use of its excellent compiler for developing and verifying the programming examples.

Finally, I'd also like to thank my other two sons, Rob Wilson and Mike Wessler. Rob has gotten me started in consulting and that is proving to be one of the best decisions I've made. Mike is a senior at Purdue University and he keeps me on my toes with his fresh ideas and unexpected outlooks on virtually everything.

Tell Us What You Think!

As the reader of this book, *you* are our most important critic and commentator. We value your opinion and want to know what we're doing right, what we could do better, what areas you'd like to see us publish in, and any other words of wisdom you're willing to pass our way.

As the Executive Editor for the Advanced Programming and Distributed Architectures team at Macmillan Computer Publishing, I welcome your comments. You can fax, e-mail, or write me directly to let me know what you did or didn't like about this book— as well as what we can do to make our books stronger.

Please note that I cannot help you with technical problems related to the topic of this book, and that due to the high volume of mail I receive, I might not be able to reply to every message.

When you write, please be sure to include this book's title and author as well as your name and phone or fax number. I will carefully review your comments and share them with the author and editors who worked on the book.

    Fax: (317) 817-7070
    Email: `programming@mcp.com`
    Mail: Tracy Dunkelberger
            Executive Editor
            Advanced Programming and Distributed Architectures Team
            Macmillan Computer Publishing
            201 West 103rd Street
            Indianapolis, IN 46290 USA

Introduction

In every technical job I have held, one or two books have always evolved into reference books of choice. They're the books I first pull down from the shelf when I encounter an unusual problem, need to do something but don't remember the details, or encounter something a little different from the norm and am curious about why and how it works that way. These books generally appear pretty worn out, have a fair number of paper clips (and lately, Post-Its) sticking out from the good parts, and contain handwritten notes and reminders that relate to my personal use of the material.

I intend for this book to be that reference book of choice for COBOL.

Is This an IBM COBOL Book or a PC COBOL Book?

It seems that most COBOL books on the market today fall into one of two groups. The first is the "IBM Mainframe COBOL" book, which generally is distinguished by lots of long listings that show samples of formatting reports and updating files of different types. This type of book discusses fun things like control breaks and different applications like financial, purchasing, inventory, and marketing. These books are pretty boring.

The second kind of book is the "PC COBOL" book. You learn a lot about the ACCEPT and DISPLAY verbs with these books because that's how COBOL interfaces with the user in an MS-DOS environment. These books generally have one or two indexed files and lots of DOS menu screens. The listings here are also pretty long and relate to different applications, such as financial, purchasing, inventory, and marketing. Unfortunately, these examples don't work very well on IBM mainframes because ACCEPT means batch system input and DISPLAY means batch system output, and neither does much for interactive programming.

So which kind of book is this? Well, it's neither or both. That's because this book emphasizes the language, which is virtually identical in both environments. In fact, it's also the same on UNIX, Unisys, CDC, VAX, and HP-3000. I know, because I've worked on them all.

If you browse through the book and look at the samples, I think you'll agree that they will work fine in your environment, whatever it is. When I'm uncertain of how a statement, structure, or function works, I've always found it pretty easy to put together a short program to compile and test to clarify things. I've done this in all the environments I just mentioned and feel that the samples presented in this book can and should be used the same way.

Why Another COBOL Book?

Even though more books probably have been written on COBOL than on any other individual topic in computers over the past 30 years, there is a definite need for this book, and there are two main reasons why.

A Good COBOL Reference Is Not Available These Days

Most books simply do not cover all the features you need to know about COBOL. Most of the books go into great detail about the applications and environments the author is familiar with, but they don't cover all the details of COBOL itself. These books also are not very good at separating environment specifics from features that are available in all environments.

Manufacturer and compiler references used to be readily available but aren't anymore. This is probably because these references are very expensive to produce, and most companies using the language won't pay the price—especially because most of their employees and consultants don't stay for very long anymore and would just take the books with them. Online help is their solution; this is helpful but is generally terse and doesn't provide the background you often need.

Lately, I've been using the 1985 ANS Standard. It has all the details I need about COBOL, but it is a bear to wade through all the compiler-writer requirements, and it is very difficult to find things unless you spend a lot of time getting familiar with the book's layout. Obviously, the book has nothing on any of the COBOL environments. It is also very poorly bound, is not readily available, and does not have anything on the intrinsic functions, which were not added until the 1989 Addendum was published.

COBOL Use Is Booming and Is Reaching into All New Technologies

I received most of my college training on computers in the late '60s. My oldest sons received their training in the early '80s, and my youngest son is now getting his degree in the late '90s. The one consistent thing across the generations is that all the professors look down their noses at COBOL. But PL-1, LISP, and SNOBOL have all faded. Ada has come and gone, and C and Pascal are beginning to fade. But COBOL remains and seems to be doing very well.

I receive questions about COBOL from people developing client/server applications with Oracle on SUN and HP UNIX machines and Windows PCs for the client side. They're using COBOL for regular application management and reporting requirements because that's the common sense way to do it. Many of the PC-based business applications are written in COBOL. Both IBM and Micro Focus have products that provide CICS VSAM interfaces for Windows and Web-based client/server applications. The new COBOL Standard currently out for public review will provide the standard interface.

Who Should Read This Book?

This book is written for the programming professional who uses COBOL. It provides quick and accurate information on all areas of the language. Although this is not a teaching book, copious examples are included so that you can readily see how things work, how you can use them, and what you can or cannot do with them.

Separate chapters and sections are included for many of the COBOL environments and interfaces. Although these chapters are not intended as complete references, they do provide enough detail to support the programmer whose mission is to provide COBOL expertise.

Although this is a technical book, management, administrative, and other professionals with some technical background also will find valuable information that provides good background and support for sound decision-making that affects the technical COBOL environment.

Although, as the author, I'm a bit prejudiced, I predict that if you work at all closely with computer technology and you deal with the software that runs on computers, you will encounter COBOL.

This is not a teach-yourself book, and it is not a textbook. But even if you're not a programmer, this book will give you some idea of what is going on with the COBOL software and how it works with most of the computer environments you're likely to encounter.

For the programmer experienced in COBOL or other languages, or the programmer just beginning to work with COBOL, this book contains most of the information you need that is not covered by textbooks and teach-yourself books.

How to Use This Book

The first three parts of this book deal entirely with the COBOL language itself. Parts I through III are based on the ANS Standard (1985) rather than any specific environment, so things will work as described anywhere. Each topic includes an introduction, a brief example, a description of how things work, and a list of the rules and standards governing its use.

Parts IV through VI cover the COBOL environments, platforms, and interfaces. Although it is not possible for these chapters to be all inclusive, the most common uses are covered, along with sufficient variations, so that most other environments and interfaces will act virtually identically to the examples given.

A portion of Part VI and all of Part VII get into the future directions of COBOL. The more I look at these possibilities, the more enthused I get about working with them. In spite of all the changes, it appears that COBOL programming will be one of those careers we'll be able to pass on to our kids so that they also can have fun with it and make good money doing so.

Part VIII deals with the year 2000. This is a critical subject area, and the treatment here cuts through the marketing and media jargon to provide an objective, technical approach. The examples show exactly what must be dealt with, what options are available to solve the problem, and what advantages and disadvantages each offers.

Finding Specific Items in This Book

An important factor to consider when determining the value of a technical reference is how easy it is to find the specific topics you need to look up. I've spent a good deal of time working on the organization and table of contents of this book so that most items are placed where they make the most sense and can be easily found under the appropriate heading or subheading.

The index is always a good place to look for a topic if you can't find it in the most likely places in the table of contents. Great care has been taken to ensure that this index will help you find items quickly and easily.

I've also come up with a third way to help you reference topics quickly. Appendix A is the COBOL language skeleton and should be helpful when you just need to find or confirm the format of a statement or clause. But I've also added a couple of other things here that will be beneficial. First, any statements or clauses that are affected by any of the COBOL Standards are so identified right in the skeleton. This will help with old programs and compilers. The skeleton also has a cross-reference back to the body of the book so that it can serve as a quick index.

Finally, I get as frustrated as anyone when I can't find a topic in a reference that should be there. So, if you do, please e-mail, mail, or fax that information to one of the addresses in the "Tell Us What You Think" section at the beginning of this book. I'll do my best to get it into the next edition.

A Short History of COBOL and the Standards

COBOL is the only language you are likely to use that is old enough to have a history. It's also the only language that is popular enough that its history can have a significant bearing on how you program with it. To illustrate this point, consider that the current COBOL Standard is ANS 1985 COBOL. However, many of the mainframe computer applications were written for the preceding standard, which is ANS 1974 COBOL. A fair number of these applications have never had compiler dependencies removed so that they could compile with the 1985 COBOL compilers. Therefore, if you need to make changes to such a program, you must limit yourself to statements that are available with 1974 COBOL. A short history of COBOL will help make such distinctions a bit more relevant. By the way, you can't feel safe if you're working on PC applications. Although most of these applications can be compiled with current compilers, many of them were developed by programmers who had not yet learned the newer features available with COBOL 85, so you still need to learn the older statements and ways of programming in order to make sense of these programs.

Line 4: The Beginnings of COBOL

The first COBOL specification was written in 1959 by a committee sponsored by the Pentagon; this group consisted of a mixture of military, manufacturing, and private-industry representatives. It was called the *Conference on Data Systems Languages* (CODASYL). Admiral Grace Hopper of the United States Navy was instrumental in this effort. It was actually a follow-up project to the development of the FORTRAN (Formula Translator) language created for scientists and engineers so that artillery and missile trajectories could be calculated more quickly in time of war.

The purpose was to show the validity of compiler software and that "words" could be translated into computer code just as readily as mathematical formulas. In fact, according to Admiral Hopper, what amazed the Pentagon was not that the compiler could translate words into computer code, but that after a hundred or so cards in some control tables were changed, the compiler could translate German (or French) just as well as it could English.

By the way, if you ever have the opportunity to see a videotape of one of Admiral Hopper's speeches, it will be well worth the time spent. She was an amazing lady who did more to further computer technology than anyone has since then. Her contributions came in the infancy of the industry and were much more critical because of this.

Four Key Events

Nothing much happened with the COBOL language until the mid-to-late 1960s. Until then, most computers were limited to government and universities for scientific purposes. When computers were used in business applications, they were not really very efficient at handling the large amounts of data required for business data processing, so assembler languages were used because that was the only way jobs could be completed in hours rather than days.

Then four significant things happened over a short period of time that determined the entire future of business data processing:

- IBM marketed its 1401 series of computers, which came with a COBOL-like compiler called Auto-coder. This was a tremendous success; it proved the viability of computers in the public marketplace and also that a text-oriented compiler could be effective in solving business data-processing problems.

- The 1968 ANS COBOL Standard was published. Although it was a very limited standard defining only the form and syntax to be used, it did establish the place for standards in the industry and defined a level of portability necessary for the industry to grow.

- At essentially the same time, the Department of Defense and the federal government in general issued policies that no new computers would be purchased for business data-processing use within the government that did not come with COBOL compilers conforming to the 1968 Standard. The policy statements also required that all new federal business applications be written with those compilers. Also, any existing applications that were converted to a new machine or in which more than a 25 percent change or enhancement was required had to be converted to the Standard COBOL. At the time, this was a major statement for the industry. The government was still the dominant computer customer then, so any manufacturer had to sell to the government to succeed. The fact that the language had to be used for large government applications ensured that the compilers would be good ones. It is a footnote to the industry's history that the Department of Defense tried to do the same thing with Ada in the late 1980s and that it was a complete, very expensive failure.

- The 1974 ANS COBOL Standard was issued. I was fortunate enough to be invited to attend its announcement, and I'll never forget it. It was the first of three times I saw Admiral Hopper speak (I believe she was a captain then), and she was truly remarkable. But the standard itself was the significant achievement. For the first time, you could take a program that was written on one machine and recompile it on a totally different one and have it work and produce the same results. This standard essentially set the limits of what had to be standardized and what did not. Your understanding of Pascal from high school still applies 10 years later on your new PC because of this. Vendors can develop and market presentation-level software that generates SQL and have it work with any number of database products because of this.

The Heyday of Mainframe Business Data Processing

Most people will identify the following 10 to 15 years as the heyday of mainframe business data processing. Although a lot happened during that period (including database technology, terminals and transaction processing, structured programming, and the establishment of minis and PCs as dominant portions of the marketplace), the establishment of the COBOL language is the most important event for the purposes of this book. Most of today's business applications were developed or were converted to standard COBOL during this period, and most of today's COBOL programmers received their training and primary experience at this time. Because of this, most of the code we have to deal with today was written to the specifications of the 1974 Standard.

The 1985 ANS COBOL Standard

The 1985 ANS COBOL Standard also has a story that had a major impact on the industry and the language. The standard was originally planned for release in 1980, but was delayed due to controversy until 1985. This standard (which is the current one) has major enhancements over the 1974 Standard that support modern block-structured programming. Had the standard been published in 1980, most business applications would look very different today. The development of the many other block-structured languages, 4GLs, and rules-based languages would likely have developed in a different manner. The controversy involving the standard involved upward compatibility, which would not have been assured, because of the removal of several statements and structures (such as the ALTER verb) that are contrary to the basic concepts of structured programming. At the same time, IBM and other vendors were guaranteeing upward compatibility to the newer machines they introduced. So what many people saw was that the very standardization that was introduced to promote portability was now preventing it.

The controversy was resolved by adding an "obsolete" list of items that would be removed with the following standard. But by 1985, too much had happened and too much code had been written, so today, many of the features now available still are not being used. Most books don't even cover many of these features. This book covers these features and treats them as integral parts of the language (it's about time). These features are included in the examples where it makes sense. The distinction between the two standards is indicated in the body of the text but is not emphasized. The differences also are shown in the language skeleton in Appendix A.

The Current Status of COBOL

A new standard is now available for public review. Although it has been called COBOL 199*x*, my understanding of the current schedule is that it won't be accepted and released officially until shortly after the year 2000. Facilities to deal with objects and a screen presentation interface are two of the primary new features. Both of these are demonstrated in this book; however, to avoid confusion, they are not treated as integral parts of the language. Items for which differences in the new standard may alter how you would want to write code today are identified. You can find the new standard and information on its status at `www.microfocus.com/Standards/` as well as on the CD-ROM accompanying this book. The reason for the `microfocus` part of the address is that the COBOL standards committees are completely voluntary, and the current chairman works for Micro Focus.

The Examples: Their Purpose and Use

I'm quite pleased with the examples used in this book. A lot of time was spent selecting examples that highlight the topic being discussed while also being relevant to the programming problems of today. However, I would like to clarify a few things to avoid possible confusion later.

This book assumes some level of programming background, so I've taken a few liberties that I feel will benefit the overall flow and usefulness of the book:

- Except for the first few examples, the Identification Division and other parts normally needed for a functioning program have been omitted. These parts are included on the CD-ROM and Web site. They were omitted from the text because they take up unnecessary space and just separate the meat of the example from the relevant text more than is desirable.

- Although most of the examples are intended to be relevant to the programming you are doing, their purpose is to illustrate the topic being covered in the text. Therefore, they are *not* full-blown programs that can be used at work with only minor changes. Instead, they tend to be blocks of code that can be inserted into production-level programs. Or, they may be the basics or skeletons that can be expanded into more complete programs to satisfy your needs.

- Some of the examples have no relevance to anything at all. There are only a few of these, and they were included only after very careful thought. These examples demonstrate the material being covered in the text extremely well and also provide a good vehicle for you to make the changes you want so that you can see exactly how the feature being presented works.

- Many books use ACCEPT and DISPLAY interfaces in examples to directly demonstrate the feature and enhance the "tinkering" potential of the example. The examples in this book are not presented in that way; such an interface does not work well for IBM mainframe batch programs. I do encourage tinkering very strongly, however, because that is a very good way of clarifying to yourself how things work. One of the easiest ways to see how the sample programs handle different data values on *any* environment is to modify the values with the (online) debugger. If you are using machines in which the keyboard and screen are the ACCEPT and DISPLAY interface, you will be interested in the versions of relevant examples on the CD-ROM.

- The examples in this book were developed with the assumption that you are an experienced programmer. Therefore, only those details relevant to the topic being covered are commented on in the text. I also assume that you will want to make any variety of refinements when applying the examples to real work situations.

- Parts I through III of this book contain nothing on how to edit, compile, and run the programs or examples. That information is covered in Part IV. Because these things vary so much, it would be confusing and prejudicial to include that information in the language portions of the book. As a courtesy to the vendor furnishing the compiler contained on the CD-ROM, a description of the installation and use of that compiler is included in "The CD-ROM," later in this introduction.

Programming Style and the Examples

Programming style is very important to the readability and maintainability of programs; perhaps the most important factor is that there is a style and that it is used consistently. Over the years, I've developed a few definite opinions on what I like to see as a part of programming style. The important opinions will become apparent as you work with the examples in this book. I also made a few conscious decisions for the unique requirements of relating the examples in this book to the related text material. These items are highlighted here:

- Paragraph numbering becomes very important to knowing where in the program you are when maintaining programs with a PC or terminal. I've included paragraph numbering in all the examples in this book.

- Many people and organizations require an exit paragraph for every main paragraph and consistently use the PERFORM *nnnn*-PARANAME THRU *nnnn*-PARANAME-EXIT. While I don't have a strong opinion one way or another on this, it does add a lot of lines and seems to detract from the purpose of the examples. So this is not used except to demonstrate how it works.

- Paragraph size is probably an area where I'll get a good deal of argument. I believe that a paragraph should contain a complete thought or a group of closely related small thoughts. This is usually somewhere between 5 and 30 lines, but in a few cases, it may be as much as 40 or 50 lines. I don't like to break a single paragraph into a number of smaller paragraphs without careful thought. Separate paragraphs tend to get separated and are usually more difficult to maintain than one larger-than-usual paragraph. I definitely get upset as the total number of paragraph names and blank lines approaches the number of statements.

- The comments regarding the examples in this book are made as part of the text instead of being included in the program code. Although this seems obvious, it introduces the subject, and I do have a few opinions to express. The first is that the program code itself should be as readable as possible. COBOL consists of English words and, in most cases, can be made very readable. When you work at it, it becomes increasingly easy. When the code is readable, comments are superfluous and unnecessary. My second opinion in this area is that when comments are placed in a program, they become part of the code and *must* be updated whenever the code is updated. If the comments aren't updated, they are worse than no comments at all. The first time I see a comment that is no longer accurate, I make a point of ignoring all other comments in that program. The result is that I feel comments should be added only when the next programmer to see the code would be seriously mislead or would develop grave doubts about your sanity without them.

- My final comments here have to do with cohesion, organization, and data-name selection. *Cohesion,* by the way, is the grouping together of related statements. These things all sound good but are somewhat more difficult to define how to accomplish. Needless to say, if these principles are followed, the program is generally pretty easy to read. If they aren't, the program is difficult to figure out. I suspect that all the other structured programming tenets will not help if these three common sense goals are ignored.

Machine Dependencies, COBOL, and This Book

Several interfaces between COBOL and its environment cannot be avoided and vary from machine to machine:

- The ASSIGN side of the SELECT *filename* ASSIGN TO *assign-name* statement. In most cases, this is the name or an alias assigned to the name of a data file that is to be read, written, or updated. Part IV of the book expands on this as needed for the different environments.

- The CALL statement and passing information between programs and subprograms or subroutines is well defined when all are COBOL. But the requirement to link them together is machine dependent and is covered in Part IV. Interfacing COBOL programs and subroutines with other languages and programming environments is very machine dependent. Interfacing to programs written in other languages (such as assembler, C, and so on) is covered in its basics in Part IV. Parts V through VII address many of the other interfaces.

- Data items with USAGE COMPUTATIONAL are described in Parts I and III. As long as these items are defined and stay in WORKING-STORAGE, the machine dependency does not need any further commentary. Their interpretation when written to data files is covered in Part IV. The ASCII and EBCDIC character sets are addressed in Part I.

- COBOL specifies that ACCEPT receives data from the computer's primary or default system input device. It also specifies that DISPLAY writes data to the computer's primary or default output device. All machines that I am aware of—except for the IBM mainframe—provide an easy interactive or conversational interface for executing COBOL (and other language) programs where the keyboard is the default input device and the screen is the default output device. On IBM mainframes, the default input device is the file given the SYSIN DD name, and the default output device is the file given the SYSOUT DD name. Exceptions to this are covered in Part IV.

- A *preprocessor* is a software product that reads a source program and manipulates it before it is processed by the compiler. This is generally done to convert COBOL-like statements that are not defined in the COBOL Standard to other statements that are acceptable. The most common example is standard SQL, where the preprocessor builds COPY statements for the data definitions in WORKING-STORAGE and CALL statements for the actual SQL statements in the PROCEDURE DIVISION. Each database vendor generally provides its own preprocessor. IBM also provides a preprocessor for its CICS transaction interface. These are covered in Parts V and VI.

- Editing, compiling, linking, and running or executing the program are obviously machine dependent. This is covered in Part IV for the different environments.

The CD-ROM

Source code for all the examples shown in the text is included on the CD-ROM that accompanies this book. The names of the codes are shown in the text, and they're located on the CD-ROM in the source directory, and are further organized by chapters. Where appropriate, test input files also are included.

We have also included several third-party tools and compilers on the CD-ROM, including the Fujitsu compiler. They are all located in the <3RDPARTY> directory. To decide what tools best fit your needs, refer to the documentation located within the individual directories. This is the same area where installation instructions can be found.

The Language—
An In-Depth Look at
"The Nucleus"

PART
I

IN THIS PART

CHAPTER 1

The Organization and Syntax of the COBOL Program

IN THIS CHAPTER

Because this is the first chapter, it covers the general material needed for the basic COBOL program. However, the purpose is *not* simply to present and explain the first program. Instead, it is to define and detail the basic requirements and formats for the program. Therefore, I will cover material that is not readily available in most books. This information should give you a much more in-depth understanding of how and why the COBOL language functions the way it does.

If you are an experienced programmer and anxious to get to the more hands-on portions of the language, you can skip the first few sections of this chapter for now and use them as reference material or bedtime reading.

The examples and the way they appear in this book are sometimes somewhat lax with regard to the COBOL format and organization. This was done on purpose in order to make things as readable as possible. The liberties taken are most frequently the removal of the line numbers and the IDENTIFICATION and ENVIRONMENT divisions where they aren't relevant to the example. After the first few sections of this chapter, you probably won't notice their presence or absence. The programs provided on the CD-ROM do include them and are ready to compile and run.

Reference Format: The Layout of the COBOL Line, Word, and Statement

Although COBOL is a freeform language, it is also the very first freeform language and therefore has some special requirements that must be clarified. By *freeform*, I mean that the compiler software does not really care where statements are placed on the line, how many spaces are inserted between words, how long user-defined words are, and which characters are used in creating user-defined words. Some of the requirements have been removed with recent compilers, and others are being removed when the next standard is approved. I will assume the 1985 Standard but make comments as appropriate.

The Layout of the COBOL Line

The COBOL line is laid out as shown in Figure 1.1.

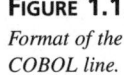

FIGURE 1.1.
Format of the COBOL line.

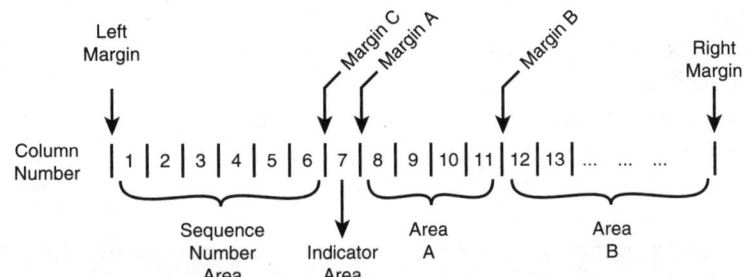

The sequence number area used to be very important in the days of card decks and before terminals were used to edit programs. All compilers still allow for the area, although most compilers essentially ignore it when compiling. When editing a program with an editor tailored for COBOL, this area usually isn't visible. However, the sequence number area is required for the compiler and must be spaces or numbers.

The indicator area is not really part of the program and is usually blank. Several characters are recognized by the compiler and can be employed for some useful purposes:

*	Signifies to the compiler that the remainder of this line is a remark and will be printed on any program listing but will not be compiled.
/	Signifies that the remainder of the line is a remark but also causes a page eject when the compile listing is printed.
-	Signifies that this line is a continuation of the preceding line and that the first nonblank character will begin immediately after the character and before the right margin of the preceding line. If the preceding line terminated within a nonnumeric literal (something surrounded by quotation marks, such as "Hi There"), the first character must be a quote, and the continuation of the literal begins with the first character following the quote. This feature is used most often for long, nonnumeric literals (there is an example in the expanded listing in the next section).
D	If debugging is turned on by the `Source-Computer` switch (see the next section), this line will be compiled with the program. If not, this line will be treated as a remark. This capability was introduced with the 1974 Standard but never became very popular. Online and interactive debugging facilities (which are *not* covered by the COBOL Standard) have largely made the function unnecessary, and it will be removed with the next version of the standard.

The actual COBOL program begins at margin A or column 8 and continues to the right margin. Notice that no actual column number is specified for the right margin. This has been the case since 1974 as far as the standard is concerned. However, a right margin is specified by the standard, and the specific column it occurs at is determined by the compiler. Most compilers specify (as a default) that the right margin is defined between columns 72 and 73.

> **NOTE**
>
> The right-margin definition is required by the standard, and any text beyond it is ignored by the compiler and is treated as remarks. Many organizations take advantage of this by identifying lines altered during maintenance upgrades in the columns beyond the right margin. Often, the date of the change and the initials of the programmer making it are entered here. If formal change-control software is used, the change-control number can also be entered here.

The distinction between areas A and B in the COBOL source program is a holdover from the first forms of COBOL. It is still important, though, and still required.

Division and section headings and paragraph names must begin in area A. Within the Data Division, the level indicators FD, SD, RD, and CD, as well as any level numbers 01 and 77, must begin in area A. The keywords Declaratives, End Declaratives, and End Program must begin in area A if they are used. Although all these items can start at any column in area A, they almost always begin at column 8. The details of what these items signify are covered in various parts of the book. At this point, suffice it to say that they are relatively important and therefore must begin in area A.

All other levels, entries, and statements must begin in area B. Although many of these do begin right at column 12, many also are indented beyond that to enhance the structure and readability of the program.

The Makeup of the COBOL Word and Upper- and Lowercase

COBOL words are made up of the letters of the alphabet, the numeric digits, and the hyphen or dash (-). Other special characters may *not* be used when defining data or procedure names. The underscore (_) is scheduled to be added with the next version of the standard. COBOL words must be 30 characters or less. When defined in the Data Division, they must contain at least one letter (otherwise, it wouldn't be possible to distinguish them from numeric literals).

Upper- and lowercase characters may be used interchangeably in COBOL words. COBOL will treat them as equal here. So `Data Division` is the same as `DATA DIVISION`; `ADD` is equal to `Add`, `add`, and `aDD`; and `My-Name` is equal to `MY-NAME` and `my-name`.

> **NOTE**
>
> Most existing COBOL programs are strictly uppercase—probably just out of habit. It has become apparent that it is much easier to enter everything in either *all* uppercase or *all* lowercase. Because COBOL was invented before lowercase existed on computers, the habit of uppercase began; programmers just turned on Caps Lock when lowercase became available, because it was easier to deal with existing programs that way. The newer languages are written pretty much in lowercase only because there was never a reason to turn on Caps Lock, and the Shift key doesn't really make any sense to anyone but English majors.

On the other hand, it is important to know that upper- and lowercase characters are *not* treated as equal when they appear in data or in nonnumeric literals. Hence, the literal `END` is *not* equal to the literal `End`, and a data element `last-name` in a record that has the value `JONES` is *not* the same as one in another record with the value `Jones`. There is a form of the `Inspect` statement that deals with this pretty nicely, as do several of the intrinsic functions.

There are a large number of reserved words in COBOL. Although the list is long, most words are not likely to be used for data or procedure names. If they are, strange compiler diagnostics will appear.

COBOL Entries, Statements, Sentences, and Other Terminology

Some terminology that is defined and used in COBOL standards publications is ignored in most books on COBOL or is described in a general, ambiguous manner. Although you can be a very good programmer without getting into this terminology, knowing the terms and how they relate will give you a better background on how COBOL entries relate to each other and therefore will help you understand how things work in the language. In a manner similar to any spoken language, you can be well-spoken without knowing the grammar of a language. But it is easier to understand and speak the language well if you do know the grammar. I'll present these definitions in a top-down order, which should help make it more apparent how they fit together:

Division

A COBOL program is composed of four divisions: the IDENTIFICATION DIVISION, the ENVIRONMENT DIVISION, the DATA DIVISION, and the PROCEDURE DIVISION. Although all except the IDENTIFICATION DIVISION are optional, most programs will contain all four divisions. Each of the divisions consists of sections and paragraphs.

Section

The ENVIRONMENT and DATA DIVISION each have pre-defined section names that you will or will not include, depending on the needs of your program. The IDENTIFICATION DIVISION does not have sections. In the PROCEDURE DIVISION, section names are optional and are defined by the programmer if they are used. If section names are used, everything in the PROCEDURE DIVISION must be included in one or another of them. A section-name is a COBOL word followed by a space, the word SECTION, and a period. It must begin in area A.

Paragraph

Paragraphs are contained in sections and divisions and are the lowest-level grouping that is given a name. In the IDENTIFICATION DIVISION and ENVIRONMENT DIVISION, the names are predefined, but the programmer determines which are needed and which aren't. In the PROCEDURE DIVISION, the programmer makes up the paragraph names. The DATA DIVISION does not have paragraphs, but instead has *description entries,* which distinguish items in a similar manner but have specialized functions that are described as the related topics are covered. A paragraph-name is a COBOL word followed by a period, and it must begin in area A.

Entry

The paragraphs and sections of all the divisions except for the PROCEDURE DIVISION are composed of entries. The entries, in turn, consist of clauses and are terminated by a period. The purpose of an entry is to form a conceptually complete definition or description. However, because of the special requirements for some definitions and descriptions, this isn't always quite true. For example, a record definition entry is terminated by a period, even though it contains a number of data-definition entries, and each of them is also terminated by a period.

Clause	The COBOL Standard defines a clause as "an ordered set of consecutive COBOL character-strings whose purpose is to specify an attribute of an entry." This is pretty circular and not much of a definition, but after working with it quite a while, I found that I couldn't do much better. In most cases, clauses contain COBOL words with an occasional literal thrown in. For example, LABEL RECORDS STANDARD and OCCURS 23 TIMES are clauses. On the other hand, some clauses contain items that are nothing more than character strings. An example is PIC Z,ZZZ,ZZ9.99CR.
Sentence	A sentence is found only in the PROCEDURE DIVISION. It consists of one or more statements and is terminated by a period.
Statement	A COBOL statement begins with a COBOL verb; contains other COBOL words, literals, and separators; and is put together in a manner that is syntactically correct and complete. For example, MOVE 25 TO COUNTER-A is a statement. Statements can include other statements. For example, READ INPUT-FILE AT END MOVE 'YES' TO INPUT-END-FILE-STATUS is a statement, but so is MOVE 'YES' TO INPUT-END-FILE-STATUS.

Paragraphs in the PROCEDURE DIVISION normally consist of sentences. But they also can contain a group of statements with none of them ending in a period:

Phrase	A phrase is an ordered set of COBOL words or character strings that form a portion of a COBOL statement (they also may form a portion of a clause). AT END is a phrase, as is UNTIL COUNT-B > 18. Note that these are meaningless by themselves, but they are necessary to make the complete statement do what is required.

Imperative and Conditional Statements

An imperative statement begins with an imperative verb and specifies an unconditional action to be taken. On the other hand, a conditional statement is one in which the action to be taken is determined by some condition that is evaluated when the program executes. ADD 25 TO COUNT-1 is an imperative statement, but ADD 25 TO COUNT-1 ON SIZE ERROR PERFORM 100-UPDATE-ERROR is a conditional statement. An imperative statement can consist of a sequence of imperative statements. Chapter 3, "Using Conditional Statements to Control Processing," discusses these two kinds of statements in more detail; at this point, it is sufficient to be aware of the distinction.

NOTE

It is not necessary to memorize this terminology and be correct in its use all the time. I often get the terms *phrase* and *clause* reversed, because each is a subordinate group of words, and they both just "add" something to an existing statement, definition, or description. The important thing is to begin getting a feel for how things are grouped together with COBOL so that the rules and requirements make some sense when they're presented.

The Organization of the COBOL Program

COBOL was originally designed with an organization that would follow that of a technical specifications document. Although time has shown many of the details to be unnecessary and also presented new items that don't fit very well into the existing structure, it does still hold and is required.

The COBOL program is divided into four divisions. These are divided into sections and paragraphs in a manner appropriate to the material required for the division. About 95 percent of the program code is entered in only two of the divisions. In addition to providing an introduction to all the divisions, this section also covers some of the details in the two lesser-used divisions.

The Basic Program Format

The most basic form of the COBOL program follows:

```
IDENTIFICATON DIVISION.
PROGRAM-ID.  program-id
[ENVIRONMENT DIVISION.]
[DATA DIVISION.]
[PROCEDURE DIVISION.]
[END PROGRAM program-id.]
```

This is an example of a language skeleton. As a review, there are a few things to notice. The first one is that all but the first two lines are surrounded by brackets ([]). This indicates that the material enclosed in them is optional and not required. If it is entered, though, it must be as specified. Hence, the smallest COBOL program is the first two lines of the skeleton. Obviously, it won't do much, and on most machines, if you compile and run it, there won't even be an indication that it has run. By the way, there is actually a use for such small programs. They're called *program stubs* and can be handy in large-scale development using subroutines and subprograms. Program stubs are covered in detail in Chapter 14, "Invoking Other Programs and Subprograms."

Notice also in the example that some of the words are entered as all capital letters and others aren't. Those that are all capitals must be entered exactly as shown when they are used. The lowercase words indicate also that something is required, and the word indicates what it is. But the actual composition is left up to the programmer.

Observe that although the term program-id is in lowercase, it is spelled identically on both the second and last lines. This means that even though the actual value is up to the programmer, the same spelling must be used in both places. So if you choose to name your program MYPROG1 on the second line, if you also want to use the END PROGRAM on the last line, you also must specify MYPROG1 there.

All the lines in the skeleton begin at the same character position of the line. Notice that this is area A or column 8. Typically, the specific position where code begins will not be shown in the examples but will become obvious because of how it is lined up and indented.

Finally, I'll comment on the END PROGRAM at the last line. When used, its purpose is to signify the end of the source program that is being compiled. On some machines in times past, this was necessary to distinguish the program from the statements that controlled the program compilation, linkage, and listings. Now most source programs are kept as separate files or *members* or *elements* in a *library* or *program file* (the nomenclature depends on the machine/environment you're working in). Now the primary purpose for END PROGRAM is to separate one of several programs that may be kept in the same file,

member, or element. When this is done, the next line (if there is one) must be the
IDENTIFICATION DIVISION of the next program. The details of this usage are covered in
Chapter 14.

The IDENTIFICATION DIVISION

The full format of the IDENTIFICATION DIVISION follows:

```
IDENTIFICATION DIVISION.
PROGRAM-ID.  program-id
[AUTHOR.   [comment-entry]...]
[INSTALLATION.  [comment-entry]...]
[DATE-WRITTEN.  [comment-entry]...]
[DATE-COMPILED.  [comment-entry]...]
[SECURITY.  [comment-entry]...]
```

Again, note that everything but the IDENTIFICATION DIVISION and PROGRAM-ID are
optional. The program-id must be a properly formed word (in other words, it must be
made up of letters, numbers, and/or the hyphen or dash and be 30 characters or less). The
program-id identifies the source program, the object program (what is produced by the
compiler), and any listings generated by the compiler. Because these are tied to the compiler and the machine or environment you're working with, other restrictions also may
apply, especially if you're working with subroutines or subprograms. Things will work
correctly on every machine I've worked on if you limit the program-id to letters and
numbers and restrict it to 8 characters or less.

The comment entries are essentially remarks and can contain any characters you want.
They can span several lines, but if they do, all the lines after the first one must begin in
area B (or after column 11).

Notice the ellipsis (...) in the example. This is frequently seen in a programming language skeleton and simply indicates that the preceding entry may be repeated as often as
needed by the programmer. In this case, the ellipsis is almost redundant; the comment
entry can contain any and as many characters as desired.

The AUTHOR and INSTALLATION paragraphs often are used, but not always, and it does not
make much difference whether or not they are. The DATE-WRITTEN paragraph is a good
idea, because it often gives a good idea of the kind of logic and structure you can expect
in the program. The DATE-COMPILED is interesting. If it is left blank, the compiler will
insert the current date here in the program listing (*not* in the source program) whenever
the program is compiled. I don't recall ever seeing the SECURITY paragraph in a real
program.

The only paragraph names allowed are the ones shown in the example, and no section names are permitted. But since everything except the `program-id` is comments, any and all comments you want may be entered in any format by simply using the asterisk (*) in column 7.

This, in fact, is commonly done with most *production-level* programs, and I strongly recommend it. The examples in the book don't have comments because the text provides more commentary than there is in the example. However, when you need to make changes to, debug, or review a program you have never seen before, a few lines indicating what the program is all about are greatly appreciated. A historical log providing a line or two identifying each change made to the program is also a very good idea, because it also indicates why the code looks the way it does and can make it a lot easier to debug or make changes to later.

A point of emphasis is that COBOL is a self-documenting language and can and should be read like a technical book when it is written properly. Therefore, by a few lines of comments, I mean just that. In almost all cases, somewhere between two and eight lines of description plus one to three lines for each change are more than sufficient. The following is a typical example:

```
IDENTIFICATION DIVISION.
PROGRAM-ID.  RSTL050D
AUTHOR.  J SMITH.
DATE-WRITTEN.  MARCH 22, 1987.
DATE-COMPILED.
********************************************************************

* THIS PROGRAM PRODUCES THE COMPANY'S SUGGESTED DISCOUNT
* SUMMARY.  IT SELECTS RECORDS FROM THE INVENTORY MASTER WHERE
* THE QUARTER TO DATE QUANTITY SOLD IS LESS THAN 40 PERCENT OF
* THE TOTAL INVENTORY AMOUNT.

********************************************************************
CHANGE HISTORY

JUN 18, 1987 - J SMITH    CHANGE NR XY19876
   CHANGED TO USE QUARTER TO DATE QUANTITY SINCE PROGRAM IS
   ONLY RUN ON END OF QUARTER.

SEP 8, 1987  - J SMITH    CHANGE NR XY19883
   CORRECT PRICE CALCULATION TO EXCLUDE OTHER DISCOUNTS

MAR 13, 1993 - W ROGERS   CHANGE NR XY22134
   INVENTORY MASTER CHANGED TO DATABASE.
********************************************************************
```

The ENVIRONMENT DIVISION

The express purpose of this division is to identify and isolate the unique compiler and manufacturer characteristics from the rest of the program. The goal is that you should be able to limit changes to this division only and then be able to recompile the program with some other compiler and run it on some other machine without making any other changes. Although this is a bit idealistic, most programs are pretty portable and can be moved from machine to machine without much trouble.

For most everyday programs in most environments, the only need for this division is to relate the program's data file definitions to actual files contained on the machine on which the program runs. These specifications are contained in the INPUT-OUTPUT SECTION and are covered in detail in Part II, "The Language—Structure Data and External Media." The remainder of the specifications is covered here. The following is the general form of the ENVIRONMENT DIVISION:

```
ENVIRONMENT DIVISION.
[CONFIGURATION SECTION.
[SOURCE COMPUTER.   [computer-name-1 [WITH DEBUGGING MODE].]
[OBJECT-COMPUTER.   [computer-name-2
    [MEMORY SIZE integer-1 {WORDS/CHARACTERS/MODULES}]
    [PROGRAM COLLATING  SEQUENCE IS alphabet-name-1].]
[SPECIAL-NAMES.
    [implementor-name-1 IS mnemonic-name-1]...
    [implementor-name-2 IS mnemonic-name-2 [{ON/OFF} STATUS IS
➥condition-name-1]...]...
    [implementor-name-3 [{ON/OFF} STATUS IS condition-name-2]...]...
    [ALPHABET alphabet-name-1 IS
➥{STANDARD-1/STANDARD-2/NATIVE/implementor-name-4/
                                alphabet-specification}]...
    [SYMBOLIC CHARACTERS {{{char-1}...{IS/ARE} {integer-2}...}
➥[IN alphabet-name-2]}]...
    [CLASS class-name IS {literal-1 [{THRU/THROUGH} literal-2]}...]...
    [CURRENCY SIGN IS literal-3]
    [DECIMAL-POINT IS COMMA].]
[INPUT-OUPUT SECTION.
FILE-CONTROL. {file-control-entry}...
[I-O-CONTROL.  [input-output-control-entry]]]
```

A few remarks on the format of the example are appropriate here. Notice that a number of the words are printed in italics. These are "noise" words that are optional and ignored by the compiler. They are allowed, though, and are recommended for the sake of clarity. Now look at the items enclosed in the braces ({ }). Here, a choice of terms is provided, and one of them must be used. Note also that there is only one period at the end of all the optional entries within each paragraph of the CONFIGURATION SECTION. If you use more periods, most compilers will produce error messages.

The SOURCE-COMPUTER specifies on which computer the program is compiled. computer-name-1 is generally a remark entry. If the DEBUGGING MODE clause is present, all lines having a D in column 7 will be compiled as part of the program. If the D is absent, such lines will be treated as remarks. When I used this in the days before interactive debug facilities, I generally placed this clause on a line by itself so it could be activated or turned off easily with an asterisk in column 7 of that one line.

The OBJECT-COMPUTER specifies the computer on which the program will be executed. computer-name-2 is generally a remark entry, but where a compiler can create different object code for different computers, this will indicate to the compiler for which of the possible target machines this program is to be compiled. The MEMORY SIZE clause is a holdover from the time when both computer memory and processor speed were both extremely limited. When smaller sizes were specified, the program would be optimized for speed, but larger sizes also could be specified where it was reasonable to sacrifice speed for the additional memory. The COLLATING SEQUENCE clause is tied to an alphabet name that would need to be defined in the SPECIAL-NAMES paragraph. When specified, it causes all comparisons of character data to be done according to the sequencing of the characters defined for that alphabet. This is used primarily when working with non-English alphabets and data, but it sometimes also comes in handy when dealing with data from both ASCII and EBCDIC environments where the sequencing of the numeric and alphabetic groups of characters differs.

Because the SPECIAL-NAMES paragraph contains a larger number of topics and some of them are used pretty frequently, I'll cover each in a separate paragraph.

implementor-name-1 is a machine-specific name that can be associated here with a COBOL word (mnemonic-name-1) that then can be used in the program. The four COBOL statements the words can be used with are ACCEPT, DISPLAY, SEND, and WRITE. The most common use is to identify special advancing characteristics, such as TOP-OF-PAGE for output (printer) files to be used with the WRITE statement (for example, WRITE record-name AFTER ADVANCING TOP-OF-PAGE). Another use is to specify the device or file to be used as the source or destination (other than the default) for the ACCEPT or DISPLAY statement (for example, ACCEPT data-name FROM mnemonic-name or DISPLAY "HELLO" UPON mnemonic-name). When the COMMUNICATIONS SECTION is used for message handling, the SEND statement also may use a similarly defined mnemonic name.

implementor-name-2 and implementor-name-3 identify binary switches that might be set to "on" or "off" values by the program and also tested by the program. Their value is that they also may be set and tested by the computer hardware or software external to the program. When mnemonic-name-2 is used, the statement SET mnemonic-name-2 TO ON/OFF will establish the specified value. Referencing condition-name-1 or condition-name-2 in an IF (or other conditional statement) will result in the appropriate statements being executed, depending on the value of the switch.

The ALPHABET clause is a means of identifying what character set is to be used for the data processed by the program. When an alphabet-name that is defined here is used in the COLLATING SEQUENCE clause of the OBJECT-COMPUTER (see the preceding example) or in the CODE-SET clause of a FILE DESCRIPTION, the sequence of the characters associated with that character set is used to determine greater and less-than conditions and the SORT/MERGE sequence. For example, if STANDARD-1 (ASCII) is specified here on an IBM mainframe, and the defined alphabet-name then is used in the COLLATING SEQUENCE clause, greater and less-than comparisons on alphanumeric data will be done according to the rules for ASCII instead of IBM's normal EBCDIC rules.

The various designations for ALPHABETs follow. As indicated earlier, STANDARD-1 identifies *American Standard Code of Information Interchange* (ASCII). STANDARD-2 identifies the *International Standards Organization* (ISO) character set. NATIVE indicates that the computer's normal default character set should be used. NATIVE is the default. On IBM mainframes, the default is EBCDIC; on most other machines, it is ASCII. implementor-name-4 allows vendors to establish other character sets for data processing with foreign languages that have different characters than are available with the American brand of English.

The alphabet specification permits programmers to define their own character sets. The format for such a specification follows:

```
{literal-1 [{THRU/THROUGH literal-2}/{ALSO literal-3}...]}...
```

Essentially, you simply list the literal values. The THRU option allows you to specify sequences of values as they are defined in the NATIVE character set. The ALSO clause allows you to "fold" several characters to the same relative position in the new alphabet.

The SYMBOLIC *CHARACTERS* clause was established for environments where lowercase characters cannot be defined in the COBOL program but do exist in the data being processed. The char-1 designation is simply a multiple character name for whatever character is associated with the integer-2 position in the specified alphabet (normally, the NATIVE one would be used). In all likelihood, this designation will be removed with the next COBOL standard.

The CLASS clause allows you to define a group (or groups) of characters that can then be tested for in conditional statements. For example, if CLASS A-VOWEL IS 'A' 'E' 'I' 'O' 'U' is defined in the SPECIAL-NAMES, the statement IF data-name IS A-VOWEL will be true only if the data name references data that consists only of the uppercase characters A, E, I, O, and U. If the literals are numbers, they represent the relative positions

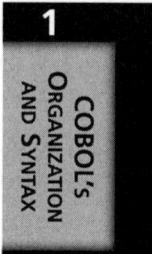

within the NATIVE character set. Otherwise, the literals need to be characters, as shown in the example.

The CURRENCY clause enables you to specify some other character to replace the dollar sign ($) in edited numeric fields. This character cannot be a character that is already defined by COBOL for use in PICTURE clauses.

The DECIMAL-POINT IS COMMA clause reverses the use of periods and commas in edited numeric PICTURE clauses and numeric literals.

As mentioned at the beginning of this section, the INPUT-OUTPUT SECTION is covered in detail in Part II of this book.

The DATA DIVISION

This section is only a brief introduction to the DATA DIVISION. A large portion of this division is covered in the next chapter, and other portions and options are introduced throughout the language chapters of the book as the relevant topics are introduced. The language skeleton follows:

```
[DATA DIVISION.

[FILE SECTION.
[file-description-entry...]
[sort-merge-description-entry...]
[report-file-description-entry]]

[WORKING-STORAGE SECTION.
[data-description-entry..]]

[LINKAGE SECTION.
[data-description-entry...]]

[COMMUNICATION SECTION.
[communication-description-entry...]]

[REPORT SECTION.
[report-description-entry...]]]
```

The FILE SECTION is covered in depth in Part II.

The WORKING-STORAGE SECTION is introduced in this chapter and is covered in more depth in the next chapter. Also, I include additional items in many of the other language chapters. This section, together with the PROCEDURE DIVISION, is where most COBOL programming is done.

The LINKAGE SECTION is covered in depth in Chapter 14.

The COMMUNICATIONS SECTION is covered in Chapter 15, "Specialty Features."

The REPORT SECTION is covered in Chapter 9, "The Report Writer Module."

Notice that all the sections are optional. Those that are present must be in the order indicated. Almost every real program I've seen has a WORKING-STORAGE SECTION. Most also have a FILE SECTION. The LINKAGE SECTION is pretty common but may not be used at all in some organizations. The REPORT SECTION is hardly used at all anymore, although the next COBOL standard currently intends that it be a required part of basic COBOL implementations. I have not seen the COMMUNICATIONS SECTION used other than in special programming situations.

The PROCEDURE DIVISION

There are two formats for the PROCEDURE DIVISION. The first format is by far the most common and is used almost exclusively in the book. The second format provides for declaratives and user-defined sections; these topics are covered in Chapter 15. The two formats follow:

Format 1:

```
[PROCEDURE DIVISION [USING {data-name}...].
{paragraph-name.
    [sentence]...}...]
```

Format 2:

```
[PROCEDURE DIVISION [USING {data-name}...].
[DECLARATIVES.
{section-name SECTION [segment-number].
    USE statement.
[paragraph-name.
    [sentence]...]...}...
 END DECLARATIVES.]
{section name SECTION [segment-number].
[paragraph-name.
    [sentence]...]...}...]
```

Notice the USING data-name clause. This is how a COBOL subprogram or subroutine receives data from the calling program (see Chapter 14). Other than that, most COBOL programs' PROCEDURE DIVISION is one or more paragraphs, each containing one or more sentences. Of course, the trick is to get the right things into the right sentences and to get them in the right order in the right paragraphs.

The next several sections introduce the basic data definitions and verbs of the language.

Introducing the Basic COBOL Program

The remainder of this chapter uses a number of basic examples to introduce the essential requirements for COBOL programs. Although these examples will be basic, I'll use them as stepping stones to elaborate on how things work with COBOL and to define the essential rules of the language. The first program is the very typical Hello There program, shown in Listing 1.1.

LISTING 1.1   BASIC1.

```
IDENTIFICATION DIVISION.
PROGRAM-ID.  Basic1.
PROCEDURE DIVISION.
0000-MAIN.
    DISPLAY 'Hello There.'.
    STOP RUN.
```

Who said COBOL programs must be large? By the way, I don't really need the STOP RUN, and many compilers will create the IDENTIFICATION DIVISION for you, so the program could be even smaller. But several topics need to be covered, so I'll use this as the example.

There are no line numbers with the listing, as shown in the text here. I did that on purpose to make it easier to see the relevant parts of the program. In general, I'll skip line numbers on short examples but use them in the longer ones so that it is easier to find items in the list that the text references. That is really the only purpose for the line numbers in this book. That is also why line numbers often consist of only four digits instead of the COBOL norm of six digits. The programs on the CD-ROM are set up with spaces in the line-number field so that they can be readily referenced by almost any compiler you choose to use.

The Hello There program is included on the CD-ROM as BASIC1. Observe how it is identified and try it out. It's a good way to make sure your compiler and the options are synchronized with what you're doing in the book.

You may receive a compiler error about the nonnumeric literal or the use of the apostrophe ('). This relates to the apostrophe character that delimits the Hello There. literal. Although the current COBOL standard specifies the quote (") as the delimiter for nonnumeric literals, most computers and compilers in the early-to-mid-'70s did not have the quote available in their character set, so the apostrophe was used instead. In order to make things easy for their customers, most vendors will accept either the quote or the apostrophe or provide an option to tell the compiler to use the apostrophe instead. I use the apostrophe because it appears to be the most common in use. If you receive the diagnostic on this program, check your compiler for the option to use the apostrophe instead of the quote. In the worst situation, use the global-change command with your editor to simply change all the apostrophes to quotes.

By definition, a *nonnumeric literal* is any character string surrounded by quote characters. The standard provides that nonnumeric literals can contain up to 160 characters. In most cases, it is best to keep these literals to 50 or so characters so that they will fit on one line. It is easy enough to concatenate, define, or string together these literals; it is easier to deal with them that way than if they span more than one line using the ' - ' continuation character in column 7. You also can use numeric literals, as you'll see later in this chapter.

The first COBOL verb I'll describe is DISPLAY. DISPLAY 'Hello There.'. is the statement, and because it ends with a period, it is also a COBOL sentence. DISPLAY is pretty simple; it causes whatever follows it to be written to the standard system output device. In most cases, this device is your PC or terminal screen. However, in other cases (including IBM mainframes), the device is the default printer device or file (SYSOUT, in the case of IBM). If Hello There. does not appear on your screen, check Part V, "COBOL Databases and Transactions (A Sampling)," and you should be able see what is happening for your specific machine. Because DISPLAY is a very common verb, your compiler documentation or "help" mechanism should readily clarify things.

> **NOTE**
>
> Because of these differences from environment to environment, this book does not rely heavily on DISPLAY as a demonstration tool. I use it in the beginning because it is a simple means of getting started, and the results are readily apparent regardless of whether the results appear on the screen or in the default system output file.

There are some additional options and rules regarding DISPLAY, and I'll expand on them as you proceed through the rest of this chapter.

STOP RUN. is also a statement and sentence. In this case STOP is the verb. This causes the program to terminate execution and control to be returned to the computer's operating system or runtime environment. This is the normal way of terminating the program execution. I indicated above that STOP RUN isn't really required for this example. The reason is that if the *last* program statement is executed without being under some other explicit control mechanism, the program will terminate execution and return control to the operating system or runtime environment. That is exactly what would happen in this example. However, we include the STOP RUN because the explicit termination and return of control is by far the preferred way of doing things. That way we can easily see exactly what will happen.

I'll briefly describe one other form of the STOP verb here. It is the statement STOP literal. In this case, the value of the literal is displayed to the computer operator, and operation of the program is suspended. The program begins execution again with the next statement after the operator completes some implementor-defined action. Although this may seem innocuous enough, especially on a PC, it is definitely no longer the way of doing things on a modern mainframe computer. This form of the STOP verb is being removed from COBOL with the next standard.

Finally, observe 0000-MAIN. This is a paragraph name. If a program has a PROCEDURE DIVISION, a paragraph name is required. Paragraph names are easy to identify, because they begin in area A, are a single word that is not a verb, and end with a period. Although the number at the beginning is not needed, it is a good habit to begin with.

Expanding on the DISPLAY Statement

You can expand the capabilities of DISPLAY in a few ways. One way involves using a number of operands instead of just one. Notice the changes to the example in Listing 1.1 (see Listing 1.2).

LISTING 1.2   BASIC2.

```
IDENTIFICATION DIVISION.
PROGRAM-ID.  Basic2.
PROCEDURE DIVISION.
0000-MAIN.
    DISPLAY 'Hello there,' ' my name is: ' 'Jon'
        ', and '.
    DISPLAY 'my ID number is: '  855.
    STOP RUN.
```

The big difference here is that instead of just one literal, I have listed several of them, one after the other. Although this is a common capability with most new computer languages, it was unique with the original COBOL compilers. It makes the verb very handy for informally showing what is happening in the program. Before online debug facilities became commonly available, this verb was invaluable. It is still commonly used in all environments for showing summary processing totals and other small amounts of information where a full report isn't necessary, but the information is still important for the user or the system-maintenance personnel.

Observe that one of the literals I used is simply the number 855. It is not surrounded by quotes because it is a numeric literal, and they do not have quotes. COBOL can distinguish numeric literals from data names, paragraph names, and other words, because all these others *must* have at least one alphabetic character in them. Although the results don't appear any different here, COBOL does handle numerics differently from nonnumeric (alphanumeric) data, and the difference is important, as you'll see shortly.

If you've compiled and executed the program, you'll also notice that my ID number is: 855 appears on a separate line. This is because these literals are part of a separate DISPLAY statement. In general, each DISPLAY statement terminates the current line and advances to the next one. As you can see, placing the literals on a separate line in the program makes no difference. The maximum number of characters you can display on one line is determined by the compiler and the computer on which you are working. If your output comes directly to the terminal/PC screen, it is probably 80 characters, and if it goes to a printer-type file or device, it is likely more than 80 characters.

An option enables you to tell COBOL to stay on the same line (if there is room): the WITH NO ADVANCING phrase. This phrase was added with the 1985 COBOL Standard, and you can see it added to the example in Listing 1.3 (WITH is optional but is included for clarity).

LISTING 1.3 BASIC3.

```
IDENTIFICATION DIVISION.
PROGRAM-ID.  Basic3.
PROCEDURE DIVISION.
0000-MAIN.
    DISPLAY 'Hello there,' ' my name is: ' 'Jon'
        ', and ' WITH NO ADVANCING.
    DISPLAY 'my ID number is: '  855.
    STOP RUN.
```

Another option is the UPON mnemonic-name phrase, which can be added to the end of the DISPLAY statement. Here, the mnemonic name is defined in the SPECIAL-NAMES paragraph of the ENVIRONMENT DIVISION. It may be used to designate one of any number of devices defined for the specific computer environment for which your program is being compiled. The main operator's CONSOLE, the default PRINTER output device, and the interactive user TERMINAL are examples I've seen used with mainframe and midrange environments. Some other examples are described in Part IV, "COBOL Platforms and Environments," but they all will be specific to the machine/compiler with which you are working.

> **NOTE**
>
> DISPLAY commonly is used to implement full screen-handling output facilities with most PC COBOL compilers, including the demonstration compiler contained on the CD-ROM. The current revision of the next (future) COBOL standard also implements these capabilities in a similar manner, and a copy of it also is included on the CD-ROM. A fairly complete description of how this works is included in Part VI, "COBOL Presentation Interfaces." However, for the first three parts, I'll stay with the current 1985 Standard definition, since that is assured with all implementations (1974 COBOL also works the same, except for WITH NO ADVANCING).

WORKING-STORAGE and Data Definitions (COBOL's Variables)

The WORKING-STORAGE SECTION in the DATA DIVISION is where the program's variables are defined. In COBOL, they're called *data definitions,* and they are kept in this distinct portion of the program's memory. This is a lengthy subject and is covered extensively in the next chapter, but I'll introduce it here so that I can define the basic concepts before presenting all the details. Instead of trying to just explain these items, I've added some data definitions to the sample program, as shown in Listing 1.4; then, I'll discuss them one at a time.

LISTING 1.4 BASIC4.

```
IDENTIFICATION DIVISION.
PROGRAM-ID.  Basic4.
DATA DIVISION.
WORKING-STORAGE SECTION.
77  MY-NAME                 PIC X(10) VALUE 'Jon'.
77  MY-ID-NR                PIC 99999 VALUE 855.
PROCEDURE DIVISION.
0000-MAIN.
    DISPLAY 'Hello there,' ' my name is: ' MY-NAME
        ', and ' WITH NO ADVANCING.
    DISPLAY 'my ID number is: '  MY-ID-NR.
    STOP RUN.
```

Four lines have been added. Two of them (DATA DIVISION and WORKING-STORAGE SEC-TION) were described in "The DATA DIVISION," earlier in this chapter, and simply identify the portion of the program with which you're dealing. The other two lines are the new data-definition entries, which I'll discuss later. Each entry is made up of four distinct parts, and although they may appear fairly obscure at first glance, after you review their makeup, they'll become pretty easy to follow.

The first thing on each line is the 77. This is the level number. It is required, and it must be two digits. In this case, the 77 indicates that the data definition is for a single, independent piece of data that is not inherently related to other data definitions. In other words, when 77 is used, the data cannot be a part of any other data definition, and it cannot include any other data definitions that are subordinate to it. When 77 is used, it must begin in area A.

The next item is the data name—how the data will be referred to throughout the program. The data name is composed of letters (at least one), numbers, and a hyphen, and it must contain 30 characters or fewer. Although you can make up any name you want, good names are important and stressed in COBOL programming. I'll try to show you reasonably good naming practices and conventions by example throughout the book. Each of these data names must be unique (data names cannot be the same as other names defined elsewhere in the program) if the data is to be referenced elsewhere in the program. The data name must begin in area B.

The third part of the data definition is the PICTURE clause, and I'll have several comments on it. It is composed of the designator PIC (or, optionally, PICTURE) and a "picture string." The PICTURE clause is necessary in almost all data definitions and describes the size and composition of the data being defined. (This wasn't the case in the original compilers, for which the complete definition could be derived from other clauses, but these became so cumbersome that most were removed from the standard.)

Notice that `PIC` is indented to the right side of the line. This is a common practice that makes `PIC`s very easy to find and interpret. Although many COBOL teachers will fail you (and most other programmers will get very upset) if you don't indent `PIC`s like this, the compilers and standard don't care at all, and things will work just fine as long as there is at least one space between the `PIC` and the data name.

The two picture strings I use in the example are `X(10)` and `99999`. The `X` in the first case specifies that the data is alphanumeric and can consist of any character in the computer's character set. In addition to letters (upper- and lowercase) and numbers, all the other special characters and other symbols also may be included. The `10` in the parentheses means that the data item is to be 10 characters long. The `9` in the second case means that the data is numeric and that numeric calculations may be done with it. For this reason, such data elements are limited to the numeric digits (many compilers also allow spaces to precede the first digit and convert them to zero automatically, but this is not guaranteed). Observe that the `9` is repeated five times. This means that the number I have defined is five digits long.

You may wonder why the size of the two items was specified in two different ways. I did this simply because they are there. In other words, it demonstrates the two ways of specifying the size of data items in the picture string. I also could have defined the first as `XXXXXXXXXX` and the second as `9(5)`. It is clearer to read the parenthetical form when the number of letters or digits is more than four or five.

NOTE

You may have observed how easy it is to specify the size of your data items—even the numeric ones. In many of the newer languages, you don't have much choice regarding the size of numeric datatypes, and it is difficult to even find out how many digits of accuracy you have. With COBOL, you simply define as many digits as you need—up to 18 digits (15 digits will define up to 9 trillion and also account for the cents).

The final phrase in these data definitions is the `VALUE` clause. It is optional, and you'll likely see it as often as not. This clause defines an initial value for the data item. If it is not there, the initial value is not always predictable, so it is important to ensure that data items in `WORKING-STORAGE` are initialized in some fashion. A number of `PROCEDURE DIVISION` statements also establish values for data items, and it will become more apparent as you go how best to initialize different data in different situations.

Notice how the number of characters (and digits) in the VALUE clauses is less than the number specified in the PICTURE string. COBOL is pretty smart and helpful here. It knows the difference between numeric and alphanumeric data, so it automatically adds the correct number of zeroes to the left of 855 to expand it to 00855 to properly align it to the decimal point. This is called *right-justified* with *zero-fill*. COBOL also knows that we generally add spaces to the right of alphanumeric data, so it will expand "Jon" to "Jon " so it is aligned to the leftmost position in the field. This is called *left-justified* with *space-fill*. This process is covered in greater detail later. In general, though, COBOL is quite carefully designed in this area and makes the assumptions you want in these cases.

Notice how the data names MY-NAME and MY-ID-NR are used in the DISPLAY statements. I've just inserted them in place of the literal value that was there previously. In this case (and many others), the two can be used interchangeably.

Finally, if you haven't compiled and executed this program, go ahead and do so. You'll notice a slight difference in the results. Something like the following will appear:

```
"Hello there, my name is: Jon        , and my ID number is: 00855"
```

Observe the extra spaces after Jon and the extra two zeroes in front of 855. This is because COBOL looks at the size of the *data item* when determining how many characters to display. Even though the results don't look very good here, this is the proper way to handle these fields, and you'll see a variety of ways to eliminate extra spaces and zeroes when you want to (most of these methods are addressed in Chapter 10, "Special Tools for Character Manipulation").

The ACCEPT Statement and Getting Data into the Program

Getting different data values into the program without having to recompile it all the time is the next subject to cover. I'll use the ACCEPT statement for this. Only minor changes to the sample program are needed to accomplish this, as shown in Listing 1.5.

LISTING 1.5   BASIC5.

```
IDENTIFICATION DIVISION.
PROGRAM-ID.  Basic5.
DATA DIVISION.
WORKING-STORAGE SECTION.
77  MY-NAME              PIC X(10) VALUE SPACES.
77  MY-ID-NR             PIC 99999 VALUE ZERO.
PROCEDURE DIVISION.
0000-MAIN.
```

```
    ACCEPT MY-NAME.
    ACCEPT MY-ID-NR.
    DISPLAY 'Hello there,' ' my name is: ' MY-NAME
        ', and ' WITH NO ADVANCING.
    DISPLAY 'my ID number is: '  MY-ID-NR.
    STOP RUN.
```

Before you compile and execute this example, you need to address a few items.

If the results from the previous examples are being shown on a printer or systems output file or device, the ACCEPT statement almost certainly will try to obtain its values from some analogous card image or system input file or device. In the case of IBM, this will be the SYSIN file. Check Part IV or your vendor information if you need more details. Once the source of the data is identified, the two values will need to be placed there either as two separate records or as two fields on the same record but separated by a space. It is worthwhile getting this to work in your normal programming environment, because DISPLAY and ACCEPT provide pretty simple means to control and monitor the operation of the program without a great deal of overhead and no extra software.

If the results from the previous examples appeared on your terminal or PC screen, then chances are when you execute this program, things will just sit and wait. That is because the program is waiting for you to enter some data. Enter up to 10 characters and press Enter. The program will wait again. Now enter a number of up to 5 digits and press Enter again. The resulting message now should appear onscreen, and the program will terminate. The changes shown in Listing 1.6 will make it a bit more apparent what is happening.

LISTING 1.6 BASIC6.

```
IDENTIFICATION DIVISION.
PROGRAM-ID.  Basic6.
DATA DIVISION.
WORKING-STORAGE SECTION.
77  MY-NAME               PIC X(10) VALUE SPACES.
77  MY-ID-NR              PIC 99999 VALUE ZERO.
PROCEDURE DIVISION.
0000-MAIN.
    DISPLAY 'Enter Your Name Please: '.
    ACCEPT MY-NAME.
    DISPLAY 'Enter Your ID Number Please: '.
    ACCEPT MY-ID-NR.
    DISPLAY 'Hello there,' ' my name is: ' MY-NAME
        ', and ' WITH NO ADVANCING.
    DISPLAY 'my ID number is: '  MY-ID-NR.
    STOP RUN.
```

There are only two real changes to the program. One is the insertion of the ACCEPT statements, and the other is the change to the VALUE clauses of the data definitions. The ACCEPT statements are pretty self-explanatory. Data is transferred from the input device (your keyboard or system input file) to the named data item.

The VALUE clause requires some explanation. The original values were removed, because they aren't needed; they will be replaced by whatever you enter. The SPACES and ZERO clear the fields to the appropriate initial values. SPACES and ZERO are termed *figurative constants*. The term *figurative* is used because their size and form is not constant but is whatever is appropriate to the field with which they are used. Hence, SPACES will become 10 blank characters because of the size of the MY-NAME field. ZERO will set the number MY-ID-NR to algebraic zero, which in this case, will clear all five digits to zero. These will commonly be used throughout the book. The term SPACE can be used interchangeably with SPACES and ZEROS, and ZEROES can be used interchangeably with ZERO.

You need to be careful when entering numeric data here because it is the responsibility of the program to ensure that input data is in the proper form. This editing of data is addressed in more detail in later chapters.

You also may observe some peculiarities when entering data here. If you enter all 10 characters for a name, for example, they may be taken and the line requesting the ID number displayed without your pressing Enter. This is because ACCEPT was designed for machine-unique input devices and therefore left a lot up to the implementor's interpretation. In general, such peculiarities will not cause a problem once you get used to them, and they won't have a significant impact on how your program operates.

The only data-entry option with ACCEPT is the FROM mnemonic-name phrase, which can be added to the end of the ACCEPT statement. Here, mnemonic-name is defined in the SPECIAL-NAMES paragraph of the ENVIRONMENT DIVISION. It may be used to designate one of any number of devices that may be defined for the specific computer environment for which your program is being compiled. The main operator's CONSOLE, the default system input device, and the interactive user TERMINAL are examples I've seen used with mainframe and midrange environments. Some others are described in Part IV, but they all will be specific to the machine/compiler you are using.

NOTE

ACCEPT commonly is used to implement full screen-handling input facilities with most PC COBOL compilers, including the demonstration compiler contained on the CD-ROM. The current revision of the future COBOL standard also implements these capabilities in a similar manner, and a copy of it also is included on the CD-ROM. A fairly complete description of how this works is included in Part VI. However, for Parts I through III, I'll stay with the current 1985 Standard definition, since that is assured with all implementations (1974 COBOL also works the same).

Obtaining Date Values Using ACCEPT

A seemingly unrelated option with ACCEPT is that it can be used to obtain current date and time information from your system. Although there is no example for this option right here, it is included in a variety of other examples throughout the book. Here is the format:

```
ACCEPT data-name FROM {DATE/DAY/DAY-OF-WEEK/TIME}
```

If DATE is specified, six digits are transferred to the data-name, and they represent the two-digit year, the two-digit month, and the two-digit day of the month. Hence, if the current date is February 3, 1998, the value 980203 will transferred to the data-name.

If DAY is specified, five digits will be transferred, and they will represent the two-digit year and the 3-digit day of the year. This is commonly called the *Julian date.* So if the current date is February 3, 1998, the value 98034 will be transferred.

If DAY-OF-WEEK is specified, one digit is transferred that represents the day of the week. Here, 1 represents Monday, 2 represents Tuesday, and so on, through 7, which represents Sunday. This option is *not* available with 1974 Standard COBOL.

If TIME is specified, eight digits are transferred, and they represent the time since midnight as the two-digit hour, two-digit minute, two-digit second, and two-digit hundredths of a second. Hence, 1:25 and 34.43 seconds p.m. would be transferred as 13253443. This commonly is termed *military time.* Midnight would be all zeroes, and the split second before midnight would be 23595999.

You've probably noticed that there is no facility here to determine the current century. This problem will be remedied with the new standard that currently is scheduled to become official in late 2000 or early 2001. However, this information also can be obtained with the intrinsic-function feature discussed in Chapter 13, "Intrinsic Functions with Emphasis on the Year 2000," and is available with all compilers containing the 1989 COBOL Addendum. This subject is discussed at much greater length in Part VIII, "Addressing the Year 2000 Issues."

Looping in COBOL, a Few More Statements, and Another Example

The purpose of this section and the example in Listing 1.7 is to present enough COBOL statements and concepts to provide a framework that will be needed for the examples in the next few chapters. I will review and explain the new statements, but I won't necessarily define them in their entirety. Hence, this section is directed primarily to experienced programmers who simply don't have a COBOL background yet.

LISTING 1.7   BASIC7.

```
IDENTIFICATION DIVISION.
PROGRAM-ID.  Basic7.
DATA DIVISION.
WORKING-STORAGE SECTION.
77  TOTAL-VALUE              PIC 99999 VALUE ZERO.
77  INPUT-VALUE              PIC 99999 VALUE ZERO.
PROCEDURE DIVISION.
0000-MAIN.
    PERFORM 0100-LOOP
        UNTIL INPUT-VALUE = 99999.
    DISPLAY 'The Total is: ' TOTAL-VALUE.
    STOP RUN.
0100-LOOP.
    DISPLAY 'Enter an Amount to Add (or 99999 if Done): '.
    ACCEPT INPUT-VALUE.
    IF INPUT-VALUE NOT NUMERIC
        DISPLAY 'Amount is NOT a Number, Re-enter'
        MOVE ZERO TO INPUT-VALUE.
    IF INPUT-VALUE NOT = 99999
        ADD INPUT-VALUE TO TOTAL-VALUE
        MOVE ZERO TO INPUT-VALUE.
```

The first statement in the program is the basic PERFORM statement. In general, it causes the statements in the identified paragraph (0100-LOOP) to be executed in order; then, after the last one is completed, control is passed to the statement following the PERFORM statement. With the UNTIL clause, the condition following it (INPUT-VALUE = 99999) is evaluated *before* the designated paragraph is PERFORMed. If this condition were true, the statements in the designated paragraph are not executed, and control passes to the statement following the PERFORM statement. If the condition is not true, the statements in the designated paragraph are executed. *Then the condition is evaluated again.* If the condition is still not true, the statements in the designated paragraph are executed again. In this manner, the statements in the designated paragraph will be executed again and again until the condition finally becomes true. When that happens, control will pass to the next statement (DISPLAY 'The Total is: ' TOTAL-VALUE.). This program, that will be immediately followed by the STOP RUN, will terminate the program execution.

There are several statements in 0100-LOOP to review. I'll cover the easiest first: the statement MOVE ZERO TO INPUT-VALUE. It does exactly what it implies—that's one of the nice things about COBOL. INPUT-VALUE is set to the algebraic value of zero. By the way, MOVE is the basic statement for moving data around in the COBOL program, and as such, it is the most commonly used statement in the language. Although there are not many options to the statement, there are a number of rules and implications involved in transferring data (these are covered in the next chapter). In this case, everything will happen exactly as you would want and expect.

The statement ADD INPUT-VALUE TO TOTAL-VALUE is one of the four basic arithmetic statements available in COBOL (SUBTRACT, MULTIPLY, and DIVIDE are the obvious other ones). Here, the value of INPUT-VALUE is added to the existing value of TOTAL-VALUE, and the new result is placed back in TOTAL-VALUE. A number of options are available with the arithmetic statements, and I'll cover them in the next few chapters. (By the way, there is also a COMPUTE statement that acts very similar to the algebraic assignment statements used in many other languages.)

There are two IF statements in this program, and each is a little different. There are several things I need to say about these statements, and that will barely scratch the surface of all the material to be covered on them.

The first thing to notice is that each of the IF statements is followed by two other statements; the first of the two is *not* followed by a period, but the second one is. In COBOL, the statements following the IF condition are executed if the condition is true, and all the statements following the condition are executed until one of several "terminators" is reached. The period is one of those terminators. So all the statements between the IF conditional and the next period will be executed when the statement is true. None of them will be executed if the statement is not true. There is a great deal to cover regarding the period as a conditional terminator, and that will be done in Chapter 3. However, it is still the most common terminator for conditionals in COBOL and pretty basic, so I'll use it for the time being.

Notice that the two statements following the IF conditional that will be executed if it is true are indented. This has absolutely no effect on the way the program operates; however, it sure makes it a lot easier for us human beings to follow. I will follow this practice throughout the book.

The first IF conditional is INPUT-VALUE NOT NUMERIC. NUMERIC is a class condition provided by COBOL. The data item being evaluated is numeric if it is a proper algebraic number—in other words, all the digits are numeric values between zero and 9. NOT simply reverses the logic. So, in this case, INPUT-VALUE NOT NUMERIC is true if something besides a number has been entered for one of the digits. Should this happen, the following two statements will be executed: the message will be DISPLAYed, and ZERO will be MOVEed to INPUT-VALUE so that the program doesn't ADD bad data to the TOTAL-VALUE.

The second conditional is INPUT-VALUE NOT = 99999. So, when INPUT-VALUE is NOT 99999, the next two statements will be executed: INPUT-VALUE will be ADDed to TOTAL-VALUE, and ZERO will be MOVEed to INPUT-VALUE (in preparation for the ACCEPT statement during the next execution of the statements in this paragraph because of the PERFORM loop). If INPUT-VALUE does = 99999, these statements will not be executed.

You may have noticed the NOT in both conditionals. Some programmers are very opposed to this and avoid the NOT at all costs because they feel it is negative reasoning. Although I agree in principle, I also believe that programming should be done in the simplest and most direct manner. And that does imply using NOT from time to time. Additional discussion of the alternatives here is presented in Chapter 3.

This sample program has been constructed to work pretty easily, regardless of how ACCEPT is handled. Just make sure that the last number has the value 99999.

Although the introduction of the new statements with this last sample program has been very brief, it should provide enough background for the next few chapters so that I can cover and illustrate the material with some reasonable (and hopefully interesting) examples.

Summary

This first chapter presented the framework for COBOL programs. I covered the organization of the program as well as the format of its statements and other entries. For those programmers who haven't worked with COBOL, some samples also were presented to show how things fit together and function.

The next chapter will get into defining data in COBOL. There is a lot of material there, but there are options available, and many of them are not possible with other languages.

Defining Data and Specifying Its Attributes

IN THIS CHAPTER

This chapter covers defining and describing data in COBOL. Specifically, you'll examine the WORKING-STORAGE SECTION where the program variables and constants are kept. Data is also defined here and in the other sections of the DATA DIVISION. That will be covered in later chapters, which deal with the topics that those sections support. The foundation concepts and approaches I cover here will also apply to those sections.

The way data is described in COBOL is unique among the programming languages. Although it seems cumbersome and complex at times, it also provides a flexibility and control over the data that isn't available with other languages. Perhaps the greatest similarities are to database definitions and some of the fourth-generation or rules-based languages.

Level Numbers and Structure Hierarchy

Data definition was introduced in the preceding chapter using the 77 level to define each item of data. You'll recall that the 77 specifies that the data item being defined is separate and independent (definition-wise) from the other data definitions.

With level numbers ranging between 01 and 49, this is not the case. They allow you to define the hierarchical structure of the data in outline form. Essentially, the lower the value of the level number, the higher it is in the hierarchy. So, a data item defined with level number 01 will "contain" all the data defined with the larger-level numbers that follow it. Data definition continues downward in this outline fashion until a definition with the same or a smaller-level number appears. That completes the previous definition and begins the new one.

Because 01 is the smallest-level number, it defines the highest-level structure or record in WORKING-STORAGE. Each 01 level definition is generally independent and separate from all the others in WORKING-STORAGE. (The REDEFINES clause provides the single exception and is covered later.) As an extension to the rule, the following is also true.

> **NOTE**
>
> An 01 level definition that has its own PICTURE clause and nothing else defined at a lower level in the hierarchy is exactly equivalent to a 77 level definition.

Manipulating Dates and Times with Structure Definitions

The short example in Listing 2.1 demonstrates how hierarchical structure works and also provides a background to discuss some implications of this form of data definition. I'll do some basic date manipulation because dates are easy to relate to and they illustrate the material pretty well.

LISTING 2.1 DATES1.

```
IDENTIFICATION DIVISION.
PROGRAM-ID.  Dates1.
DATA DIVISION.
WORKING-STORAGE SECTION.
01   THIS-DATE.
     05   THIS-YEAR          PIC XX.
     05   THIS-MONTH         PIC XX.
     05   THIS-DAY           PIC XX.

01   THIS-TIME.
     05   THIS-HOUR          PIC 99.
     05   THIS-MINUTE        PIC XX.
     05   THIS-SECOND        PIC XX.
     05   THIS-SEC-FRACT     PIC XX.
01   FORMAT-TIME.
     05   FORMAT-HOUR        PIC 99.
     05   FILLER             PIC X VALUE ':'.
     05   FORMAT-MINUTE      PIC XX.
     05                      PIC X VALUE ':'.
     05   FORMAT-SECOND      PIC XX.
     05   FILLER             PIC X VALUE '.'.
     05   FORMAT-SEC-FRACT   PIC XX.
     05   FORMAT-AM-PM       PIC XXX VALUE ' AM'.

01   DAY-OF-YEAR-INFO.
     05   THIS-DAY-OF-YEAR.
          10   THIS-DOY-YEAR      PIC 99.
          10   THIS-DOY-DAY       PIC XXX.
     05   FORMAT-DAY-OF-YEAR.
          10   FORMAT-CENTURY     PIC XX VALUE '20'.
          10   FORMAT-DOY-YEAR    PIC 99.
          10   FILLER             PIC X VALUE '.'.
          10   FORMAT-DOY-DAY     PIC XXX.

PROCEDURE DIVISION.
0000-MAIN.
     ACCEPT THIS-DATE       FROM DATE.
     ACCEPT THIS-TIME       FROM TIME.
```

continues

LISTING 2.1 CONTINUED

```
ACCEPT THIS-DAY-OF-YEAR FROM DAY.

MOVE THIS-HOUR          TO FORMAT-HOUR.
MOVE THIS-MINUTE        TO FORMAT-MINUTE.
MOVE THIS-SECOND        TO FORMAT-SECOND.
MOVE THIS-SEC-FRACT     TO FORMAT-SEC-FRACT.
IF FORMAT-HOUR > 11
    MOVE ' PM'          TO FORMAT-AM-PM.
IF FORMAT-HOUR = ZERO
    MOVE 12             TO FORMAT-HOUR.
IF FORMAT-HOUR > 12
    SUBTRACT 12         FROM FORMAT-HOUR.

MOVE THIS-DOY-YEAR      TO FORMAT-DOY-YEAR.
MOVE THIS-DOY-DAY       TO FORMAT-DOY-DAY.
IF FORMAT-DOY-YEAR > 90
    MOVE '19'           TO FORMAT-CENTURY.

DISPLAY 'TODAY IS ' THIS-MONTH '/' THIS-DAY '/'
    THIS-YEAR ' ' FORMAT-TIME.
DISPLAY '  (THE DAY OF YEAR IS: '
    FORMAT-DAY-OF-YEAR ')'.

STOP RUN.
```

First, notice how I'm handling the two dates and the time differently. I did this to illustrate some of the different features of structure definition; you normally wouldn't do this in a regular program. That is also why I have more lines of code than most programs have for date manipulation. There are also many other things you can do with dates and other ways of doing them. You'll see some of them as you proceed.

Observe how the level numbers increase in value as the definition goes deeper into the structure (the 05s are contained in the 01s, and the 10s are contained in the 05s). The fact that I've used 01, 05, and 10 is a matter of convention, and it is pretty uniform. We also could have used 01, 03, 06, or any other variety of schemes. The important thing is that the first/highest level is 01 and that you leave some gap between the succeeding lower levels. This gap allows you to insert level numbers if necessary during debugging or program maintenance without redoing the whole structure. The smartest way is to use the 01, 05, 10, ... scheme because it works well and has become a de facto standard. Don't worry about running out of numbers because you have all the way up to 49, and level numbers don't go beyond 25 or maybe 30.

Each of the lower levels is indented. This is also a convention. COBOL doesn't care, but you and I sure need it to help see how the structure is laid out.

Notice that wherever a data definition has a lower-level definition below it, the higher-level definition does *not* have a PICTURE clause. *This is required.* These higher-level definitions are called *group levels* because they contain a group of one or more lower-level data items. The lowest-level definitions that have the PICTURE clause are called *elementary levels* or *elementary items*. The elementary-level definitions *must* have a PICTURE clause.

COBOL determines the definition of all group levels, and for most definitions, the algorithm is pretty simple. First, a group level is *always* treated as alphanumeric data (characters). You cannot add, subtract, or do other arithmetic using a group level. The size of the group level is the total of the number of characters required by each of the elementary levels subordinate to it. So, if you could specify a PICTURE for FORMAT-DAY-OF-YEAR, it would be PIC X(8) (2 characters in FORMAT-CENTURY + 2 digits in FORMAT-DOY-YEAR + 1 character for the FILLER item + 3 characters for FORMAT-DOY-DAY). The calculation gets a bit more complicated with some of the special data definitions, but the principle remains the same. Also, in almost all cases, you don't even have to worry about it because COBOL does the correct calculations for you.

Notice that you can transfer data to the group levels (the ACCEPT statements), and you can process the data from the group level (the DISPLAY statements) in the same manner that you do the elementary items. Just remember that when you do, it is treated as alphanumeric data equivalent to one alphanumeric elementary item. You can include a VALUE clause for a group level, and it will be handled in the manner just described. If you do use the VALUE clause at the group level, it cannot be used with the subordinate elementary levels because that would result in an obvious conflict.

Observe the word that appears in several of the data definitions: FILLER. The intent here is as a placeholder where you need to define some data in the structure but *do not* intend to reference it as an elementary item anywhere else in the program. This is exactly what FILLER does. In the example, I use FILLER to set up constant data (such as the : and .) to help make the displays easier to read. You'll see FILLER used as a placeholder throughout just about every COBOL program ever written. Notice, though, that I've omitted it from the definition right after the FORMAT-MINUTE item in FORMAT-TIME. This also is okay. Such definitions are allowed beginning with the 1985 Standard. You probably won't see this very much because most programmers still use FILLER, as it is more explicit.

In several places, I defined the elementary items as numeric (PIC 99) instead of alphanumeric (FORMAT-HOUR and FORMAT-DOY-YEAR). These are cases in which I needed to do arithmetic with the data. In one case, I needed to subtract a 12 from the value, and in the other case, I wanted to do a numeric comparison instead of an alphanumeric comparison.

Other parts of the date are defined as alphanumeric (PIC XX). This implies that the data is stored the same with either definition but that it is just treated or viewed differently because of the definition. That is exactly the case. This provides a lot of flexibility in handling different data, and the compilers have become quite efficient in doing arithmetic on numeric-character data. However, you need to be very careful when defining data as numeric because if something besides a number gets into such an item and the program attempts to treat it as a number, bad results will occur. In this case, you don't have to worry because the date information is coming from the system and is assured to be formatted properly. You'll learn more about numeric data in "Dealing With Numeric Information in COBOL," later in this chapter.

The SUBTRACT statement is new here, but it works very similar to ADD. Here, 12 is subtracted from the value of FORMAT-HOUR, and the results are stored back in FORMAT-HOUR. Additional details and options are discussed later.

A Few Comments on Program Style

Notice the term DOY in some of the definitions under DAY-OF-YEAR-INFO. If you haven't guessed, this is short for *day of year.* In spite of what some people may say, COBOL programmers don't like to make all data names as close to 30 characters as possible. This is an example of how items are often abbreviated so that their size is manageable but the full meaning can readily be determined.

The program includes a fair number of blank lines; they're there on purpose. Notice how these blank lines tend to separate and group the data definitions and statements. For me, this makes the program a lot easier to read and follow, and it doesn't cost anything. Notice also how all the related statements are kept together. Those statements dealing with each of the dates are grouped, and so are those dealing with the time. This is just as important. Although it doesn't seem like a big deal in a small program like this, grouping such as this becomes much more important (and more difficult) in larger, more complex programs.

If you look at the definitions for THIS-TIME and FORMAT-TIME, you'll see that each is defined as an independent 01 level. On the other hand, THIS-DAY-OF-YEAR and FORMAT-DAY-OF-YEAR are each 05 group-level definitions under the 01 level DAY-OF-YEAR-INFO. Each definition will produce the desired results. The way in which you group similar data together is a matter of style. The point to stress is that in both cases, the definitions contain related data and therefore should be defined near each other.

Finally, observe how the objects in MOVE, ACCEPT, and SUBTRACT statements are indented to the right of the page. This is not nearly as common as indenting the PIC clause. I've begun doing it when a lot of data-manipulation is involved because it helps me easily check off all the data items that need to be handled. You'll see this style in many examples in the book, but certainly not everywhere.

The REDEFINES Clause

As a means of introducing the REDEFINES, I'll change my sample program so that it includes the century when it displays the current date and also displays the value of the next month. As you'll notice in Listing 2.2, the changes are highlighted in bold.

LISTING 2.2 DATES2.

```
IDENTIFICATION DIVISION.
PROGRAM-ID.  Dates2.
DATA DIVISION.
WORKING-STORAGE SECTION.
01   THIS-DATE.
     05   THIS-YEAR           PIC 99.
     05   THIS-MONTH          PIC XX.
     05   THIS-DAY            PIC XX.
01   FORMAT-MONTH-AND-YEAR.
     05   FORMAT-MAY-MONTH.
          10   FORMAT-MAY-MONTH-NUM PIC 99.
     05   FILLER              PIC X VALUE '/'.
     05   FORMAT-4DIG-YEAR-AN.
          10   FORMAT-MAY-CENT    PIC XX VALUE '20'.
          10   FORMAT-MAY-YEAR    PIC 99.
     05   FORMAT-4DIG-YEAR REDEFINES FORMAT-4DIG-YEAR-AN
                              PIC 9999.


01   THIS-TIME.
     05   THIS-HOUR           PIC 99.
     05   THIS-MINUTE         PIC XX.
     05   THIS-SECOND         PIC XX.
     05   THIS-SEC-FRACT      PIC XX.
01   FORMAT-TIME.
     05   FORMAT-HOUR         PIC 99.
     05   FILLER              PIC X VALUE ':'.
     05   FORMAT-MINUTE       PIC XX.
     05                       PIC X VALUE ':'.
     05   FORMAT-SECOND       PIC XX.
     05   FILLER              PIC X VALUE '.'.
     05   FORMAT-SEC-FRACT    PIC XX.
     05   FORMAT-AM-PM        PIC XXX VALUE ' AM'.

01   DAY-OF-YEAR-INFO.
     05   THIS-DAY-OF-YEAR.
          10   THIS-DOY-YEAR  PIC 99.
          10   THIS-DOY-DAY   PIC XXX.
```

continues

LISTING 2.2 CONTINUED

```
  05  FORMAT-DAY-OF-YEAR.
      10  FORMAT-CENTURY      PIC XX VALUE '20'.
      10  FORMAT-DOY-YEAR     PIC 99.
      10  FILLER             PIC X VALUE '.'.
      10  FORMAT-DOY-DAY      PIC XXX.

PROCEDURE DIVISION.
0000-MAIN.
    ACCEPT THIS-DATE        FROM DATE.
    ACCEPT THIS-TIME        FROM TIME.
    ACCEPT THIS-DAY-OF-YEAR FROM DAY.

    MOVE THIS-MONTH         TO FORMAT-MAY-MONTH.
    MOVE THIS-YEAR          TO FORMAT-MAY-YEAR.
    IF FORMAT-MAY-YEAR > 90
        MOVE '19'           TO FORMAT-MAY-CENT.

    MOVE THIS-HOUR          TO FORMAT-HOUR.
    MOVE THIS-MINUTE        TO FORMAT-MINUTE.
    MOVE THIS-SECOND        TO FORMAT-SECOND.
    MOVE THIS-SEC-FRACT     TO FORMAT-SEC-FRACT.
    IF FORMAT-HOUR > 11
        MOVE ' PM'          TO FORMAT-AM-PM.
    IF FORMAT-HOUR = ZERO
        MOVE 12             TO FORMAT-HOUR.
    IF FORMAT-HOUR > 12
        SUBTRACT 12         FROM FORMAT-HOUR.

    MOVE THIS-DOY-YEAR      TO FORMAT-DOY-YEAR.
    MOVE THIS-DOY-DAY       TO FORMAT-DOY-DAY.
    IF FORMAT-DOY-YEAR > 90
        MOVE '19'           TO FORMAT-CENTURY.

    DISPLAY 'TODAY IS ' THIS-MONTH '/' THIS-DAY '/'
        FORMAT-4DIG-YEAR-AN ' ' FORMAT-TIME.
    DISPLAY '  (THE DAY OF YEAR IS: '
        FORMAT-DAY-OF-YEAR ')'.

    ADD 1                   TO FORMAT-MAY-MONTH-NUM.
    IF FORMAT-MAY-MONTH-NUM > 12
        MOVE 1              TO FORMAT-MAY-MONTH-NUM
        ADD 1               TO FORMAT-4DIG-YEAR.

    DISPLAY '   NEXT MONTH IS: ' FORMAT-MONTH-AND-YEAR.

STOP RUN.
```

I've added a new data definition as `FORMAT-MONTH-AND-YEAR`. Examine the `FORMAT-4DIG-YEAR-AN` defined below that. It is set up as a group level so that you can piece together the century and the year. This is done with the new code beginning five lines after the start of the `PROCEDURE DIVISION`. But, when you determine the next month in the new code at the end of the program, you will need to be able to add 1 to this four-digit year when the current month is December and the next month is January of the following year. You can't have `FORMAT-4DIG-YEAR-AN` defined as a number because it is a group level and therefore must be alphanumeric. The `REDEFINES` clause in the definition of `FORMAT-4DIG-YEAR` enables you to solve this problem quite nicely.

`REDEFINES` essentially says that the definition for the subject of the clause (`FORMAT-4DIG-YEAR`) will *redescribe the same computer memory* that was previously defined by the object of the clause (`FORMAT-4DIG-YEAR-AN`). In this case, the data is now redescribed as `PIC 9999`, so that you can `ADD` to it. The computer's memory will still have the same values in it. But if the current year is 1998 in the first definition, it is treated as two characters for `FORMAT-MAY-CENT`, with a value of 19, and two digits with name `FORMAT-MAY-YEAR` and a value of 98. The `REDEFINE` name `FORMAT-4DIG-YEAR` treats these values as a four-digit number with a value of 1998.

Several rules and remarks pertain to the `REDEFINES` clause.

Observe that both the subject and the object in `REDEFINES` have the same level number (`05`). This is required for `REDEFINES`.

Observe also that no equal or higher-ranking (smaller-value) level numbers are between the definition of the object of `REDEFINES` and the definition with the `REDEFINES` clause. In other words, the `REDEFINES` description must appear right after the original description.

You can have a whole series of `REDEFINES` definitions if you need them, but they must all appear after each other, and the original defining data name must be the object for all of the definitions.

The `REDEFINES` definition can be a group level as well as an elementary item (as in the example).

The `REDEFINING` description *cannot* contain any `VALUE` clauses. Any initializing `VALUE`s must be specified in the original definition. This makes sense because the area of memory has already been defined; `REDEFINES` simply provides another viewpoint for it.

As you can see from the example, `REDEFINES` is not limited to `01` or the highest-structure level. This is not the case for analogous constructs in some other languages.

The `REDEFINES` definitions do not all need to be the same size. COBOL will define sufficient memory for the largest and align the others using its normal alignment rules.

Note that with the 1974 Standard, no REDEFINES definitions could be larger than the original definition.

A cautionary note is needed here. In the first days of COBOL, use of REDEFINES was very widespread, and it often was used simply as a means of reusing and therefore saving computer memory. This made for some very confusing programs. Fortunately, programmers have learned this, and the clause is currently used in a limited but very sensible manner. The clause is used in a number of problems later in this book where appropriate.

> **NOTE**
>
> Many programmers use REDEFINES whenever data must be treated as numeric in one place in the program and as alphanumeric somewhere else. In most cases, this is *not* required. Remember that a group level is by definition alphanumeric, and then look at the new definitions for FORMAT-MAY-MONTH and FORMAT-MAY-MONTH-NUM in Listing 2.2. The first is a group level (alphanumeric) containing only the second, which is defined as a number. This structure does exactly what is required but without the REDEFINES. Note also that such a structure is not possible for FORMAT-4DIG-YEAR, since it contains more than one subordinate item.

Dealing with Numeric Information in COBOL

With most modern languages, when you deal with numbers, you get a choice of integer (large, small, and sometimes very large) or floating point, where you can have 30 or 40 assumed positions before or after the decimal point, but you only have 8 or 10 digits that have actual numbers. Accountants, auditors, and IRS agents tend to want something more. They want to deal with billions or trillions of dollars, but they also want to account for them to the penny. COBOL has always been able to deal with this very nicely because it treats numbers very differently.

As you saw briefly in the preceding chapter, COBOL enables programmers to specify the number of digits required (up to 18), which provides a great deal of flexibility. However, the downside is that things are handled differently, and in some cases, more understanding and work are required on the part of the programmer. There are also a few items left over from the ancient days, and they can be a real pain on the few occasions when you have to deal with them.

Fortunately, most of the requirements make pretty good sense. I'll cover that topic first and then also review the idiosyncrasies that many COBOL programmers have to tackle.

Numeric PICTURE Clauses, Numeric Literals, and VALUE Clauses

As you saw in at the end of the preceding chapter, the digit 9 in the PICTURE clause is what describes data as being numeric, and the number of 9s specifies the number of digits the number contains. The number of digits can also be indicated by following a single 9 by the count in parentheses. For example, PIC 9(6) and PIC 999999 both represent a six-digit numeric integer. Three other characters can be used in arithmetic numeric PICTURE clauses. Note that I specified *arithmetic* here. There is a whole other group of numeric PICTURE clauses that are termed numeric *edited,* and they are very different because you can't do arithmetic with them. You'll look at these later in the chapter. Here are the three PICTURE-clause characters:

V   This character specifies the "assumed" decimal point in numeric data. The V can obviously occur only once in the PICTURE clause. For example, PIC 9999V999 describes a number with four digits before the decimal point and three digits after it. You also can specify PIC 9(6)V9(5), which describes a number having six digits before the decimal point and five digits after it. The total number of digits is still limited to 18, so if you need to support 15 digits of accuracy in front of the decimal point, you can define only three digits after it. Because many COBOL systems deal with financial data, you'll often see clauses like PIC 9(7)V99 or PIC 9(11)V99. That is how dollars and cents normally are described. The number of digits before the assumed decimal point often indicates how large (or optimistic) the company is.

     If you omit the V from a PICTURE clause, COBOL assumes that the decimal point is after the last digit to the right. This is what you would want because that is how an integer is defined and that is what you would assume in such a case. Thus, the examples to this point have dealt with integer data.

     I mentioned that the decimal point is assumed, and that is necessary to know. COBOL will keep things lined up as long as you properly define where this assumed decimal point is. Nothing needs to be placed in the number itself to tell where the decimal point is; it is the PICTURE clause that determines it. This also means that the V does not take up any space when determining the size of the data element.

S   This character specifies that the number is signed and may have positive or negative values. The numbers used in the examples to this point did not have the S in the PICTURE clause and so could not have dealt with negative numbers. When used, the S must be the first character in the clause, and it can occur only once in the clause. Unless specified differently in the SIGN clause (which I'll get to shortly), the sign information does not take up any additional space in the data definition. You must deal with a few peculiarities because of this, and I'll cover that also in the section on signed data. As a result, a number with the PICTURE clause S9(8)V99 will take up 10 character positions just like one defined as 9(10). This information is important in determining record sizes.

P   This character defines decimal-scaling positions to the left or right of the decimal point. A P is specified for each scaling position desired. It allows you to define larger numbers of decimal positions without wasting memory or disk on them. This feature is pretty limited because the total number of scaling positions plus regular digits is still limited to 18. If you define a PIC 999PPPPP, for example, then only the three digits are defined in memory, and the field only requires three characters. However, whenever an arithmetic operation is done, the value is converted to nnn00000 (where nnn is the value in the defined field) before the operation, and the five low-order digits are dropped when the value is placed back in the data field. Similarly, you can define PIC VPPPPP999 so that .00000nnn is used in calculations but only the nnn is kept in the data field. The P is one of those items that has been available in COBOL for many years but is hardly, if ever, used.

In addition to the SIGN clause I alluded to, there is also the USAGE clause, which has a bearing on how numeric data is handled. I'll also cover that a bit later.

There is one other item to cover here that is related to the PICTURE clause, and that is the VALUE clause. This will also confirm any remaining details regarding the use of numeric literals because that is what is required for the VALUE clause. To this point, only numeric digits have been used, but I can expand on that a little. The minus sign (-) can be used as the first character of a numeric literal to indicate that its value is negative. This applies only if the related data item is signed. Of course, a numeric literal without the sign is assumed to be positive. The decimal point (.) can also be included in a numeric literal; it can't be the last character of a numeric literal, though. Such a character is treated as the period ending the sentence or entry. This does not really have an effect, though, because a numeric literal without a decimal point is treated as an integer value with the assumed decimal point just after the rightmost position.

The SIGN Clause and Signed Digits

In the preceding section, you learned that, by default, the sign information is stored with the data but does not take up additional storage. The Standard allows the computer and/or compiler vendor to determine exactly how the information is stored. In most situations, this works quite well, but when handling input data or transferring data between computers, something else is often needed. The SIGN clause provides that. It can be included with the PICTURE clause in the data definition, as shown in this example:

```
[SIGN IS] {LEADING/TRAILING} [SEPARATE CHARACTER]
```

An example where this might be used follows:

```
05   INPUT-NUMBER          PIC S9(5)V99 SIGN LEADING SEPARATE.
```

The term LEADING specifies that the sign will be at the beginning of the data item. TRAILING means that it will be at the end, and that is the default. The term SEPARATE means that instead of the sign being stored as an internal part of the data item, it is to be stored as a separate character, and that character will have the value - if the value is negative and + or blank if the value is positive. In the example, a value of -123.5 will be represented as -0012350, and a value of 100 will be +0010000. Note that eight characters are required instead of the seven that would be needed without the term SEPARATE.

As implied earlier, when the SIGN clause is not used, the sign information is carried as part of the low order or rightmost digit in the data item. If a programmer only has to look at the reports produced by the programs, this might not be too important. Unfortunately, you often do have to look at data as it is stored internally, so sometimes it is necessary to decipher the sign digits. Although COBOL leaves the specific coding up to the vendor, many follow the *sign-over-punch* encoding scheme.

This scheme goes back to ancient times when a lot of data was stored or read into the computer from punched cards. Here a separate column was used for each digit, and a row was designated for each of the values 0 through 9. There were also three extra rows at the top of the card. If one of these rows was punched in addition to the row corresponding to the digit value, then a *minus-over-punch* value was indicated. Another of the top rows implied a *positive-over-punch* value. Hence the term *over-punch*. These card-punch combinations also corresponded to character values if they were interpreted as alphabetic instead of numeric, so there was a defined relationship between the characters and the sign-over-punch values. Because there was a lot of overlap between punched card equipment and computers in those days, this coding scheme managed to migrate to the early computers and into COBOL. Because it is easier to sell upward-compatible computers than to force conversions, the scheme has stayed there ever since. Table 2.1 lists the various over-punch values with their corresponding digit and sign values.

TABLE 2.1 SIGNED OVER-PUNCH VALUES.

Digit	Signed Positive	Signed Negative
0	{	}
1	A	J
2	B	K
3	C	L
4	D	M
5	E	N
6	F	O
7	G	P
8	H	Q
9	I	R

This table will be correct for all mainframe computers I'm aware of and also for most PC and midrange compilers. The program in Listing 2.3 also lists the various values. Notice how the alphanumeric definition is being DISPLAYed to ensure that the compiler doesn't convert the numeric value to a separate digit and sign as it is displayed.

LISTING 2.3 NUMBERS1.

```
IDENTIFICATION DIVISION.
PROGRAM-ID.  Numbers1.
DATA DIVISION.
WORKING-STORAGE SECTION.
01   UNSIGN-AN.
     05   UNSIGNED-DIGIT        PIC 9 VALUE ZERO.
01   NEGATIVE-AN.
     05   NEGATIVE-DIGIT        PIC S9.
01   POSITIVE-AN.
     05   POSITIVE-DIGIT        PIC S9.
PROCEDURE DIVISION.
0000-MAIN.
     DISPLAY 'DIGIT NEGATIVE POSITIVE'.
     PERFORM 0100-LOOP 10 TIMES.
     STOP RUN.
0100-LOOP.
     MULTIPLY UNSIGNED-DIGIT BY -1 GIVING NEGATIVE-DIGIT.
     MULTIPLY NEGATIVE-DIGIT BY -1 GIVING POSITIVE-DIGIT.
     DISPLAY ' ' UNSIGND-AN '       ' NEGATIVE-AN
          '             ' POSITIVE-AN.
     ADD 1 TO UNSIGNED-DIGIT.
```

There is one item here that hasn't been covered before: the statement PERFORM 0100-LOOP 10 TIMES. The 10 TIMES phrase is new, and I used it because it was a lot easier than setting up an artificial UNTIL mechanism. This will have exactly the desired effect: It will cause the statements in the paragraph 0100-LOOP to be executed 10 times. The ADD statement at the end of the paragraph will increment the digit for each subsequent iteration.

Everything else in the program should be self-explanatory.

ACCEPT and DISPLAY with Signed Numeric Data

As discussed earlier, COBOL leaves most of the specifics of how ACCEPT and DISPLAY handle data up to the individual vendors. This is especially true when you deal with numeric data. It is not really a problem or limitation because you'll very seldom need or want to deal with internal numeric values individually using ACCEPT or DISPLAY.

In most cases, numbers coming into the program come from data records or tables produced by some program, or they are part of an input record or screen and are defined as alphanumeric before being edited and transferred to the internal numeric data items. In fact, a great deal of the current terminal/screen-management software for both the mainframe and PC has built-in editing features so that by the time the numbers get to your programs, they have already been edited and converted.

On the output side, most numeric data is MOVEd to "edited" numeric fields before it is presented to the user in reports or screens. A very large variety of options is available here, and I'll discuss them a bit later in this chapter.

The reason for getting into this subject is that ACCEPT and DISPLAY are so easy to use that they are powerful tools for debugging, special testing, and dealing with small amounts of data. Furthermore, in most cases, the newer compilers handle the data quite well, so all you need to do is confirm exactly how the data is treated. The following simple programs will do that.

This first program in Listing 2.4 shows how the various numeric formats are handled by DISPLAY. Feel free to make whatever changes you want to satisfy yourself as to how the data is being handled. This program will also come in handy in the next few sections.

LISTING 2.4 NUMBERS2.

```
IDENTIFICATION DIVISION.
PROGRAM-ID.  Numbers2.
DATA DIVISION.
WORKING-STORAGE SECTION.
01   UNSIGN-9-5AN.
     05   UNSIGNED-9-5          PIC 9(5) VALUE 123.
01   UNSIGN-9-5V99AN.
     05   UNSIGNED-9-5V99       PIC 9(5)V99 VALUE 123.4.
01   NEGATIVE-9-5V99AN.
     05   NEGATIVE-9-5V99       PIC S9(5)V99 VALUE -123.4.
01   LEAD-SEP-NEG-9-5V99AN.
     05   LEAD-SEP-NEG-9-5V99   PIC S9(5)V99
                     SIGN LEADING SEPARATE VALUE -123.4.
01   TRAIL-SEP-NEG-9-5V99AN.
     05   TRAIL-SEP-NEG-9-5V99 PIC S9(5)V99
                     SIGN TRAILING SEPARATE VALUE -123.4.
PROCEDURE DIVISION.
0000-MAIN.
     DISPLAY 'UNSIGN 9(5) A/N: ' UNSIGN-9-5AN
             ', NUM: ' UNSIGNED-9-5.
     DISPLAY 'UNSIGN 9(5)V99 A/N: ' UNSIGN-9-5V99AN
             ', NUM: ' UNSIGNED-9-5V99.
     DISPLAY 'NEGATIVE 9(5)V99 A/N: ' NEGATIVE-9-5V99AN
             ', NUM: ' NEGATIVE-9-5V99.
     DISPLAY 'LEAD/SEP/NEG 9(5)V99 A/N: ' LEAD-SEP-NEG-9-5V99AN
             ', NUM: ' LEAD-SEP-NEG-9-5V99.
     DISPLAY 'TRAIL/SEP/NEG 9(5)V99 A/N: ' TRAIL-SEP-NEG-9-5V99AN
             ', NUM: ' TRAIL-SEP-NEG-9-5V99.
     STOP RUN.
```

From this example, you can see how easy it is to determine exactly how things are working in your environment. The results will appear something like the following, but don't be too surprised to see some variations—especially in the last column. You don't want to make your environment show the results that follow; instead, you want to see what it does present and why so that it is predictable in the future:

```
UNSIGN 9(5) A/N: 00123, NUM: 00123
UNSIGN 9(5)V99 A/N: 0012340, NUM: 0012340
NEGATIVE 9(5)V99 A/N: 001234}, NUM: 001234}
LEAD/SEP/NEG 9(5)V99 A/N: -0012340, NUM: -0012340
TRAIL/SEP/NEG 9(5)V99 A/N: 0012340-, NUM: 0012340-
```

In the version in Listing 2.5, data is taken into the program with the ACCEPT statement. The first time you run this, make sure that the data is entered properly. On the regular signed field (the third one), enter an unsigned number the first time. This is because the results are not specified if nonnumeric values are entered when the program is expecting a number. In some cases, the program will be terminated; an obscure error message is displayed when this happens. If you're using a system where ACCEPT data comes from a systems input file, the DISPLAYs describing what data to enter obviously are unnecessary.

LISTING 2.5 NUMBERS3.

```
IDENTIFICATION DIVISION.
PROGRAM-ID.  Numbers3.
DATA DIVISION.
WORKING-STORAGE SECTION.
01  UNSIGN-9-5AN.
    05  UNSIGNED-9-5          PIC 9(5) VALUE ZERO.
01  UNSIGN-9-5V99AN.
    05  UNSIGNED-9-5V99       PIC 9(5)V99 VALUE ZERO.
01  NEGATIVE-9-5V99AN.
    05  NEGATIVE-9-5V99       PIC S9(5)V99 VALUE ZERO.
01  LEAD-SEP-NEG-9-5V99AN.
    05  LEAD-SEP-NEG-9-5V99  PIC S9(5)V99
                    SIGN LEADING SEPARATE VALUE ZERO.
01  TRAIL-SEP-NEG-9-5V99AN.
    05  TRAIL-SEP-NEG-9-5V99 PIC S9(5)V99
                    SIGN TRAILING SEPARATE VALUE ZERO.
PROCEDURE DIVISION.
0000-MAIN.
    DISPLAY 'ENTER 5 NUMERIC DIGITS: '.
    ACCEPT UNSIGNED-9-5.
    DISPLAY 'UNSIGN 9(5) A/N: ' UNSIGN-9-5AN
            ', NUM: ' UNSIGNED-9-5.
    DISPLAY 'ENTER 9(5)V99 AS 7 NUMERIC DIGITS: '.
    ACCEPT UNSIGNED-9-5V99.
    DISPLAY 'UNSIGN 9(5)V99 A/N: ' UNSIGN-9-5V99AN
            ', NUM: ' UNSIGNED-9-5V99.
    DISPLAY 'ENTER S9(5)V99 AS 7 DIGITS AND AN OVERPUNCHED SIGN'
            ' IF DESIRED: '.
    ACCEPT NEGATIVE-9-5V99.
    DISPLAY 'NEGATIVE 9(5)V99 A/N: ' NEGATIVE-9-5V99AN
            ', NUM: ' NEGATIVE-9-5V99.
    DISPLAY 'ENTER S9(5)V99 AS LEADING +/- AND 7DIGITS: '.
    ACCEPT LEAD-SEP-NEG-9-5V99.
    DISPLAY 'LEAD/SEP/NEG 9(5)V99 A/N: ' LEAD-SEP-NEG-9-5V99AN
            ', NUM: ' LEAD-SEP-NEG-9-5V99.
    DISPLAY 'ENTER S9(5)V99 AS 7 DIGITS AND TRAILING +/-: '.
    ACCEPT TRAIL-SEP-NEG-9-5V99.
    DISPLAY 'TRAIL/SEP/NEG 9(5)V99 A/N: ' TRAIL-SEP-NEG-9-5V99AN
            ', NUM: ' TRAIL-SEP-NEG-9-5V99.
    STOP RUN.
```

2

DEFINING DATA AND SPECIFYING ITS ATTRIBUTES

The final program in Listing 2.6 demonstrates how input data can be edited to ensure that it is numeric before it is used. Because of the looping mechanism, it works best when ACCEPT receives its data from the keyboard, but it will also work with system input files if the loop is removed. You may also want to experiment with different PICTURE clauses to see how they work.

LISTING 2.6 NUMBERS4.

```
IDENTIFICATION DIVISION.
PROGRAM-ID.  Numbers4.
DATA DIVISION.
WORKING-STORAGE SECTION.
01  VALID-NUMBER              PIC X VALUE 'N'.
01  LEAD-SEP-NEG-9-5V99AN.
    05  LEAD-SEP-NEG-9-5V99   PIC S9(5)V99
                      SIGN LEADING SEPARATE VALUE ZERO.
01  LEAD-SEP-CHAR-9-5V99AN.
    05  LEAD-SEP-CHAR-SIGN    PIC X VALUE SPACE.
    05  LEAD-SEP-CHAR-9-5V99  PIC 9(5)V99 VALUE ZERO.
01  LEAD-SEP-CHAR-RESULT      PIC S9(5)V99
                      SIGN LEADING SEPARATE VALUE ZERO.
PROCEDURE DIVISION.
0000-MAIN.
    PERFORM 0100-LOOP1
        UNTIL VALID-NUMBER = 'Y'.
    DISPLAY 'THE NUMBER ENTERED IS: '
        LEAD-SEP-NEG-9-5V99.
    MOVE 'N' TO VALID-NUMBER.
    PERFORM 0200-LOOP2
        UNTIL VALID-NUMBER = 'Y'.
    MOVE LEAD-SEP-CHAR-9-5V99 TO LEAD-SEP-CHAR-RESULT.
    IF LEAD-SEP-CHAR-SIGN = '-'
        MULTIPLY LEAD-SEP-CHAR-RESULT BY -1
            GIVING LEAD-SEP-CHAR-RESULT.
    DISPLAY 'THE NUMBER ENTERED IS: '
        LEAD-SEP-CHAR-RESULT.
    STOP RUN.
0100-LOOP1.
    MOVE ZERO TO LEAD-SEP-NEG-9-5V99.
    DISPLAY 'ENTER S9(5)V99 AS +/- AND 7 DIGITS: '.
    ACCEPT LEAD-SEP-NEG-9-5V99AN.
    IF LEAD-SEP-NEG-9-5V99 NOT NUMERIC
        DISPLAY 'TRY AGAIN'.
    IF LEAD-SEP-NEG-9-5V99 NUMERIC
        MOVE 'Y' TO VALID-NUMBER.
0200-LOOP2.
    MOVE ZERO TO LEAD-SEP-CHAR-9-5V99.
    MOVE SPACE TO LEAD-SEP-CHAR-SIGN.
    DISPLAY 'ENTER S9(5)V99 AS +/- AND 7 DIGITS: '.
```

```
ACCEPT LEAD-SEP-CHAR-9-5V99AN.
MOVE 'Y' TO VALID-NUMBER.
IF LEAD-SEP-CHAR-9-5V99 NOT NUMERIC
    MOVE 'N' TO VALID-NUMBER.
IF LEAD-SEP-CHAR-SIGN NOT = '-'
    AND LEAD-SEP-CHAR-SIGN NOT = '+'
    AND LEAD-SEP-CHAR-SIGN NOT = SPACE
        MOVE 'N' TO VALID-NUMBER.
IF VALID-NUMBER = 'N'
    DISPLAY 'TRY AGAIN'.
```

Notice that here you are ACCEPTing an alphanumeric value and testing it before attempting to treat it as a number. This way, strange things won't happen when bad data is received. The user is required to keep trying again and again until an acceptable value is entered. This is pretty typical of how data is edited for numeric values in a COBOL environment. The second loop where the sign is treated as an independent character that the program controls is also a common way of handling signed values.

Special USAGE Clause Options for Numeric Data

The USAGE clause in a data definition enables you to specify how data is stored internally. For numeric information, USAGE provides a means of defining numbers in a manner that is more efficient for numeric calculations and/or takes up less storage space. The options with this clause are

```
[USAGE IS] {COMPUTATIONAL/COMP/DISPLAY/INDEX/PACKED-DECIMAL}
```

Many vendors implement two other options that I will discuss: COMP-2 and COMP-3. Notice that the term USAGE itself is optional, so in many cases, you will see definitions of the form PIC 9(5) COMP, which is perfectly legitimate. The term INDEX is limited strictly to table handling and is discussed in the relevant chapters. COMP is an abbreviation for COMPUTATIONAL, so these two terms are synonymous (and where available, COMP-2 is synonymous for COMPUTATIONAL-2, and COMP-3 is synonymous for COMPUTATIONAL-3).

If no USAGE clause is specified, DISPLAY is the default. This means that the data will be stored as character data. This is what I have used to this point, and except for special circumstances that I will identify, I'll continue to use the default. It is what is generally used for most COBOL programs in most places. It is because of this default that, in most cases, you can show numbers as either numeric or alphanumeric and still recognize the results.

The other options for USAGE are all limited to numeric data, and all specify various *internal* machine representations of the data. Therefore, if you DISPLAY a group level containing an item with such a USAGE, you will see garbage or nothing for the positions it occupies. With most compilers, if you DISPLAY the number having the USAGE clause, it will be converted to a decimal value as a part of the DISPLAY function. If you need to see the internal value for the data, you will need to look at a program "dump" or view the data with a utility that can show the machine representation.

COMPUTATIONAL is defined in the COBOL Standard and is available with all compilers and machines. It specifies that the number will be stored in a binary form for the purpose of efficient numeric calculations. It is generally specified for integer-type numbers used internally by the program for counters and subscripts. A numeric PICTURE clause is used, and the number of digits specifies the number of decimal digits the data item must be able to hold. But, because the actual value is stored in binary form, there will not be a direct correlation between the number of digits and the number of bytes of memory reserved for the data item. For most machines based on the 8-bit byte, 1 or 2 digits require 1 byte; 3 or 4 digits will be stored in 2 bytes; and 5-, 6-, or 7-digit numbers will be stored in 3 bytes. If the item is signed, an additional bit is required, and 7-digit numbers will require 4 bytes instead of 3 (the extra sign bit will not impact the size requirements for the others). It is generally not a good idea to define fractional or assumed decimal points with COMPUTATIONAL data because the *decimal* point implies base 10, which does not exactly convert to and from binary.

COMPUTATIONAL-2 is not defined in the COBOL Standard but has become a de facto USAGE for floating-point data. It uses mantissa and exponent values to represent very large or very small values. Because of this, it does not have a PICTURE clause associated with it. It is most frequently used when interfacing with other languages that use such data for special calculations. Needless to say, this is not seen in very many COBOL programs.

COMP-3 is probably the next most common USAGE after DISPLAY, even though it is not defined by the COBOL Standard. This is especially true if you program with IBM mainframes or interface with them. This representation of numeric data is usually referred to as *packed decimal,* and COBOL does define a PACKED-DECIMAL USAGE. COMP-3 and PACKED-DECIMAL are synonymous to the best of my knowledge, but the term COMP-3 is used almost exclusively to refer to it. This representation is based on the 8-bit byte, and in it, each set of 4 bits represents a decimal digit. This way, 2 digits can be stored in each byte. The exception is that the low-order 4 bits are *always* reserved for sign information. Here, a hexadecimal F (1111) represents an unsigned value, D (1101) represents a negative value, and C (1100) represents a signed positive value.

Even with the bits reserved for sign information, determining the size of a packed decimal data item is not very difficult. One digit requires 1 byte, 2 or 3 digits require 2 bytes, 4 or 5 digits require 3 bytes, 6 or 7 digits require 4 bytes, and so on. If you like formulas, the one here is to add 1 to the number of digits, divide by 2, and round up. So 12 digits plus 1 is 13, divided by 2 is 6.5, and rounded up is 7 bytes. Nine digits plus 1 is 10, divided by 2 is 5 exactly, so no rounding is needed: 5 bytes are required.

Because this representation is decimal based, assumed decimal positions are handled as easily as integer data.

I suspect that this is popular because it is based on the hexadecimal representation of the decimal digits; hexadecimal dumps or displays of this information are pretty easy to interpret. Because they always end with sign information that is always C, D, or F, the beginning and end of the fields are also usually easy to find. Most hexadecimal dumps of 8-bit byte information represent the high-order hexadecimal digit on one line and the low-order digit on the next line. Here's an example:

```
000240135000205
0013F024C001D0F
```

In this case, the first number is an 8- or 9-digit unsigned number with a value of 1234, the second is 6 or 7 digits with a value of +12345, the third is 6 or 7 digits with a value of -12, and the last is 2 or 3 digits, unsigned, with a value of 5. Simply start with the top line and read down and then back up and down again until you come to the sign position. Any assumed decimal positions need to be determined from the PICTURE clause.

PICTURE Clauses for Edited Numeric Results

The PICTURE clause provides a large variety of characters used to control the formatting of numeric data for presentation on reports and screens. Data items in which the PICTURE clause contains such characters are termed *numeric edited* or *edited numeric*. Because of these characters, they are no longer *arithmetic numeric,* and calculations cannot be done with them. Instead, they are a form of alphanumeric data. I'll describe a few of the most commonly used editing characters and provide a short sample program before defining all the other characters available for editing numeric data.

The decimal point (.) can occur once in a PICTURE clause. It is counted as a character position when determining the size of the data item and will be included with the data whenever the data item is referenced.

The character Z in the PICTURE clause indicates zero suppression (or *blanking out)* of leading digits with a value of zero. The upper- and lowercase z are equivalent. The Z character can be repeated as many times as necessary in the PICTURE clause, but it must precede any 9 values that would be entered to indicate digit positions where the actual value is to be inserted, regardless of whether it is a leading zero. The total number of Zs and 9s in a PICTURE clause cannot exceed 18. Each Z is counted as a character position for determining the size of the data item.

The comma (,) is an insertion character and is inserted between digit positions, as indicated in the PICTURE clause. As many commas as required can be included. If a comma is preceded by a Z in the PICTURE clause and the digit value is a leading zero, a space will be inserted instead of a comma. Each comma is counted as a character position.

The example in Listing 2.7 demonstrates how this works a lot better than a long explanation. Notice that the characters specified in the editing PICTURE clause are not inserted except when data is transferred to the data-name specified for it. Also, any value transferred to a group level containing an element with an edited PICTURE clause will replace whatever was previously there.

LISTING 2.7 EDITNRS1.

```
IDENTIFICATION DIVISION.
PROGRAM-ID.  EditNrs1.
DATA DIVISION.
WORKING-STORAGE SECTION.
01   CALC-NUMBER              PIC 9(5)V99 VALUE 3245.12.
01   EDIT-GRP1.
     05  EDIT-NR1             PIC 9(5).99.
01   EDIT-GRP2.
     05  EDIT-NR2             PIC Z(5).ZZ.
01   EDIT-GRP3.
     05  EDIT-NR3             PIC Z(4)9.99.
01   EDIT-GRP4.
     05  EDIT-NR4             PIC ZZ,ZZ9.99.

PROCEDURE DIVISION.
0000-MAIN.
    PERFORM 0100-DISPLAY.
    MOVE ZERO TO CALC-NUMBER.
    PERFORM 0100-DISPLAY.
    MOVE 10.54 TO CALC-NUMBER.
    PERFORM 0100-DISPLAY.
    MOVE .2 TO CALC-NUMBER
    PERFORM 0100-DISPLAY.
    STOP RUN.
0100-DISPLAY.
    MOVE CALC-NUMBER TO EDIT-NR1.
    MOVE CALC-NUMBER TO EDIT-NR2.
    MOVE CALC-NUMBER TO EDIT-NR3.
    MOVE CALC-NUMBER TO EDIT-NR4.
    DISPLAY '  9(5).99: ' EDIT-GRP1.
    DISPLAY '  Z(5).ZZ: ' EDIT-GRP2.
    DISPLAY ' Z(4)9.99: ' EDIT-GRP3.
    DISPLAY 'ZZ,ZZ9.99: ' EDIT-GRP4.
```

This example can readily be modified to see how various combinations of all the other editing options work. Some books contain a table of some form that shows all the options and attempts to classify which options can be used with which other options. With all the variations here, these tables have always seemed too much trouble to decipher. So I'll just briefly describe the options in relative order of importance and mention where they have an impact on those that were described previously. The characters involved will be identified in the first few words of the paragraph, so they should also be easy to find.

The + and - symbols can be used to show the sign of a numeric value in an edited PICTURE clause. These symbols have several options and rules associated with them. If - is used, it is shown if the value of the number is negative; no sign is shown if the value is zero or positive. If + is used, it is shown if the value is zero or positive, and - is shown if the value is negative.

When + or - is used, it must either be the leftmost character(s) or rightmost character in the PICTURE clause. When the value is used as the single leftmost character or the rightmost character, the value is shown as indicated in that position.

On the other hand, if the + or - is repeated more than once at the left of the PICTURE clause, it is treated as a *floating insertion character.* Here, any leading zeros in positions represented by the sign characters are replaced by spaces, except for the last one, where the sign value is shown as indicated by the rule just described. Hence, the sign is "floated" into the desired digit position. When the sign character is used in this manner, the Z (zero suppression) is not allowed because it would be redundant.

Each sign character is counted as a character position. The following examples clarify how this works:

PICTURE	Value	Result	Value	Result
-9(4).99	25.50	0025.50	-2.25	-0002.25
+9(4).99	25.45	+0025.45	-124.32	-0124.32
9(4).99-	12.13	0012.13	-12.13	0012.13-
+ZZ99.99	10.25	+10.25	-1.12	-01.12*
----9.99-	12.25	-12.25	-.75	-0.75
+++++.99	1256.50	+1256.56	-234.00	-234.00

This combination is allowed because the + is being used as a single insertion character instead of a floating one. (That doesn't necessarily make it a good idea.)

The characters CR and DB may also be used to depict the sign value of a number. Obviously, only one of them may be chosen for a given PICTURE clause. It must the right two character positions (for example, PIC ZZZ,ZZ9.99CR). Whichever pair is selected will be printed only if the value is negative (spaces will be shown otherwise). This will count as two character positions.

The currency symbol ($ in the United States, or the value specified in SPECIAL-NAMES in many other places) can be used as a stationary or floating insertion symbol in a manner similar to the floating sign character. This symbol will be printed regardless of the sign or value of the number. It can be specified only on the left of the PICTURE clause, and only the fixed-sign character can be placed to the left of it. If the single, fixed currency symbol is specified on the left, either the Z (zero suppress) or the floating sign character (but not both) can be specified to its right. If multiple floating currency symbols are used, the single fixed sign can be used, but the Z and floating sign may not. Each currency symbol is counted as one character.

The asterisk (*) character is a floating insertion character that works very much like the zero-suppress Z character and spaces. *Every* leading zero in a position specified by the * is replaced by the *. Any insertion commas included in the PICTURE clause and preceded by asterisks also are replaced by the *. The * can be used with the fixed sign character and the fixed currency symbol, but it cannot be used with any of the other floating insertion characters. The floating asterisk is most commonly used for formatting numeric check amounts. The clause PIC $**,***,***.00 is a common example. Each asterisk is counted as one character position.

> **NOTE**
>
> The maximum number of characters that may be strung together following PIC is 30. Even though edited numerics may get pretty large and complex, I've yet to see these strings go much beyond 20.

Alphabetic, Alphanumeric Data, and Other Data Topics

There aren't nearly as many options or subtleties involving alphanumeric data and definitions as there are with numeric data. They can come in handy, though, in certain situations.

There are also a few final topics that involve both numeric and alphanumeric data that need to be covered.

Alphanumeric Picture Clauses

You already saw the PICTURE character X used to define alphanumeric elementary items. You also saw that any group-level items (which contain one or more subordinate data definitions) are also classified and treated as alphanumeric. Almost all alphanumeric data definitions in a program are one of these two forms. There is no defined maximum size for an alphanumeric data item like there is for numeric data items. This is defined by the manufacturer or compiler and is normally not a concern to the programmer. The other options with PICTURE clauses for alphanumeric data follow.

The character A defines the associated data as alphabetic only. This implies that it is limited to the letters of the alphabet (upper- and lowercase) and the space. A data item whose PICTURE clause contains only the letter A—for example, PICTURE AAAA or PICTURE A(22)—is termed *alphabetic,* and that is the only kind of data item that is alphabetic. Because there is really no benefit to using such a definition, it is very seldom seen.

The characters B, /, and 0 (zero) are editing insertion characters that may be used as alphanumeric editing characters in PICTURE clauses. Wherever B is specified, a blank or SPACE character is inserted into the data. / and 0 are also inserted wherever they are shown in the PICTURE clause. Each occurrence of any of these characters is counted when determining the size of the data item. In addition to being used with the characters X and A, these three characters can be used in edited numeric data items. The most common example used for these characters is basic format editing for dates. For example, if the data item REPORT-DATE is defined with PIC 99/99/99, the statement ACCEPT REPORT-DATE FROM DATE will result in values such as 98/01/31.

De-Editing

De-editing occurs when an elementary item with a PICTURE clause containing editing characters is MOVEd to a similarly defined elementary item, but without the editing characters. By "similarly defined," I mean numeric edited to numeric, or alphanumeric edited to alphanumeric. When this is done, the effects of the editing are reversed, and the original value is produced and placed in the receiving field. So if an edited field has a PICTURE clause of PIC ZZ,ZZ9.99, a value of 2,876.22, and is MOVEd to a field defined as PIC 9(5)V99, it will end up with the value 0287622 (with an assumed decimal point between the 6 and the 2).

De-editing was introduced in the 1985 COBOL Standard. It is not available when using a 1974 Standard (or prior) compiler. In such a case, because edited data items are classified as alphanumeric, they are treated as such, and whatever characters are there are transferred. Needless to say, the results are not very good.

Even with new programs, de-editing is very rarely done. This is because the PICTURE edit facilities are designed for output data that is being presented to the user on screens or in reports. In most of these cases, there is no intent to reuse the data because the unedited value is readily available in the computer data file or database.

Situations in which de-editing is used occasionally are in terminal and PC screen update programs. Even here, use is normally limited to PICTURE clauses such as PIC -(7).99. This will present numbers without leading zeros and will float in a minus sign if the value is negative. When or if the user modifies the value, the program can convert it back to an arithmetic number with a simple MOVE statement. Obviously, normal editing for NUMERIC is still required in case some other characters have been entered.

USAGE DISPLAY and SYNCHRONIZED

The clause USAGE DISPLAY can be included with any numeric or alphanumeric data definition (except if a different USAGE is needed with a numeric definition). It specifies that character data will be used. Because it is the default and there are no other options for character data, it is seldom seen. I am aware of one machine where a second option was defined during the "old days" when some data could be stored in a 6-bit character mode and this needed to be distinguished from normal ASCII data.

The SYNCHRONIZED clause can be used with numeric or alphanumeric data items, but they must be elementary. The purpose of the clause is to align the data with the "natural machine boundaries" for the sake of efficiency. Its format follows:

```
{SYNCHRONIZED/SYNC} [LEFT/RIGHT]
```

SYNC is an abbreviation for SYNCHRONIZED, and the two are synonymous. If LEFT and RIGHT are omitted, the one that produces the more efficient code will be used. This clause is an old one and is based on computers designed around "word" architecture instead of the byte. With much slower processors, this provides a means of storing work fields (especially subscripts, counters, totals, and accumulators) so that they can be manipulated faster. With modern computers, it is not really needed and, in most cases, will not make any noticeable difference in the program's processing speed. If it is used, it should be limited to independent elementary items such as 77 and 01 level elementary items. The reason is that on some machines, it may cause extra bits, bytes, or half-bytes to be inserted before or after the data item, and if the data item is part of a group level, determining the size of the group level becomes completely machine-dependent and difficult for the programmer to determine.

Justification, Alignment, and Mixing Numeric and Alphanumeric

The terms *justification* and *alignment* need to be defined and explained because they are important when describing how the results are determined in MOVE and comparison statements involving various combinations of data.

The term *justification* applies only to alphabetic and alphanumeric data. By default, alphanumeric fields are *left justified*. This means that when data is MOVEd to an alphanumeric field, the first character is placed in the leftmost position, and additional characters are added to its right until either all the character positions in the field are filled or every position in the sending field has been transferred. When all the character positions of the receiving field have been filled, the MOVE is complete, and any remaining characters on the right side of the sending field are ignored or truncated. If all the character positions from the sending field are transferred before all the character positions of the receiving field have been filled, SPACES are placed in all these unfilled positions before the MOVE is completed. The term for this is *space-fill*. To illustrate, if FIELD-A is defined as PIC X(4), the statement MOVE 'ABCDEFG' TO FIELD-A will leave it with a value of ABCD. The statement MOVE 'AB' TO FIELD-A will leave it with a value of AB.

When two alphanumeric fields of unequal sizes are compared, COBOL creates a temporary field the size of the larger field. The shorter field is MOVEd to it left justified with space-fill. Then the temporary field is compared to the larger field. Thus, ABC is equal to 'ABC ' but is less than 'ABC X' (the space character is less than both numbers and characters in both ASCII and EBCDIC).

"JUSTIFIED" or "JUST" or "JUSTIFIED RIGHT" or "JUST RIGHT" is a clause that can be included in alphanumeric data definitions. All the terms have the same meaning and cause data that is MOVEd to that field to be MOVEd beginning at the right side instead of the left. Space-fill still is done as appropriate but is done on the left instead of the right. This clause is hardly ever used because the effect is not exactly what you would intuitively hope for or expect. If FIELD-B is defined as PIC X(6) JUST RIGHT, the statement MOVE 'JIM' TO FIELD-B will give the result ' JIM' as you would expect. But if FIELD-C is defined as PIC X(4) and has a value 'SUE ', the statement MOVE FIELD-C TO FIELD-B will give the result ' SUE '. Think about it. The reason this happens is that the *field* is right-justified and not the characters in it. So, when the MOVE is done, *all* the characters in FIELD-C are transferred to FIELD-B, beginning with the SPACE character on the right.

Alignment pertains only to numeric data. It refers to the fact that numbers are aligned at the decimal point when doing compares—arithmetic MOVEs. From a mathematical point of view, this is essential if the correct algebraic (or arithmetic) result is to be produced. In a MOVE statement (involving only numbers), this means that both numbers will be aligned at the decimal point, and then zeros will be added on the left and/or right side as needed where the sending field is smaller than the receiving field. Digits will also be dropped (or truncated) as needed when the sending field is larger than the receiving field. An item to note is that one MOVE statement may result in both zeros being added *and* truncated. For example, if a data item with PIC 9999V99 and a value of 2345.65 is MOVEd to a field defined with PIC 999V999, the result will be 345.650. Observe that a digit on the left is truncated, and a zero digit is added to the right.

When comparing two numeric fields, they are aligned at the decimal point, and (where necessary) temporary fields are created that will hold the largest number of digits both to the left and right of the decimal point before the compare is made. So if 2345.65 is compared with 233.678, they will be converted to 2345.650 and 0233.678 and then compared. The only restriction here is that the total size of the temporary fields is limited to 18 digits, and digits will be truncated on the right if this occurs.

Arithmetic statements are handled similarly to compare statements in preparing the operands for the arithmetic operation, and then the results are transferred to the receiving field according to the rules for the MOVE statement. For example, if FIELD-A is PIC 999V999 with value 123.456, FIELD-B is PIC 9999V99 with value 1234.45, and FIELD-C has PIC 99999V99, the statement ADD FIELD-A FIELD-B GIVING FIELD-C will be handled as follows. Temporary fields with PIC 9999V999 will be used, so 0123.456 will be added to 1234.450, producing 1357.906; but then a digit will be added to the left and truncated on the right to produce the result in FIELD-C of 01357.90. Some additional rules for special cases apply to the arithmetic statements, and they are covered with those statements, but the basic concept always applies.

Signed numbers are treated algebraically, so –100 is less than –50, and both are less than +.01 or .01.

If you've worked through this section carefully, you should agree that these rules do follow common sense and will do exactly what you want them to, even though they may not always produce the desired results if the fields are not defined with sufficient digits. Things get a bit trickier when numeric and alphanumeric data are both used in the same statement, and because of this mixing, the two generally should be avoided. The following guidelines apply to these cases.

When data is transferred, the receiving field always determines the format of the results.

When a number is MOVEd to an alphanumeric field, it is converted to alphanumeric format (if it isn't already), and then characters are transferred from left to right with space-fill at the end. Decimal-point alignment is *not* done. So a PIC 9(5) field with a value of 00123 will become 0012 when MOVEd to a PIC X(4) field. This same rule applies to numeric literals, so the numeric literal 123.45 will become 12345 with the assumed decimal point and then 1234 when transferred to the PIC X(4) field. If the PIC 9(5) value 00123 is MOVEd to a PIC X(6) field, the result will be '00123 ', and the numeric literal 123.45 will be '12345 '. Signed numeric literals can prove even more troublesome because -123.41 will be converted to 1234J (with most compilers and machines, the J is the sign-over-punch value for -1) and produce a result in the PIC X(6) field of '1234J ' and '1234' in the PIC X(4) field.

When the receiving field is numeric and the sending field is alphanumeric, the sending field is converted to a number and then decimal-point alignment rules are used to transfer it to the numeric field. If the alphanumeric field is really a numeric-edited field, the editing characters are dealt with as the conversion takes place. In all other cases, the field (including alphanumeric literals) is treated as a purely PIC X(n) field, so the handling of characters such as -, ., ,, and so on is not done. Leading spaces (those on the left) are converted to zeroes, and trailing spaces (on the right) are dropped (with many compilers). The COBOL standard does *not* guarantee this handling.

Because alphanumeric fields can contain virtually any character value, but numeric fields must contain numbers that can be used in arithmetic, MOV(E)ing (PIC X) alphanumeric data to numeric should always be avoided. Instead, the data needs to be defined or redefined as numeric (or numeric edited) in the manner that represents how it actually exists. When the data is user input or comes from a source where the values or format cannot be guaranteed, the field should be defined in the numeric form that represents how it is supposed to be presented, and that field needs to be tested for NUMERIC before it is MOVEd to another numeric field.

Arithmetic can be done only with numeric fields.

When a numeric field is compared to an alphanumeric field (or vice versa), the numeric field is converted to a temporary alphanumeric field, and an *alphanumeric* (character-by-character, beginning at the left) *comparison* is done. If the number is smaller, spaces are added to the right in the temporary field. If the number is larger, a temporary field is created for the alphanumeric field with spaces being added to the right of it. Although this seems simple enough, it can lead to a lot of confusion in greater and less-than compares and with regard to sorting. For example, a numeric field with PIC 9(5) and value 123 will be converted to an alphanumeric field as 00123. When compared to a PIC X field of any size, if the first character is 1, it will be greater, regardless of what is in the rest of the field, because the first character is greater. Signed numerics are also a problem because the sign normally is stored in the low-order position.

It should be noted that these mixed-data concerns are often not a problem with nonarithmetic numbers, such as identification numbers; ZIP codes; fully numeric telephone numbers; and dates that are in century, year, month, day format. This is because all the positions generally are valued with a numeric digit, and when this is true and because they are not signed, the comparisons will work properly whether they are numeric or alphanumeric.

The following guidelines will result in safe, predictable programs:

- Don't mix numeric and alphanumeric fields in the same statement if at all possible.
- Always use numeric literals when the other field(s) are numeric, and use alphanumeric literals when the other fields are alphanumeric. I have not seen a valid reason for doing otherwise.
- When one of the fields is numeric, define (or redefine) the other field as numeric (or numeric edited) to match the data it contains.
- When data is input from the user or some other source where nonnumeric "errors" may occur, test it for NUMERIC (with appropriate error-handling statements) before using any statements that require a numeric value.
- If these rules don't readily handle the situation, a conversion is likely required. A variety of statements to handle such conversions is covered in Chapter 10, "Special Tools for Character Manipulation."

Figurative Constants

A number of special words are defined by COBOL that take on the form of whatever data item they are associated with; therefore, the programmer doesn't need to worry about justification or alignment when using them. These are *figurative constants,* and they can be used wherever a literal is allowed (ZERO and SPACES are two I already touched on briefly). *All figurative constants have both singular and plural forms that can be used interchangeably with identical results.* When one is used, a temporary data item is created and filled with the exact number of repetitions of the figurative constant character value to match the size of the data item it is associated with in the statement (or data definition). This then is used to do whatever is specified. When there is no associated data item, such as with the DISPLAY (or STRING, UNSTRING, or INSPECT) statement, a single character is used.

ZERO, ZEROS, and ZEROES are the only figurative constants that can be used with numeric data, and when the data item is numeric, an algebraic zero is used. Because of this definition, the term can be used just as well with all the special numeric USAGEs (such as COMP, COMP-3, PACKED-DECIMAL). When ZERO is used with alphanumeric data, enough zero characters are used to match the size of the data item. So, `77 FIELD-1 PIC X(6) VALUE ZERO` and `MOVE ZERO TO FIELD-1` will both result in the value `000000` being placed in `FIELD-1`. A comparison of `FIELD-1` with `ZERO` (>, <, or = in an `IF` or `UNTIL`) will cause `FIELD-1` to be compared to `000000'`. By the way, if you need to use zero and trailing spaces (for example, `'0   '`), the literal `'0'` will do the job because space-fill is always done for alphanumeric fields.

`SPACE` or `SPACES` will fill or compare the field to all `SPACE` characters. This should be self-explanatory.

`QUOTE` or `QUOTES` represents the character used to delimit alphanumeric literals. Although it will cause an entire field to be filled with or compared to quote characters, it generally is used to specify a single quote character, since that cannot be done with the normal alphanumeric literal. For example, the statement `DISPLAY 'HELLO'` will cause HELLO to be displayed, while the statement `DISPLAY QUOTE 'HELLO' QUOTE` will cause `'HELLO'` to be displayed. Note that this will be reversed if you're using real quotes to delimit alphanumeric literals. Also, the term `QUOTE` cannot be used to delimit alphanumeric literals.

`HIGH-VALUE` or `HIGH-VALUES` represents the highest valued alphanumeric character in the specified character set. It is established so that no alphanumeric character can compare greater than it. It is especially handy in dealing with sorted data to determine whether you are at the end of it. In most environments, `HIGH-VALUES` is equivalent to all binary 1s, but that is not guaranteed by COBOL. `HIGH-VALUES` ensures that the program is dealing with the highest possible character value, regardless of the machine on which the program is running.

`LOW-VALUE` or `LOW-VALUES` represents the lowest valued alphanumeric character in the specified character set. No alphanumeric character can compare less than it. In most environments, it is represented by binary zeroes. It is commonly used to initialize fields to their lowest possible value. This is handy to ensure that certain data sorts at the beginning of a file. But it is most often used to set up key data items for indexed files and databases in order to begin processing at the beginning of a series of records. This will be covered in Chapter 7, "Advanced Techniques Using Indexed Files."

`ALL` is a term that can be used to generate a figurative constant from any character value. Thus, if `FIELD-A` is defined as `PIC X(7)`, the statement `MOVE ALL 'A' TO FIELD-A` will result in AAAAAAA to be transferred to `FIELD-A`. `IF FIELD-A > ALL 'A'` will be true if `FIELD-A` is greater than AAAAAAA. Literals larger than a single character can be used, but there is seldom a reason for that. `ALL` can be used together with any of the other figurative constants (for example, `ALL SPACES`), but it is completely redundant and makes absolutely no difference in the results.

This completes the chapter on data definition in COBOL. Almost everything has been covered. A few special topics will be covered later in specific chapters devoted to those topics. Although some of the examples have been pretty basic, the foundation has been built so that, as the examples become more complex and real-world, the data definitions used in them will make sense and be understandable. This chapter should also be a good reference when you encounter questions and unusual uses.

Using Conditional Statements to Control Processing

IN THIS CHAPTER

The first part of this chapter covers the basic imperative statements in some detail. These include the arithmetic statements (ADD, SUBTRACT, MULTIPLY, and DIVIDE), the COMPUTE statement, and the MOVE. Then you'll look in some depth at conditional processing in COBOL using the IF statement. Also, some of the significant differences between the 1974 and 1985 Standards are discussed here. Finally, the EVALUATE statement, which is new with the 1985 Standard, is covered in detail.

This chapter and the next two cover everything about basic data manipulation and program logic control. The remaining parts of COBOL fall into two categories. One is dealing with data that exists in files external to the program; this is covered in Part II, "The Language—Structure Data and External Media." The other items are grouped into feature modules and are covered in Part III, "The Language—Advanced Topics."

The Basic Imperative Statements

There are a fairly large number of imperative statements. In fact, I've already covered three of them in their entirety (ACCEPT, DISPLAY, and STOP RUN). A number of other statements are covered in other chapters that deal with the topics they help implement. In this section, I'll expand on the MOVE statement a bit and then cover the arithmetic statements. These all have a couple special features; I'll discuss these afterward, and I'll also give you a more explicit definition of the imperative statement. As you'll see, this will be necessary as you get into conditional statements in the next section. Finally, a short sample program will demonstrate how these statements frequently are used.

The MOVE Statement

The general format of MOVE follows:

```
MOVE {data-item1/literal} TO {data-item2}...
```

This statement is rather basic and has been covered pretty thoroughly in the last few chapters (the most complex subject is determining the results when the data items are of differing sizes and/or alphanumeric/numeric, and that was covered in depth in the last chapter). Notice the ellipsis following data-item2. This implies that any number of data-items may be listed after the word TO. This is true, and when it is done, each data-item2 is treated as if it were the recipient of a separate MOVE statement. The separate transfers are done in the same sequence in which the data-item2 names are listed.

The Add Statement

The ADD statement has two general forms:

```
ADD {data-item1/literal1}... TO {data-item2/literal2}
➥GIVING {data-item3}...
```

First of all, notice that the *TO* is in italics. That means it isn't needed in this format. As far as I'm concerned, in this case, that means *do not* use it for this format. *TO* implies that something is being transferred *TO* `data-item2/literal2`, and with this format, that does *not* happen. Therefore, the *TO* becomes nothing but misleading for someone reading the program.

Notice that both `data-item1/literal1` and `data-item2/literal2` are surrounded by braces (`{}`). What this boils down to is that two separate `data-item/literals` are required between `ADD` and `GIVING`. Notice also that there is an ellipsis after `data-item1/literal1`. So two or more items can be listed here. The ellipsis after `data-item3` indicates that one or more data items can be listed there.

The way this statement works is that a temporary item is set up that will hold the maximum number of digits required (according to decimal-alignment rules) for all the data items listed between `ADD` and `GIVING`. An extra digit is added to the left of the decimal to allow for the "carry" digit. The values then are added together, and the results are placed in the temporary item. The value of the temporary item then is transferred to each item listed after `GIVING` in the order in which each is listed, according to the numeric `MOVE` rules.

In human language, all the stuff between `ADD` and `GIVING` is added together, and the answer is put in all the places shown after `GIVING`.

The second format for `ADD` follows:

```
ADD {data-item1/literal1}... TO {data-item2}...
```

Again, notice the ellipses following `data-item1/literal1` and `data-item2`. This implies that statements such as `ADD NUMBER1 NUMBER2 NUMBER3 TO NUMBER4 NUMBER5` are allowed. This is true. First, a temporary storage item (`TEMP`) is set up that will hold the maximum number of digits required for all the `data-item1/literal1`s and `data-item2`s listed (according to the rules for decimal-point alignment), with an extra digit for the carry. Next, all the `data-item1/literal1`s listed are added together, and the result is stored in the `TEMP` item. Finally, the temporary `TEMP` is added together with, and the result is stored in, each `data-item2` in the order they are listed. The value of `TEMP` is not altered as this part is done. These steps are best illustrated by converting the second format for `ADD` into several format-1 `ADD` statements:

```
ADD NUMBER1 NUMBER2 NUMBER3 GIVING TEMP.
ADD TEMP NUMBER4 GIVING NUMBER4.
ADD TEMP NUMBER5 GIVING NUMBER5.
```

This format is most frequently used to accumulate totals during the course of the program or a loop within the program. For example, `"ADD 1 TO COUNTER"` will increment

COUNTER by 1 each time the statement is executed. The statement "ADD INPUT-AMOUNT TO TOTAL-AMOUNT" often is included in the paragraph that reads input records for the program. Then, when the program finishes reading the file, TOTAL-AMOUNT will contain a summary total value for the entire file. The more exotic uses of this format, such as the example for format 2 of ADD, aren't seen very often.

As a sidebar, the temporary field is used even when there is only one data-item before the TO. This is done to ensure predictability for the results fields. The rationale and details are described with the MULTIPLY statement.

The SUBTRACT Statement

There are also two formats for SUBTRACT. The first follows:

```
SUBTRACT {data-item1/literal1}...FROM {data-item2/literal2}
➥GIVING {data-item3}...
```

Although this looks similar to ADD, some subtle differences will become apparent as I go through it. The ellipses following data-item1/literal1 and data-item3 indicate that as many items as are needed may be listed at each of these places (as with the ADD statement). But, notice that FROM is *not* italicized. It is required because of how the statement works. All the items before the FROM are added together, the result is subtracted from data-item2/literal2, and the results of this are transferred to each item listed after GIVING. A temporary field is set up to hold the intermediate results, and its size is the maximum number of digits required for all the items before GIVING, according to decimal-point alignment rules, with an extra digit for any "carry." Listing multiple items before the FROM isn't done very often, so most statements are of the form SUBTRACT FIELD-1 FROM FIELD-2 GIVING FIELD-3, which is pretty easy to interpret.

Here is the second format for SUBTRACT:

```
SUBTRACT {data-item1/literal1}... FROM {data-item2}...
```

This is also similar to the second format for ADD. Note that both items may be repeated as often as needed. Like with the ADD, a temporary field is set up to hold the number of digits required for all the data-item1/literal1s, plus one extra digit. All the data-item1/literal1 values are added together, and the result is placed in the temporary field. Then the value of the temporary field is subtracted, and the result is transferred to each data-item2 in the order in which each is listed. The format-1 SUBTRACT is used much more frequently than the format-2 SUBTRACT, because it defines much more clearly what is going on. Format 2 generally is used only for statements such as SUBTRACT 1 FROM COUNTER.

The MULTIPLY Statement

The two formats for MULTIPLY are a bit more limited than ADD and SUBTRACT. The first format follows:

```
MULTIPLY {data-item1/literal1} BY {data-item2/literal2}
➥GIVING  {data-item3}...
```

The important difference here is that an ellipsis does not follow data-item1/literal1. This means that MULTIPLY with more than two operands is *not* allowed. There is a reason for this, and it involves the size of the temporary storage needed to hold the results of the MULTIPLY. For ADD and SUBTRACT, only one extra digit is needed for every 10 operands to hold any "carry" digits. (For example, 8 and 7 are each a single digit, and adding them results in a 5 for the unit's position and a "carry" of 1 to the 10's position.) However, with MULTIPLY, the number of digits needed for the result is determined by adding together the total number of digits of each operand. So multiplying three seven-digit operands would require up to 21 digits in the result. Because this would require the size of the temporary storage field to grow so quickly, more than two operands is simply not allowed. This is not much of a limitation, because the COMPUTE statement provides a general means of handling large complex calculations.

Besides the exception just described, MULTIPLY functions in a manner similar to ADD and SUBTRACT. The values of the two operands are multiplied together, and the results are placed in a temporary field. The temporary field then is transferred to each of the results fields shown after the GIVING, according to MOVE alignment rules.

Here is the second format for MULTIPLY:

```
MULTIPLY {data-item1/literal1} BY {data-item2}...
```

I generally stay away from this format, because it always seems unclear to me which of the data-items is the receiving field. In this format, data-item1/literal1 is placed in a temporary field and then is multiplied by each data-item2 in turn, with the results transferred back according to MOVE alignment rules. As in the first format, only one data-item1/literal1 is allowed. You therefore might wonder why COBOL bothers with the temporary field. The reason is to ensure predictable results. The first situation involves statements such as MULTIPLY FIELD-1 BY FIELD-1 FIELD-1 FIELD-1. Without specifying the temporary field, the final value for FIELD-1 could be unpredictable. With the temporary field, the result is ensured, and in fact, it is equivalent to raising FIELD-1 to the fourth power. (This provides a somewhat obscure means for exponentiation.) The other situation involves using a subscript both as one of the data-items and as a means of referencing one of the data-items. Such a statement might be MULTIPLY FIELD-1 (SUB-1) BY SUB-1 FIELD-2 (SUB-1). Again, specifying use of the temporary field ensures predictability. For those statements where such ambiguity does not exist, the temporary field may be optionally removed from the object program for the sake of efficiency.

The DIVIDE Statement

In order to provide semantic flexibility, COBOL provides *five* formats for DIVIDE. As much as DIVIDE is used, this seems like overkill. But since these formats have been there from day one, it's hard to get rid of any of them. Before I get into these formats, let me make a comment on dividing by zero. As with all languages, this is not allowed in COBOL, and the program essentially crashes if you divide by zero. The best option is to test the divisor for zero before the DIVIDE and to do something else appropriate if the value is zero. With COBOL, there is another way to handle this exception. It is the ON SIZE ERROR phrase that is common to all the arithmetic statements; this phrase is covered later in its own section.

The first two formats for DIVIDE follow:

```
DIVIDE {data-item1/literal1} INTO {data-item2/literal2}
➡GIVING {data-item3}...
```

and

```
DIVIDE {data-item1/literal1} BY {data-item2/literal2}
➡GIVING {data-item3}...
```

The only difference between the two formats is INTO and BY, which simply means that data-item1/literal1 is the divisor in the first format, and data-item2/literal2 is the dividend. In the second format, the two are reversed. Otherwise, the functionality is the same, and so are the results. In both cases, a temporary field of the proper size is set up, and the results of the calculation are placed in it. This result then is transferred to each data-item3 in order, using decimal-point alignment rules.

The following two formats are very similar to the first two formats but also provide the remainder result of the division:

```
DIVIDE {data-item1/literal1} INTO {data-item2/literal2}
➡GIVING data-item3 REMAINDER data-item4
```

and

```
DIVIDE {data-item1/literal1} BY {data-item2/literal2}
➡GIVING data-item3 REMAINDER data-item4
```

As with the first two formats, the only difference is the BY and INTO. There are a few differences from the first two formats. First, only one data-item3 is permitted. Second, the REMAINDER phrase provides a receiving field for the remainder value from the division to be stored. This remainder is calculated as the result of subtracting the product of `data-item3` and the divisor from the dividend. This result is transferred to `data-item4` using normal decimal-point alignment rules.

The final `DIVIDE` format follows:

```
DIVIDE {data-item1/literal1} INTO {data-item2}...
```

Here, a temporary field is set up with the value of `data-item1/literal1`. That value then is divided into each `data-item2` in sequence, and the results are transferred back to them in turn. As usual, decimal-point alignment rules are applied.

The COMPUTE Statement

`COMPUTE` provides the means to use complex arithmetic statements or formulas in COBOL. For numeric data, it is analogous to the assignment statements in many other languages that are popular today. `COMPUTE` is used only with numeric data. Its general format follows:

```
COMPUTE {data-item1}... = arithmetic-expression
```

I'll make a few observations before getting into some of the details of arithmetic expressions as they pertain to COBOL.

Notice that any number of `data-item1`s may be listed. Here, the value of the arithmetic expression is determined, and then that value is transferred to each `data-item1`. The `data-item1`s must be numeric or numeric-edited elementary items.

The arithmetic statements in their simplest form can be a numeric literal or a data item. In these cases, `COMPUTE` functions in a manner very similar to `MOVE`, except that several optional phrases that pertain only to the arithmetic statements can be used (these are covered in later sections).

All the other arithmetic statements have very explicit rules regarding the formation and use of temporary fields supporting the calculations and storing the results in the receiving fields. I summarized these rules briefly in previous sections. Such requirements do *not* apply to the `COMPUTE` statement for two reasons. As you saw with the `MULTIPLY` statement, there are situations in which the number of digits required to store all possible results can grow all out of proportion very quickly. With the open-ended nature of arithmetic expressions, such an approach is not feasible. The second reason why these requirements do not apply is that current language software technology provides standard algorithms that do an excellent job of managing the accuracy of intermediate results in evaluating arithmetic expressions. For this reason, the current standards simply specify that the compiler documentation identify the technique or algorithm being used in the evaluation of arithmetic expressions. This apparently works pretty well, because I have not run into any problems for a good number of years. However, you should be aware that COMPUTE and the other arithmetic statements are handled differently in this area.

Arithmetic expressions are formed in COBOL pretty much like other languages, but subtle differences often exist, so I'll summarize what is available with COBOL. The normal arithmetic operations and symbols follow:

Symbol	Operation
+	Addition
-	Subtraction
*	Multiplication
/	Division
**	Exponentiation

The unary operators - and + can be used immediately preceding a data item or literal to indicate multiplication by -1 or +1.

The left and right parenthesis characters—(and)—should be used in pairs to ensure that the order in which the operations are performed is not ambiguous.

All data items in arithmetic expressions in COBOL must be numeric.

Functions and function calls are not an integral part of arithmetic expressions in COBOL. Functions are available with the 1989 Addendum to the 1985 Standard and are covered in Chapter 13, "Intrinsic Functions with Emphasis on the Year 2000."

The following rules show the order in which the operations in an arithmetic expression are evaluated:

1. All the operations within the innermost set of parentheses are evaluated first. Then each outer set is evaluated, working outward, until all have been resolved. For example, in the expression (FIELD-1 * (FIELD-2 + FIELD-3)), because FIELD-2 + FIELD-3 are within the innermost parentheses, they are added together first, and then the result is multiplied by FIELD-1, because that is enclosed in the next outer set of parentheses.

2. When several operands and operations are specified without parentheses, leaving an ambiguity regarding which to evaluate first, this order of precedence is followed:

   a. Any unary plus and minus is done first (note that because these symbols are the same as addition and subtraction, which are last in this rule, it is almost imperative that these be surrounded by parentheses).

   b. Exponentiation is done next.

c. Multiplication and division are done next.

d. Addition and subtraction are done last.

As an example, look at a typical combination of addition and multiplication. The expression FIELD-A + FIELD-B * FIELD-C doesn't have any parentheses to specify the order in which the operations are to be done. Rule 2 states that multiplication and division are done before addition and subtraction. Hence, FIELD-B is multiplied by FIELD-C, and then the result is added to FIELD-A.

3. If there is still ambiguity, the operations proceed from left to right. For example, in the expression FIELD-1 + FIELD-2 + FIELD-3, FIELD-1 is added to FIELD-2, and then the result is added to FIELD-3.

A Sample Program to Demonstrate COMPUTE

The program in listing 3.1 demonstrates COMPUTE and gives a few examples of arithmetic expressions. It calculates bowling averages and handicaps, and even though this isn't sophisticated data processing, it's a good example. I've left the means of getting data into the program at a very primitive level so that the emphasis will remain with the calculations; feel free to expand on that area.

LISTING 3.1 COMPUT.

```
IDENTIFICATION DIVISION.
PROGRAM-ID.  Comput.
DATA DIVISION.
WORKING-STORAGE SECTION.
01  SIGNED-HANDICAP          PIC S999.
01  BOWLER-INFO.
    05  GAME1                PIC 999.
    05  GAME2                PIC 999.
    05  GAME3                PIC 999.
    05  OLD-HANDICAP         PIC 999.
    05  TOTAL-GAMES          PIC 999.
    05  TOTAL-PINS           PIC 9(5).
01  NEW-BOWLER-INFO.
    05  SERIES-SCORE         PIC 999.
    05  AVERAGE-SCORE        PIC 999.
    05  NEW-HANDICAP         PIC 999.
    05  SERIES-WITH-HANDICAP PIC 999.
01  BOWLER1 PIC X(20) VALUE '12518816500000000000'.
01  BOWLER2 PIC X(20) VALUE '17315618202401202045'.

PROCEDURE DIVISION.
0000-MAIN.
    MOVE BOWLER1 TO BOWLER-INFO.
*   ACCEPT BOWLER-INFO.
```

continues

LISTING 3.1 CONTINUED

```
        IF TOTAL-GAMES = ZERO
            PERFORM 0100-NEW-BOWLER.
        IF TOTAL-GAMES NOT = ZERO
            PERFORM 0200-REGULAR-BOWLER.
        PERFORM 0300-DISPLAY-RESULTS.
        MOVE BOWLER2 TO BOWLER-INFO.
*       ACCEPT BOWLER-INFO.
        IF TOTAL-GAMES = ZERO
            PERFORM 0100-NEW-BOWLER.
        IF TOTAL-GAMES NOT = ZERO
            PERFORM 0200-REGULAR-BOWLER.
        PERFORM 0300-DISPLAY-RESULTS.
        STOP RUN.


    0100-NEW-BOWLER.
        COMPUTE SERIES-SCORE TOTAL-PINS =
            GAME1 + GAME2 + GAME3.
        COMPUTE AVERAGE-SCORE = (GAME1 + GAME2 + GAME3) / 3.
        COMPUTE SIGNED-HANDICAP OLD-HANDICAP NEW-HANDICAP =
            (200 - AVERAGE-SCORE) * .8.
*           (200 - ((GAME1 + GAME2 + GAME3) / 3)) * .8.
        IF SIGNED-HANDICAP < ZERO
            MOVE ZERO TO OLD-HANDICAP NEW-HANDICAP.
        MOVE 3 TO TOTAL-GAMES.


    0200-REGULAR-BOWLER.
        COMPUTE SERIES-SCORE = GAME1 + GAME2 + GAME3.
        COMPUTE TOTAL-PINS = TOTAL-PINS + SERIES-SCORE.
*       ADD SERIES-SCORE TO TOTAL-PINS.
        ADD 3 TO TOTAL-GAMES.
        COMPUTE AVERAGE-SCORE = TOTAL-PINS / TOTAL-GAMES.
*       DIVIDE TOTAL-PINS BY TOTAL-GAMES GIVING AVERAGE-SCORE.
        COMPUTE SIGNED-HANDICAP NEW-HANDICAP =
            (200 - AVERAGE-SCORE) * .8.
*           (200 - TOTAL-PINS / TOTAL-GAMES) * .8.
        IF SIGNED-HANDICAP < ZERO
            MOVE ZERO TO NEW-HANDICAP.


    0300-DISPLAY-RESULTS.
        ADD OLD-HANDICAP TO GAME1 GAME2 GAME3.
        COMPUTE SERIES-WITH-HANDICAP =
            SERIES-SCORE + OLD-HANDICAP * 3.
        DISPLAY 'ACTUAL GAME1 GAME2 GAME3 SERIES TOTAL TOTAL   NEW '.
        DISPLAY 'SERIES W HCP W HCP W HCP W HCP   GAMES  PINS   HCP '.
        DISPLAY ' ' SERIES-SCORE ' ' GAME1 ' ' GAME2 ' ' GAME3
            ' ' SERIES-WITH-HANDICAP ' ' TOTAL-GAMES ' '
            TOTAL-PINS ' ' NEW-HANDICAP.
```

Notice that the asterisk or comment lines in the program are alternatives to the preceding line that produces the same result but in a different manner. The ACCEPT statements would allow you to enter your own data instead of using the numbers I coded for testing with BOWLER1 and BOWLER2. If you want to do that, just be careful that you enter the values correctly, or you'll get screwy results, because there is no editing in this program for valid values.

The program is based on bowling in a handicap bowling league where three games comprise a series. The handicap value is set at 80 percent of the difference between the bowler's average and 200. That's fairly common but can easily be changed if you want. Note that there is a special calculation for new bowlers who haven't bowled before. A similar program also works for golf but isn't quite as interesting, because one round of golf is played instead of three games of bowling.

In the first COMPUTE for the new bowler, the scores for the three games are added together. Since this is a new bowler, the result is both the total for that series and the grand total bowled in the league. I just listed both before the =, and the result is stored in both data-items.

In the second COMPUTE where the average score is calculated, the summing of the scores for the three games is surrounded by parentheses. This is needed because multiplication and division are done before addition and subtraction if parentheses aren't there. Such a result would be GAME3 divided by 3, added to GAME1 plus GAME2, and that is certainly not what you want.

The same rationale applies to the third COMPUTE. The difference between the average and 200 must be calculated first, so it is surrounded by parentheses. Notice that the alternative here has parentheses inside parentheses. This works quite well and produces the same results. It's just a little bit trickier to work through if you're not familiar with formulas and arithmetic expressions.

The code with the SIGNED-HANDICAP is just to ensure that bowlers with averages of over 200 don't get penalized with negative handicaps.

In the code for regular bowlers, you can see that the asterisked ADD statement is simpler and more direct when adding to cumulative totals than the COMPUTE. Both will have the same result. However, the alternative DIVIDE statement three lines below is about as simple (or complex) as the COMPUTE.

Notice in the alternative calculation for the new handicap in this paragraph that TOTAL-PINS / TOTAL-GAMES has not been surrounded by parentheses. That isn't needed, since division and multiplication are done before addition and subtraction, so the result will be the same either way. The parentheses can be added for clarity, though, and that's normally a good idea.

3

USING CONDITIONAL STATEMENTS

Observe the ADD statement in 0300-DISPLAY-RESULTS. Here, you can add the handicap to the scores for all three games with just one statement.

Finally, in the COMPUTE in this paragraph, note again that there are no parentheses, because OLD-HANDICAP will be multiplied by 3 first, and then that result will be added with the SERIES-SCORE to produce SERIES-WITH-HANDICAP. That is what you want to happen.

The ROUNDED Option

So far I've only discussed how digits may be truncated or dropped off from the left or right side of numeric results if the results field does not have sufficient digits to store them. With addition and subtraction, this is not much of a problem, and you can ensure that data fields have enough digits to store the results. But with other calculations, additional facilities sometimes are needed.

The word ROUNDED may be added after any receiving field in any arithmetic statement (ADD, SUBTRACT, MULTIPLY, DIVIDE, and COMPUTE). ROUNDED will cause the low-order positions of the temporary results fields to be rounded to the nearest value that can be stored in that results field. For example, the statement MULTIPLY DOLLAR-AMT BY .22 GIVING EMPLOYEE-TAX ROUNDED ACTUAL-TAX REPORT-TAX ROUNDED will result in rounding being done for EMPLOYEE-TAX and REPORT-TAX but not for ACTUAL-TAX.

The way COBOL does rounding is to add 5 to the intermediate results in the next lower-order position than is defined in the results field. This is done to the absolute value (or unsigned version) of the intermediate results so that rounding is always away from zero. The new intermediate result then is stored in the receiving field using normal truncation rules. The following examples show how this happens:

PICTURE	*Intermediate Result*	*Rounding Factor*	*New Result*	*Final Result*
S9(5)V99	00234.4847	.005	00234.4897	00234.48
S9(5)V99	00234.4857	.005	00234.4907	00234.49
S9(5)V99	-(00234.4857)	.005	-(00234.4907)	-00234.49
9(4)	1042.7	.5	1043.2	1043
S9V999	0.00049	.0005	0.00099	0.000
S9V999	0.00050	.0005	0.00100	0.001
S9V999	-(0.00050)	.0005	-(0.00100)	-0.001

You can see that this works like you would want. There are other rounding algorithms, and some languages use them instead, but this is the accepted mechanism for accounting and finance, and it works well in most business applications.

The `ON SIZE ERROR` Phrase

There is also a means for dealing with the truncation of high-order digits during arithmetic operations, but it must be handled differently than ROUNDED. That is because there is no obvious algorithm for dealing with losing the most significant digits in the value. COBOL provides the conditional ON SIZE ERROR phrase, which can be added to any arithmetic statement to deal with this situation. With the DIVIDE statements or division operations in COMPUTE statements, this phrase also gives the program control of the situation should division by zero occur. The following is a typical statement with the ON SIZE ERROR phrase:

```
MULTIPLY FIELD-A-3DIGITS BY FIELD-B-3DIGITS GIVING ANSWER-5DIGITS
  ON SIZE ERROR
    DISPLAY 'NOT ENOUGH DIGITS FOR RESULT'.
```

For most three-digit numbers being multiplied, a five-result field is large enough. But there are also many cases in which it may not be enough (500 * 500 = 250,000). If one field is the number of hours worked in the month, and the other is the hourly pay rate in American dollars, five digits should be plenty to hold the answer (at least for the next 5 or 10 years). The ON SIZE ERROR phrase is used to identify that the overflow situation has occurred so that appropriate changes can be made should inflation ever cause the condition to occur.

The following is the general format of arithmetic statements with the ON SIZE ERROR phrase:

```
arithmetic statement
  [ON SIZE ERROR
    imperative statement]
  [NOT ON SIZE ERROR
    imperative statement]
  [END-arithmetic verb]
```

As with ROUNDED, the arithmetic statements are ADD, SUBTRACT, MULTIPLY, DIVIDE, and COMPUTE. The END-arithmetic verb term is END-ADD, END-SUBTRACT, and so on, and it must match up the statement being used.

The NOT ON SIZE ERROR phrase and the END-arithmetic term were introduced with the 1985 COBOL Standard and generally are not available with 1974 compilers.

When the ON SIZE ERROR phrase is specified and the condition does occur, the receiving field is *not* modified by the arithmetic statement, but the statements following that phrase

3

USING CONDITIONAL STATEMENTS

are executed instead. When the condition does not occur, the results are placed in the receiving field, and the statements following any NOT ON SIZE ERROR phrase are executed.

If no ON SIZE ERROR phrase is coded, but the condition does occur, the results are *unspecified*. In most cases, the high-order digits that will not fit will be truncated (in my example, 50,000 would be placed in ANSWER-5DIGITS). But, if the data-item is defined with USAGE COMPUTATIONAL, some other result would be likely. When a DIVIDE BY ZERO occurs and no ON SIZE ERROR phrase is coded, the program is terminated abruptly in most environments.

An in-depth discussion of imperative statements is provided in "The General Definition of Imperative Statements and Some Comments on Them," later in this chapter, but this brief intuitive description introduces these statements and provides background for the sample program.

An *imperative statement* is one or more statements (other than IF) that do not have any conditional phrases (such as ON SIZE ERROR). Because MOVE, ACCEPT, DISPLAY, and STOP RUN don't have any conditional phrases, they always are considered imperative statements.

Beginning with the 1985 COBOL Standard, statements with conditional phrases that also include the statement-terminating END-verb (such as END-ADD, END-SUBTRACT, and so on) term also are considered imperative statements.

So, the following statement is allowed:

```
MULTIPLY FIELD-1 BY FIELD-2 GIVING FIELD-2
   ON SIZE ERROR
      ADD FIELD-A TO FIELD-B
      DISPLAY 'MULTIPLY ERROR'
```

However, the following statement is not allowed:

```
MULTIPLY FIELD-1 BY FIELD-2 GIVING FIELD-2
   ON SIZE ERROR
      ADD FIELD-A TO FIELD-B
         ON SIZE ERROR
            DISPLAY '???? ERROR'
      DISPLAY '???? ERROR'
```

This is because the ADD statement now contains a conditional phrase, so it is not an imperative statement. The 1985 COBOL Standard permits you to change the statement by inserting END-ADD, as follows, so that it will be acceptable:

```
MULTIPLY FIELD-1 BY FIELD-2 GIVING FIELD-2
  ON SIZE ERROR
    ADD FIELD-A TO FIELD-B
      ON SIZE ERROR
        DISPLAY 'ADD ERROR'
    END-ADD
    DISPLAY 'MULTIPLY ERROR'
```

Demonstrating the Arithmetic Statements (and Some Edited PICTURE Clauses)

The code in Listing 3.2 shows a variety of arithmetic statements as they are typically used. There's nothing fancy or sophisticated about it. You also might notice some different PIC clauses and can see the effect they have.

LISTING 3.2   ARITH.

```
IDENTIFICATION DIVISION.
 PROGRAM-ID.  Arith.
 DATA DIVISION.
 WORKING-STORAGE SECTION.
 01   TOTAL-SUPPLY-VALUE          PIC 9(6)V99 VALUE ZERO.
 01   TOTAL-ORDER-COST            PIC 9(6)V99 VALUE ZERO.
 01   WORK-COST                   PIC 9(5)V99.
 01   WORK-COUNT                  PIC 999.
 01   ORDER-RATIO                 PIC 99V99.
 01   ERROR-FLAG                  PIC X VALUE SPACE.
 01   SUPPLY-INFO.
      05   ID-NUMBER              PIC X(6).
      05   COUNT-ON-HAND          PIC 999.
      05   COST-EACH              PIC 999V99.
      05   LAST-REQUESTED-DATE    PIC X(8).
      05   LAST-REQUESTED-COUNT   PIC 999.

 01   SUGGESTED-ORDER.
      05   ORD-ID-NUMBER          PIC XXXXBXX.
      05   FILLER                 PIC XX VALUE SPACES.
      05   ORD-ON-HAND            PIC 999.
      05   FILLER                 PIC XX VALUE SPACES.
      05   ORD-LAST-REQUESTED-DATE  PIC XXXX/XX/XX.
      05   FILLER                 PIC XX VALUE SPACES.
      05   ORD-QUANTITY           PIC 999.
      05   FILLER                 PIC XX VALUE SPACES.
      05   ORD-AMOUNT             PIC ZZ,ZZ9.99.
      05   ORD-FLAG               PIC X VALUE SPACE.

 01   ITEM1 PIC X(25) VALUE 'A00101005001991998021 5002'.
 01   ITEM2 PIC X(25) VALUE 'B00201025000241997093 0010'.
```

continues

LISTING 3.2 CONTINUED

```
01   ITEM3 PIC X(25) VALUE 'B00204025025991998O115010'.
PROCEDURE DIVISION.
0000-MAIN.
     DISPLAY 'ID NUMB AVAIL  LAST USED ORDER       COST'.
     MOVE ITEM1 TO SUPPLY-INFO.
*    ACCEPT SUPPLY-INFO.
     PERFORM 0100-PROCESS.
     MOVE ITEM2 TO SUPPLY-INFO.
*    ACCEPT SUPPLY-INFO.
     PERFORM 0100-PROCESS.
     MOVE ITEM3 TO SUPPLY-INFO.
*    ACCEPT SUPPLY-INFO.
     PERFORM 0100-PROCESS.
     DISPLAY ' '.
     DISPLAY 'CURRENT SUPPLY VALUE: ' TOTAL-SUPPLY-VALUE
         ', SUGGESTED ORDER COST: ' TOTAL-ORDER-COST.
     IF ERROR-FLAG  NOT = SPACE
       DISPLAY ' * CALL PROGRAMMER'.
     STOP RUN.

0100-PROCESS.
     MOVE SPACE TO ORD-FLAG.
     MOVE ID-NUMBER TO ORD-ID-NUMBER.
     MOVE COUNT-ON-HAND TO ORD-ON-HAND.
     MOVE LAST-REQUESTED-DATE TO ORD-LAST-REQUESTED-DATE.
     MOVE ZERO TO WORK-COST.
     MULTIPLY COUNT-ON-HAND BY COST-EACH GIVING WORK-COST
       ON SIZE ERROR
          MOVE '*' TO ORD-FLAG
                      ERROR-FLAG.
     ADD WORK-COST TO TOTAL-SUPPLY-VALUE.
     MOVE ZERO TO ORDER-RATIO ORD-QUANTITY.
     ADD COUNT-ON-HAND LAST-REQUESTED-COUNT
        GIVING WORK-COUNT.
     IF LAST-REQUESTED-DATE > '19980101'
        DIVIDE WORK-COUNT INTO LAST-REQUESTED-COUNT
           GIVING ORDER-RATIO.
     MULTIPLY ORDER-RATIO BY 2 GIVING ORDER-RATIO.
     IF ORDER-RATIO > .25
        MULTIPLY WORK-COUNT BY ORDER-RATIO
           GIVING ORD-QUANTITY ROUNDED.
     MULTIPLY ORD-QUANTITY BY COST-EACH
        GIVING WORK-COST
               ORD-AMOUNT.
     ADD WORK-COST TO TOTAL-ORDER-COST.
     DISPLAY SUGGESTED-ORDER.
```

This program is a very basic supply-ordering program. Again, the means of obtaining input data is very primitive. Normally, the data on all the items kept in supply would be in a data file or database, but since I haven't gotten to handling data files yet, sample data is defined in WORKING-STORAGE. This can be expanded on readily. The important highlights are that a good variety of the arithmetic statements are used like they normally are in COBOL programs, and some of the many PICTURE editing statements also are included, so you can see some of the things they can do for you. Because the statements and logic are both self-evident, I won't make any additional comments.

The General Definition of Imperative Statements and Some Comments on Them

You've seen a good variety of imperative statements, and in the preceding section, you got a general intuitive notion of their definitions and how to distinguish them from conditional statements. You also saw a number of simplified IF statements. Before beginning an in-depth examination of conditional processing in COBOL, a more formal and complete treatment of the imperative statements is needed.

Because COBOL was standardized before the advent of structured programming principles and the development of the modern block-structure languages (such as C and Pascal), its statements were designed without a clear, definitive statement termination. The intent was that COBOL was to be a very "human-language," and that statements and sentences should not have artificial constructs or special characters introduced that might interfere with the flow of the language. The period character always has been used to terminate sentences in COBOL, but because a sentence can contain many imperative statements in addition to the complex IF structure, the period is not sufficient for a variety of programming needs. This results in ambiguities such as the one you looked at earlier:

```
MULTIPLY FIELD-1 BY FIELD-2 GIVING FIELD-2
  ON SIZE ERROR
    ADD FIELD-A TO FIELD-B
      ON SIZE ERROR
        DISPLAY '???? ERROR'
    DISPLAY '???? ERROR'
```

As you saw, the ADD statement with the ON SIZE ERROR phrase is not allowed, because with that phrase, it is not an imperative statement and therefore cannot be included in the conditional phrase of the MULTIPLY statement. The rationale is obvious, because without a clear termination of each statement, there is no way to determine with which conditional phrase the two DISPLAY statements are to be associated.

The 1985 COBOL Standard introduced the END-verb term in a manner so that it could serve as a terminator for any statement containing a conditional phrase. When a program is written completely from this premise, a rich mixture of imperative and conditional statements can be coded without ambiguity or confusion. Unfortunately, many programs are written for the 1974 Standard in this area, regardless of whether it is really necessary. The READ statement is the most obvious beneficiary of the new structure, but I've hardly ever seen it employed in production programs. Even though it's a few chapters premature, I demonstrate the newer techniques with the READ at the end of this section.

All conditional statements and phrases except for IF *may contain only imperative statements.*

There are several ways of determining whether a statement is an imperative statement. Even though most of the verbs and phrases have not yet been defined or described, they are all shown so you can find them all in one place.

Statements beginning with the following verbs always are imperative, because no conditional phrases are defined for them. This is true for both the 1985 and the 1974 Standards.

ACCEPT	DISPLAY	INITIALIZE	OPEN	SET
ALTER	ENABLE	INSPECT	PERFORM	SORT
CANCEL	EXIT	INITIATE	PURGE	STOP
CLOSE	GENERATE	MERGE	RELEASE	SUPPRESS
CONTINUE	GO TO	MOVE	SEND	TERMINATE
DISABLE				

Statements beginning with the following verbs have conditional phrases that are optional. If such phrases are not used, the statement is imperative. This is true for both the 1974 and the 1985 Standards.

ADD	DELETE	READ	START	UNSTRING
CALL	DIVIDE	RECEIVE	STRING	WRITE
COMPUTE	MULTIPLY	REWRITE	SUBTRACT	

When the associated conditional phrases are used with the statements beginning with these verbs, the statements become conditional instead of imperative. In that form, they cannot be used within other conditional phrases. For programs conforming to the 1974 Standard, there are no other options. For programs compiled with 1985 Standard compilers, the corresponding END-verb term may be used to terminate the conditional phrases and hence the statement itself. When this term is used, the statement becomes imperative again, because its scope has been explicitly terminated. In that form, it can be used within a conditional phrase of another statement. Again, the example from the previous section demonstrates this:

```
MULTIPLY FIELD-1 BY FIELD-2 GIVING FIELD-2
  ON SIZE ERROR
    ADD FIELD-A TO FIELD-B
      ON SIZE ERROR
        DISPLAY 'ADD ERROR'
    END-ADD
    DISPLAY 'MULTIPLY ERROR'
END-MULTIPLY
```

Note that END-MULTIPLY is not required to terminate the MULTIPLY statement, because it is not part of a conditional phrase. The following words identify the various conditional phrases that can be used with the verbs listed earlier (which are associated with the verbs described wherever they are fully defined). The available corresponding converse conditions also are shown:

AT END	NOT AT END
END-OF-PAGE	NOT END-OF-PAGE
INVALID KEY	NOT INVALID KEY
NO DATA	WITH DATA
ON EXCEPTION	NOT ON EXCEPTION
ON OVERFLOW	NOT ON OVERFLOW
ON SIZE ERROR	NOT ON SIZE ERROR

Four verbs are exceptions. IF and SEARCH are verbs that simply do not function without the conditional processing associated with them; therefore, no simplified form can be used within conditional phrases in 1974 Standard COBOL. END-IF and END-SEARCH statement-termination terms are defined, though, in the 1985 Standard, so if these are used, statements beginning with these verbs may be used within conditional phrases in 1985 Standard programs. EVALUATE is a new verb that is not available to 1974 COBOL. Conditional processing also is inherent to its processing, so no simplified form can be used as an imperative statement unless it is terminated by a corresponding END-EVALUATE. PERFORM is the final exception. Observe that it is listed with those verbs that always are imperative. Although this is true, there is also a new feature that was added with the 1985 Standard that enables you to list one or more imperative statements following the PERFORM and terminated by the END-PERFORM terminator. Although this is not conditional processing, the statements are bracketed in the same way. Such use of PERFORM is termed *inline* PERFORM and is covered in the next chapter.

As I promised earlier, I'll demonstrate a technique to simplify the READ statement in COBOL. READ is used to place data from an external file into program storage. The conditional phrase AT END is included when data is to be processed sequentially (one record after the other) until there is no more. The next time the READ statement is executed after

3

USING
CONDITIONAL
STATEMENTS

the last record is processed, the statements in the AT END conditional phrase are executed. Most programs keep READ statements in separate paragraphs that are PERFORMed from elsewhere in the program. This is a good idea that I support. But from here, common sense heads south with the notions "That's the way everyone else does it," and "It's always worked that way." The first example isn't too bad, but notice the redundant IF statement:

```
0100-READ-INPUT-FILE.

    READ INPUT-FILE
        AT END
            MOVE  'Y' TO END-OF-FILE-STATUS.
    IF END-OF-FILE-STATUS = 'N'
        ADD 1 TO INPUT-RECORD-COUNT.
```

The following example employs a mechanism and statements that haven't been covered yet, but if you've ever had programming classes, you know that GO TO should be avoided whenever possible:

```
0100-READ-INPUT-FILE.

    READ INPUT-FILE
        AT END
            MOVE 'Y' TO END-OF-FILE-STATUS
            GO TO 0100-EXIT.
    ADD 1 TO INPUT-RECORD-COUNT.

0100-EXIT.
    EXIT.
```

The EXIT statement, the exit paragraph, and the GO TO statement are covered in the next chapter. The following alternative is the one I prefer. Not only does it seem a bit clearer to me, but it is also more efficient:

```
0100-READ-INPUT-FILE.

    READ INPUT-FILE
        AT END
            MOVE  'Y' TO END-OF-FILE-STATUS
        NOT AT END
            ADD 1 TO INPUT-RECORD-COUNT
    END-READ.
```

By the way, I have coded all three alternatives, because it is very important to be consistent with the present style when working with existing programs. In programs of any significant size, this consistency is much more important than the slight differences in the three forms. What does upset me is when these older forms are used in brand-new production programs where there is no need at all for the older forms.

The IF Statement

IF is one of the most powerful statements in COBOL. It contains some features and capabilities that simply aren't available in other languages. But it also carries some historical baggage that can be both troublesome and confusing. To this point, I've used IF with basic comparisons (both numeric and alphanumeric). I've combined comparisons using either AND or OR (but not both). I've also used NOT to reverse the truth of my comparisons. This only scratches the surface of the capabilities IF has for organizing the logic of a program.

As with the imperative and conditional statements, there are some subtle differences between the 1974 and 1985 Standards. In order to highlight and compare the differences, I'll cover the two IF standards separately. In a sense, this distinction is artificial, because in most areas, the two are identical and coexist quite well in new programs written for the 1985 Standard. The separation will simplify the discussion, however, and highlight the impact of the differences.

The 1974 Standard IF Statement

The basic format for IF according to the 1974 Standard follows:

```
IF condition {statement-1/NEXT SENTENCE} ELSE {statement-2/NEXT SENTENCE}
```

The condition is a comparison, a combination of comparisons, and/or one of several other conditional operations where a value of either true or false can be calculated. Conditions are covered in more detail in the next section and are visited again in Chapter 5, "Advanced Conditional Features and Techniques."

statement-1 and statement-2 can be any imperative statement, a conditional statement, or an imperative statement followed by a conditional statement. Because IF is a conditional statement, this means that an IF statement can contain another IF statement. The term for this is *nesting,* and it provides one of the powerful capabilities of the IF statement. IF statements can contain other conditional statements, such as ADD FIELD-A TO FIELD-B ON SIZE ERROR DISPLAY 'ERROR'. However, because there are no statement terminators in 1974 COBOL, this was so restrictive and confusing that it was hardly ever used.

NEXT SENTENCE is used as a placeholder when there is no statement-1 or statement-2 but the IF structure still needs to be continued. Observe that this term is called NEXT SENTENCE and *not* NEXT statement. This means that when it is encountered, the next item to be executed is the statement that begins the *next sentence,* and that is the statement that follows the *next period.* (If this IF is the last item in the paragraph, the first statement of wherever control passes from the current paragraph becomes the next item to be executed.) You'll see examples shortly to understand what happens here and why.

When there is no `statement-2` and `ELSE NEXT SENTENCE` is the last phrase in the sentence (in other words, it is followed by the period), it may be omitted. I agree with this and believe that trailing `ELSE NEXT SENTENCE` phrases should be eliminated, because they do nothing to add to the clarity of the `IF` structure and only add to the program length. The following examples demonstrate this:

```
IF FIELD-A = FIELD-B
    MOVE 1 TO ANSWER-1
    IF FIELD-C = FIELD-D
        MOVE 2 TO ANSWER-1
    ELSE
        NEXT SENTENCE
ELSE
    NEXT SENTENCE.
```

In this first example, neither `IF` has an associated `statement-2`, so both `NEXT SENTENCE` phrases are superfluous and may be removed, as shown here:

```
IF FIELD-A = FIELD-B
    MOVE 1 TO ANSWER-1
    IF FIELD-C = FIELD-D
        MOVE 2 TO ANSWER-1.
```

This is not possible with the following example:

```
IF FIELD-A = FIELD-B
    MOVE 1 TO ANSWER-1
    IF FIELD-C = FIELD-D
        MOVE 2 TO ANSWER-1
    ELSE
        NEXT SENTENCE
ELSE
    MOVE 3 TO ANSWER-1.
```

Here, `NEXT SENTENCE` is needed as a placeholder. It will cause the second `ELSE` to be associated with the first `IF` statement so that 3 is `MOVE`d to `ANSWER-1` when `FIELD-A` is not equal to `FIELD-B`. (`ANSWER-1` will be left unchanged from 1 when `FIELD-A` is equal to `FIELD-B` but `FIELD-C` is not equal to `FIELD-D`.)

In general, when `IF`s are nested (as shown in the example), each `ELSE` is associated with the preceding `IF` that does not already have an `ELSE` associated with it.

The general rules regarding the processing of `IF` follow. If the `condition` is true, `statement-1` is executed in its entirety, and then control is passed to the next *sentence*. So when the `condition` is true, anything following an `ELSE` for this `IF` is ignored. If the `condition` is false, `statement-2` is executed in its entirety, and then control is passed to the next *sentence.* So when the condition is false, everything between the condition and the ELSE is ignored. The next sentence is always the statement to be executed after the next terminating period (.) is reached. When the IF is the last sentence in the paragraph, control passes to wherever it would have if the statement had been an imperative statement instead of an IF (this is the commonsense rule here). The only exception is when GO TO is part of statement-1 or statement-2, and in that case, control is passed to wherever GO TO specifies (GO TO is covered in the next chapter).

It is because of these rules that the terminating period is so important in COBOL. Prior to the 1985 Standard, the period was the only means for terminating an IF statement, and forgetting a period or inserting an extra period where it shouldn't be could cause the program to work very differently than desired. Because the character is very small, such errors also are very difficult to spot.

The following block of code illustrates the basic IF statement and also will be used to demonstrate the important limitations it has with the 1974 Standard. Even though it's not a full program, it should be more than sufficient for this purpose.

```
100-PROCESS-PAYROLL-RECORD.
    PERFORM 200-UPDATE-INFORMATION.
    IF HOURS-WORKED > ZERO
       OR SPECIAL-PAY > ZERO
         MOVE EMPLOYEE-INFORMATION TO PAYROLL-INFORMATION
         MULTIPLY HOURS-WORKED BY HOURLY-RATE
             GIVING GROSS-PAY
         ADD SPECIAL-PAY TO GROSS-PAY
         MULTIPLY GROSS-PAY BY .25
             GIVING INCOME-TAX
         SUBTRACT INCOME-TAX FROM GROSS-PAY
             GIVING NET-PAY
         PERFORM 300-WRITE-PAYROLL-RECORD.
    PERFORM 400-READ-EMPLOYEE-RECORD.
```

This is a basic IF statement with nothing special about it until the following change needs to be made: When GROSS-PAY is more than 800.00, INCOME-TAX must be calculated at 30 percent instead of 25 percent. With 1974 COBOL, there is no way to do this simply and directly, because there is no way to terminate the new IF statement without also terminating the entire sentence. The following examples show alternatives that were (and still are) used.

Alternative 1

```
100-PROCESS-PAYROLL-RECORD.
    PERFORM 200-UPDATE-INFORMATION.
    IF HOURS-WORKED > ZERO
       OR SPECIAL-PAY > ZERO
         MOVE EMPLOYEE-INFORMATION TO PAYROLL-INFORMATION
```

```
        MULTIPLY HOURS-WORKED BY HOURLY-RATE
            GIVING GROSS-PAY
        ADD SPECIAL-PAY TO GROSS-PAY
        IF GROSS-PAY  > 800
            MULTIPLY GROSS-PAY BY .30
                GIVING INCOME-TAX
            SUBTRACT INCOME-TAX FROM GROSS-PAY
                GIVING NET-PAY
            PERFORM 300-WRITE-PAYROLL-RECORD
        ELSE
            MULTIPLY GROSS-PAY BY .25
                GIVING INCOME-TAX
            SUBTRACT INCOME-TAX FROM GROSS-PAY
                GIVING NET-PAY
            PERFORM 300-WRITE-PAYROLL-RECORD.
    PERFORM 400-READ-EMPLOYEE-RECORD.
```

Alternative 2

```
100-PROCESS-PAYROLL-RECORD.
    PERFORM 200-UPDATE-INFORMATION.
    IF HOURS-WORKED > ZERO
       OR SPECIAL-PAY > ZERO
       MOVE EMPLOYEE-INFORMATION TO PAYROLL-INFORMATION
       MULTIPLY HOURS-WORKED BY HOURLY-RATE
           GIVING GROSS-PAY
       ADD SPECIAL-PAY TO GROSS-PAY
       IF GROSS-PAY > 800
           MULTIPLY GROSS-PAY BY .30
               GIVING INCOME-TAX
       ELSE
           MULTIPLY GROSS-PAY BY .25
               GIVING INCOME-TAX.
    IF HOURS-WORKED > ZERO
       OR SPECIAL-PAY > ZERO
       SUBTRACT INCOME-TAX FROM GROSS-PAY
           GIVING NET-PAY
       PERFORM 300-WRITE-PAYROLL-RECORD.
    PERFORM 400-READ-EMPLOYEE-RECORD.
```

Alternative 3

```
100-PROCESS-PAYROLL-RECORD.
    PERFORM 200-UPDATE-INFORMATION.
    IF HOURS-WORKED > ZERO
       OR SPECIAL-PAY > ZERO
           PERFORM 250-CALCULATE-PAY.
PERFORM 400-READ-EMPLOYEE-RECORD.
    .
    .
    .

  250-CALCULATE-PAY.
```

```
MOVE EMPLOYEE-INFORMATION TO PAYROLL-INFORMATION.
MULTIPLY HOURS-WORKED BY HOURLY-RATE
    GIVING GROSS-PAY.
ADD SPECIAL-PAY TO GROSS-PAY.
IF GROSS-PAY > 800
    MULTIPLY GROSS-PAY BY .30
        GIVING INCOME-TAX
ELSE
    MULTIPLY GROSS-PAY BY .25
        GIVING INCOME-TAX.
SUBTRACT INCOME-TAX FROM GROSS-PAY
    GIVING NET-PAY.
PERFORM 300-WRITE-PAYROLL-RECORD.
```

None of these alternatives is very pleasing, and the END-IF introduced with the 1985 Standard solves the problem pretty cleanly.

The 1985 Standard IF Statement (with CONTINUE)

The basic format for IF according to the 1985 Standard follows:

```
IF condition THEN {statement-1} [ELSE statement-2] {END-IF}
```

First observe the THEN, then notice that it is optional, and forget that it is available in COBOL. Neither COBOL compilers nor COBOL programmers need it to determine where the condition ends and statement-1 begins.

Notice that the NEXT SENTENCE phrase is not shown here. This does not mean that it isn't allowed in 1985 COBOL. It is. But when the END-IF is used to terminate the IF, then NEXT SENTENCE is not allowed. That is because the two are essentially contradictory. You'll see how this is resolved shortly.

The general rules regarding the processing of the 1985 IF follow. If the condition is true, statement-1 is executed in its entirety, and then control is passed to the next statement following the END-IF. So when the condition is true, anything following an ELSE for this IF is ignored. If the condition is false, statement-2 is executed in its entirety, and then control is passed to the next statement following the END-IF. So, when the condition is false, everything between the condition and the ELSE is ignored. Like the other conditional statements with END-verb termination terms, the END-IF causes everything between the IF and it to be treated as one large imperative statement. Therefore, determining which statement will be executed next would be the same as if the entire IF statement were replaced by a simple MOVE statement. The only exception is when the GO TO is part of statement-1 or statement-2, and there, control is passed to wherever the GO TO specifies (GO TO is covered in the next chapter).

3

USING CONDITIONAL STATEMENTS

Now take a look at how you can resolve the situation from the last section by using the 1985 IF structure. For good measure, I'll also do SIZE ERROR checking so that I can identify cases in which I pay employees incorrectly.

```
100-PROCESS-PAYROLL-RECORD.
    PERFORM 200-UPDATE-INFORMATION.
    IF HOURS-WORKED > ZERO
       OR SPECIAL-PAY > ZERO
         MOVE EMPLOYEE-INFORMATION TO PAYROLL-INFORMATION
         COMPUTE GROSS-PAY = HOURS-WORKED * HOURLY-RATE + SPECIAL-PAY
           ON SIZE ERROR
             DISPLAY '** PAY CALC ERROR FOR ' EMPLOYEE-INFORMATION
             MOVE 999.99 TO GROSS-PAY
         END-COMPUTE
         IF GROSS-PAY > 800
             MULTIPLY GROSS-PAY BY .30
                 GIVING INCOME-TAX
         ELSE
             MULTIPLY GROSS-PAY BY .25
                 GIVING INCOME-TAX
         END-IF
         SUBTRACT INCOME-TAX FROM GROSS-PAY
             GIVING NET-PAY
         PERFORM 300-WRITE-PAYROLL-RECORD
    END-IF.
    PERFORM 400-READ-EMPLOYEE-RECORD.
```

As I mentioned earlier, NEXT SENTENCE can't be used with 1985 IF statements, because it implies transferring control to the next *sentence,* while the END-IF implies transferring control to the next *statement.* The word CONTINUE provides a clean alternative. It was introduced with the 1985 Standard and can be used in place of the imperative statement anywhere one is required. Because statement-1 can be an imperative statement, CON-TINUE can readily serve as a placeholder there when needed. Notice that statement-2 is not mentioned; it isn't needed, because END-IF can terminate an IF without an ELSE being required. The following examples demonstrate a few situations in which CONTINUE might be used:

```
IF FIELD-A = FIELD-B
    CONTINUE
ELSE
    MOVE 1 TO ANSWER-1
    IF FIELD-C = FIELD-D
       MOVE 2 TO ANSWER-1
    END-IF
END-IF.
```

In this case, ANSWER-1 is unaltered if FIELD-A equals FIELD-B. If they're unequal, ANSWER-1 is set to 1 but is changed to 2 if FIELD-C equals FIELD-D.

```
IF FIELD-A = FIELD-B
    MOVE 1 TO ANSWER-1
    IF FIELD-C = FIELD-D
       CONTINUE
    ELSE
       MOVE 2 TO ANSWER-1
    END-IF
    IF FIELD-E = FIELD-F
       MOVE 4 TO ANSWER-1
    END-IF
ELSE
    MOVE 3 TO ANSWER-1
END-IF.
```

Here, ANSWER-1 is set to 1 if FIELD-A equals FIELD-B, but then is changed to 2 if FIELD-C does not equal FIELD-D, and then is changed to 4 if FIELD-E equals FIELD-F. ANSWER-1 is set to 3 if FIELD-A does not equal FIELD-B.

Finally, it is important to note that when END-IF is not used, the rules for the statement revert to those for the 1974 Standard. In most cases, this is not a problem, because such situations are simple IF statements where the rules are identical. The distinction does need to be made, though, to avoid any confusion. The other situation to be aware of is that because one IF statement can contain another one (nesting), it is possible for IFs conforming to the two different sets of rules to be mixed in the same sentence. Although this isn't done often and should be avoided, you must know which set of rules is being used in order to interpret the statement.

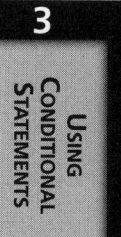

Conditions, `Condition-Names`, and the 88 Level

COBOL has a wide variety of options for expressing conditions. I cover the variations available in this section, and I revisit them and introduce additional complexity in Chapter 5. The six variations are relational, class, sign, switch, condition-name, and complex.

Relational Conditions

The relational condition simply compares two data items using any of a variety of relational operators and/or words. Most of the conditions I've used so far in this book have been of this type. The different relations that can be used follow (remember that the italicized words are optional):

```
IS [NOT] GREATER THAN
IS [NOT] >
IS [NOT] LESS THAN
IS [NOT] <
IS [NOT] EQUAL TO
IS [NOT] =
IS GREATER THAN OR EQUAL TO
IS >=
IS LESS THAN OR EQUAL TO
IS <=
```

Observe that there is both a word and special character version for each condition. Both are commonly used and are interchangeable. Items can be compared as shown here:

```
{identifier-1/literal-1/arithmetic-expression-1}
          {relational-term}
          {identifier-2/literal-2/arithmetic-expression-2}
```

Observe that arithmetic expressions can be used on either side or both sides of the relational operator. These are the same as they were defined for the COMPUTE statement. The literals and identifiers are as they were defined and described in Chapter 2, "Defining Data and Specifying Its Attributes." In most cases, numbers can be compared only with other numbers, and alphanumeric (character data) can be compared only with other alphanumeric data.

When the two items are numeric, they are aligned at the decimal point and an algebraic comparison is done. Unsigned numbers are treated as positive.

When the two items are alphanumeric (or alphabetic), if one is smaller in size (has fewer characters) than the other, it is placed in a temporary field left-justified, and spaces are added on the right so that it is of the same size as the larger item. The two items are then compared from left to right, one character at a time, according to the collating (or sort) sequence defined for that character set. Group level items always are treated as alphanumeric.

Numbers can be compared to alphanumeric data only if they are numeric integers and are not defined with any of the special USAGES (for example COMP, COMPUTATIONAL) available for numbers. In this case, the number is transferred to a temporary item and is either truncated or space-filled on the right to make it the same size as the alphanumeric data item. Then a character-by-character comparison is done, just as if they were both alphanumeric.

Class Conditions

There are five different class conditions that may be tested:

```
identifier IS [NOT] {NUMERIC/ALPHABETIC/ALPHABETIC-LOWER/ALPHABETIC-
UPPER/class-name}
```

When NUMERIC is used, the identifier must not be alphabetic. Otherwise, any operational signs must match the definition of the identifier. If the identifier is defined as alphanumeric, any sign values within the data will return a result of NOT NUMERIC. In general, if the identifier tests NUMERIC, the program must be able to do proper arithmetic with it.

With all the other class conditions, the identifier must be defined as either alphanumeric or alphabetic.

The condition ALPHABETIC means that all the characters are spaces, uppercase characters, or lowercase characters. Any special characters or numbers will give a NOT ALPHABETIC result.

ALPHABETIC-LOWER requires that all the characters be lowercase letters or spaces.

ALPHABETIC-UPPER requires that all the characters be uppercase letters or spaces.

A user-defined class-name can be used if it has been defined as such in the SPECIAL-NAMES paragraph in the ENVIRONMENT DIVISION. In this case, all the characters in the identifier must be one of those specified in the class-name definition.

Sign Conditions

This is the format for the sign conditions:

```
arithmetic-expression IS [NOT] {POSITIVE/ZERO/NEGATIVE}
```

The arithmetic expression must contain at least one variable. Because this is limited to arithmetic expressions, all data items must be numeric. This simplest form of this arithmetic expression is a single numeric data item.

If the expression is greater than zero, the sign condition POSITIVE is true. If it is less than zero, the condition NEGATIVE is true, and if it equals zero, the condition ZERO is true.

Switch Conditions

Switches may be defined in the SPECIAL-NAMES paragraph of the ENVIRONMENT DIVISION and associated with computer variables that are external to the COBOL program. Within this definition, condition-names also are defined that correspond to the "on" or "off" status of the external variable switch. When such a condition-name is referenced in an

3

USING
CONDITIONAL
STATEMENTS

IF condition, it is true when the variable is on or off as specified in the condition-name definition.

88 Level Condition-Name Conditions

The condition-names described here are quite popular with many COBOL programmers. Although these are defined in the DATA DIVISION, they are defined and described here instead of in the preceding chapter, because the definition does not make a great deal of sense unless you also see how the names are used in the PROCEDURE DIVISION.

An 88 level condition-name definition can be inserted after any data definition in the DATA DIVISION. It simply lists values and/or ranges of values for that data item. Then when that condition-name is identified in an IF (or PERFORM, EVALUATE, or SEARCH where such conditionals also are permitted), the condition is true if the current value of the data item matches one of those specified for the condition-name. Obviously, the values shown for the condition-name must correspond to the data definition of the data-item to which it pertains. The 88 level is defined as the following:

```
88  condition-name {VALUE IS/VALUES ARE}
➥{literal-1 [{THROUGH/THRU} literal-2]}...
```

VALUE and VALUES are synonymous, as are THROUGH and THRU. THRU allows a range of values to be identified. The ellipsis indicates that as many literals and/or ranges of literals can be identified as are required. Again, their form must match the data definition that the 88 level follows. Here are two examples to show how condition names can be used. You can see the first example in almost every COBOL program that handles sequential input files. Although it is a bit premature, it has to be included because it is so common.

```
WORKING-STORAGE SECTION.
01   INPUT-END-FILE-SWITCH              PIC X VALUE 'N'.
     88   END-OF-INPUT                  VALUE 'Y'.
     .
     .
     .
PROCEDURE DIVISION.
000-MAIN-CONTROL.
     .
     .
     .
     PERFORM 200-READ-INPUT-FILE.
     PERFORM 100-PROCESS-LOOP
         UNTIL END-OF-INPUT.
     .
     .
     .
     STOP RUN.
```

```
100-PROCESS-CONTROL.
    .
    .
    .
    PERFORM 200-READ-INPUT-FILE.
150-PROCESS-DETAIL.
    .
    .
    .
200-READ-INPUT-FILE.
    READ INPUT-FILE
        AT END
            MOVE 'Y' TO INPUT-END-FILE-SWITCH.
210-NEXT-PARAGRAPH.
    .
    .
    .
```

Although this is more of a skeleton than a program, you can see where the condition-name END-OF-INPUT is defined in WORKING-STORAGE and how it is associated with the data item INPUT-END-FILE-SWITCH that is defined with an initial value of N. You also can see how it is referenced in the UNTIL phrase of the PERFORM statement in 000-MAIN-CONTROL. This way, 100-PROCESS-CONTROL will continue to loop, processing and reading more records until the last one is processed and the READ statement executes the AT END conditional. This sets INPUT-END-FILE-SWITCH to Y, which matches the value defined for END-OF-INPUT, so the UNTIL END-OF-INPUT in the PERFORM 100-PROCESS-CONTROL is now true and the looping terminates.

The next example uses condition names to edit dates for a proper day value for the corresponding month. I must apologize, because the handling of leap years is not entirely correct with regard to the centuries. It is correct, though, for all years from 1901 through 2099, and that should be sufficient for the purposes of this book.

```
WORKING-STORAGE SECTION.
01   EDIT-DATE.
     05    EDIT-YEAR             PIC 9999.
     05    EDIT-MONTH            PIC 99.
        88  31-DAY-MONTH         VALUES 1 3 5 7 8 10 12.
        88  30-DAY-MONTH         VALUES 4 6 9 11.
        88  FEBRUARY             VALUE 2.
     05    EDIT-DAY              PIC 99.
        88  DAYS1-TO-31          VALUES 1 THRU 31.
        88  DAYS1-TO-30          VALUES 1 THRU 30.
        88  DAYS1-TO-28          VALUES 1 THRU 28.
        88  DAY29                VALUE 29.
01   WORK-YEAR                   PIC 9999.
01   WORK-REMAINDER              PIC 9.
        88  LEAP-YEAR            VALUE ZERO.
```

```
01  DATE-VALID-SWITCH            PIC X VALUE 'N'.
,
,
,
PROCEDURE DIVISION.
.
.
.
345-EDIT-DATE.
    MOVE 'N' TO DATE-VALID-SWITCH.
    IF 31-DAY-MONTH AND DAYS1-TO-31
        MOVE 'Y' TO DATE-VALID-SWITCH.
    IF 30-DAY-MONTH AND DAYS1-TO-30
        MOVE 'Y' TO DATE-VALID-SWITCH.
    IF FEBRUARY
        IF DAYS1-TO-28
            MOVE 'Y' TO DATE-VALID-SWITCH
        ELSE
            DIVIDE EDIT-YEAR BY 4 GIVING WORK-YEAR
                REMAINDER WORK-REMAINDER
            IF LEAP-YEAR AND DAY29
                MOVE 'Y' TO DATE-VALID-SWITCH.
```

You can see where setting up condition-names in the DATA DIVISION has made the statements in the PROCEDURE DIVISION clearer and easier to follow.

Complex Conditions

Complex conditionals are not really a separate type of conditional but instead are a means of combining any of the previously described types so that a single truth value can be calculated. I've already used AND several places, OR several places, and NOT to reverse the truth value in several other places. But so far, I've carefully kept all of them separate.

This is not really necessary, because COBOL uses an order of precedence in evaluating them, just like it does for the various operations in arithmetic statements. You also can use parentheses to clarify the order of evaluation when necessary. The order of precedence for complex conditionals follows:

1. Conditions in the innermost parentheses are evaluated first. When multiple conditionals are present at the same level within the parentheses, the following sequence applies.

2. The NOT reversal of truth value is done next.

3. Any pair of conditions separated by AND is combined to form a single truth value.

4. Any pair of conditions separated by OR is combined to form a single truth value.

5. When a series of conditions is separated by the same operator, they are combined from left to right.

These steps are repeated from the innermost parentheses outward until a single truth value for the conditional is determined. I've redone the PROCEDURE DIVISION for the date editing in the preceding section to demonstrate how conditionals can be combined (and even make sense, when you look at them carefully):

```
345-EDIT-DATE.
    MOVE 'N' TO DATE-VALID-SWITCH.
    DIVIDE EDIT-YEAR BY 4 GIVING WORK-YEAR
        REMAINDER WORK-REMAINDER.
    IF (31-DAY-MONTH AND DAYS1-TO-31)
        OR (30-DAY-MONTH AND DAYS1-TO-30)
        OR (FEBRUARY AND DAYS1-TO-28)
        OR (FEBRUARY AND LEAP-YEAR AND DAY29)
        MOVE 'Y' TO DATE-VALID-SWITCH.
```

Notice that this paragraph is much smaller than the preceding one, and it isn't difficult to figure out. The parentheses are not necessary, because all the AND combinations will be done before the ORs anyway because of the precedence order. The parentheses do make things clearer for programmers, though. You also could remove the 88 level conditionals, but that would complicate things a bit too much for this point in the book.

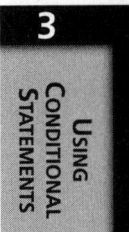

I'll get back to complex conditionals in Chapter 5 and make them even more interesting as the abbreviations COBOL allows are introduced. But first, you need to look more closely at PERFORM and the other mechanisms COBOL gives programmers to manage the flow of execution through the program; this topic is covered in Chapter 4.

Managing Program Flow and Looping

IN THIS CHAPTER

Flow control in COBOL is a large topic. When it is done well, the program is easy to write, easy to read and understand, and easy to maintain and upgrade regardless of the kinds of changes required. COBOL also has a variety of advanced features that enable you to control complex looping and process control in ways that are direct, organized, and easy to follow when the basic concepts are understood.

Process control is different in COBOL than in many other languages. When you stick to the basics and follow the guidelines for good structured programming, everything works out well. For the advanced programmer and when dealing with the variations in existing programs, though, it is very important to develop a good feel for how flow control is managed by COBOL.

The downside is that with all the features, the age of the language, the age of some programs, and the lack of understanding of some programmers, with some programs, it is very difficult to figure out what will happen in different situations. In fact, with some programs, this statement is a compliment. The terms *spaghetti code* and *spaghetti bowl* originated with this kind of program. Other analogies include giant kite-string or fishing-line tangles, or several jigsaw puzzles dumped together with pieces missing.

This chapter begins with the basics. Increasingly advanced techniques will be added, and descriptions of how things work will be presented. The final part of the chapter discusses the problem areas and presents some approaches for dealing with them. Although this chapter will not eliminate spaghetti code or allow you to maintain it easily, it will give you some options and direction so that you can deal with the problem, make progress, and eventually get the job done.

I'll use one basic sample program for illustration purposes in this chapter. Its advantage is that it is fairly short but has enough variety to demonstrate different process-control mechanisms. The program will do basic calculations with numbers that are 18 digits long; this also is useful because calculators can't handle numbers this large. A few other samples of code (with varying degrees of applicability) also are mixed in as needed.

The Basics of PERFORM and a Basic Calculator

The simplest PERFORM statement is PERFORM paragraph-name. I've already used this numerous times in the sample programs, and the essentials of how it works are simple. The statements in the referenced paragraph-name are executed in order, and then control is returned to the end of the PERFORM statement. I would like to emphasize a few items here because even though they seem obvious, it will be important to have a firm grasp of them as things get a bit more complex later. When I say that the statements in the referenced paragraph are executed, what I mean is that control is transferred to the first statement in that paragraph. A transfer back to the end of PERFORM occurs at the end of the paragraph being PERFORMed. The end of the paragraph really is defined by the name of the next paragraph. (Or the end of the program, if the paragraph being PERFORMed is the last one in the program.)

The following form of PERFORM also has been used frequently in previous examples:

```
PERFORM paragraph-name UNTIL condition
```

Here, condition can be any condition that returns a simple true or false result. Essentially, any condition (or combination of them) described in the preceding chapter can be specified here, and that by itself makes this a very flexible statement. The important comment to make here is that the condition is evaluated *before* the statements in the paragraph-name are executed. This means that if the condition is true at the start of the PERFORM, the statements in the paragraph-name will *not* be executed, and control passes immediately to the next statement following the PERFORM. If the condition is not true, the statements in the paragraph-name are executed, and then the condition is evaluated again. This process is repeated until the condition does become true, and then control is passed to the next statement.

The following form isn't used as often, but it can be very handy in special situations:

```
PERFORM paragraph-name {integer-literal/integer-data-item} TIMES
```

Here, the statements in the paragraph-name are executed the number of times specified by the integer or data-item. If the literal is used, it must be a whole number greater than zero. If a data-item is used, it also must be an integer (or whole number). But, the data-item can have a zero or negative value when the PERFORM is executed. If that happens, the statements in the paragraph-name are *not* executed. Also, when the data-item is used, its value is tested at the beginning of the statement to determine how many times to execute the statements in the paragraph-name, but it is not tested again during or between these executions. That means that altering the value of the data-item by the statements in the paragraph-name will have *no* impact on the number of times the statements are executed.

The code in Listing 4.1 demonstrates these statements.

LISTING 4.1 CALCULAT.

```
IDENTIFICATION DIVISION.
PROGRAM-ID.  Calculat.
DATA DIVISION.
WORKING-STORAGE SECTION.
01   LOOP-CONTROL                PIC X VALUE 'N'.
     88  USER-IS-DONE            VALUE 'Y'.
01   COMPUTE-INFO.
     05   FIELD-1                PIC 9(18).
     05   FILLER                 PIC X.
     05   OPERATION              PIC X.
     05   FILLER                 PIC X.
     05   FIELD-2                PIC 9(18).
01   RESULT                      PIC 9(18).
01   SHOW-RESULT      PIC ZZZ,ZZZ,ZZZ,ZZZ,ZZZ,ZZ9.


PROCEDURE DIVISION.
0100-MAIN.
     PERFORM 0200-CALCULATOR-CONTROL
         UNTIL USER-IS-DONE.
     STOP RUN.
0200-CALCULATOR-CONTROL.
     DISPLAY 'ENTER 18-DIGIT NUMBERS SEPARATED BY OPERATION AS'.
     DISPLAY '123456789012345678 X 123456789012345678'.
     ACCEPT COMPUTE-INFO.
     MOVE ZERO TO RESULT.
     IF OPERATION = '+'
        ADD FIELD-1 FIELD-2 GIVING RESULT
     ELSE
     IF OPERATION = '-'
        SUBTRACT FIELD-2 FROM FIELD-1 GIVING RESULT
     ELSE
     IF OPERATION = '*'
        MULTIPLY FIELD-1 BY FIELD-2 GIVING RESULT
     ELSE
     IF OPERATION = '/'
        DIVIDE FIELD-1 BY FIELD-2 GIVING RESULT
     ELSE
     IF OPERATION = '^'
        MOVE 1 TO RESULT
        PERFORM 0210-EXPONENT FIELD-2 TIMES.
     MOVE RESULT TO SHOW-RESULT.
     DISPLAY ' THE ANSWER IS: ' SHOW-RESULT.
     DISPLAY 'ARE YOU FINISHED WITH YOUR CALCULATIONS? (Y/N): '.
     ACCEPT LOOP-CONTROL.
0210-EXPONENT.
     MULTIPLY RESULT BY FIELD-1 GIVING RESULT.
```

Although this program is intended to be used interactively, it also works well in a "batch" mode. Listing 4.2 is a strictly batch-oriented version, so you can readily see the differences. Because the differences are small, I'll continue with only the interactive version in this chapter.

LISTING 4.2 CALCBATCH.

```
IDENTIFICATION DIVISION.
PROGRAM-ID.  CalcBat.
DATA DIVISION.
WORKING-STORAGE SECTION.
                                                     *
                                                     *

01   COMPUTE-INFO.
     05  FIELD-1              PIC 9(18).
     05  FILLER              PIC X.
     05  OPERATION           PIC X.
     05  FILLER              PIC X.
     05  FIELD-2             PIC 9(18).
     05  FILLER              PIC X.              *
     05  LOOP-CONTROL        PIC X VALUE SPACE.  *
     88  USER-IS-DONE        VALUE 'Y'.          *

01   RESULT                  PIC 9(18).
01   SHOW-RESULT      PIC ZZZ,ZZZ,ZZZ,ZZZ,ZZZ,ZZ9.

PROCEDURE DIVISION.
0100-MAIN.
     PERFORM 0200-CALCULATOR-CONTROL
         UNTIL USER-IS-DONE.
     STOP RUN.
0200-CALCULATOR-CONTROL.
                                                     *
                                                     *

     ACCEPT COMPUTE-INFO.
     MOVE ZERO TO RESULT.
     IF OPERATION = '+'
        ADD FIELD-1 FIELD-2 GIVING RESULT
     ELSE
     IF OPERATION = '-'
        SUBTRACT FIELD-2 FROM FIELD-1 GIVING RESULT
     ELSE
     IF OPERATION = '*'
        MULTIPLY FIELD-1 BY FIELD-2 GIVING RESULT
     ELSE
     IF OPERATION = '/'
        DIVIDE FIELD-1 BY FIELD-2 GIVING RESULT
     ELSE
     IF OPERATION = '^'
```

continues

4

LISTING 4.2 CONTINUED

```
        MOVE 1 TO RESULT
        PERFORM 0210-EXPONENT FIELD-2 TIMES.
    MOVE RESULT TO SHOW-RESULT.
    DISPLAY COMPUTE-INFO.                        *
    DISPLAY ' THE ANSWER IS: ' SHOW-RESULT.

                                                 *
                                                 *

0210-EXPONENT.
    MULTIPLY RESULT BY FIELD-1 GIVING RESULT.
```

You'll notice right away that there is no editing being done in this example; I will add that later. For now, you have to be very careful entering the data here. Make sure that all the digits are entered as numeric for each value. Also make sure that field-2 has a value other than zero when using the division operation.

The PERFORM...UNTIL at the beginning of the PROCEDURE DIVISION is normal. The use of the 88 level helps clarify what is being tested for.

The "^", which is the last operation value tested for, is being used to indicate exponentiation. Observe how the PERFORM 0210-EXPONENT FIELD-2 TIMES simulates exponentiation by repetitive multiplication using the looping mechanism. Don't use large values for FIELD-2 here, because the results will increase quickly.

The TEST AFTER Option (1985)

Earlier, I described how any UNTIL conditions in PERFORM statements are evaluated before the paragraph specified in the PERFORM is executed, and if the condition is true at that time, the paragraph is not executed at all. The TEST AFTER option was introduced in the 1985 Standard to give the programmer control over when the condition is evaluated. This is handy when it is known that the paragraph will always need to be performed at least one first time. Such situations are fairly common when reading external data into the program, and the condition can't really be evaluated until the first set of data has been obtained. I demonstrate this in the updated sample program at the end of this section. The format for specifying this option follows:

```
PERFORM paragraph-name
    [[WITH TEST {BEFORE/AFTER}] UNTIL condition]
```

The word WITH is optional, and the word BEFORE can be specified, although it is never really needed, because BEFORE is the default. Note here that this option can be used only when the UNTIL condition phrase is used, and then the TEST option must precede the UNTIL part of the phrase.

The Inline PERFORM Feature (1985)

The inline PERFORM functionality allows you to include the statements that are to be PERFORMed right with the PERFORM itself instead of in another paragraph somewhere else in the program. This is especially handy where a loop is required, but only a few statements are required in the loop. Here, it is inconvenient to have to set up a separate paragraph somewhere else in the program for these few statements. It also is cumbersome for the maintenance programmer to have to find such a paragraph in order to see what is going on in the loop. The 0210-EXPONENT paragraph in my sample program is an example of such a situation, and I'll remedy that in the updated version at the end of this section.

It should be noted that in most situations, when PERFORM is used to control the execution of subordinate processing and/or logic, the inline PERFORM is not necessary, and the PERFORM paragraph-name format should be used instead. The inline PERFORM functionality was added with the 1985 Standard, and its formats follow:

```
PERFORM
    imperative statement
    END-PERFORM
PERFORM
    {numeric-data-item/integer} TIMES
    imperative statement
    END-PERFORM
PERFORM
    [[WITH TEST {AFTER/BEFORE}] UNTIL condition]
    imperative statement
    END-PERFORM
```

Note that in all the forms, no paragraph name is specified. This means that the two formats are mutually exclusively. Remember also that an imperative statement can, in fact, be any number of imperative statements as long as none of them have unterminated conditional phrases.

PERFORM VARYING

PERFORM VARYING is intended primarily to support table and array handling and therefore is covered more extensively in Chapter 11, "Tables and Arrays." I'll also cover it here briefly so that it can be readily found, and because there are some situations in which it can be useful, even though tables, arrays, and subscripts are not involved. The basic format of PERFORM VARYING follows:

```
PERFORM [paragraph-name]
    [[WITH TEST {AFTER/BEFORE}]
        VARYING numeric-data-item-1 FROM
        ➥{numeric-literal-1/numeric-data-item-2}
```

```
      BY {numeric-literal-2/numeric-data-item-3}
      UNTIL condition]
[imperative-statement
  END-PERFORM]
```

This feature is involved, but it does act pretty much like you would expect from the wording that is used. Note that there is also a VARYING...AFTER phrase that can be included in this format but is not shown here. See Chapter 11 for details on how you can use it, as well as more detailed rules on exactly what you can and cannot do with the feature.

In general, the numeric-data-item-1 is set to the value of the FROM literal/data-item at the beginning. The TEST AFTER/BEFORE option can be used to specify whether the condition is to be evaluated after or before the statements are executed (BEFORE is the default, as with the regular PERFORM UNTIL). If the TEST BEFORE is specified (or implied), the condition is evaluated, and if it is true, control passes to the end of the PERFORM without the statements being executed at all. Otherwise, the statements are executed, and then the numeric-data-item-1 is incremented by the amount of the BY literal/data-item. The condition is evaluated, and if it is true, control passes to the end of the PER-FORM. Otherwise, the statements are executed again, the numeric-data-item-1 is incre-mented again, the condition is evaluated again, and this process is repeated until the condition evaluates as true and the looping ends.

This is one of those cases where the program statements are easier to follow than the explanation. I'll use this feature in the sample program in Listing 4.3 so you can see that it is easy to follow.

As with the other PERFORM formats, the inline PERFORM feature can be used or a paragraph-name can be specified, but both options cannot be combined in the same statement.

Updated Sample Program

In addition to demonstrating the PERFORM VARYING, this updated version takes advan-tages of the other items I just covered in the last few sections.

LISTING 4.3 CALCUL2—UPDATED SAMPLE PROGRAM.

```
IDENTIFICATION DIVISION.
PROGRAM-ID.  Calcul2.
DATA DIVISION.
WORKING-STORAGE SECTION.
01  LOOP-CONTROL               PIC X VALUE 'N'.
    88  USER-IS-DONE           VALUE 'Y'.
```

```
01   COMPUTE-INFO.
     05   FIELD-1              PIC 9(18).
     05   FILLER               PIC X.
     05   OPERATION            PIC X.
     05   FILLER               PIC X.
     05   FIELD-2              PIC 9(18).
01   RESULT                    PIC 9(18).
01   POWER-VALUE               PIC 9(18).
01   SHOW-RESULT     PIC ZZZ,ZZZ,ZZZ,ZZZ,ZZZ,ZZ9.
01   OVERFLOW-CONTROL          PIC X VALUE 'N'.

PROCEDURE DIVISION.
0100-MAIN.
     PERFORM 0200-CALCULATOR-CONTROL
         TEST AFTER
         UNTIL USER-IS-DONE.
     STOP RUN.
0200-CALCULATOR-CONTROL.
     DISPLAY 'ENTER 18-DIGIT NUMBERS SEPARATED BY OPERATION AS'.
     DISPLAY '123456789012345678 X 123456789012345678'.
     ACCEPT COMPUTE-INFO.
     MOVE ZERO TO RESULT.
     IF OPERATION = '+'
        ADD FIELD-1 FIELD-2 GIVING RESULT
     ELSE
     IF OPERATION = '-'
        SUBTRACT FIELD-2 FROM FIELD-1 GIVING RESULT
     ELSE
     IF OPERATION = '*'
        MULTIPLY FIELD-1 BY FIELD-2 GIVING RESULT
     ELSE
     IF OPERATION = '/'
        DIVIDE FIELD-1 BY FIELD-2 GIVING RESULT
     ELSE
     IF OPERATION = '^'
        MOVE 1 TO RESULT
        MOVE 'N' TO OVERFLOW-CONTROL
        PERFORM
            VARYING POWER-VALUE FROM 1 BY 1
            UNTIL POWER-VALUE > FIELD-2
              MULTIPLY RESULT BY FIELD-1 GIVING RESULT
                ON SIZE ERROR
                   DISPLAY 'OVERFLOW AT POWER = ' POWER-VALUE
                   SUBTRACT 1 FROM POWER-VALUE
                   DISPLAY 'VALUE AT ' POWER-VALUE ' WAS: '
                   MOVE FIELD-2 TO POWER-VALUE
              END-MULTIPLY
        END-PERFORM.
     MOVE RESULT TO SHOW-RESULT.
     DISPLAY ' THE ANSWER IS: ' SHOW-RESULT.
     DISPLAY 'ARE YOU FINISHED WITH YOUR CALCULATIONS? (Y/N): '.
     ACCEPT LOOP-CONTROL.
```

I inserted the TEST AFTER before the UNTIL condition in the PERFORM at the beginning of 0100-MAIN. Even though the program worked without this because of the way I initialized LOOP-CONTROL, I added it here, because regardless of the value of LOOP-CONTROL, I know that 0200-CALCULATOR-CONTROL must be executed at least one first time.

I made several changes in the exponent calculation. First, I eliminated the paragraph 0210-EXPONENT and replaced it with an inline PERFORM. The following would have done the job:

```
PERFORM
  FIELD-2 TIMES
    MULTIPLY RESULT BY FIELD-1 GIVING RESULT
END-PERFORM
```

However, because the result will increase so rapidly with exponentiation, the ON SIZE ERROR phrase was added so that results exceeding the number of digits available could be detected. I decided that the error message I show the user also should identify the value of the exponent where the overflow occurs. This was done by adding the variable POWER-VALUE and changing to the PERFORM VARYING. This will keep a count of the number of multiplications equal to the current exponent value. Because the value of RESULT is not changed when the ON SIZE ERROR occurs, the additional DISPLAY clarifies the meaning of the RESULT.

Finally, I MOVE FIELD-2 TO POWER-VALUE so that the looping will be terminated with this iteration. This works well here, because the VARYING form of PERFORM does fully evaluate the condition with each iteration. Although you normally should not modify the value of the variable controlled by the VARYING, this form of exception handling is a case where it is the reasonable thing to do.

Using PERFORM...THRU with the GO TO Statement and the EXIT Paragraph

Beginning with this section, I will get into some statements and structures that get beyond those recommended for good structured programming—at least as far as the structured programming purists are concerned. Those covered in this section can be misused and can lead to some very bad programming, as you'll see toward the end of this chapter. On the other side of the coin, when they're used in the manner described here, they can be kept under control and provide a powerful mechanism for dealing with some of the complexities you face in real-world programming. In fact, the structure presented here has become so commonplace that most professional programmers take it for granted.

PERFORM paragraph-1 THRU paragraph-2

So far, when PERFORMing paragraphs elsewhere in the program, the only alternative you've seen is the PERFORM paragraph-name structure. COBOL does have an extension to this concept that is unique among programming languages as far as I am aware. COBOL also provides the statement of the form PERFORM paragraph-1 THRU paragraph-2.

Here, control is passed to the beginning of paragraph-1 and is returned to the end of the PERFORM statement after it reaches the end of paragraph-2.

If you were brought up with the modern languages, such as Pascal and C, you're probably wondering what in the world is going on here because in those languages, each "procedure" is a separate, independent entity, and procedures are linked together only when one is invoked by another one. Invoking a group of procedures is contrary to their nature.

In this respect, COBOL is more similar to assembler languages, where the paragraph name is used as a "tag" to identify the starting point of a group of statements. Each group of statements (or paragraph) immediately follows the one preceding it in a contiguous manner. Because of this, if there is no PERFORM or STOP RUN statement (or a few others I'll get to later) to prevent it, program control passes from the first paragraph to the next, and the next, and so on, until it reaches the end of the program, where a STOP RUN is implied.

This notion might make you a bit nervous about how things work here—and it probably should. This is the reason why the STOP RUN is the last statement of the first paragraph of all the examples in this book (except for a couple at the end of this chapter where I demonstrate some programming techniques that are not really acceptable anymore, even though they still exist). Without the STOP RUN there, flow would "fall through" into the following paragraphs, and some strange, unexpected results could occur.

Returning to the statement PERFORM paragraph-name-1 THRU paragraph-name-2, this takes advantage of the contiguous nature of paragraphs in COBOL. Soon, you'll see how you can use it in a controlled manner to provide a flexible structure for handling programming situations that otherwise would be very complex and unwieldy. But first, a couple of other items are needed.

The EXIT Statement and the EXIT Paragraph

EXIT is a one-word statement. When it is used, it must be the only statement in the sentence (it must be followed by a period). This sentence also must be the only sentence in the paragraph. EXIT actually does nothing. It only acts as a placeholder that defines an empty paragraph. The real purpose of this statement and any paragraph that contains it is to serve as a "common exit point" for the PERFORM paragraph-name-1 THRU paragraph-name-2 structure.

I should point out parenthetically that there is also an EXIT PROGRAM statement that is in no way related to the EXIT statement. EXIT PROGRAM is used only in subroutines and sub-programs and is covered later in this book.

The GO TO Statement

The format of the GO TO is GO TO paragraph-name. The only rule for GO TO is quite simple. Control is transferred to the beginning of the referenced paragraph-name. The important inference to make is that control is not explicitly returned to anywhere. It's sort of like GO TO PARAGRAPH-X and do whatever and keep on going. This is exactly what happens.

You can imagine how tricky and confusing things can get unless GO TO is controlled in a very explicit structure and some rules are specified for its use. This is done with the PERFORM PARAGRAPH THRU PARAGRAPH-EXIT structure.

NOTE

Because of the somewhat contradictory nature of GO TO and PERFORM, it is important for the advanced programmer to also know how PERFORM works; this is covered later in the chapter.

PERFORM PARAGRAPH THRU PARAGRAPH-EXIT: Samples and Rules

To see how all this fits together, I'll quickly return to and comment on one of the commonly used read modules from the preceding chapter. Then I'll outline some important rules for using the structure. Finally, I'll employ the module in the calculator program.

The following example is from the section on conditional phrases in the preceding chapter. This structure was and is very common, because the NOT AT END and END-READ phrases were not available prior to the 1985 Standard. The module is executed with the statement PERFORM 0100-READ-INPUT-FILE THRU 0100-EXIT.

```
0100-READ-INPUT-FILE.

    READ INPUT-FILE
        AT END
            MOVE 'Y' TO END-OF-FILE-STATUS
            GO TO 0100-EXIT.
    ADD 1 TO INPUT-RECORD-COUNT.

0100-EXIT.
    EXIT.
```

Observe here how the beginning paragraph name and the exit paragraph name enclose and "bracket" all the statements in the module. Notice also that the only GO TO statement in the module "goes to" the exit paragraph. This way, you effectively limit the statement and keep it under control.

The following rules allow this structure to be employed in very complex situations and still provide assurance that the program control is maintained. You will notice that none of these rules are required by COBOL itself or are enforced by any COBOL compilers. However, they are followed very carefully by all good COBOL programmers. These are essentially the "survival rules" for working in a COBOL environment:

1. Any paragraph that contains a GO TO statement must have an EXIT paragraph, and *all* GO TO statements within the paragraph must reference *only* that EXIT paragraph.

2. *All* EXIT paragraphs must contain the EXIT statement and *only* the EXIT statement.

3. The word EXIT *must* be the last word in the name of the EXIT paragraph. The paragraphs *must* be numbered, and the number of the EXIT paragraph *must* be identical to that of the module paragraph name. The paragraph number must not be used in any other paragraph names. Some programmers simply use the entire module paragraph name and append the word EXIT to it. Others simply use the number and the word EXIT (as I did earlier). Either method works well, but one of the two should be chosen and used exclusively to avoid confusion.

4. All PERFORMS of any module having an EXIT paragraph must be of the form PERFORM nnnn-paragraph-name THRU nnnn-EXIT (or PERFORM nnnn-paragraph -name THRU nnnn-paragraph-name-EXIT if that naming method is employed).

I'll have a few comments on these rules, but first look at how the structure can be employed usefully in the calculator program shown in Listing 4.4.

LISTING 4.4 CALCUL3.

```
IDENTIFICATION DIVISION.
PROGRAM-ID.  Calcul3.
DATA DIVISION.
WORKING-STORAGE SECTION.
01   LOOP-CONTROL                PIC X VALUE 'N'.
     88  USER-IS-DONE            VALUE 'Y'.
01   DATA-VALID-INDICATOR        PIC X VALUE 'Y'.
     88  VALID-DATA              VALUE 'Y'.
01   COMPUTE-INFO.
     05  FIELD-1                 PIC 9(18).
     05  FILLER                  PIC X.
     05  OPERATION               PIC X.
     88  VALID-OPERATION         VALUE '+' '-' '*' '/' '^'.
     05  FILLER                  PIC X.
     05  FIELD-2                 PIC 9(18).
01   RESULT                      PIC 9(18).
01   POWER-VALUE                 PIC 9(18).
01   SHOW-RESULT      PIC ZZZ,ZZZ,ZZZ,ZZZ,ZZZ,ZZ9.
01   OVERFLOW-CONTROL            PIC X VALUE 'N'.
PROCEDURE DIVISION.
0100-MAIN.
     PERFORM 0200-CALCULATOR-CONTROL
         TEST AFTER
         UNTIL USER-IS-DONE.
     STOP RUN.
0200-CALCULATOR-CONTROL.
     DISPLAY 'ENTER 18-DIGIT NUMBERS SEPARATED BY OPERATION AS'.
     DISPLAY '123456789012345678 X 123456789012345678'.
     ACCEPT COMPUTE-INFO.
     MOVE ZERO TO RESULT.
     MOVE 'Y' TO DATA-VALID-INDICATOR.
     PERFORM 0300-EDIT-INPUT THRU 0300-EXIT.
     IF VALID-DATA
         PERFORM 0400-CALCULATE THRU 0400-EXIT
         MOVE RESULT TO SHOW-RESULT
         DISPLAY ' THE ANSWER IS: ' SHOW-RESULT.
     DISPLAY 'ARE YOU FINISHED WITH YOUR CALCULATIONS? (Y/N): '.
     ACCEPT LOOP-CONTROL.

0300-EDIT-INPUT.
     IF FIELD-1 NOT NUMERIC
         DISPLAY 'FIRST FIELD NOT A VALID NUMBER'
         MOVE 'N' TO DATA-VALID-INDICATOR.
     IF FIELD-2 NOT NUMERIC
         DISPLAY 'SECOND FIELD NOT A VALID NUMBER'
         MOVE 'N' TO DATA-VALID-INDICATOR.
     IF NOT VALID-OPERATION
         DISPLAY 'UNKNOWN CALCULATION'
         MOVE 'N' TO DATA-VALID-INDICATOR.
```

```
    IF NOT VALID-DATA
        DISPLAY '  RE-ENTER IF YOU WISH'
        GO TO 0300-EXIT.
    IF OPERATION = '/' AND FIELD-2 = ZERO
        DISPLAY 'DIVIDE BY ZERO NOT PERMITTED, RE-ENTER IF YOU WISH'
        MOVE 'N' TO DATA-VALID-INDICATOR.
0300-EXIT.
    EXIT.


0400-CALCULATE.
    IF OPERATION = '+'
        ADD FIELD-1 FIELD-2 GIVING RESULT
        GO TO 0400-EXIT.
    IF OPERATION = '-'
        SUBTRACT FIELD-2 FROM FIELD-1 GIVING RESULT
        GO TO 0400-EXIT.
    IF OPERATION = '*'
        MULTIPLY FIELD-1 BY FIELD-2 GIVING RESULT
          ON SIZE ERROR
            DISPLAY 'MULTIPLY OVERFLOW, SIGNIFICANT DIGITS LOST'
            MULTIPLY FIELD-1 BY FIELD-2 GIVING RESULT
            END-MULTIPLY
        END-MULTIPLY
        GO TO 0400-EXIT.
    IF OPERATION = '/'
        DIVIDE FIELD-1 BY FIELD-2 GIVING RESULT ROUNDED
          ON SIZE ERROR
            DISPLAY 'DIVIDE OVERFLOW, UNSPECIFIED RESULTS'
        END-DIVIDE
        GO TO 0400-EXIT.
    IF OPERATION = '^'
        MOVE 1 TO RESULT
        MOVE 'N' TO OVERFLOW-CONTROL
        PERFORM
            VARYING POWER-VALUE FROM 1 BY 1
            UNTIL POWER-VALUE > FIELD-2
              MULTIPLY RESULT BY FIELD-1 GIVING RESULT
                ON SIZE ERROR
                  DISPLAY 'OVERFLOW AT POWER = ' POWER-VALUE
                  SUBTRACT 1 FROM POWER-VALUE
                  DISPLAY 'VALUE AT ' POWER-VALUE ' WAS: '
                  MOVE FIELD-2 TO POWER-VALUE
              END-MULTIPLY
        END-PERFORM
    END-IF.
0400-EXIT.
    EXIT.
```

You'll notice that I added a fair number of edits and some more error checking. Even though I've placed this in separate modules, each is still fairly lengthy. But notice that the modules are still quite easy to follow. This is because you can simply and directly get out of the module as soon you're done with each particular related group of statements.

Another item to look at is in the `0300-EDIT-INPUT` module. All of the first three edits are done here before exiting the module. That way, if there is a problem with any or all of the input fields, you'll tell the user so that all the errors can be corrected at the same time. It does not make sense to do the last edit if any error is detected in the first edits. You can see how this structure gives you the flexibility to make such determinations. Anyone who has worked with edits of raw data knows how extensive they can be, and this structure is almost always used when editing data in COBOL.

Now that you've seen something approaching a real example, I have a few more comments on the rules that apply to it before I move on to the next section:

1. Some programs and programmers code an `EXIT` paragraph for *every* paragraph or module. Although this method gives a nice blocked appearance to the program, I disagree with the notion for three reasons. First, this structure is special and has a special purpose and therefore should be easily distinguishable from other modules. Second, by having this structure in place everywhere, it becomes too easy to use the `GO TO` statement to evade thorny logic problems instead of carefully working through them. The result of that is unnecessary complexity for the maintenance programmer trying to understand the program logic. Third, even though this structure places a semblance of control on the `GO TO`, the `GO TO` and `PERFORM...THRU` are still dangerous and should be avoided.

2. Some programmers will argue for allowing `GO TO` statements that go to the paragraph name of the module instead of the just the `EXIT` paragraph. This can provide for some pretty elaborate looping in the module; however, in most cases, the loops can be generated just as well with the `PERFORM...UNTIL`, and that is where everyone expects to see loop control mechanisms.

3. A surprising number of programs use `SECTION`s in the `PROCEDURE DIVISION` to accomplish the same thing as `PERFORM...THRU`. You'll see how this can be done later, but generally, you should avoid doing this because it tends to hide what is really going on and can cause real problems for the casual programmer doing maintenance.

4. Finally, even though this is a useful structure and has become quite commonplace, it is still very dangerous. The reason is simple. It is too easy for bugs to get into this kind of logic, and compounding that, these kinds of bugs are some of the most difficult to figure out. Furthermore, the bugs are also some of the ones that are most prone to get through normal program testing. As an experiment, change one

of the references to one of the EXIT paragraphs from 300 to 400 (or vice versa) in either a GO TO or PERFORM...THRU statement and see what happens (make sure that you enter values to invoke those changes). Observe how varying and confusing the results can be. If they aren't, try changing another reference. Try to predict what will happen before you run the program.

More Details on How Things Work (the Gray Areas)

In this section, I expand on the previous topics. I'll go into more detail on how things work and present some optional features and alternative ways of doing things. As with most advanced tools, these can be quite beneficial when used well, but they also can become very confusing and complicated when misapplied.

The Ordering of the Paragraphs in the Program

Unlike some other languages, COBOL does not care about what physical order the paragraphs are in. Even though you haven't done it before, you can PERFORM a paragraph preceding the paragraph containing the PERFORM statement just as well as one that follows it. So, in the preceding sample program, the paragraphs can be reordered as follows without making any difference in how the program operates:

```
0100-MAIN.
     PERFORM 0200-CALCULATOR-CONTROL
         TEST AFTER
         UNTIL USER-IS-DONE.
     STOP RUN.

0400-CALCULATE.
        .

        .
0400-EXIT.
     EXIT.
0200-CALCULATOR-CONTROL.
        .
     PERFORM 0300-EDIT-INPUT THRU 0300-EXIT.
     IF VALID-DATA
         PERFORM 0400-CALCULATE THRU 0400-EXIT
        .

0300-EDIT-INPUT.
        .

        .
0300-EXIT.
     EXIT.
```

4

You can readily see that in this case, rearranging the order of the paragraphs does nothing but make the program more confusing. In other cases, though, it is quite convenient to be able to PERFORM a paragraph from a location below where the paragraph is situated. Paragraphs that serve a "utility" function and are PERFORMed from many different places in the program are the most common examples.

There are a few rules about how COBOL "flow control" operates that have a bearing on how paragraphs are ordered:

1. Execution always begins with the first statement in the PROCEDURE DIVISION. That is why the main control paragraph always should be the first one in the program.

2. If the last sentence of a paragraph is not a GO TO and the paragraph is not being PERFORMed, control will fall through from the end of the paragraph to the first statement of the next paragraph and continue from there. This is why the first paragraph in the program always should end with the STOP RUN statement. It is also why you do not need GO TO statements immediately preceding the 0300-EXIT and 0400-EXIT paragraphs in the preceding sample program. This is also important as to why and how GO TO control logic works and is why it can easily get so confusing.

3. When the PERFORM paragraph-name-1 THRU paragraph-name-2 is used, paragraph-name-2 must be defined after paragraph-name-1. In other words, the EXIT paragraph must be located after the main paragraph.

Overlapping PERFORM Statements

You will notice that I have *not* said that paragraph-name-2 must *immediately* follow paragraph-name-2 in the PERFORM paragraph-name-1 THRU paragraph-name-2 structure. This correctly implies that any number of paragraphs may exist between paragraphs one and two. It was originally thought that this would be the most general way of doing things and would provide a capability for more efficient programs. In a modern programming environment, having any paragraphs defined between paragraph-name-1 and paragraph-name-2 causes nothing but confusion, though. Any efficiency gains are minuscule.

This fact introduces an additional rule and some comments on the PERFORM statement.

The 1985 COBOL Standard contains a number of definitions and explanations regarding the range of PERFORM statements. Buried in there is one pretty simple rule. It essentially states that an active PERFORM statement must *not* allow control to pass through the exit point of another active PERFORM statement. The following examples show what is allowed.

EXAMPLE 4.1.

```
        .
      PERFORM 0100-PARAGRAPH THRU 1100-PARAGRAPH
        .
0100-PARAGRAPH.
        .
      PERFORM 0400-PARAGRAPH THRU 0800-PARAGRAPH
        .
0400-PARAGRAPH.
        .
0800-PARAGRAPH.
        .
1100-PARAGRAPH.
        .
```

EXAMPLE 4.2.

```
        .
      PERFORM 0100-PARAGRAPH THRU 0400-PARAGRAPH
        .
0100-PARAGRAPH.
        .
      PERFORM 0800-PARAGRAPH THRU 1100-PARAGRAPH
        .
0400-PARAGRAPH.
        .
0800-PARAGRAPH.
        .
1100-PARAGRAPH.
        .
```

EXAMPLE 4.3.

```
        .
      PERFORM 0100-PARAGRAPH THRU 0800-PARAGRAPH
        .
0100-PARAGRAPH.
        .
0400-PARAGRAPH.
        .
0800-PARAGRAPH.
        .
1100-PARAGRAPH.
        .
1200-PARAGRAPH.
        .
      PERFORM 0400-PARAGRAPH THRU 1100-PARAGRAPH
```

Although none of these examples are seen (and should not be) in modern programs, COBOL will handle them, and they will work correctly. More interestingly, the following examples show what is *not* permitted.

EXAMPLE 4.4.

```
        .
    PERFORM 0100-PARAGRAPH THRU 1100-PARAGRAPH
        .
0100-PARAGRAPH.
        .
    IF A = B
            PERFORM 0400-PARAGRAPH THRU 1100-PARAGRAPH.
        .
0400-PARAGRAPH.
        .
0800-PARAGRAPH.
        .
1100-PARAGRAPH.
        .
```

EXAMPLE 4.5.

```
        .
    PERFORM 0100-PARAGRAPH THRU 0800-PARAGRAPH
        .
0100-PARAGRAPH.
        .
    IF A = B
            PERFORM 0400-PARAGRAPH THRU 1100-PARAGRAPH.
        .
0400-PARAGRAPH.
        .
0800-PARAGRAPH.
        .
1100-PARAGRAPH.
        .
```

EXAMPLE 4.6.

```
        .
0100-PARAGRAPH.
        .
    PERFORM 0400-PARAGRAPH
        .
0400-PARAGRAPH.
        .
    PERFORM 1100-PARAGRAPH
```

```
        .
1100-PARAGRAPH.
        .
    IF A = B
        PERFORM 0100-PARAGRAPH.
        .
```

EXAMPLE 4.7.

```
        .
    PERFORM 0100-PARAGRAPH
        .
0100-PARAGRAPH.
        .
    IF A = B
        PERFORM 0100-PARAGRAPH.
        .
0400-PARAGRAPH.
        .
```

The last two examples are very interesting because THRU is not even used. If you are familiar with Pascal or C, you should recognize them as being recursive. The COBOL Standard does not permit this, and it is probably a good thing because I have yet to see any real application for recursion in a business application.

Although the 1985 Standard rules do not permit the recursive and overlapping PERFORMs illustrated in the last four examples, *there are not any compilers that diagnose them as errors.* The problem is that in a program of any size or complexity, identifying such errors is extremely difficult, if not impossible. This is especially true when the PERFORMs are part of conditional phrases and there is no way for a compiler to determine whether conditions necessary to cause the conflict can ever exist with real data.

The result is that the programmer must deal with such logic and that is why this section is here. A few factors result in logic problems caused by such "runaway" control logic to be pretty rare.

The first factor is that most modern compilers use a *stack mechanism* to handle PERFORM returns. Although this doesn't eliminate bad logic, it results in most programs operating in a reasonable fashion in spite of it. I'll get into this a little more in the next section, where I briefly discuss how PERFORM works.

The second factor is to avoid logic-control problems by following good structured programming practices. Follow the primary rules in the section "PERFORM PARAGRAPH THRU PARAGRAPH-EXIT: Samples and Rules," earlier in this chapter. Additionally, *always* PERFORM down the logic path, and avoid performing paragraphs defined above the PERFORM statement.

How PERFORM Works

This section is intended to be of help in determining what is really going on when you encounter a program that is "behaving badly" and the probable cause is a PERFORM structure that is similar to one of those shown in the last for examples. The immediate solution to the programming problem is to determine what the program is supposed to accomplish and to rework the logic so that this can be done correctly. The advanced programmer also will want to determine exactly what the program is doing and why, so that the correction can be made with the confidence that the problem will not recur.

This section provides the necessary background so that such tracing can be done.

There are essentially two methods for saving the memory location to return to after the statements executed by the PERFORM are completed. I'll briefly summarize how each of them works and step through two of the examples from the previous section to illustrate exactly what will happen in each situation.

Saved Return Address (SRA) Area

This first mechanism is the older of the two, and although it is more limited, it does the job directly and is pretty easy to follow and predict. To the best of my knowledge, it currently is pretty much limited to older mainframe compilers. All the PC compilers, and other compilers written for the 1985 COBOL Standard, use the more modern stack mechanism.

With the older method, COBOL sets aside a location in its memory work area for the end of every paragraph (and section) in the program. This is the *saved return address* (SRA) area. It contains the location of the next statement to be executed after the last sentence in the paragraph (or section) has finished execution. Initially, all the locations (SRAs) are set to point to the first instruction of each next paragraph (except for the last one in the program, which is set to point to the program termination/STOP RUN procedures).

Whenever execution of the last sentence of a paragraph (or section) completes, COBOL takes control and uses the SRA for that paragraph to determine where control is to be transferred to next.

When a PERFORM statement is executed, COBOL modifies the SRA for the last paragraph (or section) referenced by the PERFORM to point to the next statement following the PERFORM. After the last sentence in that paragraph is executed, COBOL takes control. It uses the value of the SRA to determine where to transfer control. But before it does, it resets the SRA to point to the first statement in the next paragraph. This is necessary so that later, if control falls through the end of that paragraph, it will be passed to the start of the next paragraph like it should.

Now look at Example 4.8 to see what happens and why. When the PERFORM 0100-PARAGRAPH THRU 0800-PARAGRAPH is encountered, the SRA for 0800-PARAGRAPH is modified to point to the statement following this first PERFORM. Control then is transferred to the first statement in 0100-PARAGRAPH. Assuming A = B, when the PERFORM 0400-PARAGRAPH THRU 1100-PARAGRAPH is encountered, the SRA for 1100-PARAGRAPH is modified to point to the statement following this second PERFORM. Control is transferred to the beginning of the 0400-PARAGRAPH. The statements in that paragraph will be executed, and because the SRA for 0400-PARAGRAPH has never been modified from its initial value, COBOL then will transfer control to the beginning of 0800-PARAGRAPH. When the last sentence in that paragraph has been executed, COBOL will take control and retrieve the value in the SRA for the 0800-PARAGRAPH. Remember now that this had been modified to point to the statement following the first PERFORM in the example. COBOL will reset this SRA to point to the first statement in the 1100-PARAGRAPH and then transfer control to the statement following the PERFORM 0100-PARAGRAPH THRU 0800-PARAGRAPH. This is obviously *not* what was intended and is why overlapping PERFORMs *must always be avoided.* You also might observe that the SRA for the 1100-PARAGRAPH has not been reset, so if the program logic continues and falls through that paragraph, it will then "jump" back to the instruction following the PERFORM 0400-PARAGRAPH THRU 1100-PARAGRAPH instead of proceeding to the next paragraph. Assuming that there are no GO TOs to confuse the issue, the following modified example eliminates the problem. It is a good exercise to work through the SRA values to show to yourself how and why it works.

EXAMPLE 4.8.

```
    .
    PERFORM 0100-PARAGRAPH
    PERFORM 0400-PARAGRAPH
    PERFORM 0800-PARAGRAPH
    .
0100-PARAGRAPH.
    .
    IF A = B
        PERFORM 0400-PARAGRAPH
        PERFORM 0800-PARAGRAPH
        PERFORM 1100-PARAGRAPH.
    .
0400-PARAGRAPH.
    .
0800-PARAGRAPH.
    .
1100-PARAGRAPH.
    .
```

Now look at Example 4.7. This is the implied recursion example that will not work well at all with the SRA area mechanism. When the first PERFORM 0100-PARAGRAPH is encountered, COBOL modifies the SRA for the 0100-PARAGRAPH to point to the statement following this PERFORM and transfers control to the first statement in the 0100-PARAGRAPH. Assuming A = B, the second PERFORM 0100-PARAGRAPH is encountered, and COBOL now modifies that SRA to point to the statement following this second PERFORM. Control again is transferred to the beginning of the 0100-PARAGRAPH. Assuming that one of the first statements in the paragraph eventually does something to alter the value of either A or B, the remaining statements in the paragraph get executed, and COBOL takes control. (If neither value is ever modified, there is a permanent loop, and that is another issue entirely.) At this point, the SRA for 0100-PARAGRAPH is reset to point to the first instruction of the 0400-PARAGRAPH (which is the next paragraph following 0100-PARA-GRAPH), and control is transferred to the statement following the second "PERFORM 0100-PARAGRAPH" statement. The remaining statements in the 0100-PARAGRAPH are executed again, and control is passed back to COBOL. Remember that the SRA for 0100-PARA-GRAPH was just reset to point to the first statement in the 0400-PARAGRAPH, so COBOL will transfer control to fall through and into that paragraph. Control is never transferred back to the statement following the first PERFORM statement, and this again is definitely not what you want. Instead, control will fall through the remainder of the program.

The correction here is most likely a GO TO statement. In many cases, adding an EXIT paragraph at the end of 0100-PARAGRAPH and changing the second PERFORM to GO TO that EXIT paragraph and the first PERFORM to perform THRU the new EXIT paragraph is the solution. In a few cases, the original programmer may have really needed to loop back to the beginning of 0100-PARAGRAPH but was afraid to use a GO TO and so used PERFORM instead. In this case, the second PERFORM simply can be changed to GO TO. (See the section later in this chapter on GO TO logic to see how this can work.)

The Stack Mechanism

If you have a background in C or Pascal, this section will be review for you because the stack mechanism used by COBOL compilers is the same as any other. The only two minor differences are that COBOL does not need to place data or arguments on the stack but does need to track whether each paragraph exit is in PERFORM-control mode or fall-through mode.

A *stack* is essentially a list of data values. When a new value is added, it is placed at the first position in the stack, and any other values already in the stack are "pushed down" the stack. When a value is retrieved from the stack, it is the first one in the stack, and the remainder of the values in the stack are "popped up" by one position in the stack. The closest analogy I can think of is the old spring-loaded coin changer. Coins are inserted at the top, forcing other coins and the spring downward. When a coin is taken, the spring causes the coins beneath it to be pushed up to the top so that another coin is always ready.

COBOL uses the stack mechanism to save the address of the next instruction to be executed when control is returned for any PERFORM that is being executed. You generally do not have to worry about the size of the stack, except when there is a logic-control bug, or a permanent loop including PERFORMs occurs. In such cases, you may see error messages, such as `stack overflow` or `stack underflow`.

Because `stacks` is a concept not normally used in COBOL, I'll illustrate one of the correct examples from a previous section before I get into the problem examples. Some additional logic also is involved in managing whether a paragraph is under PERFORM control or in fall-through mode, but it is not necessary for these illustrations; it works properly, so you can take it for granted here.

In Example 4.2, when the first PERFORM statement PERFORM 0100-PARAGRAPH THRU 0400-PARAGRAPH is executed, the location following this statement is added to the stack, 0400-PARAGRAPH is set as being under PERFORM control, and control is transferred to the beginning of 0100-PARAGRAPH. When the statement PERFORM 0800-PARAGRAPH THRU 1100-PARAGRAPH then is executed in that paragraph, the address following that statement is added in the first position of the stack, "pushing" the address for the previous PERFORM "down" to the second position in the stack. 1100-PARAGRAPH is set as being under PERFORM control, and control is transferred to the beginning of 0800-PARAGRAPH. Because the 0800-PARAGRAPH is set to fall-through mode, execution proceeds through it and into and through 1100-PARAGRAPH. When the end of that paragraph is reached, COBOL takes control; since the paragraph is under PERFORM control, COBOL takes the address from the first position of the stack and pops the remaining entries up one position in the stack. 1100-PARAGRAPH is reset to fall-through mode, and control is transferred to the address retrieved from the stack, which is the location following the PERFORM 0800-PARAGRAPH THRU 1100-PARAGRAPH statement.

Execution proceeds through 0100-PARAGRAPH and (because it is set to fall-through mode) into and through 0400-PARAGRAPH. COBOL now takes control again (because 0400-PARAGRAPH is in PERFORM-control mode) and again retrieves the first address from the stack, popping any remaining entries up one position. This address is the location of the statement following the first PERFORM 0100-PARAGRAPH THRU 0400-PARAGRAPH. After resetting 0400-PARAGRAPH to fall-through mode, control is transferred back to the retrieved location, and everything has worked like you would want.

Now go back to Example 4.5 and see how things work with the stack mechanism.

4

MANAGING
PROGRAM FLOW
AND LOOPING

When the first PERFORM 0100-PARAGRAPH THRU 0800-PARAGRAPH statement is executed, the address of the statement is added as the first entry in the stack, pushing down any other stack entries. PERFORM-control mode is set for the 0800-PARAGRAPH, and control is transferred to the beginning of 0100-PARAGRAPH. Again, assuming that A = B, the statement PERFORM 0400-PARAGRAPH THRU 1100-PARAGRAPH is executed. The address of the statement following the PERFORM is inserted at the top of the stack, pushing down the remaining entries. After setting 1100-PARAGRAPH to PERFORM-control mode, control is transferred to the first statement in 0400-PARAGRAPH. These statements are executed, and because control has never been changed from fall-through mode, control passes through and into 0800-PARAGRAPH like you would expect.

After these statements are executed, things get interesting. The *first* PERFORM caused 0800-PARAGRAPH to be set to PERFORM control. So COBOL takes control and retrieves the first address from the stack, popping the remaining entries upward. However, *this first address* retrieved from the stack *is not the address* of the statement following *the first PERFORM statement. It is* the address of the statement following the *second* PERFORM statement, so control is transferred to that statement (the statement following PERFORM 0400-PARAGRAPH THRU 1100-PARAGRAPH), *even though no statements in 1100-PARAGRAPH were ever executed.* This is definitely *not* what you want. The confusion is compounded because this entry on the stack causes the 1100-PARAGRAPH to be returned to fall-through mode instead of 0800-PARAGRAPH.

Now following the example through, the remaining statements in 0100-PARAGRAPH are executed, and then those in 0400-PARAGRAPH and 0800-PARAGRAPH also are executed in turn, because 0100-PARAGRAPH and 0400-PARAGRAPH are in fall-through mode. Because 800-PARAGRAPH was *not* returned to fall-through mode, COBOL takes over after the last statement in it has been executed. The first address is retrieved from the stack, the remaining entries are popped up one level, and 0800-PARAGRAPH finally is reset to fall-through mode. However, again the address retrieved from the stack is the *wrong one.* It is actually the address of the statement following the *first* PERFORM statement. This means that 1100-PERFORM is never executed, even though it was the THRU paragraph of the *second* PERFORM.

In this case, the program did not quite lose control, but the intended ordering of the PERFORMs also did not occur. The conclusion here is that overlapping PERFORM...THRUs must be avoided, because although the results can be predicted, they are not those specified by the statements. It should be noted that such PERFORMs very seldom are seen in programs today.

> **NOTE**
>
> The preceding description shows how the stack mechanism for most compilers handles the COBOL logic in Example 4.5. The current Micro Focus COBOL, however, employs a mechanism designed specifically to handle the kind of example just described. It treats each paragraph in the PERFORM...THRU range as though it were PERFORMed separately. This causes things to work exactly as if the code were written as illustrated in Example 4.8.

Finally, look at how the stacking mechanism handles the recursive PERFORM illustrated in Example 4.7.

Here, the first PERFORM 0100-PARAGRAPH statement will result in COBOL placing the address of the statement following it into the stack as the first entry and pushing the other stack entries down one. The 0100-PARAGRAPH will be set to PERFORM-control mode, and control will be transferred to the first statement in that paragraph. Assuming that A = B, the PERFORM 0100-PARAGRAPH statement inside that paragraph will be executed. Here, the address of the statement following this PERFORM now will be added as the new first entry in the stack, with the remaining entries being pushed down by one. PERFORM-control mode will be set for this PERFORM of the 0100-PARAGRAPH, and control again will be transferred to the first instruction in the paragraph. If A is still = B, the PERFORM 0100-PARAGRAPH will be executed again, and the address of the next statement again will be added to the stack.

This looping will continue until either A is not = B, or the program terminates in error with a stack-overflow condition. Assuming that the program is programmed properly, A will eventually not = B. When that occurs, the PERFORM will not be executed, but instead, the last statement in the 0100-PARAGRAPH will be reached. Because the paragraph is set to PERFORM-control mode, COBOL will retrieve the first address from the stack and pop the stack up by one entry. This address points to the statement following the PERFORM 0100-PARAGRAPH statement located within the 0100-PARAGARAPH. So control will be transferred there. This is exactly what you want to happen. Note also that 0100-PARAGRAPH will remain in PERFORM-control mode, because there is still at least one outstanding PERFORM of it. Now the remaining statements in the 0100-PARAGRAPH will be executed (again). COBOL again will retrieve the first entry from the stack and, after popping the remaining entries up by one, transfer control to the statement that will again be the one following the PERFORM 0100-PARAGRAPH located within the 0100-PARAGRAPH. This process will continue until all the repetitious entries of this address have been removed.

When this happens, the next first entry in the stack will be the address of the statement following the first PERFORM 0100-PARAGRAPH statement at the beginning of the example. Because there are no more outstanding PERFORMs of this paragraph, it now will be reset to fall-through control mode, the remaining entries in the stack are popped up by one, and then control is transferred to the statement following that first PERFORM statement.

Hence, this recursive PERFORM has operated exactly like it should. However, the looping that has occurred here has a great deal of overhead, and the behavior of the paragraph as the loops progress may not be exactly what the programmer has in mind. Needless to say, you should stay away from the kind of PERFORM shown in this example (and Example 4.6), unless there is a very special need for it that cannot be satisfied in some other manner. As I stated at the beginning of this section, I haven't yet encountered a real need for recursion in any business application I've encountered.

SECTIONs and SECTION Names in PERFORM

I would rather not include this topic, because I personally feel that the SECTION is archaic, no longer serves a purpose, and causes nothing but confusion when it is used in the PROCEDURE DIVISION. However, it is an integral part of COBOL and still is used in a surprisingly large number of programs and by a fairly large number of programmers. A secondary topic on nonmemory resident SECTIONs and segmentation is covered in Chapter 15, "Specialty Features."

A section is defined in the PROCEDURE DIVISION in the same way a paragraph is, only a section is followed by a space and the word SECTION. Like the paragraph-name, the section-name must begin in area A (columns 8–11). As in the other divisions in COBOL, a PROCEDURE DIVISON section contains paragraphs.

Once one section is defined in the PROCEDURE DIVISION, all the paragraphs in the PROCEDURE DIVISION must become a part of that section or some other one.

Once sections have been defined, they can be referenced in PERFORM and GO TO statements just like paragraphs. This is one of the reasons why I don't like to use sections: It is not possible to tell whether they are sections or paragraphs unless they are looked up.

When a section is PERFORMed, control is returned to the statement following the PERFORM after the last sentence in the section is executed. Many years ago, when GO TO logic was quite common, such a mechanism was pretty useful. But with modern techniques, this results in sections devolving into a single paragraph with its exit paragraph, and in my opinion, that means that there is really very little value for them.

You also can PERFORM section-name-1 THRU section-name-2.

The PROCEDURE DIVISION of the calculator example is shown in Listing 4.5 with section names.

LISTING 4.5 CALCUL4.

```
PROCEDURE DIVISION.
S100-MAIN SECTION.
0100-MAIN.
    PERFORM S200-CALCULATOR-CONTROL
        TEST AFTER
        UNTIL USER-IS-DONE.
    STOP RUN.
S200-CALCULATOR-CONTROL SECTION.
0200-CALCULATOR-CONTROL.
    DISPLAY 'ENTER 18-DIGIT NUMBERS SEPARATED BY OPERATION AS'.
    DISPLAY '123456789012345678 X 123456789012345678'.
    ACCEPT COMPUTE-INFO.
    MOVE ZERO TO RESULT.
    MOVE 'Y' TO DATA-VALID-INDICATOR.
    PERFORM S300-EDIT-INPUT.
    IF VALID-DATA
        PERFORM S400-CALCULATE
        MOVE RESULT TO SHOW-RESULT
        DISPLAY ' THE ANSWER IS: ' SHOW-RESULT.
    DISPLAY 'ARE YOU FINISHED WITH YOUR CALCULATIONS? (Y/N): '.
    ACCEPT LOOP-CONTROL.

S300-EDIT-INPUT SECTION.
0300-EDIT-INPUT.
    IF FIELD-1 NOT NUMERIC
        DISPLAY 'FIRST FIELD NOT A VALID NUMBER'
        MOVE 'N' TO DATA-VALID-INDICATOR.
    IF FIELD-2 NOT NUMERIC
        DISPLAY 'SECOND FIELD NOT A VALID NUMBER'
        MOVE 'N' TO DATA-VALID-INDICATOR.
    IF NOT VALID-OPERATION
        DISPLAY 'UNKNOWN CALCULATION'
        MOVE 'N' TO DATA-VALID-INDICATOR.
    IF NOT VALID-DATA
        DISPLAY '  RE-ENTER IF YOU WISH'
        GO TO 0300-EXIT.
    IF OPERATION = '/' AND FIELD-2 = ZERO
        DISPLAY 'DIVIDE BY ZERO NOT PERMITTED, RE-ENTER IF YOU WISH'
        MOVE 'N' TO DATA-VALID-INDICATOR.
0300-EXIT.
    EXIT.

S400-CALCULATE SECTION.
0400-CALCULATE.
    IF OPERATION = '+'
        ADD FIELD-1 FIELD-2 GIVING RESULT
        GO TO 0400-EXIT.
    IF OPERATION = '-'
```

4

MANAGING
PROGRAM FLOW
AND LOOPING

continues

LISTING 4.5 CONTINUED

```
            SUBTRACT FIELD-2 FROM FIELD-1 GIVING RESULT
            GO TO 0400-EXIT.
        IF OPERATION = '*'
            MULTIPLY FIELD-1 BY FIELD-2 GIVING RESULT
              ON SIZE ERROR
                DISPLAY 'MULTIPLY OVERFLOW, SIGNIFICANT DIGITS LOST'
                MULTIPLY FIELD-1 BY FIELD-2 GIVING RESULT
                END-MULTIPLY
            END-MULTIPLY
            GO TO 0400-EXIT.
        IF OPERATION = '/'
            DIVIDE FIELD-1 BY FIELD-2 GIVING RESULT ROUNDED
              ON SIZE ERROR
                DISPLAY 'DIVIDE OVERFLOW, UNSPECIFIED RESULTS'
            END-DIVIDE
            GO TO 0400-EXIT.
        IF OPERATION = '^'
            MOVE 1 TO RESULT
            MOVE 'N' TO OVERFLOW-CONTROL
            PERFORM
                VARYING POWER-VALUE FROM 1 BY 1
                UNTIL POWER-VALUE > FIELD-2
                  MULTIPLY RESULT BY FIELD-1 GIVING RESULT
                    ON SIZE ERROR
                      DISPLAY 'OVERFLOW AT POWER = ' POWER-VALUE
                      SUBTRACT 1 FROM POWER-VALUE
                      DISPLAY 'VALUE AT ' POWER-VALUE ' WAS: '
                      MOVE FIELD-2 TO POWER-VALUE
                  END-MULTIPLY
            END-PERFORM
        END-IF.
    0400-EXIT.
        EXIT.
```

The Example with GO TO Logic

I had a fair number of misgivings about putting the example in Listing 4.6 in the book because programs written this way are gradually becoming more rare. However, the sample program is only a couple of pages long, and it's good to get a chance to see this kind of logic in a small program when you have a modern version with which to compare it. That way, a maintenance problem with a 1,000- or 2,000-line program with GO TO logic won't be quite as terrifying. Notice also that most of the other modern programming techniques have been removed, because they won't likely be seen in this type of program. The PERFORM VARYING also was removed, although this kind of loop has been available for a long time. The reason here is to simply show another means of looping with the GO TO statement.

LISTING 4.6 CALCUL5.

```
PROCEDURE DIVISION.
0100-MAIN.
    DISPLAY 'ENTER 18-DIGIT NUMBERS SEPARATED BY OPERATION AS'.
    DISPLAY '123456789012345678 X 123456789012345678'.
    ACCEPT COMPUTE-INFO.
    MOVE ZERO TO RESULT.
    MOVE 'Y' TO DATA-VALID-INDICATOR.
    IF FIELD-1 NOT NUMERIC
        DISPLAY 'FIRST FIELD NOT A VALID NUMBER'
        MOVE 'N' TO DATA-VALID-INDICATOR.
    IF FIELD-2 NOT NUMERIC
        DISPLAY 'SECOND FIELD NOT A VALID NUMBER'
        MOVE 'N' TO DATA-VALID-INDICATOR.
    IF NOT VALID-OPERATION
        DISPLAY 'UNKNOWN CALCULATION'
        MOVE 'N' TO DATA-VALID-INDICATOR.
    IF NOT VALID-DATA
        DISPLAY '  RE-ENTER IF YOU WISH'
        GO TO 0500-CHECK-MORE-DAYS.

    IF OPERATION = '/' AND FIELD-2 = ZERO
        DISPLAY 'DIVIDE BY ZERO NOT PERMITTED, RE-ENTER IF YOU WISH'
        GO TO 0500-CHECK-MORE-DAYS.

*   EDITING COMPLETE, BEGIN CALCULATIONS

    IF OPERATION = '+'
        ADD FIELD-1 FIELD-2 GIVING RESULT
        GO TO 0400-SHOW-RESULT.
    IF OPERATION = '-'
        SUBTRACT FIELD-2 FROM FIELD-1 GIVING RESULT
        GO TO 0400-SHOW-RESULT.
    IF OPERATION NOT = '*'
        GO TO 0200-CHECK-DIVIDE.
    MULTIPLY FIELD-1 BY FIELD-2 GIVING RESULT
        ON SIZE ERROR
            DISPLAY 'MULTIPLY OVERFLOW, SIGNIFICANT DIGITS LOST'
            MULTIPLY FIELD-1 BY FIELD-2 GIVING RESULT.
    GO TO 0400-SHOW-RESULT.

0200-CHECK-DIVIDE.
    IF OPERATION NOT = '/'
        GO TO 0300-CHECK-POWER.
    DIVIDE FIELD-1 BY FIELD-2 GIVING RESULT ROUNDED
        ON SIZE ERROR
            DISPLAY 'DIVIDE OVERFLOW, UNSPECIFIED RESULTS'.
    GO TO 0400-SHOW-RESULT.
```

4

MANAGING
PROGRAM FLOW
AND LOOPING

continues

LISTING 4.6 CONTINUED

```
0300-CHECK-POWER.
    IF OPERATION NOT = '^'
        GO TO 0400-SHOW-RESULT.
    MOVE 1 TO RESULT.
    MOVE 1 TO POWER-VALUE.

0350-POWER-LOOP.
    IF POWER-VALUE > FIELD-2
        GO TO 0400-SHOW-RESULT.
    MULTIPLY RESULT BY FIELD-1 GIVING RESULT
        ON SIZE ERROR
            DISPLAY 'OVERFLOW AT POWER = ' POWER-VALUE
            SUBTRACT 1 FROM POWER-VALUE
            DISPLAY 'VALUE AT ' POWER-VALUE ' WAS: '
            GO TO 0400-SHOW-RESULT.
    ADD 1 TO POWER-VALUE.
    GO TO 0350-POWER-LOOP.

0400-SHOW-RESULT.
    MOVE RESULT TO SHOW-RESULT.
    DISPLAY ' THE ANSWER IS: ' SHOW-RESULT.

0500-CHECK-MORE-DAYS.
    DISPLAY 'ARE YOU FINISHED WITH YOUR CALCULATIONS? (Y/N): '.
    ACCEPT LOOP-CONTROL.
    IF USER-IS-DONE
        STOP RUN.
    GO TO 0100-MAIN.
```

The Dark Side of COBOL: ALTER and GO TO...DEPENDING

These two statements will be treated very briefly, because virtually everyone agrees that they should be avoided as much as possible, and the less said about them the better. Unfortunately, these statements still are used in some programs, so a brief explanation is required.

ALTER

ALTER will be removed from COBOL when the next standard is released (shortly after the turn of the century). When you see how it works, you'll agree that this is a good idea. The format of ALTER follows:

```
ALTER paragraph-name-1 TO PROCEED TO paragraph-name-2.
```

The paragraph identified by `paragraph-name-1` must contain only one statement, and that statement must be a `GO TO` statement.

When `ALTER` is executed, the destination of the `GO TO` statement contained in `paragraph-name-1` is altered to be the first statement in `paragraph-name-2`. This means that after `ALTER` has been executed, every time `paragraph-name-1` is executed, it will transfer control to `paragraph-name-2`. This will remain in effect until the program terminates (or some other `ALTER` statement alters the destination of the `GO TO` to some other `paragraph-name-3`).

So the fact that you can have `GO TO` logic in COBOL by itself is very confusing. But now, you can modify the destination of those `GO TO` statements during the execution of the program. Fortunately, such `GO TO` statements must each be in a paragraph all by themselves and therefore are easy to spot. Also, the instances of `ALTER` are very few and far between. I doubt whether more than a dozen exist in all the PC and midrange COBOL programs (I haven't seen any), and I've only seen a couple in production mainframe programs in the past 20 years.

One other item needs to be identified at this time. The `GO TO` statement that exists by itself in a paragraph so that it can be `ALTER`ed does not need to reference a `paragraph-name`. This means that `GO TO` is allowed in these specific instances. When this is done, the implied destination of such a `GO TO` is the next paragraph (at least until an `ALTER` is executed that modifies the destination to some other `paragraph-name`).

GO TO DEPENDING

Although `GO TO DEPENDING` is also a statement to be avoided, it is interesting, because it is the precursor to the modern `CASE`-structure statements. In fact, I wouldn't be surprised if the idea didn't come from it. The format follows:

```
GO TO paragraph-name-1
     .
     .
     paragraph-name-n
    DEPENDING ON integer-name.
```

At least two `paragraph-name` entries are required. Although the statement looks a bit complicated, its operation is actually pretty easy to describe. When the statement is executed, the value of `integer-name` is evaluated. If the value is 1, control is transferred to `paragraph-name-1`. If the value is 2, control is transferred to `paragraph-name-2`, and so on for each `paragraph-name` that is listed. If `integer-name` has a zero or negative value, or it is greater than the number of `paragraph-name`s listed, control is transferred to the statement immediately following `GO TO DEPENDING`.

The same paragraph-name may be repeated any number of times in the list.

Although this statement still exists and still is used, it was never used in more than a few isolated situations. This is because of two reasons. The first is that because it is GO TO–based, it becomes very difficult to funnel all the paragraph-names listed into a common exit point. Even with programs that were constructed with a GO TO control structure, this statement was very cumbersome to use, and it also was very difficult to follow the resulting code. The second reason is that there are very few programming situations in which a simple integer can be associated with the variations needed for controlling the flow of a program or a function within the program.

Summary

Now that you've seen a variety of things available in COBOL that most people would rather not have to deal with, you should be ready to see some features that can make life easier. The next chapter gets right into that by introducing COBOL's new case-structure statement called EVALUATE.

CHAPTER 5

Advanced Conditional Features and Techniques

Conditional processing is the primary means of translating the complexities of the business requirements into the programming statements to deal with them. Conditional processing commonly is associated with the IF statement but can be used other places as well (such as the UNTIL phrase of the PERFORM statement and the EVALUATE statement, which I'll get to shortly).

Complex conditional phrases that were introduced in Chapter 3, "Using Conditional Statements to Control Processing," together with the logic control described in the preceding chapter allow the requirements of any level of complexity to be programmed. However, we learned in the '70s that that is not sufficient. People (as well as the compiler) also must be able to decipher the complex code that was written, and that is not always so easy.

Several mechanisms come into play here. COBOL allows certain items to be abbreviated (or assumed) in conditionals. This makes the program statements more "human-language"–oriented but also can make them more easy to misinterpret. The EVALUATE case-structure statement was added to COBOL in the 1985 Standard, and it provides a clear, distinct means of relating alternative processing steps to the conditions that define the alternatives.

Before getting into the details of this chapter, I'd like to make one more introductory comment that many people tend to forget. *You can't make the program any less complicated than the requirements it implements.* This means that if it takes calculus to figure the angles and amounts of thrust to put the shuttle into orbit, then the computer programs that control the shuttle rockets *must* be able to do calculus. The implication is that even though you can always break an IF statement down into several smaller statements in separate paragraphs, it sometimes is wiser to keep the complexity in one place in the same statement so that it can be dealt with all at once.

EVALUATE: The Case-Structure Statement in COBOL

Even though the EVALUATE statements you write and those you see in existing programs are quite direct and easy to follow, the general definition of this statement is one of the most complicated ones in the language. Therefore, I'll define the two most common forms (with examples) and then expand to the more general form. If you're curious, the general format of the entire statement is in the back of the book.

EVALUATE Identifier

The format for the first basic form of EVALUATE follows:

```
EVALUATE {Data-Item-1/Literal-1/Arith-Expr-1}
  {{WHEN [NOT] {Data-Item-2/Literal-2/Arith-Expr-2}
➡[THRU {Data-Item-3/Litera-3/Arith-Expr-3}]}}...
    Imperative-statement-1}...
  [WHEN OTHER Imperative-statement-2]
  [END-EVALUATE]
```

Although Literal-1 and Arith-Expr-1 work quite well, I'll restrict this initial discussion to working with Data-Item-1 only and return to discuss the other two later.

First observe the ellipsis following Imperative-statement-1. This means that any number of WHEN phrase/Imperative-statement combinations may be included in an EVALUATE. Note also that an ellipsis follows the WHEN phrase itself. This means that any number of WHEN phrases can be listed, and all will cause the same imperative statement to be executed. (Remember that the term Imperative-statement implies any one or more imperative statements.)

The type or "class" of all the data items, literals, and arithmetic expressions in the WHEN phrases must match that of Data-Item-1.

The general functioning process of EVALUATE follows. First, Data-Item-1 is compared with the value (or range of values) specified in the first WHEN phrase. If the values match, Imperative-statement-1 is executed, and the EVALUATE statement is completed. If the values don't match, the value (or range of values) in the next WHEN is tested, and if a match occurs, that imperative-statement is executed, and the EVALUATE is completed. This process continues until either a match is found or all the WHEN values have been compared without a match being found. If no match is found and a WHEN OTHER phrase is present, Imperative-statement-2 is executed, and the EVALUATE is completed. If no match is found and there is no WHEN OTHER phrase, the EVALUATE is completed without any imperative statements being executed.

Comparisons are made using COBOL's normal compare rules. When THRU is used to specify a range of values, a match is indicated if Data-Item-1 is greater than or equal to the value before the THRU and less than or equal to the value after the THRU. If the optional NOT is specified, the "not matched" condition will cause the imperative statement(s) to be executed and the EVALUATE completed.

Where multiple WHEN phrases precede an Imperative-statement-1, a match to any of the values specified in any of the WHENs is considered a match, causing the Imperative-statement-1 to be executed and the EVALUATE completed.

Because at least one WHEN phrase is required, it always will be a conditional statement that needs to be terminated by either a period or the END-EVALUATE term. (Since it is a "new" statement, you almost always will see it terminated by END-EVALUATE in existing programs.)

The following are two self-explanatory examples that demonstrate how this form of EVALUATE can be used.

```
EVALUATE TAXABLE-WAGES
    WHEN ZERO THRU 200
       MULTIPLY TAXABLE-WAGES BY .15 GIVING FEDERAL-TAXES
    WHEN 200 THRU 300
       MULTIPLY TAXABLE-WAGES BY .22 GIVING FEDERAL-TAXES
    WHEN 300 THRU 400
       MULTIPLY TAXABLE-WAGES BY .28 GIVING FEDERAL-TAXES
    WHEN 400 THRU 600
       MULTIPLY TAXABLE-WAGES BY .32 GIVING FEDERAL-TAXES
    WHEN OTHER
       MULTIPLY TAXABLE-WAGES BY .36 GIVING FEDERAL-TAXES
END-EVALUATE.
```

Note that these rates are totally fictitious.

```
EVALUATE TRANSACTION-FUNCTION
    WHEN 'DISPLAY'
       PERFORM 0100-SHOW-RECORD THRU 0100-EXIT
    WHEN 'INSERT'
       PERFORM 0200-INSERT-NEW-RECORD THRU 0200-EXIT
    WHEN 'MODIFY'
    WHEN 'UPDATE'
       PERFORM 0300-UPDATE-CONTROL THRU 0300-EXIT
    WHEN 'DELETE'
       PERFORM 0400-DELETE-RECORD THRU 0400-EXIT
    WHEN OTHER
       MOVE 'UNKNOWN FUNCTION' TO ERROR-MESSAGE
       PERFORM 0500-TRANSACTION-ERROR THRU 0500-EXIT
END-EVALUATE.
```

In this example, TRANSACTION-FUNCTION is simply a data item that specifies what action is to be taken for some arbitrary master-file record that exists in the systems database. The transaction could just as well come from batch input or an online user.

Now look at the use of Literal-1 and Arithmetic-Expression-1 as the subject of EVALUATE. You can see from this discussion and examples that neither makes a great deal of sense for most programming situations. The one possibility I can come up with would be to replace TAXABLE-WAGES with the expression ANNUAL-SALARY / 52 in the first example. Although it works, there does not seem to be much reason for it. Anyway, both options are there should you run into a situation calling for one of them.

A final note is that 88-level conditionals cannot be used with this format, even though they might seem to fit. They do work just fine in the format that follows, though.

EVALUATE TRUE (or FALSE)

Practically speaking, this second form of EVALUATE is really nothing more than a translation of the case structure IF / ELSE IF / ELSE IF–type statement to the EVALUATE format. Although there are a few extensions I'll discuss at the end of this section, the following general format covers almost all situation in which it is used:

```
EVALUATE TRUE
  {{WHEN Condition}...
      Imperative-Statement-1}...
   [WHEN OTHER
      Imperative-Statement-2]
[END-EVALUATE]
```

Notice the ellipses again. They are located as in the preceding section, so multiple WHENs and multiple WHEN/Imperative-Statement-1 combinations are implied here also.

In this case, though, no variable subject follows the word EVALUATE. This means that each WHEN condition is evaluated, and the first one that evaluates to TRUE will have its imperative statement(s) executed, and the EVALUATE will be completed at that point. You can see how similar this is to the case IF statement. You also can see that 88-level condition names will easily work in this structure. An example follows:

```
EVALUATE TRUE
    WHEN TRANSACTION-FUNCTION = 'DISPLAY'
        PERFORM 0100-SHOW-RECORD THRU 0100-EXIT
    WHEN TRANSACTION-FUNCTION = 'INSERT'
      AND USER-PERMISSION = 'UPDATE'
        PERFORM 0200-INSERT-NEW-RECORD THRU 0200-EXIT
    WHEN (TRANSACTION-FUNCTION = 'MODIFY'
      OR TRANSACTION-FUNCTION = 'UPDATE')
      AND USER-PERMISSION = 'UPDATE'
        PERFORM 0300-UPDATE-CONTROL THRU 0300-EXIT
    WHEN TRANSACTION-FUNCTION = 'DELETE'
      AND USER-PERMISSION = 'SUPER'
        PERFORM 0400-DELETE-RECORD THRU 0400-EXIT
    WHEN OTHER
        MOVE 'INVALID FUNCTION' TO ERROR-MESSAGE
        PERFORM 0500-TRANSACTION-ERROR THRU 0500-EXIT
    END-EVALUATE.
```

Observe how I've expanded the complexity by adding another variable. This is the USER-PERMISSION, and it specifies what security access the user will be allowed for your database. All users are allowed to DISPLAY or see the records in the database. Users with UPDATE permission have been specially trained and are allowed to modify records and insert new records on the database. Only a select few users have SUPER permission, which allows them to delete records from the database.

The expanded format of EVALUATE for using conditionals follows:

```
EVALUATE {Condition-1/TRUE/FALSE}
   {{WHEN {Condition-2/TRUE/FALSE}}...
       Imperative-Statement-1}...
   [WHEN OTHER
       Imperative-Statement-2]
[END-EVALUATE]
```

Even though the changes I've made don't appear to be major, they really change what you can do and what kind of statements you can write.

Notice first that you can specify FALSE instead of TRUE as the subject immediately following EVALUATE. This just reverses everything, so the WHEN condition is matched if the Condition-2 specified in the WHEN is NOT TRUE. Talk about reverse logic and negative programming; I definitely stay away from writing code this way.

Now observe that a Condition-1 can be written as the subject immediately following EVALUATE. Also, TRUE and FALSE can be written in the WHEN phrases. This means that you can essentially replace the basic IF with EVALUATE. This is demonstrated in the following example:

```
EVALUATE FIELD-A = FIELD-B
    WHEN TRUE
        PERFORM 0100-PROCESS THRU 0100-EXIT
        EVALUATE FIELD-C = FIELD-D
           WHEN TRUE
               PERFORM 0150-PROCESS THRU 0150-EXIT
        END-EVALUATE
    WHEN FALSE
        PERFORM 0200-PROCESS THRU 0200-EXIT
    WHEN OTHER
        DISPLAY 'IF YOU SEE THIS, COBOL IS BROKEN'
END-EVALUATE.
```

The implication, of course, is that you now can easily write an "IF-less" program. I don't really know what that means to the future of programming.

You also can write Condition-1 as the subject following EVALUATE and Condition-2s within the WHEN phrases. That means that when Condition-1 evaluates to true, the Condition-2s must evaluate to true in order to match, but when Condition-1 evaluates to false, the Condition-2s also must evaluate to false in order to match. Now that will produce some complicated code that I would rather not have to deal with.

Finally, you can combine TRUE/FALSE in the subject of the EVALUATE with TRUE/FALSE in one or more WHEN phrases. I don't really see a purpose for this, but there are many things that exist without purpose.

Using the Words ALSO (and ANY) and the General Format

The following format is seldom seen but could have more use if programmers were more familiar with it. The details from earlier have been reduced to the terms Evaluate-item and When-item so that the structure of the following definition can become easier to see and relate to:

```
EVALUATE Evaluate-item-1 [ALSO Evaluate-item-2]...
  {{WHEN {When-item-1/ANY} [ALSO {When-item-2/ANY}]...}...
    Imperative-statement-1}...
  [WHEN OTHER
    Imperative-statement-2]
[END-EVALUATE]
```

This statement has the same structure as the previous two, but I've added an optional, indefinite number of ALSO phrases for both the EVALUATE portion and the WHEN phrases. I've also added the term ANY as an alternative within all the WHEN phrases.

Conceptually, this allows you to specify and deal with multiple EVALUATE subjects in a structured manner.

Each Evaluate-item-1, 2, 3, and so on must correspond to a related When-item-1, 2, 3, and so on. A WHEN phrase is matched if and only if every specified Evaluate-item matches to its corresponding When-item.

The word ANY is used in place of a When-item when any value is acceptable for the corresponding Evaluate-item.

Okay, I'm a little bit confused, too, and I just wrote this. The following example should clarify things:

```
EVALUATE TRANSACTION-FUNCTION ALSO USER-PERMISSION
    WHEN 'DISPLAY' ALSO ANY
      PERFORM 0100-SHOW-RECORD THRU 0100-EXIT
    WHEN 'INSERT'  ALSO 'UPDATE'
      PERFORM 0200-INSERT-NEW-RECORD THRU 0200-EXIT
    WHEN 'MODIFY'  ALSO 'UPDATE'
    WHEN 'UPDATE'  ALSO 'UPDATE'
      PERFORM 0300-UPDATE-CONTROL THRU 0300-EXIT
    WHEN 'DELETE'  ALSO 'SUPER'
      PERFORM 0400-DELETE-RECORD THRU 0400-EXIT
    WHEN OTHER
      MOVE 'INVALID FUNCTION' TO ERROR-MESSAGE
      PERFORM 0500-TRANSACTION-ERROR THRU 0500-EXIT
    END-EVALUATE.
```

Compare this with the first example in the preceding section. The two examples do the same thing, but they sure look different. In the first WHEN, if the TRANSACTION-FUNCTION has a value of DISPLAY, ANY value will be acceptable for USER-PERMISSION, and the SHOW-RECORD procedure will be executed. In the second WHEN, if TRANSACTION-FUNCTION has a value of INSERT *and* the USER-PERMISSION has a value of UPDATE, the INSERT-NEW-RECORD procedure will be executed. Any other combination will not match that WHEN. Matching is done for the other WHENs in the same manner.

This format can be expanded to any number of ALSO phrases in a similar manner. It also can be used with the conditional items described in the preceding section.

This covers the definition of EVALUATE. There is more to be said about conditional expressions, though.

Advanced Discussion on Conditionals

Complex conditional statements and phrases are one of the powerful tools you have for defining to the computer the intricate decision requirements for processing data imposed by the real-world environment. On the other hand, these statements and phrases also can be very difficult to interpret and, in some cases, downright misleading. The following is one form of the classic deceptive IF statement that has left COBOL programmers muttering under their breath for the last 30 years:

```
IF PROCESSING-MONTH NOT = 3 OR 6 OR 9 OR 12
    PERFORM 0250-NORMAL-MONTH-END-PROCESS.
```

At first glance, it appears that 0250-NORMAL-MONTH-END-PROCESS will be PERFORMed for all months except 3, 6, 9, and 12, and that for those values, it will not be PERFORMed. That is not the case; as you'll see later in this section, the paragraph will be PERFORMed for *all* values of PROCESSING-MONTH.

Many COBOL programmers have avoided the complex conditional for years, and I've even seen textbooks that say such statements are contrary to all structured programming concepts. However, it is necessary to deal with such statements; they exist in many programs, and an increasing number of programmers are employed to maintain such programs. Additionally, more and more programmers with backgrounds in other languages now are working with COBOL, and these other languages teach complex conditionals, take them for granted, and force programmers to learn to understand them.

Complex conditionals seem so difficult to deal with for three main reasons. First, complex conditionals seldom are taught in COBOL programming classes and seldom are defined or described in books on COBOL. Second, until a few years ago, most COBOL programmers spent all their time writing programs instead of reading (maintaining) them, so it was very easy to avoid learning anything about complex conditionals. Third, COBOL provides an "abbreviation" facility that allows the programmer to skip the subject and/or the relation in conditionals in certain situations. Although this makes writing the program quicker and the resulting statement shorter and seemingly simpler, it also can make it much more difficult to interpret.

I'll deal with all these factors in this section. First, I'll define exactly how abbreviations work and how COBOL interprets conditionals. Next, I'll provide a series of steps you can use to decipher complex conditionals, together with some samples, so that you can see how they work. A skeleton program also will be presented so that you can have your own COBOL compiler verify how things are interpreted. Finally, I'll give you some tips for writing complex conditionals so they will be easier for the maintenance programmer to understand.

Abbreviations Available with COBOL

COBOL permits "abbreviations" when the subject (first data item) of a relation is repeated in the following relations. If this is the case, you may skip the subject in the relations after the first one, and COBOL will assume and use the subject from the first relation. Here's an example:

```
IF THIS-MONTH = 2
   OR THIS-MONTH > 6
   AND THIS-MONTH < 12
```

This also may be written as

```
IF THIS-MONTH = 2 OR > 6 AND < 12
```

COBOL also allows you to skip both the subject and the relational operator if both are the same. Here's an example:

```
IF THIS-MONTH = 2
   OR THIS-MONTH = 4
   OR THIS-MONTH > 6
   AND THIS-MONTH < 12
```

This also may be written as

```
IF THIS-MONTH = 2 OR 4 OR > 6 AND < 12
```

It's easy to see how terse or abbreviated this second option is. But, by examining it carefully, you can see how COBOL will expand it back to the full statement so that all the necessary comparisons will be made correctly. This is a basic illustrative example. In more complicated conditionals, COBOL has several rules for beginning and terminating the abbreviation process (these rules take for granted that the conditional is compiled without diagnostics):

1. When the subject of a relation is missing, COBOL assumes that the last subject used in this conditional is intended. When both the subject and the relation are missing, COBOL assumes that the last one of each is intended. (This summarizes the earlier examples.)

2. Conditional abbreviations must begin with a specified subject and relation. Abbreviation assumptions are terminated with the end of each full conditional. (This simply means that you can't begin with an abbreviation. So IF = 3 isn't allowed.)

3. Abbreviation assumptions are terminated when a parenthesis character is encountered. For example, IF A = B OR C AND (< D OR > E) is *not* permitted.

4. Abbreviation assumptions are terminated when the next simple conditional is encountered.

    a. If that conditional specifies a subject, relation, and object, the assumptions are set to the new values. For example, IF A = B OR C OR D = E OR F is permitted and expands to IF A = B OR A = C OR D = E OR D = F.

    b. If the new conditional is a condition-name (88 level), the assumption values are set to "null" and another conditional is required to establish new ones. For example, IF A = B OR C OR INPUT-EOF OR = 'X', where INPUT-EOF is an 88 level, is *not* permitted because COBOL has no way of knowing what to compare 'X' to.

    c. If the new conditional is a class or sign condition, the assumption value for the subject is set to the new one, but the relation assumption is set to "null." For example, IF A = B OR C OR D NUMERIC AND POSITIVE OR = SPACES is permitted and expands to IF A = B OR A = C OR D NUMERIC AND D POSITIVE OR D = SPACES.

Although these rules are a bit lengthy, they all make good common sense and are pretty easy to interpret. Essentially, they just specify that in order for COBOL to make an assumption, it must know what to assume. Generally, if you can say it without confusing someone else, COBOL won't get confused, either.

Adding the word NOT to the mix is another matter entirely. COBOL has specific rules for dealing with "NOT", and they make good sense. Unfortunately, human beings don't think that way—at least not in English (I don't know about other "human" languages). The code at the beginning of this section is a good example.

Part of the confusion stems from the fact that NOT can be used in two completely distinct roles. The first and most common is where it is part of a relation (for example, NOT =, NOT >, and so on). The second role NOT can serve is that of a logical operator that simply reverses the truth value of the conditional. For example, IF NOT (A = B OR C = D) will be false when A = B OR C = D is true, and it will be true when A = B OR C = D is false.

The following rules apply when NOT is encountered in an abbreviated conditional:

1. When NOT immediately precedes a relational operator (=, >, <, EQUAL, GREATER, LESS), it is treated as a part of that relation. Therefore, *it will be repeated* along with the rest of the relational operator when interpreting abbreviated conditionals. For example, IF A NOT = B OR C will be expanded to IF A NOT = B OR A NOT = C.

2. When NOT appears anywhere else in a conditional, it is assumed to be a logical operator, and therefore *it will not be repeated* when abbreviated conditionals are expanded. For example, IF NOT A = B OR C will be expanded to IF NOT A = B OR A = C. Also, for those who really get into this sort of thing, IF A = B OR NOT C OR D will expand to IF A = B OR NOT A = C OR A = D, because NOT *doesn't* precede a relational operator, but IF A = B OR NOT = C OR D will expand to IF A = B OR A NOT = C OR A NOT = D, because here, NOT *does* precede a relational operator.

Before you go on to the next section, look at the example from the beginning of this section:

```
IF PROCESSING-MONTH NOT = 3 OR 6 OR 9 OR 12
    PERFORM 0250-NORMAL-MONTH-END-PROCESS.
```

You now can see that this will expand to

```
IF PROCESSING-MONTH NOT = 3
  OR PROCESSING-MONTH NOT = 6
  OR PROCESSING-MONTH NOT = 9
  OR PROCESSING-MONTH NOT = 12
    PERFORM 0250-NORMAL-MONTH-END-PROCESS.
```

Look at this carefully, and you can see why the condition always will be true and the paragraph will be PERFORMed for all values of PROCESSING-MONTH. When it has a value other than 3, 6, 9, or 12, all the NOT = relations will be true, so the whole condition obviously will be true. When it has a value of 3, though, the first relation will be false, but that means that the other three relations will have to be true. So again, the whole condition will be true. The same will apply to the values 6, 9, and 12.

What you really want is for the PERFORM to be skipped when any of the relations are false. AND will do this for you:

```
IF PROCESSING-MONTH NOT = 3 AND 6 AND 9 AND 12
    PERFORM 0250-NORMAL-MONTH-END-PROCESS.
```

This will work like you want, but unfortunately, it doesn't make much sense when you read it. This expands to the following:

```
IF PROCESSING-MONTH NOT = 3
    AND PROCESSING-MONTH NOT = 6
    AND PROCESSING-MONTH NOT = 9
    AND PROCESSING-MONTH NOT = 12
        PERFORM 0250-NORMAL-MONTH-END-PROCESS.
```

The following are three other alternatives that also work the way you want but seem to read a little bit better.

EXAMPLE 5.1.

```
IF PROCESSING-MONTH NOT = 3 AND NOT = 6 AND  NOT = 9 AND NOT = 12
    PERFORM 0250-NORMAL-MONTH-END-PROCESS.
```

EXAMPLE 5.2.

```
IF PROCESSING-MONTH  = 3 OR 6 OR 9 OR 12
    CONTINUE
ELSE
    PERFORM 0250-NORMAL-MONTH-END-PROCESS.
```

EXAMPLE 5.3.

```
IF NOT (PROCESSING-MONTH = 3 OR 6 OR 9 OR 12)
    PERFORM 0250-NORMAL-MONTH-END-PROCESS.
```

I prefer the last example, but I suspect that is mostly a matter of taste and familiarity with logical operators. All the examples work like you would want, and I can relate to any of them without problems. Take your choice.

COBOL's Processing Steps for Conditionals

COBOL's order of precedence for resolving complex conditionals follows. This list is from the end of Chapter 3, but I've updated it to handle abbreviations.

1. All abbreviated conditions are fully expanded according to the rules in the preceding section.

2. Conditions in the innermost parentheses are evaluated first. When multiple conditionals are present at the same level within the parentheses, the following sequence applies.

3. NOT reversal of truth value is done next.

4. Any pair of conditions separated by AND is combined to form a single truth value.

5. Any pair of conditions separated by OR is combined to form a single truth value.

6. When a series of conditions is separated by the same operator, they are combined from left to right.

Definitions of the three logical operators follow:

NOT	This reverses the truth value of the condition. If the condition it precedes is true, the result will be false. If the condition it precedes is false, the result will be true.
OR	This combines the truth values of the two conditions it separates. If either or both of the conditions are true, the result will be true. If both of the conditions are false, the result will be false.
AND	This also combines the truth values of the two conditions it separates. If both of the conditions are true, the result is true. If either or both of the conditions are false, the result will be false.

Solving Parsing Conditionals

No matter how careful you are in writing complex conditionals and how well you understand how COBOL evaluates them, there are always some that are still very confusing and for which it is impossible to determine for sure what the result will be for a given set of values. The following is a list of steps to decompose such statements. Although the steps are a bit time-consuming, they will produce the correct result if you follow them and the rules from the preceding section correctly. I've found that by working through these steps with pencil and paper, the original intent of the program's author becomes much more obvious, and that makes the problem much easier to handle.

1. Remove all the abbreviations from the conditional using the rules for abbreviations. For example, A = B OR C will be translated to A = B OR A = C.

2. Rewrite all the simple conditionals and logical operators each on a separate line on a piece of paper. For example, A = B, OR, and A = C will each be on separate lines.

3. Add any parentheses that existed in the original conditional. Leave some space before and after them, because you probably will need some space in the next steps. I also find it handy to draw connecting lines to the right of the statements tying each beginning and ending parenthesis together. Again, leave some space, because you will use it in the next steps. This will become much clearer if you glance at the examples that follow.

4. Using the rules in the preceding section, add parentheses and "tie lines" connecting the conditionals together according to the precedence sequence COBOL uses to evaluate them. Begin with the innermost conditionals and work outward. Tie the conditionals together in pairs. At the end, one final grouping or conditional should be paired with the other remaining conditional or group of conditionals. The right side of the paper will vaguely resemble the pairing chart for a sporting tournament.

5. List each variable with its value. You do this here so that the values will not influence how you draw the diagram.

6. Using these values, determine the truth value for each simple conditional.

7. Combine the truth values according to the diagram you've drawn. Begin with the innermost pair and work outward.

8. When you've reached the outermost bracket, you will have the truth value for the entire complex conditional.

Now work through a few examples to see how this works.

Example 1

In the first example, you'll use this complex IF statement:

```
A = B OR C AND D = E AND NOT F = B OR C
```

Following the first step, you'll remove all the abbreviations, leaving the following result:

```
A  = B OR A = C AND D = E AND NOT F = B OR F = C
```

Next, following step 2 as you see in Figure 5.1, you'll spread out the statement on the page using one line for each conditional or logical operator.

FIGURE 5.1.

A = B
___OR___
A = C
___AND___
D = E
___AND___
___NOT___
F = B
___OR___
F = C

Notice how I've spread things out. This will be important, especially when you work with a pencil and scratch paper. Because the original statement had no parentheses, you can skip step 3 and go on to step 4. Because this is the first example, I'll go through this one iteration at a time following the rules in the preceding section. Parentheses aside, the first logical operator to deal with is the NOT, so you'll do that now (see Figure 5.2).

FIGURE 5.2.

A = B
___OR___
A = C
___AND___
D = E
___AND___
___(NOT___
F = B)
___OR___
F = C

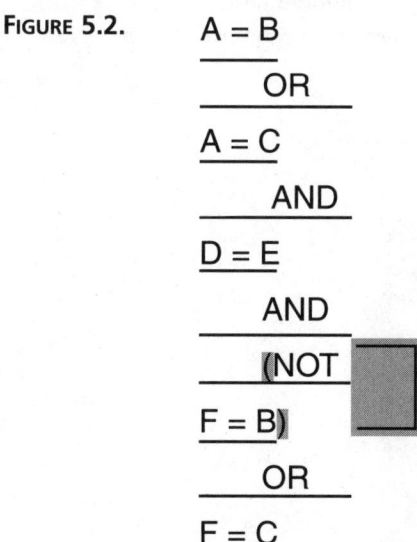

Because there are no more NOTs, the next-highest precedence item is the AND. There are two of them, so you'll do the leftmost (or first one) first (see Figure 5.3).

FIGURE 5.3.

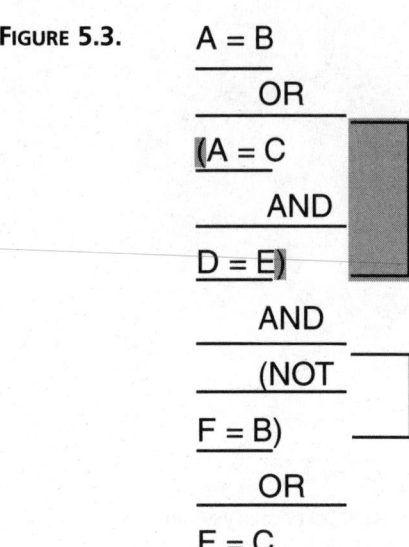

A = B

OR

(A = C

AND

D = E)

AND

(NOT

F = B)

OR

F = C

Notice how I've extended the lines a little farther to the right than before. This will make it completely obvious which conditionals to combine in what order. It isn't really necessary, because the order becomes pretty obvious as you get more familiar with the diagram. As you get to very complicated conditionals, there isn't room for it, either. Now you'll do the other AND (see Figure 5.4).

FIGURE 5.4.

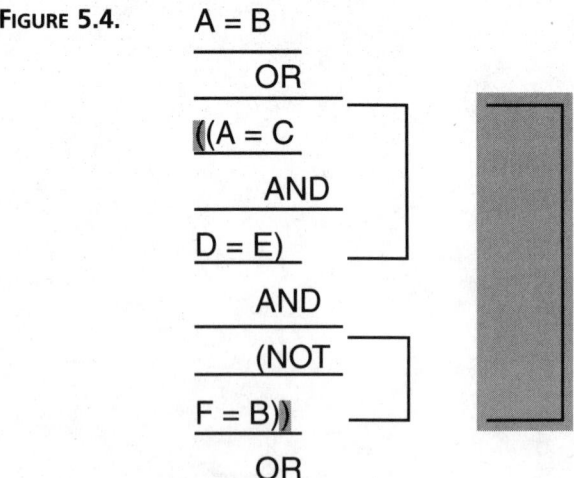

A = B

OR

((A = C

AND

D = E)

AND

(NOT

F = B))

OR

Now that you've finished with the ANDs, you'll do the ORs, beginning with the first one and finishing with the last (see Figure 5.5).

FIGURE 5.5.

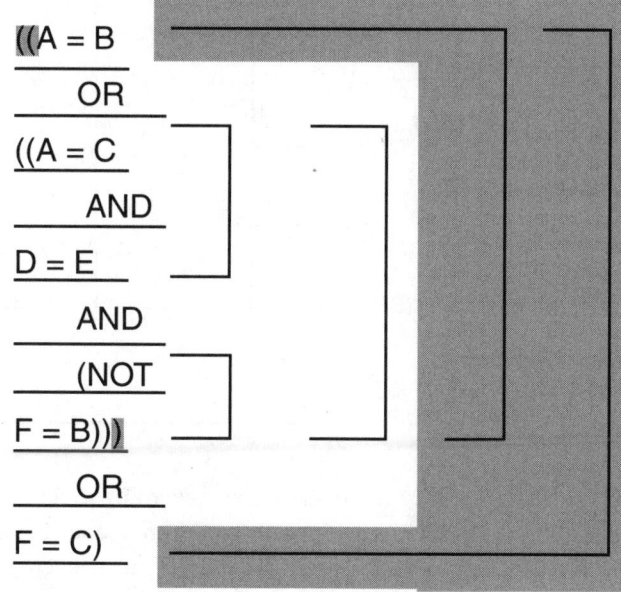

$$((A = B$$
$$OR$$
$$((A = C$$
$$AND$$
$$D = E$$
$$AND$$
$$(NOT$$
$$F = B)))$$
$$OR$$
$$F = C)$$

Now that you've completed the basic diagram, you can go on to step 5, where you determine the values of each of the variables. For this example, you have the following:

```
A = 1, B = 3, C = 1, D = 2, E = 3 and F = 1
```

If you're working with pencil and paper, you might want to make a copy of the diagram at this point. That way, it will be quite easy to try a variety of different data combinations to see how they work.

According to step 6, you now apply the values to each simple conditional to determine whether it is true or false (see Figure 5.6).

FIGURE 5.6.

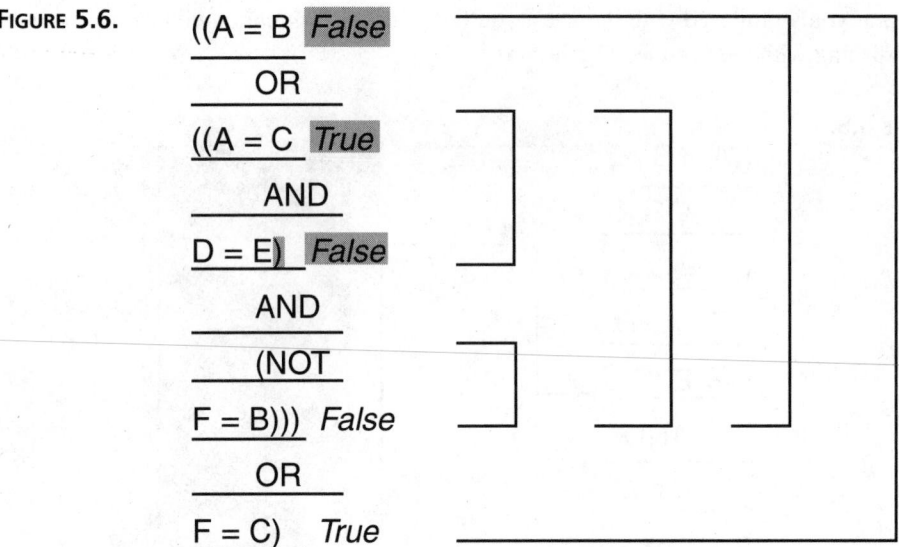

Now, according to step 7, you'll combine the values according to the rules for the logical operators in the preceding section. Again, you'll work from the inside out. First, you'll combine the innermost two. Observe that because they're independent of each other, it doesn't really matter which one you do first (see Figure 5.7).

FIGURE 5.7.

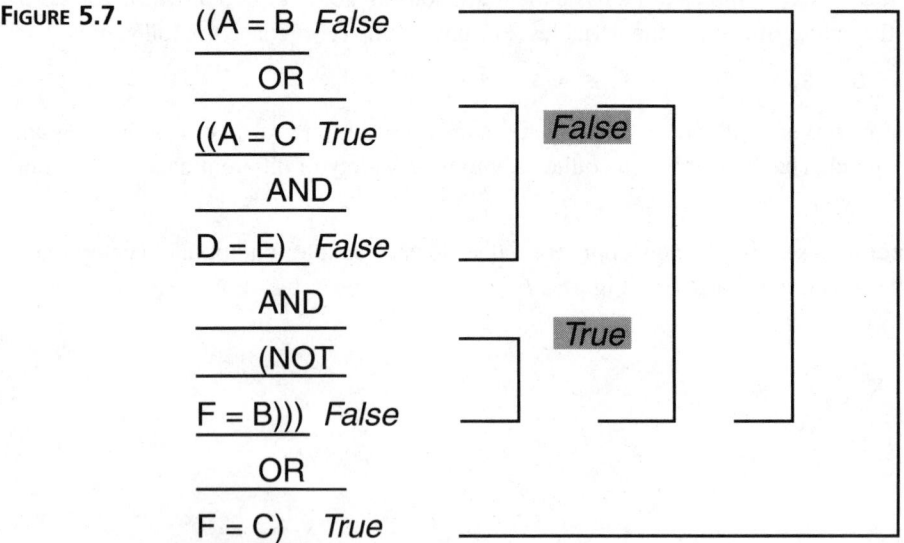

Now you'll combine the remaining conditionals (see Figure 5.8). Notice that the order in which you need to combine them is pretty obvious, both because of the lines you've drawn and because the truth values aren't there to use unless you've evaluated the previous conditionals in the correct order.

FIGURE 5.8.

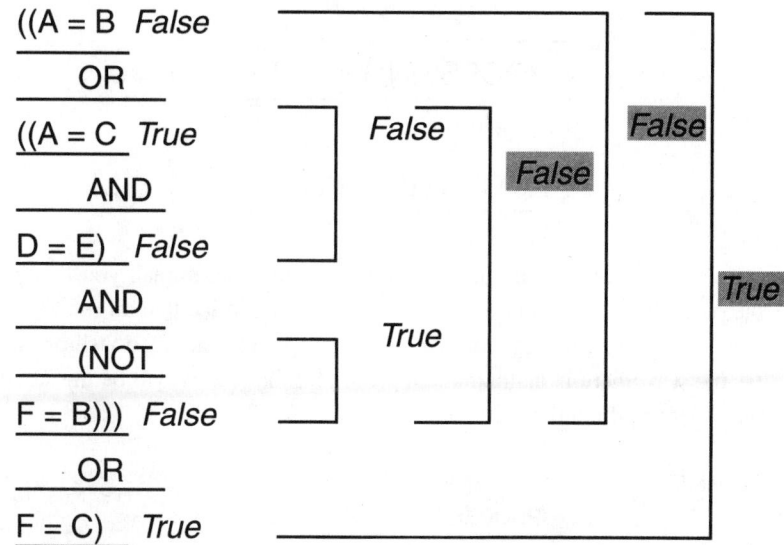

Now you're at step 8, where you see the final result. It's not really complicated at all once you've gone through a few examples. Believe me, it's a lot easier with pencil and paper than it is using a word processor.

Example 2

Now you'll return again to the conditional

```
IF PROCESSING-MONTH NOT = 3 OR 6 OR 9 OR 12
```

Although this isn't very complicated, it is instructive to work through the steps with it. Again, the first step is to remove the abbreviations:

```
IF PROCESSING-MONTH NOT = 3
   OR PROCESSING-MONTH NOT = 6
   OR PROCESSING-MONTH NOT = 9
   OR PROCESSING-MONTH NOT = 12
```

Now, according to step 2, you'll rewrite the statement on paper (see Figure 5.9). Note that because the NOT immediately precedes the =, it is part of the relational operator and therefore doesn't go on a line by itself.

FIGURE 5.9.

PROCESSING-MONTH NOT = 3

OR

PROCESSING-MONTH NOT = 6

OR

PROCESSING-MONTH NOT = 9

OR

PROCESSING-MONTH NOT = 12

Because there are no parentheses in the original conditional, you'll skip step 3 and add the parentheses and lines as indicated in step 4. Notice that all the logical operators are "OR", so you begin at the top (or left) when pairing the relationships (see Figure 5.10). By the way, there is mathematical proof that the results will be the same, regardless of the order in which they are paired.

FIGURE 5.10.

(((PROCESSING-MONTH NOT = 3

OR

PROCESSING-MONTH NOT = 6)

OR

PROCESSING-MONTH NOT = 9)

OR

PROCESSING-MONTH NOT = 12)

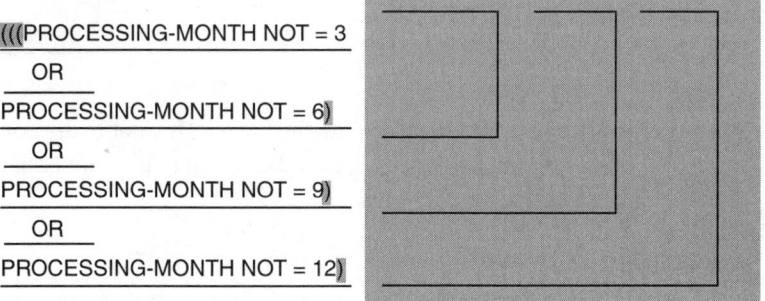

Now, at step 5, you only have one variable, so see what happens if `PROCESSING-MONTH` is 6. Because this is a basic example, you'll combine steps 7 and 8 (see Figure 5.11).

FIGURE 5.11.

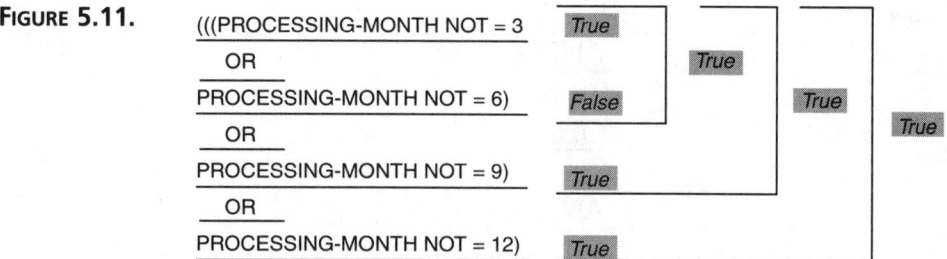

Now see what happens if the value is 12 (see Figure 5.12).

FIGURE 5.12.

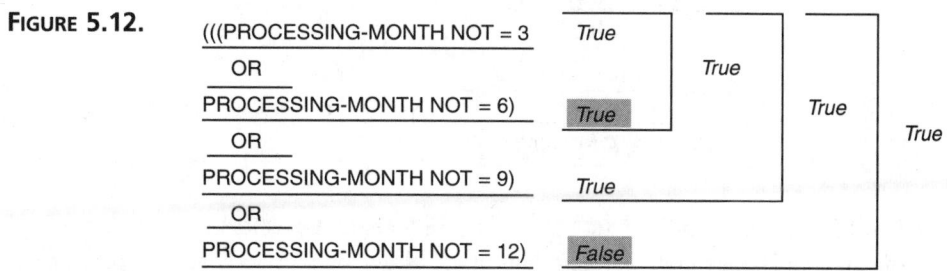

Obviously, if the value is something besides 3, 6, 9, or 12, all the truth values will be "true," making the whole statement true again. Now, for a final example, you'll complicate things a bit by adding an 88-level conditional, a class conditional, some parentheses, and some relations beside = and NOT =. You'll notice that none of these except for the parentheses really changes how you deal with the complex conditional.

Example 3

The conditional follows:

```
D = E AND (A > B OR < C AND = F) OR A = B AND NOT
➥(X NUMERIC OR EVEN-MONTH)
```

EVEN-MONTH is an 88 level defined with values 2, 4, 6, 8, 10, and 12.

The first step is to remove any abbreviations, which is pretty easy in this case, because there are only two. The resulting conditional is

```
D = E AND (A > B OR A < C AND A = F) OR A = B AND NOT
➥(X NUMERIC OR EVEN-MONTH)
```

Now you'll list the statement out as shown in Figure 5.13.

5

ADVANCED CONDITIONAL FEATURES

FIGURE 5.13.

```
    D = E
        AND
    A > B
        OR
    A < C
        AND
    A = F
        OR
    A = B
        AND
        NOT
    X NUMERIC
        OR
    EVEN-MONTH
```

Observe that the class condition (NUMERIC), the 88 level (EVEN-MONTH), and the different relations did not change how you do things at all. Now you will add back the parentheses, as indicated in step 3. Notice how you need to be careful to leave space for the work required in step 4 (see Figure 5.14).

FIGURE 5.14.

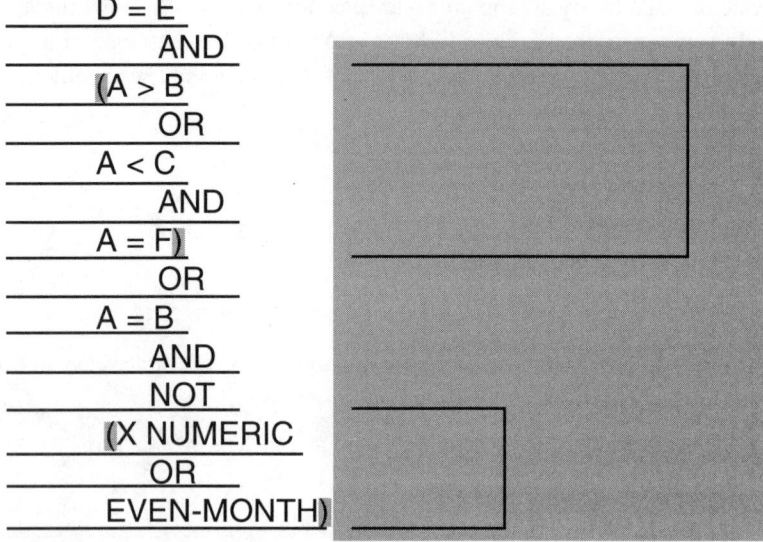

```
    D = E
        AND
    (A > B
        OR
    A < C
        AND
    A = F)
        OR
    A = B
        AND
        NOT
    (X NUMERIC
        OR
    EVEN-MONTH)
```

Extra space is left for the first parenthesis, since additional parsing will be needed there. Now you add more parentheses using the rules in the previous section as guidelines. First, you work inside the parentheses, then you do the NOT, followed by the AND, and finally the OR. The diagram is shown in two stages to make it easier to follow what is being done (see Figure 5.15).

FIGURE 5.15.

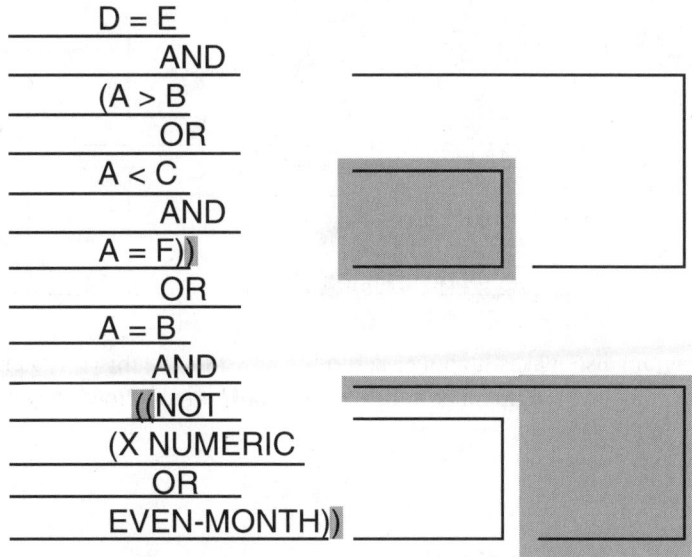

```
D = E
    AND
(A > B
    OR
A < C
    AND
A = F))
    OR
A = B
    AND
    ((NOT
(X NUMERIC
    OR
EVEN-MONTH))
```

Now you'll finish this diagram, as shown in Figure 5.16.

FIGURE 5.16.

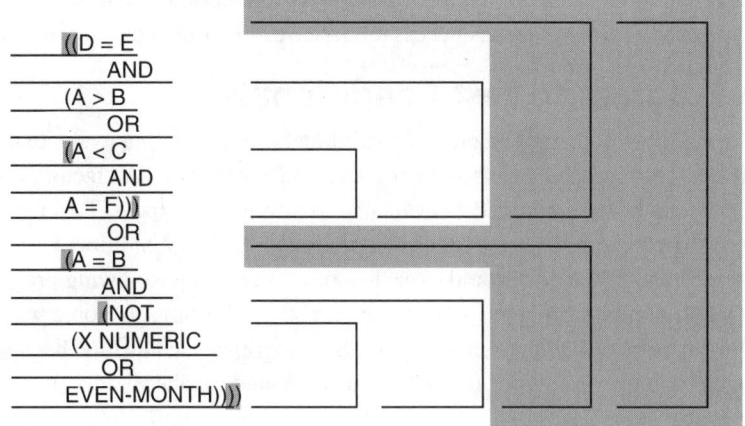

```
((D = E
    AND
(A > B
    OR
(A < C
    AND
A = F))
    OR
(A = B
    AND
    (NOT
(X NUMERIC
    OR
EVEN-MONTH))))
```

5

ADVANCED CONDITIONAL FEATURES

Now let A = 3, B = 4, C = 5, D = 1, E = 2, F = 3, and X = 3 (which is numeric). The data item associated with the 88 level EVEN-MONTH has the value 7. Now follow the results in the diagram shown in Figure 5.17.

FIGURE 5.17.

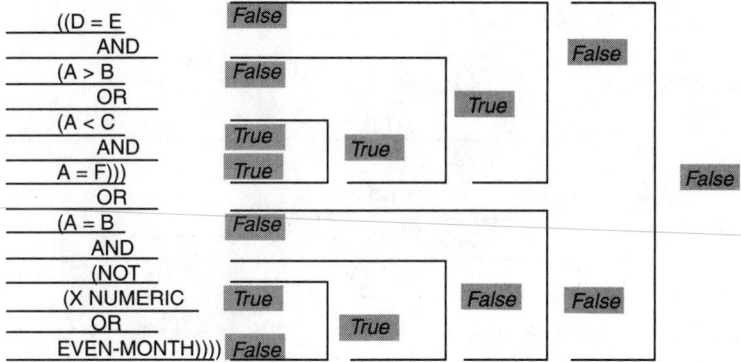

This diagram also makes it a lot easier to see how to write this IF statement, so it's a lot easier for the next programmer to figure out. Look at the following code and see how it follows the diagram:

```
IF ((D = E
    AND (A > B
          OR (A < C
              AND A = F)))
    OR (A = B
        AND (NOT (X NUMERIC
                  OR EVEN-MONTH))))
```

Most conditionals are simple enough or have a pattern to them, so placing each relation on a separate line seldom is necessary. In cases like this, however, it is well worth it.

A Program to Test Conditionals

In spite of everything, sometimes conditionals simply do not evaluate the way you expect. This usually is caused by one of two factors. The first factor is when the data is simply not being compared or evaluated as you would expect. This factor is covered in previous chapters. The other reason is that the complex conditional simply is being treated differently than you would expect—somewhere. The following program uses the COBOL compiler to help isolate what is really happening. In some ways, modern debuggers can accomplish the same thing. I like programs such as this, because they also enable you to "prototype" the code in a controlled manner before putting it into the real program.

LISTING 5.1 CONDITON.

```
IDENTIFICATION DIVISION.
PROGRAM-ID.  Conditon.
DATA DIVISION.
WORKING-STORAGE SECTION.
01  VARIABLES.
    05  A            PIC X.
    05  B            PIC X.
    05  C            PIC X.
    05  D            PIC X.
    05  E            PIC X.
    05  F            PIC X.
    05  X            PIC X.
    05  MO           PIC XX.
    88  EVEN-MONTH VALUE '02' '04' '06' '08' '10' '12'.
PROCEDURE DIVISION.
0000-MAIN.
    PERFORM 0100-IF-TEST
        TEST AFTER
        UNTIL A = 'Z'.
   STOP RUN.
0100-IF-TEST.
    DISPLAY 'ENTER VALUES ABCDEFXMO WITH A = Z TO QUIT'.
    ACCEPT VARIABLES.
    IF A NOT = 'Z'
        DISPLAY 'VALUES ENTERED WERE: ' VARIABLES
        PERFORM 0200-COMPARE.

0200-COMPARE.
   IF ((D = E
       AND (A > B
              OR (A < C
                 AND A = F))))
           DISPLAY 'D=E AND (A>B OR A<C AND A=F) IS TRUE'
     ELSE
           DISPLAY 'D=E AND (A>B OR A<C AND A=F) IS FALSE'.

     IF (A = B
          AND (NOT (X NUMERIC
                 OR EVEN-MONTH)))
          DISPLAY 'A=B AND NOT (X NUMERIC OR EVEN-MONTH) IS TRUE'
     ELSE
          DISPLAY 'A=B AND NOT (X NUMERIC OR EVEN-MONTH) IS FALSE'.

     IF ((D = E
      AND (A > B
              OR (A < C
                 AND A = F)))
        OR (A = B
```

continues

Listing 5.1 CONTINUED

```
                AND (NOT (X NUMERIC
                     OR EVEN-MONTH))))
        DISPLAY 'FULL STATEMENT TRUE'
    ELSE
        DISPLAY 'FULL STATEMENT FALSE'.
```

This program will work easily in both an interactive and batch mode. By using single characters, initial testing is quite easy. It also is easy to tinker with the IF statements and try different things. The conditionals easily can be broken down into smaller pieces where necessary to isolate what actually is happening.

Editorial Comments on Readability

As I've said earlier, I don't mind well-written complex IF statements at all. I would rather see that than to try to debug a dozen simple IF statements spread across just as many paragraphs. If you are into challenges, break down the statement in Listing 5.1 into simple IFs and PERFORMs and then try to figure out what you have.

It is extremely important to be careful when developing complex conditional statements so that others can decipher them. The following guidelines should be helpful:

1. Good data names are extremely important. When the programmer can readily relate to the data, the relations being tested often make a great deal more sense. Two of the examples in the preceding section had terrible data names. I did this to make sure that the connotations of the names did not detract from the exercise itself and so you could see how to approach such statements in a methodical manner. However, such names have no business at all in a production program.

2. Hold abbreviations to a minimum. They are fine for a simple list of OR conditions, but in most cases, they just cause unnecessary confusion. Other languages do without abbreviations entirely. It is strange that some programmers will add unnecessary EXIT paragraphs throughout the program and insert all kinds of blank lines and comment lines. But then they will use all sorts of abbreviations in the only complex IF in the program and compress it into two or three lines so that no one can figure it out.

3. Use parentheses to add clarity. Not only does this help the next programmer, but it helps ensure that COBOL interprets the statement the way you intend. But just as with everything else, don't go overboard. A list of AND or OR conditions such as (MONTH = 3 OR 6 OR 9 OR 12) does not need parentheses inside it. I've seen some statements of the form IF ((A = B) OR (C = D)), where the inner parenthesis are not needed.

4. Use indentation to highlight the hierarchy or structure of the conditional. I've never found an exact set of guidelines on how much to indent where for complex conditionals, but some careful thought usually can produce something that's pretty easy to follow. Listing 5.1 shows what a difference this can make.

5. Finally, remember that the code you write cannot be any less complex than the situation in which you are programming. The best goal is for the complexity of the program to match that of the situation.

Summary

This completes the core portion of the COBOL language itself. These are the essential tools of the language. Part II, "The Language—Stucture Data and External Media," gets into records and files, which are the main product of COBOL programming and business data processing.

The Language—
Structure Data and
External Media

PART
II

IN THIS PART

Data Structures
and Sequential I/O

by Judson McClendon

IN THIS CHAPTER

COBOL's features are designed around the needs of business programming. Although business is not often concerned with complex calculations, it is very concerned about organizing, storing, and processing large volumes of data. Along with processing all the data, business is also very interested in seeing the data presented in reports. To this end, COBOL is equipped with very powerful capabilities to describe, organize, and store data. This chapter discusses how data is described and organized into records and files; it also introduces the basic concepts of file handling, sequential I/O, and basic report printing. The next few chapters cover more advanced file-handling features.

Structure Data

One of the more powerful and useful features of COBOL is its facilities for clearly, simply, and logically defining and formatting data. This section discusses these powerful COBOL features and how to use them effectively.

Records

The most fundamental element of data in COBOL is the *field*. A field is one piece of information, such as a name, Social Security number, or salary rate. It is often very useful to be able to group several related fields together so they can be used as a unit. For example, you might want to store a customer name in separate fields for title (Dr., for example), first name, middle name or initial, last name, and suffix (Jr., for example). However, you might also want to be able to reference the entire set of name fields as a unit. COBOL provides two methods of grouping data fields. The first and most powerful is the *record,* and the second is the 66-level RENAMES clause, which is described in "66-Level RENAMES" later in this chapter. In COBOL, a *record* is a structure that collectively encompasses one or more fields defined within it. To support defining groups within groups, the COBOL record is a hierarchical structure.

Hierarchical Structure

In the simplest scenario, a record would simply contain a list of fields—and you can easily do this with records. COBOL records are capable of much greater things. Experience teaches us that the most convenient way of describing the relationships among most data is hierarchical. *Hierarchical* means *gradational.* One hierarchical structure that everyone is familiar with is the outline. In the outline, equally important elements are listed sequentially. Elements subordinate to an element are listed under the element to which they are subordinate, with each successive gradation increasingly indented—for example,

Data Structures and Sequential I/O
CHAPTER 6
177

6
DATA STRUCTURES
AND SEQUENTIAL
I/O

```
Outline
  I
    A
      1
        a
        b
      2
    B
...
```

The COBOL record structure is very analogous to the outline, but to signify different levels of subordination in the hierarchy, the elements in a COBOL record are graded by level numbers instead of A, 1, a, and so on. Entries with higher-level numbers are more subordinate than entries with lower-level numbers.

Level Numbers

Each element within a record, including the record itself, is given a level number between 01 and 49. The record itself, and only the record, must be assigned the level number 01. In COBOL, a 01 level is a record, and a record is a 01 level. Here is what the earlier sample outline structure might look like, using level numbers:

```
01 Record
  03  I
    05  A
      07  1
        09  a
        09  b
      07  2
    05  B
...
```

> **NOTE**
>
> You could have used level numbers 01, 02, 03, and so on, instead of 01, 03, 05, and so on. It is common practice to skip numbers in order to allow room for later insertion of an intermediate level, if needed. The most common skip is the odd numbers, as in the above example, but some programmers use other increments. The important thing is to be consistent.

In COBOL 85, the 01-level numbers must be in area a of the source line, column 8; the other levels must be in area b or in column 12 or greater. Other than that, COBOL does not impose any indentation rules. It is a virtually universal practice to indent each higher-level number farther. A record with no proper indenting would be extremely difficult to visually discriminate.

> **TIP**
>
> It turns out that using a four-space indentation (for example, columns 8, 12, 16, 20, 24, and so on) works well. A smaller indent is not so visually obvious, and a greater indent goes too far to the right in deeply nested fields. Most COBOL coding forms used to be printed with a heavier line every four columns, beginning with column 8. The important thing is to be consistent.

Data Names

Most of the time, a field within a record will be referenced somewhere in the program. For a field to be referenced, it must be given a data name. A *data name* is a valid COBOL word that is placed immediately following the level numbers. All data names must be uniquely qualified (see "Data Name Qualification" later in this chapter).

If a field is never referenced, it may be given the name `FILLER`. `FILLER` is a null name and can be used as often as desired. If the data name is omitted in COBOL 85, it is treated as if the name were `FILLER` (COBOL 74 requires a name). Here is an example of a record to hold the current date in both `MMDDYYYY` and `YYYYMMDD` form:

```
01   DATE-WORK-AREA.
     03   DW-TODAYS-DATE.
          05   DW-TODAYS-MONTH        PIC   9(02).
          05   DW-TODAYS-DAY          PIC   9(02).
          05   DW-TODAYS-YEAR         PIC   9(04).
     03   DW-TODAYS-YYYYMMDD.
          05   DW-TODAYS-YYYY.
               07        FILLER       PIC   9(02).
               07   DW-TODAYS-YY       PIC   9(02).
          05   DW-TODAYS-MM           PIC   9(02).
          05   DW-TODAYS-DD           PIC   9(02).
```

A reference to data name `DW-TODAYS-DATE` encompasses all three subordinate fields—`DW-TODAYS-MONTH`, `DW-TODAYS-DAY`, and `DW-TODAYS-YEAR`. Similarly, a reference to `DW-TODAYS-YYYYMMDD` encompasses subordinate fields `DW-TODAYS-YYYY` (which encompasses the century `FILLER` and `DW-TODAYS-YY`), `DW-TODAYS-MM`, and `DW-TODAYS-DD`. A reference to `DW-TODAYS-YYYY` encompasses subordinate fields the century `FILLER` and `DW-TODAYS-YY`. A reference to `DATE-WORK-AREA` encompasses subordinate fields `DW-TODAYS-DATE` and `DW-TODAYS-YYYYMMDD`.

In this example, the two-digit century field `FILLER` under `DW-TODAYS-YYYY` is not accessible as an individual field, although `DW-TODAYS-YYYY` (which includes the century) and `DW-TODAYS-YY` are both accessible.

Data Structures and Sequential I/O

CHAPTER 6

179

6

DATA STRUCTURES
AND SEQUENTIAL
I/O

Tips and Techniques

This section presents a number of tips that you should find helpful. If you do much maintenance programming, you will learn to appreciate the principles embodied in these tips.

- The word FILLER is indented from the regular data names to make it stand out visually. The reason for a program listing's existence is for human eyes to read. Format your code to make it easy for visual assimilation.

- Note the use of a consistent (nn) format for the PICTURE clauses. It is sometimes necessary to calculate the position of fields within a record. If this format is used, it is much easier to accurately determine the size of each field. But don't go overboard. For fields of more than 99 characters, use (nnn) or (nnnn) on those fields rather than break them up. With an edited PICTURE such as $Z,ZZZ,ZZZ.99, it is usually better to avoid parentheses—for example,
$(01)Z(01),Z(03),Z(03).9(02) is no improvement.

- It is good practice to assign a unique prefix to each record within a program. A mnemonic abbreviation or acronym of the record data name works well. Then use that prefix with every data name in the record. This enables you to easily discern which data names are part of the same record anywhere they appear in the program. It also helps you remember data names when coding.

- Casual programming practices that may work for small programs can break down on larger programs and projects. Consistency is always important in programming and is particularly important when working on larger projects. It is a good idea to use the same spelling of field names everywhere they are used in a project, except for the prefix, which indicates the record in which the field is located. One exception to this rule is when data that is being moved from one field to another changes its meaning. (At some point in processing, for example, CURRENT-DATE may be moved to PREVIOUS-DATE. Same data, different meaning.)

- It is a good idea to create as part of the system documentation a table of data names and abbreviations used in a large program or system, particularly if several people are working on it. When you know what the field name is, and which record it is in, you don't have to guess what the correct data name will be.

Understanding the Structure

As each successive field is defined in a record, it is placed immediately after the preceding field. The result is a contiguous group of fields, some of which may be subdivided into subfields, which may be subdivided, and so on. It is important to understand that a record itself is one contiguous group of data elements that is structured in some fashion.

Now, to see how it works, examine a structure that can be very useful in printing reports with control breaks:

```
01   CONTROL-BREAK-AREA.
     03   CBA-CURRENT.
          05   CBA-CURR-LEVEL-1.
               07   CBA-CURR-LEVEL-2.
                    09   CBA-CURR-VISIT-DATE.
                         11   CBA-CURR-VISIT-CC    PIC  9(02).
                         11   CBA-CURR-VISIT-YY    PIC  9(02).
                         11   CBA-CURR-VISIT-MM    PIC  9(02).
                         11   CBA-CURR-VISIT-DD    PIC  9(02).
               07   CBA-CURR-PAT-NBR              PIC  9(06).
     03   CBA-PREVIOUS.
          05   CBA-PREV-LEVEL-1.
               07   CBA-PREV-LEVEL-2.
                    09   CBA-PREV-VISIT-DATE.
                         11   CBA-PREV-VISIT-CC    PIC  9(02).
                         11   CBA-PREV-VISIT-YY    PIC  9(02).
                         11   CBA-PREV-VISIT-MM    PIC  9(02).
                         11   CBA-PREV-VISIT-DD    PIC  9(02).
               07   CBA-PREV-PAT-NBR              PIC  9(06).
```

The purpose of this structure is to support a two-level control break in a printed report, where the input file is sorted by visit date and patient number. As a secondary sort field, PAT-NBR (patient number) will change more frequently than VISIT-DATE. Each time a new record is read, CBA-CURRENT is moved to CBA-PREVIOUS, and fields VISIT-DATE and PAT-NBR are moved from the input record into CBA-CURR-VISIT-DATE and CBA-CURR-PAT-NBR, respectively.

If the current visit date changes from the previous visit date, this is a level 2 break and can be detected by testing (CBA-CURR-LEVEL-2 > CBA-PREV-LEVEL-2).

If the current visit date is the same as the previous visit date (the test in the preceding paragraph is false), but the current patient number has changed, this is a level 1 break and can be detected by testing (CBA-CURR-LEVEL-1 > CBA-PREV-LEVEL-1).

A level 2 break generally implies a level 1 break, so the level 1 break can be tested in the detail print loop, and the level 2 break can be tested inside the level 1 break routine.

Group Levels and Implied Handling

Every data field is either a group item or an ELEMENTARY ITEM. An ELEMENTARY ITEM is an item that has no subordinate items, and it also contains a PICTURE clause and a USAGE, although the USAGE clause may be implied. A group item is an item that does contain subordinate items, and it does not have a PICTURE clause or a USAGE clause. Because group items do not have PICTURE or USAGE clauses, COBOL rules define how they are handled in situations in which the USAGE or PICTURE clauses would affect the result.

Group items are treated as ALPHANUMERIC items. The exception to this is when moving a group item to an edited field. When a group item is moved to an edited field, it is executed as an alphanumeric-to-alphanumeric move with no editing. Here is an example:

```
03   MY-GROUP.
     05  MY-ELEM   PIC X(04) VALUE "ABCD".
03   MY-EDIT-G     PIC XXBXX.
03   MY-EDIT-E     PIC XXBXX.

MOVE MY-GROUP TO MY-EDIT-G.
MOVE MY-ELEM  TO MY-EDIT-E.
```

After these two moves, here is the result:

```
MY-EDIT-G will contain "ABCD "
MY-EDIT-E will contain "AB CD"
```

It is important to remember that in a MOVE of a group item, the group item is treated as a single ALPHANUMERIC field. No attempt is made to convert or match any subordinate field. If you move one group item to another, you must ensure that the subordinate fields are arranged correctly. The compiler will not match them or convert them for you. MOVE CORRESPONDING will match fields for you and move them individually, but the fields must have identical names and qualifications.

CAUTION

One of the most important caveats is when you MOVE to or from a group item that contains COMPUTATIONAL type data, as shown in this example:

```
03   MY-GROUP.
     05  MY-NUMBER   PIC 9999.99 COMP.
03   MY-RESULT       PIC 9999.99.


MOVE MY-GROUP TO MY-RESULT.
```

Whatever is intended by this move, the result almost certainly will not be what the programmer intended. When dealing with numeric data, it is safest to move elementary item to elementary item. Also, define both items appropriately; don't lie to the compiler about what the data looks like. Many sleepless nights have been spent debugging code in which the PICTURE did not correctly match the data.

Data Name Qualification

Every data name must be uniquely defined within in a COBOL program. COBOL provides that you can define the exact same data name more than once in a program, as long as each reference can be uniquely distinguished through qualification. *Qualification* is the specification of a unique set of group item, record, filename, report name, library name, CD name, or program name to which the data name is subordinate. Multiple qualifications can, and sometimes must, be used (each subordinate to the next), depending on the data structure. In other words, if you spell more than one data name exactly alike, each time you reference either of them, you must also specify the name of one or more levels to which the data name is subordinate, sufficient to uniquely qualify (specify) which data name you mean. Here is the format for a qualified reference to a data name:

```
data-name-1 OF data-name-2
data-name-1 [ IN data-name-2 ] ... IN file-name-1
data-name-1 [ OF data-name-2 ] ... OF data-name-3
```

The words IN and OF are equivalent; either can be used as you prefer. The following examples should make it clear:

```
01  MY-WORK-AREA.
    03  MWA-OLD-NAME.
        05  MWA-FIRST    PIC X(15).
        05  MWA-MI       PIC X(01).
        05  MWA-LAST     PIC X(15).
    03  MWA-NEW-NAME.
        05  MWA-FIRST    PIC X(15).
        05  MWA-MI       PIC X(01).
        05  MWA-LAST     PIC X(15).
```

In this structure, any reference to MWA-FIRST, MWA-MI, or MWA-LAST would need to be qualified by MWA-OLD-NAME or MWA-NEW-NAME, as shown in these references:

```
MWA-FIRST OF MWA-OLD-NAME
MWA-MI OF MWA-NEW-NAME
MWA-LAST IN MWA-OLD-NAME
```

Sometimes you need to use more than one qualification. Suppose that you have two similar structures like the one just shown:

```
01  MY-WORK-AREA.
    03  MWA-OLD-NAME.
        05  MWA-FIRST    PIC X(15).
        05  MWA-MI       PIC X(01).
        05  MWA-LAST     PIC X(15).
    03  MWA-NEW-NAME.
        05  MWA-FIRST    PIC X(15).
        05  MWA-MI       PIC X(01).
        05  MWA-LAST     PIC X(15).
```

```
01  YOUR-WORK-AREA.
    03  MWA-OLD-NAME.
        05  MWA-FIRST    PIC X(15).
        05  MWA-MI       PIC X(01).
        05  MWA-LAST     PIC X(15).
    03  MWA-NEW-NAME.
        05  MWA-FIRST    PIC X(15).
        05  MWA-MI       PIC X(01).
        05  MWA-LAST     PIC X(15).
```

In this example, qualification by MWA-OLD-NAME or MWA-NEW-NAME is not sufficient because there are two of each of them. Reference to any of the 05-level fields would need qualification by both MWA-OLD-NAME or MWA-NEW-NAME and MY-WORK-AREA or YOUR-WORK-AREA. Here are some correct qualified references:

```
MWA-FIRST IN MWA-OLD-NAME IN YOUR-WORK-AREA
MWA-NEW-NAME IN MY-WORK-AREA
MWA-MI OF MWA-LAST-NAME IN MY-WORK-AREA
MWA-OLD-NAME OF YOUR-WORK-AREA.
```

Qualification does not have to be to the first level above the referenced data name, however; it can be to any superior level that sufficiently specifies which field you mean. Consider this example:

```
01  MY-WORK-AREA.
    03  MWA-OLD-NAME.
        05  MWA-FIRST    PIC X(15).
        05  MWA-MI       PIC X(01).
        05  MWA-LAST     PIC X(15).
01  YOUR-WORK-AREA.
    03  MWA-NEW-NAME.
        05  MWA-FIRST    PIC X(15).
        05  MWA-MI       PIC X(01).
        05  MWA-LAST     PIC X(15).
```

In this example, you could qualify the 05-level items by either their 03 or 01:

```
MWA-FIRST OF MWA-OLD-NAME
MWA-LAST IN YOUR-WORK-AREA
```

> **TIP**
>
> As a general rule, it is better to spell your data names uniquely rather than use qualification, which takes coding time and can lead to errors.

CORRESPONDING Phrase

The CORRESPONDING phrase, used with MOVE, ADD, or SUBTRACT verbs, allows you to move, add, or subtract one group level to or from another group level. The result will be as if the subordinate fields had been specified individually. Here is an example:

```
01  CONTROL-BREAK-TOTALS.
    03  CBT-LEVEL-1.
        05  CBT-TOT-1    PIC  9(06).
        05  CBT-TOT-2    PIC  9(06).
    03  CBT-LEVEL-2.
        05  CBT-TOT-1    PIC  9(06).
        05  CBT-TOT-2    PIC  9(06).
```

With this structure, you can use these forms:

  a. MOVE CBT-LEVEL-1 TO CBT-LEVEL-2.

  b. ADD CBT-LEVEL-1 TO CBT-LEVEL-2.

  c. SUBTRACT CBT-LEVEL-1 FROM CBT-LEVEL-2.

The result will be as if the following respective moves had been coded instead:

  a. MOVE CBT-TOT-1 OF CBT-LEVEL-1 TO CBT-TOT-1 OF CBT-LEVEL-2.

   MOVE CBT-TOT-2 OF CBT-LEVEL-1 TO CBT-TOT-2 OF CBT-LEVEL-2.

  b. ADD CBT-TOT-1 OF CBT-LEVEL-1 TO CBT-TOT-1 OF CBT-LEVEL-2.

   ADD CBT-TOT-2 OF CBT-LEVEL-1 TO CBT-TOT-2 OF CBT-LEVEL-2.

  c. SUBTRACT CBT-TOT-1 OF CBT-LEVEL-1 FROM CBT-TOT-1 OF CBT-LEVEL-2.

   SUBTRACT CBT-TOT-2 OF CBT-LEVEL-1 FROM CBT-TOT-2 OF CBT-LEVEL-2.

However, for the individual fields to be matched successfully, they must meet several criteria. Assuming the following statement:

```
MOVE group-item-1 TO group-item-2.
ADD group-item-1 TO group-item-2.
SUBTRACT group-item-1 FROM group-item-2.
```

note these points:

- The two field data names must be exactly the same, and every superior data name up to, but not including, group-item-1 and group-item-2 must be the same.

- At least one of the two fields must be an elementary item, and the types of the fields must be such that an elementary MOVE between them is valid. For ADD CORRESPONDING and SUBTRACT CORRESPONDING, both fields must be elementary numeric data items.

- The descriptions of group-item-1 and group-item-2 must not include level numbers 66, 77, or 88, or the USAGE IS INDEX clause.

Data Structures and Sequential I/O

CHAPTER 6

185

6

DATA STRUCTURES
AND SEQUENTIAL
I/O

- Any subordinate data items will be ignored if they contain, or are subordinate to an item that contains, a REDEFINES, RENAMES, OCCURS, or USAGE IS INDEX clause.

- Each data name must have unique qualifiers (although the qualifiers below group-item-1 and group-item-2 are not explicitly stated).

You must be very careful when setting up your structures for the CORRESPONDING phrase to work as you intend. Use CORRESPONDING sparingly, if at all. You might discover that not all the fields you expected are being moved, added, or subtracted, and the compiler did not warn you. In most cases, you will spend more time writing field qualifications for your individual references than you save by using CORRESPONDING.

REDEFINES

The REDEFINES clause allows you to define the same data field or record in more than one way, as shown in this example:

```
03  MY-DATE      PIC 9(08).
03  MY-DATE-R    REDEFINES MY-DATE.
    05  MY-YEAR      PIC 9(04).
    05  MY-MONTH     PIC 9(02).
    05  MY-DAY       PIC 9(02).
```

In this example, MY-DATE and MY-DATE-R refer to the same data but are described differently. MY-DATE is numeric. MY-DATE-R is a group item, so it is inherently alphanumeric, generally equivalent to X(8), except that if you move MY-DATE-R to an edited field, the result will be as if the receiving field were alphanumeric and *not* edited. (See "Group Levels and Implied Handling" earlier in this chapter.)

This capability is very useful, particularly when handling numeric fields or fields that may or may not be numeric. In many systems, referencing a numeric field that contains nonnumeric characters can cause a program abort. Having an alphanumeric definition of that field enables you to examine it before using it and to deal with it if it is not numeric.

When you redefine a 01 record with another 01, either record can be larger, smaller, or the same size as the other. But when you redefine field-1 by field-2 at a higher-level number, field-1 must not be smaller than field-2.

TIP

Indenting the PICTURE of the redefining field and its subordinate entries visually separates the redefinition from the field it is redefining. This is useful when trying to determine the record size or position of fields within the record.

You can redefine a field any number of times, but each REDEFINES must immediately follow the field being redefined or a previous redefinition of the field. You can also redefine a field that is subordinate to a redefinition. Here is an example:

```
03  MY-DATE      PIC 9(08).
03  MY-DATE-R    REDEFINES MY-DATE.
    05  MY-YEAR      PIC 9(04).
    05  MY-CCYY      REDEFINES MY-YEAR.
        07  MY-CC       PIC 9(02).
        07  MY-YY       PIC 9(02).
    05  MY-MONTH   PIC 9(02).
    05  MY-DAY     PIC 9(02).
```

As with group-level items, redefining fields can be a source of errors if you are not careful when constructing your definitions. But REDEFINES is a very powerful feature—one for which you will find many uses.

66-Level RENAMES

The 66-level entry is associated exclusively with the RENAMES clause. The 66 level is placed immediately after the last data-description entry of a record and is used to create a group item consisting of one or more fields in the record. The formats for a 66-level entry follow:

```
66 data-name-1 REDEFINES data-name-2.
66 data-name-1 REDEFINES data-name-2 THRU data-name-3.
66 data-name-1 REDEFINES data-name-2 THROUGH data-name-3.
```

The words THRU and THROUGH are equivalent; use the one you prefer. In the first form, all the data attributes of data-name-2 become the data attributes of data-name-1. In this case, if data-name-2 is an elementary item, data-name-1 is also an elementary item. But in the other two forms (actually, the same form with a different spelling of THRU—THROUGH), data-name-1 is a group item and, as in a normal group item, is treated implicitly as an alphanumeric field, except that if it is moved to an edited field, the editing is ignored.

The 66-level entry must meet the following criteria:

- You can use any number of RENAMES entries for a record.

- The individual 66 RENAMES entries can overlap one another.

- All the RENAMES associated with a given record must immediately follow that record.

- data-name-2 and data-name-3 must be items subordinate to the associated record.

- data-name-2 cannot be the same as data-name-3, and neither can be 01-, 66-, 77-, or 88-level items.

- data-name-2, data-name-3, and all items between or subordinate to them cannot be variable-occurrence data items.

- data-name-2 must begin to the left of data-name-3, and data-name-3 must end to the right of data-name-2. data-name-3 cannot be subordinate to data-name-2.

- data-name-2 and data-name-3 can be qualified.

- You cannot qualify an item using data-name-1, and data-name-1 can be qualified only by the associated 01-level entry and the FD, CD, or SD entries. data-name-2 and data-name-3 cannot have, or be subordinate to, an item that has an OCCURS clause.

Here are examples of valid RENAMES entries:

```
01   MY-RECORD.
     03   MY-FIELD-1        PIC   X(04).
     03   MY-FIELD-2        PIC   9(10).
     03   MY-FIELD-3.
          05   MY-FIELD-3A  PIC   X(02).
          05   MY-FIELD-3B  PIC   9(04).
     03   MY-FIELD-4        PIC   X(10).
     03   MY-FIELD-5.
          05   MY-FIELD-5A  PIC   X(02).
          05   MY-FIELD-5B  PIC   X(01).
     66   MY-FIELD-2-4      RENAMES MY-FIELD-2  THRU MY-FIELD-4.
     66   MY-FIELD-1-3A     RENAMES MY-FIELD-1  THRU MY-FIELD-3A.
     66   MY-FIELD-3B-5A    RENAMES MY-FIELD-3B THRU MY-FIELD-5A.
     66   MY-FIELD-2R       RENAMES MY-FIELD-2.
     66   MY-FIELD-5R       RENAMES MY-FIELD-5
```

All these 66-level entries result in group-level data names, except for MY-FIELD-2R, which is an elementary item. Note that a reference to MY-FIELD-2R gives the exact same result as a reference to MY-FIELD-2.

77-Level Noncontiguous Items

Not all data fields in a COBOL program are part of a structure. There are two ways to set up noncontiguous (autonomous) items in COBOL. One way is to create an elementary 01 level, and the other is to create a 77-level entry. Both ways can be used, and are formatted, virtually identically:

```
77   WS-FIELD-1      PIC   X(02).
01   WS-FIELD-2      PIC   X(02).
77   WS-FIELD-3      PIC   S9(05)V9(02).
01   WS-FIELD-4      PIC   S9(05)V9(02).
```

The methods give practically the same result. In some computer architectures, 01-level entries are aligned on word boundaries in memory and 77-level entries are not. For this reason, on those systems, it may be more memory efficient to use 77-level entries than

01-level entries because extra FILLER may be added by the compiler between the 01-level entries to make them start on a word boundary. In most cases, this is not a big consideration. If it is a consideration, you can achieve the same result by creating a 01 level and placing inside it as subordinate entries all the noncontiguous fields that would normally be 77-level entries, as shown here:

```
01   NONCONTIGUOUS-FIELDS.
        03   NC-FIELD-1      PIC  X(02).
        03   NC-FIELD-2      PIC  X(02).
        03   NC-FIELD-3      PIC  S9(05)V9(02).
        03   NC-FIELD-4      PIC  S9(05)V9(02).
```

By placing all the normally noncontiguous fields inside the 01, the individual fields are placed adjacent to one another with no intervening FILLER. On some architectures, you can still get filler when you place an odd-length COMPUTATIONAL field between two DISPLAY fields. But you would probably still get those fillers using 77 level entries. Some architectures require certain fields used as arguments to built-in functions to be either 77 level or 01 level. Other than that, whether you use 77-level or 01-level entries or collect them all under 01-level entries is a matter of preference. Either method is perfectly good COBOL.

> **TIP**
>
> You can create 01-level entries for each set of related but noncontiguous fields, creating a natural logical grouping. If you follow the *unique prefix for each record* rule described earlier, the prefix will also help you identify and locate the fields in WORKING-STORAGE.

INITIALIZE

INITIALIZE is a very handy verb that was introduced in COBOL 85. INITIALIZE is used to set one field or a group of fields to predetermined values based on the field type. Its primary and default use is to move spaces or zeros to all the elementary items within a group. The format can be either of the following:

INITIALIZE identifier-1

INITIALIZE identifier-1 REPLACING {field-type DATA BY replacement-1} ...

The word DATA is optional. Here, identifier-1 is an elementary or group item, field-type is one of the types in the following list, and replacement-1 is a data name or literal.

Data Structures and Sequential I/O
CHAPTER 6

189

6

DATA STRUCTURES
AND SEQUENTIAL
I/O

field-type	*Replacing Default*
ALPHABETIC	SPACES
ALPHANUMERIC	SPACES
NUMERIC	ZEROS
ALPHANUMERIC-EDITED	SPACES
NUMERIC-EDITED	ZEROS

REPLACING phrases can be used for any or all of the types in the list, but each type can be specified only once within a given INITIALIZE statement. You cannot initialize an index data item or any item that has, or contains an item that has, the DEPENDING phrase of the OCCURS clause. identifier-1 cannot be a 66 level.

INITIALIZE operates as if a series of individual statements were used to MOVE ZEROS, SPACES, identifier-2, or literal-1 to the elementary fields subordinate to identifier-1. Here are some examples of INITIALIZE, with the result listed giving the equivalent MOVE statements:

```
77  MY-VALUE            PIC 9(01).
01  MY-RECORD.
    03  MY-FIELD-1.
        05  MY-FIELD-1A  PIC 9(04).
        05  MY-FIELD-1B  PIC X(02).
    03  MY-FIELD-2       PIC X(06).
    03  MY-FIELD-2R      REDEFINES MY-FIELD-2.
        05  MY-FIELD-2A      PIC X(04).
        05  MY-FIELD-2B      PIC 9(02).
    03      FILLER       PIC X(04).
    03  MY-FIELD-3       PIC XXBXX.
    03  MY-FIELD-4       PIC ZZ9.99.

INITIALIZE MY-RECORD
    Result: MOVE ZEROS  TO MY-FIELD-1A
            MOVE SPACES TO MY-FIELD-1B
            MOVE SPACES TO MY-FIELD-2
            MOVE SPACES TO MY-FIELD-3
            MOVE ZEROS  TO MY-FIELD-4

INITIALIZE MY-FIELD-1
    Result: MOVE ZEROS  TO MY-FIELD-1A
            MOVE SPACES TO MY-FIELD-1B

INITIALIZE MY-FIELD-2R
    Result: MOVE SPACES TO MY-FIELD-2A
            MOVE ZEROS  TO MY-FIELD-2B
```

```
INITIALIZE MY-RECORD
    REPLACING NUMERIC DATA BY MY-VALUE
                ALPHANUMERIC-EDITED BY "XYZ"
    Result: MOVE MY-VALUE TO MY-FIELD-1A
            MOVE "XYZ"    TO MY-FIELD-3
```

As you can see in the last example, if the REPLACING phrase is used, only the types specifically named are initialized. FILLER items and index data items are not initialized— nor are items containing, or subordinate to items containing, a REDEFINES clause, unless the item containing the REDEFINES clause is identifier-1 (for example, MY-FIELD-2R in the first INITIALIZE example). If a data name is used in the REPLACING clause, it should not be subordinate to identifier-1, or the result is undefined.

Sequential I/O

The most fundamental type of file structure is the sequential file. This section discusses sequential files, how they are organized, and how to use them and when. You'll also learn about a special type of sequential file, the printer, and how to use it. The next few chapters cover more advanced file structures and concepts.

The Concept of File

In computers, data is organized and stored in files. As you learned earlier, the most fundamental unit of data in a COBOL program is the *field,* or *data element.* A field is one item of data, such as a name, address, phone number, invoice number, date, and so on. A collection of related fields is called a *record.* For example, a record could be the fields associated with an employee, such as name, address, phone number, job title, salary rate, and so on. Remember that the 01-level entry is used to define the structure of a record. A collection of records is called a *file.* A file of all the employees for a company would be the collection of all the individual employee records, with each of the records a collection of all the fields associated with that employee. This grid should help you visualize how a file is structured:

```
---------------------------- FIELDS ----------------------------
          NAME            ADDRESS         CITY/STATE      PHONE NBR
RECORD#
    1     ADAMS, WILLIAM  4519 27TH ST    ATLANTA, GA     555-1234
    2     BROWN, ROBERT   123 23RD WAY    NEW YORK, NY    555-9999
    3     KENT, CLARK     1 MAIN ST       METROPOLIS, NY  555-0000
    4     SMITH, SALLY    34 ELM AVE      BOSTON, MA      555-9999
```

If you compare this grid to a spreadsheet or database table, the records correspond to rows and the fields correspond to columns.

Data Structures and Sequential I/O

CHAPTER 6

191

6

DATA STRUCTURES
AND SEQUENTIAL
I/O

The *record* is the unit of data that is input from or output to a file. When data is output to a file, always one record is written at a time. When data is input from a file, always one record is input at a time. A file is processed one record at a time.

In some devices, however, such as magnetic tape and disk, records can be grouped before being written to a file and can be read from a file in groups. This is done for efficiency, both in speed and storage space. This physical group of records is called a *block*. All I/O done to a file is done one block at a time. The COBOL *record* is often referred to as a *logical* record because it is the logical unit that the programmer is concerned with, and the *block* is often referred to as the *physical record* because it is the actual unit of data transferred during physical I/O. A block may be only one record, though, in which case, the file is said to be *unblocked*. Blocking is handled by the operating system and/or compiler-generated code, transparently to the programmer. However, the way in which a file is blocked may be (depending on the implementation) specified in the FD file-description entry (see "FD File Description" later in this chapter). In some implementations, the block structure is specified outside the program through a mechanism such as IBM's *Job Control Language* (JCL). Some implementations support variable block sizes.

Files can be structured by using a fixed record size, which is most common, or a variable record size. This attribute, along with the minimum and maximum sizes, is specified in the FD file-description entry (see "FD File Description" later in this section).

Sequential File Structure

In a sequential file, records are always accessed beginning with the first record in the file, then the second, then the next, and so on, through to the end of the file. To visualize how a sequential file works, think of a cassette tape. You must pass through the first part of the tape to access the middle or end of the tape. In a similar manner, to access a record in the middle of a sequential file, you must first read the records that precede it. In the preceding example, to access record #3 for Clark Kent, records #1 and #2 must be read first.

Using Sequential Files

In COBOL, a sequential file is defined by a SELECT clause in the FILE-CONTROL paragraph of the INPUT-OUTPUT SECTION of the ENVIRONMENT DIVISION and an FD file-description entry in the FILE SECTION of the DATA DIVISION. The SELECT clause has the following format:

```
SELECT [OPTIONAL] file-name-1 ASSIGN TO file-type
    [ RESERVE integer-1 AREA(S) ]
    [ ORGANIZATION IS ] SEQUENTIAL
    [ PADDING CHARACTER IS padding-type ]
    [ RECORD DELIMITER IS delimiter-type ]
    [ ACCESS MODE IS SEQUENTIAL ]
    [ FILE STATUS IS data-name-1 ]
```

Use of the SELECT clause can be highly implementation dependent. In some systems, the SELECT clause almost entirely determines the interface to the physical file. In other systems, the SELECT clause is almost for documentation only. Refer to your specific systems documentation for details.

file-name-1 is the logical filename used in the program to refer to the file and must be identical to the filename in the associated FD in the FILE SECTION (described later in this section). file-name-1 must be unique in the FILE SECTION.

If the OPTIONAL phrase is used, and the file is opened in a mode expecting a physical file to be present, and the physical file is not present, the effect is as if the physical file were present but containing no records.

file-type is an implementor-defined name (PRINTER, DISK, TAPE, and so on) or a non-numeric literal. The details of both these possibilities are implementor defined.

The RESERVE clause specifies the number of input/output areas (buffers) to be allocated to the file. If the RESERVE clause is omitted, the number of input/output areas assigned is implementor defined. The exact effect of this clause is implementor defined and, in some implementations, is for documentation only.

The ORGANIZATION IS SEQUENTIAL clause is used to specify a sequential file. On some implementations, there are variations to this clause, such as Micro Focus COBOL, which supports ORGANIZATION IS LINE SEQUENTIAL to specify a standard text file with trailing spaces removed from each record, compatible with a standard text file on the particular system.

In some implementations where records are *blocked* (read and written in groups for efficiency), a block can contain empty records after the last actual record in that block. These empty records can be recognized and ignored on input because they are filled with a certain character called a *padding character.* For these implementations, the PADDING CHARACTER phrase can be used to specify which padding character should be used. The padding type can be a one-character alphanumeric data element or a one-character non-numeric literal.

On some implementations, the length of variable-length records is determined by the use of a record delimiter character to terminate the record. In those implementations, the

RECORD DELIMITER clause can be used to specify the delimiter character to be used. In these cases, the delimiter type must be an implementor-defined name or an industry-standard phrase for determining the length of magnetic tape labels.

The ACCESS MODE IS SEQUENTIAL clause is optional because an ORGANIZATION SEQUEN-TIAL file can be accessed only sequentially.

The FILE STATUS clause is used to specify a two-character alphanumeric data-name-1. Each time an I/O operation is done on file-name-1, the result status code from that operation is stored in data-name-1. Status codes are discussed in more detail in the next chapter, but here is a brief list of possibilities:

Code	Meaning
00	Successful; no other details.
0x	Successful; x defines details.
1x	An AT END condition was encountered; x defines details.
3x	A permanent error was encountered; x defines details.
4x	A logic error was encountered; x defines details.
9x	Implementor-defined error; x defines details.

Here, x indicates a character that will further define what the exception or error was. Some of the values for x are standard, and some are implementor defined.

Status codes are used to handle I/O errors programmatically rather than let the default error handling deal with them. One use could be to extract all the valid records from a physical file that has one or more bad spots that can't be read because of I/O errors. Without the FILE STATUS clause, an error of that kind would usually abort the program. Using FILE STATUS, the errors can be detected programmatically, and the bad records can be skipped.

CAUTION

Be aware that if FILE STATUS is specified for a file, much of the built-in error-handling normally done by the operating system is bypassed. If you don't programmatically detect and handle any I/O errors that occur, an error could happen and not be detected.

The operation of the AT END clause of a READ statement (see "READ Statement" later in this section) on a file with a status code specified can vary between implementations. If you intend to use both on the same file, check your compiler documentation.

FD File Description

The second part of defining a file in COBOL is the FD file-description entry in the FILE SECTION of the DATA DIVISION. Following the FD entry must be one or more 01-level entries, one for each different record format. Most data files have only one record format, but print files can have many formats—one for each print line layout. All the 01 entries under one FD, except the first entry, have an implicit REDEFINES of the first 01. In other words, even if the FD is followed by several 01 entries, each of the 01 entries occupies the same record area.

The format for an FD entry follows. Each clause that has multiple formats is repeated for each format.

```
FD file-name-1

    [BLOCK CONTAINS [integer-1 TO] integer-2 RECORDS]
    [BLOCK CONTAINS [integer-1 TO] integer-2 CHARACTERS]

    [RECORD CONTAINS integer-3 CHARACTERS]
    [RECORD IS VARYING IN SIZE
        [[FROM integer-4] [TO integer-5] CHARACTERS]
        [DEPENDING ON data-name-1]]
    [RECORD CONTAINS integer-6 TO integer-7 CHARACTERS]

    [LABEL RECORD IS STANDARD]
    [LABEL RECORD IS OMITTED]
    [LABEL RECORDS ARE STANDARD]
    [LABEL RECORDS ARE OMITTED]

    [VALUE OF implementor-name-1 IS data-name-2]
    [VALUE OF implementor-name-1 IS literal-1]

    [DATA RECORD IS {data-name-3} ...]
    [DATA RECORDS ARE {data-name-3} ..]

    [CODE-SET IS alphabet-name-1].

01  record definitions ...
```

As you can see, the only required parts of the FD entry are the letters FD, file-name-1, and at least one 01 record definition. file-name-1 must have been declared in a SELECT statement in the FILE-CONTROL paragraph.

For blocked files, the BLOCK CONTAINS clause is used to specify how many records or characters are in a block. If the integer-1 TO clause is specified, the blocks are to be of variable size, with the minimum being integer-1 and the maximum being integer-2 records or characters. Use of blocks and variable blocking is implementation dependent, and for some implementations, the block size is specified using external means.

By default, the file has a fixed record size, determined by the largest 01 entry following the FD. The RECORD CONTAINS clause can be used to specify a fixed record size or to specify the limits of a variable record size. integer-4 or integer-6 specifies the lower limit, and integer-5 or integer-7 specifies the upper limit. The DEPENDING ON phrase can be used to specify a numeric field that will the actual record size when the record is output. Record size on input is determined by the physical size of the record. The value of data-name-1 must be set prior to an output statement. The value of data-name-1 is *not* changed by an input statement. For some file types on some implementations, the RECORD CONTAINS (or RECORD IS) clause is ignored. In some implementations, the specified record size is compared against the size of the largest 01 level associated with the FD, and an error is given by the compiler if the values are different.

The LABEL RECORDS clause specifies whether the (magnetic tape) file uses labels. This clause is obsolete and will be deleted from the next standard.

The VALUE OF clause specifies details of the LABEL records mentioned in the LABEL clause. Some implementations use this clause to specify the physical, external name of the file and other details of how the file is physically structured. This clause is obsolete and will be deleted from the next standard.

The DATA RECORDS clause is for documentation only because the 01-level records following the FD are the DATA records and do not need to be specified. This clause is obsolete and will be deleted from the next standard.

The CODE-SET clause is used to specify a character code convention used to represent data in the external media. One use for this clause might be to access an ASCII data file from a program running on an EBCDIC computer. For the definition of alphabet-name-1, see the ALPHABET clause of the SPECIAL-NAMES paragraph of the CONFIGURATION SECTION of the ENVIRONMENT DIVISION.

OPEN Statement

Before any I/O can be done on a file, the file must be opened. The OPEN statement essentially establishes a link between the FD in the program and the external medium that contains or will contain, the file. After the file is opened, I/O operations can be done on it. After a CLOSE statement is executed on the FD, the file is said to be *closed,* and no more I/O operations can be performed on the file unless it is opened again. Sometimes files are opened and closed more than once in a program, depending on processing requirements. One reason to do this could be to process through a sequential file more than once—for example, to create two reports from one file. The general idea is that you open a file, execute whatever I/O statements are required, and then close the file. In this section, you will learn about the OPEN, CLOSE, READ, WRITE, and REWRITE statements.

```
OPEN {INPUT file-name-1} ...
OPEN {OUTPUT file-name-1} ...
OPEN {I-O file-name-1} ...
OPEN {EXTEND file-name-1} ...
```

The word following OPEN specifies the open mode, indicating what kind of I/O is permissible on the file. The modes and their permissible I/O statements in that mode follow:

Mode	I/O Statement
INPUT	READ
OUTPUT	WRITE
I-O	READ, REWRITE
EXTEND	WRITE

The INPUT, I-O, and EXTEND modes require the file to already exist, unless the SELECT statement for that file contains the OPTIONAL clause. If it does, the result is as if the file already existed but contained no records. OUTPUT mode creates a new file.

When a sequential file is opened in I-O mode, records can be read just as in INPUT mode, but the REWRITE statement can be used to modify a record after it has been read (see "REWRITE Statement" later in this section).

OPEN EXTEND is used to append records to the end of an existing sequential file. When the OPEN is complete, the file state is as if it were in OUTPUT mode, positioned immediately after the last record preexisting in the file. All subsequent WRITE statements append records to the end of the file.

CLOSE Statement

The CLOSE statement releases the link between the FD and the external file media that was established by the OPEN statement, and it releases the file.

```
CLOSE {file-name-1 [WITH LOCK]} ...
```

If the LOCK phrase is used, the file cannot be reopened by the program.

Data Structures and Sequential I/O

CHAPTER 6

197

6

DATA STRUCTURES
AND SEQUENTIAL
I/O

READ Statement

The READ statement is used with sequential files to input the next record from a file opened in INPUT mode or I-O mode.

```
READ file-name-1 NEXT RECORD
    [INTO identifier-1]
    [AT END imperative-statement-1]
    [NOT AT END imperative-statement-2]
    [END-READ]
```

The words NEXT, RECORD, and AT are for documentation only. In sequential files, READ always attempts to read the next record.

In COBOL, you always *read a file, write a record.* The reason is that when you are reading a record from a file with more than one record type, you do not necessarily know which type record you are going to read. So the READ syntax specifies the filename. When you are writing a record to a file with more than one record type, however, you must specify which record is to be written, because it might affect the length of the physical record. The WRITE and REWRITE syntax specifies the record name.

The INTO phrase allows the next record to be read and then moved into another work area, all in one statement. However, to use INTO, there must be only one 01 entry associated with file-name-1, or all the 01 entries must be group items or alphanumeric items; also, identifier-1 must be a group or alphanumeric item.

The AT END phrase causes imperative-statement-1 to be executed if the READ was unsuccessful because there are no more records in file-name-1.

The NOT AT END phrase causes imperative-statement-1 to be executed if the READ was successful.

The END-READ phrase ends the scope of the READ statement.

WRITE Statement

The WRITE statement is used with sequential files opened in OUTPUT or EXTEND mode to output the next record to the file. Phrases with multiple forms are listed once for each form.

```
WRITE record-name-1
    [FROM identifier-1]

    [BEFORE ADVANCING integer-1 LINES]
    [AFTER ADVANCING integer-1 LINES]
    [BEFORE ADVANCING identifier-2 LINES]
    [AFTER ADVANCING identifier-2 LINES]
    [BEFORE ADVANCING PAGE]
    [AFTER ADVANCING PAGE]

END-WRITE
```

The words ADVANCING, LINES (or LINE), and AT are for documentation only.

The FROM phrase causes a MOVE of identifier-1 to record-name-1 before the WRITE is executed.

The ADVANCING phrase is used with printer files. It specifies how the paper is to be positioned by the WRITE statement. Using BEFORE causes the line to be printed, and then the paper is advanced by the number of lines specified by integer-1 or identifier-2, or to the top of the next PAGE. Using AFTER causes the paper to be advanced by the number of lines specified by integer-1 or identifier-2, or to the top of the next PAGE; then the line is printed, and the paper stays positioned over that line. If the ADVANCING phrase is omitted, AFTER ADVANCING 1 LINE is assumed.

REWRITE Statement

REWRITE is used with sequential files open in I-O mode to modify a record input from the preceding READ statement on the same file.

```
REWRITE record-name-1
    [FROM identifier-1]
    [END-REWRITE]
```

The FROM phrase causes a MOVE of identifier-1 to record-name-1 before the REWRITE is executed.

When REWRITE is used with a sequential file, the size of the record being rewritten must be exactly the same as the record it is overwriting. If the sizes do not match, the REWRITE is not done, the file remains unchanged, and the I-O status of the file is set to a value indicating the error (see the FILE STATUS clause in "Using Sequential Files" earlier in this chapter).

Example of Sequential I/O

To illustrate the use of sequential files, here is a simple program that reads a file and appends the contents onto the end of another sequential file of the same format. The program counts the records appended to the file and displays the count at the end of the job. The program is written in Micro Focus COBOL, so the SELECT statements and FD entries may be slightly different from those used by your COBOL compiler.

LISTING 6.1   APPEND

```
000100 IDENTIFICATION DIVISION.
000200 ENVIRONMENT DIVISION.
000300 INPUT-OUTPUT SECTION.
000400 FILE-CONTROL.
000500     SELECT INPUT-FILE        ASSIGN TO DISK
```

Data Structures and Sequential I/O

CHAPTER 6

199

6

DATA STRUCTURES
AND SEQUENTIAL
I/O

```
000600                           ORGANIZATION IS LINE SEQUENTIAL.
000700     SELECT OPTIONAL
000800           APPEND-FILE      ASSIGN TO DISK
000900                           ORGANIZATION IS LINE SEQUENTIAL.
001000 DATA DIVISION.
001100 FILE SECTION.
001200
001300 FD  INPUT-FILE
001400     VALUE OF FILE-ID IS "INPUT.DAT".
001500 01  INPUT-RECORD.
001600     03  INPUT-NAME          PIC  X(30).
001700     03  INPUT-ADDR-1        PIC  X(30).
001800     03  INPUT-ADDR-2        PIC  X(30).
001900     03  INPUT-PHONE         PIC  X(16).
002000
002100 FD  APPEND-FILE
002200     VALUE OF FILE-ID IS "APPEND.DAT".
002300 01  APPEND-RECORD.
002400     03  APPEND-NAME         PIC  X(30).
002500     03  APPEND-ADDR-1       PIC  X(30).
002600     03  APPEND-ADDR-2       PIC  X(30).
002700     03  APPEND-PHONE        PIC  X(16).
002800
002900 WORKING-STORAGE SECTION.
003000 77  WS-END-FLAG             PIC  9(01)      VALUE 0.
003100 77  WS-COUNT                PIC  9(06) COMP VALUE 0.
003200
003300 PROCEDURE DIVISION.
003400
003500 000000-CONTROL.
003600     PERFORM 000100-INITIALIZE.
003700     PERFORM 000200-PROCESS
003800         UNTIL (WS-END-FLAG = 1).
003900     PERFORM 000300-TERMINATE.
004000     STOP RUN.
004100
004200 000100-INITIALIZE.
004300     OPEN INPUT  INPUT-FILE
004400          EXTEND APPEND-FILE.
004500     READ INPUT-FILE
004600         AT END
004700             MOVE 1 TO WS-END-FLAG
004800     END-READ.
004900
005000 000200-PROCESS.
005100     INITIALIZE APPEND-RECORD.
005200     MOVE INPUT-NAME   TO APPEND-NAME.
005300     MOVE INPUT-ADDR-1 TO APPEND-ADDR-1.
005400     MOVE INPUT-ADDR-2 TO APPEND-ADDR-2.
005500     MOVE INPUT-PHONE  TO APPEND-PHONE.
```

continues

LISTING 6.1 CONTINUED

```
005600     WRITE APPEND-RECORD.
005700     ADD 1 TO WS-COUNT.
005800     READ INPUT-FILE
005900         AT END
006000             MOVE 1 TO WS-END-FLAG
006100     END-READ.
006200
006300 000300-TERMINATE.
006400     CLOSE INPUT-FILE
006500           APPEND-FILE.
006600     DISPLAY WS-COUNT " records".
```

In paragraph `000100-INITIALIZE`, both files are opened before processing begins. `APPEND-FILE` is opened in `EXTEND` mode, so the new records will be appended to the end of the file. The first record of `INPUT-FILE` is read, and if no records are present, `WS-END-FLAG` is set.

The program then performs paragraph `000200-PROCESS` until no more records remain in `INPUT-FILE`. If an end-of-file was detected on the first read, `000200-PROCESS` is not performed at all.

`000200-PROCESS` creates the new `APPEND-RECORD` from the record in `INPUT-RECORD` and then reads the next record from `INPUT-FILE`. This read sets `WS-END-FLAG` if end-of-file has been reached on `INPUT-FILE`.

When processing is complete, paragraph `000300-TERMINATE` is performed. The files are closed, unlinking the `FD` entries from the physical files, and the record count is displayed.

Reports

One of the most important types of sequential files is the printed report. When printing reports, flexible formatting of the data onto the printed lines and pages becomes very important. This is one of the many areas in which COBOL really shines because COBOL provides very powerful features for formatting data in files and on the printed page.

The lowest level of formatting is in editing the individual fields to appear properly on the report. The `PICTURE` clause is extremely flexible and powerful (the `PICTURE` clause is covered in detail in Chapter 2, "Defining Data and Specifying Its Attributes").

The Print Line

The next level of formatting is in positioning the individual fields on the print line. For a print file, each line is a record. In general, for each different format of print line, you will create a `01`-level record under the `FD` that defines that format.

Data Structures and Sequential I/O

CHAPTER 6

201

6

DATA STRUCTURES
AND SEQUENTIAL
I/O

NOTE

In some programming circles, it is customary to place the different record descriptions in WORKING-STORAGE, and to use READ INTO and WRITE FROM statements for I/O. The reason for this practice is operating system dependent, though, having to do with record- and buffer-handling during I/O. The examples in this chapter use 01-level entries under the FD.

Creating a print line is very similar to creating any type of output record. The 01 level contains subordinate entries that define the layout of the line. In print lines, FILLER items are often used between items to separate them and before items to position them farther to the right on the page. In processing, the print line is first cleared, usually by moving spaces to the 01 level under the FD. Next, the data items to be printed are moved to the corresponding fields under the 01 level. After the print line is complete, it is written to the file using a WRITE statement.

The Printed Page

COBOL provides some built-in capabilities to handle automated report generation and page overflow. These advanced functions are covered in Chapter 9, "The Report Writer Module."

In printed reports, keeping track of the page is important. To position to the top of the next page and print a header, it is important to know when printing reaches the bottom of the page. Often a printed page is a preprinted form, such as an invoice or license, and the data must be printed precisely in preprinted blocks on the form. This requires keeping careful track of the vertical positioning on the page. A good way to do this is to maintain a line counter in WORKING-STORAGE, increment it each time you print, and reset it when a page header is printed. Then it is always available to determine the current vertical positioning (see the sample report program in Listing 6.2).

If you need to print a variable number of lines and then skip to a specific line on the page, you can subtract the line counter from the line you must skip to, and the difference is how many lines you must advance to be at the desired line number.

Sample Report

The simple program in Listing 6.2 illustrates how to produce a report. The program produces a report from a file of names, addresses, and phone numbers.

The first step in programming a report is to create a template that shows how the finished report will look. This is a valuable tool that you can present to the person who will approve the report. Use it yourself to visualize how the report will look and as a target to program toward. Use a word processor and a monospaced font or a simple text editor to create the template. It is very useful if you can read the line and column numbers from the cursor position of the editor. This helps you calculate field sizes, filler, and so on. Here is the template for this report:

```
Date 99/99/9999          S A M P L E   R E P O R T          Page 9999

NAME- - - - - - - - - - - - - - - - - - - - - ADDRESS- - - - - - - - - - - - - - - - - - - PHONE NUMBER- - - -

XXXXXXXXXXXXXXXXXXXXXXXXXXXXXX XXXXXXXXXXXXXXXXXXXXXXXXXXXXXX XXXXXXXXXXXXXXX
                               XXXXXXXXXXXXXXXXXXXXXXXXXXXXXX

XXXXXXXXXXXXXXXXXXXXXXXXXXXXXX XXXXXXXXXXXXXXXXXXXXXXXXXXXXXX XXXXXXXXXXXXXXX
                               XXXXXXXXXXXXXXXXXXXXXXXXXXXXXX

XXXXXXXXXXXXXXXXXXXXXXXXXXXXXX XXXXXXXXXXXXXXXXXXXXXXXXXXXXXX XXXXXXXXXXXXXXX
                               XXXXXXXXXXXXXXXXXXXXXXXXXXXXXX

        ZZZ,ZZ9 records printed
```

I placed Xs, Zs, and 9s to show where alphanumeric, numeric, and edited fields will be printed.

Listing 6.2 is a program for printing this report. The program counts the records as they are printed and prints a total line at the end of the report. The program is written in Micro Focus COBOL, so the SELECT statements and FD entries may be slightly different from those used by your COBOL compiler.

LISTING 6.2   REPORT

```
000100 IDENTIFICATION DIVISION.
000200 ENVIRONMENT DIVISION.
000300 CONFIGURATION SECTION.
000400 INPUT-OUTPUT SECTION.
000500 FILE-CONTROL.
000600     SELECT INPUT-FILE      ASSIGN TO DISK
000700                            ORGANIZATION IS SEQUENTIAL.
000800     SELECT PRINT-FILE      ASSIGN TO PRINTER.
000900 DATA DIVISION.
001000 FILE SECTION.
001100
001200 FD  INPUT-FILE
001300     VALUE OF FILE-ID IS "REPORT.DAT".
001400 01  INPUT-RECORD.
001500     03  INPUT-NAME         PIC  X(30).
001600     03  INPUT-ADDR-1       PIC  X(30).
001700     03  INPUT-ADDR-2       PIC  X(30).
001800     03  INPUT-PHONE        PIC  X(16).
```

```
001900
002000 FD  PRINT-FILE.
002100 01  PRINT-RECORD            PIC  X(80).
002200 01  PRINT-LINE-1.
002300     03  PL1-NAME            PIC  X(30).
002400     03      FILLER          PIC  X(01).
002500     03  PL1-ADDR-1          PIC  X(30).
002600     03      FILLER          PIC  X(01).
002700     03  PL1-PHONE           PIC  X(16).
002800 01  PRINT-LINE-2.
002900     03      FILLER          PIC  X(31).
003000     03  PL2-ADDR-2          PIC  X(30).
003100 01  PRINT-TOTAL-LINE.
003200     03      FILLER          PIC  X(10).
003300     03  PTL-REC-COUNT       PIC  ZZZ,ZZ9.
003400     03  PTL-TOTAL-TEXT      PIC  X(16).
003500
003600 WORKING-STORAGE SECTION.
003700 77  WS-END-FLAG             PIC  9(01)      VALUE 0.
003800 77  WS-REC-COUNT            PIC  9(06) COMP VALUE 0.
003900 77  WS-MAX-LINES            PIC  9(03) COMP VALUE 57.
004000 77  WS-LINE-COUNT           PIC  9(03) COMP VALUE 0.
004100 77  WS-PAGE-COUNT           PIC  9(03) COMP VALUE 0.
004200
004300 01  DATE-WORK-AREA.
004400     03  DWA-CURRENT-DATE.
004500         05  DWA-YEAR            PIC  9(04).
004600         05  DWA-MONTH           PIC  9(02).
004700         05  DWA-DAY             PIC  9(02).
004800         05  DWA-HOUR            PIC  9(02).
004900         05  DWA-MINUTE          PIC  9(02).
005000         05  DWA-SECOND          PIC  99V99.
005100         05  DWA-GREENWICH-DIFF  PIC  X(01).
005200         05  DWA-DIFF-HOURS      PIC  9(02).
005300         05  DWA-DIFF-MINUTES    PIC  9(02).
005400     03  DWA-TODAYS-DATE         PIC  9(08).
005500     03  DWA-TODAYS-DATE-R       REDEFINES DWA-TODAYS-DATE.
005600         05  DWA-MM              PIC  9(02).
005700         05  DWA-DD              PIC  9(02).
005800         05  DWA-YYYY            PIC  9(04).
005900
006000 01  PAGE-HEADER-1.
006100     03      FILLER          PIC  X(05) VALUE "Page ".
006200     03  PH1-RUN-DATE        PIC  99/99/9999.
006300     03      FILLER          PIC  X(59) VALUE
006400         "         S A M P L E   R E P O R T          Pa
006500-        "ge ".
006600     03  PH1-PAGE-NBR        PIC  ZZZ9.
006700 01  PAGE-HEADER-2.
006800     03      FILLER          PIC  X(78) VALUE
```

continues

LISTING 6.2　CONTINUED

```
006900           "NAME----------------------- ADDRESS-----------------
007000-          "----- PHONE NUMBER----".
007100
007200 PROCEDURE DIVISION.
007300
007400 000000-CONTROL.
007500      PERFORM 000100-INITIALIZE.
007600      PERFORM 000200-PROCESS
007700           UNTIL (WS-END-FLAG = 1).
007800      PERFORM 000300-TERMINATE.
007900      STOP RUN.
008000
008100 000100-INITIALIZE.
008200      OPEN INPUT   INPUT-FILE
008300           OUTPUT PRINT-FILE.
008400
008500      MOVE FUNCTION CURRENT-DATE TO DWA-CURRENT-DATE.
008600      MOVE DWA-YEAR   TO DWA-YYYY.
008700      MOVE DWA-MONTH TO DWA-MM.
008800      MOVE DWA-DAY    TO DWA-DD.
008900      MOVE DWA-TODAYS-DATE TO PH1-RUN-DATE.
009000      PERFORM 000210-PAGE-HEADING.
009100
009200      READ INPUT-FILE
009300          AT END
009400               MOVE 1 TO WS-END-FLAG
009500      END-READ.
009600
009700 000200-PROCESS.
009800      IF (WS-LINE-COUNT > WS-MAX-LINES)
009900           PERFORM 000210-PAGE-HEADING.
010000
010100      MOVE INPUT-NAME    TO PL1-NAME.
010200      MOVE INPUT-ADDR-1 TO PL1-ADDR-1.
010300      MOVE INPUT-PHONE   TO PL1-PHONE.
010400      WRITE PRINT-RECORD BEFORE 1.
010500      MOVE SPACES TO PRINT-RECORD.
010600
010700      MOVE INPUT-ADDR-2 TO PL2-ADDR-2.
010800      WRITE PRINT-RECORD BEFORE 2.
010900      MOVE SPACES TO PRINT-RECORD.
011000      ADD 3 TO WS-LINE-COUNT.
011100
011200      ADD 1 TO WS-REC-COUNT.
011300      READ INPUT-FILE
011400          AT END
011500               MOVE 1 TO WS-END-FLAG
011600      END-READ.
011700
```

Data Structures and Sequential I/O

CHAPTER 6

205

6

DATA STRUCTURES
AND SEQUENTIAL
I/O

```
011800 000210-PAGE-HEADING.
011900     IF (WS-LINE-COUNT > ZERO)
012000         WRITE PRINT-RECORD BEFORE PAGE.
012100
012200     ADD 1 TO WS-PAGE-COUNT.
012300     MOVE WS-PAGE-COUNT TO PH1-PAGE-NBR.
012400     WRITE PRINT-RECORD FROM PAGE-HEADER-1 BEFORE 2.
012500     MOVE SPACES TO PRINT-RECORD.
012600
012700     WRITE PRINT-RECORD FROM PAGE-HEADER-2 BEFORE 2.
012800     MOVE SPACES TO PRINT-RECORD.
012900     MOVE 5 TO WS-LINE-COUNT.
013000
013100 000300-TERMINATE.
013200     MOVE WS-REC-COUNT        TO PTL-REC-COUNT.
013300     MOVE " records printed" TO PTL-TOTAL-TEXT.
013400     WRITE PRINT-RECORD BEFORE PAGE.
013500
013600     CLOSE INPUT-FILE
013700           PRINT-FILE.
```

The field WS-MAX-LINES on line 003900 is used as a constant. In a large report program, the maximum lines on a page may be tested at a number of locations in the program. Using a single variable for this can save trouble if the value needs changing.

Page headers usually contain more constant text than variable text. It is convenient to set up WORKING-STORAGE areas for page headers, such as those in lines 006000-007000.

Paragraph 000100-INITIALIZE opens the files, initializes the date in PAGE-HEADER-1, and performs the page-heading routine. It then reads the first record from INPUT-FILE and sets WS-END-FLAG if no records are in the file.

Each loop through paragraph 000200-PROCESS prints the previously read record. Before a record is printed, you want to ensure that there is room on the page, so you test WS-LINE-COUNT to check that the page has not exceeded WS-MAX-LINES.

The two print lines are created and written out, one at a time, with the appropriate ADVANCING. The print line is cleared to spaces immediately after each WRITE, so the print record is always ready to receive a new print line.

The record count is incremented, and the next record is read from INPUT-FILE, setting WS-END-FLAG if end of file is detected.

When a print file is initially opened, the printer should already be positioned at the top of the page. Every time we print a page heading in paragraph 000210-PAGE-HEADING, we want to skip to the top of the next page, except for the first time. The line counter will be zero only the first time through, so you skip to the top of the next page if WS-LINE-COUNT is greater than zero. Because you always clear the print record to spaces after every print, you know that the print record will be clear at this point.

Next, you increment the page count, move it into the page header, and print the page headers. Finally, you set WS-LINE-COUNT to 5, which is the line over which the printer is now positioned.

Paragraph 000300-TERMINATE prints the total line and then closes the files.

COPY and Replace

Most business computer systems consist of many programs, and usually, files are accessed by more than one program in the system. In addition, record structures and routines are generally used by several programs. In each of these situations, it is important to ensure that each program has the same file description, record structure, or code. Maintaining several copies of the same thing leads to errors and is time-consuming. Each time you modify one copy, you also must modify all the other copies, and each modification is an opportunity to introduce errors. To address all these issues, COBOL provides the COPY statement.

The COPY statement logically inserts (copies) COBOL text from a library of such texts into the source program for the compile, replacing itself. In other words, your COBOL compiler or third-party software has some mechanism, which varies by implementation, to create libraries of COBOL code that you can insert into a program being compiled by using the COPY statement. Often the library simply consists of COBOL source files on disk, but it can be much more elaborate, with version control and sophisticated editing and maintenance capabilities. In addition to merely inserting text from a library file into the program being compiled, the COPY statement can also modify the text as it is being inserted, by replacing words or text strings contained in the copy text.

A COPY statement can be placed anywhere in the source program where a character string or a separator (except for a closing quotation mark) can be used. COPY statements cannot be nested (a COPY text cannot contain a COPY statement).

```
COPY text-name-1 [OF library-name-1]
COPY text-name-1 [IN library-name-1]

    [REPLACING token-1 BY token-2].
```

The COPY statement must be preceded by a space and terminated by a period. As in other qualifications, the words OF and IN are synonymous. text-name-1 and library-name-1 are the names of the copy text to be inserted and the library containing the copy text, respectively. library-name-1 needs to be specified only if multiple libraries are available.

Data Structures and Sequential I/O

CHAPTER 6

207

6

DATA STRUCTURES
AND SEQUENTIAL
I/O

The format for `text-name-1` and `library-name-1` is implementor defined and usually consists of alphanumeric literals. `token-1` and `token-2` must be in one of these formats:

```
==pseudo-text-1==
identifier-1
literal-1
word-1
```

When using `pseudo-text-1`, the `==` is required as a delimiter. When `pseudo-text-1` is used as `token-1`, it must be at least one or more COBOL words, but when it is used as `token-2`, it can be empty. For comparison purposes, spaces, separator commas or semicolons, and other white space are reduced to one space per occurrence (but not within alphanumeric literals). In other words, `==(1, 2)==` is treated as `==(1 2)==`. This makes it much simpler to match text, because you don't need to be concerned about how many spaces, commas, or line breaks separate words in `pseudo-text-1`. Literals can be continued across lines.

Here are some examples.

Here are the contents of the copy text `CHRGFILE.COP`:

```
FD   CHRG-FILE.
01   CHRG-RECORD.
        03   CHRG-CHARGE-CODE      PIC   9(06).
        03   CHRG-DESC             PIC   X(30).
        03   CHRG-STD-FEE          PIC   9(03)V9(02).
```

These are COPY statements in the program using the copy text `CHRGFILE.COP`:

```
COPY "CHRGFILE.COP".
COPY "CHRGFILE.COP"
     REPLACING
             CHRG-FILE           BY CHRG2-FILE
             CHRG-RECORD         BY CHRG2-RECORD
             CHRG-CHARGE-CODE    BY CHRG2-CHARGE-CODE
             CHRG-DESC           BY CHRG2-DESC
             CHRG-STD-FEE        BY CHRG2-STD-FEE.
```

These COPY statements are used in a program that needs to open two files with an identical format. The first COPY statement copies `CHRGFILE.COP` into the program unchanged. The second COPY statement also copies `CHRGFILE.COP` into the program but replaces the filename and all the data names to avoid qualification conflicts. The result of the second COPY statement is as if `CHRGFILE.COP` had contained the following:

```
FD   CHRG2-FILE.
01   CHRG2-RECORD.
        03   CHRG2-CHARGE-CODE     PIC   9(06).
        03   CHRG2-DESC            PIC   X(30).
        03   CHRG2-STD-FEE         PIC   9(03)V9(02).
```

Here are the contents of the copy text `MYCODE.COP`:

```
MOVE ZERO         TO FIELD-1.
MOVE "MY PROGRAM" TO FIELD-2.
MOVE "MOVE ZERO"  TO FIELD-3.
IF (FIELD-4 > ZERO)
    PERFORM 000100-PARAGRAPH
END-IF.
```

This is the `COPY` statement in the program using the copy text `MYCODE.COP`:

```
COPY "MYCODE.COP"
    REPLACING
        ==MOVE ZERO==  BY ==MOVE 0==
        "MY PROGRAM" BY "YOUR PROGRAM"
        PERFORM      BY ==GO TO==.
```

The result of this `COPY` statement is as if `MYCODE.COP` had contained the following:

```
MOVE 0            TO FIELD-1.
MOVE "YOUR PROGRAM" TO FIELD-2.
MOVE "MOVE ZERO"  TO FIELD-3.
IF (FIELD-4 > ZERO)
    GO TO 000100-PARAGRAPH
END-IF.
```

Note that the word `ZERO` in the `IF` statement was not replaced because `==MOVE ZERO==` only matches the word `MOVE` followed by the word `ZERO`. Also note that the literal `"MOVE ZERO"` is unchanged because a literal is considered in its entirety as one word.

Summary

This chapter discusses the concepts and details of records. You learned about the structure of records and their uses. You also examined the structure and use of sequential files. Finally, you saw how to use the `COPY` statement. The next few chapters discuss more advanced file-handling features and techniques.

Advanced Techniques Using Indexed Files

CHAPTER 7

Indexed files in COBOL are one of the things that make COBOL such a good language for business. The indexed file mirrors the needs of business in day-to-day operations. Indexed files, when used properly, can lead to superior performance in application programming.

Setting Up the File

The first thing to decide is whether an indexed file is the best approach to solve the problem at hand. Indexed files typically require more processing and *direct access storage device* (DASD) overhead than sequential datasets. The platform you are running the application on also will figure into the determination for the requirement of an indexed file. Some platforms have very efficient sort programs available to them. If you need to access the data in a sorted sequence only for reporting purposes, an indexed file probably is not required. A sort of the data before the report would be more efficient. However, if you are constantly updating the file or performing data validations against the file, an indexed file is ideal.

> **NOTE**
>
> A *direct access storage device* (DASD) commonly is referred to as a *disk drive* or *disk storage*. DASD now encompasses any storage medium where data can be directly addressed and accessed. One modern example of a DASD that is not a disk is the PCMCIA card, which can be inserted into a PC and behaves like a disk drive.

Proper design of your indexed file data structure is very important. Before you write a line of code, you must determine the structure of your indexed files. Analysis of the user requirements is very important. The design of your program will depend largely on the design of your indexed files.

You should consider several points when designing the structure of the indexed file. Indexed files allow retrieval of data either sequentially, or randomly via the key fields. With an indexed file record, you can quickly and directly retrieve a particular record or range of records. Indexed file use is advantageous in several areas of application development:

- Quick data validation
- Individual item lookup
- Reports of similar items

When you design your indexed file structure, you need to keep in mind some of the limitations on indexed files. The actual I/O that occurs on indexed file operations is up to the implementer of the COBOL Standard. The COBOL language itself, while allowing for varying levels of performance, relies heavily on the design of the indexed file access provided by the vendor. Some COBOL vendors use indexed file structures already found on specific hardware, while others have developed their own indexed file methods. The point to remember is that COBOL insulates you from having to know too much about the details of this indexed file access. The syntax of the language statements used to access these files remains largely the same across compiler vendors.

In general, indexed files are very efficient. They usually suffer when a large quantity of records is added or when multiple complex keys exist. When designing your structure, keep these points in mind. While it might be *nice* to access the data via every conceivable possible combination of fields, it is not very efficient and will negatively impact the performance of your application.

Key Limitations

Different variants of COBOL have differing restrictions on the key field size. You should become familiar with your particular compiler to determine this limitation. It is unlikely that you will ever actually come up against this limit, unless you try to make a very large record the entire key to a file. The *primary* or *prime key* to an indexed file may not have duplicates. This key must uniquely identify a record in the file.

Alternate keys may contain duplicates. Most compilers limit the number of alternate keys that can be applied to one indexed file. Key fields must be contiguous—they must be identifiable by a single group level. In the following example, RECORD-KEY is a valid key field:

```
01  The-Record.
    03  Record-key.
        05  Last-name      PIC X(30).
        05  First-name     PIC X(20).
    03  Street-Address     PIC X(50).
```

LAST-NAME also would be valid, but you could not use RECORD-KEY and STREET-ADDRESS. Some COBOL vendors do allow the use of what is called a SPLIT KEY, where you can say the following:

```
RECORD KEY IS JOINED-KEY = LAST-NAME FIRST-NAME STREET-ADDRESS
```

It should be noted, however, that this is not part of the COBOL Standard and is not generally portable across compilers or operating platforms.

When using alternate keys, you should be aware of performance issues relating to the number of alternate keys and their content. The COBOL Standard requires that an entry be made in the index for each alternate key entry, even when filled with zeros, nulls (low values), or spaces. Use care when defining alternate key fields to avoid those fields that would have a significant number of duplicates. An additional consideration when determining your key fields is that no key fields may be of variable length.

Leaving Room for Growth

One of the things that happens in programming is future product enhancements. When defining your file layout and key structure, it is important to leave room for growth. In the past, programmers were under extreme pressure to save as much space as possible. Even considering that, the common practice was to reserve a relatively large portion of the data area as *filler* for use later. When defining key fields, you should keep this under consideration; this is especially important when it comes to defining keys.

Suppose that you are to define a file that is accessed by a customer number that is five positions long and numeric. It might seem to be a more efficient use of space to make the key field a packed decimal or binary field; the space usage would be cut in half. Someday, though, there might be a need to change that structure to allow alphabetic customer numbers. Customer number 1 might need to become customer DD1, or there might be a need to add new customers after all the existing numbers are used. One way to allow for this future growth is to define your key as the following:

```
01   The-Record.
     05   The-Record-Key.
          10   Customer-number.
               15   Numeric-format-customer PIC 9(5).
     05   Body-of-Record.....
```

This approach allows the programmer to have a field, `Customer-number`, that can be used to store alphabetic customer numbers while still retaining the current requirement for numeric customer numbers.

> **TIP**
>
> You actually could leave some expansion area in the key. This method must be weighed against performance requirements and space considerations. It would be a good idea to initialize this extra expansion area. Remember when using the `Initialize` verb that filler items are not initialized, and you should make sure that the expansion is named and not just filler.

```
01   The-Record.
     05   The-Record-Key.
          10   Customer-Number.
               15   Numeric-format customer PIC 9(5).
          10   Future-Expansion-area       PIC X(10).
     05   Body-of-Record....
```

When defining the actual fields in your file, make sure to also allow some room for future field additions and future field size changes. I remember having to do numerous file conversions and program changes when the nine-digit ZIP code was introduced. Never assume that field sizes will not change.

Determining the Key Field

Remember that the primary access key in an indexed file must be unique. When determining your primary key, keep this in mind. Generally speaking, the key field should be one that is static—it should accurately and uniquely describe the data record and should not require modification in the future. Changes to the primary key are troublesome because you cannot just *rewrite* a record after changing the primary key. First, the original record has to be deleted, and then the modified record must be written. This can lead to interesting problems if the new record's key already exists in the file, or if the delete of the old record fails. A technique for handling this type of situation is used in the sample program.

> **NOTE**
>
> Because you cannot change the primary key of a file, your only choice is to attempt to write the new record. Then, if you get a file status 22, rewrite the record and delete the original. This can cause some problems. Imagine that you are keeping a name and address file. The primary key to the file is Name. Mary Smith notifies you that she has married and her name is now Mary Jones. If you follow the logic just described, and there is a different Mary Jones in your file, you will erase her information and replace it with the old Mary Smith. That is obviously a problem. How do you handle that? One method is to check for the existence of the new record before doing the write and delete. Another is to attempt the write. Then, if a file status 22 occurs, notify the user that the name already exists in the file. This method prevents you from having two Mary Jones records in the file, however, even though they are unique individuals. You could expand the key to include some other identifying information. But there is a better way.

When dealing with data files that have keys that do not describe something necessarily unique, like driver's license or Social Security number, I use something I call a *record handle*. The record handle becomes the primary key for the file, and what was the primary key becomes the first alternate key—allowing duplicates. This record handle can be anything you want, but I use a 16-digit number that corresponds to the date and time the record was initially added. The format is YYYYMMDDHHMMSShh. When adding a record, I generate this handle and then attempt a read to make sure the record is not already on file (added by another workstation). The user never sees or is aware of this key. Then when a change is necessary to the apparent primary key, all that is necessary is a rewrite; no complex read, check status, delete original record logic is necessary. An example of this technique is included as CHAPT07.COB.

Some shops actually prohibit modifications to the primary key and require the end user to actually make the new record add and to delete the old record. An example of a poorly chosen primary key is a telephone number. When designing a name/address/phone data file, you might want to be able to look up a customer by telephone number, but the phone number for an individual might change. Name would be a better choice for the primary key in this case. Telephone number would make an excellent alternate key. You should allow duplicates for the telephone number, in case you have multiple individuals from the same family in your data file. You can make a change to an alternate key with a simple rewrite statement.

Alternate Key Selection and Maintenance

Alternate keys can provide exceptional performance advantages when accessing data stored in indexed files. Although some overhead is associated with alternate keys, the performance gain observed by the end user when an alternate key is applied properly outweighs most performance issues. When choosing an alternate key, it is important to consider how the user will be accessing the data. How can an alternate key be used to speed data access and make the application easier and faster to operate? You also need to consider whether duplicate alternate keys will be allowed or necessary.

As an example, consider an application that might be used for newspaper delivery. For billing purposes, you will need to track the name, address, and phone. You probably will be assigning an account number. Because the account number will be unique, it makes an excellent primary key. In addition to name, address, and phone, it would be nice to have the delivery order. The order can let the carrier know which paper will be delivered first and the address to which it will be delivered. As the carriers deliver papers, they might find a more efficient order in which to deliver the papers, and that can be updated in the data file. This delivery order would be a good alternate key, because it would enable you to easily and quickly generate a report showing the order of delivery for the carrier. A possible file layout would look like this:

```
01  Newspaper-master.
    05  Account-number.
        10  Account-no          PIC 9(8).
* leaving room for growth
        10  Account-filler      PIC X(8).
    05  Cust-name.
        10  Last-name           PIC X(30).
        10  First-name          PIC X(30).
    05  Street-Address          PIC X(50).
    05  City                    PIC X(30).
    05  State-or-province       PIC X(10).
    05  Country                 PIC X(30).
    05  Postal-Code             PIC X(20).
    05  Future-Expansion        PIC X(20).
    05  Delivery-Sequence       PIC 9(10).
    05  Future-Record-Expansion PIC X(50).
```

The `Select` statement for defining the key fields might look like this:

```
Select Newspaper-customer assign to NEWS-CUST
        Organization is indexed
        Access is dynamic
        Record key is Account-number
        Alternate record key is Cust-name with duplicates
        Alternate record key is Delivery-sequence
        File Status is News-cust-status.
```

Notice the duplicates on the `Cust-name` key. This allows for multiple customers with the same name to be in your data file. Also, note that `Delivery-sequence` will not allow duplicates. When you code the program, you will want to assign the delivery sequence with large increments between numbers to allow for future additions.

The use of the alternate index in this situation allows you to quickly develop an application that will allow the user to access the data via account number or name, and to list and modify the delivery sequence of the newspapers.

When considering the design of your index and alternate index structure, you need to keep performance in mind. Nothing irritates a user more than having to wait for the computer. If you design your index file structure properly, you can minimize this frustration.

Several performance issues exist. Some depend on the type of application you are developing and how the users will access the data. Others depend on the implementation of the indexed file system being accessed by your COBOL program. In some cases, multiple indexes don't actually buy any performance gains but cause the response times to suffer. In other cases, the indexed file structure can be used to make up for other shortcomings in the target operating environment.

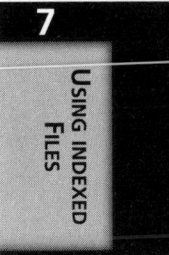

7

USING INDEXED
FILES

If your application will be sharing the data file among many users who will be simultaneously accessing the data, you should consider whether the operating environment offers record- or file-locking. When file-locking is used, the entire file usually is available to all users for inquiry, but once any user opens the file for update, the file becomes locked and no other users can access the file. This does not mean that systems requiring file locks must necessarily suffer from poor performance.

The necessity to use file-locking does not have to mean death to your application's performance. Some indexed file systems that provide for file-locking only are extremely fast and have superior performance. The lack of the necessary record-locking overhead means that your files are accessed faster and need to be open for shorter periods of time. Additionally, the open and close routines for files are optimized, and extensive buffering is used to make file access extremely fast. When coding in this environment, it is especially important to not have the files open for any time longer than absolutely necessary. Open files for I/O only while they are being updated, and close them immediately after they are used. Record-locking can be emulated using these file systems by setting an in-use flag in the records. You also must be alert for practices that could lead to deadly embrace, to which file-locking systems are more vulnerable.

If the operating environment offers record-locking, then multiple users of the data can be more easily accommodated. However, be careful: Record-locking sometimes leads to sloppy programming practice that can lead to deadly embrace and file corruption. Most systems that offer record-level locking also offer file-locking. It is inadvisable, but sometimes necessary, to mix the two types of file access. The only time a file should be locked exclusively in an environment where record-locking is the primary method of securing records for update is when an update process must be performed against the entire file, or when interruption of the process would lead to data corruption.

> **NOTE**
>
> One example of a process that might benefit from having the entire file locked when other applications rely on record locks is a *batch update*. In a batch update, transactions are applied against a file from a set of update transactions. It would not be advisable to allow users to access the file during this update, or their results could be incomplete. It is also not advisable to allow updates to the file by users when the update process is occurring. Changes made by users could erase changes made by your update process.
>
> Opening the file with exclusive access will ensure that no users are accessing the data and that no users will be able to open the file until the update process is complete.

Many indexed file systems suffer serious performance problems when massive numbers of records are added after the file is established. This is especially true of IBM's VSAM system. *VSAM is discussed in depth later in this chapter.* Some systems keep the index and data embedded in the same file. Others keep the index as a separate file and either have tools for reorganizing the index or keep the index sorted as records are added. Systems that keep the record sorted as they are added usually suffer from poor performance during the add process but access the data quickly later.

In the early days of COBOL on the PC, some of the compilers did not come with a sort option. Still today, some sort systems are very poor performers. Some require excessive space or memory to sort efficiently, and still others do not perform well at all. The platform being used also can have an impact on this speed. Many times, sort work files need to be extended. On some systems, this is simply allocating some more space to be used. On others, the operating system searches for enough freespace to hold the entire file plus the new size after extension and then moves the file to this location. This process can take a lot of time.

An alternative to sorting is to use an indexed file as your output file when a sort is required. This has the advantage of not requiring a lot of workspace and of being relatively fast. Of course, this depends on how well your indexed file system performs when adding records. This method is extremely useful when space is at a minimum or a sort is not available.

File Maintenance and Reorganization

Indexed files can provide superior application performance. However, over time, the data may become fragmented. This problem is exhibited mainly in the area of performance. An application that used to be fast may become slow. Periodic file reorganization can remedy this situation. In addition, hardware problems, power outages, or users resetting their computers during updates can corrupt the index of an indexed file. In these situations, unpredictable results may be seen in the execution of an application. Files may need to be restored from backups, reorganized, or have their index portions re-created.

Performance Tuning

Several things can impact the performance of your indexed file system. Most compiler vendors offer indexed file optimization, either at compile time or at runtime. Do not rely on the `Reserve Areas` clause of the `SELECT` statement to always increase performance, however. Many vendors ignore this clause. With many compilers, file-buffering can be defined in the SELECT statement using different language extensions. In the mainframe environment, the *Job Control Language* (JCL) can provide for much-needed file access optimization and buffering. Other vendors offer environment variables that can be set at runtime to control the buffering for a type of file or specific files.

Most modern-day indexed file methods allow the compression of data in indexed files. The compression and decompression of the data are invisible to the COBOL programmer. Data compression can either increase or decrease performance, depending on the implementation. On some local area networks, compressed files actually can decrease the amount of data moving over the wire, thus saving time and bandwidth.

When a Reorganization Is Necessary

Basically, two things can cause a file reorganization to become necessary: poor performance and file corruption. When many records have been added or deleted from a file, performance can suffer. Some indexed file structures do not remove records that are deleted, nor do they reuse the space that was occupied by these records. When many new records have been added to a file, or records have been deleted, users may start to experience slowdowns in response time. If this happens, it's likely time to reorganize the files.

Different systems offer different methods of reorganizing files. Some just rebuild the index portion of the file from the data portion. Others rebuild the entire data file and indexed portion in order to recover deleted space and to correct any corruption in the actual data.

File corruption is the other primary reason for rebuilding data files. File corruption is particularly insidious because it is not always obvious that this is what has happened. When applications that have run reliably for long periods of time start behaving strangely, the problem may not be in the program itself, but in the data file. I have seen file corruption do things from entering an endless loop when writing a backup tape to returning records out of order during sequential reads. Most systems have some way of telling that an indexed file is corrupt. However, the file status returns on these corrupt files vary from vendor to vendor. You should become familiar with the method of determining that a file is corrupt that your particular compiler vendor recommends.

File or index reorganizations can do more than just recover lost space and fix data corruption. Some vendors allow you to order the records in the indexed portion of the data file in a sequence other than primary-key sequence. This capability comes in handy particularly when you need to access data primarily via the alternate key, but the alternate key makes a poor primary key. If this is the case, you can use the vendor's reorganization utility to create the index in a different sequence than is the default.

Alternate Keys Versus Alternate Index Files

Another consideration when creating and maintaining indexed files is the alternate key. When performance becomes an issue, and the alternate keys negatively impact that performance, it might be more advantageous to use a separate index file rather than an alternate key within the same file. I have seen this method used at several installations to avoid the overhead of the alternate key. An alternate index file is a second file that is keyed by a different key, but in which each record points to the primary key of the main indexed file. This alternate index also can be used to *reverse key* the primary file so that records can be retrieved in reverse key order.

Under some circumstances, the performance overhead of maintaining an alternate index may outweigh the benefits. You might want to access the data with this index only occasionally. In this case, it might be advisable to just create a file that indexes the base file only when necessary.

Another reason to have one of these alternate index files is to assign a special key to a file that consists of noncontiguous data in the base file. Most COBOL implementations do not allow the assignation of split keys. For example, you might have a record that looks like this:

```
01   The-Record.
     03   Prime-Key.
          05  Last-Name      PIC X(30).
          05  First-Name     PIC X(20).
     03   Address            PIC X(50).
     03   City               PIC X(30).
     03   State              PIC X(2).
     03   Postal-Code        PIC X(10).
```

You might want to access this data via a key that is `Postal-Code`, `Address`, `First-Name`, `Last-Name`. You may not be able to define an alternate key using these fields because they are not contiguous in your data record. An alternate index data file would be ideal.

An alternate index file consists of a file that is keyed by your desired key and contains a pointer to the primary key in your base file. You will have to write the program that creates this alternate index file. To use the alternate index file, you perform your start and read operations first. Then, using the primary key pointer information you find, access the base file to obtain the real record. The alternate index file does not need to contain any more information than the two related keys.

7

USING INDEXED FILES

If this alternate index file is to be kept synchronized with your base file, you will have to be sure to code your programs accordingly. If the alternate index file is used infrequently, it may be more efficient to create it each time it is required for use.

TIP

Retrieving records in reverse order has been a problem with indexed files. Most compiler vendors now allow the retrieval of records in reverse key sequence, but the method and syntax vary among compiler vendors. Currently, the COBOL Standards do not describe a method for retrieving files in reverse order or descending key sequence. One way you can do this is to create an alternate index file with reverse keys.

You can do this in a few ways. One way is to use what commonly is called the *9s complement.* The key field must be numeric and less than 18 digits for this to work. What you do is subtract all 9s from the key field, and use the result as the key field value. For example, if the key is PIC S9(5), you subtract 99999 from the key. The resultant numbers will be in reverse key sequence.

Another method works whether or not the key is numeric. The key must be less than eight characters long. If it is, you can move the primary key field to a signed binary field and multiply the contents by –1. This works as long as none of the key fields has a low value in it.

One final method involves first sorting the key values in descending order, and then assigning a sequence number as the key in the alternate index file. You should leave large gaps in the numbers assigned, however, to allow room for future file additions. If you take this approach, you will be responsible for calculating and assigning a new sequence number to keys that are added.

Remember that when you create a separate alternate index file, you are responsible for keeping it in sync with the other files. Also, do not confuse alternate index files with VSAM alternate indexes. VSAM alternate indexes are closely associated with the base file and provide the standard alternate record key support found in COBOL.

Most indexed file systems today allow the retrieval of records in reverse key order. However, the existing COBOL Standard offers no way to read records in reverse order. Most compiler vendors have added their own extensions to the language in order to accommodate reading records backward. For each of these, a START statement first must be issued, followed by a READ. Some use READ PREVIOUS RECORD, and others use READ PRIOR RECORD. In IBM's CICS, an EXEC CICS command is provided to read records in reverse key order.

The Online Environment, IBM's VSAM File Structure

In the *online environment,* you can have several users accessing the indexed data files at the same time. There are different types of online environments to consider. These systems range from LAN-type environments, where a common file server processes requests, to UNIX environments, where all instances of the application run on the common processor, to IBM's CICS, where a single copy of the program runs and is reentered by the various users. Each of these offers a challenge to the programmer to provide fast and efficient access to the various data files.

It is important to note that the current COBOL Standard does not define file- or record-locking. Any locking applied to indexed files is based on the file system being used and is subject to the syntax rules of the particular compiler being used. You can use the locking description that follows as a general guide, but you should not assume that any or all of these features are available on your particular platform. It is important for you to read your COBOL and operating system manuals for information on file- and record-locking.

> **NOTE**
>
> The upcoming COBOL Standard addresses the issues of record-locking. The method currently agreed upon is the same as that described in this section.

When using file-locking, the programmer must be certain to not keep the files opened and locked for too long. Additionally, the programmer must make sure that some form of locking is in place before updating records. It is possible to code your program expecting a single user on a single machine to use it, and to later find out that multiple users will be accessing the data simultaneously. If you did not consider record- or file-locking, the files probably will become corrupted. Record-locking provides a way for the programmer to prevent multiple users from accessing the same record at the same time. In general, file-locking provides for more data integrity than record-locking. When file-locking is used, only one application or user at a time can update a file, and the file cannot be simultaneously updated by another user.

When record-locking is available, several types of locking can be applied. The most common is *lock mode automatic*. With this lock mode, when a file is open for I/O, the record is locked until it is rewritten, it is deleted, another record is read, an unlock statement is issued, or a COMMIT statement is issued. When a record is locked, other applications trying to read that record will receive the `locked record file` status. This status varies from vendor to vendor. You can determine at compile time and runtime whether the application trying to read the locked record can obtain the contents of the record. You will have to code for the locked record status in your program. The `UNLOCK` and `COMMIT` statements generally are not used when a lock mode of automatic is used. `UNLOCK` explicitly releases the held lock on the record, and `COMMIT` releases all locks held by the run unit. Automatic locking can acquire locks on multiple records. This is the exception to the use of `UNLOCK` and `COMMIT` when using automatic lock mode. When a file is open for I/O and locks on multiple records are maintained, each time a record is read, it is locked. No other application can update these records until the locks are released.

You must use caution because most systems have a maximum number of records that can be locked at one time. I remember watching an application for file maintenance be designed, coded, tested, and placed in production, only to see it fail more than a year later because someone left a `lock mode is automatic with lock on multiple records` statement in the `SELECT`. The program ran fine, until a user entered more records in one session than the system allowed to be locked at one time.

Lock mode manual gives the programmer more control over the locking and unlocking of records. Records are locked when read specifically with lock. If the programmer does not specify the `WITH LOCK` clause on the `READ` statement, the record is not locked and any other application can update it. A useful extension to manual lock mode provided by some vendors is the `WRITE LOCK` extension. This will keep a newly written record locked until an `UNLOCK` statement is issued. It should be noted that when a lock mode of manual is selected and multiple records are locked, the `UNLOCK` statement will release all record locks for the specified file, and not just the most recently obtained lock. When using lock mode manual, remember that all records where a lock is obtained remain locked until they are released with the `UNLOCK` statement or another lock is obtained—unless `lock on multiple records` is specified, in which case records remain locked until the next `UNLOCK` or `COMMIT` is issued.

The different methods for locking files and records may seem confusing and a bit over-whelming, but they do serve a very serious purpose. The integrity of your data in the multiuser environment depends on only a single user updating a single record at a time. You should consider many areas when designing your programs in the multiuser arena, and you should be alert for some pitfalls. One common problem concerns multiple users updating the same record and removing the other users' updates.

Consider the following scenario. User A calls up an inquiry screen for a customer. At the same time, user B examines the same record. User A makes a modification to the record, and the update is applied. Some time after this, user B—with the same record displayed—updates a different field and writes the same record. What happens to the changes user A made? This depends on how you coded your program. Record-locking could have prevented this problem, if you had locked the record when user A issued his read. However, this would have locked user B out of the record. What would happen if user A went to lunch with that record displayed at his workstation? User B would never have been able to process her work. User B could become frustrated, have the network rebooted, or reboot her computer and physically corrupt the data file. There are some simple things that you, as the programmer, can do to prevent this kind of problem from occurring.

First, make sure that before every update of a record, you reread the data file and compare the record for changes since your last read. If someone else has modified the record, you can notify the current user of the change and prompt for further action. If you want to make the process transparent to the user, read the record for display and save it in a hold area. Then before the update, reread the record. You will have to keep track of the fields your user has modified by comparing them to the original saved copy of the record. Then see whether any of those fields were changed by another user. If so, you have to decide which change to keep, or let the user choose. Using the last read of the record, change only the fields in the record that your particular user modified, and rewrite the record.

A different approach involves placing a flag in the record to indicate that it is being updated by a program. When you read a record, you will have to check to see whether it is marked as being viewed or updated by another user, and if so, disallow any change. The disadvantages of this approach are many, and I do not recommend it. First, if something happens to the program that last marked the record for update and it never marks the record as updated or available, then no other program will be able to update the record. The only repair that can be performed is to write a custom program to mark all records in the file as available. Second, you are dependent on every program accessing the file to update the flag. If even one program does not properly check or update this flag, you lose data integrity.

Deadly Embrace

One common problem with systems that incorporate file- or record-locking is something called *deadly embrace*. This problem is insidious and hard to track down if it is occurring. You should consider the possibility of deadly embrace in the design of your programs and systems so that it will be less likely to occur. Deadly embrace occurs when two or more programs are waiting for different resources to become available, and each program has the other program's desired resource locked.

Deadly embrace should not be confused with two applications waiting for a resource to become available when a third program has the resource locked. That situation is not truly a deadly embrace. One of the two waiting programs will gain access to the file when the third application releases it. Although the wait for the user may seem eternal, it is not. Deadly embrace is a condition that cannot be cured once it occurs, except by terminating one or both of the offending applications.

To understand deadly embrace, imagine two children fighting over a piece of candy. One child holds the candy, and the other holds the hair of the candy holder. The one holding the candy won't release the candy until his hair is let go, and the one pulling the hair won't let go until she gets sole possession of the candy! Nothing can happen until someone gives.

Some transactional and indexed file systems will wait, or the programmer has chosen to wait for a requested record or file to become unlocked, when a file-access operation is coded. When this occurs, the program continually retries the operation until it is successful. If an operation is set to time out after a certain number of retries, then deadly embrace can be avoided to some extent. However, this is only true if an application releases all of its locked resources when timing out of a file-access operation.

It is best to avoid deadly embrace at the outset. An example that could cause the condition to occur is shown in Figure 7.1. The system in question applies exclusive file-locking. Program DD reads file A and then, based on information in the record, updates file B. Assume that program DD opens file A for input. This would allow other programs to read file A, but not to open it for update. Program CH reads file B, also open for input, and then updates a record in file A. If program DD does not close file A after opening it, program CH will wait for file A to become available so that it can open it for update. However, program DD has read file A and now is attempting to open file B for update but can't, because program CH has not released its lock on file B. This same scenario can occur with record locks within a single file or multiple files.

How can deadly embrace be avoided? You can prevent the situation from occurring by using a few simple methods. First, when multiple files are accessed in an environment with file-locking, always open the files in the same order in all programs. When closing the files, close them in the reverse order in which they were opened. For example, always open file A, then file B, followed by file C. When closing, close file C, then file B, and finally, file A. This order must be followed in all programs. When using this method, it is best to open all files at the front of the program and then close them all at the end. This method generally does not lead to efficient operations, because a program could wait for a long time for the files to become available.

FIGURE 7.1.

Flow that can lead to deadly embrace.

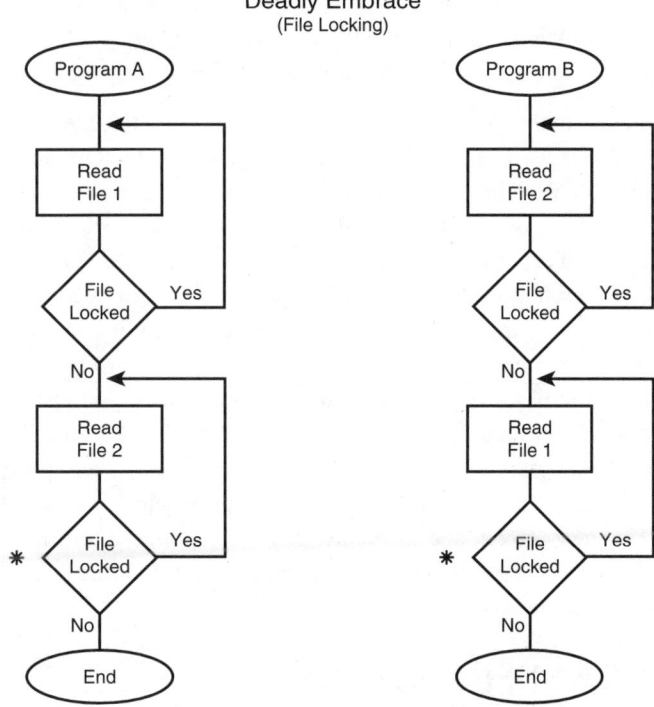

Deadly Embrace
(File Locking)

In both cases, the marked (✱) condition will always be true, and neither application can end.

Another way to avoid the problem is to only have one file open at any time, and then have it open only for the duration of the operation required. I use this technique when the file system being used has good performance. With some file systems, a tremendous overhead is associated with opens and closes, and this approach yields slow applications. I do keep files open when several sequential reads are required, and I do not close them between read operations. Whenever the screen is waiting for user input, make sure that all files are closed. Another advantage of this method is that in the event of a power failure or workstation lockup, a reboot is not as likely to corrupt your data files.

A third method is to use record-locking when it is available. You must use caution to only open files for I/O or update when you are actually going to update a record. Remember that when a file is open for I/O in an automatic record-locking environment, it will be locked until you close the file, rewrite the record, unlock the record, or obtain another lock. You can use manual locking if you are careful to remember to actually lock the records you will be updating, but you must remember to keep the method used consistent across all applications in a system. Don't try to mix manual and automatic record-locking. When using locks on multiple records, you will be susceptible to the deadly embrace problem. Make sure that the locks really are necessary and that they are applied in a consistent manner across applications. Release the locks as soon as possible.

One situation in which you might want to apply locks on multiple records is when a sequence number is assigned to any newly added records. In some instances, when a record is added, you might want to have the computer assign a part number or serial number. In this case, you could keep the last serial number assigned in a header record for the same file. In order to make sure that no other programs running against this file assign the same serial number, you will want to read the base record with LOCK. Using the serial number from this base record, you will increment it and then write your new record. Your new record will remain locked (if you specified WRITE LOCK) so no other user can access it until all your changes are complete. Next, you update your last number assigned in the header record and then rewrite the record. If lock mode automatic was specified, the header record will be automatically unlocked. Then make any changes to your newly added record. This would allow the user to select ADD, see the new serial number on his entry screen, and then enter any corresponding information. No other users would reuse the serial number, and they could not update the new record while it is in the process of being changed.

IBM's VSAM File System

No discussion of indexed files would be complete without a discussion of IBM's *Virtual Storage Access Method* (VSAM). The VSAM system actually encompasses three types of file structures: ESDS, KSDS, and RSDS. An *entry sequence dataset* (ESDS) is basically a sequential or *flat* file, a *keyed sequence dataset* (KSDS) is an indexed file, and a *relative sequence dataset* (RSDS) is a relative file. VSAM is widely used on virtually all IBM mainframe systems. In IBM's latest mainframe operating system offering, OS/390, the system-definition tables are all held in VSAM datasets. VSAM files are the underpinning of IBM's DB2 relational database on the mainframe.

VSAM files and indexes require definition external to the COBOL program in order to be used. The utility used to perform this is IDCAMS. You should become as familiar with this utility as possible if you are working with VSAM datasets.

An understanding of the internal VSAM structure will help you see why it is such a powerful and reliable file structure. This explanation is meant as an introduction to VSAM and does not contain extensive detail information. The information presented here is simplified to a great degree. VSAM datasets are stored in areas called *catalogs*. VSAM catalogs can span disk packs and contain multiple files. Within the catalogs, VSAM indexed files are made up of *clusters*. A VSAM cluster is made up of a data area and an index area. VSAM gets its performance from buffering the index and data areas in virtual storage. The data in the buffers is directly addressable, thus increasing performance.

The data area of a VSAM cluster is made up of areas called *control intervals* (CIs). Records are stored in control intervals in ascending key sequence, based on the primary key definition for the file. This feature is one of the things that makes VSAM such a good performer. When records are read, it makes it easy to buffer the records that are adjacent to each other. CIs contain the actual data records and some control information that describes the records contained in the CI. The last 4 bytes of a CI make of the *control interval definition field* (CIDF). This field contains information about the CI's size and amount of freespace. *Record definition fields* (RDFs) are 3 bytes long and are added to the CI from the *end* as records are added to the *front*. RDFs describe the length of the records and how many adjacent records of that length exist in the CI. If you are using fixed-length records, there will be one RDF per CI. Figure 7.2 shows the structure of a CI.

FIGURE 7.2.
Basic structure of a control interval.

VSAM CI Structure

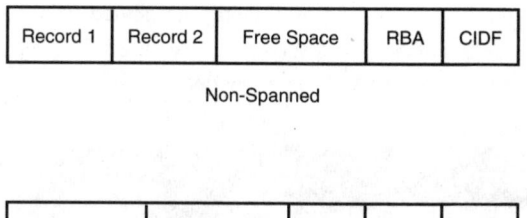

Non-Spanned

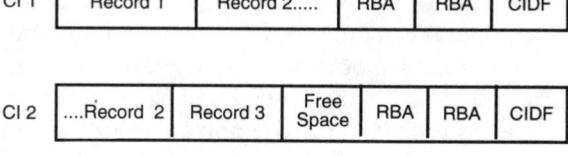

Spanned

RBAs describe differing-length records. When records are of the same length and contiguous, only a single RBA entry is necessary.

CIs are stored in areas called *control areas* (CAs). CA and CI sizes are determined when you define the VSAM file using Access Method Services. These generally are available online or from an IBM utility called IDCAMS.

Defining VSAM Files

When you define a VSAM file, you define, among other things, the CI size, the CA size, the record length, minimum and maximum, and the primary key location and size. If your file will have alternate keys, these are defined to VSAM as alternate index files. One of the reasons you usually find the key information in an index file at the front of a record description is because of VSAM. VSAM requires that the primary key be contained solely within one CI. Normally, records are not spread across CIs. A given record normally exists wholly within a control interval, whereas CIs can contain multiple records. When you define your file, you can specify that CIs are to be *spanned*, which means that records can be spread across multiple CIs. This can save space but is inefficient during reads, especially in a multiuser environment. Take care when you define your VSAM file to make the CI size large enough to hold the records.

Unlike many indexed file systems, VSAM recovers space immediately when records are deleted. When a record is deleted from a CI, the existing records in the CI are shifted down, and the excess is reassigned to freespace within the CI.

VSAM has some size limitations. The maximum size of a VSAM dataset is 4GB. Additionally, the maximum number of extents that can be allocated by a VSAM dataset is 119 to 123 per volume, depending on the storage device. When you define the primary and secondary space allocations, you need to make sure that they are not so small that the maximum number of extents will be exceeded.

> **NOTE**
>
> *Extents* are secondary file allocations. When a file is defined using VSAM, its primary and secondary allocations are specified. Depending on the type of hardware, the allocation can be in *blocks* (for FBA devices) or in *tracks* and *cylinders* for other disk types. VSAM is limited in the number of secondary allocations that can be obtained on each volume. The primary space allocation is used for the first allocation on each disk volume.

CI and CA sizes also are limited. CI size limits vary, based on whether the VSAM file is cataloged using the *Interactive Catalog Facility* (ICF). Most modern VSAM installations make use of the ICF, and it is the only method that is considered Year 2000-compliant for VSAM datasets. If not using ICF, the CI size may vary from 512 to 8192 bytes, in increments of 512 bytes. If you are not using the ICF, and your record size is larger than 8192, you must use the SPANNED parameter when defining your VSAM file, allowing VSAM to spread your record across CIs. If ICF is used, the CI size can be from 8KB to 32KB, in increments of 2KB.

When defining your VSAM file, you define the size of the areas for the data portion and the index portion. The valid CI sizes for the index portion are 512, 1024, 2048, and 4096 bytes.

CA sizes are not explicitly defined. VSAM determines the CA size based on the allocation's specifications you specify for your primary and secondary space allocations. First, VSAM considers the primary and secondary allocation sizes. If either one is less than one cylinder, the smaller of the two is used. If the RECORDS parameter is specified, the size is rounded up to complete tracks. If both the primary and secondary space allocations are larger than one cylinder, the CA size becomes one cylinder, which is the largest it can become.

VSAM data access is extremely fast, but you can suffer some performance problems if your datasets are not defined properly for the file structure and usage that you plan. When a VSAM record is read, the entire CI is read, and if it is read for update, it is locked. All other applications requesting VSAM service for any records in that CI will wait until the CI is released. Another important performance issue is *splits*. CIs and CAs can be split. When records are added to a VSAM dataset, they are inserted in key order. This means that if a record needs to be inserted before an existing record within a CI, the existing record is moved down within the CI, and the new record is inserted. If there is not enough room in the CI for the new record, instead of finding the next CI and moving all the records in it down, VSAM creates a new CI in the same control area. If there is not enough room in the CA for the new CI, the CA experiences a split. A new CA is created. CI and CA splits can move like data physically apart, making access inefficient. When suffering from excessive CI and CA splits, it is advantageous to reorganize the VSAM file. Additionally, when a CI split occurs, the entire control area is inaccessible to the other applications using the file until the split is complete.

When defining your initial file, you can specify the percentage of space in a CI that is to remain free. You also can preallocate empty CIs within the CAs. When records are inserted, the CIs will split to retain this percentage of freespace. You can alter this freespace percentage after the initial load of a VSAM file.

The way freespace is managed is very important to how your VSAM file will perform. Too much freespace can lead to excessive physical I/O as VSAM attempts to buffer records and indexes, and too little can lead to CI and CA splits. To create a new VSAM dataset, the most efficient way to load the file is to sort the data in primary key sequence and then use the Access Method Services REPRO command. This method loads the file from start to end, leaving freespace in the CIs per your VSAM definition. How much freespace to leave in the initial definition will depend on how you expect future records to be added.

7

USING INDEXED FILES

If your file will not have any records added, you can make the best use of space by leaving no freespace. If you will have only a few additions, a freespace setting of (0 5) is adequate. The first number is the minimum amount of freespace VSAM will keep in the CI after the initial load as records are added, and the second number is the percentage that will be kept free on initial load.

If your file will have a lot of insertions, you need an initial freespace setting that is a higher percentage. After the file is loaded, reduce the freespace setting to zero. That way, when many records are inserted and new CIs are created by splits, they will be filled completely before another split occurs.

If you know the key ranges where adds are likely to occur, you can load your file accordingly. First, load the file with records in the key area where you will have few adds, with a freespace setting of zero. Then alter the freespace to something like 20 percent. Then load the records in the area in which you expect to have massive additions. This will result in a file with CIs that are full in the area where insertions are not likely, and CIs with 20 percent freespace in the area where records are likely to be inserted. After the records are inserted, use the ALTER command to reduce the freespace setting.

In addition to intelligently loading your files, you can use the BUFIN statement in your JCL to control the VSAM buffer sizes. Increasing the buffer sizes can improve performance on large numbers of record adds, but not nearly as much as properly defining your percentage of freespace.

VSAM Alternate Indexes

When you need to access data via an alternate key in your COBOL program using VSAM, you must define a VSAM alternate index. You can use Access Method Services to accomplish this task. VSAM alternate indexes have some limitations you should be aware of, though.

Alternate indexes may contain nonunique data. They are made up of an index and data portion, just like any other VSAM indexed file cluster. The data portion contains information that points to the record location in the file for which the alternate index was built. There is a limit of 32,767 duplicate key entries. You can use any field on the base record for the alternate index, but the fields must be in the first segment of any spanned records.

After your alternate index is built, it must be associated with the primary file before it can be used. This is done using the DEFINE PATH statement. You will assign a name to your path and refer to the base cluster/alternate index pair using this path. This is an interesting and power feature of VSAM. This means that if you want to assign an alternate index to a VSAM file after many programs are written, you can do so. The existing programs access the base cluster using the JCL they always have, and without change to their select statements. Your new program uses JCL that references your new path, and your program uses the alternate key statement in the `select` statement. Only the programs requiring access via the alternate key need these statements.

Accessing VSAM Files

VSAM datasets can be used in batch processing, under CICS, or both. Care must be taken to properly analyze the purpose for each VSAM file defined. VSAM files can be accessed concurrently by both batch and CICS programs, but you must consider some performance and data-integrity issues. From batch, the files are accessed very simply. CICS offers many advantages in how the data can be accessed; however, the normal COBOL syntax for indexed file access is not used.

Batch Program Access

VSAM files are accessed very simply. The COBOL program uses the normal syntax for accessing indexed files. If an alternate index is used, the JCL must reference the defined path to the alternate index/base cluster pair, and the alternate record key statement is required in your `select`.

CICS Access

CICS, one of IBM's major online environments, allows access to VSAM files in a different way. In CICS programming, the programmer does not code a `select` or `FD` statement. CICS has a *file control table* (FCT) that defines the dataset names for the CICS programmer to access. CICS command-level entries are made in the COBOL program to access the data. Separate FCT entries are made to allow access of data via a VSAM alternate index. These FCT entries will point to the alternate index/base cluster combination.

Within CICS you will code CICS commands with various key words in order to access your indexed files. These commands will execute and return the specific information requested or an error that you will have to decode. Command-level CICS programming itself is beyond the scope of this chapter, but I will discuss the various CICS commands to access indexed files within your COBOL program.

The relevant CICS commands for accessing VSAM files are `STARTBR`, `ENDBR`, `RESETBR`, `READ`, `READNEXT`, `READPREV`, `DELETE`, and `WRITE`. CICS provides some very powerful methods for accessing data in a VSAM dataset.

Browsing through records under CICS is the same as issuing a `START` statement. The `STARTBR` statement is the method used for CICS. When using the `STARTBR` command, you need to remember that the browse is in effect only while the transaction is active. When using the `STARTBR`, you must specify the key field and its length. The minimum syntax for the `STARTBR` command follows:

7

USING INDEXED FILES

```
STARTBR  FILE(filename)  RIDFLD(data-area)
  KEYLENGTH(data-value)  REQID(data-value)
  GENERIC
  EQUAL¦GTEQ
```

RIDFLD is the key area for the file. KEYLENGTH is the length of the key field. It must match the actual key size of the file, unless the optional keyword GENERIC is specified. (GENERIC is discussed in detail later.) GTEQ or EQUAL specifies whether the key field where the browse will start must be equal to or greater than or equal to the specified RIDFLD key value. REQID allows you to identify a specific browse command so that you can issue multiple concurrent browses within a single transaction.

After issuing the STARTBR, you can issue subsequent READNEXT or READPREV statements. Unlike regular COBOL access, when you want to start reading in another position, you cannot issue another STARTBR. Before any other STARTBR commands can be issued, you must end the previous browse by using the ENDBR command. However, you can reposition your browsing location in the file by using the RESETBR command. This allows you to start browsing the file in a different location without having to issue an ENDBR and then another STARTBR.

The minimum syntax for READNEXT follows:

```
READNEXT  FILE(filename) INTO(data-area)
          RIDFLD(data-area)
          LENGTH(data-area)
          KEYLENGTH(data-value)
          REQID(data-value)
```

The INTO keyword specifies the data area—for example, an 01 level in working storage—into which the data is to be read. REQID is used to specify which browse is to be used when there are multiple browses in use. If only one browse is used at a time, the REQID does not need to be coded.

The syntax for READPREV is the same as READNEXT.

The syntax for ENDBR follows:

```
ENDBR  FILE(filename)
       REQID(data-value)
```

The syntax for RESETBR is the same as that for STARTBR.

When updating records within a VSAM file from CICS, you must first issue a READ with the UPDATE keyword. This locks the record and does not allow any other transactions to access it until you unlock it or complete the operation by a rewrite or delete. CICS will not allow you to rewrite records that have not been read with the UPDATE keyword. The minimum syntax for the READ command follows:

```
READ   FILE(filename)
       UPDATE
       INTO(data-area)  RIDFLD(data-area)
       LENGTH(data-area)
       KEYLENGTH(data-value) GENERIC
       EQUAL¦GTEQ
```

When deleting records from within CICS, you must specify the key field and key length. It is a good practice to issue a read with update first. However, CICS will allow you to delete records without first reading them with UPDATE. The record is locked only during the actual delete. When using the UPDATE keyword, if you determine not to complete the operation, be sure to release your lock by using the UNLOCK command.

The minimum syntax for the DELETE command follows:

```
DELETE   FILE(filename)
   RIDDFLD(data-area)
   KEYLENGTH(data-value)
   GENERIC
```

The KEYLENGTH need not be specified unless the GENERIC key word is used.

Adding records to the VSAM dataset is accomplished with the WRITE statement. VSAM writes under CICS can be slow and cause poor performance. Great numbers of adds generally are avoided. CICS does provide a method for adding numerous records to the VSAM dataset that is more efficient; this is WRITE MASSINSERT.

The minimum WRITE syntax follows:

```
WRITE   FILE(filename)   FROM(data-area)
   MASSINSERT
   RIDFLD(data-area)
   LENGTH(data-value)
   KEYLENGTH(data-value)
```

MASSINSERT is optional.

When WRITE MASSINSERT is coded, the record writes are queued so as to be added all at once. Performance gains using this method can be substantial, but *only* if the writes are performed in ascending key order. The MASSINSERT is complete, and the records are written when a WRITE MASSINSERT statement is followed by an UNLOCK command. It is *very* important to code the UNLOCK after the last MASSINSERT before any other update operation (read with update, delete) is performed on the file. If you do not, the results are unpredictable and may lead to a deadlock situation.

Generic Keys

Under CICS, you may access the data file using something called *generic keys*. Generic keys are one of the more interesting and powerful aspects of CICS programming using indexed files. By specifying a generic key, you can access information in the dataset without specifying the entire key. The GENERIC keyword can be applied to the STARTBR, READ, and DELETE commands. To specify a generic key, you use the regular RIDFLD keyword with the name of the key field, but in KEYLENGTH, you specify a smaller size, the size of the generic key information, and you add the GENERIC keyword. Suppose that your key is Last-name, and you want to browse through all of the last names that start with Mc, you would issue the CICS STARTBR command using the RIDFLD of the key field, the GTEQ keyword, Mc, a key length of 2, and the key word GENERIC. The subsequent READNEXT statements would return the records starting with Mc. Note that when using a generic key, you can browse only in a forward direction.

You also can use generic keys to delete a set of records that match the generic key with only a single DELETE command being coded. Use this with caution, because you may be deleting more records from the file than you really want. However, this is a fast and powerful way to delete records.

Another powerful aspect of the CICS command-level set for accessing indexed files is the use of the GTEQ keyword. When performing reads in the file, you do not need to specify the exact key that you require. You may use GTEQ to find the next record in the file whose key is greater or equal to the one you specify. This eliminates the need to perform a STARTBR in order to locate a record.

> **NOTE**
>
> The CICS interface for transaction processing is described more fully in Chapter 23, "CICS Transaction Interface (IBM)."

VSAM Performance Under CICS

You should remember several factors that may impact your application's performance under CICS. One of these is the fact that when a record lock is applied, the entire CI is locked. If you have stored too many records in a single CI, this can cause other applications to have to wait to access other records in the CI while you complete your update operation. If you are adding a record to a VSAM dataset, and a CI split is required that does not cause a CA split, the entire CA is locked. If a CA split is required, the entire dataset may be locked.

When updating a file via an alternate key path, the record lock is applied at the physical level in VSAM, and *no* other update operations will be allowed against the file until your update operation is complete.

Remember that VSAM stands for *Virtual Storage Access Method.* VSAM stores the buffers for the index and data portions of a cluster in virtual storage. Each request against a VSAM file under CICS requires at least one *string.* Each string contains a set of VSAM buffers. Any operation that holds the position in the file causes the string to be held, and no other application can access the file until the string is released. The following CICS commands hold the position within the file:

READ with UPDATE, WRITE MASSINSERT, and STARTBR. STARTBR releases the string when ENDBR is issued. WRITE MASSINSERT releases the string when an UNLOCK is issued, and READ releases the string when REWRITE, DELETE, or UNLOCK is specified.

You can specify the number of strings for each VSAM file in the FCT entries. Because each string acquires its own set of buffers, more memory is required when you specify many strings. The number of strings assigned needs to be balanced against performance and storage requirements.

Share Options

The other item that affects performance and data integrity is the *share options* specified for the VSAM file. Share options determine exactly how record- and file-locking occur when multiple applications access a VSAM dataset with a DISP=SHR. Share options can affect data integrity, especially when data is shared across systems between batch and CICS regions. Many shops do not allow concurrent updating of the VSAM datasets from both batch and CICS. When these datasets are updated from batch, they generally are closed to CICS. You can determine how you want your datasets to be shared by specifying the share options during definition or by altering them after a cluster is defined. In order to have good data integrity, you should specify that VSAM use the *Record Level Sharing* (RLS) access option, specified in the *Access Method Control Block* (ACB) or as a JCL parameter.

Share options consist of numeric values ranging from 1 to 4. They are specified in pairs—for example, (2 4). The first number is the Cross Region share option, and the second is the Cross System share option. A share option of 1 allows any number of applications to have read access to the dataset or will allow one application to have update access. This ensures complete data integrity and is very similar to lock mode exclusive, discussed earlier. Share option 2 allows any number of programs to have read access, and only one to have update access, but this can happen concurrently. Write integrity is guaranteed, but read integrity is not.

ENQ/DEQ should be used to guarantee that the currently read record is the one that was just updated. If ENQ/DEQ is not used, you could obtain a record that has been updated, but it will not reflect the update. Your particular shop should have standards for using

ENQ and DEQ, because these have to be applied consistently across the entire system. Share option 3 allows full sharing of all access by any number of applications. This is perhaps the most dangerous of the share options. ENQ/DEQ must be used to guarantee data integrity. If it is not, the VSAM program checks could occur and datasets could become corrupted. Share option 4, like share option 3, allows unlimited sharing, but the buffers are updated after each request. Share option 4 has better integrity than share option 3, but the user still is responsible for data integrity. When using share option 4, CA splits are disallowed unless the system is using IBM's CBUF facility. Share options are overridden by the system during a file load, and no other applications may have access to the dataset.

Share option 2 is the most commonly used. Generally, CICS is allowed to update the dataset, and batch is allowed to read it. When batch must update, the file is closed to CICS.

VSAM Reorganization

VSAM files generally are reorganized on a regular basis to ensure good performance. Using the LISTCAT command of Access Method Services, you can get a view of the status of the VSAM datasets. When you see excessive CI and CA splits, it is time to reorganize the files and perhaps consider using different CI sizes and freespace requirements. Remember that when a VSAM file is backed up and restored, its attributes do not change. The REPRO command of Access Method Services should be used to store a file that needs its CI size, freespace, or other attributes changed. Use REPRO to save the cluster, delete it, and redefine it, and then use REPRO again to load it. Any files that you back up, restore, or reorganize should be closed to CICS before processing.

CHAPTER 8

Special-Purpose Files—Relative and Extend Structures

by Judson McClendon

IN THIS CHAPTER

Most operating systems and programming languages provide two basic file types: sequential and random. Sequential files are discussed in Chapter 6, "Data Structures and Sequential I/O." In this chapter, you will examine relative files—a type of random file.

Relative Files

Not all data is stored and accessed in a sequential manner. Often data stored on disk must be accessed randomly. In other words, data is accessed in some sequence that is not dependent on the order in which the data was stored on disk. Also, records must sometimes be deleted from a file. For these situations, COBOL provides a structure called a *relative file*. In this section, you will look at the structure and use of relative files.

Relative File Concepts and Structure

Relative files differ from sequential files in two basic ways. First, relative files can be accessed by a relative key in addition to sequentially. The RELATIVE KEY is essentially a record number, beginning with 1 for the first record, 2 for the second record, and so on. Sequential access for a relative file means accessing the file in order of ascending RELATIVE KEY. The second basic difference between relative and sequential files is that in a relative file, records can be deleted. If a record is deleted, it is passed over on sequential reads, and an INVALID KEY condition is returned if a random read is done with a RELATIVE KEY value that points to a deleted record.

As with sequential files, relative files may be blocked. *Blocking* means that records are actually read and written in groups called a *block*. This is done to speed I/O, because it is quicker to physically read one block of 10 records than to do 10 individual physical reads. Blocking is also done to better use space on tape and disk. There is a gap between physical blocks on tape to allow the tape head space to start and stop, so using blocks reduces the number of inter-record gaps. On random-access devices such as a disk, the device always reads and writes in some multiple of a segment. By blocking records, the records can be made to fit more efficiently into the segment structure of the disk. However, blocking is done completely transparently to the programmer. In COBOL, you do not have to be concerned about handling the blocks. All you do is to specify what the blocking is, and the operating system handles the rest. In some implementations, some physical parameters—such as physical medium, filename, and blocking—are specified externally to the program.

Using Relative Files

Like other COBOL file types, a relative file is defined by a SELECT clause in the FILE-CONTROL paragraph of the INPUT-OUTPUT SECTION of the ENVIRONMENT DIVISION and an

FD file description entry in the FILE SECTION of the DATA DIVISION. The SELECT clause has the following format. Clauses with multiple formats are listed once for each format.

```
SELECT [OPTIONAL] file-name-1 ASSIGN TO file-type
    [RESERVE integer-1 AREA(S)]
    [ORGANIZATION IS ] RELATIVE

    [ACCESS MODE IS SEQUENTIAL [RELATIVE KEY IS data-name-1] ]
    [ACCESS MODE IS RANDOM RELATIVE KEY IS data-name-1]
    [ACCESS MODE IS DYNAMIC RELATIVE KEY IS data-name-1]

    [FILE STATUS IS data-name-2]
```

The words TO, IS, and KEY are for documentation only.

The use of the SELECT clause can be highly implementation dependent. In some systems, the SELECT clause almost entirely determines the interface to the physical file. In other systems, the SELECT clause is almost for documentation only. Refer to your specific systems documentation for details.

Here, file-name-1 is the logical filename used in the program to refer to the file; it must be identical to the filename in the associated FD in the FILE SECTION. file-name-1 must be unique in the FILE SECTION.

If the OPTIONAL phrase is used, and the file is opened in a mode expecting a physical file to be present, and the physical file is not present, the effect is as if the physical file were present but containing no records.

file-type is an implementor-defined name (for example, DISK) or a nonnumeric literal. The details of both these possibilities are implementor defined. Whatever the syntax, a relative file will be stored on a random-access medium, such as a disk.

The RESERVE clause specifies the number of input/output areas (buffers) to be allocated to this file. If the RESERVE clause is omitted, the number of I/O areas assigned is implementor defined. The exact effect of this clause is implementor defined and, in some implementations, is for documentation only.

The ORGANIZATION IS RELATIVE clause is used to specify that this is a relative file.

The ACCESS MODE clause is optional. If this clause is omitted, the default mode is SEQUENTIAL. A relative file with ACCESS MODE SEQUENTIAL operates logically very much like an ORGANIZATION IS SEQUENTIAL file, except that you can delete records (see DELETE below) and position to a given location within the file (see START below). If ACCESS MODE IS RANDOM, the target record for every I-O statement is specified by the value of data-name-1. ACCESS MODE IS DYNAMIC is the most flexible. By using specific syntax in the I-O statements, you can process the file sequentially or randomly at any time. The downside is that you must specify which type of access you want for each read operation. See the individual I-O statements that follow for more details. data-name-1 must be an integer numeric item, and its PICTURE cannot contain the P symbol. Obviously, it must be large enough to contain the highest record number you will need. It also must not be contained in any of the 01 records under the FD for this file. Some implementations may impose more restrictions on the format of data-name-1.

The FILE STATUS clause is used to specify a two-character alphanumeric data-name-1. Each time an I/O operation is done on file-name-1, the result status code from that operation is stored in data-name-1. Here is a brief list of possible status codes:

Code	Meaning
00	Successful; no other details.
0x	Successful; x defines details.
1x	An AT END condition was encountered; x defines details.
3x	A permanent error was encountered; x defines details.
4x	A logic error was encountered; x defines details.
9x	Implementor-defined error; x defines details.

Here, x indicates a character that will further define what the exception or error was. Some of the values for x are standard and some are implementor defined.

Status codes are used to handle I/O errors programmatically, rather than let the default error handling deal with them. One use of status codes could be to extract all the valid records from a physical file that has one or more bad spots that can't be read because of I/O errors. Without the FILE STATUS clause, an error of that kind would usually abort the program. Using FILE STATUS, the errors can be detected programmatically, and the bad records can be skipped.

CAUTION

Be aware that if FILE STATUS is specified for a file, much of the built-in error handling normally done by the operating system is bypassed. If you don't programmatically detect and handle any I/O errors that occur, an error could happen and not be detected.

The operation of the AT END and INVALID KEY clauses of I-O statements on a file with a status code specified can vary between implementations. If you intend to use both clauses on the same file, check your compiler documentation.

FD File Description

The second part of defining a file in COBOL is the FD file-description entry in the FILE SECTION of the DATA DIVISION. One or more 01 level entries must follow the FD entry—one for each record format. All of the 01 entries under one FD, except the first one, have an implicit REDEFINES of the first 01. In other words, even if the FD is followed by several 01 entries, each of the 01 entries occupies the same record area.

The format for the FD entry for relative files follows. Each clause that has multiple formats is repeated for each format.

```
FD file-name-1

    [BLOCK CONTAINS [integer-1 TO] integer-2 RECORDS]
    [BLOCK CONTAINS [integer-1 TO] integer-2 CHARACTERS]

    [RECORD CONTAINS integer-3 CHARACTERS]
    [RECORD IS VARYING IN SIZE
        [[FROM integer-4] [TO integer-5] CHARACTERS]
        [DEPENDING ON data-name-1]]
    [RECORD CONTAINS integer-6 TO integer-7 CHARACTERS]

    [LABEL RECORD IS STANDARD]
    [LABEL RECORD IS OMITTED]
    [LABEL RECORDS ARE STANDARD]
    [LABEL RECORDS ARE OMITTED]

    [VALUE OF implementor-name-1 IS data-name-2]
    [VALUE OF implementor-name-1 IS literal-1]

    [DATA RECORD IS {data-name-3} ...]
    [DATA RECORDS ARE {data-name-3} ...].

01  record definitions ...
```

The only required parts of the FD entry are the letters FD, file-name-1, and at least one 01 record definition. file-name-1 must have been declared in a SELECT statement in the FILE-CONTROL paragraph.

For blocked files, the BLOCK CONTAINS clause is used to specify how many records or characters are in a block. If the integer-1 TO clause is specified, the blocks are to be of variable size—with a minimum of integer-1 and a maximum of integer-2—records or characters. Use of blocks and variable blocking is implementation dependent, and for some implementations, the block size is specified using external means.

By default, the file has a fixed record size, which is determined by the largest 01 entry following the FD. The RECORD CONTAINS clause can be used to specify a fixed record size or to specify the limits of a variable record size. integer-4 or integer-6 specifies the lower limit and `integer-5` or `integer-7` specifies the upper limit. The `DEPENDING ON` phrase can be used to specify a numeric field that will specify the actual record size when the record is output. Record size on input is determined by the physical size of the record. The value of `data-name-1` must be set prior to an output statement. The value of `data-name-1` is *not* changed by an input statement. For some file types on some implementations, the `RECORD CONTAINS` (or `RECORD IS`) clause is ignored. In some implementations, the specified record size is compared against the size of the largest `01` level associated with the `FD`, and an error is given by the compiler if the values are different.

The `LABEL RECORDS` clause specifies whether the (magnetic tape) file uses labels. This clause is obsolete and will be deleted from the next standard.

The `VALUE OF` clause specifies details of the `LABEL` records mentioned in the `LABEL` clause. Some implementations use this clause to specify the physical, external name of the file and other details of how the file is physically structured. This clause is obsolete and will be deleted from the next standard.

The `DATA RECORDS` clause is for documentation only because the `01` level records following the `FD` are the data records and do not need to be specified. This clause is obsolete and will be deleted from the next standard.

OPEN Statement

Before any I/O can be done on a file, the file must be opened. The `OPEN` statement essentially establishes a link between the `FD` in the program and the external medium that contains, or will contain, the file. After the `FD` is opened, I/O operations may be done on it. After a `CLOSE` statement is executed on the `FD`, the file is said to be *closed,* and no more I/O operations may be performed on the file unless it is opened again. Sometimes files are opened and closed more than once in a program, depending on processing requirements. But the general idea is that you open a file, execute whatever `I-O` statements are required, and then close the file. In this section, you will look at the `OPEN`, `CLOSE`, `READ`, `WRITE`, `REWRITE`, `DELETE`, and `START` statements.

```
OPEN {INPUT file-name-1} ...
OPEN {OUTPUT file-name-1} ...
OPEN {I-O file-name-1} ...
OPEN {EXTEND file-name-1} ...
```

The word following `OPEN` specifies the open mode, indicating what kind of I/O is permissible on the file. Table 8.1 lists the `OPEN` modes, the `ACCESS` modes, and their permissible `I-O` statements in that mode.

TABLE 8.1 PERMISSIBLE I-O STATEMENTS BY ACCESS AND OPEN MODES.

OPEN *Mode*	*Statements*
ACCESS *Mode Sequential*	
OPEN INPUT	READ, START
OPEN OUTPUT	WRITE
OPEN I-O	READ, REWRITE, START, DELETE
OPEN EXTEND	WRITE
ACCESS *Mode Random*	
OPEN INPUT	READ
OPEN OUTPUT	WRITE
OPEN I-O	READ, WRITE, REWRITE, DELETE
OPEN EXTEND	Invalid access/open combination
ACCESS *Mode Dynamic*	
OPEN INPUT	READ, START
OPEN OUTPUT	WRITE
OPEN I-O	READ, WRITE, REWRITE, START, DELETE
OPEN EXTEND	Invalid access/open combination

The INPUT, I-O, and EXTEND modes require the file to already exist, unless the SELECT statement for that file contains the OPTIONAL clause. If it does, the result is as if the file already exists but contains no records. OUTPUT mode will create a new file. Note that if a file of the same name already exists, OPEN OUTPUT will replace the old file with the new file, and the contents of the old file will be lost. The EXTEND phrase must be used only with files having ACCESS MODE IS SEQUENTIAL phrases in their SELECT.

When a relative file is opened in I-O mode, records may be read just as in INPUT mode, but the REWRITE statement may be used to modify a record after it has been read, and the DELETE statement may be used to delete a record after it is read.

Only in OPEN EXTEND mode can OPEN EXTEND be used to append records to the end of an existing relative file. When the OPEN is complete, the file state is as if it were in OUTPUT mode, positioned immediately after the last record preexisting in the file. All subsequent WRITE statements append records to the end of the file.

CLOSE Statement

The CLOSE statement releases the link between the FD and the external file media that was established by the OPEN statement, and it releases the file.

```
CLOSE {file-name-1 [WITH LOCK]} …
```

The word WITH is for documentation only. If the LOCK phrase is used, the file cannot be reopened by the program.

READ Statement

The READ statement is used with relative files to input a RECORD from a file opened in INPUT mode or I-O mode. There are two formats for the READ statement:

Format 1:

```
READ file-name-1 [NEXT] RECORD [INTO identifier-1]
    [AT END imperative-statement-1]
    [NOT AT END imperative-statement-2]
    [END-READ]
```

Format 2:

```
READ file-name-1 RECORD [INTO identifier-1]
    [INVALID KEY imperative-statement-3]
    [NOT INVALID KEY imperative-statement-4]
    [END-READ]
```

The words RECORD, AT, and KEY are for documentation only.

Format 1 must be used with files in SEQUENTIAL access mode, in which case the word NEXT may be omitted, because it is implied. Format 1 can also be used with files in DYNAMIC access mode to read the next sequential record, in which case the word NEXT is required. When using combinations of SEQUENTIAL, DYNAMIC, and RANDOM access within a program, always using NEXT on sequential reads can make the logic clearer.

Format 2 must be used for files in RANDOM access mode and can be used with files in DYNAMIC access mode to retrieve a record by RELATIVE KEY.

The INTO phrase allows the record to be read and then moved into another work area, all in one statement. But to use INTO, there must be only one 01 entry associated with file-name-1, or all the 01 entries must be group items or alphanumeric items, and identifier-1 must be a group or alphanumeric item.

The AT END phrase causes imperative-statement-1 to be executed if the READ was unsuccessful because there are no more records in file-name-1.

The NOT AT END phrase causes imperative-statement-2 to be executed if the READ was successful.

The INVALID KEY phrase causes imperative-statement-3 to be executed if the READ was unsuccessful because the record specified by the value of the RELATIVE KEY data name does not exist in file-name-1.

The NOT INVALID KEY phrase causes imperative-statement-4 to be executed if the READ was successful.

The END-READ phrase ends the scope of the READ statement.

WRITE Statement

The WRITE statement is used with ACCESS SEQUENTIAL relative files opened in OUTPUT or EXTEND mode, or ACCESS RANDOM or DYNAMIC relative files opened in OUTPUT or I-O mode, to output a record to the file. SEQUENTIAL modes write the next record; random and DYNAMIC modes write the record specified by the RELATIVE KEY.

```
WRITE record-name-1  [FROM identifier-1]
    [INVALID KEY imperative-statement-1]
    [NOT INVALID KEY imperative-statement-2]
END-WRITE
```

The word KEY is for documentation only.

The FROM phrase causes a MOVE of identifier-1 to record-name-1 before the WRITE is executed.

The INVALID KEY phrase causes imperative-statement-1 to be executed if the WRITE was unsuccessful because the record specified by the value of the RELATIVE KEY data item already exists in file-name-1, or an attempt was made to write beyond the physical boundaries of the file, or the number of digits in the relative record number is greater than the size of the RELATIVE KEY data item.

The NOT INVALID KEY phrase causes imperative-statement-2 to be executed if the WRITE was successful.

REWRITE Statement

REWRITE is used with relative files open in I-O mode to modify a record. For ACCESS SEQUENTIAL, the record rewritten is the one input from the immediately preceding READ NEXT statement on the same file. For ACCESS RANDOM or DYNAMIC, the record rewritten is specified by the value of the RELATIVE KEY data item.

```
REWRITE record-name-1  [FROM identifier-1]
    [INVALID KEY imperative-statement-1]
    [NOT INVALID KEY imperative-statement-2]
    [END-REWRITE]
```

In COBOL, you always READ a FILE, WRITE a RECORD. The reason is that when you are reading a record from a file with more than one record type, you do not necessarily know which type record you are going to read. So the READ syntax specifies the filename. But when you are writing a record to a file with more than one record type, you must specify which record is to be written, because it may affect the length of the physical record. So the WRITE and REWRITE syntax specifies the record name.

8

SPECIAL-PURPOSE
FILES

The FROM phrase causes a MOVE of identifier-1 to record-name-1 before the REWRITE is executed.

The INVALID KEY phrase causes imperative-statement-1 to be executed if the REWRITE was unsuccessful because the record specified by the value of the RELATIVE KEY data item does not exist in file-name-1. The INVALID KEY phrase must be specified for files in RANDOM or DYNAMIC access mode and must not be specified for files in SEQUENTIAL access mode.

The NOT INVALID KEY phrase causes imperative-statement-2 to be executed if the WRITE was successful. The NOT INVALID KEY phrase must not be specified for files in SEQUENTIAL access mode.

If your compiler implements the RELATIVE I-O module at level 2, the size of the record being rewritten does not need to match the size of the record being overwritten. But if your compiler implements the RELATIVE I-O module at level 1, when REWRITE is used with a relative file, the size of the record being rewritten must be exactly the same as the record it is overwriting. If the sizes do not match, the REWRITE is not done, the file remains unchanged, and the I/O status of the file is set to a value indicating the error (see the FILE STATUS clause earlier).

START Statement

The START statement is used with relative files to logically position the file to a specific RECORD. The file must be declared with SEQUENTIAL or DYNAMIC access mode and opened in INPUT mode or I-O mode. The START statement *does not* modify the contents of the record area. The result of a successful START statement is that the following READ NEXT statement will input the record located by the START statement.

```
START file-name-1 [KEY relation-expression-1 data-name-1]
    [INVALID KEY imperative-statement-1]
    [NOT INVALID KEY imperative-statement-2]
    [END-START]
```

The word KEY is for documentation only.

relation-condition-1 can be any of the following:

IS EQUAL TO

IS =

IS GREATER THAN

IS >

IS NOT LESS THAN

```
IS NOT <

IS GREATER THAN OR EQUAL TO

IS >=
```

The words IS, TO, and THAN are for documentation only.

data-name-1 must be the data item specified in the RELATIVE KEY phrase of the ACCESS mode of the associated file control SELECT statement.

If the KEY phrase is not specified, relation IS EQUAL TO is implied.

The INVALID KEY phrase causes imperative-statement-1 to be executed if the START was unsuccessful because no record in file-name-1 satisfies the relation condition.

The NOT INVALID KEY phrase causes imperative-statement-2 to be executed if the START was successful.

The END-START phrase ends the scope of the START statement.

DELETE Statement

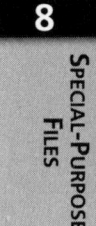

The DELETE statement removes a record from the RELATIVE file. The RELATIVE file must be opened in I-0 mode. The DELETE statement *does not* modify the contents of the record area. For RELATIVE files in SEQUENTIAL mode, the record deleted is the record obtained by the preceding READ statement, which must have been successful. For RELATIVE files in RANDOM or DYNAMIC mode, the record to be deleted is the record number determined by the value of the RELATIVE KEY data item associated with file-name-1.

```
DELETE file-name-1 RECORD
    [INVALID KEY imperative-statement-1]
    [NOT INVALID KEY imperative-statement-2]
    [END-DELETE]
```

The words RECORD and KEY are for documentation only.

The INVALID KEY and NOT INVALID KEY phrases must not be used with a RELATIVE file in SEQUENTIAL access mode.

The INVALID KEY phrase causes imperative-statement-1 to be executed if the DELETE was unsuccessful because the record was not available.

The NOT INVALID KEY phrase causes imperative-statement-2 to be executed if the DELETE was successful.

The END-DELETE phrase ends the scope of the DELETE statement.

Example of Relative I/O

To illustrate the use of relative files, Listing 8.1 shows a program that maintains a file of names, addresses, and phone numbers. Records can be added, modified, or deleted. The program is written in Micro Focus COBOL, so the SELECT statements and FD entries may be slightly different from those used by your COBOL compiler. Only portions of the program are printed here, but the entire program is on the CD-ROM in the back of this book.

LISTING 8.1   RELATIVE.

```
000200 ENVIRONMENT DIVISION.
000300 INPUT-OUTPUT SECTION.
000400 FILE-CONTROL.
000500     SELECT OPTIONAL NAME-FILE
000600                         ASSIGN TO DISK
000700                         ORGANIZATION IS RELATIVE
000800                         ACCESS MODE IS DYNAMIC
000900                         RELATIVE KEY IS
001000                             WS-NAME-KEY.
001100 DATA DIVISION.
001200 FILE SECTION.
001300
001400 FD   NAME-FILE
001500      VALUE OF FILE-ID IS "RELATIVE.DAT".
001600 01   NAME-RECORD.
001700      03   NAME-NAME            PIC   X(30).
001800      03   NAME-ADDR-1          PIC   X(30).
001900      03   NAME-ADDR-2          PIC   X(30).
002000      03   NAME-PHONE           PIC   X(16).

002200 WORKING-STORAGE SECTION.

003100 77   WS-NAME-KEY               PIC   9(06)   VALUE 0.

018100 PROCEDURE DIVISION.
018200
018300 000000-CONTROL.
018400      OPEN I-O NAME-FILE.

018900      CLOSE NAME-FILE.
019000      STOP RUN.

021700 011000-ADD-LOOP.

022400      INITIALIZE NAME-RECORD.
022500      MOVE SH-NAME-KEY TO WS-NAME-KEY.
022600      MOVE SH-NAME     TO NAME-NAME.
022700      MOVE SH-ADDR-1   TO NAME-ADDR-1.
```

```
022800          MOVE SH-ADDR-2    TO NAME-ADDR-2.
022900          MOVE SH-PHONE     TO NAME-PHONE.
023000          WRITE NAME-RECORD
023100              INVALID KEY
023200                  MOVE "DUPLICATE KEY" TO SH-ERROR-MSG
023300                  DISPLAY ERROR-SCREEN
023400                  EXIT PARAGRAPH.

025500 020100-GET-KEY.

026100          INITIALIZE NAME-RECORD.
026200          MOVE SH-NAME-KEY TO WS-NAME-KEY.
026300          START NAME-FILE
026400              KEY NOT < WS-NAME-KEY
026500              INVALID KEY
026600                  MOVE "NO RECORDS FOUND" TO SH-ERROR-MSG
026700                  DISPLAY ERROR-SCREEN
026800                  EXIT PARAGRAPH.
026900          READ NAME-FILE NEXT.

027200 020200-SELECT-LOOP.

028000          EVALUATE SH-ANSWER
028100              WHEN "N"
028200                  IF (NT-NAME(NT-SIZE) NOT = SPACES)
028300                      INITIALIZE NAME-RECORD
028400                      MOVE NT-NAME-KEY(NT-SIZE) TO WS-NAME-KEY
028500                      READ NAME-FILE
028600                      READ NAME-FILE NEXT
028700                          NOT AT END
028800                              PERFORM 020300-FORWARD
028900                      END-READ
029000                  END-IF
029100              WHEN "1" THRU "9"
029200                  IF (NT-NAME(SH-ANSWER-NUM) NOT = SPACES)
029300                      INITIALIZE NAME-RECORD
029400                      MOVE NT-NAME-KEY(SH-ANSWER-NUM) TO WS-NAME-KEY
029500                      READ NAME-FILE
029600                      PERFORM 021000-VIEW
029700                      MOVE 1 TO SH-ESCAPE-FLAG
029800                      EXIT PARAGRAPH
029900                  END-IF
030000              WHEN OTHER
030100                  EXIT PARAGRAPH
030200          END-EVALUATE.

031500 020310-NEXT-ADDR.
031600          MOVE WS-NAME-KEY  TO NT-NAME-KEY-PIC(NT-EX).
031700          MOVE NAME-NAME    TO NT-NAME          (NT-EX).
031800          MOVE NAME-PHONE   TO NT-PHONE         (NT-EX).
```

8

**SPECIAL-PURPOSE
FILES**

continues

LISTING 8.1 CONTINUED

```
031900        MOVE WS-NAME-KEY   TO NT-NAME-KEY     (NT-EX).
032000        ADD 1 TO NT-EX.
032100        READ NAME-FILE NEXT
032200            AT END
032300                MOVE 0 TO WS-NAME-PRESENT-FLAG.

038300 021310-ACCEPT-MOD.

038800        DISPLAY ERASE-ERROR-SCREEN.
038900        MOVE SH-ADDR-1   TO NAME-ADDR-1.
039000        MOVE SH-ADDR-2   TO NAME-ADDR-2.
039100        MOVE SH-PHONE    TO NAME-PHONE.
039200        REWRITE NAME-RECORD.

040200 021410-ACCEPT-DEL.

040800        EVALUATE SH-ANSWER
040900            WHEN "N"
041000                MOVE 1 TO SH-ESCAPE-FLAG
041100                EXIT PARAGRAPH
041200            WHEN "Y"
041300                DELETE NAME-FILE
041400                MOVE 1 TO SH-ESCAPE-FLAG
041500                EXIT PARAGRAPH
041600        END-EVALUATE.
```

The SELECT statement has the OPTIONAL phrase so that you can open the file the first
time through, and ACCESS MODE DYNAMIC so that you can use RANDOM or SEQUENTIAL I/O
as you want. I have created a RELATIVE KEY named WS-NAME-KEY in WORKING-STORAGE.
The FD and 01 that define the file are in the FILE SECTION.

In the PROCEDURE DIVISION, the file is opened in I-O mode so that you can use any of
the I-O statements. Of course, the file is closed at the end of job.

In paragraph 011000-ADD-LOOP, once a good record is obtained, the record area is initialized, RELATIVE KEY WS-NAME-KEY is set, the data is moved into the record, and a WRITE
statement is used to store the record in the file. The INVALID KEY clause traps duplicate
relative keys.

In paragraph 020100-GET-KEY, after the user inputs a beginning RELATIVE KEY value, a
START statement is used to position the file to that location. The INVALID KEY clause
traps a situation in which there are no records equal to or greater than your relative key.
If the START was successful, you then READ NEXT to actually read the record.

In `020200-SELECT-LOOP`, you are processing keyboard requests to display the next screen of names, or a specific name, selected by a digit 1 through 9. An `EVALUATE` statement is used to process the keyboard input. In the `WHEN "N"` (Next screen) clause, the last record in the screen table is read by a random read using the relative key, and then a sequential read is done to obtain the first record for the following screen. If the read was good (`NOT AT END`), the next screen is fetched and displayed.

Paragraph `020310-NEXT-ADDR` reads the next address record using a `READ NEXT` statement and stores it in the screen display table. The `AT END` clause traps the end of file.

Paragraph `021310-ACCEPT-MOD` accepts modifications to a record from the user and updates the record on disk. The record is updated using a `REWRITE` statement.

Paragraph `021410-ACCEPT-DEL` queries the user if a delete is really wanted, and if the answer is `'Y'`, the displayed record is deleted using the `DELETE` statement.

Listing 8.1 illustrates just about all the I/O operations on relative files. Examine the full source code on the CD-ROM.

The Report Writer Module

CHAPTER 9

The story of COBOL Report Writer goes back to 1961. At that time, the greatest single need in any data-processing project was to generate printed outputs. Business already was driven by a torrent of paperwork that still would be required, and the new data-processing technology presented endless opportunities to generate new printouts so that all the secret corners of the computer's files could be brought into the daylight. So the new *COmmercial Business-Oriented Language* (COBOL) urgently needed a way of producing printed output.

By then, COBOL already possessed basic "verbs" such as MOVE, ADD, and WRITE that could, technically at least, produce any printed output. The committee, however, with great foresight, must have considered basic COBOL much too low-level for this task. When the first *American National Standard* (ANS) COBOL appeared, Report Writer was included, and it has remained a part of every standard since then. Apart from a few differences in the ANS 1968 standard, each new standard was compatible with the preceding standard. Curiously, Report Writer was optional in the 1985 Standard.

In the new standard, Report Writer is once again a regular part of the language. At the same time, most of the additional features that had been anticipated for so long were added to the language. Several other desirable features remain available only as vendor extensions. With interest in Report Writer now beginning to revive, these features may find their way into a future standard, too.

Why Was Report Writer So Neglected?

It is a puzzle that until the latest new standard, Report Writer was hardly altered or enhanced. The original facilities were limited in scope, yet the design principles are quite sound and seem to invite enhancement. For example, it was never easy to define a printed table or an optional print field with Report Writer until the new standard introduced an OCCURS clause and conditions. This lack of development undoubtedly is linked to the fact that far less than half the users who might benefit from Report Writer have chosen to use it. There are several reasons why many people chose not to use Report Writer:

- The name *Report Writer* gives some potential users the wrong impression of the purpose of this facility. The word *report* usually suggests an ad-hoc printout produced by a dedicated report-generator program. This chapter will show that Report Writer is, in fact, a general-purpose print facility.

- The facility usually was made to seem much more complicated than it really is, because vendors often reproduce the standard definition in their programming manuals. The standard definition was written for compiler developers and certainly not for programmers—and especially not for the less technical type of programmer who might be writing a print program. You will see how simple the features really are in the next section.

- Report Writer often was omitted from COBOL programmers' courses. (Some experienced programmers still do not know the facility at all.) This deficiency has been remedied by some good online references and tutorials.

- With some notable exceptions, Report Writer has been poorly implemented in comparison to the other parts of COBOL; it has exhibited more bugs, less-rigorous syntax checking, and a go-it-alone attitude to interpreting the standard. These older versions have largely been superseded by better versions.

- Despite Report Writer's inclusion in the standard, some vendors stubbornly omitted it in the past, which presented a dilemma for any developers who needed to have portable code.

If it weren't for these external handicaps, Report Writer could have become the generally accepted method of producing all printed output in COBOL, well-known by every programmer and acquiring new features year by year.

Does COBOL Still Need a Print Facility?

In recent years, the focus has tended to be on applications that run in interactive mode and produce their output on a screen. Despite this, the need for quality printed output has expanded, as the huge sales of desktop printers demonstrate. Management increasingly has access to PCs hooked up to legacy systems to provide data queries and is asking for printed output on a regular basis. *Any* tool a COBOL programmer can use to create solid report programs (especially if it doesn't carry an additional charge) is invaluable. These legacy programs often have to be enhanced to produce new printouts—perhaps to print extra information for the century change. In addition, a "printed output" may not be a paper document, but something browsed on a screen or transmitted electronically. As a modern programming language, COBOL therefore must retain and improve its print facility.

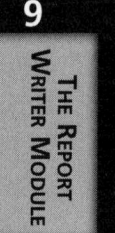

Report Writer Versus Basic COBOL

It should be made compulsory for every person who considers basic COBOL suitable for printed output to sit down one week before a scheduled vacation and code a moderate-sized print. It can be an eye-opening experience. COBOL-course students usually remember being shocked at how low-level COBOL seems to be when they need to code a print. The need to invent working-storage data items to receive the print data, with fillers between them, and then to MOVE each print item before the WRITE statement seems an outrage to the sensibilities and an appalling waste of a programmer's skill. How appealing is the prospect of being able to code something like this?

```
01  MONTHLY-SALES-LINES TYPE DETAIL.
    03  LINE PLUS 2.
        05  COLUMN 20       VALUE "Sales for".
        05  COLUMN PLUS 2  PIC XXX
            SOURCE MONTH-NAME (MONTH-NO).
        05  COLUMN 35       PIC $$$$9   SOURCE MONTHLY-SALES.
    03  LINE PLUS 1.
        05  COLUMN 20       PIC X(20) VALUE ALL "-".
 . . .
    GENERATE MONTHLY-SALES-LINES
```

Consider an average print layout with 300 print fields in 50 print lines. How many coded statements would be needed in basic COBOL (assume an average amount of totals and an average complexity)? Here are the rough totals of the data entries and statements that might be needed:

600	Data entries (including FILLER items)
200	MOVE statements
80	ADD statements
50	WRITE (or PERFORM) statements
100	Various other procedural statements
1030	Total

The procedural statements, furthermore, have to be carefully ordered and debugged like any other program code to ensure the correct result. Print layouts tend to change more than other types of files, but with this level of painstaking coding, making a change can be a nightmare. *Basic COBOL is not a practical medium for producing printed output.*

As a matter of interest, look at how these numbers change if you use Report Writer:

361	Data entries
12	Procedural statements
373	Total

Notice the sizable qualitative as well as quantitative difference. Because so much of the Report Writer coding is in the Data Division, the program is less susceptible to logical errors. It is easy to produce a logically correct program as a first draft, inspect the results, and make adjustments. It also is easy to make changes to the program later. Report Writer dramatically changes the viability of COBOL as a vehicle for applications with a printout.

Report Writer Versus Non-COBOL Report Generators

Many COBOL users accept that the basic language is too low-level for print applications but take refuge in report generators outside the language for this purpose. Most of these report generators offer excellent features and repay the investment in them many times over. However, this is not an argument against a Report Writer facility within COBOL. Those who argue that it is forget that a COBOL program *can do many things other than just print*. Because the Report Writer syntax mixes in any proportion with the rest of COBOL, it can be used in every program that prints something.

Other arguments shift the pendulum of applicability toward Report Writer:

- Most report generators are targeted toward the ad hoc type of print. COBOL Report Writer is designed for the permanent production types of applications that are written by programmers rather than end users; the layouts are more complex and are precisely specified, and report generators, in this case, generally perform less well.

- No matter how excellent the report generator is, programming teams quickly forget how to use it as new people join up. (This is the familiar flavor-of-the-month argument.) Report Writer is accepted as a part of COBOL.

- COBOL Report Writer is not a totally new language but is recognizably part of COBOL, so it has a gentler learning curve.

There seems to be a vital and quite distinct place for both technologies (Report Writer and other report generators) in the typical commercial project, just as we all need both lawyers and accountants.

Using Report Writer

After reading the analysis in the preceding section, who could be blamed for feeling a little skeptical? To substantiate these statements about the advantages of Report Writer, there is nothing better than a simple guide with a completely worked example. Readers with a knowledge of basic COBOL should feel totally at home here. After all, this is just the familiar COBOL coding style, but set at a level higher than people are used to. Newcomers to COBOL probably will be bewildered by the amount of debate that has occurred on this topic.

This guide will introduce you to the basics of Report Writer. After reading this chapter, you may be ready to use Report Writer's features, or you may want to use this guide as preparation for understanding more detailed text on the subject. The code introduced in this section will work with any of the COBOL standards.

The recipe presented here is well-tried. Here is a summary of the steps used in the example:

1. Find the report groups.
2. Decide on the type of each report group.
3. Code the `RD` entry.
4. Code the report group descriptions.
5. Code the `SELECT...ASSIGN` and `FD`.
6. Code the procedure division.

Find the Report Groups

Figure 9.1 shows an example of one imaginary report layout.

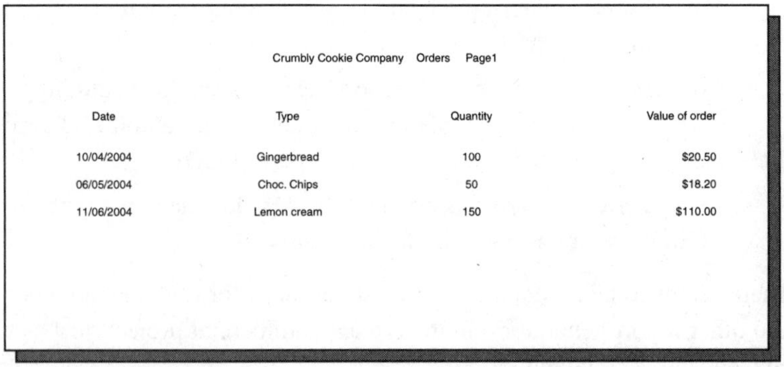

FIGURE 9.1.

A simple report layout.

	Crumbly Cookie Company	Orders	Page1	
Date	Type		Quantity	Value of order
10/04/2004	Gingerbread		100	$20.50
06/05/2004	Choc. Chips		50	$18.20
11/06/2004	Lemon cream		150	$110.00

The first task is to divide up the layout into *report groups*. A report group (or *group,* for short) is a block of lines produced in one operation. The layout can be built up from any number of different groups. The shape and contents of each group can be varied as much as desired, but if the variations become very complex, it is easier to define two different groups.

Use the following guidelines to define a group:

- The group can consist of one to any number of lines and can have any number of fields.
- The group normally fits on one page instead of being split by a page boundary.
- The group can contain fields with contents from anywhere in the Data Division, provided that all the fields are present in memory at the moment the program generates the report group.

If the report structure corresponds to records in a main file or database, unless there is a special reason for reading ahead and buffering several records, a report group should correspond to one record from the main file or database. (However, there is also a *summary reporting* feature that enables the program to output one report group that summarizes a whole set of records.)

Each group must be marked clearly. In this example, a line has been drawn after each group (see Figure 9.2).

FIGURE 9.2.

A layout showing report groups.

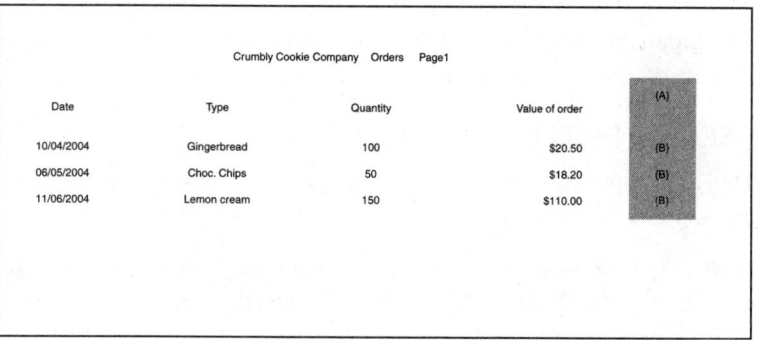

There are three instances of group (B), which all have the same structure, even though the data is different. Only one instance needs to be coded.

Decide on the Type of Each Report Group

Each report group can appear in one of seven basic positions in the report, indicated by the *TYPE* clause. Their names and positions follow.

DETAIL or DE

This is the TYPE assumed by any report group that is not one of the special six described in the following subsections. DETAIL groups usually contain the most important data in the report. They are the only groups that are explicitly generated (using a GENERATE statement). This type and the next two types are known as *body groups*. They are positioned between the PAGE HEADING and PAGE FOOTING, if any, on each page.

CONTROL HEADING or CH

This group is generated automatically at the *start* of each different value of the corresponding control field.

CONTROL FOOTING or CF

This group is generated automatically at the *end* of each different value of the corresponding control field.

PAGE HEADING or PH

This group appears at the *start* of each page.

PAGE FOOTING or PF

This group appears at the *end* of each page.

REPORT HEADING or RH

This group appears once, on a page by itself or above the first PAGE HEADING (if any), at the *very start* of the printout.

REPORT FOOTING or RF

This group appears once, on a page by itself or below the last PAGE FOOTING (if any), at the *very end* of the printout.

Each TYPE is optional. The report can contain any number of different DETAIL groups and any number of different CONTROL HEADING and CONTROL FOOTING groups (up to one of each for each control level), but only one of each of the other four groups. More complex printouts can be built up from several report descriptions written to the same file.

It now is possible to assign the correct TYPE clauses to each group in the layout (see Figure 9.3).

FIGURE 9.3.

A layout showing types of the report group.

Code the RD Entry

The report groups are described in the REPORT SECTION, which is the *last* section in the program's Data Division. The Report Section can contain any number of *report descriptions.* Each of these begins with an RD entry that starts in the A margin:

```
REPORT SECTION.
RD
```

This is followed by a chosen *report name.* This name will be used to stand for the report as a whole, so you should choose an appropriate name.

```
REPORT SECTION.
RD   STOCK-SUMMARY
```

Several clauses may follow the report name. PAGE LIMIT is required if the report is divided into *pages.* It specifies the *maximum number of lines* to be written to each page. FIRST DETAIL indicates on which line the main information of each page should start.

```
REPORT SECTION.
RD   STOCK-SUMMARY
     PAGE LIMIT 64 LINES
     FIRST DETAIL 5.
```

Code the Report Group Descriptions

Describing the report groups is the essence of the Report Writer code, so most of the coding time and effort is spent on this task.

01-Level Entries

Each report group is coded as a series of regular COBOL entries, consisting of a *level number*, an optional *data name*, any number of optional clauses, and a period. Each group must start with an 01 level number in the A margin.

If the group is a DETAIL, this level number is followed by a chosen data name, which is used to identify the group. For other types, this data name is optional. Next comes the word TYPE and the type of the group. Any number of entries can follow the 01-level entry, as you will see shortly.

```
01   TYPE PH.
     . . . etc . . .
01   COOKIE-LINE    TYPE DE.
     . . . etc . . .
```

To make the program even clearer, the TYPE clause can be spelled out in full—for example, TYPE IS PAGE HEADING.

Lines and Columns

After each group's 01-level entry, a series of LINE entries can be coded, each containing a series of COLUMN entries. (A group also can be a *dummy* group without any LINE or COLUMN clauses.)

```
01   TYPE PH.
     03   LINE . . .
          05   COLUMN . . .
```

After the LINE keyword, there are two ways to specify positioning of the line:

- *integer* is a *specific* (absolute) line on the page—for example, LINE 20. Line numbers can vary from 1 to the PAGE LIMIT value. Within a group, these numbers must increase.

- *PLUS integer* is a position *relative to the preceding line*—for example, LINE PLUS 2 specifies to use double-line spacing. On the first detail line of the page, this value is ignored, and the line is positioned instead in the FIRST DETAIL position.

You also can use a NEXT GROUP clause, which inserts additional spacing between report groups.

The clause *COLUMN integer* positions a report field within the line, counting from the lefthand side (column 1). Column numbers can vary from 1 to the width of the printer.

Report Writer writes the TYPE DETAIL report groups *vertically* down the page in the order in which they are generated. Before printing one of these groups, Report Writer verifies that the whole group can be printed on the current page; this is called a *page-fit test*. If the group will not fit on the current page, Report Writer executes an automatic *page advance*. In this example, the PAGE HEADING group will be printed automatically as part of this process.

VALUE and SOURCE

A description of the *contents* of each report field is all that is needed now to complete the description of a report group. For the earlier example, a PICTURE and two clauses suffice:

- If the contents of the report field consist of fixed text, use VALUE "literal".

- If the contents of the report field come from a data item in the Data Division, use SOURCE name-of-data-item.

The source data item can be defined in any section of the Data Division. Subscripts and qualifiers can be used, as shown here:

```
SOURCE IS BACK-PAY IN MASTER-RECORD (4)
```

The item also can be a *special register*—especially PAGE-COUNTER, which gives the number of the current page.

The PICTURE clause, as in basic COBOL, specifies the format in which the field is to be displayed. The rules are the same for the MOVE statement.

There is enough information now to complete the Data Division in the example. Suppose that the record that supplies data for the layout is defined in a standard file like this:

```
FD   COOKIE-FILE           LABEL RECORDS STANDARD.
01   COOKIE-RECORD.
     05  DEPOT             PIC X(10).
     05  ORDER-DATE        PIC 9(8).
     05  COOKIE-TYPE       PIC X(12).
     05  QTY-ORDERED       PIC 9(4) COMP.
     05  QTY-IN-STOCK      PIC 9(4) COMP.
     05  ORDER-VALUE       PIC S9(5)V99 COMP.
```

The complete report description now can be completed using these new clauses:

```
REPORT SECTION.
RD   STOCK-SUMMARY
     PAGE LIMIT 64 LINES
     FIRST DETAIL 5.
01   TYPE PH.
     03  LINE 1.
         05  COLUMN 12  PIC X(32)
                        VALUE "Crumbly Cookie Company     Orders".
         05  COLUMN 47  PIC X(4)  VALUE "Page".
         05  COLUMN 52  PIC ZZ9   SOURCE PAGE-COUNTER.
     03  LINE 3.
         05  COLUMN 7   PIC X(47) VALUE
             "Date      Type       Quantity      Value of order".
```

9

THE REPORT
WRITER MODULE

```
01   COOKIE-LINE  TYPE DE.
     03  LINE PLUS 2.
         05   COLUMN 4    PIC 99/99/9999 SOURCE ORDER-DATE.
         05   COLUMN 16   PIC X(12)      SOURCE COOKIE-TYPE.
         05   COLUMN 29   PIC ZZZ9       SOURCE QTY-ORDERED.
         05   COLUMN 41   PIC $(5)9.99   SOURCE ORDER-VALUE.
```

There is no implicit time sequence in the way these print fields will be generated. The code simply *describes* the layout required instead of trying to solve the problem of how to produce it.

Code the SELECT...ASSIGN and FD

Report Writer writes the output automatically to a regular COBOL file. So, near the start of the program, a Writer SELECT...ASSIGN clause and an FD are required. The FD entry must contain a new clause: REPORT IS name-of-report. No record description is required following it. The following code might result:

```
IDENTIFICATION DIVISION.
PROGRAM-ID.  COOKIES.
ENVIRONMENT DIVISION.
INPUT-OUTPUT SECTION.
FILE-CONTROL.
     SELECT COOKIE-FILE ASSIGN TO DATAIN.
     SELECT STOCK-PRINT ASSIGN TO LIST01.
DATA DIVISION.
FILE SECTION.
FD   COOKIE-FILE.
...  (description as above) ...
FD   STOCK-PRINT
     REPORT IS STOCK-SUMMARY.
WORKING-STORAGE SECTION.
01   WS-EOF          PIC X    VALUE "N".
```

Code the Procedure Division

Report Writer is entirely under the control of the program, but at a higher level than is the case with basic COBOL. This means that no action is taken until the program executes a Report Writer statement. There are three of these statements:

- INITIATE name-of-report initializes the report. It must be done before any other operation on the report. It does not open the file or print anything.

- GENERATE name-of-detail generates *one instance* of a DETAIL group. name-of-detail is the data name written after the 01 level number for the group. GENERATE also does a page-fit test so that a PAGE HEADING group also can be generated in this example. You can build complex report layouts by doing a GENERATE for different DETAIL groups at different points in the program.

- `TERMINATE name-of-report` ends the report and produces any final items that are required at the end of the report. It does not close the file.

As you will see, it now is possible to make extensive changes or improvements to the print layout *without any change to this Procedure Division.* For example, `TYPE REPORT HEADING` and `TYPE REPORT FOOTING` groups could be added and, if the end user wants something printed at the foot of each page, a `TYPE PAGE FOOTING` can be added (in which case, a phrase like `LAST DETAIL 62` also is required after the `PAGE LIMIT`).

For the current example, the following would be a suitable complete Procedure Division:

```
PROCEDURE DIVISION.
PROGRAM-START.
    OPEN INPUT COOKIE-FILE, OUTPUT STOCK-PRINT
    INITIATE STOCK-SUMMARY
    PERFORM NEXT-RECORD
    PERFORM UNTIL WS-EOF = "Y"
        GENERATE COOKIE-LINE
        PERFORM NEXT-RECORD
    END-PERFORM
    TERMINATE STOCK-SUMMARY
    CLOSE STOCK-PRINT, COOKIE-FILE
    STOP RUN.
NEXT-RECORD.
    READ COOKIE-FILE AT END MOVE "Y" TO WS-EOF.
```

If this code is written after the code for steps 5 and 4, in that order, a complete program results.

This sample program does nothing but printing, but Report Writer code can be inserted in a program that performs many other tasks. Because the printed data is described in the Report Section, it does not clutter up the rest of the Data Division.

Simplifications in the New COBOL Standard

The new COBOL standard, which is published, contains many improvements to Report Writer. These improvements have been available for many years via vendor extensions in widely available implementations, such as the IBM COBOL family, and in some other versions for as long as 20 years. The new standard simplifies some of the more elementary syntax, and the code already shown can be trimmed optionally as shown here:

- `COLUMN` can be written as `COL`.
- `PICTURE` is not required with `VALUE`.

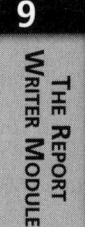

9

THE REPORT WRITER MODULE

- COLUMN can be relative, like LINE, using PLUS integer (for example, COLUMN PLUS 2 means "one space following the preceding item").

- PLUS can be written +.

This yields the following simplified version:

```
REPORT SECTION.
RD   STOCK-SUMMARY
     PAGE LIMIT 64 LINES
     FIRST DETAIL 5.
01   TYPE PH.
     03   LINE 1.
          05   COL 12   VALUE "Crumbly Cookie Company   Orders".
          05   COL 47   VALUE "Page".
          05   COL + 2 PIC ZZ9   SOURCE PAGE-COUNTER.
     03   LINE 3.
          05   COL 7   VALUE
          "Date       Type         Quantity      Value of order".
01   COOKIE-LINE   TYPE DE.
     03   LINE + 2.
          05   COL 4    PIC 99/99/9999 SOURCE ORDER-DATE.
          05   COL 16   PIC X(12)      SOURCE COOKIE-TYPE.
          05   COL 29   PIC ZZZ9       SOURCE QTY-ORDERED.
          05   COL 41   PIC $(5)9.99   SOURCE ORDER-VALUE.
```

To make for more concise code, the new standard will be used in all further sample code. Programmers who still use the older ANS 1968, 1974, or 1985 standard need to regress the shortcuts just described.

The new standard also introduces some totally new features. Some of the more basic of these follow:

- COLUMN RIGHT and CENTER.

- SOURCE can be followed by an *expression* like

  ```
  SOURCE (MONTHLY-PAY * 12) + YEARLY-BONUS ROUNDED
  ```

  or by a function like

  ```
  SOURCE FUNCTION CURRENT-DATE
  ```

- LINE, COLUMN, SOURCE, and VALUE clauses have a *multiple* form, as shown in this example:

  ```
  COLS 1, 21, 39, 48 VALUES "this year", "next year", "sometime",
  "never"
  ```

- *Error conditions* are trapped. The case in which these are needed most often is when a total field overflows. A six-digit total previously would print 1 million as zero!

Control Breaks and Totaling

Imagine now that the end user has asked for the preceding layout to be enhanced, as shown in Figure 9.4.

FIGURE 9.4.

A layout with controls and totals.

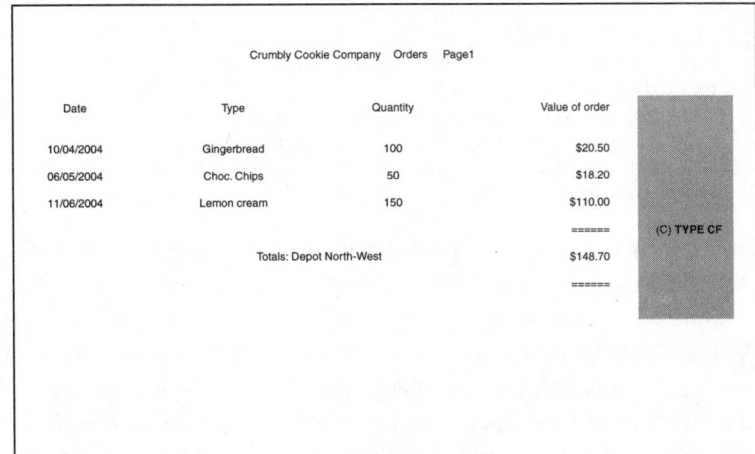

Date	Type	Quantity	Value of order
	Crumbly Cookie Company Orders Page1		
10/04/2004	Gingerbread	100	$20.50
06/05/2004	Choc. Chips	50	$18.20
11/06/2004	Lemon cream	150	$110.00
			======
	Totals: Depot North-West		$148.70
			======

The new lines constitute a single new `CONTROL FOOTING` group (see Figure 9.5).

FIGURE 9.5.

Analysis of the control footing.

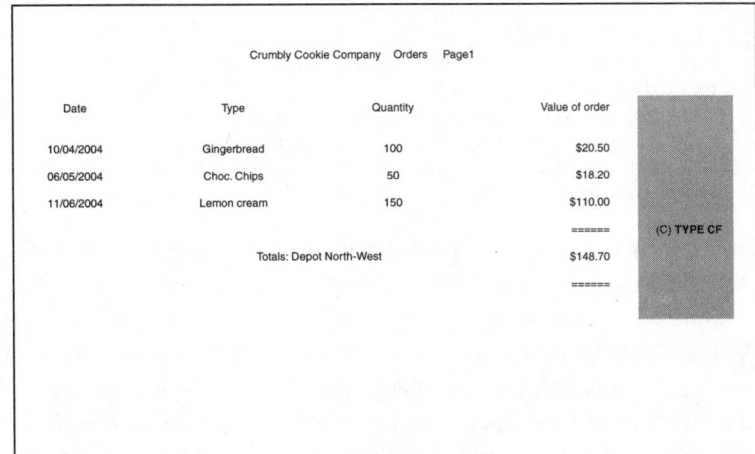

Date	Type	Quantity	Value of order
	Crumbly Cookie Company Orders Page1		
10/04/2004	Gingerbread	100	$20.50
06/05/2004	Choc. Chips	50	$18.20
11/06/2004	Lemon cream	150	$110.00
			====== (C) TYPE CF
	Totals: Depot North-West		$148.70
			======

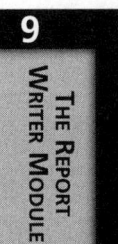

The report now has *subtotals* in a new CF (control footing) group. After each change in the value of a certain data item (DEPOT, in this case), Report Writer is required to print three lines. DEPOT is known as a *control,* and a change in its value is called a *control break.* A report can have any number of controls arranged in a hierarchy. For each control, optionally one CH (control heading) and one CF group can be defined. Visually, you can represent the data as a nested structure—for example, the report consists of all the data for 1998, followed by all the data for 1999, and so on, and then, within each year, all the data for January, followed by all the data for February...there's no limit to the number of levels.

Whenever the program performs a GENERATE, all the controls are examined (from highest down to lowest) to see whether there has been any change (a *control break*), and if so, these additional groups are printed automatically, depending on the *level* of the control break. Control headings also are printed at the start, during the first GENERATE, and control footings are printed during the TERMINATE.

CH and CF groups are treated in all other respects like DETAIL groups. (One useful exception: The page-fit test for a CF uses the FOOTING rather than the LAST DETAIL value so that subtotals can be prevented from appearing at the top of the page.) The original COBOL code can be changed as the following:

```
REPORT SECTION.
RD   STOCK-SUMMARY
     PAGE LIMIT 64 LINES
     FIRST DETAIL 5
     CONTROL IS DEPOT.
...
01   TYPE CF FOR DEPOT.
     03   LINE + 2    COL 41   VALUE "========".
     03   LINE + 1.
          05   COL 15   VALUE " Totals: Depot".
          05   COL + 2 PIC X(10)      SOURCE DEPOT.
          05   COL 41   PIC $(5)9.99  SUM OF ORDER-VALUE.
     03   LINE + 1     COL 41   VALUE "========".
```

There is also a special control name called FINAL, which is by definition higher than any other control and never undergoes a control break. It can be used when *grand totals* (over the entire report) are required. If there are two controls instead of one (for example, STATE and DEPOT), the coding here could have *four* new automatic report groups: a CH for STATE, a CH for DEPOT, a CF for DEPOT, and a CF for STATE. Note that in the CF groups, the value of the control obtained from the SOURCE is the value *before the break.* Any number of SUM clauses can be described in a report group, and they can reference each other, producing *rolling forward* and *cross-footing* effects.

While making these extensive additions to the report layout, it is comforting to recall once again that the Procedure Division does not change.

The new COBOL standard also assists here by providing the following extensions:

- `SUM` can be used in any type of report group (not just `TYPE CF`).
- *Any* numeric item can be totaled, whether in the Report Section or elsewhere, simply by coding `SUM OF name-of-item`.
- The "padding words" `OF` and `FOR`, as shown in the code, can be used.
- By adding the phrase `OR PAGE`, you can make a control-heading group appear at the top of each page, even if there has not been a control break (one of the most requested additions).

Conditionals

The end user now has requested an extra feature for the report layout, as shown in Figure 9.6.

FIGURE 9.6.
A more complex layout.

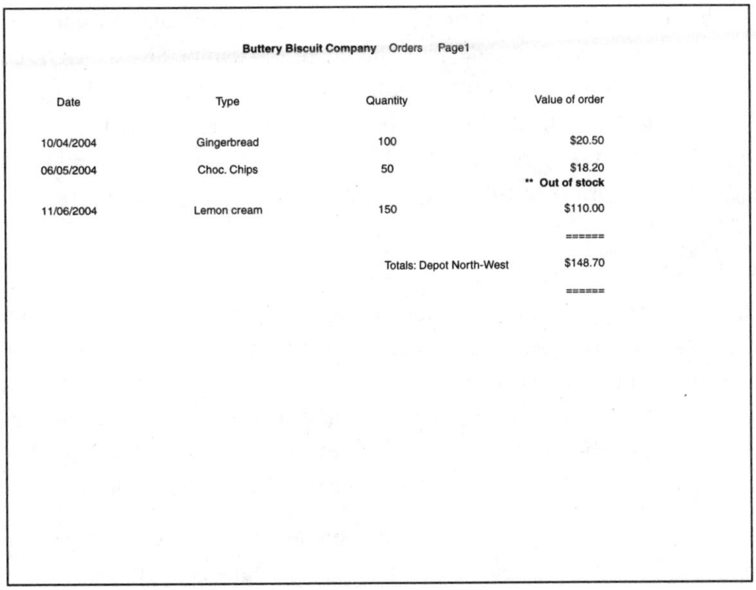

Buttery Biscuit Company Orders Page1

Date	Type	Quantity	Value of order
10/04/2004	Gingerbread	100	$20.50
06/05/2004	Choc. Chips	50	$18.20
			**** Out of stock**
11/06/2004	Lemon cream	150	$110.00
			======
		Totals: Depot North-West	$148.70
			======

Suppose that a transatlantic company (that is called "Biscuits") has undergone a merger, and its name must appear if the data item `COMPANY-ID` is equal to `"B"`. In addition, the words `Out of stock` must be printed if the quantity ordered is greater than a new item called `QTY-IN-STOCK`.

Here are the changes required to the earlier coding (study the boldface items):

```
01  TYPE PH.
    03  LINE 1.
        05  COL 11   VALUE "Buttery Biscuit Company    Orders"
            PRESENT WHEN COMPANY-ID = "B".
        05  COL 12   VALUE "Crumbly Cookie Company    Orders"
            PRESENT WHEN COMPANY-ID = "C".
             . . .
01  COOKIE-LINE  TYPE DE.
    03  LINE + 2.
             . . .
    03  LINE + 1  PRESENT WHEN QTY-ORDERED > QTY-IN-STOCK.
        05  COL 34      VALUE "** Out of stock".
```

The condition in the PRESENT WHEN clause is evaluated *before* Report Writer performs the page-fit test so that an accurate fit is obtained on the page.

The PRESENT WHEN clause represents a stage in the evolution of Report Writer equivalent to fish growing feet in the primeval mud. This clause makes possible a gallery of effects from one simple syntactic device. The *condition* can be any COBOL condition. If an item is *not* present, spaces or blank lines appear, except when the LINE or COLUMN is *relative,* in which case these spaces or blank lines get closed up. The PRESENT clause is block-structured. For example, if a LINE is not present, the entire line vanishes along with all its subordinate columns. An entire report group can be "not present."

Tables

The end is happy with the new layout, but the technical people have abolished the simple file system and introduced a database in which all the data for one depot is held in a table. Thus, the data names defined in the old record now are held in a table and must be subscripted whenever they are referenced. There is also a counter—for example, NO-OF-DEPOTS—that tells users how many entries exist. Assume also that all of a depot's data will fit on one page (if not, see the next section, "Further Extensions").

The layout is unchanged (except that each depot's data now can be guaranteed not to be split across two pages), but the COBOL code changes as shown here:

```
01  DEPOT-LINES  TYPE DE.
    03  LINE + 2 OCCURS 1 TO 20 TIMES DEPENDING ON NO-OF-DEPOTS
            VARYING ITEM-SUB FROM 1 BY 1.
        05  COL 4   PIC 99/99/9999 SOURCE ORDER-DATE (ITEM-SUB).
        05  COL 16  PIC X(12)      SOURCE COOKIE-TYPE (ITEM-SUB).
        05  COL 29  PIC ZZZ9       SOURCE QTY-ORDERED (ITEM-SUB).
        05  RS-VAL  COL 41         PIC $(5)9.99
                                   SOURCE ORDER-VALUE (ITEM-SUB).
    03  LINE + 2    COL 1          VALUE "========".
    03  LINE + 1.
        05  COL 15  VALUE " Totals: Depot".
```

```
      05   COL + 2 PIC X(10)       SOURCE DEPOT.
      05   COL 41   PIC $(5)9.99   SUM OF RS-VAL.
   03 LINE + 1      COL 1          VALUE "========".
```

The CONTROL clause no longer is required, and the Report Writer procedural code changes to GENERATE DEPOT-LINES. Note the way the numeric report item is named (RS-VAL) and then totaled (SUM OF RS-VAL) within the same report group.

The OCCURS clause, with its elegant VARYING and STEP phrases, is another spectacular addition to the features, and this example hardly does it justice.

Further Extensions

The improvements made to Report Writer in the new standard might seem sufficient for any need, but they only make up for the intervening years of neglect, and further additional features are desirable for the programming tasks that span the millennium. Furthermore, the features listed here are available as vendor extensions in all versions that offer the standard features described earlier. The most notable of these extensions follow:

- Printer attributes or "styles" provided via the STYLE clause. This clause is block-structured and applies to the COBOL entry in which it is coded. For example, STYLE HIGHLIGHT, coded with a LINE clause, prints the entire line darker or in a different color, depending on how the generic style HIGHLIGHT was chosen to be realized on the available printer.

> **NOTE**
>
> Any printer can show a few different properties: Even the old line printer could use double-hammering to represent boldface. Programmers who are not sure or want a portable program should use only generic names. For example, STYLE ALT-FONT might be implemented as italic, in red, or in courier on different physical printers.

- Variable-length report items. This feature incorporates extra symbols into the PICTURE to trim trailing spaces or leading zeros. The following code, for example, centers the name and left-aligns the numeric item:

```
05   COL CENTER 20  PIC <X(30)> SOURCE COMPANY-NAME.
05   COL LEFT 50    PIC 9<999> SOURCE NO-OF-ITEMS.
```

- A variation of the PRESENT WHEN feature that prints or a line or report field after a control break or page break. The following code, for example, prints this item both after a change in STATE and after a new page is advanced:

```
05  COL 1 PIC X(10) SOURCE STATE
          PRESENT AFTER NEW STATE OR PAGE.
```

- A multiple-choice syntax to avoid the need for a series of entries with PRESENT WHEN clauses. For example,

```
05  COL 35  VALUE "ROUGE" WHEN LANGUAGE = "F"
            VALUE "ROT" WHEN LANGUAGE = "G"
            VALYE "ROJO" WHEN LANGUAGE = "S"
            VALUE "RED" WHEN OTHER.
```

- Features to print report groups side by side (the label-printing problem, in a generalized context) and to provide snaking columns and other irregular layouts.

- A multiple control-footing feature enabling the same report group description to be used for totals, subtotals, and grand totals. The syntax here is especially elegant. You can write the TYPE clause like this, for example:

```
TYPE CF FOR STATE, COUNTY, CITY
```

Or, if all the controls are to be included, you can use this:

```
TYPE CF FOR ALL
```

- Line-wrap and page-wrap features. The WRAP clause allows the programmer to print a large table under one LINE entry or to include a large number of optional report fields (such as error messages) without any worry about over-filling the line. The MULTIPLE PAGE clause allows a report group to span several pages so that huge tables can be printed in a single operation.

- More concise code. These items are too numerous to list here, but the general result is that Report Writer code now can be very elegant and concise without losing the quality for which COBOL is valued: legibility.

- A feature to redirect Report Writer output. The previous features were all application features, but this one is concerned more with the physical nature of the report output. Many programmers of the older generation will remember having to write print records to a tape or a disk file with a special organization in order to use some particular vendor software that indexed and spooled the print data. Today, the programmer might want to incorporate the program within an online system so that the printer no longer is local but is a device controlled by the network. (Another typical use is in storing and counting the pages and then going back to each page heading and marking it as 1 of *n*, 2 of *n*, and so on.) In all these cases, the

Report Writer output is not printed by means of a traditional batch file but is passed through a special software routine or handler. This handler can be developed separately from the COBOL compiler, and the program source is transparent to it.

Summary

After reading this chapter, you probably have formed a judgment about the learning curve involved in using Report Writer. You might ask yourself these questions:

- If I need to learn Report Writer at short notice to write a new program, does the Report Writer syntax appear easy to learn?
- If I inherit a Report Writer program, will I be able to understand it and, if necessary, change it easily?

If your project depends on other people, you might consider these questions as well:

- Will my team be able to absorb this new syntax quickly and make real savings in development time?
- Will my team enjoy using the Report Writer facility and react well to it? (This item is important; too many great ideas in "productive programming" produce too much resistance among the programming staff.)

The availability of good literature in recent years has made this process of absorption much easier. I have found from practical experience that the outcome of these questions is usually extremely positive.

There are now good implementations on most operating platforms, both host and desktop. Some of these are integrated into the compiler, and others operate as a co-processor or precompiler. These latter types, such as the version for IBM VisualAge COBOL, are so closely integrated with the workbench, compiler, and debugger that the programmer is hardly aware that another process is running.

Report Writer has been described by some as COBOL's best feature. With the new standard, more people now will feel inclined to judge for themselves.

9

THE REPORT
WRITER MODULE

The Language— Advanced Topics

PART

III

IN THIS PART

CHAPTER 10

Special Tools for Character Manipulation

IN THIS CHAPTER

COBOL has three separate verbs plus the Reference Modification facility for manipulating the character and text data in alphanumeric fields. The variety is due to a combination of COBOL's age and the way its data items are named, given fixed sizes, and organized into record structures.

Not many situations in business programming call for extensive manipulation of the characters within defined fields. But when these situations do occur, these tools provide a rich variety of options to deal with them. As you'll see, the situation often calls for using several of these tools in combination to produce a good solution.

None of the current character-manipulation tools were available in the original COBOL compilers. The 1968 Standard defined only the EXAMINE verb, which was a precursor to INSPECT. EXAMINE could deal only with a single character at a time, and the counter it used was reset to zero each time the statement was executed; both these were limiting factors. Interestingly, no counter data item was specified in the TALLYING format of EXAMINE. Instead, COBOL defined its own counter, which was named TALLY, so that it could be referenced by other statements.

Because of the limitations in EXAMINE, it was removed from the 1974 Standard and replaced with INSPECT. Because many vendors continued to support it as a language extension, you still can find it in an occasional mainframe or midrange program. EXAM-INE can easily and almost directly be changed to INSPECT. The STRING and UNSTRING verbs also were added with the 1974 Standard and, in combination with INSPECT, provide the facility to accomplish most character manipulation done in business programming.

The 1985 Standard added the CONVERTING format to INSPECT. This is useful in handling uppercase and lowercase character conversions, as well as in dealing with special character requirements for some text and non-English language manipulation. Reference modification also was added at this point; it is like similar features in Pascal and BASIC and allows a single character or a group of characters within an alphanumeric data item to be treated as a separate, independent data item. This feature is quite handy for complex text manipulations; it allows alphanumeric fields to be processed one character at a time (or in groups of characters). Previously, an artificial table definition using the OCCURS clause was required for this kind of processing (see Chapter 11, "Tables and Arrays").

The INSPECT Statement

There are three general forms of INSPECT:

- INSPECT/TALLYING is used to count the number of occurrences of a character or group of characters within an alphanumeric data item.

- `INSPECT/REPLACING` is used to identify and replace occurrences of a character or group of characters with another character or group of characters.
- `INSPECT/CONVERTING` is used to compare all the characters in an alphanumeric data item to a listed group of characters. Where matches are found, they are replaced with the corresponding values in another listed group of characters.

Note that `INSPECT/TALLYING` and `INSPECT/REPLACING` can be used together in one statement when the data item being `INSPECT`ed is the same. But because the effect is the same as following one statement with the other, the value is minimal, so that form is hardly ever seen and is not discussed further in this book.

All the formats of `INSPECT` have one common thread: Each begins at the leftmost character position of the data item being `INSPECT`ed and proceeds to the right, one or more characters at a time in a looping fashion, as it does whatever the `TALLYING`, `REPLACING`, or `CONVERTING` function is specified.

`INSPECT` is interesting because even though its functions allow for some very complex character manipulations, only a few of them have proven to have any real practical value. Even though I'll cover the full statement, the forms that have shown to be useful will be highlighted.

INSPECT/TALLYING

`INSPECT/TALLYING` is used to count the number of occurrences of a character or group of characters within an alphanumeric data item. Its general format follows:

```
INSPECT alpha-num-item-1 TALLYING {numeric-item-1 FOR
    {{CHARACTERS/ALL alpha-num-item-2/LEADING alpha-num-item-3}
    [AFTER INITIAL alpha-num-item-4]
    [BEFORE INITIAL alpha-num-item-5]}...}...
```

`alpha-num-item-1` is the data item being `INSPECT`ed, and it can be any elementary- or group-level alphanumeric data item.

`numeric-item-1` specifies the counter that will be incremented each time a match is found. This must be a numeric elementary item, and `INSPECT` does *not* initialize its value.

The remaining `alpha-num-items` must be alphanumeric elementary items or literals. These items can be one or more characters in length. Figurative constants such as `SPACE(S)` or `ZERO(S)` may be used; they are treated as being one character in length.

The `FOR CHARACTERS/ALL/LEADING` phrase specifies what value is to be matched and counted.

The AFTER and BEFORE phrases allow you to specify some value to begin and/or terminate the matching process other than the leftmost and rightmost values. When AFTER is used, character(s) are compared to alpha-num-item-4, beginning with the leftmost value in alpha-num-item-1. When a match is found, the FOR matching process begins just to the right of the character (or group of characters) that matched to alpha-num-item-1. When BEFORE is used, the value of alpha-num-item-5 begins being compared as soon as the FOR matching process starts. That value is tested prior to the FOR value at each successive character position, and if a match is found, the FOR matching is completed. If a match is not found, the FOR processing is done.

When the CHARACTERS form of the FOR phrase is used, numeric-item-1 is incremented for *all* character values. So, if no AFTER or BEFORE phrase is used, the size of alpha-num-item-1 simply is added to numeric-item-1.

When the ALL form of the FOR phrase is used, numeric-item-1 is incremented by each time a match with alpha-num-item-2 is found. Note that when alpha-num-item-2 is more than one character long and a match occurs, the next attempted match begins with the character position just to the right of the last character participating in the preceding match. The examples that follow will clarify this.

When the LEADING form of the FOR phrase is used, numeric-item-1 is incremented if the first attempted match to alpha-num-item-3 is equal. If that is the case, matching continues until the first nonmatch occurs. When that happens (or if the first match was not equal), the FOR phrase is completed with no more matching being done.

Now look at some examples of INSPECT/TALLYING. These will be brief and limited, because in most cases, INSPECT/TALLYING is used in a supportive role with the other character-manipulation verbs to accomplish the overall requirement. I'll begin with some basic examples that have some practical application and finish with a few that aren't very useful but demonstrate how the various phrases work together.

In most cases, you want data to be left-justified within its field. In addition to being necessary for things to sort correctly, this also is important to the proper formatting of reports and other outputs. The following INSPECT identifies and counts any leading spaces:

```
MOVE ZERO TO LEADING-SPACE-COUNT.
INSPECT INPUT-NAME TALLYING LEADING-SPACE-COUNT FOR LEADING SPACES.
```

Obviously, you'll need some of the other character-manipulation verbs to deal with the situation. You'll see that in later sections of this chapter.

The following statements sometimes are used to handle user-input data:

```
MOVE ZERO TO MINUS-SIGN-COUNT DECIMAL-POINT-COUNT LEADING-SPACES
➥LEADING-CHARS.
INSPECT INPUT-NUMBER-ALPHA-NUM TALLYING MINUS-SIGN-COUNT FOR '-'.
INSPECT INPUT-NUMBER-ALPHA-NUM TALLYING DECIMAL-POINT-COUNT FOR '.'.
INSPECT INPUT-NUMBER-ALPHA-NUM TALLYING LEADING-SPACES FOR LEADING SPACES.
INSPECT INPUT-NUMBER-ALPHA-NUM TALLYING LEADING-CHARS FOR CHARACTERS
➥BEFORE '-'.
IF DECIMAL-POINT-COUNT > 1
    OR MINUS-SIGN-COUNT > 1
    OR LEADING-SPACES NOT = LEADING-CHARS
    PERFORM XXXX-ERROR-ROUTINE.
```

Again, additional character manipulation is needed to fully reformat the characters into a proper number. Also, on new systems, modern screen handlers and painters, together with COBOL's de-editing facility, often eliminate the need for this kind of manipulation in the COBOL program.

The following examples don't have much practical use but illustrate how some of the phrases can be used together.

Notice in the following code how the same counter is incremented whenever either of the two values is matched:

```
MOVE ZERO TO TALLY-CTR.
INSPECT ALPHA-FIELD TALLYING TALLY-CTR FOR ALL 'AB' ALL 'X'.
```

Also, the two values do not have to be the same size. If ALPHA-FIELD has a value of 'ABXBAX', TALLY-CTR will have a resulting value of 3.

Although the following example appears fairly simple, it can be deceptive:

```
MOVE ZERO TO TALLY-CTR.
INSPECT ALPHA-FIELD TALLYING TALLY-CTR FOR ALL 'B' AFTER 'AB' BEFORE 'BC'.
```

If ALPHA-FIELD has a value of 'BBABBCBB', TALLY-CTR will have a result of zero. If ALPHA-FIELD has a value of 'BBABBBCB', TALLY-CTR will have a result of 1. If ALPHA-FIELD has a value of 'BBABCBBB', TALLY-CTR will have a result of 3.

The following example illustrates how multiple TALLYING phrases are handled:

```
MOVE ZERO TO TALLY-CTR TALLY-CTR2.
INSPECT ALPHA-FIELD TALLYING TALLY-CTR FOR CHARACTERS
                    TALLY-CTR2 FOR ALL 'X'.
```

In this case, TALLY-CTR will always have a value equal to the size of ALPHA-FIELD, and TALLY-CTR2 always will be zero. That is because when a match occurs, INSPECT increments the designated counter and then continues to the next character position of ALPHA-FIELD and starts again with the first TALLYING phrase. Here, because the CHARACTER form will result in a match for every value, INSPECT will never get to the second phrase.

The following example produces a more reasonable result:

```
MOVE ZERO TO TALLY-CTR TALLY-CTR2.
INSPECT ALPHA-FIELD TALLYING TALLY-CTR FOR ALL 'X'
                    TALLY-CTR2 FOR CHARACTERS.
```

Here, `TALLY-CTR` will have a count for all occurrences of the letter `'X'`, and `TALLY-CTR2` will have a count for all the other values. (`TALLY-CTR` + `TALLY-CTR2` = size of `ALPHA-FIELD`.)

INSPECT/REPLACING

`INSPECT/REPLACING` is used to identify and replace occurrences of a character or group of characters with another character or group of characters. The format is very similar to `INSPECT/TALLYING`:

```
INSPECT alpha-num-item-1 REPLACING
    {CHARACTERS/ALL alpha-num-item-2/LEADING alpha-num-item-3}
    BY alpha-num-item-4
    [AFTER INITIAL alpha-num-item-5] [BEFORE INITIAL alpha-num-item-6]}...
```

Notice how little difference there is between `INSPECT/TALLYING` and `INSPECT/REPLACING`. Instead of the `TALLYING` counter `FOR` and the matching specification phrase, you have `REPLACING`, the matching specification phrase, and the `BY` and replacement value.

In this format, `alpha-num-item-4` must be the same size as `alpha-num-item-2` or `alpha-num-item-3`, depending on which option is used. If `CHARACTERS` is used, `alpha-num-item-4` must have a size of 1. `alpha-num-item-4` may be an elementary alphanumeric data item or a literal.

With `INSPECT/REPLACING`, the matching mechanism and the `AFTER` and `BEFORE` phrases operate in the exact same manner as they do with `INSPECT/TALLYING`. However, when a match occurs, instead of incrementing a counter, the characters in `alpha-num-item-1` that were matched are replaced with the value of `alpha-num-item-4`. A few common examples follow to demonstrate what happens.

This is probably the most common `INSPECT` statement:

```
INSPECT INPUT-NUMBER REPLACING LEADING SPACES BY ZEROES.
```

This statement converts leading spaces to zeroes in numeric input fields so that they can be used in arithmetic operations. It is curious that, in most cases, the statement isn't really necessary, because most compilers perform this conversion automatically when encountering leading spaces in a field being used in an arithmetic operation.

The following statement forces all occurrences of the letters a, b, c, and d to their upper-case equivalents:

```
INSPECT CODE-FIELD REPLACING
    ALL 'a' BY 'A'
    ALL 'b' BY 'B'
    ALL 'c' BY 'C'
    ALL 'd' BY 'D'.
```

This statement comes in handy when the program must compare for certain values and only a few different characters are used, but the user may use uppercase, lowercase, or a mixture of cases. You'll see the general form for this kind of translation in the next section.

This example is again not very practical but demonstrates how the different phrases can be mixed:

```
INSPECT ALPHA-FIELD  REPLACING
    ALL 'AB' BY 'XY'
    LEADING 'A' BY 'W'
    CHARACTERS BY SPACES.
```

Here, if ALPHA-FIELD begins with a value of 'AAABAA', it will end up with a value of 'WWXY '.

INSPECT/CONVERTING

INSPECT/CONVERTING is used to compare all the characters in an alphanumeric data item to a listed group of characters. Then, when matches are found, they are replaced with the corresponding values in another listed group of characters. The format follows:

```
INSPECT alpha-num-item-1 CONVERTING alpha-num-item-2 TO alpha-num-item-3
    [AFTER INITIAL alpha-num-item-4] [BEFORE INITIAL alpha-num-item-5]
```

In this format, the size of alpha-num-item-3 must be the same as that of alpha-num-item-2.

The AFTER and BEFORE phrases operate in the same manner as the other two formats.

Notice in this example that the rather elaborate matching phrase in the previous two formats has been replaced with the very direct CONVERTING phrase.

In the CONVERTING phrase, each character of alpha-num-item-1 is compared to each of the characters of alpha-num-item-2. When a match is found, the character in alpha-num-item-1 is replaced by the character in alpha-num-item-3 that occupies the same relative position as the matching character from alpha-num-item-2. The following example illustrates what happens:

10

SPECIAL TOOLS
FOR CHARACTER
MANIPULATION

```
INSPECT ALPHA-INPUT CONVERTING 'abcd' TO 'ABCD'.
```

By definition in the 1985 Standard, this is exactly equal to the following statement from the preceding section:

```
INSPECT ALPHA-INPUT REPLACING
    ALL 'a' BY 'A'
    ALL 'b' BY 'B'
    ALL 'c' BY 'C'
    ALL 'd' BY 'D'.
```

In both statements, every lowercase a, b, c, and d will be replaced by its uppercase equivalent. The general form to translate all lowercase characters to uppercase follows:

```
INSPECT ALPHA-INPUT CONVERTING
    'abcdefghijklmnopqrstuvwxyz'  TO
    'ABCDEFGHIJKLMNOPQRSTUVWXYZ'.
```

The reverse translation is done simply by switching the converting identifiers. Other conversions and translations can be done just as simply, and that can include very basic encoding and decoding of data. You should be aware, however, that because this conversion is done as a loop within a loop for every character, it is one of the more CPU-intensive statements in COBOL. In most applications, the difference in time isn't noticeable, but this statement can degrade performance if used indiscriminately in programs that already are performance sensitive.

The STRING Statement

The STRING statement allows you to combine serially (or to concatenate) several fields (or partial fields) into one receiving field. The format follows:

```
STRING {alpha-num-item-1... DELIMITED BY {SIZE/alpha-num-item-2}}...
    INTO alpha-num-item-3
    [WITH POINTER numeric-item-1]
    [ON OVERFLOW imperative-statement-1]
    [NOT ON OVERFLOW imperative-statement-2]
    [END-STRING]
```

The alpha-num-item-1 items are the fields that will be concatenated together, and alpha-num-item-3 is the receiving field where they will be placed. The DELIMITED phrase determines how much of each alpha-num-item-1 will be transferred. I'll describe the optional items a little later.

All alpha-num-item-1 and alpha-num-item-2 items must be alphanumeric. They can be literals, but if they are, they must be nonnumeric literals (in other words, they need to be surrounded by quotes). They can be numeric elementary data items, but in that case, they must be integers and cannot be defined with the PICTURE character P, and they cannot be COMP or COMP-3 or PACKED-DECIMAL or any other nondisplay USAGE.

alpha-num-item-3 must be alphanumeric and cannot be a literal. STRING does *not* clear this field to spaces at the beginning of the operation and does *not* space-fill any unused character positions at the end of the operation.

STRING basically operates as follows. Each successive alpha-num-item-1 character is inserted, one after the other, beginning at the leftmost position of alpha-num-item-3, one character at a time, until all characters have been inserted or no character positions are left in alpha-num-item-3. The DELIMITED BY phrase determines how much of each alpha-num-item-1 is to be transferred. When SIZE is specified, the entire field or literal is transferred. If some other value is specified, characters are transferred until a character or group of successive characters within alpha-num-item-3 match the value specified (or until the entire field has been transferred).

The following examples combine the various parts of a person's name to form the whole name in the desired format:

```
MOVE SPACES TO FIRST-NAME-FIRST.
STRING FIRST-NAME DELIMITED BY SPACE
       SPACE DELIMITED BY SIZE
       MIDDLE-INIT DELIMITED BY SIZE
       '. ' DELIMITED BY SIZE
       LAST-NAME DELIMITED BY SPACE
    INTO FIRST-NAME-FIRST.

MOVE SPACES TO LAST-NAME-FIRST.
STRING LAST-NAME DELIMITED BY SPACE
       ', ' DELIMITED BY SIZE
       FIRST-NAME DELIMITED BY SPACE
       SPACE DELIMITED BY SIZE
       MIDDLE-INIT DELIMITED BY SIZE
       '.' DELIMITED BY SIZE
    INTO LAST-NAME-FIRST.
```

The following example similarly combines the various parts of the last line of an address. Note here that the delimiter for CITY is a two-character literal ('   '), which is needed so that cities like St. Louis, San Diego, and New Bedford will be transferred completely:

```
MOVE SPACES TO LAST-ADDRESS-LINE
STRING CITY DELIMITED BY '  '
       ', ' DELIMITED BY SIZE
       STATE DELIMITED BY SPACE
       '   ' DELIMITED BY SIZE
       ZIP-CODE DELIMITED BY SIZE
    INTO LAST-ADDRESS-LINE.
```

You can see how some fairly tricky concatenation can be done pretty easily in a clear, easy-to-follow manner.

The optional POINTER phrase adds a level of generality that allows you to handle a variety of special situations. It also provides for full text-manipulation capabilities when used together with the other character-manipulation features. In other words, you can write a word processor in COBOL if you choose. You'll see a simple example of this in the next sections.

When the POINTER phrase is used, numeric-item-1 must be an elementary numeric integer item. Initially, it specifies the character position within the alpha-num-item-3 where the first character from the first alpha-num-item-1 is to be placed. From that point, it is incremented by 1 for each character that is inserted and used to determine where each next character is to be inserted. Thus, when the STRING statement is completed, its value will be one more than the last position where a character was inserted.

The following example demonstrates how this works by adding an optional last four digits of a ZIP-PLUS-4 value to the last line of the preceding address example:

```
MOVE SPACES TO LAST-ADDRESS-LINE
MOVE 1 TO ADDRESS-POINTER.
STRING CITY DELIMITED BY '  '
       ', ' DELIMITED BY SIZE
        STATE DELIMITED BY SPACE
       '  ' DELIMITED BY SIZE
        ZIP-CODE DELIMITED BY SIZE
     INTO LAST-ADDRESS-LINE
        POINTER ADDRESS-POINTER.

IF ZIP-LAST-4 NOT = ZERO
    AND ZIP-LAST-4 NOT = SPACES
    STRING '-' DELIMITED BY SIZE
           ZIP-LAST-4 DELIMITED BY SIZE
      INTO LAST-ADDRESS-LINE
           POINTER ADDRESS-POINTER.
```

Notice how I had to initialize ADDRESS-POINTER to 1 before the first STRING statement and then included the POINTER phrase in that statement. But then, if the last four digits of the ZIP-PLUS-4 are present, they simply can be added on to the end of the already inserted five-digit ZIP code.

The other optional phrase for the STRING statement is ON OVERFLOW (and corresponding NOT ON OVERFLOW). Overflow occurs in a STRING statement when there are no more character positions left in alpha-num-item-3 to place characters still left in the alpha-num-item-1 fields. If the POINTER phrase is used, overflow also will occur if numeric-item-1 has a value of zero or some other value greater than the number of positions available in alpha-num-item-3.

ON OVERFLOW isn't used a great deal with the STRING statement because the received field can be defined large enough so that it will not happen, or it is acceptable to just allow the remaining characters to be truncated (which is what happens if no overflow phrase is coded).

The END-STRING is appropriate only if one of the overflow phrases is used.

The UNSTRING Statement

UNSTRING is the inverse of STRING. Whereas STRING concatenates a list of different data items, inserting them into a single receiving field, UNSTRING separates one field into components and places them in a number of listed receiving fields.

Surprisingly, the UNSTRING statement is more complex than the STRING statement. It's surprising because normally it is much easier to take things apart than it is to put them back together again. The reason for this added complexity is that UNSTRING provides additional (optional) information about each of the receiving fields to make it easier for the program to deal with them (and possibly put the fields back together again in some other form).

The entire format for UNSTRING follows, even though I won't get to some of the optional phrases for several pages:

```
UNSTRING alpha-num-item-1
    [DELIMITED BY [ALL] alpha-num-item-2 [OR [ALL] alpha-num-item-3]...]
    INTO {alpha-num-item-4 [DELIMITER IN alpha-num-item-5]
    [COUNT IN numeric-item-1]}...
    [WITH POINTER numeric-item-2]
    [TALLYING IN numeric-item-3]
    [ON OVERFLOW imperative-statement-1]
    [NOT ON OVERFLOW imperative-statement-2]
    [END-UNSTRING]
```

alpha-num-item-1 is the field that will be separated into component parts, and it must be an alphanumeric data item. alpha-num-item-4 and alpha-num-item-5 also must be alphanumeric data items. alpha-num-item-4 also may be a numeric data item, but it must be DISPLAY USAGE (which is the default, as opposed to COMP, COMP-3, and so on) and be defined with the PIC character 'P'.

alpha-num-item-2 and alpha-num-item-3 also need to be alphanumeric, but they can be data items or alphanumeric literals.

numeric-item-1, numeric-item-2, and numeric-item-3 must all be elementary numeric integer data items.

The basic form of UNSTRING operates like this: Beginning with the first character at the left of alpha-num-item-1 (or the character position specified by the POINTER item, if it is used), characters are matched to each of the delimiter alpha-num-item-1/alpha-num-item-2 values. As long as no match occurs, the characters are transferred to a work area one at a time (with the POINTER item being incremented) until one of them is matched or the last character of alpha-num-item-1 has been transferred. The characters then are transferred from the work area to alpha-num-item-4 *according to elementary* MOVE *rules*. This means that if alpha-num-item-4 is a numeric item, it will be right-justified with zero-fill, and if alpha-num-item-4 is alphanumeric, it will be left-justified with space-fill. At this point, UNSTRING clears the work area, positions itself past the character(s) that matched the delimiter (incrementing the POINTER item), and begins the compare/transfer process again. This continues until all characters in alpha-num-item-1 have been compared/transferred or until the last of the listed alpha-num-item-4 fields has been valued.

Observe that if two characters that each match a delimiter value follow each other in alpha-num-item-1, each of them will cause a transfer to one of the INTO alpha-num-item-4 fields. That will result in the first of them being set to spaces or zeros. The ALL can be used to prevent this from happening in many situations. When ALL precedes a delimiter item, any number of consecutive occurrences of that same delimiter in alpha-num-item-1 is treated as a single delimiter. So, the commonly used DELIMITED BY ALL SPACES will result in any number of consecutive space characters being treated as a single delimiter occurrence. However, notice also that even if DELIMITED BY ALL SPACES OR ALL ',' is used, the ", " in ABC, XYZ will be treated as two separate delimiters, so the field that "ABC" is placed in will be followed by a field with spaces and then the field containing XYZ.

Observe also that the entire DELIMITED BY phrase is optional. This is really a special case of UNSTRING, and it is one I have yet to see used. In this case, data is transferred to the receiving alpha-num-item-4 fields based solely on their respective sizes. For example, in the statement UNSTRING IN-ITEM INTO OUT-ITEM1 OUT-ITEM2 OUT-ITEM3, if IN-ITEM is 20 characters long, OUT-ITEM1 is 8, OUT-ITEM2 is 4, and OUT-ITEM3 is 5, OUT-ITEM1 will receive characters 1 through 8 of IN-ITEM, OUT-ITEM2 will receive 9 through 12, and OUT-ITEM3 will receive 13 through 17.

The reason this is termed a special case is that in a normal UNSTRING statement where the DELIMITED BY phrase is used but none of the characters in alpha-num-item-1 match any of the delimiter values, a very different result will occur. In this case, the first receiving alpha-num-item-4 field will have characters transferred to it, but any remaining characters in alpha-num-item-1 will be truncated, and none of the remaining alpha-num-item-4 fields will have anything transferred to them.

Now I'll finally get to some examples. I'll begin by separating the last line of the address for which I used STRING to put together the address in the preceding section. However, assume that the data was entered at a terminal instead of put together by some other program. This forces you to come up with a more general solution. You will make the following assumptions. The city, state, and ZIP code are in the proper order, the city and state are separated by a comma and one or more spaces, the state and ZIP code are separated by one or more spaces, and if there is a full nine-digit ZIP code, the last four digits are separated from the first five by a hyphen.

```
MOVE 1 TO ADDRESS-POINTER.
UNSTRING LAST-ADDRESS-LINE DELIMITED BY ','
     INTO CITY
     POINTER ADDRESS-POINTER.

MOVE ZERO TO ZIP-LAST-4.
UNSTRING LAST-ADDRESS-LINE DELIMITED BY ALL SPACES OR '-'
     INTO STATE
          STATE
          ZIP-CODE
          ZIP-LAST-4
     POINTER ADDRESS-POINTER.
```

Notice how I separated this into two statements. This allows you to easily handle the possibility of spaces being included in the city name as well as spaces preceding the city name. It is also part of the solution to the fact that both the comma and space delimiters separate the city and state. You know that the second UNSTRING will encounter the space(s) delimiter between the two as the first characters. Therefore, nothing will be transferred to STATE in its first position, but because ALL SPACES is used as a delimiter, all the spaces will be passed, and the value of the state will be transferred to STATE in its second position. Notice that I set an initial value of zero for ZIP-LAST-4. This is needed because I don't know if anything will be transferred to it. Of course, the POINTER phrase is necessary to pick up processing in the second statement where I left off in the first one.

Before leaving this example, I'd like to point out another way of handling the two different delimiters between the city and the state. You can use the INPECT/TALLYING statement to count past the extra spaces. Notice that when you do this, you do not repeat STATE a second time in the second UNSTRING statement. The modified code follows:

```
MOVE 1 TO ADDRESS-POINTER.
UNSTRING LAST-ADDRESS-LINE DELIMITED BY ','
     INTO CITY
     POINTER ADDRESS-POINTER.

INSPECT LAST-ADDRESS-LINE TALLYING ADDRESS-POINTER
     FOR LEADING  SPACES AFTER ','.
```

```
MOVE ZERO TO ZIP-LAST-4.
UNSTRING LAST-ADDRESS-LINE DELIMITED BY ALL SPACES OR '-'
    INTO STATE
        ZIP-CODE
        ZIP-LAST-4
    POINTER ADDRESS-POINTER.
```

I should note that INSPECT cannot always be used this conveniently, mainly because it has no POINTER facility. The next example also is related to one of the previous examples. In this example, I'll have the user enter his or her name, and then I'll show how smart the program is by reversing its order and displaying the result back to the user:

```
MOVE SPACES TO FULL-NAME-INPUT.
DISPLAY 'ENTER YOUR FULL NAME PLEASE'.
ACCEPT FULL-NAME-INPUT.
INSPECT FULL-NAME-INPUT REPLACING ALL '.' BY SPACE.
MOVE 1 TO NAME-POINTER.
INSPECT FULL-NAME-INPUT TALLYING NAME-POINTER FOR LEADING SPACES.
UNSTRING FULL-NAME-INPUT DELIMITED BY ALL SPACES
    INTO FIRST-NAME
        MIDDLE-INITIAL
        LAST-NAME
    POINTER NAME-POINTER.
MOVE SPACES TO FULL-NAME-LAST-FIRST.
STRING LAST-NAME DELIMITED BY SPACES
    ', ' DELIMITED BY SIZE
    FIRST-NAME DELIMITED BY SPACE
    SPACE DELIMITED BY SIZE
    MIDDLE-INITIAL DELIMITED BY SIZE
    '.' DELIMITED BY SIZE
    INTO FULL-NAME-LAST-FIRST.
DISPLAY 'YOUR NAME WILL BE RECORDED AS: ' FULL-NAME-LAST-FIRST.
```

Notice how I use INPECT/REPLACING to eliminate any period following the middle initial if it was entered. This solves the problem of consecutive delimiters for UNSTRING. INSPECT/TALLYING is used to get past any leading spaces in the input. Even if a full middle name is entered, it is chopped down to a single initial because MIDDLE-INITIAL is only one character in length, and UNSTRING discards any additional characters between the first and the next space delimiter. Finally, remember that FULL-NAME-LAST-FIRST must be set to spaces before the STRING statement because it does not space-fill.

Now it is time to review the remaining optional phrases available with UNSTRING.

Two of these optional phrases are really subordinate to INTO phrases specifying alpha-num-item-4 fields receiving the separated results of UNSTRING. When data is stored in one of these alpha-num-item-4 fields, the fields in the corresponding optional phrases are valued at the same time if the phrase is present. If no value is stored in an alpha-num-item-4 because the end of alpha-num-item-1 already was reached, these optional fields will not be changed from their initial values, either.

The DELIMITER IN alpha-num-item-5 phrase causes the delimiter value that terminates the transfer of characters used to value the corresponding alpha-num-item-4 to be transferred to alpha-num-item-5 according to elementary item MOVE rules. If the corresponding alpha-num-item-4 is the last one to be valued because the end of alpha-num-item-1 is reached, the corresponding alpha-num-item-5 is set to spaces.

COUNT IN numeric-item-1 causes the count of the number of characters transferred from alpha-num-item-1 to the corresponding alpha-num-item-4 to be placed in numeric-item-1 (spaces or zeroes used to fill alpha-num-item-4 are not included in the count).

TALLYING IN numeric-item-3 causes numeric-item-3 to be incremented by 1 each time an alpha-num-item-4 field is valued by the UNSTRING statement. numeric-item-3 is not initialized by UNSTRING. If the program initializes it to zero before the UNSTRING, at completion, it will contain a count of the number of alpha-num-item-4 fields that were valued during the execution of UNSTRING.

The following artificial example demonstrates these phrases:

```
MOVE ZERO TO FIELD-CTR.
UNSTRING INPUT-DATA DELIMITED BY ALL SPACES OR '.' OR ','
    INTO FIELD-1 DELIMITER DELIM-1 COUNT CTR-1
         FIELD-2 DELIMITER DELIM-2 COUNT CTR-2
         FIELD-3 DELIMITER DELIM-3 COUNT CTR-3
         FIELD-4 DELIMITER DELIM-4 COUNT CTR-4
    TALLYING  FIELD-CTR.
```

If INPUT-DATA is 10 characters long and has a value of 'XY AB.CDE', these fields will have resulting values of FIELD-1='XY', DELIM-1=' ', CTR-1=2, FIELD-2='AB', DELIM-2='.', CTR-2=2, FIELD-3='CDE', DELIM-3= ' ', CTR-3=3, and FIELD-CTR=3. The values of FIELD-4, DELIM-4, and CTR-4 will be unchanged from their initial values.

An overflow condition can occur in an UNSTRING for either of the following reasons. All the receiving alpha-num-item-4 fields have been valued, but all the characters in the sending alpha-num-item-1 have not yet been processed. Or, the POINTER phrase is used, but the associated numeric-item-2 has a value of zero or a value that is greater than the number of characters in alpha-num-item-1.

In the next section, I'll get into a few full-sized programs that are largely tied to character and text manipulation.

Examples of Text Manipulation

First return to the example a few sections back involving the rearranging of peoples' names. This example works well for those of us with a first, middle, and last name. But a lot of people do not have middle names, have several middle names and want them recognized, want to use only their first initial, or have a suffix, such as "Jr." or "Sr.", following their names. I'll use a few optional phrases to help expand the example to handle up to three middle names as well as these other requirements. I'll also add WORKING-STORAGE to make the whole example more complete.

LISTING **10.1**   NAMES.

```
WORKING-STORAGE SECTION.
01   FULL-NAME-INPUT          PIC X(79).
01   FULL-NAME-SIZE           PIC 99 VALUE 79.
01   NAME-POINTER             PIC 99.
01   FIRST-NAME               PIC X(50).
01   MIDDLE-NAME-1.
     05   MIDDLE-INITIAL-1     PIC X.
     05   FILLER               PIC X(49).
01   MIDDLE-NAME-2.
     05   MIDDLE-INITIAL-2     PIC X.
     05   FILLER               PIC X(49).
01   MIDDLE-NAME-3.
     05   MIDDLE-INITIAL-3     PIC X.
     05   FILLER               PIC X(49).
01   LAST-NAME                PIC X(50).
01   SUFFIX                   PIC X(50).
     88   SUFFIX-VALUE VALUE 'JR' 'SR' 'II' 'III'
                              'IV' 'V' 'ESQ' 'Jr'
                              'Sr' 'Esq'.
01   FULL-NAME-LAST-FIRST     PIC X(79).
01   FIRST-NAME-SIZE          PIC 99.
01   NUMBER-OF-NAMES          PIC 99 VALUE ZERO.

PROCEDURE DIVISION.
0001-MAIN-PARAGRAPH.
     MOVE SPACES TO FULL-NAME-INPUT.
     DISPLAY 'ENTER YOUR FULL NAME PLEASE'.
     ACCEPT FULL-NAME-INPUT.
     INSPECT FULL-NAME-INPUT REPLACING ALL '.' BY SPACE.
     MOVE 1 TO NAME-POINTER.
     INSPECT FULL-NAME-INPUT TALLYING NAME-POINTER FOR LEADING SPACES.
     MOVE SPACES TO MIDDLE-INITIAL-1 MIDDLE-INITIAL-2 MIDDLE-INITIAL-3
                    LAST-NAME SUFFIX.
     UNSTRING FULL-NAME-INPUT DELIMITED BY ALL SPACES
          INTO FIRST-NAME COUNT IN FIRST-NAME-SIZE
               MIDDLE-NAME-1
```

```
            MIDDLE-NAME-2
            MIDDLE-NAME-3
            LAST-NAME
            SUFFIX
    POINTER NAME-POINTER
    TALLYING NUMBER-OF-NAMES
    ON OVERFLOW
        DISPLAY 'WE CAN ONLY HANDLE 3 MIDDLE NAMES'
        PERFORM 0100-EXTRA-NAMES
            UNTIL NAME-POINTER > FULL-NAME-SIZE
    END-UNSTRING.
EVALUATE NUMBER-OF-NAMES
  WHEN 1
    CONTINUE
  WHEN 2
    MOVE MIDDLE-NAME-1 TO LAST-NAME
    MOVE SPACES TO MIDDLE-NAME-1
  WHEN 3
    MOVE MIDDLE-NAME-2 TO SUFFIX
    IF SUFFIX-VALUE
        MOVE MIDDLE-NAME-1 TO LAST-NAME
        MOVE SPACES TO MIDDLE-NAME-1 MIDDLE-NAME-2
    ELSE
        MOVE MIDDLE-NAME-2 TO LAST-NAME
        MOVE SPACES TO MIDDLE-NAME-2 SUFFIX
    END-IF
  WHEN 4
    MOVE MIDDLE-NAME-3 TO SUFFIX
    IF SUFFIX-VALUE
        MOVE MIDDLE-NAME-2 TO LAST-NAME
        MOVE SPACES TO MIDDLE-NAME-2 MIDDLE-NAME-3
    ELSE
        MOVE MIDDLE-NAME-3 TO LAST-NAME
        MOVE SPACES TO MIDDLE-NAME-3 SUFFIX
    END-IF
  WHEN 5
    MOVE LAST-NAME TO SUFFIX
    IF SUFFIX-VALUE
        MOVE MIDDLE-NAME-3 TO LAST-NAME
        MOVE SPACES TO MIDDLE-NAME-3
    ELSE
        MOVE SPACES TO SUFFIX
    END-IF
  WHEN 6
    IF NOT SUFFIX-VALUE
        MOVE SUFFIX TO LAST-NAME
        MOVE SPACES TO SUFFIX
    END-IF
  END-EVALUATE.
MOVE 1 TO NAME-POINTER.
```

continues

LISTING 10.1 CONTINUED

```
    MOVE SPACES TO FULL-NAME-LAST-FIRST.
    STRING LAST-NAME DELIMITED BY SPACES
           ', ' DELIMITED BY SIZE
            FIRST-NAME DELIMITED BY SPACE
        INTO FULL-NAME-LAST-FIRST
        POINTER NAME-POINTER.
    IF FIRST-NAME-SIZE = 1
       STRING '.' DELIMITED BY SIZE
         INTO FULL-NAME-LAST-FIRST
         POINTER NAME-POINTER.
    STRING SPACE DELIMITED BY SIZE
         INTO FULL-NAME-LAST-FIRST
         POINTER NAME-POINTER.
    IF MIDDLE-INITIAL-1 NOT = SPACES
       STRING MIDDLE-INITIAL-1 DELIMITED BY SIZE
            '. ' DELIMITED BY SIZE
         INTO FULL-NAME-LAST-FIRST
         POINTER NAME-POINTER.
    IF MIDDLE-INITIAL-2 NOT = SPACES
       STRING MIDDLE-INITIAL-2 DELIMITED BY SIZE
            '. ' DELIMITED BY SIZE
         INTO FULL-NAME-LAST-FIRST
         POINTER NAME-POINTER.
    IF MIDDLE-INITIAL-3 NOT = SPACES
       STRING MIDDLE-INITIAL-3 DELIMITED BY SIZE
            '. ' DELIMITED BY SIZE
         INTO FULL-NAME-LAST-FIRST
         POINTER NAME-POINTER.
    IF SUFFIX NOT = SPACES
       STRING SUFFIX DELIMITED BY SPACE
         INTO FULL-NAME-LAST-FIRST
         POINTER NAME-POINTER.
    DISPLAY 'YOUR NAME WILL BE RECORDED AS: ' FULL-NAME-LAST-FIRST.
    STOP RUN.
0100-EXTRA-NAMES.
    MOVE SUFFIX TO LAST-NAME.
    UNSTRING FULL-NAME-INPUT DELIMITED BY ALL SPACES
        INTO SUFFIX
        POINTER NAME-POINTER.
```

Even though this example has become a bit lengthy, and there are several ways to do the same thing with fewer lines of code, it is good here because of the various ways it uses the different options in UNSTRING (and STRING and INSPECT).

In this next example, I'll do some basic text manipulation to produce standard form letters.

LISTING 10.2 FORMLETR.

```
ENVIRONMENT DIVISION.
INPUT-OUTPUT SECTION.
FILE-CONTROL.
     SELECT FORM-LETTER         ASSIGN TO FORMFILE.
     SELECT INSERTION-VALUES    ASSIGN TO VALUFILE.
     SELECT ACTUAL-LETTERS      ASSIGN TO LETTERS.
DATA DIVISION.
FILE SECTION.
FD  FORM-LETTER
    LABEL RECORDS STANDARD.
01  FORM-LINE                  PIC X(150).
FD  INSERTION-VALUES
    LABEL RECORDS STANDARD.
01  VALUE-RECORD               PIC X(150).
FD  ACTUAL-LETTERS.
01  LETTER-LINE                PIC X(80).


WORKING-STORAGE SECTION.
01  VALUES-EOF-STATUS          PIC X VALUE 'N'
    88  VALUES-EOF             VALUE 'Y'.
01  FORMS-EOF-STATUS           PIC X VALUE 'N'
    88  FORMS-EOF              VALUE 'Y'.
01  FORM-LINE-SIZE             PIC 999 VALUE 150.
01  LETTER-LINE-SIZE           PIC 999 VALUE 80.
01  FORM-POINTER               PIC 999.
01  LETTER-POINTER             PIC 999.
01  VARIABLE-INFO.
    05  VARIABLE-1             PIC X(25).
    05  VARIABLE-2             PIC X(25).
    05  VARIABLE-3             PIC X(25).
    05  VARIABLE-4             PIC X(25).
    05  VARIABLE-5             PIC X(25).
    05  VARIABLE-6             PIC X(25).
01  WORK-WORD .
    05  WORK-CHAR1-2           PIC XX.
    05  FILLER                 PIC X(50).
01  WORD-SIZE                  PIC 99.


PROCEDURE DIVISION.
0100-MAIN-CONTROL.
    OPEN INPUT INSERTION-VALUES
         OUTPUT ACTUAL-LETTERS.
    PERFORM 0800-READ-INSERTION-VALUES.
    PERFORM 0200-PRODUCE-FORMS
         UNTIL VALUES-EOF.
    CLOSE INSERTION-VALUES
          ACTUAL-LETTERS.
    STOP RUN.
```

continues

LISTING 10.2 CONTINUED

```
0200-PRODUCE-FORMS.
    OPEN INPUT FORM-LETTER.
    MOVE 'N' TO FORMS-EOF-STATUS.
    PERFORM 0820-READ-FORMS-LETTER.
    MOVE 1 TO FORM-POINTER LETTER-POINTER.
    MOVE SPACES TO LETTER-LINE.
    PERFORM 0300-GENERATE-FORM
        UNTIL FORMS-EOF.
    PERFORM 0840-WRITE-LETTER-LINE.
    MOVE SPACES TO LETTER-LINE.
    WRITE LETTER-LINE AFTER ADVANCING PAGE.
    CLOSE FORM-LETTER.
    PERFORM 0800-READ-INSERTION-VALUES.


0300-GENERATE-FORM.
    IF FORM-POINTER = 1
        INSPECT FORM-LINE TALLYING FORM-POINTER FOR LEADING SPACES
        IF FORM-POINTER > 1
            IF LETTER-POINTER > 1
                PERFORM 0840-WRITE-LETTER-LINE
                MOVE SPACES TO LETTER-LINE
            END-IF
            MOVE FORM-POINTER TO LETTER-POINTER.
            MOVE SPACES TO WORK-WORD.
    UNSTRING FORM-LINE DELIMITED BY ALL SPACE
        INTO WORK-WORD COUNT IN WORD-SIZE
        POINTER FORM-POINTER.
    IF WORK-CHAR1-2 = '$$'
        PERFORM 0400-GET-VARIABLE.
    IF WORD-SIZE + LETTER-POINTER > LETTER-LINE-SIZE
        PERFORM 0840-WRITE-LETTER-LINE
        MOVE SPACES TO LETTER-LINE
        MOVE 1 TO LETTER-POINTER.
    STRING WORK-WORD DELIMITED BY ' '
        SPACE DELIMITED BY SIZE
        INTO LETTER-LINE
        POINTER LETTER-POINTER.
    IF FORM-POINTER > FORM-LINE-SIZE
        PERFORM 0820-READ-FORMS-LETTER
        MOVE 1 TO FORM-POINTER
        IF NOT FORMS-EOF AND FORM-LINE = SPACES
            AND LETTER-LINE NOT = SPACES
            PERFORM 0840-WRITE-LETTER-LINE
            MOVE SPACES TO LETTER-LINE
            MOVE 1 TO LETTER-POINTER
            PERFORM 0820-READ-FORMS-LETTER.


0400-GET-VARIABLE.
    IF WORK-WORD = '$$1'
        UNSTRING VARIABLE-1 DELIMITED BY ' '
```

```
                INTO WORK-WORD COUNT WORD-SIZE
          ELSE
          IF WORK-WORD = '$$2'
              UNSTRING VARIABLE-2 DELIMITED BY ' '
              INTO WORK-WORD COUNT WORD-SIZE
          ELSE
          IF WORK-WORD = '$$3'
              UNSTRING VARIABLE-3 DELIMITED BY ' '
              INTO WORK-WORD COUNT WORD-SIZE
          ELSE
          IF WORK-WORD = '$$4'
              UNSTRING VARIABLE-4 DELIMITED BY ' '
              INTO WORK-WORD COUNT WORD-SIZE
          ELSE
          IF WORK-WORD = '$$5'
              UNSTRING VARIABLE-5 DELIMITED BY ' '
              INTO WORK-WORD COUNT WORD-SIZE
          ELSE
          IF WORK-WORD = '$$6'
              UNSTRING VARIABLE-6 DELIMITED BY ' '
              INTO WORK-WORD COUNT WORD-SIZE.

0800-READ-INSERTION-VALUES.
    READ INSERTION-VALUES INTO VARIABLE-INFO
         AT END
              MOVE 'Y' TO VALUES-EOF-STATUS.
0820-READ-FORMS-LETTER.
    READ FORM-LETTER
         AT END
              MOVE 'Y' TO FORMS-EOF-STATUS.
0840-WRITE-LETTER-LINE.
    WRITE LETTER-LINE AFTER 1.
```

A few general comments on this program are in order. The file FORM-LETTER contains the form letter and is read once for each letter that is produced. The file INSERTION-VALUES contains the variable information that will be inserted into the form letters to tailor them to each recipient. The file contains one record of variables for each letter that is produced. The file ACTUAL-LETTERS is the file to which the finalized form letters are written for printing.

The program is driven by two main loops. The high-level loop is the paragraph 0200-PRODUCE-FORMS, which is PERFORMed from 0100-MAIN-CONTROL. This paragraph causes one form letter to be produced for each record in the INSERTION-VALUES file. It OPENs the FORM-LETTER file, reads the first record, and after some initializing, PERFORMs the 0300-GENERATE-FORM that will actually produce the form letter. After that is complete, it writes out the last line of the form letter, CLOSEs the FORM-LETTER file so that it will be ready for the next form letter, and READs the next record of variable information from the INSERTION-VALUES file.

The main work of producing the form letter is done in the looping paragraph 0300-GENERATE-FORM. It does this by extracting one word at a time from the FORM-LETTER file and inserting each word into the ACTUAL-LETTER file. As it does this, it must determine when to write lines to the ACTUAL-LETTER file, when to read new FORM-LETTER records, and when to replace specially coded words with the variable information from the VARIABLE-INFO record.

The first thing 0300-GENERATE-FORM does is check to see whether it is at the beginning of a FORM-LETTER line. If it is, INSPECT is used to determine whether the line is indented. If the line is indented, it must be the beginning of a new paragraph, so anything still to be printed from the preceding paragraph must be written, and then the amount of indentation must be transferred to the letter being written (MOVE FORM-POINTER TO LETTER-POINTER).

The next statement, which is an UNSTRING, extracts a word from the FORM-LETTER line. Notice that the COUNT phrase is used to obtain the size of that word. The word now is compared for the value '$$' in the first two character positions. This signals that the word is a variable, so the paragraph 0400-GET-VARIABLE is PERFORMed to replace the variable code with the actual value to be used in this letter. The one item to note about this paragraph is that it uses UNSTRING to replace the value of the word with the variable value obtaining its size, and that it does this with a delimiter value of a double space, which allows single spaces to be embedded in the variable information.

Before the new word can be inserted, the routine must determine whether there is room for it on the current line. Because you know the size of the word (WORD-SIZE), and the LETTER-POINTER tells the current location on the output line, the compare is easy. If there isn't enough space, the routine simply writes out the current line and starts a new one. Now STRING can be used to insert the new word.

The only thing remaining is to see whether you've used the last word from the current line of the FORM-LETTER file. If so, you read a new one and reset to its beginning. You also need to check to see whether this is a blank line, and if so, insert a blank line in the output letter and get another input line.

Although some might want to add changes and features, this program does do the job and also demonstrates how easily text manipulation can be done with COBOL.

Reference Modification (or Part Referencing)

Reference modification allows the program to manipulate pieces and parts of almost any alphanumeric field. It was introduced with the 1985 COBOL Standard, and it is specified as the following:

```
ALPHA-NUMERIC-ITEM (STARTING-CHAR-POSITION: [LENGTH])
```

The notion of how this works is pretty simple. If `YOUR-NAME` is a data name defined as `PIC X(10)` and has a value of `'JACK JONES'`, the statement `DISPLAY YOUR-NAME (4:3)` will result in `"K J"` being displayed, because `"K"` is in the fourth position and three characters beginning there were specified for the length. The statement `MOVE 'SMITH' TO YOUR-NAME (6: 5)` will change the value of `YOUR-NAME` to `'JACK SMITH'`.

Because reference modification is so inherently simple, I suspect that a lot of us old-time programmers have been a little nervous about using it. I am beginning to see it in a lot more programs because it is such a powerful tool and a very convenient facility. The rules for reference modification follow.

`alpha-numeric-item` can be almost any group- or elementary-level data item that has a `DISPLAY USAGE` (the default). Data items with `USAGE COMP`, `COMP-3`, `PACKED-DECIMAL`, and so on are *not* allowed.

When reference modification is used, it causes the temporary creation of an artificial data item, beginning at the `starting-char-position` and with an implied `PIC X(length)`.

`alpha-numeric-item` can be a numeric or numeric-edited data item, but the artificial item created for the reference modification still has an implied `PIC X` format. So be careful here, or the results might be very strange. You also should avoid `MOV`ing values `TO` a reference-modified numeric field for this very reason.

`alpha-numeric-item` cannot be the main receiving field of `STRING (alpha-num-item-3)` or the sending field of `UNSTRING (alpha-num-item-1)`, although it can be the main field being `INSPECT`ed (`alpha-num-item-1`).

`starting-char-position` must be numeric. However, it can be an arithmetic expression as well as a numeric literal or a numeric data item. When this is evaluated, it must be an integer value between 1 and the length of the alphanumeric item. Results are unspecified if the value is something else. (With most compilers, such an invalid value causes the field to be interpreted as "null," so no data is transferred.)

The starting-char-position and the : following it are required within the parentheses for reference modification. If the : is omitted, the reference modification item(s) will be interpreted as subscript instead (see Chapters 11 and 12, "Advanced Techniques Using Tables").

length also is numeric and can be a numeric literal, a numeric data item, or an arithmetic expression. It evaluates to 1 or more. length plus starting-char-position must be equal to or less than the size of alpha-numeric-item. Results are unspecified if the value is something else. (Again, most compilers are forgiving, and if the length evaluates to zero or a similar strange value, nothing will be transferred. However, if the total is greater than the size of alpha-numeric-item, the characters from the starting-char-position to the end will be used.)

length is optional. If it is not present, COBOL assumes that the remainder of the alpha-numeric-item field is to be used. This often can be handy because the program doesn't have to keep track of how many characters are left in the field.

The following are some basic examples where reference modification can come in handy.

This example is the easiest and most common use for reference modification:

```
DISPLAY 'Are you finished with this program? (Respond Yes or No please)'.
ACCEPT ANSWER.
IF ANSWER (1:1) = 'Y' OR 'y'
    STOP RUN.
```

Here, you want to use just the first character of the field.

The following example easily eliminates leading spaces from an input field as it is transferred to the output field:

```
MOVE 1 TO TALLY-CTR.
INSPECT INPUT-FIELD TALLYING TALLY-CTR FOR LEADING SPACES.
MOVE INPUT-FIELD (TALLY-CTR: ) TO OUTPUT-FIELD.
```

The following loop will extract all the numeric digits from an input field and concatenate them together into an output field:

```
MOVE SPACES TO OUTPUT-FIELD.
MOVE 1 TO OUT-CHAR-NR.
PERFORM
    VARYING IN-CHAR-NR FROM 1 BY 1
    UNTIL IN-CHAR-NR > IN-FIELD-SIZE
      IF IN-FIELD (IN-CHAR-NR:1) NUMERIC
        MOVE IN-FIELD (IN-CHAR-NR:1) TO OUT-FIELD (OUT-CHAR-NR:1)
        ADD 1 TO OUT-CHAR-NR
      END-IF
END-PERFORM.
```

The mechanism is what is important here. Notice how easy it is to loop through all the characters in a field, testing them and doing whatever processing is needed.

The example here seems like it might be fairly handy:

```
WORKING-STORAGE SECTION.
01   UPPER-CASE PIC X(26) VALUE 'ABCDEFGHIJKLMNOPQRSTUVWXYZ'.
01   LOWER-CASE PIC X(26) VALUE 'abcdefghijklmnopqrstuvwxyz'.
01   INPUT-FIELD        PIC X(80).
01   CHAR-NR            PIC 99.
01   FIELD-SIZE         PIC 99 VALUE 80.
PROCEDURE DIVISION.
0000-DEMO-PARAGRAPH.
    ACCEPT INPUT-FIELD.
    INSPECT INPUT-FIELD CONVERTING UPPER-CASE TO LOWER-CASE.
    MOVE 1 TO CHAR-NR.
    INSPECT INPUT-FIELD TALLYING CHAR-NR FOR LEADING SPACES.
    PERFORM
      UNTIL CHAR-NR > FIELD-SIZE
        INSPECT INPUT-FIELD (CHAR-NR:1) CONVERTING LOWER-CASE TO
        ➥UPPER-CASE
        INSPECT INPUT-FIELD (CHAR-NR: ) TALLYING CHAR-NR FOR CHARACTERS
            BEFORE ' '
        IF CHAR-NR NOT > FIELD-SIZE
            INSPECT INPUT-FIELD (CHAR-NR: ) TALLYING CHAR-NR FOR LEADING
            ➥SPACES
        END-IF
      END-PERFORM.
    DISPLAY INPUT-FIELD.
    STOP RUN.
```

This example first converts all the input characters to lowercase. Then it goes through and converts the first character of each word back to uppercase. Notice that I'm using only INSPECT, and even though it doesn't have a pointer facility, I'm able to work my way through the field from left to right quite nicely by using reference modification. I can reference a single character or the entire remainder of the field without having to do any special calculations.

Summary

This about covers character manipulation. Even though this is not needed in a great many business-programming situations, the tools I've covered provide ample facility to deal with these situations effectively. I'm sure there are a good variety of other applications for these tools, and this chapter hopefully has provided a good background for them. The next chapters deal with another topic that doesn't always occur on a regular basis in business programming: arrays and tables. Again, even though many programs don't have or need any tables or arrays, it is important to be able to deal with them effectively when the situation calls for it.

Tables and Arrays

In This Chapter

Tables (or arrays, in C and Pascal) are one of the powerful tools available to the programmer. They can save many lines of code and simplify your program logic. COBOL has a wealth of structures and statements that help use the full range of table-handling capabilities. I'll start with the basics and add capabilities until, by the end of the chapter, you'll be ready for about anything you're likely to see.

The Basic Table: OCCURS and Subscripts

The idea behind tables is that you have several pieces of data that you need to use. They are all the same with regard to size and structure, but they have different values. The months of the year are probably the simplest example. There are 12 of them, and we all know that the month 03 is really March. But very few of us refer to a month by its number—we call it by name. Let's jump right in and look at some code in Listing 11.1 to see how easy it is to show dates as people expect to see them.

LISTING 11.1 MONOFYR1.

```
WORKING-STORAGE SECTION.

01   COMPUTER-DATE.
     05   THIS-YEAR            PIC XX.
     05   THIS-MONTH           PIC 99.
     05   THIS-DAY             PIC XX.

01   MONTH-LIST.
     05   FILLER PIC X(30) VALUE 'January    February   March'.
     05   FILLER PIC X(30) VALUE 'April      May        June'.
     05   FILLER PIC X(30) VALUE 'July       August     September'.
     05   FILLER PIC X(30) VALUE 'October    November   December'.
01   MONTH-TABLE REDEFINES MONTH-LIST.
     05   MONTH-NAME OCCURS 12 TIMES PIC X(10).

PROCEDURE DIVISION.

0100-SHOW-THE-MONTH.
     ACCEPT COMPUTER-DATE FROM DATE.
     DISPLAY MONTH-NAME (THIS-MONTH) THIS-DAY ', ' THIS-YEAR.
     STOP RUN.
```

This is about as easy as it gets! Only two new items are needed to make this work the way you want. First, the MONTH-NAME OCCURS line does exactly what you would want and expect. It defines the memory space for 12 iterations of the data item named MONTH-NAME, and each of them is 10 characters long. Second, the DISPLAY MONTH-NAME (THIS-

MONTH) line identifies which of the 12 MONTH-NAME iterations you want to reference by placing the numerical data item (THIS-MONTH) in parentheses right afterward. The data item referenced in parentheses is called the *subscript*. In this example, THIS-MONTH is the subscript. That's all there is to the basic table concept in COBOL!

> **NOTE**
>
> You might want to change the ACCEPT statement in this program so that you can enter the values for the date. This way, you can see what happens for dates other than whatever the current date happens to be when you work with this chapter.

You might notice a few quirks about this example, and I'll get to them shortly. But first, take a look at some basic details to see how the table works in the computer.

Basic Rules and COBOL Requirements

Some basic rules and remarks follow. For this example, they're pretty simple and obvious, but as you get into more involved examples, things can get confusing if you don't keep them in mind.

- The REDEFINES is simply a means of establishing values for the 12 OCCURRENCES of MONTH-NAME. The two 01 level definitions (MONTH-LIST and MONTH-TABLE) each describe the same portion of computer memory. The total number of characters adds up to 120 for each of them. (MONTH-LIST is made up of four FILLER definitions, with each defining 30 characters. MONTH-TABLE has 12 OCCURRENCES of 10 characters each.) Notice that when you use the VALUE clause to initialize the table, they must be in the first 01 level definition. You'll see some other ways of getting the values you need into table entries later.

- The number following the OCCURS must be a positive integer. This is because COBOL sets up the addresses for WORKING-STORAGE when it compiles the program. Some variations provide some flexibility, and you'll look at these later. In most cases, though, you'll use and see a numeric value like I've used here.

- The *subscript* must be numeric and not have any decimal positions (in other words, it must be an integer). If you use a data item with a PIC X or PIC 9V9 type of definition for a subscript, you'll get a compile error. Some compilers allow you to use a PIC S9 definition, but obviously, you don't ever want a negative value for a subscript when attempting to reference a table entry.

- When the program references a table item, the subscript must be between 1 and the number of occurrences defined for the table. If it isn't, the result is undefined. With some compilers, the program is terminated with an error message. With others, some sort of address still is calculated, but where it is cannot be predicted, and the program obviously can behave strangely if this occurs. The simple rule of thumb is to know your data. If the data is coming from user input, it must be edited properly so that an improper value cannot be entered. If the value is calculated or comes from another program, it can be assumed to be valid after the programs have been validated. If you've changed your program so that you can enter the dates you want, try entering some invalid values for the month to see what your compiler and program do with them.

  A data name that has a subscript also can be qualified, and the characters within it can be specified, using reference modification. When this is done, the subscript is specified after the qualification and before any reference modification. If MONTH-NAME also is defined in another record, for example, and you want to use only the first three characters of the month's name, you would use MONTH-NAME OF MONTH-TABLE (THIS-MONTH) (1:3).

- You easily can reference the whole table by using the data name MONTH-TABLE (or optionally, MONTH-LIST, in this example). Obviously, you don't want to include a subscript here and will get a compile diagnostic if you do. You also will get a compile diagnostic if you do not specify a subscript when referencing MONTH-NAME.

Storing and Referencing Tables

COBOL sets up tables in memory and references them pretty much as all the languages do, even though they often call them *arrays* instead. First, take a look at all the names of the months in memory as they are defined in the MONTH-LIST structure. You'll start at an arbitrary beginning memory address of 1000 (see Figure 11.1).

Notice how the J in January is located at memory address 1000, the a is at 1001, the n is at 1002, and so on. The F in February is located at 1010, and the M in March is located at 1020. You might notice that I've listed the months on three lines, which do not correspond to the four FILLER items in the listing. I can do this because the FILLER items are contiguous, and the memory addresses that are the important factors will be the same in either case. Figure 11.2 shows you how the same characters at the same memory locations can be seen differently through the redefining template with the OCCURS clause in MONTH-TABLE.

FIGURE 11.1.

Names of the months in memory (MONTH-LIST).

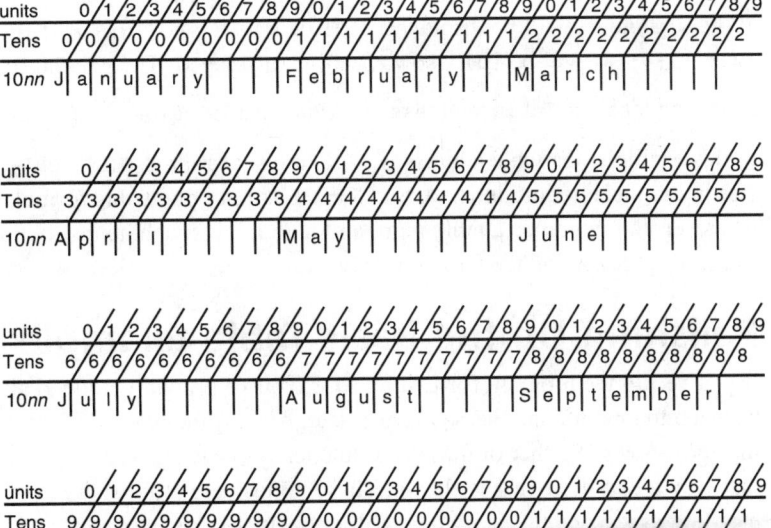

FIGURE 11.2.

Names of the months in memory (MONTH-TABLE).

	0	1	2	3	4	5	6	7	8	9
100n	J	a	n	u	a	r	y			
101n	F	e	b	r	u	a	r	y		
102n	M	a	r	c	h					
103n	A	p	r	i	l					
104n	M	a	y							
105n	J	u	n	e						
106n	J	u	l	y						
107n	A	u	g	u	s	t				
108n	S	e	p	t	e	m	b	e	r	
109n	O	c	t	o	b	e	r			
110n	N	o	v	e	m	b	e	r		
111n	D	e	c	e	m	b	e	r		

See where each occurrence of MONTH-NAME begins. Notice that the M of the name May begins at memory address 1040 in both figures. However, in Figure 11.2, you can see where COBOL can make a pretty simple calculation to determine the beginning of any MONTH-NAME, regardless of the value of THIS-MONTH. The formula for this example follows:

```
Starting address = 1000 + ((THIS-MONTH value - 1) * 10)
```

So, if THIS-MONTH is 1, (THIS-MONTH - 1) will be zero, and 1000 + (0*10) will be 1000, so January will be displayed. If THIS-MONTH is 5, (THIS-MONTH - 1) will be 4, and 1000 + (4*10) will be 1040, so May will be displayed. The general formula follows:

```
Start address = Table address + ((Subscript value - 1) * OCCURS size)
```

In this example, the table address is 1000, the subscript is THIS-MONTH, and the OCCURS size in the table definition is 10. So COBOL simply plugs this formula into the program wherever you reference a table item, and with a few machine instructions, the program can readily determine the table item you want.

Polishing Up the Basic Table Example

If you've run the program for Listing 11.1, you've probably noticed all the spaces between the month and the day of the date. Also, if the day is before the 10th, the leading zero shows. Neither of these is aesthetically pleasing. You also might have noticed that only a two-digit year is shown. These items were purposely left out so that the table-handling aspects could easily be highlighted. It is fairly easy to fix up the program. Listing 11.2 uses character-manipulation features to fix up the output. It also introduces a feature that COBOL calls the *intrinsic function* to fix up the year. Intrinsic functions are covered in detail in Chapter 15, "Specialty Features."

LISTING 11.2   MONOFYR2.

```
WORKING-STORAGE SECTION.

01   COMPUTER-DATE.
     05   THIS-YEAR              PIC XXXX.
     05   THIS-MONTH             PIC 99.
     05   THIS-DAY               PIC XX.
     05   FILLER                 PIC X(13).

01   MONTH-LIST.
     05   FILLER PIC X(30) VALUE 'January    February   March'.
     05   FILLER PIC X(30) VALUE 'April      May        June'.
     05   FILLER PIC X(30) VALUE 'July       August     September'.
     05   FILLER PIC X(30) VALUE 'October    November   December'.
01   MONTH-TABLE REDEFINES MONTH-LIST.
     05   MONTH-NAME OCCURS 12 TIMES PIC X(10).

01   DISPLAY-AREA              PIC X(40) VALUE SPACES.
01   POSITION-NUMBER           PIC 99    VALUE 1.

PROCEDURE DIVISION.
```

```
0100-SHOW-THE-MONTH.
    MOVE FUNCTION CURRENT-DATE TO COMPUTER-DATE.
    STRING MONTH-NAME (THIS-MONTH) DELIMITED BY SPACE
        ' ' DELIMITED BY SIZE
        INTO DISPLAY-AREA
        POINTER POSITION-NUMBER.
    IF THIS-DAY (1:1) = '0'
        STRING THIS-DAY (2:1) DELIMITED BY SIZE
            INTO DISPLAY-AREA
            POINTER POSITION-NUMBER
    ELSE
        STRING THIS-DAY DELIMITED BY SIZE
            INTO DISPLAY-AREA
            POINTER POSITION-NUMBER
    END-IF.
    STRING ', ' DELIMITED BY SIZE
        THIS-YEAR DELIMITED BY SIZE
        INTO DISPLAY-AREA
        POINTER POSITION-NUMBER.
    DISPLAY DISPLAY-AREA.
    STOP RUN.
```

The first statement in the PROCEDURE DIVISION references the intrinsic function
CURRENT-DATE. It simply stores the current date (and time) into the field COMPUTER-DATE
in a new format that includes the full four-digit year. The FILLER portion of the
COMPUTER-DATE definition actually has the time stored in it, but I have not given it a
name because it isn't needed by this program. The details of this, as well as the many
other intrinsic functions, are covered in Chapter 16.

This problem with the display of the year can be solved in fewer lines by using reference
modification with the DISPLAY-AREA, and it's a good exercise to convert this program to
work that way. I chose to use the STRING statement because it makes it very clear what
I'm doing. This is also the form you're most likely to see in existing programs.

Program It Yourself

The program now shows the date nicely, beginning at the left margin. However, in
numerous cases, you might want the date to be right-justified or flush with the right margin. The headings of form letters and reports are some obvious examples. Use your skills
gained from the character-manipulation chapters to construct a new version of the program that will do this. MONOFYR3 on the program disc/CD-ROM shows one way of
doing this.

Accumulating Totals: An Example Using PERFORM...VARYING

The listing that follows is an example of one of the most common uses of tables in business data processing. I'll use it and build on it to introduce a variety of features available with COBOL.

The premise of the program is that you own a company with several divisions or teams that order supplies or services from a number of other companies with which you have continuing contracts. The input data is in order by a code for the company you're ordering from and a product/service code for the specific item being ordered. The primary purpose of the program is to create the consolidated order for each of the companies. However, you also need to report the total count and amount of orders submitted by each of the organizations in your company. This is where you'll introduce tables to make your life easier.

I'd like to remark here that while this example is for purchase orders submitted and organizations submitting them, the same scenario applies to just about every programming environment. Payroll and company organization, sales orders and sales teams, inventory used and by what team, and insurance policies and agencies are just a few environments I have seen.

When looking at Listing 11.3, you'll notice that the definition and logic for producing the consolidated orders has been left out, even though they are the whole purpose for the program. The reason is that it takes many more lines than the portion you are concerned with and therefore would detract from the material being presented. I have left remark stubs so that you can see where and how the report will fit into the finished program.

LISTING 11.3 SEARCH1.

```
0010   ENVIRONMENT DIVISION.
0020   INPUT-OUTPUT SECTION.
0030   FILE-CONTROL.
0040       SELECT ORDERS-SUBMITTED   ASSIGN TO ORDFILE.
0050 *     SELECT COMPANY-ORDERS     ASSIGN TO ORDRPRT.
0060       SELECT ORDER-SUMMARY      ASSIGN TO ORDSUMM.
0070   FILE SECTION.
0080   FD  ORDERS-SUBMITTED
0090       LABEL RECORDS STANDARD.
0100   01  ORDER-RECORD.
0110       05  ORD-COMPANY           PIC X(10).
0120       05  ORD-ITEM-CODE         PIC X(10).
0130       05  ORD-ITEM-NAME         PIC X(30).
```

```
0140        05   ORD-ITEM-COUNT        PIC 9(5).
0150        05   ORD-ITEM-RATE         PIC 9(6)V99.
0160        05   ORD-ITEM-DATE         PIC X(8).
0170        05   ORD-RECIPIENT         PIC 9(5).
0180
0190 *FD   COMPANY-ORDERS.
0200  FD   ORDER-SUMMARY
0210           LABEL RECORDS STANDARD.
0220  01   ORDER-SUMMARY-LINE       PIC X(132).
0230
0240  WORKING-STORAGE SECTION.
0250  01   INPUT-EOF-CONTROL          PIC XXX VALUE 'NO '.
0260     88   END-OF-INPUT                     VALUE 'YES'.
0270
0280  01   COMPUTER-DATE.
0290        05   THIS-YEAR             PIC 9999.
0300        05   THIS-MONTH            PIC 99.
0310        05   THIS-DAY              PIC XX.
0320        05   FILLER                PIC X(13).
0330
0340  01   MONTH-LIST.
0350        05   FILLER PIC X(30) VALUE 'January    February   March'.
0360        05   FILLER PIC X(30) VALUE 'April      May        June'.
0370        05   FILLER PIC X(30) VALUE 'July       August     September'.
0380        05   FILLER PIC X(30) VALUE 'October    November   December'.
0390  01   MONTH-TABLE REDEFINES MONTH-LIST.
0400        05   MONTH-NAME OCCURS 12 TIMES PIC X(10).
0410
0420  01   ORG-SUB                    PIC 99       COMP.
0421  01   TOTAL-COUNT                PIC 9(5)     COMP VALUE ZERO.
0422  01   TOTAL-AMOUNT               PIC 9(8)V99 COMP VALUE ZERO.
0430  01   DIVISION-NAME-LIST.
0440        05   FILLER PIC X(30) VALUE 'FIRST SHIFT ASSEMBLY LINE'.
0450        05   FILLER PIC X(30) VALUE 'SECOND SHIFT ASSEMBLY LINE'.
0460        05   FILLER PIC X(30) VALUE 'EAST REGION SALES OFFICE'.
0470        05   FILLER PIC X(30) VALUE 'WEST REGION SALES OFFICE'.
0480        05   FILLER PIC X(30) VALUE 'TECHNICAL SUPPORT DIVISION'.
0490        05   FILLER PIC X(30) VALUE 'ADMINISTRATIVE DIVISION'.
0500        05   FILLER PIC X(30) VALUE 'MANAGEMENT STAFF'.
0510  01   DIVISION-NAME-TABLE REDEFINES DIVISION-NAME-LIST.
0520        05   DIVISION-NAME OCCURS 7 TIMES PIC X(30).
0530  01   DIVISION-TOTALS-TABLE.
0540        05   DIVISION-TOTAL-ENTRY OCCURS 7 TIMES.
0550           10   DIVISION-COUNT     PIC 9(5)     COMP.
0560           10   DIVISION-AMOUNT    PIC 9(8)V99 COMP.
0570
0580 *01   COMPANY-ORDER-DEFINITIONS.
0590
0600  01   SUMMARY-TITLE.
0610        05   FILLER                    PIC X(20) VALUE SPACES.
```

continues

LISTING 11.3 CONTINUED

```
0620        05  FILLER                    PIC X(38) VALUE
0630            'COMPANY ORDER SUMMARY BY DIVISION FOR '.
0640        05  SUM-TITLE-DATE            PIC X(16) VALUE SPACES.
0650   01  SUMMARY-HEADING.
0660        05  FILLER                    PIC X(50) VALUE
0670            '                        ORGANIZATION NAME'.
0680        05  FILLER                    PIC X(10) VALUE ' COUNT'.
0690        05  FILLER                    PIC X(13) VALUE '        AMOUNT'.
0700   01  SUMMARY-DETAIL.
0710        05  FILLER                    PIC X(20) VALUE SPACES.
0720        05  SUM-DTL-NAME              PIC X(30).
0730        05  FILLER                    PIC X(5)  VALUE SPACES.
0740        05  SUM-DTL-COUNT             PIC ZZ,ZZ9.
0750        05  FILLER                    PIC X(5)  VALUE SPACES.
0760        05  SUM-DTL-AMOUNT            PIC ZZ,ZZZ,ZZ9.99.
0770
0780   PROCEDURE DIVISION.
0790
0800   0100-MAIN-CONTROL.
0810        MOVE FUNCTION CURRENT-DATE TO COMPUTER-DATE.
0810        SUBTRACT 1 FROM THIS-MONTH.
0820        IF THIS-MONTH = ZERO
0830            MOVE 12 TO THIS-MONTH
0840            SUBTRACT 1 FROM THIS-YEAR.
0850        STRING MONTH-NAME (THIS-MONTH) DELIMITED BY SPACE
0860          ' ' DELIMITED BY SIZE
0870          THIS-YEAR DELIMITED BY SIZE
0880          INTO SUM-TITLE-DATE.
0890
0900        INITIALIZE DIVISION-TOTALS-TABLE.
0910
0920        OPEN INPUT ORDERS-SUBMITTED.
0930 *      OPEN OUTPUT COMPANY-ORDERS.
0940        PERFORM 0500-READ-ORDER.
0950        PERFORM 0200-MAIN-LOOP
0960            UNTIL END-OF-INPUT.
0970        CLOSE ORDERS-SUBMITTED.
0980 *      CLOSE COMPANY-ORDERS.
0990
1000        OPEN OUTPUT ORDER-SUMMARY.
1010        WRITE ORDER-SUMMARY-LINE FROM SUMMARY-TITLE
1020            AFTER ADVANCING 1 LINE.
1030        WRITE ORDER-SUMMARY-LINE FROM  SUMMARY-HEADING
1040            AFTER ADVANCING 2 LINES.
1050        MOVE SPACES TO ORDER-SUMMARY-LINE.
1060        WRITE ORDER-SUMMARY-LINE
1070            AFTER ADVANCING 2 LINES.
1080        PERFORM 0300-PRINT-SUMMARY
1090            VARYING ORG-SUB FROM 1 BY 1
```

```
1100            UNTIL ORG-SUB > 7.
1101       MOVE 'GRAND TOTAL' TO   SUM-DTL-NAME.
1102       MOVE TOTAL-COUNT TO   SUM-DTL-COUNT.
1103       MOVE   TOTAL-AMOUNT TO   SUM-DTL-AMOUNT.
1104       WRITE ORDER-SUMMARY-LINE FROM SUMMARY-DETAIL
1105           AFTER ADVANCING 3 LINES.
1110       CLOSE ORDER-SUMMARY.
1120       STOP RUN.
1130
1140   0200-MAIN-LOOP.
1150 *     PERFORM 0250-FORMAT-ORDER-LINE.
1160       ADD 1 TO DIVISION-COUNT (ORD-RECIPIENT).
1170       COMPUTE DIVISION-AMOUNT (ORD-RECIPIENT)
1171           = DIVISION-AMOUNT (ORD-RECIPIENT)
1180           + (ORD-ITEM-COUNT * ORD-ITEM-RATE).
1190       PERFORM 0500-READ-ORDER.
1200 *0250-FORMAT-ORDER-LINE.
1210   0300-PRINT-SUMMARY.
1211       ADD DIVISION-COUNT (ORG-SUB) TO TOTAL-COUNT.
1212       ADD DIVISION-AMOUNT (ORG-SUB) TO TOTAL-AMOUNT.
1220       MOVE DIVISION-NAME (ORG-SUB) TO SUM-DTL-NAME.
1230       MOVE DIVISION-COUNT (ORG-SUB) TO SUM-DTL-COUNT.
1240       MOVE DIVISION-AMOUNT (ORG-SUB) TO SUM-DTL-AMOUNT.
1250       WRITE ORDER-SUMMARY-LINE FROM SUMMARY-DETAIL
1260           AFTER ADVANCING 2 LINES.
1270   0500-READ-ORDER.
1280       READ ORDERS-SUBMITTED
1290           AT END
1300               MOVE 'YES' TO INPUT-EOF-CONTROL.
```

As you look at this program, you'll notice that there really isn't too much here that hasn't already been covered. But there are some things that look a bit different, and I would like to comment on them. In general, you can see where the program does its initialization at lines 810 through 940, does its main processing of the input file in `0200-MAIN-LOOP`, where it updates the totals for the appropriate organization at lines 1160 through 1180, and prints out the summary totals at lines 1000 through 1100.

Introductory Comments on Accumulating Totals

At lines 540 through 560, notice how the separate totals are elementary items and that the definition containing the OCCURS clause is really a group-level alphanumeric item. This is perfectly fine and is commonly done in COBOL programs. Hence, you have multiple occurrences of a data structure. There are also other things that I'll get to later.

Notice how `DIVISION-TOTALS-TABLE` is set to zero values by the `INITIALIZE` statement at line 900. By design, it will move `ZERO` to each data name for each occurrence, so it works out pretty nicely, even though `DIVISION-COUNT` and `DIVISION-AMOUNT` are defined with USAGE COMPUTATIONAL (COMP). It also will work for COMP-3. If the fields were not COMP, the statement MOVE ZEROES TO DIVISION-TOTALS-TABLE. also would have worked (at least on most machines). In fact, I could have just added a VALUE ZEROES to the definition for DIVISION-TOTALS-TABLE at line 530.

In many existing programs, you'll see code like the following to initialize tables. This is because the INITIALIZE statement was not available until the 85 COBOL Standard came out, and the code is pretty much guaranteed for all situations:

```
PERFORM XXXX-CLEAR-TABLE
        VARYING ORG-SUB FROM 1 BY 1
        UNTIL ORG-SUB > 7.
      .
      .
      .
    XXXX-CLEAR-TABLE.
     MOVE ZERO TO DIVISION-COUNT (ORG-SUB)
                  DIVISION-AMOUNT (ORG-SUB).
```

PERFORM...VARYING

Notice the PERFORM...VARYING in the preceding code and at lines 1080 through 1100 in Listing 11.3. Even though it isn't actually a part of tables, I'll discuss it here because its real value comes in controlling loops that work with tables. VARYING works exactly as you would expect. ORG-SUB is set to 1 at the beginning, and the UNTIL condition is tested before the paragraph is performed. It then is incremented by 1 before the UNTIL condition is tested in subsequent iterations of the loop. In general, the VARYING, FROM, and BY variables can all be data names (or expressions), but they all must be numeric. They do not have to reference the subscript used in the PERFORM paragraph, although in most cases, they will.

Some Additional Comments and Items for Thought

Notice that the DIVISION-COUNT, DIVISION-AMOUNT, and ORG-SUB are all defined as COMP (computational usage). This is because they are all primarily used in arithmetic- or table-referencing statements and therefore can take advantage of improved machine efficiency. It's generally a good habit to get into, although I suspect that on most modern machines, you will not notice any real difference in program execution time, whether or not you use COMP. On IBM mainframes, COMP-3 generally is used instead of COMP.

The COMPUTE statement at lines 1170 through 1180 shows how numeric items in a table can be used just like any other numeric items.

MONTH-TABLE also is included in this program, although you're using it slightly differently here.

In most programs, you'll see all the OPEN statements together in the initialization and all the CLOSE statements together in the close-out portion. I didn't do it that way here. There is a premise in structured programming that items that are logically and functionally related should be kept together. That is why the ORDERS-SUBMITTED file is closed when the program finishes processing its records, and the ORDER-SUMMARY file isn't opened until the program is ready to start writing records to it.

The definitions for DIVISION-NAME-LIST, SUMMARY-TITLE, and SUMMARY-HEADING take full advantage of the fact that COBOL always left-justifies and space-fills alphanumeric fields with literal data. This is a personal preference and seems to work more easily for me when setting up and making maintenance changes to reports in COBOL.

You might have noticed that there is no logic for page breaks in the summary report. They aren't needed at this time because only seven organizations currently exist in the company, and I've learned over the years that it is not a good idea to put in code for changes that might happen later—too many other things can happen between now and then.

Some Table-Related Items to Consider

Look carefully at the table definitions at lines 430 through 560. The names and totals are in separate tables. I've done this as a matter of convenience because it is easier to initialize the totals that way. It is only necessary to keep the names in the same positions as the numbers that refer to them. But that brings to mind the question of what happens if the names and numbers are not in the same position. Or, more likely, what happens if there is a gap in the numbers, as is likely to happen in the real world.

As shown in Listing 11.3, it is important that all the numbers in the input data be between 1 and 7, because otherwise, the program could do some seriously unpredictable things. In this case, you're getting data from another program and may assume that the organization numbers have been edited properly.

Another item for consideration is that rarely do you see an organization in which organizations and identifiers are strictly numeric values. You need to have a mechanism for dealing with this. The next section introduces the SEARCH statement, which is just the tool you need. You'll also deal with other concerns.

Indexes and the SET Statement

Now, forget the assumption that the organization number (ORD-RECIPIENT) must be a number between 1 and 7. In fact, it can be any combination of five characters. The only restriction is that the code for any organization cannot be changed without letting you know ahead of time. The program can be changed to handle this without too much trouble, and you'll use the SEARCH statement to do this. But first, you need to make some changes to your table definition for DIVISION-NAME-TABLE (and associated DIVISION-NAME-LIST) and introduce the index data type. The new table definition follows:

```
0430   01  DIVISION-NAME-LIST.
0440       05  FILLER PIC X(35) VALUE 'ASM01FIRST SHIFT ASSEMBLY LINE'.
0450       05  FILLER PIC X(35) VALUE 'ASM02SECOND SHIFT ASSEMBLY LINE'.
0460       05  FILLER PIC X(35) VALUE 'SAL01EAST REGION SALES OFFICE'.
0470       05  FILLER PIC X(35) VALUE 'SAL02WEST REGION SALES OFFICE'.
0480       05  FILLER PIC X(35) VALUE 'DIV01TECHNICAL SUPPORT DIVISION'.
0490       05  FILLER PIC X(35) VALUE 'DIV01ADMINISTRATIVE DIVISION'.
0500       05  FILLER PIC X(35) VALUE 'STAFFMANAGEMENT STAFF'.
0501       05  FILLER PIC X(5)  VALUE HIGH-VALUES.
0502       05  FILLER PIC X(30) VALUE 'UNKNOWN ORGANIZATION'.
0510   01  DIVISION-NAME-TABLE REDEFINES DIVISION-NAME-LIST.
0520       05  DIVISION-ENTRY OCCURS 8 TIMES
0521           INDEXED BY DIV-IX.        .
0522           10  DIVISION-CODE      PIC X(5).
0523           10  DIVISION-NAME      PIC X(30).
0530   01  DIVISION-TOTALS-TABLE.
0540       05  DIVISION-TOTAL-ENTRY OCCURS 8 TIMES.
0550           10  DIVISION-COUNT     PIC 9(5)    COMP.
0560           10  DIVISION-AMOUNT    PIC 9(8)V99 COMP.
```

You'll also change lines 170 and 1100 now so that you don't miss them later. The new lines follow:

```
0170       05  ORD-RECIPIENT       PIC X(5).
```

and

```
1100           UNTIL ORG-SUB > 8.
```

There are a number of changes here, so I'll mention them and then describe and define the index entry.

Comments on Changes to the Example for Indexes

Line 170 was changed from PIC 9(5) to PIC X(5) so that alphanumeric codes can be used instead of just numbers.

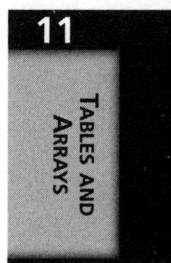

Each of the lines from 440 through 500 has been increased by five characters. By looking at the VALUE clause, you can see that this represents the new code assigned to each organization in the company.

A new eighth row has been added to the table at lines 501 and 502. Although it isn't clear how it will be used yet, it appears that you'll be identifying and accumulating totals for cases in which the ORD-RECIPIENT value does not match any that you have in your table. Note that the FILLER definition has been separated into two items so that you can value the code with HIGH-VALUES. By doing this, you can be pretty well assured that no record will ever have an ORD-RECIPIENT value matching your assigned code.

The OCCURS entry on line 520 has been increased from 7 to 8 to handle the new entry in the table. Note that the OCCURS at line 540 also has been increased to 8 so that you can accumulate totals for records that do not match any of the codes in the table. The UNTIL condition at line 1100 also has been increased from 7 to 8 so that the counts and amounts for any unrecognized organizations will be shown on the report.

Line 520 also has been changed to a group-level entry (DIVISION-ENTRY) so that the new DIVISION-CODE and DIVISION-NAME can be defined below it.

Now, look at line 521 where your new index, DIV-IX, is defined. That's right, it is *defined* in the 05 level definition for DIVISION-ENTRY. An *index* is a form of subscript that is actually a relative memory address. Its sole purpose is to efficiently reference data entries in COBOL tables that have been defined with the OCCURS clause. It does not have its own level. Furthermore, it does not have a PIC clause because it is really a memory address kind of data item and is set up specifically for the table established by the OCCURS clause for DIVISION-ENTRY.

COBOL Rules for Indexes

Because of the unique way an index is defined, a number of special rules apply.

The index is defined expressly to reference the data item established by the OCCURS clause (and any data items defined subordinate to it). So you can reference DIVISION-ENTRY (DIV-IX) or DIVISION-CODE (DIV-IX) or DIVISION-NAME (DIV-IX). However, the index *cannot* be used to reference data in another table established by a different OCCURS clause. So DIVISION-COUNT (DIV-IX) is *not* allowed.

Several indexes can be defined for the same table. Simply add the other index names to the INDEXED BY clause (for example, INDEXED BY DIV-IX DIV-IX2 DI-IY).

An index can be used by itself on either side of the comparison operator in a conditional statement. So the clause UNTIL DIV-IX > 8 will work exactly as you would expect. It also can be used like this in IF statements, although it isn't done very often. When indexes are used this way, the address is converted to the relative table occurrence number before the comparison is made. It makes sense that the value on the other side of the condition will resolve to some sort of positive number.

When indexes are used on both sides of the comparison, their values are compared directly. So IF DIV-IX = DIV-IX2 would give the kind of result you would expect. But if you define DIV-T-IX in the OCCURS clause for the DIVISION-TOTAL-ENTRY, the statement IF DIV-IX = DIV-T-IX will not give predictable results (some compilers may handle this like you would want, but the result is not guaranteed by the COBOL Standard).

Indexes *cannot* be used in arithmetic statements. Indexes cannot be used in ADD, SUBTRACT, MULTIPLY, DIVIDE, or COMPUTE. They also cannot be used in an arithmetic expression. So UNTIL DIV-IX + 1 > ORG-SUB is *not* allowed, but UNTIL DIV-IX > ORG-SUB - 1 is allowed. Remember that this rule applies only to indexes and not to the data items in the tables they reference. So if you define DIV-T-IX as an index for DIVISION-TOTAL-ENTRY, you can do arithmetic on DIV-COUNT (DIV-T-IX) or DIV-AMOUNT (DIV-T-IX) just as you would want.

There are only three ways to change the value of an index: the VARYING clause in the PERFORM statement, the SEARCH statement, and the SET statement. The VARYING clause is easy to describe. This means simply that you can say PERFORM 0300-PRINT-SUMMARY VARYING DIV-IX FROM 1 BY 1 UNTIL DIV-IX > 8. Note that this doesn't necessarily do all you want, because DIV-IX cannot be used to reference DIV-COUNT or DIV-AMOUNT. The next section defines how you can use SET to modify index values. The SEARCH statement is treated as a topic on its own.

The SET Statement

The value for an index normally is established with the statement SET *index* TO *positive integer*. *Positive integer* refers to an occurrence number within the table. It can be a numeric literal, a data name, or an arithmetic expression. The value must be an integer, be greater than or equal to zero, and not be greater than the number of occurrences in the table. You'll use SET DIV-IX TO 1 later.

The relative occurrence number associated with an index value can be converted to a regular number with the statement SET *data-name* TO *index*. Here, the data name is an elementary numeric item. The index value will be converted to a positive integer that corresponds to the occurrence number the index points to, and the data name will be set to that value.

SET *index-1* TO *index-2* also is allowed. This is how you convert the relative occurrence number in one table to the same relative occurrence number in another table. Hence, if you define DIV-T-IX as an index in the OCCURS clause for DIVISION-TOTAL-ENTRY, the statement `SET DIV-T-IX TO DIV-IX` will convert the address value for `DIV-IX` to the correct occurrence number and then convert that to the proper address for `DIV-T-IX`.

Index values can be modified with `SET` statements of the form `SET` *index* `UP BY` *integer value* or `SET` *index* `DOWN` by *integer value*. In this case, the integer value can be negative because the final value of the index is what must be equal to or greater than zero and not the amount of the increment or decrement. Note here that you cannot `SET` an index `UP` or `DOWN` by another index.

Some Final Comments Regarding Indexes

Before getting into the `SEARCH` statement, I'd like to make a few final comments about indexes.

You can define an index with its own level number. So the statement `01 SAVE-IX USAGE INDEX.` is valid. However, this isn't very helpful because you cannot reference any table items with `SAVE-IX`. It can be used to save the values of indexes defined elsewhere, but this is seldom done because it is easier to just define multiple indexes in the `OCCURS` clause for the table.

Although indexes store values in memory in an address type of format, they are *not* actual addresses, so don't think of them in the same way you would a C pointer variable. Remember that an index is relevant only to the table for which it is defined.

Indexes originally were defined in COBOL to provide an efficient means for referencing data in tables. However, with modern hardware and software, the added efficiency is hardly ever noticeable. In most new programs, regular numeric data items are defined and used as subscripts to reference table data. This is just as easy and doesn't have the inherent limitations of indexes.

Indexes are required for `SEARCH` statements. That, and the fact that they exist in a lot of older programs, is why they are covered.

The SEARCH Statement

The `SEARCH` statement is a direct means of looking at the entries in a table and finding the one that matches the value for which you're looking. Such a statement is not available in most other languages. There are a number of requirements for using `SEARCH`, but first look at the new version of `0200-MAIN-LOOP`, which incorporates the `SEARCH` into the sample program:

```
1140  0200-MAIN-LOOP.
1150 *    PERFORM 0250-FORMAT-ORDER-LINE.
1151      SET DIV-IX TO 1.
```

```
1152      SEARCH DIVISION-ENTRY
1153         AT END
1154            MOVE 8 TO ORG-SUB
1155         WHEN ORD-RECIPIENT = DIVISION-CODE (DIV-IX)
1156            SET ORG-SUB TO DIV-IX.
1160      ADD 1 TO DIVISION-COUNT (ORG-SUB).
1170      COMPUTE DIVISION-AMOUNT (ORG-SUB)
1171         = DIVISION-AMOUNT (ORG-SUB)
1180         + (ORD-ITEM-COUNT * ORD-ITEM-RATE).
1190      PERFORM 0500-READ-ORDER.
```

I've inserted lines 1151 through 1156. Line 1151 sets the initial value of DIV-IX at 1, and lines 1152 through 1156 are the SEARCH statement itself. Lines 1160, 1170, and 1171 have been changed to use ORG-SUB as the subscript instead of ORD-RECIPIENT. Those are the only changes I've made. The code reads pretty easily and looks like it will do what you want, but let's review it briefly before getting into the rules and options for SEARCH.

Analysis of the Example

First, you set DIV-IX to the value 1. SEARCH does *not* initialize the index(s) it uses, so you must assume that it has the initial value you want. This is easy to forget, and you can spend hours trying to figure out why the program is acting unpredictably when you do forget it (I have).

The (only) argument of SEARCH is the data name with the OCCURS clause.

The AT END clause allows you to do something if the value you're looking for is not found. In this case, you're setting ORG-SUB to 8, which corresponds to the entry that will contain values for UNKNOWN or unrecognized organizations.

The WHEN clause is where you tell SEARCH which values to compare. In this case, you want the occurrence number where the DIVISION-CODE matches the ORD-RECIPIENT defined in your input record.

The way the statement works is pretty basic and is what you would want. It first checks the value of DIV-IX to make sure that it refers to an occurrence in the table (if not, it does any statements in the AT END clause and exits the SEARCH statement). Next, it evaluates the WHEN condition (if it is true, it does the statements in there and exits the SEARCH statement). Finally (if neither of these things occurs) it increments DIV-IX by 1 occurrence and repeats the loop.

Notice that in both conditions, you establish values for ORG-SUB and then use it to update the values for DIVISION-COUNT and DIVISION-AMOUNT. You cannot use DIV-IX because it was defined for the DIVISION-ENTRY table and can reference only data names defined there.

The Rules for the SEARCH Statement

Now let's review the rules and options available with SEARCH.

Remember that SEARCH does *not* initialize the value for DIV-IX. The program must establish this value by some other means. Note that this is different for the SEARCH ALL statement, which is described later.

The AT END clause is optional, but if it is used, it *must precede* the WHEN clause. The compile error message you get if it is placed after the WHEN is consistently one of the most obscure set of words compiler writers can come up with.

The condition following the WHEN can be any conditional statement. It does not even have to reference anything in the table being SEARCHed. This is also different in the SEARCH ALL, which is discussed later.

Multiple WHEN clauses are allowed for SEARCH. When this option is used, the first one that results in a true condition terminates the SEARCH. (Because of this and the earlier rule, I've seen programmers use SEARCH with multiple WHENs for a sort of CASE structure before EVALUATE was introduced in the 85 Standard. It's certainly not a good thing to do because it's both confusing and inefficient. But it did work and probably still exists in some programs.)

END-SEARCHcan be used to terminate the SEARCH, and it's probably a good idea to use it because it is explicit, especially if there are multiple WHENs or the SEARCH is part of a conditional statement.

> **NOTE**
>
> There is no NOT-WHEN or WHEN OTHER. AT END provides that functionality.

SEARCH...VARYING

A VARYING clause is available with SEARCH. If you use it, or if you have more than one index defined in the OCCURS for the table being SEARCHed, the following rules are important. Note that if neither of these situations applies, the one and only index defined for the table will be updated as the SEARCH proceeds.

If VARYING is *not* used, but multiple indexes are defined in the OCCURS clause, the *first* one defined is the one that is updated as the SEARCH proceeds.

VARYING is used as SEARCH table-name VARYING name, where name is an index name or a numeric data name. If the name is an index name and is defined in the OCCURS for the table being searched, it is the index that will be used for the SEARCH process, regardless of which index is defined first.

If the VARYING name is an index name but isn't defined for the table being searched, the *first index* defined for the table being SEARCHed *will be used* for the SEARCH. But the VARYING index-name *also will be updated* at the same time and by the same amount as the SEARCH index.

If the VARYING name is a numeric data name, the first index defined for the table being SEARCHed will be used for the SEARCH. But the data name will be incremented by 1 whenever the SEARCH index is incremented.

A Search Alternative

As a final note on SEARCH, experienced programmers already may have observed that PERFORM VARYING can be used to accomplish essentially the same thing as SEARCH. The following shows how PERFORM VARYING could be used in the program:

```
1140   0200-MAIN-LOOP.
1150 *     PERFORM 0250-FORMAT-ORDER-LINE.
1152       PERFORM
1153         VARYING DIV-IX
1154           FROM 1 BY 1
1155         UNTIL ORG-RECIPIENT = DIVISION-CODE (DIV-IX)
1156           OR DIV-IX > 7
1157         CONTINUE
1158       END-PERFORM.
1159       SET ORG-SUB TO DIV-IX.
1160       ADD 1 TO DIVISION-COUNT (ORG-SUB).
1170       COMPUTE DIVISION-AMOUNT (ORG-SUB)
1171           = DIVISION-AMOUNT (ORG-SUB)
1180           + (ORD-ITEM-COUNT * ORD-ITEM-RATE).
1190       PERFORM 0500-READ-ORDER.
```

Each alternative takes about the same amount of code, each is probably about as efficient as the other, and each can be seen about as often as the other in existing programs. I generally prefer using SEARCH for this, though, because it more clearly describes what I'm trying to do.

Initializing Tables from External Data and OCCURS...DEPENDING ON

There is another enhancement that you'll want to add to your program. There are very few companies that go very long without growing and adding organizations, reorganizing the existing structure, or just changing their names. The way the program currently is written, it will have to be modified every time one of these changes occurs. You can add some additional logic to initialize the table names and codes from an external datafile or database table. Note that initializing a table in WORKING-STORAGE from a database table and using it often is preferable to reading from the database table throughout the program, because it is usually more efficient, especially if the database table is available for online updating.

Changes in the Data Division

Although almost all the additional code has been covered already, I will show an additional option with the OCCURS clause that will allow you to handle variations in the number of organizations in the company without having to alter the program.

First, you need to set up a new file that will contain all the names and codes of the organizations in the company:

```
0030   FILE-CONTROL.
0031       SELECT ORGANIZATION-LIST   ASSIGN TO ORGLIST.
0040       SELECT ORDERS-SUBMITTED    ASSIGN TO ORDFILE.
0050 *     SELECT COMPANY-ORDERS      ASSIGN TO ORDRPRT.
0060       SELECT ORDER-SUMMARY       ASSIGN TO ORDSUMM.
0070   FILE SECTION.
0071   FD  ORGANIZATION-LIST
0072       LABEL RECORDS STANDARD.
0073   01  ORGANIZATION-RECORD.
0074       05  ORG-CODE           PIC X(5).
0075       05  ORG-NAME           PIC X(30).
0080   FD  ORDERS-SUBMITTED
```

This has been done at lines 31 and 71 through 75. These end-of-file control values also are set up and added at lines 261 and 262:

```
0261   01  ORGANIZATION-EOF-CONTROL   PIC XXX VALUE 'NO '.
0262       88  END-OF-ORGANIZATIONS             VALUE 'YES'.
```

You'll also need to change your definition of the DIVISION-NAME-TABLE:

```
0419   01  ORG-LIMIT            PIC 99       COMP VALUE 50.
0420   01  ORG-SUB              PIC 99       COMP.
0421   01  TOTAL-COUNT          PIC 9(5)     COMP VALUE ZERO.
0422   01  TOTAL-AMOUNT         PIC 9(8)V99  COMP VALUE ZERO.
0510   01  DIVISION-NAME-TABLE.
0519       05  DIVISION-ENTRY OCCURS 1 TO 50 TIMES
0520           DEPENDING ON ORG-LIMIT
0521           INDEXED BY DIV-IX.
0522           10  DIVISION-CODE    PIC X(5).
0523           10  DIVISION-NAME    PIC X(30).
0530   01  DIVISION-TOTALS-TABLE.
0540       05  DIVISION-TOTAL-ENTRY OCCURS 50 TIMES.
0550           10  DIVISION-COUNT   PIC 9(5)     COMP.
0560           10  DIVISION-AMOUNT  PIC 9(8)V99  COMP.
```

Notice that the DIVISION-NAME-LIST has been removed. Because these values will be established during the program execution, initial values in WORKING-STORAGE aren't required. There are a number of differences in the OCCURS clause at lines 519 and 520. Instead of saying OCCURS 8 TIMES, the clause now states OCCURS 1 TO 50 TIMES DEPENDING ON ORG-LIMIT. Comments and rules regarding them follow.

Even though the 1 TO 50 indicates that the number of occurrences will be variable, COBOL will set up enough memory for all 50 of them, and any of the 50 can be referenced by the program.

Even though the number of occurrences in memory will remain constant at 50, the new data name ORG-LIMIT will determine how many of the occurrences should be considered active or valid. ORG-LIMIT is defined at line 419.

The real value of setting up ORG-LIMIT and the OCCURS this way is that SEARCH now will use ORG-LIMIT to determine the maximum number of occurrences in the table. You will not need to change it at all for it to work as you would like.

The number of occurrences in DIVISION-TOTALS-TABLE has been increased to 50. The form of the OCCURS has not been changed, though; you don't need to change it because there won't be any SEARCH statements used with it.

Changes for the Procedure Division

Now let's look at the code that will initialize the table. It will be inserted after line 880:

```
0881
0882        OPEN INPUT ORGANIZATION-LIST.
0883        READ ORGANIZATION LIST
0884            AT END
0885                MOVE 'YES' TO ORGANIZATION-EOF-CONTROL.
0886        PERFORM
0887            VARYING ORG-LIMIT FROM 1 BY 1
0888            UNTIL ORG-LIMIT > 49
0889                OR END-OF-ORGANIZATIONS
0890                MOVE ORG-CODE TO DIVISION-CODE (ORG-LIMIT)
0891                MOVE ORG-NAME TO DIVISION-NAME (ORG-LIMIT)
0892                READ ORGANIZATION-LIST
0893                    AT END
0894                        MOVE 'YES' TO ORGANIZATION-EOF-CONTROL
0895            END-PERFORM.
0896        CLOSE ORGANIZATION-LIST.
0897        MOVE HIGH-VALUES TO DIVISION-CODE (ORG-LIMIT).
0898        MOVE 'UNKNOWN ORGANIZATION' TO DIVISION-NAME (ORG-LIMIT).
0899
```

Observe how the READ loop automatically will increment the ORG-LIMIT and value the appropriate occurrence of the table with the input values of the organization CODE and NAME. When the loop terminates, the value of ORG-LIMIT will be 1 greater than the number of records read and inserted into the table. You'll use that occurrence to accumulate any unrecognized codes from the main input file.

Notice also what happens if there are 50 or more organization records. The program will quit reading these records after 49 of them have been moved to the table. The fiftieth occurrence will be set up for unrecognized organizations, and any codes that would have matched records 50 and beyond will be accumulated here. The recipient of the report should notice this and notify the programming staff, and the program should be modified as needed. The way these situations should be handled will vary from place to place, but they need to be addressed. Otherwise, the program will likely fail eventually, and some programmer will get called in the middle of the night to deal with the problem.

Two final changes are needed to complete the enhancements.

At line 1154, ORG-SUB needs to be set to the value of ORG-LIMIT instead of 8 in the AT END clause of the SEARCH statement:

```
1154          MOVE ORG-LIMIT TO ORG-SUB
```

At line 1100, the UNTIL is changed from 8 to ORG-LIMIT so that all the entries are included in the summary report:

```
1100          UNTIL ORG-SUB > 8.
```

The SEARCH ALL Statement

The final topic to cover with this example is the SEARCH ALL statement. As background for this example, assume that your company has been very successful and has increased in size so that it now has 40 organizations in it. It has been suggested that the program efficiency can be improved by converting the SEARCH statement to SEARCH ALL.

Remember that the SEARCH statement starts at the beginning of the table (assuming that the index has been set there) and increments through every occurrence until the WHEN condition is satisfied or the end of the table is reached. SEARCH ALL, on the other hand, presumes that the table is in a predefined sequence and, beginning in the middle of the table, employs the binary search algorithm and finds the matching value (or determines that there is no matching value) with only a minimal number of compares.

The everyday analogy is looking someone's number up in the telephone book. Because you know the spelling of the person's last name, and you know that the phone book is in alphabetical order, you don't have to begin on page 1 and read everyone's name to find the name you want. Instead, you flip through pages at a time until you find the first letter of the last name and then continue a few pages at a time until you find the page with the person's last name.

SEARCH ALL functions the same way. It compares the entry in the middle of the table with the value being looked for. If this entry is greater, it then compares the entry in the middle of the first half of the table; if the entry is not greater, it compares to the entry in the middle of the last half of the table. Based on that compare, it again looks at the middle of the relevant portion of the table. The process of finding the middle of a portion of the table and comparing it continues until a match is found or it reaches the point where the portion of the table is only one occurrence in size and it does not match the value for which you are searching.

Changes Needed for SEARCH ALL

Now let's see what changes are needed to use SEARCH ALL in the program.

The records in the file ORGANIZATION-LIST must be in sequence by the ORG-CODE field. Assume that this has been taken care of by utility SORT software.

The clause ASCENDING KEY DIVISION-CODE needs to be inserted in the OCCURS for DIVISION-ENTRY between 520 and 521.

The statement SET DIV-IX TO 1. at line 1151 can be deleted because the SEARCH software will determine the initial value.

The SEARCH DIVISION-ENTRY statement at line 1152 will be changed to SEARCH ALL DIVISION-ENTRY. The ALL is what invokes the binary searching software.

At line 1155, the WHEN condition needs to be reversed from WHEN ORD-RECIPIENT = DIVISION-CODE (DIV-IX) to WHEN DIVISION-CODE (DIV-IX) = ORD-RECIPIENT. This is because COBOL has very specific requirements for the WHEN condition, and one of those is that the data name specified in the KEY phrase in the OCCURS clause has to be on the left side of the equal (=) sign.

These are the only changes needed. Notice that there are only two noticeable changes in the program's operation. The first is that the file ORGANIZATION-LIST has to be sorted into sequence by the ORG-CODE value. The second is that the program will run more quickly.

Rules for the SEARCH ALL Statement

There are a number of rules and specifications for SEARCH ALL:

- The sequence of the table is specified by using ASCENDING/DESCENDING KEY data-name in the OCCURS clause. The data name must be the one used for the OCCURS entry or one defined at a level below the entry with the OCCURS clause. The data name is specified without a subscript here as would normally be required elsewhere in the program.

- Multiple data names and KEY clauses can be used here, but in all cases, they must conform to the preceding rule. If more than one is used, the order they appear in defines the table sequence. In other words, the first data name is the highest-order sequence key and the last one is the lowest-order key.

- If the entries are *not* in the sequence defined by the ASCENDING/DESCENDING KEY clause(s), the results of the SEARCH ALL are unspecified. In other words, the AT END path may be taken, even if there is a matching occurrence.

- If all the data names specified in the KEY clauses compare equal for two entries in the table, which of them is matched by the SEARCH ALL statement is *not* predetermined.

- The VARYING clause is not allowed in the SEARCH ALL statement. The first (or only) index specified in the OCCURS clause always will be used.

- Only one WHEN clause is allowed in the SEARCH ALL. The rules regarding it are very specific and may seem a little peculiar at first; they attempt to ensure a construction that will match the KEY phrase defined in the OCCURS clause. In almost all cases, the WHEN will be pretty much like the sample program.

- The WHEN clause can use only the equal (=) operation.

- The identifier on the left of the = can be a data name or a condition name. But in either case, the identifier *must* reference the (or one of the) data names specified in the KEY phrase of the OCCURS clause. The identifier also *must* use the first (or only) index name defined in that OCCURS clause. If a condition name is used, it must have exactly one value.

- The identifier on the right of the = essentially can be anything that can be compared to the identifier on the left with these limitations. It *must not* include any of the data names included in the KEY phrase of the OCCURS clause and it *must not* include the index name being used in the SEARCH.

- The AND can be used in the WHEN (OR is *not* allowed). When it is used, the conditional following it must conform to the previous rules. This is the mechanism used to reference other data names from the KEY phrase if more than one was specified.

There are two things to remember about the WHEN clause. The first is that it needs to identify the data names that were used to order (or sort) the entries in the table and to specify what each of them is to be compared with in order to match the appropriate occurrence. The other thing to remember is that the items in the table are referenced on the left of the =, and the items they are compared to are on the right of the =.

TIP

The final question you might ask is when to use SEARCH and when to use SEARCH ALL. Regarding the efficiency of the statement itself, the rule of thumb I generally use follows: If there are fewer than 25 entries in the table, the additional overhead of the binary SEARCH ALL software is too great for the relatively few items in the table. If there are more than 50 items, SEARCH ALL will be more efficient. For values between 25 and 50, the call could go either way, depending on a number of factors.

Of course, there is the larger question of when you even need to worry about efficiency. With the speed of modern CPUs (mainframe and PC), you don't really need to be concerned about most batch or report programs. On the other hand, I've seen numerous batch programs in which the time could be reduced from hours to minutes and online or PC screen programs in which wait times could be eliminated by a simple change here.

Updated Listing of Sample Program

Listing 11.4 is the final sample program; it incorporates all the changes made in the course of this chapter.

LISTING 11.4   SEARCH2.

```
0010    ENVIRONMENT DIVISION.
0020    INPUT-OUTPUT SECTION.
0030    FILE-CONTROL.
0031        SELECT ORGANIZATION-LIST    ASSIGN TO ORGLIST.
0040        SELECT ORDERS-SUBMITTED     ASSIGN TO ORDFILE.
0050 *      SELECT COMPANY-ORDERS       ASSIGN TO ORDRPRT.
0060        SELECT ORDER-SUMMARY        ASSIGN TO ORDSUMM.
0065
0070    FILE SECTION.
0071    FD  ORGANIZATION-LIST
```

```
0072        LABEL RECORDS STANDARD.
0073    01  ORGANIZATION-RECORD.
0074        05   ORG-CODE          PIC X(5).
0075        05   ORG-NAME          PIC X(30).
0076
0080    FD  ORDERS-SUBMITTED
0090        LABEL RECORDS STANDARD.
0100    01  ORDER-RECORD.
0110        05   ORD-COMPANY       PIC X(10).
0120        05   ORD-ITEM-CODE     PIC X(10).
0130        05   ORD-ITEM-NAME     PIC X(30).
0140        05   ORD-ITEM-COUNT    PIC 9(5).
0150        05   ORD-ITEM-RATE     PIC 9(6)V99.
0160        05   ORD-ITEM-DATE     PIC X(8).
0170        05   ORD-RECIPIENT     PIC X(5).
0180
0190   *FD  COMPANY-ORDERS.
0200    FD  ORDER-SUMMARY
0210         LABEL RECORDS STANDARD.
0220    01  ORDER-SUMMARY-LINE     PIC X(132).
0230
0240    WORKING-STORAGE SECTION.
0250    01  INPUT-EOF-CONTROL          PIC XXX VALUE 'NO '.
0260        88  END-OF-INPUT                    VALUE 'YES'.
0261    01  ORGANIZATION-EOF-CONTROL  PIC XXX VALUE 'NO '.
0262        88  END-OF-ORGANIZATIONS            VALUE 'YES'.
0270
0280    01  COMPUTER-DATE.
0290        05   THIS-YEAR         PIC 9999.
0300        05   THIS-MONTH        PIC 99.
0310        05   THIS-DAY          PIC XX.
0320        05   FILLER            PIC X(13).
0330
0340    01  MONTH-LIST.
0350        05   FILLER PIC X(30) VALUE 'January   February   March'.
0360        05   FILLER PIC X(30) VALUE 'April     May        June'.
0370        05   FILLER PIC X(30) VALUE 'July      August     September'.
0380        05   FILLER PIC X(30) VALUE 'October   November   December'.
0390    01  MONTH-TABLE REDEFINES MONTH-LIST.
0400        05   MONTH-NAME OCCURS 12 TIMES PIC X(10).
0410
0419    01  ORG-LIMIT                 PIC 99      COMP VALUE 50.
0420    01  ORG-SUB                   PIC 99      COMP.
0421    01  TOTAL-COUNT               PIC 9(5)    COMP VALUE ZERO.
0422    01  TOTAL-AMOUNT              PIC 9(8)V99 COMP VALUE ZERO.
0517    01  DIVISION-NAME-TABLE.
0518        05  DIVISION-ENTRY OCCURS 1 TO 50 TIMES
0519            DEPENDING ON ORG-LIMIT
0520            ASCENDING KEY DIVISION-CODE
0521            INDEXED BY DIV-IX.
```

continues

LISTING 11.4   CONTINUED

```
0522            10  DIVISION-CODE       PIC X(5).
0523            10  DIVISION-NAME       PIC X(30).
0530    01  DIVISION-TOTALS-TABLE.
0540        05  DIVISION-TOTAL-ENTRY OCCURS 50 TIMES.
0550            10  DIVISION-COUNT      PIC 9(5)     COMP.
0560            10  DIVISION-AMOUNT     PIC 9(8)V99 COMP.
0570
0580 *01  COMPANY-ORDER-DEFINITIONS.
0590
0600    01  SUMMARY-TITLE.
0610        05  FILLER                  PIC X(20) VALUE SPACES.
0620        05  FILLER                  PIC X(38) VALUE
0630            'COMPANY ORDER SUMMARY BY DIVISION FOR '.
0640        05  SUM-TITLE-DATE          PIC X(16) VALUE SPACES.
0650    01  SUMMARY-HEADING.
0660        05  FILLER                  PIC X(50) VALUE
0670            '                         ORGANIZATION NAME'.
0680        05  FILLER                  PIC X(10) VALUE ' COUNT'.
0690        05  FILLER                  PIC X(13) VALUE '        AMOUNT'.
0700    01  SUMMARY-DETAIL.
0710        05  FILLER                  PIC X(20) VALUE SPACE.
0720        05  SUM-DTL-NAME            PIC X(30).
0730        05  FILLER                  PIC X(5)  VALUE SPACES.
0740        05  SUM-DTL-COUNT           PIC ZZ,ZZ9.
0750        05  FILLER                  PIC X(5)  VALUE SPACES.
0760        05  SUM-DTL-AMOUNT          PIC ZZ,ZZZ,ZZ9.99.
0770
0780 PROCEDURE DIVISION.
0790
0800    0100-MAIN-CONTROL.
0810        MOVE FUNCTION CURRENT-DATE TO COMPUTER-DATE.
0815        SUBTRACT 1 FROM THIS-MONTH.
0820        IF THIS-MONTH = ZERO
0830            MOVE 12 TO THIS-MONTH
0840            SUBTRACT 1 FROM THIS-YEAR.
0850        STRING MONTH-NAME (THIS-MONTH) DELIMITED BY SPACE
0860          ' ' DELIMITED BY SIZE
0870          THIS-YEAR DELIMITED BY SIZE
0880          INTO SUM-TITLE-DATE.
0881
0882        OPEN INPUT ORGANIZATION-LIST.
0883        LIST
0884
READ ORGANIZATION-LIST
   AT END
      MOVE 'YES' TO ORGANIZATION-EOF-CONTROL.
0886        PERFORM
0887            VARYING ORG-LIMIT FROM 1 BY 1
0888            UNTIL ORG-LIMIT > 49
0889                OR END-OF-ORGANIZATIONS
0890                MOVE ORG-CODE TO DIVISION-CODE (ORG-LIMIT)
```

```
        MOVE ORG-NAME TO DIVISION-NAME (ORG-LIMIT)
        READ ORGANIZATION-LIST
            AT END
                MOVE 'YES' TO ORGANIZATION-EOF-CONTROL
        END-READ
0892
0893
0894
0895        END-PERFORM.
0896        CLOSE ORGANIZATION-LIST.
0897        MOVE HIGH-VALUES TO DIVISION-CODE (ORG-LIMIT).
0898        MOVE 'UNKNOWN ORGANIZATION' TO DIVISION-NAME (ORG-LIMIT).
0890
0900        INITIALIZE DIVISION-TOTALS-TABLE.
0910
0920        OPEN INPUT ORDERS-SUBMITTED.
0930 *     OPEN OUTPUT COMPANY-ORDERS.
0940        PERFORM 0500-READ-ORDER.
0950        PERFORM 0200-MAIN-LOOP
0960            UNTIL END-OF-INPUT.
0970        CLOSE ORDERS-SUBMITTED.
0980 *     CLOSE COMPANY-ORDERS.
0990
1000        OPEN OUTPUT ORDER-SUMMARY.
1010        WRITE ORDER-SUMMARY-LINE FROM SUMMARY-TITLE
1020            AFTER ADVANCING 1 LINE.
1030        WRITE ORDER-SUMMARY-LINE FROM SUMMARY-HEADING
1040            AFTER ADVANCING 2 LINES.
1050        MOVE SPACES TO ORDER-SUMMARY-LINE.
1060        WRITE ORDER-SUMMARY-LINE
1070            AFTER ADVANCING 2 LINES.
1080        PERFORM 0300-PRINT-SUMMARY
1090            VARYING ORG-SUB FROM 1 BY 1
1100            UNTIL ORG-SUB > ORG-LIMIT.
1101        MOVE 'GRAND TOTAL' TO  SUM-DTL-NAME.
1102        MOVE TOTAL-COUNT TO SUM-DTL-COUNT.
1103        MOVE   TOTAL-AMOUNT TO SUM-DTL-AMOUNT.
1104        WRITE ORDER-SUMMARY-LINE FROM SUMMARY-DETAIL
1105            AFTER ADVANCING 3 LINES.
1110        CLOSE ORDER-SUMMARY.
1120        STOP RUN.
1130
1140   0200-MAIN-LOOP.
1150 *     PERFORM 0250-FORMAT-ORDER-LINE.
1152        SEARCH ALL DIVISION-ENTRY
1153            AT END
1154                MOVE ORG-LIMIT TO ORG-SUB
1155            WHEN DIVISION-CODE (DIV-IX) = ORD-RECIPIENT
1156                SET ORG-SUB TO DIV-IX.
1160        ADD 1 TO DIVISION-COUNT (ORG-SUB).
```

continues

Listing 11.4 CONTINUED

```
1170        COMPUTE DIVISION-AMOUNT (ORG-SUB)
1171            = DIVISION-AMOUNT (ORG-SUB)
1180            + (ORD-ITEM-COUNT * ORD-ITEM-RATE).
1190        PERFORM 0500-READ-ORDER.
1200 *0250-FORMAT-ORDER-LINE.
1205
1210   0300-PRINT-SUMMARY.
1211        ADD DIVISION-COUNT (ORG-SUB) TO TOTAL-COUNT.
1212        ADD DIVISION-AMOUNT (ORG-SUB) TO TOTAL-AMOUNT.
1220        MOVE DIVISION-NAME (ORG-SUB) TO SUM-DTL-NAME.
1230        MOVE DIVISION-COUNT (ORG-SUB) TO SUM-DTL-COUNT.
1240        MOVE DIVISION-AMOUNT (ORG-SUB) TO SUM-DTL-AMOUNT.
1250        WRITE ORDER-SUMMARY-LINE FROM SUMMARY-DETAIL
1260            AFTER ADVANCING 2 LINES.
1265
1270   0500-READ-ORDER.
1280        READ ORDERS-SUBMITTED
1290            AT END
1295            MOVE 'YES' TO INPUT-EOF-CONTROL.
```

One final comment on this example is that the paragraph 0100-MAIN-CONTROL has become rather large. But even though it is large, it still reads pretty easily to me. Notice how the carefully placed blank lines separate the major portions of the paragraph. Also, care is taken so that the related statements are kept together. A single comment or title line surrounded by blank lines is another way to help readability.

Another obvious option is to break the paragraph up into several smaller ones, and the obvious choices of names for the new paragraphs are 0110-INITIAL and 0900-FINAL. However, I am hesitant to do that with paragraphs of this size and smaller. The reason is that these paragraphs have a tendency to get separated, and then the continuity of logic flow is lost. The way this program is laid out now, you can browse the first three or four screens of the PROCEDURE DIVISION and have a very good idea of what the program is all about. This is important to me and is something you should strive for when writing programs.

Summary

With SEARCH ALL, almost everything involving tables and arrays in COBOL has been covered. The material in this chapter deals with just about every situation you're likely to encounter. The situations simply will be variations and extensions of the structures defined here. The next chapter will take array- and table-handling a step further and give you an indication of some of the many things you can accomplish with this powerful tool.

Advanced Techniques Using Tables

This chapter examines several extensions to the concepts covered in the Chapter 11, "Tables and Arrays." Several examples are presented to show more of the range of programming problems and how you can deal with them effectively by using table-handling techniques.

Multidimensional Tables

A multidimensional table is established when the OCCURS clause is specified in the data definition at a level subordinate to another data definition that also has an OCCURS clause. This is essentially nesting one OCCURS within another. Observe the following lines of code:

```
01   ROW-NR                              PIC 99 VALUE 12.
01   COL-NR                              PIC 99 VALUE 33.
01   DISPLAY-SCREEN.
     05   SCREEN-LINE OCCURS 24 TIMES.
          10   SCREEN-CHAR OCCURS 80 TIMES PIC X.
```

This definition does exactly what you would expect. There are 24 occurrences of SCREEN-LINE (which is exactly the same as the table definitions in Chapter 12), and *each* occurrence of SCREEN-LINE contains 80 occurrences of SCREEN-CHAR.

Referencing the data is also as you would expect. DISPLAY-SCREEN references the entire table and all 1,920 characters defined in it. SCREEN-LINE (ROW-NR) references the twelfth occurrence (or row) and all 80 characters defined in it. Referencing a specific value of SCREEN-CHAR is new and requires the use of two subscripts. It looks pretty much like you would expect, though:

```
SCREEN-CHAR (ROW-NR COL-NR)
```

This will reference character 33 of the twelfth row of the table. Notice that the first subscript in the parentheses specifies the SCREEN-LINE, and the second subscript specifies the SCREEN-CHAR within SCREEN-LINE.

The general rule for referencing data in multidimensional tables is that the far left subscript identifies the highest-level occurrence definition in the table. The following subscripts identify successively lower-level occurrence definitions, until the rightmost subscript identifies the lowest-level occurrence definition that corresponds to the data name used as the identifier (SCREEN-CHAR, in this example).

COBOL permits you to define up to seven dimensions for a table. That is, you can specify up to seven OCCURS clauses in data definitions of successively lower levels of the same table definition. The programming situation requiring this kind of table would be extremely rare. I haven't seen a case where more than three levels were used. Note that the 1974 Standard only requires that up to three dimensional tables be available.

Now I'll expand this example to a program that you can tinker with a bit. It's a good example because it is pretty easy to visualize, the code is short, and the results are readily apparent. (If you're working in a batch environment, the results will appear on a system output file that generally is readily available.)

```
WORKING-STORAGE SECTION.
01   ROW-NR                            PIC 99 VALUE 1.
01   COL-NR                            PIC 99 VALUE 1.
01   CTR                          PIC 9  VALUE ZERO.
01   DISPLAY-SCREEN                           VALUE SPACES.
     05   SCREEN-LINE OCCURS 24 TIMES.
          10   SCREEN-CHAR OCCURS 80 TIMES PIC X.
PROCEDURE DIVISION.
0000-ONLY-PARAGRAPH.
     PERFORM VARYING ROW-NR FROM 3 BY 2 UNTIL ROW-NR > 9
         PERFORM VARYING COL-NR FROM 12 BY 2 UNTIL COL-NR > 18
             ADD 1 TO  CTR
             MOVE  CTR TO SCREEN-CHAR (ROW-NR COL-NR).

     PERFORM VARYING ROW-NR FROM 1 BY 1 UNTIL ROW-NR > 24
         DISPLAY SCREEN-LINE (ROW-NR).
     STOP RUN.
```

Observe how the following block of digits appears:

```
1 2 3 4
5 6 7 8
9 0 1 2
3 4 5 6
```

Work through the program logic so that you are sure how this is happening. Now reverse the first two lines in the program and see what appears. The first four lines of code should look like this:

```
     PERFORM VARYING COL-NR FROM 12 BY 2 UNTIL COL-NR > 18
         PERFORM VARYING ROW-NR FROM 3 BY 2 UNTIL ROW-NR > 9
             ADD 1 TO CTR
             MOVE CTR TO SCREEN-CHAR (ROW-NR COL-NR).
```

The results should look like this:

```
1 5 9 3
2 6 0 4
3 7 1 5
4 8 2 6
```

Observe how the count is incremented down the rows instead of across the columns. Work through why this is happening. Now, as a final example, I'll add a loop to create a diagonal mirror image of the first display. The four-line loop is inserted in the middle, and the PROCEDURE DIVISION follows:

```
0000-ONLY-PARAGRAPH.
    PERFORM VARYING ROW-NR FROM 3 BY 2 UNTIL ROW-NR > 9
        PERFORM VARYING COL-NR FROM 12 BY 2 UNTIL COL-NR > 18
            ADD 1 TO CTR
            MOVE CTR TO SCREEN-CHAR (ROW-NR COL-NR).

    PERFORM VARYING ROW-NR FROM 3 BY 2 UNTIL ROW-NR > 9
        PERFORM VARYING COL-NR FROM 12 BY 2 UNTIL COL NR > 18
            MOVE SCREEN-CHAR (ROW-NR COL-NR)
                TO SCREEN-CHAR (COL-NR ROW-NR).

    PERFORM VARYING ROW-NR FROM 1 BY 1 UNTIL ROW-NR > 24
        DISPLAY SCREEN-LINE (ROW-NR).
    STOP RUN.
```

The result should look something like this:

```
    1 2 3 4
    5 6 7 8
    9 0 1 2
    3 4 5 6
1 5 9 3
2 6 0 4
3 7 1 5
4 8 2 6
```

You should observe a few things as you work through this logic. First, notice where the COL-NR subscript is being used in the left position so that it actually will specify the SCREEN-LINE occurrence, and ROW-NR is in the right position so that it will specify the SCREEN-CHAR occurrence in that line. This is okay because both are just numbers as far as COBOL is concerned. However, 80 occurrences of SCREEN-CHAR are defined, so your programs could use values for COL-NR that are as large as 80. But if that is used to reference an occurrence of SCREEN-LINE that has only 24 occurrences defined, that will be a reference outside the defined memory for the table. This is a memory violation and, with most modern compilers, will result in the program being terminated with a more or less explanatory error message. Some compilers will allow such a reference, but that means that some other position in memory is being modified, and predicting exactly how the program will function afterward is no longer possible. Fortunately, this program does not reference any rows (or columns) beyond 24.

The second thing to observe about this program is that the ranges of values for ROW-NR (3–9) and COL-NR (12–18) do *not* overlap. This is important for this program; otherwise, the blocks of digits that are displayed would overlap each other, and the results would be very confusing.

An Example Using Multidimensional Tables

A telephone directory is a good example of when you would want to produce report pages with several columns of data, and the data is to be in sequence running down the columns. The two-dimensional table will allow you to do this easily.

LISTING 12.1   DEVELOPING A MULTIDIMENSIONAL TABLE.

```
0010   DATA DIVISION.
0020   FILE SECTION.
0030   FD   PERSONNEL-FILE
0040        LABEL RECORDS STANDARD.
0050   01   PERSONNEL-RECORD.
0060        05   INPUT-NAME               PIC X(20).
0070        05   INPUT-NUMBER             PIC X(4).
0080   FD   PHONE-LIST.
0090   01   LIST-RECORD                   PIC X(80).
0100
0110   WORKING-STORAGE SECTION.
0120   01   INPUT-EOF-STATUS              PIC XXX VALUE 'NO'.
0130      88   END-OF-FILE                        VALUE 'YES'.
0140
0150   01   COMPUTER-DATE.
0160        05   THIS-YEAR           PIC 9999.
0170        05   THIS-MONTH          PIC 99.
0180        05   THIS-DAY            PIC XX.
0190        05   FILLER              PIC X(13).
0200
0210   01   MONTH-LIST.
0220        05   FILLER PIC X(30) VALUE 'January   February   March'.
0230        05   FILLER PIC X(30) VALUE 'April     May        June'.
0240        05   FILLER PIC X(30) VALUE 'July      August     September'.
0250        05   FILLER PIC X(30) VALUE 'October   November   December'.
0260   01   MONTH-TABLE REDEFINES MONTH-LIST.
0270        05   MONTH-NAME OCCURS 12 TIMES PIC X(10).
0280
0290   01   ROW-NR                        PIC 99 VALUE 1.
0300   01   COL-NR                        PIC 99 VALUE 1.
0310   01   PHONE-NUMBERS.
0320        05   PHONE-COLUMN OCCURS 3 TIMES.
0330           10   PHONE-ENTRY OCCURS 55 TIMES.
0340              15   PHONE-NAME         PIC X(20).
0350              15   PHONE-NUMBER       PIC X(4).
0360
0370   01   DIRECTORY-TITLE.
0380        05   FILLER              PIC X(20) VALUE SPACES.
0390        05   FILLER              PIC X(40) VALUE
0400             'COMPANY TELEPHONE DIRECTORY '.
0410        05   DIR-TITLE-DATE      PIC X(20) VALUE SPACES.
0420   01   DIRECTORY-HEADING.
```

continues

LISTING 12.1 CONTINUED

```
0430      05  FILLER PIC X(27) VALUE 'NAME              NUMBER  '.
0440      05  FILLER PIC X(27) VALUE 'NAME              NUMBER  '.
0450      05  FILLER PIC X(26) VALUE 'NAME              NUMBER  '.
0460  01  DIRECTORY-DETAIL              VALUE SPACES.
0470      05  DETAIL-ENTRY OCCURS 3 TIMES.
0480          10  DET-NAME           PIC X(20).
0490          10  FILLER             PIC X.
0500          10  DET-NUMBER         PIC X(4).
0510          10  FILLER             PIC XX.
0520
0530  PROCEDURE DIVISION.
0540  0000-MAIN-CONTROL.
0550      MOVE FUNCTION CURRENT-DATE TO COMPUTER-DATE.
0560      STRING MONTH-NAME (THIS-MONTH) DELIMITED BY SPACE
0570        ' ' DELIMITED BY SIZE
0580        THIS-YEAR DELIMITED BY SIZE
0590        INTO DIR-TITLE-DATE.
0600
0610      OPEN INPUT  PERSONNEL-FILE
0620           OUTPUT PHONE-LIST.
0630      PERFORM 0600-READ-INPUT.
0640      PERFORM 0100-MAIN-LOOP
0650        UNTIL END-OF-FILE.
0660      CLOSE PERSONNEL-FILE
0670            PHONE-LIST.
0680      STOP RUN.
0690
0700  0100-MAIN-LOOP.
0705      MOVE SPACES TO PHONE-NUMBERS.
0710      PERFORM VARYING COL-NR FROM 1 BY 1
0720          UNTIL COL-NR > 3
0730            OR END-OF-FILE
0740          PERFORM 0120-LOAD-TABLE
0750            VARYING ROW-NR FROM 1 BY 1
0760            UNTIL ROW-NR > 55
0770              OR END-OF-FILE.
0780      WRITE LIST-RECORD FROM DIRECTORY-TITLE
0790        AFTER ADVANCING PAGE.
0800      WRITE LIST-RECORD FROM DIRECTORY-HEADING
0810        AFTER ADVANCING 2 LINES
0820      MOVE SPACES TO LIST-RECORD.
0830      WRITE LIST-RECORD
0840        AFTER ADVANCING 1 LINE.
0850      PERFORM VARYING ROW-NR FROM 1 BY 1
0860        UNTIL ROW-NR > 55
0870      MOVE SPACES TO DIRECTORY-DETAIL
0880        PERFORM 0140-FORMAT-ENTRY
0890          VARYING COL-NR FROM 1 BY 1
0900          UNTIL COL-NR > 3
0910        WRITE LIST-RECORD FROM DIRECTORY-DETAIL
```

```
0920              AFTER ADVANCING 1 LINE
0930         END-PERFORM.
0940
0950   0120-LOAD-TABLE.
0960       MOVE INPUT-NAME TO PHONE-NAME (COL-NR ROW-NR).
0970       MOVE INPUT-NUMBER TO PHONE-NUMBER (COL-NR ROW-NR).
0980       PERFORM 0600-READ-INPUT.
0990   0140-FORMAT-ENTRY.
1000           IF PHONE-NAME (COL-NR ROW-NR) NOT=SPACES
1010           MOVE ALL ' .' TO DET-NAME (COL-NR)
1020           STRING PHONE-NAME (COL-NR ROW-NR) DELIMITED BY ' '
1030              INTO DET-NAME (COL-NR)
1040           MOVE PHONE-NUMBER (COL-NR ROW-NR) TO DET-NUMBER (COL-NR).
1050
1060   0600-READ-INPUT.
1070      READ PERSONNEL-FILE
1080         AT END
1090            MOVE 'YES' TO INPUT-EOF-STATUS.
```

You should know several things about this program:

- When looking at the PHONE-NUMBERS table, you'll notice that three columns have been defined and that each column has 55 phone entries defined in it. This is the reverse of the DISPLAY-SCREEN table, which had 24 lines, each with 80 columns. In each case, the way the table is set up makes good sense for how it is being used. There are no exact rules regarding how to define tables. The definition simply needs to satisfy the purpose for which it is defined.

- 0100-MAIN-LOOP controls the main logic flow, and there are two major parts to it. The first part reads the PERSONNEL-FILE and moves the records into the PHONE-NUMBERS table. This continues until the table is full or there are no more records in the PERSONNEL-FILE. The second part formats and prints exactly one page of the PHONE-LIST. Even if there is only one name and number in the table, the whole page will be printed.

- Look carefully at the VARYING clauses in 0100-MAIN-LOOP. In the first part, the COL-NR is varied first, so if COL-NR equals 1, records are read and moved to each of the 55 entries in it. The next 55 records are moved into the second column, and then another 55 records are moved to the third column. In the second part, however, the ROW-NR is varied first. Therefore, the first line will contain the first entry from column 1, the first entry from column 2, and the first entry from column 3. Then the ROW-NR will be incremented so that the second entry from each column will be placed on the second line. This continues until all 55 lines are formatted and printed.

Finally, examine the nested PEFORM VARYING... statements. These are seen twice in this program and also were used in the previous example involving the screen lines and characters. Essentially, they are loops within loops, which are necessary when you need to manipulate all the entries in a multidimensional table. These programs use the inline PERFORM structure to control the looping. There are a couple of other ways to do this. The most common is to PERFORM an intermediate paragraph, which in turn PERFORMs the object paragraph. Instead of lines 850 through 930, for example, the following type of code would be used:

```
0850        PERFORM 0130-FORMAT-LINE
0860            VARYING ROW-NR FROM 1 BY 1
0860            UNTIL ROW-NR > 55.
```

Then, beginning at line 981, the new paragraph would be inserted as the following:

```
0981    0130-FORMAT-LINE.
0982        PERFORM 0140-FORMAT-ENTRY
0983            VARYING COL-NR FROM 1 BY 1
0984            UNTIL COL-NR > 3.
0985        WRITE LIST-RECORD FROM DIRECTORY-DETAIL
0986            AFTER ADVANCING 1 LINE
```

This will work just as well as the inline PERFORM, but it generally is more difficult to maintain because the loop-controlling mechanisms are separated. Over time, these mechanisms often become separated by many lines or pages. This creates much more work for the maintenance programmer to determine what looping is being done and why. The reason this mechanism is the most common is purely historic. The inline PERFORM was not a part of COBOL until the 1985 Standard and COBOL II became available, and most of the existing programs were written before then. Additionally, because the inline PERFORM is not commonly used, many programmers are not as comfortable using it.

The PERFORM VARYING...AFTER structure also will manage multiple levels of looping; it is covered in the next section.

PERFORM VARYING...AFTER

The AFTER clause of the PERFORM...VARYING statement was designed specifically to support multidimensional tables in COBOL. It pre-dates the inline PERFORM statement (which was added with the 1985 Standard) and was included in many of the earliest compilers dating back to the 1960s. Its format is fairly simple and can best be illustrated by referring back to the initial example in this chapter:

```
PERFORM
    VARYING ROW-NR FROM 3 BY 2 UNTIL ROW-NR > 9
        PERFORM VARYING COL-NR FROM 12 BY 2 UNTIL COL-NR > 18
            ADD 1 TO CTR
            MOVE CTR TO SCREEN-CHAR (ROW-NR COL-NR).
```

You can modify this code to use the VARYING... AFTER, as shown here:

```
PERFORM
     VARYING ROW-NR FROM 3 BY 2 UNTIL ROW-NR > 9
       AFTER COL-NR FROM 12 BY 2 UNTIL COL-NR > 18
         ADD 1 TO CTR
         MOVE CTR TO SCREEN-CHAR (ROW-NR COL-NR).
```

Notice how the nested inline PERFORM simply has been replaced by the word AFTER. This makes the second looping through the values for COL-NR a part of the original VARYING clause instead of an independent statement that can stand on its own.

The statement operates as you would expect. ROW-NR is set to 3, and then AFTER sets COL-NR to 12 and increments it by 2 each time the inline statements are executed until its value exceeds 18. When this occurs, ROW-NR is incremented by 2, and then (if it doesn't exceed 9) COL-NR again is set to 12 and is incremented by 2 each time the statements are executed until it (COL-NR) exceeds 18. This continues until ROW-NR exceeds 9, and then the full statement is complete.

It is important to see that multiple levels of looping and control are managed by *one* (PERFORM) statement instead of multiple, independent, nested statements.

Up to seven AFTERs can be nested under one PERFORM statement in this manner. This is related to the fact that you can have up to seven dimensional tables because COBOL allows up to seven OCCURS to be defined subordinate to each other.

I mentioned earlier that the AFTER existed in COBOL long before inline PERFORM became available. Now you'll see how that works. Look at one of the inline PERFORM structures in the telephone directory example in the previous section:

```
0710       PERFORM VARYING COL-NR FROM 1 BY 1
0720           UNTIL COL-NR > 3
0730             OR END-OF-FILE
0740           PERFORM 0120-LOAD-TABLE
0750             VARYING ROW-NR FROM 1 BY 1
0760               UNTIL ROW-NR > 55
0770                 OR END-OF-FILE.
```

This can be modified to use the AFTER:

```
0710       PERFORM 0120-LOAD-TABLE
0715           VARYING COL-NR FROM 1 BY 1
0720               UNTIL COL-NR > 3
0730                 OR END-OF-FILE
0750             AFTER ROW-NR FROM 1 BY 1
0760               UNTIL ROW-NR > 55
0770                 OR END-OF-FILE.
```

Notice how the nested inline PERFORM at line 740 has been removed and the paragraph being performed now is identified at line 710 instead. Notice also that there are no inline

12

statements for the PERFORM. Therefore, this structure will work on all compilers prior to the 1974 Standard.

Now examine the other nested inline PERFORM statement in the same example:

```
0850       PERFORM VARYING ROW-NR FROM 1 BY 1
0860           UNTIL ROW-NR > 55
0870           PERFORM 0140-FORMAT-ENTRY
0880               VARYING COL-NR FROM 1 BY 1
0890               UNTIL COL-NR > 3
0900           END-PERFORM
0910           WRITE LIST-RECORD FROM DIRECTORY-DETAIL
0920               AFTER ADVANCING 1 LINE
```

Consider how you might convert this code to use the VARYING...AFTER. It can't be done! This is because of the WRITE statement at lines 910 and 920. This is one of two statements controlled by the higher-level PERFORM at line 850 (the PERFORM at line 870 is the other). The WRITE *must* be executed each time the PERFORM at line 870 completes. The fact that the nested looping is managed by two independent statements allows this. Because AFTER manages nesting looping under the control of *one* statement, the flexibility to handle this situation is simply not there.

This situation is one of two reasons why I prefer using the inline PERFORM to control multiple loops in multidimensional tables. The other reason is simply a personal feeling that the inline PERFORM shows most clearly what is happening as the different subscripts are initialized, incremented, and tested.

OCCURS DEPENDING ON (ODO) and Variable-Sized Records

The DEPENDING ON phrase in the OCCURS clause was described in Chapter 12. However, there is a significant additional functionality provided when it is included in records that are defined in the FILE SECTION; this section addresses that functionality. First, you'll look at a sample that shows its benefits and how it is used. Then I'll provide a historical perspective and discuss its current value in programming.

Recall how the following table was defined in Chapter 11:

```
0419  01  ORG-LIMIT                  PIC 99       COMP VALUE 50.
0510  01  DIVISION-NAME-TABLE.
0519      05  DIVISION-ENTRY OCCURS 1 TO 50 TIMES
0520          DEPENDING ON ORG-LIMIT
0521          INDEXED BY DIV-IX.
0522          10  DIVISION-CODE      PIC X(5).
0523          10  DIVISION-NAME      PIC X(30).
```

The value of ORG-LIMIT is used to determine the size of the table for the purposes of the SEARCH and SEARCH ALL statements. Remember, though, that because the table is defined in WORKING-STORAGE, enough memory is defined to hold all 50 occurrences. Space for those occurrences beyond DIVISION-ENTRY (ORG-LIMIT) is there but is simply *not* considered by SEARCH or SEARCH ALL.

The key is that this table is defined in WORKING-STORAGE, which defines variables and constants in the program's memory. On the other hand, if a table of this type is defined in a record in the FILE SECTION, the situation is considerably different. Here, the record is a definition of data in a file (normally, a sequential one), and *the records can have different sizes.*

Consider a file with several million records. If the record definition can have a maximum of 50 occurrences, but the normal record only has 10 or 12, the total amount of disk or tape saved by writing only the number of occurrences required for each record is quite significant. If each occurrence requires 30 characters, and the average number of occurrences per record is 10, the savings will be 40×30 or 1200 bytes per record. If the file has 1 million records, the total savings is 1.2 billion bytes, which is a very significant amount of storage (especially three or four years ago).

Consider this programming example: Your company has a large number of salespeople, and records of each sale need to be kept so that each person's monthly commission can be determined. Each sales entry will show the sale's invoice number, the amount of the sale, the amount paid by the purchaser, and the amount credited for the preceding month's commissions. The following program calculates commissions and creates a file of commissions that will be processed by the company's accounts payable system.

LISTING 12.2 CALCULATING COMMISSIONS AND CREATING A COMMISSIONS FILE.

```
0010  DATA DIVISION.
0020  FILE SECTION
0030  FD  INPUT-SALES-FILE.
0040  01  INPUT-SALES-RECORD.
0050      05  INPSAL-SALESMAN-ID            PIC X(9).
0060      05  INPSAL-YEAR-TO-DATE-COMMIS    PIC 9(6)V99.
0070      05  INPSAL-NR-SALES               PIC 99.
0080      05  INPSA-SALES-ITEMS OCCURS 0 TO 99 TIMES
0090          DEPENDING ON INPSAL-NR-SALES.
0100          10  INPSAL-INVOICE-NR         PIC X(9).
0110          10  INPSAL-INV-AMT            PIC 9(7)V99.
0120          10  INPSAL-AMT-PAID           PIC 9(7)V99.
0130          10  INPSAL-AMT-CR-FOR-COMMIS  PIC 9(7)V99.
0140
0150  FD  OUTPUT-SALES-FILE.
0160  01  OUTPUT-SALES-RECORD.
0170      05  OUTSAL-SALESMAN-ID            PIC X(9).
0180      05  OUTSAL-YEAR-TO-DATE-COMMIS    PIC 9(6)V99.
0190      05  OUTSAL-NR-SALES               PIC 99.
0200      05  OUTSA-SALES-ITEMS OCCURS 0 TO 99 TIMES
```

continues

12

ADVANCED
TECHNIQUES
USING TABLES

LISTING 12.2   CONTINUED

```
0210                DEPENDING ON OUTSAL-NR-SALES.
0220            10  OUTSAL-INVOICE-NR        PIC X(9).
0230            10  OUTSAL-INV-AMT           PIC 9(7)V99.
0240            10  OUTSAL-AMT-PAID          PIC 9(7)V99.
0250            10  OUTSAL-AMT-CR-COMMIS     PIC 9(7)V99.
0260
0270   FD  COMMISSIONS-OWED-FILE.
0280   01  COMMIS-OWED-RECORD.
0290        05  COMMIS-SALESMAN-ID           PIC X(9).
0300        05  COMMIS-NR-ITEMS              PIC 99.
0310        05  COMMIS-AMOUNT-SUBJECT        PIC 9(7)V99.
0320        05  COMMIS-COMMISSION-AMOUNT     PIC 9(7)V99.
0330
0340   WORKING-STORAGE SECTION.
0350   01  INPUT-EOF-STATUS                  PIC XXX VALUE 'NO '.
0360        88  END-OF-INPUT                 VALUE 'YES'.
0370   01  NR-PAYING-INVOICES               PIC 99.
0380   01  TOTAL-SUBJECT-TO-COMMIS          PIC 9(7)V99.
0390   01  TOTAL-COMMISSION                 PIC 9(7)V99.
0400   01  INV-SUB                          PIC 99.
0410
0420   PROCEDURE DIVISION.
0430   0000-MAIN-CONTROL.
0440       OPEN INPUT INPUT-SALES-FILE
0450           OUTPUT OUTPUT-SALES-FILE
0460                   COMMISSIONS-OWED-FILE.
0470       PERFORM 0500-READ-SALES-FILE.
0480       PERFORM 0100-MAIN-LOOP
0490           UNTIL END-OF-INPUT.
0500       CLOSE INPUT-SALES-FILE
0510             OUTPUT-SALES-FILE
0520             COMMISSIONS-OWED-FILE.
0530       STOP RUN.
0540
0550   0100-MAIN-LOOP.
0560       MOVE ZERO TO NR-PAYING-INVOICES
0570                    TOTAL-SUBJECT-TO-COMMIS.
0580                    TOTAL-COMMISSION.
0590       MOVE INPUT-SALES-RECORD TO OUTPUT-SALES-RECORD.
0600       PERFORM 0150-ACCUMULATE-COMMISSIONS
0610           VARYING INV-SUB FROM 1 BY 1
0620           UNTIL INV-SUB > OUTSAL-NR-SALES.
0630       MOVE OUTSAL-SALESMAN-ID TO COMMIS-SALESMAN-ID.
0640       MOVE NR-PAYING-INVOICES TO COMMIS-NR-ITEMS.
0650       MOVE TOTAL-SUBJECT-TO-COMMIS TO COMMIS-AMOUNT-SUBJECT.
0660       MOVE TOTAL-COMMISSION TO COMMIS-COMMISSION-AMOUNT.
0670       WRITE COMMIS-OWED-RECORD.
0680       ADD TOTAL-COMMISSION TO OUTSAL-YEAR-TO-DATE-COMMIS.
0690       WRITE OUTPUT-SALES-RECORD.
0700       PERFORM 0500-READ-SALES-FILE.
0710
0720   0150-ACCUMULATE-COMMISSIONS.
```

```
0730            IF OUTSAL-AMT-PAID (INV-SUB) > OUTSAL-AMT-CR-COMMIS (INV-SUB)
0740               ADD 1 TO NR-PAYING-INVOICES
0750               COMPUTE TOTAL-SUBJECT-TO-COMMIS = TOTAL-SUBJECT-TO-COMMIS +
0760                  OUTSAL-AMT-PAID (INV-SUB) - OUTSAL-AMT-CR-COMMIS (INV-SUB)
0770               COMPUTE TOTAL-COMMISSION = TOTAL-COMMISSION + .07 *
0780                  (OUTSAL-AMT-PAID (INV-SUB) - OUTSAL-AMT-CR-COMMIS (INV-SUB))
0790               MOVE OUTSAL-AMT-PAID (INV-SUB) TO OUTSAL-AMT-CR-COMMIS
                   (INV-SUB).
0800        0500-READ-SALES-FILE.
0810            READ INPUT-SALES-FILE
0820               AT END
0830                  MOVE 'YES' TO INPUT-EOF-STATUS.
```

This is a normal sequential file-processing program. Several points and rules need to be described here. The rules are explicitly for using OCCURS DEPENDING ON in the FILE SECTION and are necessary to determine the record size and structure when it is read or written:

- Notice that for every record, the program loops through all the invoice occurrences; wherever something has been paid since the last commission was calculated, the program accumulates the commission information and updates the occurrence to reflect that. Observe that if there are no invoices (which is possible), the program will not go through the loop at all. It will write a commission record that reflects that zero commission was earned, however.

- The full details of the record are defined for both the input and output record definition. Although some FILLER items could be used instead, the *full* OCCURS clause and the DEPENDING ON data item *must* be defined in the record. This is necessary so that COBOL can calculate the size of the record when reading or writing it.

- The DEPENDING ON data names (INPSAL-NR-SALES and OUTSAL-NR-SALES) are defined in the records containing the OCCURS DEPENDING ON clauses. This is necessary because otherwise there would be no way to determine how many occurrences there are when the record is read. This data name also must be defined *before* the OCCURS clause; otherwise, it would not be possible to determine its location without knowing its value.

- The OCCURS DEPENDING ON level and everything subordinate to it are the last things defined in the record. There is nothing with an equal or smaller level number defined after the definition with this OCCURS clause in it. This is required because any such definitions would not be part of the OCCURS DEPENDING ON structure. But if they are defined after it, their location would be dependent on the value of the DEPENDING ON data name. This is a contradiction to both definitions and therefore is not allowed.

- Only one OCCURS DEPENDING ON definition is allowed in a record. If one were subordinate to another, the size of each of the higher defined occurrences would vary because lower defined ones would cause no end of problems. If one definition were not subordinate to the other, the preceding rule would apply to one of the definitions and disallow it.

- An OCCURS DEPENDING ON definition can contain another OCCURS clause that does not have a DEPENDING ON. In this case, the subordinate OCCURS has a constant size, so the record size can be calculated. However, an OCCURS clause *cannot* contain a subordinate OCCURS DEPENDING ON. Again, this would result in each of the higher-level occurrences having different sizes, which is not allowed.

- The maximum number of occurrences always is included in MOVE statements (or READ INTO or WRITE FROM). This is new with the 1985 Standard and avoids a number of peculiar results that did not make intuitive sense with the 1974 Standard definition. (It specified that the DEPENDING ON data name in the receiving record determined the number of occurrences that would be moved.)

- Any occurrence can be referenced by statements in the program. This is because such references are made to the program's memory and sufficient memory is always defined to hold the maximum number of occurrences. It is only when the record is read or written to (or SEARCHed) that the DEPENDING ON data name is used to determine the number of occurrences that will be processed.

When used with files, OCCURS DEPENDING ON has an interesting history. For a period of time, and in some organizations, it was (and in some cases, still is) used very extensively. In many others, it is not used at all. This warrants a few comments.

In the late 1960s and the 1970s disks, all computer memory and tape drives were at a premium. Software and compiler development also was still in its infancy, so the number of files that could be defined in a single program also was very limited. It was absolutely necessary to conserve all these elements; otherwise, the application simply would not function.

The concept of the OCCURS DEPENDING ON within the records of a file conserved all these items. Because multiple related groups of data could be combined in one record, the number of files and tape drives could be reduced, along with the extra memory needed for each additional file. Because the number of occurrences written to the output device was only the number required as specified in the DEPENDING ON data name, the total amount of disk or tape also was kept to a minimum.

This concept was used very successfully in a variety of applications. In fact, there were cases in which the entire application database was maintained in a single file. The occurrences were used to store a variety of different but related data and a series of codes used to distinguish them. The programs processing such a file needed to decode these occurrences and move the data to one of a number of different tables defined in WORKING-STORAGE before updating could take place.

Rapidly increasing disk and memory capacities during the 1980s and 1990s, as well as improved software capabilities, greatly reduced the need for efficiency mechanisms such as OCCURS DEPENDING ON. Database technology also provided both the programming mechanisms and impetus to keep data in separate files and then relate it as needed within the program.

The net result is that OCCURS DEPENDING ON is seldom, if ever, used in new applications. On the other hand, there are existing applications that use it in extremely complex and sophisticated manners.

Subscript Modification and Indirect Table Referencing

This final section covers a few features of COBOL tables that aren't used often but can be of tremendous value when the situation calls for them.

When I defined the term *subscript* in Chapter 11, I indicated that a variation existed that would be covered later. Subscript modification is that variation. This allows you to increment or decrement a subscript by an integer value when referencing an occurrence in a table. Although that increment/decrement is used to determine which occurrence in the table is to be referenced, the value of the subscript itself is *not* altered. Referring back to the first example in this chapter, if you want to copy the value of a character to the next row on the screen, the statement MOVE SCREEN-CHAR (ROW-NR COL-NR) TO SCREEN-CHAR (ROW-NR + 1 COL-NR) would do the job. The value of ROW-NR would not be changed by this statement.

Indirect table referencing is a process by which a value from one table is used as a subscript to another one. This does not involve anything new in the language, but it can be a useful technique in certain situations and merits some discussion.

I'll use an example to introduce these features. In this case, suppose that your company does telephone marketing and has a specialized computer that manages all the calls being made by the telephone solicitors. A record is written to the computer's log for each call made. In addition to the actual sales information, the record contains the solicitor's user ID, the date the call was made, and the duration of the call (in seconds). At midnight on the last day of each month, the system automatically switches to a new log file for the next month.

It is necessary to create a summary file with a record for each solicitor that shows the total calls made for each day of the month and the total time spent on those calls. This file will be downloaded to an accountant's PC to be used in a spreadsheet for a variety of purposes. There is not enough room on the disk of the telephone computer to sort the entire log for the month. Your program will run at night when calls are not being made so that there will be enough memory for a large table. However, the time available to run the program is fairly short, so the program must be pretty efficient.

LISTING 12.3 CREATING A TELEPHONE LOG.

```
0010   DATA DIVISION.
0020   FILE SECTION.
0030   FD  PHONE-LOG-FILE.
0040   01  PHONE-LOG-RECORD.
0050       05  PH-USER-ID            PIC X(8).
0060       05  PH-CALL-DATE.
0070           10  PH-CALL-YR        PIC 9999.
0080           10  PH-CALL-MO        PIC 99.
0090           10  PH-CALL-DA        PIC 99.
0100       05  PH-CALL-LENGTH        PIC 9999.
0110       05  PH-CALL-NUMBER        PIC 9(10).
0120       05  PH-SALES-INFO         PIC X(50).
0130
0140   FD  SOLICITOR-SUMMARY-FILE.
0150   01  SOLICITOR-RECORD.
0160       05  SOL-USER-ID           PIC X(8).
0170       05  SOL-DAYS-ACTIVITY OCCURS 31 TIMES.
0180           10  SOL-CALL-CT        PIC 9(4).
0190           10  SOL-CALL-TIME      PIC 9(5).
0200
0210   WORKING-STORAGE SECTION.
0220   01  INPUT-EOF-STATUS          PIC XXX VALUE 'NO '.
0230       88  END-OF-INPUT          VALUE 'YES'.
0240   01  NR-USERS                  PIC 999 COMP VALUE ZERO.
0245   01  DAY-SUB                   PIC 99  COMP VALUE ZERO.
0250   01  USER-ID-TABLE.
0260       05  USER-ID-ENTRY OCCURS   0 TO 200 TIMES
0270           DEPENDING ON NR-USERS
0275           ASCENDING KEY USER-ID
0280           INDEXED BY USR-IX USR-IX2.
0290           10  USER-ID            PIC X(8).
0300           10  USER-SUM-NR        PIC 999 COMP.
0310   01  USER-SUMMARY-TABLE.
0320       05  SUMMARY-ENTRY OCCURS 200 TIMES
0330           INDEXED BY SUM-IX.
0340           10  SUMMARY-DAY OCCURS 31 TIMES.
0350               15  SUM-COUNT      PIC 9(4).
0360               15  SUM-TIME       PIC 9(5).
0370
0380   PROCEDURE DIVISION.
0390   0100-MAIN-CONTROL.
0400       OPEN INPUT PHONE-LOG-FILE.
0410       PERFORM 0500-READ-PHONE-LOG.
0420       PERFORM 0200-INPUT-LOOP
0430           UNTIL END-OF-INPUT.
```

Advanced Techniques Using Tables

CHAPTER 12

349

12

**ADVANCED
TECHNIQUES
USING TABLES**

```
0440        CLOSE PHONE-LOG-FILE.
0450        OPEN OUTPUT SOLICITOR-SUMMARY-FILE.
0460        PERFORM 0300-WRITE-SUMMARY-RECORDS
0470            VARYING USR-IX FROM 1 BY 1
0480            UNTIL USR-IX > NR-USERS.
0490        CLOSE SOLICITOR-SUMMARY-FILE.
0500        STOP RUN.
0510
0520    0200-INPUT-LOOP.
0530        SEARCH ALL USER-ID-ENTRY
0540            AT END
0550                PERFORM 0250-ADD-USER
0560            WHEN USER-ID (USR-IX) = PH-USER-ID
0570                SET SUM-IX TO USER-SUM-NR (USR-IX).
0580        ADD 1 TO SUM-COUNT (SUM-IX PH-CALL-DA).
0590        ADD PH-CALL-LENGTH TO SUM-TIME (SUM-IX PH-CALL-DA).
0600        PERFORM 0500-READ-PHONE-LOG.
0610
0620    0250-ADD-USER.
0630        PERFORM
0640            VARYING USR-IX FROM 1 BY 1
0650            UNTIL USR-IX > NR-USERS
0660                OR PH-USER-ID < USER-ID (USR-IX)
0670                CONTINUE.
0680        PERFORM
0690         VARYING USR-IX2 FROM NR-USERS BY -1
0700         UNTIL USR-IX2 < USR-IX
0710           MOVE USER-ID (USR-IX2) TO USER-ID (USR-IX2 + 1)
0720           MOVE USER-SUM-NR (USR-IX2) TO USER-SUM-NR (USR-IX2 + 1).
0730        ADD 1 TO NR-USERS.
0740        MOVE PH-USER-ID TO USER-ID (USR-IX).
0750        MOVE NR-USERS TO USER-SUM-NR (USR-IX).
0760        SET SUM-IX TO USER-SUM-NR (USR-IX).
0770        INITIALIZE SUMMARY-ENTRY (SUM-IX).
0780
0790    0300-WRITE-SUMMARY-RECORDS.
0800        MOVE USER-ID (USR-IX) TO SOL-USER-ID.
0810        SET SUM-IX TO USER-SUM-NR (USR-IX).
0820        PERFORM
0830            VARYING DAY-SUB FROM 1 BY 1
0840                UNTIL DAY-SUB > 31
0850          MOVE SUM-COUNT (SUM-IX DAY-SUB) TO SOL-CALL-CT (DAY-SUB)
0860          MOVE SUM-TIME (SUM-IX DAY-SUB) TO SOL-CALL-TIME (DAY-SUB).
0865        0870       WRITE SOLICITOR-RECORD.
0880
0890    0500-READ-PHONE-LOG.
0900        READ PHONE-LOG-FILE
0910            AT END
0920                MOVE 'YES' TO INPUT-EOF-STATUS.
```

This program uses subscripts a good deal more than most programs ever would. But when you look at it a bit, it is not too difficult to follow, and there are not many other ways to program it that are as direct, effective, and efficient. I'll make some comments on the program and the techniques used and point out where and how subscript modification and indirect table referencing are used. Then I'll summarize the rules regarding subscript modification.

The program has two main loops invoked from `0100-MAIN-CONTROL`. The first loop accumulates the data for each solicitor as it reads the phone log records. The second loop writes out a summary record for each solicitor from the tables where the accumulation took place.

Notice that there is nothing at the beginning of the program to set up the values in the `USER-ID-TABLE`. This is because there is a high rate of turnover of solicitors. There also are some part-time solicitors who are students or retired people who often will go a month or more without working for the company. The program deals with this simply by adding new user IDs as it encounters them in the telephone log file.

Paragraph `0200-INPUT-LOOP` is the main loop that reads the input log records and accumulates the totals in the summary table for each record. Notice that `SEARCH ALL` is used; this is done for efficiency because there are a very large number of input records and a large number of solicitors. This will require that the `USER-ID-TABLE` be kept in sequence by the `USER-ID` values. To a large extent, adding new user ID entries and keeping them in sequence are what makes this program interesting.

Line 570 is where you first encounter indirect table referencing. `SUM-IX` is set to the value of `USER-SUM-NR (USR-IX)`, which is contained in the user ID table. That value is what specifies which entry in the summary table will be used to accumulate the totals for that user. You will keep track of that entry number in the user ID table, so it can be different from the entry number that contains the matching user ID in the user ID table. This provides a great deal of flexibility, and you'll see how the program takes advantage of it a little later.

Lines 580 and 590 are where the totals are accumulated in the summary table. This is a two-dimensional table, and the day of the month is used directly to specify which of the 31 totals to add the new values to.

Paragraph `0250-ADD-USER` contains most of the interesting code. Notice that the first `PERFORM` loop contains only a `CONTINUE` statement. That's okay, though, because the purpose of this paragraph is only to set `USR-IX` to the entry where the new user ID will be inserted. Remember that you must insert the new user ID in the proper place so that the table is kept in sequence for the `SEARCH ALL` statement. The loop will continue until it finds a user ID value in the table that is greater than the value of the new user ID, or the end of the table is reached because the new user ID value is greater than any of those already in the table. Notice that if the new user ID is less than all user IDs in the table, or the table is empty because this is the first input record, the PERFORM will not loop at all but will fall through with USR-IX set to 1.

Now that the location for the new user ID has been found, the entries already in the table must be shifted down in order to make room for it. This is what the second loop in this paragraph does. This is also where *subscript modification* is done. Observe at lines 710 and 720 how the values for the USER-ID and USER-SUM-NR at the USR-IX2 occurrence are moved to the next (USR-IX2 + 1) occurrence. COBOL will calculate the USR-IX2 + 1 occurrence but will not change the value of USR-IX2, which is exactly what you want here. The alternative would have been to define an additional subscript and then use a separate statement in the loop to set its value each time through the loop.

There is one other interesting thing to note about this loop. It is working *backward*. Observe that the VARYING establishes the initial value at the last entry in the table and then increments it by –1 each time, until it works back to the occurrence where the new user ID information will be inserted. This is necessary because the only occurrences not in use are at the end of the table. So the last entry can be moved to the next entry because it hasn't been used yet. After this is done, the entry before it can be moved to its previous spot, and this can continue until a spot is made for the new entry. Notice that if the new user ID is greater than all those already in the table (or for the first record read), this PERFORM does not loop at all.

Line 750 is where the value of the indirect table referencing is set for this user ID. It is simply the next available entry in the summary table. This number is placed in the user ID table and will be moved whenever the user ID is moved. But because the number is used to determine which entry in the summary table is to be used, it can stay the same throughout the program. This way, the entries in the summary table do not need to be moved around like the user ID entries each time a user ID is added. Line 760 shows SUM-IX being set to that value so the entry can be initialized and the proper totals updated in 0200-INPUT-LOOP.

The remainder of the program is pretty straightforward, so I will not comment on it here.

As you have seen, indirect table referencing is simply saving the value of an occurrence number from one table in another occurrence of some other table. Although this is a valuable technique, no special syntax or COBOL features are needed, so no special rules about it need to be discussed. Subscript modification does have a few rules, however:

- A value can only be added to or subtracted from the base subscript. This means that a full arithmetic expression is *not* allowed.

- The value to be added or subtracted must be an integer. It can be a data name, but it must be numeric, with no digits to the right of the assumed decimal place.

- The net result of the base subscript plus or minus the integer is used to determine the occurrence number in the table. The value of the base subscript is *not* modified.

- The result of the addition or subtraction must be in the range of the table and conform to all the rules for table referencing.

- The 1974 Standard allows only indexes to be used in this manner. The 1985 Standard extends the functionality to all subscripts.

Summary

I covered several concepts in this chapter that might seem a bit tricky at first, but I've found that doing a quick browse-through, followed by a more careful review a day or two later, makes the concepts much easier to deal with. None of the three major topics of multidimensional tables, OCCURS DEPENDING ON, and indirect table referencing is required on a regular basis in most COBOL environments. However, as you saw in the examples, there are situations in which these features seem to fit perfectly—as long as you know a little about their capabilities so that you can recognize the situations when they occur.

The next chapter explores an area that was added to COBOL in 1989 and is optional, even though it is available with all the common up-to-date compilers. This subject is intrinsic functions.

Intrinsic Functions with Emphasis on the Year 2000

The intrinsic functions were made available for COBOL with the release of the 1989 Addendum to the 1985 Standard. This addendum identifies intrinsic functions as an optional feature for current COBOL compilers, and that is still the case today. All the modern compilers I'm aware of do include intrinsic functions, and they will be required when the next standard is released.

Although the function is fairly new in COBOL, it has been around in other languages for many years, dating back to the old FORTRAN compilers of the 1960s. Functions are also commonly available with most spreadsheets and PC development products.

The purpose of a function is to provide single-valued data from a standard calculation in a form that is easy to reference in the program. The general concept is that whenever a statement referencing a function is executed, the reference to the function is replaced by the value it calculates. This is much easier to demonstrate than to define or explain; consider the following example:

```
WORKING-STORAGE SECTION.
01   INPUT-INFO           PIC X(40) VALUE SPACES.
01   SAVE-UPPER           PIC X(40).
PROCEDURE DIVISION.
0100-MAIN.
    DISPLAY 'Enter a message please '.
    ACCEPT INPUT-INFO.
    DISPLAY 'Your message in all caps: '
        FUNCTION UPPER-CASE (INPUT-INFO).
    DISPLAY 'Your original message: '
        INPUT-INFO.
    MOVE FUNCITON UPPER-CASE (INPUT-INFO) TO SAVE-UPPER.
    STOP RUN.
```

The intrinsic function UPPER-CASE converts all the letters in the argument in parentheses (INPUT-INFO, in this case) to their uppercase equivalent.

The value of INPUT-INFO is *not* altered by the function. Instead, the results are placed in a temporary storage field, and the program statement determines what is to be done with them. In the first reference to the function, the results are simply DISPLAYed back to the user. In the second reference, the results are MOVEd to the field SAVE-UPPER. (Note that you would normally reference only the function in the MOVE statement and DISPLAY the results from SAVE-UPPER because functions do involve some additional overhead. However, the example demonstrates how flexibly functions can be used in different statements.)

The requirements for the argument(s) and the size and type of the results are different for the various specific functions. The notion of how they are referenced and used will be pretty much the same for all of them, though.

In this chapter, I'll describe all the intrinsic functions available in COBOL, but first, you need to review the rules for using and referencing these functions. As a footnote, the next COBOL standard will provide a facility to write your own functions in COBOL (or other languages).

General Rules for Referencing Functions in COBOL

COBOL has some special rules for referencing functions that are a little different than in other languages where they are commonly used. These rules aren't really a problem but can cause some confusion if you aren't aware of them.

The word FUNCTION must precede any reference to a COBOL function. This way, the function can be easily identified without having to add the name of each function to COBOL's list of reserved words or without causing confusion on whether the program means to reference a function or a regular data item.

There are three basic types of functions in COBOL; the specific type is determined by the type of data item produced by the function. The three types are alphanumeric, numeric, and integer. In general, a specific type of function can be used only where that type of data item can be referenced. There are several rules that apply only to specific function types:

- An alphanumeric function may be used anywhere an alphanumeric elementary item is permitted.

- Numeric and integer functions may be used only within arithmetic expressions. This is a somewhat picky requirement and will be removed with the next standard.

  This rule implies that MOVE FUNCTION COS (ANGLE-VALUE) TO COSINE-RESULT *is not* allowed, but COMPUTE COSINE-RESULT = FUNCTION COS (ANGLE-VALUE) is allowed. The statement IF FUNCTION COS (ANGLE-VALUE) > X-VALUE is also permitted. (The COS function produces the value of the trigonometric cosine for the argument value.)

- A function may be used as an argument to another function as long as the function type matches the argument requirements of the function in which it is being used.

  This rule allows statements such as COMPUTE X-VALUE = Y-VALUE * FUNCTION SQRT (FUNCTION COS (ANGLE-VALUE)). (SQRT is the function that produces the square root of the argument value.)

  This is where the type of function can be important, because a numeric function *cannot* be used where an integer argument is required, even if the values returned for the specific usage will always be a whole number.

- Reference modification may be used with functions but only if they are type alphanumeric. MOVE FUNCTION UPPER-CASE (FULL-NAME) (1:5) TO FIRST-5-NAME will convert all the letters of FULL-NAME to uppercase (transferring the other characters unchanged) and MOVE the first five characters of the temporary result to FIRST-5-NAME.

- The program must specify the number of arguments required for the specific function being used, and the arguments must be in the proper sequence.

- Literals or arithmetic expressions may be used as arguments, but they must conform to the requirements specific to the function being used.

The COBOL functions provide a very nice feature for dealing with large groups of arguments that need to be included in a calculation. This involves defining the arguments in a table by using the OCCURS clause and then, rather than referencing them individually with a subscript, using the word ALL in place of the subscript when using a function to perform the required calculation. The following paragraphs summarize how this works.

There are a number of functions (primarily the statistical ones) for which an indefinite number of arguments may be specified. Examples of these are SUM (calculates the sum of the listed arguments), MEAN (calculates the average of the listed arguments), and STANDARD-DEVIATION (calculates the statistical standard deviation of the listed arguments).

If a group of numbers called SUB-TOTAL are defined in a table by using the OCCURS clause, you might use the SUM function to determine the GRAND-TOTAL of their values. Such a statement might be COMPUTE GRAND-TOTAL = FUNCTION SUM (SUB-TOTAL (1) SUB-TOTAL (2) SUB-TOTAL (3) SUB-TOTAL (4) SUB-TOTAL (5)). The simpler alternative of using ALL in place of the subscript is COMPUTE GRAND-TOTAL = FUNCTION SUM (SUB-TOTAL (ALL)).

Date Manipulation Functions

The functions described here all deal with dates having a full four-digit year. Two of the functions provide the current date and the date the source program was compiled, in an appropriate format, including the full century, year, month, day, and available time information.

The other four functions convert dates to and from an integer value that is equal to the numbers of days since December 31, 1600. The significance of this is that such an integer will represent dates up to some time after the year 4000 and will require only six digits to do it. Many computer systems needing to address the Year 2000 problem currently store date information as a two-digit year, month, and day, which also takes six digits. A conversion to this "count of days" provides a means of storing a full date without having to restructure all the records in all the files in the system.

I discuss these functions relative to the Year 2000 problem a bit more at the end of this section. Part VIII, "Addressing the Year 2000 Issues," also deals with this problem extensively.

FUNCTION CURRENT-DATE

The function CURRENT-DATE is an alphanumeric function that returns the current value of the date and time when the program executes. There are no arguments for the function, and the value returned is 21 characters in the following format.

Character Position	Value
1–4	The current four-digit year
5–6	The current two-digit month
7–8	The current two-digit day
9–10	Two digits representing the number of hours past midnight
11–12	Two digits representing the number of minutes past the hour
13–14	Two digits representing the number of seconds past the minute
15–16	Two digits representing the number of hundredths of a second past the second (or zero, if this cannot be provided)
17–21	Five characters of the form +hhmm or –hhmm representing the number of hours and minutes the preceding time is ahead of or behind Greenwich Mean Time. If this cannot be provided, positions 17–21 are set to zeroes.

FUNCTION WHEN-COMPILED

The function WHEN-COMPILED is an alphanumeric function that returns the value of the date and time when the source program was compiled. This will match the date and time shown on the listing for that specific compilation, although there may be differences in format and precision. There are no arguments for the function, and the value returned is 21 characters in the same format returned by the CURRENT-DATE function.

FUNCTION INTEGER-OF-DATE (integer-1)

The function INTEGER-OF-DATE converts a numeric integer data item of the form YYYYMMDD to an integer that equals the number of days past the date December 31, 1600. If the integer-1 data item contains the value 16010101, the value produced by the function will be 1. An integer-1 value of 16010105 will produce a value of 5, and 16010202 will produce 33. Dates between late 1998 and late 2000 will produces values between 145000 and 146000.

Again, the advantage of this function is that all the results produced by it for the next couple thousand years will require only six digits, and most current business systems have space for six digits (or characters) for date fields being kept in their files and databases.

The integer-1 value passed to the function must in the form YYYYMMDD. This is the equivalent of the formula (YYYY * 10000) + (MM * 100) + DD. This *must* be a proper date. YYYY must be between 1601 and 9999. MM must be between 1 and 12. DD must be between 1 and 31 and be a correct value corresponding to the value of MM.

Note that since the result is an integer, this function can be used only as part of an arithmetic expression or where an arithmetic expression is allowed.

FUNCTION DATE-OF-INTEGER (integer-1)

The function DATE-OF-INTEGER converts the integer-1 value (such as one produced by the function INTEGER-OF-DATE) into a date of the form YYYYMMDD. For example, if integer-1 is 1, the result returned will be 16010101. In mathematical terms, this function is the *inverse* of INTEGER-OF-DATE.

The integer-1 data item must contain a positive integer between 1 and FUNCTION INTEGER-OF-DATE (99991231).

Note that because the result is an integer, this function can be used only as part of an arithmetic expression or where an arithmetic expression is allowed.

A Simple Year 2000-Compliant Example Using the Date Functions

The example shown here is a very basic skeleton program using some of the date functions to manipulate dates containing the full four-digit years. The premise is that the program is part of a billing system, and the program updates the billing master records to reflect payments that have been received in the mail that day. I have dropped a lot of the detail code (including the entire handling of the OUTPUT-BILLING-MASTER) to save space and so that you can easily see the date manipulation. It is assumed that the file of billing master records has been converted to use the integer format of the date by a separate one-time conversion program.

```
DATA DIVISION.
 FILE SECTION.
 FD  INPUT-BILLING-MASTER.
 01  MSTR-IN-BILLING-RECORD.
     05  MSTR-IN-ACCOUNT-NR          PIC X(8).
     05  MSTR-IN-LAST-BILLED-DATE    PIC 9(6).
     05  MSTR-IN-LAST-PAID-DATE      PIC 9(6).
```

```
    Other Input Master Billing Definitions
    .
FD  DAILY-PAYMENTS.
01  PYMT-RECEIVED-RECORD.
    05  PYMT-ACCOUNT-NR        PIC X(8).
    .
    Daily Payment Information Definitions
    .
FD  PAYMENT-OVERDUE-REPORT.
01  OVRDUE-PAYMENT-RECORD.
    05  OVRDUE-ACCOUNT-NR      PIC X(8).
    05              PIC X.
    05  OVRDUE-BILLED-DATE     PIC 9(8).
    .
    Other Information for Overdue Report
    .
WORKING-STORAGE SECTION.
01  CURRENT-DATE-INFO          PIC X(21).
01  CURRENT-DATE-INFO-GROUP REDEFINES CURRENT-DATE-INFO.
    05  CURRENT-DATE-INTEGER      PIC 9(8).
    05  FILLER        PIC X(13).
01  MASTER-EOF-STATUS      PIC X VALUE 'N'.
    88  MASTER-END            VALUE 'Y'.
01  PAYMENT-EOF-STATUS    PIC X VALUE 'N'.
    88  PAYMENT-END          VALUE 'Y'.


PROCEDURE DIVISION.
0000-MAIN-CONTROL.
    OPEN INPUT  INPUT-BILLING-MASTER
                DAILY-PAYMENTS
         OUTPUT OUTPUT-BILLING-MASTER
                PAYMENT-OVERDUE-REPORT.
    MOVE FUNCTION CURRENT-DATE TO CURRENT-DATE-INFO.
    PERFORM 0800-READ-INPUT-MASTER.
    PERFORM 0820-READ-PAYMENTS.
    PERFORM 0200-UPDATE-CONTROL-LOOP
        UNTIL MASTER-END AND PAYMENT-END.
    PERFORM 0900-CLOSE-ROUTINE.
    STOP RUN.


0200-UPDATE-CONTROL-LOOP.
    IF MSTR-IN-ACCOUNT-NR > PYMT-ACCOUNT-NR
        PERFORM 0300-NO-MASTER-MATCH
        PERFORM 0820-READ-PAYMENTS
    ELSE
    IF MSTR-IN-ACCOUNT-NR < PYMT-ACCOUNT-NR
        PERFORM 0400-OUTPUT-MASTER
        PERFORM 0800-READ-INPUT-MASTER
    ELSE
        PERFORM 0500-POST-PAYMENT
        PERFORM 0820-READ-PAYMENTS.
```

13

INTRINSIC
FUNCTIONS

```
0300-NO-MASTER-MATCH.
    EXIT.

0400-OUTPUT-MASTER.
    IF MSTR-IN-LAST-BILLED-DATE < FUNCTION INTEGER-OF-DATE
    ➡ (CURRENT-DATE-INTEGER) + 25
       AND MSTR-IN-LAST-BILLED-DATE < MSTR-IN-LAST-PAID-DATE
       MOVE SPACES TO OVRDUE-PAYMENT-RECORD
       MOVE MSTR-IN-ACCOUNT-NR TO OVRDUE-ACCOUNT-NR
       COMPUTE OVRDUE-BILLED-DATE = FUNCTION DATE-OF-INTEGER
       ➡ (MSTR-IN-LAST-BILLED-DATE)
       .
Additional Overdue Report Formatting
       .
       PERFORM 0840-WRITE-OVERDUE-RECORD.
    PERFORM 0860-WRITE-OUTPUT-MASTER.

0500-POST-PAYMENT.
    IF MSTR-IN-LAST-BILLED-DATE < FUNCTION INTEGER-OF-DATE
    ➡ (CURRENT-DATE-INTEGER) + 25
       PERFORM 0520-DETERMINE-LATE-CHARGES.
    COMPUTE MSTR-IN-LAST-PAID-DATE = FUNCTION INTEGER-OF-DATE
    ➡ (CURRENT-DATE-INTEGER).
    .
Additional Payment Processing.
    .
Remainder of Program
    .
```

A brief note on the sequential update logic in 0200-UPDATE-CONTROL-LOOP is that there will be no output master record written in 0500-POST-PAYMENT and no read of the input master file, either. This allows multiple payments to be processed against the same master account if they are received on the same day.

Notice that the dates in the input master record are still six characters long. They are defined as numeric, though, because the integer/date functions require numeric integer arguments and results. The date in the overdue report record is also numeric for the same reason, but it is eight digits, so it can hold a YYYYMMDD format value (previously, it was probably X(8) and stored in a format such as MM/DD/YY).

The definition for the CURRENT-DATE-INFO is interesting. This must be an elementary alphanumeric definition for the CURRENT-DATE function. You also need an integer definition for the YYYYMMDD portion so that it can be used in the INTEGER-OF-DATE function. Because the definition of the CURRENT-DATE function ensures that this will be a numeric value, the REDEFINES and associated definition are all that is required here.

The MOVE can be used with the CURRENT-DATE function at the beginning of the program because it returns alphanumeric results and therefore can be used anywhere an alphanumeric data item is permitted. However, in `0400-OUTPUT-MASTER` and `0500-POST-PAYMENT`, you need to use `COMPUTE` statements because the functions `INTEGER-OF-DATE` and `DATE-OF-INTEGER` both produce numeric integer results and can be used only where arithmetic expressions are permitted.

Notice how the function `INTEGER-OF-DATE` is used in the `IF` statements in `0400-OUTPUT-MASTER` and `0500-POST-PAYMENT`. You need to compare the current date to the date when the bill was sent for this account. But the `MSTR-IN-LAST-BILLED-DATE` is in integer format (number of days since 1600), whereas `CURRENT-DATE-INTEGER` is in YYYYMMDD format. You can use the function to convert `CURRENT-DATE-INTEGER` right in the `IF` statement because arithmetic expressions can be used here. That way, you compare like values.

Notice also how easy it is to handle the "25 day grace period" with the + 25 right in the `IF` statements. That is because you're already dealing with a pure count of days and therefore don't need to worry about dealing with "next month" or "previous month" concerns that you would have to deal with if working with regular date formats. This is a very nice side benefit of this form of date management.

Finally, observe that `MSTR-IN-LAST-BILLED-DATE` and `MSTR-IN-LAST-PAID-DATE` can be compared directly following the `AND` in `0400-OUTPUT-MASTER`. This is because they are in the same format.

FUNCTION DAY-OF-INTEGER (integer-1)

The function `DAY-OF-INTEGER` is the same as `DATE-OF-INTEGER`, except that the result returned is in the format YYYYDDD where DDD is the day of day of the year (February 1 will result in DDD being 32).

`integer-1` needs to be a numeric integer representing the number of days since December 31, 1600, and the result returned will also be a numeric integer value.

Because the result is an integer, this function can be used only as part of an arithmetic expression or where an arithmetic expression is allowed.

FUNCTION INTEGER-OF-DAY (integer-1)

The function `INTEGER-OF-DAY` is the same as `INTEGER-OF-DATE`, except that the `integer-1` must be in the format YYYYDDD where DDD is the day of day of the year (February 1 will result in DDD being 32). YYYY must be a value between 1601 and 9999, and DDD must be from 1 to 366 (365, unless YYYY is a leap year).

The result will be a numeric integer representing the number of days since December 31, 1600. The conversion formula is (YYYY * 1000) + DDD.

Because the result is an integer, this function can be used only as part of an arithmetic expression or where an arithmetic expression is allowed.

The Value of Standard Functions in Year 2000 Conversions

Because the functions described in this section work with the full four-digit year and provide some facility for dealing with the Year 2000 situation, it is worthwhile to add a few brief comments here as to their overall value.

Using the conversion functions provided with COBOL and storing the resulting integers (representing the number of days since 1600) in files and databases instead of the current YYMMDD format dates provides the following advantages:

- Programs that use files containing the dates in the new formats but not referencing any of them do *not* need to be changed or recompiled.

- The new-format dates will still sort and compare correctly.

- Because this format doesn't rely on special or computational formats, the values can still be easily read in file lists and displayed. (It is still a count of days since 1600 that needs a calculation, but at least it is legible.)

- No additional software needs to be purchased or leased to take advantage of these functions (unless the COBOL compiler is pre-1989 or doesn't support intrinsic functions).

The following limitations and items still must be dealt with if these functions are used:

- The representation of dates as the number of days since 1600 is pretty much limited to the COBOL functions, so data containing such dates that is used with other software products must undergo a conversion if the dates are to be properly interpreted by those products.

- All the date fields in master files and databases must be converted to the new formats. This normally requires that conversion programs be written.

- All references to the date fields must still be identified and looked at. In many cases (such as simple compares), nothing will need to be done, but in many other cases, code changes will be needed. This requirement exists regardless of what algorithm is selected. A variety of software products address this need, with different degrees of success.

- Input and output date formats having the two-digit year must still be dealt with.

- Editing of dates and dealing with program internal date formats still need to be handled.

Some additional functions and features are now available with the newer COBOL compilers and provide additional capabilities for dealing with dates. Many of these are being considered for inclusion in the next standard COBOL. Unfortunately, that standard will not become official until some time after January 2000. I cover these items briefly in the last section of this chapter. If these are available with the compiler you are using and they aren't changed between now and the release of the new standard, they can simplify things even more in dealing with the Year 2000.

Alphanumeric Functions

The alphanumeric group of functions works with alphanumeric or character data. These functions can be quite useful in a variety of programming situations. Although the same result can usually be obtained by other means, most of the functions produce a simpler, more direct result.

FUNCTION UPPER-CASE (AN-data-item-1)

UPPER-CASE returns an alphanumeric item with the same number of characters as AN-data-item-1, but all the lowercase letters are converted to their uppercase equivalent. Any characters that are not letters are left unchanged.

AN-data-item-1 must be an elementary alphanumeric data item—PIC X(n)—or literal.

Because this is an alphanumeric function, it can be used anywhere an alphanumeric data item is permitted.

FUNCTION LOWER-CASE (AN-data-item-1)

LOWER-CASE returns an alphanumeric item with the same number of characters as AN-data-item-1, but all the uppercase letters are converted to their lowercase equivalent. Any characters that are not letters are left unchanged.

AN-data-item-1 must be an elementary alphanumeric data item—PIC X(n)—or literal.

Because this is an alphanumeric function, it can be used anywhere an alphanumeric data item is permitted.

FUNCTION REVERSE (AN-data-item-1)

REVERSE is an interesting but only marginally useful function that returns an alphanumeric item with the same number of characters as AN-data-item-1 but with the characters in exact reversed sequence. Therefore, if AN-data-item-1 has a value of 'ABCDEF12', REVERSE will return '21FEDCBA'. Spaces and other special characters are treated just like the letters and numbers, so '   aB.*13' will be REVERSEd to '31*.Ba   '.

AN-data-item-1 must be an elementary alphanumeric data item—PIC X(n) —or literal.

Because this is an alphanumeric function, it can be used anywhere an alphanumeric data item is permitted.

FUNCTION ORD (char-item-1)

ORD returns an integer value that represents the relative position of char-item-1 within the collating or sort sequence of the character set being used.

So, if char-item-1 has a value equal to LOW-VALUE, the result returned will be 1; if it has a value of HIGH-VALUE, the result will equal the number of characters (or collating sequence positions possible) in the character set.

The ORD function is the inverse of the CHAR function.

char-item-1 must be an elementary alphanumeric data item that is one character position in length.

Because this is an integer function, it can be used only in arithmetic expressions or where an arithmetic expression is permitted.

FUNCTION CHAR (integer-item-1)

CHAR returns a single character having a value corresponding to the ordinal position within the collating or sort sequence of the character set being used that is equal to integer-item-1.

So, if integer-item-1 has a value equal to 1, a single character of value LOW-VALUE will be returned; if it has a value equal to the number of characters in the character set, the result returned will be a single character with a value of HIGH-VALUE.

The CHAR function is the inverse of the ORD function.

integer-item-1 must be an integer data item with a value between 1 and the number of characters in the character set being used. For standard ASCII, the maximum value is 128, and for EBCDIC, it is 256.

Because this is an alphanumeric function, it can be used wherever alphanumeric data items are permitted.

FUNCTION LENGTH (data-item-1))

LENGTH returns an integer value that is equal to the size in character positions of data-item-1.

data-item-1 may be any elementary-level or group-level data item.

Because this is an integer function, it can be used only in arithmetic expressions or where an arithmetic expression is permitted.

FUNCTION NUMVAL (AN-data-item-1)

The purpose of NUMVAL is to convert an "edited" numeric value in AN-data-item-1 to its corresponding numeric value.

AN-data-item-1 can contain up to 30 characters and must be in one of the following formats:

```
[spaces] [+/-] [spaces] digits [.[digits]] [spaces]

[spaces] [+/-] [spaces] .digits [spaces]

[spaces] digits[.[digits]] [spaces] [+/-/CR/DB] [spaces]

[spaces] .digits [spaces] [+/-/CR/DB] [spaces]
```

Here, the term spaces represents zero or more spaces, and the term digits represents between 1 and 30 numeric digits.

Because this is a numeric function, it can be used only in arithmetic expressions or where an arithmetic expression is permitted.

FUNCTION NUMVAL-C (AN-data-item-1 [char-item-1])

The purpose of NUMVAL-C is also to convert an "edited" numeric value in AN-data-item-1 to its corresponding numeric value. However, in this form, the currency (or dollar) sign (cs), as well as editing commas, can be included in the character string. If char-item-1 is specified, it must be a single character and represents the currency sign to be used in the translation; otherwise, the program's default currency sign is used.

If the clause DECIMAL-POINT IS COMMA is specified in the SPECIAL-NAMES paragraph, the roles of the comma and decimal point are reversed.

AN-data-item-1 can contain up to 30 characters and must be in one of the following formats:

```
[spaces] [+/-] [spaces] [cs] [spaces] digits [, digits] ... [.[digits]]
➡[spaces]

[spaces] [+/-] [spaces] [cs] [spaces] .digits [spaces]

[spaces] [cs] [spaces] digits [, digits] ... [.[digits]] [spaces]
➡[+/-/CR/DB] [spaces]

[spaces] [cs] [spaces] .digits [spaces] [+/-/CR/DB] [spaces]
```

Here, the term spaces represents zero or more spaces, and the term digits represents between 1 and 30 numeric digits.

Because this is a numeric function, it can be used only in arithmetic expressions or where an arithmetic expression is permitted.

13

INTRINSIC
FUNCTIONS

Statistical Functions

These functions provide for the basic statistical calculations. With the exception of the RANDOM function, they all allow an indefinite number of arguments. This allows the sum, average, standard deviation, and so on to be calculated for any number of arguments.

As demonstrated at the beginning of this chapter, it is usually more convenient to store the values used in the calculation in a table and then reference the numeric OCCURS item using the term ALL instead of the subscript. This way, only a single argument needs to be specified, but all the required values will be included in the calculation. Where the number of values to be used is not known ahead of time, the DEPENDING ON numeric-item part of the OCCURS clause can be used in the table definition, and the value of the numeric-item will tell the function how many of the table items to use in the calculation. (See Chapter 12, "Advanced Techniques Using Tables," for more information on this form of the OCCURS clause.)

FUNCTION SUM ({numeric-item-1}...)

The function SUM simply returns a numeric value that is the total of values of all the numeric-item-1 arguments.

A special case of the SUM function is that it returns an integer value if *all* the numeric-item-1 definitions are also type integer. If *any* of the numeric-item-1 definitions has digits defined after the decimal point, SUM returns a non-integer numeric result.

This is one of the more useful of the intrinsic functions. A common example to calculate the grand total of all the different types of data records processed in a program might be COMPUTE GRAND-TOTAL = FUNCTION SUM (SUB-TOTAL-BY-TYPE (ALL) REJECT-TOTAL). Here, SUB-TOTAL-BY-TYPE would be defined in a table with an OCCURS clause, whereas GRAND-TOTAL and REJECT-TOTAL are other numeric items defined in WORKING-STORAGE.

Because this is a numeric (or integer) function, it can be used only in arithmetic expressions or where an arithmetic expression is permitted.

FUNCTION MEAN ({numeric-item-1}...)

The function MEAN returns a numeric value that is the average (or statistical *mean*) of the values of all the numeric-item-1 arguments.

Because this is a numeric function, it can be used only in arithmetic expressions or where an arithmetic expression is permitted.

FUNCTION MEDIAN ({numeric-item-1}...)

The function MEDIAN returns a numeric value that is the middle value of the list of all the numeric-item-1 arguments.

The determination of the middle value is made through standard algebraic comparisons of the values. If there is an even number of arguments, the value returned is calculated as the average of the two middle values.

Because this is a numeric function, it can be used only in arithmetic expressions or where an arithmetic expression is permitted.

FUNCTION RANGE ({numeric-item-1}...)

The function RANGE returns a numeric value that is the difference between the largest algebraic value of any of the arguments and the smallest algebraic value of any of the arguments.

Because this is a numeric function, it can be used only in arithmetic expressions or where an arithmetic expression is permitted.

FUNCTION MIDRANGE ({numeric-item-1}...)

The function MIDRANGE returns a numeric value that is the average of the largest algebraic value of any of the arguments and the smallest algebraic value of any of the arguments.

Because this is a numeric function, it can be used only in arithmetic expressions or where an arithmetic expression is permitted.

FUNCTION VARIANCE ({numeric-item-1}...)

The function VARIANCE returns a numeric value that is the statistical *variance* of all the numeric-item-1 arguments.

Because this is a numeric function, it can be used only in arithmetic expressions or where an arithmetic expression is permitted.

FUNCTION STANDARD-DEVIATION ({numeric-item-1}...)

The function STANDARD-DEVIATION returns a numeric value that is the statistical *standard deviation* of all the numeric-item-1 arguments. This is computed as the square root of the result of the VARIANCE function.

Because this is a numeric function, it can be used only in arithmetic expressions or where an arithmetic expression is permitted.

FUNCTION RANDOM ([integer-item-1])

The function RANDOM returns a numeric value that is a decimal fraction between 0 and 1. The specific value is determined by the "pseudo-random number generator" used by the compiler.

Random numbers are not often used in business programming. They are a main requirement in creating computer games where a degree of variation and unpredictability is desirable. They can also be employed occasionally in business programming to vary certain responses to users. For example, rather than simply display Hello *username*, you could use the RANDOM function to randomly select one of a list of several initial user greetings to display.

If integer-item-1 is specified, it must be zero or a positive value. This is the *seed value* for the random number generator used to initialize the series of random numbers the function will produce. If integer-item-1 is used, it is normally used only the first time the RANDOM function is used by the program. Each subsequent random number is determined from the preceding one, resulting in a pseudo-random series of values. This series has the same random properties as other random functions, such as dealing cards, but it can be reproduced simply by specifying the same integer-item-1 value for the first reference to the RANDOM function.

Therefore, the reason to specify an integer-item-1 value is to begin with a different series of random numbers each time the program is executed. Values such as the seconds and hundredths-of-seconds portion of the current time are usually used for integer-item-1 when it is used.

COBOL specifies that the same series of random numbers will be produced each time the same integer-item-1 value is used. The vendor determines which specific random number–generator logic is to be used and which or whether a specific series of random numbers is to be used if no integer-item-1 is referenced the first time the RANDOM function is referenced in a program execution.

Because the result returned by the FUNCTION RANDOM is a decimal fraction between 0 and 1, it normally must be converted to a more useable value in a range of acceptable values. The normal formula to accomplish this follows:

```
COMPUTE RAND-VALUE ROUNDED = LOW-RANDOM + (FUNCTION RANDOM *
➡(HIGH-RANDOM - LOW-RANDOM)).
```

Because this is a numeric function, it can be used only in arithmetic expressions or where an arithmetic expression is permitted.

Algebraic Functions

The algebraic functions produce functional results sometimes required in formulas. They all produce numeric or integer results and require one or two specific numeric or integer arguments.

FUNCTION SQRT (numeric-item-1)

The function SQRT returns a numeric value that approximates the square root of numeric-item-1.

numeric-item-1 must be zero or a positive number.

Because this is a numeric function, it can be used only in arithmetic expressions or where an arithmetic expression is permitted.

FUNCTION FACTORIAL (integer-item-1)

The function FACTORIAL returns an integer value that is equal to the factorial of integer-item-1.

If integer-item-1 is 0 or 1, the value 1 is returned. Otherwise, the formula n * (n-1) * (n-2) * ... * 1 is used to determine the result, in which n is the value of integer-item-1.

integer-item-1 must be zero or a positive integer.

Because this is an integer function, it can be used only in arithmetic expressions or where an arithmetic expression is permitted.

FUNCTION INTEGER (numeric-item-1)

The function INTEGER returns an integer value that is the greatest integer that is less than or equal to numeric-item-1.

For example, if numeric-item-1 is 1.1 or 1.5 or 1.9, the value 1 is returned. If numeric-item-1 is -1.1 or -1.5 or -1.9, the value -2 is returned.

numeric-item-1 can be any number.

Because this is an integer function, it can be used only in arithmetic expressions or where an arithmetic expression is permitted.

FUNCTION INTEGER-PART (numeric-item-1)

The function INTEGER-PART returns an integer value that is the integer portion of numeric-item-1. It is essentially the result of dropping or ignoring all the digits to the right of the decimal point.

For example, if numeric-item-1 is 1.1 or 1.5 or 1.9, the value 1 is returned. If numeric-item-1 is -1.1 or -1.5 or -1.9, the value -1 is returned.

numeric-item-1 can be any number.

Because this is an integer function, it can be used only in arithmetic expressions or where an arithmetic expression is permitted.

FUNCTION REM (numeric-item-1 numeric-item-2)

The function REM returns a numeric value that is the remainder of numeric-item-1 divided by numeric-item-2.

numeric-item-1 can be any number, and numeric-item-2 can be any number other than zero.

Because this is a numeric function, it can be used only in arithmetic expressions or where an arithmetic expression is permitted.

FUNCTION MOD (integer-item-1 integer-item-2)

The function MOD returns an integer value that is the result of integer-item-1 modulo integer-item-2. This value can be calculated by this formula:

```
integer-item-1 - (integer-item-2 * FUNCTION INTEGER
➡(integer-item-1/integer-item-2))
```

integer-item-1 can be any integer, and integer-item-2 can be any integer other than zero.

Because this is an integer function, it can be used only in arithmetic expressions or where an arithmetic expression is permitted.

Miscellaneous Functions

There are really two types of functions here, but neither group has enough functions to warrant its own section, so I've combined them here.

FUNCTION MAX ({argument-1}...)

The function MAX returns the value that is the largest of all the argument-1 values. The argument-1 values may be of any type, but the following rules apply:

- If any of the argument-1s is alphanumeric, they all must be alphanumeric. In this case, the function is treated as an alphanumeric function, and the result returned will be alphanumeric. Its size will be the number of character positions of the specific argument-1 value selected as having the maximum value. This means that different-sized results will be returned, depending on which argument-1 has the maximum value. The compares made to determine which argument-1 value is largest are the same as in any other alphanumeric compares.

- Integer and noninteger numeric argument-1s may be combined. If all of them are integers, the function is treated as an integer function and an integer result is returned. Otherwise, the function is treated as a numeric function, and a numeric result is returned. The determination of the largest value is based on standard algebraic numeric comparisons.

- If this function is used as a numeric or integer function, it can be used only in arithmetic expressions or where an arithmetic expression is permitted. If it is used as an alphanumeric function, it may be used anywhere an alphanumeric data item is permitted.

FUNCTION MIN ({argument-1}...)

The function MIN returns the value that is the smallest of all the argument-1 values. The argument-1 values may be of any type, but the following rules apply:

- If any of the argument-1s is alphanumeric, they all must be alphanumeric. In this case, the function is treated as an alphanumeric function and the result returned will be alphanumeric. Its size will be the number of character positions of the specific argument-1 value selected as having the minimum value. This means that different-sized results will be returned, depending on which argument-1 has the minimum value. The compares made to determine which argument-1 value is smallest are the same as in any other alphanumeric compares.

- Integer and noninteger numeric argument-1s may be combined. If all of them are integers, the function is treated as an integer function and an integer result is returned. Otherwise, the function is treated as a numeric function, and a numeric result is returned. The determination of the smallest value is based on standard algebraic numeric comparisons.

- If this function is used as a numeric or integer function, it can be used only in arithmetic expressions or where an arithmetic expression is permitted. If it is used as an alphanumeric function, it may be used anywhere an alphanumeric data item is permitted.

FUNCTION ORD-MAX ({argument-1}...)

The function ORD-MAX returns an integer value that corresponds to the relative position of the argument-1 whose value is the largest of all the argument-1 values.

This function is very closely related to the MAX function. The rules regarding what kinds of arguments may be grouped together are the same, and the rules on how comparisons are made are the same. The only difference is that the MAX function returns the largest value, whereas ORD-MAX returns the relative position within the argument list that has the largest value.

Note that if the term ALL" is used with a subscripted data item, the argument list is treated as if each subscript value was listed separately from left to right, beginning with the smallest subscript value first.

Because this function is an integer function, it can be used only in arithmetic expressions or where an arithmetic expression is permitted.

13

INTRINSIC
FUNCTIONS

FUNCTION ORD-MIN ({argument-1}...)

The function `ORD-MIN` returns an integer value that corresponds to the relative position of the `argument-1` whose value is the smallest of all the `argument-1` values.

This function is very closely related to the `MIN` function. The rules regarding what kinds of arguments may be grouped together are the same, and the rules on how comparisons are made are the same. The only difference is that the `MIN` function returns the smallest value, whereas `ORD-MIN` returns the relative position within the argument list that has the smallest value.

Note that if the term `ALL` is used with a subscripted data item, the argument list is treated as if each subscript value was listed separately from left to right, beginning with the smallest subscript value first.

Because this function is an integer function, it can be used only in arithmetic expressions or where an arithmetic expression is permitted.

FUNCTION ANNUITY (numeric-item-1 integer-item-1)

The `ANNUITY` function provides the standard *annuity immediate* calculation. `numeric-item-1` specifies the rate at which interest is earned, and `integer-item-1` specifies the number of periods over which the annuity is to be paid. The calculation assumes that interest is paid at the end of each period but before the annuity value for that period is paid. The value returned is numeric and approximates the amount paid at the end of each period based on an initial investment of 1. Therefore, to determine the annuity value for any initial investment amount, simply multiply it by the result returned by the `ANNUITY` function.

`numeric-item-1` must be numeric and greater than or equal to zero. `integer-item-1` must be an integer greater than zero.

Because this function is a numeric function, it can be used only in arithmetic expressions or where an arithmetic expression is permitted.

FUNCTION PRESENT-VALUE (numeric-item-1 {numeric-item-2}...)

The `PRESENT-VALUE` function returns a numeric value approximating the results of the standard *present value* calculation. `numeric-item-1` specifies the discount rate, and the various `numeric-item-2`s represent the series of future end-of-period amounts. The value returned represents the current or present total value of all the amounts, with the discount rate being applied for each period.

`numeric-item-1` must be a numeric item greater than -1. The various `numeric-item-2` values must all be numeric.

Because this function is a numeric function, it can be used only in arithmetic expressions or where an arithmetic expression is permitted.

Trigonometric Functions

The functions provided here provide standard trigonometric values and conversions. Although calculations requiring trigonometry aren't often seen in COBOL, they do occur occasionally. Previously, programs needing such values or conversions used CALLs to subroutines written in FORTRAN, PL/1, or similar languages to get the job done (see Chapter 14, "Invoking Other Programs and Subprograms," for more information on CALL).

Because these are mathematical functions, they are normally implemented with a floating-point type of number. In COBOL, this implies that a large number of digits both before and after the decimal point should be defined for both the arguments and any fields receiving the results of these functions.

Because all these functions return numeric values, they can be used only in arithmetic expressions or where arithmetic expressions are permitted.

FUNCTION SIN (number-1)

This is a numeric function requiring a single numeric argument. It returns a value representing the nearest approximation of the trigonometric sine of number-1, which is an angle (or arc) expressed in radians.

FUNCTION COS (number-1)

This is a numeric function requiring a single numeric argument. It returns a value representing the nearest approximation of the trigonometric cosine of number-1, which is an angle (or arc) expressed in radians.

FUNCTION TAN (number-1)

This is a numeric function requiring a single numeric argument. It returns a value representing the nearest approximation of the trigonometric tangent of number-1, which is an angle (or arc) expressed in radians.

FUNCTION ASIN (number-1)

This is a numeric function requiring a single numeric argument. It returns a numeric value expressed in radians representing the nearest approximation of the trigonometric arc sine of number-1.

13

INTRINSIC
FUNCTIONS

FUNCTION ACOS (number-1)

This is a numeric function requiring a single numeric argument. It returns a numeric value expressed in radians representing the nearest approximation of the trigonometric arc cosine of number-1.

FUNCTION ATAN (number-1)

This is a numeric function requiring a single numeric argument. It returns a numeric value expressed in radians representing the nearest approximation of the trigonometric arc tangent of number-1.

FUNCTION LOG (number-1)

This is a numeric function requiring a single numeric argument. It returns a numeric value representing the nearest approximation of the natural logarithm (to base *e*) of number-1.

FUNCTION LOG10 (number-1)

This is a numeric function requiring a single numeric argument. It returns a numeric value representing the nearest approximation of the logarithm to base 10 of number-1.

Useful Date-Processing Functions and Features Not Yet Available with Standard COBOL

Several functions and an extension to the ACCEPT statement are available with most new compilers that directly support dealing with the Year 2000. These are included in current drafts of the next COBOL Standard. However, because that standard has not yet been approved and published, these functions aren't official, and it's possible that they may be removed or modified in the future. Realistically, I doubt seriously that this will happen, so I describe them here in the hope that they will be of use in dealing with Year 2000 conversion.

When you look at Part VIII, you'll see how closely the functions described here tie into some of the methods described in that part of the book.

FUNCTION YEAR-TO-YYYY (integer – item-1 [integer-item-2])

The function YEAR-TO-YYYY returns a four-digit integer year that it calculates from the two-digit year in integer-item-1. integer-item-2 is used to determine the sliding window for calculating the value of the century. If integer-item-2 is not specified, a value of 50 is assumed.

`integer-item-1` must be an integer with a value between zero and 99. `integer-item-2` must be an integer that, when added to the *current* four-digit year, yields a result between 1700 and 9999.

The *sliding-window* conversion works very simply. The value of `integer-item-2` (or 50, if it is omitted) is added to the current four-digit year to produce a maximum value for the four-digit value to be calculated. A test result is calculated as the `integer-item-1` two-digit year with the century for the maximum value applied to it. If this test result is greater than the maximum value, the century of the test result is reduced by 1. This result is then the value returned.

This sliding-window calculation works nicely for all dates between now and 9900. Like all two-digit-year conversions, it cannot deal with potential date values spanning more than 100 years. The following table of values illustrates how this conversion works:

`integer-1`	`integer-2`	Current Year	Maximum Year	Test Result	Final Result
88	50	1998	2048	2088	1988
99	50	1998	2048	2099	1999
02	50	1998	2048	2002	2002
25	50	1998	2048	2025	2025
88	50	2001	2051	2088	1988
99	50	2001	2051	2099	1999
02	50	2001	2051	2002	2002
25	50	2001	2051	2025	2025
88	20	1998	2018	2088	1988
99	20	1998	2018	2099	1999
02	20	1998	2018	2002	2002
25	20	2002	2022	2025	1925
78	80	2002	2082	2078	2078

As you can see, the value 50 for `integer-item-2` works very well for dates that are close to the current date. But if the system deals with older dates, a smaller value should probably be used. If the system deals with long-range future dates, a higher value generally will work better.

Because this function is an integer function, it can be used only in arithmetic expressions or where an arithmetic expression is permitted.

FUNCTION DATE-TO-YYYYMMDD (integer − item-1 [integer-item-2])

The function DATE-TO-YYYYMMDD returns an eight-digit integer date having a four-digit year that it calculates from the six-digit date of the form YYMMDD in integer-item-1. integer-item-2 is used to determine the sliding window for calculating the value of the century. If integer-item-2 is not specified, a value of 50 is assumed.

integer-item-1 must be an integer between zero and 99999999. integer-item-2 must be an integer that, when added to the value of the current four-digit year, yields a result between 1700 and 9999.

This function converts the two-digit year to a four-digit year in exactly the same manner as the function YEAR-TO-YYYY does. The MMDD portion of integer-item-1 is then appropriately applied to this year to produce the result that is returned. No editing or modification of the MMDD portion is done.

Because this function is an integer function, it can be used only in arithmetic expressions or where an arithmetic expression is permitted.

FUNCTION DAY-TO-YYYYDDD (integer − item-1 [integer-item-2])

The function DAY-TO-YYYYDDD returns a seven-digit integer date having a four-digit year that it calculates from the five-digit date of the form YYDDD in integer-item-1. integer-item-2 is used to determine the sliding window for calculating the value of the century. If integer-item-2 is not specified, a value of 50 is assumed.

integer-item-1 must be an integer between zero and 9999999. integer-item-2 must be an integer that, when added to the value of the current four-digit year, yields a result between 1700 and 9999.

This function converts the two-digit year to a four-digit year in exactly the same manner as the function YEAR-TO-YYYY does. The DDD portion of integer-item-1 is then appropriately applied to this year to produce the result that is returned. No editing or modification of the DDD portion is done.

Because this function is an integer function, it can be used only in arithmetic expressions or where an arithmetic expression is permitted.

FUNCTION TEST-DATE-YYYYMMDD (integer − item-1)

The function TEST-DATE-YYYYMMDD returns a one-digit integer value indicating the validity of the date in integer-item-1.

`integer-item-1` is an integer of the form YYYYMMDD. The possible values returned are the following:

0	The date is valid
1	The year is not in the range 1601-9999
2	The month is not in the range 01-12
3	The day is not valid for the given year and month

Because this function is an integer function, it can be used only in arithmetic expressions or where an arithmetic expression is permitted.

FUNCTION TEST-DAY-YYYYDDD (integer – item-1)

The function TEST-DAY-YYYYDDD returns a one-digit integer value indicating the validity of the date in `integer-item-1`.

`integer-item-1` is an integer of the form YYYYDDD. The following are the possible values returned:

0	The date is valid
1	The year is not in the range 1601-9999
2	The day is not valid for the given year

Because this function is an integer function, it can be used only in arithmetic expressions or where an arithmetic expression is permitted.

Year 2000 Extension to the ACCEPT Statement

The ACCEPT statement is expanded to optionally transfer date values containing the full four-digit year. The format for this is

`ACCEPT data-item FROM {DATE [YYYYMMDD]/DAY [YYYYDDD]/DAY-OF-WEEK/TIME}`

If the new optional term YYYYMMDD is specified in the FROM DATE phrase, eight characters are transferred to the `data-item` in the YYYYMMDD form instead of the default six characters of the YYMMDD form, which was previously the only available form.

If the new optional term YYYYDDD is specified in the FROM DAY phrase, seven characters are transferred to the `data-item` in the YYYYDDD form instead of the default five characters of the YYDDD form, which was previously the only available form.

Summary

This completes the chapter on intrinsic functions. There are a lot of these functions, and it appears that some of them can provide real value in dealing with the Year 2000. These functions will not change how you program, but they should enable you to handle a variety of special requirements simply and directly.

In the next chapter, you'll get into subprograms and the CALL statement. These also enable you to reference routines outside your immediate program, and they have a much longer history in COBOL than functions. In addition to showing you how to use the CALL to reference subroutines, I'll demonstrate how to design and write your own subroutines.

Invoking Other Programs and Subprograms

In this chapter, you will find a description and demonstration of how to invoke or CALL another program from within your program. You will also learn how to write programs that can be CALLed by other programs and to define how information is passed between such programs. Finally, I'll describe and demonstrate how several programs can be combined (or nested) in one set of source code and function as a unit but with well-defined sharing of resources and clearly specified interfaces. This last item operates in a manner very similar to the procedure mechanism integral to Pascal, C, and other modern programming languages.

There are several reasons why it is useful to invoke other programs:

- To obtain or use services and functionality that otherwise are not normally available within COBOL itself. For example, the operating system often maintains information about the operating environment or the user of the program that the program might need to obtain. This information can then be used to determine how the program will function from that point on, to implement applications-level security that limits different users to different functionality within the application, or simply to record this information with other application data for future reference. As another example, many interfaces with modern database and transaction systems are implemented with the CALL facility. Some of the most common of these are covered in Part V, "COBOL Databases and Transactions: A Sampling."

- To provide standard and utility functions to all the programs in large applications. The best examples are date editing, conversion, and other manipulation facilities. Part VIII, "Addressing the Year 2000 Issue," covers some of these functions quite extensively. Other examples here include application-specific edit, conversion, and formatting functions and obtaining commonly required information from programs, indexes, or database tables.

- To break up large, cumbersome programming requirements into smaller, more manageable portions. Even though this has been done quite commonly in many places, the results have often been less than satisfactory. One reason is that good documentation describing the interfaces and their organization is not developed. (If you write programs, this problem is easy to relate to; if you've ever maintained programs, poor documentation is still totally unacceptable.) The other reason for these poor results is that COBOL was pretty limited in this area before enhancements made with the 1985 Standard—nested source programs are one of the primary enhancements with this standard.

This chapter may appear more fragmented than the other chapters. That is because it's organized differently.

Invoking other programs (and being invoked by other programs) affects a fair number of different parts of the program; most of these effects have already been described. This chapter breaks these program parts into groups and gives examples so that you don't have to deal with all the technical aspects at once before you see how these groups are used.

Invoking other programs implies that several programs will be compiled separately and put together before or when they are executed. How this happens is entirely dependent on your specific programming environment. That side of things is beyond the scope of this chapter (Part IV, "COBOL Platforms and Environments," gets into the basics of these environments), but the one-step-at-a-time approach should make these programs easier to handle.

Several vendors have developed commonly used extensions, and these need to be described briefly and kept separate from coverage of the standard implementation.

As I mentioned earlier, the 1985 Standard has added a number of new features, including nested source programs. Unfortunately, though, the Standard document and other reference books I've seen mix the features together in something resembling alphabetical order. To add to the confusion, a great many applications (especially in the mainframe environments) have not implemented any of these features. That will make all this material brand new to many who read this chapter. Although this chapter should be able to do much better by dealing with the key topics separately, some of these topics still need to be listed and described.

I'll begin the first section by describing and demonstrating the basic essentials of subprograms and subroutines.

CALLing, Being CALLed, and Passing Information Back and Forth

In this section, you'll examine the basics of CALLing and being CALLed by other programs. You'll see how these separate programs are tied together and learn what is involved in passing data from one program to another.

Because a number of different parts of the programs are involved, the complete programs are shown here.

The Basic CALL with an Example

The two source programs shown in Listings 14.1A and 14.1B are probably some of the smallest examples of one program calling or invoking another program. This process is a simple extension of the primitive "Hello There" example most learn-to-program books present first. However, these examples serve a couple of important purposes. They provide an easy way to illustrate how the two programs are tied together and what parts of them must be altered for them to work together. These listings also provide you with the simplest programs for testing your programming environment to ensure that it is putting things together properly for you.

LISTING 14.1A   MAINPRG1

```
IDENTIFICATION DIVISION.
PROGRAM-ID.  MAINPRG1.                            (1)

PROCEDURE DIVISION.
0100-MAIN.
    DISPLAY 'BEGIN MAIN PROGRAM'.
    CALL 'SUBPRG1'.                               (2)
    DISPLAY 'END OF MAIN PROGRAM'.
    STOP RUN.                                     (3)
```

LISTING 14.1B   SUBPRG1

```
IDENTIFICATION DIVISION.
PROGRAM-ID.  SUBPRG1.                             (4)

PROCEDURE DIVISION.
0100-MAIN.
    DISPLAY 'EXECUTING SUB PROGRAM'.
EXIT PROGRAM.                                     (5)
```

You should be able to compile each of these programs, link them together (if necessary for your environment), and then run the first program to produce the following results:

```
BEGIN MAIN PROGRAM
EXECUTING SUBROUTINE
END OF MAIN PROGRAM
```

If you run into problems, you can review the rest of this section and the next section for some generic background on how programs and subprograms are connected. Part IV, "COBOL Platforms and Environments," also provides details on many of the common programming environments. If you are still having trouble, you will need to check the technical information for your specific environment. Generally speaking, you should not encounter problems here because this is basic to all COBOL environments.

Now look at the line identified as (2) in Listing 14.1A. It is the only line in this program that is different from any other programs you've seen so far. This is where you invoke the second program (the subprogram or subroutine), and you use the `CALL` statement to do it. The name of the program you're calling is `'SUBPRG1'`; notice how I've enclosed it in quotes to make it a nonnumeric literal. This is how it is done in most cases, although it can also be defined as an alphanumeric data item. I've limited the length of this name to eight characters. That isn't necessary, but before the 1985 Standard, it was necessary and still is in some programming environments.

Next, look at the line identified as (4) in Listing 14.1B. This is the `PROGRAM-ID`, and it also has a value of `'SUBPRG1'`. This is required by COBOL and is how the program is identified. It generally is also how the programming environment finds the program when the `CALL` from `MAINPRG1` is resolved (during the link process or when it is executed). In some environments, this name must also be used to name the compiler output or object module. This connection between the `CALL` name in the main program and `PROGRAM-ID` in the subprogram is essential but is often overlooked. If the two don't match, both programs will still compile and, in some cases, even link and execute. They will not connect with each other and produce the desired result, however.

Finally, look at the line identified as (5) in Listing 14.1B. The statement `EXIT PROGRAM` is on the line where you normally expect to see `STOP RUN`. The `STOP RUN` can't be used here because it implies that everything is to be terminated, that any files still in an `OPEN` state are to be closed, and that all resources are to be returned to the operating system. All you want to do is return control to the program that executed the `CALL` and begin execution again with the next statement following it—hence the `EXIT PROGRAM`.

Linking: A Generic Overview

When `MAINPRG1` in the preceding section is compiled and the name `SUBPRG1` is encountered in the `CALL` statement, there is nothing with which to match the name `SUBPRG1`. Because this is a `CALL` statement, though, it knows that this is acceptable, so it simply identifies it as an unresolved reference and continues with the compile process. However, somewhere along the line before this program can execute completely and correctly, the reference must be resolved or satisfied.

Linking is the process that deals with this kind of situation. In some environments, this is called *collecting, preparing, mapping,* or something similar, but the function is still required and is still the same. Finding the proper subprogram to match the name of the program being `CALL`ed is one of a large number of items that have to be taken care of in this process. The process must also ensure that control is passed to the proper location in the subprogram and that control is returned to the proper location in the `CALL`ing program when the `EXIT PROGRAM` statement is executed.

14

INVOKING OTHER
PROGRAMS AND
SUBPROGRAMS

Linking is also the process by which differences between the different programming languages are resolved so that COBOL programs can call programs written in C, assembler, PL1, Pascal, and a larger number of other languages. Linking also enables the programs written in these languages to call COBOL programs. Passing data and other information between the CALLing and CALLed program is also handled by the linking process, as are a variety of other functions. You will look at a number of these functions as you proceed through this chapter.

There are two basic types of linking: *static* and *dynamic*. The type of linking to be done is normally an option or parameter that is specified when the linker is called to prepare the compiler-produced object module for execution. Most modern environments now allow either form of linking. All the environments default to one of the two methods, and some linkers are so unobtrusive that the programmer is not even aware of the process.

Static linking is done before the program is executed. In this case, the linker locates the CALLed program as a distinctly separate step as it prepares the CALLing program for execution. It then combines the two programs into a single entity that can then be executed. This process generally produces a more efficient program because all the work is done ahead of time before the program is executed. Static linking is typically used for online programs and software that is prepared for customers and marketed to customers by software companies. The disadvantage of static linking is that every time a change needs to be made to the subprogram, all the programs that CALL it must be relinked.

Dynamic linking is specified when the programs are prepared for execution, but it occurs while the program executes. Thus, when the main program is executing and CALLs the subprogram, that subprogram isn't there, so the linker comes in automatically, searches for and loads the subprogram, and passes control to it. After the linker executes the EXIT PROGRAM statement, it returns and transfers control back to the proper location in the CALLing program. The linker also must handle a variety of other tasks, such as passing any data between the two programs, but the tasks described here are the essentials. Even though dynamic linking is less efficient than static linking, the difference is not normally noticeable in most batch applications, and using dynamic linking is definitely worth not having to be concerned about having all applications programs linked with current versions of all the subprograms.

Passing Data Between Programs

The example in Listings 14.2A and 14.2B demonstrates how data is normally passed between the CALLing program and the CALLed program. A file has also been added to the subprogram so that the example will have everything in it that is normally required in most programming situations.

LISTING 14.2A   MAINPRG2

```
IDENTIFICATION DIVISION.
PROGRAM-ID.  MAINPRG2.
DATA DIVISION.
WORKING-STORAGE SECTION.
01   INPUT-STATE-CODE           PIC XX.
01   INPUT-LOCATION             PIC X(20).
01   CONTINUE-PROCESSING        PIC XXX VALUE SPACES.
01   READ-FUNCTION              PIC X VALUE 'R'.            (1)
01   CLOSE-FUNCTION             PIC X VALUE 'C'.            (2)
01   RETRN-CODE                 PIC XX VALUE ZERO.         (3)
01   AGENT-INFO.                                           (4)
     05  AGENT-STATE            PIC XX.
     05  AGENT-TERRITORY        PIC X(20).
     05  AGENT-NAME             PIC X(20).
     05  AGENT-PHONE-NR         PIC X(13).
     05  AGENT-ADDRESS          PIC X(70).


PROCEDURE DIVISION.
0100-MAIN.
     DISPLAY 'WELCOME TO THE ACME AGENT LOCATION SYSTEM'.
     PERFORM 0200-MAIN-LOOP THRU 0200-EXIT
         UNTIL CONTINUE-PROCESSING (1:1) = 'N' OR 'n'.
     CALL 'SUBPRG2'
         USING CLOSE-FUNCTION RETRN-CODE AGENT-INFO.        (5)
     STOP RUN.
0200-MAIN-LOOP.
     DISPLAY 'PLEASE ENTER THE STATE YOU ARE INTERESTED IN'.
     ACCEPT INPUT-STATE-CODE.
     DISPLAY 'PLEASE ENTER THE TOWNSHIP, CITY, TOWN OR COUNTY'
     ACCEPT INPUT-LOCATION.
     MOVE INPUT-STATE-CODE TO AGENT-STATE.
     MOVE INPUT-LOCATION TO AGENT-TERRITORY.
     CALL 'SUBPRG2'
         USING READ-FUNCTION RETRN-CODE AGENT-INFO.         (6)
     IF RETRN-CODE = '01'
         DISPLAY 'WE ARE UNABLE TO LOCATE AN AGENT FOR THAT AREA'
     ELSE
     IF RETRN-CODE = '00'
         DISPLAY 'NAME: ' AGENT-NAME
         DISPLAY 'PHONE NR: ' AGENT-PHONE-NR
         DISPLAY 'ADDRESS:' AGENT-ADDRESS
     ELSE
         MOVE 'N' TO CONTINUE-PROCESSING
         GO TO 0200-EXIT.
     DISPLAY 'WOULD LIKE TO LOOK UP ANOTHER AGENT? (Y/N)'.
     ACCEPT CONTINUE-PROCESSING.
0200-EXIT.
     EXIT.
```

14

INVOKING OTHER
PROGRAMS AND
SUBPROGRAMS

LISTING 14.2B   SUBPRG2

```
IDENTIFICATION DIVISION.
PROGRAM-ID.  SUBPRG2.                                        (7)
ENVIRONMENT DIVISION.
INPUT-OUTPUT SECTION.
FILE-CONTROL.
    SELECT AGENT-INFO-FILE      ASSIGN TO AGTINFO
                                ORGANIZATION INDEXED
                                ACCESS MODE DYNAMIC
                                RECORD KEY AGENT-KEY
                                FILE STATUS AGENT-STATUS.
DATA DIVISION.
FILE SECTION.
FD  AGENT-INFO-FILE.
01  AGENT-RECORD.
    05  AGENT-KEY.
        10  AGENT-STATE         PIC XX.
        10  AGENT-TERRITORY     PIC X(20).
    05  FILLER                  PIC X(103).
WORKING-STORAGE SECTION.
01  AGENT-STATUS                PIC XX VALUE '00'.
01  FIRST-TIME-STATUS           PIC X   VALUE 'Y'.            (8)
LINKAGE SECTION.                                             (9)
01  CALL-FUNCTION               PIC X.
01  CALL-RETURN                 PIC XX.
01  CALL-INFO                   PIC X(125).
PROCEDURE DIVISION USING CALL-FUNCTION CALL-RETURN CALL-INFO. (10)
0100-MAIN.
    IF FIRST-TIME-STATUS = 'N'
        PERFORM 0200-PROCESS-REQUEST
    ELSE
        MOVE 'N' TO FIRST-TIME-STATUS
        OPEN INPUT AGENT-INFO-FILE
        IF AGENT-STATUS  = '00'
            PERFORM 0200-PROCESS-REQUEST
        ELSE
            DISPLAY 'UNABLE TO OPEN AGENT FILE, STATUS: '
                AGENT-STATUS
            DISPLAY '**PLEASE CALL HELP DESK**'
            MOVE '99' TO CALL-RETURN.
    EXIT PROGRAM.                                            (11)
0200-PROCESS-REQUEST.
    EVALUATE CALL-FUNCTION
        WHEN 'C'
          CLOSE AGENT-INFO-FILE
          MOVE '00' TO CALL-RETURN
        WHEN 'R'
          PERFORM 0300-DIRECT-READ
        WHEN OTHER
          DISPLAY 'UNKNOWN REQUEST FUNCTION: ' CALL-FUNCTION
```

```
            DISPLAY '**PLEASE CALL HELP DESK**'
            MOVE '99' TO CALL-RETURN.
0300-DIRECT-READ.
    MOVE CALL-INFO TO AGENT-RECORD.
    READ AGENT-INFO-FILE INTO CALL-INFO.
    IF AGENT-STATUS = '00'
        MOVE '00' TO CALL-RETURN
    ELSE
    IF AGENT-STATUS = '23'
        MOVE '01' TO CALL-RETURN
    ELSE
        DISPLAY 'AGENT FILE SYSTEM ERROR, STATUS: ' AGENT-STATUS
        DISPLAY '**PLEASE CALL HELP DESK**'
        MOVE '99' TO CALL-RETURN.
```

In most real programming situations, both the main program and the subprogram would have more functionality. But for this example, there is still sufficient processing to see the kinds of things that are normally done in both the main program and the subprogram.

Now examine some of the details of how these programs are wired together.

The lines identified as (1), (2), (3), and (4) are the definitions of the data items that will be passed to the subprogram. Observe that these data items are defined just the same as any other data items in WORKING-STORAGE. For that matter, these data items do not even need to be defined in there. The only requirements are that they be a 01 level, a 77 level, or an elementary item (before the 1985 Standard, the elementary item option was not allowed).

The lines identified as (5) and (6) are the two places where I CALL the subprogram SUBPRG2. I added the USING phrase in both places and then identified the three data items I want to pass to SUBPRG2. This is how the CALLing program passes data items. It is important to notice that the order of the data items is the same in both cases. Even though a different data name is used for the first data item listed, it is still a single character with the purpose of telling the subprogram which function to perform. The subprogram doesn't know or care that different data names are used in the calling program. All the subprogram will see is the two different values that distinguish the different functions.

Now look at line (6) more closely. This is the main CALL to the subprogram. Just before this line, the program has established the key values in the AGENT-INFO record that the subprogram will use to READ the indexed file and retrieve agent information for. The next thing the main program does after the CALL is to check the different values of RETRN-CODE. This is where the subprogram informs the main program of its success in obtaining the requested record. A value of '00' means that the designated record was read successfully, so the main program can display the results. A value of '01' means that the specific record was not on file, so the main program informs the user of this fact. A value of '99' means that something out of the ordinary has happened, so in this case, the main program sets itself to fall immediately to the STOP RUN (other program actions might be required, depending on the application and environment).

This is a very normal situation in which data is passed to the subprogram and the results are passed back to the main program. The use of the RETRN-CODE data item by this or some other name is commonly used with COBOL subprograms to notify the CALLing program of the status of its request. There are also many situations in which such a RETRN-CODE is not needed because the subprogram will always be able to perform the requested function.

The CALL at line (6) is similar, except that here the CLOSE-FUNCTION data item is used to pass the value C as a function to the subprogram to tell it to CLOSE the file because there will be no more requests.

Line (7) in the subprogram shows the PROGRAM-ID, and here the name matches the name used in the CALL statements of the CALLing program, just as it did in the first example.

I'll skip lines (8) and (9) briefly to look at line (10) in the subprogram. This is the PROCEDURE DIVISION declaration, but observe that it contains the term USING, followed by the list of data names defined in the subprogram that match up with the data names passed by the main program in the CALL statement. *Observe carefully that even though these have different names, their definitions and functions match identically and are in the same order as was specified in the* CALL *statements.* This is critical, and things will not work well at all otherwise. Notice also that the number of characters for each matches identically (even though AGENT-INFO and CALL-INFO have differing subordinate definitions).

Now let's return to line (9). Here you see a whole new section that you haven't seen before. This is the LINKAGE SECTION, and its sole purpose is to define the data items in a subprogram that are passed to it by a CALLing program. This section is still part of the DATA DIVISION, and it needs to follow the WORKING-STORAGE SECTION and must be present in any subprogram that needs to pass data back and forth with the CALLing program. The rules for this section are the same as for WORKING-STORAGE except that *no* VALUE *clauses are allowed,* except where 88-level condition names are defined. This is because all these data items are initially valued by the CALLing program.

A few more comments about the CALL parameters are appropriate at this time. Both the main program and subprogram have changed the values of the data items with equal ease. This is the default way the CALL interface uses to work with COBOL. In fact, the COBOL Standard states that these CALL parameters are to be treated as if they are located in only one place in memory, with both the CALLing and CALLed programs having equal access to these parameters. Prior to the 1985 Standard, this was the only way CALL parameters could be handled. The 1985 Standard provides another alternative, and I'll describe it in the last section of this chapter.

Now back to line (8). Here the data item FIRST-TIME-STATUS is defined. The subprogram uses it to determine whether this is the first time it has been CALLed in this program execution. You can see this being done in the first few lines of the PROCEDURE DIVISION. In these statements, you can see why this is necessary. The first time, and only the first time, the subprogram is CALLed, it needs to OPEN the index file. The FIRST-TIME-STATUS allows this to be handled properly.

This explanation highlights another default property of COBOL subprograms. After a subprogram is initially CALLed in a program execution, a subprogram's *internal values are not reset between succeeding* CALLs. Again, this is the only way things could work before the 1985 Standard, but there is now another option, which is described in the last section of this chapter.

Line (11) contains the EXIT PROGRAM statement and is the same as in the preceding example.

I just need to make one more comment before going on to the next section. This sample subprogram has both a FUNCTION-CODE and a RETRN-CODE with different values for each having explicit meanings and implications. I briefly described those meanings earlier, and they were also easy to see from the source statements because both were listed. However, this is not generally the case in a normal development or maintenance environment. For this reason, it is extremely important to carefully document all such interfaces used with all subprograms. The best place for this documentation is in the beginning of the subprogram. People lose hard-copy documentation and forget the names of word processor documents, but almost all organizations are careful about keeping the source programs that support their production computer applications.

Some Additional Options, Statements, and Features

In this section, you'll briefly examine a few additional options available in all the subprogram environments that weren't demonstrated in the previous examples. You'll also take a look at several vendor extensions that have become so common they need to be described. Most of these extensions will be included in the next COBOL Standard.

ON OVERFLOW, CANCEL, and ENTER

The following all pertain to the 1974 Standard. I'm keeping the 1974 and the 1985 Standards separate because most applications are more or less designed for one or the other standard, without a lot of gray area between when it comes to subprograms.

CALL...ON OVERFLOW

The ON OVERFLOW is an optional phrase in the CALL statement, and the imperative statement(s) following it are executed only when an overflow condition occurs. Such a condition occurs when a CALL statement is executed, but it is not possible for the program being CALLed to be made available for execution. Determining exactly what this means is left up to the COBOL vendors, but in most cases, it is limited to the situation in which dynamic linking is being done and the program being CALLed does not exist, cannot be loaded into computer memory for some reason, does not have a valid starting address, or the USING parameters cannot be properly passed to it. In 1974 Standard implementations, the ON OVERFLOW phrase turns the CALL statement into a conditional statement. The 1985 Standard adds an END-CALL, which will properly delimit the CALL and turn it back into an imperative statement, but it does *not* provide an alternative NOT ON OVERFLOW phrase. Instead, it introduces new ON EXCEPTION and NOT ON EXCEPTION phrases, which are now the preferred phrases to use. If such a phrase is not specified, but the condition occurs, COBOL does not specify what the results will be. However, most implementations will terminate the CALLing program with an error message.

The CANCEL Statement

The CANCEL sub-program-name... is a statement that will return the specified subprogram(s) to its initial state so that if it is CALLed again in the same program execution, it will operate as if it has not been previously executed. As a part of this function, any files defined within and OPENed by the subprogram will be CLOSEd. A program may not CANCEL a subprogram that has been CALLed but has not yet executed its EXIT PROGRAM statement. This would imply that the program was attempting to CANCEL a program that had previously directly or indirectly CALLed the CANCELing program (which would really lead to a mess).

Some Additional Comments

The USING clause in the PROCEDURE DIVISION identifier and the LINKAGE SECTION are defined for subprograms to receive parameters from the programs CALLing them. From that perspective, they serve no purpose in a main program that is not CALLed by some other program. The COBOL Standard states that these are essentially meaningful only if the program is to be CALLed by some other program.

The *recursive* CALL is a term that simply means that a subprogram has CALLed either itself or some other program that currently has an actively invoked (directly or indirectly) CALL to it. The COBOL Standard (both 1974 and 1985) states that this is not allowed.

The ENTER Statement

The ENTER statement is not really a part of interprogram communication, but it fits here better than anywhere else. This statement was included in the very first compilers and standards but will be removed and no longer available when the next standard is issued. It probably doesn't matter because I haven't seen it used since about 1968. The format of the statement follows:

```
ENTER language-name [routine-name]
```

After this statement, you can write in the language specified by language-name, and COBOL will transfer control to that compiler (or assembler) to compile (or assemble) it. This other compiler (or assembler) will continue to do its thing until an ENTER COBOL statement is encountered. At that time, control is returned to the COBOL compiler. Although this seemed like a good idea at the time, it never really worked out, and I am unaware of any compilers or assemblers that can accomplish such an interface at this time.

Vendor Extensions

This section lists several extensions that I have seen in a variety of applications that involve the subprogram interface. These extensions appear to be in common use in mainframe applications in the IBM environment and PC/midrange implementations using Micro Focus COBOL. These extensions are also under consideration for implementation with the next COBOL Standard.

The ENTRY Statement

The statement ENTRY entry-name USING data-name... can be inserted in the PROCEDURE DIVISION of a subprogram and is used to define additional alternative entry points to the subprogram. When this is done, and the CALLing program invokes the other entry to the subprogram with the statement CALL entry-name USING data-name, control is still passed to the subprogram, but in this case, *execution begins in the subprogram with the statement immediately following the ENTRY statement*. It is important to note here that the list of data names in the ENTRY statement and the CALL statements invoking it must correspond to the same sequence of data names specified in the USING phrase for the PROCEDURE DIVISION of the subprogram. The same or additional EXIT PROGRAM statements are used to return control to the CALLing program from this alternative entry point.

The most common use for such ENTRY statements is to OPEN and CLOSE files used by the subprogram. For example, if the following statements were added at the end of SUBPRG2 of the previous section, the statement at line (5) in MAINPRG2 could be replaced with the simple statement CALL 'SUBPRG2C'.:

```
0300-CLOSE
     ENTRY 'SUBPRG2C'.
     CLOSE AGENT-INFO-FILE.
     EXIT PROGRAM.
```

Finally, observe that no USING names are listed in either the CALL or the ENTRY statements. This is because no additional information needs to be provided to the second entry point, so the data items do not need to be passed to it. This is allowed in most implementations because the sequence specified in the PROCEDURE DIVISION USING phrase is not really contradicted. Problems would occur, however, if the code in 0300-CLOSE were to reference one of those data names.

The GOBACK Statement

Many implementations now allow the one-word GOBACK statement to be used in place of both the STOP RUN and the EXIT PROGRAM statements. The implied meaning of the statement is to *go back to wherever you came from.* These environments are sophisticated enough to know whether the program executing the GOBACK was invoked as a main program or a subprogram. If it was invoked as a subprogram, control is simply returned to the CALLing program. If it was invoked as a main program, any OPEN files are CLOSEd, computer memory is released, and all other miscellaneous cleanup functions are accomplished before returning control to the operating system.

Receiving Parameters in a Main Program

Most IBM environments treat programs as subprograms of the operating system. This interpretation makes things very convenient for IBM's transaction and database systems. This method also provides a side benefit to batch program applications: It allows a LINKAGE SECTION and a PROCEDURE DIVISION USING phrase to become functional in what COBOL views as a main program. When these become functional, the PARM parameter in the JCL EXEC statement can be used to pass character information to the program.

Here, the USING phrase of the PROCEDURE DIVISION needs to identify one record name defined in the LINKAGE SECTION. In this definition, the first 2 bytes are four COMP digits that are set by the operating system to indicate the number of characters transferred to the program when it was executed. The remainder of this record is the PARM value itself.

Recursive CALL Mechanisms

The recursive CALL is permitted in an increasing number of implementations that use stacks to support their linking facility. This mechanism probably causes as much confusion when it is invoked mistakenly as it provides additional facilities to the business programming environment.

Nested Source Programs

As mentioned earlier, the nesting of source programs was implemented with the 1985 Standard to allow the CALL statement to be used in a manner very similar to the way procedures are used in other languages, such as C and Pascal. To support this implementation, the terms GLOBAL and COMMON were also introduced.

The COBOL Standard attempts to define nested programs, and I've seen a few books that attempt to explain nested programs. Both are confusing, and neither really shows what is happening.

Instead, I'll begin again with an example and then base my comments, descriptions, and definitions on it. By necessity, this example is lengthy, in spite of cutting it down to a bare-minimum skeleton. I hope that it is a decent compromise—full enough to show you what is really going on but small enough so that you don't become lost.

The Nested Program Example

Remember that the example in Listing 14.3 is a single program that is compiled all at one time.

LISTING 14.3   NESTPROG

```
IDENTIFICATION DIVISION.                                     (1)
PROGRAM-ID.  NESTPROG.
 ENVIRONMENT DIVISION.
 INPUT-OUTPUT SECTION.
 FILE-CONTROL.
     SELECT POLICY-INPUT       ASSIGN TO POLICYIN.
     SELECT POLICY-EDITED      ASSIGN TO POLICYED.

 DATA DIVISION.
 FILE SECTION.
 FD  POLICY-INPUT.
 01  POLICY-RECORD             PIC X(100).
 FD  POLICY-EDITED.
 01  GOOD-POLICY-RECORD        PIC X(100).
```

continues

14

LISTING 14.3 CONTINUED

```
WORKING-STORAGE SECTION.
01  POLICY-INFO                  GLOBAL.                      (2)
        05  POLICY-TYPE          PIC XXXX.
        05  POLICY-NUMBER        PIC X(12).
        05  POLICY-UPDATE-CODE   PIC XXXX.
        05  POLICY-DATE          PIC X(8).
        05  POLICY-HOLDER        PIC X(20).
        05  POLICY-MISC-INFO     PIC X(12).
        05  FILLER               PIC X(40).

01  EDIT-STATUS                  PIC X.
01  VALID-STATUS                 PIC X.
01  ERROR-CODE                   PIC 999.
01  POLICY-EOF-STATUS            PIC X VALUE 'N'.
        88  POLICY-EOF           VALUE 'Y'.
PROCEDURE DIVISION.
0100-MAIN-CONTROL.
    OPEN INPUT POLICY-INPUT
         OUTPUT POLICY-EDITED.
    PERFORM 0800-READ-POLICY-CHANGES.
    PERFORM 0200-EDIT-CONTROL
        UNTIL POLICY-EOF.
    CLOSE POLICY-INPUT
          POLICY-EDITED.
    CALL 'NSTSUB2C'                                           (3)
    CALL 'NSTSUBXC'.
    STOP RUN.
0200-EDIT-CONTROL.
    MOVE 'Y' TO EDIT-STATUS.

    CALL 'DATEEDIT' USING POLICY-DATE EDIT-STATUS.            (4)
    IF EDIT-STATUS = 'Y'
        EVALUATE POLICY-TYPE
          WHEN 'LIFE'
            CALL 'NSTSUB1' USING EDIT-STATUS                  (5)
          WHEN 'AUTO'
            CALL 'NSTSUB2' USING EDIT-STATUS                  (6)
          WHEN 'HLTH'
            CALL 'NSTSUB3' USING EDIT-STATUS                  (7)
          WHEN OTHER
            MOVE 024 TO ERROR-CODE
            CALL 'NSTSUBX' USING ERROR-CODE                   (8)
        END-EVALUATE
    ELSE
        MOVE 023 TO ERROR-CODE
        CALL 'NSTSUBX' USING ERROR-CODE                       (9)
    END-IF.
    IF EDIT-STATUS = 'Y'
        WRITE GOOD-POLICY-RECORD FROM POLICY-INFO.
```

```
        PERFORM 0800-READ-POLICY-CHANGES.
0800-READ-POLICY-CHANGES.
    READ POLICY-INPUT INTO POLICY-INFO
        AT END
            MOVE 'Y' TO POLICY-EOF-STATUS.


IDENTIFICATION DIVISION.                                        (10)
PROGRAM-ID.  NSTSUB1.
DATA DIVISION.
WORKING-STORAGE SECTION.
01  ERROR-CODE-NEW-NAME              PIC 999.
LINKAGE SECTION.
01  MY-STATUS                        PIC X.
PROCEDURE DIVISION USING MY-STATUS.
0100-MAIN-CONTROL.
    IF POLICY-HOLDER  = POLICY-MISC-INFO
        MOVE 'N' TO MY-STATUS
        MOVE 101 TO ERROR-CODE-NEW-NAME
        CALL 'NSTSUBX' USING ERROR-CODE-NEW-NAME.
    EXIT PROGRAM.
END PROGRAM  NSTSUB1.
IDENTIFICATION DIVISION.                                        (11)
PROGRAM-ID.  NSTSUB2.
DATA DIVISION.
WORKING-STORAGE SECTION.
01  ERROR-CODE                       PIC 999.
01  RECORD-FOUND                     PIC X.
LINKAGE SECTION.
01  EDIT-STATUS                      PIC X.
PROCEDURE DIVISION USING EDIT-STATUS.
0100-MAIN-CONTROL.
    CALL 'NSTSUB2A' USING RECORD-FOUND POLICY-MISC-INFO.
    IF RECORD-FOUND = 'N'
        MOVE 'N' TO EDIT-STATUS
        MOVE 201 TO ERROR-CODE
        CALL 'NSTSUBX' USING ERROR-CODE.
    EXIT PROGRAM.
0200-PASS-CLOSE.
  ENTRY 'NSTSUB2C'.
  CALL 'NSTSUB2B'.
  EXIT PROGRAM.
IDENTIFICATION DIVISION.                                        (12)
PROGRAM-ID.  NSTSUB2A.
ENVIRONMENT DIVISION.
INPUT-OUTPUT SECTION.
FILE-CONTROL.
        SELECT AUTO-FILE          ASSIGN TO AUTOINFO
                                  ORGANIZATION INDEXED
                                  ACCESS MODE DYNAMIC
                                  RECORD KEY AUTO-KEY.
```

14

INVOKING OTHER
PROGRAMS AND
SUBPROGRAMS

continues

LISTING 14.3   CONTINUED

```
DATA DIVISION.
FILE SECTION.
FD   AUTO-FILE.
01   AUTO-RECORD.
     05   AUTO-KEY                   PIC X(12).
     05   FILLER                     PIC X(68).
WORKING-STORAGE SECTION.
01   FIRST-TIME-STATUS               PIC X VALUE 'Y'.
LINKAGE SECTION.
01   FOUND-STATUS                    PIC X.
01   AUTO-TYPE-YEAR                  PIC X(12).
PROCEDURE DIVISION USING FOUND-STATUS AUTO-TYPE-YEAR.
0100-MAIN-CONTROL.
     IF FIRST-TIME-STATUS = 'Y'
        OPEN INPUT AUTO-FILE
        MOVE 'N' TO FIRST-TIME-STATUS.
     MOVE AUTO-TYPE-YEAR TO AUTO-KEY.
     MOVE 'Y' TO FOUND-STATUS.
     READ AUTO-FILE
        INVALID KEY
           MOVE 'N' TO FOUND-STATUS.
     EXIT PROGRAM.
0900-CLOSE-FILE.
     ENTRY 'NSTSUB2C'.
     IF FIRST-TIME-STATUS NOT = 'Y'
        CLOSE AUTO-FILE.
     EXIT PROGRAM.
0300-CLOSE-FILE.
   ENTRY 'NSTSUB2B'.
   IF FIRST-TIME-STATUS NOT='Y'
        CLOSE AUTO-FILE.
   EXIT PROGRAM.
END PROGRAM   NSTSUB2A.
END PROGRAM   NSTSUB2.


IDENTIFICATION DIVISION.                              (13)
PROGRAM-ID.  NSTSUB3.
DATA DIVISION.
WORKING-STORAGE SECTION.
01   ERR-CODE                    PIC 999.
LINKAGE SECTION.
01   EDIT-STATUS                 PIC X.
PROCEDURE DIVISION USING EDIT-STATUS.
0100-MAIN-CONTROL.
     IF POLICY-MISC-INFO = SPACES
        MOVE 301 TO ERR-CODE
        CALL 'NSTSUBX' USING ERR-CODE
```

```
        MOVE 'N' TO EDIT-STATUS.
    EXIT PROGRAM.
END PROGRAM   NSTSUB3.

IDENTIFICATION DIVISION.
PROGRAM-ID.  NSTSUBX  COMMON  PROGRAM.                           (14)
ENVIRONMENT DIVISION.
INPUT-OUTPUT SECTION.
FILE-CONTROL.
    SELECT ERROR-FILE          ASSIGN TO ERRINFO.
DATA DIVISION.
FILE SECTION.
FD   ERROR-FILE.
01   ERROR-RECORD.
     05   ERROR-INFO              PIC X(100).
     05   ERROR-REASON            PIC X(20).
WORKING-STORAGE SECTION.
01   FIRST-TIME-STATUS           PIC X VALUE 'Y'.
LINKAGE SECTION.
01   ERROR-CODE                  PIC 999.
PROCEDURE DIVISION USING ERROR-CODE.
0100-MAIN-CONTROL.
    IF FIRST-TIME-STATUS = 'Y'
        OPEN OUTPUT ERROR-FILE
        MOVE 'N' TO FIRST-TIME-STATUS.
    MOVE POLICY-INFO TO ERROR-INFO.
    MOVE ERROR-CODE TO ERROR-REASON.
    WRITE ERROR-RECORD.
    EXIT PROGRAM.
0300-CLOSE-FILE.
    ENTRY 'NSTSUBXC'.
    IF FIRST-TIME-STATUS NOT = 'Y'
        CLOSE ERROR-FILE.
    EXIT PROGRAM.
END PROGRAM   NSTSUBX.
END PROGRAM   NESTPROG.
```

The purpose of this program is to edit input data for each of the three types of insurance policies sold by the company. At this point, the program is not much more than a skeleton of the finished product, but it does contain all the pieces and will function properly. This makes it an excellent illustrative example. I should note that this is also an excellent beginning in program development because as requirements are received, they can easily be inserted into the appropriate module and tested. Results can then be submitted for user approval.

END PROGRAM, Programs Containing Programs, and Which Programs Call Other Programs

Observe lines (1), (10), (11), (12), (13), and (14) of Listing 14.3. These lines are the beginnings of each of the programs and subprograms that comprise the single nested program.

Notice that some of these lines are preceded by END PROGRAM name lines. The END PROGRAM is used to designate the END of the program or subprogram specified by the name. Notice that the name is the same as that of the PROGRAM-ID of a previous program.

Notice also that in some cases, no END PROGRAM line precedes the beginning of the new program or subprogram. Here, the fact that the IDENTIFICATION DIVISION begins the new program means that no more statements follow for the preceding program but that the program is not yet terminated. This leads to a very important implication for nested programs: A *program contains all the programs following it until its own* END PROGRAM *line is reached.*

Now take a look and see which programs contain which other programs. First, notice that the very last line is the END PROGRAM for the main program NESTPROG, which means that it contains *all* the other programs. Line (10) is the beginning of the subprogram NSTSUB1, and the line above line (11) is the END PROGRAM line for it, so it does *not* contain any programs. Line (11) is the beginning of subprogram NSTSUB2, but no END PROGRAM line precedes the beginning of the next subprogram that begins at line (12). Hence, NSTSUB2 *contains* the following program, which is NSTSUB2A. Now, at line (13), observe that two END PROGRAMs precede the beginning of the next subprogram. The first END PROGRAM terminates NSTSUB2A, so that subprogram doesn't contain any programs. The next END PROGRAM terminates NSTSUB2, so that subprogram does not contain any additional programs. Similarly, NSTSUB3 and NSTSUBX are each followed immediately by their END PROGRAM lines, so neither of them contains any other subprograms.

You can see the importance of the concept of programs containing other programs by considering this statement: *Within a nested group of programs, any one program may only* CALL *those other programs that it contains.* There is one exception to this rule, but I'll cover that in the next subsection. The implication of this statement is that the main program can CALL any of the others. As you can see at lines (3), (5), (6), (7), (8), and (9), it does, in fact, do that. Also, because NSTSUB2 contains NSTSUB2A, it also can and does CALL that subprogram. With the exception of line (4) and the CALLs to NSTSUBX, there are no other CALLs; they would not be permitted because none of the other subprograms contain any other subprograms.

Now, returning to line (4), this is a CALL to the subprogram called DATEEDIT. It is not one of these nested programs but is, in fact, a normal separately compiled program. The correct implication is that this, and any of the other nested subprograms in this group, may call other separately compiled programs according to the rules presented in the previous sections of this chapter.

The converse of this is more complex. Although it isn't illustrated here, I'll describe how it works. The program NESTPROG is the main program of this group, and therefore, its name is properly defined just like any other separately compiled COBOL program. For that reason, it could be CALLed by another separately compiled program, and the linking mechanism would tie the two programs together. If NESTPROG had a LINKAGE SECTION and a PROCEDURE DIVISION with a USING clause, data could be passed to NESTPROG the same as all other separately compiled subprograms. This cannot be said for the other programs contained within NESTPROG, however. This is because all those programs are *contained within* NESTPROG, and all references to them are resolved at compile time. For that reason, those programs aren't visible to the linking system.

The COMMON Subprogram

Look at line (14) in the example. This is the PROGRAM-ID for the program NSTSUBX. Observe that the term COMMON PROGRAM has been included after the name. This is an option available with nested programs and specifies that this program is to be made COMMONly available to all the other subprograms contained in the same program that directly contains it. Because NESTPROG, in fact, contains NSTSUBX, NSTSUBX can be (and is) CALLed from all the other programs contained in NESTPROG. Note, though, that NSTSUBX still could not be called by any program that *it* contains, because that would be recursive.

GLOBAL Data (Versus Local Data)

Finally, look at line (2) at the beginning of the program NESTPROG. This is the 01 level record definition for the POLICY-INFO record. Notice that the term GLOBAL has been specified here. You may have already noticed that this name and some of the others defined in its record description are commonly used in the other nested programs contained in NESTPROG. Other data definitions in NESTPROG aren't—and in fact, can't be—referenced by the other subprograms in the group. If you look closely, you'll see that some of the other subprograms have used some of these same names for their own definition without any confusion at all.

The term GLOBAL is what makes the difference and distinction. This is how it works: *By default, all data names and corresponding definitions within a subprogram (of a nested group) are considered local to that subprogram only and can be referenced only by statements in that subprogram.*

14

INVOKING OTHER
PROGRAMS AND
SUBPROGRAMS

The term GLOBAL is what defines the exception. It may be applied to any 01 level record definition, FD file description, or RD report description. *When the term GLOBAL is specified for a record, file, or report, it and all the descriptions and definitions subordinate to it are made available for reference by all the subprograms contained in the program in which the GLOBAL item is defined.*

Extension to the CANCEL Statement

Remember that the effect of the CANCEL statement is to sever any relation between the program executing the CANCEL statement and the subprogram that is the subject of the CANCEL statement. This essentially returns that subprogram to its initial state as if it had never been CALLed in the executing program.

In the case of nested subprograms, the process of being returned to the initial state is extended to all subprograms contained within the subprogram that is the subject of the CANCEL statement.

One effect of the CANCEL is to CLOSE any files that were defined in the subject subprogram and were in an OPEN state at the time of the CANCEL. This effect is also extended to any files that had similarly been defined in subprograms contained in the subject subprogram and were in an OPEN state at the time of the CANCEL.

Other Features from the 1985 Standard

A few other items were implemented with the 1985 Standard and are not a part of the nested program facility. These features are all special-purpose but can be useful when the situation calls for them.

EXTERNAL

The term EXTERNAL may be applied to an FD file description or a 01-level record definition in a program and/or subprogram(s) that it has CALLed. When this is done, the name by which it is identified and the information it contains are maintained externally to the program itself (by the linking software and execution environment). This allows the program and any subprograms that specified that same name with the term EXTERNAL to all have equal access to the referenced file and/or data.

This feature essentially allows the main program and/or one or more subprograms to all READ or WRITE records of the same file. It also allows them to have equal access to the same data record. Because the name, data, and/or file control information are the only things kept EXTERNALly, each subprogram referencing it must have its own definition of the detailed subordinate items. Because this is managed by the execution environment and linking software, it is available to all programs and CALLed subprograms, regardless of whether they were compiled separately or together as a nested unit.

Very careful management of this facility by the program is required to ensure that conflicting actions to the file/record are not taken to different subprograms.

EXTERNAL is completely distinct from and not to be confused with the term GLOBAL, which is limited to nested programs. Both terms may be applied to the same record or file.

INITIAL

The term INITIAL may be applied to the program name of a subprogram in the PROGRAM-ID paragraph of the IDENTIFICATION DIVISION (for example, PROGRAM-ID. DATEDIT *IS* INITIAL.). When this is done, that subprogram and any other subprograms it contains are set to their initial values every time it is CALLed. This is handy for a variety of utility routines, such as date editing, where every execution is independent of all others.

CALL BY REFERENCE or BY CONTENT and ON EXCEPTION

The full format of the CALL statement as defined for the 1985 Standard is

```
CALL program-name [USING [{BY REFERENCE/BY CONTENT}] data-item...]
    [ON EXCEPTION imperative-statement-1]
    [NOT ON EXCEPTION imperative-statement-2]
    [END-CALL]
```

The terms REFERENCE or CONTENT can be applied to any data item specified in a CALL statement. The term REFERENCE is the default and specifies that the data item can be freely modified by the subprogram being CALLed in the same manner discussed throughout this chapter. However, if the term CONTENT is specified for a data item, that data item as it exists in the CALLing program may *not* be modified by the CALLed subprogram. Instead, the interface or linking software must make available a storage area containing the value of the data item in the same format that is defined for it in the CALLing program; this storage area is then made available to the CALLed subprogram. This way, the CALLed program may continue to use the data item any way it requires, but the effects are limited to the special storage area so that the actual data item in the CALLing program is never actually referenced by the CALLed subprogram.

If the terms CONTENT or REFERENCE are specified for a data item, but neither is specified for a succeeding data item, the one that was specified for the first data item is assumed to also apply to the successive one.

The phrase ON EXCEPTION has the same meaning as ON OVERFLOW, which was described earlier in this chapter. However, NOT ON EXCEPTION is also defined to allow the "other side of the coin" to be specified. To review, an OVERFLOW or EXCEPTION condition exists if (at execution time) the program name specified cannot be located, loaded into memory, or have control or data passed to it as required by the CALL statement.

CHAPTER 15

Specialty Features

This chapter covers several features in COBOL that are or have been important to the language but generally aren't included among the statements and items programmers consider a main part of their toolkit.

Segmentation

Segmentation is the way a programmer defines portions of the PROCEDURE DIVISION that will not be in memory at all times with the rest of the program. The fact that segmentation is a separate chapter in the 1985 Standard indicates how recently memory availability was a major programming consideration. Hardware advances in memory-chip design and software advances in memory management have made this kind of program-level control obsolete. This is one of the few areas where obsolete technology has been removed from most programs.

COBOL uses SECTIONs defined in the PROCEDURE DIVISION as a basis for its segmentation. Chapter 4, "Managing Program Flow and Looping," introduces the use of SECTION names in the PROCEDURE DIVISION, how they are defined and work, and how they are referenced in statements such as PERFORM.

When segmentation is to be used in a COBOL program, each SECTION definition contains a two-digit number that is assigned to that section. This number follows the word SECTION in the definition. A segment then is composed of all those SECTIONs having the same two-digit number. The short sample in Listing 15.1 demonstrates this process. If the number is omitted for the SECTION definition, it is assumed to be zero.

All segments are treated in one of two (or, optionally, three) ways, depending on the value of their segment number. The first type is the *fixed portion* and contains all segments assigned the numbers 0 through 49. These segments are logically assumed to be in memory at all times. Passing control among such segments (with PERFORM, GO TO, and so on) works just the same as if no segmentation had been specified for the program.

Segments assigned segment numbers 50 through 99 are called *independent segments* and are a bit trickier to handle. These segments always are treated as if they had not been loaded in memory before and therefore are loaded in their initial state every time they are referenced (by PERFORM or GO TO). This works well, as long as these independent segments are referenced by and in turn reference only paragraphs or sections belonging in the same segment number or fixed portion of the program. If, on the other hand, another segment with a different segment number also greater than 50 is referenced by the first referenced independent segment, that segment will overlay the first segment; in doing so, the first segment's reference back to the original location of the main program is destroyed.

Modern compiler and operating system designs for memory management have essentially eliminated the need for concern about control information contained in PROCEDURE DIVISION modules. For that reason, independent segments are no longer needed and should not be used; you therefore will be able to avoid the concerns described earlier. The following sample defines independent segments because they commonly were used in older programs, but they will be referenced properly.

The third (optional) kind of segment is called *fixed overlayable*. Such segments are handled as if they were in memory at all times, but they can be overlaid by other segments to conserve memory. In order for this mechanism to work, all the segment's information regarding references to other parts of the PROCEDURE DIVISION must be kept outside the segment itself in reference tables that are established in the program's permanent memory. When segmentation first was designed for COBOL, this was considered a difficult thing to do with significant amounts of computer (CPU) overhead, so it was avoided. However, this now is the normal way to do things for a large number of reasons, so it is no longer a concern.

Defining fixed overlayable segments requires the specification of the SEGMENT-LIMIT for the program. This clause needs to be added in the computer-name-2 sentence of the OBJECT-COMPUTER paragraph, as in this example:

```
ENVIRONMENT DIVISION.
[CONFIGURATION SECTION.
[SOURCE COMPUTER.  [computer-name-1 [WITH DEBUGGING MODE].]
[OBJECT-COMPUTER.  [computer-name-2
    [MEMORY SIZE integer-1 {WORDS/CHARACTERS/MODULES}]
    [PROGRAM COLLATING  SEQUENCE IS alphabet-name-1]
    [SEGMENT-LIMIT IS segment-number].]
```

Here, segment-number is a two-digit number between 1 and 49. When SEGMENT-LIMIT is used, any segment with an assigned value between the SEGMENT-LIMIT and 49 is treated as a fixed overlayable. Segments with segment numbers below the value of the SEGMENT-LIMIT are termed *fixed permanent* and are guaranteed to be kept in memory whenever the program is in memory. Observe that the OBJECT-COMPUTER paragraph contains only one sentence and therefore only one period, which must be at the very end of the entire specification.

The short example in Listing 15.1 demonstrates a simple segmented program.

LISTING 15.1 SEGMENT.

```
IDENTIFICATION DIVISION.
PROGRAM-ID.  Segments.
ENVIRONMENT DIVISION.
CONFIGURATION SECTION.
SOURCE-COMPUTER.  BRANDXY.
OBJECT-COMPUTER.  BRANDXY
    SEGMENT-LIMIT 30.
*
*   File Control and Data Division omitted for brevity.
*
PROCEDURE DIVISION.
0000-MAIN SECTION 00.
0000-MAIN-PARA.
    PERFORM 0010-INITIAL.
    PERFORM 1000-MAIN-LOOP
        UNTIL INPUT-EOF.
    PERFORM 9010-FINAL.
    STOP RUN.

0010-INITIAL SECTION 90.
0010-INITIAL-PARA.
    OPEN INPUT MAIN-INPUT
              EDIT-TABLE-FILE
         OUTPUT EDIT-OUTPUT
               ERROR-REPORT.
    PERFORM 0100-READ-MAIN-INPUT.

0100-READ-MAIN-INPUT SECTION 00.
0100-READ-MAIN-INPUT-PARA.
    READ MAIN-INPUT
        AT END
            MOVE 'Y' TO INPUT-EOF-STATUS.

1000-MAIN-LOOP SECTION 00.
1000-MAIN-LOOP-PARA.
    EVALUATE INPUT-TYPE
        WHEN 'AUTO'
          PERFORM 2000-AUTO-POLICY-EDIT
        WHEN 'LIFE'
          PERFORM 3000-LIFE-POLICY-EDIT
        WHEN OTHER
          MOVE 1234 TO ERROR-CODE
          PERFORM 1500-HANDLE-ERROR
    END-EVALUATE.
    PERFORM 0100-READ-MAIN-INPUT.

1200-EDIT-DATES SECTION 22.
1200-EDIT-DATES-PARA.
*   Date editing routine
```

```
 1500-HANDLE-ERROR SECTION 45.
 1500-HANDLE-ERROR-PARA.
*    Format and write reject into to report

 2000-AUTO-POLICY-EDIT SECTION 60.
 2000-AUTO-POLICY-EDIT-PARA.
*    Edit details for Automobile Insurance policy transactions
*    Including:
         MOVE AUTO-RENEWAL-DATE TO DATE-FIELD.
         PERFORM 1200-EDIT-DATES.
         IF DATE-STATUS NOT = ZERO
             MOVE DATE-STATUS TO ERROR-CODE
             PERFORM 1500-HANDLE-ERROR.
*    More editing


 3000-LIFE-POLICY-EDIT SECTION 70.
 3000-LIFE-POLICY-EDIT-PARA.

*    Edit details for Life Insurance policy transactions
*    Including:
         MOVE POLICY-ACTIVATION-DATE TO DATE-FIELD.
         PERFORM 1200-EDIT-DATES.
         IF DATE-STATUS NOT = ZERO
             MOVE DATE-STATUS TO ERROR-CODE
             PERFORM 1500-HANDLE-ERROR.
*    More editing
*
 9010-FINAL SECTION 90.
 9010-FINAL-PARA.
         CLOSE MAIN-INPUT
               EDIT-TABLE-FILE
               EDIT-OUTPUT
               ERROR-REPORT.
```

This listing is a very bare skeleton of a program, but it does show how segmentation works and how a typical program using it might be "wired" together.

The paragraphs 0000-MAIN, 0100-READ-MAIN-INPUT, and 1000-MAIN-LOOP all have segment numbers of zero because they need to be kept in main memory permanently.

0010-INITIAL and 9010-FINAL are each used only once in the course of the entire program, so they don't need to be kept in memory to their given segment number 90. They will be placed in the same segment because they have the same number, and that is done because they are so small.

1200-EDIT-DATES is an "in-between" module. Because it can be used by any of the editing modules, it needs to be in fixed memory. But because it isn't a part of the main program control, it doesn't have to be in memory all the time. I've assigned it segment number 22 to keep it in main memory because all the edit routines use it.

15

SPECIALTY
FEATURES

1500-HANDLE-ERROR is also one of those in-between modules, but because it is needed only to handle error transactions, it will not be used that much. It therefore can be assigned number 45, which will make it a fixed overlayable segment.

2000-AUTO-POLICY-EDIT and 3000-LIFE-POLICY-EDIT are given numbers 60 and 70, respectively. This means they will never be in memory at the same time—that's okay because they will never need to be. These are the independent segments.

Because 2000-AUTO-POLICY-EDIT and 3000-LIFE-POLICY-EDIT are independent segments, neither one of them can perform any code in other independent segments having numbers that don't match their own. Because 1200-EDIT-DATES and 1500-HANDLE-ERROR are PERFORMed by independent segments, neither one of them can PERFORM code in an independent segment, either, or that also would result in a loss of control.

Sorting and Merging Files in COBOL

Sorting has a long and interesting history in data processing. This was one of the first areas in which independent software companies were able to develop products that competed successfully with mainframe manufacturers. COBOL's significance is that it provides a means for modifying the data going into and coming out of the actual sort process. Standalone sort utilities now do this as a matter of course, and that is one of the key reasons why they are so convenient to use. However, these utilities still cannot offer some of the same flexible options offered by the COBOL interface. In fact, in many cases, the actual sort software used from the COBOL program is the same software that does the sorting for the standalone utilities.

Several items need to be set up for sorting (and merging) within COBOL programs. Two primary interfaces need to be provided by the program. The first is access to system resources (memory and disk) that the sort software will need to accomplish the sorting and merging task. The second is a flexible interface between the program and the sort software so that the data to be sorted can be passed to the software and the resulting sorted (or merged) data can be passed back to the program for further processing.

The Sort File

The sort file is the data interface between the program and the sort software, as well as the interface to the system resources (memory and disk) the software will need in order to accomplish the sorting (or merging). To the programmer, this sort file looks very much like any other sequential file. There are a few differences that you'll learn about in this section, though.

A FILE-CONTROL entry is required in the INPUT-OUTPUT SECTION of the ENVIRONMENT DIVISION. Because this a special work area for the sort software, none of the file description clauses are appropriate, and the entry is limited to this:

```
SELECT file-name ASSIGN TO implementor-name.
```

The file-name of the sort file can be included in a SAME AREA clause of the I-O-CONTROL paragraph, but it is limited to SAME SORT AREA or SAME SORT-MERGE AREA clauses. Other files also may be included in this clause. The terms SORT and SORT-MERGE are equivalent in this clause.

The entry for the sort file in the FILE SECTION of the DATA DIVISION has several differences. Because it describes a sort-merge file, the description entry begins with the code SD instead of FD. The only two clauses allowed within this entry are the RECORD clause and the DATA RECORD clause. These two are exactly as described for sequential files, so additional comments about them aren't needed here. Other clauses are not permitted—again because the file is specifically set up for the sort software and its requirements are taken for granted.

Record definition(s) describing the record(s) being sorted or merged follow the SD entry, just as they would for any file described by an FD.

The data item(s) that will identify the sequence key information are defined in these record definition(s) following the sort-merge file description. When more than one record are described, the data items identified as keys (in the SORT or MERGE statement) are assumed to be in the same relative position in all the record descriptions. This means that the keys need to be defined in only one of the records.

The SORT Statement

The complete SORT statement follows:

```
SORT file-name-1 {ON {ASCENDING/DESCENDING} KEY {data-name-1}... }...
  [WITH DUPLICATES IN ORDER]
  [COLLATING SEQUENCE IS alphabet-name]
  {USING {file-name-2}.../INPUT PROCEDURE IS procedure-name-1
  ➡[{THRU/THROUGH} procedure-name-2]}
  {GIVING {file-name-3.../OUTPUT PROCEDURE IS procedure-name-3
  ➡[{THRU/THROUGH} procedure-name-4]}
```

Here, file-name-1 is the name of the sort-merge file described in the last section.

The data-name-1 entries specify the sequence keys for the sort and must be defined in one of the records belonging to file-name-1. They are listed from left to right in order of significance, with the first one listed being the most significant. Ascending and descending orders can be interspersed as needed, and the data-name-1 items can be defined however is required. Numeric items will be compared algebraically, and alphanumeric items will be compared by character or collating sequence order.

The DUPLICATES phrase was introduced with the 1985 Standard, and it specifies that when two records match identically based on the key information, the first record received into the sort will be the first produced out of the sort. Without this clause, the ordering of records having identical key values is unspecified.

The COLLATING SEQUENCE phrase allows you to optionally specify the collating sequence of an alternative alphabet-name that was defined in the SPECIAL-NAMES paragraph in the CONFIGURATION SECTION of the ENVIRONMENT DIVISION.

Examine the line beginning with USING... and observe that there are two alternatives here, and one of them is required. This line specifies how data will be presented to the sort software. The USING with one or more file-name-2 entries is one alternative. The INPUT PROCEDURE... is the other alternative; I'll cover this second alternative later in the chapter because it is a bit involved.

When the USING is specified, the sort software simply reads all the records from each of the files listed (in that order) and sorts them. The files listed here must all be in a closed state when the SORT statement is executed. These files can be of any type(s) or organization(s) and are regular files that might be used anywhere in any other COBOL programs. These files aren't to be confused with, and cannot be sort files of, the type described in the preceding section. If the size of the records in these files differs from that specified for the records defined for the sort file (file-name-1), the data will be transferred to file-name-1 record(s) according to the normal rules for the MOVE statement.

The last line of the definition, beginning with GIVING, is very similar to the line just described. It specifies the disposition of the records after they have been sorted. Again, the OUTPUT PROCEDURE alternative is covered in a later section.

When GIVING is specified, the records simply are written to the file-name-3 specified as their final sorted order is determined. If multiple file-name-3 entries are specified, multiple copies of the records will be produced in the indicated files. The formats of the files may be different, though, if the files have different organizations, record lengths, and so on. If the size of the records in these files differs from that specified for the records defined for the sort file (file-name-1), the data will be transferred to the file-name-3 record(s) according to the normal rules for the MOVE statement.

A Basic Sort Program Example

The code in Listing 15.2 demonstrates a basic sort program.

LISTING 15.2   SORT1.

```
IDENTIFICATION DIVISION.
PROGRAM-ID.  Sort1.
ENVIRONMENT DIVISION.
INPUT-OUTPUT SECTION.
FILE-CONTROL.
      SELECT FILLED-ORDERS        ASSIGN TO INDATA1.
      SELECT OUTSTANDING-ORDERS    ASSIGN TO INDATA2
                                   ORGANIZATION INDEXED
                                   ACCESS SEQUENTIAL
                                   RECORD KEY ORDER-KEY.
      SELECT OUTPUT-DATA           ASSIGN TO OUTDATA.
      SELECT SORT-WORK             ASSIGN TO SORTWORK.

DATA DIVISION.
FILE SECTION.
FD  FILLED-ORDERS
    LABEL RECORDS STANDARD.
01  FILLED-ORDER-RECORD           PIC X(97).

FD  OUTSTANDING-ORDERS.
01  OUTSTANDING-ORDER-RECORD.
    05  ORDER-KEY.
        10  ORDER-DATE-YYYYMMDD    PIC 9(8).
        10  ORDER-NUMBER           PIC 9(6).
    05  FILLER                     PIC X(83).

FD  OUTPUT-DATA
    LABEL RECORDS STANDARD.
01  OUTPUT-RECORD                  PIC X(97).

SD  SORT-WORK.
01  SORT-RECORD.
    05  SORT-ORDER-DATE-YYYYMMDD   PIC 9(8).
    05  SORT-ORDER-NUMBER          PIC 9(6).
    05  SORT-CUSTOMER-CODE         PIC X(6).
    05  SORT-CUSTOMER-NAME         PIC X(25).
    05  FILLER                     PIC X(20).
    05  SORT-SALESMAN-NAME         PIC X(25).
    05  FILLER                     PIC X(7).

PROCEDURE DIVISION.
0000-MAIN-PARA.
      SORT SORT-WORK
          ASCENDING KEY SORT-SALESMAN-NAME
          DESCENDING KEY SORT-ORDER-DATE-YYYYMMDD
          ASCENDING KEY  SORT-CUSTOMER-NAME
                         SORT-ORDER-NUMBER
        USING FILLED-ORDERS
              OUTSTANDING-ORDERS
        GIVING OUTPUT-DATA.
      STOP RUN.
```

15

Utility software is available on many computer systems that can do this same sort with only half a dozen control statements. This wasn't always the case, though, and because of the way this program is written, it is very easy to see exactly what is happening.

The value of the example here is to show where and how the files and keys are set up and used.

Notice how the keys are defined in the file SORT-WORK and then specified in the SORT statement. The most significant key is the first one, and the least significant key is the last one. So, all the records for each salesperson will be sorted together. Within that, the records will be sorted by the date of the order (most recent first), and for each date, the records will be ordered by customer name and order number.

The input and output files are neither OPENed nor CLOSEd. The SORT software will take care of that because you're using the USING and GIVING phrases.

Two files are included in the USING phrase, and one of them is indexed. This is no problem because of the ACCESS SEQUENTIAL (according to the ORDER-KEY).

The MERGE Statement

The complete MERGE statement follows:

```
MERGE file-name-1 {ON {ASCENDING/DESCENDING} KEY {data-name-1}... }...
   [WITH DUPLICATES IN ORDER]
   [COLLATING SEQUENCE IS alphabet-name]
   {USING file-name-2 {file-name-3}...
   {GIVING {file-name-4.../OUTPUT PROCEDURE IS procedure-name-3
[{THRU/THROUGH} procedure-name-4]}
```

The MERGE statement is very similar to the SORT statement, and the processing is related. There are some important distinctions, though.

Observe that with the exception of the verb MERGE, the first three lines of the statement are identical, and the way in which they are specified also is identical.

However, notice the key differences in the USING phrase. The first difference is that a minimum of two files must be specified after the USING. This is because the very concept of the MERGE is to merge records of two or more files.

The second difference is the implication of the term *merge.* This term implies (and in programming requires) that *the two (or more) files are already in the proper sequence and simply need to be combined together* into a single file with that sequence preserved. The keys defined in the first line of the MERGE statement specify this sequence.

The implications of this are what cause the third and final difference between the SORT and MERGE statements. This is the fact that the INPUT PROCEDURE is not permitted with the

MERGE. The reason is that the trick to successfully merging several files is determining which records are to be processed from which input file in which order. The only way MERGE can do this is by having control over reading these files, and that is why the INPUT PROCEDURE is not possible here.

Obviously, if all the input files are in the required sequence, the MERGE is much more efficient than sorting. However, this rarely occurs, so the MERGE is seen infrequently in data processing. For that reason and the fact that the format of the SORT and MERGE statements is so similar, there is no separate sample merge program.

The INPUT PROCEDURE and the RELEASE Statement

The INPUT PROCEDURE provides the program with a means of formatting, modifying, and/or building the data as it is turned over or RELEASEd to the SORT software for sorting. procedure-name-1 [THRU procedure-name-2] is the paragraph (or section) or beginning and ending paragraphs (or sections) that contain or control this logic.

The concept is exactly as if the sort software were "performing" the paragraph or paragraphs or section or group of sections. When procedure-name-2 is used, it is normally as an EXIT paragraph, which is a convenient way of getting to the end of the INPUT PROCEDURE. The way this works follows.

The SORT begins by doing its own internal initialization, which includes OPENing the sort file (file-name-1) or preparing it to receive the data that will be passed to it. Control then is turned over to the beginning statement of the procedure-name-1 paragraph or section.

The statements within the procedure-name-1 [THRU procedure-name-2] can be any regular statements (except SORT, MERGE, or RETURN). When a record has been formatted and is ready, the RELEASE statement is used to pass the record to the SORT software, which does its thing with the record and then gives control back to the statement following the RELEASE.

The logic of these INPUT PROCEDURE statements continues formatting and releasing records to the sort software until all of the records have been RELEASEd. At that point, the logic needs to pass through the last statement of the INPUT PROCEDURE so that control can be passed back to the sort software.

When the sort software receives control back from the end of the INPUT PROCEDURE, this signals that no more data will be given to it for sorting. At this point, the records are sorted and written to the GIVING file(s) or prepared to be transferred back to the program's control in the OUTPUT PROCEDURE.

15

SPECIALTY FEATURES

Note how important it is for the program logic to pass through the end of the INPUT PROCEDURE when all the data has been RELEASEd to the SORT so that control can be passed back to the sort software. If that does not happen properly, the sort software will never know that it has all the records it needs to SORT. The converse is equally important. If the last statement of the INPUT PROCEDURE is executed before all the data has been passed to the sort, it will have CLOSEd its receiving mechanism and will not be able to process the next record that may be RELEASEd to it.

The final rule about the INPUT PROCEDURE applies if the program is segmented. If the INPUT PROCEDURE, any part of it, or any procedure referenced by it is in an independent segment (segment numbers 50–99), all of it and all procedures referenced by it must be in the same independent segment (have the same segment number). In addition, if the INPUT PROCEDURE is in an independent segment, the SORT statement must be in that same segment or in a fixed segment (segment numbers 0–49). The INPUT and OUTPUT PROCEDUREs can be in different independent segments, but if and only if the SORT statement is in a fixed segment.

The RELEASE statement is quite simple; its format follows:

```
RELEASE record-name-1 [FROM data-item-1]
```

Here, record-name-1 must be the name of a record defined in the sort file (file-name-1) specified in the SORT statement. The optional FROM data-item-1 acts just as it would in a WRITE statement. This is exactly as if a MOVE data-item-1 TO record-name-1 were executed just before the RELEASE record-name-1 is executed.

As indicated earlier, the RELEASE passes the data in record-name-1 to the sort software, which does the initial processing on it and stores it away before returning control back to the statement following the RELEASE statement. At that point, the program logic can do whatever it does to obtain and build the next record to be RELEASEd. (Listing 15.3 illustrates this process.)

The OUTPUT PROCEDURE and the RETURN Statement

The OUTPUT PROCEDURE ties program logic to the sort software in the same way the INPUT PROCEDURE does, except that here, the records are RETURNed back to the program control *after* they are placed in the required sequence by the SORT software. The OUTPUT PROCEDURE also can be used with the MERGE statement, and the interface is identical.

When the sort software has ordered the data and is ready to present it back to the program logic, it OPENs the sort file for sending records back to the program and PERFORMs the OUTPUT PROCEDURE. The program logic here uses the RETURN statement to receive control of each of the records in the SORT (file-name-1) record area. At this point, the logic can manipulate the data as needed and WRITE it to output files wherever required.

Each successive record is RETURNed and processed in this fashion. After all the sorted (or merged) records have been handled, the AT END phrase of the RETURN statement is used by the sort software to signal to the program logic that there are no more records.

After completing any final processing, the OUTPUT PROCEDURE exits back to the SORT software control when the last statement in the OUTPUT PROCEDURE is executed. The sort software then CLOSEs the sort file, does its final cleanup, and passes control back to the main program logic, which is at the next statement to be executed following the SORT statement itself.

The rules regarding segmentation apply equally to the OUTPUT PROCEDURE.

Conceptually, the RETURN statement operates in the same manner as the sequential READ statement. Its format follows:

```
RETURN file-name-1 RECORD [INTO data-item-1]
    AT END imperative statement-1
    [NOT AT END imperative-statement-2]
    [END-RETURN]
```

Here, file-name-1 is the name of the sort file and is the same as the file-name-1 specified in the SORT (or MERGE) statement. The RETURN causes the sort software to place the next sequenced record into the record area for file-name-1, where it can be processed using the data definitions for the records defined for file-name-1.

The INTO data-item-1 is essentially the same as following the RETURN statement with a MOVE record-name-1 TO data-item-1 statement, where record-name-1 is the name of the appropriate-sized record defined for the file-name-1.

As with the sequential READ statement, the AT END imperative statement-1 is executed with the next RETURN after the last record has been passed to the program. Note that the AT END phrase is required. This is because a FILE STATUS data name *cannot* be defined for a sort file, so the AT END phrase is a logical necessity.

The NOT AT END and END-RETURN phrases act exactly as the corresponding phrases work with the sequential READ statement.

An Advanced Sort Program Example

The example in Listing 15.3 shows a more advanced sort program.

LISTING 15.3 SORT2.

```
IDENTIFICATION DIVISION.
PROGRAM-ID.  Sort2.
ENVIRONMENT DIVISION.
INPUT-OUTPUT SECTION.
FILE-CONTROL.
     SELECT MAILING-INFO        ASSIGN TO INDATA1.
     SELECT MAILING-OUTPUT      ASSIGN TO OUTDATA.
     SELECT SORT-WORK           ASSIGN TO SORTWORK.


DATA DIVISION.
FILE SECTION.
FD  MAILING-INFO.
     LABEL RECORDS STANDARD.
01  MAILING-INFO-RECORD.
     05  FILLER                 PIC X(27).
     05  MAILING-ADDRESS        PIC X(120).
     05  FILLER                 PIC X(50).


FD  MAILING-OUTPUT.
01  MAILING-OUTPUT-RECORD.
     05  MAIL-CONTROL-BREAK-CODE    PIC XXX.
     05  MAIL-BREAK-ZIP-CODE        PIC X(5).
     05  MAIL-BREAK-COUNT           PIC 9(9).
     05  FILLER                     PIC X(111).
01  MAILING-PRINT-RECORD           PIC X(132).


SD  SORT-WORK.
01  SORT-RECORD.
     05  SORT-FULL-ZIP-CODE     PIC X(9).
     05  SORT-MAILING-INFO      PIC X(197).


WORKING-STORAGE SECTION.
01  END-INPUT-STATUS           PIC XXX VALUE 'NO '.
     88  END-INPUT                      VALUE 'YES'.
01  END-SORT-STATUS            PIC XXX VALUE 'NO '.
     88  END-SORT                       VALUE 'YES'.
01  PREVIOUS-ZIP-CODE          PIC X(5) VALUE ZERO.
01  ZIP-CODE-COUNT             PIC 9(9) VALUE ZERO.


PROCEDURE DIVISION.
0000-MAIN-PARA.
     SORT SORT-WORK
         ASCENDING KEY SORT-FULL-ZIP-CODE
         INPUT PROCEDURE 1000-RELEASE-CONTROL
         OUTPUT PROCEDURE 2000-RETURN-CONTROL.
     STOP RUN.


1000-RELEASE-CONTROL.
     OPEN INPUT MAILING-INFO.
```

```
        PERFORM 1200-READ-MAIL-INPUT.
        PERFORM 1100-READ-RELEASE-LOOP
            UNTIL END-INPUT.
        CLOSE MAILING-INFO.


    1100-READ-RELEASE-LOOP.
        CALL 'FIND-ZIP' USING MAILING-ADDRESS SORT-FULL-ZIP-CODE.
        MOVE MAILING-INFO-RECORD TO SORT-MAILING-INFO.
        RELEASE SORT-RECORD.
        PERFORM 1200-READ-MAIL-INPUT.


    1200-READ-MAIL-INPUT.
        READ MAILING-INFO
            AT END
                MOVE 'YES' TO END-INPUT-STATUS.


    2000-RETURN-CONTROL.
        OPEN OUTPUT MAILING-OUTPUT.
        PERFORM 2200-RETURN-SORT-RECORD.
        MOVE SORT-FULL-ZIP-CODE (1:5) TO PREVIOUS-ZIP-CODE.
        PERFORM 2100-PROCESS-OUTPUT-LOOP
            UNTIL END-SORT.
        MOVE 'XXX' TO MAIL-CONTROL-BREAK-code.
        MOVE PREVIOUS-ZIP-CODE TO MAIL-BREAK-ZIP-CODE.
        MOVE ZIP-CODE-COUNT TO MAIL-BREAK-COUNT.
        WRITE MAILING-OUTPUT-RECORD.
        CLOSE MAILING-OUTPUT.


    2100-PROCESS-OUTPUT-LOOP.
        IF SORT-FULL-ZIP-CODE (1:5) NOT = PREVIOUS-ZIP-CODE
            MOVE 'XXX' TO MAIL-CONTROL-BREAK-code
            MOVE PREVIOUS-ZIP-CODE TO MAIL-BREAK-ZIP-CODE
            MOVE ZIP-CODE-COUNT TO MAIL-BREAK-COUNT
            WRITE MAILING-OUTPUT-RECORD
            MOVE ZERO TO ZIP-CODE-COUNT
            MOVE SORT-FULL-ZIP-CODE  (1:5) TO PREVIOUS-ZIP-CODE.
        PERFORM 2500-FORMAT-PRINT-OUTPUT.
        ADD 1 TO ZIP-CODE-COUNT.
        PERFORM 2200-RETURN-SORT-RECORD.


    2200-RETURN-SORT-RECORD.
        RETURN SORT-WORK
            AT END
                MOVE 'YES' TO END-SORT-STATUS.


    2500-FORMAT-PRINT-OUTPUT.
*       Formatting and printing mailing data will be done here.
        EXIT.
```

The premise for this program is the savings in mailing costs that can be realized if ZIP codes are fully used in all addresses. The first savings come from using the correct nine-digit ZIP code, and this is assured in the 1100-READ-RELEASE-LOOP, where a post office–approved commercial package is invoked with the CALL statement. The second savings are achieved by sorting the items to be mailed by that ZIP code. The final savings are obtained by packaging the items for each post office, and the "break" record in 2100-PROCESS-OUTPUT-LOOP accomplishes this. The actual formatting and printing details have been omitted.

Not many comments need to be made on this program because it is pretty direct. The sort file, key, and SORT statement are set up in the same way as the first sort example. Note how the INPUT and OUTPUT PROCEDURE phrases each function like a PERFORM statement, with the sort software controlling things before, during, and after control is passed to the paragraphs specified in these phrases.

The RELEASE statement passes records to the sort software in 1100-READ-RELEASE-LOOP, and data is received back in 2200-RETURN-SORT-RECORD. The RETURN and its AT END phrase are set up just like a sequential READ statement.

As in the previous example, there is no OPEN or CLOSE for the SORT-WORK file because the sort software handles this. However, observe that the program must OPEN and CLOSE both the input MAILING-INFO and output MAILING-OUTPUT files. This is because the program is managing the processing of this data before it is passed to the sort and after it is received back from it.

1974 Standard Requirements for the INPUT PROCEDURE and the OUTPUT PROCEDURE

The 1974 Standard had some very special rules for INPUT and OUTPUT PROCEDUREs.

When this standard was published 25 years ago, memory, disk, and computer speed were at a premium. It was common for sort programs to run six or eight hours and not uncommon for them to run longer. Additionally, the software managing these facilities and ensuring data integrity was not nearly as sophisticated as it is now.

The rules specified in the standard were designed to simplify the interface between the program logic and the sort software in a segmented program environment. Although these rules work okay where GO TO logic is employed, they do not work well at all in a structured programming framework. These rules may be part of the reason why so many programmers avoid COBOL sorts.

These rules do need to be covered because a fairly large number of programs were written to conform to them. By the early 1980s, most compilers eased up on the requirements because advances in software design made them largely unnecessary.

The first rule is that the INPUT and OUTPUT PROCEDUREs can specify only SECTIONs.

The second rule is that if the THRU procedure-name-2 is used, all the code in the INPUT or OUTPUT PROCEDURE must be contiguous between the beginning of procedure-name-1 and procedure-name-2.

The third, final, and most restrictive rule is that no PERFORM or GO TO (or ALTER) statements can reference any paragraph or section name that is not physically located between the beginning of procedure-name-1 and the end of procedure-name-2.

These rules essentially ensure that the entire procedure will be exactly one segment that can be an independent segment and loaded into memory with the appropriate sort interface software. Furthermore, because there can be no references outside the range of the procedure, this procedure will not need to interface with any other procedures until it exits and then can be removed from memory. This makes the memory-management software extremely easy to use.

Unfortunately, these same rules make it impossible to get from the beginning of the procedure to its end without GO TO logic. Additionally, this GO TO logic will have to branch around at least one (and often more) paragraph(s). This obviously is contrary to all structured programming logic control rules.

Declaratives and the USE Statement

Declaratives are statements and procedures that are *event-driven* (executed based on the occurrence of a specified event) rather than procedurally controlled by the execution flow of the program statements. The events that can be dealt with by declaratives also are managed by other facilities and, in most cases, quite effectively. For this reason, declaratives are not commonly used.

When declaratives are used, they must be specified at the beginning of the PROCEDURE DIVISION, and section names are required. A separate section needs to be defined for each event being declared, and at least one other section must contain all the other normal PROCEDURE DIVISION code. The format of this structure follows:

```
PROCEDURE DIVISION.
DECLARATIVES.
{section-name-1 SECTION.
    USE statement.
[paragraph-name-1.
    [sentence-1]...]...}...
END DECLARATIVES.
```

```
{section-name-2 SECTION.
[paragraph-name-2.
    [sentence-2]...]...}...
```

The terms DECLARATIVES and END DECLARATIVES must begin at column 8 (margin A) and must end with a period. section-name-2 starts the normal beginning of the program, and this is where execution of the program begins (except in one case, in which a debug declarative can specify an event to occur with the beginning of the program).

As many declarative sections can be coded as are required. Each of these sections begins with a USE statement that specifies the event being declared. Note that this statement precedes the first paragraph of that section. One and only one USE statement is required in each declarative section.

The paragraph(s) following the USE statement is executed each time the specified event occurs. After the last sentence of the declarative section is executed, control returns to wherever it would have gone if the declarative had not been coded. Hence, declaratives do not have a direct impact on the overall flow of the program.

Statements in a declarative section can reference paragraphs in other declarative sections, and statements in the nondeclarative portion can reference declarative paragraphs, but several rules apply. Only the PERFORM statement can be used for such references. With debug declaratives, only paragraphs in other debug declarative sections can reference each other. Statements in the referenced paragraph cannot cause an event that is specified in another declarative section and that hasn't yet returned control to the code resulting in it being invoked. (In other words, if the procedures in one declarative section cause another declarative event to occur, the code for the two events cannot overlap.)

Three kinds of declaratives can be specified; these are explained in the following subsections.

File-Processing Errors and Exceptions

The declarative USE statement to specify file-handling error or exception events follows:

```
USE AFTER STANDARD {EXCEPTION/ERROR} PROCEDURE ON
        {INPUT/OUTPUT/I-O/EXTEND/{file-name-1}...}
```

The terms EXCEPTION and ERROR are synonymous.

The paragraph(s) following this statement is executed after the implementor's normal error-handling routine after any unsuccessful file-handling statement covered by the declarative. The only exception to this rule is that if a READ statement has an AT END phrase—and that condition occurs—the AT END phrase will be executed instead of the declarative paragraph(s).

After the last statement in the declarative section has been executed, control is returned to the appropriate next statement following the file-manipulation statement that resulted in the exception if the error was not critical (as indicated by the file-status value). If the error was critical, the implementor determines what happens next.

If INPUT, OUTPUT, I-O, or EXTEND is specified, the declarative procedures will be executed for any error conditions occurring for any file-manipulation statement (OPEN, CLOSE, READ, WRITE, START, REWRITE, DELETE) involving any file OPEN (or being OPENed) in the specified mode. Such a declarative applies to all such files, regardless of their ORGANIZATION or ACCESS MODE. Each of these specifications can be used only once in the program.

If one or more file-name-1 names are specified, the declarative paragraphs are executed whenever an error condition occurs in a file-manipulation statement involving the file-name-1(s). If a file-name-1 is specified in a declarative and it also is OPEN in a mode (INPUT, OUTPUT, I-O, EXTEND) specified in another declarative statement, the declarative procedures specified for the file-name-1 will be the only ones executed if an error occurs for that file.

Any file-name-1 can be specified in only one declarative statement.

The Report Writer Declarative

The report writer declarative format follows:

```
USE BEFORE REPORTING identifier-1
```

Here, identifier-1 must reference a report group, and each identifier-1 can be referenced only in one such USE statement. The declarative procedure(s) will be executed just before the report group is produced.

The GENERATE, INITIATE, and TERMINATE statements cannot be used in a declarative procedure or in any paragraph PERFORMed by statements in the declarative procedure. Also, these statements cannot alter any control data item.

Debug Declaratives

Of the three kinds of declaratives, debug declaratives are the most involved. They provide some fairly sophisticated capabilities for tracing program logic. However, debug declaratives still cannot compete with online or interactive debug software and packages. They do have a few advantages, though. The debug declaratives can be used when interactive debug software is not available, they can be used (or turned on) in any environment and don't require any special interfaces, and they can be turned on or off at will.

Two switches can be used to turn the debug declaratives on or off.

The first is the compile time switch. The WITH DEBUGGING MODE phrase must be specified in the SOURCE-COMPUTER paragraph when the program is compiled (see Chapter 1, "The Organization and Syntax of the COBOL Program"). If this phrase is not present when the program is compiled, all the debug declaratives are treated as comment lines.

The second switch is the Object Time Switch. If the program has been compiled WITH DEBUGGING MODE, this switch also must be set when the program is executed in order for the debug declaratives to become operational. By nature, this switch must be implementor-defined. Logically, this switch can be controlled by a link time parameter or an execution time parameter.

Format of USE FOR DEBUGGING

The format of the debug declarative USE statement follows:

```
USE FOR DEBUGGING ON {procedure-name-1/ALL PROCEDURES/file-name-1/
➥cd-name-1/
            [ALL REFERENCES OF] data-item-1}...
```

In general, the declarative procedure is executed whenever the specified item(s) is referenced in the PROCEDURE DIVISION statements of the program. References by statements in declarative procedures are *not* considered.

When debug declaratives are used, they must precede any other types of declaratives.

The phrase ALL PROCEDURES can be used only once in a program. If it is used, other declaratives specifying any procedure-name-1 are not allowed because that would be redundant.

Statements in debug declarative procedures can reference only paragraph names in debug declarative procedures, and that can be done only with the PERFORM statement. Paragraph names defined within debug declarative sections cannot be referenced by any statements that are not in debug declarative sections.

Any item identified in a debug declarative USE statement (procedure-name-1, file-name-1, cd-name-1, data-item-1) can be referenced only once in that statement and cannot be referenced in any other debug USE declarative.

Definition of DEBUG-ITEM

When a debug procedure is executed, COBOL provides additional information about the item specified in the USE statement. This is placed in the various fields of a record defined within COBOL and called the DEBUG-ITEM. Each time a debug declarative section is executed, this record is cleared to spaces, and then the appropriate values are stored in the applicable fields by COBOL before transferring control to the declarative procedure. DEBUG-ITEM and all its related subfields are reserved words. They are set up for reference by the statements in debug declarative paragraphs. Reference to them by other statements in the program is not permitted.

The layout of `DEBUG-ITEM` follows:

```
01   DEBUG-ITEM.
        05   DEBUG-LINE            PIC X(6).
        05   FILLER                PIC X VALUE SPACE.
        05   DEBUG-NAME            PIC X(30).
        05   FILLER                PIC X VALUE SPACE.
        05   DEBUG-SUB-1           PIC S9999 SIGN LEADING SEPARATE.
        05   FILLER                PIC X VALUE SPACE.
        05   DEBUG-SUB-2           PIC S9999 SIGN LEADING SEPARATE.
        05   FILLER                PIC X VALUE SPACE.
        05   DEBUG-SUB-3           PIC S9999 SIGN LEADING SEPARATE.
        05   FILLER                PIC X VALUE SPACE.
        05   DEBUG-CONTENTS        PIC X(n).
```

`DEBUG-LINE` is set to the line number of the source statement causing the debug declarative section to be executed. The specifics of how this number is related to the source statement (whether it is a sequential number on the compile listing or a number related to the source file) are left to the implementor.

`DEBUG-NAME` is set to the name of the `procedure-name-1`, `PROCEDURE`, `file-name-1`, `data-item-1`, or `cd-name-1` in the source statement, causing the debug declarative section to be executed.

The values of the other items depend on the type of debug `USE` statement. The following sections describe how the various types of debug declaratives operate.

Procedure Name DEBUG Declaratives

If `procedure-name-1` or `ALL PROCEDURES` is specified in the `USE FOR DEBUGGING` statement, the procedures in the debug section are executed just before control is passed to the indicated procedure. `DEBUG-LINE` will be set to the line number of the statement causing the transfer of control to the indicated procedure, and that name is stored in `DEBUG-NAME`. If this statement is a `PERFORM`, `DEBUG-CONTENTS` will be set to `PERFORM LOOP`. If it is a `SORT INPUT`, `OUTPUT PROCEDURE`, or a `MERGE OUTPUT PROCEDURE`, `DEBUG-CONTENTS` is set to `SORT INPUT`, `SORT OUTPUT`, or `MERGE OUTPUT`, respectively. If this is the start of the program, `DEBUG-CONTENTS` is set to `START PROGRAM`. If it is a `USE` procedure of some nondebug declarative, `DEBUG-CONTENTS` is set to `USE PROCEDURE`. If the paragraph (or section) is entered by "falling into it" from the previous paragraph (or section), `DEBUG-CONTENTS` is set to `FALL THROUGH`. If a `GO TO` statement caused the transfer of control, `DEBUG-CONTENTS` also is set to indicate this. If `ALTER` is the statement causing the execution of the debug procedure, `DEBUG-CONTENTS` is set to the name of the paragraph that the paragraph identified in `DEBUG-NAME` is being `ALTER`ed `TO PROCEED TO`.

`file-name` and `cd-name` DEBUG Declaratives

If a `file-name-1`(s) is specified in the `USE FOR DEBUG` declarative, the declarative procedure is executed *after* any `OPEN`, `CLOSE`, `READ`, `START`, or `DELETE` statement referencing the `file-name-1`(s) (`WRITE` and `REWRITE` aren't included because they reference a `record-name` and not a `file-name`). If any `USE AFTER ERROR/EXCEPTION` declaratives were specified for the `file-name-1`(s), and they are executed, the debug declarative procedures are executed after the `ERROR` declarative procedures. If the statement is a `READ`, and an `AT END` or `INVALID KEY` phrase is executed instead of the record being read, the debug declarative procedure is *not* executed. If a `READ` statement caused the debug procedure to be executed, `DEBUG-CONTENTS` is set to the value of the *entire record* that was read. `DEBUG-LINE` is set to the line number of the statement causing the procedure to be executed, and `DEBUG-NAME` is set to the `file-name-1` name.

`cd-name-1` is the name of a communications description entry; this is discussed briefly in the next section. In this case, the declarative procedure is executed whenever a `SEND`, `ENABLE`, `DISABLE`, or `ACCEPT MESSAGE COUNT` statement referencing `cd-name-1` is executed, and whenever a `RECEIVE` that does not result in a `NO DATA` condition is executed. `DEBUG-CONTENTS` is set to the value of the area associated with the `cd-name-1` in all cases.

Specifying Data Items in DEBUG Declaratives

When `data-item-1`(s) is specified, several remarks apply.

It is important to note that the references to the *data name* cause the debug procedure to be executed and not references or changes to its *contents*. This means that if `data-item-1` is an `01`-level record name, references to subordinate-level data items defined within it will *not* cause the debug procedure to be executed, unless all the references also are specified in its `USE` declarative statement.

If the `ALL REFERENCES OF` clause is specified, any statement referencing the `data-item-1` will cause the debug procedure to be executed. If this clause is not included, only those statements modifying the contents of `data-item-1` will cause the debug procedure to be executed. If `data-item-1` is the record being written or rewritten, the procedure will be executed, regardless of whether it is being modified by using the `FROM` phrase.

In general, the debug procedure is executed after the statement referencing the `data-item-1` has been executed so that any change in value will be available to it. In the case of `GO TO DEPENDING`, `PERFORM VARYING`, `AFTER`, or `UNTIL`, where the `data-item-1` is referenced in the `DEPENDING`, `VARYING`, `AFTER`, and `UNTIL` phrases, the debug procedure is executed *after* the phrase itself is executed but *before* any transfer of control takes place. In the case of the `WRITE` and `REWRITE` statements, the debug procedure is executed after any `FROM` phrase is processed but before the record actually is written or rewritten.

data-item-1 must not be specified with reference modification in the USE declarative.

If data-item-1 contains an OCCURS clause or is subordinate to an item defined with an OCCURS clause, it still must be specified in USE FOR DEBUGGING declaratives without subscripts or indexes. This means that the declarative procedures will be executed for all references to any occurrence numbers. However, the relative occurrence numbers will be stored in DEBUG-SUB-1 (and DEBUG-SUB-2 and DEBUG-SUB-3, if multidimensional subscripting is being used).

DEBUG-LINE will be set to the value of the line number of the statement causing the debug procedure to be executed. DEBUG-NAME will be set to the name of data-item-1. DEBUG-CONTENTS will be set to the value of data-item-1 at the time of the execution of the debug procedure.

A Short Example of DEBUG Declaratives

The following example shows the basic use of debug declaratives in trapping a problem where you know that the program logic begins doing unusual things sometime after 11,000 input records are handled correctly:

```
WORKING-STORAGE SECTION.
01   INPUT-RECORD-COUNT        PIC 9(6) VALUE ZERO.
01   OUTPUT-RECORD-COUNT       PIC 9(6) VALUE ZERO.
01   SEQUENCE-KEY              PIC X(20) VALUE LOW-VALUES.
01   DEBUG-PREV-KEY            PIC X(20) VALUE LOW-VALUES.
     .
     .
     .
PROCEDURE DIVISION.
DECLARATIVES.
0000A-INPUT-FILE-DECL SECTION.
     USE FOR DEBUGGING ON INPUT-FILE.
0000A-INPUT-FILE-PROC.
     ADD 1 TO INPUT-RECORD-COUNT.
     IF INPUT-RECORD-COUNT > 11000
         DISPLAY '**RECORD: ' INPUT-RECORD-COUNT
         DISPLAY ' ' DEBUG-ITEM.
0000B-PROCEDURE-DECL SECTION.
     USE FOR DEBUGGING ON ALL PROCEDURES.
0000B-PROCEDURE-PROC.
     IF INPUT-RECORD-COUNT > 11000
         DISPLAY ' ' DEBUG-ITEM.
0000C-DATA-DECL SECTION.
     USE FOR DEBUGGING ON SEQUENCE-KEY ALL OUTPUT-RECORD
              OUTPUT-RECORD-COUNT.
0000C-DATA-PROC.
     IF DEBUG-PREV-KEY > SEQUENCE-KEY
         DISPLAY '***SOMETHING IS REALLY SCREWY***'
```

```
                     ', PREV KEY: ' DEBUG-PREV-KEY
            DISPLAY '  SEQUENCE KEY: ' SEQUENCE-KEY
            DISPLAY DEBUG-ITEM.
        MOVE SEQUENCE-KEY TO DEBUG-PREV-KEY.
        PERFORM 0000B-PROCEDURE-PROC.
    END DECLARATIVES.
    0100-MAIN-PROGRAM SECTION.
    0100-MAIN-CONTROL.
        OPEN INPUT INPUT-FILE.
              OUTPUT OUTPUT-FILE.
              .
              .
              .
```

Notice that even though the declaratives are executed for every instance, information is DISPLAYed only after record 11,000 has been read (except if the sequence key gets out of sequence). Notice also how the DISPLAYs of the DEBUG-ITEM are indented, whereas the others are not. These things will help you find your way through the output created by the debug procedures, which can be quite large in many cases.

If you're careful, this kind of debugging can be included in a production program that has problems from time to time and simply turned on and rerun when the problem occurs. That kind of debugging is often not possible with interactive debug software.

The Communications Module

The communications module provides a connection to a computer's *message control system* (MCS) and through it to its communications devices. The module involves accessing, processing, and creating messages that are routed to and from these communications devices.

Although the 1974 Standard has 23 pages covering this module, and the 1985 Standard has 30, I have not yet seen or heard of an applications system using this module. Although the communications module provides interfaces to the systems communications environment, it does so at a primitive level, and all the systems I'm aware of have more sophisticated means of interfacing with remote terminals and other devices.

This section summarizes the contents of the communications module, although you will need much more detailed information from an implementing vendor in order to develop a functioning application.

The COMMUNICATION SECTION

The COMMUNICATION SECTION can contain communications description entries (CD entries) in three formats. These entries define the data interface with the *message control system* (MCS). The data items comprising the interface can be in clauses within the CD entry itself or as data items of an exactly specified 01-level record definition. I'll show three alternatives, even though one is sufficient.

Format 1:

```
CD   cd-name-1 FOR [INITIAL] INPUT
     [[SYMBOLIC QUEUE IS data-name-1]
      [SYMBOLIC SUB-QUEUE-1 IS data-name-2]
      [SYMBOLIC SUB-QUEUE-2 IS data-name-3]
      [SYMBOLIC SUB-QUEUE-3 IS data-name-4]
      [MESSAGE DATE IS data-name-5]
      [MESSAGE TIME IS data-name-6]
      [SYMBOLIC SOURCE IS data-name-7]
      [TEXT LENGTH IS data-name-8]
      [END KEY IS data-name-9]
      [STATUS KEY IS data-name-10]
      [MESSAGE COUNT IS data-name-11]].

01   cd-record-name-1.
     05   data-name-1      PIC X(12).      (SYMBOLIC QUEUE)
     05   data-name-2      PIC X(12).      (SYMBOLIC SUB-QUEUE-1)
     05   data-name-3      PIC X(12).      (SYMBOLIC SUB-QUEUE-2)
     05   data-name-4      PIC X(12).      (SYMBOLIC SUB-QUEUE-3)
     05   data-name-5      PIC 9(6).       (MESSAGE DATE)
     05   data-name-6      PIC 9(8).       (MESSAGE TIME)
     05   data-name-7      PIC X(12).      (SYMBOLIC SOURCE)
     05   data-name-8      PIC 9(4).       (TEXT LENGTH)
     05   data-name-9      PIC X.          (END KEY)
     05   data-name-10     PIC XX.         (STATUS KEY)
     05   data-name-11     PIC 9(6).       (MESSAGE COUNT)
```

The INPUT CD information is the data interface between the MCS and the program about the message that is being handled.

The INITIAL clause can appear only in one CD in any program and cannot appear in a subprogram.

When the program is scheduled by the MCS, the CD entry specified as INITIAL will have data-name-1 through data-name-4 set to values to define the queue structure that causes the program to be scheduled. These values are set before the execution of the first PROCEDURE DIVISION statement.

The RECEIVE statement causes the MCS to transfer the message according to the values specified in data-name-1 through data-name-4. If the subqueues are blank, the values pertaining to the message are supplied by the MCS. The MCS also values the other data items when the RECEIVE statement is executed.

Format 2:

```
CD    cd-name-1  FOR OUTPUT
      [DESTINATION COUNT IS data-name-1]
      [TEXT LENGTH IS data-name-2]
      [STATUS KEY IS data-name-3]
      [DESTINATION TABLE OCCURS integer-1 TIMES
          [INDEXED BY {index-name-1}…]]
      [ERROR KEY IS data-name-4]
      [SYMBOLIC DESTINATION IS data-name-5].

01    cd-record-name-1.
      05    data-name-1        PIC 9(4).        (DESTINATION COUNT)
      05    data-name-2        PIC 9(4).        (TEXT LENGTH)
      05    data-name-3        PIC XX.          (STATUS KEY)
      05    data-name OCCURS integer-1 TIMES.   (DESTINATION TABLE)
            10    data-name-4  PIC X.           (ERROR KEY)
            10    data-name-5  PIC X(12).       (SYMBOLIC DESTINATION)
```

The OUTPUT CD is used in the SEND, PURGE, ENABLE OUTPUT, and DISABLE OUTPUT statements to pass information between the program and the MCS about the destination(s) and message. Results are unspecified if the value of data-item-1 is larger than integer-1. The STATUS KEY is updated to reflect the results of the statement.

Format 3:

```
CD    cd-name-1  FOR [INITIAL] I-O
      [[MESSAGE DATE IS data-name-1]
         [MESSAGE TIME IS data-name-2]
      [SYMBOLIC TERMINAL IS data-name-3]
      [TEXT LENGTH IS data-name-4]
      [END KEY IS data-name-5]
      [STATUS KEY IS data-name-6]]

01    cd-record-name-1.
      05    data-name-1        PIC 9(6).        (MESSAGE DATE)
      05    data-name-2        PIC 9(8).        (MESSAGE TIME)
      05    data-name-3        PIC X(12).       (SYMBOLIC TERMINAL)
      05    data-name-4        PIC 9(4).        (TEXT LENGTH)
      05    data-name-5        PIC X.           (END KEY)
      05    data-name-6        PIC XX.          (STATUS KEY)
```

The I-O CD is used for input/output devices, such as terminals. The comments regarding INITIAL also apply here. Here, the device and destination are specified by the SYMBOLIC TERMINAL instead of the queue/subqueue structure; once this value is established, it must not be changed.

The various values returned in STATUS KEY follow:

00	Successful completion
10	One or more destinations disabled
15	Symbolic source or one or more queues or destinations already disabled/enabled
20	One or more destinations unknown
21	Symbolic source unknown
30	Destination count invalid
40	Password invalid
50	Text length exceeds size of `indentifier-1`
60	Portion requested to be sent has text length of zero, or `identifier-1` is absent
65	Output queue capacity exceeded
70	One or move destinations do not have portions associated with them
80	A combination of at least two status-key conditions 10, 15, and 20 has occurred
9x	Implementor defined

The various values returned in `ERROR KEY` follow:

0	No error
1	Symbolic destination unknown
2	Symbolic destination disabled
4	No partial message with referenced symbolic destination
5	Symbolic destination already enabled/disabled
6	Output queue capacity exceeded
A-Z	Implementor-defined condition

The possible values of `END KEY` follow:

0	Less than a full message is transferred
2	End of message has been detected
3	End of group has been detected

PROCEDURE DIVISION Statements Interfacing to the MCS

The `ACCEPT` statement causes the `MESSAGE COUNT` item to be updated with the number of complete messages that currently exist in the queue structure specified (data names 1 through 4):

```
ACCEPT cd-name-1 MESSAGE COUNT
```

Here, cd-name-1 must be an INPUT CD. The STATUS KEY also is updated as appropriate.

The DISABLE statement tells the MCS to terminate the data transfer between the queue structure and the device (for INPUT or OUTPUT cd-name-1s) or between the program and terminal for I-O cd-name-1 values:

```
DISABLE {INPUT [TERMINAL]/I-O TERMINAL/OUTPUT} cd-name-1
➡[WITH KEY data-item-1]
```

The type of cd-name-1 must correspond to the term specified in the DISABLE statement. The result of this statement is a logical disconnection of the device.

The WITH KEY phrase has been designated as obsolete and no longer will be available when the next standard is published. If the phrase is used, the data-item-1 will be matched to a password maintained by the MCS, and the DISABLE will be processed only if they are equal.

The STATUS KEY is updated to reflect the results of the statement.

The ENABLE statement tells the MCS to allow data transfer between the queue structure and the device (for INPUT or OUTPUT cd-name-1s) or between the program and terminal for I-O cd-name-1 values:

```
ENABLE {INPUT [TERMINAL]/I-O TERMINAL/OUTPUT} cd-name-1
➡[WITH KEY data-item-1]
```

The type of cd-name-1 must correspond to the term specified in the ENABLE statement. The result of this statement is a logical connection of the device with the MCS and the program.

The WITH KEY phrase has been designated as obsolete and no longer will be available when the next standard is published. If the phrase is used, the data-item-1 will be matched to a password maintained by the MCS, and the ENABLE will be processed only if they are equal.

The STATUS KEY is updated to reflect the results of the statement.

The PURGE statement eliminates a partial message from the MCS that had previously been released by one or more SEND statements:

```
PURGE cd-name-1
```

cd-name-1 must be an OUTPUT or I-O CD.

The RECEIVE statement transfers a message (or portion of it) to identifier-1 from the MCS:

```
RECEIVE cd-name-1 {MESSAGE/SEGMENT} INTO identifier-1
    [NO DATA imperative-statement-1]
    [WITH DATA imperative-statement-2]
    [END-RECEIVE]
```

cd-name-1 must be an INPUT or I-O CD.

The various data items of cd-name-1 are used by the MCS to identify the message to be transferred, and other appropriate data items are updated to reflect the results of the RECEIVE statement.

No message or portion of it is transferred until the MCS has received the entire message from the designated device. More than one full message is never transferred. If SEGMENT is specified, more than a full segment is never transferred.

identifier-1 is not space-filled if the message (or segment) contains fewer characters than the size of identifier-1.

The SEND statement transfers the message contained in identifier-2 to the MCS:

```
SEND cd-name-1 FROM identifier-1
```

or

```
SEND cd-name-1 [FROM identifier-1] WITH {identifier-2/ESI/EMI/EGI}
    [{BEFORE/AFTER} ADVANCING {identifier-3 LINES/PAGE/mnemonic-name-1}
    [REPLACING LINE]
```

From there, the MCS will transfer the message to the device specified in the cd-name-1. The MCS will not transfer anything to the device until it receives the entire message from the program.

cd-name-1 must be an OUTPUT or I-O CD. The data items defined there specify the message destination and show the results as indicated by the MCS.

The *WITH* phrase in the second format specifies which indicator is to be sent with the message. These values follow:

identifier-2	*Indicator*	*Meaning*
0	- -	Portion of a message or segment
1	ESI	End of segment
2	EMI	End of message
3	EGI	End of group of messages

15

SPECIALTY FEATURES

If the first format is used, the identifier-1 value is treated as a portion of the designated message or segment.

If the second format is used but no identifier-1 is specified, then only the specified end indicator is transferred.

The ADVANCING phrase is applicable only to printer devices, and the specifications are the same as described for printer files in Chapter 6, "Data Structures and Sequential I/O."

The REPLACING LINE phrase results in the characters being transmitted by the SEND statement replacing any characters that may have previously been transmitted to the same line. This applies to character-imaging devices where characters may be transmitted to the same line and be superimposed over or replace characters previously transmitted.

Summary

This completes the language portion of this book. You've looked at everything integral to COBOL itself, and everything to this point (except as noted) is available regardless of which computer or compiler you are using. However, there is a lot more to be covered. These are the interfaces and extensions that allow programs to work with databases, terminals, screens, and the various computer environments themselves. This book could never cover all these areas at anywhere near the level of detail applied to the language itself. Many books have been written on some items (such as DB2, Oracle, SQL, CICS) that this book only summarizes in a single chapter. Parts IV through VI are targeted to cover the most significant and common interfaces at a level that will give you a good idea of how to work with these interfaces. Expert knowledge of any of these areas, however, requires more in-depth coverage, which is beyond the scope of this book.

COBOL Platforms and Environments

PART

IV

IN THIS PART

Mainframe and Mini Environments

CHAPTER 16

COBOL has traditionally been thought of as a language that was written for mainframe or minicomputers and batch processing. Typically, COBOL is good for processing large amounts of data to create reports or bills for customers. However, COBOL has evolved over the years to provide more powerful language constructs, such as intrinsic functions, and functionality that makes the language similar in some ways to other languages, such as C. It can also call modules written in other languages, such as RPG and C.

This chapter compares the way in which you use COBOL on three of the main COBOL platforms: Unisys, VM, and AS/400. It also introduces you to VAX COBOL and COBOL for the HP 3000 so that you will note the similarities that make programming in a mainframe or mini-environment different from using COBOL in a client/server or workstation environment.

Editing, Compiling, and Running Programs

The basic tasks a programmer needs to be familiar with before programming on a specific platform are editing, compiling, and debugging. This section looks at performing those tasks in the three sample environments.

Editing Programs

Each environment has its own editor. Some are page editors, whereas others are line editors. These editors usually are dual-purpose, too. You can use them to create text documents or programs. These editors usually have some functionality that makes creating programs easier.

Editing in the Unisys Environment

In a Unisys environment, you can use the A Series Editor or the *Command and Edit* (CANDE) system from a terminal emulator. Using the Series A Editor (hereafter referred to as *the Editor*), you can do the basic functions, such as enter text, display text from more than one file or a range of lines, print, and save. You can also format text; delete, insert, move, and copy text (including blocks of text); perform search-and-replace operations; number and resequence lines; and restore text using an UNDO (or OOPS) command. The Editor also has advanced functions that you can use. The most important of these are features that allow you to compile and run jobs from the Editor and use macros. Compiling and running programs is described in more detail in "Compiling in the Unisys Environment" and "Running Programs in the Unisys Environment," later in this chapter. The other advanced features, such as spell checking, are more useful if you are using the Editor to create documents.

If you use CANDE in page mode, some of the features are similar to those found in the Series A Editor. However, the editors are distinctly different for the most part.

Editing in the VM Environment

In a VM/ESA (hereafter referred to as VM) environment, you use the XEDIT editor. XEDIT is a line editor (with some page-mode functionality) that allows you to do the same things you can do in other editors, such as the tasks described in the preceding section, "Editing in the Unisys Environment." However, you cannot compile and run your programs from XEDIT.

In addition to the editing functions, XEDIT allows you to keep track of the changes you make to a file as you edit. These changes include deletions, replacements, additions, and so on. Using XEDIT in update mode, you can make modifications to a source program without affecting the original source file, record all the changes made in separate files created in update mode, identify and time stamp the changes in the update files, and apply or remove your changes as needed. You use a control file to itemize which update files should be applied to a source file, and in which order.

Editing in the AS/400 Environment

In an AS/400 environment, you edit source code using the *Source Entry Utility* (SEU), which is a part of the larger product Application Development Toolset for AS/400. SEU is a line editor that allows you to directly type in your code; it also supplies display prompts that correspond to COBOL coding forms if you need help placing your code within the proper columns.

SEU provides all the regular editing functions the Unisys Editor provides (refer to "Editing in the Unisys Environment," earlier in this chapter). You cannot compile or run your source from SEU, however. You can do this from another AS/400 utility, however, called *Programming Development Manager* (PDM), from which you can also invoke SEU.

In addition to the regular editing functions, SEU provides syntax checking. The syntax checker goes through the syntax of each line as it is added or changed. If SEU detects an error, it displays an error message, which allows you to correct the syntax error before compiling the source. However, only syntax errors within single statements can be detected. You can turn off syntax checking if you want to use SEU to work with languages for which syntax checking is not available.

Compiling Programs

Programs are usually compiled in batch in a mainframe or mini-environment. Batch processing uses the resources of a mainframe or minicomputer to its best advantage.

Some sort of *Job Control Language* (JCL) is available to submit your program for batch compilation. However, programs can be compiled interactively, too. Depending on your development environment, though, you probably will want to compile in batch mode to minimize the use of system resources.

Compiling in the Unisys Environment

The Unisys COBOL compiler takes three main kinds of input files (CARD, SOURCE, and COPYFILES) and compiles them to create a CODE, NEWSOURCE, LINE, ERRORFILE, and XREFFILE. Any of the input files can reside on a disk, even though the name of the CARD file implies that it is a card deck. (This name is left over from earlier days when programs were written on computer cards.)

The CARD file is the primary input source file of the program. The SOURCE file is optional; it contains only source statements that are to be merged with the SOURCE file. The INCLUDE statement can be used to temporarily redirect compiler input to another source. When the INCLUDE compiler option is encountered, processing of the program is suspended until all the statements in the INCLUDE file are processed.

The INITIALCCI file is an optional input file that you can use to specify the initial compiler settings. Different initial settings can be invoked, depending on where the compilation is started. Here is an example:

```
$ OPTION (SET USERDEBUG)
 .
 .
 .
$ IF USERDEBUG
MOVE ERR-CODE TO DEBUG-CODE.
PERFORM WRITE-DEBUG-INFO.
$ ELSE
PERFORM NONFATAL-ERR-RECOVERY.
$ END
```

After the compile is completed, from one to four files are created, depending on the compile options specified. The CODE file is created unless the compiler option was set for syntax checking only. It contains the executable object code of the program. The NEWSOURCE file is created only if the NEW option is set to TRUE; it contains the source input from the CARD and SOURCE files. The LINE file is created by default, depending on where the compilation was started. The context of the LINE file depends on how the CODE option was set. The maximum amount of information it can contain is the source code used as input, code-segmentation information, and error information.

Programs are compiled using job files. The following is an example of a job file that could be used to compile a program:

Mainframe and Mini Environments

CHAPTER **16**

439

16

MAINFRAME AND
MINI
ENVIRONMENTS

```
?BEGIN JOB EXAMPLE;
COMPILE <program title> WITH COBOL85 LIBRARY;
COMPILER DATA CARD
<COBOL85 source program>
?END JOB;
```

You can also compile programs from the editors using the COMPILE command. You can run your compilation from the editors in batch mode so that you can continue editing while the jobs are running. If errors are detected during the compilation, the error report is displayed in the Editor, starting at the first error. The actual error message is displayed on the command line, and the source code line that contains the error is flagged.

Compiling in the VM Environment

In the VM environment, you invoke the compiler using the command that corresponds to the type of COBOL you are using. For example, you use the COBOL2 command to compile a program in VS COBOL II. VM searches all your minidisks, your reader, or a tape for all the input files in the normal search order. After the compilation is completed, the compiler creates an output listing file with a file type of LISTING and a text deck file with the file type of TEXT.

After you compile your program, you have to load it into storage. You can do this by using the LOAD or INCLUDE command. If you use more than one INCLUDE command in succession, the loader tables are not reset. However, if you use the LOAD command, the tables are reset. You can use as many INCLUDE commands as necessary following a LOAD command. After the LOAD and INCLUDE commands have executed, they produce a loadmap that is created on your A disk. In addition to these commands, you can issue the GENMOD command to create an executable module or the LKED command to create an executable program that is stored as a load module in a member of a CMS LOADLIB.

In addition to the options provided by the LOAD and INCLUDE commands, you can use loader-control statements. These statements can be inserted into TEXT files using XEDIT. You use these statements to set the location counter to control the load address of the next load module (TEXT file), modify instructions and constants in a load module (patch a program), change the entry point to a load module, and nullify an external reference.

You can also compile a program in batch mode, which allows you to continue performing other tasks while you wait for the compilation to complete. You can send jobs to batch by reading the real punched card input into the system card reader or by spooling a user's virtual punch to the virtual reader of the virtual batch machine. When you spool virtual punch to the batch machine's virtual reader, you need to punch the virtual cards. Here is an example of an EXEC that does that for you:

```
/JOB JOBNAME 012345
CP LINK USERID 291 291 RR SECRET
ACCESS 291 B/A
LONDON
```

Compiling in the AS/400 Environment

On the AS/400, you can create and compile programs for two types of environments: *Original Program Model* (OPM) and *Integrated Language Environment* (ILE). The ILE environment is available in later releases of COBOL.

To compile a program in the OPM environment, you compile a program using the Create COBOL Program (CRTCBLPGM) command. The AS/400 supplies prompts for every command in its operating system. If you want a display that can help you with the compiler options you can enter with this command, press F4 over top of the command as you have typed it on the command line. Typically, an OPM program is a main source file that copies in other program source files using the COPY statement.

After the compilation has completed, a spooled output file is created that contains information about the compiler options that were used, counts of verbs used, a data-division map, a cross-reference, and a report of error messages generated. The output file also contains a program listing with expanded COPY statements and error flagging. You can access this file by issuing the Work with Spooled Files (WRKSPLF) command.

To compile a program in ILE, you first compile all the individual modules that make up your program using the Create COBOL Module (CRTCBLMOD) command. You can also write modules in other ILE languages, such as RPG, and bind them with the COBOL modules to create a program. After you compile all the modules, you use the Create Bound COBOL (CRTBNDCBL) command to bind all the program's modules together to create the program. An output file is created that is similar to the one described for the OPM compilation. You can bind programs that were written in other ILE languages, such as ILE RPG or ILE C.

You might also want to create a service program to contain a collection of runable procedures and data items to be used by other ILE program objects. To create a service program, you use the Create Service Program (CRTSRVPGM) command to bind together modules of command procedures and data items. (These modules would have been previously compiled using the CRTCBLMOD command.) The only difference between a service program and a bound program is that a service program does not contain an entry point, which means that it cannot be called or canceled.

You can also compile OPM and ILE programs from the *Programming Development Manager* (PDM). PDM invokes the appropriate compiler based on the file type of the source file. OPM source files have a file type of CBL; ILE source files have a file type of CBLLE.

You can compile programs in batch mode on the AS/400 by setting up the appropriate queues and options in your user profile.

Running Programs

You can run programs interactively or in batches, depending on the type of program. If you are running a program that needs input from a user, you run this type of program interactively. Programs that only process data can be run in batch mode.

If you are testing a program with a small amount of data, you might resort to running that program interactively. However, in production mode, when you are running the program live and processing a large amount of data, you definitely should run the program in batch. Using batch mode also allows the job to be scheduled at a time when the system has a lighter level of use.

Running Programs in the Unisys Environment

In the Unisys environment, you can run programs using *Work Flow Language* (WFL) or an editor. An example of using WFL to create a job file to run a program follows:

```
?BEGIN JOB RUN/A/PROGRAM;
RUN SAMPLE/PROGRAM;
?END JOB;
```

You can use the same job file to compile and run a program. However, if server errors are received from the compilation that prevent the executable object code (`CODE` file) from being created, the job file terminates and the program does not run.

Programs can also be run from an editor. The `RUN` or `UTILITY` command runs a program from an editor. You can specify options with either of these commands. If you do not specify the name of the program that you want to run, the commands run the editor's work file. If you enter the `RUN` command and the file has not been compiled first, this command compiles the file and then runs it.

If a program is run from an editor and ends abnormally, the editor loads the stack history of the program. You can view the stack history by using the `STACK` command.

Running Programs in the VM Environment

In the VM environment, you can run programs in three ways. The method you use to run a program depends on the method you used to create the load module.

If you created the load module using only the `LOAD` or `INCLUDE` command, you use the `START` command to run the program. For example, you could enter the following series of commands in this situation to load and run the program:

```
load yourProgramName
start
```

If you created your load module using the GENMOD command (issued after the LOAD or INCLUDE command), you type the filename of the module to run the program. You could enter the following series of commands in this situation to create the load module and run the program:

```
load yourProgramName
genmod yourProgramName
yourProgramName
```

If you created your load module using the LKED command (the link-edit method), after you create the load module, you can optionally use the GLOBAL command to identify all the load libraries that need to be searched when your program is run. Then you issue the OSRUN command to run the program.

You can also run your programs using the batch facility. If your program uses input and output files, you need to include the file definitions in the job file. If you expect printed or punched output from your job, you might also need to include the spooling commands required to control the output. For example, the following job file prepares the environment (CP LINK and ACCESS commands), defines the input and output files (FILEDEF commands), defines how the output is to be spooled (CP SPOOL command), and runs the program (yourProgramName):

```
CP LINK ARDEN 391 391 RR FOREST
ACCESS 391 B/A
FILEDEF INFILE DISK VITAL STAT B
FILEDEF OUTFILE PUNCH
CP SPOOL PUNCH TO MCGUIRE
yourProgramName
```

Running Programs in the AS/400 Environment

You can run a program in the AS/400 environment in several ways. You can call the program using a CL command (the system Command Language), a *High Level Language* (HLL) CALL statement, a menu-driven application, or a user-created command.

To run a program using a CL command, you type CALL PGM(*program-name*) on the command line, or you can type CALL and press F4 to prompt for the arguments you can use with the CALL command. If you are calling a program in batch that uses a Format 1 ACCEPT statement, you need to include the input data right after the CALL statement. You can pass parameters to the program using the PARM argument of the CALL command. If you are using the PARM argument, the syntax of the command becomes the following:

```
CALL PGM(program-name) PARM(parameter-1 parameter-2 parameter-3)
```

Using an HLL CALL statement to call a program means that you can use the CALL statement in an ILE COBOL program to call another ILE COBOL program. Alternatively, an

Mainframe and Mini Environments

CHAPTER 16

443

16

MAINFRAME AND
MINI
ENVIRONMENTS

ILE C program, a Visual Age C++ for AS/400 (an ILE-compatible C++) program, or an ILE RPG program can call an ILE COBOL program. You can also call OPM programs from ILE programs or other OPM programs.

You can create a menu to call an ILE COBOL application in several ways. You can create a menu using DDS, for example, or you can create a menu using CL commands. For more information about interacting with a program using menus and displays, see "Interacting with a Program in the AS/400 Environment," later in this chapter.

Finally, you can call an ILE COBOL program from a user-created command. A *command definition* is a system object of type `*CMD` that contains the command name, the command parameters, and validity-checking information.

Interacting with the Program (ACCEPT and DISPLAY)

Some compilers allow users to interact with your COBOL programs using special formats of the `ACCEPT` and `DISPLAY` statements. These statements allow you to create primitive displays that accept input from users. They are not sophisticated enough to handle events the way *graphical user interfaces* (GUIs) do.

Most COBOL programming environments allow you to create programs that can interact with displays or forms, however. This functionality usually also allows the data to be formatted for display. For example, some environments allow displayed data to be highlighted.

Interacting with a Program in the Unisys Environment

In a Unisys environment, COBOL85 does not provide `ACCEPT` and `DISPLAY` statements that can create and manipulate displays and menus. However, you can use a tool called *Screen Design Facility* (SDF). SDF language extensions are available to allow you to write a program that interacts with SDF forms or displays. (SDF Plus extensions are also available.) The following statements are part of the SDF language extensions:

- `DICTIONARY` statement
- `FORM-KEY` function
- `FROM DICTIONARY` clause
- `READ FORM` statement
- `REDEFINES` clause

- SAME RECORD AREA clause
- WRITE FORM statement

You use the DICTIONARY statement to identify the SDF form library that you want to use. The DICTIONARY statement identifies the library attribute FUNCTIONNAME, which is the same FUNCTIONNAME you identified in your SDF session when you created the form.

Next, you must code a special data-description entry to identify the form-record library that you want to invoke and to specify certain characteristics of that form library. This special type of data-description entry uses the FROM DICTIONARY phrase to identify specific information about the form-record library.

The READ FORM statement allows you to read data from a form as input to your program. The WRITE FORM statement allows you to write data back to a form. When you use the READ FORM statement, it not only reads the form, but it also validates the record and performs screen error handling, passes the valid record or the detected error condition back to the record, and updates the file status associated with the file. The WRITE FORM statement also handles error conditions and file statuses.

SDF also supports the use of program control flags. Flags are set by the form library when a program performs a read operation or a write operation, depending on the type of flag. Flags are set before the first write operation and retain those values throughout the execution of the program unless you reset them.

You can also use the basic functionality of the standard ACCEPT and DISPLAY statements to create menus and prompts. This functionality is described in the next section.

Interacting with a Program in the VM Environment

In the VM environment, the fancy screen design tools and language constructs are not available to create and manipulate displays from COBOL programs. However, you can use the basic formats of the ACCEPT and DISPLAY statements to create simple menus and displays.

You can create a simple menu using several DISPLAY statements, for example. The following example shows you how you can do this for a simple tape-library program for an Operations department:

```
DISPLAY "          1. Request Tape".
DISPLAY "          2. Delete Tape".
DISPLAY "          3. Add Tape".
DISPLAY "                        ".
DISPLAY "          Make a Selection:'.
ACCEPT MENU-SELECTION FROM CONSOLE.
```

These statements produce the following menu:

```
1. Request Tape
2. Delete Tape
3. Add Tape

Make a Selection:_
```

The DISPLAY statements create the menu. The cursor positions itself at the end of the last display statement encountered before an ACCEPT statement and waits until the user presses Enter. There are no fancy ways to ensure that the user enters a valid value, except for the validity-checking code you can add. After the ACCEPT statement, for example, you could add code to test whether MENU-SELECTION is greater than or equal to 1 but less than or equal to 3.

After the user presses Enter, the value the user entered (if it passes the validity check) is passed to the program and accepted into the variable MENU-SELECTION, where it is used to decide which procedure in the program should be performed. If the user entered 1, for example, the procedure that randomly selects an available tape from the tape library is performed. If the user entered 3, the procedure that allows the user to add his or her own tape to the tape library database is performed.

This simpler method of interacting with programs is also available in the Unisys and AS/400 environments.

Interacting with a Program in the AS/400 Environment

In an AS/400 environment, you can use the Format 7 ACCEPT statement (workstation I/O) with the Format 3 DISPLAY statement (workstation I/O). Or you can use *data description specifications* (DDSs) to create displays and menus and incorporate them into your COBOL programs using the COPY DDS statement. A tool called *Screen Design Aid* (SDA, a part of the Application Development Toolset for AS/400) is available to help you create the DDS for displays and menus.

The ACCEPT and DISPLAY statements support a 24-line by 80-column display format. It is the programmer's responsibility to ensure that each field is positioned on the screen in such a way that fields do not overlap. If the size of the data accepted will not fit on the display, any numeric data is not displayed and any alphanumeric data is truncated. The AT phrase defines the starting line and column for the fields that will be accepted or displayed. The changed values of the display are accepted from the display and transferred to the program after the user presses Enter. Many display formatting attributes are available with these statements. Some of the available attributes are BELL, BLINK, HIGHLIGHT, REQUIRED, and REVERSE-VIDEO.

Here is an example of a DDS that defines a display:

```
....+....1....+....2....+....3....+....4....+....5....+....6....+....7....
    A* DISPLAY FILE
    A* DSPFILE
    A                                    INDARA
    A          R FORMAT1                 CF01(99 'END OF PROGRAM')
    A                                    CF05(51 'DAILY REPORT')
    A                                    CF09(52 'MONTHLY REPORT')
    A*
    A                              10 10'DEPARTMENT NUMBER:'
    A          DEPTNO         5   I 10 32
    A    01                       20 26'PRODUCE MONTHLY REPORTS'
    A                                    DSPATR(BL)
    A*
    A                              24 01'F5 = DAILY REPORT'
    A                              24 26'F9 = MONTHLY REPORT'
    A                              24 53'F1 = TERMINATE'
    A          R ERRFMT
    A    98                         6  5'INPUT-OUTPUT ERROR'
```

The R FORMAT1 keyword describes the record format of the display file. R ERRFMT describes the format of the error record. DEPTNO is an input field in the display, and CF01, CF05, and CF09 define the function keys for the display. Indicators are used in a COBOL program to interact with the function keys.

Depending on which option you specify on the COPY DDS statement, the data field names that are brought into the COBOL program are the same as those specified in the internal DDS, or they are the data field names identified by the ALIAS keyword in the DDS. The ALIAS keyword identifies the alternative data field names you can use in your COBOL program.

You can also use SDA to create the DDS for you. SDA prompts you to define the display record and the input and output fields you want to use on the display. These can be obtained from a data file, if one already exists. SDA also provides you with a blank screen interface that works like a canvas. You type your prompts and display attributes on this canvas. Later SDA prompts you to map the data fields to the appropriate places on the display.

Setting Up for Input and Output Files

To gain access to a file in COBOL, a program must specify both the organization and access mode of the file. There are three types of file organization: *sequential, indexed,*

Mainframe and Mini Environments

CHAPTER 16

447

16

MAINFRAME AND
MINI
ENVIRONMENTS

and *relative.* There are three types of access modes: *sequential, random,* and *dynamic.* Both the organization and access mode of a file are defined in the SELECT clause of the FILE-CONTROL paragraph.

COBOL programs process logical records, which may or may not be the same as the physical file. For example, a logical record may contain parts of several physical records. A logical record acts like a database view of one or more physical records or their parts.

The organization of a file describes how the file's records are related to each other. In a sequential file, the order of the records is based on the time they were written to the file. The first record in a sequential file is the first record that was written to that file, for example. This order never changes unless records are deleted. You should use sequential files when you have to process most of the records in a file. Examples of sequential files are tape files and printer files.

Relative file organization makes the random processing of records easier. The relative key defines the relative position of the records in the file. (The records may not physically be in the same sequence as the sequence defined by the relative key.) In a relative file, records are located by a relative record number. You should use relative files when you want to access records randomly and they must be disk files.

An indexed file contains records that can be accessed by more than one criterion. For example, in an indexed inventory file of books, records could be accessed by their title or their number. With indexed files, you can access records sequentially by key, randomly by key, or by using their relative record number. Indexed files generally require more space and are slower to access because they require more I/O overhead. They can only be disk files.

Access modes define how the records in a file are processed. Not all the access modes can be used with each of the types of file organization. A sequential- or random-access mode can be used with a sequential file organization. You can use a sequential-, random-, or dynamic-access mode with both relative and indexed file organizations.

The way you define files in your programs varies depending on the environment in which you are programming. The next sections focus on defining your files in a few of the COBOL environments.

Setting Up Files in the Unisys Environment

In the Unisys environment, you name each sequential file used in the program with a SELECT statement and use the ASSIGN clause of this statement to assign to a type of hardware. You use SEQUENTIAL in both the ORGANIZATION IS and ACCESS MODE clauses.

To declare the physical attributes for a file, as well as to specify the filename, you can specify LOCAL or COMMON and RECEIVED BY REFERENCE. Using LOCAL identifies the file as a formal parameter of a procedure. Using COMMON indicates that the file was declared in another module to which the program is bound. Using RECEIVED BY REFERENCE indicates that you want two or more programs to access the file.

You can assign the following physical devices to a file:

- DISK: A *disk* file is a file on a mass-storage device.
- PORT: A *port* file is used to communicate across a BNA network.
- PRINTER: A *printer* file sends output to a printer.
- READER: A *reader* file reads input from a card reader.
- REMOTE: A *remote* file accesses a remote station.
- TAPE: A *tape* file reads or writes data to a tape.

For files with a relative organization, you name each relative file used in the program with a SELECT statement and use the ASSIGN clause of this statement to assign it to DISK (the only type of hardware to which you can assign a relative file). You use RELATIVE in the ORGANIZATION IS, and SEQUENTIAL, RANDOM, or DYNAMIC in the ACCESS MODE clause. To declare the physical attributes of a relative file, you can specify the same clauses as you can when specifying the physical attributes of sequential files (described earlier).

For files with an indexed organization, the same rules described for relative files apply, except that you specify INDEXED in the ORGANIZATION IS clause.

You need to use the appropriate I/O statement for the type of files you have defined in your program. To access data in a file with an organization of SEQUENTIAL and an access mode of SEQUENTIAL, for example, you use the READ statement with the AT END phrase.

Setting Up Files in the VM Environment

In the VM environment, you can access files in *Queued Sequential Access Method* (QSAM) or *Virtual Storage Access Method* (VSAM) format. A file of sequential organization can be QSAM or VSAM; a file of indexed or relative organization can be VSAM.

Here is an example of how you can define file information in a program:

```
IDENTIFICATION DIVISION.
    .
    .
    .
ENVIRONMENT DIVISION.
INPUT-OUTPUT SECTION.
  FILE-CONTROL.
```

```
SELECT file-name ASSIGN TO assignment-name
ORGANIZATION IS org-type ACCESS MODE IS access-mode
FILE STATUS IS file-status.
      .
      .
      .
DATA DIVISION.
  FILE SECTION.
  FD file-name
  01 recordname
      nn . . . field-length & field-type
      nn . . . field-length & field-type
   .
   .
   .
WORKING-STORAGE SECTION
 01 file-status PICTURE 99.
```

You would supply the following information to the statements in this example:

- *file-name* is any name you choose. You must use the same name on the SELECT clause and the FD entry.

- *assignment-name* is also any name you choose. The assignment name is defined in a DD statement in the job file that runs your program or by a FILEDEF system command.

- The *org-type* can be SEQUENTIAL, INDEXED, or RELATIVE. This clause is optional for QSAM files because the organization must be SEQUENTIAL.

- The *access-mode* can be SEQUENTIAL, RANDOM, or DYNAMIC. This clause is optional for sequential file processing.

- *file-status* is the two-character COBOL FILE STATUS key. This name is also defined in the WORKING-STORAGE SECTION.

- *recordname* is any name you want to give the record. This name is used in WRITE and REWRITE statements.

- *field-length* is the logical length of the field.

- *field-type* must match the file's record format.

- *iomode* is INPUT, OUTPUT or EXTEND, or I-O. If you are just reading from a file, you should specify INPUT. If you are writing to a file, you should specify OUTPUT or EXTEND. If you are doing both, you should specify I-O.

QSAM Files

If you are using QSAM files, you define the files in your program as QSAM, which means that you specify SEQUENTIAL for both the ORGANIZATION and ACCESS MODE clauses. In the FD entry, you specify a RECORDING MODE, which can be one of the following:

- F for fixed-length records
- V or D (D is used with tape files) for variable-length records
- S for spanned records (records that can span across physical blocks)
- U for records with undefined or unspecified characteristics

You need to use the appropriate format of the I/O statements when working with QSAM files.

VSAM Files

If you are using indexed or relative file organization in your program, you must use VSAM files. The organization of a VSAM file is considerably different from the organization of other files. VSAM files are held in control intervals and control areas, and their size is determined by the method used to access them.

The typical coding of the SELECT clauses for VSAM files follows.

The first scenario shows how to code a VSAM sequential file or an *entry-sequenced dataset* (ESDS):

```
SELECT S-FILE
    ASSIGN TO SEQUENTIAL-AS-FILE
    ORGANIZATION IS SEQUENTIAL
    ACCESS IS SEQUENTIAL
    FILE STATUS KEY IS FSTATUS-CODE VSAM-CODE.
```

The second scenario shows the statements for a VSAM indexed file or *key-sequenced dataset* (KSDS) that will be accessed dynamically:

```
SELECT I-FILE
    ASSIGN TO INDEXED-FILE
    ORGANIZATION IS INDEXED
    ACCESS IS DYNAMIC
    RECORD KEY IS IFILE-REC-KEY
    ALTERNATE RECORD KEY IS IFILE-ALTREC-KEY
    FILE STATUS KEY IS FSTATUS-CODE VSAM-CODE.
```

The third scenario is for a *relative-record dataset* (RRDS) to be accessed randomly by the value placed in the relative key, ITEM-NO:

```
SELECT R-FILE
    ASSIGN TO REL-FILE
    ORGANIZATION IS RELATIVE
    ACCESS IS RANDOM
    RELATIVE KEY IS RFILE-REL-KEY
    FILE STATUS KEY IS FSTATUS-CODE VSAM-CODE.
```

The Data Division entries define whether the VSAM file has fixed- or variable-length records. You define records as fixed length by specifying the RECORD CONTAINS clause, or by omitting this clause but defining all the level-01 record-description entries associated with this file as being the same length and not using the OCCURS DEPENDING ON clause.

You define records as variable length by doing one of the following:

- Specifying the RECORD IS VARYING clause
- Specifying the RECORD CONTAINS integer-1 TO integer-2 clause
- Omitting the RECORD clause and defining all the level-01 record-description entries associated with this file as having different lengths
- Using the OCCURS DEPENDING ON clause

You have to predefine VSAM files using the DEFINE command. Because most of the information about a VSAM file is in the catalog, you only need to specify minimal JCL to define it.

You need to use the appropriate format of the I/O statements for working with VSAM files.

Setting Up Files in the AS/400 Environment

In the AS/400 environment, you can assign the following physical devices to a file:

- DISK: A *disk* file is a file on a mass-storage device.
- DATABASE: A *database* file is used to define a database or *Distributed Data Management* (DDM) file.
- PRINTER: A *printer* file sends output to a printer.
- FORMATFILE: A *format file* is used for externally described printer files—those printer files defined using *Data Description Specifications* (DDSs).
- DISKETTE: A *diskette* file reads or writes data to a disk.
- TAPEFILE: A *tape file* reads or writes data to a tape.
- WORKSTATION: A *workstation* file defines a display file or an *Intersystems Communication File* (ICF).

These device keywords prefix the filename and end in a hyphen. For example, you can define a DISK file as shown here:

```
SELECT file-name
    ASSIGN TO DISK-disk-file-name
    ORGANIZATION IS SEQUENTIAL
    ACCESS MODE IS SEQUENTIAL.
```

DISK files are associated with a single physical or logical database file. You use a DATABASE file if you want to use the database extensions in your program, such as commitment control, duplicate record keys, record formats, or externally described files (those files described using DDS).

You name each sequential file used in the program with a SELECT statement and use the ASSIGN clause of this statement to assign a device type to it. You use SEQUENTIAL in both the ORGANIZATION IS and ACCESS MODE clauses. Printer files, tape files, disk files, and display files are defined with an organization of SEQUENTIAL.

For files with a relative organization, you name each relative file used in the program with a SELECT statement. You use RELATIVE in the ORGANIZATION IS clause, and you use SEQUENTIAL, RANDOM, or DYNAMIC in the ACCESS MODE clause. To declare the physical attributes of a relative file, you can specify the same clauses you can when specifying the physical attributes of sequential files (described earlier).

For files with an indexed organization, the same rules described for relative files apply, except that you specify INDEXED in the ORGANIZATION IS clause.

In an AS/400 environment, you can specify TRANSACTION in the ORGANIZATION IS clause and in the ACCESS MODE clause. If you are using a transaction file, you first must acquire the device using the ACQUIRE statement. Display files and ICF files are defined with an organization of TRANSACTION.

You can use disk files with fixed- or variable-length records, but these can be only files defined with the device name DISK. The maximum and minimum lengths of the records are defined in the FD entry.

You need to use the appropriate I/O statement for the type of files you have defined in your program. To access data in a file with an organization of SEQUENTIAL and an access mode of SEQUENTIAL, for example, you use the READ statement with the AT END phrase.

Using Debugging Facilities

Most COBOL programming environments also supply debugging support. After all, where is a programmer without a debugger? Many functions are standard to those environments that offer full-fledged debuggers. However, some environments also offer COBOL language constructs that help you debug your programs.

Using Debugging Facilities in the Unisys Environment

In the Unisys environment, you use the *Test and Debug System* (TADS) to debug programs. With TADS you can display and change program data, set breakpoints, trace the flow of a program, perform paragraphs and sections interactively, specify and maintain conditions, obtain commands from a disk file, route diagnostic information, and count loops.

Before you can debug a program, you need to prepare it for debugging. To do this you need to include the TADS compiler control option ($SET TADS) before the first program statement and compile the program. The release level of TADS must match the release level of the compiler, or you will get a version mismatch error.

Several commands are available that allow you to display and change program data:

- CHANGE: Modifies file attributes
- DISPLAY: Evaluates expressions and interrogates attributes
- MOVE: Transfers data from one data area to one or more data areas
- COMPUTE: Calculates arithmetic expressions and stores the result

You can also set breakpoints in the program you are debugging to stop its execution. Breakpoints can occur at various times:

- At the beginning of a TADS session
- At specific statements in the program (these can be conditional)
- After the STEP command has been processed
- As a request from the editor to suspend the session
- If a program fault is encountered from which the program cannot recover

You cannot issue breakpoints for conditional command expressions, condition-accepting command expressions, or a language statement that is entered during the debug session.

You can use the HISTORY, TRACE, and AT commands to trace the logic flow of a program. The HISTORY command provides the history of active programs, sections, or paragraphs; and the TRACE command identifies the current position of execution within the program. The AT command allows you to set trace conditions at the beginning of a program.

You can perform paragraphs or sections of your program interactively by using the RUN command. You can use the EXIT command to halt the execution of the program that you started using the RUN command.

You can conditionally specify other TADS commands using the AT, ON, WHEN, and FROM commands. You can use other commands to monitor and administer the conditions that are in effect during the debug session.

You can use some commands to gather statement-execution statistics: CLEAR, COVERAGE, FREQUENCY, MERGE, and SAVE. To use these commands, you must compile the program with the FREQUENCY TADS compiler option.

To use commands that have been previously defined, you can use the DO command. You can use the OUTPUT command to create a command file for later use.

If you want to route diagnostic information, you can use the OUTPUT command to send the session information to a task file or disk file. If you are using TADS interactively, session information is displayed on your terminal by default. If you are using TADS in batch, session information is sent to the printer.

Using the integer-valued runtime variables, you can count the number of times a program executes a block of code without having to add extra source-code statements. To do this, you need to initialize the counters to zero by typing a statement such as the following at the command line:

```
AT 27510 ONCE MOVE ZERO TO TADSVAR (1)
```

Then you need to establish a condition that increments the value of the loop counter each time execution of the program passes through the designated block of code. You can do this by using a statement such as the following:

```
AT 27530 COMPUTE TADSVAR (1) = TADSVAR (1) + 1
```

Then you can display the contents of the loop counter at any time using a statement such as this:

```
DISPLAY "LOOP COUNT =", TADSVAR (1)
```

You can use the CALL SYSTEM DUMP statement from within a COBOL program to call the dump facility to capture the contents of the memory area that the program is currently using. Only the DUMP option can be used with this type of call statement.

In a Unisys environment, you can also use the WITH DEBUGGING MODE clause and the USE AFTER STANDARD EXCEPTION phrase (which is similar to the USE EXCEPTION/ERROR phrase used in the VM or AS/400 environment) on I/O statements. These coding techniques are described in the next section.

Using Debugging Facilities in the VM Environment

`DEBUG-ITEM` is a special register that you can access to provide information for a debugging declarative procedure regarding the conditions that caused the debugging section to be executed. `DEBUG-ITEM` has the following implicit definition:

```
01 DEBUG-ITEM.
02 DEBUG-LINE PICTURE IS X(6).
02 FILLER PICTURE IS X VALUE SPACE.
02 DEBUG-NAME PICTURE IS X(30).
02 FILLER PICTURE IS X VALUE SPACE.
02 DEBUG-SUB-1 PICTURE IS S9999 SIGN IS LEADING SEPARATE CHARACTER.
02 FILLER PICTURE IS X VALUE SPACE.
02 DEBUG-SUB-2 PICTURE IS S9999 SIGN IS LEADING SEPARATE CHARACTER.
02 FILLER PICTURE IS X VALUE SPACE.
02 DEBUG-SUB-3 PICTURE IS S9999 SIGN IS LEADING SEPARATE CHARACTER.
02 FILLER PICTURE IS X VALUE SPACE.
02 DEBUG-CONTENTS PICTURE IS X(n).
```

The contents of `DEBUG-ITEM` follow:

- `DEBUG-ITEM` contains the source statement sequence number that caused execution of the debugging section.
- `DEBUG-NAME` contains the first 30 characters of the name that caused execution of the debugging section.
- `DEBUG-SUB-1`, `DEBUG-SUB-2`, and `DEBUG-SUB-3` contain (if the `DEBUG-NAME` is subscripted or indexed) the occurrence number of each level, which is entered in the respective `DEBUG-SUB-n`.
- `DEBUG-CONTENTS` contains information about procedures that caused the debugging section to be executed.

You can include source statements in your program that will be used only for debugging. When you enter these statements in your program, you preface them with a `D` in column 7. Then you just need to specify the `WITH DEBUGGING MODE` clause on the `SOURCE-COMPUTER` statement to activate these statements.

You can also use the `READY TRACE` statement to isolate code that is to be used only for debugging purposes. When you run the program with the `DEBUG` option, the code in the `READY TRACE` statements is executed. You can also use the `USE FOR DEBUGGING` declarative to do the same thing.

Other program statements you use to help debug your program follow:

- `DISPLAY` statements to trace the flow of logic
- `USE EXCEPTION`/`ERROR` phrases on I/O statements to provide information about file errors
- Class tests to validate data types
- File-status keys to provide information about the success of I/O statements

Information from your output listings can also help you debug your programs. For example, a data-division map or cross-reference listing can be useful for tracking the way in which variables are used.

If you want to use an interactive tool to debug your programs, Debug Tool is available as a component of the CODE/370 product. You can use Debug Tool in full-screen mode, line mode, or batch mode.

Before you can use Debug Tool, though, you need to compile your program with the `TEST` compile option.

Debug Tool offers features such as session logging, program testing, debugging of mixed-language programs, dynamic patching, use of macros, dynamic breakpoints, stepping functionality, program frequency information, and other program information.

With session logging, you can log a debug session in a file. Later you can edit or play back this file to help pinpoint program errors. You can also use Debug Tool as a test tool; you can use the logs of previous debug sessions as input to test that the code changes you make do not introduce more errors into the program. In this way, Debug Tool is useful as a regression-testing tool. You can also use Debug Tool to debug programs that use more than one language (for example, you could debug a program that uses C and COBOL code).

By using the commands that are a part of Debug Tool, you can alter the value of variables or declare new variables to patch a program as it is being debugged. Using macros can make it easier to use these commands.

You can also use dynamic breakpoints and the stepping functionality provided with Debug Tool. You can set simple or complex breakpoints to monitor the contents of variables and to watch for the occurrence of specified exceptions and conditions during the execution of a program. You can remove or disable breakpoints at any time. You can also step through a program one line at a time or several lines at a time.

Debug Tool can also be useful to count the number of times that a statement or verb has been processed in a program. It can also display program and environment information, such as information about how a program was compiled and information about its structure.

16

Debug Tool also provides functionality that is specific to COBOL. It offers commands that are a subset of the COBOL language, for example. This makes the commands easy to remember and use. Debug Tool supports all the variable types available in COBOL; it also allows you to assign values to variables and display the contents of variables, as well as to declare temporary variables. You can also use the set of variables supplied with Debug Tool. For example, the %EPA variable returns the address of the primary entry point in the currently interrupted program. As far as COBOL expressions are concerned, Debug Tool interprets these according to COBOL rules. You can use the LIST command to display the results of arithmetic expressions.

Using Debugging Facilities in the AS/400 Environment

In the AS/400 environment, you can use all the coding techniques described in the preceding section, "Using Debugging Facilities in the VM Environment," except for the READY TRACE statement. You can also debug programs interactively in the AS/400 environment using the Start Debug (STRDBG) and End Debug (ENDDBG) AS/400 commands. These commands start and stop the ILE source debugger. You can debug both ILE and OPM programs using the ILE source debugger, and you can interact with the ILE source debugger using debug commands or the display interface.

You can also use the *Interactive Source Debugger* (ISDB), which is a part of the Application Development Toolset for AS/400 product. ISDB is based on the ILE source debugger and can do many of the same things. However, this tool is not being updated to incorporate the enhancements that are being made to the ILE source debugger. More emphasis is being placed on workstation application development tools. However, you can start this debugger using the STRISDB command. The rest of this section discusses the ILE source debugger.

Before you can debug a program using the ILE source debugger, you have to prepare it for debugging. You can create three views of the program you want to debug. You create the listing view by compiling the program with the *LIST or *ALL value of the DBGVIEW compile parameter. The listing view is similar to the listing portion of a compile listing. You can create the source view using the *SOURCE value of the DBGVIEW parameter. The source view contains references to the source statements of the source member. If the source member contains multiple compilation units, the source view contains all the source code of all the compilation units, even if only one of them can be debugged. You can create the statement view using the *STMT value of the DBGVIEW parameter. The statement view contains line numbers and statement numbers. You must debug in the statement view along with a hard-copy listing of the program.

You can run a program from a debug session in several ways, and you can add or remove program objects to or from a debug session after it has been started. Here are some of the other functions you can perform with the ILE source debugger:

- View program source (change the views that are shown).
- Set and remove conditional and unconditional breakpoints.
- Set and remove watch conditions. (A *watch condition* sets a breakpoint when the contents of a specified variable change.)
- Step through a program (including step over and step into).
- Display variables, expressions, records, group items, and arrays.
- Change the value of variables.
- Equate a name with a variable, expression, or command.

Other Unique Features

Well, it's true. Not all COBOL compilers are alike. This section describes some of the features that are unique to each sample COBOL environment.

Other Unique Features in the Unisys Environment

In the Unisys environment, several clauses, statements, and sections are unique. Some of these clauses follow:

ACTUAL KEY	Specifies the logical ordinal position of a record in a file
CAUSE	Initiates specified events
CHANNEL	Specifies a channel number that is to be referenced by a SEND or WRITE statement
DISK SIZE	Specifies the amount of disk space to be used for a sort
LIBRARY-SECTION	Defines the interface between a user program and a library program
LOCK	Locks a common data storage area so that other processes cannot get it
LOWER-BOUNDS	For array parameters that generate a stack item, can be used to pass the lower bound of the array

ODT	Defines an *operator display terminal* to be used in an ACCEPT or DISPLAY statement
PROCESS	Initiates another program as a separate asynchronous process
RECEIVE	Receives data asynchronously
SEND	Sends data asynchronously
SET (Format 5)	Sets a file attribute
USAGE IS EVENT	Specifies that the data item is an event item to be used to provide synchronization and common interlocks between two or more tasks

You can also use intrinsic functions in the Unisys environment like you can in the other environments. However, this environment has a few functions that are unique:

DIV	Returns the integer part of the quotient of N1/N2 (where N1 is divided by N2)
EXP	Returns the exponent
FIRSTONE	Returns the bit number, plus 1, of the leftmost nonzero bits in the numeric argument supplied
FORMATTED-SIZE	Returns the formatted size of an argument
ONES	Returns the number of nonzero bits in the numeric argument supplied

The description supplied for intrinsic functions available in the VM environment in the next section, "Other Unique Features in the VM Environment," also applies to the Unisys environment.

Several language extensions are provided in addition to the SDF (and SDF Plus) language extensions described in "Interacting with a Program in the Unisys Environment," earlier in this chapter:

Language Extension	Enables You To
Advanced Data Dictionary System (ADDS)	Centrally create and maintain data descriptions.
Communications Management System (COMS)	Communicate with COMS through direct windows.
Data Management System II (DSMII)	Invoke a database and maintain relationships among the various data elements in the database.
TransIT Open/OLTP	Do transaction processing.

Other Unique Features in the VM Environment

In the Unisys environment, several paragraphs, clauses, and statements are unique. Some of these clauses follow:

APPLY WRITE-ONLY	Applies the write permission to a file
EXIT METHOD	Specifies the end of an invoked method
REPOSITORY paragraph	Defines the name of the classes you can use in a class definition or program
YEARWINDOW	Returns the starting century of the Century window

In the VM environment, you can also use the *System Object Model* (SOM), which is an object-oriented programming technology that allows the interface for a class to be described in a standard language called the *Interface Definition Language* (IDL). Unlike the object model found in formal object-oriented programming languages, SOM is language neutral. It preserves the key object-oriented programming characteristics of encapsulation, inheritance, and polymorphism, but the implementor or user (in both cases, these are programmers) of a SOM class does not have to use the same programming language.

Class definitions are stored in a database called a SOM *Interface Repository* (IR). All the classes that are referenced by a program are declared in the REPOSITORY paragraph of the CONFIGURATION SECTION. The IR files to be used are also defined externally using an environment variable. When a program is compiled with IDL generation, SOM compiles the IDL (which populates the SOM interface repository); compiles the COBOL program again with type checking; and then prelinks, link-edits, and executes the application.

You can make some changes to SOM classes without having to recompile the program. You can add new methods, change the size of an object by adding or deleting instance data, insert new parent classes in the class hierarchy, and relocate methods to a higher position in the class hierarchy.

In the VM environment you can also reenter a program that is currently running recursively. All you have to do is specify the RECURSIVE phrase on the PROGRAM-ID clause. However, the RECURSIVE phrase can be coded only in the outermost program.

In the VM environment, you can also separately compile more than one program and link the programs together to create a single, larger program. You can also use other language environment languages to code these subprograms. You can use several methods to transfer control to another program. You can make calls to nested programs, static calls, or dynamic calls. When you terminate the execution of any of the programs using the EXIT PROGRAM or GOBACK statement, the program is left in its last-used state. When the terminated program is called again, the internal values are in the state in which they were

Mainframe and Mini Environments

CHAPTER **16**

461

16

MAINFRAME AND
MINI
ENVIRONMENTS

left when the program was exited, except for the return values for PERFORM statements, which are reset to their first value.

Another feature is the availability of intrinsic functions, which can allow you to do such things as numeric calculations without having to code an algorithm. For example, you can use the ANNUITY intrinsic function to calculate an annuity; ACOS, ASIN, or ATAN to calculate just what their names imply; or intrinsic functions that will calculate STANDARD-DEVIATION, MEAN, or MEDIAN. You can choose from many more intrinsic functions as well.

Other Unique Features in the AS/400 Environment

You can use the following clauses and statements in the AS/400 environment in addition to the standard COBOL clauses, intrinsic functions, and statements:

ADD-DURATION	Adds a date and time duration.
CONSOLE	Specifies whether ACCEPT and DISPLAY statements are to be extended or whether the Dynamic Screen Manager APIs are to be accessed.
CONVERT-DATE-TIME	Converts other data types to a date-time data type.
EXTRACT-DATE-TIME	Returns part of a date, time, or timestamp item.
LOCALE-DATE	Returns a date in a culturally appropriate format.
LOCALE-TIME	Returns a time in a culturally appropriate format.
SET statements	Manipulate pointers.
SUBTRACT-DURATION	Subtracts a date and time duration.
TEST-DATE-TIME	Determines whether a data item is a valid date-time data item.

User-Defined Data Types

User-defined data types refer to data-description entries that can be used as templates to be copied and applied to other data-description entries. The initial data-description entry is defined using the TYPEDEF clause. Other identical data-description entries (except for the name) can then be created using the TYPE clause, which references the name of any data-description entry that was defined using the TYPEDEF clause.

Locales

Locales refer to culturally specific formats that can be applied to culturally specific, numeric-formatted data, such as dates and times, and money. Locales are defined in the FORMAT clause of the SPECIAL-NAMES paragraph. These map to locales that reside on the AS/400 system. Locales that are defined in the SPECIAL-NAMES paragraph then can be applied to PICTURE clauses in data-description entries in order to apply the required culturally specific formatting attributes to these data items.

Overview of VAX COBOL

Although the VAX manuals were not available at the time this chapter was written, this section provides an overview of programming with COBOL in a VAX environment.

You can access database files using VAX COBOL. VAX COBOL interfaces with the Oracle DBMS Data Management System.

VAX COBOL includes various extensions to COBOL, such as the following:

- Extended ACCEPT and DISPLAY statements
- File extensions for segmented keys, descending keys, and duplicate primary keys
- RMS-STS, RMS-STV, and RMS-FILENAME special registers that can be examined to assist in debugging
- Conditional compilation to make debugging easier
- File-sharing and record-locking features
- A COPY FROM DICTIONARY statement to allow access to common record descriptions stored in the Oracle repository

VAX COBOL has several unique statements, clauses, and constructs, such as these:

- CALL statement extensions: BY VALUE, BY DESCRIPTOR, OMITTED, and GIVING.
- VALUE IS EXTERNAL allows you to access link-time constants.
- USAGE IS POINTER allows you to define an address data type.
- VALUE IS REFERENCE allows you to specify compile-time address evaluation.
- SET TO REFERENCE allows you to specify runtime address evaluation.
- SUCCESS and FAILURE are used for class conditions.
- 31-character usernames.
- ACCEPT AT END statement.
- Single-quote–delimited, nonnumeric literals.
- Hyphen/underscore equivalence in usernames.
- Nonnumeric literal argument passing.

The VAX COBOL compiler produces an object module from a source program. The compiler produces a source listing with embedded diagnostics, such as a machine-language listing, a filename map, a data-name map, a procedure-name map, an external–program name map, database subschema information, and a cross-reference listing.

VAX COBOL also provides support for using the error diagnostics and cross-reference information in the DEC Language-Sensitive Editor/Source Code Analyzer. Additionally, you can process pseudocode and design comments that are used by the DEC Language-Sensitive Editor/Source Code Analyzer to create low-level program design documents.

Finally, you can link object modules produced by the compiler with other object modules produced by many other OpenVMS VAX compilers, including VAX BASIC and DEC FORTRAN. VAX COBOL is supported by both the OpenVMS VAX Common *Run Time Library* (RTL) and the Symbolic Debugger for OpenVMS VAX.

Micro Focus COBOL for HP 3000

Micro Focus COBOL for HP 3000 is a cross-platform COBOL compiler. You can create new applications in a networked environment and develop applications that run across multiple platforms. There are also some key new features.

Support has been enhanced for converted macros, function prototypes, external data definitions, and C typedef to COBOL typedef structures. This means that you can use C header files, such as the operating system APIs.

Besides supporting `int` and `a.out` executable forms, the new compiler supports the native dynamically loadable form (`snt`), which may mean that data takes up less space in a multiuser environment.

Executable programs now are built with shared HP Micro Focus COBOL libraries, which will make them smaller.

HP Micro Focus COBOL/iX has a high-performance native code generator, integrated SQL preprocessor support, and productivity tools that support the development process. HP Micro Focus COBOL/iX also supports portable source code and intermediate code.

UNIX-Based Platforms

CHAPTER

17

This chapter focuses on developing COBOL programs in the UNIX environment.

You'll start by examining some important UNIX environment variables. You'll look at the password and group files, and you'll learn about reading and manipulating a file's permissions. Next, you'll learn what a program is in UNIX; you'll see a working program and learn how to compile and execute it. Then you'll look at some useful UNIX commands and development tools that UNIX provides as part of its environment. Keep in mind that UNIX is a hugely complex and powerful system and that you need to make full use of your system's documentation when developing systems.

UNIX Environment

The command shell is a program present during your login session that executes the commands you enter at the terminal or in any shell scripts you run. Generally speaking, UNIX supports numerous types of shells. Each shell offers common functionality while allowing you to take advantage of the shell's unique capabilities. You also have the capability to switch shells at the command line, which you can do by entering the shell's program name at the shell prompt.

Here are the more popular shells (you can find these commands in Volume 1 of the UNIX Reference Manual):

csh	The C-Shell uses a C-like command syntax and, like the other two shells, provides for job control and command history. The C Shell is the default for Sun systems.
ksh	The K-Shell, or Korn Shell, is also a powerful programming language and commands shell. It also supports job control and provides a command-history mechanism. This shell is made the default shell on some systems because of its popularity and powerful programming capabilities.
sh	The POSIX Shell is POSIX.2 compliant. This usually is the default shell assigned to a new user by the administrator. It offers job control and a shell-command history. This shell is not to be confused with the older non–POSIX compliant Bourne Shell (sh). This shell lacks the many POSIX features of today's newer UNIX operating systems. You still can invoke this shell, but keep in mind that it is being phased out of UNIX.

Although it seems as though there is not much difference between these shells, they all support not only the generic shell commands available in UNIX but also contain their own specific language and commands that make each one a very powerful programming language.

If you want to invoke a different shell than your current one (as defined in the /etc/passwd entry for your login ID), simply enter its name at the prompt. Suppose that you want to run the Korn shell; you type ksh. This places you at a $ prompt, which is the prompt that usually signifies the ksh.

Every shell, whether it is a parent or a child (subshell), has two main data areas associated with it. The two areas, *environment space* and *local variables,* hold all the variables in a string format and are used to transfer data to a program, to customize the executing program, and to retain information that is important to the current program.

As a programmer, you need to understand the difference between parent and child programs and how they affect the environment space and the local variables. A local variable is specific to the shell in which it was created and cannot be passed to a child program. This variable may be construed as private to the creating program. An environment space variable is global and therefore is passed from a parent program to a child program, which makes the passing of information from one program to another very convenient and straightforward.

A typical local variable looks like this:

```
TERM=vt100
```

Exporting the variable makes it global:

```
export TERM
```

Making the variable global simply moves the variable from the local variable environment to the environment space.

Predefined variables are associated with each type of shell. These variables are initialized at startup in the .profile (.login in the csh) file located in the user's home directory. Six basic variables are common to all shells:

$HOME	Specifies the full pathname to your home directory
$MAIL	Specifies the full pathname to your mail directory
$PATH	Searches path directories
$SHELL	Specifies the full pathname to your login shell
$TERM	Defines your terminal type
$USER	Specifies your user ID as entered at login

You can find these variables in the .profile file, and you can change them by simply editing the .profile file.

The following is the output from env, which shows all the variables that are set from the command line, the .profile file, or a script or program:

```
MANPATH=/usr/share/man/%L:/usr/share/man:/usr/contrib/man/%L:/usr/contrib/
➡      man:/usr/local/man/%L:/usr/local/man:/opt/omni/lib/man:/opt/
➡      hpnp//man:/opt/perf/man
PATH=/usr/devbin:/usr/bin:/usr/ccs/bin:/usr/contrib/bin:/opt/nettladm/bin:/
➡      opt/upgrade/bin:/usr/bin/X11:/usr/contrib/bin/X11:/opt/hpnp//bin:/
➡      opt/perf/bin:/opt/omni/bin:/home/piercew:/usr/devbin:/usr/local/
➡      bin:/bin:/home/piercew/bin:.
COLUMNS=132
EDITOR=vi
LOGNAME=wgpierce
MAIL=/var/mail/wgpierce
ERASE=^H
SHELL=/usr/bin/ksh
HOME=/home/wgpierce
TERM=vt100
PWD=/home/wgpierce
TZ=EST5
LINES=25
```

You must consider the various UNIX environment variables when developing an application. Micro Focus COBOL, for example, requires that you set certain environment variables (for example, COBDIR, COBLIB) prior to invoking the COBOL compiler. Be sure that you read the vendor documentation before using the product.

Password File

The basic unit of security for UNIX systems is the password. It is the key that opens the door for system access. Access is granted by the *system administrator* (SA) at the time the user is granted system access. When the user ID is created, the SA must also enter an initial password. The user must change this password after his or her initial login to the system. Otherwise the SA will probably execute a script that will deactivate the user ID if it isn't changed within a predefined time span.

The password file (/etc/passwd) usually can be read by anyone and can be written to only by a user with root capabilities. Because users can change their own password and they don't have root access, you might wonder whether this statement is correct. Yes, special permissions allow this process without requiring root capabilities. You might want to read about setuid and the passwd command for more information.

The password file is a colon-delimited, seven-field record broken into the following fields:

Username	User's login name.
Password	Encrypted/encoded password.
UserId (UID)	Unique integer associated with the username. (The system uses the UID, and the username is for human convenience.)
GroupId (GID)	Unique integer associated with the user's primary group.
Personal Description_	Pertinent user information.
Home_Directory	Full pathname to user's home directory. This directory can be the application developer's working directory. Here working directory refers to the directory where the programs are edited and compiled. Virtually any directory can be a working directory. If this account happens to be the application account, developers use this home directory as the application's working directory.
Startup	Shell that is run at login.

A typical entry looks like this:

```
piercew:kslsuertqwczx:317:20:,,,:/home/piercew:/bin/ksh
    1              2    3  4  5         6          7
```

Notice that in field 5, there are three commas indicating that no personal data was entered. Because this is the only field with subfields, the comma is implemented as a subfield delimiter.

The password file is one of the most important files on the system. If this file becomes corrupted or destroyed, it causes extensive work for the system administrator, and access to the system is denied during the time of the restoration or re-creation of the file. Remember to protect this file at all times. What this means to you as a developer is that you cannot access the system until the password file is repaired or restored.

Group and Group File

Part of UNIX security is to separate classes of users into groups that are functional and allow shared access by common groups and restrict access to nongroup members. This is done not only for administrative and organizational purposes but also to assist in resource-access protection.

Three major classes of users exist for access to system resources: file owner, group owner, and all other users. Resource access is controlled by the effective user ID and group ID of the resources creator and the system umask. In the next section, "Permissions," you will see how these classes/groups are implemented so that the file-protection scheme can control resource access.

The file /etc/group defines all information related to groups and the associated users. This file is maintained by the SA through the use of a system administration tool(s) or simply by editing the ASCII text file. The SA can grant the user access to several of the groups or restrict the user to the primary group. The primary group is located in field 4 of the /etc/passwd file and is depicted by the *group ID number* (GID). All users must have an association with at least one group; that group is the user's *primary group*.

The group file is a colon-delimited four-field record, with field 4 having subfields that are delimited by commas. Here are the fields you will find in a group file:

Group_Name	A unique name established by the SA
Group_Password	An encrypted password established by the SA; should not be implemented because it can cause security problems
GID	A group identifier that is a unique integer
Group_Members	A comma-delimited field

Here is a typical group file with attached users:

```
root::0:root
other::1:root,hpdb
bin::2:root,bin
sys::3:root,uucp,dbadmin,dboper,piercew,woodb
adm::4:root,adm,piercew,wilsond,piercejb
daemon::5:root,daemon
mail::6:root
lp::7:root,lp,pierce
tty::10:
nuucp::11:nuucp
users::20:root,piercew,woodw,wilsond,spb,fifo,piercejb
```

As this example indicates, the user piercew has access to groups sys, adm, users, and lp. If you check the example in the preceding section, "Password File," you will see that piercew has a primary group of 20. Now check the group file here, and you will see that group 20 is group users. Everything checks, so user piercew will have system access.

Permissions

This section uses file permissions to explain the concept of permissions. You already know that when a file is created, the effective user ID and group ID become the owner and group, respectively, for that file. The access permissions are related to the umask as defined by the system or user.

File permissions are maintained in the first field of the entry, beginning with character 1 and ending with character 10. The first character identifies the type of entry—whether it's a file, directory, special file, or link. The hyphen (-) indicates that the entry is an ordinary file. The next nine characters, in groups of three, represent owner, group, and other permissions. An r represents read permission, w represents write permission, x represents execute/search permission, and - means permission denied. Each three-character group identifier has a numeric value, which is determined by adding the read, write, and execute permissions together. Read permission is always 4, write permission is always 2, execute/search is always 1, and the hyphen is always 0.

In the following example, the numeric value for File Owner is 7, Group is 5, and Other is 2. The permissions therefore can be represented as 752 instead of rwxr-x-w-, although either format is correct.

```
-rwxr-x-w-   1 piercew     users        0 Mar  6 09:14 develop.doc

rwx                 File owner    4+2+1 = 7
    r-x             Group         4+1   = 5
        -w-         0ther         2       = 2
```

When you create a file, the permissions are set using the system- or user-defined umask. That way, all files are created the same way by default, which gives uniformity to the system. Files frequently need to have different permissions to satisfy different requirements; this can be accomplished by using the chmod command. There are several ways to change permissions. The first thing to remember is that only the owner or superuser (root) can change permissions. Using the earlier example, suppose that the permissions are 752 or rwxr-x-w-, and you want to remove execute permission from Owner and add read permission for Other. You can accomplish this by using numeric values or character values.

If you use the character-option technique, use the following conventions to make the changes:

Owner permissions	u
Group permissions	g
Other permissions	o
Add a permission	+
Remove a permission	-
Assign permissions	=
Read	r
Write	w
Execute	x

Here are two examples of changing permission settings with the character and numeric methods:

Character method	chmod u -x develop.doc	Removes execute from Owner
Numeric method	chmod 652 develop.doc	
Character method	chmod o+r develop.doc	Adds read for Other
Numeric method	chmod 656 develop.doc	

Multiple permissions can be removed at the same time by doing the following:

| Character method | chmod u -rx Filename | Removes execute and read from Owner |
| Numeric method | chmod 252 develop.doc | Removes execute and read but leaves write |

As you can see, understanding the way UNIX handles file permissions is an important part of successfully developing programs in this environment.

UNIX Programs

An executing program in UNIX is called a *process*. A process can be an executing shell script or a compiled program (for example, COBOL); either one uses system resources to perform meaningful work. In this section, you will examine an executable program to see how a program comes to life in UNIX.

The first step is to decide what your program needs to do. UNIX offers a very rich set of tools and libraries that enable you to build extremely powerful programs. Add to that the various vendor-supplied libraries, and you have the means of writing robust applications to support your organization. You can use the Micro Focus COBOL suite of tools along with Oracle's database and tools, for example, to build world-class applications. Because UNIX is considered an "open system," you can take this application and with minimal effort port it between competing UNIX vendors' machines; this is not easily accomplished when coding for the more proprietary mainframe environments. This is one reason why so many companies are migrating some or all of their applications to the open systems environment.

After you perform the necessary analysis and determine what it is that you need to write, you can use the standard tools supplied with your environment to begin coding. You can start by invoking the standard UNIX editor, vi. The vi editor is supplied as part of your UNIX environment and is the editor of choice for most UNIX programmers. If you don't feel the need to learn vi because of its terse command structure, you can use emacs or your PC's editor and then upload the program source file to your UNIX platform by using FTP.

Suppose that you have successfully mastered the vi editor and you are staring at your first COBOL program source code written for a UNIX environment. You now need to invoke the compiler to produce an executable. The examples here show you how I did this by using HP Micro-Focus COBOL/UX 4.0 on a Hewlett-Packard *Symmetric Multiprocessor* (SMP) system. The operating system is HP-UX 10.X.

Suppose that you have a program that copies one datafile to another datafile. Listing 17.1 shows the source code for this program, which is named copy-file.cob.

LISTING 17.1 A COBOL PROGRAM THAT MAKES A COPY OF A FILE.

```
IDENTIFICATION DIVISION.
PROGRAM-ID.
    COPY_FILE.
ENVIRONMENT DIVISION.
INPUT-OUTPUT SECTION.
FILE-CONTROL.
    SELECT TEXT-IN-FILE ASSIGN TO DISK "filein.dat".
    SELECT TEXT-OUT-FILE ASSIGN TO "FILEOUT.DAT".
DATA DIVISION.
FILE SECTION.
FD  TEXT-IN-FILE
    LABEL RECORDS ARE OMITTED.
01  TEXT-IN-RECORD           PICTURE X(80).
FD  TEXT-OUT-FILE
    LABEL RECORDS ARE OMITTED.
01  LINE-OUT-RECORD          PICTURE X(80).
WORKING-STORAGE SECTION.
01  OUT-OF-DATA-FLAG         PICTURE X(1).
PROCEDURE DIVISION.
    OPEN INPUT TEXT-IN-FILE
         OUTPUT TEXT-OUT-FILE.
    MOVE 'N' TO OUT-OF-DATA-FLAG.
    READ TEXT-IN-FILE
        AT END MOVE 'Y' TO OUT-OF-DATA-FLAG.
    PERFORM B010-PROCESS-WRITE-READ
        UNTIL OUT-OF-DATA-FLAG = 'Y'.
    CLOSE TEXT-IN-FILE
          TEXT-OUT-FILE.
    STOP RUN.
B010-PROCESS-WRITE-READ.
    MOVE TEXT-IN-RECORD TO LINE-OUT-RECORD.
    WRITE LINE-OUT-RECORD.
    READ TEXT-IN-FILE
        AT END MOVE 'Y' TO OUT-OF-DATA-FLAG.
```

Notice that "filein.dat" is in lowercase. This program reads from a UNIX file named filein.dat and writes to a file named FILEOUT.DAT. Remember that UNIX is case-sensitive.

To compile this program using the HP Micro Focus COBOL/UX compiler, you enter the following at the UNIX prompt:

```
$ cob -v -V -x -o copy-file copy-file.cob
```

Here is the screen output that results from this command:

```
cob -C nolist -v -V -x -o copy-file copy-file.cob
version @(#)cob.c        1.101
PRN=21UPK/BMF:8a.1a.12.01
PTI=NLS
* Micro Focus COBOL for UNIX        V4.0 revision 005 Compiler
* Copyright  1984-1994 Micro Focus Ltd.
* Accepted - verbose
* Accepted - nolist
* Compiling copy_file.cob
* Total Messages:     0
* Data:        772    Code:       538
* Micro Focus COBOL/2              v4.0 revision   Code generator
* Copyright  1984-1994 Micro Focus Ltd.
* Accepted - verbose
* Accepted - hpoptimize(1)
* Generating copy-file.int
* Data =       944 Code =       0 Literals =       48 Dictionary =    2027
cob: Entry points defined in module: copy-file.o
        *copy0file
        COPY0FILE
        _HP_copy0file
as: HP92453-03 UX.10.20.05 (DAVIS) PA-RISC 2.0 Assembler
ld: 92453-07 linker linker ld B.10.27 970417
as: HP92453-03 UX.10.20.05 (DAVIS) PA-RISC 2.0 Assembler
```

You can see from this output that the compile was successful. By executing an ls -al copy-file*, you should see the COBOL source file(s) and COBOL executable(s), as well as other intermediate files associated with the program:

```
$ ls -al copy-file*
-rwxrwxrwx   1 dwilson     users       81984 Feb 21 19:41 copy-file
-rw-rw-rw-   1 dwilson     users        1054 Feb 21 19:39 copy-file.cob
-rw-rw-rw-   1 dwilson     users        2816 Feb 21 19:40 copy-file.int
-rw-rw-rw-   1 dwilson     users        4536 Feb 21 19:40 copy-file.o
```

Notice that the executable program has the same name that you gave it on the command line when you compiled the copy-file.cob file. The o (the letter o) option allows you to name the executable at compile time.

HP Micro Focus COBOL/UX is a full-featured enterprise class compiler. It is necessary that you read and understand the documentation prior to developing your application. You will save hours of frustration by learning your compiler and development environment before writing your first program. Remember that UNIX is a complex environment that uses a rather cryptic and terse set of commands. As when using most computer systems, if you don't understand what you're doing, you can end up spending days doing what would have taken hours if you had only read the documentation.

Useful UNIX Commands

This section presents the fundamental commands necessary for you to navigate through your UNIX environment. UNIX commands are case-sensitive. For example, you could have two separate hypothetical commands named abc and ABC; each would be considered a different command in UNIX. Be careful not to use the Caps Lock key in this environment. It causes problems not only in the vi editor but also in the command shell interpreter—better known simply as the *shell*.

Now that you understand what the shell does for you (handling the execution of your commands), take a look at some commands you need to know to successfully navigate the UNIX environment.

env(1)

This command obtains the current environment variables that exist for your current session. In UNIX, certain variables must be preset so that programs can run successfully. To run a specific program, for example, you need to know where it is located or have its directory placed in your PATH. Here is an example:

At the command prompt $, type env:

```
$ env
```

As you can see from the output, you automatically have numerous global variables pre-assigned to your session (you learned about the environment at the beginning of this chapter):

```
PATH=/usr/bin:/opt/ansic/bin:/bin:/opt/cobol/bin:.
EDITOR=vi
LOGNAME=nancy_gordon
MAIL=/var/mail/ngordon
ERASE=^H
SHELL=/usr/bin/sh
HOME=/Oracle/Practice_Manager/ngordon
TERM=vt100
PWD=/Oracle/Indy/ngordon
TZ=CST6CDT
```

Now suppose that you want to execute a COBOL program called READ_CUSTOMERS that reads data from an Oracle database, and that program resides in /Oracle8/COBOL/APPS. You can see from the preceding output that Oracle8/COBOL/APPS does not reside in your PATH variable. You can add it to the global PATH variable, or you can execute /Oracle8/COBOL/APPS/READ_CUSTOMERS in the command shell. As long as you have the appropriate directory and file permissions, the program will execute.

My preference is to use the export command to append /Oracle8/COBOL/APPS to your current PATH variable:

```
$ export PATH=$PATH:/Oracle8/COBOL/APPS
```

By issuing the env command after the PATH has been changed, you see the following output:

```
PATH=/usr/bin:/opt/ansic/bin:/bin:/opt/cobol/bin:/Oracle8/COBOL/APPS:.
EDITOR=vi
LOGNAME=nancy_gordon
MAIL=/var/mail/ngordon
ERASE=^H
SHELL=/usr/bin/sh
HOME=/Oracle/Practice_Manager/ngordon
TERM=vt100
PWD=/Oracle/Indy/ngordon
TZ=CST6CDT
```

You can see that the directory containing the READ_CUSTOMERS program is in your PATH, and you now can execute it simply by entering READ_CUSTOMERS at the shell prompt. Otherwise, you would have had to enter the full path and program name to execute the program:

```
'/Oracle8/COBOL/APPS/ READ_CUSTOMERS'.
```

ps(1)

The ps command returns a report about the UNIX processes currently running on your system. See your UNIX Systems Manual for a complete list of options to use with the ps command. You can use this command to see whether your program is running or whether another program is active that your program needs in order to execute. If you need a database to run against, for example, you can use the ps command to verify that it's available prior to starting your job. Now look at an example. If your Oracle database is named apps, you can issue the ps -ef command to see whether it is running. (Note: grep is used as a filter to exclude every line not containing the word apps.)

The command

```
$ ps -ef | grep apps
```

generates this listing:

```
oracle 25205    1   0   Feb  2   ?           0:01  ora_reco_apps
oracle 25201    1   0   Feb  2   ?           1:58  ora_ckpt_apps
oracle 25194    1   0   Feb  2   ?           3:37  ora_dbwr_apps
oracle 25192    1   0   Feb  2   ?           2:13  ora_pmon_apps
oracle 25203    1   0   Feb  2   ?           0:11  ora_smon_apps
oracle 25199    1   0   Feb  2   ?           2:27  ora_lgwr_apps
```

This listing shows that your database is up and running.

ls(1)

You can use the `ls` command to generate a listing of all the files in a directory. If you want to see what is in your home directory, for example, you can issue the following command from your home directory:

```
$ ls -al
```

This generates the following output:

```
drwxrwxrwx   2 dwilson      users       1024 Feb 15 12:25 .
drwxr-xr-x   6 root         root        1024 Nov 21 07:16 ..
-rw-r--r--   1 avjohnson    users        814 Nov 21 07:16 .cshrc
-rw-r--r--   1 avjohnson    users        347 Nov 21 07:16 .exrc
-rw-rw-rw-   1 avjohnson    users         97 Feb 15 11:37 .glancerc
-rw-r--r--   1 avjohnson    users        341 Nov 21 07:16 .login
-rw-r--r--   1 avjohnson    users        446 Nov 21 07:16 .profile
-rw-r--r--   1 avjohnson    dba          890 Nov 21 07:56 .profile.oracle
-rw-------   1 avjohnson    users       3218 Feb 15 15:11 .sh_history
-rwxrwxrwx   1 avjohnson    users      81984 Feb  2 20:35 db_reader
-rw-rw-rw-   1 avjohnson    users       1051 Feb  2 20:35 db_reader.cob
-rw-rw-rw-   1 avjohnson    users       8192 Feb  2 19:33 db_reader.idy
-rw-rw-rw-   1 avjohnson    users       2816 Feb  2 20:35 db_reader.int
-rw-rw-rw-   1 avjohnson    users       4496 Feb  2 20:35 db_reader.o
-rw-rw-rw-   1 avjohnson    users       1051 Feb 15 12:23 file_reader.cob
-rw-rw-rw-   1 avjohnson    users       2816 Feb 15 12:25 file_reader.int
-rw-rw-rw-   1 avjohnson    users       4496 Feb 15 12:25 file_reader.o
```

In this listing, you see all the files in the current (your home) directory. Notice files that begin with a dot (.). These files don't show up during a standard `ls`; you must add the a option to your `ls` to see these files. The dot (.) and dot-dot (..) files are the current and parent directories, respectively. See your UNIX documentation for options for this command.

find(1)

This command searches directories in a hierarchical fashion for files that you provide as part of the command. The command is smart enough to descend through directories and subdirectories searching for a match. Now look at a few examples.

First, check for COBOL source files in your home directory:

```
$ pwd
/home/mcoffey
$ find . -name "*.cob" -print
./act.cob
./reader.cob
./readerx.cob
$
```

As you can see, the `find` command located three COBOL source program files in your home directory. The format of the output can be interpreted as the following:

. (dot)	Specifies the current directory. You told `find` to begin its search in the current directory.
/	Denotes directory hierarchical location.
file_name	The file(s) the command found a match with from the list you provided.

You also can use the `find` command to see where any other COBOL source files are located. The following example begins at the current directory:

```
$ pwd
/home/dselby

$ find . -name "*.cob" -print
./reader.cob
./readerx.cob
./COBOL/APP1.cob
./COBOL/APP2.cob
./COBOL/APP3.cob
$
```

You also can enter the following command to see the same files in a different way:

```
$ find /home/dselby -name "*.cob" -print
```

This generates the following output:

```
/home/dselby/reader.cob
/home/dselby/readerx.cob
/home/dselby/COBOL/APP1.cob
/home/dselby/COBOL/APP2.cob
/home/dselby/COBOL/APP3.cob
$
```

As you can see, the two commands return the same base COBOL files, but they are displayed with different directory information. The first command tells find to use the current directory (.). The find command simply prepends each file match with the implicit dot (.). This tells you that relative to your current directory, the find command found the following files in the current directory as well as these other subdirectories. The second example explicitly tells find to begin its search at /home/delby and to continue downward along the directory tree until it finishes. As you can see, it prepends the found files with the beginning /home/dselby directory path.

cpio(1)

You use this command to copy files and/or directories to tape or new locations. Most UNIX programmers use cpio to archive their directories to tape. You will look at examples of both uses here.

Begin by looking at an example of the cpio command being used with the find command. Suppose that you need to copy your source code to a backup directory. This directory is a common directory used by your team as the source directory for storing files that will be archived to tape. Instead of using cp to copy each individual file over to the backup directory, you use the find and cpio commands in the same command line.

The backup directory is located in /COBOL_APPS/backup/. The programs you want to copy to that directory are located in /home/dbaber/APPS. You will start by looking at the /COBOL_APPS/backup directory to see the files that have already been placed there.

The command

```
$ ls -al /COBOL_APPS/backup
```

generates this output:

```
total 15
drwxrwxrwx   2 root        sys         1024 Feb 21 10:47 .
drwxrwxrwx   3 root        sys         1024 Feb 21 10:44 ..
-rw-rw-rw-   1 dwilson     apps          29 Feb 21 10:47 acct1.cob
-rw-rw-rw-   1 twilson     apps          10 Feb 21 10:47 acct2.cob
-rw-rw-rw-   1 ewilson     apps          20 Feb 21 10:47 acct12.cob
-rw-rw-rw-   1 awilson     apps          30 Feb 21 10:47 acct22.cob
-rw-rw-rw-   1 bpierce     apps          40 Feb 21 10:47 acct32.cob
-rw-rw-rw-   1 jpierce     apps          40 Feb 21 10:47 acct24.cob
-rw-rw-rw-   1 jjpierce    apps          50 Feb 21 10:47 acct25.cob
-rw-rw-rw-   1 mwessler    apps          10 Feb 21 10:47 acct26.cob
-rw-rw-rw-   1 mcbhugheyr  apps          80 Feb 21 10:47 acct28.cob
-rw-rw-rw-   1 cspretnjak  apps          70 Feb 21 10:47 acct29.cob
-rw-rw-rw-   1 rblum       apps          90 Feb 21 10:47 acct62.cob
-rw-rw-rw-   1 sjohnson    apps         100 Feb 21 10:47 acct3.cob
-rw-rw-rw-   1 bwessler    apps         200 Feb 21 10:47 acct45.cob
$
```

Now move your program files over to the `/COBOL_APPS/backup` directory:

```
$ pwd
/home/dbaber

$ find . -name "*.cob" ¦ cpio -pdmlv /COBOL_APPS/backup
```

You then see the following output:

```
/COBOL_APPS/backup/reader.cob
/COBOL_APPS/backup/readerx.cob
/COBOL_APPS/backup/COBOL/APP1.cob
/COBOL_APPS/backup/COBOL/APP2.cob
/COBOL_APPS/backup/COBOL/APP3.cob
$
```

Do an `ls -al` on the `/COBOL_APPS/backup` directory to see your newly added files, as shown in this sample output:

```
drwxrwxrwx  2 root        sys         1024 Feb 21 10:47 .
drwxrwxrwx  3 root        sys         1024 Feb 21 10:44 ..
-rw-rw-rw-  1 bwessler    apps         200 Feb 21 10:47 acct45.cob
-rw-rw-rw-  1 dwilson     apps          29 Feb 21 10:47 acct1.cob
-rw-rw-rw-  1 twilson     apps          10 Feb 21 10:47 acct2.cob
-rw-rw-rw-  1 ewilson     apps          20 Feb 21 10:47 acct12.cob
-rw-rw-rw-  1 awilson     apps          30 Feb 21 10:47 acct22.cob
-rw-rw-rw-  1 bpierce     apps          40 Feb 21 10:47 acct32.cob
-rw-rw-rw-  1 jpierce     apps          40 Feb 21 10:47 acct24.cob
-rw-rw-rw-  1 jjpierce    apps          50 Feb 21 10:47 acct25.cob
-rw-rw-rw-  1 mwessler    apps          10 Feb 21 10:47 acct26.cob
-rw-rw-rw-  1 bhugheyr    apps          80 Feb 21 10:47 acct28.cob
-rw-rw-rw-  1 cspretnjak  apps          70 Feb 21 10:47 acct29.cob
-rw-rw-rw-  1 rblum       apps          90 Feb 21 10:47 acct62.cob
-rw-rw-rw-  1 sjohnson    apps         100 Feb 21 10:47 acct3.cob
-rw-rw-rw-  1 dbaber      apps         200 Feb 25 11:57 reader.cob
-rw-rw-rw-  1 dbaber      apps         300 Feb 25 11:57 readerx.cob


/COBOL_APPS/backup/COBOL:
total 4
drwxrwxrwx  2 root        sys         1024 Feb 25 11:57 .
drwxrwxrwx  3 root        sys         1024 Feb 25 11:57 ..
-rw-rw-rw-  1 dbaber      apps         100 Feb 25 09:17 APP1.cob
-rw-rw-rw-  1 dbaber      apps         200 Feb 25 09:18 APP2.cob
-rw-rw-rw-  1 dbaber      apps         300 Feb 25 09:18 APP3.cob
$
```

Notice that not only did you move your program files from your current directory over to `/COBOL_APPS/backup`, but you also copied your program files from your subdirectory `COBOL` over as well. As you can see, by combining UNIX commands, you can simplify complex problems.

chown(1)

The `chown` command allows you to change the ownership of a file you own to that of another user. You might be wondering why you would want to do that. One answer is that you might have a number of developers on your team. Each developer has his or her own user ID. Each developer creates numerous data and program files that will comprise the whole application. The common practice in UNIX is to have what is called an *application ID* or *application account*. This ID or account is the owner of all the program and data files that exist for the application. By assigning each developer's program and data files to this common application account, you can simplify the management of the application. For example, instead of each developer establishing file and directory permissions for files in the application that he or she is responsible for, a global approach can be implemented for the application account, and management becomes relatively simple.

Now look at an example of this. Suppose that you have tested your programs and are ready to move the executables over into production. You can use `chown` to change the ownership of the executables to that of the application account.

```
$ ls -al ./COBOL
-rw-rw-rw-   1 dwilson    users          45987 Feb 21 09:17 APP1.cob
-rw-rw-rw-   1 dwilson    users           2342 Feb 21 09:18 APP2.cob
-rw-rw-rw-   1 dwilson    users          35678 Feb 21 09:58 APP3.cob
-rw-rw-rw-   1 dwilson    users           1008 Feb 21 09:20 APP1
-rw-rw-rw-   1 dwilson    users         256677 Feb 21 09:21 APP2
-rw-rw-rw-   1 dwilson    users         236978 Feb 22 09:36 APP3
```

You can see from this list that this directory contains both COBOL source files and executables.

You can simply change ownership of the executables by issuing the following command:

```
$ chown appl_id APP?
```

An `ls -al` shows the results of this:

```
-rw-rw-rw-   1 dwilson    users          45987 Feb 21 09:17 APP1.cob
-rw-rw-rw-   1 dwilson    users           2342 Feb 21 09:18 APP2.cob
-rw-rw-rw-   1 dwilson    users          35678 Feb 21 09:58 APP3.cob
-rw-rw-rw-   1 appl_id    users           1008 Feb 21 09:20 APP1
-rw-rw-rw-   1 appl_id    users         256677 Feb 21 09:21 APP2
-rw-rw-rw-   1 appl_id    users         236978 Feb 22 09:36 APP3
```

The `?` in the preceding command has the effect of a wildcard character. It informs `chown` to change ownership of all files in the current directory that have APP and any single character in the fourth position of the filename to `appl_id`.

Now you need to change the group ID to that of the `appl_id` group. You can do this by using the `chgrp` command:

```
$ ls -al ./COBOL

-rw-rw-rw-   1 dwilson    users           45987 Feb 21 09:17 APP1.cob
-rw-rw-rw-   1 dwilson    users            2342 Feb 21 09:18 APP2.cob
-rw-rw-rw-   1 dwilson    users           35678 Feb 21 09:58 APP3.cob
-rw-rw-rw-   1 appl_id    users            1008 Feb 21 09:20 APP1
-rw-rw-rw-   1 appl_id    users          256677 Feb 21 09:21 APP2
-rw-rw-rw-   1 appl_id    users          236978 Feb 22 09:36 APP3
```

This listing shows you the directory as it exists after you execute the chown command. You now can execute the chgrp command to change your group ID of the executables:

```
$ chgrp appl_grp APP?

$ls -al ./COBOL

-rw-rw-rw-   1 dwilson    users           45987 Feb 21 09:17 APP1.cob
-rw-rw-rw-   1 dwilson    users            2342 Feb 21 09:18 APP2.cob
-rw-rw-rw-   1 dwilson    users           35678 Feb 21 09:58 APP3.cob
-rw-rw-rw-   1 appl_id    appl_grp         1008 Feb 21 09:20 APP1
-rw-rw-rw-   1 appl_id    appl_grp       256677 Feb 21 09:21 APP2
-rw-rw-rw-   1 appl_id    appl_grp       236978 Feb 22 09:36 APP3
```

As you can see, you again used the wildcard character substitution with the preceding chgrp command.

Now that you know how to use both chown and chgrp to alter your files' user and group IDs, take a look at how you can simplify the whole process by relying on chown to change both the owner and group IDs:

```
$ chown appl_id:appl_grp APP?
```

If you had executed this command on your COBOL directory first, you would have ended up with the same results as executing both the chown and chgrp one after another. Again, you see the power of the UNIX command set that you have available to simplify your job as a developer.

Additional UNIX Utilities

As a programmer, you should know about two additional UNIX utilities: make(1) and RCS(1). This section provides a brief discussion of each utility; each one could have a complete chapter devoted to it, but because this is a book on COBOL, I'll just provide an overview of each utility.

It is no secret that development projects of any real size require more than one file. As projects become larger with more files being created and modified by multiple developers, the inherent complexity of the project increases. When those files become dependent on each other, the situation becomes even more complex. Because files are often dependent on each other, a change to one file will have an impact on the execution of other files. If one program is modified, all the connected programs need to be recompiled and relinked as necessary.

A classic example is a program that calls several outside modules written by multiple people on a development team. Suppose that a developer tests a program that calls several outside modules created and maintained by another team member. The program seems to run fine, so the developer moves on to something else. Meanwhile, one of the called modules is modified by another team member. Later that day, the first developer runs the compiled code from earlier and gets the same results. But these results are not necessarily up-to-date! Why? Obviously the newly modified module needs to be recompiled and relinked with the current main program. The first developer, who is hopefully aware of the new modification, will need to recompile and relink the main module and all the supporting modules to get current results. If only a few modules are involved, this is simply an inconvenience. On the other hand, if the main program calls many modules that in turn are dependent on even more modules, this situation obviously gets out of control very quickly. Fortunately, UNIX provides a command to keep these problems to a minimum.

The make Utility

The make utility tracks, recompiles, and relinks a set of files as needed whenever any one of the files is modified. The purpose is to allow for the easy recompilation and linking of all files that are dependent on each other without having to address each file separately. For example, if program A calls (is dependent on) module B, make recompiles B and relinks to A if B has been modified. This occurs because A is dependent on B. The make command does not recompile or relink files that have not been modified and are not dependent on a newly modified file. For example, if program A calls only module B and both are unmodified, a change in a module C generates a recompile and relink only for module C when the make command is issued. On the other hand, if modules A, B, and C have been modified but are not dependent on each other, make recompiles all three modules because they have been modified, even though they are not dependent on each other. The benefits of the make command boil down to being able to recompile and relink a group of programs if there is a belief that they may have been modified. The make utility, rather than the developer, goes to the trouble of identifying modified files and determining their dependencies so that only those modified and/or dependent files are recompiled and relinked.

The make utility requires the existence of a file that contains all the files to be checked for modification and their dependencies. This file is called a *makefile*. The developer (often using vi) writes this file to specify for the make utility which files need to be checked and whether any dependencies exist. Note that the idea behind make is to keep the application modules current when programs are compiled and linked. See the next section, "The Revision Control System," for information on program version control.

The make utility has several options you can use to provide more information about the execution of the makefile; Table 17.1 summarizes these options.

TABLE 17.1   make OPTIONS.

Option	Function
-d	Displays the reason why make is regenerating files and which dependent files have been modified
-dd	Displays in detail the dependency check and processing of the makefile
-D	Displays the makefile text
-DD	Similar to the -D option but provides more details
-e	Allows environment variables to override assignments made within makefiles
-f makefile	Works as normal but searches for a makefile when no makefile exists in the current working directory
-i	Ignores any error codes generated from within the makefile
-k	Continues the makefile process even if an error status occurs or a rule is not found
-K	Uses the state file statefile
-n	Prints commands but does not execute any commands unless the command references the $(MAKE) macro or lines that start with + when POSIX is in effect
-p	Prints all macro definitions and target descriptions
-P	Prints file dependencies but does not enforce them
-q	Returns a zero or nonzero code depending on whether the target file is current
-r	Does not use default makefile/usr/share/lib/make/make.rules
-s	Does not print command lines before execution
-S	Undoes the effect caused by the -k option and stops processing when an error status is found
-t	Brings target files up-to-date but does not perform their processing rules
-V	make enters into SysV mode

You enter the desired option after the `make` command. For example, if you use the `-d` option, the output looks like this:

```
$ make -f makefile
```

The `make` utility and its associated makefiles are a valuable tool for developers. Files can be easily recompiled and relinked when changes are made. Although this is helpful for programs that are only one file, it is especially useful in environments where programs are dependent on many files that in turn may have additional dependencies. You saw what a simple makefile looks like, what it does, and some of the options available for the `make` command. By implementing and then expanding on what has been discussed in this section, you will be able to reduce the confusion and problems inherent when working with multiple program files.

The Revision Control System

The *Revision Control System* (RCS) is a feature that stores and protects files in a "library" so that they can be "checked in" and "checked out" by qualified programmers for modification. Although RCS can be used in a nonprogramming environment with a single user, it is most beneficial in situations where multiple programmers are working on projects with many interdependent modules. Each program module is placed into or "checked into" the RCS library. There it is given an identifying version number. Any time you want to modify that module, you must check out that particular module from the RCS library file. You then can make modifications only to that module. After the modifications (revisions) are made, you check the newly updated module back into the RCS library file. Before you actually check the module back in, you must describe what changes were made to the module in a log that is stored with the module. This log contains the revision number of the module, name of the programmer, date of modification, and description of changes made. The module then can be checked out again for use or modification by any other programmer. Thus RCS acts as a library of modules, but it is a library where the "books" can be changed after they are checked out. The essence of RCS in a programming environment therefore is the maintenance of a library of modules that must be checked in and out by programmers any time a modification is made so that everyone is using the newest versions of each module.

Every module stored with RCS is given a revision number starting at 1.1. Any time a module is checked out, modified, and checked back in, that copy of the module becomes the newest version available and has its version number incremented by .1. For example, if a programmer checks out version 1.3 of a program module, modifies it, and checks it back in, it will be version 1.4, which denotes that it is different and newer than the older 1.3 version. On the other hand, if a module is checked out but not modified, it does not receive a new version number when checked back in; it reverts to the current version number. You can check out any previous version of a module for use or modification.

Suppose that the modifications in version 1.4 of your program module were wrong and now the complete program no longer works. The developers of the program can simply revert to using version 1.3 without any problems. They can simply ignore version 1.4 by never checking it out for use. Version 1.3 can be checked out, modified, and checked back in to form a revision branch of 1.3.1.1. Now changes can be made off the version 1.3 branch without affecting any other version of the module (1.2, for example). This creation of revision branches allows modules to be modified and used for separate projects without overlapping changes but to still be stored in the same RCS library file. Unless otherwise specified during the checkout process, the newest version of the module is what is checked out.

RCS provides a file-locking option for every module checked out. If the option is selected when the module is checked out, only the programmer who checked out the module has write permission to that particular version while it is checked out. Other programmers can check out that version at the same time, but they will have read-only access. Similarly, if the file-locking option is not selected at checkout time, the file is checked out with read-only access. This may be useful if an individual only wants to view the contents of a module rather than make any modifications.

The actual process of implementing RCS is quite simple. Suppose that you have a `copyfile.cob` program for which you want to create an RCS file. The RCS file will contain a list of every version of that module, when it was created, who it was created by, whether there are any existing branches, a user-created description for that particular version, and the most current version number. Simply create the initial RCS file by checking in the file. The system automatically creates the RCS file using your original filename with a `,v` at the end. It asks you to enter a description of what your module is; this description also is stored in the RCS file. Your copy of the module disappears because you now can access it only through RCS starting at version 1.1.

```
expert.cc.purdue.edu% ci copy-file.cob
copy-file.cob,v  <--  copy-file.cob
enter description, terminated with single '.' or end of file:
NOTE: This is NOT the log message!
>> This is a hello world program module
>> This statement creates a new RCS file for copy-file.cob
>> Copy-file.c will be replaced by copy-file.cob,v
>> .
initial revision: 1.1
done
expert.cc.purdue.edu%
```

A quick check of the directory shows that `copy-file.c` has been replaced with `copyfile.cob,v`, which is the RCS file.

```
expert.cc.purdue.edu% ls
copy-file.cob,v
expert.cc.purdue.edu%
```

Note that `copy-file.cob` now can be accessed only by checking it out through RCS. A look at `copy-file.cob,v` shows the following RCS information:

```
head     1.1;
access;
symbols;
locks; strict;
comment @ * @;


1.1
date     98.02.22.23.54.20;       author wesslerm;        state Exp;
branches;
next     ;


desc
@This is a hello world program module
This statement creates a new RCS file for copy-file.cob
Copy-file.cob will be replaced by copy-file.cob,v
@


1.1
log
@Initial revision
@
text
@
    * Please reference  the source code from figure 1. Edited for brevity.

@
```

To check out a copy of `copy-file.cob` with a lock, enter the following:

```
expert.cc.purdue.edu% co -l copy-file.cob
copy-file.cob,v  -->  copy-file.cob
revision 1.1 (locked)
done
expert.cc.purdue.edu%
```

Now you have read, write, and execute privileges for version 1.1 of `copy-file.cob`. You can make changes to the file as though it were any other file. Suppose that you decide not to modify the program and want to check the module back in. Note how RCS handles this:

```
expert.cc.purdue.edu% ci copy-file.cob
copy-file.cob,v  <--  copy-file.cob
file is unchanged; reverting to previous revision 1.1
done
expert.cc.purdue.edu%
```

On the other hand, if you had decided to change the code (using vi, for example), RCS would have created a new version number and prompted you for a description of the newer module. This information would have been stored in the copy-file.cob,v RCS file:

```
expert.cc.purdue.edu% ci -l copy-file.cob
copy-file.cob,v  <--  copy-file.cob
new revision: 1.2; previous revision: 1.1
enter log message, terminated with single '.' or end of file:
>> This is a newly modified version.
>> It will get a new version number.
>> .
done
expert.cc.purdue.edu%
```

Notice that the –l locking option was used for the check-in process. This creates a new version number and automatically checks it out so that you can continue to make modifications on the newest version. A check of the directory verifies this fact:

```
expert.cc.purdue.edu% ls
copy-file.cob    copy-file.cob,v
expert.cc.purdue.edu%
```

However, if the –l locking option were not used for the check-in process, the copy-file.cob file would have disappeared from the current directory after the new version was created. This is because the module would have been checked back in but not automatically checked back out. You would have to check out the new version separately.

```
expert.cc.purdue.edu% ci copy-file.cob
copy-file.cob,v  <--  copy-file.cob
new revision: 1.3; previous revision: 1.2
enter log message, terminated with single '.' or end of file:
>> This is the newest version.
>> Checked in without the -l option.
>> Will Not automatically be checked out.
>> .
done
expert.cc.purdue.edu% ls
copy-file.cob,v
expert.cc.purdue.edu%
```

The average programmer can most likely get by with the features described here, particularly once file locking and version numbers are fully understood. Additional options for

RCS files do exist, such as changing the access list or locking options. Various options also exist for both check-in and checkout. The importance of these additional options really becomes apparent in larger programming environments. These options can better be described by typing man ci or man co and then focusing on the desired option, rather than attempting a comprehensive description of them all within this text.

In review, the Revision Control System is a valuable tool when programming with multiple modules. Because modules are constantly changing in a large programming environment and because many different people are often making these changes, a system to keep track of every revision is needed. RCS keeps track of every change made to a module, who made it, when it was made, and what was done. RCS can make sure that only one copy of a version is available for update at a time and creates new versions as needed. RCS can create revision branches to allow separate projects to access and modify different versions of the same module without conflict. Any previous version of the module can also be accessed. The two basic commands in RCS are check-in (ci) and checkout (co). Specific versions of modules are checked out and checked back into RCS almost as if they were books in a library; the key difference is that the programmer can modify these "books" as needed.

Summary

As you can see, UNIX is a very powerful programming and development environment. It offers you many powerful tools and programs that ease the development process. However, you must understand that if you do not spend the time to learn how the UNIX environment works, you will be limited in your ability to take advantage of the full power of UNIX. By learning as much as you can up front, you can combine the tools already available with UNIX with other third-party software to develop world-class software. Fortunately, if you are willing to take the time and effort to master UNIX, you can look forward to programming in an environment that will be around for years to come.

The Personal Computer

IN THIS CHAPTER

There are several good reasons for using COBOL on a PC. A modern PC is very fast and offers an enticing work environment compared to the standard mainframe environment. Some major reasons for working with COBOL on a PC follow:

- You can use the PC for editing and unit testing of programs to be uploaded later to a mainframe. For example, the ultimate run environment might be a mainframe, but you might want to take advantage of the PC environment for its immediate response. This topic is covered in detail in Chapter 19, "Mainframe Development Offloading."

- You can use a COBOL compiler on the PC as a tool for learning basic COBOL syntax or to explore an intricate algorithm and get it right before uploading the program to a mainframe.

- You can build a COBOL-based application to actually run on a PC; you might want to take advantage of its graphical user interface or connectivity to the Internet.

Major COBOL vendors cater to both a mainframe-centric view by making their compilers closely mainframe compatible and to a PC-centric view by offering extensions to the COBOL language (usually in the form of callable modules) that allow access (an API) to PC-specific functions.

The PC Environment

The PC environment is very rich and quite different from the mainframe environment. The difference is apparent both when developing a program and when running it. Even on a PC, there are a variety of environments to cope with: DOS, Windows 3.*x*, Windows 98/95/NT, OS/2, and various flavors of UNIX (in particular, Linux). This chapter excludes UNIX, although it is an excellent, stable development platform. See Chapter 17, "UNIX-Based Platforms," for a discussion of COBOL on UNIX platforms.

Evolution of the PC Environment

Over time the PC environment has become very powerful, now rivaling the processing power of the mainframe of only a decade ago. The COBOL compilers that vendors offer for the PC have been able to absorb that extra processing power in a most remarkable way; as a result, the compilation time has stayed almost constant even as the processing power of the PC has increased a hundredfold. This means that no matter what PC you have, no matter how old or resource-limited it is, you can find a COBOL compiler that runs on that PC. Most of the older DOS-based compilers may be a bit hard to come by because vendors tend to promote their latest and greatest versions.

JCL (or the Lack Thereof)

There is no *Job Control Language* (JCL) in the classical sense on a PC. JCL normally serves two important functions: allocation of resources and sequencing of job steps within a job. In DOS you can use a batch file for primitive sequencing. In OS/2 a command file allows somewhat better control, but in Windows the situation is not very good. In Windows 3.*x*, you are out of luck. Finally, Windows 98/95/NT allows you to start 32-bit programs from the command line or a batch file in a DOS box, but it is cumbersome for a running COBOL program to communicate back to the batch file.

The lack of JCL and true batch processing is at the same time a strength—it makes working a lot easier and more immediate—but also a serious weakness because it limits the degree of automation you can build into an application.

Development Environment

You have two choices when working with COBOL on a PC: a command-line environment and an *Integrated Development Environment* (IDE). With a command-line environment, you basically use a DOS box to launch the compiler, librarian, linker, and finally, the program itself. With an IDE, all this takes place from within the IDE itself by using a point-and-click interface. Both choices have their strong points and weak points; ideally, you want a compiler that lets you use both choices.

Development Tools

Because COBOL has always supported separate compilation units, the classical development cycle involves editing the program, compiling it, placing it in an object library, and possibly linking it with other COBOL programs and system routines to produce an executable load module. The following separate tools generally are needed:

- **An editor.** Any text editor will do, but the best solution is to use an editor that is COBOL aware. The compiler vendors usually supply special COBOL editors that help with keyword recognition, indentation, syntax checking, outlining, and other productivity enhancements. If you are working as part of a team, you may also need (or have to live with!) some form of version control system.

  Some editors even completely emulate popular mainframe and minicomputer editors so that the learning curve is very flat. On the other hand, you take less advantage of the PC environment if you only use it to emulate the mainframe.

- **A compiler.** The compiler produces the object module and other needed modules—for example, symbol tables for debugging.

- **A librarian.** The librarian manages object libraries, usually in the standard PC format. The compiler vendor usually supplies some version of the LIB.EXE program.

- **A linker.** The linker extracts object modules from the libraries and produces an executable or another loadable module. The compiler vendor usually supplies some version of the LINK.EXE program. Microsoft also supplies a librarian and linker with many of its language offerings.

With the advent of Windows and OS/2, there are now two distinct forms of executable modules: the EXE file, which is always the starting point of a run-unit; and the *Dynamic Link Library* (DLL), which may contain subprograms, icons, and other resources needed at runtime. Modern COBOL compilers can produce modules in these forms as well, but the library management and linking process have become dauntingly complex as a result. IDEs purport to hide most of that complexity but unfortunately just shift the complexity elsewhere—the various options have to be defined *somewhere*.

Compiler options that control elements such as the format of computational data items, source-program format, optimization, type of COBOL dialect, and so on can often be stored in a special file or included in the source text itself as a special comment line before the program proper. Some compilers have a multitude of options, making the learning curve steeper. At the time of this writing, for example, the popular Micro Focus compiler has 183 options (called *directives*).

Some compilers do not produce standard object modules at all, so library management and linking are nonissues. AccuCobol is the foremost example of this approach; the result of the compilation is in a proprietary binary format that is interpreted by a runtime system.

An Example of Command-Line Compilation

After you figure out all the options and settings you need (and this is the *hard* part), you hide all that in a batch or command file so that the only thing you have to do to produce a DLL, for example, from your source file is issue this single command:

```
cobol myprog
```

To give you an idea of what is involved, here is the cobol.bat file for the Fujitsu 32-bit compiler:

```
@echo off
::COBOL - compilation using FUJITSU COBOL
echo Compiling %1...
%lib%\cobol32 -i %etkdir%\cobol85.cbi %1.cob > %1.err
if exist %1.obj goto linkup
```

```
:error
type %1.err ¦ more
goto end

:linkup
echo making DLL %1...
echo LIBRARY %1 >  %1.exp
echo EXPORTS %1 >> %1.exp
upper<%1.exp>%1.def
%lib%\lib/nologo /def:%1.def /out:%1.lib /machine:ix86 %1.obj  > nul
%lib%\link/nologo %1.obj %1.exp /dll /out:%1.dll @%etkdir%\f3libs

if exist %1.def   del   %1.def > nul
if exist %1.exp   del   %1.exp > nul
if exist %1.lib   del   %1.lib > nul
if exist %1.obj   del   %1.obj > nul
if exist %1.err   del   %1.err > nul
:end
```

Working with an IDE

With an IDE, you usually work with a *project*. After you set up the project, you build an executable just by clicking an appropriate button or icon. The IDE looks enticing enough. The real problem is setting up the project and all its appropriate properties.

COBOL Compiler Requirements

COBOL compilers for the PC come in all sizes, ranging from simple DOS-based compilers that fit on a single floppy disk to full-featured 32-bit workbenches that come on one or more CD-ROMs, take several hundred megabytes of your disk space, and require 32MB of RAM to work efficiently. Amazingly, there is little difference in capabilities between the two extremes; the main difference is that the large 32-bit compilers work about 10 times slower than the "lean and mean" DOS-based compilers.

The CD-ROM accompanying this book includes a sampling of full 32-bit Windows 98/95/NT-based compilers. The documentation supplied with those compilers shows how to compile and run programs.

Runtime Environment

COBOL has always had an ENVIRONMENT division where differences in runtime environments can be addressed. You can still specify some items here, notably for file handling, but most other issues must be dealt with elsewhere. Here are the main environmental issues:

- **File handling:** This deals with associating a COBOL file with an actual file on the PC. Examples of the issues here include the name of the file (including the path to the file), the file type (often specified using a certain extension to the name, such as `.txt` for text files), and performance-related issues such as buffering and sharing.

- **Screen handling:** If your COBOL program is a batch program, you probably only need support for simple `DISPLAY` and `ACCEPT` statements, which generally are supported as going to and coming from a console that can be a DOS box or a simple window with scrolling text. If you plan on using a full-screen forms mode to interact with your program (an online program), the PC offers a rich set of possibilities, from a simple text-based form to a full-fledged GUI window or even a Web page.

- **Command-line parameters:** Batch programs often need a small amount of control information. On a PC you can supply this information as parameters to the program call. Other external values of great interest in a PC environment are the environment variables, which are kept in memory for the running process. The capability to access parameters and environment variables is important when your program must interface with other subsystems on a PC.

- **Printing and spooling:** The traditional COBOL printer is a line printer with very simple form control. On a PC this will still work, but some COBOL compilers also support sophisticated overlay or presentation formats, such as support for fonts and font sizes. Print spooling is accomplished by simply directing all the print output to a file for later printing.

- **Interfacing to other languages:** The capability to call C, C++, and other PC-centric languages enhances the value of your COBOL system by allowing integration with standard PC-based applications. Also, DOS interrupts and the Windows API usually are accessed by calling system routines supplied by the COBOL system and linked to your application.

File Handling

The main problem to solve here is not allocation of the file—this is a concept foreign to the PC environment—but rather specification of where in the hierarchical file system the file is located. You can assign a name to a file in three ways:

- Use an environment variable to externally assign a file, including a full pathname:

```
SELECT MY-FILE ASSIGN TO MYFILE
```

You then should set an environment variable to define `MYFILE`:

```
SET MYFILE=C:\MYDIR\FILE1.DAT
```

This is similar to attaching a dataset using JCL on a mainframe.

- Use a hard-coded explicit filename:

```
SELECT MY-FILE ASSIGN TO "C:\MYDIR\\FILE.DAT"
```

- Use a filename stored in a data item:

```
SELECT MY-FILE ASSIGN TO VARYING DATA-NAME-1
...
WORKING-STORAGE SECTION.
01  DATA-NAME-1                 PIC X(128).
...
PROCEDURE DIVISION.
...
    MOVE "C:\MYDIR\FILE1.DAT" TO DATA-NAME-1
    OPEN INPUT MY-FILE
...
```

Syntax Differences

Even for these simple examples, various compilers use different syntax. The examples here use the CA-Realia compiler syntax. For the Micro Focus compiler, the three ASSIGN clauses would look like this:

```
ASSIGN TO EXTERNAL MYFILE
ASSIGN TO "C:\MYDIR\FILE1.DAT"
ASSIGN TO DYNAMIC MYFILE
```

I will not show the syntactical differences between all the compilers available for the PC here; enough differences (some obvious and some more subtle) exist to make life miserable for someone trying to write a COBOL program that can be compiled by more than one compiler. In Chapter 19 you learn how to cope with and overcome this problem.

Directory Structure

Files on a PC are organized in directories (also called *folders)* that reside on drives. Drives can be local on your PC or on a network connected to your PC. Directories can have subdirectories to any reasonable depth. At any given time, a *current* directory (also called the *working directory*) exists. Programs usually are executed out of the current directory, although the PATH environment variable can specify a search list of directories to go through in order to locate a program.

Unfortunately, there is no analogous data path to locate files. It is up to the application to implement its own search strategy. Any errors encountered, such as file not found, write error, and so on, must also be dealt with by the application. Some COBOL compilers generate code to stop the run-unit in case of file-access failure. You usually can trap these conditions and do your own error handling—for example, with a DECLARATIVES section.

Screen Handling

Some COBOL systems support a SCREEN SECTION within the language itself. The SCREEN SECTION contains syntax that enables you to do the following:

- Specify the exact position of fields.
- Accept data typed at specified positions.
- Define screen attributes such as colors and underlining.

Here is a simple SCREEN SECTION:

```
WORKING-STORAGE SECTION.
01   CUSTOMER-NO          PIC X(8).

SCREEN SECTION.
01   CUSTOMER-SCREEN      BLANK SCREEN..
       02   VALUE         X"    Customer No.    :"
                          LINE 10  COLUMN 10.
       02   S-CUSTOMER-NO LINE 10  COLUMN 30
                          PIC X(8) USING CUSTOMER-NO AUTO.

PROCEDURE DIVISION.
...
       DISPLAY CUSTOMER-SCREEN
       ACCEPT CUSTOMER-SCREEN
...
```

The SCREEN SECTION is fine for controlling a text-based form but does not lend itself to a GUI or Web page format. It therefore has fallen into disuse. Also, although the SCREEN SECTION is part of the X/OPEN standard, its implementation tends to be spotty at best. For simple COBOL programs, you are better off using the teletype-style DISPLAY and ACCEPT statements. Major applications should not be targeted at a text-based user interface anymore.

GUI support usually is handled by external modules you can call from your COBOL program. A thriving third-party market exists for such modules.

Command-Line Parameters

Access to the command line can be through an extension of the ACCEPT verb, as shown here:

```
ACCEPT PROGRAM-COMMAND-LINE FROM COMMAND-LINE
```

Another popular mechanism is to use a fictitious LINKAGE SECTION, as shown here:

```
LINKAGE SECTION.

01   PROGRAM-COMMAND-LINE.
     02   PROGRAM-COMMAND-LENGTH       PIC S9(4)   COMP-4.
     02   PROGRAM-COMMAND-ARG.
          03   FILLER                  PIC X   OCCURS 1 TO 120
               DEPENDING ON            PROGRAM-COMMAND-LENGTH.

PROCEDURE DIVISION
     USING PROGRAM-COMMAND-LINE.
BEGIN-OF-PROGRAM.
     ...
```

The syntax is compiler specific. The syntax shown here is for the CA-Realia compiler. For that same compiler, access to environment variables is possible with a call to a run-time routine:

```
01   ENV-STRING-NAME             PIC X(nnn).
01   ENV-STRING-VALUE            PIC X(nnn).
...
CALL "DOS-GET-ENV-STRING"
     USING ENV-STRING-NAME
           ENV-STRING-VALUE
```

Even if you are programming for a 32-bit Windows target, the WIN32 API supplies support for command-line parameters and environment variables.

Printing and Spooling

Typically you assign the keyword PRINTER to the print file, as shown here:

```
FILE-CONTROL.
   SELECT MY-PRINT-FILE
          ASSIGN TO PRINTER.
```

This causes the output to be sent to the system default printer.

Alternatively, you can assign a specific printer to the file, as shown here:

```
FILE-CONTROL.
   SELECT MY-PRINT-FILE
          ASSIGN TO "PRTNAME:Canon LBP-A40E".
```

As usual, the exact syntax for the printer name varies from compiler to compiler. If the printer is on a network, the network software handles the spooling.

For some compilers, you can specify printing information in the ENVIRONMENT DIVISION. Here is an example for the Fujitsu compiler:

18

THE PERSONAL
COMPUTER

```
PRINTING MODE printing-mode-name
    IN SIZE literal-1 POINT
    AT PITCH literal-2 CPI
    WITH FONT font-name
    AT ANGLE integer-1 DEGREES
    BY FORM form-name.
```

There are a couple of alternative approaches to using compiler-supplied extensions. One is to embed your own control codes for printer control and then have a special print conversion program that deals with control codes for specific printers. A better alternative is to produce output in a widely used external format such as HTML. This approach enables you to leverage existing (and powerful) technology.

Interfacing to Other Languages

It is vital that your COBOL system can call programs and modules written in other languages. This is the only way you can access operating system–specific routines that are not built in to the COBOL runtime library, and in these days of rapid and unpredictable changes, you need this open back door. At the very least, you should be able to call an Assembler routine that in turn can manipulate the stack and registers to fit the calling conventions of the routines you want to call.

Using Assembler may limit you to a specific platform and hamper porting an application from an Intel-type PC to an Alpha-type Windows NT platform. Today it is better to call a C module to maintain portability.

Several different calling conventions control how parameters are placed on the call stack and who removes them from the stack. In a mainframe COBOL environment, program calls normally are not handled with a stack mechanism, so the call-stack concept may be somewhat alien to you. This concept is fundamental to the way a program running on the PC accesses the Windows system services.

Parameters can be passed BY REFERENCE (which is the normal COBOL mechanism), BY CONTENT, or BY VALUE corresponding to what the called routine expects. A return value (variously called RETURN-CODE or PROGRAM-STATUS) is used to signal the result of the call, as shown here:

```
CALL "SYS01" WITH C LINKAGE
    USING BY REFERENCE SYS-PAR-1
          BY VALUE     SYS-PAR-2

IF PROGRAM-STATUS = ZEROES
    ...
END-IF
```

Advanced System Services

System services generally are platform specific. Some compilers come with assorted system calls that are built in as functions or are available as callable modules in a system library. Alternatively, you can "roll your own" if the compiler allows calls to other languages. This is usually the most flexible approach because it allows you to take advantage of any system feature without being dependent on support from your COBOL compiler vendor.

Here is some sample C++ code for advanced file manipulation, such as getting the attributes for a file, deleting, and renaming a file (the full source code is available on the CD-ROM with this book):

```
typedef struct
{// Format of Control
  char  Operation;    // selects Function
  char  Feedback;     // space if OK
  int   ErrorCode;    // 32 bit error code if any
  int   Number;       // depends on Operation
  char  Text[256];    // depends on Operation
}p;

extern "C" // to preserve names
void _stdcall _export ETK2SYST (char* Control, char* Buffer);
void _stdcall _export ETK2SYST (char* Control, char* Buffer)
{// begin
p* pControl = (p*) Control;

SetLastError(0);
switch (pControl->Operation)
{// switch
case 'A':
 {// File Attributes
    unsigned int Attributes;
    Attributes = GetFileAttributes (pControl->Text);
    pControl->Number = Attributes;
    if (Attributes & (FILE_ATTRIBUTE_DIRECTORY |
                      FILE_ATTRIBUTE_HIDDEN     |
                      FILE_ATTRIBUTE_SYSTEM))
        pControl->Feedback = 'N';
    else
        pControl->Feedback = ' ';
 break;}
case 'D':
 {// Delete a File
    if (DeleteFile (pControl->Text))
        pControl->Feedback = ' ';
    else
        pControl->Feedback = 'E';
```

```
  break;}
case 'R':
 {// Rename a File
    if (MoveFile (pControl->Text, Buffer))
        pControl->Feedback = ' ';
    else
        pControl->Feedback = 'E';
 break;}

default:
 {// Otherwise
    pControl->Feedback = 'O';
 break;}
}// Switch
if (pControl->Feedback == ' ')
    pControl->ErrorCode = 0;
else
    pControl->ErrorCode = GetLastError();
} //end
```

You compile this code to a DLL using any C++ compiler. You then can call these functions from a COBOL program, as shown here:

```
01   ETK2SYST-CONTROL.
        02   ETK2SYST-OPERATION        PIC X.
        02   ETK2SYST-FEEDBACK         PIC X.
        02   ETK2SYST-ERROR-CODE       PIC S9(9)   COMP-5.
        02   ETK2SYST-NUMBER           PIC S9(9)   COMP-5.
        02   ETK2SYST-TEXT.
             03   ETK2SYST-TEXT-CHAR   PIC X       OCCURS 256 TIMES.

01   ETK2SYST-BUFFER.
        02   ETK2SYST-BUFFER-CHAR      PIC X       OCCURS 256 TIMES.
...
DELETE-FILE.
     MOVE "DELETE" TO ETK2SYST-OPERATION
     MOVE "C:\MYAPP\DATA1" & LOW-VALUE TO ETK2SYST-TEXT
     PERFORM CALL-ETK2SYST
     IF ETK2SYST-FEEDBACK > SPACE
         PERFORM SIGNAL-ERROR-DELETING

         .

CALL-ETK2SYST.
     CALL "ETK2SYST" WITH STDCALL LINKAGE
          USING ETK2SYST-CONTROL
                ETK2SYST-BUFFER

         .
```

In this way, you have full access to any facility your platform offers. To make it really useful, you should encapsulate the system services once more so that you call yet another COBOL program to actually call the system service provider. Then you are truly portable and protected against changes in the environment. The one lesson we have all learned the hard way? As soon as you rely directly on system-specific functions in your application programs, you have a legacy program, so you always encapsulate such functionality (which you, of course, must have and cannot do without) as external subprograms.

Runtime Control of the Program

Most compilers allow you to control the runtime behavior of your program. This is in addition to the specific requirements your program might have. Some compilers use environment variables for this, some use switches appended to the program name when you execute the program, and others use the simple (and platform-independent) device of reading the control information from a configuration file.

Here is a sample configuration file for a program (ETK) compiled with the Fujitsu compiler:

```
[ETK]
@IconName=COB85EXE
@CnslWinSize=(81,24)
@CnslFont=(LUCIDA CONSOLE,12)
@CnslBufLine=240
@WinCloseMsg=OFF
@EnvSetWindow=UNUSE
@AllFileExclusive=NO

[ETK.ENTRY]
SCRNWIN=ETK2SCRN.DLL
```

Fine control at the level of individual programs carries a cost, though: Now you have to distribute and maintain the configuration files as well.

Mainframe Development Offloading

This chapter discusses using *personal computer* (PC) workstations for the development of COBOL applications that are targeted to run on other platforms. Although much of the discussion focuses on using the IBM PC platform to develop and maintain COBOL applications that run on IBM mainframes, many of the issues described here apply to developing applications for other environments as well. The term that is widely used to describe the use of PC workstations to perform IBM mainframe targeted development is *mainframe development offloading.*

A Brief History of Mainframe Offloading

This section contains a great deal of technical information presented in an historical fashion. If you take the time to read and digest this section, you should come away with a keen understanding of the issues involved in developing COBOL applications on one platform that are intended to run on a different platform for production purposes. Although many of the issues noted are directly related to IBM mainframe EBCDIC environments versus PC ASCII environments, you will find that understanding these issues will greatly help you to recognize the same types of problems if you are using a PC to develop COBOL applications for a production UNIX system.

I was actually on the front lines on day one of attempts to use microprocessor-based computers to perform mainframe COBOL development offloading. This need was driven by several well-known facts regarding mainframe application development:

- The IBM mainframe environment was and still is a very expensive environment.

- IBM mainframes were generally designed for production purposes—to run the business on rather than provide optimal development environments for developing applications on.

- IBM mainframe application developers generally compete with production applications for mainframe time and resources—and the production applications are generally given higher priority. This often leaves developers waiting for hours for compile turnaround and many seconds for response time when editing.

- IBM mainframe environments are not graphical and are not highly interactive by nature. They typically provide character-mode terminal interfaces with somewhat basic and noninteractive development and testing tools. Although some mainframe advocates may argue that editors such as IBM's ISPF are very powerful, the truth is that the very architecture of mainframe terminal communications makes for slow response time and nongraphical interaction.

- Because of the very design of the mainframe terminal communications system, mainframe-based interactive debuggers are tedious at best and are seldom used given their enormous costs in resources. This means that many critical business applications are simply batch tested (also known as *black-box* testing).

- Users of IBM's IMS and CICS OLTP and DMBSs often are forced to wait days or even weeks for certain supporting technical tasks to be completed. For example, if a COBOL programmer needs to add a new segment to an IMS database, he or she typically must submit the request to the database administration team, get it to create the appropriate assembler macros, and wait for the next time that IMS is stopped and restarted to perform the IMSGEN, which might be once a week or once a month. Using a PC, programmers can take care of this task themselves in a few minutes, affecting only themselves, and then be allowed to continue development without waiting.

The major fact that has spurred on the growth of the mainframe offloading market is the rather simple fact that if you can remove the development process from the mainframe (or at least some portion of it), you free up these mainframe resources to apply to production application use. The idea of not purchasing or upgrading a mainframe, which costs millions of dollars, and instead simply purchasing some far cheaper microprocessor-based computer workstations for developers is very desirable to MIS managers. The additional fact that in doing this, mainframe resources are freed up to apply to production applications, thus postponing a mainframe purchase or upgrade, is a double boon.

This dual payback benefit made the use of micro-based computers with development tools very cost-effective. In the early days of this technology evolution, it cost roughly $10,000 to $15,000 to equip a single developer with the required hardware and software to perform mainframe development on a microprocessor-based computer. Today this cost has dropped to between $5,000 and $10,000, depending on the software required.

The Early Players

As mainframe costs soared and production systems ate up more and more mainframe resources, a few individuals in the industry began to look at providing standalone mini- or micro-based workstations to offload COBOL development. This idea came up in the late 1970s and early 1980s as micro-based computers began to emerge for widespread use.

SOLOsystems

The mainframe development offloading industry began when two former Silicon Valley executives, Mitch Gooze (*goo-say*) and Henry Davis, put together a business plan to found a company named SOLOsystems Inc. around 1980. Mitch and Henry were successful in securing venture capital financing to begin this effort. At its height, SOLOsystems employed around 100 people in the U.S.

The basis for SOLOsystems was the design of a high-end dual Motorola 68000 microprocessor-based workstation called a SOLOstation. The SOLOstation was capable of running up to 12 processes concurrently and provided a character windowing interface. SOLOsystems designed a proprietary operating system (SOLOS) for it. Additionally, SOLOsystems helped to fund other startups, such as SyQuest Technology, Inc. SyQuest delivered to SOLOsystems some of the world's first removable mini–hard disk storage systems, which were incorporated into the SOLOStation. The original SyQuest removable disks held 5MB of data. Later 10MB and 20MB removable disks were delivered. SOLOsystems additionally offered an add-on Winchester disk pod that stored 100MB of data. SOLOsystems provided a high-level encryption technology to encode data to specific SOLOstations for security reasons.

SOLOsystems later developed the world's first IBM OSVS compatible COBOL system off an IBM mainframe. This is somewhat arguable because the SOLOsystems "compiler" was not a full compiler that generated normal executable files. Instead, it generated a kind of pseudocode that was interpreted by a debugger. For example, there was not a real file system that could read and write mass numbers of records to real files.

The original price for a single SOLOstation was $45,000 in 1983. Even with this high price, SOLOsystems generated an enormous amount of interest in corporate America and was tested in large COBOL development shops such as Ford Motor Company and Allstate Insurance Company, among others.

SOLOsystems' eventual demise came in 1984 when it was refused a third round of venture capital. The company was shut down and liquidated. None of the technology survives in today's market, although SyQuest went on to become successful. There have been quite a few discussions about what went wrong at SOLOsystems. It is generally accepted that its design of an expensive and highly proprietary microcomputer and operating system, the limited usefulness of its software, and IBM's announcement of the 3270PC around 1983 doomed SOLOsystems.

In 1983, General Dynamics Corp. put out a *request for proposal* (RFP) to the computer industry looking for a microcomputer- or minicomputer-based workstation for offloading mainframe COBOL development. SOLOsystems responded, along with Apple Computer (which curiously submitted an early Lisa computer with no COBOL software on it) and Micro Focus (which had a non–IBM OSVS compliant ANSI 74 compiler on an IBM PC). This proposal provided a stimulus to the general industry to address this area. Evidently, IBM had previously been trying to protect its mainframe sales revenues and refused to push the PC as a mainframe development offloader. Micro Focus had previously built a $20 million company based on selling COBOL development tools on microprocessor-based and mini-computers but had no mainframe COBOL experience.

Realia

Along this same timeline, a small company named Realia was formed in Chicago by Marc Sokol. Realia had the honor of marketing the first real IBM OSVS–compatible COBOL compiler on a PC around 1984.

Micro Focus

In 1985, as a result of its experience with General Dynamics' needs, Micro Focus unleashed version 1 of its COBOL Workbench product, which was IBM OSVS compatible. To make a long story short, Realia had a fast and tight OSVS COBOL–compatible compiler, debugger, and runtime. However, the Micro Focus product—with its advanced debugger and its later mainframe compatibility add-ons, such as IMS and CICS (which Realia later tried to duplicate with some success)—was too much to compete with. As a result, Realia was acquired by Pansophic, which was later acquired by *Computer Associates* (CA). Although there are some small pockets of Realia users still out there, the Micro Focus COBOL Workbench product is the dominant technology in the marketplace for mainframe COBOL development offloading. Micro Focus' revenues last year were in the $150 million range, showing just how lucrative this niche has become.

IBM

Micro Focus' rise to market dominance in this area was assisted by IBM's own endorsement of the technology in the late 1980s. IBM itself had taken a crack at this market in the mid-1980s by introducing the 370-PC, which was an IBM PC look-alike that claimed to have a mainframe model 370–compatible microprocessor and could run a cutdown version of IBM's VM operating system and development tools—including the real IBM OSVS COBOL compiler. This was a startling announcement, but it seemed that every large corporation in America had exactly one of these new 370-PCs, which were generally found to be less than ideal for this mission. IBM later countered with the 9370 minicomputer, which was somewhat of a replacement for its older 8100 series of minis. The 9370 also proved to be a less than effective mainframe COBOL development offloading platform, leaving the crux of the market to standalone PCs. Micro Focus took great advantage of IBM's initial reluctance to enter this market, as well as IBM's later pitfalls. IBM's attempts to become a dominant player in this market ended (arguably) with the death of AD/CYCLE in the early 1990s. AD/CYCLE was a grandiose framework for managing enterprise application development on a large scale and actually initially incorporated various third-party tools. AD/CYCLE was built around the concept of a single large repository (or the *R-word,* as many IBMers later described it after its failure).

IBM actually marketed the Micro Focus COBOL Workbench product line for a number of years both as a separate product and as part of its AD/CYCLE initiative. The reason for this was twofold. First of all, IBM wanted a piece of the offloading revenue pie. Second, the marketplace for the COBOL Workbench product was corporate America—the traditional IBM mainframe shops that had thousands of COBOL programmers. These programmers had IBM 3270 terminals on their desks, and there was an enormous opportunity to replace these 3270 terminals with real PCs. IBM sold thousands of its PS/2s to these shops along with the Micro Focus COBOL Workbench for mainframe COBOL development offloading. Several other PC manufacturers made friends with Micro Focus in an effort to get a piece of this new hardware market. Today Micro Focus sits atop the software portion of this market almost unchallenged.

Issues Related to Offloading Mainframe COBOL Development

A number of issues are related to offloading mainframe COBOL development. Some of these issues are quite obvious, whereas a number are less obvious.

> **NOTE**
>
> One of my favorite comments regarding the Micro Focus COBOL Workbench is that in 1985, Micro Focus delivered IBM OSVS (and later VS COBOL II and COBOL370 compatibility by supporting the syntax in its COBOL compiler) and then spent the next 10 years getting it to work correctly.

Elementary and Obvious Differences

There are a number of rather obvious differences between the IBM mainframe EBCDIC environment and the PC-based ACSII environment.

Character Sets and Collating Sequences

To understand some of the challenges in emulating mainframe behavior on a PC, you first must realize that IBM mainframes are EBCDIC-based environments as opposed to the ASCII environment of the PC world. EBCDIC defines up to 256 values to represent data in a single 8-bit byte. ASCII defines up to 128 character values and an additional 128 values used for control codes and special character representations in a single 8-bit byte.

For example, the letter A in EBCDIC is represented by the hexadecimal value C1, whereas in ASCII, the letter A is represented by the hexadecimal value 41. In EBDCIC, the digit 1 is represented by the hexadecimal value F1, whereas in ASCII, the same 1 is represented by the hexadecimal value 31. If you examine the hexadecimal representation for A and 1 in EBCDIC versus ASCII, you may see a rather interesting difference that is not so obvious. If you are doing a SORT operation or a comparison operation in EBCDIC, 1 is greater than A (the hexadecimal F1 is greater than the hexadecimal C1), but on an ASCII system, 1 is less than A (the hexadecimal 31 is less than the hexadecimal 41).

The order in which character values are sorted and compared on a given system is known as a *collating sequence.* As you may have guessed or already known, the collating sequence is quite different between EBCDIC and ASCII. This presents a number of problems in trying to create a mainframe development environment on a PC. In the early days, Micro Focus' approach was to have customers convert their data files from EBCDIC into ASCII and use their ASCII COBOL compiler on the ASCII PC. Micro Focus (as well as other COBOL vendors, such as Fujitsu) supports the capability to specify a different collating sequence in its compiler. The EBCDIC collating sequence is available, which allows the application to run in ASCII using ASCII data but treats sorts and comparisons as if you are running on an EBCDIC system. This works for some applications, but a number of interesting problems crop up.

For example, the collating problem exists in three areas. The first area is in the file system. If you are reading records and comparing values using START and READ NEXT commands with an indexed file, for example, records are retrieved in a different order on the PC than on the mainframe. It is a common programming technique on an IBM mainframe to create a record with a key value of all nines (for example, 9999999) to indicate when the end of file has been reached. On an ASCII PC, a record with a value of 9999999 is found in sequential order before any records containing characters (for example, AAAAAAA). Specifying an EBCDIC collating sequence in the compiler has no effect on the ASCII file system and does not solve the collating problem.

The second area of potential trouble comes with the use of COBOL SORTs, which sort files in different orders depending on the collating sequence. The final problem area caused by the difference in collating sequences is conditional logic within the actual COBOL program. Anywhere in a COBOL program where two character values are being compared (for example, IF and EVALUATE statements) is a candidate for incorrect branching based on the difference in the collating sequences. Consider the following example of COBOL code:

```
IF "1" < "A"
        DISPLAY "I must be running on a PC!"
    ELSE
        DISPLAY "I must be running on a mainframe!"
    END-IF.
```

19

MAINFRAME
DEVELOPMENT
OFFLOADING

If this program is compiled, linked, and executed on a PC, it displays the string I must be running on a PC! because in ASCII, the character 1 (represented in ASCII as a hexadecimal 31) is less than the character A (represented in ASCII as a hexadecimal 41). The same program, however, when compiled, linked, and executed on an IBM mainframe, displays the string I must be running on a mainframe!. This is because on a mainframe, the character 1 (represented in EBCDIC as a hexadecimal F1) is greater than the character A (represented in EBCDIC as a hexadecimal C1).

You can see from the preceding example that programs may easily behave very differently when executed in ASCII versus EBCDIC. This created a major challenge for Micro Focus soon after it released its initial COBOL Workbench product in 1985.

Another major area of difficulty related to data files stems from the fact that nearly all COBOL applications running on IBM mainframes access date files, whether they are flat sequential files, relative record (RSDS) files, indexed (VSAM) files, or part of a proprietary database management system (DBMS), such as IMS/DB.

Format Differences in File Transfers and Lack of Supporting Utilities

When PC connectivity to IBM mainframes began to appear in the market in the early 1980s, file transfer programs typically transferred files to and from the PC in one of two formats. The first format was *text,* which meant that the file transfer program looked at every character in the file and converted it from EBCDIC to its ASCII equivalent (or vice versa, depending on the direction in which you were transferring the file between the PC and mainframe). The file then appeared as a text file on the platform to which it was being transferred. The second option was to transfer the file in pure binary doing no conversion at all.

This presented a couple of problems in transferring data files to and from the mainframe. The first problem relates to the various file types and formats found on the mainframe. If you are familiar with indexed files on the mainframe, for example, you know that the *Virtual Storage Access Method* (VSAM) is commonly used. VSAM creates indexed files as clusters that contain separate data and index components. Alternative indexes are found in separate files. Unfortunately, VSAM did not exist on the PC in 1985, when COBOL Workbench was first introduced. In fact, it does not exist today, although IBM did at one time bring out a PC-VSAM package. Micro Focus' COBOL Workbench product originally included an indexed file system known as C-ISAM.

Micro Focus provided nearly flawless compatibility with VSAM for *relative sequenced dataset* (RSDS) and *key sequenced dataset* (KSDS) but did not provide support for the rarely used *entry sequenced dataset* (ESDS). The runtime behavior of the Micro Focus indexed files closely mimicked mainframe VSAM. The problem, however, was that

C-ISAM and VSAM were completely different designs and structures, and users could not simply transfer a VSAM file from the mainframe to the PC and use it. Instead users were forced to use the IDCAMS REPRO utility (part of VSAM) to extract an indexed file and create a sequential flat file. Users then were forced to transfer it to the PC, converting it into ASCII.

Micro Focus, however, did not initially provide the equivalent of an IDCAMS REPRO utility in COBOL Workbench. Instead, users were forced to write individual programs to read each newly transferred sequential file and write it out to a C-ISAM indexed file.

Going through this process quickly flushed out two more serious problems in transferring data files from the mainframe to the PC environment. The first of these problems relates to the fact that many data files used by COBOL programs contain data that consists of both text (display) fields along with fields in other data type formats. For example, binary data fields (COMP), packed decimal (COMP-3), and even floating-point data (COMP-1 and COMP-2) are data types often intermixed with text data in data files.

Micro Focus' initial COBOL compiler and runtime required text fields to be in ASCII. On a mainframe using packed decimal (COMP-3), the individual numeric digits (0 to 9) are represented in half bytes (four bits). And the rightmost four bits will contain a sign. If the field is unsigned, the rightmost four bits will always contain a hexadecimal F. If the field is signed and the value is positive, the rightmost four bits will contain a hexadecimal C. If the field is signed and contains a negative value, the rightmost four bits will contain a hexadecimal D. Micro Focus' initial COBOL compiler and runtime in 1985 used a hexadecimal C in all cases for positive or unsigned pack decimal fields and a hexadecimal D for signed negative fields. The hexadecimal F for unsigned fields was not to be found. Additionally, Micro Focus initially used the leftmost four bits to store the sign in a packed decimal field. Micro Focus later changed this behavior to mimic the IBM mainframe packed decimal format, and this is not an issue today.

You should be well able to imagine just how difficult it may have been to get in and fiddle with half-bytes to convert mainframe packed decimal to PC packed decimal in the early days.

Binary Number Representations

Another problem related to data types revolves around the representation of binary data (COMP) on the mainframe versus the PC. There are two major differences. On the mainframe, binary data is stored from right to left, with the rightmost byte being the least significant. On the PC, binary data typically is stored using the native Intel format in reverse byte order—the least significant byte is the leftmost byte. The second difference is that IBM mainframes align binary data on half-word boundaries (known as *synchronization* in COBOL terms). The PC environment does not require this, which means that data items are stored on two-byte, four-byte, or eight-byte boundaries, depending on the word size. This means that on an IBM mainframe, a two-digit number stored in binary always takes up two bytes to align on the half-word boundary. On an Intel-based PC, however, the same two-digit number takes up only a single byte of physical space because the numeric range of a two-digit field (0 to 99) can easily be fit into the possible 256 values of a single 8-bit field. Even when you have a signed two-digit field to represent in binary, a single physical byte can represent both the positive (0 to 99) and the negative (–1 to –99) values.

Signed Fields

Finally, yet another difference was found in the representation of display numeric fields that contained signs. The signed display (Pic S999) number +123 on an IBM mainframe in hexadecimal is F1 F2 C3. On the PC (in ASCII), +123 is represented as hexadecimal 31 32 33. The signed display number -123 is represented on the mainframe as hexadecimal F1 F2 D3, whereas on the PC under Micro Focus, it is represented in ASCII in hexadecimal as 31 32 73.

So in retrospect, users were faced with the problems of data types being stored physically in a variety of formats and even in varying amounts of physical space for the same representations when taking mainframe data and attempting to transport it to the PC. Micro Focus alleviated some of the problem by implementing the compiler directives IBMCOMP (which forced binary data alignment on half-word boundaries like the mainframe) and SIGN(EBCDIC) (which forced display numeric signs to behave like the mainframe). Micro Focus also changed its default physical storage format for COMP (binary) data items to be the same as the mainframe and implemented a new data type (COMP-5) to represent native Intel reverse byte order binary format.

Variable Record Delimiters

One final problem related to data files revolved around variable-length records (COBOL record definitions that contained OCCURS DEPENDING ON or ODO phrases). As you may have guessed, the physical file format of a variable-length file on the mainframe is quite different from the Micro Focus COBOL physical format on the PC. Another not-so-obvious problem cropped up involving variable-length files and various file transfer programs on the market. Some of these file transfer programs could read variable-length data files on the mainframe, but as you may already know, the actual record length that is physically placed at the start of each record is dropped off when the record is read into a program (and the file transfer utility was simply a program). This meant that variable-length records would be read from the mainframe file and written to the PC file being created by the file transfer with no record-length information. Users thus received a "glob" of data on the PC that was generally useless because the individual record-length information was missing. Mike Fidel of Micro Focus addressed this problem in the late 1980s by writing a mainframe utility program called VRECGEN, which Micro Focus now ships with COBOL/2 Workbench. VRECGEN simply reads variable-length records, ascertains each record's length (LRECL), and appends it to the front of each record being transferred to the PC. A second PC-based utility then reads a VRECGEN-created file and generates a true variable-length file in Micro Focus format. Prior to VRECGEN, users were forced to write specialized programs to convert and unconvert variable-length files to fixed record sizes for file transfer purposes, and then to write programs on the PC to reverse this process.

I actually wrote Micro Focus' first IDCAMS-like file-conversion facility around 1987. The utility converted sequential files to indexed files and vice versa. It used Micro Focus COBOL's rather spiffy external file handler technology. Micro Focus later encompassed this utility in the more comprehensive *Workbench File Loader* (WFL) utility that is found in COBOL/2 Workbench today.

Even after the file-conversion utilities appeared, there was still one glaring problem that made transporting data files from the mainframe to the PC (and back) quite miserable for users. This problem relates back to the discussion on data types having different physical representations and storage requirements. It became quite obvious that it was physically impossible to create some neat utility that could simply parse through any EBCDIC data file, recognize all the various data types as they are encountered, and simply convert them into proper ASCII text and/or Micro Focus numeric data types.

If the reason for this is not obvious, consider the contents of a single byte of information located anywhere within a given data file. There is no way you can examine the contents of a single byte (or even a series of bytes) and determine whether the bit pattern contained therein is a valid EBCDIC character, part of a binary number, or part of a packed decimal number. Basically, data is data and bits are bits. You cannot distinguish data types by examining the actual physical data. Instead you must have some external knowledge of the record layout (such as a COBOL data record definition) to identify specific fields and data types for conversion. Given the additional fact that the physical storage formats of numeric data types vary between the mainframe and the PC, such a conversion utility additionally would have to contain a great deal of detailed knowledge of data type layouts in it if it were to work correctly.

Enter IBM mainframe IMS wizards Bruce Zupek and Mike McQuaid of Stingray Software Inc. (a company that Micro Focus later acquired). Stingray provided the first intelligent file-conversion utility around 1987. This facility actually reads in and parses through complex COBOL record definitions, generates the required information, and then performs the file conversion. Micro Focus later encompassed this capability within its WFL product.

Logic Branching Differences with Performs and Exits

At this point, users now had the needed utilities available to perform data-file conversion. Once users were able to convert data files and transfer them to and from the mainframe, it seemed that all would be well. Unfortunately, this did not hold to be true. Users began running into sometimes vague and obscure problems related to both IBM 370 mainframe runtime behavior and actual bugs in the OSVS COBOL compiler. An example of an IBM 370 mainframe runtime behavioral difference with the PC environment relates to the way program code branching and returns are implemented. To oversimplify a complex discussion, on the mainframe, actual return addresses are tracked during program execution. On the PC, a perform stack is used.

To understand this difference, consider the following COBOL sample code:

```
Procedure Division.
        Perform Para-A Thru Para-A-Exit.
        Display "I'm Back From Para-A".
        Stop Run.

    Para-A.
        Display "I'm In Para-A".
        Perform Para-B Thru Para-B-Exit.
        Display "I'm Back in Para-A".

    Para-B.
        Display "I'm in Para-B".
    Para-A-Exit.
        Exit.
    Para-B-Exit.
        Exit.

        Display "I've Fallen through!".
```

When executing this program on an IBM mainframe, the program branches to Para-A and then branches to Para-B via the PERFORM statement. When the EXIT statement after PARA-A-EXIT is encountered, the program branches all the way back up to the DISPLAY statement just prior to the STOP RUN statement because the initial PERFORM statement instructed the program to branch and PERFORM only through A-EXIT, and A-EXIT is encountered shortly after the second PERFORM branch to PARA-B.

The logic flow on the PC, however, is quite different given the fact that a perform stack is being maintained by the Micro Focus COBOL runtime. Because the program has branched around one of the exits, the perform stack gets corrupted, and the program logic simply falls through to the next executable statement because no valid return address is on the perform stack. The program actually continues execution through to the bottom and abends there.

Although the sample program's structure is a bit odd, these types of scenarios do exist between the mainframe and the PC. Micro Focus later implemented a compiler (Micro Focus actually calls its compiler the *checker)* directive called PERFORMTYPE(OSVS) to alleviate this problem. When this directive is used, the Micro Focus COBOL runtime system actually marks and rewinds the perform stack automatically to prevent this corruption.

Subscript and Boundary Checking

An example of an actual bug in OSVS COBOL that Micro Focus was actually forced to implement for compatibility purposes centers around subscripting out of range. In COBOL, you can define a data type as a table (like an array in other languages) using the OCCURS phrase. For example, consider the following COBOL data definition:

```
01 My-Table.
    03 My-Item       Pic X(10) Occurs 10 Times.
01 Next-Data-Item  Pic X(10).
```

In COBOL, to access the individual members of this table, you add a subscript, as shown here:

```
Display My-Item(5).
```

This displays the fifth element in the table. Now consider what happens if you place too large a number in the subscript area, as in this example:

```
Display My-Item(11).
```

You would typically expect to receive an error at compile time or runtime. In fact, Micro Focus' COBOL runtime suspends execution and displays an error message similar to this:

```
RTS Error 153: Subscript out of Range
```

Believe it or not, OSVS COBOL running on an IBM mainframe will typically not encounter an error. Instead it actually displays the next 10 bytes of data in Working-Storage that immediately follow the table definition (Next-Data-Item). Not only is this a bug in the OSVS COBOL compiler, but it is a very useful bug that programmers actually have taken advantage of. The maximum single data item size on an IBM mainframe under OSVS COBOL is 32KB. When programmers ran into this limitation and needed larger tables, they simply defined another dummy data item immediately proceeding the table and subscripted out of range to access this area as if they had a larger table.

In the early days of COBOL Workbench, the Micro Focus runtime stopped these developers dead with a subscript out of range error. Unfortunately, this became a serious compatibility error with mainframe applications, so Micro Focus was forced to actually implement an IBM OSVS bug! (How's this for true compatibility?)

19

MAINFRAME
DEVELOPMENT
OFFLOADING

Operating System Extensions and Additions

As Micro Focus began to experience these sorts of compatibility issues, it became obvious that mainframe compatibility was much more of a job technically than anyone had ever imagined. Simply implementing OSVS COBOL syntax in its compiler was only the tip of the iceberg for Micro Focus, effortwise.

> **NOTE**
>
> Sometime in 1987 or so, I had the pleasant experience of meeting Micro Focus runtime guru Ben Wint, who was visiting Micro Focus' Palo Alto office from his home base in Newbury, England (home of Micro Focus' expert development staff). This meeting was purely by chance and occurred around midnight. I was visiting the Palo Alto office as well from my home base then of Chicago. I had come into the office late to find that the locks had been changed and my key no longer worked. I then went around the various offices in the building beating on the doors in the hopes that someone might be working late and would let me in.
>
> From behind one of these doors emerged Ben Wint. At the time, I had been working as a senior systems engineer at COBOL Workbench customer sites, encountering many of the problems I described earlier in this chapter. I had been an IBM mainframe systems programmer and was one of the few mainframe knowledgeable employees at Micro Focus at this time. In introducing himself, Ben immediately posed the following question to me: "So, Howard, if you could have any enhancement in the COBOL runtime that you could choose, what would it be?"
>
> Without thinking, I immediately responded "An EBCDIC runtime system!" Later that month Ben returned to England, where he designed and implemented the world's first EBCDIC runtime on a PC. Ben worked hand in hand with Micro Focus' COBOL compiler expert and visionary, Robert Sales, and Micro Focus' debugger whiz, Clive Beavis, to implement a system that proved to be the single most significant step in the evolution of mainframe COBOL development offloading.

Micro Focus' EBCDIC runtime for COBOL Workbench first appeared around 1987. It provided two very key benefits. COBOL applications actually ran in EBCDIC, and their data was stored and manipulated in EBCDIC. This allowed for much smoother 370 mainframe emulation. Second, data files were stored in native EBCDIC: Data files no longer needed to go through the data type conversion process from EBCDIC to ASCII text, along with all the earlier mentioned data type conversions required. A fixed-length sequential file could be transferred from the mainframe completely intact—in binary without any conversion required—and used directly by a COBOL program compiled and running under the EBCDIC runtime system. Relative record and indexed files still needed to be REPROed out to sequential files and transferred to the PC in binary and then reindexed using the WFL utility, but this was a very straightforward point-and-shoot type of operation because no data type conversions were required.

It now seemed as though the major issues involving offloading mainframe COBOL development to PCs had been solved, but not so. After Micro Focus made it realistic to transfer COBOL applications and their data files to the PC for development, customers began doing just that—and then began to run into a new level of technical challenges.

Databases and Transaction Processing

The first challenge related to the fact that only a portion of existing mainframe COBOL applications consisted of simple batch programs accessing data files. Instead, many of these mainframe applications were running under the auspices of an *online transaction processing* (OLTP) system such as CICS or IMS/DC.

The second challenge was the fact that many COBOL applications used a database management system such as IMS/DB (DL/1) or DB/2, and even DATACOM/DB or IDMS. These database systems existed only on the IBM mainframe, and the vendors of these database systems had no intention of porting them to the PC environment. To make matters worse, they often required the use of a special macro language or programming API that required a specialized preprocessor to translate into a more complex low-level programming API. This meant that COBOL programs containing these macro languages (for example, EXEC SQL) would not even compile using Micro Focus COBOL because they were not COBOL compliant and no preprocessor existed on the PC for them.

Macro Language Reprocessors

One early solution was to run these programs containing macro language commands through the preprocessor on the mainframe and then transfer down the post-processed COBOL program to at least syntax check it and get it through the Micro Focus compiler. This often proved to be unwieldy, however, because a single change on the PC required transfer back to the mainframe for preprocessing again and then transfer of the results back down. An additional problem was the fact that programmers were forced to wade through the output code from the preprocessor, which is typically ugly and quite large.

Runtime Support for OLTPs and DBMSs

Additionally, there was no runtime support for debugging these programs because the actual DBMS did not exist on the PC. The same problems held true for the OLTPs, IMS and CICS, although IBM did later release CICS/OS2, which was a port of its CICS OLTP to the PC environment.

About the same time Micro Focus was faced with the problem of OLTPs and DBMSs, customers began to run into architectural limitations of the DOS operating system on an Intel PC. Large mainframe COBOL applications simply would not execute on 640KB DOS-based PCs. Micro Focus initially addressed this problem in 1986 or so when it released COBOL Workbench 1.3, which implemented a 32-bit runtime. The main feature of this runtime system (which came prior to the EBCDIC runtime noted earlier) was its capability to page to disk COBOL application code segments (the executable portion of an application). This allowed an application much larger than the available 640KB of memory to run in some cases. The drawback was that it could not page data segments (the COBOL Data Division) of COBOL applications to disk. Another problem that aggravated this 640KB memory limitation was the fact that Micro Focus' excellent debugger, Animator, had grown to require more than 350KB of memory just for itself.

In attempting to address the problem of providing complex mainframe DBMSs and OLTPs, Micro Focus quickly realized that it had neither the expertise nor the bandwidth to create these mainframe emulation products. Micro Focus thus decided to seek help from the outside and to instead concentrate on solving the EBCDIC runtime issues and the memory-limitation problems of the DOS-based Intel PC.

NOTE

Micro Focus was very fortunate to hook up with the exceptionally talented mainframe CICS expert Cary Teraji of Innovative Solutions Inc. (a company that Micro Focus later acquired) around this time. Cary had developed the world's first BMS screen painter on a PC (CO-Maps), which allowed programmers to paint CICS screens and automatically generate BMS macros. Micro Focus and Cary entered into a joint venture in which Cary created the world's first CICS emulator (CICSVS86) on a PC.

Around the same time, Micro Focus was additionally fortunate to hook up with IBM IMS experts Mike McQuaid and Bruce Zupek of Stingray Software Co. Bruce and Mike had been designing a complete IMS DB/DC system for use with Realia COBOL. It was I who first approached Bruce and Mike with a request to change their efforts over to Micro Focus. I can't resist noting that Bruce actually collected Corvettes (thus the company name Stingray), and Mike was beloved by every car salesperson in Cedarburg, Wisconsin, given his "talent" at totaling cars. After some time, Stingray agreed and delivered the world's first IBM DB/DC emulator on a PC.

Bruce, Mike, and Cary proved to be immensely brilliant individuals, and their mainframe emulation add-ons were marketed by Micro Focus as options for the COBOL Workbench. Their mainframe knowledge additionally made its way into the Micro Focus COBOL compiler and runtime, making life much easier for mainframe developers who used this product.

One of the final missing pieces was a DB/2 emulation product for relational database development. One of the early adopters en masse of Micro Focus' COBOL Workbench was Ford Motor Company's Parts and Service Division.

> **NOTE**
>
> John Hrubes of Ford made the initial decision to go forward with COBOL Workbench, and George Amin was the programmer who later became the overall technical expert for Ford. At the time, this represented the largest single deployment of the COBOL Workbench technology in the world (initially, 85 copies). Ford later became a user of several hundred copies of COBOL Workbench. The corporate point man at Ford was Jim Graves, who later left Ford and developed his own reusable code manager to market, called RCM. It was Jim who had been desperately seeking a DB/2 solution for Ford and had come across a very small software company named Systems Software Technology Inc., founded by University of Maryland Professor Dr. Bing Yao. It seems that Jim and Dr. Yao had actually been roommates during their college years. Jim pointed Micro Focus at Dr. Yao's company, which had developed a DB/2-like DBMS on the PC. After some negotiation, Dr. Yao agreed to develop an interface for Micro Focus COBOL. The resulting product was known as XDB, and Dr. Yao later changed the name of his company to XDB as well. Micro Focus very recently acquired XDB.

With the XDB product on the market, Micro Focus now offered CICS, IMS DB/DC, and DB/2 emulation products for COBOL on the PC platform.

Memory Barriers

The final major problem Micro Focus needed to solve was the architectural limitations imposed by the 640KB DOS operating system. This problem was made worse by the fact that the CICS, IMS, and DB/2 emulators took up even more of the limited memory available on 640KB DOS machines.

Enter Micro Focus runtime guru Ben Wint again. Ben had been examining the actual chip architecture of the newer Intel 80286 and 80386 microprocessors. Ben had deduced that it was indeed fully possible to run much larger applications on these microprocessors than the 640KB that DOS allowed. The key technical term was *protect mode,* which was a mode that the 80x86 CPUs could be placed into to perform 32-bit memory addressing. Around the same time, IBM came to the same realization and began working with Microsoft Corporation to develop the OS/2 operating system. Ben decided, however, that an entirely new operating system was not required to solve the problem that Micro Focus customers were facing and instead designed arguably the world's first protect mode DOS extender—XM (Extended Memory).

Using XM on an 80386-based PC with appropriate memory, the Micro Focus COBOL runtime system running under the DOS operating system could address up to 16MB of real memory. Given the Micro Focus COBOL runtime's 32-bit architecture and the fact that it already implemented a virtual storage paging to disk paradigm, massive COBOL applications now could be run on the PC with the full use and benefit of the Micro Focus COBOL Workbench toolset and the add-on mainframe emulation products. It is interesting to note that at this time (around 1987), it was actually possible to execute a larger COBOL application on a standalone PC costing a few thousand dollars than could be executed on an IBM mainframe running MVS that cost millions of dollars.

With the later advent of IBM's OS/2 and Microsoft's Windows 95 and Windows NT 32-bit operating systems, the need for XM disappeared; the Micro Focus Workbench runs natively as a true 32-bit application under these operating systems today.

After users were able to transfer complex applications from the mainframe and edit, compile, and test them on the PC, thousands of copies of the Micro Focus COBOL Workbench were sold into a number of Fortune 1000 companies. The challenge of getting this technology to work began to shift somewhat from Micro Focus to the customers themselves in implementing a strategy to manage the use of this technology. Micro Focus, however, has been kept plenty busy implementing new versions of COBOL, such as IBM's VS COBOL II and COBOL 370, as well as the new ANSI extensions to COBOL, including object-oriented COBOL. Micro Focus also has worked diligently to offer a number of impressive year-2000 millennium tools to aid in finding and correcting year-2000 bugs. Micro Focus recently announced its Mainframe Maintenance Product, which allows users to access mainframe-based resources such as programs and data files transparently.

NOTE

Not long after all of this was in place, corporate America began investing heavily in this technology. In the late 1980s, within a few square miles of Hartford, Connecticut, more than 10,000 copies of COBOL Workbench soon existed in daily use at four of the largest insurance companies in America.

Challenges in Implementing COBOL Development on PCs

As noted earlier, users of this technology began to feel challenged to come up with solutions for managing this technology. It is a daunting task to replace 3270 terminals with Intel-based PCs running a Microsoft Windows operating system and then add in the Micro Focus software.

One of the early challenges was the replacement of the IBM mainframe ISPF character-mode development environment with the highly graphical OS/2 or Windows environment. Micro Focus countered this by offering an alternative front end for the COBOL Workbench developed by Stingray Software known as AD/MVS. AD/MVS is basically an ISPF copycat interface that allows mainframers to use a PC but to access the Micro Focus technology in a manner they are already familiar with (an ISPF interface). AD/MVS even includes an ISPF-like editor from which you can submit batch jobs and supports MVS JCL for controlling applications.

> **NOTE**
>
> There was a massive argument within the market and within Micro Focus about the need for an ISPF look-alike. American Express Co. actually demanded this look-alike, and some people at Stingray were ISPF fanatics and leveraged American Express' need to go ahead and deliver this product. One thing that can be said for ISPF on the PC is that PCs represented a daunting learning curve to many mainframe COBOL programmers, given their complete difference at almost every level from the mainframe (for example, file system, user interface). The AD/MVS ISPF interface was so "lifelike" that American Express claimed it saved more than two weeks of additional training for each programmer (2 weeks times 1,000 programmers is a significant cost savings in productivity and training costs).

19

MAINFRAME
DEVELOPMENT
OFFLOADING

For users already accustomed to today's Windows PCs, Micro Focus offers a graphical interface that was actually developed in Micro Focus' Object COBOL. The vast majority of Micro Focus' COBOL Workbench is written in Micro Focus COBOL, which says a lot about the power of COBOL as a modern PC-based development language.

Source Code Control

One of the major issues that users of this technology face is the management of their actual application and source code across a large number of users. In the early days, this problem was even more significant because mainframe library management systems such as Panvalet, Endeavor, and Librarian were not initially designed with the concept of PC workstations in place. Instead, these *source code control systems* (SCCSs) were tightly integrated with the mainframe-based development facilities such as ISPF, both usability-wise and security-wise. It was a difficult process to extract an application from one of these systems and transfer it to the PC without going through several steps.

Today almost every major SCCS offers a PC-based component for extending the library management system to the PC workstation. It is highly recommended that users look at and fully understand the capabilities and requirements of these systems before imple-menting PC-based workstations in their environments. Additionally, there are a number of newer generation SCCSs, such as Intersolv's PVCS, Microsoft's Source Safe, and Fujitsu's PowerGEM, that were developed on or for PCs and networked PCs in an enter-prise environment. Micro Focus itself includes a sophisticated SCCS as part of its COBOL Workbench product.

Implementing a tight SCCS can alleviate a number of headaches caused by the potential mistakes of multiple programmers accessing and updating the same programs or com-mon copy files. A good SCCS will track this process and all changes and allow users to step back to prior versions of code if an individual update creates problems down the road.

Application Component Dependencies

One of the major challenges in transferring an application from the mainframe for main-tenance on the PC workstation is identifying all of the needed pieces (for example, all the programs, called *subprograms*, and copy files), along with other required application components such as data files, database definition files, and IMS- or CICS-related assembler macros (such as BMS or MFS maps). Once again, using a good SCCS can help alleviate this process of identifying an application's related files and components and, more important, make it easier to find them.

Using a LAN for Application Development and Management

Making good use of a *local area network* (LAN) to centralize and share common compo-nents such as COBOL copy files is highly desirable as well. This prevents problems encountered when multiple users have downloaded individual copies of the same file, such as a COBOL copy file containing a record layout definition. If this file is updated, it can become a real headache trying to figure out who has an older version of it on their individual PC and ensuring that the new version gets copied to each user who is currently using it. Using a LAN with shared network drives to centralize COBOL copy files goes a long way toward organizing this process. Micro Focus COBOL Workbench provides an environment variable called COBCPY, which you can set to point at multiple paths. When specified, the COBOL compiler searches each of these directories for copy files when it encounters a COBOL copy statement. This allows you to place copy files in shared network directories and to point individual PCs at these in the search order you prefer.

Another excellent use of a LAN is for centralizing called subprograms. Many COBOL shops have a large number of already tested programs that may be called by various applications as they execute. Instead of being forced to transfer an entire application to an individual PC and then compiling the entire application, it is useful to be able to transfer only those individual programs on which you are working. After you edit and compile these programs and want to debug the application, it is very useful to already have access to all the rest of the application without any additional transfers or compiles. By placing compiled modules in shared directories on a LAN, you can give individual PCs access to the modules using the environmental variable COBDIR.

Program Architecture

It is important to understand the actual Micro Focus COBOL architecture to fully understand the options available for distributing compiled executables and possibly sharing them. Most language compilers read in source code and create a native machine language object module (for example, an .obj file). These object files then are taken into a linkage editor that outputs an executable file (for example, an .exe or .dll file). Although Micro Focus COBOL supports this paradigm, it is not the paradigm that mainframe COBOL programmers use. In fact, the capability to generate .obj files was a later addition to Micro Focus COBOL, forced on Micro Focus by IBM in building IBM's COBOL/2 for OS/2 in the late 1980s.

Micro Focus' Abstract Machine Architecture

Micro Focus COBOL was actually founded on the concept of an abstract machine. COBOL is highly portable to a large number of environments, including mainframes, minis, and PCs. COBOL is found running under a wide variety of operating systems on a large number of hardware platforms. One of the challenges in porting COBOL compilers and development environments to various platforms is the fact that the underlying hardware often varies dramatically, and the host operating systems offer varying programming APIs. Some PCs are based on a 16-bit architecture, for example, whereas others are 32-bit. Also, the size and number of registers varies across hardware platforms. If you are writing a COBOL compiler, this can become a real nightmare as you port this compiler to new or different environments. When Micro Focus chose to implement its first 8-bit COBOL compiler on an early microcomputer in 1976, it recognized that massive changes were in store for the micro-based computer industry.

Given these facts, Micro Focus decided to create an abstract machine architecture. You can think of this as a kind of imaginary computer—with some fixed number of registers and other fixed features. Micro Focus thus implemented an abstraction layer of software (the COBOL runtime system) that provides a level of interpretation for COBOL programs that are compiled to a kind of imaginary object code, which Micro Focus calls *intermediate code* or .int code. This intermediate code is a Micro Focus–specific pseudo object code that is interpreted by the Micro Focus runtime system. This intermediate code thus is highly portable to the hundreds of environments on which Micro Focus has implemented its COBOL runtime system. The tradeoff of using this intermediate code is performance, although it is highly optimized. The fact that it is being interpreted adds overhead and thus affects performance.

As noted earlier, the Micro Focus compiler is actually called the *checker.* This checker reads COBOL source code and produces an intermediate code module. It also produces a sort of super data dictionary file known as an .idy file. The .idy file is used by various Micro Focus utilities during the development process, such as the Animator debugger. The .idy file is not required to simply execute the application. It is required, however, for debugging with Animator, because it contains all the data structures and their definitions, along with other information required by Animator.

If you follow the evolution of programming languages, you might note that the abstract machine approach has been taken for one of the most exciting new arrivals: Sun Microsystems' Java.

NOTE

In April 1996, I attended a major industry conference highlighting Java in San Francisco's Moscone Center. I signed up for a Java quick-start session out of curiosity. The demand was so intense for this session that hundreds of people were turned away and a second quick-start session was scheduled. The orator of this session, a college professor from a university in New York, opened the session "humorously" with the line "Welcome to the interpretive COBOL session."

The week prior to this conference, I had the great pleasure of meeting for a few hours with the "father" of Java, the somewhat extraordinary Sun Microsystems' engineer (and Sun Fellow) James Gosling. James noted during our meeting that he had worked with COBOL early in his career. This is not to imply that the idea of Java came from Micro Focus; the UCSD Pascal system, which was based on an abstract machine as well, was in existence at about the same time Micro Focus COBOL first emerged in the mid-1970s. It's interesting to note, however, that the Micro Focus approach to portability bears a striking resemblance to the Java architecture. In fact, Micro Focus' Panels/2 portable GUI architecture predated the Java AWT (Java's equivalent) by several years. Micro Focus' founder, former chairman, and visionary, Brian Reynolds, had recognized the potential of a truly portable language across the Internet prior to Java's arrival and attempted to focus Micro Focus' development resources on such an effort. Micro Focus development was unfortunately too involved with and committed to the current Micro Focus technology to react to this potential opportunity and has proven to be successful in deriving ongoing large revenues from its traditional market.

Interpreted Code

To address the performance concerns with intermediate code, Micro Focus implemented native code generators that read in the intermediate code and generate high-performance object code. Micro Focus has implemented its own sort of global object code known as .gnt (generated) code. This .gnt code still requires a Micro Focus runtime system but is significantly faster than intermediate code. The Micro Focus native code generator also can produce native object code (.obj) files for the host platform, which can be linked into standard executables (.exe or .dll files), which then can be executed without the Micro Focus runtime system being present. The one drawback to generating .gnt files is that they may not be stepped through line by line in the debugger. Note that Micro Focus has been promising Animator debugging support for .gnt files for some time and may have delivered such by the time this book is published.

Subprogram Execution

One other rather nice architectural feature of Micro Focus COBOL is that `.int` and `.gnt` modules are dynamically callable, which means that no linkage editor process is required. This is a very powerful feature for developers of large-scale mainframe applications for two reasons. The first is that developers are not forced to have an entire application (all of the subprograms) available to build and execute a single program because no linkage is required. When a developer changes a single program in a large application, he or she only needs to recompile (check) that individual program before executing or debugging the application. The second major feature here is the fact that Micro Focus dynamically loadable `.int` or `.gnt` modules may exist in separate locations, and Micro Focus provides two additional environmental variables (`COBDIR` and `COBIDY`) to specify multiple paths and the search order. `COBDIR` is used by the COBOL runtime to search for called programs. `COBIDY` is used to search for `.idy` files associated with `.int` modules for debugging purposes. The Micro Focus Animator (now known as Animator/2) provides some useful behavior in this area that aids mainframe application developers. When you are debugging a program and your program calls another COBOL program, the COBOL runtime system first searches for a file named `progname.gnt` (where `progname` is the name of the program being called). If `progname.gnt` is found, it is executed at machine speed (you do not see its source code in the Animator) and control is returned to the calling program's next executable statement after the `CALL` statement. If the COBOL runtime system does not find a `progname.gnt` file, it searches for a `progname.int` file. If `progname.int` is found, it checks to see whether a file named `progname.idy` is also available (`progname.cbl`, which is the actual source code file that must also be available if you want to step through the source code). If this file is available, Animator positions you on the source code for the first executable statement in `progname`. If the `.idy` file is not available, `progname.int` is executed at machine speed, and control is returned to the calling program's next executable statement after the `CALL` statement.

This highly dynamic and easily customizable behavior is very useful to shops that have large numbers of programs and/or complex COBOL applications. It is not uncommon, for example, for COBOL development shops to have multiple renditions (sometimes called *steps*) of the same application. For example, a production version may exist. A separate test version may exist with multiple integration levels, depending on the progress of individual developers working on the same project. Being able to test a newly developed or updated module against multiple versions of a larger application by simply changing the called program search locations using environmental variables is a very nice feature. It is not unlike the concatenation of libraries that takes place on the mainframe to achieve the same purpose. The fact that the application does not require linking all of the modules together makes this a very nice feature indeed when dealing with large applications.

Using a LAN to Share Subprograms

Many shops will create sharable network directories on their LAN containing common COBOL modules compiled into .int for debugging purposes, and separate network directories containing common modules compiled in .gnt modules. They need only switch the COBDIR environment variable to point at the desired directory or directories to pick up the desired versions of called programs.

Managing Data Files and External Resources

Another major issue is the initial setup of data files, databases, and OLTP support, if used. In some cases, programmers working on individual PCs will want all the data files local on their machine, because during testing they may be modifying these files by writing and deleting records. For read-only files, multiple users can share these concurrently. Because only one user can write to a file at a time, it is desirable to have such a file locally on the user's PC. This means that shops may want to store master copies of downloaded and converted files on their LAN somewhere and allow them to be copied to end-user PCs for testing purposes. Read-only files may be centralized and shared off the LAN. Because applications that read and write records change the state of data files, it is desirable in any case to have easily assessable master copies available on the LAN. Many shops will designate an individual as a file administrator whose job it is to transfer, convert, and place the data files on a LAN server. This person then provides appropriate location information to end users to allow them to update their environment settings.

To use data files, it is important to understand the Micro Focus behavior with COBOL SELECT...ASSIGN TO statements.

Suppose that you have the following COBOL SELECT statement:

```
SELECT PAY-FILE ASSIGN TO UT-S-PAYROLL
```

The Micro Focus COBOL runtime ignores the UT-S- portion of the filename and concentrates on PAYROLL as the external name of the file. You have a couple of options for equating PAYROLL with an actual file on a PC. The first option is that you may define a Working-Storage data item, as shown here:

```
01 PAYROLL    Pic X(24) Value "C:\datafiles\payroll.dat".
```

The COBOL runtime automatically looks for this definition and finds the file. This is not typically a desirable technique for mainframe programs because it requires a change to the source code. This change will not affect the behavior of the program when it is moved back to the mainframe, however. Some shops actually create a COBOL copy file

19

MAINFRAME
DEVELOPMENT
OFFLOADING

containing all the filenames used in SELECT statements, with COBOL data definitions for each containing VALUE phrases specifying the location of each file. A single COPY statement then is added to each program's Working-Storage section to copy these definitions in. On the mainframe, this COPY statement points to a dummy copy file containing only a comment. This allows you to transfer programs back and forth without any additional changes.

A second option available is to hard code the actual filename in the SELECT statement, which must be surrounded by quotes, as this example shows:

```
SELECT PAY-FILE ASSIGN TO "C:\datafiles\payroll.dat".
```

The COBOL runtime then finds the file directly. The downside of this is that this change is not compatible with the mainframe.

The third option is a bit more desirable. It requires a special compiler directive— ASSIGN(EXTERNAL)—to work. Consider the following SELECT statement:

```
SELECT PAY-FILE ASSIGN TO UT-S-PAYROLL
```

Remember that the COBOL runtime ignores the UT-S- portion and concentrates on looking for a file identifier of PAYROLL (the DD name). If you specify the ASSIGN(EXTERNAL) compiler directive, the COBOL runtime looks externally for the file definition in two places. It first searches the paths specified in the COBDIR environmental variable for a file named MFEXTMAP.DAT. This is a simple text file that contains the actual file DD names and their locations. For example, the Micro Focus sample program VSAMDEMO (which I wrote) has several SELECT statements for various files. The MFEXTMAP.DAT file appears as shown here:

```
SORTWRK C:\mfcob32\demo\mdedemo\SORTWORK.DAT
SALEDATA C:\mfcob32\demo\mdedemo\SALEDATA.DAT
BADDATA C:\mfcob32\demo\mdedemo\BADDATA.DAT
INQUIRY C:\mfcob32\demo\mdedemo\SALESINQ.DAT
FRGNVSAM C:\mfcob32\demo\mdedemo\FRGNVSAM.DAT
EASTVSAM C:\mfcob32\demo\mdedemo\EASTVSAM.DAT
WESTVSAM C:\mfcob32\demo\mdedemo\WESTVSAM.DAT
```

This simple text format is ideal for entering the needed information for pointing the COBOL runtime system to actual data files on the PC or a LAN. Note that MFEXTMAP.DAT must be placed in a directory pointed to by the COBDIR environment variable, and you can have only one MFEXTMAP.DAT file at a time. This means that you might want to put all of your shop's standard DD names in a single MFEXTMAP.DAT file.

Add-On Emulation Products

A final setup issue relates to the various add-on products that may be needed for IMS, CICS, and DB/2 applications. All these mainframe emulation products support centralized locations for their supporting facilities. Using the IMS emulator, for example, you have to download DBD and PSB macros and generate them on the PC. Instead of forcing each individual COBOL programmer to become his or her own local database administrator, many shops designate an individual or team to set up this environment properly and ensure that individual COBOL programmers are pointed at the centralized results.

In some cases, though, it may be desirable to allow individual programmers to perform their own generations (such as BMS and MFS macros) and add transaction IDs (TRIDs). It is important to make sure that everyone is "reading from the same page" when assigning these types of resources, to prevent problems down the road when everyone's work is merged together.

After you install all the software and go through the tasks of downloading and converting data files and setting up any required add-on emulation environments, such as IMS or CICS, you are ready to begin development using the Micro Focus COBOL Workbench.

Using the Micro Focus COBOL Workbench

In this section, you will take a brief tour of some of the tools and facilities contained in Micro Focus' COBOL Workbench product. The Workbench comes with an older style text interface, a common *graphical user interface* (GUI), and the advanced GUI.

Figure 19.1 shows the Micro Focus advanced GUI for Micro Focus Workbench version 4. This interface uses a drag-and-drop paradigm. Application folders may be defined and then dragged and dropped on any tool available to begin a task. As an alternative, you can start a tool by double-clicking it. You can open tool folders to expose their tools by double-clicking them.

The heart and soul of the Micro Focus Workbench is the advanced Animator/2, which was the brainchild of Clive Beavis. Clive proposed what he described as "one-stop programming" some years back when Micro Focus decided to create the next generation of its popular Animator COBOL debugger.

FIGURE 19.1.
The Micro Focus advanced GUI.

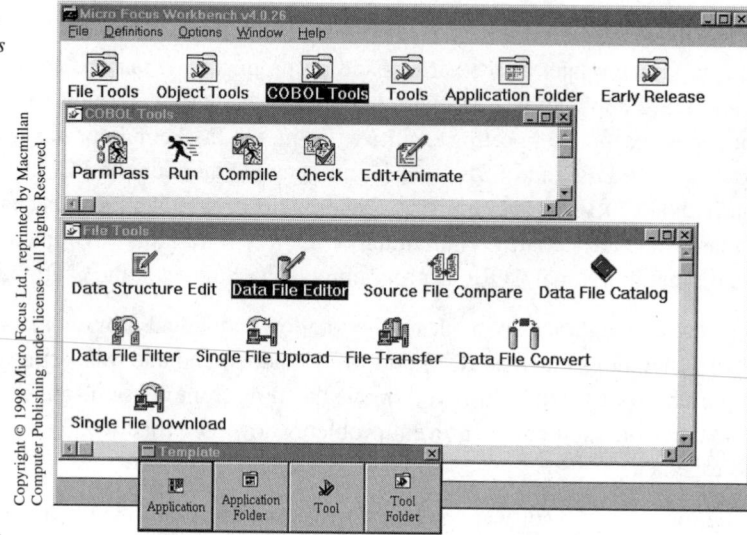

The general concept behind Clive's design was the fact that most COBOL programmers go through a continuous loop of *edit-compile-debug* (ECD) when developing or maintaining applications. In most cases, the editor, compiler, and debugger in this model represent three wholly separate facilities and three wholly separate steps. Programmers typically invoke an editor on a COBOL program, save their changes, exit the editor, and then manually invoke a compiler. If they receive any errors, they are forced to reinvoke the editor and start over. After they receive a clean compile, they invoke a debugger. During debugging, if a change to the source code is required, you must exit the debugger, restart the editor, and begin the process from square one again.

Clive came up with the somewhat revolutionary concept that programmers should instead be able to stay inside an advanced editor, invoke a compiler within the editor that handshakes with the editor to allow users to fix errors, and then jump into debug mode within the same editor using the same source code. Clive's Advanced Animator/2 delivered just this capability. This means that programmers spend a great deal of their development time within Animator/2 when editing, compiling, and debugging COBOL programs. Figure 19.2 shows Animator/2 in action on the VSAMDEMO sample program that ships with COBOL Workbench.

FIGURE 19.2.

Workbench Animator/2 in action.

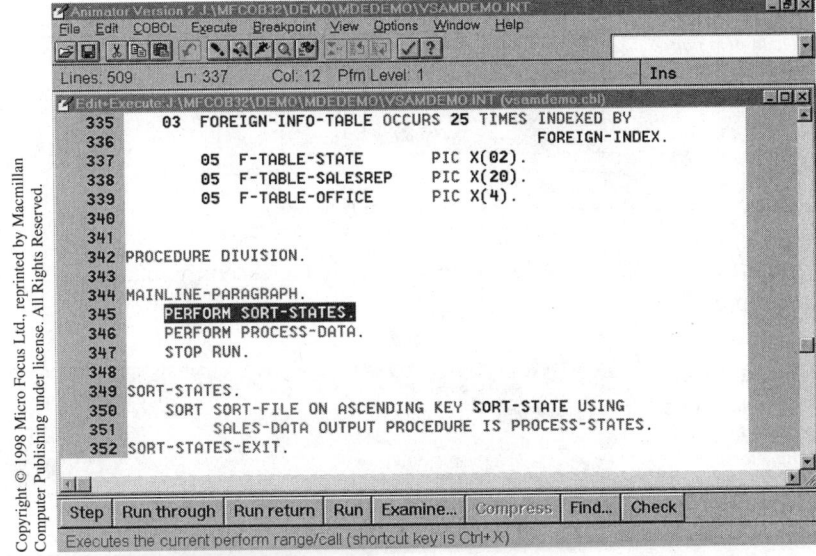

If you examine Figure 19.2, some very useful features are immediately obvious. The COBOL program's source code display makes extensive use of colors to identify source-code components. COBOL data items appear in red, for example, and COBOL reserved words and syntax appear in green. Data file references are displayed in a tan color, whereas labels appear in aqua. These colors are customizable. The Animator/2 is *language sensitive*. This means that as you enter and change COBOL source code, Animator/2 examines it, syntax checks it, and colorizes it without any required user interaction. You will find this feature quite useful because if you misspell something like a data name, it will not be colorized and you will know instantly that a problem exists. Note that before data items are colorized, you must go through the check (compile process) once to populate the data dictionary (.idy file) used by Animator/2. You can accomplish this by checking a partial program or one with errors; data item definitions still are added to the .idy file if they are valid.

The Animator/2 offers programmers some additional high-level facilities. For example, you can perform a find operation on a data item, and every occurrence of the data item found is highlighted. Figure 19.3 shows an example of a data item being found. The pop-up window displays some detailed information about the data, such as whether it gets modified in the program and how many places it appears.

19

MAINFRAME DEVELOPMENT OFFLOADING

FIGURE 19.3.

A data item pop-up window in Animator/2.

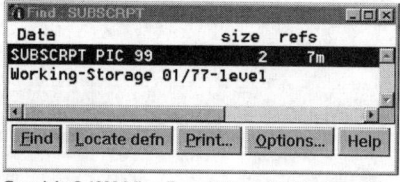

You then can collapse the listing to show only the currently found items, as demonstrated in Figure 19.4.

FIGURE 19.4.

A dynamic listing of data items in Animator/2.

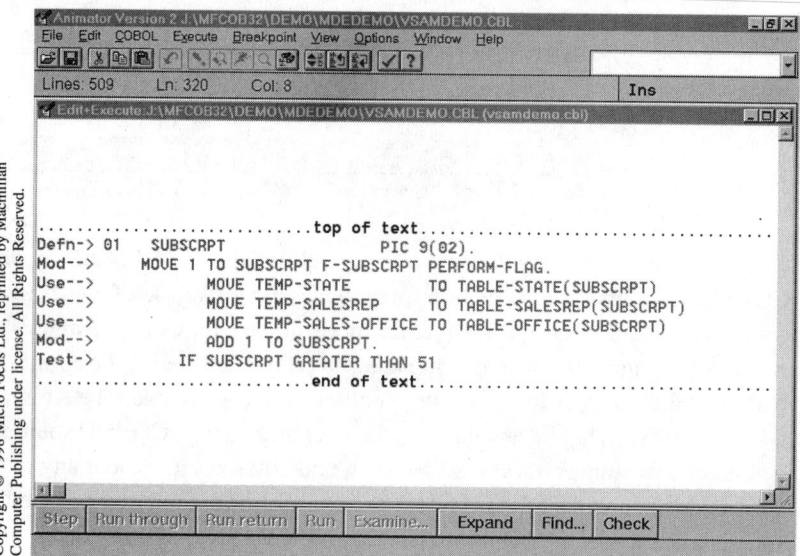

If you examine Figure 19.4 in more detail, you will note that along the left-hand column, informational tags identify the action that each line of code containing the found data item performs on the item. For example, `Defn` specifies that this is where the data item is defined. `Mod` indicates lines of code where the data item is being modified in the program. `Use` means that the data item is being referenced but not changed. `Test` indicates that the value of the data item is being tested (perhaps the item is being compared within a conditional statement, for example). If you have ever spent hours pouring over a program trying to figure out where a certain data item is being mysteriously changed, think of the benefit of clicking on a single `find` command and having all lines of code where the item is being modified displayed for you!

Animator/2 can also display valuable statistics (accessible from the COBOL pull-down menu) about your program, as Figure 19.5 shows.

FIGURE 19.5.

Program statistics in Animator/2.

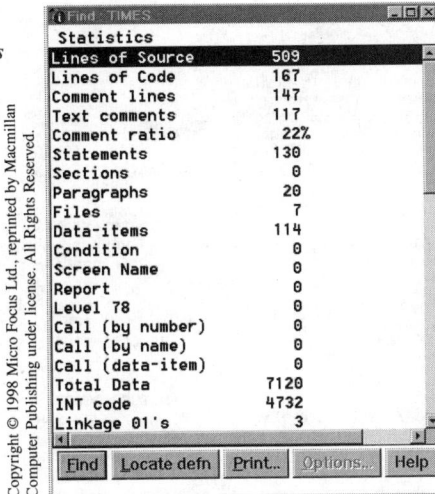

```
Find : TIMES                       _ □ X
Statistics
Lines of Source      509
Lines of Code        167
Comment lines        147
Text comments        117
Comment ratio        22%
Statements           130
Sections               0
Paragraphs            20
Files                  7
Data-items           114
Condition              0
Screen Name            0
Report                 0
Level 78               0
Call (by number)       0
Call (by name)         0
Call (data-item)       0
Total Data          7120
INT code            4732
Linkage 01's           3

 Find   Locate defn   Print...  Options...  Help
```

Additional features identify COBOL verb usage, dead data, unreferenced data (see Figure 19.6) and procedures, undeclared procedures, copy files used, end scopes, all input and output, and program exits. All these features are available from the COBOL pull-down menu.

FIGURE 19.6.

Additional features in Animator/2.

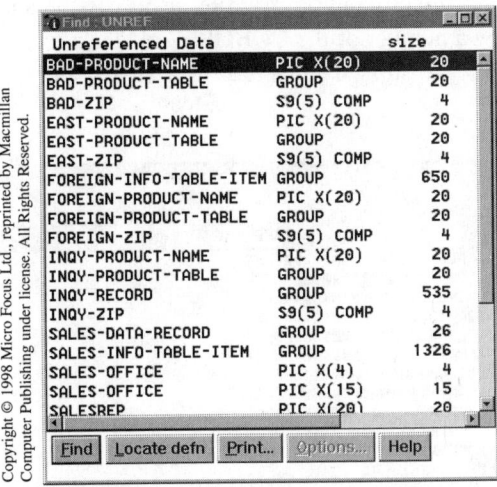

```
Find : UNREF                                 _ □ X
Unreferenced Data                       size
BAD-PRODUCT-NAME          PIC X(20)       20
BAD-PRODUCT-TABLE         GROUP           20
BAD-ZIP                   S9(5) COMP       4
EAST-PRODUCT-NAME         PIC X(20)       20
EAST-PRODUCT-TABLE        GROUP           20
EAST-ZIP                  S9(5) COMP       4
FOREIGN-INFO-TABLE-ITEM   GROUP          650
FOREIGN-PRODUCT-NAME      PIC X(20)       20
FOREIGN-PRODUCT-TABLE     GROUP           20
FOREIGN-ZIP               S9(5) COMP       4
INQY-PRODUCT-NAME         PIC X(20)       20
INQY-PRODUCT-TABLE        GROUP           20
INQY-RECORD               GROUP          535
INQY-ZIP                  S9(5) COMP       4
SALES-DATA-RECORD         GROUP           26
SALES-INFO-TABLE-ITEM     GROUP         1326
SALES-OFFICE              PIC X(4)         4
SALES-OFFICE              PIC X(15)       15
SALESREP                  PIC X(20)       20

 Find   Locate defn   Print...  Options...  Help
```

The COBOL Workbench contains a number of other powerful and useful tools to aid in COBOL development. For example, the powerful source file comparator compares two source programs and highlights all differences, as shown in Figure 19.7.

FIGURE 19.7.

The Micro Focus source code comparator in action.

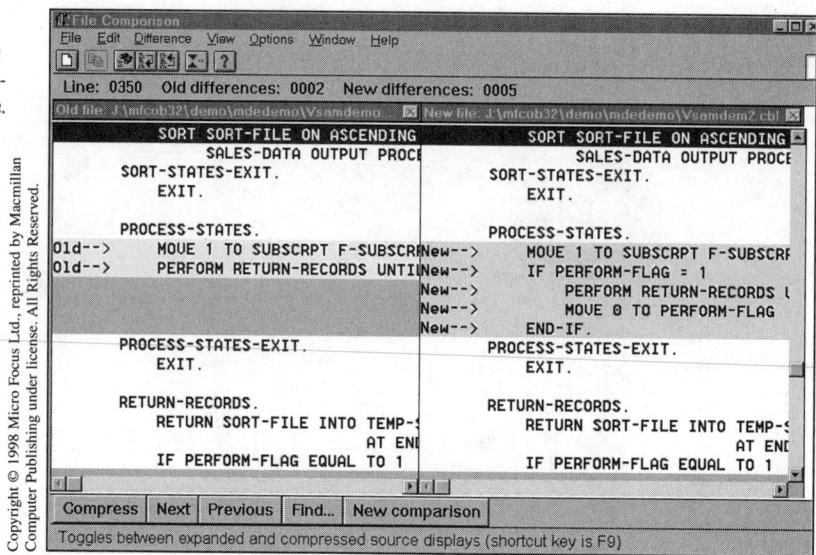

A sophisticated *data file editor* (DFED) is also included, as shown in Figure 19.8. DFED not only allows you to edit any COBOL data file type in text and hexadecimal but also to view data and change it easily. A data structure catalog facility is included that can look up compiled data file structures directly out of .idy files. This catalog and the included structures then can be used by a number of the COBOL Workbench tools. DFED can reference these cataloged structures to show data records in a labeled and formatted display, as shown in Figure 19.9.

FIGURE 19.8.

The Micro Focus data file editor (DFED).

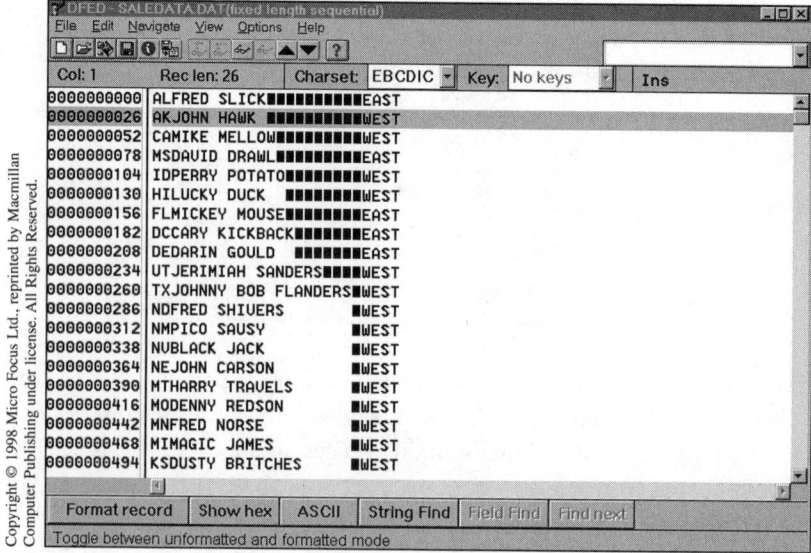

FIGURE 19.9.
A formatted display in the data file editor.

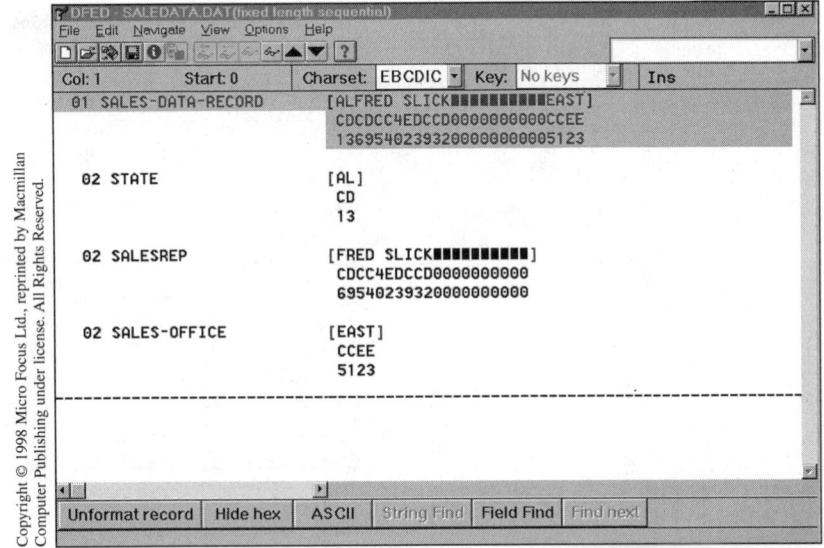

A Parmpass utility allows developers to set up parameters to be automatically passed into programs when they are initialized. This is useful for JCL-driven programs that expect parameters to be passed in from the JCL. I actually wrote the first version of the parm passer in the early 1980s.

As noted earlier, one of the challenges facing programmers who want to transfer applications from the mainframe to the PC for development activities is finding and transferring all of the pieces (files). A single large COBOL program may reference dozens of copy files and called subprograms. Trying to manually identify, list, and transfer all the files that are needed can be a very tedious and time-consuming process. Micro Focus recognized this bottleneck and provides a file transfer aid utility. I actually developed the very first version of this utility. The file transfer facility allows users to create file transfer profiles that list files to be transferred and preserves both their mainframe and PC locations and names (see Figure 19.10). More important, this facility optionally scans source files being transferred to identify other needed files and builds subsequent transfer commands to perform this operation. The scanning capability looks for a number of methods by which external files are referenced in the COBOL world, including COPY, CALL, and proprietary source code management facilities (refer to Figure 19.10). It will actually interact with PC, LAN, and mainframe-based source code control systems.

19

MAINFRAME
DEVELOPMENT
OFFLOADING

FIGURE 19.10.

The file transfer facility scanning transfer files.

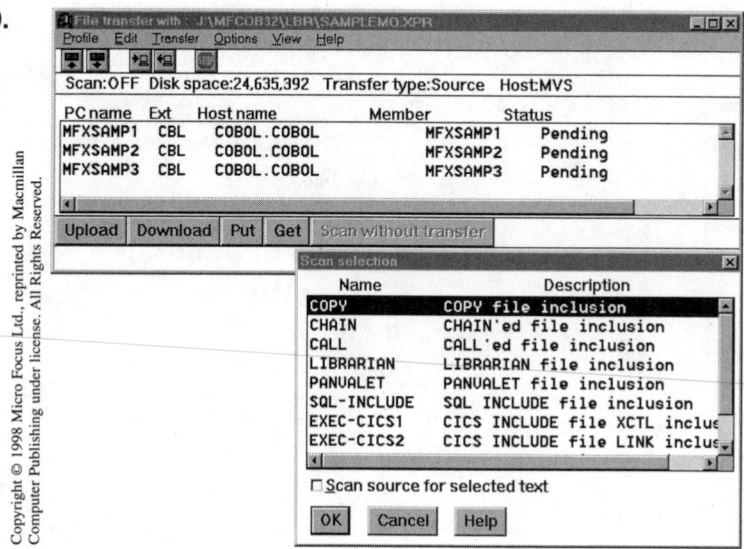

Finally, as was also previously noted, the COBOL Workbench includes a sophisticated source code management facility, as shown in Figure 19.11.

FIGURE 19.11.

The Micro Focus source code management facility.

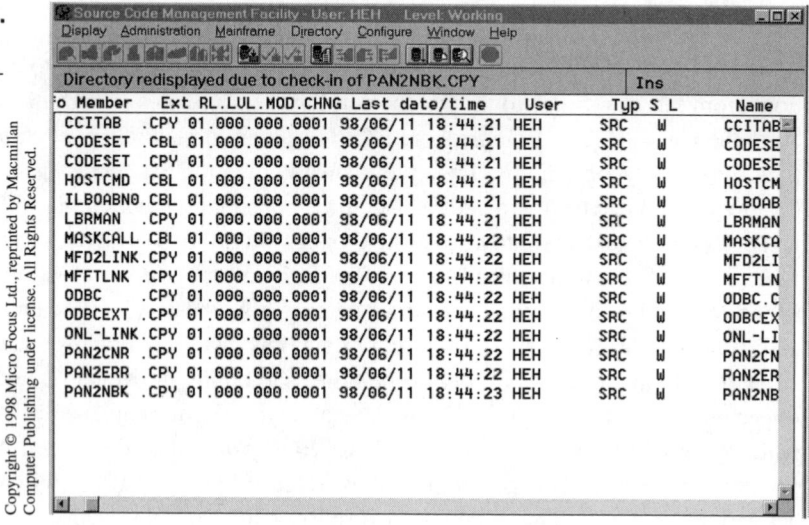

You now hopefully have a keen understanding of the issues involved in offloading mainframe COBOL development to PC workstations.

COBOL Databases and Transactions (A Sampling)

PART
V

Writing DB2 Applications in COBOL

CHAPTER 20

IN THIS CHAPTER

DB2 is IBM's family of relational database products that offers database management for decision support, transaction processing, and an extensive range of business applications. Members of the DB2 family run on IBM mainframes, AS/400 systems, RISC System/6000 hardware, IBM-compatible PCs, and hardware from Hewlett-Packard and Sun Microsystems.

This chapter gives you a quick overview of some fundamental DB2 concepts and then explains some basic information on writing and preparing COBOL programs that access DB2 databases.

The simplest way to think of a relational database is as one or more tables, each consisting of rows and columns. To make changes to or query the database, you write statements in the *Structured Query Language* (SQL), which you embed in your COBOL application program.

Using SQL to Work with a DB2 Table

This section demonstrates how to use SQL statements to define a DB2 table, modify that definition, put data in the table, modify selected rows, extract information, delete selected rows, and drop the table.

For this introduction to SQL, assume that you have access to an application, such as SPUFI or DSNTEP2, that accepts one or more SQL statements (terminated by semicolons), processes them, and returns the result to you. In later sections, you'll look at creating such a program.

Creating a Table

To create a table, you must give DB2 this minimum information:

- Name of the table
- Name of each column
- Type and length of the data in each column
- Whether each column accepts null values

Suppose that you want to create a table to inventory the books in your personal library. For each book, you want to store the following information:

- Title
- Author's last name

- Number of pages
- Price
- Date purchased
- A short description of the book

Each item will become a column of your table. You use the following CREATE TABLE statement to define the table to DB2:

```
CREATE TABLE MY_BOOKS
     (TITLE            VARCHAR(30) NOT NULL,
      AUTHOR           VARCHAR(15),
      NUM_PAGES        INTEGER,
      PRICE            DECIMAL(5,2),
      DATE_PURCHASED   DATE,
      DESCRIPTION      VARCHAR(40)  );
```

Altering a Table

Suppose that after thinking about your definition some more, you decide that you need a field to rate the book, and you want the rating to be an integer between 1 and 5. To add a column for the rating, execute an ALTER TABLE statement like this:

```
ALTER TABLE MY_BOOKS
  ADD RATING SMALLINT NOT NULL DEFAULT 3
    CHECK RATING BETWEEN 1 AND 5;
```

This statement adds a short integer column called RATING that does not accept nulls but replaces null values with a value of 3, which you assume to be an average rating. The clause that begins with CHECK is called a *check constraint;* it limits the values in the RATING column to numbers between 1 and 5.

Inserting Rows into a Table

Now that you have your table set up the way you want it, you can begin to put information in the table. Use a SQL INSERT statement to do that. For example, the first book you want to enter has the following characteristics:

Title	Bears in the Wild
Author	Ursine
Number of pages	125
Price	15.95
Date purchased	12/19/1991
Description	Case studies of wild bear behavior
Rating	4

20

WRITING DB2
APPLICATIONS IN
COBOL

To enter this information in the table, use the following INSERT statement:

```
INSERT INTO MY_BOOKS
VALUES ('Bears in the Wild', 'Ursine', 125, 15.95, '12/19/1991',
➤ 'Case studies of wild bear behavior', 4);
```

To indicate that a value is a character value, surround the value with quotes. Notice that although DATE_PURCHASED is a date field, you insert a character string into the field. COBOL does not have a data type of date, so DB2 handles the conversion from character to date type.

After entering a few more book titles, you find a book for which you know neither the date of purchase nor the price. Because both the DATE_PURCHASED field and the PRICE field accept null values, you still can enter the rest of the information for the book and enter the value NULL for the field values you do not know:

```
INSERT INTO MY_BOOKS
VALUES ('French Cooking for Amateurs',
➤ 'LaForet', 500, NULL, NULL, 'Good recipes—NOT for amateurs', 2);
```

Updating Rows

Later, you find the receipt for *French Cooking for Amateurs,* so you want to update the purchase date in your table. To do this, use an UPDATE statement:

```
UPDATE MY_BOOKS
    SET DATE_PURCHASED='5/10/1994'
    WHERE TITLE='French Cooking for Amateurs';
```

Committing and Rolling Back Changes

After you use SQL statements to make changes to your table, those changes are not yet permanently in the table. If you want to make those changes permanent, execute the COMMIT statement:

```
COMMIT;
```

COMMIT makes all changes you have made since you last executed COMMIT permanent.

If you have not committed a set of changes yet, and you want to back out of them, execute the ROLLBACK statement:

```
ROLLBACK;
```

After you commit changes, you cannot use ROLLBACK to back out of those changes.

Selecting Rows

Suppose that after you have entered book entries into your table for several hours, you want to see a list of all entries you have made so far. To do that, execute this SQL statement:

```
SELECT * FROM MY_BOOKS;
```

The set of rows and columns that DB2 returns from any SELECT statement is called the *result table*. If you have made entries for 20 books in MY_BOOKS, this SELECT statement returns a result table with 20 rows and 7 columns.

You also can execute SELECT statements to return a result table that contains a subset of the rows and columns in your table. For example, to check whether you have made an entry for *French Cooking for Amateurs* in your MY_BOOKS table, execute this SQL statement:

```
SELECT TITLE, AUTHOR FROM MY_BOOKS
    WHERE TITLE='French Cooking for Amateurs';
```

DB2 returns a result table that consists of one row and two columns:

French Cooking for Amateurs   Laforet

Deleting Rows

Suppose that after you finish entering all your books, you decide that you want to donate all your cookbooks to the library, so you need to delete all cookbook entries from your table. Because all your cookbooks have the word "cook" in the title, you can determine which books are cookbooks by deleting all entries with "cook" in the title. Do that with the following DELETE statement:

```
DELETE FROM MY_BOOKS
    WHERE TITLE LIKE '%Cook%' OR TITLE LIKE '%cook%';
```

This statement tells DB2 to delete all rows with the string "Cook" or "cook" anywhere in the title.

Dropping a Table

Suppose that you get involved in so many other projects that you decide to abandon your personal library inventory. To delete the table MY_BOOKS and all of its contents, you execute this SQL statement:

```
DROP TABLE MY_BOOKS;
```

20

WRITING DB2
APPLICATIONS IN
COBOL

Now that you have been introduced to a few fundamentals of SQL, you will move on to putting that SQL into COBOL applications.

Writing Static SQL Applications in COBOL

All of the SQL examples so far have shown *dynamic* SQL, where DB2 compiles the SQL statements when the program runs. You'll look at coding programs for dynamic SQL later. In this section, you'll examine *static* SQL, where you embed SQL statements in your COBOL program, and DB2 prepares the SQL statements before the program runs. If you want to change a static SQL statement after you have prepared an application program, you must prepare the program again.

To write a COBOL static SQL application program, you need to do the following things:

1. Declare special COBOL variables called *host variables* to hold the values you send to DB2 or retrieve from DB2.

2. Declare special COBOL variables called *indicator variables* to keep track of null values.

3. Declare a *SQL communications area* (SQLCA) to record the status of the most recently executed SQL statement.

4. Write static SQL statements to access DB2.

I discuss each of these steps in more detail in the following sections. For a complete example of a DB2 COBOL static SQL program, see DB2STAT.COB in directory \SOURCE\CHAP20 on your *COBOL Unleashed* CD-ROM.

Declaring Host Variables

Just as in other parts of your COBOL program, you need to be able to use variables in your SQL statements. Variables you use in SQL statements are called *host variables*. You declare COBOL host variables along with all of your other variables in the WORKING-STORAGE section or LINKAGE section. When you use a host variable in a SQL statement, you must precede the host variable with a colon.

Before you can declare host variables, you need to know which host variables are compatible with which DB2 data types. Table 20.1 lists the most common DB2 data types and their COBOL host variable equivalents.

TABLE 20.1   DB2 DATA TYPES AND COBOL HOST VARIABLE EQUIVALENTS.

DB2 Data Type	COBOL Host Variable Declaration
CHAR(*n*)	01 *var-name* PIC X(*n*).
DATE	01 *var-name* PIC X(10).
DECIMAL(*p,s*)	01 *var-name* PIC S9(*p-s*) V9(*s*) COMP-3.
DOUBLE or FLOAT	01 *var-name* USAGE IS COMP-2.
INTEGER	01 *var-name* PIC S9(9) COMP.
REAL or FLOAT	01 *var-name* USAGE IS COMP-1.
SMALLINT	01 *var-name* PIC S9(4) COMP.
TIME	01 *var-name* PIC X(8).
TIMESTAMP	01 *var-name* PIC X(26).
VARCHAR(*n*)	01 *var.*
	49 *var-length* PIC S9(4) COMP.
	49 *var-text* PIC X(*n*).

Notes:

n *is the maximum number of bytes that the variable occupies.*

p *is the precision of a decimal number.*

s *is the scale of a decimal number.*

You can use the information in Table 20.1 to declare host variables for all the columns in MY_BOOK. The declarations look like this:

```
*      HOST VARIABLE FOR TITLE (VARCHAR(30))
    01  HV-TITLE.
        49 HV-TITLE-LEN  PIC S9(4) USAGE COMP.
        49 HV-TITLE-TEXT PIC X(30).
*      HOST VARIABLE FOR AUTHOR (VARCHAR(15))
    01  HV-AUTHOR.
        49 HV-AUTHOR-LEN  PIC S9(4) USAGE COMP.
        49 HV-AUTHOR-TEXT PIC X(15).
*      HOST VARIABLE FOR NUM_PAGES (INTEGER)
    01  HV-NUM-PAGES      PIC S9(9) USAGE COMP.
*      HOST VARIABLE FOR PRICE (DECIMAL(5,2))
    01  HV-PRICE          PIC S9(3)V9(2) COMP-3.
*      HOST VARIABLE FOR DATE_PURCHASED (DATE)
    01  HV-DATE-PURCHASED PIC X(10).
*      HOST VARIABLE FOR DESCRIPTION (VARCHAR(40))
    01  HV-DESCRIPTION.
        49 HV-DESC-LEN    PIC S9(4) USAGE COMP.
        49 HV-DESC-TEXT   PIC X(40).
*      HOST VARIABLE FOR RATING (SMALLINT)
    01  HV-RATING         PIC  S9(4) USAGE COMP.
```

With declarations like these, you can specify the individual host variables in SQL statements. To obtain all data about your book about wild bears, for example, you can execute a SQL statement like this:

```
EXEC SQL SELECT * INTO :HV-TITLE, :HV-AUTHOR, :HV-NUM-PAGES,
    :HV-PRICE, :HV-DATE-PURCHASED, :HV-DESCRIPTION, :HV-RATING
    FROM MY_BOOKS WHERE TITLE='Bears in the Wild'
END-EXEC.
```

This can be cumbersome, especially if your table has a lot of columns. To simplify SELECT statements like these, you can create a host structure that contains the host variable declarations. A host structure for the MY_BOOK declarations looks like this:

```
01  HV-BOOK.
    10  HV-TITLE.
        49 HV-TITLE-LEN  PIC S9(4) USAGE COMP.
        49 HV-TITLE-TEXT PIC X(30).
    10  HV-AUTHOR.
        49 HV-AUTHOR-LEN  PIC S9(4) USAGE COMP.
        49 HV-AUTHOR-TEXT PIC X(15).
    10  HV-NUM-PAGES     PIC S9(9) USAGE COMP.
    10  HV-PRICE         PIC S9(3)V9(2) COMP-3.
    10  HV-DATE-PURCHASED PIC X(10).
    10  HV-DESCRIPTION.
        49 HV-DESC-LEN   PIC S9(4) USAGE COMP.
        49 HV-DESC-TEXT  PIC X(40).
    10  HV-RATING        PIC  S9(4) USAGE COMP.
```

With a host structure like this, you can select all values for a row by specifying the host structure name, like this:

```
EXEC SQL SELECT * INTO :HV-BOOK
    FROM MY_BOOKS WHERE TITLE='Bears in the Wild'
END-EXEC.
```

Declaring Indicator Variables

With the variable declarations you have so far, you cannot obtain all information about *French Cooking for Amateurs* without getting an error. The reason is that the row for *French Cooking for Amateurs* contains a null value for PRICE. When you use host variables to perform SQL operations on rows with null values, you must specify *indicator variables* to keep track of the null values. You declare an indicator variable in COBOL like this:

```
01 ind-var-name PIC S9(4) COMP.
```

For each column in a SQL statement that can accept a null value, you need an indicator variable. If you refer to a host structure in a SQL statement, and one or more host variables in that structure can receive a null value, you must declare an *indicator array* for the structure. The indicator array contains as many indicator variables as there are host variables in the structure. An indicator array for the HV-BOOK structure looks like this:

```
01 IND-BOOK.
         02 IND-BOOK-VARS PIC S9(4) COMP OCCURS 7 TIMES.
```

Before you perform a SELECT statement to retrieve a row in which some column values might be null, you need to set the values of all indicator variables to 0. Then, in the SELECT statement, for each host variable that might retrieve a null value, follow the host variable name with an indicator variable name. After the SELECT statement completes, examine the contents of the indicator variables. If an indicator variable contains -1, the corresponding host variable retrieves a null value. When you select into a host structure, you follow the host structure name with the indicator array name. For example, to select the *French Cooking for Amateurs* row, execute this statement:

```
EXEC SQL SELECT * INTO :HV-BOOK:IND-BOOK-VARS
    FROM MY_BOOKS WHERE TITLE='French Cooking for Amateurs'
END-EXEC.
```

When you select data from a DB2 table into a host structure with an indicator array, DB2 treats only the variables in the indicator array that correspond to nullable columns in the table as indicator variables. In this example, columns 2 through 6 in MY_BOOKS (AUTHOR, NUM_PAGES, PRICE, DATE_PURCHASED, and DESCRIPTION) can contain null values, so DB2 treats the second through sixth variables in indicator array IND-BOOK-VARS as indicator variables and ignores the rest of the variables in the array. Therefore, when you check the results of the SELECT for null values, you must check only the second through sixth variables in IND-BOOK-VARS.

Declaring the SQL Communications Area (SQLCA)

So far, these examples have assumed that all SQL statements complete successfully. Because this is not a realistic assumption, you need a means of tracking the success or failure of your SQL statements. In every application program you write, you must define an SQLCA. The easiest way to define this area is to include this SQL statement in your WORKING-STORAGE section or LINKAGE section:

```
EXEC SQL INCLUDE SQLCA END-EXEC.
```

This tells DB2 to put a structure into your source code that looks like this:

```
01 SQLCA.
   05  SQLCAID    PIC X(8).
   05  SQLCABC    PIC S9(9) COMP.
```

```
05  SQLCODE    PIC S9(9) COMP.
05  SQLERRM.
    49  SQLERRML PIC S9(4) COMP.
    49  SQLERRMC   PIC X(70).
05  SQLERRP    PIC X(8).
05  SQLERRD    OCCURS 6 TIMES PIC S9(9) COMP.
05  SQLWARN.
    10  SQLWARN0 PIC X.
    10  SQLWARN1    PIC X.
    10  SQLWARN2 PIC X.
    10  SQLWARN3 PIC X.
    10  SQLWARN4 PIC X.
    10  SQLWARN5 PIC X.
    10  SQLWARN6 PIC X.
    10  SQLWARN7 PIC X.
05  SQLEXT.
    10  SQLWARN8 PIC X.
    10  SQLWARN9 PIC X.
    10  SQLWARNA PIC X.
    10  SQLSTATE PIC X(5).
```

After a SQL statement executes, you check the values in the SQLCA fields to determine whether the SQL statement was completely successful, partially successful, or a failure. Table 20.2 shows the fields in the SQLCA that you normally need to check.

TABLE 20.2 SQLCA FIELDS.

SQLCA Field	Function
SQLCODE	Contains the SQL return code. This field can be used to locate the fixed part of a message in a DB2 messages and codes manual. 0 means that the statement executed successfully. A positive value means that a warning occurred and you need to check the SQLWARN fields. A negative value means that the statement failed.
SQLERRM	The variable part of an error message. DB2 messages and codes manuals show you the fixed part of the message. The variable part consists of tokens separated by X'FF'. SQLERRML gives you the total length of the variable part of the message.
SQLWARN0-SQLWARNA	If a SQL statement receives a positive SQLCODE, SQLWARN0 and one or more of the other SQLWARNn fields contains 'W'. Check which fields contain 'W' to determine more about the warning.
SQLSTATE	Like the SQLCA, this is a return code that indicates whether the SQL statement succeeded or failed, as well as the nature of the error. SQLSTATE values are common to all relational databases.

Including Static SQL Statements in Your COBOL Program

You can include any SQL statement in a static SQL application program. To include a SQL statement in your application program as a static SQL statement, you begin the statement with EXEC SQL and end it with END-EXEC, as shown in this example:

```
EXEC SQL UPDATE MY_BOOKS
    SET DATE_PURCHASED='5/10/1994'
    WHERE TITLE='French Cooking for Amateurs'
END-EXEC.
```

Using a Cursor to Select One Row at a Time

You have learned that you use a SQL SELECT statement to retrieve rows from a table. However, selecting rows in an application program is a little more complicated than just executing a SELECT statement. When you execute a SELECT statement, DB2 returns zero or more rows from a table, but an application program can receive only one row at a time. You therefore need a way to select rows one by one. A *cursor* lets you do that.

To use a cursor, you first must define it to DB2 using a DECLARE CURSOR statement. The DECLARE CURSOR statement gives the cursor a name and identifies an associated SELECT statement. For example, to declare a cursor to retrieve a list of titles and authors of the books in your library, use this statement:

```
EXEC SQL DECLARE CRSR CURSOR FOR
    SELECT TITLE, AUTHOR FROM MY_BOOKS
END-EXEC.
```

The next thing you need to do before you can start selecting rows from your table is to tell DB2 to ready the cursor to retrieve those rows. You do this with the OPEN statement. To ready cursor CRSR to select rows from MY_BOOKS, use this statement:

```
EXEC SQL OPEN CRSR END-EXEC.
```

Now you can start selecting rows using the FETCH statement. To select the first title and author from your list of books, execute this statement:

```
EXEC SQL FETCH CRSR INTO :HV-TITLE, :HV-AUTHOR END-EXEC.
```

If you want to retrieve a complete list of titles and authors, you can execute FETCH statements in a loop. After each FETCH, check the SQLCODE, and when the SQLCODE is +100, which indicates that there are no more rows to retrieve, exit the loop:

```
PERFORM GET-LIST UNTIL SQLCODE IS EQUAL TO 100.
...
GET-LIST.
```

```
EXEC SQL FETCH CRSR INTO :HV-TITLE, :HV-AUTHOR END-EXEC.
PERFORM PRINT-ITEM.
```

When you have finished using the cursor, tell DB2 to deactivate it by executing the CLOSE statement, as shown here:

```
EXEC SQL CLOSE CRSR END-EXEC.
```

Writing Dynamic SQL Applications in COBOL

Static SQL applications are fine for situations in which you know at compile time which SQL statements you want to execute. However, if you want your program to be able to read in SQL statements and execute them at runtime, you need *dynamic* SQL.

To write the most flexible dynamic SQL application, you need to do these things:

1. Define a SQLCA for error handling (the same one you use for static SQL applications).

2. Define a SQLDA to hold descriptions of SQL statements and host buffers for those SQL statements. A *host buffer* is an area your program allocates for DB2 to send data to or receive data from this area. Host buffers serve the same purpose as host variables.

3. Declare a host variable to hold the source form of SQL statements you read in and a SQL variable to hold the compiled form of those SQL statements. (See step 6.)

4. Declare a cursor for any SELECT statements you read in. (See step 9.)

5. Read a SQL statement into the host variable you declared in step 3.

6. Execute the PREPARE statement to compile the source SQL statement and put the compiled form into the SQL variable you declared in step 3.

7. Execute the DESCRIBE statement on the compiled SQL statement to put information about the statement in the SQLDA you defined in step 2. This information includes the statement type (SELECT or non-SELECT) and, for a SELECT, the types of host buffers the statement needs.

8. If the statement is not a SELECT statement, perform the EXECUTE statement on the compiled form of the SQL statement.

9. If the statement is a SELECT statement, modify the SQLDA that DB2 populated in step 7 and execute FETCH statements with the cursor you declared in step 4.

You'll learn about this process in detail in the following section. For a complete example of a DB2 COBOL program that performs dynamic SQL, see the sample programs

DB2ALLC.COB and DB2DYNM.COB in directory \SOURCE\CHAP20 on your *COBOL Unleashed* CD-ROM.

Defining the SQL Descriptor Area (SQLDA)

The SQLDA is a structure you define in your COBOL program to exchange information with DB2 about SQL statements that you execute dynamically. The simplest form of a SQLDA for COBOL is defined like this:

```
01   sqlda-name.
     05   SQLDAID     PIC X(8).
     05   SQLDABC     PIC S9(9) BINARY.
     05   SQLN        PIC S9(4) BINARY.
     05   SQLD        PIC S9(4) BINARY.
     05   SQLVAR      OCCURS 0 to n TIMES DEPENDING ON SQLN.
          10   SQLTYPE  PIC S9(4) BINARY.
          10     SQLLEN PIC S9(4) BINARY.
          10 FILLER      REDEFINES SQLLEN.
             15   SQLPRECISION PIC X.
             15   SQLSCALE     PIC X.
          10 SQLDATA    POINTER.
          10 SQLIND     POINTER.
          10 SQLNAME.
             49 SQLNAMEL PIC S9(4) BINARY.
             49 SQLNAMEC PIC X(30).
```

This SQLDA consists of a header section, followed by zero or more SQLVAR sections. The number of SQLVAR sections you need for a SQL statement is equal to the number of host buffers used by that SQL statement.

Generally, you allocate an SQLDA big enough to describe the largest number of host buffers you expect to have in any statement. The SQLDA holds *descriptions* of host buffers, not the host buffers themselves. See "Executing DESCRIBE to Put SQL Statement Information in an SQLDA," later in this chapter, for information on what is stored in a SQLDA.

Declaring Variables to Hold SQL Statements

You need to declare two types of variables to hold SQL statements you execute dynamically:

- A host variable to hold SQL statements you read in. Define this host variable as a structure that is equivalent to a DB2 VARCHAR type, as shown in this example:

```
10   SRCSTMT.
     49   SRCSTMT-LEN  PIC S9(4) USAGE COMP.
     49   SRCSTMT-TEXT PIC X(100).
```

This host variable can hold SQL statements of up to 100 bytes.

- A SQL variable to hold the compiled form of SQL statements, as shown in this example:

```
EXEC SQL DECLARE OBJSTMT STATEMENT END-EXEC.
```

If you execute each SQL statement before you read in the next SQL statement, you need to declare only one host variable for the source forms of all SQL statements and only one SQL variable for the compiled forms of all SQL statements.

Declaring a Cursor for SELECT Statements

Because your program might read in SELECT statements that retrieve more than one row, you need a cursor to execute those SELECT statements. For dynamic SQL, you declare the cursor for the compiled form of the SQL statement. For example, to declare cursor CRSR for compiled statement OBJSTMT, use this statement:

```
EXEC SQL DECLARE CRSR CURSOR FOR OBJSTMT END-EXEC.
```

If you execute a SQL statement before you read in the next SQL statement, you need to declare only one cursor for all compiled SQL statements.

Obtaining the Compiled Form of a SQL Statement

After you read a SQL statement into a host variable, you need to obtain the compiled form of the SQL statement. Execute the SQL PREPARE statement to do this. For example, to compile the SQL statement in host variable SRCSTMT and place the result in SQL variable OBJSTMT, execute this statement:

```
EXEC SQL PREPARE OBJSTMT FROM :SRCSTMT END-EXEC.
```

Executing DESCRIBE to Put SQL Statement Information in an SQLDA

After you compile your SQL statement using PREPARE, you can execute DESCRIBE to put information about that statement in an SQLDA. Before you execute DESCRIBE, however, you need to tell DB2 how big the SQLDA is. To do this, set the SQLN field in the SQLDA to the number of SQLVAR structures you defined when you declared your SQLDA. For example, if you have defined an SQLDA called BKSQLDA that contains 10 SQLVAR structures, set SQLN in BKSQLDA to 10.

After the value of SQLN is set, execute the DESCRIBE statement on your compiled SQL statement to fill the SQLDA with information about that statement. Table 20.3 shows the information DB2 puts into a SQLDA after you execute DESCRIBE.

TABLE 20.3 CONTENTS OF AN SQLDA AFTER DESCRIBE.

SQLDA Field	*What DB2 Puts in this Field After* DESCRIBE
	Header Information
SQLDAID	Eye-catcher 'SQLDA '.
SQLDABC	The size of this SQLDA: SQLN*44+16.
SQLN	DB2 does not modify this field. Before you execute DESCRIBE, you enter the number of SQLVAR sections you have allocated.
SQLD	If the statement being described is a SELECT, this is the number of columns in the result table; otherwise, it is 0.
	SQLVAR *Fields*
SQLTYPE	A number that indicates the data type of a result table column and whether the column can contain nulls. Columns that can contain nulls have odd SQLTYPE values; columns that cannot contain nulls have even SQLTYPE values.
SQLLEN	The length of a result table column.
SQLDATA	For a character or graphic column, information about the character set ID of the column.
SQLIND	Reserved.
SQLNAME	The name of a result table column.

Suppose that OBJSTMT contains the compiled form of this statement:

```
UPDATE MY_BOOKS SET DATE_PURCHASED='5/10/1994'
   WHERE TITLE='French Cooking for Amateurs'
```

To place information about OBJSTMT into the SQLDA named BKSQLDA, execute this statement:

```
EXEC SQL DESCRIBE OBJSTMT INTO :BKSQLDA END-EXEC.
```

Your SQLDA now contains this information:

Field	Contents
SQLDAID	'SQLDA '
SQLDABC	456=10*44+16
SQLN	10
SQLD	0

Because SQLD is 0, you know that there are no SQLVAR sections used and that the statement is not a SELECT statement.

Executing a Non-SELECT Statement Dynamically

After you learn from the SQLD value in the SQLDA that a statement is not a SELECT statement, all you have to do is execute the compiled form of the statement, which you obtained when you prepared the statement. To execute the compiled SQL statement in OBJSTMT, do this:

```
EXEC SQL EXECUTE OBJSTMT END-EXEC.
```

Executing a SELECT Statement Dynamically

If, after you execute DESCRIBE, the SQLD value in your SQLDA tells you that a SQL statement is a SELECT statement, you need to follow these steps to execute the statement:

1. Examine each SQLVAR section in the SQLDA to determine the type and length of each host buffer you need and whether you also need a corresponding buffer to keep track of null values. If the data type in SQLTYPE is an odd number, the corresponding column can contain nulls, so you need a null buffer to go with the host buffer.

2. Allocate a data area for each host buffer and null buffer.

3. For each SQLVAR section in the SQLDA, put the address of the host buffer in SQLDATA. If the host buffer requires an associated null buffer, put the address of the null buffer in SQLIND.

4. Open the cursor you declared for the compiled statement.

5. Fetch rows using the SQLDA until the SQLCODE indicates that there are no more rows left to fetch.

6. Close the cursor.

Suppose that you have read the SQL statement that follows into host variable SRCSTMT:

```
SELECT TITLE, PRICE FROM MY_BOOKS
```

You also have executed PREPARE to put the compiled form of the statement in OBJSTMT, and executed DESCRIBE on OBJSTMT to put information about the statement into BKSQLDA.

After DESCRIBE completes, BKSQLDA contains this information:

Field	Contents
SQLDAID	'SQLDA '
SQLDABC	456=10*44+16
SQLN	10
SQLD	2
SQLTYPE	448
SQLLEN	30
SQLNAME	'TITLE'
SQLTYPE	485
SQLLEN	5 in byte 1 2 in byte 2
SQLNAME	'PRICE'

Because SQLD is 2, you know that the statement is a SELECT statement that requires two host buffers. The values in the SQLTYPE, SQLLEN, and SQLNAME fields give you this information about the host buffers:

- The first host buffer receives values from column TITLE. This buffer receives values of a varying character type (448) that are never null (448 is even) and have a maximum length of 30.
- The second host buffer receives values from column PRICE. This buffer receives values of a decimal type (485) that can be null (485 is odd) and have a precision of 5 and a scale of 2.

You therefore need to allocate three buffers:

- A 32-byte buffer to hold each value you retrieve from column TITLE. The first two bytes hold the length of the retrieved value, and the following 30 bytes hold the characters.
- A 3-byte buffer to hold each value you retrieve from column PRICE. The buffer holds the packed decimal form of the retrieved value.
- A 2-byte buffer that will contain -1 if the value retrieved from the PRICE column is null.

Suppose that you allocate the buffers and call them T, P, and IP. Now you need to put the address of each buffer in the appropriate place in BKSQLDA:

Field	Contents
SQLDAID	'SQLDA '
SQLDABC	456=10*44+16
SQLN	10
SQLD	2
SQLTYPE	448
SQLLEN	30
SQLDATA	Address of T
SQLIND	Unused
SQLNAME	'TITLE'
SQLTYPE	485
SQLLEN	5 in byte 1 2 in byte 2
SQLDATA	Address of P
SQLIND	Address of IP
SQLNAME	'PRICE'

Now BKSQLDA is set up to receive data. The remaining steps are to open the cursor you declared for compiled SELECT statements, execute FETCH statements using BKSQLDA until there are no more rows to fetch, and then close the cursor:

```
EXEC SQL DECLARE CRSR CURSOR FOR OBJSTMT END-EXEC.
...
EXEC SQL OPEN CRSR END-EXEC.
PERFORM GET-LIST UNTIL SQLCODE IS EQUAL TO 100.
EXEC SQL CLOSE CRSR END-EXEC.
...
GET-LIST.
    EXEC SQL FETCH CRSR USING DESCRIPTOR :BKSQLDA END-EXEC.
    PERFORM PRINT-ITEM.
...
```

After every FETCH for which the PRICE column value is not null, areas T and P contain the values of TITLE and PRICE for the current row. When the PRICE column value is null, area P contains the value of TITLE for the current row, and area IP contains -1.

Writing DB2 COBOL Client/Server Applications

All of the DB2 products contain support for *Distributed Relational Database Architecture* (DRDA), which lets relational database applications access tables at remote locations (servers). Therefore, you can write DB2 COBOL applications that can access tables at any server that also supports DRDA.

To access data at a server, your program must execute these steps:

1. Connect to the server.
2. Execute SQL statements.
3. Disconnect from the server at a commit point.

To connect to a server, you execute this SQL statement:

```
EXEC SQL CONNECT TO location-name END-EXEC.
```

Here, `location-name` is a 1- to 16-byte name that identifies a relational database system and is defined when that database system is installed. You can execute CONNECT only as a static SQL statement. For example, to connect to remote location REMOTEBOOKS, execute this SQL statement:

```
EXEC SQL CONNECT TO REMOTEBOOKS END-EXEC.
```

You also can put the location name in a host variable and execute the CONNECT statement with the host variable:

```
MOVE 'REMOTEBOOKS' TO CURRENT-LOCATION.
EXEC SQL CONNECT TO :CURRENT-LOCATION END-EXEC.
```

You can connect to more than one server at a time. The server to which you connected most recently is called the *current server.*

After you are connected to a server, you can execute any SQL statement that the server's database system supports, either through static or dynamic SQL. In general, most relational database systems support at least SELECT, INSERT, UPDATE, DELETE, DECLARE CURSOR, and FETCH.

Suppose that there is a personal library inventory table called MY-BOOKS at location REMOTEBOOKS, and you lend your copy of *French Cooking for Amateurs* to that library. You need to remove the row for that book from your MY-BOOKS table and add it to the MY-BOOKS table at REMOTEBOOKS. To do that, you can execute SQL statements like these:

```
EXEC SQL SELECT * INTO :HV-BOOK:IND-BOOK
    FROM MY_BOOKS WHERE TITLE='French Cooking for Amateurs'
END-EXEC.
EXEC SQL DELETE FROM MY_BOOKS
  WHERE TITLE='French Cooking for Amateurs'
END-EXEC.
EXEC SQL CONNECT TO REMOTEBOOKS END-EXEC.
EXEC SQL INSERT INTO MY_BOOKS
  VALUES (:HV-BOOK:IND-BOOK)
END-EXEC.
```

When you finish accessing a table at a server, you need to disconnect from that server. To do that, execute the RELEASE statement. RELEASE causes DB2 to disconnect from the server at the next commit point.

For example, to disconnect from server REMOTEBOOKS, execute these statements:

```
EXEC SQL RELEASE REMOTEBOOKS END-EXEC.
EXEC SQL COMMIT END-EXEC.
```

You also can specify a host variable in the RELEASE statement:

```
MOVE 'REMOTEBOOKS' TO CURRENT-LOCATION.
EXEC SQL RELEASE :CURRENT-LOCATION END-EXEC.
```

If you are connected to several locations and want to disconnect from all of them at the next commit point, you can execute this statement:

```
EXEC SQL RELEASE ALL END-EXEC.
```

Writing DB2 COBOL Stored Procedures

One problem with accessing tables at remote locations is that every time you execute a SQL statement at a remote location, your local DB2 must exchange messages with the remote location, which can make applications perform more slowly than you might like. To decrease the amount of network traffic and thus improve performance, you can execute your SQL statements at the server in a *stored procedure*.

Figure 20.1 shows the difference in the amount of network traffic when you execute remote SQL statements directly and when you use a stored procedure.

A stored procedure is a DB2 application program that you define, prepare, and store at a server and access from a client using the SQL CALL statement.

You can write a stored procedure and the program that calls the stored procedure (the client program) in a number of languages, including COBOL. Your client program and stored procedure do not have to be written in the same language.

FIGURE 20.1.

Network traffic with and without a stored procedure.

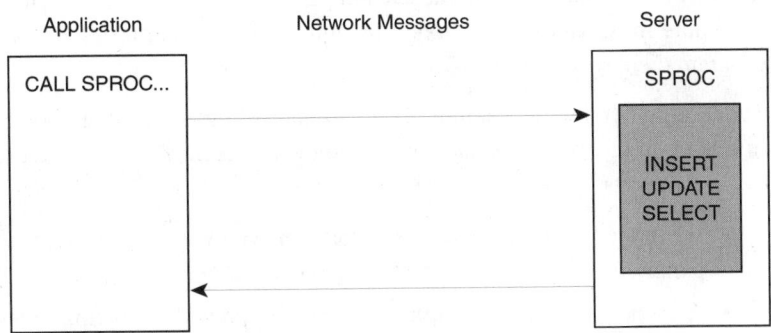

Remote SQL Execution through a Stored Procedure

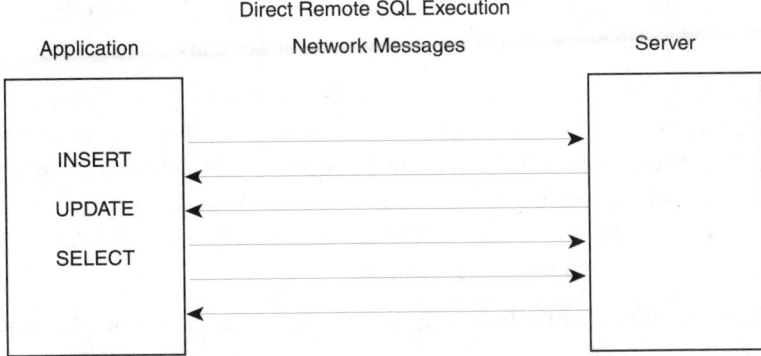

For a complete example of a COBOL stored procedure and a client program that calls the stored procedure, see sample programs DB2SPROC.COB and DB2CLIEN.COB in directory \SOURCE\CHAP20 on your *COBOL Unleashed* CD-ROM.

A COBOL stored procedure is much like any other DB2 COBOL program. You can include any SQL statements in your stored procedure except these (this list varies with the version of DB2 on which you run the stored procedure):

- CALL
- COMMIT
- CONNECT
- RELEASE
- SET CONNECTION
- SET CURRENT SQLID

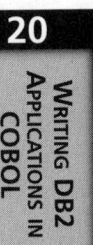

20

WRITING DB2
APPLICATIONS IN
COBOL

The other difference between stored procedures and other DB2 application programs is that stored procedures do not do I/O. Therefore, the client program must read in information that the stored procedure needs and pass it to the stored procedure, and the stored procedure must pass information to be output to the client program and let the calling program display or print it.

Suppose that you write a stored procedure named DB2SPROC that updates the description of a book in the MY_BOOKS table at location REMOTEBOOKS. The stored procedure accepts these parameters:

- An input parameter of varying character type with a maximum length of 30. This parameter holds a value of TITLE from MY_BOOKS.

- An input parameter of varying character type with a maximum length of 40. This parameter holds a value of DESCRIPTION from MY_BOOKS.

- An output parameter of small integer type. This parameter returns a value to the calling program that indicates the number of rows in MY_BOOKS updated. If no rows in MY_BOOKS are updated, this parameter contains a null value.

For stored procedure parameters, you keep track of null values just as you do when you execute SQL statements: You use indicator variables. For example, because you might pass null values for a book title and description to DB2SPROC, you define null indicators for the two input parameters. Similarly, because you want to pass a null value to the calling program if no rows of MY_BOOKS at REMOTEBOOKS are updated, you also define an indicator variable for the output parameter.

In stored procedure DB2SPROC, the parameter declarations look like this:

```
LINKAGE SECTION.

01   BK-TITLE.
     10   BK-TITLE-LEN  PIC S9(4) USAGE COMP.
     10   BK-TITLE-TEXT PIC X(30).
01   BK-DESCRIPTION.
     10   BK-DESC-LEN  PIC S9(4) USAGE COMP.
     10   BK-DESC-TEXT PIC X(40).
01   UPDATED PIC S9(4) USAGE COMP.
01   INDICATORS.
     10   IND-VAR1  PIC S9(4) USAGE COMP.
     10   IND-VAR2  PIC S9(4) USAGE COMP.
     10   IND-VAR3  PIC S9(4) USAGE COMP.
...
PROCEDURE DIVISION USING BK-TITLE, BK-DESCRIPTION, UPDATED, INDICATORS.
```

In DB2SPROC, you first need to check your input indicator variables, IND-VAR1 and IND-VAR2, to determine whether BK-TITLE and BK-DESCRIPTION have null values. If the input values are not null, you copy BK-TITLE and BK-DESCRIPTION to local host variables HV-TITLE and HV-DESCRIPTION. You then can execute this SQL statement to determine how many rows are to be updated:

```
EXEC SQL SELECT COUNT(*) INTO :MATCH
    FROM MY_BOOKS
    WHERE TITLE=:HV-TITLE
END-EXEC.
```

If the value in host variable MATCH is greater than 0, you can update MY_BOOKS with the description in HV-DESCRIPTION for the title in HV-TITLE:

```
EXEC SQL UPDATE MY_BOOKS
    SET DESCRIPTION=:HV-DESCRIPTION
    WHERE TITLE=:HV-TITLE
END-EXEC.
```

If the UPDATE statement is successful, you return the number of rows updated in UPDATED and set IND-VAR3 to 0. If the UPDATE statement is unsuccessful, you set IND-VAR3 to -1.

Calling a Stored Procedure

To call a stored procedure, you first connect to the location that has the stored procedure, and then you execute the SQL CALL statement to invoke the stored procedure. In the CALL statement, you pass a parameter list that includes information to be passed to and from the stored procedure. Suppose that you have written the stored procedure described earlier and defined and prepared it at REMOTEBOOKS. To call the stored procedure, the calling program first initializes indicator variables and sets values for input parameters, and then it connects to REMOTEBOOKS and executes the CALL statement:

```
MOVE 0 TO IND-VAR1.
MOVE 0 TO IND-VAR2.
MOVE 0 TO IND-VAR3.
MOVE 'French Cooking for Amateurs' TO HV-TITLE-TEXT.
MOVE 27 TO HV-TITLE-LEN.
MOVE 'Great cookbook, even for professionals' TO
  HV-DESCRIPTION-TEXT.
MOVE 38 TO HV-DESCRIPTION-LEN.
EXEC SQL CONNECT TO REMOTEBOOKS END-EXEC.
EXEC SQL
    CALL DB2SPROC(:HV-TITLE:IND-VAR1,
                  :HV-DESCRIPTION:IND-VAR2,
                  :UPDATED:IND-VAR3)
END-EXEC.
```

You cannot execute the COMMIT statement in a stored procedure. Therefore, to commit any changes you make in the stored procedure, execute the COMMIT statement in your client program after you execute the CALL statement.

Preparing a DB2 COBOL Application to Run

Before you can run a DB2 COBOL application, you need to prepare that application to run. In addition to compiling and link-editing the COBOL code, you must generate an executable form of the DB2 code. For applications that access remote sites, you also must generate executable DB2 code at those remote sites. Figure 20.2 shows the DB2 program preparation process.

FIGURE 20.2.

The DB2 program preparation process.

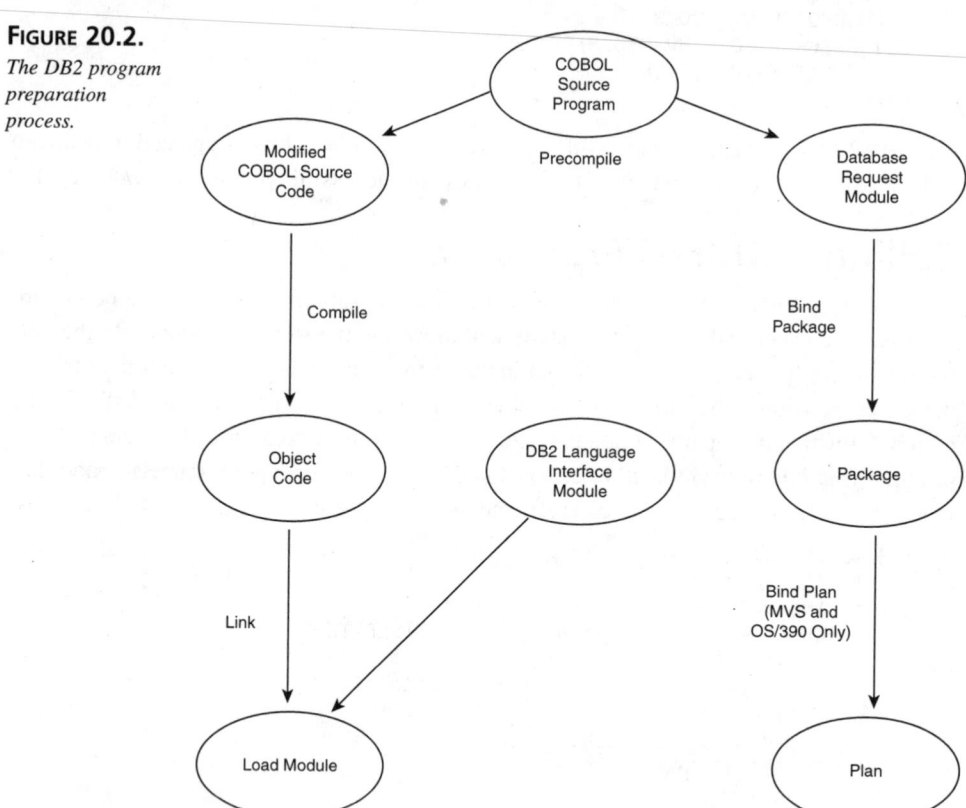

These are the basic steps for preparation of a DB2 COBOL application:

1. *Precompile* the application. This step performs two functions:

   It removes the SQL statements from the program and places information about them in a *database request module* (DBRM).

   It replaces the SQL statements with calls to a DB2 language interface module.

2. Compile and link-edit the precompiler output to generate an executable COBOL program. Unless you dynamically load the DB2 language interface module, you need to link-edit that module with your program. If the program is a stored procedure, you must compile and link-edit the stored procedure at the location where the stored procedure runs.

3. *Bind* the DBRM into a *package* that contains instructions to DB2 on how to access DB2 tables. If the application accesses data at remote locations, you need to bind a package at each of those locations. For a stored procedure that contains SQL statements, you must bind a package for the stored procedure at the location where the stored procedure runs.

4. For versions of DB2 that run on MVS or OS/390, bind all packages associated with the program into a *plan.*

When you invoke the application program, you specify the plan or packages that go with your COBOL load module. This tells DB2 which set of instructions for getting to your DB2 data belongs with your COBOL program.

Each version of DB2 comes with batch files or procedures to help you perform the program preparation process. With versions of DB2 for MVS or OS/390, for example, you receive *Job Control Language* (JCL) procedures such as DSNHICOB, which precompiles, compiles, links, and binds DB2 COBOL applications. To use DSNHICOB to prepare the DB2STAT sample application program shipped on your *COBOL Unleashed* CD-ROM, use JCL statements like those in Listing 20.1.

LISTING 20.1   JCL TO PREPARE THE DB2STAT PROGRAM FOR EXECUTION.

```
//DB2STAT JOB ...
//************************************************************//
//*  PRECOMPILE, COMPILE, AND LINK DB2STAT USING        *//
//*  THE DSNHICOB JCL PROCEDURE.                        *//
//************************************************************//
//COBPREP  EXEC DSNHICOB,MEM=DB2STAT,
//         PARM.PC=('HOST(IBMCOB)',APOST,APOSTSQL,NOSOURCE,NOXREF,
//         'STDSQL(NO),DEC(31)'),
//         PARM.COB='APOST,XREF,NODYNAM,SOURCE'
//************************************************************//
//*  DATA SETS USED FOR PREPARING DB2STAT:              *//
//*    USER.DBRMLIB.DATA HOLDS THE DBRM                 *//
//*    USER.SRCLIB.DATA HOLDS THE SOURCE PROGRAM AND    *//
//*     ANY INCLUDE FILES NEEDED AT PRECOMPILE TIME     *//
//*    USER.RUNLIB.LOAD HOLDS THE LOAD MODULE           *//
//************************************************************//
//PC.DBRMLIB   DD DSN=USER.DBRMLIB.DATA(DB2STAT),
```

continues

LISTING 20.1   CONTINUED

```
//           DISP=SHR
//PC.SYSLIB  DD DSN=USER.SRCLIB.DATA,
//           DISP=SHR
//PC.SYSIN   DD  DSN=USER.SRCLIB.DATA(DB2STAT),
//           DISP=SHR
//LKED.SYSLMOD DD DSN=USER.RUNLIB.LOAD(DB2STAT),
//           DISP=SHR
//LKED.RUNLIB DD DSN=USER.RUNLIB.LOAD,
//           DISP=SHR
//LKED.SYSIN DD  *
    INCLUDE SYSLIB(DSNELI)
//*
//BIND     EXEC PGM=IKJEFT01,DYNAMNBR=20
//**********************************************************//
//* BIND THE DBRM FOR DB2STAT INTO A PACKAGE, THEN    *//
//* BIND THE PACKAGE INTO A PLAN ON DB2 SUBSYSTEM DSN.  *//
//**********************************************************//
//DBRMLIB  DD DSN=USER.DBRMLIB.DATA,DISP=SHR
//SYSTSPRT DD  SYSOUT=*
//SYSPRINT DD  SYSOUT=*
//SYSUDUMP DD  SYSOUT=*
//SYSTSIN  DD  *
 DSN SYSTEM(DSN)
 BIND PACKAGE(COBTEST) MEMBER(DB2STAT) -
   ACTION(REPLACE) ISOLATION(CS)
 BIND PLAN(COBTEST) PKLIST(*.COBTEST.COBTEST) -
   ACTION(REPLACE) ISOLATION(CS)
 END
//*
```

Summary

In this chapter, you learned how you can access DB2 data from your COBOL applications. You received a short introduction to DB2 and the SQL language. You learned the difference between static and dynamic SQL and explored examples of each. You received a brief introduction to DB2 client/server processing with COBOL and learned how you can use stored procedures for more efficient client/server processing. Finally, you learned about the DB2 program preparation process, which is the process you use to transform COBOL source code that contains SQL statements into an executable COBOL program that accesses DB2 databases.

Using COBOL with
Oracle

CHAPTER 21

Database users generally use SQL to manipulate information in a database. By using Oracle precompilers, you can embed these SQL statements within a 3GL and combine the ease of use of *Structured Query Language* (SQL) with the power of a procedural 3GL application.

Using Oracle Precompilers

An Oracle precompiler is a programming tool that enables you to embed SQL statements in a host language source program (C, Pascal, FORTRAN, COBOL, PL/1, and ADA).

Oracle precompilers allow development of highly customized user interfaces, batch processing, and data-intensive applications. As a result, companies can retain their investment in 3GL applications and skills development and at the same time allow them to transfer data into Oracle.

The Pro*COBOL precompiler enables you to do the following:

- Write COBOL applications.
- Use embedded SQL that conforms to the ANSI/ISO standard. Functions, joins, inserts/updates/deletes, queries, and so on are all supported.
- Use dynamic SQL. This refers to the capability to build the SQL statement within the 3GL application itself. For example, the WHERE clause may not exist on a query embedded in a 3GL; however, it is built depending on how the application proceeds.
- Automatically convert between Oracle8 internal datatypes and COBOL datatypes.
- Improve performance by embedding PL/SQL transaction processing blocks in COBOL applications.
- Specify precompiler options.
- Precompile modules separately and then link them into one executable program.
- Use arrays as input and output program variables.
- Interface with tools such as Oracle Forms and Oracle Reports via *user exits*. User exits are 3GL applications that are integrated closely with these Oracle tools. For example, values in screen fields of Oracle Forms application can be passed to a COBOL program, manipulated and changed, and then passed back to the screen field. This allows programmers to use the advanced features of both the COBOL program and the Oracle tool.
- Handle errors and warnings using the ANSI-approved status variables SQLSTATE and SQLCODE and/or the *SQL Communications Area* SQLCA and WHENEVER statement.

- Use diagnostics provided by *Oracle Communications Area* (ORACA).
- Use distributed processing with multiple concurrent connection support and multiple database transaction support.
- Use DB2 compatibility options:

  Optional `DECLARE` section

  Support for `COMP-4`, zoned decimal

  Support for group items as host variables

  Support for implicit `VARCHAR`

  Explicit control of end-of-fetch code

  Support for `Declare Cursor .. With Hold`

  Explicit control over close-on-commit

  Support for `DSNTIAR`

- Use other options:

  Nested program support

  Support for `REDEFINES` and `FILLER`

  Capability to define default mapping for `PIC X(n)`

  Capability to change password while connected

NOTE

The default mapping for `PIC X(..)` variables has changed from `VARCHAR2` (variable length blank padded) to `CHARF` (fixed length blank padded). Therefore, when you upgrade, make sure to specify `PICX=VARCHAR2`; otherwise, you'll insert blank padded strings into the database.

Oracle's Pro*COBOL Precompiler and the Micro Focus COBOL Compiler

The precompiler provided by Oracle on most UNIX systems goes through the embedded SQL statements in their COBOL code and converts them to COBOL calls to Oracle library functions. Micro Focus is currently the largest supplier of COBOL compilers to UNIX systems and has ported its compilers across a wide variety of architectures. You can use Micro Focus COBOL to create two types of executable programs: *statically linked* and *dynamically loaded*.

In static linking, a standard UNIX executable object module is created by compiling your code; it then can be linked to other objects and library procedures (such as the COBOL libraries, the Oracle libraries, and the C libraries that Oracle calls) into a standalone, complete executable. The static-linking method of compiling and running COBOL programs is easier for users who are accustomed to using C, FORTRAN, or other programming languages on UNIX to understand. The compiled objects are modular and can be linked easily with procedures from other languages as well.

> **NOTE**
>
> Statically compiled modules are the only way to add Pro*COBOL user exits to SQL*Forms.

Modularity and ease of linking in other procedures make static linking the best choice for larger, multiple-procedure COBOL programs.

Using this method, creation of a runable COBOL program takes slightly more time, and the executable takes up more disk space. However, because the code is complete and in binary executable form, it runs faster, uses less memory, and shares the code in memory between concurrent users.

On the other hand, in a dynamically loaded executable, either a COBOL intermediate code file or a COBOL-generated code file is created. The program is run by executing a separate runtime procedure that interprets and performs the COBOL code.

> **NOTE**
>
> Small COBOL programs generally are run using the dynamically loaded method.

The runtime system has the COBOL libraries already linked into it (and Oracle adds its own libraries as well). This allows individual programs to be small and quick to make and test.

Procedures that are not contained in the program code itself but are called from it need to be compiled and statically linked to the runtime system. These procedures can be shared and called by any COBOL program run by the new runtime system executable.

CAUTION

Dynamic loading will not work if your COBOL procedure needs to be called by other programs, such as when a Pro*COBOL user exit is called by SQL*Forms.

NOTE

Dynamic loading allows you to use Micro Focus Animator, a runtime debugger provided by Micro Focus.

The COBOL/Oracle Interface

When you want to use COBOL intermediate code (INT/GNT code) for modules that make calls to ORACLE or you want to animate your COBOL code, you need to supply an interface to resolve the calls to Oracle. This interface is available from Micro Focus. The interface comes in the form of a loadable file called `CBL2ORA.DLE`, `CBL2ORA.DLW`, or `CBL2ORA.DLL`, depending on whether you are running on DOS, Windows, or OS/2, respectively.

You can load the interface in three ways:

- Before you attempt any database access, add a line to the COBOL code to call the correct module. For example, if your application is DOS-based, add this line:

```
CALL 'CBL2ORA.DLE'
```

If your program calls other COBOL modules, the `CBL2ORA` interface only needs to be called at the top level of execution.

- Use the compiler directive `INITCALL` when compiling the program. For example, enter this command:

```
COBOL program.COB INITCALL'CBL2ORA.DLW'
```

If your program calls other COBOL modules, you just need to use the `INITCALL` directive when compiling the main COBOL module.

- Modify the application's configuration (`.cfg`) file to preload the `CBL2ORA` module. For example, in the `APPLIC-INSTALL` section of the application's `.cfg` file, place this line:

```
APPLIC-INSTALL[
CBL2ORA
```

Installing the Correct Options for Oracle Database Support

You should select the following two options when installing the Micro-Focus COBOL product set. If these options are not set, you will have unresolved external or undefined symbol errors during linking:

- SQL Database Interface Support: You must select this option if you will be embedding calls to Oracle in your COBOL programs.

- Mixed-Language Programming Support: Oracle database is written in the C programming language; therefore, making calls to Oracle from within a COBOL application requires that you set the mixed-language option in order for those calls to be resolved.

Embedded SQL Statements

Embedded SQL refers to the use of SQL statements from within the application program, which is referred to as the *host program*. The language in which the program is written is called the *host language*. Embedded SQL includes all the interactive SQL statements and several others that allow you to transfer data between Oracle and the host (COBOL) program. There are two types of embedded SQL statements (see Table 21.1):

- **Executable:** These SQL statements generate calls to the database and include all the queries, *Data Manipulation Language* (DML), *Data Definition Language* (DDL), and *Data Control Language* (DCL) statements.

- **Declarative:** These statements do not make calls to SQLLIB and do not operate on the database. They are used to declare Oracle objects, communications areas, and SQL variables.

TABLE 21.1 SQL STATEMENTS THAT CAN BE EMBEDDED.

Statement	Use
Declarative SQL	
ARRAYLEN	Use host tables with PL/SQL
BEGIN DECLARE SECTION END DECLARE SECTION	Declare host variables
DECLARE	Name Oracle objects
INCLUDE	Copy files in the code
VAR	Equivalence variables
WHENEVER	Handle runtime errors

Statement	Use
Executable SQL	
ALLOCATE	
ALTER	
ANALYZE	
AUDIT	
COMMENT	
CONNECT	
CREATE	
DROP	
GRANT	
NOAUDIT	
RENAME	
REVOKE	
TRUNCATE	
CLOSE	Define and control Oracle data
DELETE	
EXPLAIN PLAN	
FETCH	
INSERT	
LOCK TABLE	
OPEN	
SELECT	
UPDATE	Query and manipulate data
COMMIT	
ROLLBACK	
SAVEPOINT	
SET TRANSACTION	Transaction processing
DESCRIBE	
EXECUTE	
PREPARE	Dynamic SQL
ALTER SESSION	
SET ROLE	Session control

Listing 21.1 shows an example of a simple COBOL program using embedded SQL to communicate with Oracle.

LISTING 21.1   USING EMBEDDED SQL WITH COBOL.

```
IDENTIFICATION DIVISION.
 PROGRAM-ID. QUERY.
 ENVIRONMENT DIVISION.
 DATA DIVISION.
 WORKING-STORAGE SECTION.

     EXEC SQL BEGIN DECLARE SECTION END-EXEC.
         01   USERNAME          PIC X(10) VARYING.
         01   PASSWD            PIC X(10) VARYING.
         01   EMP-REC-VARS.
             05   PRODUCT-NAME       PIC X(20) VARYING.
             05   PRODUCT-ID     PIC S9(4) COMP VALUE ZERO.
             05   UNIT-PRICE         PIC S9(5)V99 COMP-3 VALUE ZERO.

     EXEC SQL END DECLARE SECTION END-EXEC.

     EXEC SQL INCLUDE SQLCA END-EXEC.

         01   DISPLAY-VARIABLES.
             05   D-PRODUCT-NAME    PIC X(20).
             05   D-UNIT-PRICE      PIC Z(4)9.99.

         01  D-TOTAL-QUERIED     PIC 9(4) VALUE ZERO.

 PROCEDURE DIVISION.
 BEGIN-PGM.
     EXEC SQL
         WHENEVER SQLERROR DO PERFORM SQL-ERROR
     END-EXEC.
     PERFORM LOGON.

 QUERY-LOOP.
     DISPLAY " ".
     DISPLAY "ENTER PRODUCT ID TO SEARCH (0 TO QUIT): " WITH NO ADVANCING.
     ACCEPT PRODUCT-ID.
     IF (PRODUCT-ID = 0) PERFORM SIGN-OFF.
     MOVE SPACES TO PRODUCT-NAME-ARR.
     EXEC SQL
         WHENEVER NOT FOUND GOTO NO-PROD
     END-EXEC.
     EXEC SQL
         SELECT PRODNAME,UPRICE
         INTO :PRODUCT-NAME, :UNIT-PRICE
         FROM PRODUCTS
         WHERE PRODID = :PRODUCT-ID
```

```
        END-EXEC.
        PERFORM DISPLAY-INFO.
        ADD 1 TO D-TOTAL-QUERIED.
        GO TO QUERY-LOOP.

NO-PROD.
        DISPLAY "NOT A VALID PRODUCT ID - TRY AGAIN.".
        GO TO QUERY-LOOP.

LOGON.
        MOVE "SCOTT" TO USERNAME-ARR.
        MOVE 5 TO USERNAME-LEN.
        MOVE "TIGER" TO PASSWD-ARR.
        MOVE 5 TO PASSWD-LEN.
        EXEC SQL
            CONNECT :USERNAME IDENTIFIED BY :PASSWD
        END-EXEC.
        DISPLAY " ".
        DISPLAY "CONNECTED TO ORACLE AS USER: ", USERNAME-ARR.
DISPLAY-INFO.
        DISPLAY " ".
        DISPLAY "PRODUCT UNIT-PRICE".
        DISPLAY "-------------- ----------------".
        MOVE PRODUCT-NAME-ARR TO D-PRODUCT-NAME.
        MOVE UNIT-PRICE TO D-UNIT-PRICE.

SIGN-OFF.
        DISPLAY " ".
        DISPLAY "TOTAL NUMBER QUERIED WAS ", D-TOTAL-QUERIED, ".".
        DISPLAY " ".
        EXEC SQL
            COMMIT WORK RELEASE
        END-EXEC.
        STOP RUN.

SQL-ERROR.
        EXEC SQL
            WHENEVER SQLERROR CONTINUE
        END-EXEC.
        DISPLAY " ".
        DISPLAY "ORACLE ERROR DETECTED:".
        DISPLAY " ".
        DISPLAY SQLERRMC.
        EXEC SQL
            ROLLBACK WORK RELEASE
        END-EXEC.
        STOP RUN.
```

This program logs on to the database, prompts the user for a product ID, and then queries the database table PRODUCTS for the product's name and unit price. The selected results are stored in the host variables PRODUCT-NAME and UNIT-PRICE. The paragraph DISPLAY-INFO then displays the result. When the user enters 0 for the product ID, the program stops. If an error occurs, paragraph SQL-ERROR is performed, and the SQLCA is used for error handling.

The COBOL variables USERNAME, PASSWD, and PRODUCT-NAME are declared using the VARYING clause, which allows you to use a variable-length string external Oracle datatype called VARCHAR.

> **NOTE**
>
> The BEGIN DECLARE SECTION and END DECLARE SECTION statements used are optional, unless you set the precompiler option DECLARE_SECTION to YES.

Programming with COBOL Against an Oracle Database

You can use the following guidelines when programming with COBOL against Oracle:

- **Abbreviations:** You can use the standard COBOL abbreviations, such as PIC for PICTURE IS and COMP for USAGE IS COMPUTATIONAL.

- **Case-insensitivity:** Pro*COBOL precompiler options and values, as well as all EXEC SQL statements, inline commands, and COBOL statements are not case-sensitive.

- **COBOL versions:** Pro*COBOL supports the standard implementation of COBOL for your operating system (usually, COBOL-85 or COBOL-74).

- **Coding area:** Code EXEC SQL and EXEC ORACLE statements in columns 12 through 72 (columns 73 through 80 are ignored).

- **Commas:** In SQL, you must use commas to separate list items, whereas in COBOL, you can use commas or blanks to separate list items.

- **Comments:** You can place COBOL comment lines within SQL statements in several ways:

    Use COBOL comment lines starting with an asterisk (*) in column 7.

    Place ANSI SQL-style comments (-- ...) within SQL statements at the end of a line (but not after the last line of the SQL statement).

    Place C-style comments (/* ... */) in SQL statements.

- **Continuation lines:** You can continue SQL statements from one line to the next, according to the rules of COBOL, as shown in this example:

```
EXEC SQL SELECT PROD-NAME, UNIT-PRICE INTO :PRODNAME, :UPRICE
                 FROM PRODUCTS
      WHERE PROD_ID = :PRODID
END-EXEC.
```

> **NOTE**
>
> No continuation indicator is needed. To continue a string literal from one line to the next, code the literal through column 72. On the next line, code a hyphen (-) in column 7, a quote in column 12 or beyond, and then the rest of the literal.

- **Delimiters:** The LITDELIM option specifies the delimiters for COBOL string constants and literals. LITDELIM=APOST specifies that apostrophes be used when generating COBOL code, whereas LITDELIM=QUOTE (default) specifies that quotation marks be used.

> **NOTE**
>
> Pro*COBOL generates the delimiter specified by the LITDELIM value, regardless of which delimiter is used in the Pro*COBOL source file.

- **Embedded SQL syntax:** You can embed SQL statements in your Pro*COBOL application by preceding the SQL statement with the EXEC SQL clause and ending the statement with the END-EXEC keyword.

- **Host variable names:** You can use any valid standard COBOL identifier as a host variable. Only the first 30 characters of the variable names are significant, though.

- **Hyphenated names:** You can use hyphenated host variable names in static SQL statements but not in dynamic SQL.

- **Nulls:** In SQL, a null represents a missing, unknown, or inapplicable column value; it equates neither to zero nor to a blank. Null values can be manipulated in several ways:

  Using the NVL function to convert nulls to non-null values

  Using the IS [NOT] NULL comparison operator to search for nulls

  Using Indicator variables to insert and test for nulls

- **Relational operators:** COBOL relational operators differ from their SQL equivalents, as shown in Table 21.2.
- **FILLER is allowed:** The word FILLER is used to specify an elementary item of a group that cannot be referred to explicitly. Host variable declarations can use the word FILLER.

TABLE 21.2 COBOL RELATIONAL OPERATORS.

SQL Operators	COBOL Operators
! =	=, EQUAL TO
< >, !=, ^=	NOT=, NOT EQUAL TO
>	>, GREATER THAN
<	<, LESS THAN
>=	>=, GREATER THAN OR EQUAL TO
<=	<=, LESS THAN OR EQUAL TO

Errors and Warnings

Pro*COBOL provides the following mechanisms to handle errors and warnings that result from embedded SQL statements:

- **SQLCODE/SQLSTATE status variables:** After a SQL statement is executed, the Oracle Server returns a status code to a variable named SQLCODE or SQLSTATE. The status code indicates whether the SQL statement executed successfully or caused an error or warning condition.
- **SQLCA status variable:** The SQLCA is a data structure that defines program variables used by Oracle to pass runtime status information to the program. Using the SQLCA, you can take different actions based on feedback from the server.
- **WHENEVER statement:** With the WHENEVER statement, you can specify reactive steps that should be taken automatically when Oracle detects an error or warning condition. These actions can be any of the following:

  Continue with the next statement.

  Call a subroutine.

  Branch to a labeled statement.

  Stop execution.

- **ORACA:** You can use the ORACA data structure when you need more information than is provided by SQLCA. Oracle communication is handled by the ORACA. It contains the following:

  Cursor statistics

  Information about the current SQL statement

  Option settings

  System statistics

Automatic Logons

Oracle enables you to use operating-system authentication so that you can log on to Oracle automatically with the user ID:

```
<prefix><username>
```

Here, `prefix` is the value of the Oracle initialization parameter `OS_AUTHENT_PREFIX` (default: `OPS$`), and username is your operating system user or task name.

For example, if the prefix is `OPS$`, your username is `COBUSER`, and `OPS$COBUSER` is a valid Oracle user ID, you log on to Oracle as user `OPS$COBUSER`.

To take advantage of the automatic logon feature, pass a slash (/) character to Pro*COBOL, as shown here:

```
EXEC SQL BEGIN DECLARE SECTION END-EXEC.
    01 ORACLEID   PIC X.
...
EXEC SQL END DECLARE SECTION END-EXEC.
...
MOVE '/' TO ORACLEID.
EXEC SQL CONNECT :ORACLEID END-EXEC.
```

> **NOTE**
>
> You can use the precompiler option `AUTO_CONNECT` to log on to the default database without using the `CONNECT` statement. When `AUTO_CONNECT=YES`, as soon as Pro*COBOL encounters an executable SQL statement, your program logs on to Oracle automatically with the user ID `OPS$username`. However, you must use the `CONNECT` statement to log on to Oracle if `AUTO_CONNECT = NO`.

Cursors

You can use cursors to manipulate the result set of a query when it returns multiple rows.

A cursor identifies the current row in the set of rows returned by the query. The following statements let you define and manipulate a cursor:

- **CLOSE:** When you are done with the cursor, you can use this statement to disable the cursor.

- **DECLARE:** You can use DECLARE to name a cursor and associate it with a query.

- **FETCH:** You can use this statement to retrieve the current row in the active set one by one, unless you use host arrays.

- **OPEN:** This statement executes the query and identifies all the rows that meet the query search conditions. These rows form the active set of the cursor.

Basic SQL Statements

The following SQL statements let you query and manipulate Oracle data:

- SELECT returns rows from one or more tables. In the following example, you query the EMP table:

```
EXEC SQL SELECT ENAME, JOB, SAL
    INTO :emp_name, :JOB-TITLE, :SALARY
    FROM EMP
    WHERE EMPNO = :EMP-NUMBER
END-EXEC.
```

- INSERT adds new rows to a table. In the following example, you add a row to the EMP table:

```
EXEC SQL INSERT INTO EMP (EMPNO, ENAME, SAL, DEPTNO)
    VALUES (:EMP_NUMBER, :EMP-NAME, :SALARY, :DEPT-NUMBER)
END-EXEC.
```

- UPDATE modifies rows in a table. In the following example, you update the SAL and COMM columns in the EMP table:

```
EXEC SQL UPDATE EMP
    SET SAL = :SALARY, COMM = :COMMISSION
    WHERE EMPNO = :EMP-NUMBER
END-EXEC.
```

- DELETE removes rows from a table. In the following example, you delete all employees in a given department from the EMP table:

```
EXEC SQL DELETE FROM EMP
    WHERE DEPTNO = :DEPT-NUMBER
END-EXEC.
```

The program in Listing 21.2 logs on to Oracle, declares and opens a cursor, fetches the names and unit prices of all the products, displays the results, and then closes the cursor.

LISTING 21.2 AN EXAMPLE: USING CURSORS.

```
IDENTIFICATION DIVISION.
PROGRAM-ID. CURSORS-EXAMPLE.
ENVIRONMENT DIVISION.
DATA DIVISION.
WORKING-STORAGE SECTION.
    EXEC SQL BEGIN DECLARE SECTION END-EXEC.
        01  USERNAME            PIC X(10) VARYING.
        01  PASSWD              PIC X(10) VARYING.
        01  EMP-REC-VARS.
            05  PRODUCT-NAME    PIC X(20) VARYING.
            05  UNIT-PRICE      PIC S9(6)V99
                            DISPLAY SIGN LEADING SEPARATE.
        EXEC SQL VAR UNIT-PRICE IS DISPLAY(8,2) END-EXEC.
     EXEC SQL END DECLARE SECTION END-EXEC.

    EXEC SQL INCLUDE SQLCA END-EXEC.

        01  DISPLAY-VARIABLES.
            05  D-PROD-NAME    PIC X(10).
            05  D-UPRICE       PIC Z(4)9.99.

PROCEDURE DIVISION.

BEGIN-PGM.
    EXEC SQL
        WHENEVER SQLERROR DO PERFORM SQL-ERROR
    END-EXEC.
    PERFORM LOGON.
    EXEC SQL
        DECLARE PRODUCTSNAME CURSOR FOR
        SELECT PROD_NAME, UNIT_PRICE FROM PRODUCTS
    END-EXEC.
    EXEC SQL
        OPEN PRODUCTSNAME
END-EXEC.
    DISPLAY "PRODUCT-NAME    UNIT-PRICE".
    DISPLAY "----------------------    ------------------".

FETCH-LOOP.
    EXEC SQL
        WHENEVER NOT FOUND DO PERFORM SIGN-OFF
    END-EXEC.
    EXEC SQL
        FETCH PRODUCTSNAME
```

continues

LISTING 21.2   CONTINUED

```
        INTO :PROD-NAME, :UPRICE
    END-EXEC.
    MOVE PROD-NAME-ARR TO D-PROD-NAME.
    MOVE UPRICE TO D-UPRICE.
     DISPLAY D-PROD-NAME, "      ", D-UPRICE.
    MOVE SPACES TO PROD-NAME-ARR.
    GO TO FETCH-LOOP.

LOGON.
    MOVE "SCOTT" TO USERNAME-ARR.
    MOVE 5 TO USERNAME-LEN.
    MOVE "TIGER" TO PASSWD-ARR.
    MOVE 5 TO PASSWD-LEN.
    EXEC SQL
        CONNECT :USERNAME IDENTIFIED BY :PASSWD
    END-EXEC.
    DISPLAY " ".
    DISPLAY "CONNECTED TO ORACLE AS USER: ", USERNAME-ARR.
    DISPLAY " ".

SIGN-OFF.
    EXEC SQL
        CLOSE PRODUCTSNAME
    END-EXEC.
    DISPLAY " ".
    EXEC SQL
        COMMIT WORK RELEASE
    END-EXEC.
    STOP RUN.

SQL-ERROR.
    EXEC SQL
        WHENEVER SQLERROR CONTINUE
    END-EXEC.
    DISPLAY " ".
    DISPLAY "ORACLE ERROR DETECTED:".
    DISPLAY " ".
    DISPLAY SQLERRMC.
    EXEC SQL
        ROLLBACK WORK RELEASE
    END-EXEC.
    STOP RUN.
```

Using the Animator

The Animator is a useful tool for debugging COBOL code. This tool helps you step through your code line by line. Using this tool, you can narrow down a problem as something wrong with the environment settings or your COBOL code. Because Animator provides you with the information at runtime, you can get real values used by your program.

> **NOTE**
>
> The Animator is not available with the statically linked method.

To compile the COBOL code for interpretation by the Animator, use the +A option instead of the -u option:

```
cob +A -C IBMCOMP testprog.cob
```

This code creates `testprog.int`, a compiled intermediate file ready for execution with the Animator.

> **NOTE**
>
> The option to use for the Animator varies with different platforms. See the COBOL documentation for your specific platform. You also can find information in the $COBDIR/docs directory and in the man page for cob.

Then, you need to make sure that the Animator is enabled by setting the COBSW environment variable to +A:

In the Korn or the Bourne Shell, use this:

```
COBSW=+A; export COBSW
```

In the C-Shell, use this:

```
setenv COBSW +A
```

Now you can execute your COBOL program:

```
$COBDIR/rts32 testprog.int      (older versions of Animator)
```

or

```
rtsora testprog.int             (newer versions of Animator)
```

This code runs your program with the Animator.

User Exits for Oracle Forms on UNIX Platforms

A *user exit* is a function written in (or usually precompiled into) a third-generation language like C, COBOL, FORTRAN, and so on to do special-purpose processing, which is linked into the Oracle Forms executable files. User exits can be used in several circumstances, such as these:

- Performance of complex data manipulation
- Control of real-time devices or processes
- Data manipulation that requires excessive procedural capabilities
- Special file I/O operations

You can embed SQL and PL/SQL into the user exit. The user exit is called from the form by using an Oracle Forms trigger, and processing control is passed to the user exit. When the user exit completes its processing, it returns an integer value to the form indicating success, failure, or fatal error.

> **NOTE**
>
> You can call a user exit from a PL/SQL block with the USER_EXIT function.

> **NOTE**
>
> User exits are more complicated to write and implement than SQL, PL/SQL, or Oracle Forms commands. Therefore, you should use these exits only to do processing that is beyond the scope of these commands.

Steps in Developing a User Exit Using Pro*COBOL and Linking It to a Form

The following steps are involved in developing an Oracle Forms user exit:

1. Write the user exit in Pro*COBOL.
2. Precompile and compile the source code into an object file.
3. Create the `iapxtb.c` file and include the name of the user exit function in it.
4. Create a new Oracle Forms executable by linking the standard Oracle Forms modules, your user exit object, and the `iapxtb.o` file.
5. In the form, define a trigger to call the user exit.
6. Run the form with the user exit linked to it.

Precompiler Options for Memory Use

HOLD_CURSOR and RELEASE_CURSOR are precompiler options that allow you to specify how the precompiler uses memory. HOLD_CURSOR refers to memory areas (cursors) in the program, whereas RELEASE_CURSOR refers to memory areas in the Oracle database (or shadow) process.

There are several combinations of these option settings:

* HOLD_CURSOR=no and RELEASE_CURSOR=no

  This is the default and usually is sufficient for most programs.

* HOLD_CURSOR=yes

  When this option is set, it specifies that each memory area allocated for a SQL statement be retained. Therefore, extra work is not done when you reissue a SQL statement.

* RELEASE_CURSOR=yes

  For implicit cursors, the memory area allocated for a SQL statement is released immediately; for explicit cursors, the memory area is released as soon as the cursor is closed. When this option is set, it reduces the memory used by the program but has a performance problem, because a new memory area has to be allocated each time any SQL statement is executed.

> **NOTE**
>
> HOLD_CURSOR=yes and RELEASE_CURSOR=yes cannot be set simultaneously.

The MAXOPENCURSORS parameter specifies the optimum number of cursor areas for the program to maintain. It is relevant only when HOLD_CURSOR=no and RELEASE_CURSOR=no. The maximum number of cursors that can be used is not defined by the MAXOPENCURSORS parameter but by the OPEN_CURSORS database parameter. In general, keep the maximum setting of MAXOPENCURSORS less than the value of OPEN_CURSORS.

Modifying Precompiler Make Files

Oracle provides a sample make file with all releases of the precompiler. This make file can be used as a basis for your application's make file.

In version 7.2 and prior releases, the sample make file is in the $ORACLE_HOME/prox-xxx/demo directory. On most platforms, you can use the following command to build any program based on a single source file:

```
make -f proc.mk <exename>
```

To modify the sample make file for an application, create new rules; one of the samples can be used as a basis, adding any extra libraries or flags. Each time the database is upgraded, the definitions of the Oracle libraries need to be modified.

In version 7.3 and higher releases, the make file is in the `$ORACLE_HOME/precomp/demo/proxxxx` directory. It is called `procxxxx.mk` in 7.3 and `demo_proxxxx.mk` in version 8. This make file includes a base file, `$ORACLE_HOME/precomp/env_precomp.mk`, which contains definitions for required Oracle objects, such as the library list.

> **CAUTION**
>
> The file `env_precomp.mk` should not be modified, because Oracle intends to replace this file in each new server release. The following commands can be used to build executables based on one or more source files:
>
> ```
> For Pro*Cobol:
>         Make -f procob.mk build EXE=<exename> COBS="<src1>.cob <src2>.cob _"
> ```

Using `EXEC SQL AT`

The precompiler provides functionality so that a single program can maintain more than one connection to the database at one time. Oracle provides the capability to issue `EXEC SQL AT dbname` in order for this to work. You can use one of the following statements to connect the precompiler program to a remote database:

```
EXEC SQL CONNECT :uid IDENTIFIED BY :pwd USING :connstr
```

or

```
EXEC SQL CONNECT :upwcs;
```

where upwcs contains a string of the form

```
'username/password@connectstring'
```

Or, you can use this:

```
EXEC SQL CONNECT :uid IDENTIFIED BY :pwd;
```

This relies on the `TWO_TASK` environment variable setting on UNIX or the `LOCAL` registry entry setting for Windows NT.

NOTE

Any statement not using AT uses the default connection.

TIP

You often need to pass empty strings of data to character columns when migrating to Pro*COBOL programs from another RDBMS to Oracle. The default behavior of the Oracle precompiler is to strip spaces from the end of character variables before insert; however, this transforms an empty string into a NULL string. If you want to force spaces to be passed to the server, you should specify the character variable as PIC X(n) VARYING. This creates a group structure after precompilation containing a LEN element and an ARR element. You can use the LEN element to specify to Oracle the desired number of characters to load.

Common Problems and Solutions

You might encounter several problems when using the Oracle precompiler for COBOL. This section discusses the most common problems, along with some solutions and workarounds to these issues. A lot of problems are encountered when trying to animate or link Pro*COBOL programs (see Table 21.3).

Unable to Load rtsora

You are trying to use rtsora with Micro Focus COBOL and Oracle 7.3.2, and you get the following error:

Example:

```
$ORACLE_HOME/bin/rtsora sample4.int

Could not load program/u11/oracle/7.3.2/app/oracle/product/7.3.2/bin/
rtsora
Could not load library libcobol.2.0.a[shr.o]
Error was: No such file or directory
```

Solution:

There are three steps to take:

1. Set the following:

    LIB_PATH set to $COBDIR/coblib:

    ```
    setenv LIB_PATH $COBDIR/coblib
    ```

COBDIR set to /usr/lib/cobol:

```
setenv COBDIR /usr/lib/cobol
```

COBSW = +A (if you want to use the Animator):

```
setenv COBSW +A
```

2. Make sure that no shared libraries have been moved from other machines.

3. Create a new rtsora by executing the following command:

```
make -f int_precomp.mk rtsora
```

Failure During Animation of COBOL Code Files

While using Oracle 7.3.2 and Micro Focus COBOL 3.2, and you are trying to animate or run the resulting executable, you get this error:

```
load error : file 'SQLADR'
```

Solution:

The runtime module rts32 is not linked with Oracle.

Most of the UNIX platforms support the use of Micro Focus COBOL. On such platforms, Oracle provides a program called rtsora. This is a customized version of the COBOL runtime system. You can do the following with rtsora:

- You can run programs compiled to COBOL intermediate code level (.int or .gnt).
- In a Micro Focus environment, you can use intermediate files to allow animation of the program. To do this, you must use the customized runtime system; otherwise, RTS 173 occurs:

```
       RTS 173 _ Called Program File not found in drive/directory
(SQLADR.GNT)
```

You can use these two lines of code to create rtsora in Oracle 7.3.2:

```
cd $ORACLE_HOME/precomp
make -f ins_precomp.mk rtsora
```

If you are using Micro Focus COBOL 3.2, the runtime module is rts32, not rtsora, located in the $COBDIR directory; therefore, you use these two lines:

```
mv $COBDIR/rts32 $COBDIR/rts32.orig
cp rtsora $COBDIR/rts32
```

To actually animate a program, follow these steps:

1. Set (and export) the environmental variable COBSW to +A in the Korn or Bourne Shell:

```
COBSW=+A; export COBSW
```

Or, if you are in the C-Shell, use this:

```
setenv COBSW +A
```

2. Enter the following code:

```
anim <program_name>
```

To run the program, do this:

1. Set the COBSW environmental variable to -A. If you're in the Korn or Bourne Shell, type this:

```
COBSW=-A; export COBSW
```

If you're in the C-Shell, type this:

```
setenv COBSW -A
```

2. Use the following code:

```
cobrun <program_name>
```

Or, invoke the program directly (./<program_name>).

Errors During Compilation of Sample Programs

You are trying to compile the sample Pro*COBOL programs on the DEC Alpha OSF/1 platform. You type

```
% make -f procob.mk sample1
```

and receive the following errors during the relinking process:

```
error "echodo: cob: not found"

/usr/users/cobol> make -f procob.mk sample1
cobol -ansi -align -L/app01/dbs/oracle/product/7.1.6/lib -o sample1
sample1.cobm
ld: Can't locate file for: -lsort
cobol: Severe: Failed while trying to link.
 *** Exit 1
Stop.
/usr/users/cobol> make -f procob.mk sample1 >>x.x
ld: Can't locate file for: -lsort
Stop.
/usr/users/cobol> make -f procob.mk sample1 > y.y
ld: Can't locate file for: -lsort
Stop.
/usr/users/cobol>
```

Messages displayed when compiling:

```
cobol -ansi -align -L/app01/dbs/oracle/product/7.1.6/lib -o sample1
sample1.cob
-lsql -locic /app01/dbs/oracle/product/7.1.6/lib/osntab.o -lsqlnet -lora -
```

```
➥losn
-
lora -lsqlnet -lora -losn -lora -lnlsrtl -lcv6 -lcore -lnlsrtl -lcv6 -
➥lcore
-lm
-lrt -lm
cobol: Severe: Failed while trying to link.
*** Exit 1
```

Solution:

The sample programs will not compile, because the library `libsort.a` cannot be found and specific subsets are missing.

The following subsets must be installed prior to the installation of Pro*COBOL:

- DFARTL
- OSFBASE
- OSFCMPLRS
- OSFPGMR
- SORLIB

After these subsets are installed, the sample programs will compile.

Undefined Symbols *Errors During Linking of Sample Programs*

With Micro Focus COBOL 3 and Oracle 7 (Pro*COBOL), you cannot build the samples; instead, you get the error

```
undefined symbol _GLOBAL_OFFSET_TABLE_
```

during the link phase.

Solution:

Edit your `$COBDIR/coblib/cobusym` file and add this line:

```
_GLOBAL_OFFSET_TABLE_  .
```

Adding this entry makes MF COBOL ignore this symbol and proceeds to a successful link.

Unable to Load COBOL Library

You are unable to load the library `libcobol.so.1.0` when running Pro*COBOL programs.

Solution:

Micro Focus COBOL 3.2 and higher versions are linked as shared.

Make sure that you include $COBDIR/coblib in LD_LIBRARY_PATH.

If you do this but shared library errors still occur, you must rebuild rtsora using the following commands:

```
cd  $ORACLE_HOME/precomp
make -f ins_precomp.mk relink EXENAME=rtsora
```

Embedded SQL Not Commented By the Compiler

The precompiler output, which is a COBOL program, is not commenting out the SQL statements (EXEC SQL) in the procedure division.

Solution:

You have two alternatives:

- Assign the hexadecimal value of the identifier to the variable.

- Enclose the statement in a special EXEC SQL option.

Suppose that this is the actual COBOL line:

```
88  TRIG            VALUE '"'.
```

Enclose this line within the following statements:

```
EXEC ORACLE OPTION (LITDELIM=APOST) END-EXEC.
```

In other words,

```
88  TRIG            VALUE '"'.
EXEC ORACLE OPTION (LITDELIM=QUOTE) END-EXEC.
```

TABLE 21.3 COMMON ERRORS ENCOUNTERED AND THEIR CAUSES.

Oracle Error	Cause
ORA-01001: invalid cursor	1. You either closed the cursor explicitly or closed it by a commit when using MODE=ANSI.
	2. You did not open the cursor.
	3. You did not trap an error that occurred earlier in cursor processing.
	4. You are using a dynamic cursor, but you did not specify HOLD_CURSOR=YES.

continues

TABLE 21.3 CONTINUED

Oracle Error	Cause
ORA-01002: fetch out of sequence	ORA-1002 is a program logic error. The most common cause is attempting to fetch from a cursor when it already has reached the end of the fetch. It also can be caused by attempting to fetch from a cursor declared using SELECT .. FOR UPDATE across a commit. For example, the commit occurs in a called routine or is caused by a DDL statement, such as CREATE TABLE.
ORA-01041: internal error. HOSTDEF extension does not exist	ORA-1041 is a misleading error message. It usually is accompanied by ORA-03113. It indicates that the local environment has been corrupted and the connection with the Oracle shadow process is lost because of database or network errors. Force the precompiler to reset its environment by logging off cleanly. EXEC SQL ROLLBACK WORK RELEASE
ORA-01405: fetched column value is NULL	ORA-1405 is a result of the implementation of stricter rules that govern fetching variables in Oracle7 Server. Oracle recommends that all newly written programs use indicator variables to indicate when a NULL value is fetched. If you are upgrading programs that are not written to this standard, precompile your programs with DBMS=V6 (or UNSAFE_NULL=yes from version 7.3 and higher).

> **NOTE**
>
> The error code for the end of fetch is POSITIVE, whereas all other Oracle error codes are NEGATIVE.

> **NOTE**
>
> The Oracle interface library (libsql.a on UNIX) contains the calls generated by the earlier versions of the precompiler, as well as any new calls introduced with the current version; therefore, you do not need to recompile your programs. However, precompiling ensures that you benefit from any performance improvements.

CHAPTER 22

IDMS

Overview of Network Databases

A *database management system* (DBMS) is an advanced method of maintaining data. Many sites have abandoned sequential and random files and develop all new systems under a DBMS.

There are three types of DBMSs:

- **Relational (such as DB2/SQL or Oracle):** Relational databases deal with "tables" where the COBOL program can issue SQL commands to select and join from various tables. Each table is similar to a flat file, and each "row" in the table is the same as a record in the flat file.

- **Hierarchical (such as IMS):** A hierarchical database establishes a parent-child relationship between records.

- **Network (such as IDMS):** A network database is similar to a hierarchical database but is more flexible because the relationships can be more complex. For example, a child record can have more than one parent.

Many companies adopted IDMS as the database of choice in the '80s. Although in the late '90s, most companies are using relational databases, IDMS still has a strong foothold in major corporations around the world. It often costs millions of dollars to convert a system from one DBMS technology to another, so many companies continue to run older systems until they are obsolete or can be rewritten. Other companies still believe that IDMS is a better choice than today's relational alternatives. IDMS was originally marketed by a company called Cullinet but now is sold and supported by Computer Associates.

Why a DBMS?

A DBMS typically has the following benefits over sequential and VSAM files:

- Centralized control, often with a data dictionary or repository for the meta-data (the data about the data); controlled by the database administration group

- Concurrent batch and online update and retrieval

- Improved recovery (backout or rollback procedures)

- Improved record locking to prevent simultaneous update of the same record(s) and to allow programs to wait for a lock to be released and then continue execution

> **NOTE**
>
> With release 12.0 of IDMS, a SQL option became available as an extra-cost product. One of the unique aspects of the IDMS/SQL option is that SQL can be used against an IDMS/relational database or an IDMS/network database. Another advantage of the SQL option is the ODBC capability to download data to PCs or to access IDMS mainframe data on client/server platforms.

IDMS Architecture Overview

In IDMS terminology, a parent record is called an *owner,* and a child record is called a *member.* Records are connected to each other via *sets.* All database relationships are predefined in a *schema.* A *subschema* is a smaller view of the schema that a COBOL program uses to access the database. Some sites have one large global subschema, whereas other sites have many small subschemas. When dealing with IDMS, a *database administration* (DBA) group usually is responsible for defining the databases (and for keeping the production databases well-organized).

IDMS records are stored in IDMS areas, each of which has a physical page range. The page range and page size of each area determines how much space is available in any given area. Usually each area is mapped to one physical file (dataset), but in the case of large areas, one area may be mapped to a series of dataset names. It is also possible for one physical dataset to contain several areas. In IDMS 12.0 and later versions, several related areas are grouped together to form a *segment.* Segments, buffering, and journaling are defined in a *Device Media Control Language* (DMCL) created by the DBA.

When each IDMS record occurrence is stored, it is assigned a DBKEY, which consists of the page number and line index (usually between 1 and 256). DBKEYs are referenced as an S9(8) COMP field in COBOL. To convert this number to a page and line number, the DBKEY usually is divided by 256 to get the page number, and the remainder is the line number (see the sample IDMS programs on the CD-ROM with this book for a program that converts DBKEYs from one format to another and gives full details).

An IDMS system is called a *Central Version* (CV). It is common to say that the test CV will come down at 9 p.m. and back up at 6 a.m. When the IDMS CV is down, IDMS programmer testing may be limited. Some sites have different CVs for different applications—for example, a development CV, a maintenance CV, a Y2K conversion CV, and a production CV.

IDMS programs can run in local mode or under the CV. When running under the CV, all database I/O is done by the Central Version (one task running on the computer). For the sake of speed, retrieval-only jobs usually run in local mode, and update jobs run under the CV to allow for concurrent update and record locking. Although update jobs can be run in local mode, this feature is seldom used because the areas must be varied out of update mode—thus preventing online and other batch jobs from concurrent update. This sometimes is done on weekends to speed up long-running batch jobs. Running under the CV incurs typical DBMS overhead, such as journaling, buffering, and record locking. All online programs always run under the CV. Most sites use the presence of a //SYSCTL JCL statement to indicate that the job is running under the CV.

Over the years, IDMS has gone through many releases and revisions. The basic network COBOL programming and navigation has changed very little. The material in this chapter is applicable to all releases—from 10.0 to 14.0 (and beyond).

IDMS Schema or Bachman Diagram

Most IDMS sites publish a book or chart of schema diagrams, also called *Bachman diagrams* (after Charles Bachman, one of the pioneers in database technology). Each IDMS record type is illustrated by a box. A set relationship is shown by connecting two records. All sets represent a one-to-many relationship (where the point of the arrow indicates the child relationship). Figure 22.1 shows an IDMS schema diagram.

IDMS records can be stored in three location modes:

CALC	A randomly assigned hash key based on any logical key(s) in the record.
VIA	Physically stores records near their owner record (this allows for extremely rapid access).
DIRECT	This storage mode is most commonly used for audit trails. The record can be stored with the highest DBKEY in the area. Or a specific DBKEY can be provided, and the record is stored at that location.

Each Bachman record box consists of four lines:

Line 1	Contains the record name.
Line 2	Contains the record ID:

F	Fixed
FC	Fixed Compressed
V	Variable
VC	Variable Compressed

Also contains the record length (in bytes) and the location mode (CALC, VIA, or DIRECT).

FIGURE 22.1.

An IDMS schema diagram (Employee Demo database).

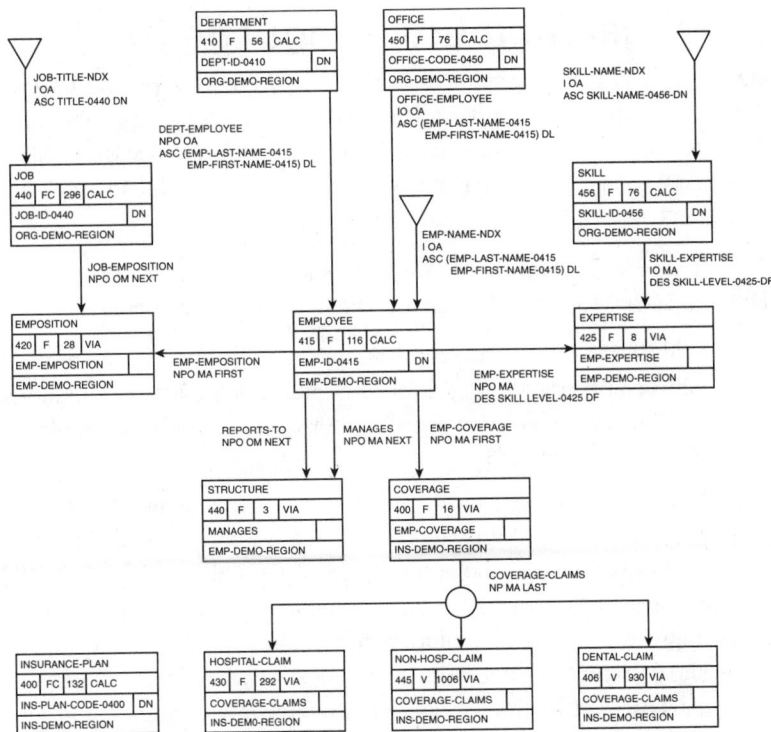

Line 3	Contains the CALC key or VIA SET-NAME, followed by the Duplicates option:
	DN Duplicates Not Allowed
	DF Duplicates First
	DL Duplicates Last
Line 4	Contains the physical AREA-NAME. Some sites add the approximate record occurrence count on line 4. This sometimes helps the programmer to create a faster navigation path.

Usually a copy of the IDMSRPTS utility is used with the schema diagram. This report contains the same information that is on the diagram, along with a full listing of all the elements in each record.

A triangle symbol on a schema diagram represents an *indexed set.* This is a set that has a predefined sort key assigned. Indexes are used as rapid access entry points into the database based on logical key values and as a means of quickly displaying sorted data on an online retrieval transaction.

22

IDMS

Data Manipulation Language (DML)

IDMS databases are maintained by executing *Data Manipulation Language* (DML) commands. The same commands can be used from COBOL, Assembler, PL/1, and even FORTRAN. The DML commands allow you to navigate the database (using OBTAIN commands) and to make changes by issuing simple commands such as MODIFY, STORE, and ERASE.

The differences between DML and SQL show that there are two primary differences between an IDMS network database and a relational database:

- With IDMS, all the set relationships are predefined. A program cannot issue a JOIN between two record types, for example. A predefined set relationship must exist between the two record types (and this set relationship is drawn on the schema diagram).

- With IDMS you choose the preferred database navigation strategy (which hopefully is the fastest). With relational databases, you just query for the desired data, and the DBMS chooses the access logic. Thus as the metrics of an IDMS database change, a program's DML navigation may become slower. Sometimes you can improve the program's runtime by changing the DML navigation path. For example, it might be better to walk an index set when there are only 100 records in the database, but when there are 1 million records, it might be faster to do an area sweep for the same records.

Two Useful Tools

Computer Associates (CA) has an additional-cost product called DMLO, which stands for *Data Manipulation Language Online*. A competitor product called DBOL *(Database Online)* is sold by Allen Systems Group. These two products allow you to issue and practice DML commands online and interactively. Programmers often use these products for the following purposes:

- To test a DML navigation path before writing a COBOL program
- To help debug a COBOL program by verifying DML navigation or values of fields in a database

Although there are more than 40 manuals that describe how IDMS works, the manuals listed in Table 22.1 are most useful to COBOL programmers. Beginning with IDMS 14.0, these manuals are available on CD-ROM. These application programming manuals have not changed significantly since release 10.2 of IDMS, so even older manuals are still applicable.

TABLE 22.1   RECOMMENDED IDMS MANUALS FOR COBOL PROGRAMMERS.

Book Name in IBM/READER for CA-IDMS 14.0	Order Number	Manual Name
CAIDDMLC	R005/&F0CBE	CA-IDMS DML Reference—COBOL
CAIDNDML	R005/&F0NPE	CA-IDMS DML Navigational DML Programming
CAIDMSGR005/&F0M1E	R005/&F0M2E R005/&F0M3E R005/&F0M4E	CA-IDMS Messages and Codes (Volumes 1 through 4)
CAIDQPRG	RC05/&F0PQE CA-IDMS	Programming Quick Reference

The DML Precompiler

The DML precompiler, also called the DML preprocessor, converts high-level DML statements to standard COBOL calls to the appropriate IDMS subroutine.

A normal compile for IDMS consists of the following steps:

1. **DML precompiler:** Your COBOL source code is input to ddname SYSIPT, and the COBOL source is expanded and written to ddname SYSPCH.

2. **COBOL compiler:** This takes expanded code from the DML preprocessor and compiles it.

3. **Linkage editor:** This links the program.

A sample *Job Control Language* (JCL) to execute the preprocessor, COBOL compiler, and linkage editor is located in the COMPJCL file on the CD-ROM that accompanies this book.

Listings 22.1 and 22.2 show the DML code before and after expansion by the DML precompiler. Because OBTAIN CALC is not recognized by COBOL, the DML precompiler converts this statement to a CALL 'IDMS' statement with the appropriate using parameters. Most programmers to do not need to understand the format of the CALL 'IDMS', because the code is maintained in the high-level DML language.

Note two things about this example:

- The OBTAIN CALC statement remains in the program but is commented out.

- A unique DML-SEQUENCE number is assigned to each CALL to IDMS. This DML-SEQUENCE number is displayed in the IDMS ERROR-STATUS routine; thus, if the program fails with a bad IDMS status, the DML-SEQUENCE number is used to identify which IDMS DML verb caused the problem.

LISTING 22.1 CODE SUBMITTED TO THE DML PREPROCESSOR.

```
028400          1000-OBTAIN-EMPLOYEE.
028500              MOVE '123456789' TO EMPLOYEE-NUM
028600              OBTAIN CALC EMPLOYEE-REC
028800              IF DB-REC-NOT-FOUND
028900                  PERFORM 1100-EMP-NOT-FOUND THRU 1100-EXIT
029000              ELSE
029010                  PERFORM IDMS-STATUS
029100                  PERFORM 1200-EMP-FOUND THRU 1200-EXIT
029200              END-IF
029300                  .
029400          1000-EXIT. EXIT.
```

LISTING 22.2 CODE OUTPUT FROM THE DML PREPROCESSOR.

```
000332          1000-OBTAIN-EMPLOYEE.
000333              MOVE '123456789' TO EMPLOYEE-NUM
000334      *     OBTAIN CALC EMPLOYEE-REC
000335                  MOVE 4 TO DML-SEQUENCE
000336                  CALL 'IDMS' USING SUBSCHEMA-CTRL
000337                          IDBMSCOM (32)
000338                          SR2001
000339                          IDBMSCOM (43);
000340              IF DB-REC-NOT-FOUND
000341                  PERFORM 1100-EMP-NOT-FOUND THRU 1100-EXIT
000342              ELSE
000343                  PERFORM IDMS-STATUS
000344                  PERFORM 1200-EMP-FOUND THRU 1200-EXIT
000345              END-IF
000346                  .
000347          1000-EXIT. EXIT.
```

Precompiler Options

Precompiler options tell the precompiler how to do its work:

```
*RETRIEVAL

*DMLIST

*NODMLIST
```

Note: These three lines are standard COBOL comments (the asterisk should begin in column 7).

A feature of the DML precompiler is that it can update the IDMS *Integrated Data Dictionary* (IDD) each time the program is compiled. This can be both a blessing and a curse. The advantage is that detailed information about the program is automatically documented in the dictionary. The disadvantage is that large programs can create a large number of record locks on the dictionary, causing other IDD users and program precompiles to slow down or to abend with deadlocks.

Listing 22.3 shows a sample of program information that is automatically stored in IDD by the precompiler. This information is available within the online task IDD or by running a batch IDD job.

LISTING 22.3   AN IDD DISPLAY PROGRAM.

```
DIS PROG DBATDEMO AS SYN.
      ADD
      PROGRAM NAME IS DBATDEMO VERSION IS 1
*+        DATE CREATED IS       04/14/98
*+        DATE LAST COMPILED IS 04/14/98
*+        NUMBER OF TIMES COMPILED IS 1
          PUBLIC ACCESS IS ALLOWED FOR ALL
          ESTIMATED LINES ARE 339
          PROGRAM CALLED IS IDMS VERSION IS 1
          PROGRAM CALLED IS IDMSERR1 VERSION IS 1
          PROGRAM CALLED IS ABORT VERSION IS 1
          MODULE USED IDMS-STATUS VERSION IS 11 LANGUAGE IS COBOL
          RECORD COPIED SUBSCHEMA-CTRL VERSION IS 2
          RECORD COPIED EMPLOYEE-REC VERSION IS 1
          RECORD COPIED DB-STATISTICS VERSION IS 1
          SUBSCHEMA IS DBATSS01 OF SCHEMA DBATSC01 VERSION IS 1
              AREA DBATEST1-AREA READIED FOR UPDATE
              RECORD EMPLOYEE-REC BIND
              RECORD EMPLOYEE-REC OBTAIN
          MODE IS BATCH
          LANGUAGE IS COBOL
              .
```

Listing 22.4 shows how the IDD can also cross-reference records back to programs.

LISTING 22.4   AN IDD DISPLAY RECORD.

```
DIS REC EMPLOYEE-REC WITH PROGRAMS AS SYN.
      ADD
      RECORD NAME IS EMPLOYEE-REC VERSION IS 1
          RECORD NAME SYNONYM IS EMPLOYEE-REC VERSION 1
*+            COPIED INTO PROGRAM DBATDEMO VERSION 1
          .
```

22

IDMS

Most cross-reference information can also be obtained by scanning the source code (using TSO/ISPF 3.14, PANSCAN for Panvalet, or a Librarian Scan for Librarian). Therefore, many sites disable the auto-update of the dictionary by including the *RETRIEVAL command at the top of each program. This often is done by your compile PROC, which concatenates a one-line member that contains just the line *RETRIEVAL. An advantage of running in RETRIEVAL mode is that the program can run in local mode rather than CV mode.

> **NOTE**
>
> The precompiler runs very fast for small subschemas, but when a subschema contains 50 or 100 or 150 records, the precompiler can run for several minutes.

The *DMLIST or *NODMLIST option specifies that the source listing it to be displayed as output from the preprocessor. The default is *NODMLIST. A listing of error messages is always produced. However, the errors typically point to the line number of the error, and with *NODMLIST, it can be difficult to find the error.

Precompiler Directives

Precompiler directives also affect the way the DML precompiler works.

ENVIRONMENT DIVISION

The first required directive is the IDMS-CONTROL SECTION in the ENVIRONMENT DIVISION and is shown in Listing 22.5.

LISTING 22.5   THE PRECOMPILER/ENVIRONMENT DIVISION.

```
008700          ENVIRONMENT DIVISION.
008800          INPUT-OUTPUT SECTION.
009000          FILE-CONTROL.
009100              SELECT INPUT1-FILE ASSIGN TO INPUT1.
009200
009300          IDMS-CONTROL SECTION.
009400          PROTOCOL.    MODE IS BATCH DEBUG
009500                       IDMS-RECORDS MANUAL.
```

In place of the word BATCH (in Listing 22.5), specify IDMS-DC for online programs (programs that will use IDMS services such as MAPIN/MAPOUT) or DC-BATCH for programs that run in batch but require DC services such as GET QUEUE or CICS-AUTOSTATUS.

Table 22.2 lists several common operating modes. Check with the DBA or reference manual for a complete listing. Some sites also may have defined their own customized modes.

TABLE 22.2   COMMON OPERATING MODES.

Mode	Description
BATCH	Typical batch program
BATCH-AUTOSTATUS	Typical batch program with AUTOSTATUS on
CICS	Typical CICS program
CICS-AUTOSTATUS	Typical CICS program with AUTOSTATUS on
DC-BATCH	For batch programs that need some typically online services such as GET, QUEUE, or PUT QUEUE
IDMS-DC	For online IDMS programs that will use IDMS services such as MAP IN, MAP OUT, READ TERMINAL, or GET QUEUE

The word DEBUG is optional (but almost always used) and causes the DML-SEQUENCE numbers to be generated for each DML verb. The AUTOSTATUS protocols are discussed in "Error Handling," later in this chapter.

The IDMS RECORDS MANUAL clause specifies that the program will manually include the required COPY IDMS statements in the WORKING-STORAGE or LINKAGE SECTION. If IDMS RECORDS WITHIN WORKING-STORAGE is specified instead, all records in the entire subschema are copied into the program. This works fine for small subschemas but may be inappropriate for larger subschemas.

DATA DIVISION: SCHEMA SECTION and WORKING-STORAGE

Listing 22.6 shows where the SCHEMA SECTION is added to the program and how to copy IDMS records into the program.

LISTING 22.6   THE PRECOMPILER/DATA DIVISION.

```
010000          DATA DIVISION
010100          FILE SECTION.
010200          FD  INPUT1-FILE
010300              LABEL RECORDS ARE STANDARD
010400              BLOCK CONTAINS 0 RECORDS.
010500          01  INPUT1-REC          PIC X(80).
010600
010700          SCHEMA SECTION.
```

continues

LISTING 22.6 CONTINUED

```
011000        DB DBATSS01 WITHIN DBATSC01.
011100
011200        WORKING-STORAGE SECTION.
011300
011400        COPY IDMS SUBSCHEMA-CONTROL.
011500        COPY IDMS RECORD EMPLOYEE-REC.
011600        COPY IDMS DB-STATISTICS.
```

The SCHEMA SECTION simply identifies the name of the schema and subschema. Each source program can only access one schema (a called subroutine can be used to access data from a different schema).

In the WORKING-STORAGE section, COPY IDMS statements are used to build the required record layouts from the data dictionary (IDD). (If the IDMS RECORDS WITHIN WORKING-STORAGE clause was used, all subschema records are copied and COPY IDMS record statements do not need to be coded.)

The SUBSCHEMA-CONTROL is actually a special code word for four record names: SUB-SCHEMA-CTRL, SUBSCHEMA-RECNAMES, SUBSCHEMA-SETNAMES, and SUBSCHEMA-AREANAMES. Every program must include these because they are used in the CALL 'IDMS' statements.

DB-STATISTICS is an optional record used with the ACCEPT STATISTICS command. Many programs ACCEPT and DISPLAY the IDMS statistics at the end of the program. This information is extremely useful for debugging and/or improving performance of a program.

PROCEDURE DIVISION Declaratives

Listings 22.7 and 22.8 show how and where the COPY IDMS SUBSCHEMA-BINDS (the first listing is before the DML precompiler, and the second listing is after the expansion by the precompiler).

LISTING 22.7 PRECOMPILER DIRECTIVES IN THE PROCEDURE DIVISION.

```
025800        0500-INITIALIZE.
025900
026000            ACCEPT TODAYS-DATE FROM DATE.
026100            ACCEPT TODAYS-TIME FROM TIME.
026200            DISPLAY 'START: DBATDEMO - RELOAD AUDHST-RECS '
026300            DISPLAY 'DATE = ' TODAYS-DATE
026400                   ' TIME = ' TODAYS-TIME.
026700
026710            COPY IDMS SUBSCHEMA-BINDS.
028000        0500-EXIT.
028100            EXIT.
```

LISTING 22.8 LISTING 22.7 AFTER PRECOMPILER EXPANSION.

```
0500-INITIALIZE.
      ACCEPT TODAYS-DATE FROM DATE.
      ACCEPT TODAYS-TIME FROM TIME.
      DISPLAY 'START: DBATDEMO - RELOAD AUDHST-RECS '
      DISPLAY 'DATE = ' TODAYS-DATE
              ' TIME = ' TODAYS-TIME.

*     COPY IDMS SUBSCHEMA-BINDS.
            MOVE 'DBATDEMO' TO PROGRAM-NAME
*           BIND RUN-UNIT
            MOVE 1 TO DML-SEQUENCE
            CALL 'IDMS' USING SUBSCHEMA-CTRL
                    IDBMSCOM (59)
                    SUBSCHEMA-CTRL
                    SUBSCHEMA-SSNAME;
*           BIND JOB-REC
            MOVE 2 TO DML-SEQUENCE
            CALL 'IDMS' USING SUBSCHEMA-CTRL
                    IDBMSCOM (48)
                    SR2003
                    JOB-REC;
*           BIND EMPLOYEE-REC.
            MOVE 3 TO DML-SEQUENCE
            CALL 'IDMS' USING SUBSCHEMA-CTRL
                    IDBMSCOM (48)
                    SR2001
                    EMPLOYEE-REC.

      0500-EXIT.
          EXIT.
```

The COPY IDMS SUBSCHEMA-BINDS accomplishes three things:

- The program name from the PROGRAM-ID statement is moved to a field called PROGRAM-NAME. This is useful to the DBA when monitoring the system.

- The BIND RUN UNIT statement is generated.

- A BIND RECORD statement is generated for each database record (either each record in the subschema or each record included in the program with COPY IDMS statements).

This COPY statement does *not* generate a READY statement for each database area.

Error Handling

Because the use of IDMS in COBOL basically consists of calls to subroutines, it is important for the COBOL program to handle errors that the subroutine might return. IDMS always returns a four-character ERROR-STATUS, but there are several methods of handling these errors.

AUTOSTATUS Versus Non-AUTOSTATUS

Note that some modes contain the word AUTOSTATUS (refer to Table 22.2). This causes the precompiler to generate a PERFORM IDMS-STATUS statement after each DML command. It is a matter of a site's coding standards or a programmer's personal preference as to whether AUTOSTATUS is used.

Some people prefer AUTOSTATUS, because if a programmer forgets to check the ERROR-STATUS and the program keeps running, logic errors occur that can be difficult to debug. Some people prefer to not use AUTOSTATUS because the code looks cleaner. Use of AUTOSTATUS requires coding an ON statement for any "allowable" errors. For example, an ERROR-STATUS of 0326 or DB-REC-NOT-FOUND is common when doing an OBTAIN CALC DML command. Thus, when using AUTOSTATUS, the programmer must code one ON error statement for each anticipated status.

Listing 22.9 shows a program coded to use AUTOSTATUS, and Listing 22.10 shows the same code after it is expanded by the DML precompiler.

Several COBOL 88-level WORKING-STORAGE variables are defined for the most common IDMS error codes. (Listing 22.12 shows the definition of these 88 levels.)

LISTING 22.9 A SAMPLE OBTAIN WITH AUTOSTATUS.

```
028400          1000-OBTAIN-EMPLOYEE.
028500              MOVE '123456789' TO EMPLOYEE-NUM
028600              OBTAIN CALC EMPLOYEE-REC
028700              ON DB-REC-NOT-FOUND
028800                  PERFORM 1100-EMP-NOT-FOUND THRU 1100-EXIT
028900              .
029000              PERFORM 1200-EMP-FOUND THRU 1200-EXIT
029100              .
029200          1000-EXIT. EXIT.
```

The code in Listing 22.9 is translated to the code shown in Listing 22.10.

LISTING 22.10 LISTING 22.9 AFTER PRECOMPILER EXPANSION.

```
000336          1000-OBTAIN-EMPLOYEE.
000337              MOVE '123456789' TO EMPLOYEE-NUM
000338     *        OBTAIN CALC EMPLOYEE-REC
000339     *        ON DB-REC-NOT-FOUND
000340            MOVE 4 TO DML-SEQUENCE
000341                  CALL 'IDMS' USING SUBSCHEMA-CTRL
000342                          IDBMSCOM (32)
000343                          SR2001
000344                          IDBMSCOM (43)
000345              IF NOT DB-REC-NOT-FOUND PERFORM IDMS-STATUS;
000346              ELSE
000347              PERFORM 1100-EMP-NOT-FOUND THRU 1100-EXIT
000348              .
000349              PERFORM 1200-EMP-FOUND THRU 1200-EXIT
000350              .
000351          1000-EXIT. EXIT.
```

Listing 22.11 shows the same code as Listing 22.10 when not using AUTOSTATUS. You should code the appropriate PERFORM IDMS-STATUS after each DML verb (after checking for any normally expected errors, such as the DB-REC-NOT-FOUND condition). Note the addition of line 28950.

LISTING 22.11 NON-AUTOSTATUS.

```
028400          1000-OBTAIN-EMPLOYEE.
028500              MOVE '123456789' TO EMPLOYEE-NUM
028600              OBTAIN CALC EMPLOYEE-REC
028700              IF DB-REC-NOT-FOUND
028800                  PERFORM 1100-EMP-NOT-FOUND THRU 1100-EXIT
028900              .
```

continues

LISTING 22.11   CONTINUED

```
028950              PERFORM IDMS-STATUS
029000              PERFORM 1200-EMP-FOUND THRU 1200-EXIT
029100              .
029200          1000-EXIT. EXIT.
```

Some programmers will code a variation of Listing 22.11 as shown in Listing 22.12
(note the addition of line 28910). This avoids performing the IDMS-STATUS paragraph
unless needed but results in two lines of error-checking code instead of one. Listing
22.13 shows the result after the precompiler.

LISTING 22.12   ERROR-STATUS AND 88 LEVELS.

```
028400          1000-OBTAIN-EMPLOYEE.
028500              MOVE '123456789' TO EMPLOYEE-NUM
028600              OBTAIN CALC EMPLOYEE-REC
028700              IF DB-REC-NOT-FOUND
028800                  PERFORM 1100-EMP-NOT-FOUND THRU 1100-EXIT
028900              .
028910              IF DB-ANY-ERROR
028950                  PERFORM IDMS-STATUS.
029000              PERFORM 1200-EMP-FOUND THRU 1200-EXIT
029100              .
029200          1000-EXIT. EXIT.
```

LISTING 22.13   ERROR-STATUS AND 88 LEVELS AFTER THE PRECOMPILER.

```
        *COPY IDMS SUBSCHEMA-CONTROL.
        01  SUBSCHEMA-CTRL.
            03  PROGRAM-NAME            PIC X(8)
                                        VALUE  SPACES.
            03  ERROR-STATUS            PIC X(4)
                                        VALUE  '1400'.
                88  DB-STATUS-OK
                    VALUE  '0000'.
                88  ANY-STATUS
                    VALUE  '    ' THRU '9999'.
                88  ANY-ERROR-STATUS
                    VALUE  '0001' THRU '9999'.
                88  DB-END-OF-SET
                    VALUE  '0307'.
                88  DB-REC-NOT-FOUND
                    VALUE  '0326'.
            03  DBKEY                   PIC S9(8) COMP SYNC.
```

IDMS-STATUS Routines

Listing 22.14 shows the common code that is copied into all batch IDMS programs. Your site may have made minor modifications to this code. The code itself is stored on the data dictionary (IDD) as a module with source code. The CALL 'ABORT' statement results in the ABEND U2222, as shown in Listing 22.15.

LISTING 22.14 IDMS-STATUS.

```
*COPY IDMS IDMS-STATUS.
 **********************************************************************
  IDMS-STATUS.
 *********************** V 33 BATCH-AUTOSTATUS *******************
 *IDMS-STATUS-PARAGRAPH.
         IF NOT DB-STATUS-OK
             PERFORM IDMS-ABORT
             DISPLAY '*************************'
                     ' ABORTING - ' PROGRAM-NAME
                     ', '             ERROR-STATUS
                     ', '             ERROR-RECORD
                     ' **** RECOVER IDMS ****'
                     UPON CONSOLE
             DISPLAY 'PROGRAM NAME ------ ' PROGRAM-NAME
             DISPLAY 'ERROR STATUS ------ ' ERROR-STATUS
             DISPLAY 'ERROR RECORD ------ ' ERROR-RECORD
             DISPLAY 'ERROR SET -------- ' ERROR-SET
             DISPLAY 'ERROR AREA ------- ' ERROR-AREA
             DISPLAY 'LAST GOOD RECORD -- ' RECORD-NAME
             DISPLAY 'LAST GOOD AREA ---- ' AREA-NAME
             DISPLAY 'DML SEQUENCE--------' DML-SEQUENCE
 * IN-HOUSE CUSTOMIZATION - CHANGED "ROLLBACK"
 * TO A HARD-CODED CALL - TO AVOID "AUTOSTATUS"
 * ADDING A "PERFORM IDMS-STATUS" AFTER THE ROLLBACK COMMAND
 * AND THUS CREATING AN ENDLESS LOOP IN THIS PARAGRAPH
 * (WHICH WOULD NOW FLOOD THE CONSOLE WITH THE IDMSERR1 MESSAGES).
 *          ROLLBACK
             CALL 'IDMS' USING SUBSCHEMA-CTRL
                 IDBMSCOM (67)
             IF ANY-ERROR-STATUS
                DISPLAY 'ROLLBACK FAILED WITH STATUS='
                        ERROR-STATUS
                DISPLAY 'ROLLBACK FAILED WITH STATUS='
                        ERROR-STATUS UPON CONSOLE
             END-IF
             CALL 'ABORT'
             .
 IDMS-ABORT SECTION.
 IDMS-ABORT-EXIT.
     EXIT.
```

Several versions of the IDMS-STATUS routine exist, and the appropriate one is copied from the IDD based on the MODE IS clause of the PROTOCOL statement. A site may have custom tailored this routine to provide additional functionality.

The IDMS-STATUS routine should be performed after each DML verb after checking for anticipated errors. An example of an anticipated error is 0326 or DB-REC-NOT-FOUND. This occurs frequently, and the program should handle such an error. If there is an unexpected error, the program aborts with a U2222 (also called a USER 2222 ABEND). An example of an unexpected error might be an 0069 or 1469, which means that the IDMS/Central Version went down and thus the program cannot continue. In the case of a U2222 ABEND, the programmer must look at the DISPLAY statements found in the //SYSOUT and the job log.

MVS Job Log

Listing 22.15 shows the MVS output of a batch job with a U2222 ABEND. The key error messages are shown in bold.

LISTING 22.15 ERRORS IN MVS JOB LOG.

```
The job log on MVS would look something like this:
   J E S 2   J O B   L O G  --  S Y S T E M   G S L P  --  N O D

10.15.37 JOB05801   IRR010I   USERID USERID1       IS ASSIGNED TO THIS JOB.
10.15.38 JOB05801   ICH70001I USERID1      LAST ACCESS AT 10:13:47 ON
      WEDNESDAY, JULY
10.15.38 JOB05801   $HASP373 NRWDTSTE STARTED - INIT   12 - CLASS N - SYS
➥ABCD
10.15.38 JOB05801   IEF403I NRWDTSTE - STARTED - TIME=10.15.38
10.16.45 JOB05801   +IDMS DB347011 dbname XXXXXXXX invalid - binding
➥subschema is
10.16.46 JOB05801   +************************* ABORTING - TESTERR1, 1477,
10.16.46 JOB05801   +IDMS RUN-UNIT CANCELLED DUE TO PROGRAM REQUEST
10.16.46 JOB05801   IEA995I SYMPTOM DUMP OUTPUT
                      USER COMPLETION CODE=2222
                      TIME=10.16.45  SEQ=04261  CPU=0000  ASID=0031
                      PSW AT TIME OF ERROR  078D1000   851000DE  ILC 2  INTC 0D
                        ACTIVE LOAD MODULE          ADDRESS=05100080
➥OFFSET=0000
                        NAME=IDMSCANC
              DATA AT PSW  051000D8 - 00181610  0A0D1814  0A0D0700
                        GPR  0-3  80000000  800008AE  0000CB08  00006D60
                        GPR  4-7  000008AE  0004B298  051000B4  851000A4
                        GPR  8-11 80012BE0  0000A6A0  0004ACC0  851000A4
                        GPR 12-15 80012662  0004AFE8  80012BDE  00000000
                      END OF SYMPTOM DUMP
```

```
10.16.46 JOB05801   IEC130I SYSABOUT DD STATEMENT MISSING
10.16.46 JOB05801   +IGZ043I A 'SYSABOUT' error occurred.  The ABEND
➥information
10.16.46 JOB05801   +         incomplete.
10.16.47 JOB05801   +IGZ057I An ABEND was intercepted by the COBOL run-time
   ABEND
10.16.46 JOB05801   +         It is described by a corresponding IEA995I
➥message.
10.16.46 JOB05801   IEF450I NRWDTSTE STEP01 - ABEND=S000 U2222
➥REASON=00000000
                              TIME=10.16.46
10.16.46 JOB05801   *END STEP STEP01   OF NRWDTSTE TIME 10:16       ****
➥ABEND U2222
10.16.46 JOB05801   IEF404I NRWDTSTE - ENDED - TIME=10.16.46
10.16.46 JOB05801   JOB NRWDTSTE END DATE 96.213 CPU  0.002 75085AA
➥8000XXXA TIM
10.16.46 JOB05801   $HASP395 NRWDTSTE ENDED
------ JES2 JOB STATISTICS ------
  31 JUL 1996 JOB EXECUTION DATE
          379 CARDS READ
```

The Program's SYSOUT

Listing 22.16 shows a sample of the //SYSOUT.

LISTING 22.16   ERRORS IN THE PROGRAM'S SYSOUT.

```
PROGRAM NAME ------ TESTERR1
ERROR STATUS ------ 0301
ERROR RECORD ------ EMPLOYEE-REC
ERROR SET --------                   .
ERROR AREA -------- USER-AREA-NAME   .
LAST GOOD RECORD --
LAST GOOD AREA ----
DML SEQUENCE--------0000000008
```

IDMS ERROR-STATUS

The IDMS ERROR-STATUS is a four-byte code. The first two bytes are the major code and the last two bytes are the minor code. The major code always indicates the verb number (for example, 03=OBTAIN, 09=READY). The minor code indicates the problem, such as 26=RECORD NOT FOUND or 66=AREA NOT AVAILABLE. Consult the IDMS manuals for a full explanation of each error code (refer to Table 22.1).

IDMS Retrieval Commands

There are three retrieval commands: FIND, GET, and OBTAIN. About 95 percent of programmers use only the OBTAIN command, because an OBTAIN does a FIND plus a GET. A FIND command sets database currency and retrieves the data but does not put the data into COBOL's WORKING-STORAGE records. A GET presumes that a FIND command has already been done and simply moves the data from the IDMS buffer space to the designated record name in COBOL's WORKING-STORAGE. Occasionally, a programmer will just do a FIND to save a small amount of computer time.

You can find a completed sample IDMS retrieval program in file EMPDEMO1 on the CD-ROM that accompanies this book.

There are six formats of the FIND/OBTAIN command:

- FIND/OBTAIN CALC/DUPLICATE
- FIND/OBTAIN CURRENT
- FIND/OBTAIN DBKEY
- FIND/OBTAIN OWNER WITHIN set-name
- FIND/OBTAIN WITHIN SET USING SORT KEY
- FIND/OBTAIN WITHIN SET/AREA

Database currency refers to where the program is positioned in the database. There are four types of currency:

- Database currency (one only)
- Area currency (one for each area)
- Record currency (one for each record)
- Set currency (one for each set)

When a command like OBTAIN NEXT WITHIN ABC-AREA is issued, the area currency for area ABC-AREA is used to obtain the next record in the area. Likewise, when a command like OBTAIN NEXT WITHIN XYZ-SET is issued, the set currency for the XYZ-SET is used to obtain the next record in the set. Beginning programmers can easily get lost when navigating a database if they lack a good understanding of database currency. Unfortunately, this topic deserves an entire chapter of its own.

FIND/OBTAIN CALC/DUPLICATE

If a record is stored with a location mode of CALC, the fastest way to retrieve that record is to OBTAIN it by using its CALC key. A typical scenario would be an EMPLOYEE-RECORD where the CALC KEY might be EMPLOYEE-NUM or EMP-SOCIAL-SECURITY-NUM. A record can have only one CALC KEY, but it might consist of several noncontiguous field names. Listing 22.17 shows a code fragment that demonstrates the OBTAIN CALC command.

LISTING 22.17   AN OBTAIN CALC EXAMPLE.

```
         MOVE '123456789' TO EMPLOYEE-NUM
         OBTAIN CALC EMPLOYEE-REC
         IF DB-REC-NOT-FOUND
            DISPLAY ' EMPLOYEE-NUM=' EMPLOYEE-NUM ' WAS NOT FOUND'
         ELSE
            PERFORM IDMS-STATUS
            DISPLAY ' EMPLOYEE-NUM=' EMPLOYEE-NUM
                    ' EMPLOYEE-NAME=' EMPLOYEE-NAME
         END-IF
```

Duplicates are rare on CALC KEYS, but if the CALC record was defined as DUPLICATES FIRST or DUPLICATES LAST, the program can continue to get the remaining records with the same CALC KEY by performing a loop. Listing 22.18 shows a code fragment that demonstrates the OBTAIN CALC DUPLICATE command.

LISTING 22.18   AN OBTAIN CALC DUPLICATE EXAMPLE.

```
     1000-GET-EMPLOYEE.
         OBTAIN CALC EMPLOYEE-REC
         PERFORM IDMS-STATUS
         PERFORM 2100-DISPLAY-RESULT THRU 2100-EXIT
         PERFORM 2000-GET-DUP-EMPLOYEES THRU 2000-EXIT
            UNTIL DB-REC-NOT-FOUND.
     1000-EXIT. EXIT.

     2000-GET-DUP-EMPLOYEES.
         OBTAIN CALC EMPLOYEE-REC DUPLICATE.
         IF NOT DB-REC-NOT-FOUND
            PERFORM IDMS-STATUS
            PERFORM 2100-DISPLAY-RESULT THRU 2100-EXIT
            .
     2000-EXIT. EXIT.

     2100-DISPLAY-NAME.
         IF DB-REC-NOT-FOUND
            DISPLAY ' EMPLOYEE-NUM=' EMPLOYEE-NUM
                    'WAS NOT FOUND'
         ELSE
            DISPLAY ' EMPLOYEE-NUM=' EMPLOYEE-NUM
                    ' EMPLOYEE-NAME=' EMPLOYEE-NAME
         END-IF.
     2100-EXIT. EXIT.
```

22

IDMS

FIND/OBTAIN CURRENT and FIND/OBTAIN NEXT WITHIN SET/AREA

The FIND/OBTAIN NEXT command is used to get the first or next record in the area or set. If the database area is more than 50 percent full, the fastest way to retrieve all of a certain record type from the database is to do an AREA SWEEP. This process might also be called an *extract job*. This involves getting the FIRST record in the area and then performing the OBTAIN NEXT command until the DB-END-OF-SET condition is reached.

FIND/OBTAIN NEXT WITHIN SET is used to "walk a set." Usually the program obtains the owner record and then processes each member of the set.

FIND/OBTAIN CURRENT is used to reposition database currency back to a prior location. This is very common when sweeping a database for record 1 while walking a set for record 2. If the program is not careful, it can lose currency. For example, the OBTAIN NEXT EMPLOYEE-REC WITHIN AREA statement will start from the area of currency and go forward in the area looking for the next EMPLOYEE-REC. If the current database position is not on the last EMPLOYEE-REC, this can cause the program to omit records in an extract or to go into a loop rereading the same series of records over and over.

Listing 22.19 demonstrates the FIND/OBTAIN CURRENT command and the FIND/OBTAIN NEXT WITHIN SET and AREA commands.

LISTING 22.19 AN OBTAIN CURRENT AND OBTAIN NEXT EXAMPLE.

```
      1000-GET-EMPLOYEE.
          MOVE ZERO TO RECORD-COUNT
          PERFORM 2000-GET-NEXT-EMPLOYEE THRU 2000-EXIT
              UNTIL DB-END-OF-SET.
      1000-EXIT. EXIT.

      2000-GET-NEXT-EMPLOYEE.
          IF RECORD-COUNT = 0
              OBTAIN FIRST EMPLOYEE-REC WITHIN EMPLOYEE-AREA
          ELSE
              OBTAIN NEXT EMPLOYEE-REC WITHIN EMPLOYEE-AREA
          END-IF
          IF DB-END-OF-SET
              GO TO 2000-EXIT
          END-IF
          PERFORM IDMS-STATUS
          PERFORM 3000-GET-NEXT-JOBHIST THRU 3000-EXIT
              UNTIL DB-ANY-ERROR.
      *SET CURRENCY BACK TO LAST EMPLOYEE-REC
      *THE "FIND" IS USED INSTEAD OF THE "OBTAIN" BECAUSE THE PROGRAM
      *IS NO LONGER INTERESTED IN THE DATA FROM THAT RECORD.
```

```
        FIND CURRENT EMPLOYEE-REC
        PERFORM IDMS-STATUS
        .
    2000-EXIT. EXIT.

    3000-GET-NEXT-JOBHIST.
        OBTAIN NEXT JOBHIST WITHIN EMP-JOBHIST
        IF NOT DB-END-OF-SET
            PERFORM 4000-WRITE-OUT-DATA THRU 4000-EXIT
        END-IF
        .
    3000-EXIT. EXIT.
```

With the OBTAIN WITHIN SET/AREA command, there are five options:

- OBTAIN FIRST
- OBTAIN NEXT
- OBTAIN LAST
- OBTAIN PRIOR
- OBTAIN ws-number, where ws-number is the nth record desired (this option is rarely used)

FIND/OBTAIN DBKEY

FIND/OBTAIN DBKEY command is used to retrieve a record based on a DBKEY that was saved from a prior retrieval of that record. This is the fastest possible way to retrieve a record because IDMS will only have to do one I/O.

CAUTION

If the database administrator reorganizes or resizes the physical database, all the DBKEYs will change. Therefore, it is unwise to save DBKEYs in sequential files for processing that will occur more than a few hours later in the same day.

TIP

A DBKEY consists of a page number and a line number. In COBOL, a DBKEY is defined as an S9(8) COMP field.

continues

DBKEYs can be displayed three ways:

Method	Example
page:line_number	50,123:49
COBOL number	12831537 (which equals 50,123 * 256 + 49)
Hexadecimal	00C3CB31 (where X'00C3CB' converts to 50,123 and X'31' converts to 49)

Here are some advanced notes on DBKEYs:

- Large DBKEYs over 8,388,608 appear as negative numbers in an S9(8) COMP field and require special processing to convert to page/line number. A callable COBOL program called DBKEY is available on the CD-ROM that accompanies this book.

- 99 percent of all databases are defined to allow 255 records per page; thus, the number 256 is used in converting DBKEYs to page/line numbers. The database administrator has the power to change the radix of the DBKEY, and occasionally a different computation must be used.

- There is a field called DBKEY in the SUBSCHEMA-CTRL record. This field always contains the value of the DBKEY of the last database record accessed and thus can be used in a MOVE statement in lieu of an ACCEPT command.

FIND/OBTAIN DBKEY is almost useless without the ACCEPT DBKEY statement, which saves the current DBKEY in a WORKING-STORAGE variable. Note: The DBKEY can also be saved by doing a move of the field DBKEY in the SUBSCHEMA-CTRL to a WORKING-STORAGE variable. Listing 22.20 shows a code fragment that demonstrates the OBTAIN DBKEY command.

LISTING 22.20 AN OBTAIN DBKEY EXAMPLE.

```
77  WS-SAVE-DBKEY    PIC S9(8) COMP.

    ACCEPT WS-SAVE-DBKEY FROM CURRENCY.
    PERFORM IDMS-STATUS
*     (or ACCEPT WS-SAVE-DBKEY FROM EMPLOYEE-REC CURRENCY.)
*     (or MOVE DBKEY TO WS-SAVE-DBKEY)
*      . . . misc other processing here . . .
    OBTAIN EMPLOYEE-REC DBKEY IS WS-SAVE-DBKEY.
    PERFORM IDMS-STATUS.
```

FIND/OBTAIN OWNER WITHIN SET-NAME

The FIND/OBTAIN OWNER command allows you to navigate up a hierarchy by moving from a member (child) record to its owner (or parent). Although an OBTAIN OWNER statement may be coded with checking for ownership first, this can cause bad program logic and make debugging difficult. It therefore should be standard procedure to always use the IF MEMBER statement first. Technically, this is only needed for OPTIONAL sets, but always coding the IF MEMBER gives you the flexibility to change a site's set options without having to worry about recoding programs.

In Listing 22.21, the program has already obtained a JOBHIST record and needs to OBTAIN the owner EMPLOYEE-REC within the EMPLOYEE-JOBHIST set.

LISTING 22.21   AN IF SET-NAME MEMBER EXAMPLE.

```
IF EMPLOYEE-JOBHIST MEMBER
   OBTAIN OWNER WITHIN EMPLOYEE-JOBHIST
   DISPLAY 'OWNER-EMPLOYEE-NUM=' EMPLOYEE-NUM
ELSE
    DISPLAY 'WARNING: JOBHIST IS NOT A MEMBER OF EMPLOYEE-JOBHIST'
END-IF
```

FIND/OBTAIN WITHIN SET USING SORT KEY

FIND/OBTAIN WITHIN SET USING SORT KEY is used when a sorted set is available and the program is aware of the value of the sort key of a desired member record. Suppose that the EMPLOYEE-JOBHIST set is sorted by START-DATE. In other words, the START-DATE is the day the employee began working on a certain job. The query is "What job did employee 123456789 start on the date of 19970501?" Listing 22.22 shows a code fragment that demonstrates this command.

LISTING 22.22   AN OBTAIN USING SORT KEY EXAMPLE.

```
    MOVE '123456789' TO WS-SEARCH-EMP-NUM
* NOTE: THE EMPLOYEE DEMO-DATABASE IS NOT Y2K COMPLIANT
    MOVE '970501'   TO WS-SEARCH-DATE

    MOVE WS-SEARCH-EMP-NUM TO EMPLOYEE-NUM
    OBTAIN CALC EMPLOYEE-REC
    IF DB-REC-NOT-FOUND
       DISPLAY ' EMPLOYEE-NUM=' EMPLOYEE-NUM ' WAS NOT FOUND'
    ELSE
       PERFORM IDMS-STATUS
       DISPLAY ' EMPLOYEE-NUM=' EMPLOYEE-NUM
```

continues

LISTING 22.22   CONTINUED

```
                ' EMPLOYEE-NAME=' EMPLOYEE-NAME
        MOVE WS-SEARCH-DATE TO START-DATE
        OBTAIN JOBHIST WITHIN EMPLOYEE-JOBHIST USING START-DATE
        IF DB-REC-NOT-FOUND
            DISPLAY 'NO JOBHIST FOUND FOR DATE=' START-DATE
        ELSE
            DISPLAY 'START DATE=' START-DATE
                    ' JOB-TITLE=' JOB-TITLE
        END-IF
    END-IF
```

IDMS Update Commands

Table 22.3 shows the five simple commands used to update an IDMS database.

TABLE 22.3   IDMS UPDATE COMMANDS.

Command	Function
CONNECT	Connects a database record to an optional set
DISCONNECT	Disconnects a database record from an optional set
ERASE	Erases (deletes) the record from the database (after OBTAINING a record)
MODIFY	Modifies (replaces) the record in the database (after OBTAINING a record and changing the values of the fields in the record)
STORE	Stores (adds) a new record to the database (after setting the WORKING-STORAGE values for a record)

MODIFY

Listing 22.23 shows a code fragment that demonstrates the MODIFY command.

LISTING 22.23   A MODIFY EXAMPLE.

```
MOVE '123456789' TO WS-SEARCH-EMP-NUM
MOVE 'JONES' TO WS-NEW-LAST-NAME

MOVE WS-SEARCH-EMP-NUM TO EMPLOYEE-NUM
OBTAIN CALC EMPLOYEE-REC
IF DB-REC-NOT-FOUND
    DISPLAY ' EMPLOYEE-NUM=' EMPLOYEE-NUM ' WAS NOT FOUND'
ELSE
    PERFORM IDMS-STATUS
    MOVE EMPLOYEE-LAST-NAME TO WS-OLD-LAST-NAME
```

```
      MOVE WS-NEW-LAST-NAME TO EMPLOYEE-LAST-NAME
      MODIFY EMPLOYEE-REC
      PERFORM IDMS-STATUS
      DISPLAY ' EMPLOYEE-NUM=' EMPLOYEE-NUM
        ' LAST-NAME CHANGED FROM: '
        ' TO: ' EMPLOYEE-LAST-NAME
   END-IF
```

STORE

Listing 22.24 shows a code fragment that demonstrates the STORE command.

LISTING 22.24   A STORE EXAMPLE.

```
INITIALIZE EMPLOYEE-REC
MOVE '1231231234' TO EMPLOYEE-NUM
MOVE 'JONES' TO EMPLOYEE-LAST-NAME
MOVE 'JOHN' TO EMPLOYEE-FIRST-NAME
STORE EMPLOYEE-REC
PERFORM IDMS-STATUS
```

Note: If you attempt to store a child record (into a mandatory automatic set; see Table 22.4), you must be current on the owner record in that set. IDMS automatically connects the member record to the current owner record. If no record is current, you get an ERROR-STATUS 1225.

ERASE

The ERASE command has four options, as shown in Table 22.4. These options provide flexibility and safety when deleting OWNER records. When dealing with a record that is not the owner of any set, you can use the simplest option (option 1 in Table 22.4).

TABLE 22.4   VARIATIONS OF THE ERASE COMMAND.

Option	Function
ERASE record-name	Erases only the specified record (but if the record has children, ERASE fails)
ERASE record-name PERMANENT MEMBERS	Erases the specified record and all mandatory member records
ERASE record-name SELECTIVE MEMBERS	Erases the specified record and all optional member records
ERASE record-name ALL MEMBERS	Erases the specified record and all mandatory and optional member records

> **CAUTION**
>
> When dealing with a database that has a hierarchical structure (record A owns B owns C owns D), if the top record in the hierarchy is erased, all member records below (including C and D) might also be erased, depending on the ERASE options specified.

If the ERASE EMPLOYEE-REC command is used and the EMPLOYEE-JOBHIST set is not empty, the program gets an IDMS ERROR-STATUS=0230 (an attempt has been made to erase the owner record of a nonempty set).

It is often practical to check for members before attempting an ERASE. You can do this with the IF MEMBER command. Listing 22.25 illustrates the IF MEMBER statement and the ERASE command.

LISTING 22.25 AN ERASE EXAMPLE.

```
MOVE WS-SEARCH-EMP-NUM TO EMPLOYEE-NUM
OBTAIN CALC EMPLOYEE-REC
IF DB-REC-NOT-FOUND
  DISPLAY ' EMPLOYEE-NUM=' EMPLOYEE-NUM ' WAS NOT FOUND'
ELSE
   PERFORM IDMS-STATUS
   DISPLAY ' EMPLOYEE-NUM=' EMPLOYEE-NUM
   IF EMPLOYEE-JOBHIST NOT EMPTY
      DISPLAY 'CANNOT ERASE UNTIL MEMBERS ARE DELETED'
   ELSE
      ERASE EMPLOYEE-REC
      PERFORM IDMS-STATUS
   END-IF
END-IF
```

CONNECT and DISCONNECT

The CONNECT and DISCONNECT commands are used less frequently than the other IDMS update commands. The majority of IDMS sets are MANDATORY AUTOMATIC.

It is important to understand the meaning of these set options. These options always come in a pair, where there are two possible values for the first part of the pair and two possible values for the second part of the pair. The four combinations of set options usually are abbreviated by their initials (MA, MM, OM, OA). Tables 22.5 and 22.6 explain these set options.

TABLE 22.5 THE FIRST SET OPTIONS.

Option	Specifies
MANDATORY	The member record cannot be disconnected from the set; therefore, the DISCONNECT command is *not* allowed.
OPTIONAL	The member record can be disconnected from the set.

TABLE 22.6 THE SECOND SET OPTIONS.

Option	Specifies
AUTOMATIC	The member record will be connected to the set when the member record is stored.
MANUAL	The member record will *not* be connected to the set when the member record is stored.

The CONNECT command can be executed on any record that is not connected to its owner by the set relationship. This can be a record that was stored and never connected (OM or MM set options) or a record that had been disconnected by the DISCONNECT command (OA or OM set options). A program can never do a CONNECT or DISCONNECT when the set options are MANDATORY-AUTOMATIC (MA). Listing 22.26 shows an example of the CONNECT verb.

LISTING 22.26 A CONNECT EXAMPLE.

```
IF NOT EMPLOYEE-JOBHIST MEMBER
    CONNECT JOBHIST TO EMPLOYEE-JOBHIST
    PERFORM IDMS-STATUS
END-IF
```

It is common for a member record to be disconnected from one owner and then reconnected immediately to another owner. A record that is disconnected from one owner but is not reconnected to another owner sometimes is called an *orphan* record. Listing 22.27 shows an example of the DISCONNECT verb.

LISTING 22.27 A DISCONNECT EXAMPLE.

```
DISCONNECT JOBHIST FROM EMPLOYEE-JOBHIST
PERFORM IDMS-STATUS
```

Other Required Commands

A few other commands are important to COBOL programmers, although they neither retrieve nor store data. They are the READY, BIND, FINISH, ROLLBACK, and COMMIT commands. Table 22.7 summarizes each of these commands.

TABLE 22.7 OTHER REQUIRED COMMANDS.

Command	Function
BIND	This command has two formats:
	BIND RUN-UNIT establishes a run-unit with IDMS.
	BIND RECORD specifies an area of working storage to be used for retrieving and updating each database record.
COMMIT	Indicates that all database updates are final and releases all update (exclusive) locks but does *not* end the run-unit.
FINISH	Indicates that all database updates are final and ends the run-unit.
READY	Readies IDMS areas in retrieval or update mode.
ROLLBACK	Indicates that all database updates since the start of the program or the last commit (whichever is most recent) should be reversed or rolled out and the run-unit ended.

READY

The READY command deals with the program's intentions as to how an IDMS area is to be used. If the area is readied in retrieval mode, any updates against that area will fail. It is wise to ready each area in the lowest possible ready mode. This reduces locking and contention. The READY AREA statement is extremely useful in production job scheduling. Typically the job schedulers need to know whether two programs can run at the same time, or whether the database administrator can run a reorganization job against area X while program B is running on a weekend. Thus a SCAN utility often is run against the COBOL source code to identify how each program readies each IDMS area.

The format of the READY statement follows:

```
READY area-name  USAGE-MODE IS PROTECTED/EXCLUSIVE RETRIEVAL/UPDATE.
```

Usually the PROTECTED and EXCLUSIVE options are omitted because they limit the capability of other programs to run concurrently against the same IDMS areas. PROTECTED UPDATE indicates that this program will be the only program allowed to update the area.

After the program starts, any other program that attempts to ready the same area in update mode will fail with an IDMS ERROR-STATUS=0966.

PROTECTED UPDATE has one main advantage: It avoids deadlocks. To understand deadlocks, you must understand IDMS locking. When an IDMS program readies an area in update mode, every record retrieved has a SELECT lock (also called an INQUIRE lock) turned on. This lock is released when another record of the same record name is retrieved. Any record that is updated has an UPDATE lock (also called an EXCLUSIVE lock) turned on. This lock is released when the program does a COMMIT or when the run-unit terminates (via a ROLLBACK or FINISH). When program B requests a record that program A has locked, program B goes into a DBKEY WAIT. If two programs access different data in the same area, there is no problem. But when two programs tend to use the same data records, performance usually decreases because one program goes into WAIT until the lock is freed by the other program. When program A needs a record locked by program B, and program B needs a record that is locked by program A, a deadlock occurs. IDMS returns the xx29 ERROR-STATUS, causing one of the two programs to abend.

COMMIT

Deadlocks often can be avoided by increasing the COMMIT frequency. A program typically has a record-update counter, and when that counter reaches a certain point, the program performs a commit.

Listing 22.28 shows how to code COMMIT frequency logic in an update program.

LISTING 22.28   A COMMIT FREQUENCY EXAMPLE.

```
*THIS PROGRAM READS A SEQUENTIAL FILE CONTAINING
*AN EMPLOYEE-ID AND A CHANGE TO THE EMPLOYEE'S LAST-NAME.

     03  WS-UPDATE-COUNTER     PIC S9(4) COMP VALUE ZERO.
     03  WS-COMMIT-COUNTER     PIC S9(4) COMP VALUE ZERO.
     03  WS-COMMIT-FREQ        PIC S9(4) COMP VALUE +100.

     PERFORM 1000-UPDATE-LOOP THRU 1000-EXIT
        UNTIL WS-YN-INPUT1-EOF = 'Y'
     DISPLAY 'NUMBER OF UPDATES=' WS-UPDATE-COUNTER.

 1000-UPDATE-LOOP.
     READ INPUT1-FILE
           AT END MOVE 'Y' TO WS-YN-INPUT1-EOF
                  GO TO 1000-EXIT
     END-READ
     MOVE INPUT1-EMP-ID TO EMPLOYEE-EMP-ID
```

continues

LISTING 22.28 CONTINUED

```
      OBTAIN CALC EMPLOYEE-REC
      IF DB-REC-NOT-FOUND
        DISPLAY 'RECORD NOT FOUND EMP-ID=' INPUT1-EMP-ID
        GO TO 1000-EXIT
      END-IF
      PERFORM IDMS-STATUS
      MOVE INPUT1-LAST-NAME TO EMPLOYEE-LAST-NAME
      MODIFY EMPLOYEE-REC
      PERFORM IDMS-STATUS
      ADD 1 TO WS-UPDATE-COUNTER
      ADD 1 TO WS-COMMIT-COUNTER
      IF WS-COMMIT-COUNTER NOT < WS-COMMIT-FREQ
          PERFORM 8000-COMMIT THRU 8000-EXIT
      END-IF
      .
 1000-EXIT. EXIT.

 8000-COMMIT.
     COMMIT.
     PERFORM IDMS-STATUS.
     MOVE ZERO TO WS-COMMIT-COUNTER.
 8000-EXIT. EXIT.
```

The program in Listing 22.28 is incomplete because it does not handle the case of an ABEND and restart logic. Suppose that there are 500 records in the input file and that the program abends when processing record #325. What happens? Because the commit counter is set for every 100 records, 300 records have been written to the database. In the case of a simple modify-only program, as shown here, the program could be restarted and could simply reprocess all 500 records.

However, if the program is storing records instead of modifying them, the restart logic becomes more difficult. You could change the program in two ways:

- The program could check to see whether each record exists and only store new records.

- The program could spin past the first 300 records and begin its STORE logic right where it left off, at record #301 (realizing that records #301 to #325 were rolled out when the program abended).

The second approach is more elegant but also is more difficult to code. This means that the program must save the current record counter each time it does a commit. This could be done by adding logic, as Listing 22.29 shows. A complete sample IDMS update program with commit and restart logic is located in the EMPDEM02 file on the CD-ROM that accompanies this book.

LISTING 22.29   A COMMIT EXAMPLE (WHERE UPDATE-COUNTER IS SAVED).

```
*THIS TECHNIQUE ASSUMES THAT THE COMMIT1-FILE EXISTS
*AND THAT DISP=SHR IS SPECIFIED IN THE MAINFRAME MVS
*JCL (JOB CONTROL LANGUAGE).
  8000-COMMIT.
     COMMIT.
     PERFORM IDMS-STATUS.
     MOVE ZERO TO WS-COMMIT-COUNTER.
     OPEN OUTPUT COMMIT1-FILE
     MOVE WS-UPDATE-COUNTER TO COMMIT1-UPDATE-COUNTER.
     WRITE COMMIT1-REC
     CLOSE COMMIT1-FILE.
  8000-EXIT. EXIT.
```

The program now writes the update counter to a sequential file. By opening and closing the file each time, the last record written is overlaid. Now that the program saves this counter, it also needs restart logic, which is shown in Listing 22.30.

LISTING 22.30   A COMMIT/RESTART EXAMPLE.

```
0000-INIT.
    OPEN INPUT INPUT1-FILE
    PERFORM 8500-CHECK-RESTART THRU 8500-EXIT.
    PERFORM 1000-UPDATE-LOOP THRU 1000-EXIT
        UNTIL WS-YN-INPUT1-EOF = 'Y'
    DISPLAY 'NUMBER OF UPDATES=' WS-UPDATE-COUNTER.


8500-CHECK-RESTART.
    OPEN INPUT COMMIT1-FILE
    READ COMMIT1-FILE
        AT END MOVE 'Y' TO WS-YN-COMMIT1-EOF
    END-READ
    IF WS-YN-COMMIT1-EOF = 'Y'
       DISPLAY '8500 NO RESTART REQUIRED'
    ELSE
       DISPLAY '8500 RESTARTING AT UPDATE-COUNTER='
                COMMIT1-UPDATE-COUNTER
       PERFORM 8510-SKIP-INPUT1-REC THRU 8510-EXIT
           COMMIT1-UPDATE-COUNTER TIMES
       MOVE COMMIT1-UPDATE-COUNTER TO WS-UPDATE-COUNTER
    END-IF.
    CLOSE COMMIT1-FILE.
8500-EXIT. EXIT.


8510-SKIP-INPUT1-REC.
    READ INPUT1-FILE
        AT END MOVE 'Y' TO WS-YN-INPUT1-EOF
```

continues

LISTING 22.30   CONTINUED

```
                        DISPLAY '8510: ERROR //INPUT1 EOF ON RESTART'
                        MOVE 16 TO RETURN-CODE
                        STOP RUN
           END-READ.
8510-EXIT. EXIT.
```

BIND

The BIND RUN-UNIT statement is used to establish a run-unit. A *run-unit* is an IDMS term that describes a program that has issued a BIND but has not yet issued a FINISH or ROLLBACK. A run-unit establishes communication with the IDMS database server and creates all necessary control blocks to communicate with IDMS.

The following precompiler directive builds the BIND RUN-UNIT statement and a BIND for each record type:

```
COPY IDMS SUBSCHEMA-BINDS.
```

This statement was discussed in "PROCEDURE DIVISION Declaratives," earlier in this chapter. Prior to release 12.0 of IDMS, sites using multiple DBNAMEs would code the DBNAME on the BIND RUN-UNIT statement. But with 12.0, the DBNAME is usually specified external to the program in the //SYSIDMS file. (DBNAMEs allow the same program to run against different copies of the same database. For example, a USA Payroll database and a CANADA Payroll database could be maintained by the same programs, although the data in each database would be entirely different. This is often called *segmentation* or *segmented databases.*)

One BIND record statement must be issued for each record the program will access. Each BIND record statement provides addressability to the COBOL WORKING-STORAGE section for each record layout. If the precompiler directive COPY SUBSCHEMA BINDS (refer to Listing 22.7) is not used, your BINDs and READYs could be coded as shown in Listing 22.31.

LISTING 22.31   A BIND EXAMPLE.

```
BIND RUN-UNIT
PERFORM IDMS-STATUS
BIND JOB
PERFORM IDMS-STATUS
BIND EMPOSITION
PERFORM IDMS-STATUS
BIND EMPLOYEE
PERFORM IDMS-STATUS
READY EMP-DEMO-REGION USAGE-MODE RETRIEVAL.
```

```
PERFORM IDMS-STATUS.
READY ORG-DEMO-REGION USAGE-MODE RETRIEVAL.
PERFORM IDMS-STATUS.
```

> **TIP**
>
> It is always wise to do the PERFORM IDMS-STATUS after each statement. This ensures that you get the proper error as soon as possible rather than a misleading error later.

FINISH and ROLLBACK

The FINISH command is used to complete the IDMS run-unit and to make permanent all the changes to the database (since the last COMMIT). As IDMS updates are written to the actual database files, before and after images are also written to the IDMS journal files. If the program abends or issues the ROLLBACK command, these journal images are used to reverse the changes made to the actual database.

If the program fails to include a FINISH or a ROLLBACK, a ROLLBACK is assumed (however, the DML precompiler issues a warning). If you run a test program and then discover that the updates did not happen, it is likely that the program did not include the FINISH statement.

After the program does a FINISH or ROLLBACK, the run-unit is terminated, and it cannot do any further DML commands (resulting in a bad ERROR-STATUS, such as nn77).

IDMS Online Programming

Online programming involves creating screens (called *maps*) that allow COBOL programs to communicate with mainframe 3270 terminals (or PC programs that emulate 3270 terminals). Literals and database variables are presented on the terminal, and the application end users use function keys, transaction codes, and/or menus to access the desired programs and data. Online programming involves skills above and beyond batch COBOL programming.

Here are the four most common means of writing online programs for IDMS databases:

- IDMS *Application Development System* (ADS)
- IBM's Customer Information System (CICS)
- IDMS/DC–IDMS TP commands
- TSO/ISPF panels

IDMS also includes IDMS/DC (Data Communications) as a separate product option, which provides teleprocessing capabilities (sometimes called a *TP/Monitor*). This allows IDMS online programs using interactive screens to access or update an IDMS database.

Online programming is usually done in full-screen (mapping) mode but also can be done in line mode. IDMS full-screen maps are created in an IDMS task called MAPC (Mapping Compiler for IDMS 12.0 and after) or OLM (Online Mapping for IDMS pre–12.0 releases). CICS maps are created with an IBM CICS mapping language called *Basic Mapping Support* (BMS).

Sample IDMS DC commands follow:

Full-screen

```
INQUIRE MAP
MAP IN
MAP OUT
MAP OUTIN
```

Line mode

```
READ LINE FROM TERMINAL
READ TERMINAL
WRITE LINE TO TERMINAL
```

Other DC commands

```
ENQUEUE/DEQUEUE
GET QUEUE/PUT QUEUE
GET SCRATCH/PUT SCRATCH
POST
SEND MESSAGE
SET TIMER
SNAP
STARTPAGE
WAIT
```

These DC commands allow IDMS/DC programs to do almost anything CICS programs can do. IDMS software called *Universal Communication Facility* (UCF) allows IDMS/DC programs to run under CICS, or a site might run IDMS/DC and not use CICS at all.

Overview of ADS

ADS is a separate product and an entire programming language but one that is totally integrated with IDMS. Many sites have adopted it as their primary online development system. ADS is often referred to as *ADSO* (ADS/Online), but ADS also has batch capabilities (ADS/Batch). ADS is rarely used for batch reporting; most sites choose COBOL, Online Query (OLQ/BATCH), CULPRIT, or *fourth-generation language* (4GL) report writers such as FOCUS, SAS, Data-Analyzer, or Easytrieve-Plus.

ADS programs are written as module text and stored on the IDMS *Integrated Data Dictionary* (IDD). ADSO programmers usually have the authority to create work records and elements on the IDD. ADSO programs are typically built online using the Application Generation and Application Compiler. An ADSO program is called a *dialog*, which usually consists of a map, a subschema, a premap process, and several response processes.

Overview of CICS

CICS programs use CICS command-level language and go through a CICS precompiler in addition to the DML precompiler. A CICS/IDMS program is designed by specifying a proper mode statement in the ENVIRONMENT DIVISION, as shown in Listing 22.32.

LISTING 22.32 A CICS MODE IS EXAMPLE.

```
009200          ENVIRONMENT DIVISION.
009300          IDMS-CONTROL SECTION.
009400          PROTOCOL.    MODE IS CICS-AUTOSTATUS
009500                       IDMS-RECORDS MANUAL.
```

Some sites use only CICS to create online programs (instead of IDMS/DC or ADS) for these reasons:

- CICS programmers might be easier to find and/or the company has a larger base of CICS experience.
- Other in-house programs use CICS/VSAM or sophisticated CICS menuing systems, and the end users want a consistent method of accessing data.

Overview of IDMS/DC

IDMS/DC programs use the same DML precompiler as batch programs. An online IDMS/DC program is designated by specifying a proper mode statement in the ENVIRONMENT DIVISION, as shown in Listing 22.33.

LISTING 22.33 AN IDMS/DC MODE IS EXAMPLE.

```
009200          ENVIRONMENT DIVISION.
009300          IDMS-CONTROL SECTION.
009400          PROTOCOL.    MODE IS IDMS-DC
009500                       IDMS-RECORDS MANUAL.
```

Native VSAM

Native VSAM files can be defined to IDMS schemas so that an IDMS/DC or IDMS/batch program can read or update a VSAM file using DML commands.

Files on the CD-ROM

The following files are located on the CD-ROM that accompanies this book:

EMPDEMO1	COBOL source	Sample report program that reads sequential files and creates a detailed employee/job-history report for each employee ID specified.
EMPDEMO2	COBOL source	Sample update program. Reads sequential files containing OFFICE-CODE, DEPT-ID, EMP-ID, EMP-LAST-NAME, and EMP-FIRST-NAME and stores them on the database. This program has complete COMMIT and restart logic.
EMPDEMO3	COBOL source	Sample update program that deletes all employees with an EMP-ID between 1000 and 2000 (those employees added by the program EMPDEMO2). This is used to clean up the database so that EMPDEMO2 can be run again without getting duplicates. This program also writes a zero counter to the COMMIT file.
XMPDEMO1	Execution JCL	*Job Control Language* (JCL) and INPUT data to demonstrate report program EMPDEMO1.
XMPDEMO2	Execution JCL	JCL and INPUT data to demonstrate EMPDEMO2. JCL comments explain what each step does. JCL is set up to cause an ABEND after x records are processed, so the restart logic can be demonstrated in the next step.
XMPDEMO3	Execution JCL	JCL demonstrates the delete program EMPDEMO3.
COMPJCL	Execution JCL	Sample JCL for DML preprocessor and COBOL compile and link. Check with your site for the actual COBOL JCL or compile PROC to be used.
PMPDEMO1	Printout of execution	From EMPDEMO1.

PMPDEMO2	Printout of execution	From EMPDEMO2.
DBKEY		A COBOL subroutine that formats a DBKEY for user-friendly display (for example, converts a DBKEY to a formatted page and line number).

22

IDMS

CHAPTER 23

CICS Transaction Interface (IBM)

COBOL is a programming language based on the English language. Until now, you have examined COBOL in a *batch processing environment.* A batch processing environment processes transactions that have been collected together, placed into batches, and then processed together at the same time. In effect, batch processing happens without user intervention—noninteractively. The roots of batch processing go back to the early days of computers when punched cards were used.

The *Customer Information Control System* (CICS) is a *transaction processor.* A transaction processor processes transactions, one at a time, as they occur. Designers of application systems strive to capture the transactions as close to the source as they can. The closer to the source the transaction can be captured and processed, the fewer the number of errors, and the more up-to-date the information is.

Differences between batch processing and transaction processing, also known as *online processing,* are described in this chapter.

Batch Processing

You collect and process a batch of transactions by following these steps:

1. Document the transaction on paper.
2. Collect the transactions in piles (batches).
3. Count the transactions and accumulate the control totals per batch.
4. Enter the transactions into a computer (data entry).
5. Balance the transaction counts and control totals.
6. Process the batch of transactions with a COBOL program.
7. Correct errors from the error report.

As you can see, this is a time-consuming and error-prone process. Companies end up with bad information, and the information those companies make their decisions on is out-of-date.

Online Transaction Processing

An online processing system such as CICS processes transactions using these steps:

1. It enters the transaction into CICS as it is generated.
2. It checks the transaction for errors as it is entered.
3. It corrects errors as the transactions are entered.

The online process is quick, and errors are corrected as they are entered. The information is current and up-to-date. Now it is up to the decision makers to arrive at the correct decisions based on current and up-to-date information.

In Figure 23.1, the person at the terminal is processing COBOL CICS transaction programs. If errors occur, an error message appears onscreen and the user corrects the errors.

FIGURE 23.1.

Online processing.

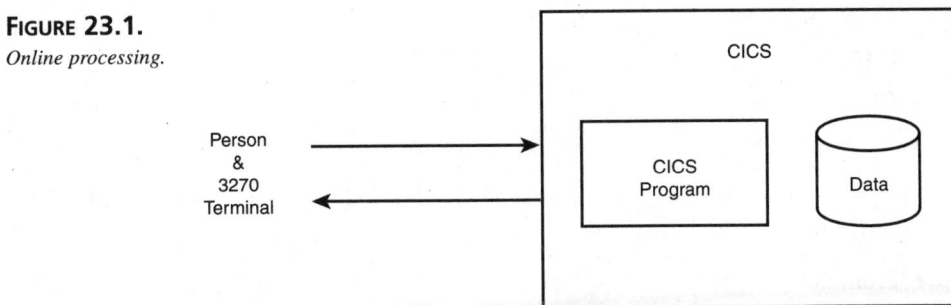

Batch Programming Versus Online Programming

Table 23.1 shows the differences between batch programming and online programming.

TABLE 23.1 BATCH PROGRAMMING VERSUS ONLINE PROGRAMMING.

Batch Programming Characteristics	Online Programming Characteristics
JCL-driven	Event-driven
Started by JCL	Started by arrival of message
Processes all transactions in batch	Processes one transaction as it arrives
Generates error report	Enables you to correct errors during entry
Working storage counters and accumulators available for all transactions of batch	Working storage counters and accumulators available during processing of one transaction only
External save area not needed	External save area needed to store counters and accumulators between transactions
Program terminates at end of job	Program terminates at end of transaction
Program designed to process all transactions of batch at one time	Program designed to process one transaction at a time

CICS Family of Products

CICS is a family of products. Versions of CICS are available for the following:

- CICS for MVS/ESA
- CICS for VSE/ESA
- CICS Transaction Server for NT, OS/2, and AIX
- CICS for Solaris
- CICS for HP-UX
- CICS for OS/2
- CICS for AIX

CICS is being enhanced for the environment of today and the future. You can expect CICS programs to be executed in these ways:

- From the Internet
- By Java programs
- From CICS clients on different PC platforms

CICS functions in a centralized environment or a distributed environment. CICS functions in large mainframe environments using 3270 terminals distributed over the world and processing thousands of transactions in a centralized environment. CICS also processes in a workgroup environment using Window 95 clients and a Windows NT Server.

CICS scales from a small Windows NT environment up to an MVS ESA mainframe environment.

Each member of the CICS family can operate in a distributed and shared environment. A program executing in one CICS system can execute another program in another CICS system. All you have to code is a simple CICS LINK command. The same program can read a file located on the local CICS system and then read a file located on another CICS system across the country. You code the same simple CICS READ command in both cases.

Figure 23.2 shows different members of the CICS family. The programmers use COBOL CICS commands, not network commands. CICS does the rest.

FIGURE 23.2.
CICS family.

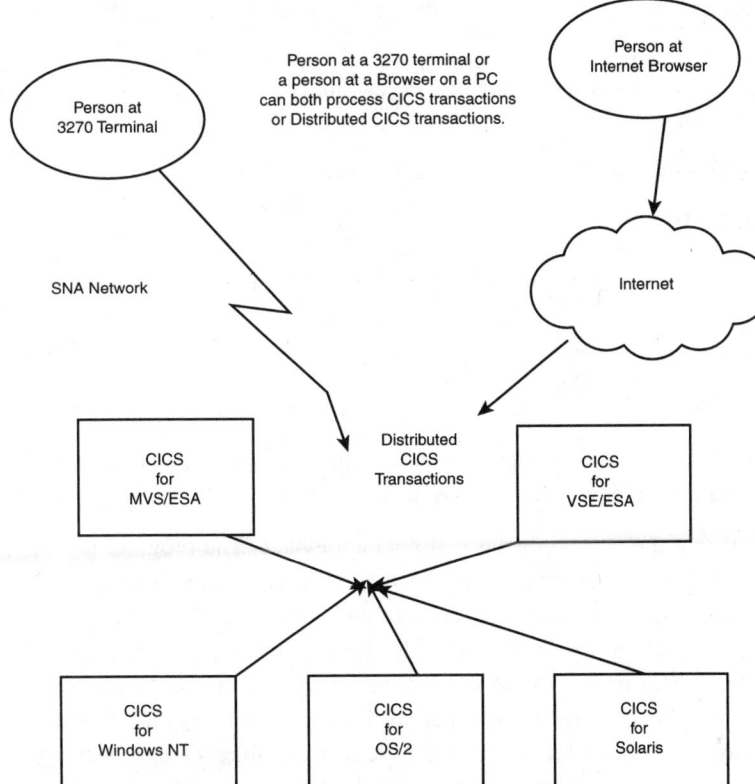

23

CICS Command-Level Programming

COBOL is the easiest programming language to read because it is based on the English language. CICS builds on this ease of use by using the *CICS command level.*

CICS command-level programming uses commands based on the English language. A simple COBOL CICS program does the following:

1. RECEIVEs input message
2. MOVEs input message to output message
3. SENDs output message

The Procedure Division of the COBOL program would contain the following COBOL and CICS command-level commands. CICS commands start with EXEC CICS and end with END-EXEC.

```
MOVE length of Input-Message to Input-Message-Length.
EXEC CICS RECEIVE
          INTO (Input-Message)
          LENGTH (Input-Message-Length)
          END-EXEC.

MOVE Input-Message to Output-Message.

EXEC CICS SEND
          FROM (Output-Message)
          LENGTH (Length of Output-Message)
          END-EXEC.

EXEC CICS RETURN
          END-EXEC.
STOP RUN.
```

This COBOL CICS program executes the same way in a mainframe CICS system as it does in a Windows NT CICS system.

Note that the program is built around a message. The program is loaded into a CICS region because a message was received by CICS. CICS associates the message with a program and loads that program into the memory of the computer managed by CICS. The program reads the message because its entire purpose is to process messages as they arrive. CICS programs are event-driven; they execute because a message (the event) arrives. The message is the input portion of the transaction. The processing of the transaction is based on the arrival and processing of the message. The output message created by the processing of the input message is the result of the processing of the transaction. CICS is a transaction processor.

COBOL and CICS

CICS command-level programming is a natural fit for COBOL. Both are based on the English language, so they can be read by almost anyone. You do not have to be a professional programmer to read a COBOL CICS command-level program.

The programmer codes CICS commands within the COBOL program. Because the CICS commands are not COBOL statements supported by COBOL, these commands must be converted from CICS syntax to COBOL syntax. This is the job of the CICS translator.

Because CICS processes the program, the program must use CICS commands instead of COBOL commands. The results will be unpredictable if a program bypasses CICS and talks to the operating system (see Figure 23.3).

FIGURE 23.3.
The CICS program versus COBOL verbs.

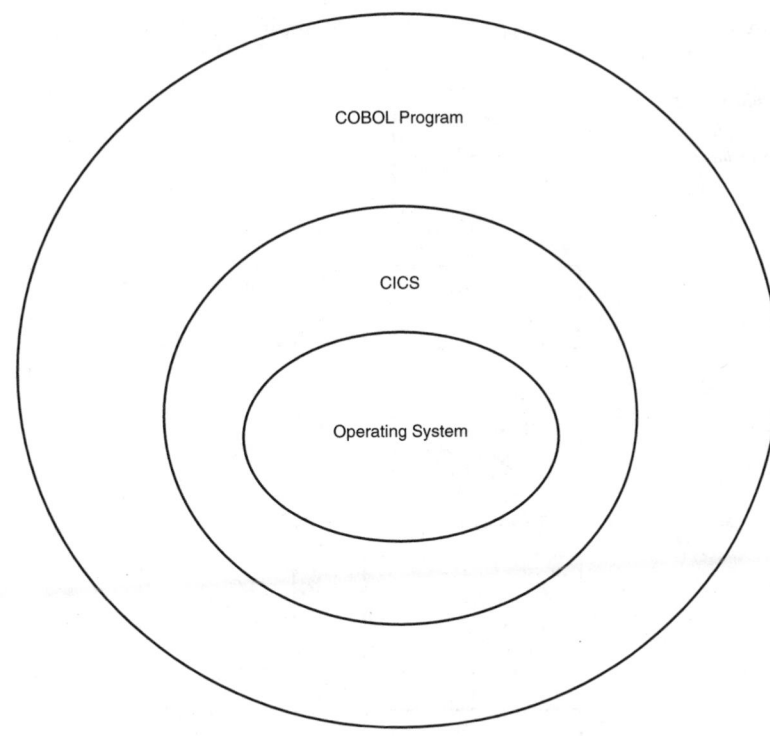

COBOL Program

CICS

Operating System

The CICS Translator

The job of the CICS translator is to convert the CICS commands that cannot be processed by the COBOL compiler into COBOL language syntax that can be processed by the COBOL compiler.

The programmer codes the COBOL program with the CICS commands included. The source program then is input to the CICS translator. The CICS translator converts the CICS commands into COBOL syntax. The CICS translator follows these steps:

1. It comments out CICS commands.
2. It replaces CICS commands with COBOL MOVE statements and calls.
3. It inserts variables into the WORKING-STORAGE section of the COBOL program.
4. It inserts a CICS control block called the *Execute Interface Block* (EIB) into the Linkage section of the COBOL program.
5. It produces error messages as appropriate.
6. It produces a COBOL program, which is then input into the COBOL compiler.

Figure 23.4 shows the steps necessary to compile a COBOL CICS program.

FIGURE 23.4.

The CICS translator.

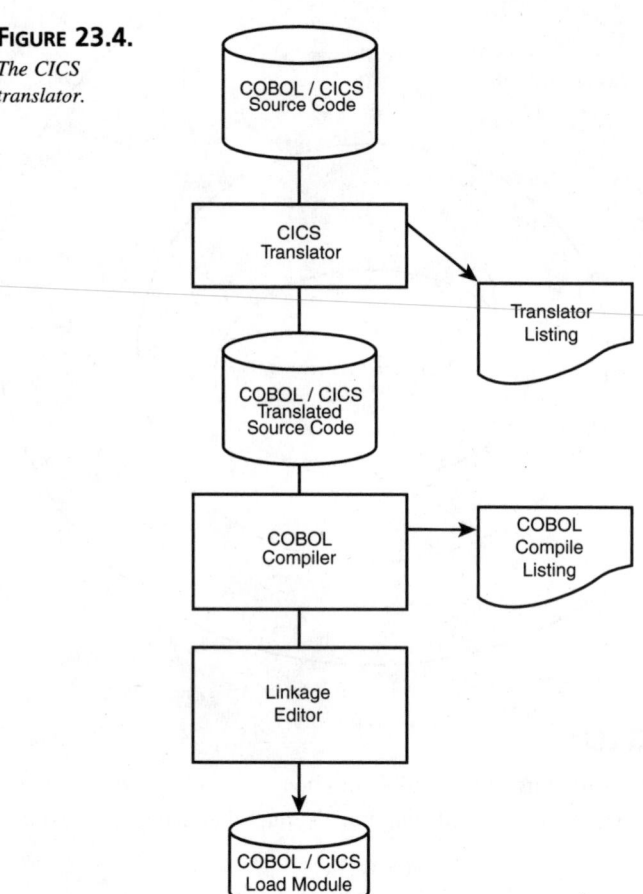

Exception Conditions

When CICS commands are executed, the results can be one of the following:

- Normal
- Warning or informational
- Errors

The process known as *status checking* in many programming environments is called *exception condition checking* in the CICS environment.

Exception conditions in a CICS program can be checked in a variety of ways. Modern CICS programs use one of these methods:

- Handle condition
- Response code

Response code is the preferred method today. It is based on the status-code method used by many programming environments. Response code is also a structured technique, unlike the handle-condition technique.

The programmer issues a CICS command and then checks the response code established by the command to check the results of the command. If the results are normal, processing continues in a normal fashion. If the results are a warning or informational, the programmer takes the appropriate action. If an error response is obtained, error messages are generated based on the standards of the organization, and an error response is given to the user.

It seems that CICS has been around forever, and many programs use the handle-condition technique. A CICS programmer should be equally at ease with both techniques.

Operator and CICS Communication

People process CICS transactions. Users sign on to CICS and start to perform the business of the corporation. They enter a CICS transaction code and receive a formatted CRT screen. They may be using a green screen (a 3270 terminal), a personal computer that emulates a 3270 screen, or a Windows GUI. Users enter information on the screen, press Enter or a *program function key* (PFK), and get the result.

CICS applications are designed for speed, and CICS users should get the response back within a second or so. The main thing is that for each entry of a transaction performed by a user, that user should receive a positive response indicating that the transaction was processed correctly or an error message.

The user and CICS are in a conversation. The user speaks and CICS speaks. Together, they process the business of the corporation.

The 3270 terminal contains an Enter key and 12 PFKs. Enter generally is used to indicate normal mainline processing, and the PFKs are used by the operator to indicate other functions to be executed based on the design of the application.

For example, the different keys could be used as shown here:

Enter	Employee inquiry
PF1	Help function

PF2	Add new employee
PF3	Change information on current employee
PF4	Delete current employee
PF5	Process another application

The user controls which transaction to process, and CICS reacts based on what the user enters. This is called *event-driven programming;* CICS programmers have been doing this type of programming for the past 25 years.

The CICS programmer checks to see which key the user pressed and then causes the appropriate action to take place.

Program Control

Transactions that drive the business of most corporations today are processed by CICS transaction-processing programs. CICS transaction-processing programs are mostly written in COBOL, but other languages, such as C, FORTRAN, and Assembler, are also used.

Remember that CICS programs are scheduled because a message has arrived in the CICS region. The CICS program is scheduled to process that message (transaction). The program starts to execute, reads the message, processes the message, and returns a response back to the user. The program then ends and stops processing.

The program still remains in the memory of the computer controlled by CICS storage control. The program stays in memory until CICS needs that memory to execute other programs. If the program processes frequently enough, the program will always be resident in memory and will provide an even faster response time. If the program is removed from memory because of nonuse, it is reloaded when required.

The same program is executed by each different concurrent user. If 10 people enter the same transaction at the same time from 10 terminals, the same program executes each transaction. Each user is given his or her own copy of the COBOL WORKING-STORAGE section but uses the same copy of the executable program. This quasi-re-entrant method of processing enables CICS to support a high number and wide variety of users at the same time with a minimal amount of resources.

Program Control Commands

Program Control is one of the CICS management modules; it is responsible for management programs within the CICS environment. Program Control uses the *Processing*

Program Table (PPT). Each program must be defined in the CICS region before the program can execute.

The primary Program Control commands follow:

- LINK
- XCTL
- RETURN

LINK

The LINK command enables one CICS program to execute another CICS program. After the linked-to program finishes execution, it issues a CICS RETURN command, and control returns the next instruction to the linking program after the LINK command. The linked-to program can be said to be *performed* or *called*. You can pass data from the linking program to the linked-to program by using the communications area, also called the COMMAREA.

The LINK command is a powerful feature because the program you are linking to can reside on the local system or a remote system. Suppose that program A links to program B. Program A resides on a Windows NT computer running CICS somewhere in the world. Program B resides on a mainframe computer running MVS ESA and CICS in St. Louis. Both programs combine to perform a business function that spreads across two different computers processing CICS on two different operating systems. This is power in action.

23

CICS
TRANSACTION
INTERFACE (IBM)

XCTL

The XCTL command enables one CICS program to transfer control to another CICS program. After the control is transferred, the program transferring the control terminates, and the program to which the control is transferred starts to execute. You can pass this data from one program to another by using the COMMAREA.

RETURN

The RETURN command in a CICS program is equivalent to a GOBACK in a COBOL program. It terminates execution of the CICS program. RETURN also causes control to be returned up one logical level.

Logical Levels

The LINK command causes control to go down one logical level. The XCTL command has no effect on logical levels. If a program is at logical level 1, the RETURN command causes control to be returned to CICS. If a program is at logical level 3, the RETURN command causes control to be returned to a logical level 2 program.

Consider the example in Figure 23.5. When program A issues a RETURN command, control is returned back to CICS. When program F issues a RETURN command, control is returned back to program E. When program E issues a RETURN command, control is returned to program C. When program C issues a RETURN command, control is returned back to program A.

FIGURE 23.5.

Logical levels.

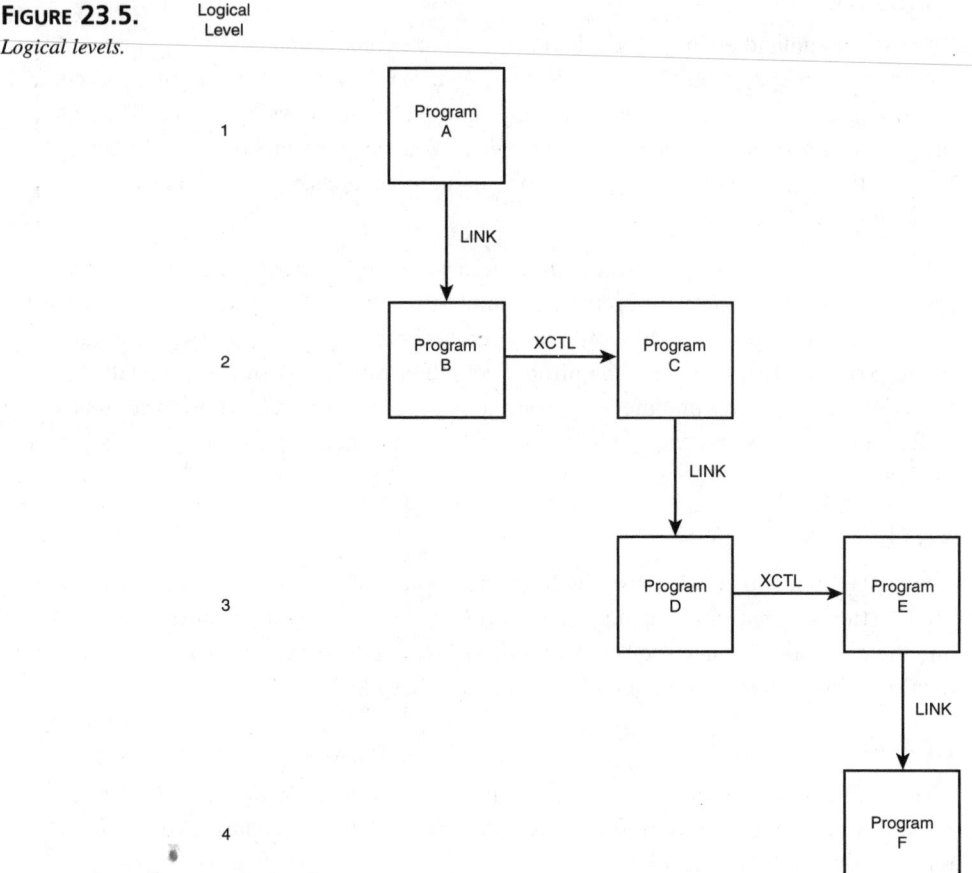

Conversational Modes

CICS COBOL programs usually are written in one of three modes:

- Nonconversational

- Pseudo-conversational
- Conversational

Nonconversational

Nonconversational mode consists of one input message, one process, and one output message. The objective of the nonconversational program is to process one message and terminate. An example is a simple inquiry program. The user enters a transaction code, followed by a space, followed by an account number. The program responds with information on the account entered and terminates by issuing a RETURN statement with no options. The user receives the account information. If the user wants to process another transaction, he or she clears the screen and enters another transaction code.

Conversational Versus Pseudo-Conversational

Table 23.2 compares the conversational and pseudo-conversational modes. Note that the results are the same to the user. The pseudo-conversational method is more efficient, because CICS resources are not being used during the user's "think time."

TABLE 23.2 CONVERSATIONAL MODE VERSUS PSEUDO-CONVERSATIONAL MODE

Conversational	*Pseudo-Conversational*
User enters transaction code.	User enters transaction code.
Program receives message.	Program receives message.
Program processes message.	Program processes message.
Program issues the CONVERSE command, which is a SEND, followed by an implied WAIT, followed by a RECEIVE command.	Program sends response.
	Program issues a RETURN statement using the TRANSID option.
User receives message from program.	User receives message from program.
User enters information and presses Enter.	User enters information and presses Enter.
Program wakes up and gets control with the statement after the CONVERSE command.	Program pointed to by the TRANSID option is scheduled and issues a RECEIVE command to get the message.
Program processes the message.	Program processes the message.
Program issues the CONVERSE command, which is a SEND, followed by an implied WAIT, followed by a RECEIVE command.	Program sends response.

continues

TABLE 23.2 CONTINUED

Conversational	Pseudo-Conversational
Process repeats until the user indicates that the conversation is over.	Process repeats until the user indicates that the conversation is over.
Program sends terminate message.	Program sends terminate message.
Program issues RETURN command.	Program issues RETURN command.
User receives terminate message. Conversation is complete.	User receives terminate message. Conversation is complete.

Distributed CICS

CICS has evolved over the years from a transaction processor processing on IBM system 360 and 370 computers. The 360 and 370 computer systems were large computers in their era. They are small systems based on today's large-scale computing systems.

The major thing to remember is that large yesterday is small today. CICS evolved over the years from a standalone transaction processor running in one address space on one computer at one location to processing in multiple address spaces in multiple computers in different locations running different operation systems.

MRO and ISC

The distributed CICS system of today uses the *Multiregion Option* (MRO) and *Intersystem Communication* (ISC) to communicate between different CICS regions on different computing systems. MRO is used to communicate between different CICS address spaces on a single computer. ISC is used to communicate between different CICS systems processing on different computers in different locations. ISC uses the network to communicate between the different systems.

The CICS system implemented in many corporations today might look something like Figure 23.6. Note the *Terminal Owning Region* (TOR). All terminals are defined to the TOR. The TOR looks at the transaction code and then routes the transaction to the appropriate *Application Owning Region* (AOR), which processes that particular transaction. The different AORs can be on the same computer or on different computers. When a program issues a READ command, the correct file is read based on the location of the file. If the file or queue is on a remote system, the request is function shipped to the appropriate system. Again, this is done by CICS and not by the programmer.

FIGURE 23.6.
TOR and AOR.

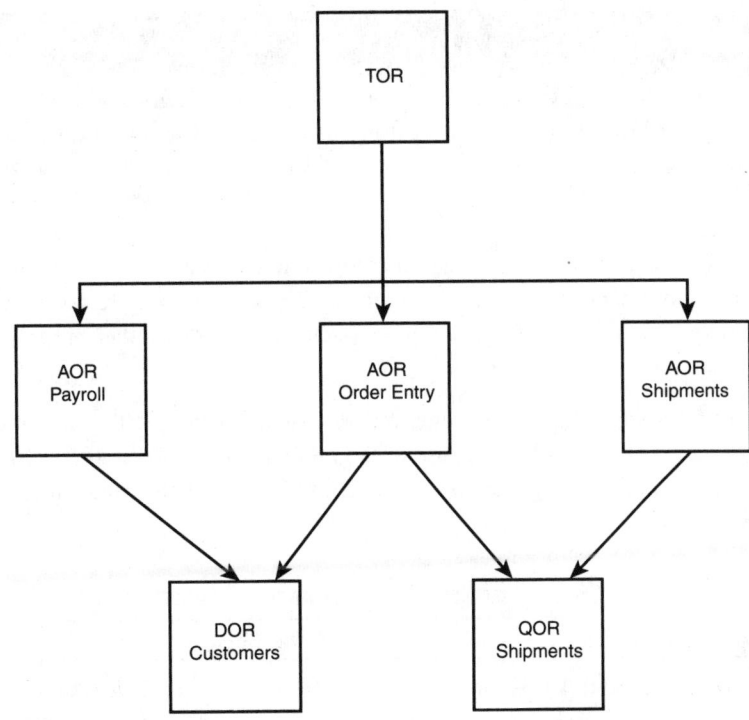

Note the *Data Owning Region* (DOR) and the *Queue Owning Region* (QOR). You can think of the DOR as a file server—as the application programs in the different AOR regions issue file-control commands to access VSAM files, the request is function shipped from the AOR to the appropriate DOR, where the VSAM file requests are satisfied. You can think of the QOR as *transient data* (TD) queue servers handling TD queue requests from the different AORs.

This is power in action.

CICS Tables

Programmers do not know or care where the program or files reside. They just code the program as if it will process in one computer in one CICS system. They do not program for the distributed environment.

> **NOTE**
>
> The CICS systems programmers are responsible for the CICS tables. Even though the application programmers do not need to know anything to do distributed programming, it makes for a better design if they plan for reality.

Transient data queues and temporary storage queues can also participate in the distributed environment and can reside in a local CICS system or a remote CICS system. Additionally, a program in one CICS system can START another program in the local system or a remote system just as easily.

Don't forget the distributed program LINK discussed earlier. The distributed and centralized features are possible because of the relationship between the CICS management modules and the tables they use. Table 23.3 lists the CICS management modules and the tables they use.

TABLE 23.3 CICS MANAGEMENT MODULES AND THE TABLES THEY USE.

CICS Management Module	Table Used
Transaction or Task Control	Program Control Table (PCT)
Program Control	Processing Program Table (PPT)
File Control	File Control Table (FCT)
Terminal Control	Terminal Control Table (TCT)
Transient Data	Destination Control Table (DCT)
Temporary Storage	Temporary Storage Table (TST)

> **NOTE**
>
> The application programmer has to communicate all of the information to the systems programmer so that the appropriate CICS table entries can be defined to the CICS systems.

Basic Mapping Support

The primary purpose of CICS is to process transactions. The transactions arrive from the network in the form of messages. The messages are processed by CICS, and a response message is sent back to the location from which they came. The messages may come from another program running on a PC or a mainframe computer. In most cases, the messages come from a person sitting in front of an IBM 3270 terminal.

The 3270 is a dumb terminal connected to a controller, connected to a network, connected to the mainframe via a communications processor such as the IBM 3745. The 3270 terminal became the standard input device used in online systems. Even today the 3270 terminal is being emulated by software programs running on PCs. In many cases, the sole justification for the PC was to replace the 3270 terminal.

> **NOTE**
>
> The power of the PC is conducive to a much more productive environment and is better used than the 3270 terminals. Programmers and users like to pretty up their CICS screens by using color. Imagine what they would come up with if they could use the power of HTML on the PC with the Internet.

Basic Mapping Support (BMS) is a software program used with CICS to keep the complexities of physical terminals from the programmers who are writing COBOL CICS programs. COBOL CICS programmers want to simply read the terminal and receive an input message from the terminal, much like they want to read a file or database to receive a record. The programmer wants to deal with fields contained in messages and not with hardware issues.

Figure 23.7 shows the relationship between a message read from the terminal using BMS and a record read from a file. A formatted record is read in both cases. The programmer is dealing with fields within a record and not physical input/output devices.

The standard format of the 3270 terminal is 24 lines of 80 characters each. Designing all the information needed to process a business function such as adding a new customer to your customer database is not an easy task. The information must fit on screens of 24 lines of 80 characters each, should contain literals or constants that describe the data fields, and must contain the necessary data fields for the business function being accomplished.

The screens that contain the information required to process the business function on the 3270 screens are called *maps*. You can think of a map as a template that defines the attributes of each field onscreen.

BMS screens (maps) are created and assembled separately from the program. The following Assembler macros are used to build BMS maps:

DFHMSD	Mapset definition
DFMMDI	Map definition
DFHMDF	Field definition

FIGURE 23.7.

Terminal messages versus file messages.

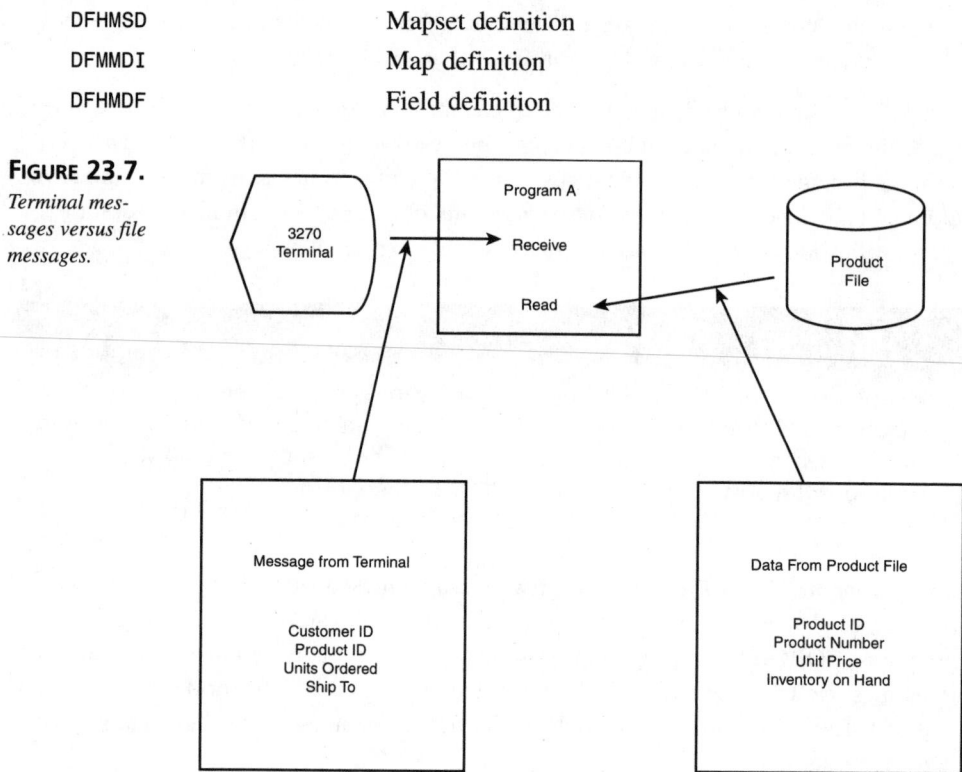

Mapsets

You need one mapset definition for each mapset. A *mapset* is a CICS load module and must be defined to CICS in the PPT table. A mapset contains one or more maps. Today's CICS environment normally consists of one mapset containing one map that is processed by one program.

Maps

Each mapset contains one or more maps. Each field on the screen—both data fields and constant fields—is defined within the map. For example, a map for a 3270 screen contains 24 lines with 80 characters on each line. In this case, the mapset contains one map.

Fields

The fields that appear onscreen (and some that are hidden) are defined within a map on a mapset. The designer decides on the different attributes of each field. The attributes used most often follow:

Name	If data field
Type	Alpha or numeric
Location	Specified by line and column number
Intensity	Normal, highlighted, or hidden
Protection	Protected or unprotected
Initial Value	If desired
Cursor Location	Initial location when map is sent to terminal
Color	If supported by terminals being used

If a field is given a name, the field appears both in the physical map and the symbolic map. If a field is not given a name, it appears on the physical map but does not appear on the symbolic map. The following occurs during a mapset assembly:

- The physical map is placed in the CICS Load library.
- The symbolic map is placed in the CICS COBOL Copy library.

The COBOL program will contain a COPY statement that will copy the CICS symbolic map definition during program compile. Each data field—those given a name on the map—is defined on the symbolic map (Copy Book).

During execution, the user enters information into the 3270 terminal and presses Enter or a PFK. The information entered into the 3270 terminal is sent to the CICS region. BMS intercepts the message, makes the appropriate adjustments based on the attributes of each data field (as defined by the DFHMDF macro for that field), and places the message into a *terminal input/output area* (TIOA). CICS then schedules the appropriate COBOL program. The COBOL program starts to execute, does an EXEC CICS command to get the message the program was scheduled for, and receives the message into the Copy Book that was copied into the program.

File Control

File Control is the CICS Management module responsible for handling files for CICS. The File Control program uses the *File Control Table* (FCT). Each file accessed by a CICS program must be defined in the FCT before the file can be used by a CICS program.

Files are defined to CICS. Files are not defined in the COBOL program using the SELECT statement, and the file description (FD) is not defined in the CICS COBOL program. The record layout is defined in WORKING-STORAGE. Each file is referred to by its FCT name while being accessed by the COBOL program. Here are some attributes defined in the FCT for each file:

Filename	Filename as defined to CICS
Dataset Name	Dataset name as known to the operating system
Log	Log before and after images of changes
Actions	Read, write, rewrite, and delete allowed

VSAM is the primary file-access method used by CICS programs today. VSAM supports direct-access, sequential-access, and indexed-access methods. The VSAM access methods replace earlier versions of the direct-, sequential-, and indexed-access methods. The primary method used is the *Keyed Sequential Dataset* (KSDS). KSDS is the replacement for ISAM.

Here are the file-control commands:

- READ
- WRITE
- REWRITE
- DELETE
- BROWSE

Reading Files

The READ command is used to retrieve a record from a file owned by CICS. An example of a CICS COBOL program reading a file in a random fashion follows:

```
MOVE    INPUT-KEY                  TO    NAME-OF-KEY-FIELD.
MOVE    LENGTH OF VSAM-RECORD      TO    RECORD-LENGTH.

EXEC CICS READ
          FILE      ('FILENAME')
          RIDFLD    (NAME-OF-KEY-FIELD)
          INTO      (VSAM-RECORD)
          LENGTH    (RECORD-LENGTH)
          RESP      (WS-RESPONSE)
          END-EXEC.

    EVALUATE TRUE
        WHEN WS-RESPONSE = DFHRESP(NORMAL)
            PERFORM 3000-PROCESS-RECORD
        WHEN WS-RESPONSE = DFHRESP(NOTFND)
            PERFORM 3100-RECORD-NOT-ON-FILE
        WHEN OTHER
            PERFORM 9000-STANDARD-ERROR
    END-EVALUATE
```

Here is an explanation of the program:

- FILENAME is the name of the file you are reading; it is defined in the FCT.
- NAME-OF-KEY-FIELD is the name of a field in the WORKING-STORAGE section of the program. The value of the key for the record you want to read is moved here from the input message read by the program. The file is indexed by this key.
- VSAM-RECORD is the name of a storage area defined in the WORKING-STORAGE section. It is copied in from a Copy Book to ensure that all programmers call the same fields in the same file the same name.
- RECORD-LENGTH contains the length of the record read from the file. If this value is exceeded by the length of the record, an error status is returned.
- WS-RESPONSE is the field used by the program to check the status of the read.

As the programmer, after you issue the CICS READ command, you are responsible for checking the status of the read. You do this by checking the WS-RESPONSE key. Notice how the preceding program uses structured program techniques to make the program easy to read and change.

If a normal response is returned, the record is processed normally. If a NOTFND condition is raised, you send back a message response stating that the record the user wants to read is not on the file. Otherwise, you send back an error message.

Updating Files

After a record is read, you have several options. If all you want to do is read the record, the preceding code is the code to use.

If you want to update the record, you add the UPDATE parameter to the call. This causes CICS to lock the record. The lock placed on the record is released when the program terminates or takes a SYNCPOINT. By default, CICS programs take a SYNCPOINT during task termination.

This lock is held on the record for a specific reason. When a program indicates the intent to update a record, no one else can be allowed to access the record. If another program tries to obtain the record being locked, it goes into a wait state until the program that locked the record takes a SYNCPOINT. This process prevents one program from losing a change made to a record by another record.

Remember that the reason you are developing online systems is because many people are processing the same transactions or different transactions and using the same files at the same time. When multiple transactions want the same record at the same time in an update application, they must single thread through the access and subsequent update of the file.

The programs should process within one or two seconds. They must get the message, process the message, send the response back, and get out. The shorter the amount time during which locks are held, the faster the response time is. A large number of transactions can be processed at the same time if the designers of the system know what they are doing and design the system accordingly.

You would not want to know the number of online systems or client/server systems that failed because they were not designed for a large number of users trying to access and update the same information at the same time.

Rewriting a Record

After a record is read for update by the program issuing a CICS READ command using the UPDATE option, the record can be replaced with a REWRITE command. You move the changed information to the VSAM-RECORD layout in WORKING-STORAGE and issue the REWRITE command. An example follows:

```
EXEC CICS REWRITE
          FILE        ('FILENAME')
          FROM        (VSAM-RECORD)
          LENGTH      (LENGTH OF VSAM-RECORD)
          RESP        (WS-RESPONSE)
          END-EXEC.

    EVALUATE TRUE
        WHEN WS-RESPONSE = DFHRESP(NORMAL)
            PERFORM 3000-PROCESS-RECORD
        WHEN OTHER
            PERFORM 9000-STANDARD-ERROR
    END-EVALUATE
```

Adding and Deleting Records

You use the WRITE command to add a new record to a file owned by CICS. You format the VSAM-RECORD in WORKING-STORAGE and issue the CICS WRITE command to add the record.

You use the DELETE command to delete an existing record from a file owned by CICS. You either issue the CICS DELETE command after reading the record for update first or issue the CICS DELETE command without first reading the record.

In both cases, you use the same parameters you use in the CICS READ and REWRITE commands.

Browsing Files

CICS also supports reading files sequentially. The sequential reading of files in a CICS program is called *browsing*. The CICS browsing commands follow:

- STARTBR
- READNEXT
- READPREV
- RESETBR
- ENDBR

The CICS STARTBR command is similar to the READ command, except the purpose of the browse command is to obtain a position before a set of records in sequence that you want to read in a sequential fashion. The STARTBR command does not retrieve a record; it simply obtains the position that will be used by a CICS READNEXT or a CICS READPREV command.

You use the CICS READNEXT command to read the next record. The first READNEXT command after a STARTBR command retrieves the record that the STARTBR command positioned. The next READNEXT command retrieves the next record in sequence. You use READPREV to read backward and READNEXT to read forward.

Use ENDBR to end a browse, and use RESETBR to end the current browse and start another browse.

Database Support

CICS is IBM's general-purpose transaction processor. CICS is used by most large corporations throughout the world. Suppose that you are a database vendor and you want to increase the market size for your database product. You would develop an interface between your database product and CICS. That is exactly what many database vendors did. As a result, most major database vendors in the mainframe world are accessible from CICS programs.

IMS

Information Management System (IMS) from IBM is IBM's other transaction processor. IMS comes in multiple versions. One version is IMS DC, which is the transaction-processing part of IMS. The other version of IMS is IMS DB.

IMS DB is a major database management system used by many of the world's largest corporations. IBM has built an interface for IMS DB into CICS. Another name for IMS DB is DL/1.

DB2

DB2 is IBM's relational database product. DB2 contains a family of products like CICS and runs on multiple platforms. Versions of DB2 follow:

- DB2 for MVS/ESA
- DB2 for AS/400
- DB2 Universal Server

DB2 was one of the earliest relational database products. It is a set-of-records processor instead of a record processor like VSAM and IMS databases.

You tell DB2 what records you want to deal with, and it deals with that set of records for you. You tell it which set of records to process but not how to obtain the records for you. You have to tell VSAM and IMS DB not only what record you want, but you also have to specify how to access the record.

Relational database technology is a large step forward in database technology.

Other CICS Facilities

Several other CICS facilities deserve mentioning:

- Temporary storage
- Transient data
- Interval control

This section describes these facilities.

Temporary Storage Queues

Temporary storage is exactly what it sounds like: It is a temporary place for a COBOL program to store data for later processing. Temporary storage often is used as a *scratch-pad area* (SPA) or as a temporary place to queue up items.

An SPA is like a note pad. When you are having a meeting with someone, you take notes. When the meeting is over, you place the note pad in a drawer for later retrieval. When you and that person have another meeting, you retrieve the note pad, refer to it during the meeting, update it as appropriate, and return it its storage place. At some point, you throw away the notes because the meeting topic is complete.

Temporary storage is also used as a queue. The CICS COBOL program can queue up records for later processing. After the records are queued, the same program or a different program can retrieve the records from a *temporary storage* (TS) queue. After a temporary storage queue is created, it is retained by CICS until you delete it or until CICS does a cold start.

Temporary storage queues are dynamic. They consist of items. When you write a record to a TS queue, the queue is created if it does not exist, and item 1 is written to the queue. If the queue does exist, the item count is increased by 1, and that item is written to the queue. When you delete the queue, the queue and its contents are deleted. An item in the queue can be read more than once by the same program or different programs.

An example of a TS queue being used both as an SPA and as a queue is an order-processing application. Suppose that you are taking an order over the phone or the Internet. When an item of an order is entered, it has to be stored somewhere before it can be processed in its entirety. Each time an item is entered, it is stored as an item in a TS queue. Each item of the order has to be handled on its own and processed all the way through or not at all.

The order is the same way. The order cannot be processed in full, with the inventory removed and the items shipped, until the complete order is entered and the buyer confirms that the order should be sent. When the order is complete, each item is read from the TS queue that contains the items, deducted from inventory, and sent on its way.

The temporary storage commands follow:

- `WRITEQ TS`
- `READQ TS`
- `DELETEQ TS`

Transient Data Queues

Transient data is another method of creating queues of items in CICS. Two types of transient data queues exist:

- Intrapartition queues
- Extrapartition queues

Intrapartition queues are queues that are processed inside CICS. They are used for *automatic task initiation* (ATI). ATI is how one program, by writing a record to a queue, can cause another program to execute. Some people call this *background message processing;* others call it *message switching.*

The primary reason to use ATI is to write something to a TD queue, notify the user at the terminal that the job is done, and then terminate. The user thinks the job is done and does not have to wait until the job is actually done. However, in most cases, the record written to the TD queue causes another program to execute. The program reads the message from the TD queue, processes the message, and terminates. In many cases, the background job is done when the user gets the response that the job is done. If it isn't, it will probably complete shortly and will not cause a problem.

Another use of ATI is when you want to write something to an online printer, but you do not want the user's terminal to hang up waiting for a response because the printer is out of paper or turned off. In this case, the TD queue being written to is associated with a printer. If the printer is not available when the record is written to the TS queue, the record is held in the queue until the printer is ready. When the printer is ready, a program is invoked to read the queue, print the record, and terminate.

In the first case, a trigger level is associated with a queue. When the number of records in the queue reaches the trigger level, a transaction is triggered to process the record(s) in the queue. After a record is processed successfully, the record in the queue is deleted.

Extrapartition TD queues are the sequential file-processing facility of CICS. Extrapartition queues are input sequential files or output sequential files. You can issue transient data READ and WRITE commands to read the files.

The CICS transient data commands follow:

- WRITEQ TD
- READQ TD
- DELETEQ TD

Figure 23.8 shows program A writing a record to a TD queue named Orders. When the number of records in the queue reaches the trigger level, the transaction pointed to by the queue is activated. It reads the queue, processes the record, and terminates. After the transaction processes successfully, the record in the TD queue is deleted.

Interval (Time) Control

The Interval Control is the facility of CICS that enables you to do things based on time. You can START another task (program) based on time, for example. You can cause the program to execute right now, in x amount of time, or at a specific time. You can start the program now, in 10 minutes, or at 1400 hours.

FIGURE 23.8.

Transient data.

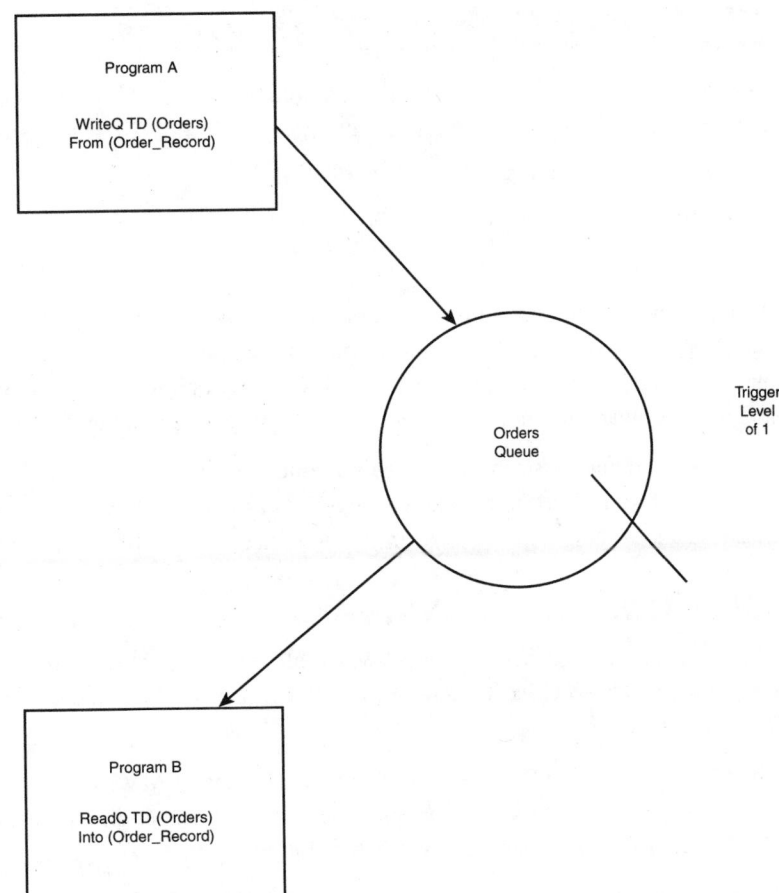

The START command is an Interval Control command. You use START to begin another program on the local CICS system or on a remote CICS system. You simply issue the following CICS command:

```
EXEC CICS START
          TRANSID    ('A133')
          END-EXEC.
```

This CICS command executes the CICS program associated with transaction code A133. The program executes on a local or remote CICS system. The local or remote system being executed on is based on the parameters of the command or the parameters in the PPT table for the program being executed.

The power and simplicity of CICS continue to amaze me.

CICS on Other Platforms

CICS not only processes on mainframe computers—it also processes on Windows NT and OS/2. The following products execute in a Windows NT or OS/2 environment:

- CICS Transaction Server from IBM
- The CICS Option from Micro Focus
- UniKix

Application development and application maintenance are the real costs of using computers. People who build applications that run only on one operating system or on only one hardware system are making a major mistake, in my opinion. They have tied themselves and their company to one vendor and are at the mercy of that vendor.

It makes good business sense to develop applications using standard APIs and standard languages. Using COBOL as a language, CICS as a transaction processor, and SQL as a database access language keeps open the options of your applications and your company.

CICS Transaction Server

The CICS Transaction Server from IBM enables you to create a distributed client/server environment. The CICS Transaction Processor from IBM is included in the CICS Transaction Series.

The CICS Transaction Server enables you to extend your MVS/ESA or VSE/ESA CICS systems across the Enterprise. You have the power and capability to develop a COBOL CICS DB2 application and deploy it across the Enterprise.

With the advent of the CICS Transaction Server and the Universal Database, you are no longer constrained to the mainframe. You can build the application the way it should be built and implement it the way it should be implemented.

Micro Focus COBOL—The CICS Option

The CICS option of Micro Focus COBOL is a product that enables you to develop and execute COBOL CICS programs on PCs running Windows NT.

You can develop the resulting application programs using Micro Focus COBOL on Windows NT. VSAM files and DB2 relational databases are supported. The Micro-Focus Animator is the best debugging tool I have used for COBOL programs. IMS DB databases are also supported using the IMS option.

Micro Focus products enable you to develop COBOL CICS DB2 applications on the PC and then deploy them where you want.

UniKix

UniKix is a transaction-processing monitor. It supports the CICS API and runs on UNIX and Windows NT systems.

Application systems built using COBOL and the CICS API are supported by UniKix. VSAM files and DB2 databases are also supported. Application programs written using COBOL, CICS, and SQL can run on UniKix.

UniKix can be used as a development environment or as a production environment.

UniKix enables you to develop COBOL CICS DB2 applications in UNIX and deploy them where you want.

Summary

CICS is a transaction processor from IBM. CICS command-level programming and COBOL programming go hand in hand. They are based on the English language. Relative to other programming languages, they are easy to read and maintain.

COBOL CICS programs are designed to process transactions in an online environment. In this environment, many people are processing the same transactions that access and update the same file or database at the same time. Short and quick transactions are the rule. CICS can operate in a centralized or distributed environment; it achieves the same results. You write CICS commands and do not need to know where the programs and files or databases actually reside. Data integrity is ensured as long as you design the applications properly.

COBOL CICS DB2 programs are a natural fit with each other. You can design and code COBOL CICS DB2 programs using CICS standards and ANSI COBOL and ANSI DB2 standards, and the program will execute on all supported programs the same way and achieve the same results.

Today, for the first time, application developers can build applications the way they are meant to be built. You do not have to put the application on the mainframe. You do not have to put it on the PC. You can build it the way it should be built and implement it the way it should be implemented.

If you were building a new application today, you could say that a third of it belongs on the desktop, a third of it belongs on a centralized processor like a mainframe, and you might have to even think about the other third.

COBOL CICS programs not only execute in the distributed environment of today—they do it well. In today's world, COBOL and CICS programs function very well together.

Client/Server
Transaction
Interface

CHAPTER 24

This chapter introduces client/server programming as it relates to the COBOL language, as well as *Open Database Connectivity* (ODBC)—the database connectivity standard from Microsoft.

Later in this chapter you will take a look at an example of a simple COBOL program that accesses an ODBC database. You then will review the individual ODBC calls in the program and other available COBOL options.

What Is Client/Server Computing?

Client/server, as the name implies, is a programming environment in which the program logic is split between a client program and a server program. When running in the production environment, these programs normally execute on different computers connected across a network. Client/server programs are often initially tested and developed on a single computer to make the programming task easier.

Client/server applications sometimes are called *distributed* or *networked* systems because in almost all cases, they execute across a computer network. However, the terms *client* and *server* are still used to refer to the individual programs that make up the application regardless of where the programs execute. Put simply, the *client* program contains the client logic or statements that display and accept screen data, and the *server* program contains the database logic. *Client computers* traditionally have been personal computers running Microsoft Windows or IBM OS/2 but today also include Internet- or intranet-connected PCs running Web browsers (such as Netscape and Internet Explorer). This setup provides substantial opportunities for increases in client/server computing in the future.

In the client/server computing paradigm, it is important to consider the design of the program more carefully than with traditional development. When writing COBOL programs, it usually is not necessary to consider where logic is placed; even a structured COBOL program can mix the various functions within the same section or paragraph. For example, a simple program involves input, process, and output, and a good programmer ensures that these processes are logically separate in the program. This formal style of programming makes it easier to fix or maintain the program even if the task is completed by another programmer. Today it is even more important to keep the individual parts of the program separate, because the program could later be converted to a client/server architecture or migrated to a different operating system altogether.

In the traditional online terminal program, there are three basic parts to the program: the user interface, business rules, and database access. Generally you should be able to determine in which of these three groups each programming statement belongs. Database or file logic can easily be identified, as well as logic that communicates with the end user via the terminal. The remaining logic, which is harder to define, is termed *business rules*. This logic usually consists of calculations and algorithms of one sort or another that are important to the business.

In the client/server environment, the user interface logic obviously must be placed within the client program, and the database logic must be placed in the server program. The business rules can be specified in either program or split between both. The result of this placement of business rules identifies the client program as a *thin* or *thick* client. Originally most client programs were thick clients, because almost all logic was placed on the client computer. More recently, interest has been in thin client computing, where most logic now is placed on the server.

The final type of logic specific to client/server computing is the logic that permits the client and server program to talk to each other. This is the communications logic. Although you could write this yourself to the TCP/IP, SNA, or other communications protocol, it is normal to use a higher level *Application Programming Interface* (API) called *middleware*.

Middleware is the network glue and may be provided by a database vendor, supplied with a transactional system such as IBM CICS, or sold as a separate product. There are many examples of middleware products, but one of the best known is MQ/Series from IBM, which connects computers of all types with a simple programming interface.

Client/Server Benefits

Although client/server applications can be more complex to develop, they do provide many benefits. Debugging client/server applications can be difficult, however, depending on the development tool being used.

Client/server applications should be easier to maintain than traditional applications because of the split in the program logic described earlier. Also, the server program can encapsulate the database(s) accessed from within the program, which then becomes the single point of connection to the database—no other programs can access the database without invoking the server program. The server program then insulates client programs from future changes in the database.

Thin client applications can be downloaded from a server computer rather than stored on the client computer's hard disk. This makes the applications easier to maintain and distribute and reduces personal computer purchase and support costs. Although ODBC applications usually are thick client, stored procedures can reduce the amount of logic found on the client (stored procedures are discussed later in this chapter in "Types of ODBC Programs"). Client/server programming can involve the use of objects or components. The idea is that the client program or process communicates with objects or components that provide a service to the client, such as database lookup. Microsoft's ActiveX components, for example, provide a standard interface for clients that want to communicate with components that follow the Microsoft *Component Object Model* (COM) and *Distributed Component Object Model* (DCOM). The *Object Management Group* (OMG), which consists of several computer organizations (notably, IBM) has introduced *Common Object Request Broker Architecture* (CORBA), which is an architecture that defines the interoperability between components.

Client/Server History

Client/server probably gets its name from using personal computers on a *Local Area Network* (LAN). The PC had to run "client" software supplied by a network vendor such as Novell to access data held on the server computer. This provided services such as data sharing and network printing. The client software running on each PC connected the PC to the network using a network protocol such as TCP/IP or Novell IPX.

The basic principle of client/server computing goes back much further, however, even if the technology wasn't known by this name. Twenty years ago it wasn't uncommon for large organizations to use a minicomputer (a nonmainframe computer such as a DEC, NCR, or Tandem) to provide local computing services to a group of related computer terminals. If data or processing capability was needed from the mainframe computer, the minicomputer passed the user request to the mainframe computer, often unknown to the end user. An example is a bank in which several branches are connected to an area office, which in turn is connected to the head office mainframe computer. Another example is the first point-of-sale terminals in supermarkets, which normally would not be connected directly to the mainframe computer.

This sort of client/server (or master-to-slave) relationship has really been present in one form or another for some time. The concept is that the client computer requests the services of the server computer as they are needed, but the client program is in control and always makes the requests and the server program always responds. If the service required by the end user can be processed locally, this saves time and server processing cycles.

COBOL and Client/Server Computing

COBOL is a latecomer to modern client/server computing, although it is rapidly catching up. Still today, however, job advertisements appear for COBOL programmers or client/server programmers—rarely "COBOL client/server" programmers. Many people think of PC products such as Microsoft Visual Basic, Borland Delphi, and Sybase

PowerBuilder when talking about client/server computing, but all these products place the emphasis on the client with no real server program capability provided and therefore are not truly client/server even if they do support ODBC databases.

Larger-scale or enterprise client/server computing considers the client to be the tip of the iceberg, because most of the business processes and data are hidden away and locked up in a UNIX or mainframe computer room. This is the area where COBOL has always been the dominant language, and the new client/server tools should increase its use across the complete enterprise. There are many benefits in using the same programming language (and programmers) for both client and server development; it enables the code and subroutines to be moved between the client and server program, thus optimizing system performance. Having the same programmers working on the complete development also helps to reduce the specification complexity of the project. This capability to reposition logic between client and server programs is called *application partitioning.*

One of the reasons for COBOL being late in the client/server development world is probably because of its lack of availability and visibility on the PC. For many years, COBOL compilers and tools were much more expensive than the C, Basic, or Pascal equivalents; this led to COBOL being used in a minority of PC applications while being dominant in other areas. Microsoft's Visual Basic (and other products) makes it so easy to write impressive-looking Windows programs that it is wrongly assumed that this also applies to building complete client/server applications.

The client program is just a small part of the total application, however. Tools must be provided to build server programs as well as to connect the client and server programs together. Like many COBOL programmers, I am pleased to say that this situation is changing with the availability of COBOL across the complete programming enterprise.

Many COBOL compilers and tools now are available at a low cost for PC and Windows development, and some provide real client/server and networking capability. More advanced COBOL tools provide higher levels of productivity; simplify Windows development of the client programs; and assist with communications, server-program functionality, and database-access functionality.

You can find a fairly complete list of COBOL software compilers and tools at

```
http://www.infogoal.com/cbd/cbdtol.htm
```

GUI Client/Server Systems

As you learned earlier in this chapter, like most computer technologies, client/server is not really new. One of the main reasons for its popularity is the availability and desire for *graphical user interfaces* (GUIs) and the proliferation of computer networks.

Old black-and-white (green-screen) terminals, even with color capability, could never compete with a well-designed graphical interface. IBM did provide graphics terminals many years ago, but the response time was slow, mainly because of limited processing power and low network speeds. GUI screens did not become a reality until Apple, Microsoft Windows, and IBM OS/2 appeared on the scene. Mainframe terminals were slowly replaced by PCs pretending to be mainframe terminals by running "emulation" software. Even then, personal computers running mainframe applications still looked just like the old terminals. Users could run PC applications at the same time as these text-based applications, of course, but the mainframe and PC systems remained firmly separate for some time, and this situation continues today.

The obvious interest to end users was to link these powerful interfaces with the back-office systems already in place on mainframe and UNIX computers running a line of business applications. First a technique called *screen scraping* promised a quick fix. COBOL tools from companies like Micro Focus were among the first to offer this new solution, which became popular for a time.

Screen-scraping tools broadly allowed GUIs to mainframe systems without altering the original system on the mainframe. This functionality was achieved by writing a PC program, often using a scripting language, to provide a GUI that used exactly the same connection to the original mainframe system. These products, although more sophisticated, are still around today. Is this client/server computing? Well, possibly if the new "client" program provides some programming functionality such as providing comprehensive help facilities or providing local validation or reformatting of user data. It generally is believed that true client/server systems require a different design style and that to gain the full benefits of this type of application development, it is necessary to redesign the system. Of course, using COBOL client/server tools *will* allow the reuse of all the business rules, reducing the effort significantly.

Another, more complex, technique for turning traditional systems into client/server systems is to provide a *wrapper* around the original program. A wrapper basically provides a new interface to the original program that allows the program to be used in a sort of server mode. This technique requires more programmer or designer effort because it is necessary to fully understand the inputs and outputs of the original program and the interrelationships between those programs, even if the internal logic does have to be understood. Still, it does mean that the original programs are reused without having to develop the systems from scratch, but maintenance of the original programs could become a nightmare. Some programmers call it plastic surgery—providing cosmetic but not business process improvements.

Early systems developed explicitly for client/server computing were very simple and are still being developed today and run in company departments all over the world. Whether these systems can be described as client/server is open to debate, because often no real server programming is involved. These systems are called *two-tier client/server* because the program runs on a PC (the client), with the database and data running on the server computer. When writing the database part of the program, the programmer uses non-COBOL special statements in the program to read and write data held in the remote database. It is the responsibility of the database vendor (Oracle, SQL Server, DB2, and so on) to provide both the database software and the connection to the client program, often through the use of a precompiler to convert these proprietary statements to COBOL calls. The precompiler (or preprocessor) comments the proprietary statements and replaces them with COBOL calls to routines provided by the vendor.

The ODBC standard mentioned earlier and covered in some detail later in this chapter is the principal published interface for connecting programs to databases and was conceived and provided by Microsoft. Other interfaces are proprietary to the database vendor.

How Many Tiers?

Client/server systems include two-tier, as mentioned earlier, three-tier, or even *n*-tier applications. Each *tier* refers to a computer platform where part of the application logic executes. Although terms differ, usually *two-tier client/server* refers to an application where the database software and data are placed on a server platform (database server), and the client platform contains the logic that interacts with the user along with the business rules. The *business rules* are the part of your program that is not concerned with communicating with the user, accessing data in a database, or communicating with another program. Business rules sometimes are described as the "added value" that differentiates computer systems from competing companies. An example is an algorithm used to calculate an insurance quotation.

In client/server programming, the logic sometimes is split across three or more platforms and includes systems that use a transaction monitor, such as IBM CICS. The middle tier is often some form of "gateway" computer or "application server" that links the client and server computers to provide translation between differing network protocols or to handle performance or security issues. Windows NT often is used to fulfill this requirement and is called a *mid-tier server*. Sometimes local data is downloaded to a database on the mid-tier server at the start of daily processing and then is used as read-only data during the day.

Two-tier client/server programs are typically database applications where all the client processing relates to handling the user interface and the business rules. The data and the database software are placed on a server computer usually on the LAN. In the client program, COBOL calls or non-COBOL statements are used to access the remote database. ODBC is an example of a two-tier client/server and is a database standard that can be used with almost all databases. Other proprietary interfaces are available for specific databases, such as DB2, Oracle, and Sybase.

An alternative technique used in some compilers, such as AcuCorp (formally AcuCobol), is to extend the use of the standard READ/WRITE COBOL statements to enable manipulation of data held in remote databases and file systems not normally available to a COBOL program. This provides a simple if proprietary solution to accessing remote databases in COBOL.

Finally, because *Structured Query Language* (SQL) is the de facto standard for accessing databases, some database precompilers or compilers allow you to type standard SQL (embedded SQL or ESQL) into your client program, which then is converted to ODBC calls or proprietary database calls. Two examples are the Fujitsu and Micro Focus compilers, which convert standard ESQL statements to ODBC calls during the compile process, thus simplifying the specification of the database access logic.

Where Is the Data?

Client/server programs provide data-access or data-manipulation facilities to an end user. In the simplest systems, data exists under the control of a database installed on your local hard drive or LAN server. However, in the most complex systems, the users need access to data stored in several computer systems involving different hardware, operating systems, and database architectures. This is called *heterogeneous data;* I mention it because the requirement for accessing heterogeneous data is becoming more common as a result of company mergers or takeovers.

It therefore is not always possible to place the server program and the data on the same computer. DB2, the original relational database from IBM, provides sophisticated facilities to allow the update of data held in many computers from a single point of access. As a programmer, you should not have to worry about this problem; you can rely on databases and/or middleware.

The RPC Call—An Example

The basic request from a client program to a server program is typically a *remote procedure call* (RPC). With an RPC, the client program requests that a procedure be executed on the server platform.

When the RPC is issued, it causes the server program to execute on the remote platform. It is the responsibility of the middleware to perform this scheduling. The server program must have been written specifically to provide a service such as passing back an account balance for a customer bank account. The client program should tell the server program the account number, and the server program should pass back the current balance or other information if the account number is wrong or the account has been closed.

The message exchanged between the client program and the server program as part of the RPC call is just a list of COBOL variables or often a COBOL structure or array. Here is an example:

```
01  CLIENT-SERVER-MESSAGE.
    03 HEADER-SECTION.
        05  CLIENT-COMPUTER-NAME     PIC X(25).
        05  CLIENT-USERID            PIC X(8).
        05  CLIENT-PASSWORD          PIC X(8).
        05  CLIENT-PROGRAM-NAME      PIC X(8).
        05  SERVER-PROGRAM-NAME      PIC X(8).
        05  SERVER-ERROR-CODE        PIC X(4).
        05  USER-SECTION-LENGTH      PIC 9(4) COMP-5.
    03 USER-SECTION.
        05  ACCOUNT-NUMBER           PIC 9(12).
        05  ACCOUNT-BALANCE          PIC S9(6)V99 COMP-5.
```

In this example, the first part of the message passed between the client and server programs could be included in all messages as a standard header that all client programs and server programs expect. The second part of the message varies, depending on the function provided by the server program and could have "occurs" values for multiple data, such as when requesting a list of overdrawn accounts.

If you think that this all sounds a bit familiar, that's because you probably have been writing this style of program for some time or perhaps reading about it in this book—calling subroutines in COBOL. You name the parameters in the call, then make sure that you define the *same* parameters in the LINKAGE SECTION of the subroutine, and list them in the PROCEDURE DIVISION USING statement making sure that they are in the *correct* order.

The client program would have the structure defined in the WORKING-STORAGE section and the following call:

```
CALL "SERVER1" USING CLIENT-SERVER-MESSAGE

IF SERVER-ERROR-CODE NOT = 0
   DISPLAY "Error occurred in SERVER1"
ELSE
   DISPLAY "The balance is" ACCOUNT-BALANCE
END-IF
```

The server program running as a subroutine would have this structure defined in the LINKAGE section with the following PROCEDURE DIVISION statement:

```
PROCEDURE DIVISION USING CLIENT-SERVER-MESSAGE
```

24

CLIENT/SERVER TRANSACTION INTERFACE

Using one variable has its benefits: You cannot get the variables crossed over between the main program and subroutine. (Fixing this problem wastes a lot of time for COBOL programmers.)

Passing information between client and server programs is almost the same technique, and it is obviously a good idea to use the same COBOL COPY statement in both programs to make sure that the messages match. It is also possible to test COBOL client/server programs in this way and then add the middleware statements later and test across a network. Can you see why client/server programming is easier when all the programs are written in the same language?

> **NOTE**
>
> When you call a subroutine, you pass a list of addresses. In client/server computing, you do not pass the address of the data because the server program could be running on a different computer. Also be aware that although most computers store data using ASCII representation, computers such as IBM mainframes and AS/400 computers use the EBCDIC character representation. When connecting dissimilar computers, it is the responsibility of the middleware to dynamically translate the data. This can be difficult when the data consists of a mixture of character and binary numeric data.

Synchronous or Asynchronous RPC Calls

Some middleware—such as the CICS *External Call Interface* or ECI (the latest releases of IBM CICS include the ECI middleware)—allows for synchronous and nonsynchronous calls to server programs. In the examples you have seen so far, you expect the client to wait until the call to the server program returns. This can be somewhat frustrating for the Windows end user, because the "busy" icon could appear for several seconds.

When using asynchronous processing, as soon as the server call parameters are validated, control is returned to the client computer, which then can continue with other processing. Later, when the server program returns the data, a special Windows message is sent to the client program that causes an event to be executed. If the client program is waiting for this event, processing now can take place to display the data onscreen.

Consider a motor insurance application. You can have an onscreen form with many questions for the customer to answer. In the client application, it might be necessary to link to two remote computers to get enough data to provide the quotation for insuring the car. In the synchronous example, the user answers all the questions, and the client program then calls the first server program. When the response returns from the first server program, it can call the second server program. Finally, when all the data or responses have been returned, it can calculate the premium. Not very user-friendly!

In the asynchronous example, the client program continually checks which fields have been entered. As soon as enough data is received, one or more of the server programs is called asynchronously while the user is still completing the form. Finally, when all the server programs have responded, a premium is displayed. Of course, a good program designer will place the questions on the form in such an order that the server can be called as early as possible.

Obviously the asynchronous example is considerably more sophisticated and powerful. Depending on the program design, the end user still can do useful tasks within the application while waiting for the server response. Therefore, this is a much smoother user interface.

Not all middleware supports asynchronous calls, and if this capability is not provided, multiple thread capability may be needed in the client program to achieve this behavior. This is again subject to the middleware providing multithread access. Not all COBOL compilers (or ODBC drivers) support multithreading.

> **NOTE**
>
> It is more complicated to program a Windows client program that connects a single client to multiple server programs asynchronously. Casegen COBOL for Distributed CICS, a COBOL software tool, supports this advanced functionality using simple screen controls and COBOL event logic.

Client/Server Performance

One reason why client/server projects have not always been successful is because of poor performance in the completed project when a full load is placed on the system or as a result of increased volume over time. Certain client/server architectures can never support high volumes or large numbers of concurrent users because of defects in the design of the system or because the capabilities of the chosen architecture have been exceeded.

The capability of a client/server application to grow while still giving good response times to its end users is called its *scaleability*. For example, building a client/server system to read a small database by a few client computers should not be a problem for any database or client/server tool. However, trying to run the same application with 1,000 users and adding database update capability using a simple PC database product on a LAN obviously is not going to work very well.

If an increase in use is planned or suspected, you must consider the scaleability of the chosen solution. COBOL is very strong in this area because of its capability to run on almost all platforms and should be chosen with a database, development tools, and middleware that can be migrated from the smallest server to the largest mainframe computer.

Some of the main limitations to performance in a high-volume system follow:

- **Poor database design:** In any multiuser system where data is updated in a database, a full understanding of how locking occurs in the chosen database is needed. This is a complex subject and requires an experienced database designer.

- **Exceeding database software capability:** Databases vary. You need to pick a high-performance database if response time is important and many concurrent clients are attached now or are planned in the future. (Some specialized databases give very impressive performances, but only for read-only processing.)

- **Excessive network traffic:** This is a common problem with client/server systems that is often overlooked when using ODBC or PC programming tools. It is very important that the programmer be able to control the size and number of messages exchanged between the client and server computer. A basic problem with most ODBC and proprietary two-tier client/server systems is that every database call is sent across the network. Consider a client/server application that is used in a car dealership to process credit requests for car purchases. The application needs to seek a lot of information from the potential client and then access many databases to establish the client's credit rating. This could be as many as 20 to 30 database calls. In a true client/server system, where a server program exists, the client data is sent to the server program, which then executes all the calls—sending a yes or no response to the client program. Obviously, the second alternative is a better solution with less network traffic. Stored procedures were introduced to solve this problem in two-tier implementations. (You will learn about stored procedures in "Types of ODBC Programs," later in this chapter.)

- **Slow client performance:** Another misconception is the assumption that the client PC has a great deal of spare CPU and memory and therefore will execute the client program without any response-time delays. Before you start blaming the server for poor performance, try running the client program with test data inside the program and the middleware or ODBC calls commented. If this provides an inadequate response time, imagine the performance when waiting for the server to respond. Windows 95 and NT applications can soak up a lot of power, especially if the client program is poorly designed or using the wrong tools. If you require extensive validation with many graphics onscreen and/or whole screen refresh, you need to use a fast development tool executing native code, not a 4GL or RAD tool that uses interpretive code. COBOL is a good choice for fast performance at the client.

I recently had a COBOL client/server system in which each time data was typed into controls on the Windows screen, a 500-line COBOL subroutine was executed for *every* character typed. What was the performance like? Excellent, because the whole application was written in COBOL, and you could not even tell when it was executing the subroutine! The subroutine, by the way, was written for IBM mainframe use, but it worked just as well on the PC without any changes necessary.

- **Inadequate hardware:** Obviously it is important to ensure that both the client and server hardware are powerful enough. Watch out for great performance, but on the largest NT or UNIX box you can buy. What happens when the volumes increase?

Introduction to ODBC

The second part of this chapter describes *Open Database Connectivity* (ODBC)—the standard introduced by Microsoft that can be placed anywhere on the network to connect programs to databases.

The database can be relational or nonrelational, and even a simple text PC file can be connected. ODBC databases can exist on almost any personal computer, minicomputer, or mainframe. The format of the data, database platform, location, and network protocols are irrelevant to the programmer, who is concerned only with coding ODBC calls in the program. ODBC provides the interface (API) to the programmer that allows this independence.

ODBC is closely tied to SQL, which has become the main standard for accessing databases, whether or not they are relational. The concept of the relational model figures prominently in the design of the interface. The relational model uses tables made up of columns and rows and establishes relationships between tables where data values match for given columns. Anyone who has ever used a spreadsheet or a bus or train timetable should feel comfortable with this concept.

All the complexity of the network protocols or communications software needed to access the remote data is hidden from the programmer and is seen purely as a data source. A *data source* is an arbitrary name such as "Aircraft Division Payroll" that has some meaning to an end user. It is the responsibility of ODBC to be aware of the relationship between a data source and the location of the physical data, its network address, and its server location. This implementation of a data source is called a *driver* by ODBC, and the relationship is maintained in Windows in the Control Panel. Check for a 32bit

24

**CLIENT/SERVER
TRANSACTION
INTERFACE**

ODBC icon in the Control Panel on your Windows 95/98 or Windows NT PC, and check what data sources and drivers are installed. You can add new data sources and define which ODBC drivers they are connected to by using the 32bit ODBC dialog box.

For software houses writing applications for customers who use many different computer platforms, ODBC provides an important independence from their customers' chosen database. Prior to ODBC, programmers had to write versions of their software for every customer database and were forced to continually *port* (modify an application to work with different hardware/software) the application to new databases as they became available. With ODBC, the database logic should be standard for all databases, but minor differences in behavior have caused improvements or tightening of the ODBC standard and the introduction of different levels of conformance to the standard.

Although ODBC is not true client/server because of its inability to execute native server programs, certain facilities are available to partially compensate for this. These facilities include stored procedures, which are discussed in the next section.

The benefit of ODBC is that almost all databases support the standard, either through native facilities or third-party ODBC drivers from companies that bring ODBC capability to the database. The standard allows application developers to use ODBC calls in their programs without worrying about which database is being accessed and even where the database physically exists. It is not even necessary to recompile or link the application to use different database drivers for a given data source coded in the program.

ODBC has been criticized for its lack of performance, and therefore proprietary database access statements still exist that require a precompiler to convert the statements to COBOL calls. Also, as you will see in the sample COBOL ODBC program later in this chapter, the syntax is not particularly easy to understand and can be rather strange to COBOL programmers because it was designed for the C language. As the program shows, though, it is perfectly possible to write these applications, and several COBOL tools make the task less arduous.

ODBC also provides a very useful facility to enable tracing of ODBC calls during the execution of a program. In the Windows Control Panel, the 32bit ODBC dialog box has a tab page that allows tracing to be enabled for a given data source. This is a very useful and easy-to-use facility for debugging.

Finally, ODBC provides the facility for the application program to query an ODBC driver as to whether a particular feature of the ODBC API is supported by that driver. The program then can use the most efficient calls in the program while still supporting less-capable ODBC drivers. If DB2, for example, supports certain advanced SQL statements, they still can be used in an ODBC application. A less-capable database could use simpler, less efficient ODBC calls by using a different code path in the program.

Types of ODBC Programs

Three types of ODBC calls can be used in a program, although the first two are closely related. ODBC is a *Call Level Interface* (CLI) used to access a *Database Management System* (DBMS), so several ODBC calls are added to the COBOL program to enable database access to be performed.

The simplest type of ODBC access is ODBC initialization that is completed by issuing several calls and then connecting to the data source. Then ODBC calls are issued that refer to the complete SQL statement, which then is executed. This type of call, `SQLExecDirect`, is the simplest mechanism and is useful for a single SQL statement that is to be executed once in the program. `SQLExecDirect` can be used many times but does not give the best performance.

In the sample program shown later in this chapter, I chose the most complicated but more efficient Prepare/Execute model. This model uses a `SQLPrepare` statement to prepare the SQL call for execution and then the `SQLExecute` statement to physically perform the statement. This model performs better and should be used when the SQL statement is to be performed repeatedly in the program. Optimizing the SQL statement in the DBMS occurs only once for the `SQLPrepare` statement and not for every `SQLExecute` statement.

The third type of model is stored procedures, which were mentioned earlier in this chapter. Stored procedures provide (almost) true client/server functionality and two important performance advantages:

- Stored procedures allow several SQL statements, along with procedural logic, to be executed at the server platform. Stored procedures give maximum performance and decrease network traffic with reduced wait/schedule/load times.

- Stored procedures usually allow *static SQL* to be executed. Static SQL offers big performance improvements in the database calls because the SQL statements can be *bound* to the database. This means that database optimization can take place before the program executes. However, static SQL does lack some of the flexibility provided in the alternative, dynamic SQL, where the SQL statement can be constructed entirely at execution time. Dynamic SQL must be used by end user query products, which often are supplied by database vendors. These software tools allow you to type or automatically construct SQL statements and then immediately execute them.

ODBC in COBOL Programs

There are easier ways to connect and use ODBC databases. The Fujitsu and Microsoft compilers enable standard *embedded SQL* (ESQL) to be typed by the programmer into the source code, which then is converted to ODBC calls by a precompiler contained within the compiler. Look at Sample Program 10 provided with the Fujitsu compiler on the accompanying CD-ROM for an example.

The Casegen COBOL for Windows Professional, Fujitsu Power COBOL, and Micro Focus NetExpress products go one step further. As well as providing a visual Windows screen designer, they provide a wizard to assist in specifying the SQL.

Other compilers and tools may also provide assistance in simplifying the specification of SQL in your COBOL program.

ODBC Standards

Although ODBC provides a standard, different levels of conformity exist to that standard. A minimal level, for example, provides the most basic facilities, although some database vendors may have exceeded or anticipated the next standard. As a programmer, it is important that you make sure you are using standards generally available, especially if you expect full database independence in your program.

ODBC—Getting Started

I used SQL Anywhere Professional 5.0 with Fujitsu COBOL Compiler 4 to build and test the sample program in this chapter, although any 32-bit COBOL compiler and ODBC database should work.

If you follow the default installation for both products, no setup should be necessary; the program accesses the sample database provided with SQL Anywhere.

Connecting to a Database

In ODBC programs, the program connects to an ODBC data source, usually specifying a user ID and password. In Windows 95/98 and Windows NT, the Control Panel has a 32bit ODBC icon. The dialog box this icon presents describes the ODBC data sources and their associated drivers. You can also specify ODBC tracing using this facility to find out what is really happening when the program executes.

ODBC Programming Example

This example shows a relatively simple COBOL ODBC program accessing an ODBC database. I tested this program using Fujitsu COBOL and SQL Anywhere, although it should work with little change for any COBOL compiler or ODBC database.

If the example looks rather lengthy for a simple COBOL program, this is the cost of ODBC's independence. There are much easier ways to write ODBC programs with sophisticated COBOL tools, but this at least provides an independent COBOL example.

For simpler development of ODBC programs, look at the ODBC facilities provided in some of the compilers and tools. Fujitsu and Micro Focus enable you to type standard *embedded SQL* (ESQL), which then is converted to ODBC calls by the compiler. Casegen COBOL for Windows, Micro Focus NetExpress, and IBM Visual Age also provide a SQL Assistant facility to simplify SQL specification, as well as graphical screen design capabilities.

The sample program is shown in Listing 24.1, and you can find it on the accompanying CD-ROM as `ODBCSAMP.COB`.

Program Overview

The program initializes the ODBC environment and then connects to a data source and displays the name of the data source in the console window. You can type an ID number to find out the associated name. To quit the program, type -1.

The first line is specific to the Fujitsu compiler, telling it to maintain the mixed-case calls to subroutines. A similar specification may be necessary for other COBOL compilers.

ODBC Calls in the Sample Program

Table 24.1 lists the calls contained in the sample program.

TABLE 24.1 ODBC CALLS IN THE SAMPLE PROGRAM.

Call	Function
`SQLAllocEnv`	Allocates and reserves memory for an environment handle and initializes the ODBC Call Level Interface. There is only one environment per program.
`SQLAllocConnect`	Allocates memory for a connection handle. A program can have multiple connections.
`SQLConnect`	Establishes a connection to a data source and loads a driver. The name of the data source is passed as a string, along with its length, the user ID, the password, and the ID and password lengths.
`SQLAllocStmt`	Allocates memory for a SQL statement handle and associates it with a connection. Passes the connection handle and a reference to the statement and returns a handle.
`SQLPrepare`	Prepares a SQL statement for execution. Passes a handle to the statement and the SQL string (with a question mark (?) in place of any parameters). The ? is like a wildcard and is the variable data that will be supplied during statement execution.

continues

24

CLIENT/SERVER
TRANSACTION
INTERFACE

TABLE 24.1 CONTINUED

Call	Function
SQLBindParameter	Binds the COBOL variable(s) to the parameters in the pre-pared SQL statement.
SQLExecute	Executes the prepared statement using the current bound parameters. You could us SQLExecDirect for an unpre-pared statement.
SQLFetch	Fetch a row of data from a result set into ODBC.
SQLGetData	Gets each column value from the fetched row (one call for each column).
SQLError	Returns error or status information to the application program.
SQLFreeStmt	Stops processing for a specific statement handle and can free resources.
SQLDisconnect	Disconnects the connection for the data source with this handle.
SQLFreeConnect	Releases a conneciton handle and frees all memory associated.
SQLFreeEnv	Frees the environment handle and all memory associated.

You can find more information about ODBC calls in *ODBC Programmer's Reference and SDK Guide,* published by Microsoft Press (ISBN: 1-55615-658-8), or in other references.

LISTING 24.1 ODBCSAMP.COB LETS YOU QUERY THE SQL ANYWHERE SAMPLE DATABASE.

```
@OPTIONS NOALPHAL

IDENTIFICATION DIVISION.
PROGRAM-ID. ODBC-EXAMPLE.

DATA DIVISION.

WORKING-STORAGE SECTION.

* ODBC defined values
01 SQL-PARAM-INPUT          PIC S9(4) COMP-5 VALUE 1.
01 SQL-INTEGER              PIC S9(4) COMP-5 VALUE 4.
01 SQL-C-LONG               PIC S9(4) COMP-5 VALUE 4.

* ODBC handles
01 ODBC-HENV                PIC S9(9) COMP-5 VALUE 0.
```

```
01  ODBC-HDBC                       PIC S9(9) COMP-5 VALUE 0.
01  ODBC-HSTMT                      PIC S9(9) COMP-5 VALUE 0.

* ODBC return code
01  ODBC-RETCODE                    PIC S9(4) COMP-5 VALUE 0.

* ODBC error message
01  ODBC-ERRMSG                     PIC X(512).

* Connection information
01  DATA-SOURCE                     PIC X(23)
      VALUE "SQL Anywhere 5.0 Sample".
01  DATA-SOURCE-LEN                 PIC S9(4) COMP-5 VALUE 23.
01  USER-NAME                       PIC X(20) VALUE "dba".
01  USER-PASSWORD                   PIC X(20) VALUE "sql".

* Status flags - initially set to OK
01  CONNECTION-FLAG                 PIC 9 VALUE 1.
      88 CONNECTION-OK              VALUE 1.
      88 CONNECTION-FAILED          VALUE 0.
01  SQL-FLAG                        PIC 9 VALUE 1.
      88 SQL-OK                     VALUE 1.
      88 SQL-FAILED                 VALUE 0.

* The SQL statement to be executed
01  SQL-STATEMENT                   PIC X(40)
      VALUE "SELECT * FROM CONTACT WHERE ID = ?".
01  PARAM-LEN                       PIC S9(9) COMP-5.

* User input
01  ID-INPUT                        PIC S9(9) COMP-5.

* Data retrieval variables
01  COL-NO                          PIC S9(5) COMP-5.
01  DATA-LEN                        PIC S9(9) COMP-5.
01  DATA-IN                         PIC X(256).


PROCEDURE DIVISION.

MAIN SECTION.

PERFORM CONNECTION
    IF CONNECTION-OK
        DISPLAY "Connected to " WITH NO ADVANCING
        DISPLAY DATA-SOURCE
        PERFORM PREPARE-SQL
        IF SQL-OK
            DISPLAY "Enter ID number or -1 to Quit -> "
                WITH NO ADVANCING
```

continues

LISTING 24.1   CONTINUED

```
                ACCEPT ID-INPUT
                PERFORM UNTIL ID-INPUT = -1
                    PERFORM DO-QUERY
                    DISPLAY "-> " WITH NO ADVANCING
                    ACCEPT ID-INPUT
                END-PERFORM
            ELSE
                DISPLAY "SQL call set-up failed"
            END-IF
            PERFORM DISCONNECTION
        ELSE
            DISPLAY "Connection to data source failed"
        END-IF

        EXIT PROGRAM.

 ********************************************************************
 *           Initialize ODBC and connect to data source          *
 ********************************************************************
  CONNECTION SECTION.

 * Allocate environment handle
        MOVE 0 TO RETURN-CODE
        CALL "SQLAllocEnv" WITH STDCALL USING
            BY REFERENCE ODBC-HENV
        MOVE RETURN-CODE TO ODBC-RETCODE
        IF ODBC-RETCODE NOT = 0 AND NOT = 1
            DISPLAY "Cannot allocate environment handle"
            SET CONNECTION-FAILED TO TRUE
        END-IF
        IF NOT CONNECTION-FAILED
 * Allocate connection handle
            CALL "SQLAllocConnect" WITH STDCALL USING
                BY VALUE ODBC-HENV
                BY REFERENCE ODBC-HDBC
            MOVE RETURN-CODE TO ODBC-RETCODE
            IF ODBC-RETCODE NOT = 0 AND NOT = 1
                DISPLAY "Cannot allocate connection handle"
                CALL "SQLFreeEnv" WITH STDCALL USING
                    BY VALUE ODBC-HENV
                SET CONNECTION-FAILED TO TRUE
            END-IF
        END-IF
        IF NOT CONNECTION-FAILED
 * Connect to data source
            CALL "SQLConnect" WITH STDCALL USING
                BY VALUE ODBC-HDBC
                BY REFERENCE DATA-SOURCE
                BY VALUE DATA-SOURCE-LEN
```

```
                BY REFERENCE USER-NAME
                BY VALUE LENGTH OF USER-NAME
                BY REFERENCE USER-PASSWORD
                BY VALUE LENGTH OF USER-PASSWORD
            MOVE RETURN-CODE TO ODBC-RETCODE
            IF ODBC-RETCODE NOT = 0
                PERFORM DO-ERRMSG
                IF ODBC-RETCODE NOT = 1
                    SET CONNECTION-FAILED TO TRUE
                END-IF
            END-IF
        END-IF

        CONTINUE.

   ******************************************************************
   *         Disconnect from data source and free handles          *
   ******************************************************************
    DISCONNECTION SECTION.

        IF ODBC-HSTMT NOT = 0
   * Statement handle was allocated
            CALL "SQLFreeStmt" WITH STDCALL USING
                BY VALUE ODBC-HSTMT
                BY VALUE 1
        END-IF
        CALL "SQLDisconnect" WITH STDCALL USING
            BY VALUE ODBC-HDBC
        CALL "SQLFreeConnect" WITH STDCALL USING
            BY VALUE ODBC-HDBC
        CALL "SQLFreeEnv" WITH STDCALL USING
            BY VALUE ODBC-HENV

        CONTINUE.

   ******************************************************************
   *         Allocate statement handle and prepare SQL call         *
   ******************************************************************
    PREPARE-SQL SECTION.

   * Allocate statement handle
        CALL "SQLAllocStmt" WITH STDCALL USING
            BY VALUE ODBC-HDBC
            BY REFERENCE ODBC-HSTMT
        MOVE RETURN-CODE TO ODBC-RETCODE
        IF ODBC-RETCODE NOT = 0 AND NOT = 1
            DISPLAY "Cannot allocate statement handle"
            SET SQL-FAILED TO TRUE
        END-IF
        IF NOT SQL-FAILED
```

continues

LISTING 24.1 CONTINUED

```
* Prepare SQL statement
        CALL "SQLPrepare" WITH STDCALL USING
            BY VALUE ODBC-HSTMT
            BY REFERENCE SQL-STATEMENT
            BY VALUE LENGTH OF SQL-STATEMENT
        MOVE RETURN-CODE TO ODBC-RETCODE
        IF ODBC-RETCODE NOT = 0
            PERFORM DO-ERRMSG
            IF ODBC-RETCODE NOT = 1
                SET SQL-FAILED TO TRUE
            END-IF
        END-IF
    END-IF
    IF NOT SQL-FAILED
* Bind where clause parameter
        CALL "SQLBindParameter" WITH STDCALL USING
            BY VALUE ODBC-HSTMT
            BY VALUE 1
            BY VALUE SQL-PARAM-INPUT
            BY VALUE SQL-INTEGER
            BY VALUE SQL-C-LONG
            BY VALUE 0
            BY VALUE 0
            BY REFERENCE ID-INPUT
            BY VALUE 0
            BY REFERENCE PARAM-LEN
        MOVE RETURN-CODE TO ODBC-RETCODE
        IF ODBC-RETCODE NOT = 0
            PERFORM DO-ERRMSG
            IF ODBC-RETCODE NOT = 1
                SET SQL-FAILED TO TRUE
            END-IF
        END-IF
    END-IF

    CONTINUE.

*******************************************************************
*                      Execute the query                         *
*******************************************************************
 DO-QUERY SECTION.

* Execute the statement
    CALL "SQLExecute" WITH STDCALL USING
        BY VALUE ODBC-HSTMT
    MOVE RETURN-CODE TO ODBC-RETCODE
    IF ODBC-RETCODE NOT = 0
        PERFORM DO-ERRMSG
    END-IF
```

```
* If successfully executed, display result
IF ODBC-RETCODE = 0 OR 1
        CALL "SQLFetch" WITH STDCALL USING
            BY VALUE ODBC-HSTMT
        MOVE RETURN-CODE TO ODBC-RETCODE
        IF ODBC-RETCODE NOT = 0
            PERFORM DO-ERRMSG
        END-IF
        IF ODBC-RETCODE = 0 OR 1
* Display ID
            DISPLAY "   " WITH NO ADVANCING
            MOVE 1 TO COL-NO
            PERFORM GETDATA
* Display first name
            DISPLAY " Name: " WITH NO ADVANCING
            MOVE 3 TO COL-NO
            PERFORM GETDATA
* Display last name
            MOVE 2 TO COL-NO
            PERFORM GETDATA
            DISPLAY " "
        ELSE
            DISPLAY "  Record not found."
        END-IF
    END-IF
* Re-set the statement
    CALL "SQLFreeStmt" WITH STDCALL USING
        BY VALUE ODBC-HSTMT
        BY VALUE 0

    CONTINUE.


*******************************************************************
*                    Get and display a value                     *
*******************************************************************
 GETDATA SECTION.

    CALL "SQLGetData" WITH STDCALL USING
        BY VALUE ODBC-HSTMT
        BY VALUE COL-NO
        BY VALUE 1
        BY REFERENCE DATA-IN
        BY VALUE LENGTH OF DATA-IN
        BY REFERENCE DATA-LEN
    MOVE RETURN-CODE TO ODBC-RETCODE
    IF ODBC-RETCODE = 0 OR 1
        DISPLAY DATA-IN WITH NO ADVANCING
        DISPLAY " " WITH NO ADVANCING
        MOVE LOW-VALUES TO DATA-IN
    END-IF
```

24

CLIENT/SERVER
TRANSACTION
INTERFACE

continues

LISTING 24.1 CONTINUED

```
        CONTINUE.

******************************************************************
*                      Display error message                     *
******************************************************************
    DO-ERRMSG SECTION.

        EVALUATE ODBC-RETCODE
            WHEN 1
*   SQL_SUCCESS_WITH_INFO
                DISPLAY "ODBC Warning:"
            WHEN -1
*   SQL_ERROR
                DISPLAY "ODBC Error:"
        END-EVALUATE
*   If some other return value, there could still be a message
*   Get and display ODBC message
        CALL "SQLError" WITH STDCALL USING
            BY VALUE ODBC-HENV
            BY VALUE ODBC-HDBC
            BY VALUE ODBC-HSTMT
            BY VALUE 0
            BY VALUE 0
            BY REFERENCE ODBC-ERRMSG
            BY VALUE LENGTH OF ODBC-ERRMSG
            BY VALUE 0
        MOVE RETURN-CODE TO ODBC-RETCODE
        IF RETURN-CODE = 0 OR 1
            DISPLAY ODBC-ERRMSG
        END-IF

        CONTINUE.

    END PROGRAM ODBC-EXAMPLE.
```

Sample Output

Listing 24.2 shows the sample output at the Windows console after the program is executed.

LISTING 24.2 ODBCSAMP.COB SAMPLE OUTPUT.

```
Connected to SQL Anywhere 5.0 Sample
Enter ID number or -1 to Quit -> 1
1  Name: Jane Hildebrand
-> 2
2  Name: Larry Simmon
-> 11
```

```
11  Name: William Kelly
-> 100
Record not found
-> -1
```

COBOL Client/Server Products

This section presents a list of some COBOL client/server vendors and gives a short description of their products. Although I have used some of these tools, I must stress that this section is based on information provided by the respective vendors about products that currently are available and is by no means an exhaustive list. I therefore can take no responsibility for the accuracy of this information. The Web page at

`http:/www.infogoal.com/cbd/cbdtol.htm`

should contain a more complete list, or you can contact the vendors directly.

AcuCorp (Formally AcuCobol)

AcuCorp provides a COBOL compiler that executes on more than 600 platforms with COBOL syntax extensions to handle GUI development. AcuCorp also provides extensions to COBOL syntax to support access to many remote databases, as well as ESQL support for Oracle, Informix, and Sybase. Internet client capability exists through CGI/HTML functionality and native browser COBOL programs.

Casegen Systems

Casegen has developed COBOL client/server products for ODBC and many database and transactional environments such as DB2, CICS, and IMS; its products are designed for use by traditional COBOL programmers. Casegen supports the Windows 95/98 and Windows NT client environment through visual GUI specification and COBOL event logic. Support is provided for IBM CICS ECI and MQ/Series middleware as well as simple SQL specification. Generated client and server programs fully support recent COBOL standards.

Fujitsu

Fujitsu provides a COBOL compiler for many platforms, including Windows 95/98, Windows NT, and the Internet. The compiler converts embedded SQL in the program to ODBC calls and provides support for additional proprietary database connectivity. The Fujitsu Power COBOL product provides extensive GUI functionality for building both 16- and 32-bit Windows programs. Additionally, Fujitsu Form provides the capability to create graphical printed forms that can be formatted and printed from within COBOL programs.

IBM

IBM provides VisualAge COBOL, a 32-bit COBOL compiler with built-in *assistants*. These assistants simplify the specification of CICS ECI middleware calls (Transaction Assistant), SQL static calls and visual programming (Data Assistant), and the building of Windows or OS/2 graphical screens (GUI Assistant). VisualAge COBOL is available on all IBM platforms and facilitates program testing in a distributed client/server environment.

Liant Software Inc.

Liant provides RM COBOL, a COBOL compiler, with the Relativity product, which provides ODBC connections to many different database types and GUI form-building capability. VanGui, Liant's Internet product, provides the capability to build Internet clients.

Micro Focus Ltd.

Micro Focus provides the NetExpress product for both Windows and Internet client/server systems based on its original Visual Object COBOL compiler and Dialog System tools. It provides tools to develop and execute Internet applications as well as Windows clients. The ESQL Assistant simplifies SQL statements, which are converted to ODBC by the compiler. The Micro Focus AAI middleware is provided with the product.

Summary

The client/server programming environment, especially with the promise of Internet and intranet connectivity, will remain an important area of programming for the future. I have only been able to cover the subject material in this chapter at a high level, but many books have been written to cover this area in more depth.

COBOL Presentation Interfaces

PART
VI

CHAPTER 25

Character- and Screen-Based Interfaces

With the exception of certain specialized computer systems, such as embedded control systems, virtually all computers earn their keep by taking data input by human operators, processing the data, and then presenting the processed results in human readable form. In addition, programs often require direction on how to process data or format output. Moreover, programs often need to display runtime error or status messages for operator action or information. Printers are great for bulk hard copy output, but for communicating directly with a program, you need a more intimate interface. This chapter deals with the character-based interface, and Chapter 26, "Messages, Events, and GUI," deals with the *graphical user interface* (GUI). You'll start with the simplest interface mode—the line-based interface—and then look at the much more powerful screen-based interface.

Line Interface

Most programs must communicate directly with the operator or user. The text line–based interface is used for immediate, low-volume data—for example, entering runtime parameters such as a date range or the version of a report to print, displaying an error message, or interfacing with the operator to align preprinted forms in a line printer. This type of interface is very easy to program, and this section explains the COBOL statements and concepts you will need to program this type of simple but important operator interface.

The Operator Console

To make it simple for a program to communicate with the computer operator or user, the concept of *operator console* was created—an ideal device for this purpose. Support for the operator console was the first step in making computers interactive with the operator. Later, additional terminals were added so that multiple users could simultaneously access the expensive mainframe resources, bringing in the era of timesharing. Eventually, as computers became smaller and cheaper, the personal computer was born, bringing interactivity to its highest level to date. On mainframe computers, the console is usually a terminal, with a screen and keyboard. On personal computers, the console is usually a combination of a display device and a keyboard. COBOL and most other programming languages provide commands to interface with the operator console. In fact, the classic "Hello World" program has come to mean the standard minimal program in a given programming language.

COBOL provides the two statements ACCEPT and DISPLAY to communicate with the console. Logically enough, the ACCEPT statement is used to receive data entered from the console, and the DISPLAY statement is used to display data on the console. The basic forms of both statements are very simple, intuitive, and easy to use. You will examine each of these statements and then see how to use them together to solve a common real-world problem. ACCEPT and DISPLAY can be used for more than simple interfacing with the console, but in this section, you will be concerned only with the simple line-based console interface function of each statement. The more powerful forms of these commands are discussed in the section "Character-Based Screen Interface" later in this chapter.

The DISPLAY Statement

One DISPLAY statement can display one or more data fields or literals on the console. Data fields can be of the type DISPLAY or COMPUTATIONAL, numeric (unsigned integer only) or nonnumeric, and the DISPLAY statement will format them properly.

> **CAUTION**
>
> If you display a group item, be sure there are no COMPUTATIONAL items within it, or the results will be undefined and probably not what you want.

If only one field or literal is specified, it will be displayed on a line by itself, as shown here:

```
Display "Hello World!"
```

If more than one field is specified, the fields are displayed one after another in left-to-right order as they appear in the DISPLAY statement, with no intervening spaces or other extra characters. Look at this example:

```
03 RECORD-COUNT   PIC 9(6) COMP VALUE 123.
Display "Processed " RECORD-COUNT " records."
```

The DISPLAY statement would display Processed 000123 records. on the console. Note that a space is included after the word Processed and before the word records to separate those words from the digits of RECORD-COUNT.

> **TIP**
>
> If you want to display a negative or non-integer numeric field in edited form (for example, $9,999.99), first move the numeric field to an edited WORKING-STORAGE field and then display the edited field.

The ACCEPT Statement

The ACCEPT statement receives one input field from the console. The basic format of ACCEPT is simple:

```
03 MY-FIELD    PIC X(20).

Accept MY-FIELD.
```

The program will be suspended until the input is supplied by the operator. Input data is placed in the receiving field (MY-FIELD, in this example) from left to right. If the input is larger than the field size, the far right characters will be truncated. If the input is smaller than the field size, more data will be requested until the field is filled. Details of this process vary among compiler implementations, so check with your COBOL manual to verify how short input is handled.

CAUTION

You might need to initialize the receiving field before the ACCEPT statement. Not all compilers clear the field if no characters are input, and the field could still hold its previous contents after the ACCEPT.

In general, you should always ACCEPT data into a field of the type DISPLAY and then scan or edit the data into numeric or computational fields as needed. As with all human input, you should validate the data before using it. This is true especially for any field used in computation or subscripting.

COBOL 85, as updated in 1989, supports the functions NUMVAL and NUMVAL-C, which convert a number coded as a string into a numeric value. However, these functions, at least on some platforms, return a floating-point number for non-integers. This can cause binary-to-decimal fractional round-off errors for decimal fractions, which cannot be expressed exactly in binary. Those who do not have a suitable FUNCTION NUMVAL or NUMVAL-C available, including those using COBOL 74, might want to use the routine shown in Listing 25.1. This routine is called GETNUM and extracts a signed decimal number from a free-form display field. The comment block at the top of the listing explains how to use the routine.

LISTING 25.1   GETNUM

```
000100*************************************************************************
000200*                                                                      *
000300*                      G E T   N U M B E R                             *
```

```
000400*                                                            *
000500*      CONVERTS A NUMBER IN FREE FORMAT DISPLAY FORM:          *
000600*         FOR EXAMPLE:                                        *
000700*                                                            *
000800*            "999,999,999,999.999999 "                        *
000900*            "-999,999,999,999.999999"                        *
001000*            "              -23.61   "                        *
001100*            "                      4"                        *
001200*            "0                      "                        *
001300*            "      .000001          "                        *
001400*            "0000000000123456789.10-"                        *
001500*            "                       "  BLANK IS VALID = 0     *
001600*                                                            *
001700*      INTO FIXED NUMERIC FORM:                               *
001800*                                                            *
001900*         PIC S9(12)V9(06)                                    *
002000*                                                            *
002100*                                                            *
002200*      USAGE:  MOVE <FREE FORM NUMBER> TO NW-WORK-NBR.         *
002300*              PERFORM 001000-GET-NBR                          *
002400*                 THRU 001000-EXIT.                            *
002500*                                                            *
002600*      RESULT: NW-NBR-ERROR-FLAG = 0 INPUT IS A VALID NUMBER   *
002700*                                  1 INPUT NOT A VALID NUMBER  *
002800*                                                            *
002900*         IF NW-NBR-ERROR-FLAG = 0 THEN:                      *
003000*                                                            *
003100*            NW-EXTRACTED-NBR  = NUMBER AS:  PIC S9(12)V9(06)  *
003200*                                                            *
003300*            NW-DEC-PLACES     = NUMBER OF DIGITS TO THE RIGHT *
003400*                                OF THE DECIMAL POINT (0=NONE) *
003500*                                                            *
003600*            NW-BLD-SIGN       = +1 OR -1 AS:  PIC S9(01)      *
003700*                                                            *
003800*            NW-BLD-INTEGER    = INTEGER DIGITS AS:  PIC  9(12) *
003900*                                                            *
004000*            NW-BLD-DECIMAL    = DECIMAL DIGITS AS:  PIC V9(06) *
004100*                                                            *
004200*****************************************************************
004300
004400 01  NUMBER-WORK-AREA.
004500     03  NW-NBR-ERROR-FLAG      PIC  9(01).
004600     03  NW-WORK-NBR.
004700         05  NW-WORK-CHAR       OCCURS 25 TIMES
004800                                INDEXED BY NW-WX
004900                                          NW-WLIM.
005000             07  NW-WORK-DIGIT    PIC  9(01).
005100     03  NW-DEC-PLACES         PIC  9(02).
005200     03  NW-BLD-SIGN           PIC S9(01).
005300     03  NW-BLD-NBR            PIC  9(12)V9(06).
```

continues

LISTING 25.1 CONTINUED

```
005400      03  NW-BLD-NBR-SPLIT          REDEFINES NW-BLD-NBR.
005500          05  NW-BLD-INTEGER        PIC  9(12).
005600          05  NW-BLD-DECIMAL        PIC V9(06).
005700              88  NW-RESULT-INTEGER              VALUE ZERO.
005800          05  NW-BLD-DEC-DIGITS     REDEFINES NW-BLD-DECIMAL.
005900              07  NW-BLD-DEC-DIGIT          OCCURS 6 TIMES
006000                                            INDEXED BY NW-BDX
006100                                                      NW-BDLIM
006200                                            PIC  9(01).
006300      03  NW-EXTRACTED-NBR          PIC S9(12)V9(06).
006400
006500 001000-GET-NBR.
006600      MOVE 0       TO NW-NBR-ERROR-FLAG.
006700      MOVE ZERO    TO NW-EXTRACTED-NBR.
006800      MOVE 0       TO NW-DEC-PLACES.
006900      MOVE ZERO    TO NW-BLD-NBR.
007000      MOVE +1      TO NW-BLD-SIGN.
007100      SET NW-BDX   TO 1.
007200      SET NW-WLIM TO 25.
007300      SET NW-WX    TO 1.
007400      SEARCH NW-WORK-CHAR
007500          WHEN NW-WORK-CHAR(NW-WX) NOT = SPACE
007600              PERFORM 001010-DECODE-NBR
007700      END-SEARCH.
007800      IF (NW-WORK-NBR NOT = SPACES)
007900          MOVE 1 TO NW-NBR-ERROR-FLAG
008000      ELSE
008100          COMPUTE NW-EXTRACTED-NBR = NW-BLD-NBR * NW-BLD-SIGN
008200      END-IF.
008300
008400 001010-DECODE-NBR.
008500      IF (NW-WORK-CHAR(NW-WX) = "-")
008600          MOVE -1     TO NW-BLD-SIGN
008700          MOVE SPACE TO NW-WORK-CHAR(NW-WX)
008800          SET NW-WX UP BY 1
008900      END-IF.
009000      PERFORM 001020-GET-INTEGER-PART
009100          UNTIL (NW-WX > NW-WLIM).
009200      SET NW-DEC-PLACES TO NW-BDX.
009300      SUBTRACT 1 FROM NW-DEC-PLACES.
009400
009500 001020-GET-INTEGER-PART.
009600      IF (NW-WORK-CHAR(NW-WX) NUMERIC)
009700          IF (NW-BLD-INTEGER > 99999999999)
009800              SET NW-WX TO NW-WLIM
009900          ELSE
010000              COMPUTE NW-BLD-INTEGER =
010100                  NW-BLD-INTEGER * 10 + NW-WORK-DIGIT(NW-WX)
```

```
010200                    MOVE SPACE TO NW-WORK-CHAR(NW-WX)
010300                END-IF
010400          ELSE
010500              IF (NW-WORK-CHAR(NW-WX) = ".")
010600                  MOVE SPACES TO NW-WORK-CHAR(NW-WX)
010700                  SET NW-WX UP BY 1
010800                  PERFORM 001030-GET-DECIMAL-PART
010900                      UNTIL (NW-WX > NW-WLIM)
011000              ELSE
011100                  IF (NW-WORK-CHAR(NW-WX) = ",")
011200                      MOVE SPACE TO NW-WORK-CHAR(NW-WX)
011300                  ELSE
011400                      SET NW-WX TO NW-WLIM
011500                  END-IF
011600              END-IF
011700          END-IF.
011800          SET NW-WX UP BY 1.
011900
012000 001030-GET-DECIMAL-PART.
012100      IF (NW-WORK-CHAR(NW-WX) NUMERIC)
012200          IF (NW-BDX > 6)
012300              SET NW-WX  TO NW-WLIM
012400          ELSE
012500              MOVE NW-WORK-DIGIT(NW-WX) TO NW-BLD-DEC-DIGIT(NW-BDX)
012600              MOVE SPACES TO NW-WORK-CHAR(NW-WX)
012700              SET NW-BDX UP BY 1
012800          END-IF
012900      ELSE
013000          IF (NW-WORK-CHAR(NW-WX) = "-")
013100              MOVE -1     TO NW-BLD-SIGN
013200              MOVE SPACE TO NW-WORK-CHAR(NW-WX)
013300              SET NW-WX  TO NW-WLIM
013400          ELSE
013500              SET NW-WX  TO NW-WLIM
013600          END-IF
013700      END-IF.
013800      SET NW-WX UP BY 1.
```

Using ACCEPT and DISPLAY

One frequent use of the line interface is in communicating with the computer operator or user to align continuous preprinted forms on a line printer. Printers that use continuous (or fanfold) paper have adjustments to move the paper up or down and left or right, with respect to the print mechanism. When the printer is used to print data onto preprinted forms, the forms must first be aligned so that printed data falls onto the proper spaces on the form. Here is an example of how this is done:

```
77  SH-ANSWER                    PIC  X(01) VALUE SPACE.

0100-ALIGN-FORMS.
    PERFORM WITH TEST AFTER
            UNTIL (SH-ANSWER = "N")
        DISPLAY "PRINT AN ALIGNMENT FORM (Y/N)?"
        MOVE SPACE TO SH-ANSWER
        ACCEPT SH-ANSWER
        IF (SH-ANSWER = "Y")
            PERFORM 0110-PRINT-ALIGNMENT-FORM
        END-IF
    END-PERFORM.
```

The paragraph 0110-PRINT-ALIGNMENT-FORM should print one or more forms—enough to project far enough above the printer mechanism that the operator can see when the forms are properly aligned.

TIP

Each alignment form should be populated in every field with XXXXXX, 99,999, 99,999.99, and so on for the maximum field sizes. This allows the operator to see any points where the printed field may extend outside the proper space on the form.

TIP

If the forms are checks or some other prenumbered form, the program should first accept the number of the first form that will actually be printed on, and increment the form number for each alignment form. Note that the first form to be printed on may not be the first form from the box because some printers need several leading inches of paper for their tractor mechanisms.

Character-Based Screen Interface

The interface requirements of some programs are more complex than can be easily handled with the simple line interface. One example is data entry applications, in which users enter screens full of data through the keyboard. These applications are the bread and butter of much business programming. On mainframe computers, this interface is usually done using separate communications software that interfaces with many terminals or PCs running terminal-emulation software. The communications software handles many of the details of interfacing with the terminals, and the application program generally receives the data already formatted into a single record structure. However, on most PCs and minicomputers, and on some mainframes, the application program interfaces directly with the user at a video screen and keyboard. The capability to position descriptive text and input fields onscreen, and to enter data into those fields, is enormously useful. The current COBOL Standard (COBOL 85) does not include syntax for this type of interface. However, a reasonably consistent syntax for this facility has developed among a number of COBOL vendors, and the latest ISO Draft COBOL Standard (July 1997) does include this syntax. For consistency, I will use the syntax in the ISO Draft Standard. A copy of the 1997 ISO Draft Standard is on the CD-ROM that comes with this book. Some of the more pertinent sections of the document for screens follow:

Section	Title
9.2	Screens
12.2.6	SPECIAL-NAMES Paragraph
13.16	Screen Description Entry
13.17	Data Division Clauses
14.10.1	ACCEPT Statement
14.10.10	DISPLAY Statement

If your COBOL compiler provides a SCREEN SECTION and the expanded ACCEPT and DISPLAY syntax, it will likely be very similar to the draft standard.

Screen-handling syntax in COBOL only now is being proposed in the current draft standard, but mainframe computers have had to deal with screen-handling issues for many years. Many mainframe systems provide some sort of proprietary capability, such as IBM's CICS, which works with the COBOL compiler, communications software, and operating system. Sometimes this function is also accomplished by third-party or in-house software. In general, here is how such screen-handling software might function, using the Unisys A Series computers as a model.

Communications between the mainframe and user terminals are handled by communications software called COMS, which takes care of the details of shipping data between the terminal and the mainframe, including line and terminal protocols. Usually, mainframe terminals support some sort of primitive forms capability, which allows a form to be painted onscreen, allowing fields where the user can input data. Some terminals can filter for numeric or alpha data, and some can't. On the A Series, when the form is transmitted to the mainframe, what is sent is only the data that is in the fields themselves. All the data (fields) onscreen are transmitted to the mainframe at one time. COMS examines the data and makes a determination as to which application program should process the data. COMS then packages the data from the terminal with other information, such as the terminal ID that transmitted the message, and puts it into a queue for the online application program.

The application program stays in a loop, waiting for an input screen and processing the screen over and over, until it receives a command to end execution. When an input screen is received, the program examines the data to see what type of transaction it is and performs the appropriate routine to handle it. As the transaction is processed, usually at least one return screen is prepared as a response and is passed back to COMS with the appropriate terminal ID so that COMS can route the screen back to the terminal. At this point, the field data is merged into the screen template (form), which is sent to the terminal. This is done by some interface in which the application program specifies a form name that is automatically fetched from disk and merged with the data, or the application program merges the data into the form itself.

When COMS receives the data from the application program, it places the data into an output queue for the terminal. As soon as the terminal is free to receive the data, the data is transmitted to the terminal, and the terminal displays the data for the user. Note that in this model, the interactivity with the user is far less than with a screen-based model, as described in this chapter.

For screens, the concept of the *screen record* is introduced. The screen record is essentially the monitor screen, or some window or other subset of the monitor screen, as supported by the particular operating system software and compiler.

In this section, you'll see how screens are defined in the SCREEN SECTION, how to use the enhanced ACCEPT and DISPLAY statements, and finally, how to use the powerful screen-record feature in useful ways.

The SCREEN SECTION

The SCREEN SECTION is part of the DATA DIVISION, and it is used to describe the screens used in a program. Each screen definition is a template that defines each element in the screen, with syntax to position text and data fields anywhere onscreen and to assign attributes such as color, blinking, highlighting, secure fields, and so on. Data fields can be output to and/or input from the screen with PICTURE editing. One of the very powerful features of screens is that they allow a whole screen full of data to be output to the screen with one DISPLAY statement, and a whole screen full of data to be input with only one ACCEPT statement. Consistent with other COBOL data structures, screens use a hierarchical structure of numeric levels. Like any other COBOL record, the highest level is the 01 screen description, with subordinate items using higher level numbers. Here, you will create a data input screen and a menu screen to see how a screen is designed.

The first step in designing a screen is to create a simple screen template with all the screen elements in place. You can use a programmer's editor to create a simple text file, but any type of editor or word processor program will work, as long as you use a monospaced font. It is very useful if the editor can display line and column numbers.

This template is very important for a number of reasons:

- It enables you to see what the screen will look like.

- You can print the template and show it to users or clients for their approval. This is much faster and cheaper than creating a prototype program, although a prototype may be required in some instances.

- The process of changing the template until the design pleases the user is very quick and easy.

- The template makes an easy and exact target to program.

- The template can be copied into your documentation, saving time and increasing accuracy.

Here is the template for the sample screen:

```
Date 99/99/9999              E M P L O Y E E   A D D

        Employee Code:    XXXX

        Employee Name:    XXXXXXXXXXXXXXXXXXXXXXXXXXXXXX

        Social Security: 999 99 9999

        Hourly Rate:      99.99
```

This is a simple screen for adding new employees to an employee file. Note the positioning of the areas where the input data will be entered. The Xs represent alphanumeric data, and the 9s represent numeric data. You might code that screen in the SCREEN SECTION of your program like this:

```
01   EMPL-ADD-SCREEN
         FOREGROUND-COLOR WC-FG-NORM
         BACKGROUND-COLOR WC-BG-NORM
         BLANK SCREEN.
     03  LINE 01   COLUMN 01   VALUE "Date ".
     03  PIC  99/99/9999       FROM DW-TODAYS-DATE.
     03            COLUMN 29   VALUE
         "E M P L O Y E E   A D D".
     03  LINE 03   COLUMN 09   VALUE "Employee Code:   ".
     03  PIC  X(04)            USING EMPL-CODE.
     03  LINE 05   COLUMN 09   VALUE "Employee Name:   ".
     03  PIC  X(30)            USING EMPL-NAME.
     03  LINE 07   COLUMN 09   VALUE "Social Security: ".
     03  PIC  999B99B9999      USING SOC-SEC.
     03  LINE 09   COLUMN 09   VALUE "Hourly Rate:     ".
     03  PIC  99.99            USING HOUR-RATE.
```

The screen is called EMPL-ADD-SCREEN, as indicated in the 01 level. The statement DISPLAY EMPL-ADD-SCREEN places all the elements on the screen record, and the statement ACCEPT EMPL-ADD-SCREEN accepts input from the user into the specified data fields. In general, you first DISPLAY the screen to place all the text and data fields onto the screen record, and then you do an ACCEPT to allow input of the input data fields.

The entries FOREGROUND-COLOR and BACKGROUND-COLOR specify the colors used for the characters and background, respectively. WC-FG-NORM and WC-BG-NORM are 78 level constants, but they could be numeric literals or variables. Because the colors are specified at the 01 level, all the subordinate items inherit the colors. Colors can also be specified at subordinate levels. BLANK SCREEN causes the entire screen to be cleared to the specified colors. The color numbers must be integers with any of the following values:

0	Black
1	Blue
2	Green
3	Cyan
4	Red
5	Magenta
6	Brown/Yellow (Yellow = Brown with HIGHLIGHT)
7	White

On monochrome devices, colors are displayed in shades of gray.

TIP

Color perception and color preference vary a great deal from person to person. It is a good idea to use global 78 level constants or variables to specify colors for different uses, such as normal, highlight, error, and so on. Using 78 level constants enables you to change the colors by changing the constants and recompiling. Using variables enables you to store the color variables in a file that can be modified by the user.

CAUTION

If you store color variables in a file, be careful to prevent the user from changing both foreground and background colors to the same value, or the text will be invisible!

> **CAUTION**
>
> Not all color combinations provide enough contrast to be clearly seen when displayed on monochrome displays.

All the subordinate items are processed sequentially from top to bottom. The first subordinate 03 item blanks the screen; positions the cursor at line 1, column 1; and displays the literal `"Date "`. A data name can be assigned to any elementary item (and must be assigned to group items) if you want to reference that item independently. The next item does not contain the `LINE` and `COLUMN` positioning clauses, so it will be displayed immediately after the preceding item. It displays the contents of numeric field `DW-TODAYS-DATE` with `PIC 99/99/9999`. If the value were `12011998`, for example, the display would be `12/01/1998`. Note the word `FROM`. This indicates that data is moved only `FROM` the field to the screen on `DISPLAY` and does nothing on `ACCEPT`. In other words, output only. Other choices are `TO`, which receives data from the screen `TO` the field on `ACCEPT` but takes no action on `DISPLAY` (input only), and `USING`, which displays and accepts data between the field and screen (input and output). The next item has only a `COLUMN` position clause, so the text is displayed on the same line, beginning in column 29. The next item positions to line 3, column 9 and displays `Employee Code:`. The following item displays (and will input on `ACCEPT`) the field `EMPL-CODE` with `PIC XXXX`. One by one, each of the other fields is displayed in the same manner.

> **NOTE**
>
> It is good to remember the top-to-bottom display sequence. At times during `ACCEPT`, you might not want to process the fields from left to right, top to bottom. The fields can be arranged in the screen definition in the order in which you want them processed, but the line and column numbers can be in any order. You might want to use two vertical columns of fields, for example, but you want to process down the first column and then down the second column. Place the entire first column of fields together in the screen definition, followed by the second column of fields.

The `LINE` and `COLUMN` position clauses may be specified with a `PLUS` or `MINUS` option. The `PLUS` and `MINUS` options interpret the values as offsets from the `LINE` or `COLUMN` at the end of the preceding field, as shown in this example:

```
03  LINE PLUS 2 COLUMN MINUS 3 VALUE "Hello".
```

The word *Hello* will be positioned two lines down and three columns to the left of where it would have been positioned without LINE and COLUMN.

> **CAUTION**
>
> Be careful that you do not exceed the line and column limits of the display device. This would cause an exception condition when the DISPLAY or ACCEPT is executed. You should carefully document such code so that the intent is clear to you and others who might work with the program later.

Now take a look at a sample menu screen. A menu screen is simply for the purpose of selecting a function from a list of possibilities. Menu screens are very important, and a well-designed menu structure can make a program or system much more intuitive, easy to use, and convenient for the user. Again, you start with a screen template:

```
Date 99/99/99   E M P L O Y E E   F I L E   M A I N T A I N E N C E


                  Press: A = Add Employee
                         F = Find Employee
                         L = List Employees

                         X = Exit: X
```

The X after Exit: is to show where the menu selection will be entered. Here is the earlier template coded in the SCREEN SECTION:

```
01   EMPL-MENU-SCREEN
         FOREGROUND-COLOR WC-FG-NORM
         BACKGROUND-COLOR WC-BG-NORM
         BLANK SCREEN.
     03  LINE 01  COLUMN 01  VALUE "Date ".
     03  PIC  99/99/99       FROM DW-TODAYS-DATE.
     03            COLUMN 18  VALUE
         "E M P L O Y E E   F I L E   M A I N T A I N E N C E".

     03  LINE 04  COLUMN 24  VALUE "Press: A = Add Employee".
     03  LINE 05  COLUMN 31  VALUE "F = Find Employee".
     03  LINE 06  COLUMN 31  VALUE "L = List Employees".
     03  LINE 08  COLUMN 31  VALUE "X = Exit: ".
     03  PIC  X(01)          USING SH-ANSWER  AUTO.
```

As in the data screen, when the menu screen is displayed, it sets the default colors and clears the screen, and then it displays the date, screen heading, and menu choices. When the screen is accepted, the only input field is one position field SH-ANSWER with the AUTO clause. The AUTO clause causes the cursor to automatically advance to the next input field during ACCEPT when the field is filled. Because SH-ANSWER is the last (only) input field, the ACCEPT is completed by the one key.

In general, to process screens, you first initialize the input and output data fields and then use DISPLAY to show the screen. Next, you do a PERFORM loop that uses ACCEPT to input the data and validate it. The loop continues until the input data is validated or the user aborts the loop by using an escape control key, as defined by the vendor. In the case of menus, the loop usually continues until the exit key is entered. On each loop, the function specified by the input character is performed. The next section discusses this process in more detail with examples.

Here is a list of some of the other attributes you can assign to a screen item and what they do:

Attribute	*Function*
BELL	Causes an audio tone (beep) to be sounded when the screen item is processed by a DISPLAY statement. Only one tone is sounded, no matter how many fields specify BELL within a screen. This is useful for displaying error messages.
BLANK LINE	Clears the current line to spaces. It is often convenient to use the last line of the display (usually line 24 or 25) for status and error messages. BLANK LINE is useful in clearing that line when you display the next message or clear the previous one.
BLANK WHEN ZERO	Causes a numeric field to be displayed as spaces if its value is zero.
BLINK	Causes each character of the displayed field to blink. Use this attribute sparingly because many people find blinking text to be extremely annoying. You might want to use this attribute for a severe error or warning that really demands attention!
ERASE END OF LINE	Clears spaces from the current cursor position to the end of the current line. You may also use the alternate spelling ERASE EOL.
ERASE END OF SCREEN	Clears spaces from the current cursor position to the end of the screen. You may also use the alternative spelling ERASE EOS. This option can be very useful in programming layered screens. For example, the top part of the display could show a customer, the middle part of the screen could show an invoice, and the lower part of the screen could display items on the invoice. You can program logic to move between invoices or scroll through items without having to clear the whole screen.

Attribute	*Function*
FULL	Specifies that the operator must leave the field completely empty or fill it entirely with data during an ACCEPT. This can be useful in accepting Social Security numbers, zip codes, or other codes that are always full length.
HIGHLIGHT	Causes the specified field to appear onscreen with the highest level of intensity. HIGHLIGHT is useful for marking fields or text for attention. You can use this attribute for error messages, but using a different color such as red has more impact.
IS GLOBAL	Specifies that the screen name is a global name and may be referenced by every program within the program that declares it.
JUSTIFIED RIGHT	Causes the data to be right-justified within a screen item. May be abbreviated as JUST.
LOWLIGHT	Causes the specified field to appear onscreen with the lowest level of intensity. You can use this attribute in a way that is similar to how Windows grays a menu selection when it is not available.
OCCURS	Screen subordinate entries may contain an OCCURS clause and be subscripted. This is very useful in using a screen to display or accept a subscripted table, as long as all the elements of the table can fit onto one screen. If the screen item is subscripted, the subscript to the associated data name does not need to be subscripted, and the number of OCCURS in the table and screen must be the same. This can eliminate the need for multiple screen entries, one for each OCCURS in the table. Define one screen entry and then use relative (PLUS/MINUS) LINE and/or COLUMN positioning.

```
WORKING STORAGE SECTION:

03  WS-TABLE        OCCURS 10 TIMES.
    05  WS-FIELD  PIC  X(05).

SCREEN SECTION:

03  SCREEN-ENTRY        OCCURS 10 TIMES.
    05  LINE PLUS 01  COLUMN 05
        PIC X(05)       USING WS-FIELD.
```

Attribute	Function
REQUIRED	Specifies that the user must enter at least one character in this field during ACCEPT. When the user is entering this field during the ACCEPT, the user cannot position to the next or preceding field if this field is empty, unless the operator uses a terminate key to terminate the ACCEPT.
REVERSE-VIDEO	Causes this field to be displayed with the foreground and background colors reversed. This is useful for highlighting error messages or input fields that are invalid.
SECURE	Prevents the contents of the field from being displayed onscreen during the ACCEPT of input-only fields. If the field is both input and output, the previous contents of the data name are displayed, but the operator cannot modify the contents. The major use of this field is to accept passwords or other confidential information.
UNDERLINE	Causes the field to be underlined when it is displayed onscreen.

Enhanced ACCEPT and DISPLAY Statements

In accordance with the enhanced capabilities embodied in the SCREEN SECTION, the ACCEPT and DISPLAY statements also have enhanced syntax and functions. Essentially, the changes support the positioning of the screen template onto the screen record and detect exception conditions occurring during ACCEPT and DISPLAY. The following is the syntax for the enhanced ACCEPT and DISPLAY statements:

```
ACCEPT screen-name-1
  [ AT LINE NUMBER {identifier-1 ¦ integer-1}
      COLUMN NUMBER {identifier-2 ¦ integer-2} ]
  [ ON EXCEPTION imperative-statement-1 ]
  [ NOT ON EXCEPTION imperative-statement-2 ]
  [ END-ACCEPT ]

DISPLAY screen-name-1
  [ AT LINE NUMBER {identifier-1 ¦ integer-1}
      COLUMN NUMBER {identifier-2 ¦ integer-2} ]
  [ ON EXCEPTION imperative-statement-1 ]
  [ NOT ON EXCEPTION imperative-statement-2 ]
  [ END-DISPLAY ]
```

Within a screen definition, the LINE and COLUMN position clauses refer to the position relative to the screen record, with LINE 1 being the topmost line and COLUMN 1 being the leftmost column. When the LINE and COLUMN clauses of the ACCEPT and DISPLAY statements are used, that position becomes LINE 1 and COLUMN 1 for that screen description during that ACCEPT or DISPLAY. For example, if you DISPLAY a screen definition at LINE 3 COLUMN 5, then for that DISPLAY, the screen definition LINE and COLUMN positions are shifted down two lines and to the right four columns. If the screen definition uses LINE 4 COLUMN 1, the position shifts to LINE 6 COLUMN 5. This can be useful because it allows you to define a screen using locations that are local to it, and then you can ACCEPT or DISPLAY that screen at any point on the actual physical screen. Later, if you need to change the location, you only have to change the ACCEPT and DISPLAY statements, or the variables used by ACCEPT and DISPLAY for LINE and COLUMN. The screen definition does not need to be modified.

> **CAUTION**
>
> Be careful that you do not exceed the line and column limits of the display device. This causes an exception condition when the DISPLAY or ACCEPT is executed.

You can use the ON EXCEPTION and NOT ON EXCEPTION clauses to test whether there was an exception during the ACCEPT or DISPLAY. To find out what kind of exception occurred, you can use FUNCTION EXCEPTION-STATUS to get an alphanumeric exception name. You can also examine the contents of the CRT status and CURSOR data names (see sections 9.2.3 and 12.2.6 in the ISO Draft Standard) to determine how the ACCEPT was terminated. Some of the specific details are implementor defined, and your COBOL implementation may provide other means for this purpose. For example, Micro Focus COBOL supports syntax to query what kind of key terminated an ACCEPT. This feature is very useful for programming an interface that responds to keys such as Tab, the up and down arrows, and so on. Check your COBOL manual for specifics.

Using Screens

This section is the most fun of all because you will find that using screens is easy and intuitive. You will now create a program to maintain a list of names, addresses, and phone numbers. This program demonstrates how to do almost anything you need to do with screens.

The first step is to create the screen templates and data file layout. Data files are covered in other sections, so this section focuses on the screen templates. This program will perform several functions, including adding new names, searching for names, modifying and deleting names, and printing a list of the name file. A menu screen will be needed to select the appropriate function.

```
              N A M E   P R O G R A M

        Press: A = Add Name
               F = Find Name
               P = Print Names

           or X = Exit Program: X



        Find Name: XXXXXXXXXXXXXXXXXXXXXXXXXXXXX
        Ready printer and press a key (Esc=Exit) X
               9999 records printed
```

This menu should make it obvious to the user that the program is expecting one key to be pressed, as well as which functions will be invoked by which keys. The last three lines will not be displayed at first. These lines will be used by the Find and Print functions, and each of the lines will actually be displayed on the same screen line at different times as needed. The Print function will display the `Ready printer` line and wait for a key to be pressed. If any key but Esc is pressed, the entire file of names will be printed. As each name is printed, a running count will be displayed using the format of the last line. Next, you need a template for the add screen:

```
               A D D   N A M E

     Name:    XXXXXXXXXXXXXXXXXXXXXXXXXXXXXXX

     Addr1:   XXXXXXXXXXXXXXXXXXXXXXXXXXXXXX
     Addr2:   XXXXXXXXXXXXXXXXXXXXXXXXXXXXXX

     Phone:   XXXXXXXXXXXXXXX

     Comment: XXXXXXXXXXXXXXXXXXXXXXXXXXXXXX


               Esc=Exit
```

Here, you have allowed fields for the name, two lines of address, a phone number, and a comment. The data file should be arranged to match. At the bottom of the screen, you display `Esc=Exit` as a reminder that the user can press Esc to exit from the Add function. Which function key accomplishes this may vary between implementations, so check your COBOL manual for specifics. This example uses Esc. This key is detected by using the

ON EXCEPTION clause of the ACCEPT statement. When Find is selected from the menu, you display the Find Name: prompt and accept a name, which can be spaces. You then display a screen of names in alphabetical order, beginning with the first name equal to or greater than the name entered. Here is a template for the select screen:

```
                        S E L E C T    N A M E

NAME- - - - - - - - - - - - - - - - - - - - - PHONE- - - - - - - - - COMMENT- - - - - - - - - - - - - - - - - - - -
1 XXXXXXXXXXXXXXXXXXXXXXXXXXXX XXXXXXXXXXXXXX XXXXXXXXXXXXXXXXXXXXXXXXXXXXXXXX
2 XXXXXXXXXXXXXXXXXXXXXXXXXXXX XXXXXXXXXXXXXX XXXXXXXXXXXXXXXXXXXXXXXXXXXXXXXX
3 XXXXXXXXXXXXXXXXXXXXXXXXXXXX XXXXXXXXXXXXXX XXXXXXXXXXXXXXXXXXXXXXXXXXXXXXXX
4 XXXXXXXXXXXXXXXXXXXXXXXXXXXX XXXXXXXXXXXXXX XXXXXXXXXXXXXXXXXXXXXXXXXXXXXXXX
5 XXXXXXXXXXXXXXXXXXXXXXXXXXXX XXXXXXXXXXXXXX XXXXXXXXXXXXXXXXXXXXXXXXXXXXXXXX
6 XXXXXXXXXXXXXXXXXXXXXXXXXXXX XXXXXXXXXXXXXX XXXXXXXXXXXXXXXXXXXXXXXXXXXXXXXX
7 XXXXXXXXXXXXXXXXXXXXXXXXXXXX XXXXXXXXXXXXXX XXXXXXXXXXXXXXXXXXXXXXXXXXXXXXXX
8 XXXXXXXXXXXXXXXXXXXXXXXXXXXX XXXXXXXXXXXXXX XXXXXXXXXXXXXXXXXXXXXXXXXXXXXXXX
9 XXXXXXXXXXXXXXXXXXXXXXXXXXXX XXXXXXXXXXXXXX XXXXXXXXXXXXXXXXXXXXXXXXXXXXXXXX

          1-9=Select Name, N=Next Page, P=Prev Page, Esc=Exit: X
```

With this screen, the user can page forward or backward through the names until the desired name is found. The desired name can then be selected by pressing the digit (1 through 9) that corresponds to the name displayed onscreen. The selected name and associated data will be displayed on the view screen. Pressing Esc will exit to the menu. Because you are displaying the same data that was entered in the add screen, you can use the same format for the view screen to your advantage:

```
                        V I E W    N A M E

          Name:   XXXXXXXXXXXXXXXXXXXXXXXXXXXXXX

          Addr1:  XXXXXXXXXXXXXXXXXXXXXXXXXXXXXX
          Addr2:  XXXXXXXXXXXXXXXXXXXXXXXXXXXXXX

          Phone:  XXXXXXXXXXXXXXX

          Comment: XXXXXXXXXXXXXXXXXXXXXXXXXXXXXX


      N=Next Name, P=Prev Name, M=Modify Name, D=Delete Name, Esc=Exit: X
```

From the view screen, the user can display the next or previous names, modify or delete this name, or press Esc to exit to the menu. Continuing with the same data layout, here is the template for the modify screen:

```
                        M O D I F Y    N A M E

          Name:   XXXXXXXXXXXXXXXXXXXXXXXXXXXXXX
```

```
Addr1:  XXXXXXXXXXXXXXXXXXXXXXXXXXXXXX
Addr2:  XXXXXXXXXXXXXXXXXXXXXXXXXXXXXX

Phone:  XXXXXXXXXXXXXXX

Comment:  XXXXXXXXXXXXXXXXXXXXXXXXXXXXXX


                    Esc=Exit
```

This screen allows the user to modify the fields or to exit by pressing Esc. The last template is for the delete screen, also using the same data layout:

```
               D E L E T E   N A M E

Name:   XXXXXXXXXXXXXXXXXXXXXXXXXXXXXX

Addr1:  XXXXXXXXXXXXXXXXXXXXXXXXXXXXXX
Addr2:  XXXXXXXXXXXXXXXXXXXXXXXXXXXXXX

Phone:  XXXXXXXXXXXXXXX

Comment:  XXXXXXXXXXXXXXXXXXXXXXXXXXXXXX


    Do you REALLY want to delete this name (Y/N)? X
```

When performing a Delete function or any function that makes substantial changes to a file, you should ask the user to verify that a key was not pressed in error. You want to do that on this screen. To make the program intuitive and consistent, you should also exit if Esc is pressed, even though it is not specifically mentioned.

Now you will put all this together into a functioning program, NAMES, which is located in its entirety on the CD-ROM that accompanies this book.

Because printing and data files are covered in other chapters of this book, this chapter is concerned primarily with screen handling. But briefly, looking at NAME-RECORD, you can see that the fields have been declared to match the screen templates:

```
001400 FD   NAME-FILE
001500      VALUE OF FILE-ID IS "NAME.DAT".
001600 01   NAME-RECORD.
001700      03  NAME-NAME              PIC  X(30).
001800      03  NAME-ADDR-1            PIC  X(30).
001900      03  NAME-ADDR-2            PIC  X(30).
002000      03  NAME-PHONE             PIC  X(16).
002100      03  NAME-COMMENT           PIC  X(30).
```

Note the color constants that are used in the screen definitions. By making decisions about which functions you want to support by colors, and placing those colors in constants, you provide a way for the color choices to be easily changed. A more flexible but elaborate technique is to store the colors in a data file and allow the user to modify the colors:

```
003500 78  WC-FG-DEFAULT        VALUE  7.
003600 78  WC-BG-DEFAULT        VALUE  0.
003700 78  WC-FG-NORM           VALUE  7.
003800 78  WC-BG-NORM           VALUE  1.
003900 78  WC-FG-HILITE         VALUE  2.
004000 78  WC-BG-HILITE         VALUE  1.
004100 78  WC-FG-ERROR          VALUE  2.
004200 78  WC-BG-ERROR          VALUE  1.
```

Although it is possible to code the screens to use the fields in the data record, it is more flexible to use an intermediate area such as this. It is also a convenient place to put other screen-related fields, such as the error message. All the name data fields have been grouped under SH-NAME-DATA to make it easier to reference the fields collectively. In a more complex application, this might not be possible or convenient.

```
005000 01  SCREEN-HOLD-AREA.
005100     03  SH-ERROR-FLAG         PIC  9(01)  VALUE 0.
005200     03  SH-ESCAPE-FLAG        PIC  9(01)  VALUE 0.
005300     03  SH-ERROR-MSG          PIC  X(70)  VALUE SPACES.
005400     03  SH-ANSWER                         VALUE SPACES.
005500         05  SH-ANSWER-NUM     PIC  9(01).
005600     03  SH-NAME-DATA.
005700         05  SH-NAME           PIC  X(30)  VALUE SPACES.
005800         05  SH-ADDR-1         PIC  X(30)  VALUE SPACES.
005900         05  SH-ADDR-2         PIC  X(30)  VALUE SPACES.
006000         05  SH-PHONE          PIC  X(16)  VALUE SPACES.
006100         05  SH-COMMENT        PIC  X(30)  VALUE SPACES.
```

Here is the table used to store the list of names for the select screen. Filler characters are used so that only one screen item is needed to display the whole entry.

```
006300 78  NT-SIZE              VALUE 9.
006400 01  NAME-TABLE.
006500     03  NT-ENTRY             OCCURS NT-SIZE TIMES.
006600         05  NT-NAME          PIC  X(30).
006700         05     FILLER        PIC  X(01).
006800         05  NT-PHONE         PIC  X(16).
006900         05     FILLER        PIC  X(01).
007000         05  NT-COMMENT       PIC  X(30).
007100     03  NT-EX            PIC  9(02)  VALUE 0.
```

The SELECT-SCREEN screen definition displays the names from NAME-TABLE as described in the preceding code:

```
010800 01  SELECT-SCREEN
010900         FOREGROUND-COLOR WC-FG-NORM
```

```
011000              BACKGROUND-COLOR WC-BG-NORM
011100              BLANK SCREEN.
011200      03  LINE 01   COLUMN 30   VALUE
011300          "S E L E C T    N A M E".
011400      03  LINE 03   COLUMN 03   VALUE
011500          "NAME---------------------- PHONE---------- COMMENT-
011600-         ----------------------".
011700      03  LINE 04   COLUMN 01   VALUE "1 ".
011800      03  PIC  X(78)            FROM NT-ENTRY(1).
011900      03  LINE 05   COLUMN 01   VALUE "2 ".
012000      03  PIC  X(78)            FROM NT-ENTRY(2).
012100      03  LINE 06   COLUMN 01   VALUE "3 ".
012200      03  PIC  X(78)            FROM NT-ENTRY(3).
012300      03  LINE 07   COLUMN 01   VALUE "4 ".
012400      03  PIC  X(78)            FROM NT-ENTRY(4).
012500      03  LINE 08   COLUMN 01   VALUE "5 ".
012600      03  PIC  X(78)            FROM NT-ENTRY(5).
012700      03  LINE 09   COLUMN 01   VALUE "6 ".
012800      03  PIC  X(78)            FROM NT-ENTRY(6).
012900      03  LINE 10   COLUMN 01   VALUE "7 ".
013000      03  PIC  X(78)            FROM NT-ENTRY(7).
013100      03  LINE 11   COLUMN 01   VALUE "8 ".
013200      03  PIC  X(78)            FROM NT-ENTRY(8).
013300      03  LINE 12   COLUMN 01   VALUE "9 ".
013400      03  PIC  X(78)            FROM NT-ENTRY(9).
013500      03      FOREGROUND-COLOR WC-FG-HILITE
013600              BACKGROUND-COLOR WC-BG-HILITE.
013700          05  LINE 14   COLUMN 13   BLANK LINE   VALUE
013800          "1-9=Select Name, N=Next Page, P=Prev Page, Esc=Exit: ".
013900          05  PIC  X                TO SH-ANSWER AUTO.
```

If it were not for the need to place numbers by each name, you could have used one entry to display all nine lines:

```
03  LINE PLUS 01   COLUMN 03   PIC X(78)   FROM NT-ENTRY   OCCURS 9 TIMES.
```

The next screen definition is used to clear the display screen to the default colors on program exit:

```
014100 01   CLEAR-DEFAULT-SCREEN
014200              FOREGROUND-COLOR WC-FG-DEFAULT
014300              BACKGROUND-COLOR WC-BG-DEFAULT
014400              BLANK SCREEN.
```

The next several screen definitions are used in combination to build the add, view, modify, and delete screens. I could have taken either of two basic approaches here. I could have defined a complete screen for each of the function screens. The advantage of that approach is simplicity, but the disadvantage is redundant code. Any time there was a change in the data fields, all of the screens would need modification. Not so bad for a program like this, but a much more complicated set of data fields would increase maintenance time and possible errors. I chose ease of maintenance, and I wanted to demonstrate how you can use multiple screen parts to build a more complex screen on-the-fly. Another advantage of this approach is that less data is transferred between the program and the display. In some hardware configurations, this can be a noticeable advantage. You might use either or both techniques, depending on circumstances and your own preferences.

```
014600 01   CLEAR-NORM-SCREEN
014700          FOREGROUND-COLOR WC-FG-NORM
014800          BACKGROUND-COLOR WC-BG-NORM
014900          BLANK SCREEN.
015000
015100 01   ADD-HEADER-SCREEN
015200          FOREGROUND-COLOR WC-FG-NORM
015300          BACKGROUND-COLOR WC-BG-NORM.
015400      03  LINE 01   COLUMN 34  BLANK LINE   VALUE
015500          "A D D    N A M E".
015600
015700 01   DELETE-HEADER-SCREEN
015800          FOREGROUND-COLOR WC-FG-NORM
015900          BACKGROUND-COLOR WC-BG-NORM.
016000      03  LINE 01   COLUMN 30  BLANK LINE   VALUE
016100          "D E L E T E    N A M E".
016200
016300 01   MODIFY-HEADER-SCREEN
016400          FOREGROUND-COLOR WC-FG-NORM
016500          BACKGROUND-COLOR WC-BG-NORM.
016600      03  LINE 01   COLUMN 30  BLANK LINE   VALUE
016700          "M O D I F Y    N A M E".
016800
016900 01   VIEW-HEADER-SCREEN
017000          FOREGROUND-COLOR WC-FG-NORM
017100          BACKGROUND-COLOR WC-BG-NORM.
017200      03  LINE 01   COLUMN 32  BLANK LINE   VALUE
017300          "V I E W    N A M E".
017400
017500 01   DATA-SCREEN
017600          FOREGROUND-COLOR WC-FG-NORM
017700          BACKGROUND-COLOR WC-BG-NORM.
017800      03  LINE 03   COLUMN 09  VALUE "Name:   ".
017900      03  PIC  X(30)          USING SH-NAME   REQUIRED.
018000      03  LINE 05   COLUMN 09  VALUE "Addr1: ".
018100      03  PIC  X(30)          USING SH-ADDR-1.
018200      03  LINE 06   COLUMN 09  VALUE "Addr2: ".
018300      03  PIC  X(30)          USING SH-ADDR-2.
018400      03  LINE 08   COLUMN 09  VALUE "Phone: ".
018500      03  PIC  X(16)          USING SH-PHONE.
018600      03  LINE 10   COLUMN 09  VALUE "Comment: ".
018700      03  PIC  X(30)          USING SH-COMMENT.
018800
```

```
018900 01  VIEW-MENU-SCREEN
019000         FOREGROUND-COLOR WC-FG-HILITE
019100         BACKGROUND-COLOR WC-BG-HILITE.
019200     03  LINE 13  COLUMN 05  BLANK LINE  VALUE
019300         "N=Next Name, P=Prev Name, M=Modify Name, D=Delete Name,
019400-        "Esc=Exit: ".
019500     03  PIC  X(01)          TO SH-ANSWER  AUTO.
019600
019700 01  ESCAPE-SCREEN
019800         FOREGROUND-COLOR WC-FG-HILITE
019900         BACKGROUND-COLOR WC-BG-HILITE.
020000     03  LINE 13  COLUMN 32  BLANK LINE  VALUE
020100         "Esc=Exit".
020200
020300 01  QUERY-DELETE-SCREEN
020400         FOREGROUND-COLOR WC-FG-HILITE
020500         BACKGROUND-COLOR WC-BG-HILITE.
020600     03  LINE 13  COLUMN 15  BLANK LINE  VALUE
020700         "Do you REALLY want to delete this name (Y/N)? ".
020800     03  PIC  X(01)          TO SH-ANSWER  AUTO.
```

The screen definition CLEAR-NORM-SCREEN in lines 14600 through 14900 is used to clear the screen to your normal display colors before building a screen.

The screen definitions ADD-HEADER-SCREEN, DELETE-HEADER-SCREEN, MODIFY-HEADER-SCREEN, and VIEW-HEADER-SCREEN in lines 15100 through 17300 are used to display the headings for the add, delete, modify, and view screens, respectively. Because these headings clear only the top line of the display, they can be used to overwrite whatever heading is already there.

The screen definition DATA-SCREEN in lines 17500 through 18700 is the common data screen used for the add, delete, modify, and view screens. Because you do not allow the name to be changed on a modify, you could have created a separate screen definition for the modify screen that did not allow input on the Name field.

NOTE

In general, when writing modify screens, you do not allow the user to modify the primary key of the record. There are a number of reasons for this, having to do with database capabilities and multiuser system architectures. To modify a primary key directly, you normally need a screen with both old and new primary keys, and this is often done as a separate function. More simply, you can "modify" the primary key by deleting the old record and re-adding the record with the new primary key.

The next three screen definitions are all located on line 13 of the display, which looks nice with your data template. But on a larger, more complex application with more complex data screens, you might want to place these screen definitions at the bottom line of the display (usually 24 or 25) instead. This will allow the maximum flexibility of using one menu-type screen definition such as these with a number of data screens.

The VIEW-MENU-SCREEN screen definition in lines 18900 through 19500 is used with the view screen.

The ESCAPE-SCREEN screen definition in lines 19700 through 20100 is used with the modify screen.

The QUERY-DELETE-SCREEN screen definition in lines 20300 through 20800 is used with the delete screen. You should always ask for verification before deleting records or making significant modifications to a data file—especially when the function is invoked by pressing a single key, as it is here. Otherwise, it is too easy to strike a key accidentally and wipe out valuable, even irreplaceable, data.

The next two screen definitions, WAIT-PRINTER-SCREEN and PRINTING-SCREEN, in lines 21000 through 22200, are used by the Print function.

The screen definitions ERROR-SCREEN and ERASE-ERROR-SCREEN in lines 22400 through 23300 are used by several functions to display and clear error messages.

In the PROCEDURE DIVISION, the file is opened and the menu is displayed. Then paragraph 000100-PROCESS is performed until the ending condition is set. Finally, the screen is cleared, the file is closed, and the program ends. The program stays in a loop waiting for a menu command, and all functions are performed from that loop as the user enters the command keys.

```
023700 000000-CONTROL.
023800     OPEN I-O NAME-FILE.
023900     DISPLAY MENU-SCREEN.
024000     PERFORM 000100-PROCESS
024100         UNTIL (WS-END-FLAG = 1).
024200     DISPLAY CLEAR-DEFAULT-SCREEN.
024300     CLOSE NAME-FILE.
024400     STOP RUN.
```

Paragraph 000100-PROCESS first clears SH-ANSWER of any previous value and then waits on an ACCEPT from the menu screen. When a key is pressed, the ACCEPT is completed and the program converts SH-ANSWER to uppercase to simplify testing. The EVALUATE statement tests SH-ANSWER and if it contains a valid function character, performs the appropriate paragraph. If SH-ANSWER contains X, the end condition is set and you exit the paragraph. Other screens use Esc to exit, but you do not use Esc to exit this screen, because it would exit the program. This change of exit modes makes a nice full stop. When you drill down several levels of menus and want to quickly exit, it is useful to be able to rapidly press Esc several times, knowing that it will exit only to the main menu, and not exit the program. After EVALUATE, the menu screen is displayed in case the screen has been changed by a paragraph performed in the EVALUATE.

```
024600 000100-PROCESS.
024700     MOVE SPACE TO SH-ANSWER.
024800     ACCEPT MENU-SCREEN.
024900     INSPECT SH-ANSWER
025000         CONVERTING WC-LOWER-CASE
025100                 TO WC-UPPER-CASE.
025200     EVALUATE SH-ANSWER
025300         WHEN "A"
025400             PERFORM 010000-ADD
025500         WHEN "F"
025600             PERFORM 020000-FIND
025700         WHEN "P"
025800             PERFORM 030000-PRINT
025900         WHEN "X"
026000             MOVE 1 TO WS-END-FLAG
026100             EXIT PARAGRAPH
026200         WHEN OTHER
026300             EXIT PARAGRAPH
026400     END-EVALUATE.
026500     DISPLAY MENU-SCREEN.
```

Paragraph 010000-ADD is performed when an *A* is entered at the menu. You are about to add a new record, so you initialize SCREEN-HOLD-AREA in preparation. Using the partial screens described earlier, the add screen is displayed. You then add records using paragraph 011000-ADD-LOOP until the user terminates the process with Esc.

```
026700 010000-ADD.
026800     INITIALIZE SCREEN-HOLD-AREA.
026900     DISPLAY CLEAR-NORM-SCREEN.
027000     DISPLAY ADD-HEADER-SCREEN.
027100     DISPLAY DATA-SCREEN.
027200     DISPLAY ESCAPE-SCREEN.
027300     PERFORM 011000-ADD-LOOP
027400         WITH TEST AFTER
027500         UNTIL (SH-ESCAPE-FLAG = 1).
```

Paragraph 011000-ADD-LOOP clears the escape indicator and accepts input using DATA-SCREEN. You convert the data to uppercase in this example for simplicity to avoid complications of uppercase and lowercase collating order. You erase any error message you may have displayed earlier. If the data needs validation, it would be done at this point. Your only requirements are that the name not be blank, which the REQUIRED clause in DATA-SCREEN enforces, and that there be no duplicate names, which the INVALID KEY clause of the WRITE statement detects. The name record is cleared, the fields are populated from SCREEN-HOLD-AREA, and the record is written to the data file. If an INVALID KEY occurs, an error message is displayed and you exit the paragraph. Because the escape indicator is not set, the PERFORM at line 27300 loops back to the top of the paragraph to ACCEPT changes to the data. The error message will be erased when the ACCEPT is complete. After the record is successfully written to the data file, the display is reset for the next add.

```
027700 011000-ADD-LOOP.
027800     MOVE 0 TO SH-ESCAPE-FLAG.
027900     ACCEPT DATA-SCREEN
028000         ON EXCEPTION
028100             MOVE 1 TO SH-ESCAPE-FLAG
028200             EXIT PARAGRAPH.
028300     INSPECT SH-NAME-DATA
028400         CONVERTING WC-LOWER-CASE
028500                 TO WC-UPPER-CASE.
028600     DISPLAY ERASE-ERROR-SCREEN.
028700
028800     INITIALIZE NAME-RECORD.
028900     MOVE SH-NAME    TO NAME-NAME.
029000     MOVE SH-ADDR-1  TO NAME-ADDR-1.
029100     MOVE SH-ADDR-2  TO NAME-ADDR-2.
029200     MOVE SH-PHONE   TO NAME-PHONE.
029300     MOVE SH-COMMENT TO NAME-COMMENT.
029400     WRITE NAME-RECORD
029500         INVALID KEY
029600             MOVE "DUPLICATE NAME" TO SH-ERROR-MSG
029700             DISPLAY ERROR-SCREEN
029800             EXIT PARAGRAPH.
029900
030000     INITIALIZE SCREEN-HOLD-AREA.
030100     DISPLAY DATA-SCREEN.
030200     DISPLAY ERASE-ERROR-SCREEN.
```

Paragraph 020000-FIND displays GET-NAME-SCREEN below the menu screen and loops paragraph 020100-GET-NAME until a valid name is found or the user escapes. If a name is found, the SELECT-SCREEN is prepared and displayed by paragraph 020300-FORWARD. Then you PERFORM paragraph 020200-SELECT-LOOP until an escape is detected.

```
030400 020000-FIND.
030500     INITIALIZE SCREEN-HOLD-AREA.
030600     DISPLAY GET-NAME-SCREEN.
030700     MOVE 0 TO SH-ESCAPE-FLAG.
030800     MOVE 0 TO WS-NAME-PRESENT-FLAG.
030900     PERFORM 020100-GET-NAME
031000         WITH TEST AFTER
031100         UNTIL (SH-ESCAPE-FLAG = 1)
031200             OR
```

```
031300                    (WS-NAME-PRESENT-FLAG = 1).
031400         IF (WS-NAME-PRESENT-FLAG = 1)
031500             PERFORM 020300-FORWARD
031600             MOVE 0 TO SH-ESCAPE-FLAG
031700             PERFORM 020200-SELECT-LOOP
031800                 UNTIL (SH-ESCAPE-FLAG = 1).

034100 020200-SELECT-LOOP.
034200     MOVE SPACE TO SH-ANSWER.
034300     ACCEPT SELECT-SCREEN
034400         ON EXCEPTION
034500             MOVE 1 TO SH-ESCAPE-FLAG
034600             EXIT PARAGRAPH.
034700     DISPLAY ERASE-ERROR-SCREEN.
034800     INSPECT SH-ANSWER
034900         CONVERTING WC-LOWER-CASE
035000                 TO WC-UPPER-CASE.
035100     EVALUATE SH-ANSWER
035200         WHEN "N"
035300             IF (NT-NAME(NT-SIZE) NOT = SPACES)
035400                 INITIALIZE NAME-RECORD
035500                 MOVE NT-NAME(NT-SIZE) TO NAME-NAME
035600                 READ NAME-FILE
035700                 READ NAME-FILE NEXT
035800                     NOT AT END
035900                         PERFORM 020300-FORWARD
036000                 END-READ
036100             END-IF
036200         WHEN "P"
036300             IF (NT-NAME(1) NOT = SPACES)
036400                 INITIALIZE NAME-RECORD
036500                 MOVE NT-NAME(1) TO NAME-NAME
036600                 READ NAME-FILE
036700                 READ NAME-FILE PREVIOUS
036800                     NOT AT END
036900                         PERFORM 020400-BACKWARD
037000                 END-READ
037100             END-IF
037200         WHEN "1" THRU "9"
037300             IF (NT-NAME(SH-ANSWER-NUM) NOT = SPACES)
037400                 INITIALIZE NAME-RECORD
037500                 MOVE NT-NAME(SH-ANSWER-NUM) TO NAME-NAME
037600                 READ NAME-FILE
037700                 PERFORM 021000-VIEW
037800                 MOVE 1 TO SH-ESCAPE-FLAG
037900                 EXIT PARAGRAPH
038000             END-IF
038100         WHEN OTHER
038200             EXIT PARAGRAPH
038300     END-EVALUATE.
038400     DISPLAY SELECT-SCREEN.
```

```
038600 020300-FORWARD.
038700     INITIALIZE NAME-TABLE.
038800     MOVE 1 TO NT-EX.
038900     MOVE 1 TO WS-NAME-PRESENT-FLAG.
039000     PERFORM 020310-NEXT-ADDR
039100         UNTIL (NT-EX > NT-SIZE)
039200                 OR
039300                  (WS-NAME-PRESENT-FLAG = 0).
039400     DISPLAY SELECT-SCREEN.
039500
039600 020310-NEXT-ADDR.
039700     MOVE NAME-NAME    TO NT-NAME    (NT-EX).
039800     MOVE NAME-PHONE   TO NT-PHONE   (NT-EX).
039900     MOVE NAME-COMMENT TO NT-COMMENT(NT-EX).
040000     ADD 1 TO NT-EX.
040100     READ NAME-FILE NEXT
040200         AT END
040300             MOVE 0 TO WS-NAME-PRESENT-FLAG.
```

After each name is printed and the counter is incremented, PRINTING-SCREEN is displayed to show the user a running total of the records printed. If your file structure allows you to easily determine the number of records to be printed, you could display that here as well. Some systems permit you to query the keyboard to see whether a key has been pressed. You can use this capability to permit the user to cancel a print by pressing Esc.

Summary

Screens are a very useful and powerful capability. They are easy to use and enable you to create very user-friendly interfaces for your programs. You can easily define how text and data fields are to be arranged onscreen, and you can easily control the display, input, and validation of data.

In recent years, much emphasis has been placed on the *graphical user interface* (GUI). GUIs provide flexibility beyond what is available through character-based interfaces, but at the cost of added complexity. The next chapter covers how GUIs are used with COBOL.

CHAPTER 26

Messages, Events, and GUIs

In this chapter, you will learn about using COBOL in the *graphical user interface* (GUI) environment.

COBOL GUI development environments are typically proprietary implementations of GUI painters that use a specialized programming *Application Programming Interface* (API), aided by a proprietary scripting language. The examples in this chapter focus on the Microsoft Windows environment, but much of the terminology and mindset will be applicable across a wide number of operating systems that offer GUIs.

Fujitsu's PowerCOBOL GUI development environment is discussed here for the purpose of illustrating high-level GUI development using COBOL, aided by a COBOL-like scripting language. Free evaluation copies of Fujitsu's 16-bit PowerCOBOL 2 and 32-bit PowerCOBOL 3 are included on the CD-ROM that accompanies this book. You should install this on your system now if you want to follow along and gain a better understanding of the examples in this chapter.

Note that by the time this book is published, Fujitsu should have released PowerCOBOL 4. You will look at version 4 near the end of this chapter.

If you are running under Microsoft Windows 3.*x*, you should install the 16-bit version of PowerCOBOL by running the Setup program from the CD-ROM. If you are running under Microsoft Windows 95, Windows 98, or Windows NT, you should install the 32-bit version of PowerCOBOL by running the Setup program from the CD-ROM.

A Brief History of COBOL and the GUI

Although there has been some argument over the inventor of the GUI, most people credit Xerox *Palo Alto Research Center* (PARC) with having developed the first real GUI in the early 1980s. GUI interfaces also were made available on UNIX minicomputers using X Window and other variations. These interfaces required specialized graphics terminals; later, standalone graphics workstations were developed for individual use.

IBM mainframes were even equipped with add-on graphics capabilities, but at great cost to customers—most later opted for less expensive mini- or desktop workstations. IBM mainframes did not offer a GUI for the operating systems itself; instead, you could create graphics programs.

Apple Computer introduced the Lisa computer in the early 1980s. This was the first micro-based desktop system containing a GUI. The Lisa's success was modest, given its price and limitations. Soon after, Apple introduced the Macintosh, which became the first widely marketed micro-based desktop computer containing a GUI. Apple actually contracted Micro Focus to port a COBOL compiler to the Macintosh in the 1980s, and Micro Focus delivered MacCOBOL, which allowed for some graphical development using COBOL on the Macintosh. This product (which produced interpretive code only) was found to be less than desirable for this market and was withdrawn by Micro Focus not long after being released. However, it was the first COBOL development environment targeted at a platform that allowed GUI development.

Not long after (around 1987 or so), Micro Focus was contracted by IBM to develop IBM COBOL/2 for its new OS/2 operating system. The GUI for OS/2 was known as *Presentation Manager* (PM). IBM previously had licensed Microsoft's COBOL to sell as IBM COBOL on the DOS operating system platform, and the newer Micro Focus COBOL/2 became a replacement. Microsoft later withdrew its COBOL and licensed Micro Focus' COBOL/2 as well. Both IBM and Microsoft later declined to renew their licenses with Micro Focus. IBM released Visual Age COBOL in its place in 1995. Microsoft currently does not offer a COBOL development environment, although it partners with Fujitsu in some aspects.

IBM's Visual Age COBOL claims close mainframe compatibility and was the first COBOL compiler to offer IBM mainframe object-oriented COBOL compatibility on a PC. It also contains IBM's cross-language GUI builder that is found in other Visual Age language-development environments. This product has suffered from the fact that it was designed to encompass multiple languages. Thus, the learning curve typically is steep for native COBOL programmers who are not familiar with C and C++.

Micro Focus' COBOL/2 for OS/2 included two key new features. One was its capability to generate native object code (.OBJ files) that could be linked into true executables, as compared to interpretive code. The second new feature was its capability to call the native PM APIs to perform low-level tasks. This laid the groundwork for writing low-level COBOL applications that could create and use GUIs. To accomplish this task, Micro-Focus created both recursion and pointers in its implementation of COBOL.

The Micro Focus PMHELLO sample program (a simple COBOL application that popped up a graphical window with the text "Hello COBOL World" in it) was a bit less than 150 lines of COBOL code. The more sophisticated Micro Focus PMCALC2 sample program (a graphical scientific calculator program) contained more than 2,000 lines of COBOL code. Micro Focus later ported COBOL/2 to the Windows 3.x, Windows 95, and Windows NT platforms. The Windows equivalents of the sample applications (WINHELLO and WINCALC), which were developed later, called the native Windows APIs and contained even more lines of code.

Given the high degree of complexity when developing and testing low-level GUI programs under both OS/2 and Windows, Micro Focus created a higher-level GUI programming API known as *Panels/2*. Micro Focus' Panels/2 API took on two challenges. One was to provide a higher-level API that took a great deal of the low-level programming burden off the COBOL developer. A second key feature was to provide cross-platform compatibility. One of the key considerations in developing low-level GUI API applications is that they are not portable to other GUI platforms. OS/2 PM programs will not run under Windows, for example, and they will not run under UNIX.

Micro Focus invested a great deal of time and effort in developing a portable GUI API that would allow users to write GUI COBOL applications that would run on multiple platforms without changes to the code and, in many instances, without recompiling. Micro Focus was arguably the first language vendor to address the GUI portability problem between these noncompatible operating system GUIs. It is interesting to note that a COBOL vendor led the rest of the industry in addressing this problem.

Panels/2 reached a reasonable level of success in this area, and Micro Focus itself used Panels/2 to develop an even higher-level GUI development product for its COBOL known as *Dialog System*. Using Dialog System, users could abstract out of their applications the user-interface code and replace it with simple calls to a GUI manager (the Dialog System runtime). Micro Focus estimates that some 60 percent of code in a GUI application is specific to handling user-interface aspects. By removing this burden from the application, development should be easier, and maintenance should be simplified greatly.

Micro Focus later released a Visual Object COBOL product that allowed GUI development in a more C/C++–like fashion, but this product was less than successful and more recently was replaced with its current NetExpress product (which includes the current rendition of Dialog System). Other COBOL vendors followed suit. ACUCOBOL released ACUCOBOL-GT not long ago and has continued to make improvements to its GUI COBOL, striving for cross-platform compatibility.

An interesting note is the answer to the often-asked question, "Why hasn't one of the COBOL language vendors released a product named Visual COBOL?" The answer is that somebody already has. MBP (a German-based company acquired by Micro Focus in the mid-1990s) trademarked the term *Visual COBOL* in the 1980s. MBP's Visual COBOL, however, was not a GUI product. Instead, the company was referring to its COBOL debugger, which was called *Follow the Source* and allowed developers to step through their actual COBOL source code while debugging. It is rumored that Microsoft purchased the rights to the Visual COBOL trademark from MBP prior to Micro Focus acquiring MBP.

Fujitsu COBOL, a dominant product in Asia, was ported to an American-English version and delivered to the American market in 1996. The Fujitsu product has an impressive

Messages, Events, and GUIs

CHAPTER 26

725

26

MESSAGES,
EVENTS, AND
GUIs

legacy, given that it grew up on IBM-compatible Fujitsu mainframes and, later, on IBM mainframes as well. It later was ported to UNIX and the PC DOS and Windows environments. Fujitsu's PowerCOBOL is a newer, high-level GUI development environment that sits on top of Fujitsu's COBOL compiler.

Fujitsu has taken a rather interesting approach to bringing COBOL programmers into modern development technology. As noted earlier, Micro Focus released a Visual Object COBOL product a few years back that it later withdrew. IBM and even Hitachi have released object-oriented COBOL development products. Object orientation is a very new and exciting addition to the development world. Micro Focus and IBM pioneered Object COBOL, and Micro-Focus released the first Object COBOL compiler in the early 1990s.

Unfortunately, object orientation (as you will see in other chapters in this book) is not a simple update to the COBOL language. Instead, OO is a very complex area, and the learning curve for traditional COBOL programmers is very steep. Because of this fact, object-oriented COBOL has not taken off in the same fashion that C++ took off with C programmers. The irony here is that some of the COBOL-language vendors have put massive resources into creating Object COBOL development environments, and object orientation brings some very significant capabilities and advantages into the COBOL realm.

While other COBOL-language vendors have marketed and touted the wonders of object-oriented COBOL, Fujitsu has quietly implemented object orientation into its COBOL compiler. Evidently, Fujitsu also has realized the arguable lack of success in getting mass numbers of traditional COBOL programmers to make the effort to learn and use object orientation in COBOL. In designing Fujitsu PowerCOBOL, Fujitsu decided to make extensive use of object-oriented COBOL extensions but, more importantly, not to force developers to learn object-oriented COBOL. When you develop applications in PowerCOBOL, you code regular non–object-oriented COBOL. PowerCOBOL, however, generates object-oriented COBOL out the back end and compiles it. The developer, in effect, never sees any of the object-oriented COBOL, although the actual source file is out on disk and can be viewed. More important, when debugging, the user never sees the object-oriented COBOL code. Fujitsu uses a sophisticated preprocessor technology to achieve this. PowerCOBOL is the first COBOL development environment on the market that allows users to develop object-oriented GUI COBOL applications without knowing anything about object-oriented COBOL extensions.

PowerCOBOL 3 (included on the CD-ROM than accompanies this book) is a powerful and feature-rich product. The upcoming PowerCOBOL 4—with its new interface, capability to create OLE/ActiveX components and controls, and additional new features—promises to bring COBOL programmers into the top tier of GUI application development.

Understanding the Message and Event-Driven Program Paradigm

Most GUI operating systems are structured in a similar fashion. This structure is not unlike the *online transaction processing systems* (OLTPs) that originated on IBM mainframes such as CICS and IMS. One of the main differences between the IBM mainframe systems and the newer GUI PC operating systems is the amount of user-interface information they must manage. A 3270 Model 2 terminal display on an IBM mainframe is typically 80 characters by 25 lines in size. This means that the operating-system code that manages the terminal display (VTAM, for example) must keep track of 80 times 25 possible character positions on the screen ($80 \times 25 = 2,000$ character positions). Note that a 3278 Model 4 terminal supports 80 characters by 43 lines, and a Model 5 actually supports 132 character lines. Each character position may have one or more attributes associated with it, such as underlining or highlighting the text, auto-skipping over the field, and so on.

Although this might seem like a lot of information to keep track of, consider a graphical PC screen. In a GUI environment, the operating system must not only keep track of all character positions on a screen; it also must keep track of every pixel (a *pixel* is a single small dot that makes up part of an image on the display). If you are not familiar with pixels, pick up a newspaper and take a close look at any of the pictures in it; they are all made up of small dots of varying colors—pixels. Additionally, given GUI application complexity, there are many more potential attributes to keep track of (known in GUI programming as *properties*). On a simple VGA resolution screen *(resolution* means how many pixels are in a square inch; the more the pixels, the better the image, and thus the higher the resolution), there are 640×480 pixels for a total of 307,200! And consider that most PC users run their displays at higher resolutions, such as 800×600 pixels or even 1024×768 pixels.

Typically, PC monitors also are multicolor (instead of the typical green-on-black mainframe terminals). Does this mean that the operating system must keep track of color information for each pixel? The answer is not exactly. This responsibility actually is divided up between the operating system and the application. In a nutshell, the operating system typically has the responsibility of recognizing when an application's window has been overlaid by another window and sending a message to the application alerting it of this fact. The application then must process this repaint message request and repaint its window as needed.

Therefore, in most cases, the individual applications must keep track of their current displays. Keeping track of color is an interesting topic and one worth exploring. The lowest non-black-and-white color depth (the number of unique colors supported) is 16. Few systems run with 16 colors (which takes 4 bits to store for each pixel, incidentally). Some systems run with 256 colors (known as 8-bit color, because it takes 8 bits to store up to 256 combinations). You also may come across 32KB colors (known as 16-bit color), 64KB colors (known as 24-bit color) and 16MB colors (known as 32-bit color or *true color*). Believe it or not, the human eye can distinguish between 16 million colors! If you want to multiply this out, one pixel times up to 16 million colors times the display resolution, you can see that this is a tremendous amount of information to track.

To make this even more of a challenge, consider that displays often are changing quite rapidly, because many different applications may come up and down at the same time in these multiprocessing environments. Consider what happens to a display when a full-motion, 30–frames-per-second, 16-million–color video clip is played on it!

Managing all of the possible application windows and user interactions against them with a mouse or keyboard (or other input device) is a processor-intensive job in itself. You now may understand why so many graphics-accelerator boards are on the market for PCs to help take some of this load off the CPU. GUI operating systems typically are completely in charge of all resources but rely heavily on the applications to keep things tidy on the display. To accomplish this, these operating systems are known as *message-driven* or *event-driven,* which means that the operating system always remains in control. When a GUI application first is executed, it is registered to the operating system and provides a list of required procedure pointers and data structures that are shared with the operating system. The operating systems will return *handles* (unique system identifiers) for certain objects to be referenced later.

One of the required procedures an application must supply to a procedure pointer is known as its *WindProc* (Window procedure). The WindProc is a procedure that processes event messages for a given application. When the operating system is requested to dispatch a message for some event that has transpired, it must know which application is interested in this message and which WindProc to send the message to for processing. A *procedure pointer* is a pointer to an offset in the application—typically, to a specialized function or procedure. You can equate this somewhat to an entry point in a COBOL program, although COBOL has implemented procedure pointers for this task from an operating system's point of view.

To implement a message or event-driven architecture, the operating system manages the physical display and all input devices. When user interaction occurs (known as an *event*), the operating system determines what happened and sends an appropriate message to the appropriate application notifying it of the event. If a user clicks the mouse on a Close pushbutton in an application window, for example, the operating system sends a message to the application that "owns" the window containing the Close pushbutton indicating that this event has occurred. However, if the user selects Close from the system menu (by clicking the mouse on the system icon, if it exists, in the upper left corner) or clicks the Close icon (the x in the upper right corner), the operating system recognizes this as a user-initiated close action and sends a special WM_DESTROY message to the application's message handler.

It is important to realize, however, that the operating system does not know that clicking the Close pushbutton is a signal to close the application. Instead, all the operating system cares about is that a user clicked the mouse on a particular pushbutton; the system then sends a message to the application indicating that this has occurred. It is the application's responsibility to realize that this is a signal to close the application and to perform all the necessary tasks. This might include closing open files and issuing any warning messages to the user before sending a message back to the operating system to terminate the application. This means that the application must be cognizant of messages that may be sent to it and ready to handle each type appropriately.

The operating system deals with the various GUI controls as independent *objects*. These objects have their own *methods* and *properties* associated with them at the application level. Event messages therefore are created in response to interactions with these objects and are sent to the related application(s) that will deal with these messages.

The bad news here is that a wide variety of event messages exists, and some are quite specialized (for example, dynamic data exchange, or DDE, messages). It is possible, for example, that some user intervention with your application or even another application will cause some specific message to be generated and sent to your application that you never considered. The good news is that most GUI operating systems provide a default message handler that you can pass unhandled requests to for processing. This means that you can implement message-handling in your application only for those messages that actually concern you.

In some cases, if you do not have code defined in your application to handle a specific message type, and you do not redirect the message to the operating system's default message handler, your application can hang or have unpredictable results, because the operating system may be waiting for you to process this message. The default message handler usually deals appropriately with the message—if you are sure that you do not want to do anything special as a result of the event.

Another important point to understand is just how many messages may be sent to your application. Consider what happens if a user clicks the left mouse button while the cursor is somewhere in your application window and moves it around. Your application will receive a mouse-down (the left mouse button is down) event message and a mouse moved (the mouse moved over this part of your application window) event message for every pixel the user moves across. Your application then receives a mouse-up (the mouse button is back up after the user releases it) event message. This could add up to hundreds or even thousands of event messages if the user moves the mouse around your application window. In fact, numerous mouse-moved event messages are sent if the user simply moves the mouse pointer across your application window without even clicking on it.

You might think this is a bit silly because your application does not care whether a user moves a mouse over it without clicking on something. Consider, however, how many applications you may use daily that display ToolTips. ToolTips are the information that pops up automatically when you position the mouse over some icon or other interesting part of a window. To implement a ToolTip in your application, you need to know when a user has moved the mouse over a specific area of your screen. Therefore, you could be very interested in the mouse-moved (sometimes referred to as the *mouse-over*) event message.

You now should begin to realize the relationship that exists between events (user actions) and event messages being sent to an application that are a result of an event. This is where the terms *event-driven* and *message-driven* programming originated. Be aware, however, that events are not raised only by user interaction. A number of events are raised without any user interaction. For example, you may load and play an audio file as part of your application. When the file stops playing because it reaches the end, a message may appear alerting your application to this development.

If you use a Timer control, each time the timer goes off, an event is generated to alert you to this fact. You will use a Timer control later in this chapter to implement a clock display with ticking seconds. To implement this clock, a Timer control is set to generate an event every half-second. The application is sent a message alerting it to each event so that it can obtain the current time and display it, thus implementing the ticking seconds in the display. No user interaction is required to keep the clock ticking constantly.

A Low-Level "Hello World" Application in COBOL

You may begin to realize that a GUI application is a very busy bit of code, receiving and processing all these messages. Given the size and complexity of an entire low-level COBOL GUI application, this chapter will just focus on a few pieces of code to illustrate certain points. If you want to actually see a complete low-level GUI COBOL application, you should check with your COBOL vendor for a sample and read the documentation. Each vendor tends to implement GUI interaction with the operating system in a proprietary manner. The examples that follow were created with the Micro Focus COBOL implementation in mind.

In most low-level COBOL GUI applications, the initial procedural code initializes a proprietary API interface into the operating system and first calls the `FindWindow` operating system API to determine whether the application window has been registered. Remember that many GUI applications can be executed more than once concurrently, so multiple instances of the application could be resident on the system at any given time. The application next begins to register its window(s) to the operating system by calling these operating system APIs:

1. `LoadIcon` (loads an icon for use by the application)
2. `LoadCursor` (loads a mouse cursor for the application)
3. `GetStockObject` (obtains a graphics object, such as a brush used to paint the window's background)
4. `RegisterClass` (to register the application with a procedure pointer to its `WindProc`—the procedure that will handle operating system–dispatched messages)

After an application is registered successfully, it is ready to create its initial window, which is accomplished by calling the operating system API `CreateWindow`.

Note that creating a window does not cause it to be displayed, however; it simply creates a blank window. Other API calls are required to create and place additional controls into the newly created window, if required. To display the newly created window, the operating system APIs `ShowWindow` and `UpdateWindow` must be called.

After all of this, a window finally appears on the display. The application then must immediately begin to process messages using its message loop. To create such an application, a message loop is set up inside the application. This portion of the program gets control and stays in a continuous loop until it receives the message that signifies that the user wants to terminate the application.

The message loop typically consists of a COBOL `EVALUATE` statement (or a multiple `IF...THEN...ELSE` statement), and each message sent to it by the operating system is checked to determine whether the application cares about that message. If the application cares about a particular message, a procedure is executed and control returns to the message loop, which then processes the next message. If the application does not care about the message, the default GUI operating system message handler is called and passed the message. The message thus is effectively passed along to be dealt with by the operating system (which often means that the message is ignored or discarded).

> **NOTE**
>
> If you have programmed on an IBM mainframe using CICS or IMS/DC, you might sense a bit of familiarity here, although both CICS and IMS/DC maintain the message queue internally instead of leaving this responsibility up to the individual applications.

A sample message loop might appear shown here:

```
Move 1 To WindReturn
Perform Until WindReturn = 0
    Call WINAPI Api-GetMessage Using By Reference WindMsg
                                By Value 0
                                By Value 0
                                By Value 0
                       Returning WindReturn
    If WindReturn Not = 0
        Call WINAPI Api-TranslateMessage Using
                                    By Reference WindMsg
        Call WINAPI Api-DispatchMessage Using
                            By Reference WindMsg
    End-If
End-Perform.
Stop Run.
```

You might notice that no COBOL EVALUATE statement is contained in this snippet of code. The reason for this may not be obvious, because another step is required. If you examine this sample code, you will note that a procedure called Api-TranslateMessage is being called. This is a procedure provided by the operating system that translates certain aspects of a message to make it more easily readable by the application. In the case of some messages, certain keyboard messages may be translated, but in the case of the vast majority of messages, nothing is changed.

Next, note that a procedure called Api-DispatchMessage is being called with the translated message. This call asks the operating system to pass the message to the proper message handler for the window specified in the message's structure. Remember that it is the initial responsibility of a GUI application to provide a procedure pointer to a WindProc procedure for each application window that actually handles the messages. The dispatch message operating system function will look this up and call the appropriate WindProc, passing the current translated message into it. A sample WindProc for a "Hello World" program might appear as shown here:

```
Entry "TheWindProc" Using By Value WindHandle
                         By Value WindMsg
                         By Value WindParm
```

```
                      By Value Lparm.
          Move 0 To WindProc-Return.
          Evaluate WindMsg
              When WM-PAINT
                   Call WINAPI Api-BeginPaint
                            Using By Value WindHandle
                            By Reference WindPaint
                       Returning HandlePs

                   Call WINPAI Api-FillRect
                       Using By Value HandlePs
                            By Reference RectXY
                            By Value HbrBackground

                   Call WINAPI Api-GetClientRect
                       Using By Value WindHandle
                            By Reference RectXY

                   Call WINAPI Api-DrawText
                       Using By Value HandlePs
                            By Reference "Hello World"
                            By Value 11
                            By Reference RectXY
                            By Value 0

                   Call WINAPI Api-EndPaint
                       Using By Value WindHandle
                            By Reference WindPaint

              When WM-DESTROY
                   Call WINAPI Api-PostQuitMessage
                            Using By Value 0
              When Other
                   Call WINAPI Api-DefWindowProc
                            Using By Value WindHandle
                            By Value WindMsg
                            By Value WindParm
                            By Value Lparm
                       Returning WindProc-Return
          End-Evaluate.
          Exit Program Returning WindProc-Return.
```

The `WindProc` shown in this code is concerned about two event messages that may be
sent to it. One is the repaint message (`WM_PAINT`). In the case of this application, a graphical window already has been created with the text string "Hello World" displayed in
the upper left corner of the window. A `WM-PAINT` event message is passed in when the
window has been overlaid and needs to be repainted on the display. It is possible after a
window is created on the display for it to be overlaid by another application, or some
other combination of events may occur that later brings the window back into view.

When this happens, the operating system alerts the application that the window needs to be repainted on the display. Remember that the operating system does not keep track of this information.

When a repaint message is dispatched to the WindProc, five separate operating system APIs are called:

- BeginPaint: Creates a paint session and returns a handle to it (HandlePS).
- FillRect: Fills in the background of the window with the current background color that is contained in HbrBackground. Note that the RectXY data item is a group data item containing two sets of x,y coordinates defining the portion of the window to fill (as a rectangle). One pair of x,y coordinates specifies the top left corner of the rectangle, and the second pair specifies the bottom right corner of the rectangle.
- GetClientRect: Uses the window's handle and returns the current size of the client area of the window as two sets of x,y coordinates specifying a rectangle (top left corner and bottom right corner).
- DrawText: Draws the text "Hello World" in the upper left corner of the client area of the window.
- EndPaint: Closes the paint session.

The other event message the application is interested in is the WM_DESTROY message, which is sent after the user selects the Close option from the system menu or clicks the Close icon in the upper right corner of the window (the x icon). This gives the application the opportunity to perform cleanup work before the operating system terminates the application. All other event messages are sent to the default operating system message handler (DefWindowProc) to be handled.

Using a High-Level COBOL GUI Development Facility

This section illustrates the use of a high-level COBOL GUI development facility. For the examples that follow, Fujitsu's PowerCOBOL 3 is referenced. This product is included on the CD-ROM that accompanies this book, and you can install it to follow along with the examples. The main purpose of using a high-level COBOL GUI development facility is to take much of the tedious and complex work described earlier in this chapter and put it into a much more intuitive and simple process. COBOL GUI development facilities typically include a form (window) painter with a tool palette that contains available controls. Controls are selected from the tool palette and dropped onto the form.

Most of these facilities implement the concept of *objects, properties,* and *methods.* An *object* typically refers to a control on a window (the window, or form, itself is also an object). For example, a pushbutton or a label is a control and can be referred to as an object. *Objects* typically have *properties* and *methods* associated with them. *Properties* sometimes are referred to as *settings.* These settings define certain current characteristics about the object.

A form (window) object, for example, has a background color property that defines its current background color, its size property, and so on. A label control has a current font type, font size, and font-style property. It also has background and foreground color properties. Some objects have only a few available properties, whereas others have a large number. Some properties are known as *static* properties, meaning that they are defined during the development process and cannot be changed at runtime. Other properties are *dynamic,* meaning that they can be changed at runtime as desired. The background color property of a form (window), for example, can be changed as easily as moving a new value to it at runtime.

Methods are available functions that interact on an object. Many objects (controls) have supplied Move methods, for example, that move the objects to new positions on the window or display. You call a method to perform a task (also known as *invoking* a method), sometimes passing it parameters. Methods can be quite simple, such as a Move method, or they can be quite complex. PowerCOBOL supplies a `GetFileName` method. This method presents users with a standard dialog box that enables them to choose a file on the system. This includes the capability to navigate to different drives and down any path to search for a file. When finished, this method returns the name of the file selected by the user, including drive and path information. Using the `GetFileName` method when requesting the user for a file to open or save to does away with the need to write all this code yourself. It also uses a standard and well-tested function to provide this functionality, which further enhances your application.

The combination of properties and methods provides a very powerful and useful technique for creating GUI applications. A number of high-level GUI development tools for COBOL are available on the market from ACUCOBOL, Computer Associates, Fujitsu, IBM, and Micro Focus. Some of these tools are targeted at cross-platform portability (for example, writing GUI COBOL applications that run on both UNIX and Windows unchanged). Other tools attempt to bring users into the object-oriented COBOL world.

Using any of these tools typically will speed up your development process and make application maintenance a much more pleasant task when developing COBOL GUI applications. Creating the sample "Hello World" low-level COBOL GUI application discussed earlier would take an unexperienced programmer several hours using

Messages, Events, and GUIs

CHAPTER 26

735

26

MESSAGES,
EVENTS, AND
GUIS

documentation. The programmer would have to determine the architecture of such an application, identify the API calls required and the order in which to call them, look up those API calls, define the needed data structures, and code and test the application. Using the higher-level development facility described in this section, it is possible for an inexperienced programmer to create such an application in a few minutes, as you will see.

In fact, to implement a simple "Hello World!" application, the user only needs to code a single line of COBOL code using Fujitsu's PowerCOBOL. You now will see how quick and easy it is to develop a simple application that contains a label field displaying the text Begin and a pushbutton. After you click the pushbutton, the text displayed in the label changes from Begin to Hello World!. PowerCOBOL implements the *object, properties, and methods* paradigm. Additionally, PowerCOBOL organizes your GUI application for you. Instead of writing a single large program, you typically write individual *event procedures,* which are stored and managed automatically by PowerCOBOL.

An *event procedure* is a small snippet of code to handle some specific event. For example, in the "Hello World!" application, after the user clicks the pushbutton, the text in the label displayed should change from Begin to Hello World!. This change in the label's text should occur after the user clicks the pushbutton, which means that you are interested in executing some specific code to change the text after the Click event for the pushbutton takes place.

In PowerCOBOL, you write an event procedure for the Click event of the pushbutton object. You do not need to be concerned with the overall program or where this Click event procedure should be inserted into the overall application—PowerCOBOL will take care of this. Having the freedom to move easily around a form (window) you have created and to write and modify event procedures on-the-fly greatly aids the development process, as you will see.

Creating the "Hello World!" Application

If you have installed Fujitsu's PowerCOBOL 3, go ahead and start it by selecting PowerCOBOL from the Fujitsu folder. You are presented with the initial PowerCOBOL development environment, as shown in Figure 26.1.

If you are executing PowerCOBOL for the first time, you will not see all of the windows shown in Figure 26.1. To correct this, open the Window menu and choose Status Box | Item Box | Color Box | Font Box to bring up these additional windows. You can move these windows around the desktop by left-clicking the mouse on the title bar while moving the mouse. PowerCOBOL initializes with a blank window (also known as a *form* or *sheet*). This blank sheet will be your application window, and you will use it as the basis for the "Hello World" application.

FIGURE 26.1.

The PowerCOBOL development facility.

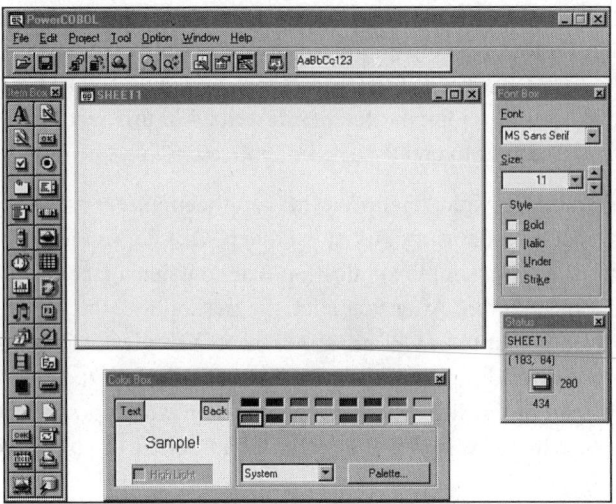

The Item Box shown on the left in Figure 26.1 is a tool palette. It enables you to select any of the controls by clicking the appropriate icon and then moving back over the sheet to drop the selected control onto the sheet. Go ahead and click the pushbutton icon in the Item Box (the second icon down in the right column). Move the mouse back over the sheet, and a pushbutton outline will appear and move with the mouse. Move the pushbutton near the bottom center of the sheet and click the mouse again to drop the pushbutton in place. If you do not like the position of a control on the sheet, you can easily move it by clicking and dragging it to a new position. Let up on the mouse button to drop the control into the new position.

The next task is to place a label field in which to display the text on the sheet. Move the mouse back over to the Item Box and click the Label icon (the top icon in the left column). Move the mouse back over the sheet and position the label near the top center of the sheet; click again to drop it into place. The label appears on the form, and the text LABEL appears in its top left corner.

Your sheet now should appear as shown in Figure 26.2.

To give you an idea of the flexibility of this high-level development environment, you next will change the font size of the text currently displayed in the label field. Make sure that the label is selected as the current object (the current object on a sheet is denoted by a set of bars around it called *handles*). Move the mouse to the Font Box (the box to the right of the sheet), and open the Size drop-down box. Select the font size of 16. The text displayed in the label on the sheet should instantly change to the larger size.

Messages, Events, and GUIs

CHAPTER 26

737

26

MESSAGES,
EVENTS, AND
GUIs

FIGURE 26.2.

The new sheet after placing a label and a push-button on it.

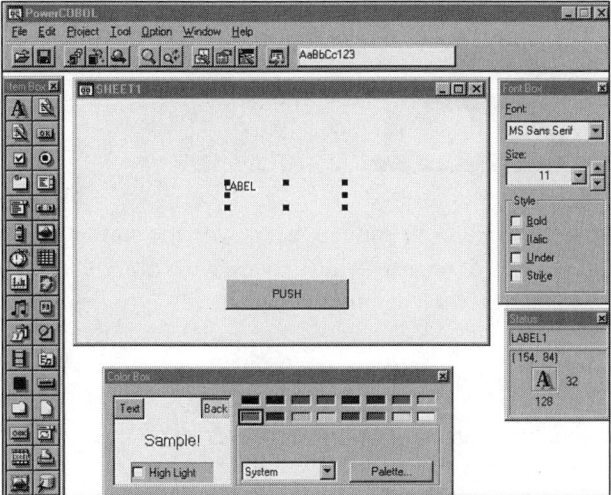

You now will change some additional properties of the label object you've placed on the sheet. Make sure that the label is still selected as the current object and right-click it. Choose Style from the context menu that appears. The Style dialog box for the label field appears. Move to the Text field and change the current text "Label" to "Begin." Now move the mouse to the Horz frame and select the Center option. Move to the Vert frame and select the Center option. The Style dialog box now appears, as shown in Figure 26.3.

FIGURE 26.3.

The Style dialog box for the label control.

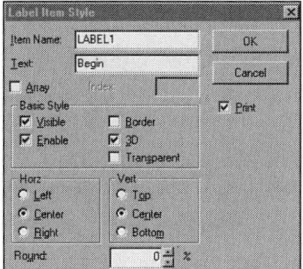

Click OK to close the Style dialog box. Now it is time to create the event procedure code for the pushbutton's Click event. Select the pushbutton as the current object by clicking it. Now right-click the pushbutton and choose Procedure from the context menu that appears. The Choose Event dialog box appears. Make sure that PUSH1 is selected on the left side and that the CLICK event is selected on the right side, as shown in Figure 26.4.

FIGURE 26.4.

The Choose Event dialog box.

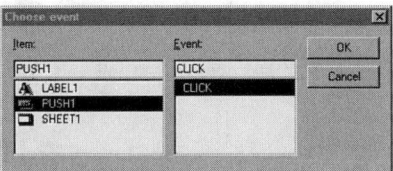

Click OK, and the PowerCOBOL editor appears with the current code for the Click event (which will be three lines of nonexecutable code). Now move the cursor to the first blank line in the `Procedure Division` and tab to column 12. Type the following line of COBOL code:

```
Move "Hello World!" To POW-TEXT Of Label1.
```

The editor now should appear as shown in Figure 26.5.

FIGURE 26.5.

The PowerCOBOL editor on the pushbutton's Click event procedure.

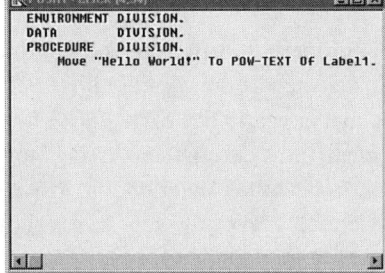

Click the Close icon in the editor window's upper right corner (x) to close the edit session. This is the only line of code you will need to enter for this entire application! Now you are ready to save and build the application into an executable. Move the mouse up to the PowerCOBOL menu bar and open the File menu. Choose Save As; then type **Hello1** for the name of the sheet (window) to save and click the Save pushbutton. Now open the Project menu and choose Build. An informational dialog box appears, indicating that PowerCOBOL is going to create a project by the same name as the window you just saved. Click OK.

The project now is compiled and linked into an executable. If you receive any errors, correct the code you typed and repeat the build process until it completes without error. You will notice that a new Project box has popped up on your desktop. This shows all the current components of your project. At the moment, the only component that appears in the Project box is the sheet name—`Sheet1.win`.

You can use the Project box to navigate between sheets in a multiwindow project. You now have a fully executable application named Hello1.exe in the same directory in which you saved the window (sheet) and project. You can execute this application just like any other executable in the Windows environment. You also can execute this program directly from the PowerCOBOL development environment. Go ahead and choose Run from the Project menu to launch the Hello1.exe program you just created.

You first are presented with the PowerCOBOL Runtime Environment Setup dialog box. This dialog box enables you to specify runtime options. You do not need to do this, so simply click OK. Any time this dialog box appears as you follow the rest of this chapter, simply click OK. You might want to minimize the PowerCOBOL development environment by clicking the minimize (-) icon near the upper right corner of the PowerCOBOL menu bar. The application should appear as shown in Figure 26.6.

FIGURE 26.6.

Executing the "Hello World!" application.

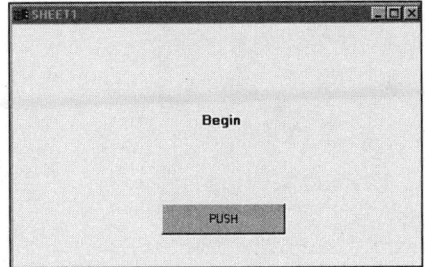

Go ahead and click the PUSH button; the text should change from Begin to Hello World, as shown in Figure 26.7.

FIGURE 26.7.

The Hello World! application after clicking the PUSH button.

When you are finished, close the application by clicking its Close icon in the upper right corner (x). Bring the PowerCOBOL development environment back up if you minimized it previously.

Enhancing the "Hello World!" Application

You now are going to see how easy it is to modify your GUI application to enhance its functionality. The capability to create, build, and execute quickly and to drop back into development mode is exceptionally handy when developing complex GUI applications.

Select the sheet as the current object by clicking anywhere on its background that does not contain a control. You know the sheet is the current object when no other control on it is surrounded by bars. Now right-click on the sheet's background in a location not occupied by a control and choose Style from the context menu that appears. This brings up the Style dialog box for the sheet (window) itself. Change the text in the Title field from Sheet1 to Hello!. The display now should appear as shown in Figure 26.8.

FIGURE 26.8.

The Sheet Style dialog box.

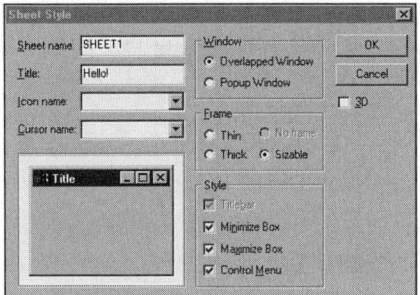

Click OK to close the Sheet Style dialog box. Make sure that the sheet still is selected as the current object. You are going to change its background color. Move the mouse to the Color Box below the sheet. Make sure that the Back button is in the down position (this selects the background color property), and click on a different color to change the background of the sheet (see Figure 26.9).

Notice that although the background color of the sheet changed, the background colors of the label and pushbutton controls did not change. This is because controls typically have their own background color properties. This makes sense for the pushbutton, which should remain gray, but the label looks a bit odd with its white background. You could change the label's background to the same color you just selected for the sheet's background by selecting the label as the current object and changing the color in the Color Box. Instead, however, you will change the background color property to Transparent to ensure that the label control will blend in with any color background on the sheet if it changes again.

Select the label control as the current object by clicking it. Now right-click it and choose Style from the context menu that appears. Enable the Transparent check box. You should notice that the background of the label now blends in with the sheet's background. Click OK to close the Style dialog box. Select the pushbutton as the current object by clicking it. Right-click the pushbutton and choose Style from the context menu. This brings up the Style dialog box for the pushbutton control. Change the Text field from Push to Say Hello. This changes the text displayed on the actual pushbutton, as shown in Figure 26.10.

FIGURE 26.9.

Changing the background color for the sheet.

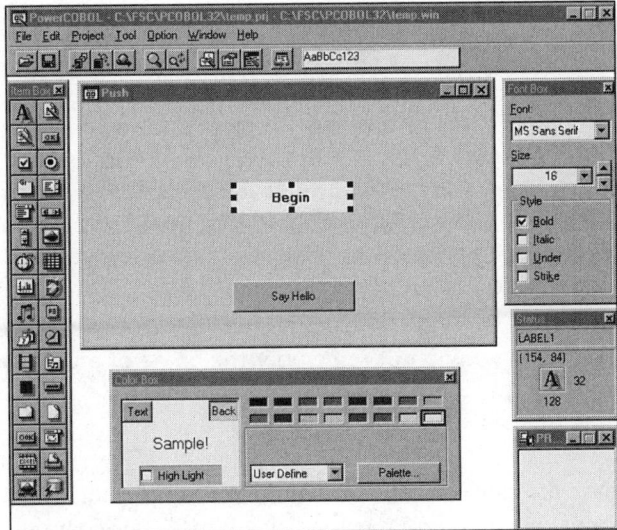

FIGURE 26.10.

The Style dialog box for the push-button with the changed text.

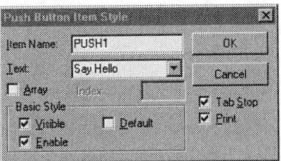

Click OK to close the Style dialog box. Choose Save from the File menu to save the sheet. Then choose Build from the Project menu to rebuild the project. When you have a clean build, choose Run from the Project menu to execute the application. You should notice the enhancements you just made. Close the application when you are finished experimenting with it by clicking the Close icon in the upper right corner.

Using Dynamic Properties at Runtime

Now you will add some programming code to the application to learn about using dynamic properties.

Bring up the event procedure code for the pushbutton's Click event; do this by selecting the pushbutton as the current object by clicking it. Now right-click the pushbutton and choose Procedure from the context menu. The event procedure for the Click event should appear in the editor. Move the cursor down to line 5 (the first blank line) and tab over to column 12. Type the name of the sheet (Sheet1). Now highlight this text by clicking the first letter and dragging to the right to highlight all of the Sheet1 text.

> ### TIP
>
> PowerCOBOL provides a very useful drag-and-drop programming feature. Instead of typing the name of the sheet in the editor window, you could have left-clicked on the sheet's background. Then, while continuing to hold down the left mouse button, you could have moved the mouse back over the editor window, as if you were dragging the sheet into the editor. When you released the mouse button, the name of the sheet would have appeared in the editor window at the location of the cursor.
>
> This drag-and-drop facility works for any control on a sheet as well. This feature is useful especially if you do not remember the name of a particular control while editing event procedure code.

Now that you have the name of the sheet highlighted in the editor, right-click the highlighted text to bring up the Insert Property dialog box for this control (the sheet), as shown in Figure 26.11.

FIGURE 26.11.

The Insert Property dialog box for the Sheet1 *object.*

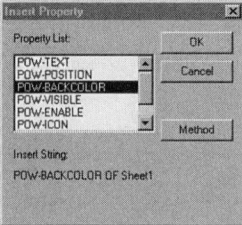

Given the number of controls and considering their individual properties and methods, you might realize that it can be a daunting task to remember which properties or methods are available for which controls. This task becomes even more complex when you consider that properties have various data types associated with them, and that methods often take one or more parameters in their calls—some of which may be optional. The online help system in PowerCOBOL provides detailed information on all of this. Using the

Messages, Events, and GUIs

CHAPTER 26

743

26

MESSAGES,
EVENTS, AND
GUIs

Insert Property dialog box can be even more invaluable. This dialog box displays all the available properties for the currently highlighted object in the editor.

Now you will use the BACKCOLOR property to change the sheet's background color at run-time. Highlight the BACKCOLOR property in the dialog box and click OK. The Insert Property dialog box disappears, and some new COBOL code is inserted into the editor session. Go ahead and modify this line of code to read as shown here:

```
Move POW-WHITE TO POW-BACKCOLOR Of Sheet1
```

Close the edit session. Now save the file and choose Build from the Project menu. Choose Run from the Project menu when you have a clean build to execute the application. After you click the pushbutton, the text in the label changes as before, but now the background color of the sheet changes as well. When you are finished experimenting, close the application. As you can see, modifying properties at runtime can add a great deal of flexibility to your application.

Using Methods

Most COBOL GUI development environments provide a number of useful methods to simplify GUI development. Although you are able to close the current application when executing it by clicking the Close icon in the upper right corner, most applications include a standard Close pushbutton near the bottom right of the window.

Now you will add a second pushbutton and set up a Close event procedure. Move the mouse over to the Item Box and click the pushbutton icon. Drag the mouse back over near the bottom right corner of Sheet1 and drop the new pushbutton in a convenient location on the sheet. Resize the new pushbutton as appropriate by selecting the handles on either side and dragging them inward. Right-click the new pushbutton and choose Style from the context menu that appears to bring up the Style dialog box. Change the Text field from Push to Close and click OK to close the Style dialog box. Right-click again on the new pushbutton and choose Procedure from the context menu that appears. Make sure that Push2 and Click are selected in the Choose Event dialog box that appears, and click OK to bring up an editor session.

You now are going to create an event procedure for the new pushbutton's Click event. Move the cursor down to the first blank line under the Procedure Division and tab over to column 12. Type Sheet1 and highlight this text. Right-click on this highlighted text to bring up the Insert Property dialog box. This shows all the available properties for this control. Now click the Method pushbutton. This changes the dialog box from Insert Property to Insert Method and lists all the available methods for the currently highlighted control. Select the CLOSESHEET method and click OK. You will see some COBOL text inserted into your editor session. This text includes some optional parameters surrounded by brackets to indicate that they are optional. Delete the optional parameters and brackets so that the line of code looks like this:

```
Call CLOSESHEET Of Sheet1.
```

This calls the `CLOSESHEET` method that will properly terminate the application. That's all there is to it. The editor session should appear as shown in Figure 26.12.

FIGURE 26.12.

The event procedure for the Close pushbutton's Click event.

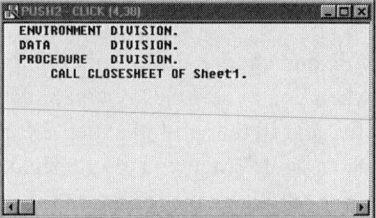

Close the editor session, save the file, and build the application again. Run the application and try out the new feature. When you are finished, close the application.

You now will enhance the Close event procedure. Most applications display a warning dialog box when you attempt to close them to prevent you from accidentally closing them and losing work. You are going to add this feature to the current application by using the `DISPLAYMESSAGE` method. Bring up the event procedure for the Close pushbutton in the editor by right-clicking the Close pushbutton and choosing Procedure from the context menu. Change the procedural code for this event procedure from

```
Call CLOSESHEET Of Sheet1.
```

to

```
CALL DISPLAYMESSAGE OF Sheet1
              USING "Exit Hello Application?"
                    "Close"
                    POW-DMYESNO.
If Program-Status = POW-DMRYES
    Call CLOSESHEET of Sheet1
End-If.
```

The `DISPLAYMESSAGE` method will display the text contained in the first parameter in a dialog box that it presents. The second parameter (`Close`) will become the title of the dialog box to be displayed. The third parameter specified (`POW-DMYESNO`) is a PowerCOBOL-defined constant. Most GUI development environments provide a number of predefined constants that you can use, so you do not have to remember data types and values for complex operations. You already have used one such constant (`POW-WHITE`, the system setting for the white color attribute), which is actually a bit pattern. `POW-DMYESNO` defines the style of the dialog box to be presented. In this case, it specifies that you want to present a dialog box with the text specified in the first parameter and both a Yes and a No pushbutton for the user.

You can choose from a number of styles for a dialog box, such as a single OK pushbutton, a Cancel pushbutton, and so on. You can look these up in the PowerCOBOL help system under the DISPLAYMESSAGE method. You will notice that after returning from the DISPLAYMESSAGE method call, a system-supplied data item named Program-Status is checked for another PowerCOBOL-defined constant value named DMRYES. DMRYES is the value for a DISPLAYMESSAGE return code indicating that the user has clicked the Yes pushbutton when asked whether he or she really wanted to exit the application. You should realize how useful this method is; it saves you from creating a second window and writing all of the code to manage it.

Go ahead and close the edit session, save the file, and build the application again. Execute the application and click the Close button. The application should appear as shown in Figure 26.13.

FIGURE 26.13.

The DISPLAY-
MESSAGE *method*
in action.

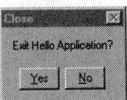

When you are finished experimenting, close the application.

Adding a Clock Display to the Sheet

The final enhancement to the application will be the addition of a clock to the form. This will be in the form of a digital display showing hours, minutes, and seconds, with the seconds ticking.

To implement the clock, you will use a Timer control. This will illustrate event-handling for events that are not invoked by a user. To implement a clock with seconds that tick on the display, the application needs to somehow check the time on a consistent interval and update the display. The Timer control does just the trick; it is a control that does not itself display at runtime but simply generates a Timer event every *nn* seconds (where *nn* can be less than a second). Because the control generates a Timer event on a consistent basis, you can use it to create an event procedure that checks the system time every *nn* seconds and updates a label with the current time.

Move the mouse over to the Item Box and click the Timer control (the icon that looks like a clock—the seventh icon down from the top in the left column of the Item Box).

Drag the mouse back over the sheet and drop the Timer control near the top left corner of the sheet. It does not matter where you place this control, because it will not display at runtime. Now right-click this new control and choose Style from the context menu that appears to bring up its Style dialog box. Enable the Activate check box to indicate that you want the timer to activate as soon as the application begins. Change the Interval field to 500 msec. The Style dialog box now should look like Figure 26.14.

FIGURE 26.14.

The Style dialog box for the Timer control.

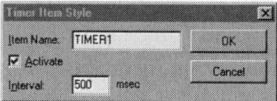

Click OK to close the Style dialog box. Now you need a second label to display the time on the sheet. Move the mouse back to the Item Box and select the Label icon. Drag the mouse back over near the upper right corner of the sheet and drop the label in a convenient location. Right-click the new label and choose Style from the context menu to bring up its Style dialog box. Blank out the text in the Text field. Enable the Transparent check box. Select the Center radio buttons in the Horz and Vert frames. Click OK to close the Style dialog box.

The actual event procedure code will be placed under the Timer control's Timer event. Select the Timer control as the current object by clicking it. Now right-click it and choose Procedure from the context menu that appears. Make sure that `Timer1` and `Timer` are highlighted in the Choose Event dialog box that appears, and click OK to bring up an editor session on the Timer event. Modify the event procedure in the editor, as shown in Figure 26.15.

FIGURE 26.15.

The event procedure for the Timer event.

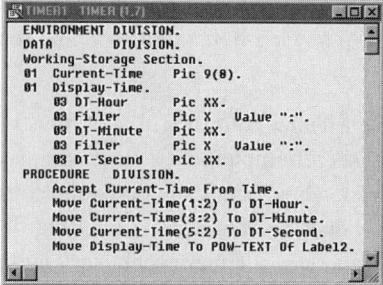

```
ENVIRONMENT DIVISION.
DATA        DIVISION.
Working-Storage Section.
01  Current-Time    Pic 9(8).
01  Display-Time.
    03  DT-Hour      Pic XX.
    03  Filler       Pic X    Value ":".
    03  DT-Minute    Pic XX.
    03  Filler       Pic X    Value ":".
    03  DT-Second    Pic XX.
PROCEDURE   DIVISION.
    Accept Current-Time From Time.
    Move Current-Time(1:2) To DT-Hour.
    Move Current-Time(3:2) To DT-Minute.
    Move Current-Time(5:2) To DT-Second.
    Move Display-Time To POW-TEXT Of Label2.
```

Close the editor session, save the file, and build the application again. Execute the application. You should see a digital clock display in the new label field with the seconds ticking, as shown in Figure 26.16.

FIGURE 26.16.

The application with a ticking clock displayed in the new label field.

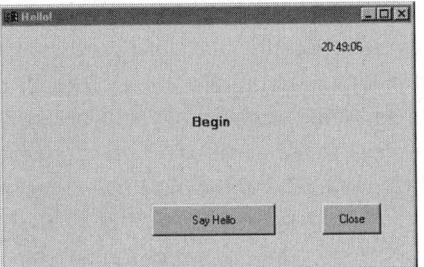

Debugging a GUI Application

PowerCOBOL comes with a very useful GUI debugger. To use it, you must make a simple change to your project's current settings. Choose Compile from the Option menu in the PowerCOBOL menu bar. Enable the Build Program for Debug check box, and then click OK to close the dialog box. Now choose Compile from the Project menu to recompile the application for debugging. Choose Build from the Project menu to rebuild the application.

To start the PowerCOBOL debugger, choose Debug from the Project menu. Click OK after the Runtime Environment Setup window appears, and then click OK after the Ready to Debug dialog box appears. The Debug menu bar appears. It is important to note that the application has not been executed yet; the debugger is waiting for you to begin execution. Choose Single Step from the Run menu to load and execute the current line of procedural code in the application. The application window will appear, and the source code for the Timer event procedure will appear in a separate window, as shown in Figure 26.17.

FIGURE 26.17.

The debug session for the application showing the Timer event procedure.

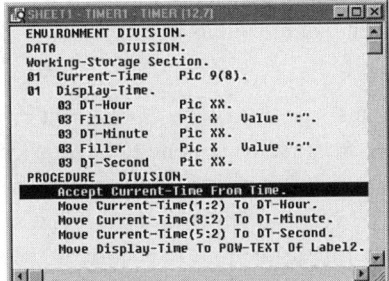

The reason the Timer event procedure appears in a separate window is because the Timer event already has occurred (remember that you set it to occur every 500ms). In fact, this event already has occurred numerous times, and event messages are beginning to stack up. You can select the Single Step option multiple times to execute down the Timer event procedure, but you will be thrown right back into the same procedure, because it is stacking up multiple times given that the event triggers every 500ms. This presents an irritating situation and also illustrates some of the potential dangers of debugging GUI applications. Think back for a moment to the previous discussion regarding low-level GUI programming using a message loop. One of the most irritating mistakes a developer can make is stepping the debugger into the message loop. Once you step into the message loop, many messages are stacked up (many of which the developer does not care about, such as mouse moves). In this case, developers are forced to stay in this seemingly infinite loop waiting for a useful message to come along to branch them out to their WindProc procedure. In the early days, you were lucky if you could even force the debugger to terminate without rebooting the operating system after you stepped a debugger into the message loop. GUI debugging was indeed a tricky and dangerous process.

The fact that the higher-level GUI development facilities remove the message loop from the debugging equation makes this task a bit less tricky. You must be cognizant of the potential pitfalls, however. In the case at hand, the Timer event has taken over the debug session. The PowerCOBOL debugger offers a workaround for this type of pitfall. This comes from the capability to set breakpoints at the places in your application with which you are concerned.

After you are convinced that the Timer event procedure is executing properly, you do not need to see it again (especially when it pops up every half-second!). You get around the Timer event by setting breakpoints at the locations in which you want to see the event code execute step by step and running the application at machine speed. Move the mouse to the Debug menu bar and open the Break menu. Choose Set. The Set Breakpoint dialog box appears. The system currently is positioned within the Timer event procedure code, and you do not want to set a breakpoint here. Select the Change Proc. option. In the Item drop-down list, select Push1. The event can remain as Click. Click OK to close the dialog box.

This method just set a breakpoint on the first line of the Click event procedure for the first pushbutton (Push1). Choose Run from the Run menu to begin executing the application at machine speed. The application window now becomes active, as indicated by the ticking clock. The event procedure code for the Timer event still is displayed. You may close it if you prefer. Click the Say Hello pushbutton. Execution is suspended, and the source code for the Click event for this pushbutton is displayed in a separate window, as shown in Figure 26.18.

Messages, Events, and GUIs

CHAPTER 26

749

26

MESSAGES,
EVENTS, AND
GUIs

FIGURE 26.18.

The event procedure for the Push1 Click event during debugging.

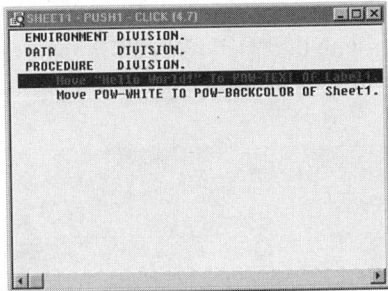

```
SHEET1 - PUSH1 - CLICK (4.7)                    _□×
ENVIRONMENT DIVISION.
DATA         DIVISION.
PROCEDURE    DIVISION.
   Move "Hello World" To POW-TEXT Of Label1.
      Move POW-WHITE TO POW-BACKCOLOR OF Sheet1.
```

You can single-step through this code or run it. You also can choose Set from the Data menu to examine, change, and monitor data-item values at any time.

> **TIP**
>
> Note that when specifying a data item in the Set dialog box, you must enter the name of the data item in all uppercase, regardless of whether the data item is specified in lowercase or mixed case.
>
> PowerCOBOL generally does not care whether data-item names are in lowercase, uppercase, or mixed case. The Data facility in the PowerCOBOL debugger, however, only recognizes data names if you type them in all uppercase for some unknown reason. This is a bug that I have reported to Fujitsu.
>
> You cannot use the debugger's Data facility to view or manipulate property names such as POW-BACKCOLOR or POW-TEXT Of Label1.

When you are finished experimenting with the debugger, close it. This concludes the section on creating a GUI application using a high-level GUI development facility.

A Quick Look at Fujitsu PowerCOBOL 4

Fujitsu will have released version 4 of its PowerCOBOL product by the time this book is available. You can obtain more information on PowerCOBOL 4 by visiting the Fujitsu Web site at

```
http://www.adtools.com
```

This new release includes a new interface that incorporates a new Project Manager to help manage complex projects. A new project Build facility will even create custom

Setup programs to install your application on other machines. Figure 26.19 shows the new PowerCOBOL Project Manager with the "Hello World!" application you just completed loaded into it (PowerCOBOL 4 accepts version 3–created projects):

FIGURE 26.19.

The Fujitsu PowerCOBOL 4 Project Manager.

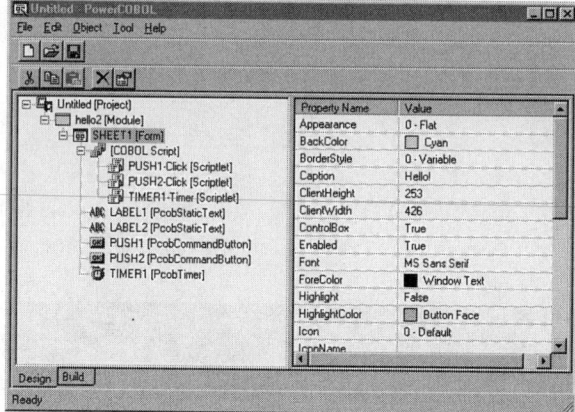

You can see in Figure 26.19 that the project's objects are nicely represented in a hierarchical tree in the left windowpane. You can select any of these objects and perform available operations on them from the Project Manager. The available properties and their current values for the selected object are displayed in the right windowpane. You can click on any of these properties and change them on-the-fly.

PowerCOBOL 4 includes a more sophisticated language-sensitive source code editor for editing event procedures. The Form Editor (window painter) contains several new features (see Figure 26.20).

FIGURE 26.20.

The Fujitsu PowerCOBOL 4 Form Editor.

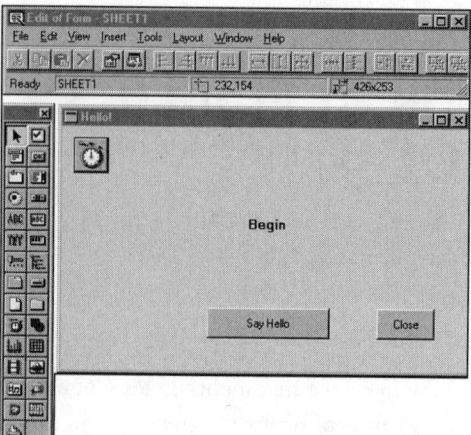

Messages, Events, and GUIs

CHAPTER 26

751

26

MESSAGES,
EVENTS, AND
GUIs

One of the most powerful new features of PowerCOBOL 4 is its capability to create OLE and ActiveX controls. You can use these controls in other development environments as well. You can place them on a Web page, for example. You can create custom properties, methods, and events that can be exposed to other applications—even applications that are not written in COBOL. Additionally, you can use OLE and ActiveX controls supplied with the operating system or with other resident software packages in PowerCOBOL applications. You can insert a custom control right into a PowerCOBOL Toolbox palette by selecting it from the appropriate menu, as shown in Figure 26.21.

FIGURE 26.21.

Selecting a custom control to add to the PowerCOBOL For Editor's Toolbox palette.

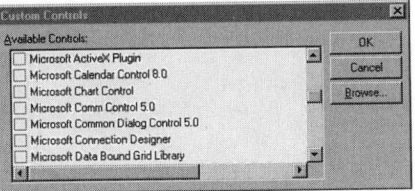

After you add an external control to the Toolbox palette, you can click it and drop it on a PowerCOBOL form, just like any other control. This new control's properties and methods will be available from your COBOL event procedures, just like regular properties and methods. This feature enables you to develop using the building-block approach—what Microsoft refers to as *component* (COM) development.

Finally, PowerCOBOL 4 comes with a more sophisticated graphical debugger. Figure 26.22 shows this new debugger running the "Hello World!" project you created.

FIGURE 26.22.

The PowerCOBOL 4 debugger.

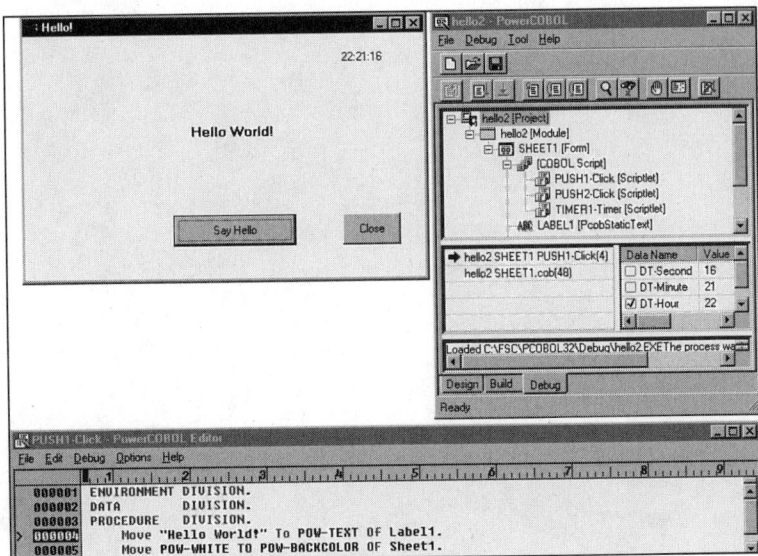

COBOL—Its Future Directions

PART

VII

Object-Oriented COBOL—Concepts

CHAPTER 27

Although object-oriented programming dates back to the late 1960s, the field generally was not recognized until the 1980s. Since then, the object-oriented view of programming has undergone a tremendous increase in popularity.

The next standard of COBOL definitely will contain a language extension for object-oriented programming. Object orientation first was raised as an issue for COBOL in 1989. In November 1989, a symposium was called by the CODASYL COBOL Committee in Scottsdale, Arizona. At the same time, the committee formed the *Object-Oriented COBOL Task Group* (OOCTG). When the CODASYL COBOL Committee disbanded in 1992, a subgroup of X3J4 (the COBOL standardization committee) was founded to continue the task of the OOCTG—to show that object orientation and COBOL is a viable combination and to propose a draft specification for corresponding extensions to the COBOL language. In 1994, object-oriented COBOL products became available on the market.

This chapter provides a small tutorial on the various principles behind object orientation, such as encapsulation, inheritance, and polymorphism. Although this chapter presents object orientation to COBOL programmers, the explanations here are not tied to COBOL or any other language because the emphasis is on concepts rather than syntax. However, COBOL terminology and fragments of ANSI85 COBOL are used occasionally to give you an idea of the concepts or to indicate the limitations of programming without object orientation.

The next chapter discusses in some detail the object-oriented extensions to the COBOL language. Thus, both chapters should be regarded as a unit. Both chapters sketch a banking application as a running example. This fictional bank deals with many individual accounts. The kinds of accounts may vary; for example, there may be interest accounts and checking accounts. Each of the bank's customers has one or more accounts. The bank employees include tellers and managers.

Motivation

The interest in object orientation stems from its benefits, such as modularity, reusability, accurate models, high quality, readability, maintainability, and so on; all result in high productivity. What is *object orientation* (OO)? What does it mean for a programming language to be object-oriented? What is an object-oriented application? Why does object orientation improve the modularity and reusability of software? Here, you'll consider such general questions before you look at the fundamental tenet of object orientation.

Object-oriented programming means to develop applications as sets of interacting (software) objects. A (software) *object* models an object of the real world—for example, a customer in our banking application or a rather abstract entity like an account or a printer job. An object consists of *attributes* (or properties) in the form of data items and *methods* operating on the attributes in the form of procedures accessing data items. Attributes model the internal state of an object, whereas methods model the services an object can supply. Another way of looking at it is that methods model the behavior of an object. An account object, for example, has attributes for the owner of the account, the account number, and the actual balance, and it has methods to deposit money into the account and to withdraw money from the account. Figure 27.1 shows the structure of an account.

FIGURE 27.1.

The structure of an account object.

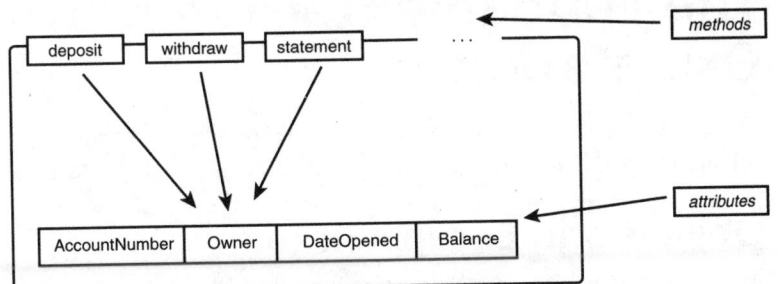

The most critical principle of OO is that an object *encapsulates* its data. Thereby, the data is protected against undesirable changes by users of the object. Only methods of the object can access the data; other objects and procedures cannot access the data. An account object, for example, can be invoked to perform a withdrawal based on the method `withdraw`, but the actual balance cannot be modified directly from outside. So keep in mind that users of an object only know the names and parameters of the methods. This system also protects the users of an object, because they are well-shielded from changes to the attributes and method implementations. Thereby, you achieve a much better adaptability than you get by using other techniques. To put it differently, an object can be regarded as a module, where some data is bundled with the corresponding services. Because the methods are part of the object, an object knows how to supply a certain service. Thereby, interchangeability is supported, because program code depends on the *interface* of an object, or only its method's profiles.

In ANSI85 COBOL, you write programs, procedures, and reusable subprograms. In contrast, you use object-oriented programming to describe classes. A *class* defines the attributes and methods common to all objects of a certain kind. The class `Account`, for example, defines the attributes and methods common to all account objects. You can think of a class as a stamp or blueprint for objects; by instantiating a class at runtime, you can obtain arbitrarily many objects of a certain kind.

By no means can you adapt procedures and subprograms in a language like ANSI85 COBOL without code duplication. In contrast, the concept of *inheritance* provides you with a powerful tool for the reuse of object-oriented software. You can derive a class that inherits, or reuses, all the attributes and methods of a given class or even several given classes. The resulting class can be extended, and inherited method implementations can be overridden. Consider a checking account for which the class can be regarded merely as an extension of the class Account, for example.

The Fundamental Tenet of Object Orientation

Object orientation builds on three fundamental principles: encapsulation, inheritance, and polymorphism. Understanding these features is the key to understanding object orientation.

Objects and Encapsulation

As you learned earlier, an object is a unit of attributes and methods. Because attributes are just data, and the implementations behind method profiles are pieces of procedural code, an object is somehow similar to a COBOL subprogram. The only way to use a subprogram is to call it. In contrast, you can *invoke* all the different methods of an object. Thus, an object can understand several messages in contrast to a subprogram. A *message* is a request sent to an object to obey one of its methods. A message consists of the method name and parameters, much like a subprogram call.

An account object, for example, has attributes such as an account number, an owner, the date the account was opened, and the actual balance. Suppose that you have the following data declarations for these attributes in the sense of ordinary WORKING-STORAGE data:

```
01 AccountNumber PIC 9(8).
01 Owner        PIC 9(8).
01 DateOpened   PIC 9(8).
01 Balance      PIC S9(10)V9999.
```

There are methods to deposit money into the account, to withdraw money from the account, and to print a statement of the account. (Refer to Figure 27.1 to see the structure of an account object.) You can think of the following procedure code associated with the withdraw method:

```
IF Balance > Amount
 SUBTRACT Amount FROM Balance
 MOVE Amount TO Given
ELSE
```

Object-Oriented COBOL—Concepts

CHAPTER 27

759

27

OBJECT-ORIENTED
COBOL—
CONCEPTS

```
  INITIALIZE Given
  END-IF.
```

The method has two parameters: `Amount` denotes the amount of money to withdraw, whereas `Given` indicates the result of the method invocation—the amount actually granted for the withdrawal. As an example, take a look at the following data declarations corresponding to the method parameters, much like the parameters of a subprogram. Actually, you can consider the following fragment as a kind of method profile for the `withdraw` method:

```
* parameters for the withdraw method
  DATA DIVISION.
  ...
  LINKAGE SECTION.
  01  Amount PIC S9(10)V9999.
  01  Given  PIC S9(10)V9999.
  PROCEDURE DIVISION USING Amount RETURNING Given.
  ...
```

The very important principle of *encapsulation* says that other programs, objects, methods, and so on cannot directly access the attributes of an object. Users only know the interface of the class, the method profiles, which consist of the method name and the types of parameters. Hiding the data (and the implementation of methods) provides two valuable benefits. The object is protected, in a sense, because it has complete control over its data. Also, the user of an object is protected from changes to the attributes and the implementation details of methods. The code using an object will continue to function even if the attributes and methods are changed, as long as the names and the parameters of the methods are left unchanged.

COBOL programmers are familiar with encapsulation up to a certain extent; if you compare procedures and subprograms, you realize that there is an important difference concerning the visibility of data. The data of a `DATA DIVISION` is available to all procedures of the `PROCEDURE DIVISION` of the same program. All items from the `DATA DIVISION` are *global* to the corresponding `PROCEDURE DIVISION`. In contrast, the data declarations of a subprogram are *local* to the subprogram—the *scope* of the declarations is restricted to the subprogram. The main program calling the subprogram cannot directly access the corresponding data. The data of a main program calling a subprogram also is local to the main program. To pass data back and forth between a main program and a subprogram, you use parameters according to a `LINKAGE SECTION`. In the same sense, the attributes of an object are local to the methods of the object.

To work out the limitations of COBOL subprograms, investigate the exact relationship between COBOL subprograms and objects. To model services for an account, consider a COBOL subprogram of the following structure:

```
1        DATA DIVISION.
2         WORKING-STORAGE SECTION.
3          01 Account.
4           05 AccountNumber PIC 9(8).
5           05 Owner         PIC 9(8).
6           05 DateOpened     PIC 9(8).
7           05 Balance       PIC S9(10)V9999.
8
9         LINKAGE SECTION.
10         01  Operation      PIC 99.
11             88 deposit-op    VALUE 01.
12             88 withdraw-op   VALUE 02.
13             88 statement-op  VALUE 03.
14             ...
15         01  Parameters.
16          05 AccountNumber PIC 9(8).
17          05 Owner         PIC 9(8).
18          05 DateOpened     PIC 9(8).
19          05 Balance       PIC S9(10)V9999.
20          05 Amount        PIC S9(10)V9999.
21
22        PROCEDURE DIVISION USING Operation Parameters.
23         EVALUATE TRUE
24          WHEN deposit-op    PERFORM deposit
25          WHEN withdraw-op   PERFORM withdraw
26          ...
27         END-EVALUATE.
28         GOBACK.
29         ...
30        withdraw SECTION.
31         IF Balance IN Account > Amount IN Parameters
32          SUBTRACT Amount IN Parameters FROM Balance IN Account
33         ELSE
34          INITIALIZE Amount IN Parameters
35         END-IF.
36         ...
```

The actual account data (lines 3–7) is local to the subprogram, because it is located in the WORKING-STORAGE SECTION of the subprogram. The actual service to be supplied is selected with the parameter Operation (lines 10–14). Input or output parameters for the respective services are modeled by the group item Parameters (lines 15–20). Note that because a COBOL subprogram usually has only a single entry point, you have to apply a general LINKAGE SECTION (lines 9–20) that can cope with the parameters of all methods. The actual implementation of withdrawals in the withdraw SECTION (lines 30–35) uses the parameter Amount as input for the amount to withdraw and as output to return the amount actually granted for the withdrawal.

Information-hiding works almost perfectly in this subprogram. However, a serious problem still must be solved before you can consider full encapsulation: This subprogram models only a single account. In ANSI85 COBOL, it is not possible to use a program more than once at runtime. More precisely, you cannot have several instantiations of the subprogram, particularly of its DATA DIVISION, at the same time. In contrast, your banking application must cope with any number of accounts. A COBOL programmer might suggest that you regard the account data as LINKAGE data rather than as WORKING-STORAGE data. Thus, the modified subprogram would serve for any account passed to it as a parameter. Unfortunately, you no longer would have encapsulation because you would not have a *unit* of account data and services on that data. This problem is insurmountable in ANSI85 COBOL.

Note that there is another very serious problem with this COBOL subprogram concerning how the owner of the account is modeled. An owner is an object. Thus, the account object somehow should contain the owner object. In contrast, you included only the owner's number (refer to the data item Owner in line 5) in the account data. To include all of the owner's data in the WORKING-STORAGE (or LINKAGE) SECTION would not be a solution at all—not only because encapsulation would not hold in that case, but because the owner might have several accounts, so the owner's data would have to be copied into all accounts, presenting obvious problems of redundancy. In a general sense, ANSI85 COBOL does not provide you with a tool for containment of objects or for multiple references to an object.

The key to object orientation is encapsulation—bundling data and services on the data in objects. Users of the objects can send messages to the object only to access the data. To get the balance of an account object, for example, there must be a corresponding method. The balance will be modified essentially by methods to deposit money into the account and to withdraw money from the account. In a non–object-oriented language like ANSI85 COBOL, you are forced to separate data and services on it, which leads to a number of problems. Two of the most obvious problems follow:

- Procedure code operating on data relies heavily on the concrete representation of the data.
- The programmer must take care to apply the appropriate procedure code to perform a certain service on some data.

Object-oriented languages such as Smalltalk, C++, Java, and OO COBOL support encapsulation by particular language features.

Classes and Inheritance

Although objects are the active agents of an object-oriented application in the sense that they pass messages to each other, you must look for a way to describe in general the structure and behavior of objects. To facilitate dealing with different kinds of software objects, objects are organized into classes. In the banking application, you have different classes of account objects—for example, interest accounts and checking accounts. Moreover, there are classes for customers, employees, and so on. Consequently, all objects belong to certain classes. All objects of a certain class have a common data structure as far as the names and types of attributes, and the objects use exactly the same methods. Figure 27.2 shows the attributes and methods declared in the class Account.

FIGURE 27.2.

Attributes and methods common to account objects.

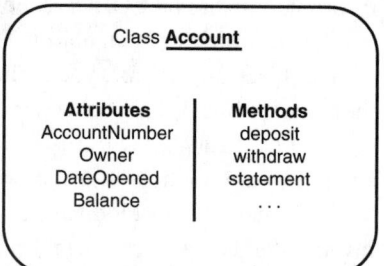

Class **Account**

Attributes	Methods
AccountNumber	deposit
Owner	withdraw
DateOpened	statement
Balance	. . .

The data and the procedural code of objects of a certain class are described once and for all in a class definition. A class can repeatedly be *instantiated* at runtime to obtain any number of objects of the class. In contrast, a COBOL subprogram encapsulates only a single data structure.

This is probably a good time to consider the *lifetime* of an object. As you know, an object is created during runtime. The lifetime continues until the run-unit terminates or the object becomes unreachable (it cannot be used any longer, or the object is explicitly destroyed by the programmer).

You also should consider persistent objects that remain in existence from one run to the next. The language environment or the programmer must put extra effort into achieving persistency: Somehow, objects must be saved and re-created in the next run. It is interesting to note that persistent objects provide an alternative to long-term storage in traditional COBOL programs. An important part of usual applications is their data model in the sense of files, or a database, if you prefer. For each single file, you need to describe the record structure, the access mode, and the organization. The application code is full of procedures operating on single records (or rows). Taking the object-oriented point of view, objects as units of data and methods become the central entities. Here, COBOL files are just one means (besides relational databases and others) of implementing objects that survive the end of a run-unit.

To facilitate reuse and to develop classification structures, the important notion of inheritance enters the game. Inheritance should be regarded as a relation to classes. One class inherits another class—for example, you will see that the class InterestAccount inherits the class Account. In general, one class may even inherit several other classes. What does it mean for a class to inherit another class? What is actually inherited from the superclass? The *subclass*—InterestAccount, in the example—reuses, or inherits, all attributes and methods from its *superclass*—Account, in this example. Further attributes and methods can be added, and inherited methods can be overridden. Figure 27.3 shows the exact relationship between Account and InterestAccount.

FIGURE 27.3.

InterestAccount *inherits* Account.

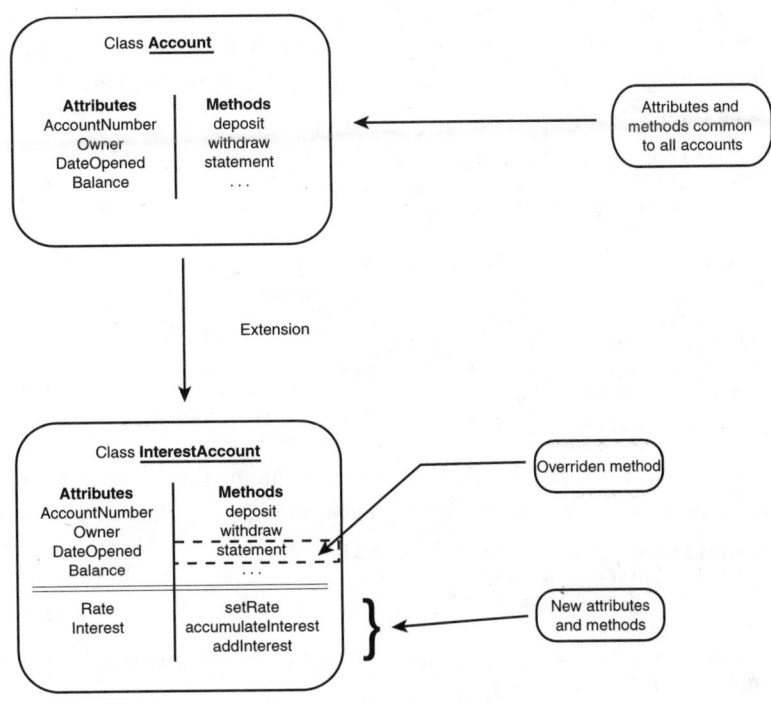

Now consider accounts in more detail. The class Account serves the purpose of figuring out the data and the behavior common to all accounts in a dedicated class. Then, all other specific kinds of accounts—for example, interest accounts and checking accounts—inherit from the basic class Account. The class InterestAccount, for example, inherits Account. Thus, all attributes (Balance) and methods (deposit) of Account are present in InterestAccount as well. To cope with interest, the following extensions are necessary:

- A further attribute, Rate, is needed to store the actual interest rate for the account. The interest rate can be initialized by a corresponding new method, setRate.

- Assume that the interest should be computed every day. In some way, the interest must be accumulated. An auxiliary attribute, Interest, serves this purpose. The daily action to add some interest is modeled by the new method accumulateInterest.

- At the end of the year, the account will be credited with the accumulated interest. A new method, addInterest, does that.

As you learned earlier, you derive a class definition by inheritance and usually add attributes and methods, but you also can override methods. All the methods from Account seem to be suitable for InterestAccount. However, the statement method of an interest account also should print out the information available in addition to the statement of a basic account. Suppose that the statement method of the class Account is responsible for printing the account number, the balance, and so on, as indicated by the following code fragment:

```
* auxiliary data fields for formatting
 01 PrettyAmount  PIC -Z(9)9.9999.
 01 PrettyDate    PIC 99/99/9999.

* procedure code for printing statement (class Account)
 DISPLAY "Account number: " AccountNumber.
 DISPLAY "Owner number: " Owner.
 MOVE DateOpened TO PrettyDate.
 DISPLAY "Date opened: " PrettyDate.
 MOVE Balance TO PrettyAmount.
 DISPLAY "Balance: " PrettyAmount.
```

The refined version of the statement method in the class InterestAccount also should print the interest rate and the accumulated interest, as indicated by this code fragment:

```
* auxiliary data fields for formatting
 01 PrettyRate     PIC Z9.9(10).
 01 PrettyInterest PIC -Z(9)9.9999.

* add (!) this procedure code for printing statement
 MOVE Rate TO PrettyRate.
 DISPLAY "Interest rate: " PrettyRate.
 MOVE Interest TO PrettyInterest.
 DISPLAY "Accumulated interest: " PrettyInterest.
```

Consequently, the statement method of the class Account must be overridden—the inherited implementation must be replaced. Actually, that is a rather disciplined form of overriding: The new implementation extends the original implementation, because a statement for an interest account is an extension of a statement for a basic account.

Single inheritance means that a class inherits from only one other class. For example, `InterestAccount` inherits from `Account` only, as shown in Figures 27.3 and 27.4. When a class inherits from more than one class, you have *multiple inheritance.* A type of account that should be regarded as both an interest account and a checking account is a good example. To derive a corresponding class by inheritance, you need multiple inheritance.

FIGURE 27.4.

A class hierarchy for accounts.

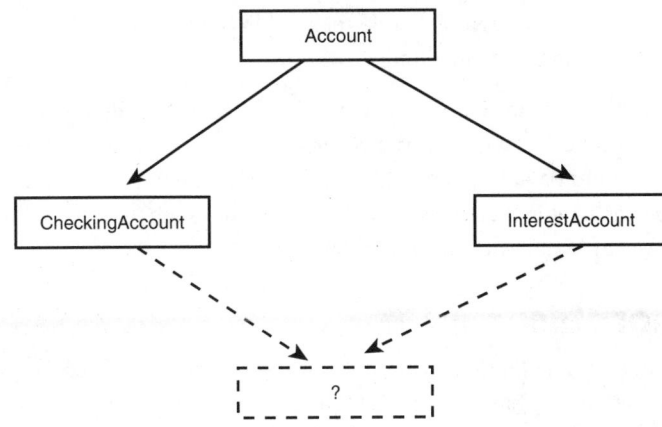

Some languages provide support for single inheritance only—for example, the current Java. There is no general agreement on whether multiple inheritance is essential; it seems that for almost every model requiring multiple inheritance, there is a suitable alternative based on single inheritance only. Multiple inheritance is a bit difficult because of the diamond problem. (Refer to Figure 27.4 to see a diamond-shaped inheritance relation.) A class inherits from several classes that may have an ancestor class in common. The class at the bottom of Figure 27.4 inherits twice from `Account`, for example. Somehow, you must decide how to deal with (or how to avoid) multiple instances of attributes and methods.

How can you avoid multiple inheritance in Figure 27.4? Well, the problem is that you modeled kinds of accounts in the example. Instead, you should consider accounts with a number of roles. Single inheritance is appropriate for classifying different roles, such as the role of a checking account or another role of an interest account. An account object, in turn, will contain an attribute suitable to hold a set of account roles. Some other classes in the banking application may be related to each other by means of inheritance. Managers are employees. Thus, the class `Manager` inherits the class `Employee`. Employees and customers are persons. Thus, the classes `Employee` and `Customer` inherit the class `Person`. Again, roles of persons might be more sensible than subclasses of persons, because a person can be both an employee and a customer.

The proper identification of classes is crucial for achieving a sensible design. Technically, inheritance provides you with an operation on classes suitable to develop hierarchies of classes where common features of several classes can be expressed at some level of the hierarchy. However, inheritance is an appropriate design tool only if the subclass can be regarded as a kind of the superclass. Moreover, a proper class hierarchy presents the conceptual structure of an application domain as proposed by the philosophy behind Simula67, the first object-oriented programming language. Inheritance should not be used too often just to facilitate code reuse; this point of view dates back to the birth of the programming language Smalltalk.

Finally, a class should preserve the behavior of its ancestor classes. This property is crucial, because whenever an object of a certain class is expected, an object of its descendant classes should be able to be used as well. An interest account, for example, understands at least the same messages as a basic account. Such an interchangeability is yet another powerful feature of object orientation.

Polymorphism

It is interesting to note that the same message can be sent to different objects. For example, all account objects have a `statement` method. More precisely, all objects of the class `Account` will have the same `statement` method. All objects of descendant classes of `Account`—for example, `InterestAccount`—have a suitable `statement` method as well. Note that the implementation of the `statement` method in the class `Account` is different from the implementation in `InterestAccount`. All the other methods of `Account` are present in `InterestAccount` as well. Interest accounts preserve the behavior of basic accounts.

Such an interchangeability allows object-oriented programmers to write safe code without knowing exactly in advance which object will be invoked. It is even not necessary that the class of the object is statically known. This is another key principle of object orientation, which is called *polymorphism*. If the exact class of the invoked object is statically known, this is called *static binding*. In contrast, *dynamic binding* is when the method code cannot be determined at compile time, but only at runtime. Of course, an invocation requiring dynamic binding will take longer, but dynamic binding is essential for polymorphism.

To check method invocations at compile time, the possible classes of invoked objects are restricted by the programmer to classes implementing certain method profiles. In contrast, in a language such as ANSI85 COBOL, you are used to hard-wiring the structural decomposition of the application in terms of `PERFORM` statements and subprogram calls.

Object-Oriented COBOL—Concepts

CHAPTER 27

767

27

OBJECT-ORIENTED
COBOL—
CONCEPTS

Consider another example in more detail to contrast the non–object-oriented style of programming with the object-oriented style exploiting polymorphism. Suppose that you want to calculate the salaries for all types of employees in your bank—tellers, salespeople, and managers. The salary probably is calculated in a different way for each kind of employee. Some employees are paid according to a rate system, overtime pay may be relevant, profit-sharing affects the salary of a salesperson, and so on. In ANSI85 COBOL, you probably would approach the problem by using a subprogram to calculate the salary of an employee in which the employee's data is passed to the subprogram as a parameter. Thus, the code performing the calculation takes the following form:

```
CALL "calculateSalary" USING EmployeeData RETURNING Salary
```

Now, suppose that another kind of employee must be modeled. The first disadvantage of the preceding approach results from the missing encapsulation. The definition of the group item `EmployeeData` needs to be adapted, and the application at least needs to be recompiled. The second problem with this approach is that you have to adapt the subprogram `calculateSalary`. Of course, you can avoid the adaptation of the subprogram, but then you have to replace the preceding subprogram call by a suitable distinction of cases. In any case, either in the subprogram itself or in all the occurrences where it is called, you have to maintain a distinction of cases as shown here:

```
EVALUATE TRUE
WHEN EMPLOYEE-IS-TELLER
  ...
WHEN EMPLOYEE-IS-SALESMAN
  ...
WHEN EMPLOYEE-IS-MANAGER
  ...
END-EVALUATE.
```

Such distinctions inflate the code and burn all kinds of employees in the program. There is no way out. You have to adapt existing program code as the application development evolves, particularly if a calculation schema needs to be added or adapted. That is obviously error-prone and inconvenient. In contrast, because of encapsulation, every specific employee object knows itself how to calculate the salary. Thus, if you want to compute the salary of an employee, you can use object-oriented code like this:

```
INVOKE AnEmployee "calculateSalary" RETURNING Salary
```

The `INVOKE` statement looks quite similar to the subprogram call to calculate the salary. Instead of passing the employee's data back and forth, as in the subprogram call, you invoke an employee object. In the subprogram call, `calculateSalary` serves as the name of the subprogram, whereas it must be regarded as a method name in the invocation. *Polymorphism* means that the data item `AnEmployee` can refer to any kind of employee object. Thus, the corresponding code does not have to be changed, even if a new kind of employee is added, and programs do not have to be recompiled. This fact points out other advantages of object orientation: Programs do not have to bother with distinctions of cases, and programs can be extended more easily.

It is safe to accept an object of a descendant class of a certain class A, because all descendant classes implement the interface of A. The term *interface* denotes a list of method profiles. Descendant classes of A can only add methods and override implementations. Thus, the interface is preserved per definition. However, polymorphism is not restricted to classes related to each other by inheritance. This gives you more freedom with invocation, because the object to be invoked at runtime is restricted only by a certain interface, in contrast to a certain class (including its descendant classes). Imagine a program fragment suitable to edit names of entities, such as persons or products. Objects that can be used by such a fragment are restricted only by the following interfaces:

- **getName:** No input parameters, the current name as result.
- **setName:** One input parameter for the new name, no result.

Explaining polymorphism in terms of interfaces rather than in terms of inheritance is a modern point of view supported by the features of languages such as OO COBOL and Java. Without the concept of the interface, a programmer must adapt the inheritance relation to permit polymorphism in a desirable way. Then multiple inheritance is really essential.

Object Orientation Improves Reusability

In this section, you'll learn how object orientation improves reusability. First, you'll look at some technical and design issues concerning class hierarchies. Second, you'll compare certain forms of reuse with other forms.

Fewer Lines of Code: Class Hierarchies

Object-oriented programming is all about writing and using classes. The structure of applications and libraries is expressed by class hierarchies. After the application domain has been thoroughly analyzed, the establishment of class hierarchies and the actual use of class libraries are the keys to reusability in object-oriented programming. In this section, you'll examine the terms *abstract class* and *parameterized class* as descriptive tools for the organization of class hierarchies. You'll then get a short overview of several kinds of class libraries.

In a meaningful class hierarchy, the classes at the root and at the next few levels often are called *abstract classes*. You are not permitted to create objects of an abstract class, because such a class usually has some method profiles without an implementation behind it. However, a class may inherit an abstract class. Therefore, suitable implementations can be added. With abstract classes, you can draw the structure of a class hierarchy, leaving open some details for concrete applications. The class `Employee` in the banking application, for example, probably will be an abstract class, because any particular employee will belong to a certain kind of employee, and there is no general schema for the calculation of a salary.

So far, I have presented inheritance as an operation yielding classes. There is another way to derive classes from *generic* or *parameterized classes*. Consider a container that is expected to hold objects of a certain class—for example, `Account`. For every specific class, you can derive such a container class from a parameterized container class.

When designing an application, you have to map the functionality to certain classes. Different kinds of classes can be distinguished, as shown in Figure 27.5. Some parts of the application are very specific to each class. The remaining functionality is not that specific to the application, but you probably can identify classes that are common for the application domain. Finally, part of the application is nonspecific, because the corresponding classes can be regarded as high-level abstractions from common programming problems.

Figure 27.5.

Mapping functionality to classes.

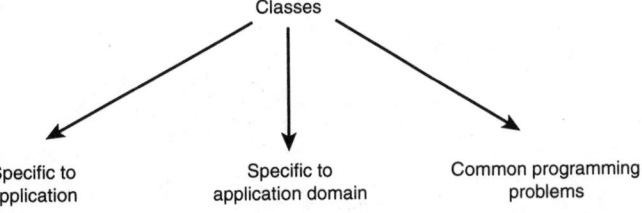

Object-oriented *frameworks* are class hierarchies supporting application-oriented programming. A framework offers several mostly abstract classes modeling an application domain. The starting pointing for a good design of an object-oriented application is a suitable framework. Then programming can be understood as a refinement of the given framework.

Vendors of object-oriented programming environments and toolsets for application development offer *class libraries* covering the following aspects that correspond to common programming problems:

- Graphical user interfaces (GUIs), forms processing
- Programming with threads, event-handling
- Internationalization
- Data storage (for example, indexed files)
- Persistency
- Communications services (for example, interprocess communication)
- Containers or collections

Forms of Reuse

This section contrasts non–object-oriented forms of reuse with object-oriented forms; see Figure 27.6 for an overview. It should become apparent to you that the object-oriented forms surpass—or complete—the conservative techniques.

FIGURE 27.6.

Different forms of reuse.

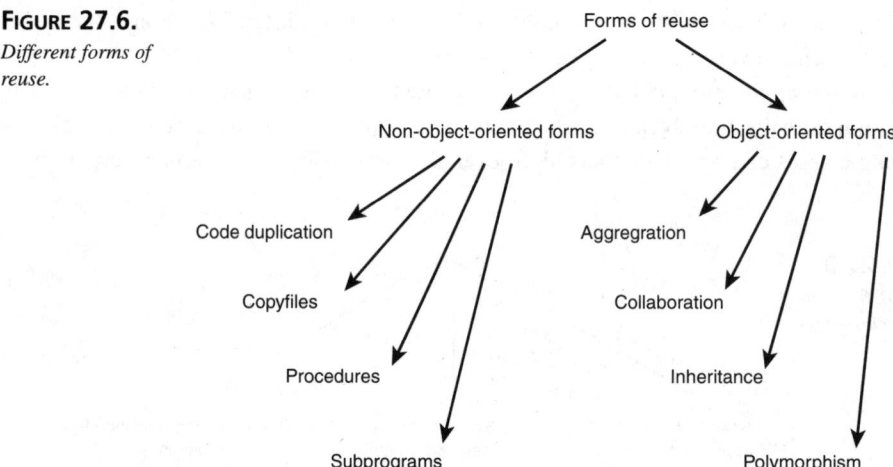

As a COBOL programmer, you know the objectives of structured programming. You are used to decomposing an application into procedures and subprograms that can be coded and tested almost independently of one another. Subprograms support a better reusability than procedures, because they have local data and can be compiled separately. Nevertheless, reusability is seriously limited, because a procedure or a subprogram can be reused only as-is.

Inheritance as an object-oriented form of reuse surpasses conservative techniques, but the applicability of inheritance should not be overvalued. Inheritance—in particular, multiple inheritance—has been used in design and programming in many cases when other techniques turned out to be more appropriate—for example, the interfaces mentioned earlier in this chapter, as well as the aggregation and collaboration discussed later in this section.

Although code duplication was mentioned as a kind of reuse in Figure 27.6, it should be clear that this is a poor form. However, in ANSI85 COBOL, you have no other choice when a subprogram is almost reusable but not as-is. To see why code duplication is poor form, consider the following situations in system maintenance. First, there is a need for a new application module with a design that is very similar to an existing module. To implement that design, you duplicate the code and adapt it accordingly. Later on, the existing module needs to be adapted for some reason. You then have to go through the new module as well to ensure that the similarities in design are retained.

The use of *copyfiles* also is a well-known technique for figuring out common data declarations and procedure code. Unfortunately, using copyfiles must be regarded as a low-level technique that does promote structured programming or systematic reuse. It is a very pragmatic technique: If a code pattern tends to be used more than once, try to figure it out into a new copyfile.

In contrast, aggregation and collaboration are suggested in the object-oriented paradigm. In *aggregation,* one object contains another object. For example, an account has an owner—an object of class Account contains an object of class Person. You should distinguish between real containment and object references that allow multiple clients to refer to the referenced object. *Collaboration* means that a method invokes a collaborator object to implement its service. To print a statement of a checking account, for example, you collaborate with the owner object to retrieve the actual name of the owner. Because the actual object, even the actual class, can change at runtime, such a delegation of responsibilities supports modularity and flexibility of code. Obviously, both aggregation and collaboration are useful in programming, but these concepts should be regarded as design tools as well. When designing an object-oriented application, you are not only concerned with the class hierarchy that is expressed in terms of the inheritance relation, but you also should identify the aggregation relation and the collaborators of methods.

Summary

This chapter explained the central principles of object orientation to give you a good foundation for the implementation presented in Chapter 28. This tutorial should make it easier for you to see why a certain construct is being presented in the next chapter.

It would be an interesting subject to compare object-oriented programming languages and environments. The most prominent languages are C++, Smalltalk, and Java.

Surprisingly, the OO extension of COBOL turns it into a very competitive and modern language. OO COBOL supports multiple inheritance, interfaces, parameterized classes, static- and dynamic-type checking, garbage collection, factories (metaclasses), and more—a combination of concepts not found in any other prominent language. OO COBOL also is applicable in the field of distributed applications—particularly client/server applications.

Object-Oriented COBOL— Implementation

Now it's time to present the object-oriented language extension of COBOL. The concepts, which were presented at an abstract level in Chapter 30, will be instantiated for OO COBOL. Again, the banking application will be used as a running example. First, you'll examine the structure of an OO COBOL program and the central OO COBOL language constructs. Then, you'll look at more secondary constructs and principles. Finally, you'll apply OO COBOL to particular programming problems in the context of your banking application.

As of this writing, the final version of the next COBOL standard, including the object-oriented language extension, was scheduled for the year 2000. However, for the topics covered in this chapter and the corresponding source code, changes are highly unlikely. Several vendors of COBOL environments offer object-oriented COBOL products.

The Essence of OO COBOL

The essence of OO COBOL follows:

- You need class definitions to describe the common structure of all objects of a certain class. A class definition is the object-oriented counterpart of an ordinary COBOL program.

- There is a new form of COBOL data item for object references. Such a data item is suitable to hold a reference to an object (or an object handle, or a kind of pointer, if you prefer), similar to the way in which a numeric data item is suitable to hold a numeric value. Data items for object references are used for invocation—when a message is passed to an object. This new form of data item also is relevant for other language constructs, as you will see later in this chapter.

- Objects are essentially dynamic entities created during runtime. Thus, you need a statement for the creation of objects. There is a new verb, INVOKE, for that purpose.

- An object-oriented application can be regarded as a set of interacting objects. Consequently, you need a new statement for the invocation of objects. The INVOKE-verb is used not only for the creation but also for the invocation of objects.

These issues are discussed in greater detail later in this chapter.

Class Definitions

It is clear that a class definition must describe the attributes and methods common to the objects of the class. Figure 28.1 shows the rough structure of a class definition in OO COBOL.

FIGURE 28.1.

Nested structure of a class definition.

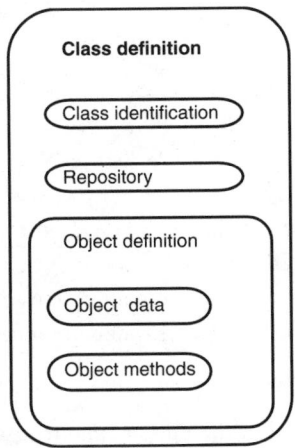

A class definition consists of the following components:

- The class identification is similar in intent to an ordinary program identification from the IDENTIFICATION DIVISION. In contrast to a program identification paragraph, not only the name of a class is fixed, but superclasses are enumerated as well.

- There is a new REPOSITORY paragraph as part of the CONFIGURATION SECTION in the ENVIRONMENT DIVISION. Essentially, this paragraph associates class names with external names. The repository is similar in purpose to SELECT ... ASSIGN clauses for files, where you also use internal names throughout the program, but you have to associate them with external names of the operating/file system.

- The *object definition* defines the data and methods common to the objects of the class. The data is defined within a DATA DIVISION as it is in an ordinary program. The methods are defined within a PROCEDURE DIVISION. (The syntactical structure of a method is explained in more detail later.) Obviously, you need to fix the method's profile (the name of it), as in an identification division; the types of the parameters; and the optional result, as in the LINKAGE SECTION of a subprogram.

The class definition of the class Account looks like this:

```
1       CLASS-ID. Account INHERITS Base.
2         ENVIRONMENT DIVISION.
3          CONFIGURATION SECTION.
4           REPOSITORY.
5            CLASS Account AS "account".
6     * object definition
7           OBJECT.
8            DATA DIVISION.
```

28

OBJECT-ORIENTED
COBOL—
IMPLEMENTATION

```
9      * object data; see below
10          ...
11        PROCEDURE DIVISION.
12     * object methods; see below
13          ...
14       END OBJECT.
15      END CLASS Account.
```

The class identification specifies that the name of the class is `Account` and that the class inherits `Base`, denoting the root class of any OO COBOL class hierarchy. The COBOL standard defines some basic features supported for descendant classes of `Base`. Here is another class identification; it concerns the class `InterestAccount` inheriting `Account`:

```
CLASS-ID. InterestAccount INHERITS Account.
```

Now look at object definitions in more detail. For the class `Account`, use the following object data:

```
1       WORKING-STORAGE SECTION.
2         01 AccountNumber PIC 9(8) VALUE ZERO.
3         01 Owner         USAGE OBJECT REFERENCE Person.
4         01 DateOpened    PIC 9(8) VALUE ZERO.
5         01 Balance       PIC S9(10)V9999 VALUE ZERO.
```

The definition of the data item `Owner` (line 3) will be made clear later in this chapter. For now, just assume that `Owner` is suitable to hold a reference to an object of class `Person`. Remember that you want to provide methods to deposit money into an account, to withdraw money from an account, to print a statement of the account, and so on. Examine the following syntactical structure for any method definition, which is similar to a subprogram:

```
1       METHOD-ID. ... .
2
3       DATA DIVISION.
4        WORKING-STORAGE SECTION.
5          ...
6        LINKAGE SECTION.
7          ...
8
9        PROCEDURE DIVISION USING ... RETURNING ... .
10         ...
11        EXIT METHOD.
12
13      END METHOD ... .
```

Thus you have an identification paragraph to fix the name of the method. Then there is a `DATA DIVISION` divided into a `WORKING-STORAGE` and a `LINKAGE SECTION` much like an ordinary subprogram. The `WORKING-STORAGE` data is local to a method invocation. The

LINKAGE SECTION defines the data items for parameters and the optional result. COBOL subprograms use the LINKAGE SECTION, the USING ..., and the RETURNING phrases of the PROCEDURE DIVISION in the same way. The actual procedure code is given in the PROCEDURE DIVISION, which is similar to the procedure code of a program or subprogram. The construct to finalize a method execution is EXIT METHOD. *Class browsers* of OO COBOL environments provide tool support to navigate through the class hierarchy and to edit the fragments of a class definition, including the methods.

Consider two methods in the banking example: deposit and withdraw. In the complete class definition of Account, these methods are part of the PROCEDURE DIVISION in the object definition:

```
1      METHOD-ID. deposit.
2
3      DATA DIVISION.
4       LINKAGE SECTION.
5        01 Amount PIC S9(10)V9999.
6
7      PROCEDURE DIVISION USING Amount.
8         ADD Amount TO Balance.
9         EXIT METHOD.
10
11     END METHOD deposit.
```

The method deposit is quite simple. The amount supplied as the only parameter Amount is added to the current balance modeled by the attribute Balance. The method withdraw described in the following code is simple, too. Because a withdrawal may fail if the balance is insufficient, the method returns the amount actually granted for the withdrawal.

```
1      METHOD-ID. withdraw.
2
3      DATA DIVISION.
4       LINKAGE SECTION.
5        01 Amount PIC S9(10)V9999.
6        01 Given  PIC S9(10)V9999.
7
8      PROCEDURE DIVISION USING Amount RETURNING Given.
9         IF Balance > Amount
10          SUBTRACT Amount FROM Balance
11          MOVE Amount TO Given
12        ELSE
13          INITIALIZE Given
14        END-IF.
15        EXIT METHOD.
16
17     END METHOD withdraw.
```

28

OBJECT-ORIENTED COBOL— IMPLEMENTATION

Obviously, a class definition may contain a method overriding a method with the same name and the same parameters defined in some of its ancestor classes. The `statement` method of the class `Account`, for example, must be overridden in the class `InterestAccount`.

Data Items for Objects

An object has a unique identifier that is generated by the COBOL runtime system when the object is created. This identifier serves as a reference to that specific object. OO COBOL supports a new datatype, `OBJECT REFERENCE`; a data item of this datatype can hold an object identifier or an object reference. The internal representation of object references is hidden completely from the programmer.

Remember the attributes of a simple account in the banking application. Among other attributes, you need an attribute modeling the owner of the account. Because owners are persons, and persons are objects of a corresponding class `Person`, the attribute `Owner` must be regarded as a data item suitable to hold a reference to an object of class `Person`. Thus, the attribute `Owner` can be declared as the following:

```
01 Owner USAGE OBJECT REFERENCE.
```

Next, you'll examine a statement form based on the `SET`-verb to transfer object references from one data item to another. In the next subsection, you will see the result of your object creation: A new object identifier is placed in a data item of type `OBJECT REFERENCE`. First, note the initialization of data items of type `OBJECT REFERENCE`: A reference to a special `NULL` object, which does not understand a single method, is placed in every data item of type `OBJECT REFERENCE` when storage for the data item is allocated.

Now return to the attribute `Owner`. You know that valid owner objects must be objects of the class `Person`, or maybe of descendant classes of `Person`. Indeed, you can restrict the data item in a corresponding manner in OO COBOL:

```
01 Owner USAGE OBJECT REFERENCE Person.
```

This definition says that the data item can hold only object identifiers of the class `Person` and its descendant classes. Therefore, certain checks are performed at compile time and runtime. If you try to store inappropriate object identifiers in the data item, you get a compiler message if the problem can be detected at compile time; otherwise, you get a runtime error. You can even restrict data items to a single class by a trailing `ONLY` after the class.

There is a statement form based on the `SET`-verb suitable to transfer an object identifier from one data item to another data item. Consider two data items, `Handle1` and `Handle2`, of data type OBJECT REFERENCE. You can set Handle2 equal to Handle1 by using this statement:

SET Handle2 TO Handle1.

You should not use the MOVE-verb for the transfer of object identifiers. Note another restriction: You should not specify data items of the type OBJECT REFERENCE in a file section; there is no sense in storing object references in files because they are meaningful only to the respective run.

Object Creation

The class definition, or class program, serves as a template from which instances, namely objects, can be created during runtime. Of course, you can create multiple objects of a given class. Suppose that you want to create an account in your application where the corresponding object identifier should be stored in the following data item:

01 AnAccount USAGE OBJECT REFERENCE Account.

Objects are created at runtime by INVOKE statements. To create an object of the class Account and to store the new object identifier in AnAccount, for example, the following statement is appropriate:

INVOKE Account "NEW" RETURNING AnAccount.

Figure 28.2 shows the general syntax for object creation. By default, the data items of a created object are initialized according to VALUE clauses.

FIGURE 28.2.
Object creation.

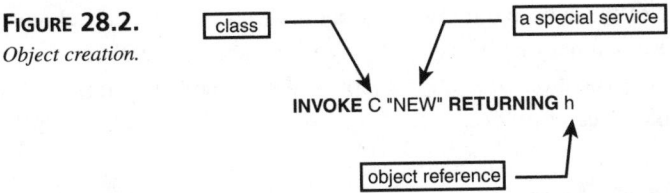

Remember that the data item AnAccount also can hold object identifiers for objects of descendant classes of Account. If you prefer to create an object of class InterestAccount, the following statement is appropriate:

INVOKE InterestAccount "NEW" RETURNING AnAccount.

Object Invocation

Object invocation means to pass a message to an object. A message consists of a method name and parameters, possibly including a data item for the result. INVOKE statements are used to code object invocation; see Figure 28.3 for the syntax. Object-oriented programming is all about interacting objects. Thus, an object-oriented program is not much more than a list of INVOKE statements.

FIGURE 28.3.
Object invocation.

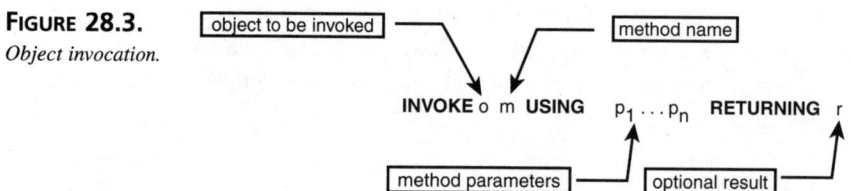

Assume that the data item AnAccount refers to an account object. To invoke the method deposit of the object, you can use the following INVOKE statement:

```
INVOKE AnAccount "deposit" USING SomeAmount.
```

Assume that the following definitions of data items are used in the INVOKE statement:

```
01 AnAccount     USAGE OBJECT REFERENCE Account.
01 SomeAmount    PIC S9(10)V9999.
```

To understand the use of results in method invocation, consider an invocation of the method withdraw:

```
INVOKE AnAccount "withdraw" USING SomeAmount RETURNING GivenAmount.
```

Overall, the syntax for object invocation is quite similar to a subprogram call. The essential difference is the way in which the code to be performed is identified: A subprogram call contains the name of the subprogram, whereas an invocation enumerates both the object and the method. Remember that because of polymorphism, the actual code to be performed according to an invocation generally cannot be determined at compile time, but a dispatch must take place at runtime.

Elaborate Issues

You now know about defining classes in OO COBOL, dealing with object references in the DATA DIVISION and the PROCEDURE DIVISION, and creating and invoking objects. These are the basics. Now you'll look at more elaborate constructs and principles, such as the following:

- Predefined object identifiers SELF and SUPER
- Factories as a way to associate services with classes rather than objects
- Certain features to retain readability in OO COBOL
- The migration of legacy code

SELF and SUPER

There are two predefined object identifiers, SUPER and SELF, which have some important applications. SELF and SUPER refer to the object on which the current method is executing. The difference concerns the way method resolution takes place.

If SELF denotes the object to be invoked, method resolution is based on the whole set of methods defined for the runtime class of the object on which the current method is executing. Consequently, SELF is useful if the code of an object's method must refer to other methods of the same object. Consider the addInterest method for interest accounts that follows. The method is used to credit an account with the accumulated interest (line 5), and after the interest has been credited, the corresponding data item must be initialized for subsequent accumulation (line 6). SELF is necessary because the implementation of the method addInterest refers to the deposit method of the same object.

```
1      * part of the InterestAccount class definition
2      METHOD-ID. addInterest.
3
4        PROCEDURE DIVISION.
5         INVOKE SELF "deposit" USING Interest.
6         INITIALIZE Interest.
7         EXIT METHOD.
8
9        END METHOD addInterest.
```

SUPER refers to the object on which the current method is executing as well. In contrast to SELF, the method resolution ignores all the methods defined in the class containing the invocation. Thus, the method code that will be executed is definitely found in some ancestor class.

As an example, consider the statement method of class InterestAccount that follows. It overrides the statement method of class Account. Remember that InterestAccount is a subclass of Account. The statement of an interest account is merely an extension of the statement of a basic account. Thus, you would like to refer to method code of basic accounts when you implement the statement method of interest accounts. The object identifier SUPER is needed for that purpose; see line 13.

```
1      * part of the InterestAccount class definition
2      METHOD-ID. statement.
3
4        DATA DIVISION.
5         WORKING-STORAGE SECTION.
6          01 PrettyRate     PIC Z9.9(10).
7          01 PrettyInterest PIC -Z(9)9.9999.
8
9         LINKAGE SECTION.
10
11        PROCEDURE DIVISION.
```

```
12    * extend (!) the statement of the superclass
13         INVOKE SUPER "statement".
14         MOVE Rate TO PrettyRate.
15         DISPLAY "Interest rate: " PrettyRate.
16         MOVE Interest TO PrettyInterest.
17         DISPLAY "Accumulated interest: " PrettyInterest.
18         EXIT METHOD.
19
20      END METHOD statement.
```

Think about the difference between SELF and SUPER: If you used SELF in line 13, you would refer to the code that is executing, which is obviously nonsense. You really want to execute the statement method of the superclass.

In the presence of multiple inheritance (the INHERITS clause of the class identification specifies more than one class), the use of SUPER must be qualified by the actual super-class *id* used for method resolution. Then the object identifier takes the following form: *id* OF SUPER.

Factories

You have examined the rough structure of a class definition with the object definition as the central part. An object definition defines a kind of a template for the data and the methods of objects to be regarded as instances of the class. Depositing money into an account and printing a statement of an account are services to be supplied by particular account objects. These services are described in the class definition once and for all. Sometimes, services cannot be naturally associated with ordinary objects. Creating a new account object cannot be regarded as a method for account objects, for example, because an object cannot create itself. Look at another example: Generating a new valid account number is a service somehow related to accounts, but you end up with a wrong design if the service is regarded as a method of any account object. Instead, it is a service to be done only during the creation and initialization of an account object. To facilitate the association of data and methods with the class itself instead of with objects, OO COBOL supports *factories*.

You need to understand how object creation is modeled as a service associated with classes instead of objects. You invoke the class to create a new object and to return its identifier. Note that ordinary object invocation and object creation have the same shape. In the first case, you use an ordinary object identifier to refer to the object to be invoked. In the second case, you use the class identifier. Object creation is regarded as the factory method NEW associated with any class. Actually, the factory method NEW is inherited from the class Base, the root class of any class hierarchy in OO COBOL. To deal with data and methods associated with the class, the structure of a class definition is extended; see Figure 28.4 for the corresponding completion.

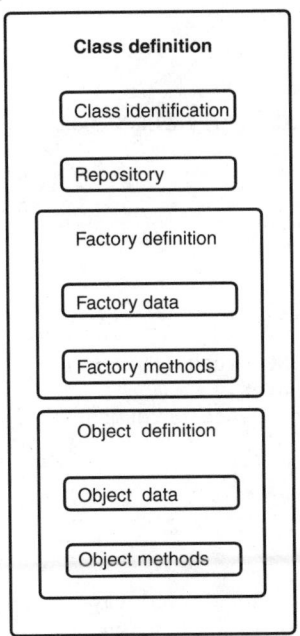

FIGURE 28.4.

The complete structure of a class definition.

Factories are characterized in OO COBOL as described here:

- You distinguish two kinds of objects: *instance objects* and *factory objects*. Whenever you see in this text the word *object* alone, it refers to an instance object. Factory objects are used primarily to create instance objects (thus the term *factory*).

- For each class, a single factory object is created automatically when the class program is loaded. Remember that the class program provides only a template from which instance objects can be created. Invoking factory methods is very similar to the way you call a subprogram. In contrast, ordinary methods cannot be invoked without first instantiating the class.

- A run-unit can create multiple instance objects during runtime, but there is only one factory object.

Your banking application provides a good example of factories. Whenever you create a new account, you probably have to take care of generating valid account numbers. To keep the example simple, assume that you get new valid account numbers by incrementing a counter every time a new account needs to be created. In the factory definition that follows, you have a data item, AccountNumberCounter, to be regarded as factory data, and a factory method, freshAccountNumber, intended to return a fresh account number.

```
1          FACTORY.
2
3          DATA DIVISION.
4           WORKING-STORAGE SECTION.
5            01 AccountNumberCounter PIC 9(8) VALUE ZERO.
6
7          PROCEDURE DIVISION.
8
9           METHOD-ID. freshAccountNumber.
10           DATA DIVISION.
11            LINKAGE SECTION.
12             01 AccountNumber-L PIC 9(8).
13
14            PROCEDURE DIVISION RETURNING AccountNumber-L.
15            ADD 1 TO AccountNumberCounter.
16            MOVE AccountNumberCounter TO AccountNumber-L.
17            EXIT METHOD.
18
19           END METHOD freshAccountNumber.
20
21         FACTORY.
```

To make sure that this method is really used in the desired way whenever a new account is created, suppose that you prefer to override the predefined factory method NEW; see the code fragment that follows. First line 12 performs elementary object creation, referring to the inherited factory method NEW. Actually NEW is inherited from the system class Base. Then lines 13–14 invokes the factory method to obtain a fresh account number. Finally line 15 stores the new account number in the account just created by using ordinary object invocation.

```
1      * class Account; factory definition
2          METHOD-ID. NEW.
3
4           DATA DIVISION.
5            WORKING-STORAGE SECTION.
6             01 TempAccountNumber PIC 9(8).
7
8            LINKAGE SECTION.
9             01 THE-OBJECT USAGE OBJECT REFERENCE.
10
11           PROCEDURE DIVISION RETURNING THE-OBJECT.
12           INVOKE SUPER "NEW" RETURNING THE-OBJECT.
13           INVOKE ACCOUNT "freshAccountNumber"
14           RETURNING TempAccountNumber.
15           INVOKE THE-OBJECT "setAccountNumber" USING TempAccountNumber.
16           EXIT METHOD.
17
18         END METHOD NEW.
```

It is interesting to notice that line 13 uses the class identifier ACCOUNT instead of SELF in order to invoke the factory method for generating a fresh account number. This choice is necessary if the account numbers of all accounts (also accounts of descendant classes of ACCOUNT), is to be administered centrally in the factory object of ACCOUNT.

Although factories support a cleaner design, the concept is not strictly necessary. Services that should not be associated with instance objects could be coded as ordinary COBOL code, or you can introduce auxiliary classes, where you probably create only a single instance of such a class. These auxiliary objects can serve much the same purpose as factory objects. The only exception concerns pure object creation. If you did not have factories, you would need a special language construct for object creation.

Retaining Readability

Object-oriented programming is all about passing messages to objects—invoking objects. Consequently, a COBOL program making extensive use of object orientation can become little more than a collection of INVOKE statements. In the good ole days, COBOL was designed with readability as a major factor in mind. To retain readability, you need further notation as an alternative to simple INVOKE statements. You can use the following approaches:

- The concept of inline method invocation allows an invocation to be placed anywhere where the result of the invocation could be used.

- Often, methods are needed for access to the encapsulated data of an object. Consequently, there are invocations to get a value from the object or to pass a value to the object. *Object properties* provide a simple mechanism to support such invocations with a special syntax.

- It is possible to support a flexible syntax for method invocation. The syntax will not be based on the INVOKE verb but rather on a verb specific for the method. Micro-Focus has coined the term *use skeletons* in that context.

The following example illustrates inline method invocation. Suppose that you want to calculate the balance of all the accounts of a certain customer. The sum is stored in the data item SomeAmount. To add the balance of a certain account whose object identifier is stored in the data item AnAccount, you need to use the following statement sequence:

```
INVOKE AnAccount "getBalance" RETURNING Balance-W.
ADD Balance-W TO SomeAmount.
```

Thus, you use a temporary data field, Balance-W, to hold the result of the method invocation. In a second step, the value of the field is added to SomeAmount. Using inline method invocation, the preceding code segment reads as this:

```
ADD AnAccount :: "getBalance" TO SomeAmount.
```

28

OBJECT-ORIENTED COBOL— IMPLEMENTATION

Inline method invocation makes sense only for methods that have a RETURNING clause. Anywhere a data item of the result type of the method can be used, an inline method invocation can be used as well. In contrast to ordinary invocations based on the INVOKE verb, you use a special notation for inline method invocations: The object and message are separated from each other by ::. Of course, the messages may contain parameters. The notation is the same as for using intrinsic functions; the parameters are specified inside parentheses separated by commas or spaces. Consider the following code fragment intended to display the result of a withdrawal:

```
INVOKE AnAccount "withdraw" USING SomeAmount RETURNING GivenAmount.
MOVE GivenAmount To PrettyAmount.
DISPLAY PrettyAmount.
```

PrettyAmount is a data item with a PICTURE clause suitable to display amounts. With inline method invocation, you get the following fragment:

```
MOVE AnAccount :: "withdraw" (SomeAmount) To PrettyAmount.
DISPLAY PrettyAmount.
```

You also can use nested inline method invocation when the result of an invocation is an object reference that can be used for a further invocation. Suppose that you want to display the name of the owner of an account. Here is a fragment using ordinary syntax:

```
INVOKE AnAccount "getOwner" RETURNING SomeOwner.
INVOKE SomeOwner "getName" RETURNING SomeName.
DISPLAY SomeName.
```

By using nested inline method invocation, you get the following fragment:

```
DISPLAY AnAccount :: "getOwner" :: "getName".
```

Now consider object properties in more detail. These properties support a kind of method particularly suited for getting a value from an object (GET methods) or passing a value to an object (SET methods).

As a consequence of encapsulation, you cannot access attributes directly, but you can implement methods that serve this purpose. Consider the following method, getBalance, for the class Account, which is suitable to return the current value of the attribute Balance:

```
1      METHOD-ID. getBalance.
2
3        DATA DIVISION.
4          LINKAGE SECTION.
5            01 Balance-L PIC S9(10)V9999.
6
7        PROCEDURE DIVISION RETURNING Balance-L.
8          MOVE Balance TO Balance-L.
9          EXIT METHOD.
```

```
10
11      END METHOD getBalance.
```

No application will ever depend on the actual internal representation of the balance. Applications depend only on the profile of the method. You can add a PROPERTY clause to an attribute definition to point out that you assume implicit definitions of a GET method and a SET method for this attribute. As an example, consider the following definition of the attribute Owner of the class Account:

```
01 Balance PIC S9(10)V9999 VALUE ZERO PROPERTY.
```

Here, a corresponding GET method—a method such as getBalance—is defined implicitly. Another method—the SET method—is defined implicitly as well. The SET method for Balance is suitable to pass a balance to an object of class Account.

If the implicit definitions become inappropriate, they can be overridden. If you need to change the internal representation of an attribute, for example, the method profile can be kept as-is if the explicit definition performs the necessary conversion. Thus, all the clients of the corresponding classes are well-shielded from the potential ripple effect of changes. There is a special form of the METHOD-ID paragraph for the SET and GET methods, but I will not discuss the details here.

The GET and SET methods contribute to readability, because there is a special form of invocation for them: it's a kind of inline method invocation. Suppose that o is an object, and a is an attribute of o. Anywhere a value of the type of a can be used, the form a OF o can be used as well. The form denotes the inline method invocation of the GET method for a. Using ordinary syntax, you move the balance of an account to a data item by the following invocation:

```
INVOKE AnAccount "getBalance" RETURNING SomeAmount.
```

Using the special notation for GET methods, the same effect is achieved by the following line of code:

```
MOVE Balance Of AnAccount TO SomeAmount.
```

Actually, whether a OF o denotes the inline method invocation of the GET method depends on the context. It also can denote the inline method invocation of the SET method for a if it is used in a context where a data item (and not just a value) of a's type is needed.

Finally, you should sketch a form of notational support based on a flexible syntax for method invocation. The general idea is that a method definition can be extended by some skeleton for method invocation based on user-defined verbs and keywords. Statements following the skeleton then can be used for method invocation instead of statements using the INVOKE verb. Thereby readability is improved.

To deposit money into an account, you might use proper English instead of a statement with the INVOKE verb:

```
DEPOSIT SomeAmount INTO AnAccount.
```

This statement corresponds to the following invocation:

```
INVOKE AnAccount "deposit" USING SomeAmount.
```

Reusing Legacy Code

When writing new applications, you should apply object orientation to gain all the benefits of it. For existing applications, or legacy code, you must ask two questions:

- How can object orientation help to improve legacy code? You might want to bring the benefits of object orientation to existing applications.
- How can legacy code be reused in an object-oriented context? Obviously, you can't and don't want to rewrite huge business applications from scratch. You have to consider hybrid applications consisting of legacy code and new object-oriented code.

The hybrid nature of the new COBOL language is a key feature to support evolution of software: Each ANSI85 COBOL program will continue to function. You can reuse procedural code in an object-oriented application—for example, by calling subprograms in method code. In maintaining or improving procedural code, you can start to employ object orientation in the following ways:

- You can use object-oriented parts of the application by adding invocations to the previous procedural code.
- You can identify certain parts of the functionality of an existing legacy application and package the corresponding data and services, yielding an object that serves as a kind of wrapper. In this way, you achieve encapsulation and can possibly reuse the extracted functionality.

How can you migrate legacy code to object-oriented code or at least qualify legacy code for further use in an object-oriented context? There is a sort of correspondence between programs and classes, as shown in Figure 28.5: A program becomes a class. WORKING-STORAGE data items become attributes. PERFORM statements are converted into INVOKE statements.

FIGURE 28.5.

The migration of legacy code.

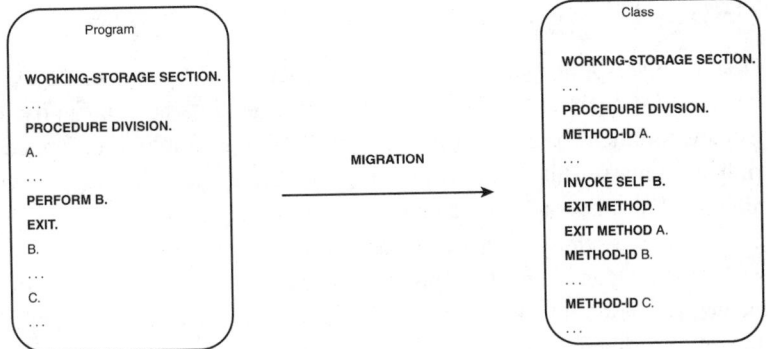

Such a migration supports reusability of the legacy code:

- You can develop clients of the legacy code that perform single procedures of the program. Actually, you invoke methods.

- By replacing PERFORMs with INVOKEs, you get rid of the requirement that the procedure being performed must be in the same program.

- You can change procedures in the program without changing the code of the program. Inheritance provides you with the expressive power to derive variants of a program.

Micro-Focus even provides compiler functionality, performing a kind of transformation similar to Figure 28.5 on-the-fly during compilation.

Object-Oriented COBOL in Action

The first two examples of object-oriented programming built on services that are likely to be supported by the class library supplied with any concrete OO COBOL language environment. Here, you'll look at collections in more detail and briefly examine the development of graphical user interfaces. The actual code samples are based on Micro-Focus Personal COBOL, but the examples easily can be adapted to other environments. A third example sketches an approach to achieve *persistency*—when objects can remain in existence from one run to the next.

Collections

Designing an application usually can be divided into a part specific to the application and other, more general, parts. Among the more general parts, you can try to identify classes that are common for the application domain—for example, financial concerns—and possibly even classes that are much more general in the sense that they can be regarded as high-level abstractions from common programming problems—for example, collection classes. A *collection* is a group of related objects. Collection classes support services such as adding an element to and removing an element from a collection and looking up an element based on a key or index. More sophisticated services support the creation of a suitably restricted copy of a collection or the subsequent invocation of each element of a collection using the same message. Prominent examples of collections follow:

- **Bags:** Groups of objects where duplicates are permitted
- **Sets:** Groups of objects where duplicates are not permitted
- **Ordered collections:** For example, stacks modeling the first-in, last-out behavior of adding and removing elements

In your banking application, there are several services that aren't associated with a particular object but instead with all objects of a certain kind—for example, a collection of objects:

- If you want to accumulate the balance of all accounts as a kind of cash check, you must have access to all the accounts.
- To log the actions performed on an account in order to be able to print out an exact statement of an account, you have to manage all the actions in a corresponding collection, possibly ordered historically.

To attack the first problem, use an ordered collection to keep track of all accounts. If an account is created, the corresponding object identifier is added to the collection. If an account is liquidated, the corresponding object identifier is removed from the collection. The code fragment that follows demonstrates the creation of a collection object (lines 1–3). Then, one object is added to the collection (line 4). Here, you assume that AnAccount is a data item of data type OBJECT REFERENCE Account.

```
1        MOVE 0 TO CollectionSize.
2        INVOKE OrderedCollection "ofReferences" USING CollectionSize
3                                            RETURNING AnOrderedCollection.
4        INVOKE AnOrderedCollection "add" USING AnAccount.
```

In the given class library, the class OrderedCollection is useful for dynamically growing collections, where the actual elements in the collection can be addressed through an index. You create a collection (lines 2–3) with the initial size 0 (line 1). The factory method ofReferences is a certain variant of NEW. The collection is extended automatically whenever an entry is added (line 4). The next fragment iterates the entries of the collection and adds each balance to a data item Amount:

```
1       INVOKE AnOrderedCollection "size" RETURNING CollectionSize.
2       INITIALIZE Amount.
3       PERFORM VARYING LoopCount FROM 1 BY 1
4              UNTIL LoopCount > CollectionSize
5        INVOKE AnOrderedCollection "at" USING LoopCount
6        RETURNING SomeHandle
7        INVOKE SomeHandle "getBalance" RETURNING Balance
8        ADD Balance TO Amount
9       END-PERFORM.
```

You first retrieve the current number of entries (line 1) using the method size. You can access each entry by its index (lines 5–6) by using the method at.

Now consider another kind of collection: *dictionaries*. A dictionary stores key/data pairs of associations. You need dictionaries in the following situation. An operator usually enters the account number to identify an account. In contrast, the program code uses the object identifier of the corresponding account object to deal with the account. Thus you need a translation from account numbers to object identifiers. The details for creating a suitable dictionary are a bit technical, but essentially you have some code such as the following:

```
INVOKE Dictionary "ofValues" USING ... RETURNING AccountDictionary.
```

The factory method ofValues can be regarded as a variant of NEW. What is probably more interesting is the way in which you access a dictionary: You add a pair consisting of an account number, AccountNumber, and the corresponding object identifier, AnAccount, in the following way:

```
INVOKE AccountDictionary "atPut" USING AccountNumber AnAccount.
```

Given an account number, you get the corresponding object identifier by the following invocation of atOrNil. Note that if no pair matches the given key, the NULL object is returned.

```
INVOKE AccountDictionary "atOrNil" USING AccountNumber
RETURNING AnAccount.
```

Graphical User Interfaces

The development of *graphical user interfaces* (GUIs) is involved in almost every business programming project. This section does not claim to provide even the shortest tutorial on the development of GUIs, but the subject is discussed here with an emphasis on the object-oriented point of view. What are the usual objects in an application containing GUI functionality? What kind of interaction takes place?

Consider the simple modal window in Figure 28.6 as a running example. The operator will see the Deposit window if a deposit action for a certain account has been requested—for example, by a menu item or by a pushbutton in a parent window. The modal dialog is finished with the OK or the Cancel button. If the OK button was clicked, the appropriate deposit message must be sent to the account object under consideration.

FIGURE 28.6.

A modal window to deposit money into an account.

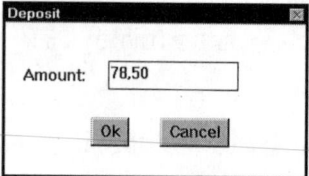

A class library facilitating GUI development must offer classes for all kinds of GUI objects. For this modal window, classes were used for modal windows, entry fields, pushbuttons, and text labels. This section will not describe all the trivial details of how to end up with a window like the one in Figure 28.6; it is just a sequence of invocations passing positions, dimensions, labels, and other straightforward parameters to the GUI widgets. This window is a window object providing the following services based on corresponding methods: The window can be shown, it can be hidden, it can moved on the screen, and the amount entered in the entry field can be retrieved.

There is an important technique for how real application objects (accounts, persons, and so on) and GUI objects (windows, pushbuttons, and so on) interact with each other. An application with a GUI usually is event-driven. The behavior is not hard-wired by a certain sequence of method invocations. Instead, the invocations are performed by a central authority, depending on certain events triggering the corresponding invocations. What you need is the concept of a *callback*. A callback is an object storing a message that may be invoked later. Callbacks understand the message invoke to invoke the stored message. Consider the action to be taken when the OK pushbutton is clicked in the window. The corresponding procedure code is regarded as the method okButtonPushed of the application object Handler:

```
1      METHOD-ID. okButtonPushed.
2        PROCEDURE DIVISION.
3      * retrieve the current value of the entry field
4          INVOKE DepositWindow "getAmount" RETURNING SomeAmount.
5      * perform the actual deposit action
6          INVOKE currentAccount "deposit" USING SomeAmount.
7      * hide the modal window
8          INVOKE DepositWindow "hide".
9          EXIT METHOD.
10     END METHOD okButtonPushed.
```

You must tell the pushbutton that the event ButtonClicked should trigger the preceding method:

```
MOVE ButtonClicked TO Event.
INVOKE OkButton "setEventTo" USING Event Handler "okButtonPushed ".
```

As you can see, the pushbutton objects offer the method setEventTo to associate an event with a message. An event manager, the central authority in an event-driven application, will invoke the stored message according to the events taking place. Event managers are supported by the class library as well. An application first creates some initial GUI objects and associates some events with suitable callbacks. Then control is passed to the event handler, which can be thought of as a simple loop looking all the time for events with an associated callback. Closing the main window of your application should terminate the event handler and thereby the application. Thus you have the following architecture:

```
* Create the main window and do other initialization
    INVOKE MainWindowClass "NEW" USING Oo-desktop RETURNING MainWindow
* Create an EventManager object
    INVOKE EventManager "NEW" RETURNING AnEventManager.
* Register initial events
    ...
* Show window and start processing events
    INVOKE MainWindow "show".
    INVOKE AnEventManager "run".
    EXIT PROGRAM.
```

Persistent Objects

Without further precautions, all objects (and with them, their data) disappear if the run-unit terminates. Obviously, such behavior is not sensible for many objects. Account objects or person objects, for example, certainly should remain in existence from one run to the next. Such objects, which are passed from one run to the next, are called *persistent objects,* as shown in Figure 28.7.

FIGURE 28.7.

Persistency.

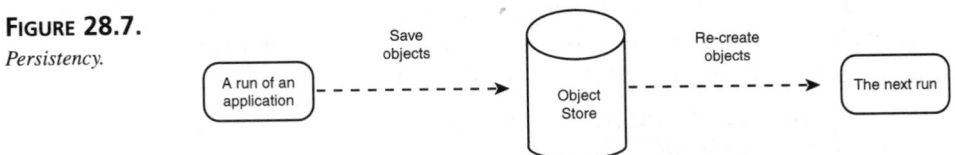

The standard for OO COBOL does not cover support for persistent objects. On the other hand, it is likely that concrete OO COBOL environments support persistency in one way or another. Here, you'll look at an approach by which persistency is achieved based on

COBOL's files. The application will be extended with code responsible for extracting data from the relevant objects to write it out to a file. Then, during initialization of the next run of the application, the application will read the data back in from the file to put it back into suitably created objects. Note that this technique is not only worth mentioning in the context of persistency, but also gives some insight as to how an object-oriented application might access files and tables of a relational or object-oriented database. The concrete examples use indexed COBOL files as the object store, but it should be apparent that the architecture could be reused even if a database needs to be accessed—for example, by means of embedded SQL.

What kind of services do you need to support persistent objects?

- The application must be able to write out an object's data to an object store—for example, to a particular indexed file dedicated to the respective class. You have the problem that object references cannot be written out in a file, because they have no meaning beyond a run-unit, similar to a pointer to a memory cell. Instead, you must use an ordinary key to identify the actual object in the object store—for example, an account number identifies an account.

- In the next run, you can "re-create" saved objects by loading their data and putting the data back into suitably created objects. Placing data in an object's attributes often is referred to as *population.*

- If an object is destroyed or updated, you must ensure that the object store is modified accordingly. There are plenty of optimization issues that should be addressed. It is not sensible, for example, to update the object store for every single change of an object's state. Finally, some machinery may be needed to cope with transactions and with committing changes in a multiuser environment.

An ideal persistency would be based on the objects themselves including their object identifier. The actual location of the objects—for example, memory or an object store—would be of no interest to the application programmer. Here, persistency is only simulated based on storing an object's data using ordinary keys instead of object references.

Now consider how you get persistent objects of class Account. First, you present the FILE-CONTROL paragraph and the FILE SECTION of an ordinary indexed file, AccountFile, which can be regarded as the object store for the class Account:

```
1        ENVIRONMENT DIVISION.
2          INPUT-OUTPUT SECTION.
3           FILE-CONTROL.
4            SELECT AccountFile ASSIGN TO "./account.dat"
5             ORGANIZATION IS INDEXED
6             ACCESS IS RANDOM
7             RECORD KEY IS AccountNumber.
8
```

```
9       DATA DIVISION.
10       FILE SECTION.
11        FD AccountFile.
12        01  AccountRecord.
13         05 AccountNumber PIC 9(8).
14         05 OwnerNumber   PIC 9(8).
15         05 DateOpened    PIC 9(8).
16         05 Balance       PIC S9(10)V9999.
```

You don't want to decide yet what the appropriate location of this code might be; it could be located in the factory or the object definition of Account. Using an external class could be sensible as well. Note that this record description deviates from the object data definition in how the owner of the account is identified: You use the number of the person instead of an object reference.

When you create an object, you can force that some initialization is performed. When you create a new account object, for example, you initialize the account with a fresh account number. Such initialization probably will make no sense for fresh objects that will be populated anyway using the data from the object store. Consequently, I suggest a factory method, fresh, that has no other purpose than to create an object suitable for subsequent population:

```
1       METHOD-ID. fresh.
2
3       DATA DIVISION.
4         LINKAGE SECTION.
5          01 AnAccount USAGE OBJECT REFERENCE.
6
7       PROCEDURE DIVISION RETURNING AnAccount.
8     * Invoke the method NEW of the Base class
9         INVOKE SUPER "NEW" RETURNING AnAccount.
10        EXIT METHOD.
11
12      END METHOD fresh.
```

Given an account number AccountNumber, the corresponding object is reestablished by reading back the data from the file in the following manner:

```
1           read-and-populate SECTION.
2             INITIALIZE AccountRecord.
3             MOVE AccountNumber TO AccountNumber IN AccountRecord.
4             READ AccountFile
5              INVALID KEY
6               SET AnAccount TO NULL
7              NOT INVALID KEY
8               INVOKE Account "fresh" RETURNING AnAccount
9               MOVE AccountNumber TO AccountNumber OF AnAccount
10              MOVE DateOpened    TO DateOpened    OF AnAccount
11              MOVE Balance       TO Balance       OF AnAccount
12      * Translate the person's number into an object identifier.
```

```
13        * That possibly includes loading the object from the object store.
14              INVOKE ... "readPerson" USING OwnerNumber RETURNING Owner-Temp
15              MOVE Owner-Temp   TO Owner          OF AnAccount
16           END-READ.
```

Note that population is coded here using the object property syntax.

Before you look at more details, you should consider two possible ways to associate the preceding services needed for persistency with an OO COBOL application. Writing an object to the object store can be modeled by a method of the object. Re-creating an object by looking up the object store could be regarded as a factory method of the corresponding class. I prefer to place all the services in a separate class, providing a kind of *database interface* (DBI). For an ordinary class like Account, there will be a DBI class—for example, AccountDBI. All the services will be handled by the factory object of the DBI class. You therefore can achieve persistency without adapting the underlying class definition—for example, Account.

Here is the factory method writeAccount of the class AccountDBI writing out an account object to the corresponding file:

```
1        METHOD-ID. writeAccount.
2
3        DATA DIVISION.
4         WORKING-STORAGE SECTION.
5          01 Owner-Temp USAGE OBJECT REFERENCE Person.
6
7         LINKAGE SECTION.
8          01 AnAccount        USAGE OBJECT REFERENCE Account.
9
10       PROCEDURE DIVISION USING AnAccount.
11        INITIALIZE AccountRecord.
12        MOVE AccountNumber OF AnAccount
13        TO AccountNumber   IN AccountRecord.
14        MOVE DateOpened    OF AnAccount
15        TO DateOpened      IN AccountRecord.
16        MOVE Balance       OF AnAccount
17        TO Balance         IN AccountRecord.
18        MOVE Owner         OF AnAccount   TO Owner-Temp.
19        IF Owner-Temp NOT = NULL
20         MOVE PersonNumber OF Owner-Temp
21         TO OwnerNumber    IN AccountRecord.
22        WRITE AccountRecord
23         INVALID KEY
24          REWRITE AccountRecord
25        END-WRITE.
26        EXIT METHOD.
27
28       END METHOD writeAccount.
```

Object property syntax is used to read the object's data. The object identifier for the owner of the account is translated first to the person's number used as the key value in the object store for persons, similar to the way in which account numbers identify account objects.

The factory method `readAccount` of the class `AccountDBI` is useful to re-create an account object. Essentially, the method performs the `read-and-populate` SECTION that was discussed earlier. However, you should make sure that an object is not re-created more than once. To keep track of the objects re-created so far, you use a dictionary—a special kind of collection. The entries of the dictionary are pairs, each consisting of an account number and the corresponding object identifier. Thus the code that follows first looks up the dictionary to see whether the object has been re-created already (lines 12–13); if not, the object is loaded and the dictionary is extended:

```
1       METHOD-ID. readAccount.
2
3        DATA DIVISION.
4         WORKING-STORAGE SECTION.
5          01 Owner-Temp USAGE OBJECT REFERENCE Person.
6
7         LINKAGE SECTION.
8          01 AccountNumber   PIC 9(8).
9          01 AnAccount        USAGE OBJECT REFERENCE Account.
10
11       PROCEDURE DIVISION USING AccountNumber RETURNING AnAccount.
12         INVOKE AccountDictionary "atOrNil" USING AccountNumber
13         RETURNING AnAccount.
14         IF AnAccount = NULL
15          PERFORM read-and-populate
16          IF AnAccount NOT = NULL
17           INVOKE AccountDictionary "atPut"
18           USING AccountNumber AnAccount.
19         EXIT METHOD.
20
21        read-and-populate SECTION.
22  * see above
23         ...
24
25       END METHOD readAccount.
```

Obviously you have to initialize the DBI: The file must be opened, and the dictionary must be initialized. Assume that the corresponding service is provided by the factory method `openAccount` of `AccountDBI`; the corresponding code fragments have been omitted.

COBOL and the Web

CHAPTER 29

This chapter is an introduction to developing COBOL applications that take advantage of Internet technology. The first part provides some general information on the Web, the Internet, and client/server design. Following this is a look at developing Web-enabled business systems. Finally, you'll examine the *Common Gateway Interface* (CGI) in some detail using COBOL examples.

The CGI examples in this chapter assume that you have a basic understanding of *Hypertext Markup Language* (HTML) forms and sufficient experience with COBOL to understand the coding examples. Numerous reference books and Web sites cover both CGI and HTML in greater detail.

The CGI examples were developed and tested using Micro Focus COBOL 4.0.32 under Windows NT Service Pack 3 using Microsoft Peer Web Services 3.0.

What Is the Web?

The Web is a system for sharing information. It consists of a collection of linked documents.

The Web is a client/server application containing Web servers that publish information and Web browsers that format HTML documents for presentation. The *World Wide Web* (WWW) is one of many applications that run on the Internet. Webs can be deployed on a smaller scale within corporations as an intranet or on a single computer.

The *Hypertext Transfer Protocol* (HTTP) was developed to define an addressing scheme and provide a standard means of describing the type of data being transmitted. HTTP makes it possible for the client and server programs to exchange and process information, such as text, HTML, images, executables, or any data type they mutually agree on. The addressing scheme is based on a *uniform resource locator* (URL). For example, http://www.mcp.com signifies a Web server. Data types are defined using *Multipart Internet Mail Extensions* (MIME) headers. MIME headers were created to facilitate sending multimedia and other nontext files as email attachments.

With HTTP, a client makes a request by contacting a server using its URL. The server returns a document or a status message. The contents of the document can be anything from simple text to an executable program. The contents are defined by the MIME header. This is discussed in more detail later in this chapter.

> **NOTE**
>
> The WWW is a good source of information for COBOL programmers. Numerous Web sites provide information on COBOL and application development. All the major compiler vendors have an Internet presence, as do most software development tool vendors.
>
> Usenet newsgroups such as `comp.lang.cobol` and `alt.cobol` provide a forum for exchanging information with other COBOL programmers and gleaning pearls of wisdom. Strictly speaking, Usenet is not an Internet application, but it is rare to find an Internet service provider that does not also provide a newsfeed.
>
> Many newsgroups have a *frequently asked questions* (FAQ) list that should be checked before posting a question. You can search for old news articles at `http://www.dejanews.com`. The document `http://www.cis.ohio-state.edu/htbin/rfc/rfc1855.html` provides comprehensive information on newsgroup etiquette.

Where Does COBOL Fit?

Languages such as Java and Perl get most of the media attention when it comes to developing Web-based applications. Contrary to this perception, COBOL can be used to write Web-enabled programs and client/server applications that use Internet technologies.

Client/Server Application Development

Client/server programming entails separating a program into multiple components, each with a specific role. In general terms, the server program processes client requests. Usually, server programs involve some form of data access, although this is not a requirement. The client is often a user interface such as a character-based screen, graphical window, or Web browser. However, a client is any program that makes use of the server; it does not require human input.

The differentiation of duties between client and server can be made in a number of arbitrary ways. Either the server or the client can do most of the work. At one end of the spectrum are *distributed databases* where clients do all the work, including the data access, which is redirected to a remote database. At the other end of the spectrum are *thin clients* that handle presentation and navigation but have little or no knowledge of the business rules or database.

29

COBOL AND THE
WEB

Thin clients usually are limited to presenting data, navigating between programs in a family of related programs, and perhaps performing some minimal algorithmic validation of data. The business logic and data storage are the roles of the server exclusively. Web browsers can be considered to be thin clients.

Another example of a thin client is a 3270 terminal with a BMS map defining the data on the screen. The terminal does some basic validation, such as testing for allowed keystrokes in a numeric field. The business function is the role of a transaction that runs after a user presses a function key.

The client/server model is not limited to a two-tier application consisting of a client and a server. It is common to define three or more architectural layers between the client and the database. The architecture defines the role of each layer. The intermediate layers are both clients and servers, because they respond to requests from other programs and initiate requests from other servers. One of the original intentions of the Common Gateway Interface was to act as an intermediary between a browser and another application, such as an existing business system—hence the name.

Server Programs Written in COBOL

Server programs can be written in any language. The programming language should be chosen based on issues such as maintainability and the skill set of the development staff. The communications interface is a small part of an application and often can be implemented as a single program that calls other programs to satisfy the client request. Most of the server code in any system larger than a simple "Hello World" program accesses databases, performs calculations, and validates and reformats user input.

Server programs should be *stateless*. That is, they should treat every client request in isolation, with no recollection of what has gone before or expectations of what will come. The responsibility for keeping track of the current state or setting the next state falls to the client program.

If you are familiar with transaction programming in CICS or IMS, this is not a new concept. Think of the 3270 terminal as the client. Each time a user presses a function key, a transaction runs that receives the information from the terminal, processes it, and returns a screen image to the terminal before terminating.

With Web clients, each request is a brand-new session. The server program remembers nothing about the client. Each time the client contacts a server program, it must provide all the information required to complete the request. The difference between this and traditional transaction programming is one of degree.

In CICS, for example, a number of resources exist that may be associated with the user and the user's current session. A user opens a session by logging on. As the session starts up, information such as the user's name, access rights, and personal preferences are initialized and saved for future use. This information persists from transaction to transaction.

On the other hand, server programs for Web clients are not designed to remember anything about a client from one request to the next. Each request must reestablish all the security and database access information. The client must store any information that must persist from transaction to transaction and return it to the server with each request.

Some server programs are written to keep user profile information. However, the client still is responsible for providing the key the server can use to look up the profile. Online banking applications may use this technique to enhance security. Encryption keys are created dynamically by the server when the customer logs on. One key is returned to the client, and the other key is known only to the server. The key is used to uniquely identify the client and to associate the transaction with the client's bank account, eliminating the need to transmit personal information over the Internet. The client key can be used only for a limited time. Once a key is invalidated, the customer must log on again to get another valid key.

> **NOTE**
>
> The Web browser has a number of ways to save information. Short-term persistence is accomplished by placing the information in the body of the document or as additional parameters on the browser's command line. *Cookies* can be used to save information indefinitely on the client's disk drive.

Web Browser Clients

A Web browser requests and displays documents. These documents may contain anything from plain text to HTML to interactive virtual reality models with full sound and video. Web browsers also can send information to server programs on the command line, as HTML form data, or via embedded Java applets that can provide their own communications layer.

Effective business applications can be developed using HTML forms that interact with CGI servers; this technique is covered in more detail later in this chapter. Basically, the client makes a request that the server responds to by providing a document that contains an HTML form. The HTML form contains a set of controls that enable the end user to provide information as text or selections of predefined values.

HTML forms have been compared to *dumb terminals,* because early browsers did not provide any way to perform client-side processing. The advent of browser scripting languages, such as JavaScript, greatly enhances the limited functionality of HTML forms. The combination of HTML forms and JavaScript produces very sophisticated user interfaces that are far from *dumb.* For example, performing client-side validation, reformatting user input, and even allowing the user to change the user interface are all possible.

> **NOTE**
>
> Another way Web browsers can be used as clients to COBOL servers is via Java applets. Most browsers are licensed to run the Java virtual machine developed by Sun Microsystems Inc. The Java programming language enables the development of sophisticated client programs that will run within a Web browser. Java clients can communicate directly with any server program that supports the TCP/IP communications protocol. This means that a mainframe server program can connect directly with a Java client without the need for a gateway program, a gateway machine, or other middleware.

> **NOTE**
>
> It now may be possible to write COBOL programs that will run on a Web browser. Fujitsu's NetCOBOL product claims to be able to compile COBOL source code into Java byte-code that runs on a Java virtual machine. If the product lives up to claims, this means that COBOL programmers can take advantage of the features of Java applets without having to learn Java.

New Life for Legacy Systems

Many existing business systems are written in COBOL. These systems and the source code written to implement them represent a substantial investment. Companies considering enhancing these systems to be accessible via Web browsers can take comfort in knowing that they can get more mileage out of their existing systems. Furthermore, the bridge program between the Web and existing applications can be written and maintained in the same language—COBOL.

COBOL is a good choice for writing CGI scripts or client/server applications where part of the solution is an existing system that was written in COBOL. Maintenance is simplified, because the application code uses the same language from end to end.

A transaction-based program, such as those written for CICS or IMS/DC, has many of the design elements required for a CGI server. The programs perform a well-defined task. A single run of the transaction represents a complete unit of work.

Figure 29.1 shows one possible way of establishing a link between a Web browser and an existing system that may not support running a Web server. The client connects to a Web browser that accesses an existing mainframe application via a gateway program. The gateway program uses a communications protocol that the existing system supports. For IBM mainframes, this can be an SNA protocol, such as APPC or CPI-C, over an LU6.2 connection.

FIGURE 29.1.

A connection model for a Web-enabled legacy system.

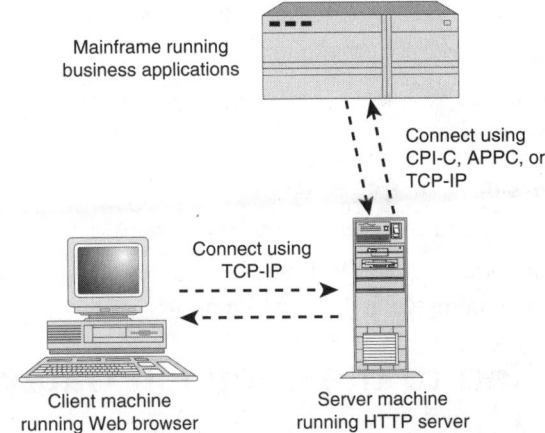

Mainframe running business applications

Connect using CPI-C, APPC, or TCP-IP

Connect using TCP-IP

Client machine running Web browser

Server machine running HTTP server

29

COBOL AND THE WEB

NOTE

If the legacy system is a CICS application, another solution is to use IBM's CICS application server to handle the communications between the Web server and the host system for the legacy application. CICS implementations exist for Windows NT, OS/2, AIX, and a number of other platforms that also support Web servers. A CICS region on the Web server can handle transactions or redirect the request to a CICS on the mainframe.

A CGI program initiates a CICS transaction from outside the CICS region and formats the response returned by the transaction using one of the external program interfaces that CICS supports.

It is possible to convert BMS maps to HTML forms. A CGI program can appear to be a 3270 terminal to the CICS region. The CGI program converts the terminal

continues

datastream to a form and vice versa. Existing character-based screens appear as HTML forms within a Web browser. This makes it possible for existing programs to continue to run on the mainframe as-is, yet appear as forms within the Web browser.

Using COBOL to Write CGI Programs

In this section, you'll explore the *Common Gateway Interface* (CGI). Sample programs illustrate various aspects of gateway programming.

Gateway programs run on the Web server. As such, the programmer needs to know certain things about the Web server:

- The operating system of the Web server
- Which directory has been configured for CGI programs
- Any other security issues or other configuration issues that may keep a guest user from successfully running the gateway program

An Introduction to the Common Gateway Interface

The CGI implements a standard method for exchanging data between client and server programs, regardless of the operating system. The term *gateway* suggests that a CGI program serves as a bridge between the Web and a system that has no inherent Web support. Figure 29.2 illustrates a typical CGI transaction.

FIGURE 29.2.

A typical CGI transaction.

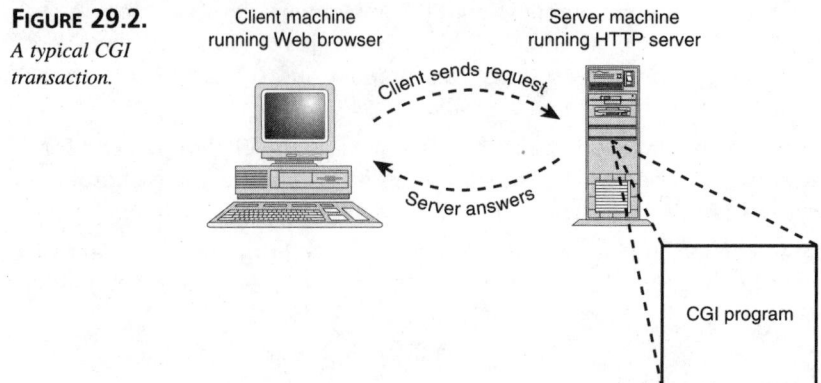

The steps for a CGI transaction follow:

1. The Web browser (client) formats the request as a URL-encoded string and sends it to the Web server.

2. The Web server receives the request, sets up the appropriate environment variables, and invokes the CGI program.

3. The CGI uses the environment variables and the standard input buffer to receive the client information. It processes the request and responds using the standard output buffer. The response includes a MIME header that describes the type of data contained in the response.

4. The Web server sends the response to the client. The connection between the client and the server is closed.

CGI programs do not contain code to handle communicating with the client browser. The CGI implementation assumes that the Web server will handle this task.

Programming Basics

All CGI programs receive data from STDIN or environment variables and return data using the standard output buffer. Different techniques may be required, depending on the compiler. The Micro Focus compiler supports reading and writing from standard buffers in a variety of ways. The most natural technique for COBOL programmers is to treat these buffers as sequential files. With other compilers, it may be necessary to make calls to the operating system API to perform I/O on the standard buffers.

Common Environment Variables

The Web server makes information about itself and the current client request available to CGI programs via environment variables. Some of these variables provide information about the Web server that is answering the request and invoking the gateway program. Other variables provide information about the current request and the client that initiated the request.

These environment variables are set for all requests:

GATEWAY_INTERFACE	Version of the CGI specification supported by the Web server; format: CGI/version.
SERVER_NAME	Hostname, *domain name server* (DNS) alias, or IP address of the Web server.
SERVER_SOFTWARE	Name and version of the Web server that invoked the CGI program; format: name/version.

These environment variables are dependent on the client request:

AUTH_TYPE	If the server supports user authentication, and the script is protected, this is the protocol-specific authentication method used to validate the user.
CONTENT_LENGTH	Length of the data sent by the client.
CONTENT_TYPE	For queries that have attached information, such as HTTP POST and PUT, this is the content type of the data.
PATH_INFO	Additional information that follows the virtual pathname used to reference this script. The information is URL encoded.
PATH_TRANSLATED	Physical path as derived by translating the virtual path.
QUERY_STRING	URL-encoded information that follows the ? in the URL that referenced the script.
REMOTE_ADDR	IP address of the host making the request.
REMOTE_HOST	Hostname making the request (client host).
REMOTE_IDENT	If the server supports RFC 931 identification, this variable is set to the remote username retrieved from the server. Use of this variable should be limited to logging only.
REMOTE_USER	If the server supports user authentication and the script is protected, this is the username.
REQUEST_METHOD	Method used for the request; usually, GET or POST.
SCRIPT_NAME	Virtual path to the script being executed.
SERVER_PORT	Port number to which the request was sent.
SERVER_PROTOCOL	Name and version of the information protocol used by the request; format: name/version.

Any header lines received from the client may be placed into environment variables of the form HTTP_ followed by the header name:

HTTP_ACCEPT	A Web browser may provide information about the MIME headers it can accept. A CGI program can use this information to decide what to send back. For example, if the Web browser can support audio, the CGI program can send an audio file; otherwise, it may send a text transcription of the audio file.
HTTP_USER_AGENT	Some Web browsers identify themselves. A CGI program can use this information to enable features supported by a particular browser.

The sample program CGISHOW.EXE is a simple CGI program that displays the values of environment variables. The source code is in CGISHOW.CBL. You might want to experiment by linking to CGISHOW.EXE from the command line with additional path information and additional query-string information. Figure 29.3 shows the sample output for a POST operation. The source code is available on the CD-ROM that accompanies this book.

> **NOTE**
>
> The source code on the CD-ROM was written and tested using Micro Focus COBOL 4.0.32 on Windows NT Workstation 4.0 running Microsoft's Peer Web Services 3.0.
>
> The source code can be compiled using the batch file BUILD.BAT, which also is included on the CD-ROM. The file CGI_NT.DIR defines the MF COBOL directives that were used to test the program.
>
> The executables, HTML documents, and *server-side includes* (SSI) document should be placed in a directory that is defined to the Web server with *execute* and *read* access.
>
> Because WWW server is a system service, environment variables such as PATH or COBSW must be set at the system level rather than the user level.
>
> Security can be an issue as well, because the WWW client has limited privileges that are different than those of the developer.

FIGURE 29.3.

CGISHOW.EXE *shows environment variables passed by a Web server to a CGI program.*

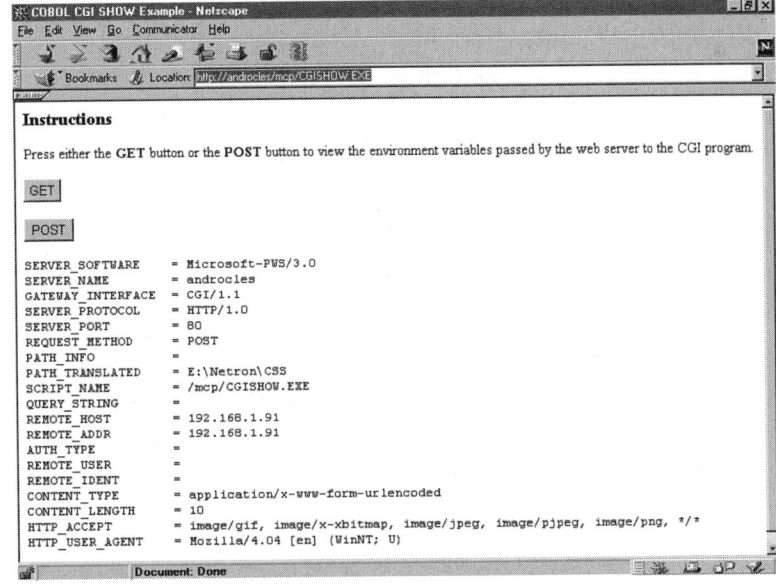

> **NOTE**
>
> You can find more information about CGI environment variables at
>
> `http://hoohoo.ncsa.uiuc.edu/cgi/env.html`

Reading from Standard Input

When the request method is POST, the client information arrives in the standard input buffer. The length of the incoming message is available from the environment variable CONTENT_LENGTH.

Handling URL-Encoded Strings

The client formats data as a URL-encoded string, as shown in this example:

```
FIELD1=This+is+field+1%21&FIELD2=This+is+field+2
```

The spaces in the string are replaced by the plus symbol (+). Certain characters are encoded as their ASCII hexadecimal values. In the example, %21 resolves to an exclamation point (!). The decoded string follows:

```
FIELD1=This is field 1!&FIELD2=This is field 2
```

When the information is from an HTML form, the ampersand (&) separates the name/value pairs. The equal sign (=) is a separator between the name and the value for a given name/value pair.

The sample programs provide a couple of algorithms for converting any URL-encoded string to an ASCII string.

Writing to Standard Output

The standard output buffer is a datastream. The stream consists of ASCII data. Lines end with a *carriage return* and *line feed* (CRLF). CRLF has the hexadecimal value 0D0A.

The Micro-Focus compiler supports writing to the standard output stream as a SEQUENTIAL or LINE SEQUENTIAL file. The SEQUENTIAL format requires the program to provide the CRLF characters. With LINE SEQUENTIAL files, trailing spaces are removed, and the CRLF is provided by the compiler.

Depending on the compiler, it may be necessary to make calls to operating system functions to write to the standard output queue, or to use routines provided with the compiler to perform byte-stream file I/O.

MIME Headers

MIME headers are the means by which Web clients determine what to do with the information they are receiving. MIME headers consist of a descriptor followed by a blank line. For most CGI applications, the MIME header will likely be in this format:

```
Content-type: text/html
```

This format indicates that the document consists of HTML text, which includes formatting information and other hypertext tokens. See `CGIGET.CBL`, `CGIPOST.CBL`, or `CGIMAINT.CBL` for an example.

The following code indicates that the document is plain text and should be displayed as-is (don't forget the blank line after the descriptor):

```
Content-type: text/plain
```

This MIME header redirects the client to the document specified by the URL:

```
Location: http://www.mcp.com
```

Again, don't forget to add the blank line after the descriptor. See `CGILOC.CBL` for an example.

> **CAUTION**
>
> The MIME header consists of two lines. The second line must be completely blank. If a CGI program runs properly from the command line but fails to return results when invoked by a Web server, one likely cause is an invalid MIME header.

URL Redirection Example

> **NOTE**
>
> The sample programs contain as little extraneous code as possible. The samples do not check for common error conditions that any well-written business application normally would handle. Optional COBOL syntax is avoided.
>
> The sample programs deliberately use different COBOL syntax to accomplish the same task. The intent is to provide a few options, because some techniques
>
> *continues*

29

COBOL AND THE
WEB

> depend on the compiler. Coding styles vary. I prefer to have one period per paragraph, because it forces me to write structured code.
>
> In the interest of space, the program listings are abbreviated. The complete program source is available on the CD-ROM that accompanies this book.

`CGILOC.CBL` is perhaps the simplest CGI program possible. It redirects the client to a different URL. It ignores any client input and returns only a MIME header. The full code is shown in Listing 29.1.

LISTING 29.1 CGILOC.CBL.

```
        IDENTIFICATION DIVISION.
        PROGRAM-ID.  CGILOC.

        ENVIRONMENT DIVISION.
        INPUT-OUTPUT SECTION.
        FILE-CONTROL.
            SELECT  STDOUT ASSIGN  "STDOUT"
                ORGANIZATION SEQUENTIAL
                ACCESS       SEQUENTIAL
                FILE STATUS  STDOUT-FILESTATUS.

        DATA DIVISION.
        FILE SECTION.
        FD  STDOUT LABEL RECORDS STANDARD.
        01  STDOUT-RECORD          PIC X(256).

        WORKING-STORAGE SECTION.
        01  STDOUT-FILESTATUS      PIC XX.

      * ASCII Carriage return/Line Feed
        01  CRLF                   PIC XX VALUE X"0D0A".

        PROCEDURE DIVISION.

        MAIN.
            OPEN OUTPUT STDOUT
            INITIALIZE STDOUT-RECORD
            STRING "Location: http://www.mcp.com" CRLF CRLF
                DELIMITED SIZE INTO STDOUT-RECORD
            END-STRING
            WRITE STDOUT-RECORD
            CLOSE STDOUT
            STOP RUN
            .
```

A GET Method Example

When REQUEST_METHOD is GET, the environment variable QUERY_STRING provides the input data as a URL-encoded string. Running CGIGET.EXE from within a Web browser yields the screen shown in Figure 29.4.

FIGURE 29.4.

The result of running CGIGET.EXE for some arbitrary input.

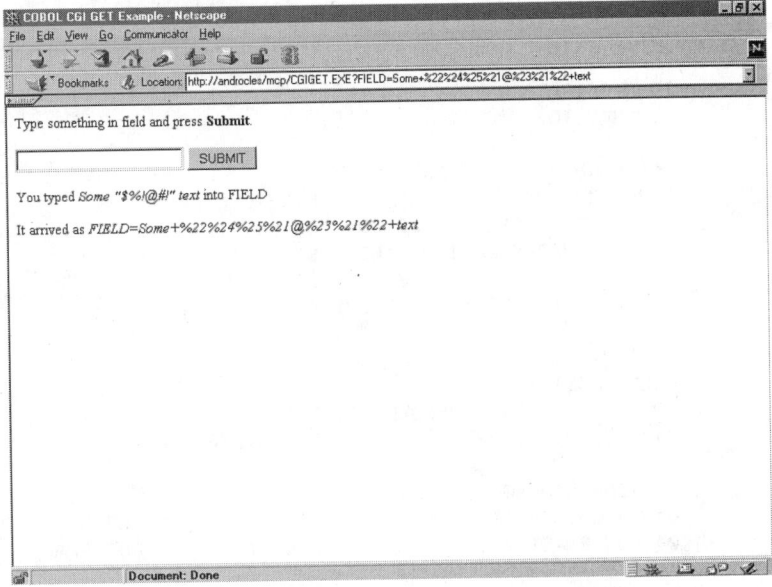

Listing 29.2 shows code fragments from CGIGET.CBL that highlight some coding techniques.

The SELECT STDOUT clause uses a Micro-Focus extension to define a line-sequential data file. The compiler trims each record for length, and it appends carriage-return and line-feed characters.

29

COBOL AND THE WEB

The mainline consists of two steps, GET-INPUT and PUT-OUTPUT. The GET-INPUT paragraph uses an X/OPEN extension to the DISPLAY and ACCEPT verbs to retrieve the values of environment variables.

The algorithm for decoding the URL string in the DECODE-URL-STRING paragraph (not shown) can be implemented in a variety of ways. CGIGET.CBL scans the input string one character at a time from left to right. It moves all the characters before the equal symbol (=) to FIELD-NAME and all the characters following the equal symbol to FIELD-VALUE. Plus symbols (+) are replaced by spaces as they are encountered, and encoded symbols (%##) are converted to their corresponding characters. A different version of the DECODE-URL-STRING paragraph appears in full in the POST method example that follows.

PUT-OUTPUT emits the required MIME headers and then emits an HTML document. It is abbreviated in the listing. The process involves writing HTML text to STDOUT. The Web server sends the resulting document to the client when the standard output queue is closed.

LISTING 29.2 CGIGET.CBL (EXCERPTS).

```
        IDENTIFICATION DIVISION.
        PROGRAM-ID.  CGIGET.

        ENVIRONMENT DIVISION.
        INPUT-OUTPUT SECTION.        FILE-CONTROL.
           SELECT  STDOUT ASSIGN  "STDOUT"
                 ORGANIZATION LINE SEQUENTIAL
                 ACCESS        SEQUENTIAL
                 FILE STATUS   STDOUT-FILESTATUS.

        DATA DIVISION.
        FILE SECTION.
        FD  STDOUT LABEL RECORDS STANDARD.
        01  STDOUT-RECORD          PIC X(256).

        WORKING-STORAGE SECTION.
        01  REQUEST-METHOD         PIC X(4)    VALUE SPACE.
        01  QUERY-STRING           PIC X(256)  VALUE SPACE.

        01  FIELD-NAME             PIC X(10)   VALUE SPACE.
        01  FIELD-VALUE            PIC X(249)  VALUE SPACE.
        01  QS-PTR                 PIC 9(4) BINARY.
        01  FN-PTR                 PIC 9(4) BINARY.
        01  FV-PTR                 PIC 9(4) BINARY.

        01  CHAR-ENCODED.
           05  CHAR-ENCODED-BINARY PIC 99 BINARY OCCURS 2.
        01  CHAR-DECODED           PIC X.
```

```
01   CHAR-DECODED-BINARY REDEFINES CHAR-DECODED
                                 PIC 99 BINARY.
01   CHAR-PTR              PIC 99 BINARY.

01   STDOUT-FILESTATUS     PIC XX.

PROCEDURE DIVISION.
MAIN.
     PERFORM GET-INPUT
     PERFORM PUT-OUTPUT
     STOP RUN
     .

GET-INPUT.
     DISPLAY "REQUEST_METHOD" UPON ENVIRONMENT-NAME
     ACCEPT  REQUEST-METHOD   FROM ENVIRONMENT-VALUE
     IF REQUEST-METHOD = "GET"
         DISPLAY "QUERY_STRING"  UPON ENVIRONMENT-NAME
         ACCEPT QUERY-STRING     FROM ENVIRONMENT-VALUE
         PERFORM DECODE-URL-STRING
     ELSE
         MOVE "Unexpected REQUEST_METHOD" TO FIELD-VALUE
     END-IF
     .

   .
   .
   .

PUT-OUTPUT.
     OPEN OUTPUT STDOUT
* The reply starts with a mime header followed by a blank line
     MOVE "Content-type: text/html" TO STDOUT-RECORD
     WRITE STDOUT-RECORD
     MOVE SPACE       TO STDOUT-RECORD
     WRITE STDOUT-RECORD
     MOVE "<HTML><HEAD><TITLE>COBOL CGI GET Example"
         TO STDOUT-RECORD
     WRITE STDOUT-RECORD
     MOVE "</TITLE></HEAD></HTML>" TO STDOUT-RECORD
     WRITE STDOUT-RECORD

... more of the same to create an HTML document

   .
   .
   .

     CLOSE STDOUT
     .
```

A POST Method Example

When REQUEST_METHOD is POST, the input data arrives in the standard input buffer. The environment variable CONTENT_LENGTH contains the length of the input string.

Listing 29.3 shows most of the code from CGIPOST.CBL.

The standard input queue maps to a variable-length *line sequential* file, with the record length determined by the CONTENT_LENGTH environment variable. This example uses the intrinsic function NUMVAL() to convert CONTENT-LENGTH-X to a numeric value.

The algorithm for decoding URL-encoded strings in the DECODE-URL-STRING uses UNSTRING and INSPECT. If it were not for the encoded characters, the algorithm would be very simple. Because the encoded character takes up 3 bytes (%##), which resolve to a single byte, the complexity increases.

The CONVERT-TO-CHARACTER paragraph uses INSPECT CONVERTING to convert each of the ASCII characters to a numeric equivalent. For example, the encoded character %2B is stored as hexadecimal 3241. The INSPECT converts this to hexadecimal 0211. The COMPUTE yields (16 * 2) + 11 = 43, which is stored as hexadecimal 2B or the character +.

When a Web browser loads a CGI program from the command line or as a link, the REQUEST_METHOD is GET. CGIPOST.CBL uses this fact in the PUT-OUTPUT paragraph to return a different HTML document, assuming that it is the first time the client invoked the CGI program.

LISTING 29.3 CGIPOST.CBL.

```
IDENTIFICATION DIVISION.
PROGRAM-ID. CGIPOST.

ENVIRONMENT DIVISION.
INPUT-OUTPUT SECTION.
FILE-CONTROL.
    SELECT  STDIN ASSIGN  "STDIN"
        ORGANIZATION LINE SEQUENTIAL
        ACCESS        SEQUENTIAL
        FILE STATUS   STDIN-FILESTATUS.
    SELECT  STDOUT ASSIGN   "STDOUT"
        ORGANIZATION LINE SEQUENTIAL
        ACCESS        SEQUENTIAL
        FILE STATUS   STDOUT-FILESTATUS.

DATA DIVISION.
FILE SECTION.
FD  STDIN LABEL RECORDS STANDARD.
01  STDIN-RECORD.
```

```
    05  FILLER                  PIC X OCCURS 1 TO 256
                                DEPENDING ON CONTENT-LENGTH.


FD  STDOUT LABEL RECORDS STANDARD.
01  STDOUT-RECORD               PIC X(256).

WORKING-STORAGE SECTION.
01  REQUEST-METHOD              PIC X(4)    VALUE SPACE.
01  CONTENT-LENGTH-X            PIC X(4).
01  CONTENT-LENGTH              PIC 9(4).

01  FIELD-NAME                  PIC X(10)   VALUE SPACE.
01  FIELD-VALUE                 PIC X(249)  VALUE SPACE.
01  FV-PTR                      PIC 9(4) BINARY.
01  TEMP-VALUE                  PIC X(249)  VALUE SPACE.
01  TEMP-PTR                    PIC 9(4) BINARY.
01  TEMP-CNT                    PIC 9(4) BINARY.

01  CHAR-ENCODED.
  05  CHAR-ENCODED-BINARY       PIC 99 BINARY OCCURS 2.
01  CHAR-DECODED.
  05  CHAR-DECODED-BINARY       PIC 99 BINARY.
01  CHAR-HEX                    PIC X(16) VALUE "0123456789ABCDEF".
01  CHAR-DECIMAL                PIC X(16) VALUE
                                X"000102030405060708090A0B0C0D0E0F".

01  STDIN-FILESTATUS            PIC X(2).
01  STDOUT-FILESTATUS           PIC X(2).

PROCEDURE DIVISION.

MAIN.
    PERFORM GET-INPUT
    PERFORM PUT-OUTPUT
    STOP RUN
    .


GET-INPUT.
    DISPLAY "REQUEST_METHOD" UPON ENVIRONMENT-NAME
    ACCEPT  REQUEST-METHOD  FROM ENVIRONMENT-VALUE
    IF REQUEST-METHOD = "POST"
        DISPLAY "CONTENT_LENGTH" UPON ENVIRONMENT-NAME
        ACCEPT  CONTENT-LENGTH-X FROM ENVIRONMENT-VALUE
        MOVE FUNCTION NUMVAL(CONTENT-LENGTH-X) TO CONTENT-LENGTH
        IF CONTENT-LENGTH > 0
            OPEN INPUT STDIN
            READ STDIN
            CLOSE STDIN
            PERFORM DECODE-URL-STRING
```

continues

LISTING 29.3. CONTINUED

```
            END-IF
        END-IF
        .


    DECODE-URL-STRING.
* Parse the name from the string
        UNSTRING STDIN-RECORD DELIMITED ALL "=" OR "&"
            INTO FIELD-NAME
                 TEMP-VALUE
        END-UNSTRING

* STDIN-RECORD is preserved to display later otherwise
* the following INSPECT could be performed upon STDIN-RECORD
* instead of each field value.
        INSPECT TEMP-VALUE REPLACING ALL "+" BY SPACE

* Now parse the field value for all encoded characters
        MOVE 1 TO TEMP-PTR FV-PTR
        PERFORM UNTIL TEMP-PTR >= CONTENT-LENGTH
            UNSTRING TEMP-VALUE DELIMITED ALL "%"
                INTO    FIELD-VALUE (FV-PTR:)
                COUNT   TEMP-CNT
                POINTER TEMP-PTR
            END-UNSTRING
            ADD TEMP-CNT TO FV-PTR
            IF TEMP-PTR < CONTENT-LENGTH
                MOVE TEMP-VALUE (TEMP-PTR:2) TO CHAR-ENCODED
                PERFORM CONVERT-TO-CHARACTER

* Put the character back in TEMP-VALUE and reposition
* the pointer to start at the character. The converted character
* will be picked up by the next UNSTRING
                MOVE CHAR-DECODED TO TEMP-VALUE (TEMP-PTR + 1:1)
                ADD 1 TO TEMP-PTR
            END-IF
        END-PERFORM
        .


    CONVERT-TO-CHARACTER.
* This routine returns CHAR-DECODED given an encoded CHAR-ENCODED
        INSPECT CHAR-ENCODED CONVERTING CHAR-HEX TO CHAR-DECIMAL
        COMPUTE CHAR-DECODED-BINARY =
            (16 * CHAR-ENCODED-BINARY (1)) + CHAR-ENCODED-BINARY (2)
        END-COMPUTE
        .


    PUT-OUTPUT.
        OPEN OUTPUT STDOUT
* The reply starts with a mime header followed by a blank line
```

```
      MOVE "Content-type: text/html" TO STDOUT-RECORD
      WRITE STDOUT-RECORD
      MOVE SPACE          TO STDOUT-RECORD
      WRITE STDOUT-RECORD

* Minimal HTML header
      MOVE "<HTML>"    TO STDOUT-RECORD
      WRITE STDOUT-RECORD
      MOVE "<HEAD>"    TO STDOUT-RECORD
      WRITE STDOUT-RECORD
      MOVE "<TITLE>COBOL CGI POST Example</TITLE>" TO STDOUT-RECORD
      WRITE STDOUT-RECORD
      MOVE "</HEAD>"   TO STDOUT-RECORD
      WRITE STDOUT-RECORD
      MOVE "<BODY>"    TO STDOUT-RECORD
      WRITE STDOUT-RECORD

* Prompt the user for input
      MOVE "Type something in field and press " TO STDOUT-RECORD
      WRITE STDOUT-RECORD
      MOVE "<STRONG>Submit</STRONG>." To STDOUT-RECORD
      WRITE STDOUT-RECORD

* Create a form for the user to enter information
      MOVE "<FORM METHOD=POST ACTION=CGIPOST.EXE>" TO STDOUT-RECORD
      WRITE STDOUT-RECORD
      MOVE "<INPUT NAME=FIELD MAXLENGTH=80>" TO STDOUT-RECORD
      WRITE STDOUT-RECORD
      MOVE "<INPUT TYPE=SUBMIT VALUE=SUBMIT>" TO STDOUT-RECORD
      WRITE STDOUT-RECORD
      MOVE "</FORM>"   TO STDOUT-RECORD
      WRITE STDOUT-RECORD

* When this program is invoked the first time, the request method
* is 'GET'.  This edit prevents the error message from appearing
* the first time the page is created.
      IF REQUEST-METHOD = "GET"
          CONTINUE
      ELSE
          IF FIELD-VALUE = SPACE
              MOVE "<P>You did not type anything in "
                  TO STDOUT-RECORD
              WRITE STDOUT-RECORD
              MOVE FIELD-NAME     TO STDOUT-RECORD
              WRITE STDOUT-RECORD
          ELSE
*     Echo the user's input
              MOVE "<P>You typed <EM>" TO STDOUT-RECORD
              WRITE STDOUT-RECORD
```

29

COBOL AND THE
WEB

continues

LISTING 29.3. CONTINUED

```
                         MOVE FIELD-VALUE          TO STDOUT-RECORD
                         WRITE STDOUT-RECORD
                         MOVE "</EM> into "        TO STDOUT-RECORD
                         WRITE STDOUT-RECORD
                         MOVE FIELD-NAME           TO STDOUT-RECORD
                         WRITE STDOUT-RECORD
                         Move "<P>The length is " TO STDOUT-RECORD
                         WRITE STDOUT-RECORD
                         MOVE CONTENT-LENGTH-X     TO STDOUT-RECORD
                         WRITE STDOUT-RECORD

*     Echo the URL encoded string
                         MOVE "<P>It arrived as <EM>" TO STDOUT-RECORD
                         WRITE STDOUT-RECORD
                         MOVE STDIN-RECORD    TO STDOUT-RECORD
                         WRITE STDOUT-RECORD
                         MOVE "</EM>"             TO STDOUT-RECORD
                         WRITE STDOUT-RECORD
                    END-IF
              END-IF

*  HTML footer
          MOVE "</BODY>"   TO STDOUT-RECORD
          WRITE STDOUT-RECORD
          MOVE "</HTML>"   TO STDOUT-RECORD
          WRITE STDOUT-RECORD
          CLOSE STDOUT
          .
```

A File Maintenance Example

This program puts it all together to actually do something sort of useful. CGIMAINT.EXE is a simple file maintenance program that uses an HTML form as the user input screen. Figure 29.5 shows the client view in a Web browser.

NOTE

The data file CONTACT.DAT can be created using MKCONT.CBL.

When CGIMAINT.EXE is invoked from the Web browser's command line or as an HTML link, the REQUEST_METHOD is GET. In this instance, CGIMAINT.EXE sends the form defined by CGIMAINT.HTM without any values defined for the fields. The user is prompted to provide information and select an action. Subsequent actions depend on the button that is pressed. Each button assigns a different value to the CLIENT_REQUEST field.

FIGURE 29.5.

The CGIMAINT.EXE *client in a Web browser.*

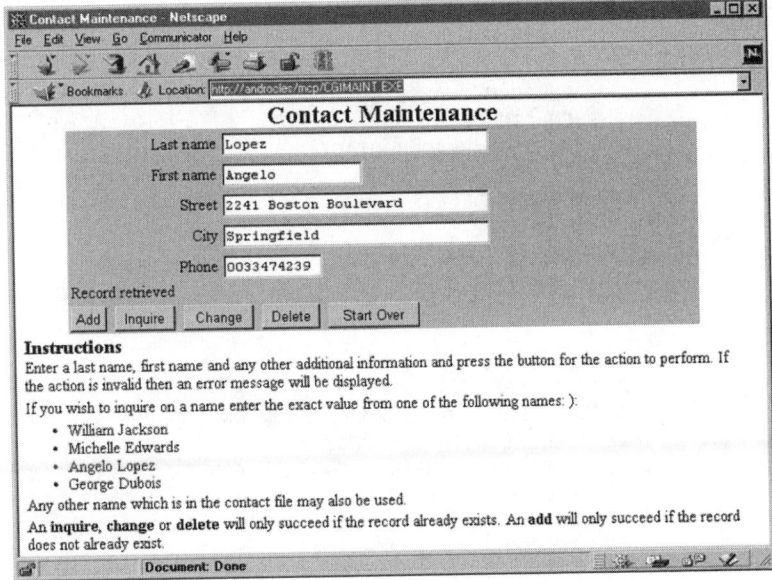

Much of the CGI-related code is identical to that in CGIPOST.CBL, so Listing 29.4 is abbreviated.

The FILL-CONTACT-RECORD section parses STDIN-RECORD using a version of DECODE-URL-STRING that is basically the same as that in CGIPOST.CBL. The differences in the algorithm are due to the fact that the input stream contains more than one name/value pair, and there is no need to preserve the contents of STDIN-RECORD.

Instead of creating reams of code to emit the HTML document, PUT-OUTPUT reads from the template file CGIMAINT.HTM and writes it STDOUT. CGIMAINT.HTM is essentially an HTML text document with a few unusual lines that contain special tokens. These lines are replaced with additional HTML based on the current client request. Only a small portion of the document changes each time.

LISTING 29.4 CGIMAINT.CBL (EXCERPTS).

```
MAIN.
    PERFORM GET-INPUT
    EVALUATE FUNCTION UPPER-CASE(CLIENT-REQUEST)
```

continues

29

COBOL AND THE WEB

LISTING 29.4 CONTINUED

```cobol
                WHEN SPACE
                  MOVE "Please read the instructions" TO STATUS-MESSAGE
                WHEN "ADD"
                  PERFORM WRITE-CONTACT
                WHEN "CHANGE"
                  PERFORM CHANGE-CONTACT
                WHEN "INQUIRE"
                  PERFORM READ-CONTACT
                WHEN "DELETE"
                  PERFORM DELETE-CONTACT
            END-EVALUATE
            PERFORM PUT-OUTPUT
            STOP RUN
            .

        GET-INPUT.
            DISPLAY "REQUEST_METHOD" UPON ENVIRONMENT-NAME
            ACCEPT  REQUEST-METHOD    FROM ENVIRONMENT-VALUE
            IF REQUEST-METHOD = "POST"
                DISPLAY "CONTENT_LENGTH" UPON ENVIRONMENT-NAME
                ACCEPT  CONTENT-LENGTH-X FROM ENVIRONMENT-VALUE
                MOVE FUNCTION NUMVAL(CONTENT-LENGTH-X) TO CONTENT-LENGTH
                IF CONTENT-LENGTH > 0
                    MOVE SPACE TO STDIN-RECORD
                    OPEN INPUT STDIN
                    READ STDIN
                    CLOSE STDIN
                    INITIALIZE CONTACT-RECORD
                    PERFORM FILL-CONTACT-RECORD
                END-IF
            END-IF
            .

        FILL-CONTACT-RECORD.
            MOVE 1 TO IN-PTR
            PERFORM UNTIL IN-PTR > CONTENT-LENGTH
                PERFORM DECODE-URL-STRING
                EVALUATE FIELD-NAME
                  WHEN "CLIENT_REQUEST"
                    MOVE FIELD-VALUE    TO CLIENT-REQUEST
                  WHEN "LAST_NAME"
                    MOVE FIELD-VALUE    TO CONTACT-LAST-NAME
                  WHEN "FIRST_NAME"
                    MOVE FIELD-VALUE    TO CONTACT-FIRST-NAME
                  WHEN "STREET"
                    MOVE FIELD-VALUE    TO CONTACT-STREET
                  WHEN "CITY"
                    MOVE FIELD-VALUE    TO CONTACT-CITY
                  WHEN "PHONE"
```

```
                 MOVE FUNCTION NUMVAL(FIELD-VALUE) TO CONTACT-PHONE
              END-EVALUATE
         END-PERFORM
         .


     WRITE-CONTACT.
         OPEN I-O CONTACT
         IF CONTACT-IO-OK
             WRITE CONTACT-RECORD
             IF CONTACT-IO-OK
                 MOVE "Record added"     TO STATUS-MESSAGE
             ELSE
                 MOVE "Record not added" TO STATUS-MESSAGE
             END-IF
             CLOSE CONTACT
         ELSE
             MOVE "Error opening contact file" TO STATUS-MESSAGE
         END-IF
         .

     READ-CONTACT.
         OPEN INPUT CONTACT
         IF CONTACT-IO-OK
             READ CONTACT
             IF CONTACT-IO-OK
                 MOVE "Record retrieved" TO STATUS-MESSAGE
             ELSE
                 MOVE "Record not found" TO STATUS-MESSAGE
             END-IF
             CLOSE CONTACT
         ELSE
             MOVE "Error opening contact file" TO STATUS-MESSAGE
         END-IF
         .

     CHANGE-CONTACT.
         OPEN I-O CONTACT
         IF CONTACT-IO-OK
             MOVE CONTACT-RECORD TO CONTACT-RECORD-SAVE
             READ CONTACT LOCK
             IF CONTACT-IO-OK
                 MOVE CONTACT-RECORD-SAVE TO CONTACT-RECORD
                 REWRITE CONTACT-RECORD
             END-IF
             IF CONTACT-IO-OK
                 MOVE "Record changed" TO STATUS-MESSAGE
             ELSE
```

29

COBOL AND THE WEB

continues

LISTING 29.4 CONTINUED

```
                    MOVE "Unable to change record" TO STATUS-MESSAGE
                END-IF
                CLOSE CONTACT
            ELSE
                MOVE "Error opening contact file" TO STATUS-MESSAGE
            END-IF
                .

    DELETE-CONTACT.
        OPEN I-O CONTACT
        IF CONTACT-IO-OK
            DELETE CONTACT
            IF CONTACT-IO-OK
                MOVE "Record deleted" TO STATUS-MESSAGE
            ELSE
                MOVE "Unable to delete record" TO STATUS-MESSAGE
            END-IF
            CLOSE CONTACT
        ELSE
            MOVE "Error opening contact file" TO STATUS-MESSAGE
        END-IF
            .

    PUT-OUTPUT.
        OPEN OUTPUT STDOUT
* The reply starts with a mime header followed by a blank line
        MOVE "Content-type: text/html" TO STDOUT-RECORD
        WRITE STDOUT-RECORD
        MOVE SPACE        TO STDOUT-RECORD
        WRITE STDOUT-RECORD

* Read the basic form from the DOCTPL template file and apply
* customizations as required.
        OPEN INPUT DOCTPL
        PERFORM UNTIL NOT DOCTPL-IO-OK
        INITIALIZE STDOUT-RECORD
           READ DOCTPL
           IF DOCTPL-IO-OK
                EVALUATE DOCTPL-RECORD
                  WHEN "%%LAST_NAME%%"
                    IF CONTACT-LAST-NAME NOT = SPACE
                        MOVE CONTACT-LAST-NAME TO OUTPUT-VALUE
                        PERFORM WRITE-VALUE-STDOUT
                    END-IF
                  WHEN "%%FIRST_NAME%%"
                    IF CONTACT-FIRST-NAME NOT = SPACE
                        MOVE CONTACT-FIRST-NAME TO OUTPUT-VALUE
                        PERFORM WRITE-VALUE-STDOUT
                    END-IF
```

```
                WHEN "%%STREET%%"
                   IF CONTACT-STREET NOT = SPACE
                        MOVE CONTACT-STREET TO OUTPUT-VALUE
                        PERFORM WRITE-VALUE-STDOUT
                   END-IF
                WHEN "%%CITY%%"
                   IF CONTACT-CITY NOT = SPACE
                        MOVE CONTACT-CITY TO OUTPUT-VALUE
                        PERFORM WRITE-VALUE-STDOUT
                   END-IF
                WHEN "%%PHONE%%"
                   IF CONTACT-PHONE NOT = ZERO
                        MOVE CONTACT-PHONE TO OUTPUT-VALUE
                        PERFORM WRITE-VALUE-STDOUT
                   END-IF
                WHEN "%%PROMPT%%"
                   MOVE STATUS-MESSAGE TO STDOUT-RECORD
                WHEN OTHER
                   MOVE DOCTPL-RECORD TO STDOUT-RECORD
             END-EVALUATE
             WRITE STDOUT-RECORD
       END-IF
    END-PERFORM
    CLOSE DOCTPL
    CLOSE STDOUT
       .

WRITE-VALUE-STDOUT.
    PERFORM VARYING OUT-PTR FROM LENGTH OF OUTPUT-VALUE BY -1
       UNTIL OUT-PTR < 1
       OR    OUTPUT-VALUE (OUT-PTR:1) NOT = SPACE
         CONTINUE
    END-PERFORM
    MOVE QUOTE TO OUTPUT-VALUE (OUT-PTR + 1:1)

    STRING "VALUE="
           QUOTE
           OUTPUT-VALUE DELIMITED SIZE INTO STDOUT-RECORD
    END-STRING
    WRITE STDOUT-RECORD
       .
```

29

COBOL AND THE
WEB

Server Design Issues

CGIMAINT.EXE is a stateless server. Each client request is treated as an isolated event. The server will respond to a *change* request whether or not an *inquire* request was received. If the user ought to retrieve a record before updating, the client is responsible for enforcing this state dependency.

All the actions necessary to change a record occur in a single invocation of the program. The concept is referred to as a *logical unit of work* (LUW). An LUW may involve updating multiple related files or multiple records within a single file. In this case, the LUW includes all the activity required to access and update a single file record.

> **CAUTION**
>
> CGIMAINT.CBL does not provide any code to detect and prevent *concurrent update* problems. A concurrent update problem occurs when two users try to change the same record at the same time.
>
> With conversational programs, concurrent record updates are prevented by having one user *lock* the record when it is read. This technique should not be used with stateless servers or pseudo-conversational programs, because it violates the idea of an LUW. There is no guarantee that a client will ever release the lock.

> **NOTE**
>
> A pseudo-conversational program appears to be a conversation to the client. In actuality, the client invokes the server multiple times. Each invocation is a complete transaction. From the end user's perspective, it appears as one continuous program.

> **CAUTION**
>
> One way to get around the dilemma of concurrent updates is to include a field in the record that indicates when the record was last updated. This field can be a version number that is incremented or, more commonly, a time stamp that is updated each time a record changes. The client reads the record and stores the time stamp. When the server processes an update, it compares the client's time stamp with the time stamp of the record. If the time stamps do not match, somebody has changed the record, because the client last read it, and an exception results.

Server-Side Includes

Server-side includes (SSI) are another technique used to merge the new values with a standard form. With server-side includes, special HTML comments are added to the base document, such as this:

```
<!-- #include virtual="/mcp/mydoc.htm" -->.
```

The Web server merges the referenced document into the base document as it transmits to the client. Usually, the server provides this processing based on the file extension of the base document. For example, Microsoft's PWS will provide SSI processing for files with an .STM extension.

CGIMAINT.CBL can be rewritten to use server-side includes (CGISSI.CBL). Each value clause is written to a different file (LASTNAME.HTM, FIRSTNAME.HTM, STATUSMSG.HTM, and so on). The base document contains a #include for each file. The MIME becomes Location: CGISSI.STM, and the entire PUT-OUTPUT paragraph would resemble the code in CGILOC.CBL. Listing 29.5 shows excerpts from CGIMAINT.CBL required to support SSI. CGISSI.CBL contains the full code.

LISTING 29.5 CGISSI.CBL PUT-OUTPUT PARAGRAPH FOR SSI.

```
    PUT-OUTPUT.
        * Create #include files used by CGISSI.STM
         MOVE "LAST_NAME.htm"    TO SSI-FILESPEC
         MOVE CONTACT-LAST-NAME  TO SSI-VALUE
         PERFORM WRITE-VALUE-SSI

         MOVE "FIRST_NAME.htm"    TO SSI-FILESPEC
         MOVE CONTACT-FIRST-NAME TO SSI-VALUE
         PERFORM WRITE-VALUE-SSI

         MOVE "STREET.htm"    TO SSI-FILESPEC
         MOVE CONTACT-STREET TO SSI-VALUE
         PERFORM WRITE-VALUE-SSI

         MOVE "CITY.htm"     TO SSI-FILESPEC
         MOVE CONTACT-CITY   TO SSI-VALUE
         PERFORM WRITE-VALUE-SSI

         MOVE "PHONE.htm"     TO SSI-FILESPEC
         MOVE CONTACT-PHONE  TO SSI-VALUE
         PERFORM WRITE-VALUE-SSI

         MOVE "PROMPT.htm"     TO SSI-FILESPEC
         OPEN OUTPUT SSI
```

29

COBOL AND THE WEB

continues

LISTING 29.5. CONTINUED

```
        MOVE STATUS-MESSAGE TO SSI-RECORD
        WRITE SSI-RECORD
        CLOSE SSI

*  Redirect client to SSI document
        OPEN OUTPUT STDOUT
        MOVE "Location: CGISSI.STM" TO STDOUT-RECORD
        WRITE STDOUT-RECORD
        MOVE SPACE          TO STDOUT-RECORD
        WRITE STDOUT-RECORD
        CLOSE STDOUT
        .

    WRITE-VALUE-SSI.
        OPEN OUTPUT SSI
        PERFORM VARYING SSI-PTR FROM LENGTH OF SSI-VALUE BY -1
          UNTIL SSI-PTR < 1
          OR    SSI-VALUE (SSI-PTR:1) NOT = SPACE
             CONTINUE
        END-PERFORM
        MOVE QUOTE TO SSI-VALUE (SSI-PTR + 1:1)

        INITIALIZE SSI-RECORD
        STRING "VALUE="
               QUOTE
               SSI-VALUE DELIMITED SIZE INTO SSI-RECORD
        END-STRING
        WRITE SSI-RECORD
        CLOSE SSI
        .
```

CAUTION

There may be some danger using server-side includes if the Web server handles more than one client at the same time. It is possible that a client could receive part of a response destined for another client.

It also is possible to create an infinite loop by including a document that includes itself recursively.

Debugging Techniques

CGI programs can be run from the computer's command line or within an interactive debugger. Environment variables can be set prior to running the CGI program. CGI programs can return error messages to a client program. However, avoid using DISPLAY statements, because they may cause problems with writing to the standard output buffer.

When run from the command line, the standard input buffer is usually the keyboard. You also can pipe a text file to the standard input buffer. The following works on Windows NT:

```
SET REQUEST_METHOD=POST
SET CONTENT_LENGTH=80
CGISHOW <TEST.TXT
```

The contents of TEST.TXT follow:

```
FIELD=this+was+piped+to+the+standard+input+buffer+from+TEST.TXT%21
```

If the CGI program runs from the command line but fails to run from the Web browser, it may be due to one or more of the following:

- The directory is not defined to the Web server.
- The directory is defined, but the Web server has not enabled execute access to a Web user.
- The Web server or Web client may not share the same privileges as your user account. Security may prohibit a Web client from accessing resources.
- The CGI program may be a dynamically linked subroutine that is not on the PATH as defined to the Web server.
- The MIME header may be incorrect, or the second line may not be blank.
- The program may become stuck reading from the standard input buffer. If you are using file-mapped I/O, make sure that the standard input buffer file is declared as LINE SEQUENTIAL.

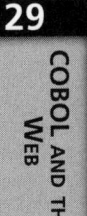

29

COBOL AND THE WEB

Addressing the Year 2000 Issues

PART
VIII

CHAPTER 30

The Technical Problem and Dealing with It

For most of us, the Year 2000 problem is creeping up faster than we would care to admit. As time draws nearer to the turn of the century, reports about the possible effects that Year 2000 computer glitches can have on our everyday lives are increasing. In this chapter, you'll explore the Year 2000 problem so that you can put some of those reports into perspective.

The chapters in Part VIII provide more detailed information about the Year 2000 problem. In this part of the book, you'll examine the following issues:

- The technical issues surrounding the Year 2000 problem, the options available for dealing with the problem, and some of the tools available to help make fixing code easier (this chapter)

- The issues that management needs to be aware of, such as obtaining extra resources, planning, project management, testing, legal issues, and more (Chapter 31)

- The symptoms that will start appearing if the Year 2000 problem isn't fixed, the impact these symptoms may have, and the attitudes of certain governments and their agencies (Chapter 32)

For information in addition to what is supplied in this book, you can refer to any of the following Internet Web pages:

```
http://www.ibm.com/IBM/year2000
```

```
http://www.microsoft.com/CIO/Articles/YEAR2000FAQ.htm
```

```
http://www.year2000.com
```

```
http://www.Y2K.com
```

```
http://www.infogoal.com/cbd/cbdhome.htm
```

```
http://www.mitre.org/research/y2k
```

This chapter provides you with an introduction to the Year 2000 problem, explains some of the more popular solutions you can use to make your programs Year 2000-compliant, and describes some of the tools available to help you do this.

An Introduction to the Year 2000 Problem

The *Year 2000 problem,* also known as the *two-digit date problem* or the *millennium problem,* refers to the inability of most computers and applications to tell the difference between the year 1900 and the year 2000. This problem must be fixed before the turn of the century (December 31, 1999).

Computers were only introduced in this century and only became popular in the 1980s. It is just within the past few years that hardware vendors and some of the major software vendors have begun to make their hardware and software Year 2000-compliant. This means that most computers, operating systems, and software packages manufactured before 1996 will not be able to handle dates when the next century rolls over.

It is estimated that the Year 2000 problem will affect about 80 percent of the world's computer systems and cost $300 billion to $600 billion to fix. Some of the work already has been completed, though. Companies that need to project dates into the future in order to conduct their business (such as credit card companies) have been running into Year 2000 problems for several years now. These companies have a head start or have even finished fixing the problem. Other proactive companies may have completed most, if not all, of their conversions by now.

Most of the problem boils down to the inability of computer hardware and software to process a four-digit date. The industry, for the most part, uses applications with dates that have a two-digit year. The year 1995, for example, is represented in a computer or computer program by the digits 95. As the century rolls over, the two-digit year will turn from 99 to 00. Because the century is not included in the year, the computer will not be able to distinguish between events happening in the year 1900 and in the year 2000.

When this occurs, many things will start happening. If the government agency that tracks births does not get its computer fixed in time, for example, the first baby born in the year 2000 will be registered as being the first baby born in the year 1900. This obviously would create a major problem for the individual and his or her parents.

Century Support in COBOL Compilers

Century support has been added to most COBOL compilers by now. You should be sure to check that the version of the compiler you are using supports the year 2000, though. It would be disappointing to find out that the COBOL compiler you are using does not support the year 2000 after you have completed all of your Year 2000 conversion work.

Century support usually involves some type of pivot date that has been added to allow the compiler to interpret dates that come before a certain two-digit year as falling into the next century. When the pivot date is encountered by software such as a compiler, it prefixes the dates that come before the pivot date with the digits 20. Any dates that come after the pivot year are prefixed with the digits 19.

In IBM COBOL compilers, for example, the pivot date is 40. This means that the compiler will prefix any dates that are less than 40 with the digits 20. So, if you retrieve the date 98, it is prefixed with 19, because it is greater than 40. If you retrieve the date 00, it is prefixed with 20, because it is less than 40.

This *default window,* as it often is referred to, works with other features that have been added to compilers to support the year 2000. These features include enhanced ACCEPT statements, intrinsic functions, and windows that you can set at compile time. The enhanced ACCEPT statements and intrinsic functions are described briefly in the next section. Windows that you can set at compile time are described in "Windowing—Fixed and Sliding" and "IBM Millennium Language Extensions," later in this chapter.

Year 2000 Solutions

This section describes some of the most popular Year 2000 solutions available (other solutions may be available):

- Date expansion
- Windowing (fixed and sliding)
- Date compression
- Date encapsulation
- Encoding the century
- Bridge programs

Date Expansion

> **TIP**
>
> The date-expansion solution is permanent, straightforward, and works with sorts. However, it takes time to implement, and you must convert your data.

The date-expansion solution involves finding all the places in your system's programs where two-digit date fields are used and permanently changing their descriptions to four-digit dates. This solution requires you to have access to all of the source code for your system so that you can change the date fields. It also requires you to update your data files, displays, and reports to use four-digit date fields.

Where your data files are involved, changing the size of the date field requires you to change the size of your data records and also might require you to change the format of your data records. Where your displays and reports are involved, changing the size of the date also might require you to move other fields around on the displays and reports to accommodate the new size of the date field.

This solution is the cleanest, because the code and data will represent dates in their correct format; no conversion or decoding takes place behind the scenes, as it does in other solutions, such as windowing. Also, this solution is permanent. You do not have to modify the conversion work you have done to make it continue to work.

However, this solution is the one that probably requires the most amount of resources and time to implement. If you have large systems and you have not started your Year 2000 conversion project yet, you probably should consider using this solution in combination with another solution, or you should just choose another solution entirely.

Areas of Code to Look For

In the `WORKING-STORAGE SECTION`, a data item that uses a two-digit year is defined in a COBOL program using code similar to this:

```
01 CURRENT-DATE-ITEM.
     05 CURRENT-YEAR        PIC 9(2).
     05 CURRENT-MONTH       PIC 9(2).
     05 CURRENT-DAY         PIC 9(2).
```

Using the date-expansion solution, the code is modified to something like the following:

```
01 CURRENT-DATE-ITEM.
     05 CURRENT-CENTURY     PIC 9(2).
     05 CURRENT-YEAR        PIC 9(2).
     05 CURRENT-MONTH       PIC 9(2).
     05 CURRENT-DAY         PIC 9(2).
```

Or, you could just make the two-digit century a part of the year by increasing the size of the year field from two digits to four digits, as shown here:

```
01 CURRENT-DATE-ITEM.
     05 CURRENT-YEAR        PIC 9(4).
     05 CURRENT-MONTH       PIC 9(2).
     05 CURRENT-DAY         PIC 9(2).
```

If you increase the size of your date fields, you also have to increase the size of the date fields defined in your data records. These are defined in the `FILE SECTION` of your program.

For example, the current data record might be defined as shown here:

```
FILE SECTION.
FD CURRENT-INPUT-FILE
                RECORD CONTAINS 80 CHARACTERS.
```

```
01 CURRENT-INPUT-RECORD.
    05 CURRENT-INPUT-FILE-YEAR      PIC 99.
    05 CURRENT-INPUT-FILE-MONTH     PIC 99.
    05 CURRENT-INPUT-FILE-DAY       PIC 99.
    05 OTHER-STUFF                  PIC X(74).
```

You have to increase the size of the CURRENT-INPUT-FILE-YEAR field or add a new field for the century. At any rate, this means that you would have fewer characters in the record for OTHER-STUFF. Not only would you have to change the record size in your programs, but you also would have to change the record size in your data files. You could write a simple COBOL program to do this conversion.

If you currently have characters in the record that aren't being used (in other words, they are defined as FILLER items), you could recover a couple of characters by reducing the size of the FILLER item and adding those characters to the date item. If you do have unused characters in your records, you do not have to change the record size of your data files.

After the date fields have been changed, you have to search through all your programs to find the date fields that

- Move data to the new date fields
- Receive moved data from the new date fields
- Are used in sort keys
- Are used in sort records
- Are used in displays
- Are received from the system using ACCEPT statements

Some of these date fields may be hard to find if they were not given names that indicate they are date fields.

You also need to search your programs for more obscure places where dates are being manipulated. For example, your program might be moving a hard-coded century (the digits 19) into a constant date field for use in displays or forms.

Enhanced ACCEPT Statements

Some COBOL languages have enhanced their ACCEPT statements to handle the four-digit year. For example, IBM's ILE COBOL for AS/400 added two phrases to its ACCEPT statement that allow you to accept four-digit dates in the Gregorian date format YYYYMMDD or the Julian date format YYYYDDD. The syntax for these statements follows:

```
ACCEPT system-date FROM DATE YYYYMMDD

ACCEPT system-date FROM DAY YYYYDDD.
```

These enhanced ACCEPT statements work with a compiler's default window. Default windows are described in "Century Support in COBOL Compilers," earlier in this chapter.

Intrinsic Functions

Some COBOL languages also have added intrinsic functions that allow you to convert dates that use a two-digit year to dates that use a four-digit year. These functions also enable you to retrieve the current date with a four-digit year. Again, IBM's ILE COBOL for AS/400 added the following intrinsic functions to provide this date functionality:

```
DATE-TO-YYYYMMDD
DAY-TO-YYYYDDD
YEAR-TO-YYYY
CURRENT-DATE
DATE-OF-INTEGER
DAY-OF-INTEGER
```

These intrinsic functions work with a compiler's default window. Default windows are described in "Century Support in COBOL Compilers," earlier in this chapter.

Steps to Implementing Date Expansion

You can follow these general steps to implement the date-expansion solution in your COBOL programs:

1. Use the tools described in "Inventory Tools" and "Impact-Analysis Tools," later in this chapter, to assess the amount of work you need to do and to get an idea of where the required changes are located in your source.

2. Restore or re-create any missing source modules.

3. Ask your management to create a specification for you and your fellow programmers to follow.

   This specification should describe the coding that management suggests you use to convert the different coding situations uncovered in step 1. If management wants you to use intrinsic functions, for example, the specification should indicate which ones to use and in which situations.

4. Convert your applications using the date-expansion method.

5. Convert your data to expand the date fields.

6. Test your applications.

   See "Testing Tools," later in this chapter, for more information about some of the tools available to help make testing your Year 2000 changes easier. Also, see the next chapter for more information about the testing processes you should use.

7. Fix any errors that were uncovered during the testing phase.

8. Repeat steps 6 and 7 until you have completed all of your testing phases and you are sure your programs are working the way they should.

9. If you have the resources, set up a test system to mimic your live system and do a live system test.

This is a good step to get the users of your system involved in the process. Because they use the system, they can provide valuable feedback during the testing phase.

Windowing—Fixed and Sliding

> **TIP**
>
> This solution is permanent (if you use a sliding window), costs less than date expansion, doesn't affect how your applications are used, and doesn't require you to convert your data. However, it only allows you to work with dates in a 100-year range, it doesn't sort in some situations, and eventually, it will have to be replaced with another solution (if you use the fixed window).

If you cannot change all your applications and data before the year 2000, the windowing solution might be the solution for you. The windowing solution cannot solve all your problems, though. Windowing does not allow you to manipulate a two-digit year to calculate a length of time greater than 100 years, for example, because the size of the window can be only a maximum of 100 years.

The fixed- or sliding-window solution doesn't require you to modify the two-digit date fields in your systems. Instead, you can choose a 100-year period and let the compiler do the windowing using either of the following window definitions:

• A default window (default windows are described in "Century Support in COBOL Compilers," earlier in this chapter)

• An option at compile time (such as the one used in "IBM Millennium Language Extensions," described later in this chapter)

Or, you can introduce program logic into your systems to test two-digit date fields based on your 100-year window, and assign the correct century accordingly.

Fixed Versus Sliding Windows

The only difference between the fixed-window solution and the sliding-window solution is the permanency of the window. For fixed-window solutions, you choose a static 100-year period. This permanent window acts as a temporary solution until the current year approaches the high range of the window you chose (some time in the next century). However, the sliding window uses a 100-year period that changes as the current year changes. It always keeps the same number of years in the past and present. The sliding window is useful in industries that always need to look ahead and behind the same number of years.

Letting the Compiler Do the Windowing

If you want the compiler to do the windowing for you, you probably will have to first convert your numeric or character date fields to date data items. If you are using ILE COBOL for AS/400, for example, you will have to do this.

You also could use the compiler option to change the window at compile time. If you need to implement a sliding window, this compiler option comes in handy. All you need to do each year is recompile all your programs using a new window definition; you do not need to make any more changes to your source code. The windowing compiler option is described in more detail in "IBM Millennium Language Extensions," later in this chapter.

Doing Your Own Windowing

If you want to do your own fixed windowing, you can use the enhanced ACCEPT statements or intrinsic functions to work with dates that have four-digit years. If these are not available in the compiler you are using, you can create a module with your own program logic that tests dates against a pivot date. If the date turns out to be less than the pivot date you chose, you prefix the two-digit date with 20. If the date turns out to be greater than the pivot date you chose, you prefix the two-digit date with 19.

Doing the windowing yourself requires that you change more code than if you let the compiler do the windowing. However, the changes you need to make still are less than if you implement the date-expansion method (remember that the windowing method doesn't require you to change your data, either).

Steps to Implement Windowing

You can follow these general steps to implement the windowing solution in your COBOL programs:

1. Use the tools described in "Inventory Tools" and "Impact-Analysis Tools" to assess the amount of work you need to do and to get an idea of where the required changes are located in your source.

2. Restore or re-create any missing source modules.

3. Ask your management to create a specification for you and your fellow programmers to follow.

   This specification should describe the coding that management wants you to use to convert the different coding situations uncovered in step 1. If you have to add code to do the windowing, for example, the specification needs to describe things such as the pivot year that has been chosen and the logic to use when testing dates against that pivot year. The specification could even provide you with a module or template with the code to use. This would make it easier for you and help to standardize the coding that is used.

4. Convert your applications using the windowing method.

NOTE

If you are letting the compiler do the windowing, you might have to first convert your numeric and character date fields to date data types.

---

5. If you are using the window compile option, remember to recompile your programs with this option.

6. Test your applications.

   See "Testing Tools" for more information about some of the tools available to help make testing your Year 2000 changes easier. Also, see the next chapter for more information about the testing processes you should use.

7. Fix any errors you uncovered during the testing phase.

8. Repeat steps 6 and 7 until you complete all of your testing phases and you are sure that your programs are working the way they should.

9. If you have the resources, set up a test system to mimic your live system and do a live system test.

   This is a good step to get the users of your system involved in the process. Because they use the system, they can provide valuable feedback during the testing phase.

10. If you are using a sliding window, and you are using the compiler option to change the sliding window every year, you and your management should set up a process

to ensure that all the programs are recompiled with the appropriate window definition at the beginning of each year.

Date Compression

> **TIP**
>
> The date-compression solution does not require additional disk space, and it gives you a wider range of years to work with. However, it is not intuitive to implement, your data files must be converted, it might slow the performance of your programs, and it could cause problems if you share your data with other companies.

Date compression consists of modifying the data type of the four-digit year values so that they can be represented in two-digit fields. Instead of storing four-digit years in numeric or alphabetic fields, they are stored as two-digit numbers in a different format.

If you use the date-compression method, you only have to create a couple of small programs that convert the dates between the compressed format and the real dates that they represent. You could call this program from your existing programs where I/O statements are processed.

However, you also have to migrate your existing data so that it is represented in the compressed format. This causes problems if you share data with other companies that are not using the same solution.

You can use several formats for date compression, and there may be more. This section describes how you can compress your four-digit dates into the following formats:

- Hexadecimal
- CYYDDD (centuries, years, days)
- DDDDDD (days)

Hexadecimal Format

One format you can use is hexadecimal format, where the two-digit hexadecimal number represents the offset value from a base year that you choose. For example, if you choose a base year of 1900, you would represent the year 1998 and the year 2006 as shown here:

```
* THE OFFSET REPRESENTING THE CURRENT YEAR (98) IS DEFINED
* AS 62 IN HEX
01 CURRENT-YEAR     PIC XX      VALUE "62".
```

```
* THE OFFSET REPRESENTING THE YEAR 2006 (106) IS DEFINED
* AS 6A IN HEX
01 YEAR2006          PIC XX       VALUE "6A".
```

Using the hexadecimal numbering system with date compression gives you a range of 255 years to work with. This means that if you use a base year of 1900, your programs could handle dates up until the year 2155.

CYYDDD Format

The CYYDDD compression method uses the year 1900 as a starting point (or any other year that you choose) and counts the number of centuries, years, and days that have elapsed since that date. The first digit, C, holds the number of centuries that have elapsed since 1900, and the second and third digits, YY, hold the number of years that have elapsed, which is the same as the two-digit year for that century. The last three digits, DDD, hold the number of days that have elapsed since the beginning of the year, in the same fashion that a Julian date would.

Starting with 1900 as the base year, the following code shows how you would represent January 1, 2000:

```
01 FIRST-DAY-YEAR2000   PIC 9(6)   VALUE 10101.
```

If you use this date-compression method, you can handle dates that occur within a 100-year range (10 centuries, 99 years, and 365 days) from your base date.

DDDDDD Format

The DDDDDD compression is similar to the CYYDDD compression method, except that instead of counting the number of centuries, years, and days that have elapsed, you just count the number of days that have elapsed. If your base year is 1900, for example, and you want to compress the date January 1, 2000 using this method, you would represent the date as the following:

```
01 FIRST-DAY-YEAR2000   PIC 9(6)   VALUE 036526.
```

If you use this date-compression method, you can handle dates that occur up until 2700 years from your base date.

The storage you save because you don't have to expand the field is also a bonus. Contrast that with the number of dates you could handle if you used the same six digits to represent the date in the YYMMDD format: that would be only the dates that fall between January 1, 1900 and December 31, 1999.

Steps to Implementing Date Compression

You can follow these general steps to implement the date-compression solution in your COBOL programs:

1. Use the tools described in "Inventory Tools" and "Impact-Analysis Tools" to assess the amount of work you need to do and to get an idea of where the required changes are located in your source.

2. Restore or re-create any missing source modules.

3. Ask your management to create a specification for your and your fellow programmers to follow.

   This specification should describe the coding you should use to convert the different coding situations uncovered in step 1. For example, it should describe the date-compression method being used, and it should supply any additional information that would make translating the dates easier. If dates are being compressed into hexadecimal format, for example, a table should be provided that shows the hexadecimal and decimal representations of the years starting from your base year.

4. Convert your applications using the date-compression method.

5. Convert your data.

6. Test your applications.

   See "Testing Tools" for more information about some of the tools available to help make testing your Year 2000 changes easier. Also, see the next chapter for more information about the testing processes you should use.

7. Fix any errors that were uncovered during the testing phase.

8. Repeat steps 6 and 7 until you complete all your testing phases and are sure that your programs are working the way they should.

9. If you have the resources, set up a test system to mimic your live system and do a live system test.

This is a good step to get the users of your system involved in the process. Because they use the system, they can provide valuable feedback during the testing phase.

You might find it helpful to use a utility that enables you to see the date data in decimal format. If you already have a utility that can do this, make sure that it is Year 2000-compliant. If not, some of the testing tools will enable you to work with dates in decimal format.

Date Encapsulation

> **TIP**
>
> The date-encapsulation solution isolates code changes to areas where I/O state-ments are executed, doesn't affect how your applications are used, and doesn't impact the performance of your applications. However, data coming into your organization has to be converted before you use it, and data that leaves your organization will be incorrect if not fixed; this is something that will need to be communicated to the organizations receiving your data.

Date encapsulation involves adding or subtracting the number of years it takes the Gregorian calendar to repeat itself from the dates you currently have stored in your data files.

The Gregorian calendar repeats itself every 28 years. This means that the days and dates in 1998 will be exactly the same as they were in 1970. The same is true for the years 1999 and 1971, the years 2000 and 1972, and so on. Using this method, you will be able to process dates up until the year 2027.

The calendar will continue to repeat itself after this date. If you want to continue to use this solution after the year 2027, you have to modify the value you subtract (add 28 to this value each time you reach the end of a 28-year period), or change your data (add 28 to the date values and store them back into the database at the end of each 28-year period). For example, to accommodate dates in the second 28-year period (the 28-year period following the year 2027), you subtract 56 (28 + 28). To accommodate dates in the next 28-year period, you subtract 84 (56 + 28).

To implement this method, you only have to modify areas of code where I/O statements, such as READs or WRITEs, are used. Every time a date is read in from a data file, you add 28 to it. Every time a date is written to a data file, you subtract 28 from it.

The date 080998 (August 9, 1998), for example, would be stored as 080970, where 28 is subtracted from 98, giving the year 70 as the last two digits of the year. When the same date is read back in by a program, 28 is added back to 70, giving the original date of 080998.

The following example shows you how this solution would work:

.
.
.

```
DATA DIVISION.
FILE SECTION.
FD DATA-IN.
01 DATA-IN-REC.
     05 INV-TYPE        PIC X.
     05 INV-DAY         PIC 99.
     05 INV-MONTH       PIC 99.
     05 INV-YEAR        PIC 99.
     05 FILLER          PIC X(73).

FD DATA-OUT.
01 DATA-OUT-REC.
   05 DATA-OUT-RECORD   PIC X(80).
   .
   .
   .
PROCEDURE DIVISION.
     READ DATA-IN
          AT END
               SET AT-END-OF-FILE TO TRUE
          NOT AT END
               MOVE INV-TYPE TO WORK-INV-TYPE
               ADD 28 TO INV-YEAR.
     DISPLAY "The inventory year is: " INV-YEAR.
   .
   .
   .
     SUBTRACT 28 FROM INV-YEAR.
     WRITE DATA-OUT-REC.

     STOP RUN.
```

Steps to Implementing Date Encapsulation

You can follow these general steps to implement the date-encapsulation solution in your COBOL programs:

1. Use the tools described in "Inventory Tools" and "Impact-Analysis Tools" to assess the amount of work you need to do and to get an idea of where the required changes are located in your source.

2. Restore or re-create any missing source modules.

3. Ask your management to create a specification for you and your fellow programmers to follow.

   This specification should describe the coding you should use to convert the different coding situations uncovered in step 1. For example, it should describe the coding that should be used to implement the solution and the places in the programs where you should place the coding.

4. Convert your applications using the date-encapsulation method.

5. Convert your data.

6. Test your applications.

   See "Testing Tools" for more information about some of the tools available to help make testing your Year 2000 changes easier. Also, see the next chapter for more information about the testing processes you should use.

7. Fix any errors that were uncovered during the testing phase.

8. Repeat steps 6 and 7 until you complete all your testing phases and you are sure that your programs are working the way they should.

9. If you have the resources, set up a test system to mimic your live system and do a live system test.

This is a good step to get the users of your system involved in the process. Because they use the system, they can provide valuable feedback during the testing phase.

Encoding the Century

> **TIP**
>
> Encoding the century is a solution that isolates code changes to areas where I/O statements are executed, doesn't affect how your applications are used, and doesn't require extra disk space. However, it is not simple to implement, and your data has to be converted. Also, shared data coming into your organization has to be converted before you use it, and data that leaves your organization will be incorrect if not fixed. This is something you will need to communicate to the organizations receiving your data.

This method uses a clever way to encode Year 2000 months or days in your already existing month (MM) or day (DD) fields. You do not really add an extra bit for the century. Instead, months and days in the next century are represented with a different first digit. The century indicator is hidden in the value of the first digit of the days or months field. This solution can be useful if you cannot expand your data fields.

To show you how this solution works, consider the day field. The first digit for the days in a calendar is a 1, 2, or 3 for the days 01 through 31 (the maximum). To represent days in the next century, you would use different first digits, such as 4, 5, and 6. This means that the next century's days would be represented as 41 through 61, corresponding to the real days 01 through 31. Your programs would have to include extra code around the I/O statements, such as READs and WRITEs, to encode and decode the dates.

Similarly, if you encode the century in the months field, you use the digits 2 and 3 as the first digit for months in the next century.

The magic number you add or subtract to encode and decode these dates would be 20 if you are using the month field and 40 if you are using the day field. For example, the first real month of a year has the numeric value 01, and the corresponding encoded month for the next century would have the numeric value 21. To get the encoded month back to its original value, you would subtract 20 from it:

```
21 - 20 = 01
```

Similarly, if you are encoding the days field, the encoded value for the first day of a month in the next century would be 41. To get the encoded month back to its original value, you would subtract 40 from it:

```
41 - 40 = 01
```

The following example shows you how this solution works for the days field:

```
WORKING-STORAGE SECTION.
01 DATE-WITH-CENTURY.
   05 CC PIC 9(2).
   05 YY PIC 9(2).
   05 MM PIC 9(2).
   05 DD PIC 9(2).
01 TWO-DIGIT-YEAR-DATE.
   05 YY PIC 9(2).
   05 MM PIC 9(2).
   05 DD PIC 9(2).
      .
      .
      .
* You would read a 6-digit date from a file
      MOVE CORRESPONDING TWO-DIGIT-YEAR-DATE TO DATE-WITH-CENTURY.
      IF DD OF TWO-DIGIT-YEAR-DATE > 31
          SUBTRACT 40 FROM DD OF DATE-WITH-CENTURY
          MOVE 20 TO CC OF DATE-WITH-CENTURY
      ELSE
          MOVE 19 TO CC OF DATE-WITH-CENTURY
      END-IF.
      .
      .
      .
* Before you write a date back to a file
      MOVE CORRESPONDING DATE-WITH-CENTURY TO TWO-DIGIT-YEAR-DATE.
      IF CC OF DATE-WITH-CENTURY > 19
          ADD 40 TO DD OF TWO-DIGIT-YEAR-DATE
      END-IF.
```

Steps to Encoding the Century

You can follow these general steps to encode the century in the month or days fields of your COBOL programs:

1. Use the tools described in "Inventory Tools" and "Impact-Analysis Tools" to assess the amount of work you need to do and to get an idea of where the required changes are located in your source.

2. Restore or re-create any missing source modules.

3. Ask your management to create a specification for you and your fellow programmers to follow.

   This specification should describe the coding you should use to convert the different coding situations uncovered in step 1. For example, the specification should describe whether a century indicator is going to be added to month or day fields, and it could supply templates of modules to make the conversion easier and to standardize the coding.

4. Convert your applications using the century-indicator method.

5. Convert your data.

6. Test your applications.

   See "Testing Tools" for more information about some of the tools available to help make testing your Year 2000 changes easier. Also, see the next chapter for more information about the testing processes you should use.

7. Fix any errors that were uncovered during the testing phase.

8. Repeat steps 6 and 7 until you complete all your testing phases and you are sure that your programs are working the way they should.

9. If you have the resources, set up a test system to mimic your live system and do a live system test.

This is a good step to get the users of your system involved in the process. Because they use the system, they can provide valuable feedback during the testing phase.

Bridge Programs

> **TIP**
>
> The bridge-program solution can buy you time while you finish converting all of your applications, but it usually is not considered permanent.

A bridge program allows you to convert data between different formats before processing it by your programs. Bridge programs are not a new concept; they have been used for many other types of data conversion in the past. Using a temporary bridge program as part of your Year 2000 solution can allow you to convert your most critical applications now using another solution and buy you some time while you finish converting your other applications.

Bridge programs usually are considered temporary because they do not fix the problem. They keep things working until the real data and code fixes can be finished. If you consider your bridge programs to be a permanent solution (somewhat like patching up an application, which is not the best solution), you might be surprised when something in your company changes down the road. For example, what will happen if your company starts a new relationship with another company and decides to share its data? The Year 2000 problem still will be there in some form. The same is true for some of the other solutions, such as fixed windowing, that have to be maintained at a later date to keep them current.

Bridge programs also can be useful in situations where the logic of your converted programs still will cause Year 2000 problems for a short window of time. Suppose that you are converting your applications using windowing, and due to the event horizons of your business, you are going to have to deal with dates outside of your 100-year window for a short period of time. You can implement a bridge program to handle the conversion of these dates that fall outside the window, and when the period of time when the dates fall outside the window passes, you can remove the bridge program.

Bridge programs also can be useful if you share data with other companies. This could be data coming into your organization or data that you are sending out to another company. Suppose that you used a windowing solution to convert your applications and you are sharing data with a company that used date expansion; you would have to write a bridge program to convert their four-digit dates to two-digit dates so that you could use the dates in your applications. Whether it is you or the other company that writes the bridge program, you will have to work out a plan between yourselves to take care of the conversion that will be required. However, if the company you deal with is not being proactive about finding a solution to the data-sharing problem, you might need to take the initiative to ensure that the bridge program gets written in order to protect yourself.

Summary of Year 2000 Solutions

As you can see, you can choose from several solutions to solve your Year 2000 problems. You can even combine solutions, if necessary. To contrast the differences between these solutions, Table 30.1 summarizes the highlights.

Table 30.1. Characteristics of the year-2000 solutions.

Solution	Longer to Implement	Permanent	Data Conversion	Works with Sorts	Difficult to Implement
Date Expansion	Yes	Yes	Yes	Yes	No
Fixed Window	No	No	No	No	No
Sliding Window	No	Yes	No	No	No
Date Compression	Yes	No	Yes	No	Yes
Date Encapsulation	No	No	No	Yes	No
Century Encoding	No	No	Yes	Yes	Yes
Bridge Programs	No	No	No	Yes	No

Year 2000 Tools

Many of the Year 2000 tools available to you are described in this section. They are divided into the following categories:

- Inventory
- Impact analysis
- Testing
- Data conversion
- Editing
- Source recovery
- Toolsets
- IBM COBOL Millennium Language Extensions
- Date routines

These categories group the tools according to the different situations you would use them in. The Millennium Language Extensions and the date routines would be used in your code, and the other tools would be used at different stages in the Year 2000 conversion process as indicated by their category name.

Inventory Tools

This section describes some of the inventory tools available to help you asses the number of programs you have, their sizes, and their contents.

IBM OPTI-AUDIT

OPTI-AUDIT, created by IBM, is a tool you can use in the VSE environment to take inventory and assessment of existing COBOL applications that providing the capability to do the following:

- Capture and build an inventory of all programs running on a VSE system.
- Extract job/program/file cross-reference information by monitoring the running of batch and online sessions.
- Scan source.
- Create reports that can be used in your Year 2000 conversion project.

SoftAudit/2000 and SoftAudit/One

SoftAudit/2000 and SoftAudit/One, created by IBM, work on MVS to provide an inventory of source modules that comprise your applications. They also relate load modules with application sources. These relationships can uncover unused source or unused load modules, which can reduce the amount of code you need to convert. These tools also produce the following types of reports:

- A list of lines of code per application, which includes the number of unused lines of code
- A load-library report that lists which applications have load modules in libraries on the system
- A load-module report that lists each load module on the system, along with the product and library associated with each load module
- A list that flags duplicate modules
- Product reports that list every module in each application in every load library
- A list of the number of jobs that have used each application

GILES

GILES, created by Global Software, Inc., runs in an IBM MVS environment and can gain information by searching through the following types of sources:

Copybooks

Transactions in CICS

Load modules

Programs

Display definitions

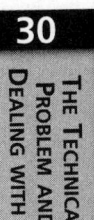

Job Control Language (JCL)

Link-edit decks

After analyzing all of your sources, GILES has knowledge about how date variables are compared and moved. Date variables that are recognized are those defined as type DATE, or those variables that are directly or indirectly loaded from a DATE variable.

YR2K Management System

YR2K Management System, created by Double E. Computer Systems, creates an inventory of software on a PC. A disk with YR2K Management System is placed in each computer in the company, and a utility on the disk identifies every piece of software installed on the PC. The disks then are returned to Double E. Computer Systems, where reports are generated. This tool can help you identify the most commonly used programs in your company.

ADPAC Inventory

ADPAC Inventory, created by ADPAC Corporation, uses JCL and load libraries to create an inventory of initial programs to be converted. Then the tool analyzes the CALL structure to create a more complete list of programs.

ADPAC also can create lists of programs that it finds are related, based on I/O records, COPYLIB structure, and JCL. By identifying groups of programs that are closely associated, project management can better assess the implications of changing specific programs and assign these groups of programs to programmers who will be working closely together.

Impact-Analysis Tools

This section describes some of the impact-analysis tools available to help you assess how much conversion work you need to do.

Edge Portfolio Analyzer

When used with a source-code scanner, the Edge Portfolio Analyzer enables you to identify the following:

- Source modules, without their corresponding load modules, so you do not end up converting programs that are not executed

- Load modules, without their corresponding source modules, so you can decide whether the program is critical enough to be replaced or whether it can be eliminated

- Compiler options used to create the load module, which can help reduce the testing efforts by anticipating differing output results due to different compiler options used

- The language, compiler version, and release used when you last compiled your applications, enabling you to plan changes required for applications and programs that were created with obsolete compilers

NA2000 SCAN

NA2000 is a tool that finds and scans source files on a PC for references to dates. This tool can search up to 500 files at a time, and you also can filter the files to be scanned by searching only those files named with a specific extension.

After NA2000 is used to scan the source files, it creates a report that lists programs, as well as specific line numbers of the code within those programs, that need to be changed. Another report can be generated to estimate the amount of time that would be required to make all of the changes the previous report listed.

Revolve/2000

Revolve/2000, developed by Micro Focus, operates on a desktop PC and evaluates code on an MVS system by tracking the following:

- Variables and data elements and their relationships with other variables and data elements

- The program logic that compares these data elements

- The fields in data records that they relate to

Resolve/2000 can trace through a program and create a flow-control diagram. It also can create a report that estimates the cost and effort required to complete a Year 2000 conversion. This estimate is based on the number of date data elements within a program, combined with the program's complexity. You specify the parameters on which the estimate is based.

SEARCH2000

SEARCH2000, developed by IBM, works in an AS/400 environment to help you evaluate the impact of date fields used in your database files. You can use SEARCH2000 to help you identify dates in your database files, the programs that use these dates, and the format of the dates. SEARCH2000 has an interface into IBM BYPASS2000 for AS/400, which is described in "BYPASS2000," later in this chapter.

Maintenance 2000

Maintenance 2000, developed by IBM, is a tool that helps you understand and analyze a large number of existing MVS application programs in your MVS or OS/390 environment. The program statically analyzes the following:

- PL/I source programs, including files and macros
- COBOL source programs and COPYBooks
- CA-Easytrieve Plus programs and macros
- JCL and cataloged procedures

You should use Maintenance 2000 during the find-and-fix phase of your Year 2000 project. Maintenance 2000 is a TSO application that you run as a batch job. You can view the output in ISPF panels on the host or download it to a workstation and use it for coding and testing.

Testing Tools

This section describes some of the testing tools available to help you test your programs after they have been converted.

DataAger/400

DataAger/400, created by Visionet Systems Inc., helps with AS/400 Year 2000 testing. DataAger/400 is a comprehensive toolset that allows data to be aged and allows the processor's date to be simulated as a future date.

This tool is useful if you want to do Year 2000 testing in a virtual future environment. DataAger/400 is designed to simplify and automate the data-aging process so that you can do this type of testing more quickly and efficiently.

DataAger/400 supports a wide variety of date formats, including these:

*MDY	CMDY
YMD	CYMD
DMY	CDMY
MDYY	YM
YYMD	YYMM
DMYY	All YYYY or YYYY*

More formats can be added as an option.

Dates can be aged by days, months, years, or based on user-defined rules. Also, dates in several formats are supported: packed, decimal, and character variables.

WITT Year2000

IBM Workstation Interactive Test Tool Year2000 for OS/2 Version 3.0 (WITT Year2000) is a set of test tools to help with the testing effort in your Year 2000 project. WITT Year2000 can assist you in finding out where date fields appear on your displays and can help you automate test cases so that regression testing that you conduct after your Year 2000 conversion will take less time. With WITT Year2000, you can test MVS and VM applications that use 3270 displays on OS/2, AS/400 applications that use 5250 displays on OS/2, and OS/2 applications that use OS/2 GUI and text windows.

HourGlass 2000

HourGlass 2000, created by MainWare, is a date-simulation product that works in an MVS/ESA operating environment. When you install the simulator, you can selectively list the programs in which you want to use the simulated date; the rest of your programs will use the old dates. Date simulation is not restricted to working at the system level. Individual users can simulate their own set of dates, enabling you to spread testing across many people.

TICTOC

TICTOC, created by Isogon, simulates dates for the OS/390 ESA and MVS/XA environments. You do not have to change any code or JCL in order to use the simulated dates, and you can selectively pick which programs you want to receive the simulated dates.

VIA/ValidDate

VIA/ValidDate, created by Viasoft, allows you to set a date in the past or future for any program you run. Programs that have been run with simulated dates are listed in a log, which can be used for verification of the testing process. Prerequisite operating systems for VIA/ValidDate are IBM MVS/ZA or MVS/ESA.

Conversion Tools

This section describes some of the conversion tools available to help you do the actual conversion work.

BYPASS2000

BYPASS2000, created by IBM, converts AS/400 application dates to handle the year 2000 with minimal manual intervention. BYPASS2000 locates and changes the areas of an application that need to be changed to accommodate four-digit years. After the changes are complete, the program source and data files can be recompiled and tested to ensure that the application continues to work as it should.

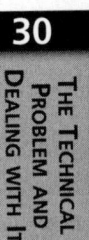

INTO2000

INTO2000, created by INTO2000 Inc., runs on PCs attached to AS/400s to automate the conversion of AS/400 applications. With INTO2000, you can choose to convert your applications using the windowing or the date-expansion solution. Depending on the needs of the solution you choose, INTO2000 will add code to the logic of programs that store dates, without changing how these stored dates are displayed. INTO2000 also adds a marker anyplace where the code is changed, so you can go back later and check it. INTO2000 also can help you convert existing databases.

TransCentury Analysis

TransCentury Analysis, created by Platinum Technology Inc., works on MVS and AS/400 systems. It identifies all the occurrences of dates in source-code files, including obvious references as well as code that is dependent on these obvious references. TransCentury Analysis also can be used to generate reports that estimate the cost and resources required to make your Year 2000 conversions.

After you use TransCentury Analysis to define all the code that needs to be changed, you can use it to make the changes. It contains a library of calendar routines that you put in place of your current date references, which will save on the overall time required for the conversion.

File-Aid

File-Aid, created by Compuware Corp., runs in an MVS operating environment and allows you to reformat data in a file so that it can be expanded to hold century bits and modified to hold initial date values that you specify.

Vantage Year2000

Vantage Year2000, created by Millennium Dynamics Inc., is a suite of tools that run in a PC or mainframe environment. Using this suite of tools, you can upgrade data files by inserting century values, and you can return files back to their original state, if necessary.

HotDate 2000/CONVERT

HotDate 2000/CONVERT, developed by SOFTWORKS Inc., is an automated code-conversion tool for COBOL applications in MVS environments. It automatically inserts expansion, windowing, or encoding code for handling the Year 2000 in COBOL programs. HotDate 2000/CONVERT can increases productivity while cutting the costs of manual conversion. It provides consistent and accurate code changes and automatically propagates the changes to any other application components that are affected.

Editing Tools

This section describes some of the editors available to help you edit your programs for Year 2000 conversion.

PREDITOR

PREDITOR, created by Compuware, has several features that are worth noting. This product works in a windowed environment, which means that you can work on several files at once; it also uses color highlighting for the different syntax elements of computer languages, emulates other editors, handles wide records and very large files, and performs search-and-replace operations on multiple files. PREDITOR also performs the following tasks:

- Handles UNIX end-of-line characters
- Supports the use of bookmarks
- Prints source files in both portrait and landscape modes

ICE

Intelligent Code Editor (ICE), created by Rasmussen Software, can be used in DOS and UNIX environments. ICE works in a windowed environment, which means that you can work on several files at once; it also uses color highlighting for the different syntax elements of computer languages, emulates other editors, handles wide records and very large files, and performs search-and-replace operations on multiple files. ICE also offers these capabilities:

- Allows you to compare different versions of the same files
- Records both DOS and UNIX record delimiters
- Supports file-locking while a file is being edited
- Performs the matching of programming language keywords and symbols, such as ELSEs, IFs, and brackets

Source-Recovery Tool

This section describes a tool available to help you recover source code that is missing.

Source Recovery

Source Recovery, from Source Recovery Company, Inc., can help you recover COBOL source code from object code created for the following environments:

- BMS MAPS
- CICS
- DB2
- IMS
- MVS/VSE/VM programs

Toolsets

Several toolsets are available that may offer you a more complete solution. They include tools that will do several jobs, such as take inventory, do impact analysis, make code changes, and help with testing. A couple of these toolsets are mentioned here.

YEAR2000.EXE

YEAR2000.EXE, created by NetVersant Technologies, consists of an intelligent COBOL analyzer and converter, related impact analysis and validator programs, and a date-simulation module. This toolset supports both the date-expansion and sliding-window Year 2000 solutions. There are YEAR2000.EXE toolsets for converting ANSI COBOL for DOS, Microsoft Windows 3.*x*, Windows 95, Windows NT, and SCO UNIX.

Piercom 2000

Piercom 2000, developed by Piercom Ltd., works on Digital applications running in VAX and Alpha systems. It has tools that assess your applications and tools that then help you make the required code changes.

Piercom 2000 recommends change scenarios that can be accepted or revised, and after the corrections are complete, the product can generate new source code that implements a windowing or date-expansion solution to fix the problem areas. You also can create reports that provide useful metrics for project-management purposes.

IBM Millennium Language Extensions

The IBM Millennium Language Extensions introduce windowing capabilities to their Year 2000–ready COBOL compilers. If windowing is the solution you have chosen, the COBOL Millennium Language Extensions may help reduce the amount of effort required to make your code Year 2000–compliant.

These extensions allow data items to be flagged as dates within a COBOL program. When a flagged date data item is referenced within the program, its value is converted automatically to a data representation that suits its implied representation within the statement. If the statement is comparing a windowed date with a four-digit year, for example, the windowed date is expanded to four digits.

The code samples in Listings 30.1a and 30.1b show how a COBOL program might be enabled for the year 2000 using Millennium Language Extensions. Listing 30.1a is the sample of code before it is updated with the Millennium Language Extensions.

LISTING 30.1A CODE BEFORE IT IS UPDATED WITH THE MILLENNIUM LANGUAGE EXTENSIONS.

```
77 TODAYS-DATE            PIC 9(6).
...
01 POLICY-RECORD.
...
   05 MATURITY-DATE        PIC 9(6).
...

   ACCEPT TODAYS-DATE FROM DATE
      IF TODAYS-DATE IS GREATER THAN OR EQUAL TO MATURITY-DATE
         DISPLAY 'Policy is mature, updating benefits record:'.
```

Listing 30.1b shows the code sample after it has been updated with the Millennium Language Extensions. (The syntax of the statements or process statement options will vary, depending on which COBOL compiler you are using.)

LISTING 30.1B CODE AFTER IT IS UPDATED WITH THE MILLENNIUM LANGUAGE EXTENSIONS.

```
process WINDOW(1950), MLEPROC
77 TODAYS-DATE            PIC 9(6)     DATE YYMMDD.
...
01 POLICY-RECORD.
...
   05 MATURITY-DATE        PIC 9(6)     DATE YYMMDD.
...

   ACCEPT TODAYS-DATE FROM DATE
      IF TODAYS-DATE IS GREATER THAN OR EQUAL TO MATURITY-DATE
         DISPLAY 'Policy is mature, updating benefits record: '.
```

The updates made to the sample code to implement the language extensions follow:

- Addition of the WINDOW process statement option (a way of embedding compiler options within the COBOL source code), which identifies 1950 as the base year of the window.

- Addition of the MLEPROC process statement option, which tells the compiler to flag the data items that have been specified as dates using the DATE phrase.

- After this code is recompiled, any dates that were flagged as DATEs (TODAYS-DATE and MATURITY-DATE, in this example) will be processed using the window. Thus, if a two-digit date—for example, 02—is introduced into either of these data items, it first is compared to the base WINDOW year. If it is less than the base year (which the two-digit year 02 is), it will be treated as being in the next century (making the four-digit expanded year 2002).

Millennium Language Extensions are available for the following COBOL products:

- COBOL for OS/390 & VM
- COBOL for VSE
- COBOL Set for AIX
- ILE COBOL for AS/400
- VisualAge COBOL (OS/2 and Windows NT)

> **NOTE**
>
> If you currently are using AS/400 COBOL in an OPM environment, you do not have to rewrite your AS/400 COBOL programs to work in the ILE environment (although they will not be taking full advantage of the ILE environment); they only need to be recompiled using a different command.

Date Routines

This section describes a date routine available for you to use in your programs as part of your Year 2000 solution.

TransCentury Calendar Routines

TransCentury Calendar Routines, created by Platinum Technology Inc., can be used in any COBOL program to perform the following tasks:

- Test the format of the current date.
- Obtain a date in relation to another date in the month.
- Calculate a date duration (past or future).
- Reformat dates.
- Find out what day of the week a future date will fall on.
- Test the validity of a date.
- Work with days that are work days (for example, Monday through Friday).

Summary

This chapter introduced you to the Year 2000 problem. You learned about some of the Year 2000 support that has been added to compilers, some of the more popular solutions that you can use to solve your Year 2000 problem, and some of the tools and code samples available to help you convert your applications.

The next chapter describes some of the management issues that will be important in a Year 2000 project. Some of these issues include planning; testing; obtaining extra resources; and handling legal issues, insurance issues, and tax issues.

CHAPTER 31

Managing a Year 2000 Project for Success

Helping your company make its business applications Year 2000-compliant is one of the most important projects you probably will ever undertake. Many problems can be caused by an inaccurate century appearing anywhere in the applications that you write and maintain for your company. But it's not just your job to ensure that your applications are made Year 2000-compliant. The management team in your company also needs to play a significant role in your Year 2000 project in order for it to be successful.

This chapter describes some of the issues the management team in your company should be addressing. If they are not, you might want to bring some of these issues to their attention so that they can deal with any potential problems now rather than later. Remember: Forewarned is forearmed.

Has Your Company Planned Its Year 2000 Project?

Now here's that word you've heard before: *Planning.* You might be wondering whether planning ever really occurs or whether it's just some kind of make-work task that project managers occupy themselves with. Or maybe you are wondering why people even bother trying to plan, because it only seems to get in the way of real coding. The Year 2000 problem has such a large impact on all businesses and can cause such catastrophic problems if it is left unfixed that it probably will change your mind about the importance of planning before the project is complete.

Before the actual job of converting the company's programs begins, the project-management team should have completed some planning tasks. Figure 31.1 illustrates these planning tasks.

Approaches to Technical and Management Issues

The project-management team should determine the approach the Year 2000 conversion project is going to take to the following technical and management issues:

- Hardware inventory
- Software inventory, including operating systems and vendor applications
- Assessment of the company's computer operations and computer administration tasks

- Selection of a date-conversion strategy
- Investigation of data issues, including data dictionaries, data definitions, data sharing, and data-modeling
- Selection of the Year 2000 tools you will use to help with the planning and conversion
- Review of processes to ensure that they will meet the needs of the Year 2000 project
- Analysis of development issues, such as migrating to and bridging with the new Year 2000 systems, prototyping, and parallel development
- Review or implementation of the project test cycle
- Updates to the documentation
- Estimation of the cost to maintain the new system

FIGURE 31.1.

The suggested planning process for a Year 2000 conversion project.

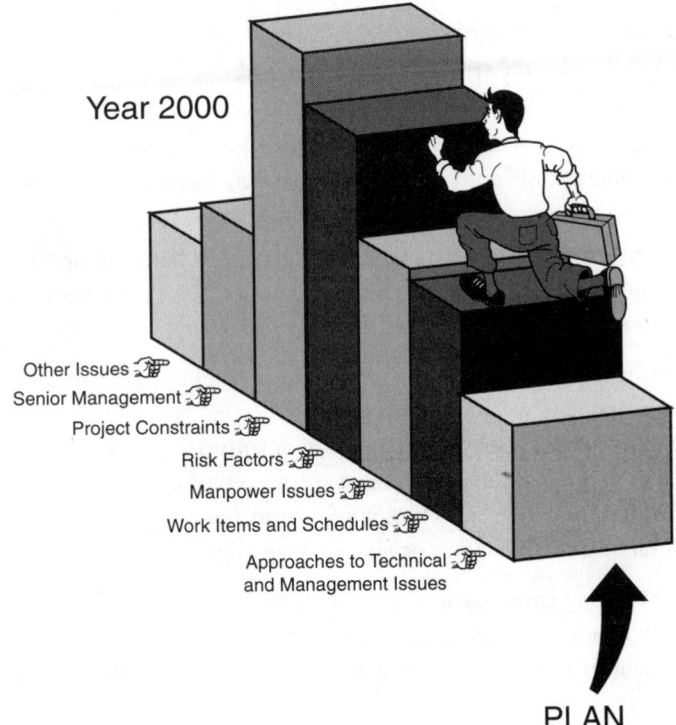

An Inventory of the Hardware

If all of the hardware your company uses is not Year 2000-compliant, the software never will be, either. This is a good place to start taking inventory.

You need a list of all the systems in your business by location. This list should include information such as model, year purchased, and vendor's name. After you complete the list, you should contact all the vendors so that they can verify which hardware, if any, needs to be upgraded.

Your inventory list should not only include the multiuser systems, but it also should include all the personal computers in the company. PCs need to be included because they contain *Basic Input/Output System* (BIOS) chips, which do not handle four-digit dates correctly. It is not easy to tell whether a PC's BIOS is going to cause a problem when the year 2000 rolls over without conducting a couple of tests. Someone should be assigned to conduct the following tests on all of the PCs used in the company:

- Change the date and time on each PC to December 34, 1999 at 12:59. Wait a couple of minutes, and if the date and time roll over correctly to January 1, 2000, the PC has passed this test.

  If your PC passes this test, you also should try setting the date in the same way, but turning the PC off until its internal clock has had time to roll over to the year 2000. When you turn some PCs back on after this test, the date displayed is wrong.

- The second test determines whether the PC will hold a Year 2000 date after it has been turned off. Change the date to January 1, 2000, and turn off the PC. If the date is still January 1, 2000 when it is turned back on, the PC has passed this test.

If a PC passes the first test, all you need to do is reset the date manually when January 1, 2000 arrives; the date will not roll over itself. If a PC did not pass the second test, you will have to replace the PC's BIOS or install a software package that automatically compensates for the error in the date. Such a software package will make the PC date appear if it is actually the correct date. For more information about how to change a computer's BIOS, contact the manufacturer or visit its Web page.

Even if the funding currently is not available for you to purchase the hardware, an estimate of how much of the existing hardware needs to be replaced must be available before you can finalize the plans and present them to senior management.

An Inventory of the Software, Including Operating Systems and Vendor Applications

You also need to take an inventory of the company's operating systems and third-party software packages. Only in the last few years have vendors started making the necessary changes to their software to enable it to handle four-digit dates. You should use the list you created of the hardware systems as the starting point for the list of operating systems and third-party software that the company uses.

Software inventory should proceed on a system-by-system basis, listing the software used on each system as it appears on the hardware list. After you complete the list, you should contact the software vendors so that they can verify which software, if any, needs to be upgraded.

Data Exchanged with Other Companies

If you do not investigate and plan early before exchanging data with other companies, you can foul up your company's capability to become Year 2000-compliant. You need to track down the data sources passed from your company to another or received by your company from another company. You can exchange data in several ways. It is usually put on tape, disk, or CD-ROM; or, it is transferred electronically.

You need to investigate all sources of data transfer—even those that the company's Information Systems department might not know about. Senior management may need to be involved in this process if a large amount of data is being transferred to other companies outside of the processes that have been set up within the company transferring the data.

After you track down the data sources exchanged between your company and other companies, you need to analyze them to assess how many date-related fields they contain. You can use the results of the analysis to estimate the amount of work that will need to be done to convert the date fields used in the data.

If the exchanged data is transferred to your company from another company, you have to work with that other company to ensure that it also will migrate its date-related fields to be Year 2000-compliant. The format to which it migrates also must be compatible with the Year 2000 solution your company chooses.

Assessment of Computer Operations and Computer Administration Tasks

You also need to consider some issues for the people who support and maintain the company's computer systems. If part of your company's Year 2000 solution requires bridge programs, for example, the computer operators probably will be responsible for starting, stopping, and monitoring these jobs every day. If the Year 2000 applications are going to be tested using date simulators, the computer-operations staff probably will have extra duties during the testing period to monitor these simulators. During the final testing stages, are two systems going to be run concurrently—one live production system and one test system using live data? If so, the operations department will have extra duties in order to be able to look after the second system.

If new systems are being purchased for the year 2000, these probably will have to be configured, and systems that work with these new systems also may have to be reconfigured.

These decisions will be made during the planning phase of the Year 2000 project and will depend on other factors, such as available resources. Date simulators are handy tools to use in a Year 2000 project, for example, but the decision to use them at your company may depend on whether enough funding is available to purchase the tool.

Date-Conversion Strategy

Before you select the date-conversion strategy, you need to thoroughly investigate the business's needs. Here are some examples of the types of issues you need to consider when deciding on a Year 2000 solution (these issues and others are described in more detail in this chapter):

- The time required by each solution for implementation.

  There isn't much time left, so this will be an important factor.

- The skills that can be pooled together to complete the work.

  If the solution requires that a large amount of code be rewritten, and enough people who are experienced with the code are not available, it may take more time than remains to implement the solution.

- The number of lines of code that need to be changed.

  For example, will the solution fit the budget?

- The impact on data used by the company, both in-house and from sources outside the company.

  If the application systems use a large database, it may or may not be a good idea to convert the data to support the Year 2000 format. You could use bridge programs to do some of the conversion, and you could complete the rest of the data conversion after the year 2000 arrives. Or, it might be more practical to convert the data as part of the Year 2000 solution. Also, if data is used from outside the company, you will have to choose a solution that can accommodate the format this data will take in the year 2000.

Choosing which date-conversion strategy is going to be used is a very important decision that needs to be made. The Year 2000 solutions are described in more detail in Chapter 33, "What Will Really Happen." Your management team should review this chapter along with someone who has a technical knowledge of the company's systems before committing to a Year 2000 solution at this stage.

Data Considerations

Now here's a topic a little closer to your everyday concerns. Your project-management team may be asking you to provide input on some of these issues.

Some of the data considerations you need to look at involve the following areas:

- Data dictionary formats
- Procedures for creating and updating data definitions
- Procedures for data sharing
- Data modeling

Data Dictionary Formats

A *data dictionary* is a file or database that documents the electronic data used by an organization. It includes information such as the following:

> Data name
>
> Description of its purpose or use
>
> Data type (for example, integer or floating-point)
>
> Size (for example, character 8, numeric 8, or single-precision floating-point)
>
> Programs that own the fields
>
> Database where the data object is stored
>
> Valid values (for example, numeric only or integer greater than 7)
>
> Synonyms, or the other names, by which this data object is known

If your organization currently is not using a data dictionary, you should suggest that one be implemented for your Year 2000 project. The data dictionary can be a useful tool during development and testing to help you and the testers perform tasks such as locating data fields, writing test cases, and creating test data. Tools are available that can help automate the process of creating a data dictionary, as well as providing an interface to search and modify it. Also, after the data dictionaries are in place, they will be around after the Year 2000 conversion is finished to be used again and again.

Procedures for Creating and Updating Data Definitions

The date-conversion strategy your company chooses to follow will dictate the data types with which the programs are going to be updated. Constructing procedures for creating and updating data definitions can make things run much smoother.

For example, if you, as developers, work independently from each other to create new data definitions for Year 2000-compliance, you could end up with a situation in which the data definitions being used do not match up with each other.

Fixing this problem after it has happened takes a substantial amount of effort. To make things easier, you should implement a procedure for creating and updating data definitions before you start the Year 2000 project.

Procedures for Data Sharing

In most organizations, applications do not work in isolation; they interact with other systems by passing data to and from them. For example, an inventory system would update data locally at stores where merchandise is sold and then download it regularly to remote mainframe systems where it would be used to update the main inventory database. If erroneous data is passed between systems, it can corrupt customer data and erode the organization's revenues.

Before the Year 2000 project starts, you should create a procedure to ensure that the integrity of the data passed between systems remains intact. After the year 2000 arrives, these procedures can be carried on into the next century.

Data Modeling

Data modeling is a method you can use to analyze the data requirements for an organization. Data that is relevant, timely, consistent, and accessible has increased value to an organization.

Effective data modeling can maximize the value of the company's data by increasing shared use of it and can help avoid data redundancy. Also, data modeling can improve the design of the company's databases, which can result in information being more readily available to users, a reduction in application-maintenance costs, and improved database performance.

If your company's Year 2000 solution requires you to make substantial database design changes, you should consider doing some data modeling before finalizing the changes you are going to make to your data.

Which Year 2000 Tools Are Going to Be Used?

Refer to the preceding chapter, "The Technical Problem and Dealing With It," for more information about some of the Year 2000 tools available. After project management analyzes the applications, estimates the amount of work that needs to be done, decides which date solution is going to be used, and decides on some testing strategies, it should work with you to decide which tools will help you complete your planned Year 2000 conversion.

A Review of the Processes

Now here's a well-loved word: *process*. Ouch! Take a deep breath and read on. The oxygen still flows in a process-driven environment.

If development and test processes are not already in place at your company, the management team should implement processes for your Year 2000 project. If these processes already are in place, you should check them to ensure that they are working.

A *process* is a set of guidelines and checkpoints that create a framework in which the team members (whether they are developers, testers, documentation writers, or team members in some other function in your company) can complete their work. A process should address the phases of a project cycle, such as these:

- Planning
- Scheduling
- Ownership
- Requirements for checkpoints and deliverables
- Checkpoints (deliverables associated with, frequency, quality criteria for each)
- Reviews
- Deliverables
- Sign-offs (from groups that supply input)

The project-management team should work with you, the developer, to implement a new process or update an existing one. You are the one who will be using the process, and you can supply valuable information to the project-management team about how things actually work in your department.

After a new process is approved, it should be well-documented, communicated to all team members who will be using it, and available in a central place so that all the team members can refer to it throughout the duration of the Year 2000 project.

This book discusses the testing procedures in more detail, because it is the most important phase of a Year 2000 project. See the section "A Suggested Test Cycle," later in this chapter.

Development Issues

Now here are some topics that you can help plan. The project-management team should at least consult you on these issues.

Some of the development issues you should consider are migration to and bridging with Year 2000 systems, prototyping, and parallel development.

Migration To and Bridging With Year 2000 Systems

After all the applications have been converted and thoroughly tested, the migration from the Year 2000 system to the live system can begin.

Prototyping

Prototyping is a step in the development cycle when a model or preliminary implementation of a product or system is created so that it can be evaluated with the following points in mind: design, performance, production potential, and usability.

You should create the prototype early in the development cycle so that you will have time to address any problems or design changes it uncovers.

For your part in the Year 2000 project, you might find that creating a prototype will help you implement your Year 2000 changes. This is especially true if you are going to be making changes to the design of your system. However, if you do not have a large amount of resources or you are short of time (which is going to be the case for many Year 2000 projects), you might want to skip this step. You need to weigh the benefits against the drawbacks before making this decision.

Parallel Development

Parallel development allows the Year 2000 team to work on the Year 2000 conversion while making other enhancements to the company's applications. However, to control the source changes that will be made to the applications in a parallel development environment, a good version-control (also called *configuration-management*) tool needs to be implemented if one is not already being used. The version-control tool should have the following characteristics:

- The capability to trace the evolution of a single component along multiple and simultaneous development paths.
- Support for emergency fixes.
- Versioning of a wide variety of development objects (not just source files). These objects can be source files, object code, documentation, project plans, spreadsheets, file system name spaces, directory hierarchies, and so on.
- Support for multiple projects, especially if you are going to add enhancements to your product in addition to doing the Year 2000 conversion work.

Managing a Year 2000 Project for Success

CHAPTER 31

875

31

MANAGING A
YEAR 2000
PROJECT

A Suggested Test Cycle

Because the testing phase of a Year 2000 project is the most important phase, I have included a description of a suggested test cycle (see Figure 31.2). The following subsections outline a suggested test cycle for a Year 2000 project.

FIGURE 31.2.

The suggested testing process for a Year 2000 conversion project.

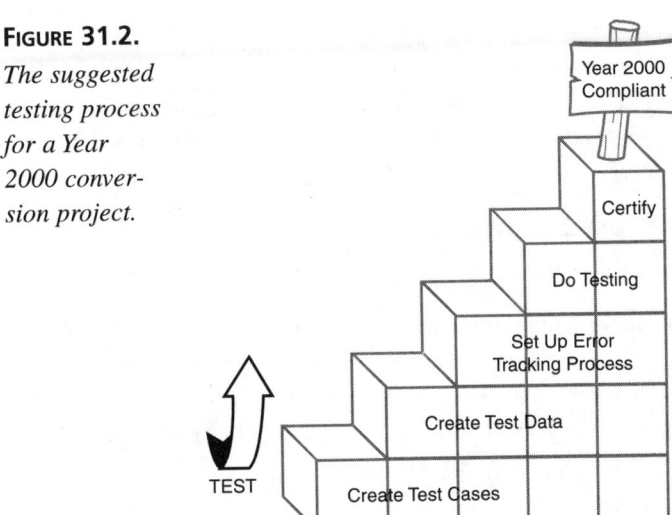

Create Test Cases

Good testing should have two qualities: It must be repeatable, and it must be as exhaustive as possible. For these reasons, you need to do the following:

- Document the test cases created, stating the expected result clearly.
- Create test cases that will cover as many of the scenarios that will be unique to the century rollover as possible.

Normal testing of the systems should continue as well; even if a piece of an application may not be affected by Year 2000 code changes, it could. Don't wait until the year 2000 to find out that something is missed.

Also, you should test your contingency plans and any new recovery procedures you have created. For more information about recovery procedures and contingency plans, see "Recovery Procedures and Contingency Plans," later in this chapter.

Possible Test Case Template

Test cases need to be clearly documented so that they can be repeated at any time. Also, the documentation for each test case must be so clear that even someone who is unfamiliar with the test scenario could complete it objectively. Test cases should include the following types of information:

- Description of the purpose
- Description of the steps of the application that will be executed in the test, including input data
- Expected results
- Any other details a tester needs to know to complete the test case accurately (such as location of any auxiliary files or communication links that need to be set up before conducting the test)

Suggested Year 2000 Test Scenarios

Here are some of the more common Year 2000 test scenarios:

- **Century ambiguity.** Century ambiguity is the most common Year 2000 technical problem. This problem refers to the situation that arises when an application that uses two-digit dates cannot tell whether a date is in the 20th ($19xx$) or 21st ($20xx$) century. The following are examples of scenarios in which century ambiguity can occur:

  A user interface rejects a four-digit date.

  Sorting leaves dates in the 20th and 21st centuries in jumbled order.

  Date periods (for example, stale dates) are calculated incorrectly.

  A comparison between a date in the 20th century and a date in the 21st century assumes that both dates are in the same century.

- **Extended semantics.** Extended semantics refers to a situation in which certain dates are reserved for special processing. For example, 99/99/1999 has the meaning "does not expire" in some financial applications. When the system date actually reaches 1999, there may be errors in the application. If a new "does not expire" date is chosen, it has to be tested to make sure that it adequately replaces the old "does not expire" date without causing application errors.

Managing a Year 2000 Project for Success

CHAPTER 31

877

31

MANAGING A
YEAR 2000
PROJECT

- **Calendar errors.** Calendar errors include problems such as failing to treat the year 2000 as a leap year and doing incorrect conversions between date representations, such as between Gregorian (YYYYMMDD) and Julian (YYYYDDD). You need to create test cases to test that February 29, 2000 is an acceptable date in an application and that all dates and days of the week after that date also are correct. Also, you need to test all the situations in which your company's applications do conversions between Julian and Gregorian dates.

- **Date overflow.** Date overflow refers to the method certain applications use to represent their dates as offsets to a base date rather than an actual date. Hardware integers that hold these dates can overflow past their maximum corresponding date, which may lead to undefined behavior. Some symptoms of this problem may be negative dates or an application that fails because of a data error.

- **Inconsistent semantics.** Inconsistent semantics refers to a situation in which two applications interface with each other, but each assumes different semantics for the data being passed. The same types of assumptions are made about two-digit years.

Create Test Data

The quality of the test data plays a large part in the success of the Year 2000 testing effort. Inadequate test data can cause missed errors, thereby opening the company up to some Year 2000 surprises.

You should create data that is similar in amount and diversity to that of the data the company currently has in its production system. Diverse data is more likely to uncover obscure problems than data that isn't diverse.

Here is some sample Year 2000 data that needs to be tested:

> December 31, 1998
> January 1, 1999
> December 31, 1999
> January 1, 2000
> January 2, 2000
> February 28, 2000
> February 29, 2000
> March 1, 2000
> December 31, 2000
> January 1, 2001
> February 28, 2001
> February 29, 2001 (not a valid date)
> March 1, 2001

December 31, 2001

January 1, 2002

February 29, 2004 (the next leap year after 2000)

If the Year 2000 solution your company is using includes windowing, ensure that the dates on both the upper and lower edges of the window are included. For example, if the window spans from January 1, 1940 to January 1, 2039, you should include the following dates in the test data:

December 31, 1939

January 1, 1940

January 2, 1940

December 31, 2038

January 1, 2039

January 2, 2039

Another area to concentrate on is the days of week that your company's applications may target. If the employees in your company get paid biweekly on a Thursday, for example, include test days that are Thursdays in the year 2000. Because the year 2000 is a leap year, you also need to add data to test whether the applications can tell correctly what day of the week it is after February 29, 2000.

No matter what dates you use, the data should resemble normal production data as closely as possible. You could save off your data just before you start setting up your test system and then modify it to use dates that fall into both this century and the next.

Set Up a Process to Track Errors Found in Testing

If a system is not already set up to track problems that testing uncovers in the applications, you definitely should set one up for the Year 2000 conversion project. The system should be available to all people on the project who have access to the applications in the system throughout the different stages of the project. Some of the functions your error reporting system should handle follow:

- Opening error reports with the following information:

  Opener's name

  Version of the system build on which the error was found

  A priority, so the more severe errors can be dealt with first

  A description of what the user or tester did before the error occurred (the description should include enough detail for a programmer to be able to duplicate the problem)

  The date the error report was opened

Managing a Year 2000 Project for Success

CHAPTER 31

879

31

MANAGING A
YEAR 2000
PROJECT

- Answering error reports
- Transferring error reports to other people
- Rejecting these reports if it turns out that they are not real problems
- Verifying these reports so that responses and fixes can be checked

Do Functional Testing

Functional testing, or *unit testing*, as it is also called, is the first level of testing. It is concerned with testing a single unit of code—usually, a module. Often, you, as the programmer, are responsible for performing this level of testing, because you are familiar with the program and the change that was made. Shortly after you make the change, the code should be unit tested. The testing of the code acts as the completion of the developer's change process, and no other changes should be made unless they are tracked through error-tracking reports. Any other errors have to be found in the other testing stages that follow.

Do Integration Testing

Integration is the next level of testing after functional testing. It is concerned with testing how all the modules in the application work together. A change in one module might appear to work fine when it is tested in an isolated setting, for example, but when that module is tested in a situation in which it has to interact with other modules in the application, the changed module might produce a different kind of error.

Also, it is possible that one module might have been modified by more than one programmer. In this situation, the individual tests that programmers perform will not necessarily test how all the changes in the module interact with each other.

Programmers do not usually perform integration testing because they do not have the wider scope of knowledge about the whole application that it requires. Also, they do not have the objectivity that good testers should have. For example, programmers often assume that they know what needs to be tested in their code because they made the change to it. But they often don't think of testing situations that are out of the scope of the common testing situations, and they can be so familiar with the fix that they do not test its limits. For these reasons, integration testing usually is done by the project test team or the company's *Quality Assurance* (QA) group.

Do System Testing

System testing tests the whole system, which is made up of several applications working together. This is the next level of testing after integration testing. System testing also is done by the project test group or the QA group. The system test phase runs all the test cases that were run for the integration test phase, but it runs them against the whole system instead of just against individual applications.

Do Acceptance Testing

The project-management team may or may not want to do acceptance testing. Acceptance testing is usually the same testing that was done for the system test phase, except that it is done by the client instead of the project test group or QA group.

Acceptance criteria might be substituted to act as a signal to stop the system test phase. An example of an acceptance criterion is the point at which 90 percent or more of the test cases run successfully. Of course, the test cases that fail have to be examined to make sure that they are not testing functionality that could cause Year 2000 problems. Another criterion could be a review of the list of outstanding error-tracking reports, which also can be used to help decide whether it is safe to end the system test phase.

Do Regression Testing

The regression test phase tests that the changes you have made to the code do not create errors in other parts of the system. By fixing a date in A, for example, you might cause another unrelated problem in B. Without going through the regression test phase, you might never uncover the error in B. To complete the regression test phase, you actually have to run your whole suite of test cases, which is usually a large number. Also, the test cases might have to be run several times to reach an acceptable success rate. For these reasons, the test cases usually are automated for the regression test phase. For more information about the tools you can use for Year 2000 testing, see the preceding chapter, "The Technical Problem and Dealing With It."

Certify That the Converted Software Is Year 2000-Compliant

Finally, certification testing can be done as the last phase of testing. This phase tests that the whole system will work in a Year 2000 environment. At this level, you should use dates from the year 2000, as well as the historical dates your business normally would process. Ideally, you should simulate a live business situation for a few weeks. This live situation should approximate, as closely as possible, the real-life environment in which your system will be running in the year 2000.

Documentation

Because the applications are going to be modified for Year 2000 compliance, the documentation also has to be modified. You should consider the following areas for documenting:

- Any application changes and testing information must be documented for future internal reference.

- Any changes to data needs to de documented for internal use and external use by any other companies that share your company's data. For more information about using data dictionaries to document the characteristics of the data objects to be used in the applications, see "Data Dictionary Formats," earlier in this chapter.

- If the company's applications have online help, those panels that describe how to use the new date fields may have to be updated. If the help references field lengths and formats, for example, it has to be updated with descriptions of the characteristics of the new Year 2000-compliant date fields.

- If the company's applications are shipped for customers' use (internal or external), the customer manuals also may have to be updated.

Cost of Future Maintenance

The Year 2000 work does not necessarily stop when all the applications are finished being converted to be Year 2000-compliant. If new programs have been added to deal with the Year 2000 problem, for example, these will add to the maintenance effort. Also, if the Year 2000 conversion effort has not been completed entirely (for example, because bridge programs were used or cosmetic changes were left until later, due to time constraints), you will have to factor this work into future maintenance costs.

Because Year 2000 changes to applications are going to have a wide impact on the company's systems, comprehensive testing might not uncover all the problems. Any problems that come up after the year 2000 arrives also will have to be fixed.

Recovery Procedures and Contingency Plans

A recovery procedure is simpler than a contingency plan. A recovery procedure usually is related to recovering from the errors created by completing a single task. If your Year 2000 test data becomes corrupted, for example, you need to have a recovery procedure in place to enable you to get a copy of the uncorrupted data back. This recovery procedure would likely involve restoring the data from a recent backup. If you are creating new recovery procedures, they need to be tested to ensure that they will work.

A contingency plan identifies the actions your company will take in the event that you encounter Year 2000 problems in the next century. It is more complex than a recovery procedure. A Year 2000 problem could affect your company's business or some other company's business, and some Year 2000 problems will be more critical than others. Your contingency plan needs to predict all the things that could go wrong and supply the courses of action to be taken if any of these problems are encountered. Your plan also must be tested to ensure that it will work.

For example, if a mission-critical system fails (such as a reservation system, electronic fund-transfer system, or interest-calculation system), and a contingency plan is not in place, the consequences could be disastrous to a business. Developing a contingency plan is like investing in insurance to protect a business.

It is wise to identify and prioritize the processes that are crucial to sustaining the business. Long-, medium-, and short-term plans should be developed that identify how individuals and those with a recovery role are to react during and after an unplanned disruption.

Also, your company could audit its suppliers to ensure that they have the appropriate Year 2000 contingency plans in place. The contingency plans your company's suppliers adopt could affect the supply chain.

Work Items and Schedules

The project management team should identify the required work items and schedules for the following categories:

Hardware

Software, including operating systems and vendor applications

Data exchanged with other companies

Documentation

Education

Operations and administration

Work Item Prioritization from Most Critical to Least Critical

After you assess all the work items that need to be done to complete the Year 2000 conversion, you should prioritize them from most critical to least critical. Then the most-critical conversion tasks should be done first, followed by the less-critical tasks. This approach also is referred to as *triage*.

Triage

Triage is a term borrowed from a hospital emergency room and refers to the order in which patients are treated. Patients are treated in order of urgency: Those with the most life-threatening injuries are treated first, regardless of when they were admitted. A patient who goes to the emergency room for an earache, for example, might wait several hours to get treated, whereas a patient who goes to the emergency room with a bullet wound most likely will be treated immediately.

Managing a Year 2000 Project for Success

CHAPTER 31

883

31

MANAGING A
YEAR 2000
PROJECT

The same analogy can be applied to a Year 2000 conversion project, where the amount of work that needs to be done is massive, and time and resources are limited. Obviously, all the Year 2000 problems will need to be fixed, but some could be considered critical, whereas others could be considered minor. A displayed date does not need to be corrected immediately, for example, if it appears only for cosmetic reasons and has no impact on the data being processed by an application. You should work triage into your overall Year 2000 strategy to ensure that all the critical applications are converted first.

Manpower Issues

So, after all the planning is done and the decisions are made, who's going to do the work? Is it going to be the same people who are currently doing the work on the applications? Not likely. Some of you will be involved, but the company is very likely going to need more help in addition to the current staff.

Some of the manpower issues the project-management team needs to investigate follow:

- What types of job assignments need to be filled?
- Where can people be found to do the work?
- How can the company's interests be protected?
- What types of employee incentives need to be put into place?
- What type of employee training needs to be set up?
- What are the resource estimates for completing the Year 2000 project?

Making Job Assignments

The people assigned to any project can make or break it, as the saying goes. But for a project as critical and with such a hard-and-fast date like the Year 2000 conversion project, it is extremely important that the right people are chosen to do the job.

Here are some guidelines your project-management team can use to select the people to be in charge of the project, to do the actual conversion work on the applications, and to provide support services for the project.

Selecting the Person to Head Up the Project

If you or anyone you know is interested in being in charge of the Year 2000 project, you'll need to know about some of the skills necessary for the job.

The person put in charge of the project will be one of the most important members on the team. Not only will he or she need to have many good leadership qualities, but he or she also will need to be able to persevere with the project and see it through to its completion, no matter what problems he or she may encounter. This is because the due date for the Year 2000 conversion project is fixed, and if the work is not complete, the consequences to the company could be disastrous.

Some of the qualities the person in charge of the project should have follow:

- Ability to set and achieve goals
- Resourcefulness at solving problems
- Good organization
- Good at motivating people
- Good communicator
- Technically knowledgeable

Selecting People to Do the Conversion Work

The people chosen to do the conversion work should be as technically qualified as possible to actually make and test the changes required for the Year 2000 conversion project. As the scope of the Year 2000 project becomes more apparent, a good balance must be established between the number of the current employees that can be assigned to the project and the number of outside people who need to be acquired.

The company's current employees have valuable experience with the company, the processes, and the product, which will be valuable in such a critical project. Also, they can pass this knowledge on to employees who are hired from outside the company for the Year 2000 project.

Establishing Support Services

To complement the work the main Year 2000 conversion team is doing, support services may be required to contribute to the Year 2000 project. You should consider the role the following people will play in the Year 2000 project:

- Analysts who provide technical information
- Area managers who help mobilize areas of the company and provide information about system ownership, processes, and so on
- Senior management that provides support for the goals of the Year 2000 project and disseminates this support throughout the rest of the company
- System administrators and operators who perform support services for the project
- Business analysts who advise senior management on the areas of the business that may be affected by the Year 2000
- End users who provide feedback about how the system is used and the design of the Year 2000-compliant system

Managing a Year 2000 Project for Success

CHAPTER 31

885

31

MANAGING A
YEAR 2000
PROJECT

Finding People to Do the Work

There are various ways that a number of people with the skill sets required can be obtained for the Year 2000 project. This section tells you about some of the places the project-management team can look for skilled people.

Programmers Currently Employed By the Company

A certain number of the company's own employees should be assigned to the Year 2000 project. After all, they know how the company works, they know the applications, and they have a vested interest in making the Year 2000 conversion a success. Their future, along with the future of the company, depends on it.

The number of the company's own employees put on the Year 2000 project needs to be balanced against any plans underway to make other enhancements to the programs. If the company can defer other enhancements and put all its resources toward the Year 2000 project, that would be the ideal situation. However, if the business requires that these other enhancements be made, these enhancements need to be managed properly within the scope of the Year 2000 project; otherwise, the success of the Year 2000 project might be jeopardized.

Individual Contractors and Consultants

Contractors and consultants are an attractive resource to choose, because they are employed by a company for only as long as they are needed, and they come with skills. When the Year 2000 project is finished, their contracts can be ended, and the company is left with the same amount of employees it had before the Year 2000 project started. This means the company will not have to face the downsizing issues it would have to face if it hired full-time permanent employees to do the job.

However, there are some drawbacks to choosing contractors and consultants:

- They are more expensive than full-time regular employees, because they have specialized skills and do not receive any company benefits.
- The more time that passes before the Year 2000 project is started, the less the number of contractors and consultants that will be available for your company.

Consulting Companies

Consulting companies offer more help than just individuals to a company trying complete its Year 2000 conversion. Consulting companies also take on other aspects of the whole project, including managing it, writing the plans, and providing all the programmers. But again, the company needs to decide whether this is the staffing solution it wants to use. As time goes on, consulting companies may become booked up.

Conversion Houses

Conversion houses operate off-site and take your company's code, convert it, and test it before handing it back to you. Most conversion houses are experienced in other types of conversion and have adapted their business to handle Year 2000 conversion. Be careful here, though. Your company should make sure that it uses a good conversion house, and when it comes to the contract, it should make sure that it agrees on an acceptable set of exit criteria with the conversion house—the criteria by which the quality of its conversion is judged. If the exit criteria turn out to be unreliable, the in-house programmers may end up having to do some cleanup work to get the applications working the way they should.

Protecting the Company's Interests

Before hiring contractors and consultants or entering into business with a consulting company or conversion house, your company needs to make sure that its interests are protected. It should consider addressing the following issues and obtaining the following agreements:

- Nondisclosure agreements to prevent new hires from leaking out information about a company's systems to its competitors

- No-hire agreements to protect consulting firms from hiring your full-time permanent staff away from the company that originally hired the consultants

- Securing sensitive data, such as employee data, lists of clients, and marketing plans

- Guarantees and warranties to ensure that the quality of work received from the new hires is acceptable

- A penalty clause to cover the cost of damages, if they occur

Using Employee Incentives

OK: Here's where you cash in, right? Well, first you'll have to convince the management at your company to adopt some of these incentives, if it isn't already using them.

Motivation is important. If the members of a team feel motivated, they most likely will work harder, do better work, and stay with the project until it is completed. These behaviors can only help the team reach its goals in a Year 2000 conversion project.

Some of the top motivators follow:

- More money (which can be presented to employees in many ways—as a salary increase, a bonus, or part of an award)

- Allowing employees more involvement in the planning of the project

Managing a Year 2000 Project for Success

CHAPTER 31

887

31

MANAGING A
YEAR 2000
PROJECT

- Promotions
- Flex time
- Casual dress
- Work-from-home arrangements
- Giving employees more time to complete tasks so that they feel they have added their own touch of quality

The project-management team should keep these incentives in mind in case employee motivation becomes an issue on the Year 2000 project.

Training Employees

You need to get involved here, too. If your management is not providing you with the education you need to do the Year 2000 conversion work, you need to convince management that this education would be very useful to you.

This is because the Year 2000 project, in many ways, requires employees to have new skills. New tools may be introduced in all phases of the project, and their use will be required to implement the changes. And, if the decision has been made to redesign some of the systems, instead of migrating the old ones, employees may have to be trained in new programming languages and methods.

Because of the importance of this project, a company may decide that it needs to refine its processes to accommodate the importance of the Year 2000 conversion project; in this case, the employees would have to be trained in using the new process. It is very important that all employees know what is expected of them if the number of problems that appear along the way is to be minimized.

Education will need to be provided in several areas:

- Programmers, regarding coding new date routines using the strategy that has been chosen
- Programmers, regarding the legacy code that may not have been updated for years
- Customers, regarding user interface updates that will be made to products your company sells
- Operations staff, regarding system software changes

Estimating Year 2000 Resources Required

The resource estimates that need to be made include employees, time (schedule), and money. Before the resources can be estimated, the project-management team needs to know the following:

- Which solution is going to be used to solve the Year 2000 problem?
- What tools or methods will be used to estimate the lines of code you, the developer, are going to have to change?
- What sort of testing effort will be required?
- What sort of data conversion will have to be completed?

For more information about solutions to the Year 2000 problem and the tools available to help, see the preceding chapter, "The Technical Problem and Dealing With It."

Risk Factors

Some of the risk factors you need to consider are the complexity of the task, the resource and time constraints, the length of time left to complete the project, and the critical skills required.

A risk assessment also should identify any possible financial and legal risks to the business. Systems that fall into these categories of risk are usually those used to procure or track revenue, to service customers, or through their use, to ensure the survival of an organization in some other way. Any systems that pose a major risk to an organization should be added to the mission-critical list.

Project Constraints

Any issues your project-management team knows about that will limit the scope the Year 2000 solution can take should be noted. The Year 2000 project will have to be planned within these constraints. Here are some examples of project constraints:

- Budget
- Number of people who can be hired to do the conversion
- Legal obligations
- Customer obligations
- Dependencies on data shared with other companies

Getting Senior Management Involved

After all the investigations and preliminary planning are complete, the Year 2000 strategy should be presented to senior management. For such a critical project, it is desirable to

Managing a Year 2000 Project for Success

CHAPTER 31

889

31

MANAGING A
YEAR 2000
PROJECT

have all the heads in an organization focused on the success of the Year 2000 conversion. Getting the support of senior management is the best way to do this, because these people influence a broad range of business goals. Convincing senior management of the importance of the Year 2000 project may be easier today than it would have been a couple of years ago, because of the recent media exposure the Year 2000 problem has received.

Other Management Issues

This section describes other issues and concepts management should be aware of, such as legal concerns, income tax-related concerns, and the idea of creating a Year 2000 central committee to focus the Year 2000 effort.

Legal Concerns

Just completing a Year 2000 project does not necessarily mean that a company's worries are over. Some legal issues need to be considered, in case a company's converted programs do not run without errors after the year 2000 arrives.

This section describes some of the legal concerns companies should be aware of; there may be more.

Risks to Companies for Not Being Able to Deliver Goods and Services

Suppose that a manufacturing company is trying to fill orders that were received before the year 2000 but are due to be delivered after the turn of the century (January 1, 2000). If its systems do not process the new century correctly, its orders for the new century may not get filled because the dates indicate that they are old orders. If customers depend on receiving goods from a company so that they can fill orders for their own customers, they could bring legal action against a company for not being able to fill their orders, and for the subsequent damage that it caused to their business.

Disclaimers Included in Software That Is Sold

The disclaimer should indicate that the software being sold is Year 2000-compliant. If the software being sold to others turns out to have Year 2000 bugs in it, and these bugs cause damage to any of the businesses that bought the software, the company selling the software could be held liable and face litigation.

Software vendors could be required to "represent" and "warrant" the product as being Year 2000-compliant. This would legally entitle customers who buy problematic Year

2000 software to both equitable remedies (such as rescission of the contract) for a breach of the representation and remedies (such as money) for damages caused by a breach of warranty.

Disclaimers Included with Software Purchased from Other Vendors

The products companies buy to save their businesses from potential damage after the year 2000 arrives should be tested. Damages could take the form of a lawsuit against the company buying the problematic software (if it causes that company to conduct business that causes damage to another company) or against the company selling the problematic software (if it causes damage to the business of the company that bought the software).

However, if the year 2000 rolls around and a software package that has been purchased is not Year 2000-compliant, as it claims to be, legal action may be brought against the vendor by the purchaser. The purchaser should be prepared to demonstrate, though, that it followed the software purchase agreement and did not modify the software in any way or copy it onto other machines that did not have a license to use it.

Contracts Made with Consulting Individuals or Firms

If Year 2000 problems arise after any of these people have completed their work, the hiring company may be tempted to bring legal action against them. However, nobody should start a Year 2000 project with this attitude in mind. It is best to just concentrate on working together to handle any problems as they arise and successfully completing the project.

Data Passed to Companies Outside an Organization

If the data a company generates on its computers is passed on to other companies to use, and this data turns out to be incorrect because of Year 2000 problems, legal suits could be filed against the company that exported the erroneous data if it caused damage to other businesses.

Insurance Policies May Not Compensate for Year 2000 Problems

Companies should check with their insurance agent to find out just how much Year 2000 coverage they have. If they find that they are not covered under their current insurance policy, they can contact companies that will actually sell insurance designed to protect them against Year 2000 failures.

Financial Disclosure

Public companies are required to disclose information about themselves in annual reports that are available to their customers and the general public. Individuals could legally expose themselves, if they are an officer of a public company and that company does not disclose the following:

- The cost of converting a business to be Year 2000-compliant
- The fact (if this turns out to be the case in the year 2000) that a business is not Year 2000-compliant

Shareholders might not be happy with the return on their investments. If Year 2000 problems cause a business to begin to falter, and the shareholders start to see the value of their shares going down, they might decide to bring a lawsuit against that company (or a public officer of that company) for not making the business Year 2000-compliant in time. In other words, you would be considered as not having exercised sufficient "care" of the company.

Income Tax-Related Concerns

If a company is going to be spending so much money on making its business Year 2000-compliant, it probably expects to be able to deduct a substantial portion of it from its company's income tax as expenses. In the United States, for example, a decision currently is being made as to whether Year 2000 costs to companies should be capitalized or expensed. If the costs are *capitalized,* they will have to be amortized (written off) over a number of years, splitting the total deduction into smaller deductions that cannot all be made against the year in which the expenses were incurred. This means that a company would have to absorb the expenses, much as it would for the acquisition of a new asset. Because so much money is being spent for a project that does not really move the company ahead technologically, companies would prefer a shorter period of amortization so that they could recover their costs as soon as possible.

If the decision is made to allow Year 2000 costs to be *expensed,* companies will be able to deduct all of their costs as expenses. This would be more beneficial to companies, because they could recover their costs in approximately the same time frame as the money was spent. Also, their financial records would return more quickly to the state they were in before the Year 2000 project started, which means that companies could begin to make other business improvements sooner.

Although expensing Year 200 costs is good for companies, it might not be good for governments. If companies are allowed to expense their Year 2000 costs, more money will be deducted from their income tax, and they will end up paying less to the government. Now this might not sound like a bad idea. The government gets too much of our money as it is. However, because the Year 2000 problem is so widespread (it affects approximately 80 percent of businesses in the U.S.), if all the companies end up paying less income taxes, it could have a dramatic effect on the U.S. government's income for that year. This, in turn, would affect the amount the government could provide to the public in the form of social programs and services.

The interpretation of other tax-law statutes also could have other effects on companies and governments. Here is an example using the U.S. tax laws.

Suppose that U.S. Corporation A enters into a contract with another company, Corporation B, to perform Year 2000-compliance work on its business applications. Corporation A structures within its agreements to make these costs deductible. Based on the interpretation of the income-tax law made by the Internal Revenue Service (IRS), Corporation B could reverse a substantial part of the deduction if it feels that other companies receiving benefits from the service have not paid for it. In other words, suppose that other companies use data that was generated by Corporation B as a main part of their business. The U.S. government could interpret these other companies as benefiting from the work that Corporation A did without having paid for it. In this case, the IRS would not allow Corporation B to deduct all its Year 2000 costs as expenses.

Year 2000 Corporate Committees

Because the Year 2000 conversion effort potentially spans an entire organization, as the project progresses, it might become difficult to retain cooperation among the various departments affected by the conversion effort. It often is hard for interested parties from different departments to drop their own interests for the sake of something else that is in the company's best interest. This kind of scenario isn't just business as usual for lower levels of management, in which the main focus is the individual departments.

By centralizing the project management and troubleshooting in a Year 2000 corporate committee, the focus of the Year 2000 project's goals can be maintained, which is more likely to bring success to the project. Also, employees who are assigned to a committee are less likely to be divided between work going on in their department and Year 2000 work.

The centrality of a Year 2000 committee makes it easier for senior management to know how the project is progressing, and for members of the Year 2000 committee to bring problems to senior management for resolution. Opening up a direct communications channel between senior management and the Year 2000 project management (which would form part of the committee) would speed up the problem-resolution process.

Summary

This chapter described the issues the management team in your company should spend most of its time handling. You learned about planning aspects, such as strategies and tools, development issues, testing, scheduling, manpower, risk management, and getting senior management involved. You also looked at other issues management should be aware of, such as legal issues, tax issues, and setting up a central Year 2000 committee.

The next chapter describes who and what are affected by the Year 2000 problem, some of the symptoms that will start appearing if the Year 2000 problem is not fixed, the attitudes and progress of some of the world's governments, and the situations and progress that some of the private industries are experiencing.

CHAPTER 32

What Will Really Happen

It has been said that the Year 2000 problem will be the single most significant event in the information technology services industry over the next few years, and it will likely have a lasting effect on the industry well into the next millennium. You cannot really predict what will happen in the Year 2000; you will have to wait until it actually arrives. But you can look at the some of the progress that has been made so far (in those situations where information has been made available) and some of the predictions that have been made.

In this chapter, you'll take a look at the scope of the problem, the symptoms that will start appearing where the Year 2000 problem is not fixed, and the progress being made to find solutions throughout the world and in a sample of governments, government services, and industries.

The Problem

The Year 2000 problem exists because most data, and the programs that process the data, use a two-digit year instead of a four-digit year. In the early 1960s, external storage devices were expensive and data entry was labor intensive, so it was more efficient to use a date with fewer characters. Hence, the six-digit date field was used (with the two-digit year). The six-digit date field accounted for the day, month, and year of the date; the century was implied but not explicitly stored.

This date-field format worked for this century (20th), but it will not work for dates in the next century (21st). Programs will not have the capability to distinguish between dates in the 20th century and dates in the 21st century, because the first two digits of the year are not stored. For example, a date using the mm/dd/yy format, such as August 9, 1900 will be stored exactly the same as August 9, 2000 (08/09/00).

Other aspects of the Year 2000 make it more complicated for computers to deal with; those areas are explored in this section.

Special Aspects of the Problem

The aspects of the Year 2000 that make this date more complicated for computers and programs to deal with follow:

- It starts with a 2.

  Many programs recognize only those years that begin with a 1.

- It ends with zeros.

  Some programs, such as random-number generators, take the system date, truncate it to its last two numbers, and then divide it into another number. Programs can end abnormally when they try to divide by 00.

- It starts on a Saturday.

  Some software does specific things, depending on which day of the week it is. A company's paychecks may be issued on Mondays, for example. If the day of the week is calculated by the computer by using the last two digits (which many do), the computer will treat January 1, 2000 as a Monday, because January 1, 1900 was a Monday. This means that it will issue the paychecks on the first day of the year 2000 (which is a Saturday), because it thinks it is Monday.

- It's a leap year.

  Every fourth turn-of-the-century year is a leap year, but some programmers did not code this logic into their programs because they were not aware of that fact. Other programmers did code this logic in because they thought every turn-of-the-century year was a leap year. Computer programs were not around for the previous turn of the century, so this experience base was missing.

The Size of the Problem

The predicted cost to address the Year 2000 problem could be a significant barrier to fixing the problem around the world.

At this time, the Gartner Group, an information technology research firm, estimates that 30 percent of all computer applications will not be Year 2000 compliant in time and that it will cost $300 billion to $600 billion to fix the problem.

The Gartner Group also estimates that 180 billion lines of COBOL code worldwide will be affected by the date change. Although COBOL remains one of the major languages used throughout the world, code in other computer languages also will have to be fixed.

The estimated cost is based on an estimate of slightly more than $1 per line of code, and this cost is expected to grow by as much as 50 percent per year as the deadline approaches. It is difficult to verify this estimate until more information about actual conversion costs becomes available, but even a conservative estimate of $200 billion could match what is forecasted for the revenue of worldwide information systems through to the year 2000. Put another way, starting with the estimate that the total American information services marketplace spends around $150 billion annually, the Year 2000 software conversion would represent anywhere from one-third to one-half of the dollars spent for information systems in one year.

Other estimates have been made indicating that the number of applications affected within companies could be as high as 90 percent, and that the percentage of a company's technology budget spent on fixing the Year 2000 problem could be as high as 50 percent. It is expected that large companies could spend an average of more than $45 million on their Year 2000 solutions, and that medium-sized companies could spend from $3.6 million to $4.2 million to make the software conversion.

UNIX Systems Should Not Be Hit

People who use a UNIX operating system should not be hit by the Year 2000 problem, but some UNIX COBOL programs may be. Because the date is calculated differently in UNIX, January 19, 2038 will be the date when 32-bit UNIX systems run out of room to store the current date and time correctly. On this date, the system will reset everything back to the date when it started accumulating time, which was January 1, 1970. Although not all UNIX systems will work this way, most will.

If your COBOL programs store the UNIX date in a format that uses a two-digit year, however, you still might have Year 2000 code changes to make. Also, if you use an end-of-file indicator of 999,999,999 in your UNIX COBOL programs, these programs could misinterpret this end-of-file indicator as a date (more specifically, the date September 8, 2001), instead. This means that these programs could cause delayed Year 2000 problems, which would show up in the autumn of 2001.

What Is Affected?

The Year 2000 problem affects mainframe, midrange, and PC computers. The two-digit–year field can be found in microcode, operating systems, software compilers, applications, database queries, procedures, displays, databases, and data.

Within the logic of applications and systems, the Year 2000 bug affects computations that perform these tasks:

- Calculate age
- Sort by date
- Compare dates
- Perform other specialized tasks

Complexity of Fixing the Problem

The complexity of fixing the problem comes mostly from the high volume of programming changes required and the widespread interdependence of systems that exchange data. Besides volume, there are other complicating factors.

An estimated 15 percent of existing production code is modified on an annual basis, which means that the majority of source code can remain untouched for years.

Also, the problem is not limited to legacy mainframe applications as is often thought. Some companies also are finding that their client/server applications are not Year 2000 compliant, either. Sharing data can be a problem as well.

Some technical issues also may complicate the problem, such as these:

- Missing source code (so that the problem cannot be fixed)
- Unsupported languages
- Special licensing fees

Coding standards used within companies can be diverse or virtually nonexistent, which can make updating code difficult. And, because the data problem affects most of the applications within a company, all system interfaces in an organization must be tested.

Engaging in relationships with outsourcing and package vendors will not solve the problem. The Year 2000 problem is outside the scope of most existing outsourcing agreements.

Legacy Code

Many companies have done a poor job of managing their source-code libraries and repositories. It is estimated that most companies are missing about 5 percent of their source code or do not have the latest version of the code. As applications are rewritten to fix the Year 2000 problem, application systems may no longer work if they use source that no longer exists. This means that companies may be forced to rewrite entire applications from scratch.

Embedded Systems

Embedded systems are systems that contain a computer or a computer-like device and are used for purposes such as controlling the operation of a plant, machinery, or equipment. For example, a paper mill may use an embedded process-control system to gauge the width of the paper its machinery produces. Embedded systems also are used in consumer products, such as cars, washing machines, photocopiers, and bedside alarm clocks.

When the Year 2000 arrives, some of the computers used in embedded systems may not work properly because of the way they store date information. They may not process the two-digit year 00 properly and may not be able to deal with operational cycles, such as "do X every 100 days."

According to a Gartner Group estimate, 50 million embedded system devices worldwide will have some kind of Year 2000 problem. It seems that very few companies have recognized the magnitude of problems that can be caused in embedded systems by their failure to be able to recognize the Year 2000. Most embedded systems do not have a look-ahead time of more than one month, so failures will occur late in 1999, if they occur at all.

Programs Can Be Zapped in Embedded Systems

The Year 2000 problem can even zap, or delete, programs in embedded systems. A company in England that searches for and fixes Year 2000 problems in embedded systems already has seen one system that deletes new programs for a process-control robot. When a new program is saved with a date greater than 2000, the system deletes the new program, because it assumes that it is an ancient 1900 program instead.

What Are the Symptoms?

In specific terms, the failure of systems to operate properly because of the Year 2000 problem could mean anything from minor inconveniences to major problems. For example, licenses and permits might not be issued; payroll and social services checks might not get cut; personnel, medical, and academic records might start to malfunction; errors in banking and finance might start to occur; accounts might not get paid or received; inventory might not get maintained; weapon systems might not function properly.

And the list goes on.

In general terms, the symptoms will appear as

- Misinterpreted dates
- Dates, and the information and transactions associated with them, that get misplaced
- Year 2000 viruses

Misinterpreted Dates

Dates can end up being misinterpreted when they are used in comparisons or moves. If date formats that still use a two-digit year end up being used in comparisons, the two-digit year (00 in the year 2000) will appear as 0 instead of 2000, and a correct comparison will not be made.

To test the expiration date of a credit card, for example, a program might test whether the current year (1998, for this example) is greater than the expiration date (the year 2000, for this example). If the logic that performed this test was not converted to be Year 2000 compliant, the test will pass instead of fail, which puts a valid credit card into early expiration.

Here are some examples of what might happen when a date is misinterpreted:

- Your local bank may stop crediting your account with the correct interest, or it may cancel your outstanding financial transactions prematurely. Financial service firms also may lose the capability to clear and settle trades on a T+3 (three days after the trade) basis, as well as lose the capability to process automated teller machine (ATM) and direct-deposit transactions.

- On January 3, 2000 (which is the first business day in the year 2000), an accounting department may be unable to enter journal entries in its general ledger, because a posting date is required and 00 is an invalid year.

- A food manufacturer that produces a vacuum-packed product with a four-year shelf life may calculate an expiration date of 00 for its latest product run and issue recall notices to its retailers, because the expiration date appears as if it has already passed.

- The "rework date" on automotive parts could cause automated just-in-time inventory systems to improperly return parts, which could shut down an automobile production line for days.

Table 32.1 lists some future dates that could cause problems in computer systems. The dates listed are not only Year 2000 dates.

TABLE 32.1 DATES THAT CAN CAUSE COMPUTER PROBLEMS.

Date	Problem
1998	In some older programs, this date (expressed as 98) is used to indicate a break in a file or sequence, especially when 99 is used to indicate end-of-file.
08/22/1999	For geographical positioning systems used in satellites, this is the date when the clocks reach their maximum and roll over to start counting time all over again.
December 1999	This is a period of maximum solar activity, which could affect communications devices and systems.
1999	In older systems, this date (expressed as 99) is used to indicate end-of-file.
09/09/1999	This date often is used to indicate end-of-file.
12.2	In older systems, this is used to indicate end-of-file.
12/31/1999	A Year 2000 problem. Also, in older systems, it is used to indicate end-of-file.
01/01/2000	A Year 2000 problem.
02/28/2000	A leap-year problem.

continues

TABLE 32.1   CONTINUED

Date	Problem
02/29/2000	A leap-year problem.
03/01/2000	A leap-year problem.
02/28/2004	A leap-year problem.
02/29/2004	A leap-year problem.
2030	This date is used as the breakpoint in the date-window algorithm used by Microsoft in a large number of its products. On these systems, 29 implies 2029 and 30 implies 1930.
2040	This date is used as the breakpoint in the date-window algorithm used by IBM in a large number of its products. On these systems, 39 implies 2039 and 40 implies 1940.
01/18/2038 01/19/2038	At 03:14:08 on Tuesday, January 19, 2038, the second counter used for date and time information in UNIX, C, and C++ will reach 2,147,483,647, which is the largest number that can be stored as a 32-bit signed integer. As a result, an overflow problem will occur, making the value of the next number unpredictable. Time differences will mean that this will appear to happen earlier in the Americas (Monday, January 18, 2038 at 22:14:07 EST).
	There also will be a discrepancy of a few seconds between system clocks and astronomical time, because the system will not have taken into account leap-second discrepancies.
	The Java programming language (which in many respects, closely resembles C++) will not have this problem.
03/01/2101	Claims have been made that systems that are compliant up to this date will be totally and permanently date compliant.

Date Information That Gets Misplaced

Because many computer functions interface with one another, the arrival of the new millennium not only could cause computer systems to misinterpret dates, but it also could cause them to misplace information associated with them.

Consider what would happen if a customer submits a request in late December 1999 for an order they need filled by January 12, 2000. In a system that is not Year 2000 compliant, the date would be processed by the system as 1/12/00, and the computer would think that 00 means 1900. As a result, the computer would not generate the documents related to the order (as it usually does), and the customer's order would not be filled.

In some cases, computer systems may not operate at all with Year 2000 dates. In fact, some computer functions, such as forecasting, planning, and materials management already may be affected by Year 2000 glitches.

Year 2000 Data Viruses

Unfortunately, fixing the Year 2000 problem does not end with fixing a company's own systems. Many companies' data is shared with other companies' systems. Especially with today's global economy, data can be shared around the world. If erroneous date data is imported by an organization, it can corrupt its own data, which in turn can corrupt the data of other organizations to which that data is passed.

Inheriting corrupted data from another company is not as difficult as many think, especially with the expansion of Web-based processing. More and more, companies are becoming interrelated.

Year 2000 data viruses are a threat to the Year 2000 economy, because many businesses are not as aware of this problem. Even if they fix their own data problems, they will not necessarily isolate themselves from the data problems they will receive from companies with which they share data.

Legal Ramifications of Year 2000 Data Problems

Year 2000 data problems also can lead to legal liabilities. Before claiming Year 2000 compliance, companies must ensure that they have tested their systems thoroughly and ensure that they are not going to be responsible for passing bad data to other companies when the year 2000 arrives.

If companies cannot be sure that they are 100 percent Year 2000 compliant, they should be careful about claiming to be compliant. If a company that claims to be Year 2000 compliant transfers corrupted Year 2000 data to another company, and that data is shown to have compromised a major system or transactions process, the liability could be enormous. Companies that have forgotten to consider working with the companies they share data with to ensure that everyone is Year 2000 compliant will be the target of Year 2000 lawsuits after the year 2000 arrives.

How Prepared Are People?

The symptoms of the problem will not likely appear all at once. They will continue to appear after midnight, December 31, 1999 arrives. A recent survey done by the Gartner Group found that approximately one-fourth of the companies and government agencies around the world have not even started fixing their Year 2000 problems, and half of the people who responded have no plans to test their Year 2000 solutions.

This section takes a general look at the progress being made on the Year 2000 problem around the world. The next section, "How Are Governments, Government Services, and Private Industries Handling the Problem?" takes a closer look at the unique requirements that some government services and some private industries have regarding their Year 2000 problems, as well as some of the progress they have made.

North America

North America seems to be farther ahead than most other countries in the world. But because people in North American countries also are more open about discussing their Year 2000 problems and the progress they have made, they simply may appear to be farther ahead than other countries. It is hard to tell. However, they do have some problems too.

Approximately 50 percent of North American companies have started their Year 2000 projects. However, the Gartner Group predicts that when the year 2000 arrives, 20 percent of companies still will not have undertaken any efforts, either because they have little or no Year 2000 risk, or because they will try to "ride it out."

Europe

Parts of Europe, such as the United Kingdom, the Netherlands, and Scandinavia are making good progress on their Year 2000 conversion projects. But, according to the Gartner Group, other European countries are lagging behind. Part of the problem is that European governments currently are occupied with making changes in their systems to accommodate the common European currency.

If Europe doesn't finish its Year 2000 conversions in time, U.S. companies may be put at risk, because U.S. companies do a substantial amount of business with European companies.

In Europe, the attitude of smaller businesses is more of a problem than the attitude of larger corporations. Many small businesses think the millennium bug affects only mainframe computers, which is not true.

Also, some businesses are skeptical that the Year 2000 problem could cause serious damage. The attitude is that the global economy will not come to a screeching halt, so why worry? Many feel that delays in products will occur, though, and that financial transactions will be mishandled.

There are some very positive signs. The larger British groceries, for example, have formed a network to help 1,400 smaller grocers solve their Year 2000 problems. Also, French public companies that post shares on the French stock market will be forced to inform shareholders of their Year 2000 vulnerability in 1998 annual reports.

Asia

Experts have said that an unknown number of companies in Thailand, Taiwan, and even Japan believe that they are not going to have a Year 2000 problem because their computers are programmed to recognize traditional cultural calendars rather than the Western calendar.

Consider these examples:

- According to Thailand's traditional calendar, the year 1998 is really 2541. Many businesses and government offices use the traditional calendar instead of the Western Gregorian calendar, and they do not foresee any problems until the year 2600.
- According to Taiwan's traditional calendar, the year 1998 is really 1987. Many people still believe that they have 11 more years before they need to start fixing the Year 2000 problem.
- In Japan, a small amount of businesses may be using the Imperial Datebook, which makes the year 1998 Heisei 10.

However, using traditional calendars will not allow the misinformed companies within these countries to escape computer operating system dates that follow the Western calendar.

Asian companies are much less prepared for the Year 2000 than their American and European counterparts. Their current economic troubles are eating up money that corporations and governments could otherwise spend on fixing their Year 2000 problems. Many companies are just tying to get through to a point of stability in the short-term before worrying about spending money to fix the Year 2000 problem.

In Hong Kong, large banks and businesses have been working on solving the problem for a few years, but smaller businesses are not taking the same kind of action. A survey taken in 1997 indicated that two-thirds of the companies surveyed have no plans to fix the problem, and about 40 percent did not even know the problem existed. Although the average number of computers used within smaller companies only amounts to a few PCs, if these Year 2000 problems are ignored, the impact they could have on the economy could be substantial.

In general, Asian businesses are getting a slow start on fixing their Year 2000 problems.

Third-World Countries

Analysts know that most Latin American, African, and Eastern European nations are months behind in fixing their Year 2000 computer problems. Although these countries do not have a large technology infrastructure to deal with, that doesn't mean that the systems that are being used will not cause major problems if they aren't fixed.

The rest of the world also would be affected, because about 40 percent of the world's gross domestic product comes from developing countries for goods such as coffee, insulin, and manganese (used to make steel).

There is some good news, though. The banks in Brazil, Mexico, and Colombia, for example, are well on their way to becoming Year 2000 compliant.

How Are Governments, Government Services, and Private Industries Handling the Problem?

This section takes a look at the progress some governments, government services, and private industries have made toward their solution to the Year 2000 problem, as well as some special issues that some of them have to handle.

Governments and Government Services

Government agencies are not even close to being Year 2000 compliant. They are well behind their corporate counterparts in solving their Year 2000 problems. Some world governments are farther ahead than others.

This section looks at the situations in which a few of the Western governments find themselves. "Other Governments" summarizes the situation of the governments in the rest of the world. This section also describes the Year 2000 situations faced by a few of the governments and government services.

U.S. Government

According to government auditors in the U.S., federal agencies are far from being prepared for the Year 2000 computer bug. Because time is closing in, they now must abandon their attempts to get all systems ready and instead concentrate on preparing mission-critical systems. Currently, only about 35 percent of federal agencies' mission-critical systems are Year 2000 compliant.

Also, a report stated that it seemed possible that not all of the mission-critical systems would be fixed in time, and U.S. government agencies were urged to put contingency plans into place. The hopes are that these contingency plans will be monitored by the Year 2000 Council created by the President.

As an example, the IRS is well behind in its efforts to fix the problem, and this could adversely affect the IRS's capability to process tax returns after 1999. The IRS's target date for completing the Year 2000 work is January 1999. It also plans to finish fixing related systems, such as a communications network, and to rewrite software to reflect tax-law changes before the year 2000.

Australian Government

In Australia, the Federal Cabinet has agreed to spend $127 million extra to avoid computer system failures and service blackouts flowing from the millennium bug. This extra money was put into the government's Year 2000 project because it was felt that the problem wasn't being taken seriously enough.

The government's officials expressed concern that significant international economic and social disruption might result if the appropriate compliance steps were not taken as soon as possible.

Canadian Government

A member of the Institute of Electrical and Electronics Engineers (IEEE) reported that the Canadian government didn't have a successful start to fixing its Year 2000 problems. However, a recent report issued by the Auditor General of Canada noted that at the end of 1997, a number of Year 2000 activities were launched that could indicate that the situation has been turned around.

Most departments are well behind where they would like to be in their Year 2000 activities, except for Revenue Canada, which is in charge of all federal tax collection, as well as customs and excise taxes. This government department is well ahead of its counterparts.

Other Governments

European governments are in even worse shape than North American governments, because they are trying to make changes to accommodate the common European currency at the same time. And third-world countries, most Asian countries, and Eastern European governments are even farther behind.

Prisons

Some prisons might not escape the effects of the Year 2000 problem. Those prisons that use computer systems to control such things as the locking of doors may find that doors will suddenly unlock, releasing prisoners from their cells. The Scottish Prison Service, for example, has started investigating the possibility that its prison computers will malfunction when the year 2000 rolls over.

Traffic Signals

Traffic signals should not cause a problem when the year 2000 arrives. Most systems were designed to use a 99-year calendar that started ticking in the mid-1970s, when computerized traffic controls were starting to be used. In other words, those systems should cause no problem until the year 2070 or so.

Private Industries

This section describes the progress some private industries have made toward solving their Year 2000 problems and some of the unique aspects of those problems.

Real Estate

Owners and tenants also could be affected by the Year 2000 problem, because many building systems are controlled by embedded systems software that might have trouble recognizing the year 2000. The building systems that could be affected follow:

- Air conditioning
- Elevators
- Lighting
- Security
- Fire detection
- Telecommunications services
- Building-access systems, such as main doors and parking

The legal and safety implications are staggering.

Other problems could arise if rental agreements are computerized. Imagine the outcry if tenants get billed for 95 years of back rent or find that their lease is mysteriously canceled in the year 2000.

The Building Owners and Managers Association has begun a campaign to urge all of its members, as well as the rest of the real estate industry, to begin assessing the impact of the Year 2000 problem and to start putting plans in place as soon as possible.

Auto Industry

In the automobile industry, budgeting and forecasting systems process dates as far as five years into the future, so some problems already are surfacing. Some of the major automobile companies are planning to have their computer systems Year 2000 compliant by the end of 1998. Also, the Automotive Industry Action Group (AIAG) will be approving a set of Year 2000 standards for the automobile industry to follow.

Securities Firms

Securities firms buy and sell financial securities in forums such as the stock exchange. The types of transactions they deal in have the following characteristics:

- Trade transactions must be posted and reconciled after each day.
- Transactions project into the past or the present.
- Accounts must be settled in a timely and accurate fashion.
- Transactions involve types of calculations such as interest and dividend payments.
- Accounts need to be accessed on an ongoing basis.

The date issues involved in the data used in the securities industry are complicated, because a large amount of the data it uses is shared. All of this is magnified by the fact that the data is very time-sensitive and used for high-speed, high-volume transactions.

Banks

Banks tend to have several large mainframe systems that work with smaller client/server systems for distributed processing. The mix of systems means that a broader range of solutions is required for the banking industry. Also, the banking industry has the same problem as the insurance industry and could benefit with some streamlining of overlapping systems.

Mortgage-processing functions have been updating to accommodate 15-year and 30-year mortgages, but the solution that was implemented does not fix the Year 2000 problem. This means that the real solution to the Year 2000 problem could be more complicated, because time is required to decipher the mortgage update logic and then rework it to fit into the Year 2000 solution that is chosen.

Another problem banks face is the calculation of multiyear loans. When the year 2000 arrives, the test will be to see whether interest rates continue to be compounded correctly.

Automated teller machines (ATMs) have been well received by banking customers and are now very widespread. However, some of the chips and microcode used in the existing ATMs will not handle four-digit dates, which means that they will not work at all when the year 2000 arrives. Therefore, many of these machines will need to be upgraded and tested.

Finally, banks share a large amount of data with other banks around the world on a daily basis. This data is very time sensitive. This means that it will be a challenge to migrate the data while coordinating this migration with the migration that also needs to occur around the rest of the world.

Healthcare

The Food and Drug Administration (FDA) requires the manufacturers it regulates to investigate and correct problems with medical devices that present a significant risk to public health. To ensure the continued safety and effectiveness of medical devices in the year 2000 and beyond, the FDA recommends that manufacturers take the following actions:

- Ensure that medical devices submitted for premarket approval can perform date-recording and computations that will not be affected by the Year 2000 problem.

- Conduct hazard and safety analyses on currently manufactured devices to determine whether device performance could be affected by the Year 2000 problem, and if so, take appropriate steps to correct production and help customers who have purchased such devices.

- Check design, production, and quality control processes to ensure Year 2000 compliance.

Insurance Firms

Compared to other industries, the insurance industry uses a large amount of data and has a large number of applications that have to be updated to be Year 2000 compliant. Because of the large number of systems that need to be converted, insurance companies are faced with deciding which systems are the most important to their business and then upgrading them.

Because mergers often occur in the insurance industry, many insurance companies have overlapping or duplicate systems. By identifying which systems overlap or are duplicates, the insurance industry can decrease the number of systems that need to be converted for Year 2000 compliance.

Insurance data uses a larger time-projection window (the future forecast) and backward-looking window (historical view) than other industries. Insurance brokers project three or more years into the future to calculate the expiration dates of policies. They also look backward to work with the birth dates of their policyholders. Because people can live to be 100 years or older, this is a very large window. The size of these windows, and the fact that the insurance industry deals with so much data, makes insurance companies very vulnerable to Year 2000 problems.

Pharmaceutical Industry

The pharmaceutical industry faces potential lawsuits if the labels on the drugs it dispenses do not express the year as a four-digit year. Also, the systems that pharmacies use internally for any other processing also need to be updated to use a four-digit year. The industry as a whole is being very quiet about the whole Year 2000 issue—probably because they deal with human lives, and their lawyers have told them it is in their best interest to say as little as possible.

Utilities

Utilities, which include power, electric, gas, water, and other companies, have large legacy systems. Rates and billing structures are based on historical data. Utilities have a shorter event horizon (about one year), however, compared to other industries. Taking into account that any forward logic these companies' applications use also must be fixed, the target date they would need to meet would be approximately one year before the year 2000. However, downsizing and regulatory actions that are common to utility companies are obstacles to solving the Year 2000 problem.

Computer systems also are used to control the operations of nuclear power stations. Some Western countries, such as America, Britain, and France, are acting quickly to address possible problems. However, there are worries that the Soviet bloc countries may not be taking the necessary action, which could lead to a nuclear meltdown such as the one that took place in Chernobyl years ago.

The Nuclear Regulatory Commission has issued a warning to all American power plants about the risk of computer systems that control room display systems, monitor radiation, and signal emergencies.

Transportation Industry

The data the transportation industry uses involves a large number of dates. Most of the dates used are for scheduling and have fairly short windows. This means that short-term workaround solutions can be used for this data. Other data the transportation industry uses may have larger windows—for example, maintenance data for aircraft, trains, buses, and so on. However, because the window for the scheduling data is so small (for example, date projections are made one year into the future at most), the problems associated with this data will be a risk only for a short time—only for the period of time that these dates span this and the next century. As soon as the data begins to fall into one century again, there will be very little risk of scheduling problems.

Telecommunications Companies

Telecommunication companies include companies that provide local telephone service, as well as the long-distance service providers. Many of these companies still use legacy systems.

Utilities commissions regulate the operation of telecommunications companies in areas such as service rates, service options, and billing-related issues. In the U.S., regulatory commissions operate at the state level, which means that a different set of guidelines can be established for the operation of a telecommunications company, depending on the state(s) in which it operates. It would be difficult to integrate all the systems that manage these different guidelines before correcting the Year 2000 problem.

The long-distance service providers also may face problems with getting management to focus on the need for Year 2000 conversions. Long-distance service providers market their products differently than the telecommunications companies that also provide local telephone service. If no direct customer benefit can be linked to a Year 2000 expenditure, it might not get the attention it requires in order to be implemented.

Manufacturers

The data and systems used in the manufacturing sector are fewer than in other industries, and the amount of date-sensitive processing these systems do is minimal. This means that the effort required to fix the Year 2000 problem will require less resources than it will in other industries.

These companies tend not to have large computer departments or budgets, however, and systems these companies own that are date sensitive may be overlooked. For example, process-control systems may use microchips that do not support the next century. These process-control systems may be hard to replace, because they are costly, out of date, or overlooked entirely because they are not on the main list of computer systems owned by the company.

Fortunately, not all of the burden of identifying the problematic process-control systems lies with the companies that use them. The manufacturers also play some role in making manufacturers aware that they are using problematic process-control systems.

To make matters worse, if the systems manufacturers use fail to process the new century properly, these manufacturers may become the subject of lawsuits brought on by their customers. The legal responsibility lies with the manufacturer if goods they produce fail. Some people are wondering whether

- Cars that use computerized chips will start in the year 2000
- Trains and airplanes that use these chips will continue to operate properly

Finally, many manufacturing companies rely heavily on packaged applications instead of applications they develop in-house. The cost of inventorying and upgrading this software can be more greater and more time consuming than just upgrading applications that are produced in-house.

Software Vendors

Software vendors produce two main types of software: operating systems and applications. Most software vendors are making their products Year 2000 compliant according to a schedule they have set. For example, IBM has published a Year 2000 white paper that documents its schedule for making various products Year 2000 compliant. It is important that the software upgrades companies make are coordinated with the Year 2000 compliance schedules that software vendors are following.

Because most companies probably will not switch to another vendor's software, vendors can benefit greatly from the Year 2000 problem if they can make their software Year 2000 compliant in time. Many companies that have foregone upgrades until now will be forced to upgrade their Year 2000 systems. Software vendors probably will profit in the short term.

Many software vendors operate on small profit margins, which means that the amount of money they can invest in solving the Year 2000 problem is tied to their software sales. That means that software vendors that are not Year 2000 compliant probably are keeping quiet about it in order to keep their software sales from declining. On the other hand, software vendors that successfully upgrade their software products to be Year 2000 compliant can use this as a factor to promote the sale of their products.

Small Businesses

Small businesses are on the increase these days as a popular alternative to a corporate job, especially when many corporations are downsizing. Small businesses range from your local dentist or doctor to franchise outlets and local grocers. These small businesses tend to use PCs that run applications produced by software vendors. If the systems are customized, it may be unlikely that the software vendors will be able to upgrade these systems for the year 2000.

Other small companies may find that upgrading their applications to be Year 2000 compliant will cost them many times more than the budgets they have. This means that the solutions these small companies choose to correct the Year 2000 problem will be very different than the solutions larger companies will choose. For example, it may be more cost-effective to scrap old systems and upgrade to smaller-sized computer systems that are Year 2000 compliant.

Small businesses are basically left to fend for themselves, because the major focus of Year 2000 planning has been for large organizations. There has not been a substantial amount of public education for small businesses, including home offices.

Legal Battles

In the United States, legal experts are predicting that damage claims arising from the effects of Year 2000 problems will fill up their courts, and the resulting amount of money that will be paid out to claimants could be as high as hundreds of billions of dollars. Australian lawyers are estimating that year 2000 legal consequences could be huge. Apparently, in the U.S., new law firms are being established just to litigate Year 2000 cases. People need to understand that lawyers probably will encourage lawsuits if there are any grounds whatsoever.

Pleading ignorance of the problem will not likely be an acceptable defense in legal cases brought about by the Year 2000 problem. Directors have clear duties to their shareholders, and if they ignore the Year 2000 problem or fail to fix it, shareholders could take legal action against them if they find that the value of the business decreases because of Year 2000 problems.

Also, directors cannot simply delegate their problems, and they must make the appropriate resources available to fix their Year 2000 problems. If the directors do not do this, they may be accused of not acting with what is called "due care" when dealing with their company's Year 2000 solution.

Limiting Legal Liability

Companies such as Intel Corp. and the California Chamber of Commerce are joining a coalition formed by the Association for California Tort Reform, which is a business-backed group that seeks to limit corporate lawsuit liability. Other companies are thinking of doing the same thing. Companies hope that if they limit lawsuits now, they will not have to fight costly courtroom battles later.

Some people disagree that companies should be able to limit their legal liability, though. They feel that this would be like knowingly selling faulty goods and then claiming after they were sold that they were not responsible.

Disclosing Risks

The Securities and Exchange Commission has issued a revised mandate that requires public companies to make complete disclosure regarding their Year 2000 risk. Companies also are responsible for coordinating with other entities with which they electronically interact (both domestically and globally), including suppliers, customers, creditors, borrowers, and financial-service organizations.

At this time, few companies have issued disclosures, and those that have usually define their exposure to risk in very narrow terms. Also, most of these companies do not assess the internal risk they present from embedded systems used in places such as security systems, heating, cooling, communications equipment, manufacturing controls, and so on. Nor do they mention the potential disruptions that could occur from the effects of problems within the public infrastructure or within their vendor-client chain.

Insurance Claims

Many people believe that the regular insurance policies used to cover business interruptions will not cover business interruptions caused by Year 2000 problems. A Year 2000 problem would result from a computer operating as it was designed, instead of because of unexpected reasons.

Year 2000 insurance is being offered to provide coverage in areas such as these:

- Business interruption or profit losses resulting from the unsuccessful conversion of a company's own systems
- Costs resulting from the impact another company's unsuccessful or incompatible conversion may have
- Third-party liability, which describes the legal liability that would result from a conversion effort done by an outside company

Some insurance companies are starting to offer Year 2000 insurance. One insurance company is offering up to $100 million in coverage, with premiums ranging from 65 percent to 85 percent of the coverage amount. If companies that purchase the insurance do not end up having any Year 2000 problems, they will get back 85 percent to 95 percent of their premium. Another insurance company is offering coverage up to $200 million, with premiums that range from 2 percent to 10 percent of the coverage selected. Premiums usually are based on information gained from audits of companies applying for Year 2000 insurance.

It has been estimated that the cost of business disruptions and the resulting litigation that will be caused by Year 2000 problems will be around $1 trillion.

Contingency Plans

Companies should create a contingency plan for each of its critical business scenarios. Backup systems probably will not help with Year 2000 problems, as they would with other disasters, because backup systems use the same hardware, applications, and data.

If companies are smart, they will have realized that they probably will not be able to find all of their Year 2000 problems, and they will apply fixes before the year 2000 arrives. The companies that have thought ahead and implemented a contingency plan will be in much better shape to get through the transition to the year 2000. At this time, even though most companies recognize that year 2000–related failures are inevitable, they do not have contingency plans in place.

A recent survey found that only 62 percent of respondents said they are developing contingency plans, and many of them said they are still in the earliest phases of developing their plans. This absence of contingency plans is likely to seriously cripple some companies.

An Expert's Prediction

Computer consultant Ed Yourdon lies awake nights thinking about the New Year's Eve of 2000, but he isn't planning his millennial bash. Instead, he's worrying about what might be the biggest crash in the history of computers.

According to Yourdon, a specialist in the Year 2000 computer crisis and co-author of the book *Time Bomb 2000*, the Year 2000 problem is so massive that it cannot possibly be completely fixed in time to prevent all of the potential Year 2000 problems from occurring. It is more a question of how many things will go wrong, how long will the problems last, and how severe will the disruption be.

Some of Yourdon's concerns follow:

- The American Transportation Department might not complete its Year 2000 changes before 2020.
- The Internal Revenue Service's Year 2000 project is in trouble.
- A possible shutdown of the Social Security system could occur.
- Failures in the Federal Aviation Administration's radar-control systems could occur.
- State and local governments might be in even worse shape than the federal government.
- Embedded systems, such as elevators, commercial heating, air conditioning, and automobiles, may be overlooked.

Unfortunately, no one will really know how big the problem will be until the first day of the year 2000 actually arrives. Yourdon has a pessimistic view, though. He envisions situations in which people will be concentrating on how to get the basic necessities of life, and the only people who will be free from the effects of the Year 2000 problem are those who do not depend on automation, such as the rural Chinese.

Appendix

IN THIS PART

Composite Language Skeleton

SECTION V: COMPOSITE LANGUAGE SKELETON

1. GENERAL DESCRIPTION

This section contains the composite language skeleton of Standard COBOL.   It is intended to display complete and syntactically correct formats.

The leftmost margin on pages V-2 through V-4 and pages V-8 through V-19 is equivalent to margin A in a COBOL source program. The first indentation after the leftmost margin is equivalent to margin B in a COBOL source program.

On pages V-20 through V-33 the leftmost margin indicates the beginning of the format for a new COBOL verb. The first indentation after the leftmost margin indicates continuation of the format of the COBOL verb. The appearance of the italic letter S, R, I, or W to the left of the format for the verbs CLOSE, OPEN, READ, and WRITE indicates the Sequential I-O module, Relative I-O module, Indexed I-O module, or Report Writer module in which that general format is used.

The following is a summary of the formats shown on pages V-2 through V-40:

- Page V-2: General format for Identification Division
- Pages V-3 and V-4: General format for Environment Division
- Pages V-5 through V-7: General formats for file control entry
- Page V-8: General format for Data Division
- Pages V-9 through V-12: General formats for file description entry
- Pages V-13 and V-14: General formats for data description entry
- Pages V-15 and V-16: General formats for communication description entry
- Pages V-17 and V-18: General formats for report description entry
                        and report group description entry
- Page V-19: General format for Procedure Division
- Pages V-20 through V-33: General formats for COBOL verbs
- Page V-34: General format for COPY and REPLACE statements
- Pages V-35 and V-36: General format for conditions
- Page V-37: General format for qualification
- Page V-38: Miscellaneous formats
- Page V-39: General format for nested source programs
- Page V-40: General format for a sequence of source programs

GENERAL FORMAT FOR IDENTIFICATION DIVISION

IDENTIFICATION DIVISION.   CH 1

PROGRAM-ID. program-name $\left[\text{IS}\ \left\{\left|\begin{array}{c}\underline{\text{COMMON}}\\ \underline{\text{INITIAL}}\end{array}\right|\right\}\ \text{PROGRAM}\right]$

[AUTHOR. [comment-entry] ...]

[INSTALLATION. [comment-entry] ...]

[DATE-WRITTEN. [comment-entry] ...]

[DATE-COMPILED. [comment-entry] ...]

[SECURITY. [comment-entry] ...]

A

COMPOSITE
LANGUAGE
SKELETON

V-2

	When Introduced	*Chapter Reference*

GENERAL FORMAT FOR ENVIRONMENT DIVISION

[ENVIRONMENT DIVISION.   CH 1

[CONFIGURATION SECTION.

[SOURCE-COMPUTER. [computer-name [WITH DEBUGGING MODE].]]

[OBJECT-COMPUTER. [computer-name

$$\left[\underline{\text{MEMORY}} \text{ SIZE integer-1} \left\{\begin{array}{l}\underline{\text{WORDS}}\\\underline{\text{CHARACTERS}}\\\underline{\text{MODULES}}\end{array}\right\}\right]$$

[PROGRAM COLLATING SEQUENCE IS alphabet-name-1]

[SEGMENT-LIMIT IS segment-number].]]

[SPECIAL-NAMES. [[implementor-name-1

$$\left.\begin{array}{l}\left\{\begin{array}{l}\text{IS mnemonic-name-1 [}\underline{\text{ON}}\text{ STATUS IS condition-name-1 [}\underline{\text{OFF}}\text{ STATUS IS condition-name-2]]}\\\text{IS mnemonic-name-2 [}\underline{\text{OFF}}\text{ STATUS IS condition-name-2 [}\underline{\text{ON}}\text{ STATUS IS condition-name-1]]}\\\underline{\text{ON}}\text{ STATUS IS condition-name-1 [}\underline{\text{OFF}}\text{ STATUS IS condition-name-2]}\\\underline{\text{OFF}}\text{ STATUS IS condition-name-2 [}\underline{\text{ON}}\text{ STATUS IS condition-name-1]}\end{array}\right\}\end{array}\right] \ldots$$

[ALPHABET alphabet-name-1 IS

$$\left\{\begin{array}{l}\underline{\text{STANDARD-1}}\\\underline{\text{STANDARD-2}}\\\underline{\text{NATIVE}}\\\text{implementor-name-2}\\\left\{\text{literal-1}\left[\left\{\begin{array}{l}\underline{\text{THROUGH}}\\\underline{\text{THRU}}\end{array}\right\}\text{literal-2}\right]\left[\{\underline{\text{ALSO}}\text{ literal-3}\}\ldots\right]\right\}\ldots\end{array}\right\} \ldots$$

$$\left[\underline{\text{SYMBOLIC}}\text{ CHARACTERS}\left\{\{\text{symbolic-character-1}\}\ldots\left\{\begin{array}{l}\text{IS}\\\text{ARE}\end{array}\right\}\{\text{integer-1}\}\ldots\right\}\ldots\right.$$
$$\left.[\underline{\text{IN}}\text{ alphabet-name-2}]\right\}\ldots$$

$$\left[\underline{\text{CLASS}}\text{ class-name-1 IS}\left\{\text{literal-4}\left[\left\{\begin{array}{l}\underline{\text{THROUGH}}\\\underline{\text{THRU}}\end{array}\right\}\text{literal-5}\right]\right\}\ldots\right]\ldots$$

[CURRENCY SIGN IS literal-6]

[DECIMAL-POINT IS COMMA].]]]

	When Introduced	Chapter Reference

GENERAL FORMAT FOR ENVIRONMENT DIVISION

[INPUT-OUTPUT SECTION.   CH 6

  FILE-CONTROL.

    {file-control-entry} ...

[I-O-CONTROL.

$$\left[\left[\text{RERUN}\left[\text{ON}\left\{\begin{matrix}\text{file-name-1}\\\text{implementor-name-1}\end{matrix}\right\}\right]\text{ EVERY }\left\{\begin{matrix}\left\{[\text{END OF}]\left\{\begin{matrix}\text{REEL}\\\text{UNIT}\end{matrix}\right\}\right\}\text{ OF file-name-2}\\\text{integer-1 RECORDS}\\\text{integer-2 CLOCK-UNITS}\\\text{condition-name-1}\end{matrix}\right\}\right]\dots$$

$$\left[\text{SAME}\left[\begin{matrix}\text{RECORD}\\\text{SORT}\\\text{SORT-MERGE}\end{matrix}\right]\text{ AREA FOR file-name-3 }\{\text{file-name-4}\}\dots\right]\dots$$

    [MULTIPLE FILE TAPE CONTAINS {file-name-5 [POSITION integer-3]} ...] ... .]]]]

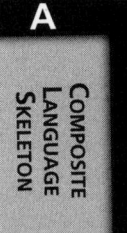

A

COMPOSITE
LANGUAGE
SKELETON

	When Introduced	Chapter Reference

GENERAL FORMAT FOR FILE CONTROL ENTRY

SEQUENTIAL FILE: CH 6

SELECT [OPTIONAL] file-name-1

   ASSIGN TO $\begin{Bmatrix} \text{implementor-name-1} \\ \text{literal-1} \end{Bmatrix}$ ...

   $\left[\text{RESERVE integer-1} \begin{bmatrix} \text{AREA} \\ \text{AREAS} \end{bmatrix} \right]$

   [[ORGANIZATION IS] SEQUENTIAL]

   $\left[\text{PADDING CHARACTER IS } \begin{Bmatrix} \text{data-name-1} \\ \text{literal-2} \end{Bmatrix} \right]$

   $\left[\text{RECORD DELIMITER IS } \begin{Bmatrix} \text{STANDARD-1} \\ \text{implementor-name-2} \end{Bmatrix} \right]$

   [ACCESS MODE IS SEQUENTIAL]

   [FILE STATUS IS data-name-2].

RELATIVE FILE: CH 8

SELECT [OPTIONAL] file-name-1

   ASSIGN TO $\begin{Bmatrix} \text{implementor-name-1} \\ \text{literal-1} \end{Bmatrix}$ ...

   $\left[\text{RESERVE integer-1} \begin{bmatrix} \text{AREA} \\ \text{AREAS} \end{bmatrix} \right]$

   [ORGANIZATION IS] RELATIVE

   $\left[\text{ACCESS MODE IS } \begin{Bmatrix} \text{SEQUENTIAL} & \text{[RELATIVE KEY IS data-name-1]} \\ \begin{Bmatrix} \text{RANDOM} \\ \text{DYNAMIC} \end{Bmatrix} & \text{RELATIVE KEY IS data-name-1} \end{Bmatrix} \right]$

   [FILE STATUS IS data-name-2].

	When Introduced	Chapter Reference

GENERAL FORMAT FOR FILE CONTROL ENTRY

INDEXED FILE: ANS 74   CH 7

SELECT [OPTIONAL] file-name-1

   ASSIGN TO $\begin{Bmatrix} \text{implementor-name-1} \\ \text{literal-1} \end{Bmatrix}$ ...

   $\left[\text{RESERVE integer-1} \begin{bmatrix} \text{AREA} \\ \text{AREAS} \end{bmatrix} \right]$

   [ORGANIZATION IS] INDEXED

   $\left[\text{ACCESS MODE IS} \begin{Bmatrix} \text{SEQUENTIAL} \\ \text{RANDOM} \\ \text{DYNAMIC} \end{Bmatrix} \right]$

   RECORD KEY IS data-name-1

   [ALTERNATE RECORD KEY IS data-name-2 [WITH DUPLICATES]] ...

   [FILE STATUS IS data-name-3].

SORT OR MERGE FILE: CH 15

SELECT file-name-1 ASSIGN TO $\begin{Bmatrix} \text{implementor-name-1} \\ \text{literal-1} \end{Bmatrix}$ ... .

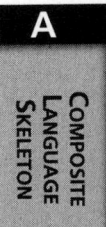

A

COMPOSITE
LANGUAGE
SKELETON

	When Introduced	Chapter Reference

GENERAL FORMAT FOR FILE CONTROL ENTRY

REPORT FILE:

SELECT [OPTIONAL] file-name-1

    ASSIGN TO $\begin{Bmatrix} \text{implementor-name-1} \\ \text{literal-1} \end{Bmatrix}$ ...

    $\left[\text{RESERVE integer-1} \begin{bmatrix} \text{AREA} \\ \text{AREAS} \end{bmatrix} \right]$

    [[ORGANIZATION IS] SEQUENTIAL]]

    $\left[\text{PADDING CHARACTER IS} \begin{Bmatrix} \text{data-name-1} \\ \text{literal-2} \end{Bmatrix} \right]$

    $\left[\text{RECORD DELIMITER IS} \begin{Bmatrix} \text{STANDARD-1} \\ \text{implementor-name-2} \end{Bmatrix} \right]$

    [ACCESS MODE IS SEQUENTIAL]

    [FILE STATUS IS data-name-2].

CH 9

V-7

	When Introduced	Chapter Reference

GENERAL FORMAT FOR DATA DIVISION

[DATA DIVISION.

[FILE SECTION.

$$\left[\begin{array}{l} \text{file-description-entry \{record-description-entry\} ...} \\ \text{sort-merge-file-description-entry \{record-description-entry\} ...} \\ \text{report-file-description-entry} \end{array} \right] ... \right]$$

CH 8
CH15
CH 9

[WORKING-STORAGE SECTION.

CH 2

$$\left[\begin{array}{l} \text{77-level-description-entry} \\ \text{record-description-entry} \end{array} \right] ... \right]$$

[LINKAGE SECTION.

CH 14

$$\left[\begin{array}{l} \text{77-level-description-entry} \\ \text{record-description-entry} \end{array} \right] ... \right]$$

[COMMUNICATION SECTION.

CH 15

[communication-description-entry [record-description-entry] ...] ...]

[REPORT SECTION.

CH 9

[report-description-entry {report-group-description-entry} ...] ...]]

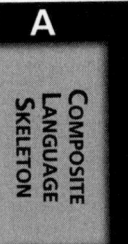

A

COMPOSITE
LANGUAGE
SKELETON

	When Introduced	Chapter Reference

GENERAL FORMAT FOR FILE DESCRIPTION ENTRY

<u>SEQUENTIAL FILE</u>:   CH 6

<u>FD</u> file-name-1

  [IS <u>EXTERNAL</u>]   ANS 85   CH 14

  [IS <u>GLOBAL</u>]   ANS 85   CH 14

  [<u>BLOCK</u> CONTAINS [integer-1 <u>TO</u>] integer-2 $\begin{Bmatrix} \underline{RECORDS} \\ CHARACTERS \end{Bmatrix}$]   CH 6

$\left[\underline{RECORD} \begin{Bmatrix} CONTAINS\ integer\text{-}3\ CHARACTERS \\ IS\ \underline{VARYING}\ IN\ SIZE\ [[FROM\ integer\text{-}4]\ [\underline{TO}\ integer\text{-}5]\ CHARACTERS] \\ \quad [\underline{DEPENDING}\ ON\ data\text{-}name\text{-}1] \\ CONTAINS\ integer\text{-}6\ \underline{TO}\ integer\text{-}7\ CHARACTERS \end{Bmatrix} \right]$ CH 6

$\left[\underline{LABEL} \begin{Bmatrix} \underline{RECORD}\ IS \\ \underline{RECORDS}\ ARE \end{Bmatrix} \begin{Bmatrix} \underline{STANDARD} \\ \underline{OMITTED} \end{Bmatrix} \right]$ CH 6

$\left[\underline{VALUE}\ \underline{OF} \quad \left\{ implementor\text{-}name\text{-}1\ IS \begin{Bmatrix} data\text{-}name\text{-}2 \\ literal\text{-}1 \end{Bmatrix} \right\} \dots \right]$ CH 6

$\left[\underline{DATA} \quad \begin{Bmatrix} \underline{RECORD}\ IS \\ \underline{RECORDS}\ ARE \end{Bmatrix} \{data\text{-}name\text{-}3\} \dots \right]$ CH 6

$\left[\underline{LINAGE}\ IS \begin{Bmatrix} data\text{-}name\text{-}4 \\ integer\text{-}8 \end{Bmatrix} LINES \left[WITH\ \underline{FOOTING}\ AT \begin{Bmatrix} data\text{-}name\text{-}5 \\ integer\text{-}9 \end{Bmatrix} \right] \right.$ CH 6

$\left. \left[LINES\ AT\ \underline{TOP} \begin{Bmatrix} data\text{-}name\text{-}6 \\ integer\text{-}10 \end{Bmatrix} \right] \left[LINES\ AT\ \underline{BOTTOM} \begin{Bmatrix} data\text{-}name\text{-}7 \\ integer\text{-}11 \end{Bmatrix} \right] \right]$ CH 6

[<u>CODE-SET</u> IS alphabet-name-1].   CH 6

	When Introduced	Chapter Reference

GENERAL FORMAT FOR FILE DESCRIPTION ENTRY

RELATIVE FILE: CH 8

FD file-name-1

    [IS EXTERNAL]   ANS 85   CH 14

    [IS GLOBAL]   ANS 85   CH 14

$$\left[\underline{\text{BLOCK}} \text{ CONTAINS } [\text{integer-1 } \underline{\text{TO}}] \text{ integer-2 } \left\{\begin{array}{l}\underline{\text{RECORDS}}\\ \text{CHARACTERS}\end{array}\right\}\right]$$ CH 8

$$\left[\underline{\text{RECORD}} \left\{\begin{array}{l}\text{CONTAINS integer-3 CHARACTERS}\\ \text{IS } \underline{\text{VARYING}} \text{ IN SIZE } [[\text{FROM integer-4}] \ [\underline{\text{TO}} \text{ integer-5}] \text{ CHARACTERS}]\\ \quad [\underline{\text{DEPENDING}} \text{ ON data-name-1}]\\ \text{CONTAINS integer-6 } \underline{\text{TO}} \text{ integer-7 CHARACTERS}\end{array}\right\}\right]$$ CH 8

$$\left[\underline{\text{LABEL}} \left\{\begin{array}{l}\underline{\text{RECORD}} \text{ IS}\\ \underline{\text{RECORDS}} \text{ ARE}\end{array}\right\} \left\{\begin{array}{l}\underline{\text{STANDARD}}\\ \underline{\text{OMITTED}}\end{array}\right\}\right]$$ CH 8

$$\left[\underline{\text{VALUE}} \ \underline{\text{OF}} \left\{\text{implementor-name-1 IS } \left\{\begin{array}{l}\text{data-name-2}\\ \text{literal-1}\end{array}\right\}\right\} \dots\right]$$ CH 8

$$\left[\underline{\text{DATA}} \left\{\begin{array}{l}\underline{\text{RECORD}} \text{ IS}\\ \underline{\text{RECORDS}} \text{ ARE}\end{array}\right\} \{\text{data-name-3}\} \dots\right].$$ CH 8

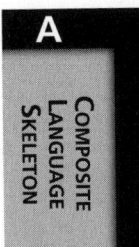

A

COMPOSITE
LANGUAGE
SKELETON

	When Introduced	Chapter Reference

GENERAL FORMAT FOR FILE DESCRIPTION ENTRY

	When Introduced	Chapter Reference
INDEXED FILE:	ANS 74	CH 7
FD file-name-1		
[IS EXTERNAL]	ANS 85	CH 14
[IS GLOBAL]	ANS 85	CH 14
[BLOCK CONTAINS [integer-1 TO] integer-2 { RECORDS / CHARACTERS }]	ANS 74	CH 7
[RECORD { CONTAINS integer-3 CHARACTERS / IS VARYING IN SIZE [[FROM integer-4] [TO integer-5] CHARACTERS] [DEPENDING ON data-name-1] / CONTAINS integer-6 TO integer-7 CHARACTERS }]	ANS 74	CH 7
[LABEL { RECORD IS / RECORDS ARE } { STANDARD / OMITTED }]	ANS 74	CH 7
[VALUE OF { implementor-name-1 IS { data-name-2 / literal-1 } } ...]	ANS 74	CH 7
[DATA { RECORD IS / RECORDS ARE } {data-name-3} ...] .	ANS 74	CH 7

	When Introduced	*Chapter Reference*

GENERAL FORMAT FOR FILE DESCRIPTION ENTRY

SORT-MERGE FILE: CH 15

SD   file-name-1

$$\left[\text{RECORD} \begin{cases} \text{CONTAINS integer-1 CHARACTERS} \\ \text{IS } \underline{\text{VARYING}} \text{ IN SIZE [[FROM integer-2] [}\underline{\text{TO}}\text{ integer-3] CHARACTERS]} \\ \quad [\underline{\text{DEPENDING}}\text{ ON data-name-1]} \\ \text{CONTAINS integer-4 } \underline{\text{TO}} \text{ integer-5 CHARACTERS} \end{cases} \right]$$

$$\left[\underline{\text{DATA}} \begin{Bmatrix} \underline{\text{RECORD}} \text{ IS} \\ \underline{\text{RECORDS}} \text{ ARE} \end{Bmatrix} \{\text{data-name-2}\} \dots \right] \ .$$

REPORT FILE: CH 9

FD   file-name-1

[IS <u>EXTERNAL</u>]   ANS 85   CH 14

[IS <u>GLOBAL</u>]   ANS 85   CH 14

$$\left[\underline{\text{BLOCK}} \text{ CONTAINS } [\text{integer-1 } \underline{\text{TO}}] \text{ integer-2 } \begin{Bmatrix} \underline{\text{RECORDS}} \\ \text{CHARACTERS} \end{Bmatrix} \right]$$ CH 9

$$\left[\underline{\text{RECORD}} \begin{Bmatrix} \text{CONTAINS integer-3 CHARACTERS} \\ \text{CONTAINS integer-4 } \underline{\text{TO}} \text{ integer-5 CHARACTERS} \end{Bmatrix} \right]$$ CH 9

$$\left[\underline{\text{LABEL}} \begin{Bmatrix} \underline{\text{RECORD}} \text{ IS} \\ \underline{\text{RECORDS}} \text{ ARE} \end{Bmatrix} \begin{Bmatrix} \underline{\text{STANDARD}} \\ \underline{\text{OMITTED}} \end{Bmatrix} \right]$$ CH 9

$$\left[\underline{\text{VALUE}} \ \underline{\text{OF}} \ \begin{Bmatrix} \text{implementor-name-1 IS} \begin{Bmatrix} \text{data-name-1} \\ \text{literal-1} \end{Bmatrix} \end{Bmatrix} \dots \right]$$ CH 9

[<u>CODE-SET</u> IS alphabet-name-1]   CH 9

$$\begin{Bmatrix} \underline{\text{REPORT}} \text{ IS} \\ \underline{\text{REPORTS}} \text{ ARE} \end{Bmatrix} \{\text{report-name-1}\} \dots \ .$$ CH 9

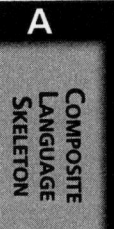

A

COMPOSITE LANGUAGE SKELETON

	When Introduced	Chapter Reference

GENERAL FORMAT FOR DATA DESCRIPTION ENTRY

FORMAT 1:

level-number $\left[\begin{array}{l}\text{data-name-1}\\\text{FILLER}\end{array}\right]$	ANS 85	CH 2
[REDEFINES data-name-2]		CH 2
[IS EXTERNAL]	ANS 85	CH 14
[IS GLOBAL]	ANS 85	CH 14
$\left[\left\{\begin{array}{l}\text{PICTURE}\\\text{PIC}\end{array}\right\}\text{ IS character-string}\right]$		CH 2
$\left[\text{USAGE IS}\left\{\begin{array}{l}\text{BINARY}\\\text{COMPUTATIONAL}\\\text{COMP}\\\text{DISPLAY}\\\text{INDEX}\\\text{PACKED-DECIMAL}\end{array}\right\}\right]$		CH 2
$\left[\text{SIGN IS}\left\{\begin{array}{l}\text{LEADING}\\\text{TRAILING}\end{array}\right\}\text{ [SEPARATE CHARACTER]}\right]$	ANS 74	CH 2
OCCURS integer-2 TIMES		CH 11
$\qquad\left[\left\{\begin{array}{l}\text{ASCENDING}\\\text{DESCENDING}\end{array}\right\}\text{ KEY IS \{data-name-3\} ... }\right]$ ...		
$\qquad$ [INDEXED BY {index-name-1} ...]		
OCCURS integer-1 TO integer-2 TIMES DEPENDING ON data-name-4		CH 11
$\qquad\left[\left\{\begin{array}{l}\text{ASCENDING}\\\text{DESCENDING}\end{array}\right\}\text{ KEY IS \{data-name-3\} ... }\right]$ ...		
$\qquad$ [INDEXED BY {index-name-1} ...]		
$\left[\left\{\begin{array}{l}\text{SYNCHRONIZED}\\\text{SYNC}\end{array}\right\}\left[\begin{array}{l}\text{LEFT}\\\text{RIGHT}\end{array}\right]\right]$		CH 2
$\left[\left\{\begin{array}{l}\text{JUSTIFIED}\\\text{JUST}\end{array}\right\}\text{ RIGHT}\right]$		CH 2
[VALUE IS literal-1].		CH 2

	When Introduced	Chapter Reference

GENERAL FORMAT FOR DATA DESCRIPTION ENTRY

FORMAT 2:

66 data-name-1 RENAMES data-name-2 $\left[\begin{Bmatrix} \text{THROUGH} \\ \text{THRU} \end{Bmatrix} \text{data-name-3} \right]$ CH 6

FORMAT 3:

88 condition-name-1 $\begin{Bmatrix} \text{VALUE IS} \\ \text{VALUES ARE} \end{Bmatrix}$ $\begin{Bmatrix} \text{literal-1} \left[\begin{Bmatrix} \text{THROUGH} \\ \text{THRU} \end{Bmatrix} \text{literal-2} \right] \end{Bmatrix}$ CH 3

A

COMPOSITE
LANGUAGE
SKELETON

	When Introduced	Chapter Reference

GENERAL FORMAT FOR COMMUNICATION DESCRIPTION ENTRY

FORMAT 1:

CD cd-name-1

ANS 74   CH 15

```
      [[SYMBOLIC QUEUE IS data-name-1]

        [SYMBOLIC SUB-QUEUE-1 IS data-name-2]

        [SYMBOLIC SUB-QUEUE-2 IS data-name-3]

        [SYMBOLIC SUB-QUEUE-3 IS data-name-4]

        [MESSAGE DATE IS data-name-5]

        [MESSAGE TIME IS data-name-6]

        [SYMBOLIC SOURCE IS data-name-7]

FOR [INITIAL] INPUT   [TEXT LENGTH IS data-name-8]

        [END KEY IS data-name-9]

        [STATUS KEY IS data-name-10]

        [MESSAGE COUNT IS data-name-11]]

  [data-name-1, data-name-2, data-name-3,

     data-name-4, data-name-5, data-name-6,

     data-name-7, data-name-8, data-name-9,

     data-name-10, data-name-11]
```

V-15

	When Introduced	Chapter Reference

<u>GENERAL FORMAT FOR COMMUNICATION DESCRIPTION ENTRY</u>

<u>FORMAT 2</u>:

<u>CD</u>   cd-name-1 FOR <u>OUTPUT</u>   ANS 74   CH 15

    [<u>DESTINATION</u> <u>COUNT</u> IS data-name-1]

    [<u>TEXT</u> <u>LENGTH</u> IS data-name-2]

    [<u>STATUS</u> <u>KEY</u> IS data-name-3]

    [<u>DESTINATION</u> <u>TABLE</u> <u>OCCURS</u> integer-1 TIMES

        [<u>INDEXED</u> BY {index-name-1} ...]]

    [<u>ERROR</u> <u>KEY</u> IS data-name-4]

    [SYMBOLIC <u>DESTINATION</u> IS data-name-5].

<u>FORMAT 3</u>:

<u>CD</u>   cd-name-1   ANS 74   CH 15

```
              ⎡[[MESSAGE DATE IS data-name-1]                  ⎤
              ⎢   [MESSAGE TIME IS data-name-2]                ⎥
              ⎢   [SYMBOLIC TERMINAL IS data-name-3]           ⎥
  FOR [INITIAL] I-O  ⎢ [TEXT LENGTH IS data-name-4]            ⎥
              ⎢   [END KEY IS data-name-5]                     ⎥
              ⎢   [STATUS KEY IS data-name-6]]                 ⎥
              ⎢ [data-name-1, data-name-2, data-name-3,        ⎥
              ⎣   data-name-4, data-name-5, data-name-6]       ⎦
```

	When Introduced	*Chapter Reference*

GENERAL FORMAT FOR REPORT DESCRIPTION ENTRY

```
RD  report-name-1                                                          CH 9

   [IS GLOBAL]

   [CODE literal-1]

   ⎡⎧CONTROL IS  ⎫  ⎧{data-name-1} ...      ⎫⎤
   ⎣⎩CONTROLS ARE⎭  ⎩FINAL [data-name-1] ...⎭⎦

   ⎡      ⎡LIMIT IS  ⎤            ⎡LINE ⎤                ⎤
   ⎢PAGE  ⎢LIMITS ARE⎥  integer-1 ⎢LINES⎥ [HEADING integer-2]
   ⎣      ⎣          ⎦            ⎣     ⎦                ⎦

        [FIRST DETAIL integer-3]  [LAST DETAIL integer-4]

           [FOOTING integer-5].
```

GENERAL FORMAT FOR REPORT GROUP DESCRIPTION ENTRY

FORMAT 1:

```
01  [data-name-1]                                                          CH 9

    ⎡                ⎧integer-1 [ON NEXT PAGE]}⎫⎤
    ⎢LINE NUMBER IS  ⎨PLUS integer-2           ⎬⎥
    ⎣                ⎩                         ⎭⎦

    ⎡               ⎧integer-3      ⎫⎤
    ⎢NEXT GROUP IS  ⎨PLUS integer-4 ⎬⎥
    ⎣               ⎩NEXT PAGE      ⎭⎦

              ⎧⎧REPORT HEADING⎫                     ⎫
              ⎪⎩RH            ⎭                     ⎪
              ⎪                                     ⎪
              ⎪⎧PAGE HEADING⎫                       ⎪
              ⎪⎩PH          ⎭                       ⎪
              ⎪                                     ⎪
              ⎪⎧CONTROL HEADING⎫  ⎧data-name-2⎫     ⎪
              ⎪⎩CH             ⎭  ⎩FINAL      ⎭     ⎪
    TYPE IS   ⎨⎧DETAIL⎫                             ⎬
              ⎪⎩DE    ⎭                             ⎪
              ⎪                                     ⎪
              ⎪⎧CONTROL FOOTING⎫  ⎧data-name-3⎫     ⎪
              ⎪⎩CF             ⎭  ⎩FINAL      ⎭     ⎪
              ⎪⎧PAGE FOOTING⎫                       ⎪
              ⎪⎩PF          ⎭                       ⎪
              ⎪⎧REPORT FOOTING⎫                     ⎪
              ⎩⎩RF            ⎭                     ⎭

    [[USAGE IS] DISPLAY].
```

V-17

	When Introduced	Chapter Reference

GENERAL FORMAT FOR REPORT GROUP DESCRIPTION ENTRY

FORMAT 2:

level-number [data-name-1]   CH 9

$$\left[\underline{LINE}\ NUMBER\ IS\ \left\{\begin{array}{l} integer-1\ [ON\ \underline{NEXT}\ \underline{PAGE}]\\ \underline{PLUS}\ Integer-2 \end{array}\right\}\right]$$

[[USAGE IS] DISPLAY].

FORMAT 3:

level-number [data-name-1]   CH 9

$$\left\{\begin{array}{l}\underline{PICTURE}\\ \underline{PIC}\end{array}\right\}\ IS\ character\text{-}string$$

[[USAGE IS] DISPLAY]

$$\left[[\underline{SIGN}\ IS]\ \left\{\begin{array}{l}\underline{LEADING}\\ \underline{TRAILING}\end{array}\right\}\ \underline{SEPARATE}\ CHARACTER\right]$$

$$\left[\left\{\begin{array}{l}\underline{JUSTIFIED}\\ \underline{JUST}\end{array}\right\}\ RIGHT\right]$$

[BLANK WHEN ZERO]

$$\left[\underline{LINE}\ NUMBER\ IS\ \left\{\begin{array}{l}integer-1\ [ON\ \underline{NEXT}\ \underline{PAGE}]\\ \underline{PLUS}\ integer-2\end{array}\right\}\right]$$

[COLUMN NUMBER IS integer-3]

$$\left\{\begin{array}{l}\underline{SOURCE}\ IS\ identifier-1\\ \underline{VALUE}\ IS\ literal-1\\ \{\underline{SUM}\ \{identifier-2\}\ ...\ [\underline{UPON}\ \{data\text{-}name-2\}\ ...\ ]\}\ ...\\ \left[\underline{RESET}\ ON\ \left\{\begin{array}{l}data\text{-}name-3\\ \underline{FINAL}\end{array}\right\}\right]\end{array}\right\}$$

[GROUP INDICATE].

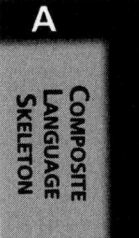

A

COMPOSITE LANGUAGE SKELETON

	When Introduced	Chapter Reference

<u>GENERAL FORMAT FOR PROCEDURE DIVISION</u>

<u>FORMAT 1</u>:

[<u>PROCEDURE DIVISION</u> [<u>USING</u> {data-name-1} ...].

CH 1, 14

[<u>DECLARATIVES</u>.

CH 15

{section-name <u>SECTION</u> [segment-number].

    USE statement.

[paragraph-name.

    [sentence] ...] ... } ...

<u>END DECLARATIVES</u>.]

{section-name <u>SECTION</u> [segment-number].

CH 4, 15

[paragraph-name.

    [sentence] ...] ... } ...]

<u>FORMAT 2</u>:

[<u>PROCEDURE DIVISION</u> [<u>USING</u> {data-name-1} ...].

                                                                                    ANS 85   CH 1, 14

{paragraph-name.

    [sentence] ... } ...]

	When Introduced	Chapter Reference

GENERAL FORMAT FOR COBOL VERBS

<u>ACCEPT</u> identifier-1 [<u>FROM</u> mnemonic-name-1] — CH 1

<u>ACCEPT</u> identifier-2 <u>FROM</u> $\left\{\begin{array}{l}\underline{\text{DATE}}\\\underline{\text{DAY}}\\\underline{\text{DAY-OF-WEEK}}\\\underline{\text{TIME}}\end{array}\right\}$ — ANS 74 — CH 1

<u>ACCEPT</u> cd-name-1 MESSAGE <u>COUNT</u> — ANS 74 — CH 1

<u>ADD</u> $\left\{\begin{array}{l}\text{identifier-1}\\\text{literal-1}\end{array}\right\}$ ... <u>TO</u> {identifier-2 [<u>ROUNDED</u>]} ... — CH 3

  [ON <u>SIZE</u> <u>ERROR</u> imperative-statement-1]

  [<u>NOT</u> ON <u>SIZE</u> <u>ERROR</u> imperative-statement-2] — ANS 85

  [<u>END-ADD</u>] — ANS 85

<u>ADD</u> $\left\{\begin{array}{l}\text{identifier-1}\\\text{literal-1}\end{array}\right\}$ ... TO $\left\{\begin{array}{l}\text{identifier-2}\\\text{literal-2}\end{array}\right\}$ — CH 3

  <u>GIVING</u> {identifier-3 [<u>ROUNDED</u>]} ...

  [ON <u>SIZE</u> <u>ERROR</u> imperative-statement-1]

  [<u>NOT</u> ON <u>SIZE</u> <u>ERROR</u> imperative-statement-2] — ANS 85

  [<u>END-ADD</u>] — ANS 85

<u>ADD</u> $\left\{\begin{array}{l}\underline{\text{CORRESPONDING}}\\\underline{\text{CORR}}\end{array}\right\}$ identifier-1 <u>TO</u> identifier-2 [<u>ROUNDED</u>] — CH 6

  [ON <u>SIZE</u> <u>ERROR</u> imperative-statement-1]

  [<u>NOT</u> ON <u>SIZE</u> <u>ERROR</u> imperative-statement-2] — ANS 85

  [<u>END-ADD</u>] — ANS 85

<u>ALTER</u> {procedure-name-1 <u>TO</u> [<u>PROCEED</u> <u>TO</u>] procedure-name-2} ... — CH 4

<u>CALL</u> $\left\{\begin{array}{l}\text{identifier-1}\\\text{literal-1}\end{array}\right\}$ $\left[\,\underline{\text{USING}}\,\left\{\begin{array}{l}[\text{BY }\underline{\text{REFERENCE}}]\quad\{\text{identifier-2}\}\ ...\\\text{BY }\underline{\text{CONTENT}}\quad\{\text{identifier-2}\}\ ...\end{array}\right\}\ ...\right]$ — CH 14

  [ON <u>OVERFLOW</u> imperative-statement-1]

  [<u>END-CALL</u>] — ANS 85

A

COMPOSITE
LANGUAGE
SKELETON

	When Introduced	Chapter Reference

GENERAL FORMAT FOR COBOL VERBS

CALL {identifier-1 / literal-1} [USING {[BY REFERENCE] {identifier-2} ... / BY CONTENT {identifier-2} ... } ...]   CH 14

    [ON EXCEPTION imperative-statement-1]   ANS 85

    [NOT ON EXCEPTION imperative-statement-2]   ANS 85

    [END-CALL]   ANS 85

CANCEL {identifier-1 / literal-1} ...   ANS 74   CH 15

SW CLOSE {file-name-1 [{REEL / UNIT} [FOR REMOVAL] / WITH {NO REWIND / LOCK}]} ...   CH 6, 9

RI CLOSE {file-name-1 [WITH LOCK]} ...   CH 7, 8

COMPUTE {identifier-1 [ROUNDED]} ... = arithmetic-expression-1   CH 3

    [ON SIZE ERROR imperative-statement-1]

    [NOT ON SIZE ERROR imperative-statement-2]   ANS 85

    [END-COMPUTE]   ANS 85

CONTINUE   ANS 85   CH 3

DELETE file-name-1 RECORD   CH 7, 8

    [INVALID KEY imperative-statement-1]

    [NOT INVALID KEY imperative-statement-2]   ANS 85

    [END-DELETE]   ANS 85

DISABLE {INPUT [TERMINAL] / I-O TERMINAL / OUTPUT} cd-name-1 [WITH KEY {identifier-1 / literal-1}]   ANS 74   CH 15

	When Introduced	Chapter Reference

GENERAL FORMAT FOR COBOL VERBS

<u>DISPLAY</u> $\begin{Bmatrix} \text{identifier-1} \\ \text{literal-1} \end{Bmatrix}$ ... [<u>UPON</u> mnemonic-name-1] [WITH <u>NO</u> <u>ADVANCING</u>]

CH 1

<u>DIVIDE</u> $\begin{Bmatrix} \text{identifier-1} \\ \text{literal-1} \end{Bmatrix}$ <u>INTO</u> {identifier-2 [<u>ROUNDED</u>]} ...

CH 3

    [ON <u>SIZE</u> <u>ERROR</u> imperative-statement-1]

    [<u>NOT</u> ON <u>SIZE</u> <u>ERROR</u> imperative-statement-2]   ANS 85

    [<u>END-DIVIDE</u>]   ANS 85

<u>DIVIDE</u> $\begin{Bmatrix} \text{identifier-1} \\ \text{literal-1} \end{Bmatrix}$ <u>INTO</u> $\begin{Bmatrix} \text{identifier-2} \\ \text{literal-2} \end{Bmatrix}$

CH 3

    <u>GIVING</u> {identifier-3 [<u>ROUNDED</u>]} ...

    [ON <u>SIZE</u> <u>ERROR</u> imperative-statement-1]

    [<u>NOT</u> ON <u>SIZE</u> <u>ERROR</u> imperative-statement-2]   ANS 85

    [<u>END-DIVIDE</u>]   ANS 85

<u>DIVIDE</u> $\begin{Bmatrix} \text{identifier-1} \\ \text{literal-1} \end{Bmatrix}$ <u>BY</u> $\begin{Bmatrix} \text{identifier-2} \\ \text{literal-2} \end{Bmatrix}$

CH 3

    <u>GIVING</u> {identifier-3 [<u>ROUNDED</u>]} ...

    [ON <u>SIZE</u> <u>ERROR</u> imperative-statement-1]

    [<u>NOT</u> ON <u>SIZE</u> <u>ERROR</u> imperative-statement-2]   ANS 85

    [<u>END-DIVIDE</u>]   ANS 85

<u>DIVIDE</u> $\begin{Bmatrix} \text{identifier-1} \\ \text{literal-1} \end{Bmatrix}$ <u>INTO</u> $\begin{Bmatrix} \text{identifier-2} \\ \text{literal-2} \end{Bmatrix}$ <u>GIVING</u> identifier-3 [<u>ROUNDED</u>]

CH 3

    <u>REMAINDER</u> identifier-4

    [ON <u>SIZE</u> <u>ERROR</u> imperative-statement-1]

    [<u>NOT</u> ON <u>SIZE</u> <u>ERROR</u> imperative-statement-2]   ANS 85

    [<u>END-DIVIDE</u>]   ANS 85

A

COMPOSITE LANGUAGE SKELETON

	When Introduced	Chapter Reference

GENERAL FORMAT FOR COBOL VERBS

<u>DIVIDE</u> $\begin{Bmatrix} \text{identifier-1} \\ \text{literal-1} \end{Bmatrix}$ <u>BY</u> $\begin{Bmatrix} \text{identifier-2} \\ \text{literal-2} \end{Bmatrix}$ <u>GIVING</u> identifier-3 [<u>ROUNDED</u>]   CH 3

   <u>REMAINDER</u> identifier-4

   [ON <u>SIZE ERROR</u> imperative-statement-1]

   [<u>NOT</u> ON <u>SIZE ERROR</u> imperative-statement-2]   ANS 85

   [<u>END-DIVIDE</u>]   ANS 85

<u>ENABLE</u> $\begin{Bmatrix} \text{INPUT [\underline{TERMINAL}]} \\ \text{\underline{I-O} TERMINAL} \\ \text{\underline{OUTPUT}} \end{Bmatrix}$ cd-name-1 $\left[\text{WITH } \underline{\text{KEY}} \begin{Bmatrix} \text{identifier-1} \\ \text{literal-1} \end{Bmatrix}\right]$ CH 15

<u>ENTER</u> language-name-1 [routine-name-1].   CH 14

<u>EVALUATE</u> $\begin{Bmatrix} \text{identifier-1} \\ \text{literal-1} \\ \text{expression-1} \\ \underline{\text{TRUE}} \\ \underline{\text{FALSE}} \end{Bmatrix}$ $\left[\underline{\text{ALSO}} \begin{Bmatrix} \text{identifier-2} \\ \text{literal-2} \\ \text{expression-2} \\ \underline{\text{TRUE}} \\ \underline{\text{FALSE}} \end{Bmatrix}\right]$ ...   ANS 85   CH 5

   $\{\{\underline{\text{WHEN}}$

   $\begin{Bmatrix} \underline{\text{ANY}} \\ \text{condition-1} \\ \underline{\text{TRUE}} \\ \underline{\text{FALSE}} \\ [\underline{\text{NOT}}] \begin{Bmatrix} \text{identifier-3} \\ \text{literal-3} \\ \text{arithmetic-expression-1} \end{Bmatrix} \left[\begin{Bmatrix}\underline{\text{THROUGH}} \\ \underline{\text{THRU}}\end{Bmatrix} \begin{Bmatrix} \text{identifier-4} \\ \text{literal-4} \\ \text{arithmetic-expression-2} \end{Bmatrix}\right] \end{Bmatrix}$

   $[\underline{\text{ALSO}}$

   $\begin{Bmatrix} \underline{\text{ANY}} \\ \text{condition-2} \\ \underline{\text{TRUE}} \\ \underline{\text{FALSE}} \\ [\underline{\text{NOT}}] \begin{Bmatrix} \text{identifier-5} \\ \text{literal-5} \\ \text{arithmetic-expression-3} \end{Bmatrix} \left[\begin{Bmatrix}\underline{\text{THROUGH}} \\ \underline{\text{THRU}}\end{Bmatrix} \begin{Bmatrix} \text{identifier-6} \\ \text{literal-6} \\ \text{arithmetic-expression-4} \end{Bmatrix}\right] \end{Bmatrix}\}\}$ ... $\}$ ...

   imperative-statement-1} ...

   [<u>WHEN</u> <u>OTHER</u> imperative-statement-2]

   [<u>END-EVALUATE</u>]

	When Introduced	Chapter Reference

<u>GENERAL FORMAT FOR COBOL VERBS</u>

<u>EXIT</u>
                    CH 4

<u>EXIT</u> <u>PROGRAM</u>
        ANS 74   CH 14

<u>GENERATE</u> {data-name-1 / report-name-1}
    CH 9

<u>GO</u> TO [procedure-name-1]
    CH 4

<u>GO</u> TO {procedure-name-1} ... <u>DEPENDING</u> ON identifier-1
    CH 4

<u>IF</u> condition-1 THEN {{statement-1} ... / <u>NEXT</u> <u>SENTENCE</u>} {<u>ELSE</u> {statement-2} ... [<u>END-IF</u>] / <u>ELSE</u> <u>NEXT</u> <u>SENTENCE</u> / <u>END-IF</u>}
  ANS 85   CH 3, 5

<u>INITIALIZE</u> {identifier-1} ...
  ANS 85   CH 6

    [<u>REPLACING</u> {(<u>ALPHABETIC</u> / <u>ALPHANUMERIC</u> / <u>NUMERIC</u> / <u>ALPHANUMERIC-EDITED</u> / <u>NUMERIC-EDITED</u>)} DATA <u>BY</u> {identifier-2 / literal-1} ...]

<u>INITIATE</u> {report-name-1} ...
    CH 9

<u>INSPECT</u> identifier-1 <u>TALLYING</u>
  ANS 74   CH 10

    { {<u>CHARACTERS</u> [{<u>BEFORE</u> / <u>AFTER</u>} INITIAL {identifier-4 / literal-2}] ... / identifier-2 <u>FOR</u> {<u>ALL</u> / <u>LEADING</u>} {identifier-3 / literal-1} [{<u>BEFORE</u> / <u>AFTER</u>} INITIAL {identifier-4 / literal-2}] ... } ... } ...

<u>INSPECT</u> identifier-1 <u>REPLACING</u>
  ANS 74   CH 10

    { <u>CHARACTERS</u> <u>BY</u> {identifier-5 / literal-3} [{<u>BEFORE</u> / <u>AFTER</u>} INITIAL {identifier-4 / literal-2}] ... / {<u>ALL</u> / <u>LEADING</u> / <u>FIRST</u>} {{identifier-3 / literal-1} <u>BY</u> {identifier-5 / literal-3} [{<u>BEFORE</u> / <u>AFTER</u>} INITIAL {identifier-4 / literal-2}] ... } ... } ...

	When Introduced	*Chapter Reference*

GENERAL FORMAT FOR COBOL VERBS

```
INSPECT identifier-1 TALLYING                                              ANS 74        CH 10

  {identifier-2 FOR  (CHARACTERS  [{BEFORE} INITIAL {identifier-4}] ...
                     (            [{AFTER }       {literal-2  }]

                     (ALL    ) {identifier-3} [{BEFORE} INITIAL {identifier-4}] ...) ...) ...
                     (LEADING) {literal-1  }  [{AFTER }        {literal-2  }]

  REPLACING

  (CHARACTERS BY {identifier-5} [{BEFORE} INITIAL {identifier-4}] ...
               {literal-3  } [{AFTER }        {literal-2  }]

  (ALL     ) {identifier-3} BY {identifier-5} [{BEFORE} INITIAL {identifier-4}] ...) ...
  (LEADING ) {literal-1  }    {literal-3  }  [{AFTER }        {literal-2  }]
  (FIRST   )
```

```
INSPECT identifier-1 CONVERTING {identifier-6} TO {identifier-7}           ANS 85        CH 10
                                {literal-4  }    {literal-5  }

  [{BEFORE} INITIAL {identifier-4}] ...
   {AFTER }         {literal-2  }
```

```
MERGE file-name-1 {ON {ASCENDING } KEY {data-name-1} ...} ...              ANS 74        CH 15
                     {DESCENDING}

  [COLLATING SEQUENCE IS alphabet-name-1]

  USING file-name-2 {file-name-3} ...

  {OUTPUT PROCEDURE IS procedure-name-1 [{THROUGH} procedure-name-2]}
  {                                     [{THRU   }                 ]}
  {GIVING {file-name-4} ...}
```

```
MOVE {identifier-1} TO {identifier-2} ...                                                CH 3
     {literal-1  }
```

```
MOVE {CORRESPONDING} identifier-1 TO identifier-2                                        CH 6
     {CORR         }
```

```
MULTIPLY {identifier-1} BY {identifier-2 [ROUNDED]} ...                                  CH 3
         {literal-1  }

  [ON SIZE ERROR imperative-statement-1]

  [NOT ON SIZE ERROR imperative-statement-2]                              ANS 85

  [END-MULTIPLY]                                                          ANS 85
```

V-25

	When Introduced	Chapter Reference

<u>GENERAL FORMAT FOR COBOL VERBS</u>

<u>MULTIPLY</u> $\begin{Bmatrix} \text{identifier-1} \\ \text{literal-1} \end{Bmatrix}$ <u>BY</u> $\begin{Bmatrix} \text{identifier-2} \\ \text{literal-2} \end{Bmatrix}$ CH 3

   <u>GIVING</u> {identifier-3 [<u>ROUNDED</u>]} ...

   [ON <u>SIZE</u> <u>ERROR</u> imperative-statement-1]

   [<u>NOT</u> ON <u>SIZE</u> <u>ERROR</u> imperative-statement-2]   ANS 85

   [<u>END-MULTIPLY</u>]   ANS 85

S <u>OPEN</u> $\begin{Bmatrix} \underline{\text{INPUT}} \ \{\text{file-name-1}\ \begin{bmatrix} \underline{\text{REVERSED}} \\ \text{WITH } \underline{\text{NO}}\ \underline{\text{REWIND}} \end{bmatrix}\} \cdots \\ \underline{\text{OUTPUT}} \ \{\text{file-name-2} \ \ [\text{WITH } \underline{\text{NO}}\ \underline{\text{REWIND}}]\} \cdots \\ \underline{\text{I-O}} \ \{\text{file-name-3}\} \cdots \\ \underline{\text{EXTEND}} \ \{\text{file-name-4}\} \cdots \end{Bmatrix} \cdots$ CH 6

     ANS 74

RI <u>OPEN</u> $\begin{Bmatrix} \underline{\text{INPUT}} \ \{\text{file-name-1}\} \cdots \\ \underline{\text{OUTPUT}} \ \{\text{file-name-2}\} \cdots \\ \underline{\text{I-O}} \ \{\text{file-name-3}\} \cdots \\ \underline{\text{EXTEND}} \ \{\text{file-name-4}\} \cdots \end{Bmatrix} \cdots$ CH 7, 8

     ANS 74

W <u>OPEN</u> $\begin{Bmatrix} \underline{\text{OUTPUT}} \ \{\text{file-name-1} \ [\text{WITH } \underline{\text{NO}}\ \underline{\text{REWIND}}]\} \cdots \\ \underline{\text{EXTEND}} \ \{\text{file-name-2}\} \cdots \end{Bmatrix} \cdots$ CH 9

<u>PERFORM</u> $\left[\text{procedure-name-1} \ \left[\begin{Bmatrix} \underline{\text{THROUGH}} \\ \underline{\text{THRU}} \end{Bmatrix} \text{procedure-name-2}\right]\right]$ CH 4

   [imperative-statement-1 <u>END-PERFORM</u>]   ANS 85

<u>PERFORM</u> $\left[\text{procedure-name-1} \ \left[\begin{Bmatrix} \underline{\text{THROUGH}} \\ \underline{\text{THRU}} \end{Bmatrix} \text{procedure-name-2}\right]\right]$ CH 4

   $\begin{Bmatrix} \text{identifier-1} \\ \text{integer-1} \end{Bmatrix}$

   <u>TIMES</u> [imperative-statement-1 <u>END-PERFORM</u>]   ANS 85   CH 4

<u>PERFORM</u> $\left[\text{procedure-name-1} \ \left[\begin{Bmatrix} \underline{\text{THROUGH}} \\ \underline{\text{THRU}} \end{Bmatrix} \text{procedure-name-2}\right]\right]$ CH 4

   $\left[\text{WITH } \underline{\text{TEST}} \ \begin{Bmatrix} \underline{\text{BEFORE}} \\ \underline{\text{AFTER}} \end{Bmatrix}\right]$ <u>UNTIL</u> condition-1   ANS 85

   [imperative-statement-1 <u>END-PERFORM</u>]   ANS 85

A

COMPOSITE LANGUAGE SKELETON

	When Introduced	Chapter Reference

GENERAL FORMAT FOR COBOL VERBS

```
PERFORM [procedure-name-1 [{THROUGH}  procedure-name-2]]                    CH 4
                           {THRU   }

         [WITH TEST {BEFORE}]                                ANS 85
                    {AFTER }

         VARYING {identifier-2} FROM {identifier-3}
                 {index-name-1}      {index-name-2}
                                     {literal-1   }

                 BY {identifier-4} UNTIL condition-1
                    {literal-2   }

              [AFTER {identifier-5} FROM {identifier-6}
                     {literal-3   }      {index-name-4}
                                         {literal-3   }

                 BY {identifier-7} UNTIL condition-2] ...
                    {literal-4   }

         [imperative-statement-1 END-PERFORM]                ANS 85


     PURGE cd-name-1                                         ANS 74    CH 15


SRI  READ file-name-1 [NEXT] RECORD [INTO identifier-1]               CH 6, 7, 8

         [AT END imperative-statement-1]

         [NOT AT END imperative-statement-2]                ANS 85

         [END-READ]                                         ANS 85


  R  READ file-name-1 RECORD [INTO identifier-1]                      CH 8

         [INVALID KEY imperative-statement-3]

         [NOT INVALID KEY imperative-statement-4]           ANS 85

         [END-READ]                                         ANS 85
```

	When Introduced	Chapter Reference

GENERAL FORMAT FOR COBOL VERBS

I <u>READ</u> file-name-1 RECORD [<u>INTO</u> identifier-1]   ANS 74   CH 7

    [<u>KEY</u> IS data-name-1]

    [<u>INVALID</u> KEY imperative-statement-3]

    [<u>NOT</u> <u>INVALID</u> KEY imperative-statement-4]   ANS 85

    [<u>END-READ</u>]   ANS 85

    <u>RECEIVE</u> cd-name-1 $\begin{Bmatrix} \underline{MESSAGE} \\ \underline{SEGMENT} \end{Bmatrix}$ <u>INTO</u> identifier-1   ANS 74   CH 15

    [<u>NO</u> <u>DATA</u> imperative-statement-1]

    [WITH <u>DATA</u> imperative-statement-2]

    [<u>END-RECEIVE</u>]   ANS 85

    <u>RELEASE</u> record-name-1 [<u>FROM</u> identifier-1]   CH 15

    <u>RETURN</u> file-name-1 RECORD [<u>INTO</u> identifier-1]   CH 15

    AT <u>END</u> imperative-statement-1

    [<u>NOT</u> AT <u>END</u> imperative-statement-2]   ANS 85

    [<u>END-RETURN</u>]   ANS 85

S <u>REWRITE</u> record-name-1 [<u>FROM</u> identifier-1]   ANS 74   CH 6

RI <u>REWRITE</u> record-name-1 [<u>FROM</u> identifier-1]   ANS 74   CH 7, 8

    [<u>INVALID</u> KEY imperative-statement-1]

    [<u>NOT</u> <u>INVALID</u> KEY imperative-statement-2]   ANS 85

    [<u>END-REWRITE</u>]   ANS 85

A

COMPOSITE
LANGUAGE
SKELETON

	When Introduced	Chapter Reference

GENERAL FORMAT FOR COBOL VERBS

SEARCH identifier-1 $\left[\underline{VARYING} \begin{Bmatrix} \text{identifier-2} \\ \text{index-name-1} \end{Bmatrix} \right]$ CH 11

    [AT <u>END</u> imperative-statement-1]

    $\begin{Bmatrix} \underline{WHEN} \text{ condition-1} \begin{Bmatrix} \text{imperative-statement-2} \\ \underline{NEXT} \underline{SENTENCE} \end{Bmatrix} \end{Bmatrix} \ldots$

    [END-SEARCH]   ANS 85

SEARCH ALL identifier-1 [AT <u>END</u> imperative-statement-1]   CH 11

    $\underline{WHEN} \begin{Bmatrix} \text{data-name-1} \begin{Bmatrix} \text{IS } \underline{EQUAL} \text{ TO} \\ \text{IS } = \end{Bmatrix} \begin{Bmatrix} \text{identifier-3} \\ \text{literal-1} \\ \text{arithmetic-expression-1} \end{Bmatrix} \\ \text{condition-name-1} \end{Bmatrix}$

    $\left[\underline{AND} \begin{Bmatrix} \text{data-name-2} \begin{Bmatrix} \text{IS } \underline{EQUAL} \text{ TO} \\ \text{IS } = \end{Bmatrix} \begin{Bmatrix} \text{identifier-4} \\ \text{literal-2} \\ \text{arithmetic-expression-2} \end{Bmatrix} \\ \text{condition-name-2} \end{Bmatrix} \right] \ldots$

    $\begin{Bmatrix} \text{imperative-statement-2} \\ \underline{NEXT} \underline{SENTENCE} \end{Bmatrix}$

    [END-SEARCH]   ANS 85

<u>SEND</u> cd-name-1 <u>FROM</u> identifier-1   ANS 74   CH 15

<u>SEND</u> cd-name-1 [<u>FROM</u> identifier-1] $\begin{Bmatrix} \text{WITH identifier-2} \\ \text{WITH } \underline{ESI} \\ \text{WITH } \underline{EMI} \\ \text{WITH } \underline{EGI} \end{Bmatrix}$ ANS 74   CH 15

    $\left[\begin{Bmatrix} \underline{BEFORE} \\ \underline{AFTER} \end{Bmatrix} \text{ ADVANCING} \begin{Bmatrix} \begin{Bmatrix} \text{identifier-3} \\ \text{integer-1} \end{Bmatrix} \begin{bmatrix} \text{LINE} \\ \text{LINES} \end{bmatrix} \\ \begin{Bmatrix} \text{mnemonic-name-1} \\ \underline{PAGE} \end{Bmatrix} \end{Bmatrix} \right]$

    [<u>REPLACING</u> LINE]

<u>SET</u> $\begin{Bmatrix} \text{index-name-1} \\ \text{identifier-1} \end{Bmatrix} \ldots \underline{TO} \begin{Bmatrix} \text{index-name-2} \\ \text{identifier-2} \\ \text{integer-1} \end{Bmatrix}$ CH 11

	When Introduced	*Chapter Reference*

<u>GENERAL FORMAT FOR COBOL VERBS</u>

<u>SET</u> {index-name-3} ... $\left\{ \begin{matrix} \underline{UP}\ \underline{BY} \\ \underline{DOWN}\ \underline{BY} \end{matrix} \right\}$ $\left\{ \begin{matrix} identifier-3 \\ integer-2 \end{matrix} \right\}$ CH 11

<u>SORT</u> file-name-1 $\left\{ ON\ \left\{ \begin{matrix} \underline{ASCENDING} \\ \underline{DESCENDING} \end{matrix} \right\}\ KEY\ \{data-name-1\} ...\ \right\}$ ...   CH 15

    [WITH <u>DUPLICATES</u> IN ORDER]

    [COLLATING <u>SEQUENCE</u> IS alphabet-name-1]

    $\left\{ \begin{matrix} INPUT\ \underline{PROCEDURE}\ IS\ procedure-name-1\ \left[\begin{matrix} \underline{THROUGH} \\ \underline{THRU} \end{matrix} \right]\ procedure-name-2 \\ \underline{USING}\ \{file-name-2\} ... \end{matrix} \right\}$

    $\left\{ \begin{matrix} \underline{OUTPUT}\ \underline{PROCEDURE}\ IS\ procedure-name-3\ \left[\begin{matrix} \underline{THROUGH} \\ \underline{THRU} \end{matrix} \right]\ procedure-name-4 \\ \underline{GIVING}\ \{file-name-3\} ... \end{matrix} \right\}$

<u>START</u> file-name-1 $\left[\underline{KEY} \left\{ \begin{matrix} IS\ \underline{EQUAL}\ TO \\ IS\ = \\ IS\ \underline{GREATER}\ THAN \\ IS\ > \\ IS\ \underline{NOT}\ \underline{LESS}\ THAN \\ IS\ \underline{NOT}\ < \\ IS\ \underline{GREATER}\ THAN\ \underline{OR}\ \underline{EQUAL}\ TO \\ IS\ >= \end{matrix} \right\} data-name-1 \right]$ ANS 74   CH 7, 8

    [<u>INVALID</u> KEY imperative-statement-1]

    [<u>NOT</u> <u>INVALID</u> KEY imperative-statement-2]   ANS 85

    [<u>END-START</u>]   ANS 85

<u>STOP</u> $\left\{ \begin{matrix} \underline{RUN} \\ literal-1 \end{matrix} \right\}$ CH 1

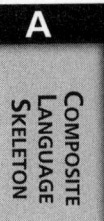

A

COMPOSITE
LANGUAGE
SKELETON

	When Introduced	*Chapter Reference*

GENERAL FORMAT FOR COBOL VERBS

STRING $\begin{Bmatrix} \text{identifier-1} \\ \text{literal-1} \end{Bmatrix}$ ... DELIMITED BY $\begin{Bmatrix} \text{identifier-2} \\ \text{literal-2} \\ \text{SIZE} \end{Bmatrix}$ ...   ANS 74   CH 10

  INTO identifier-3

  [WITH POINTER identifier-4]

  [ON OVERFLOW imperative-statement-1]

  [NOT ON OVERFLOW imperative-statement-2]   ANS 85

  [END-STRING]   ANS 85

SUBTRACT $\begin{Bmatrix} \text{identifier-1} \\ \text{literal-1} \end{Bmatrix}$ ... FROM {identifier-3 [ROUNDED]} ...   CH 3

  [ON SIZE ERROR imperative-statement-1]

  [NOT ON SIZE ERROR imperative-statement-2]   ANS 85

  [END-SUBTRACT]   ANS 85

SUBTRACT $\begin{Bmatrix} \text{identifier-1} \\ \text{literal-1} \end{Bmatrix}$ ... FROM $\begin{Bmatrix} \text{identifier-2} \\ \text{literal-2} \end{Bmatrix}$ CH 3

  GIVING {identifier-3 [ROUNDED]} ...

  [ON SIZE ERROR imperative-statement-1]

  [NOT ON SIZE ERROR imperative-statement-2]   ANS 85

  [END-SUBTRACT]   ANS 85

SUBTRACT $\begin{Bmatrix} \text{CORRESPONDING} \\ \text{CORR} \end{Bmatrix}$ identifier-1 FROM identifier-2 [ROUNDED]   CH 6

  [ON SIZE ERROR imperative-statement-1]

  [NOT ON SIZE ERROR imperative-statement-2]   ANS 85

  [END-SUBTRACT]   ANS 85

SUPPRESS PRINTING   CH 9

TERMINATE {report-name-1} ...   CH 9

	When Introduced	Chapter Reference

GENERAL FORMAT FOR COBOL VERBS

```
UNSTRING  identifier-1                                              ANS 74        CH 10
    [DELIMITED BY [ALL] {identifier-2}  [OR [ALL] {identifier-3}] ...]
                        {literal-1   }              {literal-2  }
    INTO {identifier-4 [DELIMITER IN identifier-5] [COUNT IN identifier-6]} ...

    [WITH POINTER identifier-7]

    [TALLYING IN identifier-8]

    [ON OVERFLOW imperative-statement-1]

    [NOT ON OVERFLOW imperative-statement-2]                        ANS 85

    [END-UNSTRING]                                                  ANS 85

                                                {file-name-1} ...
SRI USE [GLOBAL] AFTER STANDARD {EXCEPTION} PROCEDURE ON {INPUT   }
                                {ERROR    }              {OUTPUT  }              CH 15
                                                         {I-O     }
                                                         {EXTEND  }

                                                {file-name-1} ...
W USE AFTER STANDARD {EXCEPTION} PROCEDURE ON {OUTPUT     }
                     {ERROR    }              {EXTEND     }                      CH 15

    USE [GLOBAL] BEFORE REPORTING identifier-1                                  CH 15

                          {cd-name-1                         }
                          {[ALL REFERENCES OF] identifier-1  }
    USE FOR DEBUGGING ON  {file-name-1                       } ...
                          {procedure-name-1                  }   ANS 74         CH 15
                          {ALL PROCEDURES                    }
```

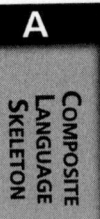

A

COMPOSITE
LANGUAGE
SKELETON

	When Introduced	Chapter Reference

GENERAL FORMAT FOR COBOL VERBS

S WRITE record-name-1 [FROM identifier-1]   CH 6

$$\left[\begin{Bmatrix} \underline{BEFORE} \\ \underline{AFTER} \end{Bmatrix} \text{ ADVANCING } \begin{Bmatrix} \begin{Bmatrix} identifier\text{-}2 \\ integer\text{-}1 \end{Bmatrix} \begin{bmatrix} LINE \\ LINES \end{bmatrix} \\ \begin{Bmatrix} mnemonic\text{-}name\text{-}1 \\ \underline{PAGE} \end{Bmatrix} \end{Bmatrix}\right]$$

$$\left[AT \begin{Bmatrix} \underline{END\text{-}OF\text{-}PAGE} \\ \underline{EOP} \end{Bmatrix} imperative\text{-}statement\text{-}1 \right]$$ ANS 74

$$\left[\underline{NOT} \; AT \begin{Bmatrix} \underline{END\text{-}OF\text{-}PAGE} \\ \underline{EOP} \end{Bmatrix} imperative\text{-}statement\text{-}2 \right]$$ ANS 85

[END-WRITE]   ANS 85

RI WRITE record-name-1 [FROM identifier-1]   CH 7, 8

[INVALID KEY imperative-statement-1]

[NOT INVALID KEY imperative-statement-2]   ANS 85

[END-WRITE]   ANS 85

	When Introduced	Chapter Reference

<u>GENERAL FORMAT FOR COPY AND REPLACE STATEMENTS</u>

$$\underline{COPY} \text{ text-name-1} \left[\begin{Bmatrix} \underline{OF} \\ \underline{IN} \end{Bmatrix} \text{ library-name-1} \right]$$

CH 6

$$\left[\underline{REPLACING} \left\{ \begin{Bmatrix} \text{==pseudo-text-1==} \\ \text{identifier-1} \\ \text{literal-1} \\ \text{word-1} \end{Bmatrix} \underline{BY} \begin{Bmatrix} \text{==pseudo-text-2==} \\ \text{identifier-2} \\ \text{literal-2} \\ \text{word-2} \end{Bmatrix} \right\} \dots \right]$$

$\underline{REPLACE}$ {==pseudo-text-1== $\underline{BY}$ ==pseudo-text-2==} ...   ANS 85   CH 6

$\underline{REPLACE} \ \underline{OFF}$ ANS 85   CH 6

A

COMPOSITE
LANGUAGE
SKELETON

V-34

	When Introduced	Chapter Reference

GENERAL FORMAT FOR CONDITIONS

RELATION CONDITION:

$$\left\{ \begin{array}{l} \text{identifier-1} \\ \text{literal-1} \\ \text{arithmetic-expression-1} \\ \text{index-name-1} \end{array} \right\} \left\{ \begin{array}{l} \text{IS [NOT] GREATER THAN} \\ \text{IS [NOT] >} \\ \text{IS [NOT] LESS THAN} \\ \text{IS [NOT] <} \\ \text{IS [NOT] EQUAL TO} \\ \text{IS [NOT] =} \\ \text{IS GREATER THAN OR EQUAL TO} \\ \text{IS >=} \\ \text{IS LESS THAN OR EQUAL TO} \\ \text{IS <=} \end{array} \right\} \left\{ \begin{array}{l} \text{identifier-2} \\ \text{literal-2} \\ \text{arithmetic-expression-2} \\ \text{index-name-2} \end{array} \right\}$$

CH 3

ANS 85

ANS 85

CLASS CONDITION:

$$\text{identifier-1 IS [NOT]} \left\{ \begin{array}{l} \text{NUMERIC} \\ \text{ALPHABETIC} \\ \text{ALPHABETIC-LOWER} \\ \text{ALPHABETIC-UPPER} \\ \text{class-name-1} \end{array} \right\}$$

ANS 85

ANS 85

CH 3

CONDITION-NAME CONDITION:

condition-name-1

CH 3

SWITCH-STATUS CONDITION:

condition-name-1

CH 3

SIGN CONDITION:

$$\text{arithmetic-expression-1 IS [NOT]} \left\{ \begin{array}{l} \text{POSITIVE} \\ \text{NEGATIVE} \\ \text{ZERO} \end{array} \right\}$$

ANS 74

CH 3

NEGATED CONDITION:

NOT condition-1

CH 5

	When Introduced	Chapter Reference

GENERAL FORMAT FOR CONDITIONS

COMBINED CONDITION:

condition-1 $\left\{ \left\{ \begin{matrix} \underline{AND} \\ \underline{OR} \end{matrix} \right\} \quad condition\text{-}2 \right\}$ ...   CH 3, 5

ABBREVIATED COMBINED RELATION CONDITION:

relation-condition $\left\{ \left\{ \begin{matrix} \underline{AND} \\ \underline{OR} \end{matrix} \right\} \quad [\underline{NOT}] \quad [relational\text{-}operator] \quad object \right\}$ ...   CH 5

A

COMPOSITE
LANGUAGE
SKELETON

V-36

	When Introduced	Chapter Reference

GENERAL FORMAT FOR QUALIFICATION

FORMAT 1:

$$\begin{Bmatrix} \text{data-name-1} \\ \text{condition-name-1} \end{Bmatrix} \begin{Bmatrix} \begin{Bmatrix} \text{IN} \\ \text{OF} \end{Bmatrix} \text{data-name-2} \\ \begin{Bmatrix} \text{IN} \\ \text{OF} \end{Bmatrix} \begin{Bmatrix} \text{file-name-1} \\ \text{cd-name-1} \end{Bmatrix} \end{Bmatrix} \dots \left[\begin{Bmatrix} \text{IN} \\ \text{OF} \end{Bmatrix} \begin{Bmatrix} \text{file-name-1} \\ \text{cd-name-1} \end{Bmatrix} \right]$$

CH 6

FORMAT 2:

paragraph-name-1 $\begin{Bmatrix} \text{IN} \\ \text{OF} \end{Bmatrix}$ section-name-1

CH 6

FORMAT 3:

text-name-1 $\begin{Bmatrix} \text{IN} \\ \text{OF} \end{Bmatrix}$ library-name-1

ANS 74   CH 6

FORMAT 4:

LINAGE-COUNTER $\begin{Bmatrix} \text{IN} \\ \text{OF} \end{Bmatrix}$ file-name-2

CH 6

FORMAT 5:

$\begin{Bmatrix} \text{PAGE-COUNTER} \\ \text{LINE-COUNTER} \end{Bmatrix}$ $\begin{Bmatrix} \text{IN} \\ \text{OF} \end{Bmatrix}$ report-name-1

CH 9

FORMAT 6:

data-name-3 $\begin{Bmatrix} \begin{Bmatrix} \text{IN} \\ \text{OF} \end{Bmatrix} \text{data-name-4} \left[\begin{Bmatrix} \text{IN} \\ \text{OF} \end{Bmatrix} \text{report-name-2} \right] \\ \begin{Bmatrix} \text{IN} \\ \text{OF} \end{Bmatrix} \text{report-name-2} \end{Bmatrix}$

CH 9

	When Introduced	Chapter Reference

<u>MISCELLANEOUS FORMATS</u>

<u>SUBSCRIPTING</u>:

$$\begin{Bmatrix} \text{condition-name-1} \\ \text{data-name-1} \end{Bmatrix} \quad (\quad \begin{Bmatrix} \text{integer-1} \\ \text{data-name-2 } [\{\pm\} \text{ integer-2}] \\ \text{index-name-1 } [\{\pm\} \text{ integer-3}] \end{Bmatrix} \quad \dots \quad)$$

CH 11, 12

<u>REFERENCE MODIFICATION</u>:

data-name-1 (leftmost-character-position: [length])

ANS 85   CH 10

<u>IDENTIFIER</u>:

$$\text{data-name-1} \quad \begin{bmatrix} \begin{Bmatrix} \underline{\text{IN}} \\ \underline{\text{OF}} \end{Bmatrix} \text{ data-name-2} \end{bmatrix} \quad \dots \quad \begin{bmatrix} \begin{Bmatrix} \underline{\text{IN}} \\ \underline{\text{OF}} \end{Bmatrix} \begin{Bmatrix} \text{cd-name-1} \\ \text{file-name-1} \\ \text{report-name-1} \end{Bmatrix} \end{bmatrix}$$

[({subscript} ...)] [(leftmost-character-position: [length])]

A

COMPOSITE
LANGUAGE
SKELETON

V-38

	When Introduced	Chapter Reference
GENERAL FORMAT FOR NESTED SOURCE PROGRAMS		
IDENTIFICATION DIVISION.	ANS 85	CH 14

```
IDENTIFICATION DIVISION.

PROGRAM-ID.  program-name-1  [IS INITIAL PROGRAM].

[ENVIRONMENT DIVISION.  environment-division-content]

[DATA DIVISION.  data-division-content]

[PROCEDURE DIVISION.  procedure-division-content]

[[nested-source-program] ...

END PROGRAM program-name-1.]
```

	When Introduced	Chapter Reference
GENERAL FORMAT FOR NESTED-SOURCE-PROGRAM	ANS 85	CH 14

```
IDENTIFICATION DIVISION.

PROGRAM-ID.  program-name-2  [IS {| COMMON  |} PROGRAM] .
                                {| INITIAL |}

[ENVIRONMENT DIVISION.  environment-division-content]

[DATA DIVISION.  data-division-content]

[PROCEDURE DIVISION.  procedure-division-content]

[nested-source-program] ...

END PROGRAM program-name-2.
```

	When Introduced	Chapter Reference
<u>GENERAL FORMAT FOR A SEQUENCE OF SOURCE PROGRAMS</u>	ANS 85	CH 14

```
{ IDENTIFICATION DIVISION.
  PROGRAM-ID.  program-name-3  [IS INITIAL PROGRAM].
 [ENVIRONMENT DIVISION.  environment-division-content]
 [DATA DIVISION.  data-division-content]
 [PROCEDURE DIVISION.  procedure-division-content]
 [nested-source-program] ...
  END PROGRAM program-name-3.} ...
  IDENTIFICATION DIVISION.
  PROGRAM-ID.  program-name-4  [IS INITIAL PROGRAM].
 [ENVIRONMENT DIVISION.  environment-division-content]
 [DATA DIVISION.  data-division-content]
 [PROCEDURE DIVISION.  procedure-division-content]
 [[nested-source-program] ...
  END PROGRAM program-name-4.]
```

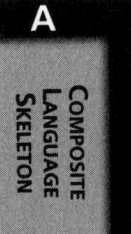

A

COMPOSITE
LANGUAGE
SKELETON

	When Introduced	*Chapter Reference*
Intrinsic Functions		
FUNCTION ACOS (number-1)	ANS 89	CH 13
FUNCTION ANNUITY (numeric-item-1 integer-item-1)	ANS 89	CH 13
FUNCTION ASIN (number-1)	ANS 89	CH 13
FUNCTION ATAN (number-1)	ANS 89	CH 13
FUNCTION CHAR (integer-item-1)	ANS 89	CH 13
FUNCTION COS (number-1)	ANS 89	CH 13
FUNCTION CURRENT-DATE	ANS 89	CH 13
FUNCTION DATE-OF-INTEGER (integer-1)	ANS 89	CH 13
FUNCTION DATE-TO-YYYYMMDD (integer item-1 [integer-item-2])	ANS 200x	CH 13
FUNCTION DAY-OF-INTEGER (integer-1)	ANS 89	CH 13
FUNCTION DAY-TO-YYYYDDD (integer item-1 [integer-item-2])	ANS 200x	CH 13
FUNCTION FACTORIAL (integer-item-1)	ANS 89	CH 13
FUNCTION INTEGER (numeric-item-1)	ANS 89	CH 13
FUNCTION INTEGER-OF-DATE (integer-1)	ANS 89	CH 13
FUNCTION INTEGER-OF-DAY (integer-1)	ANS 89	CH 13
FUNCTION INTEGER-PART (numeric-item-1)	ANS 89	CH 13
FUNCTION LENGTH (data-item-1)	ANS 89	CH 13
FUNCTION LOG (number-1)	ANS 89	CH 13
FUNCTION LOG10 (number-1)	ANS 89	CH 13
FUNCTION LOWER-CASE (AN-data-item-1)	ANS 89	CH 13
FUNCTION MAX ({argument-1})	ANS 89	CH 13
FUNCTION MEAN ({numeric-item-1})	ANS 89	CH 13
FUNCTION MEDIAN ({numeric-item-1})	ANS 89	CH 13
FUNCTION MIDRANGE ({numeric-item-1})	ANS 89	CH 13
FUNCTION MIN ({argument-1})	ANS 89	CH 13
FUNCTION MOD (integer-item-1 integer-item-2)	ANS 89	CH 13

	When Introduced	Chapter Reference
FUNCTION NUMVAL (AN-data-item-1)	ANS 89	CH 13
FUNCTION NUMVAL-C (AN-data-item-1 [char-item-1])	ANS 89	CH 13
FUNCTION ORD (char-item-1)	ANS 89	CH 13
FUNCTION ORD-MAX ({argument-1})	ANS 89	CH 13
FUNCTION ORD-MIN ({argument-1})	ANS 89	CH 13
FUNCTION PRESENT-VALUE (numeric-item-1 {numeric-item-2})	ANS 89	CH 13
FUNCTION RANDOM ([integer-item-1])	ANS 89	CH 13
FUNCTION RANGE ({numeric-item-1})	ANS 89	CH 13
FUNCTION REM (numeric-item-1 numeric-item-2)	ANS 89	CH 13
FUNCTION REVERSE (AN-data-item-1)	ANS 89	CH 13
FUNCTION SIN (number-1)	ANS 89	CH 13
FUNCTION SQRT (numeric-item-1)	ANS 89	CH 13
FUNCTION STANDARD-DEVIATION ({numeric-item-1})	ANS 89	CH 13
FUNCTION SUM ({numeric-item-1})	ANS 89	CH 13
FUNCTION TAN (number-1)	ANS 89	CH 13
FUNCTION TEST-DATE-YYYYMMDD (integer item-1)	ANS 200x	CH 13
FUNCTION TEST-DAY-YYYYDDD (integer item-1)	ANS 200x	CH 13
FUNCTION UPPER-CASE (AN-data-item-1)	ANS 89	CH 13
FUNCTION VARIANCE ({numeric-item-1})	ANS 89	CH 13
FUNCTION WHEN-COMPILED	ANS 89	CH 13
FUNCTION YEAR-TO-YYYY (integer item-1 [integer-item-2])	ANS 200x	CH 13

A

COMPOSITE
LANGUAGE
SKELETON

INDEX

G

CASEGEN Systems

End-to-End ™ COBOL for the Enterprise

CASEGEN high-performance COBOL tools give programmers the edge when it comes to developing real-world applications. These are tools that do not detract from the flexibility of the language, but get you up and running quickly, generating high-quality COBOL code that you would like to have written yourself.

With CASEGEN, you can write applications requiring high technical skills, such as 32-bit Windows programming, ODBC, and multi-tier client/server applications, without the long learning curve these environments demand. CASEGEN is designed for COBOL programmers to get up and running quickly, while still giving you that complete flexibility and performance that you expect from COBOL.

Why not review our "starter" product on the accompanying CD and check out our Web site at www.casegen.co.uk or email sales@casegen.co.uk for more details.

Get an edge over the competition—get CASEGEN skills on your CV...

What's on the Disc

The companion CD-ROM contains all of the authors' source code and samples from the book and many third-party software products.

Windows 3.1 and Windows NT 3.5.1 Installation Instructions

1. Insert the CD-ROM disc into your CD-ROM drive.

2. From File Manager or Program Manager, choose Run from the File menu.

3. Type `<drive>\README.TXT` and press Enter, where `<drive>` corresponds to the drive letter of your CD-ROM. For example, if your CD-ROM is drive D:, type `D:\README.TXT` and press Enter.

4. The README.TXT file contains information concerning installing the author's source code and third-party programs.

Windows 95/98/NT4 Installation Instructions

1. Insert the CD-ROM disc into your CD-ROM drive.

2. From the Windows 95 desktop, double-click the My Computer icon.

3. Double-click the icon representing your CD-ROM drive.

4. Double-click the icon titled SETUP.EXE to run the installation program.

NOTE

If Windows 95 is installed on your computer and you have the AutoPlay feature enabled, the SETUP.EXE program starts automatically whenever you insert the disc into your CD-ROM drive.